'I am lost in admiration both at its comprehensiveness and at the
breadth of judgement and scholarship it shows.'
MAURICE LINDSAY

'What an immense achievement! What labour and understanding
must have gone into the making of your Anthology!'
GEORGE BRUCE

'I'm very glad – and proud – to know that work of mine will
be included.'
HAMISH HENDERSON

'[This] is a scholarly, well-presented work which will be invaluable
to students and researchers alike.'
SHEENA BLACKHALL

'All who like Scottish writing should be grateful to you
for having done this.'
ALASDAIR GRAY

'It is a wonderful resource.'
DOUGLAS DUNN

'I marvel at your achievement . . . My pleasure lies in
being included.'
STEWART CONN

'The scale of work involved takes my breath away.'
DUNCAN GLEN

Published in 2002 by
SCOTTISH CULTURAL PRESS
Unit 13d, Newbattle Abbey Business Annexe
Newbattle Road, DALKEITH EH22 3LJ Scotland
Tel: +44 (0)131 660 6366 • Fax: +44 (0)131 660 6414
Email: info@scottishbooks.com
website: www.scottishbooks.com

The publisher acknowledges subsidy from the
Scottish Arts Council
towards the publication of this volume

BRITISH LIBRARY CATALOGUING IN PUBLICATION DATA
A catalogue record for this book is available from the British Library

ISBN: 1 84017 042 5

Printed and bound by Bell & Bain Ltd, Glasgow

SCOTTISH LITERATURE IN THE TWENTIETH CENTURY

~

AN ANTHOLOGY

~

EDITED BY
DAVID M\cCORDICK

SCOTTISH CULTURAL PRESS

Table of Contents

The Plan of this Book

This is Volume III of the first comprehensive anthology of English-language Scottish literature. It follows the format of the first two volumes in that it interprets 'Scottish' quite broadly and 'literature' includes poetry, fiction, essay and drama of a wide variety. Volume I covers the period from the early Middle Ages to circa 1775; Volume II continues from 1775 to 1900, and this Volume covers the whole of the twentieth century to the present day.

In this book, a Scottish writer is any person who has lived long enough in Scotland to consider himself Scottish; and Scottish literature includes any writing done by all such persons, regardless of style or subject matter.

Literary excellence has again been the prime criterion for inclusion, though some selections were chosen to emphasise Scottish genres or subjects, or to facilitate comparisons with other materials already chosen.

This volume follows the practice of the other two in avoiding excerpts wherever possible. Some items have been taken from longer works, but nothing has been presented here which is not genuinely free-standing. (A possible exception is Lorimer's translation of the New Testament into Scots.) Of course this means many fine works could not be represented at all.

Once more the editor must express regret over the exclusion of Gaelic writers. To represent the achievements of such luminaries as Sorley MacLean would simply require more space than was reasonable, given the many other English-language (i.e., English and Scots) works of distinction which demanded inclusion, not to mention the inevitable failure of translations to represent the real achievement of the modern Gaelic writers. A fourth volume, devoted exclusively to Scottish Gaelic authors over the centuries, would be the proper solution.

Even those who feel they know Scottish literature will be impressed by the sheer number of fine writers represented here. But it is a sign of the true riches of this field that of course many good writers have had to be left out. Anthologising on this scale is the art of the possible. No project of such size is financially tenable except under the terms of the most generous co-operation from authors and publishers. Only one writer declined to be included. Tom Leonard is the regretted omission. Mr Leonard, known as a man of strong convictions, would have nothing to do with this project, for personal reasons. Permissions from the agents acting for Alfred Douglas, Compton Mackenzie, Muriel Spark, Alasdair Maclean and William Boyd were also not feasible. And several other writers or estates could simply not be located even though two years was allocated for the purposes of obtaining permissions.

Each reader who loves Scottish literature will have his or her own candidates to be listed among our regretted and inexplicably missing writers. But, though admittedly some authors were simply not obtainable, even more had to be left out simply for lack of space. This editor's chief regret for a single work, for example, is for 'John Brandane's' *The Glen is Mine*, the rights to which could not be pinned down. Yet had we obtained that permission, we would have had to eliminate forty pages of material already selected. And so on. The field is rich.

Some writers were excluded, for example, chiefly because they wrote works of a kind already well represented, though the writers' talent and accomplishment were otherwise well up to the standards of the book. Donald Campbell's splendid *Widows of Clyth* should have had a place, as should Liz Lochhead's *Mary Queen of Scots Got her Head Chopped Off*, but each of these fine works examines themes well represented in the included play, *Bondagers*. Even a book of this size cannot do justice to the wonderful accomplishments of twentieth-century Scottish literature. Another first-rate book of this same size but with entirely different writers could easily have been put together. (And it should be.)

Introduction to Modern Scottish Literature

Scotland has participated rather fully in the pluralist currents of modern literature – in our century's explosion of styles and subject matter. Attempting to categorise the last one hundred years of Scottish literature is therefore doomed to shallowness and contradiction. But if such an attempt be at least mildly useful, here is a quick outline. One may divide the Scottish twentieth century into three main phases. (Writers whose dates are given in parenthesis are represented in this book. In some instances more background material is provided in their individual introductions.)

I. The Continuation of Nineteenth-century Literary Traditions

The later nineteenth century was dominated by two opposite literary movements: post-romanticism and realism. They each lingered on into much of the new century. They combined to form the now thoroughly discredited 'kailyard' (cabbage patch) school of sentimental Scottish small-town life. The main kailyarder was the extraordinarily talented James Barrie (1860–1937), through his sketches, short stories and novels (at least those set in Scotland). Besides Barrie, this volume's representative of that school is Samuel Crockett (1860–1914) with his 'Last Anderson of Deeside'.

Another expression of the late romantic is the vestige of the dreamland, the Celtic twilight, etc., as exemplified by William Sharp, who ended the last volume. Perhaps the major representative at the beginning of this century is Barrie again with the otherworldly *Mary Rose* (1920), and his Never Never Land. Kenneth Grahame, with his short stories of *The Golden Age* (1895) and the splendid *Wind in the Willows* (1908) – usually considered a children's novel – is another example. The golden world survives too in the fallen Eden of the troubled poems of Edwin Muir (1887–1959).

The rousing adventure-tale tradition of Walter Scott and Robert Louis Stevenson has remained a major factor throughout the century. Notable practitioners are the internationally famous Arthur Conan Doyle and John Buchan (1875–1940), or the more contemporary best-seller, Alasdair Maclean. Even the world-famous Klondike ballads of Robert Service (1874–1958) could probably be fitted in here.

Finally, a third aspect of romanticism is the delight in nature and the tendency to associate nature with God, mystical states, or at least profound truths. Hundreds of minor Scottish poets devoted themselves to this tradition. Perhaps the chief major poet who may be placed in this category is Andrew Young (1885–1971), but almost every Scottish poet has been at least influenced by it.

Perhaps a final feature of the nineteenth-century romanticism – its late aestheticism, world-weariness and decadence – appears, if not too prominently, in Scotland as well. Its most obvious Scottish practitioner is probably Alfred Douglas.

The second major feature of nineteenth-century literature is realism, which may be defined as the literary technique of employing 'real life' characters, dialogue and situations, together with a strongly determinist philosophy (i.e., that we are what our heredity and our environment make us). It appears in a sentimental and much muted form in the kailyard novelists (where is it rather like the realism of the American illustrator Norman Rockwell), but first explodes into prominence in Scottish literature with the tragic grandeur of George Douglas' great anti-kailyard novel, *The House with the Green Shutters* (1901), and its depiction of the actual banality, pettiness and brutality of small-town life in Scotland. We can see realism also in the working-class urban themes of John Davidson (1857–1909), and his interest in the new science. It appears in the realistic novel of manners, as practiced by the Findlater sisters, among others. Finally, Scotland joined a by now universal preoccupation with big-city slums and social conditions with the Gorbals stories of Edward Gaitens (1897–1966). Realism remains an essential feature of modern Scottish literature.

II. The 'Scottish Renaissance'

This is the twentieth-century movement for which Scotland may be most celebrated. It was led by Hugh MacDiarmid (1892–1978) in the 1920s. Tired of what he considered the effete, shallow, conventional and pithless 'Burns tradition' of Scottish diction and subject matter, MacDiarmid demanded a fresh, contemporary but still uniquely Scottish literature, fuelled by a newly invigorated Scots and which took as its subject matter the entire world, and which included all the new experimental themes and techniques which were then spreading across Europe. He ransacked old Scottish literature, Scots dictionaries, and the spoken language of the Scottish working classes to produce poems of startling brilliance which were simultaneously deeply Scottish, yet absolutely modern and European. His long philosophical poem, *A Drunk Man Looks at the Thistle* (1926), is the masterpiece of this movement and is surely one of the major artistic achievements of the twentieth century. Its linguistic and thematic variety, intellectual complexity and resonance from a wide range of literary sources made clear that everything was possible in Scots and that Scotland itself was neither a provincial subject nor an exhausted one.

Several Scottish poets had been doing rather distinguished, if much less ambitious, work in Scots before MacDiarmid, as for example Violet Jacob (1863–1946), Charles Murray (1864–1930), Marion Angus (1866–1946), and Helen Cruickshank (1886–1975). MacDiarmid's example prompted a wave of serious and adventurous new poets in Scots, such as William Soutar (1898–1943), Robert Garioch (1909–1981), Douglas Young (1913–1973), Sydney Smith (1915–1975), and Tom Scott (1918–1995). Smith's epic series of love stories, *Under the Eildon Tree* (1948), was, like *A Drunk Man*, an ambitious and successful fusing of the new Scots with the great traditions of European literature. But one can surely trace MacDiarmid's influence in prose writers as well – notably in the trilogy of novels by Lewis Grassic-Gibbon, *A Scot's Quair* (1932–1934), usually considered the major twentieth-century work of Scottish fiction. Grassic-Gibbon wrote the book in a rhythmic Scots which, like MacDiarmid's, was partly of his own making. This great work is a fusion of ideas and energy of the Scottish Renaissance with the realistic mode and the traditional Scottish preoccupation with their land and its history.

The most important Scottish novelist of our century is usually said to be Neil Gunn (1891–1973), whose long series of novels on Scottish themes, while only slightly 'vernacular', may surely also be said to reflect the influence of MacDiarmid in their combination of Scottish setting and universality of theme and insight. Indeed it would be very difficult to deny the influence of MacDiarmid on any Scottish writer who came after him, including those who wrote in standard English and even those who eschewed Scottish themes. He is the major presence in modern Scottish literature. As well as a splendid poet, who led by his own brilliant example, MacDiarmid was a tireless propagandist for the cause of a new Scottish literature, who kept the dream alive with countless speeches, articles and editorial efforts.

III. Post-war Eclecticism

Since the Second World War, literature everywhere has followed what seems to be every available path. Experimentation is the rule, shock is (paradoxically) a common feature, and social protest assumed. Scotland has not been at the forefront of modern literary experiment, but it has participated in most literary movements. There are some 'Scottish schools' if one cares to identify them as such, though mainly because of setting or language.

One of the most notable features of Scottish literature is the neo-realistic 'Glasgow' school, featuring the works of such writers as Tom Leonard, William McIlvanney (1936–), James Kelman (1946–), Alan Spence (1947–), Irvine Welsh (1958–), and Duncan McLean (1964–). The term 'Glasgow' is applied here because the school started in Glasgow and is still centred there, though one of its most spectacular practitioners, Irvine Welsh, writes of Edinburgh life, and any big city, including London, will now do. The characteristics of the Glasgow school are verisimilitude of detail, working-class subject matter, heavy use of Scots, and social protest (against the degradation of the working classes, against the emptiness of modern life). And, as is traditional for realism, we see a constant search for new, often shocking subject-matter (drugs, unusual sex, crime, violence, corruption).

Running parallel with the MacDiarmid-led emphasis upon Scots, but opposite to it, is what one may call the school of the well-made English verse. The fine poet Edwin Muir, certainly as serious and as well-read as MacDiarmid, if not as original in his thinking or his writing, ignored Scots and produced first-rate, thoughtful poetry in standard English. He was much interested in current ideas in psychology and anthropology and in such avant-garde literary experiments as the expressionism of Franz Kafka, whose work he and his wife translated. Norman MacCaig (1910–1996), a close friend of MacDiarmid, wrote in English throughout his career. MacDiarmid never seems to have reproved him for it. Like Muir, MacCaig wrote carefully controlled, rather neat verse, often on the standard themes poets have loved – the countryside, mutability, loss. Well-made, wide-ranging poetry in English has been produced by a remarkable group of other Scottish poets. In fact history may conclude this English verse was the real strength of modern Scottish literature. One can mention Iain Smith (1928–1999) – perhaps the most praised recent Scottish poet – George Bruce (1909–), Stewart Conn (1936–), Douglas Dunn (1942–), Valerie Gillies (1949–), John Burnside (1955–) and the remarkable Don Paterson (1963–) as writers whose works can also be called 'chiselled'. Most of these writers are capable of quite a range of poetic styles from a granite simplicity and stolidity to a complexity of symbol, idea, or even syntax. In the case of a Don Paterson, the density of idea and symbol is astonishing.

A major feature of Scottish literature since its beginning has been the fantastic. In our century that feature has been remarkable. Alasdair Gray (1934–), George MacBeth, D. M. Black (1941–), Margaret Elphinstone (1948–), Ron Butlin (1949–) can all be mentioned as sometime writers of the fantastic or grotesque. Alasdair Gray's Lanark is one of the major works of fantasy, or science fiction, of our century. And both David Lindsay, and Iain Banks[1] have achieved major distinction in the field of science fiction. Lindsay's *A Voyage to Arcturus* (1920) is in fact a fantasy classic.

Sometimes as part of this fantastic motif, Scotland has produced a stream of writers or works which may be labelled, 'experimental' or even deconstructionist: Muriel Spark, Edwin Morgan (1920–), W. S. Graham (1918–1986), Alexander Hutchison (1938–), Frank Kuppner (1951–), Janice Galloway (1956–), Robert Crawford (1959–), Gordon Legge (1961–), A. L. Kennedy (1965–), and Alan Warner may all be mentioned in this context. Here we find a deep interest in experiments in form, sometimes in the irrational and very often in the ambiguities of language. Spark's *The Prime of Miss Jean Brodie* (1961), probably the most internationally praised modern Scottish novel, is an ambitious experiment with

---

[1] Banks, a major writer (with a flair for the grotesque) in mainstream fiction, writes overt science fiction under the name 'Iain M. Banks'.

narrative form, restricted point of view and what can only be called a remarkable combination of the calculatedly banal and the bizarre, but it is no more experimental in these ways than scores of modern Scottish works.

Scotland's long-time interest in regional or anthropological-historical writings continues under various twentieth-century influences. The major 'regional' author is the Orkneyman, George Mackay Brown (1921–1996), who has made of Orkney a microcosm. Like other Scottish writers much influenced by setting, such as George Bruce, Edwin Muir, or Iain Smith, Brown writes in a style which is usually deceptively simple, but like them he shows a constant awareness of literary and historical tradition. Naomi Mitchison's (1897–1999) many anthropological/historical stories and novels reveal her as another who sees the Scottish setting against the long backdrop of historical process. The same is true for at least some of the works of Eric Linklater (1899–1974), who has written in many modes, but who is perhaps at his best in this category.

Mentioned above under the label of post-romantic influence is the adventure novel, *a la* R. L. Stevenson, and what we may call Empire fiction. This literary stream modulates today into this present ('regional-historical') category, as with writers like Robin Jenkins (1912–), or the comic novelist George Macdonald Fraser. In both his Scottish novels and his Empire novels, Jenkins combines the romantic love for the unusual with the perspective of history (as with Walter Scott), to which he adds a dose of twentieth-century cynicism. And Fraser's satiric novels of British military life are pretty much intended to stand the Empire novel on its head.

The Struggle for a Scottish Theatre

In the nineteenth century theatre was a popular entertainment, rather on the order of films today, and tastes were low. First rate writers ignored the Theatre or wrote closet dramas. Before Ibsen and the little-Theatre moment of its last decade or so, very little Theatre in the nineteenth century had literary merit. Scotland saw a succession of stock companies, pantomimes and literary adaptations, especially of the novels of Walter Scott. A fairly vigorous Scottish flavour was present in these popular entertainments, but the invention of the railroad made possible the playing of London-based touring companies, with their London stars, and by the late nineteenth century, Scotland had become mostly a outpost of the London stage.

The battle since that time for a truly Scottish Theatre has been long, sporadic and only slightly successful.

James Barrie (1860–1937) is the first important Scottish playwright, but he wrote primarily for the English stage. He is still the finest dramatist Scotland has produced, though his plays, *Peter Pan* excepted, have rather fallen out of the repertory. Some of his dramas, like *What Every Woman Knows* or *Mary Rose*, have Scottish elements and indeed his first major success for the stage was his own adaptation of his Scottish novel *The Little Minister* (1897). However, his London successes did nothing to further a Scottish Theatre.

The repertory movement which began to sweep through Europe in the early years of our century made possible the Glasgow Repertory Theatre (1909–1914), which produced at least one minor Scottish classic, John Ferguson's one-act, *Campbell of Kilmohr*.

Then, more importantly and also in Glasgow, came the Scottish National Players (1921–1936) who sought to present plays of 'Scottish life and characters'. This organisation produced the works of thirty Scottish dramatists, including John Brandane and James Bridie (1888–1951). Brandane's *The Glen is Mine* (1923), is one of Scotland's finest comedies. But Bridie is the first important 'Scottish' dramatist. Some of his plays were successful in London, but he wrote primarily for the Theatre in Scotland.

The relative success of the Players encouraged a number of other Theatre organisations, some of them largely amateur. The amateur Theatre movement produced a number of new plays, especially the proletarian dramas of Joe Corrie (1894–1968), whose social protest one-acts, written from 1926, were popular.

In 1943 Bridie and others founded the Glasgow Citizens' Theatre. It continues today. The Citizens is rather more European than Scottish in its outlook, but it, and the Lyceum in Edinburgh, are the unofficial National Theatres.

The Citizens revived David Lyndsay's sixteenth-century *Satire of the Three Estates* to great acclaim at the Edinburgh festival in 1948. The Festival was not originally intended to emphasise drama, but the presence there of the rapidly growing 'fringe' Theatres has made the Edinburgh Festival probably the most notable drama festival in the world. Though there is no particular emphasis on Scottish works (the Fringe does whatever it likes), the Festival has undoubtedly increased the awareness of Scotland as a theatre venue.

In 1963 the 'off-Broadway' moment reached Scotland with the founding of the Traverse Theatre in Edinburgh. This very tiny Theatre has been the most important source of new drama in Scotland. A steady stream of new plays and playwrights has come from this source. It is refreshing to report that the Traverse has recently moved to a new theatre space, not quite so tiny.

Scotland's third 'National' Theatre, the Edinburgh Civic Theatre Company, started in 1965 at the Lyceum, by which name it is now generally known. Like the Citizens, however, it is not especially Scottish in outlook.

After the Second World War, the British government began its present policy of heavily subsidising the arts. The Scottish Arts Council has provided significant funds towards the support of the Theatre in Scotland. And BBC Scotland has provided a major outlet for television and radio plays. But only a handful of 'little Theatres' are genuinely Scottish in character, and it cannot be said that Scottish drama is healthy. There have been many fine Scottish plays written in the last twenty years or so, but no major Scottish playwright has emerged. The closest is C. P. Taylor, but even Taylor moved to England to sustain his work. It is difficult for a Scottish playwright to practice his craft. The little Theatres do not generate enough money or enough attention. Even a Scottish playwright has to eat. And while Theatres such as the Traverse produce quite a number of Scottish plays, they do not keep them in the repertory. Even the most admired plays can not become classics and do not enter the permanent consciousness of audiences or students of literature. And nowhere near enough effort has been spent on keeping Scottish plays in print. Thus, the world outwith Scotland has not been exposed to them.

Prominent Themes in Modern Scottish Literature

To some degree, all the old Scottish themes carry over. The most salient is Scotland itself. Some Scottish writers have denied this, but it may be said that Scottish writers are more concerned with being Scottish than, say, most English writers are concerned with being English, or Canadian writers with being Canadian. What it means to be Scottish is still a major literary theme, not a hair less, one may assert, than it was in the nineteenth century.

Naturally, this leads to many works which describe the country itself, the romance of its past (or the defeats or the shallowness of its past), its topography, climate, its viability as a political or cultural entity.

It is not possible for a Scottish writer to select a dialect[1] for his writing without

---

[1] The word 'dialect' itself is a political word choice, as to many Scots it implies an inferior or non-standard offshoot of a proper or educated speech and is therefore an insult to the speaker or writer whose language is so described. However, the term is used here in its neutral, scholarly sense as meaning simply a type or variety of speech, by which usage any person's English – whether that of an Australian sheep farmer, a Glasgow publican or a London BBC announcer – is a form or 'dialect' of the language.

committing a political act. The Glasgow writers especially seem to be insisting that their use of Scots as it is spoken in Glasgow is a reaffirmation of the dignity and the culture of the working classes. In a sense, therefore, to write of such people without using their diction is to insult them. Other 'regional' authors have made virtually similar political/artistic statements with the Northeast diction, or even the language of the Shetlands.

And of course there is the ever-present Gaelic factor. Even this Anthology, in restricting its authors to those who write in some form of English, has been received in parts of Scotland as a political statement (i.e., insulting to Gaelic speakers or to Scotland itself). There are only about fifty thousand Gaelic speakers, but as Gaelic may be described as the most 'Scottish' of Scotland's languages, strong political forces are trying to keep it alive. There are Gaelic BBC broadcasts, Gaelic books and newspapers, and Gaelic classes in the schools. Thus Gaelic appears as a theme of modern Scottish literature, either when it is used as the medium of communication, or when its loss is bemoaned.

The interest in Scotland itself, its languages, its history, its survivability as a discrete political/cultural unit has often taken a despairing or at least nostalgic turn, where it dovetails with the disappearance of 'the good old days' of rural homogeneity, simplicity and the like. We see much of this in Edwin Muir, for example, as we do in Iain Smith. That the old world is dying, or has died, is a common theme, sometimes treated comically, but sometimes quite bitterly.

Scotland is unusual among Western countries in its working-class emphasis. An amazing amount of its prose is devoted to proletarian subject matter and ideology. This editor, for example, once attended a festival of award-winning one-act plays given at Edinburgh's Traverse Theatre. Theatre is a notoriously middle-class medium, but of the eleven plays presented by Scottish authors, ten were written in working-class Scots. Politically, Scotland has been quite left-wing in recent years and its literature reflects such a commitment. Social protest is a Scottish commonplace, in stories of disaffected youth, joblessness, uncaring government bureaucracies, monotonous public housing estates, a vapid cultural milieu (Hollywood, television), and so on.

The feminist movement arrived in Scotland a bit late, but has been a major factor since its emergence. A sizeable number of Scotland's major writers in our day are women, and what might be called the woman's point of view is now omnipresent. One associates Liz Lochhead (1947–), Janice Galloway (1956–), and Kathleen Jamie (1962–) with this movement, but examples are legion.

Finally, in common with twentieth-century literature everywhere, there is occasional emphasis upon nihilism – sometimes seen in just the fashionable (and profitable) themes of illicit drugs and crime, but sometimes a real sense of the irrationality of language and behaviour in the modern world, as in the bizarre works of Alasdair Gray, Alan Warner, or Frank Kuppner (1951–). Like everyone else, Scottish writers are a little mad.

J[ames] Keir Hardie (1856 – 1915)

Hardie was one of Scotland's most influential political thinkers and speakers. Along with Robert Cunninghame Graham, he founded the Scottish Labour Party, and is considered one of the fathers of the Socialist movement in Britain. In 1892, he was elected to Parliament. The brief Parliamentary address which follows was the first Socialist proposal brought before that legislative body. (See R. C. Graham's tribute to Hardie, 'With the North East Wind', Vol. II. 1223.)

On the Necessity for Socialism

I rise to move the motion that stands in my name.[1] After the discussion to which we have just listened, in which one section of the community has claimed support from the State and shown that German steamship lines have an advantage over British lines because they are subsidised by the State, I trust the House will listen to the logical outcome of these arguments.

I make no apology for bringing the question of Socialism before the House of Commons. It has long commanded the attention of the best minds in the country. It is a growing force in the thought of the world, and whether men agree or disagree with it, they have to reckon with it, and may as well begin by understanding it. In the German Empire, Socialism is the one section of political thought which is making headway, and to an extent which is, I believe, alarming the powers that be. Over fifty Socialist members occupy seats in the German Reichstag, between forty and fifty in the Chamber of Deputies in France, and between thirty and forty in the Belgian Parliament. Socialism on the Continent therefore is an established and recognised fact so far as its entry into politics is concerned, and if it be argued that while that may be true of the Continent it is not true of this country, I reply that the facts and conditions now existing in this country are such as to make it extremely probable that the progress of Socialism in this country will be at a more rapid pace than in any other country in Europe.

Needless to say, at this hour of the evening[2] it is impossible for me to treat this subject adequately, and I will therefore summarise briefly the principal arguments that it was my intention to submit to the House had time permitted. I begin by pointing out that the growth of our national wealth, instead of bringing comfort to the masses of the people, is imposing additional burdens on them. We are told on high authority that some 300 years ago the total wealth of the English nation was £100,000,000 sterling. At the beginning of the last century it had increased to £2,000,000,000, and this year it is estimated to be £13,000,000,000. While our population during the last century increased three and a half times, the wealth of

---

[1] 'That considering the increasing burden which the private ownership of land and capital is imposing upon the industrious and useful classes of the community, the poverty and destitution and general moral and physical deterioration resulting from a competitive system of wealth production which aims primarily at profit making, the alarming growth of trusts and syndicates able by reason of their great wealth to influence governments and plunge peaceful nations into war to serve their interests, this House is of the opinion that such a condition of affairs constitutes a menace to the well-being of the Realm, and calls for legislation designed to remedy the same by inaugurating a Socialist Commonwealth founded upon the common ownership of land and capital, production for use and not for profit, and equality of opportunity for every citizen.'

[2] 11:35.

the community increased over six times.

But one factor in our national life remained with us all through the century and is with us still, and that is that at the bottom of the social scale there is a mass of poverty and misery equal in magnitude to that which obtained 100 years ago. I submit that the true test of progress is not the accumulation of wealth in the hands of a few, but the elevation of a people as a whole.

I admit frankly that a considerable improvement was made in the condition of the working people during the last century. At the beginning of the nineteenth century the nation industrially was sick almost unto death. It was at that time passing from the old system of handicraft, under which every man was his own employer and his own capitalist and traded direct with his customer, to the factory system which the introduction of machinery brought into existence. During these 100 years the wealth of the nation accumulated, and the condition of the working classes as compared with the early years of the century improved, but I respectfully submit to the House that there was more happiness, more comfort, and more independence before machinery began to accumulate wealth. ['No.']

'No' is not an argument. I ask honourable Gentlemen opposite to listen and refute my statements if they are incorrect. I will quote an authority on this point whose words deserve respect. I mean the late Professor Thorold Rogers, who supports that view in his *Six Centuries of Work and Wages*. The high standard of comfort reached by the labouring classes at the end of the last century has not brought them that happiness which obtained in England 300 years ago when there was no machinery, no large capitalists, no private property in land as we know it today, and when every person had the right to use the land for the purpose of producing food for himself and his family.

I said that an improvement was made during the last century, but I would qualify that statement in this respect – that practically the whole of that improvement was made during the first seventy-five years. During the last quarter of the century the condition of the working classes has been practically stationary. There have been slight increases of wages here and reductions of hours there, but the landlord with his increased rent has more than absorbed any advantage that may have been gained. I could quote figures, if that statement is disputed, showing that in all the industrial parts of the country rents during the past twenty years have been going up by leaps and bounds. I will refer to one authority whom even honourable Gentlemen opposite will not dare to call into question. Viscount Goschen, when First Lord of the Admiralty, in defending the Government for refusing to give increased wages to labourers at Woolwich Arsenal, said on the 14th of April, 1899:

> If the position of the labourers at Woolwich and Deptford was as described, it was rather due to sweating landlords than to the rate of wages. The wages had been raised 20 per cent in the last ten years, and the house rents 50 per cent. It was constantly the case in those districts that the increase of wages only led to a larger sum going into the pockets of the landlords, and he was even told that some of the men who were locally the loudest in the cry for justice to the labourers were owners of cottage property who would benefit if the wages were raised.

In view of a statement of that kind, made by such an authority, I submit that my assertion is not without substance.

I come now to the causes which have forced thinking people of all ranks of society to reconsider their attitude towards Socialism. I refer particularly to the great and alarming growth of what are known as trusts and syndicates in connection with industry. We have hitherto been accustomed to regard a trust as a distinctively American product. That cannot be said any longer. Let me name a few of the trusts and combinations which have been formed in this country within recent years. Amongst others there are the Cotton Thread Trust, with capital of £9,750,000; the Fine Cotton Spinners and Doublers, with a capital of over £5,000,000; the Bradford Dyers, £3,750,000; the Bleachers' and Calico Printers' Association, £14,000,000; Cory and Co., London, £2,600,000; Rickett and Co., London,

£900,000; Armstrong, Whitworth, and Co., engineers, over £4,000,000; the Associated Cement Makers, over £7,000,000; the well-known Castle Line, £2,000,000; the Wilson, Furness, and Leyland Line and the Leyland Line, between them, £3,450,000.

These are figures which might well give the House of Commons pause and cause it to reconsider its attitude towards the whole question of political economy. So long as industry is conducted by individuals competing one with another there is a chance of the article produced being supplied at an approximation to its market value, but competition has been found to be destructive of the interests of the owners and possessors of capital in this as in every other country. Three or four firms which formerly entered one market and competed with each other find it conducive to their interests to combine, thereby creating a monopoly which enables them to charge whatever price they like and to treat their workpeople in any way that seems good to them.

I approach this question of trusts from two points of view: first, from that of the consumer, who is at the mercy of an uncontrolled and, it may be, perfectly unscrupulous combination which cares only for dividends; and secondly – and this is to me of greater concern – from that of the worker. The consumer may protect himself, but the worker is helpless. I could quote instance after instance of the most scandalous and shameless persecution of workmen by these big trusts and combinations, railway monopolies and the like. I will refer only to one case, which occurred last year in connection with the Great Eastern Railway. An employee was elected to serve on the Poplar Borough Council, exercising a right conferred upon him by this House, and being elected to a body created by this House. He was dismissed from his employment because he had permitted himself to be elected to apply a part of his own time to the public welfare without having obtained the leave of his employers. As John Stuart Mill – himself a convert to Socialism, despite the fact that as a political economist of the older school he had written against the system before he understood its full meaning and the necessity for it – wrote:

> The social problem of the future we consider to be how to unite the greatest liberty
> of action with a common ownership in the raw material of the globe and an equal
> participation in all the benefits of combined labour. [*Autobiography* (1873)]

We are rapidly approaching a point when the nation will be called upon to decide between an uncontrolled monopoly, conducted for the benefit and in the interests of its principal shareholders, and a monopoly owned, controlled, and manipulated by the State in the interests of the nation as a whole. I do not require to go far afield for arguments to support that part of my statement concerning the danger which the aggregation of wealth in a few hands is bringing upon us. This House and the British nation knows to their cost the danger which comes from allowing men to grow rich and permitting them to use their wealth to corrupt the press, to silence the pulpit, to degrade our national life, and to bring reproach and shame upon a great people, in order that a few unscrupulous scoundrels might be able to add to their ill-gotten gains. The war in South Africa is a millionaires' war. Our troubles in China are due to the desire of the capitalists to exploit the people of that country as they would fain exploit the people of South Africa. Much of the jealousy and bad blood existing between this country and France is traceable to the fact that we went to war in Egypt to suppress a popular uprising seeking freedom for the people, in order that the interest of our bondholders might be secured.

Socialism, by placing land and the instruments of production in the hands of the community, eliminates only the idle, useless class at both ends of the scale. Half a million of the people of this country benefit by the present system; the remaining millions of toilers and businessmen do not. The pursuit of wealth corrupts the manhood of men. We are called upon at the beginning of the twentieth century to decide the question propounded in the Sermon on the Mount as to whether or not we will worship God or Mammon. The present day is a Mammon-worshipping age. Socialism proposes to dethrone the brute-god Mammon and to lift humanity into its place.

I beg to submit in this very imperfect fashion the resolution on the Paper, merely premising that the last has not been heard of the Socialist movement either in the country or on the floor of this House, but that, just as sure as Radicalism democratised the system of Government politically in the last century, so will Socialism democratise the country industrially during the century upon which we have just entered.

Pittendrigh Macgillivray (1856 – 1938)

Glances

O weel I mind the bonnie morn,
Richt early in the day,
When he cam' in by oor toun end
To buy a sou o' hay.

For O he was a handsome lad,
An' weel did cock his beaver. –
He gar't★ my heart play pit-a-pat;   made
Yet – speered★ but for my faether!   asked

I turned aboot and gied a cast
That plainly said – 'Ye deevil! –   10
Although ye be a braw young lad
Ye needna be uncevil!'

He glower't at me like ane gaen wud★ –   mad
Wi' his daurin' rovin' e'en;
At that I leuch★ and wi' a fling   laughed
Flew roun' the bourtree screen.

The Return
(A Piper's Vaunting)

Och hey, for the splendour of tartans!
And hey for the dirk and the targe★!   shield
The race that was as the Spartans
Shall return again to the charge.

Shall come back again to the heather,
Like eagles, with beak and with claws
To take and to scatter for ever
The Sasunnach★ thieves and their laws.   English

Och, then, for the bonnet and feather! –
The pipe and its vaunting clear;   10
Och, then, for the glens and the heather!
And all that the Gael holds dear.

Desire

Would she were on horseback and I with her.
Facing fleetly this wind by wood and shore,
Through sun-fleck and shadow – on, evermore;
Heart a-throbbing to this day's storm and fire –
Beating like wind and wave, in wild desire. –
The lift, the lilt – hoof-clink, and forest roar.
Old days behind – a life set free before –
Free! as the Wind sings to her pine-wood lyre.

Oh, to be riding so with her this day. –
Could we but cross the march of Elfin land,   10
Where time runs not by the measure of sand:
Or, enchanted ride on some endless way;
Kissed by the winds tasting of salt sea spray –
Lovers love-lost, by unknown wold and strand.

John Davidson (1857 – 1909)

Davidson was one of the major Scottish poets of the late nineteenth century. He wrote in most genres – novels, plays, essays, short stories, and a wide variety of verse forms. He is one of the first 'modern' Scottish poets, much interested in the new ideas of his day – such as the poverty of the working class and the conflict of science and religion. The colloquial diction and social protest of his most famous poem, 'Thirty Bob a Week', has caused him to be considered rather a poetic realist, but it represents only a small part of his range. In fact, much of his work is in the end-of-the-century style of The Yellow Book, to which he was a contributor. He was a restless experimenter for most of his career. Bedevilled for a good part of his lifetime by poverty, illness, and – as he saw it – literary failure, he committed suicide in 1909. His Scottish themes are few, as he spent much of adult life in England, especially London.

Thirty Bob a Week

I couldn't touch a stop and turn a screw,
And set the blooming world a-work for me
Like such as cut their teeth – I hope, like you –
On the handle of a skeleton gold key;
I cut mine on a leek, which I eat it every week:
I'm a clerk at thirty bob as you can see.

But I don't allow it's luck and all a toss;
There's no such thing as being starred and crossed;[1]
It's just the power of some to be a boss,
And the bally power of others to be bossed: 10
I face the music, sir; you bet I ain't a cur;
Strike me lucky if I don't believe I'm lost.

For like a mole I journey in the dark,
A-travelling along the underground*   subway
From my Pillared Halls and broad Suburban Park,
To come the daily dull official round;
And home again at night with my pipe all alight,
A-scheming how to count ten bob a pound.

And it's often very cold and very wet,
And my missis stitches towels for a hunks;   20
And the Pillared Halls is half of it to let –
Three rooms about the size of travelling trunks.
And we cough, my wife and I, to dislocate a sigh,
When the noisy little kids are in their bunks.

But you never hear her do a growl or whine,
For she's made of flint and roses, very odd;
And I've got to cut my meaning rather fine,
Or I'd blubber, for I'm made of greens and sod:
So p'r'aps we are in Hell for all that I can tell,
And lost and damned and served up hot to God.   30

I ain't blaspheming, Mr Silver-tongue;
I'm saying things a bit beyond your art:
Of all the rummy starts you ever sprung,
Thirty bob a week's the rummiest start.
With your science and your books and your the'ries about spooks,
Did you ever hear of looking in your heart?

I didn't mean your pocket, Mr, no:
I mean that having children and a wife,
With thirty bob on which to come and go,
Isn't dancing to the tabor and the fife: 40
When it doesn't make you drink, by Heaven! it makes you think,
And notice curious items about life.

I step into my heart and there I meet
A god-almighty devil singing small,
Who would like to shout and whistle in the street,
And squelch the passers flat against the wall;
If the whole world was a cake he had the power to take,
He would take it, ask for more, and eat it all.

And I meet a sort of simpleton beside,
The kind that life is always giving beans;   50

---

[1] 'Star-crossed' or ill-fated.

With thirty bob a week to keep a bride
He fell in love and married in his teens:
At thirty bob he stuck; but he knows it isn't luck:
He knows the seas are deeper than tureens.

And the god-almighty devil and the fool
That meet me in the High Street on the strike,
When I walk about my heart a-gathering wool,
Are my good and evil angels if you like.
And both of them together in every kind of weather
Ride me like a double-seated bike.   60

That's rough a bit and needs its meaning curled.
But I have a high old hot un in my mind –
A most engrugious notion of the world,
That leaves your lightning 'rithmetic behind –
I give it at a glance when I say 'There ain't no chance,
Nor nothing of the lucky-lottery kind.'

And it's this way that I make it out to be:
No fathers, mothers, countries, climates – none;
Not Adam was responsible for me,
Nor society, nor systems, nary one: 70
A little sleeping seed, I woke – I did, indeed –
A million years before the blooming sun.

I woke because I thought the time had come;
Beyond my will there was no other cause;
And everywhere I found myself at home,
Because I chose to be the thing I was;
And in whatever shape of mollusk or of ape
I always went according to the laws.

I was the love that chose my mother out;
I joined two lives and from the union burst;   80
My weakness and my strength without a doubt
Are mine alone for ever from the first:
It's just the very same with difference in the name
As 'Thy will be done.' You say it if you durst!

They say it daily up and down the land
As easy as you take a drink, it's true;
But the difficultest go to understand,
And the difficultest job a man can do,
Is to come it brave and meek with thirty bob a week,
And feel that that's the proper thing for you.   90

It's a naked child against a hungry wolf;
It's playing bowls upon a splitting wreck;
It's walking on a string across a gulf
With millstones fore-and-aft about your neck;
But the thing is daily done by many and many a one;
And we fall, face forward, fighting, on the deck.

The Rev. Habakkuk McGruther of Cape Wrath, in 1879

God save old Scotland! Such a cry
Comes raving north from Edinburgh.
It shakes the earth, and rends the sky,
It thrills and fills true hearts with sorrow.
'There's no such place, by God's good grace,
As smoky hell's dusk-flaming cavern?'
Ye fools, beware, or ye may share
The hottest brew of Satan's tavern.

Ye surely know that Scotland's fate
Controls the whole wide world's well-being;   10
And well ye know her godly state
Depends on faith in sin's hell-feeing.
And would ye then, false-hearted men,
From Scotland rape her dear damnation?
Take from her hell, then take as well
From space the law of gravitation.

A battle-cry for every session
In these wild-whirling, heaving last days:
'Discard for ever the Confession;
Abolish, if you choose, the Fast-days;   20
Let Bible knowledge in school and college
No more be taught – we'll say, 'All's well.'
'Twill scarcely grieve us, if you but leave us
For Scotland's use, in Heaven's name, Hell.'

The Wastrel

An eyesore to the tourist on the shoulder of the knock
Above the green-fledged larches where the squirrel keeps its house,
The pale dissenting chapel, like a pharos on a rock,
With strong, pathetic preaching that the very dead might rouse,
Was lighted for an hour and twenty minutes by the clock,
While the cushats moaned and muttered deep among the rustling boughs.

With Conybeare-and-Howson laid on thick for local hue,
And Meyer's and Lange's comments to elucidate the text,
The minister exhibited a panoramic view
Of the story of the wastrel and the father that he vext: 10
Of little but his Bible and his creed the preacher knew,
And dogma like a razor his emotions had unsexed.

Then came the modern instance, and the congregation stirred,
And scrutinised the pew in which the preacher's family sat.
'I knew it,' thought each member, 'at the very opening word!'
And felt as perspicacious as a dog that smells a rat:
The preacher's wife and daughters seized their Bibles when they heard;
And his son, as red as poppies, stooped and glanced at this and that.

'But recently,' the preacher said, 'to London town there went
A youth from our vicinity against his father's wish;   20
To make a fortune – honestly, if possible – he meant,
Forgetting quite how God examines both sides of the dish:
Unless a holy life exhale to Heaven a savoury scent,
We know how very profitless the loaves are and the fish.' . . .

The wife and daughters shrivel up and shut their eyes and cry,
As the preacher drives the lancet home and lays their heart-strings bare;
But the wastrel, cool and clammy, feels a wind of fate go by,
And hears his pulses clank above monition, praise and prayer –
'Oho, for London Town again, where folk in peace can die,
And the thunder-and-lightning devil of a train that takes me there!'

In Romney Marsh

As I went down to Dymchurch Wall,
I heard the South sing o'er the land;
I saw the yellow sunlight fall
On knolls where Norman churches stand.

And ringing shrilly, taut and lithe,
Within the wind a core of sound,
The wire from Romney town to Hythe
Alone its airy journey wound.

A veil of purple vapour flowed
And trailed its fringe along the Straits;   10
The upper air like sapphire glowed;
And roses filled Heaven's central gates.

Masts in the offing wagged their tops;
The swinging waves pealed on the shore;
The saffron beach, all diamond drops
And beads of surge, prolonged the roar.

As I came up from Dymchurch Wall,
I saw above the Downs' low crest
The crimson brands of sunset fall,
Flicker and fade from out the west.   20

Night sank: like flakes of silver fire
The stars in one great shower came down;
Shrill blew the wind; and shrill the wire
Rang out from Hythe to Romney town.

The darkly shining salt sea drops
Streamed as the waves clashed on the shore;
The beach, with all its organ stops
Pealing again, prolonged the roar.

Spring Song

About the flowerless land adventurous bees
Pickeering hum; the rooks debate, divide,
With many a hoarse aside,
In solemn conclave on the budding trees;
Larks in the skies and ploughboys o'er the leas
Carol as if the winter ne'er had been;
The very owl comes out to greet the sun;
Rivers high-hearted run;
And hedges mantle with a flush of green.

The curlew calls me where the salt winds blow;   10
His troubled note dwells mournfully and dies;
Then the long echo cries
Deep in my heart. Ah, surely I must go!
For there the tides, moon-haunted, ebb and flow
And there the seaboard murmurs resonant;
The waves their interwoven fugue repeat
And brooding surges beat
A slow, melodious, continual chant.

The Boat Is Chafing

The boat is chafing at our long delay,
And we must leave too soon
The spicy sea-pinks and the inborne spray,
The tawny sands, the moon.

Keep us, O Thetis, in our western flight.
Watch from thy pearly throne
Our vessel, plunging deeper into night
To reach a land unknown.

The Unknown

To brave and to know the unknown
Is the high world's motive and mark,
Though the way with snares be strewn.

The earth itself alone
Wheels through the light and the dark
Onward to meet the unknown.

Each soul, upright or prone,
While the owl sings or the lark,
Must pass where the bones are strewn.

Power on the loftiest throne   10
Can fashion no certain ark
That shall stem and outride the unknown.

Beauty must doff her zone,
Strength trudge unarmed and stark
Though the way with eyes be strewn.

This only can atone,
The high world's motive and mark,
To brave and to know the unknown
Though the way with fire be strewn.

A Ballad of Hell

'A letter from my love today!
Oh, unexpected, dear appeal!'
She struck a happy tear away,
And broke the crimson seal.

'My love, there is no help on earth,
No help in heaven; the dead-man's bell
Must toll our wedding; our first hearth
Must be the well-paved floor of hell.'

The colour died from out her face.
Her eyes like ghostly candles shone;   10
She cast dread looks about the place,
Then clenched her teeth and read right on.

'I may not pass the prison door;
Here must I rot from day to day,
Unless I wed whom I abhor,
My cousin, Blanche of Valencay.

'At midnight with my dagger keen,
I'll take my life; it must be so.
Meet me in hell tonight, my queen,
For weal and woe.'   20

She laughed, although her face was wan;
She girded on her golden belt;
She took her jewelled ivory fan,
And at her glowing missal knelt.

Then rose, 'And am I mad?' she said.
She broke her fan, her belt untied;
With leather girt herself instead,
And stuck a dagger at her side.

She waited, shuddering in her room,
Till sleep had fallen on all the house.   30
She never flinched; she faced her doom;
The two must sin to keep their vows.

Then out into the night she went,
And stopping crept by hedge and tree;
Her rose-bush flung a snare of scent,
And caught a happy memory.

She fell, and lay a minute's space;
She tore the sward in her distress;
The dewy grass refreshed her face;
She rose and ran with lifted dress.   40

She started like a morn-caught ghost
Once when the moon came out and stood
To watch; the naked road she crossed,
And dived into the murmuring wood.

The branches snatched her streaming cloak;
A live thing shrieked; she made no stay.
She hurried to the trysting-oak.
Right well she knew the way.

Without a pause she bared her breast,
And drove the dagger home and fell,   50
And lay like one that takes her rest,
And died and wakened up in hell.

She bathed her spirit in the flame,
And near the centre took her post.
From all sides to her ears there came,
The dreary anguish of the lost.

The devil started at her side,
Comely, and tall, and black as jet.
'I am young Malespina's bride;
Has he come hither yet?'   60

'My poppet, welcome to your bed.'
'Is Malespina here?'
'Not he! Tomorrow he must wed
His cousin Blanche, my dear.'

'You lie, he died with me tonight.'
'Not he, it was a plot.' 'You lie.'
'My dear, I never lie outright.'
'We died at midnight, he and I.'

The devil went. Without a groan
She, gathered up in one fierce prayer,   70
Took root in hell's midst all alone,
And waited for him there.

She dared to make herself at home
Amidst the wail, the uneasy stir.
The blood-stained flame that filled the dome,
Scentless and silent, shrouded her.

How long she stayed I cannot tell;
But when she felt his perfidy,
She marched across the floor of hell;
And all the damned stood up to see.   80

The devil stopped her at the brink.
She shook him off; she cried, 'Away!'
'My dear, you have gone mad, I think.'
'I was betrayed; – I will not stay.'

Across the weltering deep she ran;
A stranger thing was never seen:
The damned stood silent to a man.
They saw the great gulf set between.

To her it seemed a meadow fair;
And flowers sprang up about her feet.   90
She entered heaven; she climbed the stair;
And knelt down at the mercy-seat.

Seraphs and saints with one great voice
Welcomed that soul that knew no fear;
Amazed to find it could rejoice,
Hell raised a hoarse half-human cheer.

A Ballad of a Nun

From Eastertide to Eastertide
For ten long years her patient knees
Engraved the stones – the fittest bride
Of Christ in all the diocese.

She conquered every earthly lust;
The abbess loved her more and more;
And, as a mark of perfect trust,
Made her the keeper of the door.

High on a hill the convent hung,
Across a duchy looking down,   10
Where everlasting mountains flung
Their shadows over tower and town.

The jewels of their lofty snows
In constellations flashed at night;
Above their crests the moon arose;
The deep earth shuddered with delight.

Long ere she left her cloudy bed,
Still dreaming in the orient land,
On many a mountain's happy head
Dawn lightly laid her rosy hand.   20

The adventurous sun took Heaven by storm;
Clouds scattered largesses of rain;
The sounding cities, rich and warm,
Smouldered and glittered in the plain.

Sometimes it was a wandering wind,
Sometimes the fragrance of the pine,
Sometimes the thought how others sinned,
That turned her sweet blood into wine.

Sometimes she heard a serenade
Complaining sweetly far away: 30
She said, 'A young man woos a maid';
And dreamt of love till break of day.

Then would she ply her knotted scourge
Until she swooned; but evermore
She had the same red sin to purge,
Poor, passionate keeper of the door.

For still night's starry scroll unfurled,
And still the day came like a flood;
It was the greatness of the world
That made her long to use her blood.   40

In winter-time when Lent drew nigh,
And hill and plain were wrapped in snow,
She watched beneath the frosty sky
The nearest city nightly glow.

Like peals of airy bells outworn
Faint laughter died above her head
In gusts of broken music borne;
'They keep the Carnival,' she said.

Her hungry heart devoured the town:
'Heaven save me by a miracle!   50
Unless God sends an angel down,
Thither I go though it were Hell.'

She dug her nails deep in her breast,
Sobbed, shrieked, and straight withdrew the bar:
A fledgling flying from the nest,
A pale moth rushing to a star.

Fillet and veil in strips she tore;
Her golden tresses floated wide;
The ring and bracelet that she wore
As Christ's betrothed, she cast aside.   60

'Life's dearest meaning I shall probe;
Lo, I shall taste of love at last!
Away!' She doffed her outer robe,
And sent it sailing down the blast.

Her body seemed to warm the wind;
With bleeding feet o'er ice she ran:
'I leave the righteous God behind;
I go to worship sinful man.'

She reached the sounding city's gate;
No question did the warder ask: 70
He passed her in: 'Welcome, wild mate!'
He thought her some fantastic mask.

Half-naked through the town she went;
Each footstep left a bloody mark;
Crowds followed her with looks intent;
Her bright eyes made the torches dark.

Alone and watching in the street
There stood a grave youth nobly dressed;
To him she knelt and kissed his feet;
Her face her great desire confessed.   80

Straight to his house the nun he led:
'Strange lady, what would you with me?'
'Your love, your love, sweet lord,' she said;
'I bring you my virginity.'

He healed her bosom with a kiss;
She gave him all her passion's hoard;
And sobbed and murmured ever, 'This
Is life's great meaning, dear, my lord.

'I care not for my broken vow;
Though God should come in thunder soon,   90
I am sister to the mountains now,
And sister to the sun and moon.'

Through all the towns of Belmarie
She made a progress like a queen.
'She is,' they said, 'whate'er she be,
The strangest woman ever seen.

'From fairyland she must have come,
Or else she is a mermaiden.'
Some said she was a ghoul, and some
A heathen goddess born again.   100

But soon her fire to ashes burned;
Her beauty changed to haggardness;
Her golden hair to silver turned;
The hour came of her last caress.

At midnight from her lonely bed
She rose, and said, 'I have had my will.'
The old ragged robe she donned, and fled
Back to the convent on the hill.

Half-naked as she went before,
She hurried to the city wall,   110
Unnoticed in the rush and roar
And splendour of the carnival.

No question did the warder ask:
Her ragged robe, her shrunken limb,
Her dreadful eyes. 'It is no mask;
It is a she-wolf, gaunt and grim.'

She ran across the icy plain;
Her worn blood curdled in the blast;
Each footstep left a crimson stain;
The white-faced moon looked on aghast.   120

She said between her chattering jaws,
'Deep peace is mine, I cease to strive;
Oh, comfortable convent laws,
That bury foolish nuns alive!

'A trowel for my passing-bell,
A little bed within the wall,
A coverlet of stones; how well
I there shall keep the Carnival.'

Like tired bells chiming in their sleep,
The wind faint peals of laughter bore;   130
She stopped her ears and climbed the steep,
And thundered at the convent door.

It opened straight; she entered in,
And at the wardress' feet fell prone:
'I come to purge away my sin;
Bury me, close me up in stone.'

The wardress raised her tenderly;
She touched her wet and fast-shut eyes:
'Look sister; sister, look at me;
Look, can you see through my disguise?'   140

She looked and saw her own sad face,
And trembled, wondering, 'Who are thou?'
'God sent me down to fill your place:
I am the Virgin Mary now.'

And with the word, God's mother shone:
The wanderer whispered, 'Mary, hail!'
The vision helped her to put on
Bracelet and fillet, ring and veil.

'You are sister to the mountains now,
And sister to the day and night;   150
Sister to God.' And on the brow
She kissed her thrice, and left her sight.

While dreaming in her cloudy bed,
Far in the crimson orient land,
On many a mountain's happy head
Dawn lightly laid her rosy hand.

A Runnable Stag

When the pods went pop on the broom, green broom,
And apples began to be golden-skinned,
We harboured a stag in the priory coomb★,   valley
And we feathered★ his trail up-wind, up-wind,   chased
     We feathered his trail up-wind –
     A stag of warrant, a stag, a stag,
     A runnable stag, a kingly crop★,   of antlers
     Brow, bay and tray and three on top,[1]
     A stag, a runnable stag.

---

[1] Brow, bay and tray are the first, second and third branches on the antler.

Then the huntsman's horn rang yap, yap, yap,   10
And 'Forwards' we heard the harbourer★ shout;   starter
But 'twas only a brocket[1] that broke a gap
In the beechen underwood, driven out,
From the underwood antlered out.
    By warrant and might of the stag, the stag,
    The runnable stag, whose lordly mind
    Was bent on sleep, though beamed and tined
    He stood, a runnable stag.

So we tufted★ the covert till afternoon   beat, drove
With Tinkerman's Pup and Bell-of-the-North;   20
And hunters were sulky and hounds out of tune
Before we tufted the right stag forth,
Before we tufted him forth,
    The stag of warrant, the wily stag,
    The runnable stag with his kingly crop,
    Brow, bay and tray and three on top,
    The royal and runnable stag.

It was Bell-of-the-North and Tinkerman's Pup
That stuck to the scent till the copse was drawn.
'Tally ho! tally ho!' and the hunt was up,   30
The tufters whipped and the pack laid on,
The resolute pack laid on,
    And the stag of warrant away at last,
    The runnable stag, the same, the same,
    His hoofs on fire, his horns like flame,
    A stag, a runnable stag.

'Yet your gelding be – if you check or chide
He stumbles at once and you're out of the hunt;
For three hundred gentlemen, able to ride,
On hunters accustomed to bear the brunt,   40
Accustomed to bear the brunt,
    Are after the runnable stag, the stag,
    The runnable stag with his kingly crop,
    Brow, bay and tray and three on top,
    The right, the runnable stag.'

By perilous paths in coomb and dell,
The heather, the rocks, and the river-bed,
The pace grew hot, for the scent lay well,
And a runnable stag goes right ahead.
    The quarry went right ahead –   50
    Ahead, ahead, and fast and far;
    His antlered crest, his cloven hoof,
    Brow, bay and tray and three aloof,
    The stag, the runnable stag.

---

[1] Immature stag.

For a matter of twenty miles and more,
By the densest hedge and the highest wall,
Through herds of bullocks he baffled the lore
Of harbourer, huntsman, hounds and all,
Of harbourer, hounds and all –
    The stag of warrant, the wily stag,   60
    For twenty miles, and five and five,
    He ran, and he never was caught alive,
    This stag, this runnable stag.

When he turned at bay in the leafy gloom,
In the emerald gloom where the brook ran deep
He heard in the distance the rollers boom,
And he saw in a vision of peaceful sleep
In a wonderful vision of sleep,
    A stag of warrant, a stag, a stag,
    A runnable stag in a jewelled bed,   70
    Under the sheltering ocean dead,
    A stag, a runnable stag.

So a fateful hope lit up his eye,
And he opened his nostrils wide again,
And he tossed his branching antlers high
As he headed the hunt down the Charlock glen,
As he raced down the echoing glen –
    For five miles more, the stag, the stag,
    For twenty miles, and five and five,
    Not to be caught now, dead or alive,   80
    The stag, the runnable stag.

Three hundred gentlemen, able to ride,
Three hundred horses as gallant and free,
Beheld him escape on the evening tide,
Far out till he sank in the Severn Sea,
Till he sank in the depths of the sea –
    The stag, the buoyant stag, the stag
    That slept at last in a jewelled bed
    Under the sheltering ocean spread,
    The stag, the runnable stag.

Closes and Courts and Lanes

Closes and courts and lanes,
Devious, clustered thick,
The thoroughfare, mains and drains,
People and mortar and brick,
Wood, metal, machinery, brains,
Pen and composing stick:
Fleet Street,[1] but exquisite flame

---

[1] Traditionally, the home of London's chief newspapers.

In the nebula once ere day and night
Began their travail, or earth became,
And all was passionate light.   10

Networks of wire overland,
Conduits under the sea,
Aerial message from strand to strand
By lightning that travels free,
Hither in haste to hand
Tidings of destiny
These tingling nerves of the world's affairs
Deliver remorseless, rendering still
The fall of empires, the price of shares,
The record of good and ill.   20

Tidal the traffic goes
Citywards out of the town;
Townwards the evening ebb o'erflows
This highway of old renown,
When the fog-woven curtains close,
And the urban night comes down,0
Where souls are spilt and intellects spent
O'er news vociferant near and far,
From Hesperus hard to the Orient,
From dawn to the evening star.   30

This is the royal refrain
That burdens the boom and the thud
Of omnibus, mobus, wain,
And the hoofs on the beaten mud,
From the Griffin at Chancery Lane
To the portal of old King Lud –
Fleet Street, diligent night and day,
Of news the mart and the burnished hearth,
Seven hundred paces of narrow way,
A notable bit of the earth.   40

London

Athwart the sky a lowly sigh
From west to east the sweet wind carried;
The sun stood still on Primrose Hill;
His light in all the city tarried;
The clouds on viewless columns bloomed
Like smouldering lilies unconsumed.

'Oh sweetheart, see! How shadowy,
Of some occult magician's rearing,
Or swung in space of heaven's grace
Dissolving, dimly reappearing,   10
Afloat upon ethereal tides
St Paul's above the city rides!'

A rumour broke through the thin smoke,
Enwreathing abbey, tower, and palace,
The parks, the squares, the thoroughfares,
The million-peopled lanes and alleys,
An ever-muttering prisoned storm,
The heart of London beating warm.

Snow

I
'Who affirms that crystals are alive?'
I affirm it, let who will deny: –
Crystals are engendered, wax and thrive,
Wane and wither; I have seen them die.

Trust me, masters, crystals have their day,
Eager to attain the perfect norm,
Lit with purpose, potent to display
Facet, angle, colour, beauty, form.

II
Water-crystals need for flower and root
Sixty clear degrees, no less, no more;   10
Snow, so fickle, still in this acute
Angle thinks, and learns no other lore:

Such its life, and such its pleasure is,
Such its art and traffic, such its gain,
Evermore in new conjunctions this
Admirable angle to maintain.

Crystalcraft in every flower and flake
Snow exhibits, of the welkin free:
Crystalline are crystals for the sake,
All and singular, of crystalry.   20

Yet does every crystal of the snow
Individualise, a seedling sown
Broadcast, but instinct with power to grow
Beautiful in beauty of its own.

Every flake with all its prongs and dints
Burns ecstatic as a new-lit star:
Men are not more diverse, fingerprints
More dissimilar than snowflakes are.

Worlds of men and snow endure, increase,
Woven of power and passion to defy   30
Time and travail: only races cease,
Individual men and crystals die.

III

Jewelled shapes of snow whose feathery showers,
Fallen or falling wither at a breath,
All afraid are they, and loath as flowers
Beasts and men to tread the way to death.

Once I saw upon an object-glass,
Martyred underneath a microscope,
One elaborate snow-flake slowly pass,
Dying hard, beyond the reach of hope.   40

Still from shape to shape the crystal changed,
Writhing in its agony; and still,
Less and less elaborate, arranged
Potently the angle of its will.

Tortured to a simple final form,
Angles six and six divergent beams,
Lo, in death it touched the perfect norm
Verifying all its crystal dreams!

IV

Such the noble tragedy of one
Martyred snow-flake. Who can tell the fate   50
Heinous and uncouth of showers undone,
Fallen in cities! – showers that expiate

Errant lives from polar worlds adrift
Where the great millennial snows abide;
Castaways from mountain-chains that lift
Snowy summits in perennial pride;

Nomad snows, or snows in evil day
Born to urban ruin, to be tossed,
Trampled, shovelled, plowed and swept away
Down the seething sewers: all the frost   60

Flowers of heaven melted up with lees,
Offal, recrement, but every flake
Showing to the last in fixed degrees
Perfect crystals for the crystal's sake.

V

Usefulness of snow is but a chance
Here in temperate climes with winter sent,
Sheltering earth's prolonged hibernal trance:
All utility is accident.

Sixty clear degrees the joyful snow,
Practising economy of means,   70
Fashions endless beauty in, and so
Glorifies the universe with scenes

Arctic and Antarctic: stainless shrouds,
Ermine woven in silvery frost, attire
Peaks in every land among the clouds
Crowned with snows to catch the morning's fire.

Miss Armstrong's Circumstances

After all, my friends have been mistaken; my experiences are not nearly so exciting as they appeared to be when I saw them through their spectacles. They insisted that I had only to write down an exact chronicle of the days of the years of my life to be the author of a record as interesting as any novel. I was pretty well persuaded of the truth of their judgement when I began to write my history; but I had not proceeded far when doubts began to spring up, and by the time I had arrived at my seventh chapter, and the end of my seventeenth year, I was so tired of writing, and of my subject, that I threw my pen in the fire, and stowed away my papers in an old bandbox, out of sight and out of mind.

I have read somewhere that if a woman once falls in love, and then falls out of it, she has no peace until she is again swimming for life in a high sea of passion. (I had better state here that I am just nineteen. The English master used to object to my figures of speech; but I am writing this entirely for my own satisfaction, and mean to give my imagination free scope.) It seems to me that literary composition is like love. When one has begun to write something of one's own, it doesn't matter how disgusted one may become, one returns to the ink-pot like a drunkard to his cups. So, after three months, I unearthed the bandbox, and read over my seven chapters. There were only two interesting pages in the whole manuscript, and those were the two last. All the early incidents in my life which my friends thought so wonderful were of no moment to me. My birth in Paris during the siege; the death of my father, a Scotch Socialist, on a barricade; my French mother's penniless journey to London; our life as beggars; my mother's second marriage to a philanthropic City man; my running away when I was seven, and my wanderings for a fortnight; my attempt to poison my baby-brother with matches; my attack on my philanthropic step-papa with a poker; my exile to a suburban boarding school; my step-papa's fraudulent bankruptcy and disappearance, and the deaths of my poor mother and her little boy – all this was narrated in a dull, frigid manner, quite up to the degree of stupidity that would have registered 'Excellent' on Mr Standard the English master's meter. (I wonder what he would think of that metaphor!) A great deal, doubtless, might be made out of my early life, and when I am older I may be able to embody it in some readable way; but in the mean-time it is impossible for me to put myself in the place of the little girl I was. This is simply because I did not begin to be self-conscious until I was seventeen. When my life ceases to be as full as it has been of late, I shall doubtless be able to study myself from the beginning. At present I am driven as if by some power outside me to write an account of a certain day in my life. I don't like writing, so I am going to make it as short as I can.

First of all, I shall quote the last two pages of my manuscript:

'It was at the age of seventeen, when I found myself in a position of dependence in the house of a relative of my stepfather's, that I first began to look upon myself as a *circumstance*. Doubtless this notion arose from something I had read, but I have never been able to trace its origin. One night while I was sitting alone in my room, the thought came to me that the whole world was an experiment. Here was I, a tall, handsome girl, already a woman in appearance, thrust by circumstances into a family that would have preferred to do without me. Were circumstances playing off a serio-comic practical joke on this family and me? But my fancy took a higher flight. I saw circumstances in the shape of the professor of chemistry and his lean assistant shaking up folk and families, and towns and countries, in bottles and beakers; braying stubborn folks like me in mortars; precipitating, calcining, sifting, subliming, filtering powers and principalities, companies and corporations; conducting a stupendous qualitative analysis of the world.

'I thought, "Since it's all an experiment, how can we help it if we're miserable?" "By joining the experimenters," came the answer pat. This warmed me, and I began to pace my room. "I will be an experimenter," I said to myself. "I will be a circumstance, and cause things." I marched up and down for awhile, thinking how much greater I was than the Prime Minister, who had simply been tossed up there by circumstances; he was only a bit of the experiment, but I was going to be a circumstance. Suddenly I saw that my metaphor had misled me. Circumstances, I perceived, *are* the experiment; everybody and everything is a circumstance. "You donkey!" I said to myself. "You don't need to become a circumstance; you are one." Then I marched up and down the room again, feeling very miserable indeed, till I hit upon an epigram. "People are divided into two classes," I said triumphantly, as I prepared for bed: "those who are circumstances without knowing it, and those who are conscious of the fact." I lay awake for long, overpowered by the tremendous responsibility which this discovery had laid on me. The load was lifted, and I fell asleep the moment I resolved not to submit tamely like a solution or a salt, which is boiled with this, and burned with that, but to have a hand in my own experiment.'

Two remarks I must make with regard to this paragraph. The first is about myself. I say that I was 'a tall, handsome girl, already a woman in appearance.' A romantic statement: the simple truth is that I was big, and rather stout, with a lot of brown, curly hair, pink cheeks, grey eyes, and generally pleasant to look at – at least, I know I liked to look at myself. The second remark is about the chemists who taught in the school where I was done something to, not educated. I had, and have, no ill will to these men; it was simply impossible that I could help thinking of them in the connection. The only one of my teachers whom I disliked, and of whom I still cherish hard thoughts, is Mr Standard, who condemned my compositions, and objected strongly to my metaphors.

Well, on the morning after my great discovery, while I was engaged in a large half-furnished room teaching the three little boys of my stepfather's relative, a loud knock came to the door, and was followed immediately by the entrance of William Somers, the eldest son. There had come between him and the oldest of my charges three children, but they were dead. I was much astonished to see him, because, although we were on the frankest terms, we seldom met. My astonishment increased, I even felt indignant at his masterful manner, as he gave his little brothers sixpence each, and said:

'Be off with you! They deserve a holiday, don't they, Miss Armstrong?'

The three little scapegraces needed no second bidding; they were halfway downstairs before I had recovered my presence of mind. William Somers closed the door, and came up straight to me as if he had been sent for on important business. I stared at him blankly, and he stood dumb and blushing within a yard of me. At last he said:

'I have a holiday. Will you come with me?'

It was evidently not the thing he had intended to say.

'What have you a holiday for?' I asked.

'It's a Bank Holiday,' he said.

'A Bank Holiday!' I exclaimed with scorn, determined to pay him off for his intrusion. 'What slaves you are, you and the whole of this toiling London! Your very holidays you must take when they come. You can't do anything else.'

'What do you mean?' he said, crestfallen.

'Are you aware that you are a circumstance?' I asked severely.

I deeply resented the laugh, quickly smothered as it was, with which he greeted this question. I see now that it must have sounded funny to him, although after my meditation of the previous night it was a natural thing for me to say in all sincerity.

'I see that you have never realised that you are a circumstance,' I continued coldly. 'The best thing you can do with your holiday is to spend it, the whole of it, hour by hour, minute by minute, in the intensest contemplation possible to you of the fact that you are a circumstance.'

He looked at my eyes for fully half a minute, until I was forced to wink.

'You are not mad,' he said; 'and you don't seem to be joking. Still, I mean to say what I have come to say. Will you sit down?'

His coolness – which was, however, assumed and his determined tone aggravated me.

'No,' I said; 'I will not sit down. I wish you to understand that I have fully realised that I am a circumstance, and I am not going to submit except to such other circumstances as please me. You are a circumstance, and don't know it. And what a circumstance! Something in the City – a broker's clerk, I suppose. You needn't tell me; I don't want to know. The prop and stay of your widowed mother and your three little brothers! Did it never strike you what a disagreeable circumstance you are? A good, respectable young man, who never misspends a penny. The very thought of you is like the taste of yarn.'

Now, I didn't mean all I said; I was simply angry without a sufficient reason, as girls and older people will sometimes be. He changed colour at my tirade, and held up his hand deprecatingly; but I went on.

'Don't interrupt me!' I cried. 'And what is it all for, all your toiling and moiling? To feed the mouths of four other circumstances, as unconscious of what they are as if they didn't exist. That's all. You're not causing anything. You're just doing exactly as thousands of others are doing – exactly as circumstances will do with you, never realising that, in all regarding yourself, you are the main circumstance. An explorer, an artist, a poet, even a prime minister, attempts to cause something that is unnecessary, and that he needn't do except of his own motion – but you!'

'Miss Armstrong,' he said steadily, as I paused for breath, 'you are very excited. Won't you sit down?'

'No,' I almost shouted. 'Don't you see that I have made up my mind not to submit? I won't be experimented on with impunity. I should like to sit down, that's true; but I refuse to yield to such a miserable circumstance. I won't be experimented on with impunity,' I repeated, liking the sound of the sentence, and thinking, with what I suppose I must call feminine inconsistency, that it would have pleased Mr Standard.

William Somers looked very much annoyed – grieved, even. I ought to say that he was a tall man of twenty-three, with reddish beard and hair, and hazel eyes. I had not paid much attention to men up to that time, and did not know how handsome William Somers was. The trouble in his face did put me about; but, again, if paltry circumstances were not to be combated, how was I to challenge and overcome the great ones which hemmed me in on all sides?

'I see some meaning in what you say, Miss Armstrong,' he said; 'but I think it is stated a little wildly.'

I felt on the point of crying, so I laughed. He looked at me inquiringly.

'Do you know,' he said, 'I never heard your age. How old are you?'

'I was seventeen two months ago.' That staggered him. 'I suppose you thought I was thirty?'

'No; but I thought you were twenty until you laughed just now, and then I saw that you must be younger. How precocious you are!' he added.

I laughed again, and he saw what a stupid remark he had made.

'I mean – your figure – ' he stammered and stuck.

'Mr Somers,' I said, being now mistress of the situation, 'I will not go with you for a holiday; but you will come with me, and escort me in my first assault on circumstances. Observe that I make a concession in having a squire. It is a bad omen.'

'Your causing a bad omen is just another circumstance for you to overcome,' he said, yielding to my humour.

'I'll be ready in ten minutes. Will you please get a hansom?' I said, as we left the room.

He had not succeeded in saying what he came to say.

Mrs Somers, a very bright, quiet little lady, looked askance at the hansom, but wished us a pleasant holiday as we drove off.

It was my first ride in a hansom, a fact which I concealed from William Somers as long as I could – about one minute, not any more.

'You have never been in a hansom before,' he said, looking at me in a quizzical way.

'How do you know?'

'At first I didn't know, you jumped in so smartly, and told the driver where to go with such aplomb; but then, when we started, in spite of yourself, a half-happy, half-frightened look shot across your face, you sighed, and sank back, and embraced yourself.'

'How dare you!' I said hotly.

My feelings had never been examined to my face before, and I felt outraged, just as I did once when I was posting a letter at a druggist's, and a ruffian laid his dirty hand on my shoulder, and turned me round, saying, 'By Jove! a strapper and a beauty.'

'I dare do all that may become a man,' said William Somers priggishly.

'Don't talk to me any more just now,' I said.

'Very well,' he replied; and, leaning his arms on the door, he tilted back his hat, and looked with unaffected interest at everybody and everything we passed.

I have a great liking for mysteries, and often stop people who begin to explain things to me, because I really don't want to know. A great London mystery of mine is that smooth, elastic, carpet-like roadway along which our hansom glided so stealthily. I admit having thought about its composition, but I have succeeded in overcoming the desire to know of what it is made. It seemed that when we jolted over the stones, we were being wound up in some curious, uncomfortable sort of way; and then, when we reached a stretch of that London turf, I felt as if we had been discharged, and were shooting along through space. (I'm thinking of a crossbow, Mr Standard.) Really, everything appeared to me delightful and interesting.

I perceived for the first time what a picturesque city London is – all of it we saw that morning. The fantastic stacks of chimneys, like hieroglyphics wrought in the air, the mellow, antique streets of dwelling-houses; brick, and plaster, and paint; umber, red, and dull gold, splashed with creeping green; the squares, and graveyards, and crescents, with their trees, and sunflowers, and fountains as if Nature were elbowing a way through the crowded buildings, Mr Standard; and the unknown streets of shops and booths where, even on a Bank Holiday, the butchers and the fishmongers cry their wares, and the little children tumble about among mouldy old furniture on the pavements, like dirty Cupids in the lumber-room of Olympus, Mr Standard; and the Parks with their glades, and avenues, and lakes, where Don Quixote and Sancho Panza lurk, and Robin Hood and Maid Marian, too, Mr Standard, if you had eyes to see; and the Thames – but we didn't see the Thames that morning; and while my thoughts were still revelling in the beauty of the City, we stopped, with a jerk that dislocated my imagination, at the house of Herr Herman Neunzehn, Wellpark Terrace, Bayswater. When I got out, and told the driver to wait, Mr Somers sat very still and attentive. He said nothing to me, and I said nothing to him; but I turned on the steps, and nodded my head encouragingly.

Herr Herman had been my music-master in the boarding-school, and had always had a word of praise for my efforts both in playing and composing. He was dusting his coat with his gloves preparatory to going out when I entered his room, but he received me kindly and said he could afford a few minutes.

'I have come on business,' I said.

'Have you?'

'Yes, Mr Neunzehn. I wish to make a start in life.'

Mr Neunzehn's little bright eyes dashed for a moment close up to his spectacles like silver fish in a miniature aquarium, and then became dim again in the depths as he prepared a cigarette.

'I have brought with me,' I said, displaying a roll: 'two songs, the words and music both by myself.'

Mr Neunzehn's fish darted past his pebbles, and he lit his cigarette.

'Will you oblige me by looking over them? and if you think them good enough, will you give me an introduction to a music-publisher?'

'I will,' said Mr Neunzehn, taking my manuscripts, and opening them out with his diabolical fingers. He was all diabolical, but his fingers were the most diabolical thing about him – long, knotty, sinewy, as if made for strangling.

'Thank you very much,' I said, moving towards the door.

'Wait,' he replied. 'I will do it just now.'

I stood stock still and watched him as he glanced rapidly through my scores. He was much more expeditious than I liked. How could he possibly comprehend in a few seconds the full beauty of my melodies, every individual note of which had been chosen with such care out of the old cottage piano's yellow keyboard, and thumped, and stroked, and listened to, positively for hours, alone, and in conjunction with the others of its phrase, until each separate sound had become so charged with emotion that I couldn't hear one of them without quivering! And my chords! and the counterpoint in my symphonies! He couldn't possibly grasp the full harmony and subtlety of these without at least playing the tunes over once.

The silver fish dashed to and fro behind their glasses, and the smoke curled up through a long, thick, grey moustache as if to cure the fish; but no change in the diabolical expression hinted at a decision one way or other. When he had turned over the last page, he rolled up my manuscripts and handed them back to me, rubbed his shaved cheeks, blew a cloud of smoke that hid his face, and said:

'No, my child.'

'Why?' I faltered.

'Because they are not good enough.'

'Oh, but try them!'

'I have read them through.'

'But let me play them to you;' and I made a dash at the piano.

'No,' he said, closing the instrument. 'It would be of no use. Your music is wrong, and it would not make it right to play it.'

I said to myself: 'The battle has begun; here's a circumstance with a vengeance: don't give in.' Then aloud:

'If you show me the mistakes I will correct them.'

'You couldn't.'

'Will you correct them, then?' I suggested faintly.

'I never correct music except for fools whose money might get into worse pockets than mine.'

I thought I understood now.

'But I will pay you, Mr Neunzehn,' I said sweetly, with a sudden burst of patronage, hope flaming up in my heart.

'You're a stupid little girl' – I was a foot taller than he. 'Listen.' He seized a newspaper and read; 'Some prank them up with oaken leaves; some small-pox hospitals, and banished as far as pos-tribution of articles of clothing to the heads of-pensations to large cities.'

He read slowly, making pauses and inflections as if the matter had been important; then his cigarette glowed and crackled faintly like a squib, and a cloud of smoke enveloped him, from which he emitted hoarsely the terrible sentence:

'That is your music.'

'How?' I whispered, stammering. 'I do not understand. Will you read it again?'

He showed me the newspaper, and with his diabolical finger tracked a line of type, straight across three columns and a half. He read also, but without attempting to make it sound like sense.

'That is your music,' he repeated. 'My dear young lady, amateurs come to me every week with things like that – parts of remembered words and phrases, correctly spelt as a rule, and each phrase or sentence quite grammatical, and sometimes containing bits and bobs of the most unconnected meanings; and they think they have made music. It just needs a little polishing, they know; and that is so easy for me. Look at these words again. See: out of four columns on four different subjects! Would you take that to Mr Standard, and ask him to polish it for you, to make it into one clear sentence? Read it again. 'Some prank them up with oaken leaves; some small-pox hospitals, and banished as far as pos-tribution of articles of clothing to the heads of-pensations to large cities.' You might by taking a few words and rejecting all the others invent a sentence. But that won't do for my amateurs. They bring me notes, and I supply the music, the meaning; but it must be with their notes. They select nonsense, and I must make it sense. I never can make it sense; but it pleases them, and I make them pay for it, I can tell you. You are young and sensible, and can learn a lesson.'

The cigarette had gone out; the fish were pressed close to the glasses, and there seemed to be more water in the aquarium than usual. The old man was pitying me, I had turned so white.

'My dear child,' he continued, 'you must not be downcast. I am like a surgeon. You come to me and ask me if you have a disease, and I tell you that you have not; that you are not a musician, and will never be one. You ought to be very glad.'

Here he sighed, and I saw that he was pitying himself. I pronounced with difficulty a heartless 'Thank you,' for I felt he was right. Then a new idea occurred to me in a flash.

'Mr Neunzehn,' I said, 'did you look at the words of my songs?'

'Here and there.'

'What do you think of them?'

'Nothing; I am no judge.'

'Will you look at them, and if you like them set them to music and publish them?'

'No. Look here.'

He opened a press and showed me a pile of manuscript.

'There are fifty songs composed by me – the best music I have written; and I cannot get one of them published. It is not my reputation. My reputation is that of a composer of pianoforte pieces.'

But I didn't give in. I said:

'Can you introduce me to anyone who might buy my songs?'

'I can. Howard Dapper lives three doors from here on the right.'

My heart bounded at the name of the famous composer, and I could have kissed old Neunzehn as he wrote me an introduction.

'My time is more than up,' he said, handing me the letter. 'We will go out together.'

He took no notice of the hansom, and I gave Mr Somers another encouraging nod.

'Dapper may be stiff,' said Mr Neunzehn at the door of the great man's house; 'but never mind. If your songs please him he'll buy them.'

Having knocked and rung, my old music-master left me in a great hurry.

'Courage, you miserable, trembling circumstance!' I said to myself, kicking my heels in the hall till Mr Dapper should have read the letter.

Again a little fellow, less than Mr Neunzehn! I thought of the tall, straight, auburn-haired man waiting in the hansom; but I plunged into business. Mr Dapper had received me stiffly, and I was just as stiff.

'I have with me the songs to which Mr Neunzehn refers,' I said. 'May I read them to you?'

'I prefer to read them myself.'

'Unfortunately, I have them set to music here, and as the music is bad, it might affect your opinion of the verses.'

'It might.'

'I know the words by heart. Shall I repeat them?'

Mr Dapper bowed, and I recited my songs very badly indeed. My auditor's pale, oily face and purple eyes, like a plain suet-pudding into which two raisins had got by mistake, had a dispiriting effect. The songs, which I still think fair productions for a girl of seventeen, were both pathetic: in the one a deserted maiden died; in the other, a mother's only child. When I had done, Mr Dapper coughed, puckered his dumpling face, and delivered a short address in a juicy voice.

'Miss Armstrong' – glancing at the letter to make sure of my name – 'your songs, I am sorry to say, do not suit me. I will be glad to look at any other verses you may have, here or elsewhere, suitable for pathetic ballads, with a little story; but death I never like introduced.

If you have a sort of musical duologue, say, to occupy about half an hour, with a good, rather startling, plot, and a little fun, I shall be glad to look at it. Or if you have a cantata for female voices only, I shall be glad to look at that; but, remember, I always like something with a story in it; and one thing I always object to – death, in the broad sense; that is, description.'

'But death is a circumstance,' I said, at my wit's end. 'It happens always.'

'We will not argue the point,' he replied, with a wave of his hand. 'If you are really anxious to succeed as a writer of words for music, you must be guided entirely by the requirements of the composer, but – and you must not take it unkindly – I do not think you will ever succeed in that way. If you wish to try, send me a cantata, or songs, or a duologue to occupy half an hour – these are things I need immediately – but I advise you not to.'

'I will,' I cried; 'I will go and write them at once.'

'I advise you not to. I am almost certain that they wouldn't suit me.'

'Why?'

'I will tell you.'

Mr Dapper had gradually dropped his professional tone and air. Some humanity had slipped into him covertly, wrinkling his brow and softening his mouth. His face looked liker a pudding than ever – a pudding that had been boiled in a cloth and creased; but no longer a plain suet pudding; rather a plum-pudding, with the graciousness and sweetness of that Christmas delicacy. A light also shone in his eyes, as if the cook had lit some brandy, and I expected every minute to see a sprig of holly appear in his hair. His voice was still juicy, not with the tallowy juiciness of a suet-dumpling, but with the rich and fragrant sap of the Yule haggis – for I must 'derange my epitaphs,' Mr Standard.

'Miss Armstrong,' he said, 'however clever you may be, you are much too young to succeed in this kind of work. It takes a very practiced writer to make a song, or else a special talent, which I don't think you have. I shall tell you how to graduate in the school of song-making. Write a tragedy, and publish it; write an epic in twelve books, and publish it; write a volume of miscellaneous verse, and publish it; write a great novel, and publish it. The sale of these remarkable works will teach you what not to do; and besides having acquired facility with your pen, you will have expended all your idealism. Then you will be in a condition to write six original songs, which no composer will take. Then you will write one song – about sitting by the river in the moon, or walking in the wood when May is young – and a composer – this composer, possibly – will give you a guinea for it; and while you are dying of consumption and starvation your song will be sung at every concert and in every drawing room, and be well forgotten before the dandelions have grown on your grave. But' – and here, as if he had been a conjurer who performed culinary tricks with his own head, he shifted his face back into a plain suet-pudding – 'but if you have a cantata for female voices only, or a duologue for a lady and gentleman to occupy about half an hour, or songs for pathetic ballads, I will be glad to look at them; only, death I always object to – naked, absolute death, or even a broad hint.'

I don't remember getting out of Mr Dapper's house and getting into the hansom. At seventeen hope is very fierce and reckless, and is always staking happiness against some old song or other. I wakened up out of a blank dream in the midst of the very street where, an hour before, the picturesqueness of London had dawned on me. Prisons the houses seemed, the leprous bricks stained with blood, the scanty creepers striving pitifully to cover up the loathsomeness. The fluent roll of the hansom – was it a hansom, or some dragon-car, sweeping along a pavement of good intentions? *'Facilis,'*[1] I began to myself, when Mr Standard's face in ebony, surmounted by ram's horns, flashed in at the window. My own special, private butt become a demon to torment me! What a war he had waged against quotations from pocket dictionaries! *'Fortiter in re,'*[2] I said aloud, in frantic defiance of the

---

[1] Facilis [descensus Averni]: the descent to Hades is easy [i.e., getting up again is not so easy].
[2] Strongly in action.

fiend. *'Respice finem,*[1] *Ad libitum,*[2] *Cui bono!'*[3] The ebony visage vanished; but another was peering into mine – a fresh face, with wondering hazel eyes. I was frightened at it, and turned away – to think about myself again. Why, I had only had the opinion of two men – the one old and soured with his half-success; the other middle-aged and cynical from prosperity. My music was doubtless as bad as Mr Neunzehn said, and my songs too maudlin for Mr Dapper; but as meaningless music and more lachrymose songs were bought and sold and sung every day, I would visit all the music-publishers in London. I laughed, and, stopping the cab, told the driver to go to one of them.

'Closed, ma'am. Holiday.'

Then I burst into tears, and Mr Somers directed the driver to take us home.

I drew myself together and cried quietly. The first comforting thought that came to me was, that if this had not been a holiday I would have kept William and myself on the rack for hours yet. I had given in. I did make an attempt to return to my own side. 'Circumstances,' I thought, 'are against you. Tomorrow isn't a holiday, and you can resume the fight. You can even post your music.' But, deep down in my own heart, I knew I had made a mistake about myself; and gradually that thought came up, and up, and up, until I writhed and wriggled on it as if I had been impaled.

I then perceived this was something very like remorse, and, feeling how unworthy it was of one who had determined to fight circumstances to go on suffering when the thing was over, I looked up at William. He was staring out of the window, with his brows knotted and his mouth set. There was pain in his eyes, and I thought at first he was ill. As I watched him a new idea came stealing on me like some melancholy music, unheard before, but strangely familiar. It filled all my senses like the smell of roses in the evening, and made my body feel as light as my soul. This was the new idea: he, here beside me, was not miserable for himself; he was suffering for me. A great desire seized me to lay my head down on this man's shoulder, to feel his arms about me, and sleep or faint away; and this desire would, I am afraid have had its course had we not arrived home before it overpowered me.

That night, in the half furnished room, William said to me what he had failed to say in the morning. How he said it, and how I replied to him, shall never be written down. We said things that men and women say to each other only once – things high and sweet that ink would soil, and an eavesdropper mock . . .

'Ho-ho, boy!'

I must end now. A little circumstance for which William and I are responsible – I *have* helped to cause something – is shouting in the next room for what nobody can give him but me.

James Barrie (1860 – 1937)

Apart from Scott and Stevenson, perhaps the most commercially successful Scottish writer in the nineteenth century was James Barrie. There is no more problematical subject for an anthologist in Scottish literature than the place of James Barrie. Barrie was a sentimentalist, who wrote a series of short stories and novels about life in remote Scottish villages, set usually some decades in the past. Like most Scottish writers of the nineteenth century, he turned his back on the Industrial Revolution,

---

[1] Look to the end [purpose].
[2] [As much] as you wish.
[3] For whom is it good? [That is, who is profiting from this crime and consequently likely to be guilty of it? – Roman legal jargon.]

with its big-city slums and factories, to write about a quaint Scotland which in the judgement of the realistic and cynical age which followed him had never existed. The last century saw a tremendous vogue for such tales about picturesque but good-hearted country people. The style existed long before Barrie turned his hand to it (Walter Scott himself is partly responsible for the trend), but he was the most popular writer of this type of story, referred to by critics as 'kailyard' (cabbage-patch) literature. The coming of the twentieth century saw a severe reaction against kailyard writers, including Barrie, who is almost the only writer of that group still read, but whose critical reputation is to some degree held hostage for the behaviour of his supposed followers. Many critics cannot accept Barrie's works as 'literature' at all. Barrie's range is unquestionably limited. But the judgement here is that Barrie, for all his faults and ellipses, is one of the finest writers Scotland has produced. A true genius, with remarkable gifts of imagination, pathos, style and wit, he is almost beyond academic criticism. His sentimentality is notable, but it is not significantly thicker than that of Charles Dickens, whose place in world literature is assured. Barrie's long short story, 'Farewell, Miss Julie Logan', published as recently as 1931, is perhaps his best piece of fiction, and the best short story by a Scot in our century.

Barrie was not only a popular writer of novels, short stories and sketches, but the first Scottish dramatist to achieve a major reputation (though now also uncertain). To compound the problem for the Scottish critic, almost all of Barrie's plays were written for the London stage where they had a great success. Only a few have a Scottish theme. Nonetheless, Barrie is a major playwright, the best Scotland has produced. *What Every Woman Knows*, a comedy of manners and a remarkable study of the Scottish character, is one of his best.

Barrie is perhaps the most notable writer of one-act plays in English. *Barbara's Wedding*, sentimental but brilliantly structured, is also one of his finest.

The Schoolhouse

Early this morning I opened a window in my schoolhouse in the glen of Quharity, awakened by the shivering of a starving sparrow against the frosted glass. As the snowy sash creaked in my hand, he made off to the waterspout that suspends its 'tangles' of ice over a gaping tank, and, rebounding from that, with a quiver of his little black breast, bobbed through the network of wire and joined a few of his fellows in a forlorn hop round the henhouse in search of food. Two days ago my hilarious bantam-cock, saucy to the last, my cheeriest companion, was found frozen in his own water-trough, the corn-saucer in three pieces by his side. Since then I have taken the hens into the house. At meal-times they litter the hearth with each other's feathers; but for the most part they give little trouble, roosting on the rafters of the low-roofed kitchen among staves and fishing-rods.

Another white blanket has been spread upon the glen since I looked out last night; for over the same wilderness of snow that has met my gaze for a week, I see the steading of Waster Lunny sunk deeper into the waste. The schoolhouse, I suppose, serves similarly as a snowmark for the people at the farm. Unless that is Waster Lunny's grieve foddering the cattle in the snow, not a living thing is visible. The ghostlike hills that pen in the glen have ceased to echo to the sharp crack of the sportsman's gun (so clear in the frosty air as to be a warning to every rabbit and partridge in the valley); and only giant Catlaw shows here and there a black ridge, rearing its head at the entrance to the glen and struggling ineffectually to cast off his shroud. Most wintry sign of all, I think as I close the window hastily, is the open farm-stile, its poles lying embedded in the snow where they were last flung by Waster Lunny's herd.[1] Through the still air comes from a distance a vibration as of a tuning-fork: a robin, perhaps, alighting on the wire of a broken fence.

---

[1] Shepherd or cowherd.

In the warm kitchen, where I dawdle over my breakfast, the widowed bantam-hen has perched on the back of my drowsy cat. It is needless to go through the form of opening the school today; for, with the exception of Waster Lunny's girl, I have had no scholars for nine days. Yesterday she announced that there would be no more schooling till it was fresh, 'as she wasna comin''; and indeed, though the smoke from the farm chimneys is a pretty prospect for a snowed-up schoolmaster, the trudge between the two houses must be weary work for a bairn. As for the other children, who have to come from all parts of the hills and glen, I may not see them for weeks. Last year the school was practically deserted for a month. A pleasant outlook, with the March examinations staring me in the face, and an inspector fresh from Oxford. I wonder what he would say if he saw me today digging myself out of the schoolhouse with the spade I now keep for the purpose in my bedroom.

The kail grows brittle from the snow in my dank and cheerless garden. A crust of bread gathers timid pheasants round me. The robins, I see, have made the coalhouse their home. Waster Lunny's dog never barks without rousing my sluggish cat to a joyful response. It is Dutch courage with the birds and beasts of the glen, hard driven for food; but I look attentively for them in these long forenoons, and they have be-gun to regard me as one of themselves. My breath freezes, despite my pipe, as I peer from the door; and with a fortnight-old newspaper I retire to the ingle-nook. The friendliest thing I have seen today is the well-smoked ham suspended from my kitchen rafters. It was a gift from the farm of Tullin, with a load of peats, the day before the snow began to fall. I doubt if I have seen a cart since.

This afternoon I was the not altogether passive spectator of a curious scene in natural history. My feet encased in stout 'tackety' boots, I had waded down two of Waster Lunny's fields to the glen burn: in summer the never-failing larder from which, with wriggling worm or garish fly, I can any morning whip a savoury breakfast; in the winter-time the only thing in the valley that defies the ice-king's chloroform. I watched the water twisting black and solemn through the snow, the ragged ice on its edge proof of the toughness of the struggle with the frost, from which it has, after all, crept only half victorious. A bare wild rosebush on the further bank was violently agitated, and then there ran from its root a black-headed rat with wings. Such was the general effect. I was not less interested when my startled eyes divided this phenomenon into its component parts, and recognised in the disturbance on the opposite bank only another fierce struggle among the hungry animals for existence: they need no professor to teach them the doctrine of the survival of the fittest. A weasel had gripped a water-hen (whit-rit and beltie they are called in these parts) cowering at the root of the rose-bush, and was being dragged down the bank by the terrified bird, which made for the water as its only chance of escape. In less disadvantageous circumstances the weasel would have made short work of his victim; but as he only had the bird by the tail, the prospects of the combatants were equalised.

It was the tug-of war being played with a life as the stakes. 'If I do not reach the water,' was the argument that went on in the heaving little breast of the one, 'I am a dead bird.' 'If this water-hen,' reasoned the other, 'reaches the burn, my supper vanishes with her.' Down the sloping bank the hen had distinctly the best of it, but after that came a yard of level snow, and here she tugged and screamed in vain. I had so far been an unobserved spectator; but my sympathies were with the beltie, and, thinking it high time to interfere, I jumped into the water. The water-hen gave one mighty final tug and toppled into the burn; while the weasel viciously showed me his teeth, and then stole slowly up the bank to the rose-bush, whence, 'girning',[1] he watched me lift his exhausted victim from the water, and set off with her for the schoolhouse. Except for her draggled tail, she already looks wonderfully composed, and so long as the frost holds I shall have little difficulty in keeping her with me.

On Sunday I found a frozen sparrow, whose heart had almost ceased to beat, in the disused pig-sty, and put him for warmth into my breast-pocket. The ungrateful little scrub bolted without a word of thanks about ten minutes afterwards to the alarm of my cat, which

---

[1] Grimacing, whining.

had not known his whereabouts.

I am alone in the schoolhouse. On just such an evening as this last year my desolation drove me to Waster Lunny, where I was storm-stayed for the night. The recollection decides me to court my own warm hearth, to challenge my right hand again to a game at the 'dambrod' against my left. I do not lock the schoolhouse door at nights; for even a highwayman (there is no such luck) would be received with open arms, and I doubt if there be a barred door in all the glen. But it is cosier to put on the shutters. The road to Thrums has lost itself miles down the valley. I wonder what they are doing out in the world. Though I am the Free Church precentor in Thrums (ten pounds a year, and the little town is five miles away), they have not seen me for three weeks. A packman whom I thawed yesterday at my kitchen fire tells me, that last Sabbath only the Auld Lichts held service. Other people realised that they were snowed up. Far up the glen, after it twists out of view, a manse and half a dozen thatched cottages that are there may still show a candle light, and the crumbling gravestones keep cold vigil round the grey old kirk. heavy shadows fade into the sky to the north. A flake trembles against the window; but it is too cold for much snow to-night. The shutter bars the outer world from the schoolhouse.

The House on the Brae

On the bump of green round which the brae twists, at the top of the brae, and within cry of T'nowhead Farm, still stands a one story house, whose whitewashed walls, streaked with the discolouration that rain leaves, look yellow when the snow comes. In the old days the stiff ascent left Thrums behind, and where is now the making of a suburb was only a poor row of dwellings and a manse, with Hendry's cot to watch the brae. The house stood bare, without a shrub, in a garden whose paling did not go all the way round, the potato pit being only kept out of the road, that here sets off southward, by a broken dyke of stones and earth. On each side of the slate coloured door was a window of knotted glass. Ropes were flung over the thatch to keep the roof on in wind.

Into this humble abode I would take any one who cares to accompany me. But you must not come in a contemptuous mood, thinking that the poor are but a stage removed from beasts of burden, as some cruel writers of these days say; nor will I have you turn over with your foot the shabby horse hair chairs that Leeby kept so speckless, and Hendry weaved for years to buy, and Jess so loved to look upon.

I speak of the chairs, but if we go together into the 'room' they will not be visible to you. For a long time the house has been to let. Here, on the left of the doorway, as we enter, is the room, without a shred of furniture in it except the boards of two closed-in beds. The flooring is not steady, and here and there holes have been eaten into the planks. You can scarcely stand upright beneath the decaying ceiling. Worn boards and ragged walls, and the rusty ribs fallen from the fireplace, are all that meet your eyes, but I see a round, unsteady waxcloth covered table, with four books lying at equal distances on it. There are six prim chairs, two of them not to be sat upon, backed against the walls, and between the window and the fireplace, a chest of drawers, with a snowy coverlet. On the drawers stands a board with coloured marbles for the game of solitaire, and I have only to open the drawer with the loose handle to bring out the dambrod. In the carved wood frame over the window hangs Jamie's portrait; in the only other frame a picture of Daniel in the den of lions, sewn by Leeby in wool. Over the chimney-piece with its shells, in which the roar of the sea can be heard, are strung three rows of birds' eggs. Once again we might be expecting company to tea.

The passage is narrow. There is a square hole between the rafters, and a ladder leading up to it. You may climb and look into the attic, as Jess liked to hear me call my tiny garret room. I am stiffer now than in the days when I lodged with Jess during the summer holiday I am trying to bring back, and there is no need for me to ascend. Do not laugh at the newspapers with which Leeby papered the garret, nor at the yarn Hendry stuffed into the windy holes. He did it to warm the house for Jess. But the paper must have gone to pieces and the yarn rotted decades ago.

I have kept the kitchen for the last, as Jamie did on the dire day of which I shall have to tell. It has a flooring of stone now, where there used only to be hard earth, and a broken pane in the window is indifferently stuffed with rags. But it is the other window I turn to, with a pain at my heart, and pride and fondness too, the square foot of glass where Jess sat in her chair and looked down the brae.

Ah, that brae! The history of tragic little Thrums is sunk into it like the stones it swallows in the winter. We have all found the brae long and steep in the spring of life. Do you remember how the child you once were sat at the foot of it and wondered if a new world began at the top? It climbs from a shallow burn, and we used to sit on the brig a long time before venturing to climb. As boys we ran up the brae. As men and women, young and in our prime, we almost forgot that it was there. But the autumn of life comes, and the brae grows steeper; then the winter, and once again we are as the child pausing apprehensively on the brig. Yet are we no longer the child; we look now for no new world at the top, only for a little garden and a tiny house, and a hand loom in the house. It is only a garden of kail and potatoes, but there may be a line of daisies, white and red, on each side of the narrow footpath, and honeysuckle over the door. Life is not always hard, even after backs grow bent, and we know that all braes lead only to the grave.

This is Jess' window. For more than twenty years she had not been able to go so far as the door, and only once while I knew her was she ben in the room. With her husband, Hendry, or their only daughter, Leeby, to lean upon, and her hand clutching her staff, she took twice a day, when she was strong, the journey between her bed and the window where stood her chair. She did not lie there looking at the sparrows or at Leeby redding[1] up the house, and I hardly ever heard her complain. All the sewing was done by her; she often baked on a table pushed close to the window, and by leaning forward she could stir the porridge. Leeby was seldom off her feet, but I do not know that she did more than Jess, who liked to tell me, when she had a moment to spare, that she had a terrible lot to be thankful for.

To those who dwell in great cities Thrums is only a small place, but what a clatter of life it has for me when I come to it from my schoolhouse in the glen. Had my lot been cast in a town I would no doubt have sought country parts during my September holiday, but the schoolhouse is quiet even when the summer takes brakes full of sportsmen and others past the top of my footpath, and I was always lighthearted when Craigiebuckle's cart bore me into the din of Thrums. I only once stayed during the whole of my holiday at the house on the brae, but I knew its inmates for many years, including Jamie, the son, who was a barber in London. Of their ancestry I never heard. With us it was only some of the articles of furniture, or perhaps a snuff mull, that had a genealogical tree. In the house on the brae was a great kettle, called the boiler, that was said to be fifty years old in the days of Hendry's grandfather, of whom nothing more is known. Jess' chair, which has carved arms and a seat stuffed with rags, had been Snecky Hobart's father's before it was hers, and old Snecky bought it at a roup[2] in the Tenements. Jess' rarest possession was, perhaps, the christening robe that even people at a distance came to borrow. Her mother could count up a hundred per-sons who had been baptised in it.

Every one of the hundred, I believe, is dead and even I cannot now pick out Jess and Hendry's grave; but I heard recently that the christening robe is still in use. It is strange that I should still be left, after so many changes, one of the three or four who can today stand on the brae and point out Jess' window. The little window commands the incline to the point where the brae suddenly jerks out of sight in its climb down into the town. The steep path up the commonty[3] makes for this elbow of the brae; and thus, whichever way the traveller

---

[1] Tidying.
[2] Auction.
[3] Community pasture.

takes, it is here that he comes first into sight of the window. Here, too, those who go to the town from the south get their first glimpse of Thrums.

Carts pass up and down the brae every few minutes, and there comes an occasional gig. Seldom is the brae empty, for many live beyond the top of it now, and men and women go by to their work, children to school or play. Not one of the children I see from the window today is known to me, and most of the men and women I only recognise by their likeness to their parents. That sweet faced old woman with the shawl on her shoulders may be one of the girls who was playing at the game of palaulays when Jamie stole into Thrums for the last time; the man who is leaning on the commonty gate gathering breath for the last quarter of the brae may, as a barefooted callant,[1] have been one of those who chased Cree Queery past the poor house.

I cannot say; but this I know, that the grandparents of most of these boys and girls were once young with me. If I see the sons and daughters of my friends grown old, I also see the grandchildren spinning the peerie[2] and hunkering at I-dree-I-dree – I-droppit-it – as we did so long ago. The world remains as young as ever. The lovers that met on the commonty in the gloaming are gone, but there are other lovers to take their place, and still the commonty is here. The sun had sunk on a fine day in June, early in the century, when Hendry and Jess, newly married, he in a rich moleskin waistcoat, she in a white net cap, walked to the house on the brae that was to be their home. So Jess has told me. Here again has been just such a day, and somewhere in Thrums there may be just such a couple, setting out for their home behind a horse with white ears instead of walking, but with the same hopes and fears, and the same lovelight in their eyes. The world does not age. The hearse passes over the brae and up the straight burying ground road, but still there is a cry for the christening robe.

Jess' window was a beacon by night to travellers in the dark, and it will be so in the future when there are none to remember Jess. There are many such windows still, with loving faces behind them. From them we watch for the friends and relatives who are coming back, and some, alas! watch in vain. Not every one returns who takes the elbow of the brae bravely, or waves his handkerchief to those who watch from the window with wet eyes, and some return too late. To Jess, at her window always when she was not in bed, things happy and mournful and terrible came into view. At this window she sat for twenty years or more looking at the world as through a telescope; and here an awful ordeal was gone through after her sweet, untarnished soul had been given back to God.

How Gavin Birse Put It to Mag Lownie

In a wet day the rain gathered in blobs on the road that passed our garden. Then it crawled into the cart tracks until the road was streaked with water. Lastly, the water gathered in heavy yellow pools. If the on-ding still continued, clods of earth toppled from the garden dyke into the ditch.

On such a day, when even the dulseman had gone into shelter, and the women scudded by with their wrappers over their heads, came Gavin Birse to our door. Gavin, who was the Glen Quharity post, was still young, but had never been quite the same man since some amateurs in the glen ironed his back for rheumatism. I thought he had called to have a crack[3] with me. He sent his compliments up to the attic, however, by Leeby, and would I come and be a witness?

Gavin came up and explained. He had taken off his scarf and thrust it into his pocket, lest the rain should take the colour out of it. His boots cheeped, and his shoulders had risen to his

---

[1] Lad.
[2] Spinning top.
[3] Chat.

ears. He stood steaming before my fire.

'If it's no ower muckle to ask ye,' he said, 'I would like ye for a witness.'

'A witness! But for what do you need a witness, Gavin?'

'I want ye,' he said, 'to come wi' me to Mag's, and be a witness.'

Gavin and Mag Birse had been engaged for a year or more. Mag was the daughter of Janet Ogilvy, who was best remembered as the body that took the hill (that is, wandered about it) for twelve hours on the day Mr Dishart, the Auld Licht minister, accepted a call to another church.

'You don't mean to tell me, Gavin,' I asked, 'that your marriage is to take place today?'

By the twist of his mouth I saw that he was only deferring a smile.

'Far frae that,' he said.

'Ah, then, you have quarrelled, and I am to speak up for you?'

'Na, na,' he said, 'I dinna want ye to do that above all things. It would be a favour if ye could give me a bad character.'

This beat me, and, I dare say my face showed it.

'I'm no' juist what ye would call anxious to marry Mag noo,' said Gavin, without a tremor.

I told him to go on.

'There's a lassie oot at Craigiebuckle,' he explained, 'workin' on the farm – Jeanie Luke by name. Ye may hae seen her?'

'What of her?' I asked, severely.

'Weel,' said Gavin, still unabashed, 'I'm thinkin' noo, 'at I would rather hae her.'

Then he stated his case more fully.

'Ay, I thocht I liked Mag oncommon till I saw Jeanie, an' I like her fine yet, but I prefer the other ane. That state o' matters canna gang on forever, so I came into Thrums the day to settle't one way or another.'

'And how,' I asked, 'do you propose going about it? It is a somewhat delicate business.'

'Ou, I see nae great difficulty in't. I'll speir at Mag, blunt oot, if she'll let me aff. Yes, I'll put it to her plain.'

'You're sure Jeanie would take you?'

'Ay; oh, there's nae fear o' that.'

'But if Mag keeps you to your bargain?'

'Weel, in that case there's nae harm done.'

'You are in a great hurry, Gavin?'

'Ye may say that; but I want to be married. The wifie I lodge wi' canna last lang, an' I would like to settle doon in some place.'

'So you are on your way to Mag's now?'

'Ay, we'll get her in atween twal' and ane.'

'Oh, yes; but why do you want me to go with you?'

'I want ye for a witness. If she winna let me aff, weel an' guid; an' if she will, it's better to hae a witness in case she should go back on her word.'

Gavin made his proposal briskly, and as coolly as if he were only asking me to go fishing; but I did not accompany him to Mag's. He left the house to look for another witness, and about an hour afterward Jess saw him pass with Tammas Haggart. Tammas cried in during the evening to tell us how the mission prospered.

'Mind ye,' said Tammas, a drop of water hanging to the point of his nose, 'I disclaim all responsibility in the business. I ken Mag weel for a thrifty, respectable woman, as her mither was afore her, an' so I said to Gavin when he came to speir me.'

'Ay, mony a pirn has 'Lisbeth filled to me,' said Hendry, settling down to a reminiscence.

'No to be ower hard on Gavin,' continued Tammas, forestalling Hendry, 'he took what I said in guid part; but aye when I stopped speakin', to draw breath, he says, 'The question is, will ye come wi' me?' He was michty made up in 's mind.'

'Weel, ye went wi' him,' suggested Jess, who wanted to bring Tammas to the point.

'Ay,' said the stone breaker, 'but no in sic a hurry as that.'

He worked his mouth round and round, to clear the course as it were for a sarcasm.

'Fowk often say,' he continued, "at 'am quick beyond the ordinar' in seein' the humourous side o' things.'

Here Tammas paused and looked at us.

'So ye are, Tammas,' said Hendry. 'Losh, ye mind hoo ye saw the humourous side o' me wearin' a pair o' boots 'at wisna marrows! No, the ane had a toe piece on, an' the other hadna.'

'Ye juist wore them sometimes when ye was delvin',' broke in Jess; 'ye have as guid a pair o' boots as ony in Thrums.'

'Ay, but I had worn them,' said Hendry, 'at odd times for mair than a year, an' I had never seen the humourous side o' them. Weel, as fac as death (here he addressed me), Tammas had juist seen them twa or three times when he saw the humourous side o' them. Syne I saw their humourous side, too, but no till Tammas pointed it oot.'

'That was naething,' said Tammas, 'naething ava to some things I've done.'

'But what aboot Mag?' said Leeby.

'We wasna that length, was we?' said Tammas. 'Na, we was speakin' aboot the humourous side. Ay, wait a wee, I didna mention the humourous side for naething.'

He paused to reflect.

'Oh, yes,' he said at last, brightening up, 'I was sayin' to ye hoo quick I was to see the humourous side o' onything. Ay, then, what made me say that was 'at in a clink (flash) I saw the humourous side o' Gavin's position.'

'Man, man,' said Hendry, admiringly, 'an' what is it?'

'Oh, it's this: there's something humourous in speirin' a woman to let ye aff so as ye can be married to anither woman.'

'I daur say there is,' said Hendry, doubtfully.

'Did she let him aff?' asked Jess, taking the words out of Leeby's mouth.

'I'm comin' to that,' said Tammas. 'Gavin proposes to me after I had ha'en my lauch – '

'Yes,' cried Hendry, banging the table with his fist, 'it has a humourous side Ye're richt again, Tammas.'

'I wish ye wadna blatter (beat) the table,' said Jess, and then Tammas proceeded:

'Gavin wanted me to tak paper an' ink an' a pen wi' me, to write the proceedin's doon, but I said, 'Na, na, I'll tak paper, but nae ink nor nae pen, for there'll be ink an' a pen there.' That was what I said.'

'An' did she let him aff?' asked Leeby.

'Weel,' said Tammas, 'aff we goes to Mag's hoose, an' sure enough Mag was in. She was alane, too; so Gavin, no to waste time, juist sat doon for politeness' sake, an' sune rises up again; an' says he, "Marget Lownie, I hae a solemn question to speir at ye, namely, this, Will you, Marget Lownie, let me, Gavin Birse, aff?"'

'Mag would start at that?'

'Sal, she was braw an' cool. I thocht she maun hae got wind o' his intentions aforehand, for she juist replies, quiet-like, "Hoo do ye want aff, Gavin?"'

'"Because," says he, like a book, "my affections has undergone a change."'

'"Ye mean Jean Luke?" says Mag.

'"That is wha I mean," says Gavin, very straitforrard.'

'But she didna let him aff, did she?'

'Na, she wasna the kind. Says she, "I wonder to hear ye, Gavin, but 'am no goin' to agree to naething o' that sort."'

'"Think it ower," says Gavin.

'"Na, my mind's made up," said she.

'"Ye would sune get anither man," he says earnestly.

'"Hoo do I ken that?" she speirs, rale sensibly, I thocht, for men's no sae easy to get.

'"Am sure o' 't," Gavin says, wi' michty conviction in his voice, "for ye're bonny to look at, an' weel kent for bein' a guid body."

'"Ay," says Mag, "I'm glad ye like me, Gavin, for ye have to tak me."'

'That put a clincher on him,' interrupted Hendry.

'He was loth to gie in,' replied Tammas, 'so he says, "Ye think 'am a fine character, Marget Lownie, but ye're very far mista'en. I wouldna wonder but what I was lossin' my place some o' thae days, an' syne whaur would ye be? – Marget Lownie," he goes on, "am nat'rally lazy an' fond o' the drink. As sure as ye stand there, 'am a reg'lar deevil!"'

'That was strong language,' said Hendry, 'but he would be wantin' to fleg (frighten) her.'

'Juist so, but he didna manage 't, for Mag says, "We a' hae oor faults, Gavin, an' deevil or no deevil, ye're the man for me!"'

'Gavin thocht a bit,' continued Tammas, 'an' syne he tries her on a new tack. "Marget Lownie," he says, "ye're father's an auld man noo, an' he has naebody but yersel' to look after him. I'm thinkin' it would be kind o' cruel o' me to tak' ye awa frae 'im."'

'Mag wouldna be ta'en in wi' that; she wasna born on a Sabbath,' said Jess, using one of her favourite sayings.

'She wasna,' answered Tammas. 'Says she, "Hae nae fear on that score, Gavin; my father's fine willin' to spare me!"'

'An' that ended it?'

'Ay, that ended it.'

'Did ye tak' it doon in writin?' asked Hendry.

'There was nae need,' said Tammas, handing round his snuff mull. 'No, I never touched paper. When I saw the thing was settled, I left them to their coortin'. They're to tak a look at Snecky Hobart's auld hoose the nicht. It's to let.'

What Every Woman Knows

Perhaps more than any playwright, Barrie liked to direct his scripts at the reader, with a steady stream of author-asides and elaborate, chatty stage directions, a practice very much out of style at the present. He even from time to time adopts the device of printing some of his dialogue as it would appear in a novel.

ACT ONE

James Wylie is about to make a move on the dambrod, and in the little Scotch room there is an awful silence befitting the occasion. James with his hand poised – for if he touches a piece he has to play it, Alick will see to that – raises his red head suddenly to read Alick's face. His father, who is Alick, is pretending to be in a panic lest James should make this move. James grins heartlessly, and his fingers are about to close on the 'man' when some instinct of self preservation makes him peep once more. This time Alick is caught: the unholy ecstasy on his face tells as plain as porridge that he has been luring James to destruction. James glares; and, too late, his opponent is a simple old father again. James mops his head, sprawls in the manner most conducive to thought in the Wylie family, and, protruding his underlip, settles down to a reconsideration of the board. Alick blows out his cheeks, and a drop of water settles on the point of his nose.

You will find them thus any Saturday night (after family worship, which sends the servant to bed); and sometimes the pauses are so long that in the end they forget whose move it is.

It is not the room you would be shown into if you were calling socially on Miss Wylie. The drawing room for you, and Miss Wylie in a coloured merino to receive you; very likely she would exclaim, 'This is a pleasant surprise!' though she has seen you coming up the avenue and has just had time to whip the dust cloths off the chairs, and to warn Alick, David and James, that they had better not dare come in to see you before they have put on a dickey. Nor is this the room in which you would dine in solemn grandeur if invited to drop in and take pot luck, which is how the Wylies invite, it being a family weakness to pretend that they sit down in the dining room daily. It is the real living room of the house, where Alick, who will never get used to fashionable ways, can take off his collar and sit happily in his stocking soles, and James at times would do so also: but catch Maggie letting him.

There is one very fine chair, but, heavens, not for sitting on; just to give the room a social standing in an emergency. It sneers at the other chairs with an air of insolent superiority, like a haughty bride who has married into the house for money. Otherwise the furniture is homely; most of it has come from that smaller house where the Wylies began. There is the large and shiny chair which can be turned into a bed if you look the other way for a moment. James cannot sit on this chair without gradually sliding down it till he is lying luxuriously on the small of his back, his legs indicating, like the hands of a clock, that it is ten past twelve; a position in which Maggie shudders to see him receiving company.

The other chairs are horsehair, than which nothing is more comfortable if there be a good slit down the seat. The seats are heavily dented, because all the Wylie family sit down with a dump. The draughtboard is on the edge of a large centre table, which also displays four books placed at equal distances from each other, one of them a Bible, and another the family album. If these were the only books they would not justify Maggie in calling this chamber the library, her dogged name for it; while David and James call it the west room and Alick calls it 'the room', which is to him the natural name for any apartment without a bed in it. There is a bookcase of pitch pine, which contains six hundred books, with glass doors to prevent your getting at them.

No one does try to get at the books, for the Wylies are not a reading family. They like you to gasp when you see so much literature gathered together in one prison house, but they gasp themselves at the thought that there are persons, chiefly clergymen, who, having finished one book, coolly begin another. Nevertheless it was not all vainglory that made David buy this library: it was rather a mighty respect for education, as something that he has missed. This same feeling makes him take in the *Contemporary Review* and stand up to it like a man. Alick, who also has a respect for education, tries to read the *Contemporary,* but becomes dispirited, and may be heard muttering over its pages, 'No, no use, no use, no,' and sometimes even 'Oh hell.' James has no respect for education; and Maggie is at present of an open mind.

They are Wylie and Sons of the local granite quarry, in which Alick was throughout his working days a mason. It is David who has raised them to this position; he climbed up himself step by step (and hewed the steps), and drew the others up after him. 'Wylie Brothers,' Alick would have had the firm called, but David said No, and James said No, and Maggie said No; first honour must be to their father; and Alick now likes it on the whole, though he often sighs at having to shave every day; and on some snell mornings he still creeps from his couch at four and even at two (thinking that his mallet and chisel are calling him), and begins to pull on his trousers, until the grandeur of them reminds him that he can go to bed again. Sometimes he cries a little, because there is no more work for him to do for ever and ever; and then Maggie gives him a spade (without telling David) or David gives him the logs to saw (without telling Maggie).

We have given James a longer time to make his move than our kind friends in front will give him, but in the meantime something has been happening. David has come in, wearing a black coat and his Sabbath boots, for he has been to a public meeting. David is nigh forty years of age, whiskered like his father and brother (Alick's whiskers being worn as a sort of cravat round the neck), and he has the too brisk manner of one who must arrive anywhere a little before any one else. The painter who did the three of them for fifteen pounds (you may observe the canvases on the walls) has caught this characteristic, perhaps accidentally, for David is almost stepping out of his frame, as if to hurry off somewhere; while Alick and James look as if they were pinned to the wall for life. All the six of them, men and pictures, however, have a family resemblance, like granite blocks from their own quarry. They are as Scotch as peat for instance, and they might exchange eyes without any neighbour noticing the difference, inquisitive little blue eyes that seem to be always totting up the price of things.

The dambrod players pay no attention to David, nor does he regard them. Dumping down on the sofa he removes his 'lastic sides, as his Sabbath boots are called, by pushing one foot against the other, gets into a pair of hand sewn slippers, deposits the boots as according to rule in the ottoman, and crosses to the fire. There must be something on David's mind tonight, for he pays no attention to the game, neither gives advice (than which nothing is more maddening) nor exchanges a wink with Alick over the parlous condition of James's crown. You can hear the wag-at-the-wall clock in the lobby ticking. Then David lets himself go; it runs out of him like a hymn:

DAVID Oh, let the solid ground
      Not fail beneath my feet,
      Before my life has found
      What some have found so sweet.

        This is not a soliloquy, but is offered as a definite statement.
        The players emerge from their game with difficulty.

ALICK *(with* JAMES*'s crown in his hand)* What's that you're saying, David?
DAVID *(like a public speaker explaining the situation in a few well chosen words)* The thing I'm speaking about is Love.
JAMES *(keeping control of himself)* Do you stand there and say you're in love, David Wylie?
DAVID Me; what would I do with the thing?
JAMES *(who is by no means without pluck)* I see no necessity for calling it a thing.

    They are two bachelors who all their lives have been afraid of nothing but Woman. DAVID *in*
    his sportive days – which continue – has done roguish things with his arm when conducting a
    lady home under an umbrella from a soiree, and has both chuckled and been scared on
    thinking of it afterwards. JAMES, *a commoner fellow altogether, has discussed the sex over a*
    glass, but is too canny to be in the company of less than two young women at a time.

DAVID *(derisively)* Oho, has she got you, James?
JAMES *(feeling the sting of it)* Nobody has got me.
DAVID They'll catch you yet, lad.
JAMES They'll never catch me. You've been nearer catched yourself.
ALICK Yes, Kitty Menzies, David.
DAVID *(feeling himself under the umbrella)* It was a kind of a shave that.
ALICK *(who knows all that is to be known about women and can speak of them without a tremor)* It's a curious thing, but a man cannot help winking when he hears that one of his friends has been catched.
DAVID That's so.
JAMES *(clinging to his manhood)* And fear of that wink is what has kept the two of us single men. And yet what's the glory of being single?
DAVID There's no particular glory in it, but it's safe.
JAMES *(putting away his aspirations)* Yes, it's lonely, but it's safe. But who did you mean the poetry for, then?
DAVID For Maggie, of course.

    You don't know DAVID *and* JAMES, *till you know how they love their sister* MAGGIE.

ALICK I thought that.
DAVID *(coming to the second point of his statement about Love)* I saw her reading poetry and saying those words over to herself.
JAMES She has such a poetical mind.
DAVID Love. There's no doubt as that's what Maggie has set her heart on. And not merely love, but one of those grand noble loves; for though Maggie is undersized she has a passion for romance.
JAMES *(wandering miserably about the room)* It's terrible not to be able to give Maggie what her heart is set on.

The others never pay much attention to JAMES, *though he is quite a smart figure in less important houses.*

ALICK *(violently)* Those idiots of men!

DAVID Father, did you tell her who had got the minister of Galashiels?

ALICK *(wagging his head sadly)* I had to tell her. And then I – I – bought her a sealskin muff, and I just slipped it into her hands and came away.

JAMES *(illustrating the sense of justice in the Wylie family)* Of course, to be fair to the man, he never pretended he wanted her.

DAVID None of them wants her; that's what depresses her. I was thinking, father, I would buy her that gold watch and chain in Snibby's window. She hankers after it.

JAMES *(slapping his pocket)* You're too late, David; I've got them for her.

DAVID It's ill done of the minister. Many a pound of steak has that man had in this house.

ALICK You mind the slippers she worked for him?

JAMES I mind them fine; she began them for William Cathro. She's getting on in years, too, though she looks so young.

ALICK I never can make up my mind, David, whether her curls make her look younger or older.

DAVID *(determinedly)* Younger. Whisht! I hear her winding the clock. Mind, not a word about the minister to her, James. Don't even mention religion this day.

JAMES Would it be like me to do such thing?

DAVID It would be very like you. And there's that other matter: say not a syllable about our having a reason for sitting up late tonight. When she says it's bed time, just all pretend we're not sleepy.

ALICK Exactly, and when –

Here MAGGIE *enters, and all three are suddenly engrossed in the dambrod. We could describe* MAGGIE *at great length. But what is the use? What you really want to know is whether she was good looking. No, she was not. Enter* MAGGIE, *who is not good looking. When this is said, all is said. Enter* MAGGIE, *as it were, with her throat cut from ear to ear. She has a soft Scotch voice and a more resolute manner than is perhaps fitting to her plainness; and she stops short at sight of* JAMES *sprawling unconsciously in the company chair.*

MAGGIE James, I wouldn't sit on the fine chair.

JAMES I forgot again.

But he wishes she had spoken more sharply. Even profanation of the fine chair has not roused her. She takes up her knitting, and they all suspect that she knows what they have been talking about.

MAGGIES You're late, David, it's nearly bed time.

DAVID *(finding the subject a safe one)* I was kept late at the public meeting.

ALICK *(glad to get so far away from Galashiels)* Was it a good meeting?

DAVID Fairish. *(With some heat.)* That young John Shand would make a speech.

MAGGIE John Shand? Is that the student Shand?

DAVID The same. It's true he's a student at Glasgow University in the winter months, but in summer he's just the railway porter here; and I think it's very presumptuous of a young lad like that to make a speech when he hasn't a penny to bless himself with.

ALICK The Shands were always an impudent family, and jealous. I suppose that's the reason they haven't been on speaking terms with us this six years. Was it a good speech?

DAVID *(illustrating the family's generosity)* It was very fine; but he needn't have made fun of me.

MAGGIE *(losing a stitch)* He dared?

DAVID *(depressed)* You see I can not get started on a speech without saying things like 'In rising for to make a few remarks.'

JAMES What's wrong with it?

DAVID He mimicked me, and said 'Will our worthy chairman come for to go for to answer my questions?' and so on; and they roared.

JAMES *(slapping his money pocket)* The sacket.[1]

DAVID I did feel bitterly, father, the want of education. *(Without knowing it, he has a beautiful way of pronouncing this noble word.)*

MAGGIE *(holding out a kind hand to him)* David.

ALICK I've missed it sore, David. Even now I feel the want of it in the very marrow of me. I'm shamed to think I never gave you your chance. But when you were young I was so desperate poor, how could I do it, Maggie?

MAGGIE It wasn't possible, father.

ALICK *(gazing at the book shelves)* To be able to understand these books! To up with them one at a time and scrape them as clean as though they were a bowl of brose. Lads, it's not to riches, it's to scholarship that I make my humble bow.

JAMES *(who is good at bathos)* There's ten yards of them. And they were selected by the minister of Galashiels. He said –

DAVID *(quickly)* James.

JAMES I mean – I mean –

MAGGIE *(calmly)* I suppose you mean what you say, James. I hear, David, that the minister of Galashiels is to be married on that Miss Turnbull.

DAVID *(on guard)* So they were saying.

ALICK All I can say is she has made a poor bargain.

MAGGIE *(the damned)* I wonder at you, father. He's a very nice gentleman. I'm sure I hope he has chosen wisely.

JAMES Not him.

MAGGIE *(getting near her tragedy)* How can you say that when you don't know her? I expect she is full of charm.

ALICK Charm? It's the very word he used.

DAVID Havering[2] idiot.

ALICK What is charm, exactly, Maggie?

MAGGIE Oh, it's – it's a sort of bloom on a woman. If you have it, you don't need to have anything else; and if you don't have it, it doesn't much matter what else you have. Some women, the few, have charm for all; and most have charm for one. But some have charm for none.

> *Somehow she has stopped knitting. Her men folk are very depressed.* JAMES *brings his fist down on the table with a bang.*

JAMES *(shouting)* I have a sister that has charm.

MAGGIE No, James, you haven't.

JAMES *(rushing at her with the watch and chain)* Ha'e, Maggie.

> *She lets them lie in her lap.*

DAVID Maggie, would you like a silk?

MAGGIE What could I do with a silk? *(With a gust of passion.)* You might as well dress up a little brown hen.

> *They wriggle miserably.*

JAMES *(stamping)* Bring him here to me.

MAGGIE Bring whom, James?

JAMES David, I would be obliged if you wouldn't kick me beneath the table.

MAGGIE *(rising)* Let's be practical; let's go to our beds.

---

[1] Rascal (general term of abuse).
[2] Speaking nonsense.

This reminds them that they have a job on hand in which she is not to share.

DAVID *(slyly)* I don't feel very sleepy yet.

ALICK Nor me either.

JAMES You've just taken the very words out of my mouth.

DAVID *(with unusual politeness)* Good night to you, Maggie.

MAGGIES *(fixing the three of them)* All of you unsleepy, when, as is well known, ten o'clock is your regular bed time?

JAMES Yes, it's common knowledge that we go to our beds at ten. *(Chuckling.)* That's what we're counting on.

MAGGIE Counting on?

DAVID You stupid whelp.

JAMES What have I done?

MAGGIE *(folding her arms)* There's something up. You've got to tell me, David.

DAVID *(who knows when he is beaten)* Go out and watch, James.

MAGGIE Watch?

> JAMES *takes himself off, armed, as* MAGGIE *notices, with a stick.*

DAVID *(in his alert business way)* Maggie, there are burglars about.

MAGGIE Burglars? *(She sits rigid, but she is not the kind to scream.)*

DAVID We hadn't meant for to tell you till we nabbed them; but they've been in this room twice of late. We sat up last night waiting for them, and we're to sit up again tonight.

MAGGIE The silver plate.

DAVID It's all safe as yet. That makes us think that they were either frightened away these other times, or that they are coming back for to make a clean sweep.

MAGGIE How did you get to know about this?

DAVID It was on Tuesday that the polissman called at the quarry with a very queer story. He had seen a man climbing out at this window at ten past two.

MAGGIE Did he chase him?

DAVID It was so dark he lost sight of him at once.

ALICK Tell her about the window.

DAVID We've found out that the catch of the window has been pushed back by slipping the blade of a knife between the woodwork.

MAGGIE David.

ALICK The polissman said he was carrying a little carpet bag.

MAGGIE The silver plate is gone.

DAVID No, no. We were thinking that very likely he has bunches of keys in the bag.

MAGGIE Or weapons.

DAVID As for that, we have some pretty stout weapons ourselves in the umbrella stand. So, if you'll go to your bed, Maggie.

MAGGIE Me? and my brothers in danger.

ALICK There's just one of them.

MAGGIE The polissman just saw one.

DAVID *(licking his palms)* I would be very pleased if there were three of them.

MAGGIE I watch with you. I would be very pleased if there were four of them.

DAIVD And they say she has no charm!

> JAMES *returns on tiptoe as if the burglars were beneath the table. He signs to every one to breathe no more, and then whispers his news.*

JAMES He's there. I had no sooner gone out than I saw him sliding down the garden wall, close to the rhubarbs.

ALICK What's he like?

JAMES He's an ugly customer. That's all I could see. There was a little carpet bag in his hand.

DAVID That's him.

JAMES He slunk into the rhodydendrons, and he's there now, watching the window.

DAVID We have him. Out with the light. *(The room is beautified by a chandelier fitted for three gas jets, but with the advance of progress one of these has been removed and the incandescent light put in its place. This alone is lit.* ALICK *climbs a chair, pulls a little chain, and the room is now but vaguely lit by the fire. It plays fitfully on four sparkling faces.)*

MAGGIE Do you think he saw you, James?

JAMES I couldn't say, but in any case I was too clever for him. I looked up at the stars, and yawned loud at them as if I was tremendous sleepy.

> *There is a long pause during which they are lurking in the shadows. At last they hear some movement, and they steal like ghosts from the room. We see* DAVID *turning out the lobby light; then the door closes and an empty room awaits the intruder with a shudder of expectancy. The window opens and shuts as softly as if this were a mother peering in to see whether her baby is asleep. Then the head of a man shows between the curtains. The remainder of him follows. He is carrying a little carpet bag. He stands irresolute; what puzzles him evidently is that the Wylies should have retired to rest without lifting that piece of coal off the fire. He opens the door and peeps into the lobby, listening to the wag-at-the-wall clock. All seems serene and he turns on the light. We see him clearly now. He is* JOHN SHAND, *age twenty-one, boots muddy, as an indignant carpet can testify. He wears a shabby topcoat and a cockerty bonnet; otherwise he is in the well-worn corduroys of a railway porter. His movements, at first stealthy, become almost homely as he feels that he is secure. He opens the bag and takes out a bunch of keys, a small paper parcel, and a black implement that may be a burglar's jemmy. This cool customer examines the fire and piles on more coals. With the keys he opens the door of the bookcase, selects two large volumes, and brings them to the table. He takes off his topcoat and opens his parcel, which we now see contains sheets of foolscap paper. His next action shows that the 'jemmy' is really a ruler. He knows where the pen and ink are kept. He pulls the fine chair nearer to the table, sits on it, and proceeds to write, occasionally dotting the carpet with ink as he stabs the air with his pen. He is so occupied that he does not see the door opening, and the Wylie family staring at him. They are armed with sticks.*

ALICK *(at last)* When you're ready, John Shand.

> JOHN *hints back, and then has the grace to rise, dogged and expressionless.*

JAMES *(like a railway porter)* Ticket, please.

DAVID You can't think of anything clever for to go for to say now, John.

MAGGIE I hope you find that chair comfortable, young man.

JOHN I have no complaint to make against the chair.

ALICK *(who is really distressed)* A native of the town. The disgrace to your family. I feel pity for the Shands this night.

JOHN *(glowering)* I'll thank you, Mr Wylie, not to pity my family.

JAMES Canny, canny.

MAGGIE *(that sense of justice again)* I think you should let the young man explain. It mayn't be so bad as we thought.

DAVID Explain away, my billie.

JOHN Only the uneducated would need an explanation. I'm a student, *(with a little passion)* and I'm desperate for want of books. You have all I want here; no use to you but for display; well, I came here to study. I come twice weekly. *(Amazement of his hosts.)*

DAVID *(who is the first to recover)* By the window.

JOHN Do you think a Shand would so far lower himself as to enter your door? Well, is it a case for the police?

JAMES It is.

MAGGIE *(not so much out of the goodness of her heart as to patronise the Shands)* It seems to me it's a case for us all to go to our beds and leave the young man to study; but not on that chair. *(And she wheels the chair away from him.)*

JOHN Thank you, Miss Maggie, but I couldn't be beholden to you.

JAMES My opinion is that he's nobody, so out with him.

JOHN Yes, out with me. And you'll be cheered to hear I'm likely to be a nobody for a long time to come.

DAVID *(who had been beginning to respect him)* Are you a poor scholar?

JOHN On the contrary, I'm a brilliant scholar.

DAVID It's sillier, then?

JOHN *(glorified by experiences he has shared with many a gallant soul)* My first year at college I lived on a barrel of potatoes, and we had just a sofa-bed between two of us; when the one lay down the other had to get up. Do you think it was hardship? It was sublime. But this year I can't afford it. I'll have to stay on here, collecting the tickets of the illiterate, such as you, when I might be with Romulus and Remus among the stars.

JAMES *(summing up)* Havers.

DAVID *(in whose head some design is vaguely taking shape)* Whisht, James. I must say, young lad, I like your spirit. Now tell me, what's your professors' opinion of your future.

JOHN They think me a young man of extraordinary promise.

DAVID You have a name here for high moral character.

JOHN And justly.

DAVID Are you serious minded?

JOHN I never laughed in my life.

DAVID Who do you sit under in Glasgow?

JOHN Mr Flemister of the Sauchiehall High.

DAVID Are you a Sabbath-school teacher?

JOHN I am.

DAVID One more question. Are you promised?

JOHN To a lady?

DAVID Yes.

JOHN I've never given one of them a single word of encouragement. I'm too much occupied thinking about my career.

DAVID So. *(He reflects, and finally indicates by a jerk of the head that he wishes to talk with his father behind the door.*

JAMES *(longingly)* Do you want me too?

But they go out without even answering him.

MAGGIE I don't know what maggot they have in their heads, but sit down, young man, till they come back.

JOHN My name's Mr Shand, and till I'm called that I decline to sit down again in this house.

MAGGIE Then I'm thinking, young sir, you'll have a weary wait.

While he waits you can see how pinched his face is. He is little more than a boy, and he seldom has enough to eat. DAVID *and* ALICK *return presently, looking as sly as if they had been discussing some move on the dambrod, as indeed they have.*

DAVID *(suddenly become genial)* Sit down, Mr Shand, and pull in your chair. You'll have a thimbleful of something to keep the cold out? *(Briskly.)* Glasses, Maggie. *(She wonders, but gets glasses and decanter from the sideboard, which* JAMES *calls the chiffy.* DAVID *and* ALICK, *in the most friendly manner, also draw up to the table.)* You're not a totaller, I hope?

JOHN *(guardedly)* I'm practically totaller.

DAVID So are we. How do you take it? Is there any hot water, Maggie?

JOHN If I take it at all, and I haven't made up my mind yet, I'll take it cold.

DAVID You'll take it hot, James?

JAMES *(also sitting at the table but completely befogged)* No, I –

DAVID *(decisively)* I think you'll take it hot, James.

JAMES *(sulking)* I'll take it hot.

DAVID The kettle, Maggie.

> JAMES *has evidently to take it hot so that they can get at the business now on hand, while* MAGGIE *goes kitchenward for the kettle.*

ALICK Now, David, quick, before she comes back.

DAVID Mr Shand, we have an offer to make you.

JOHN *(warningly)* No patronage.

ALICK It's strictly a business affair.

DAVID Leave it to me, father. It's this – *(But to his annoyance the suspicious* MAGGIE *has already returned with the kettle.)* Maggie, don't you see that you're not wanted?

MAGGIE *(sitting down by the fire and resuming her knitting)* I do, David.

DAVID I have a proposition to put before Mr Shand, and women are out of place in business transactions.

> *The needles continue to click.*

ALICK *(sighing)* We'll have to let her bide, David.

DAVID *(sternly)* Woman. *(But even this does not budge her.)* Very well then, sit there, but don't interfere, mind. Mr Shand, we're willing, the three of us, to lay out £300 on your education if –

JOHN Take care –

DAVID *(slowly, which is not his wont)* On condition that five years from now, Maggie Wylie, if still unmarried, can claim to marry you, should such be her wish; the thing to be perfectly open on her side, but you to be strictly tied down.

JAMES *(enlightened)* So, so.

DAVID *(resuming his smart manner)* Now, what have you to say? Decide.

JOHN *(after a pause)* I regret to say –

MAGGIE It doesn't matter what he regrets to say, because I decide against it. And I think it was very ill done of you to make any such proposal.

DAVID *(without looking at her)* Quiet, Maggie.

JOHN *(looking at her)* I must say, Miss Maggie, I don't see what reasons you can have for being so set against it.

MAGGIE If you would grow a beard, Mr Shand, the reasons wouldn't be quite so obvious.

JOHN I'll never grow a beard.

MAGGIE Then you're done for at the start.

ALICK Come, come.

MAGGIE Seeing I have refused the young man –

JOHN Refused!

DAVID That's no reason why we shouldn't have his friendly opinion. Your objections, Mr Shand?

JOHN Simply, it's a one sided bargain. I admit I'm no catch at present; but what could a man of my abilities not soar to with three hundred pounds? Something far above what she could aspire to.

MAGGIE Oh, indeed.

DAVID The position is that without the three hundred you can't soar.

JOHN You have me there.

MAGGIE Yes, but –

ALICK You see you're safe guarded, Maggie; you don't need to take him unless you like, but he has to take you.

JOHN That's an unfair arrangement also.

MAGGIE I wouldn't dream of it without that condition.

JOHN Then you are thinking of it?

MAGGIE Poof.

DAVID It's a good arrangement for you, Mr Shand. The chances are you'll never have to go on with it, for in all probability she'll marry soon.

JAMES She's tremendous run after.

JOHN Even if that's true, it's just keeping me in reserve in case she misses doing better.

DAVID *(relieved)* That's the situation in a nutshell.

JOHN Another thing. Supposing I was to get fond of her?

ALICK *(wistfully)* It's very likely.

JOHN Yes, and then suppose she was to give me the go-by?

DAVID You have to risk that.

JOHN Or take it the other way. Supposing as I got to know her I could not endure her?

DAVID *(suavely)* You have both to take risks.

JAMES *(less suavely)* What you need, John Shand, is a clout on the head.

JOHN Three hundred pounds is no great sum.

DAVID You can take it or leave it.

ALICK No great sum for a student studying for the ministry!

JOHN Do you think that with that amount of money I would stop short at being a minister?

DAVID That's how I like to hear you speak. A young Scotsman of your ability let loose upon the world with £300, what could he not do? It's almost appalling to think of; especially if he went among the English.

JOHN What do you think, Miss Maggie?

MAGGIE *(who is knitting)* I have no thoughts on the subject either way.

JOHN *(after looking her over)* What's her age? She looks young, but they say it's the curls that does it.

DAVID *(rather happily)* She's one of those women who are eternally young.

JOHN I can't take that for an answer.

DAVID She's twenty-five.

JOHN I'm just twenty-one.

JAMES I read in a book that about four years' difference in the ages is the ideal thing. *(As usual he is disregarded.)*

DAVID Well, Mr Shand?

JOHN *(where is his mother!)* I'm willing if she's willing.

DAVID Maggie?

MAGGIE There can be no 'if' about it. It must be an offer.

JOHN A Shand give a Wylie such a chance to humiliate him? Never.

MAGGIE Then all is off.

DAVID Come, come, Mr Shand, it's just a form.

JOHN *(reluctantly)* Miss Maggie, will you?

MAGGIE *(doggedly)* Is it an offer?

JOHN *(dourly)* Yes.

MAGGIE *(rising)* Before I answer I want first to give you a chance of drawing back.

DAVID Maggie.

MAGGIE *(bravely)* When they said that I have been run after they were misleading you. I'm without charm; nobody has ever been after me.

JOHN Oho!

ALICK They will be yet.

JOHN *(the innocent)* It shows at least that you haven't been after them.

His hosts exchange a self conscious glance.

MAGGIE One thing more; David said I'm twenty-five, I'm twenty-six.

JOHN Aha!

MAGGIE Now be practical. Do you withdraw from the bargain, or do you not?

JOHN *(on reflection)* It's a bargain.

MAGGIE Then so be it.

DAVID *(hurriedly)* And that's settled. Did you say you would take it hot, Mr Shand?

JOHN I think I'll take it neat. *(The others decide to take it hot, and there is some careful business here with the toddy ladles.)*

ALICK Here's to you, and your career.

JOHN Thank you. To you, Miss Maggie. Had we not better draw up a legal document? Lawyer Crosbie could do it on the quiet.

DAVID Should we do that, or should we just trust to one another's honour?

ALICK *(gallantly)* Let Maggie decide.

MAGGIE I think we would better have a legal document.

DAVID We'll have it drawn up tomorrow. I was thinking the best way would be for to pay the money in five yearly installments.

JOHN I was thinking, better bank the whole sum in my name at once.

ALICK I think David's plan's the best.

JOHN I think not. Of course if it's not convenient to you –

DAVID *(touched to the quick)* It's perfectly convenient. What do you say, Maggie?

MAGGIE I agree with John.

DAVID *(with an odd feeling that* MAGGIE *is now on the other side)* Very well.

JOHN Then as that's settled I think I'll be stepping. *(He is putting his papers back in the bag.)*

ALICK *(politely)* If you would like to sit on at your books –

JOHN As I can come at any orra[1] time now I think I'll be stepping. (MAGGIE *helps him into his topcoat.)*

MAGGIE Have you a muffler, John?

JOHN I have. *(He gets it from his pocket.)*

MAGGIE You had better put it twice round. *(She does this for him.)*

DAVID Well goodnight to you, Mr Shand.

ALICK And good luck.

JOHN Thank you. The same to you. And I'll cry in at your office in the morning before the 6.20 is due.

DAVID I'll have the document ready for you. *(There is the awkward pause that sometimes follows great events.)* I think, Maggie, you might see Mr Shand to the door.

MAGGIE Certainly. (JOHN *is going by the window.)* This way, John. *(She takes him off by the more usual exit.)*

DAVID He's a fine frank fellow; and you saw how cleverly he got the better of me about banking the money. *(As the heads of the conspirators come gleefully together.)* I tell you, father, he has a grand business head.

ALICK Lads, he's canny. He's cannier than any of us.

JAMES Except maybe Maggie. He has no idea what a remarkable woman Maggie is.

ALICK Best he shouldn't know. Men are nervous of remarkable women.

JAMES She's a long time in coming back.

DAVID *(not quite comfortable)* It's a good sign. H'sh. What sort of a night is it, Maggie?

MAGGIE It's a little blowy.

> She gets a large dust cloth which is lying folded on a shelf, and proceeds to spread it over the fine chair. The men exchange self conscious glances.

DAVID *(stretching himself)* Yes – well, well, oh yes. It's getting late. What is it with you, father?

ALICK I'm ten forty-two.

JAMES I'm ten forty.

DAVID Ten forty-two.

---

[1] Odd.

They wind up their watches.

MAGGIE It's high time we were bedded. *(She puts her hands on their shoulders lovingly, which is the very thing they have been trying to avoid.)* You're very kind to me.

DAVID Havers.

ALICK Havers.

JAMES *(but this does not matter)* Havers.

MAGGIE *(a little dolefully)* I'm a sort of sorry for the young man, David.

DAVID Not at all. You'll be the making of him. *(She lifts the two volumes.)* Are you taking the books to your bed, Maggie?

MAGGIE Yes. I don't want him to know things I don't know myself.

She departs with the books; and ALICK *and* DAVD, *the villains, now want to get away from each other.*

ALICK Yes – yes. Oh yes – ay, man – it is so – umpha. You'll lift the big coals off, David.

He wanders away to his spring mattress. DAVID *removes the coals.*

JAMES *(who would like to sit down and have an argy-bargy)* It's a most romantical affair. *(But he gets no answer.)* I wonder how it'll turn out? *(No answer.)* She's queer, Maggie. I wonder how some clever writer has never noticed how queer women are. It's my belief you could write a whole book about them. *(*DAVID *remains obdurate.)* It was very noble of her to tell him she's twenty-six. *(Muttering as he too wanders away.)* But I thought she was twenty-seven.

DAVID *turns out the light.*

ACT TWO

Six years have elapsed and John Shand's great hour has come. Perhaps his great hour really lies ahead of him, perhaps he had it six years ago; it often passes us by in the night with such a faint call that we don't even turn in our beds. But according to the trumpets this is John's great hour; it is the hour for which he has long been working with his coat off; and now the coat is on again (broadcloth but ill fitting), for there is no more to do but await results. He is standing for Parliament, and this is election night.

As the scene discloses itself you get, so to speak, one of John Shand's posters in the face. Vote for Shand. Shand, Shand, Shand. Civil and Religious Liberty, Faith, Hope, Freedom. They are all fly-blown names for Shand. Have a placard about Shand, have a hundred placards about him, it is snowing Shand tonight in Glasgow; take the paste out of your eye, and you will see that we are in one of Shand's committee rooms. It has been a hairdresser's emporium, but Shand, Shand, Shand has swept through it like a wind, leaving nothing but the fixtures; why shave, why have your head doused in those basins when you can be brushed and scraped and washed up for ever by simply voting for Shand?

There are a few hard chairs for yelling Shand from, and then rushing away. There is an iron spiral staircase that once led to the ladies hair dressing apartments, but now leads to more Shand, Shand, Shand. A glass door at the back opens on to the shop proper, screaming Civil and Religious Liberty, Shand, as it opens, and beyond is the street crammed with still more Shand pro and con. Men in every sort of garb rush in and out, up and down the stair, shouting the magic word. Then there is a lull, and down the stair comes MAGGIE WYLIE, decidedly over dressed in blue velvet and (let us get this over) less good looking than ever. She raises her hands to heaven, she spins round like a little teetotum. To her from the street, suffering from a determination of the word Shand to the mouth, rush ALICK and DAVID. ALICK is thinner (being older), DAVID is stouter (being older), and they are both in tweeds and silk hats.

MAGGIE David – have they – is he? quick, quick!

DAVID There's no news yet, no news. It's terrible.

The teetotum revolves more quickly.

ALICK For God's sake, Maggie, sit down.

MAGGIE I can't, I can't.

DAVID Hold her down.

They press her into a chair; JAMES darts in, stouter also. His necktie has gone; he will never again be able to attend a funeral in that hat.

JAMES *(wildly)* John Shand's the man for you. John Shand's the man for you. John Shand's the man for you.

DAVID *(clutching him)* Have you heard anything?

JAMES Not a word.

ALICK Look at her.

DAVID Maggie *(he goes on his knees beside her, pressing her to him in affectionate anxiety).* It was mad of him to dare.

MAGGIE It was grand of him.

ALICK *(moving about distraught)* Insane ambition.

MAGGIE Glorious ambition.

DAVID Maggie, Maggie, my lamb, best be prepared for the worst.

MAGGIE *(husky)* I am prepared.

ALICK Six weary years has she waited for this night.

MAGGIE Six brave years has John toiled for this night.

JAMES And you could have had him, Maggie, at the end of five. The document says five.

MAGGIE Do you think I grudge not being married to him yet? Was I to hamper him till the fight was won?

DAVID *(with wrinkled brows)* But if it's lost? *(She can't answer.)*

ALICK *(starting)* What's that?

The three listen at the door; the shouting dies down.

DAVID They're terrible still; what can make them so still?

*JAMES spirits himself away. ALICK and DAVID blanch to hear
MAGGIE speaking softly as if to JOHN.*

MAGGIE Did you say you had lost, John? Of course you would lose the first time, dear John. Six years. Very well, we'll begin another six tonight. You'll win yet. *(Fiercely.)* Never give in, John, never give in!

The roar of the multitude breaks out again and comes rolling nearer.

DAVID I think he's coming.

JAMES is fired into the room like a squeezed onion.

JAMES He's coming!

They may go on speaking, but through the clang outside none could hear. The populace seem to be trying to take the committee room by assault. Out of the scrimmage a man emerges disheveled and bursts into the room, closing the door behind him. It is JOHN SHAND in a five guinea suit, including the hat. There are other changes in him also, for he has been delving his way through loamy ground all those years. His right shoulder, which he used to raise to pound a path through the crowd, now remains permanently in that position. His mouth tends to close like a box. His eyes are tired, they need some one to pull the lids over them and send him to sleep for a week. But they are honest eyes still, and faithful, and could even light up his face at times with a smile, if the mouth would give a little help.

JOHN *(clinging to a chair that he may not fly straight to heaven)* I'm in; I'm elected. Majority two hundred and forty-four; I'm John Shand, M.P.

> *The crowd have the news by this time and their roar breaks the door open.* JAMES *is off at once to tell them that he is to be Shand's brother-in-law. A teardrop clings to* ALICK'S *nose;* DAVID *hits out playfully at* JOHN, *and* JOHN *in an ecstasy returns the blow.*

DAVID Fling yourself at the door, father, and bar them out. Maggie, what keeps you so quiet now?

MAGGIE *(weak in her limbs)* You're sure you're in, John.

JOHN Majority 244. I've beaten the baronet. I've done it, Maggie, and not a soul to help me; I've done it alone. *(His voice breaks; you could almost pick up the pieces.)* I'm as hoarse as a crow, and I have to address the Cowcaddens Club yet; David, pump some oxygen into me.

DAVID Certainly, Mr Shand. *(While he does it,* MAGGIE *is seeing visions.)*

ALICK What are you doing, Maggie?

MAGGIE This is the House of Commons, and I'm John, catching the Speaker's eye for the first time. Do you see a queer little old wifie sitting away up there in the Ladies' Gallery? That's me. Mr Speaker, sir, I rise to make my historic maiden speech. I am no orator, sir; voice from Ladies' Gallery, 'Are you not, John? you'll soon let them see that'; cries of 'Silence, woman,' and general indignation. Mr Speaker, sir, I stand here diffidently with my eyes on the Treasury Bench; voice from the Ladies' Gallery, 'And you'll soon have yours coat-tails on it, John'; loud cries of 'Remove that little old wifie,' in which she is forcibly ejected, and the honourable gentleman resumes his seat in a torrent of admiring applause.

> ALICK *and* DAVID *waggle their proud heads.*

JOHN *(tolerantly)* Maggie, Maggie.

MAGGIE You re not angry with me, John?

JOHN No, no.

MAGGIE But you glowered.

JOHN I was thinking of Sir Peregrine. Just because I beat him at the poll he took a shabby revenge; he congratulated me in French, a language I haven't taken the trouble to master.

MAGGIE *(becoming a little taller)* Would it help you, John, if you were to marry a woman that could speak French?

DAVID *(quickly)* Not at all.

MAGGIE *(gloriously)* Mon cher Jean, laissez moi parler le français, voulez-vous un interprète?

JOHN Hullo!

MAGGIE Je suis la soeur française de mes deux frères écossais.[1]

DAVID *(worshipping her)* She's been learning French.

JOHN *(lightly)* Well done.

MAGGIE *(grandly)* They're arriving.

ALICK Who?

MAGGIE Our guests. This is London, and Mrs John Shand is giving her first reception. *(Airily)*. Have I told you, darling, who are coming tonight? There's that dear Sir Peregrine. *(To* ALICK.) Sir Peregrine, this is a pleasure. Avez-vous. . . So sorry we beat you at the poll.

JOHN I'm doubting the baronet would sit on you, Maggie.

MAGGIE I've invited a lord to sit on the baronet. Voilà!

DAVID *(delighted)* You thing! You'll find the lords expensive.

---

[1] My dear John, let me speak French, do you want an interpreter?/I am the sister of my two Scottish brothers.

MAGGIE Just a little cheap lord. (JAMES *enters importantly.*) My dear Lord Cheap, this is kind of you.

JAMES *hopes that* MAGGIE'S *reason is not unbalanced.*

DAVID *(who really ought to have had education)* How de doo, Cheap?
JAMES *(bewildered)* Maggie –
MAGGIE Yes, do call me Maggie.
ALICK *(grinning)* She's practicing her first party, James. The swells are at the door.
JAMES *(heavily)* That's what I came to say. They are at the door.
JOHN Who?
JAMES The swells; a carriage and pair. *(He gives* JOHN *three cards.)*
JOHN 'Mr Tenterden'.
DAVID Him that was speaking for you?
JOHN The same. He's a whip and an Honourable. 'Lady Sybil Tenterden'. *(Frowns.)* Her! She's his sister.
MAGGIE A married woman?
JOHN No. 'The Comtesse de la Briére'.
MAGGIE *(the scholar)* She must be French.
JOHN Yes; I think she's some relation. She's a widow.
JAMES But what am I to say to them? *('Mr Shand's compliments, and he will be proud to receive them' is the very least that the Wylies expect.)*
JOHN *(who was evidently made for great ends)* Say I'm very busy, but if they care to wait I hope presently to give them a few minutes.
JAMES *(thunderstruck)* Good God, Mr Shand!

But it makes him JOHN'S *more humble servant than ever, and he departs with the message.*

JOHN *(not unaware of the sensation he has created)* I'll go up and let the crowd see me from the window.
MAGGIE But – but – what are we to do with these ladies?
JOHN *(as he tramps upwards)* It's your reception, Maggie; this will prove you.
MAGGIE *(growing smaller)* Tell me what you know about this Lady Sybil?
JOHN The only thing I know about her is that she thinks me vulgar.
MAGGIE You?
JOHN She has attended some of my meetings, and I'm told she said that.
MAGGIE What could the woman mean?
JOHN I wonder. When I come down I'll ask her.

With his departure MAGGIE'S *nervousness increases.*

ALICK *(encouragingly)* In at them, Maggie, with your French.
MAGGIE It's all slipping from me, father.
DAVID *(gloomily)* I'm sure to say 'for to come for to go.'

> *The newcomers glorify the room, and* MAGGIE *feels that they have lifted her up with the tongs and deposited her in one of the basins. They are far from intending to be rude; it is not their fault that thus do swans scatter the ducks. They do not know that they are guests of the family, they think merely that they are waiting with other strangers in a public room; they undulate enquiringly, and if* MAGGIE *could undulate in return she would have no cause for offence. But she suddenly realises that this is an art as yet denied her, and that though* DAVID *might buy her evening gowns as fine as theirs (and is at this moment probably deciding to do so), she would look better carrying them in her arms than on her person. She also feels that to emerge from wraps as they are doing is more difficult than to plank your money on the counter for them. The* COMTESSE *she could forgive, for she is old; but* LADY SYBIL *is young and beautiful and comes lazily to rest like a stately ship of Tarsus.*

COMTESSE *(smiling divinely, and speaking with such a pretty accent)* I hope one is not in the way. We were told we might wait.

MAGGIE *(bravely climbing out of the basin)* Certainly – I am sure – if you will be so – it is – *(She knows that* DAVID *and her father are very sorry for her.)*

A high voice is heard orating outside.

SYBIL *(screwing her nose deliciously)* He is at it again, Auntie.

COMTESSE Mon Dieu! *(Like one begging pardon of the universe.)* It is Mr Tenterden, you understand, making one more of his delightful speeches to the crowd. Would you be so charming as to shut the door?

This to DAVID *in such appeal that she is evidently making the petition of her life.* DAVID *saves her.*

MAGGIE *(determined not to go under)* J'espère que vous – trouvez – cette – réunion – intéressante?

COMTESSE Vous parlez français? Mais c'est charmant! Voyons, causons un peu. Racontezmoi tout de ce grand homme, toutes les choses merveilleuses qu'il a faites.

MAGGIE I – I – Je connais[1] – *(Alas!)*

COMTESSE *(naughtily)* Forgive me, Mademoiselle, I thought you spoke French.

SYBIL *(who sinows that* DAVID *admires her shoulders)* How wicked of you, Auntie. *(To* MAGGIE.*)* I assure you none of us can understand her when she gallops at that pace.

MAGGIE *(crushed)* It doesn't matter. I will tell Mr Shand that you are here.

SYBIL *(drawling)* Please don't trouble him. We are really only waiting till my brother recovers and can take us back to our hotel.

MAGGIE I'll tell him.

She is glad to disappear up the stair.

COMTESSE The lady seems distressed. Is she a relation of Mr Shand?

DAVID Not for to say a relation. She's my sister. Our name is Wylie.

But granite quarries are nothing to them.

COMTESSE How do you do. You are the committee man of Mr Shand?

DAVID No, just friends.

COMTESSE *(gaily to the basins)* Aha! I know you. Next, please! Sybil, do you weigh yourself, or are you asleep?

LADY SYBIL *has sunk indolently into a weighing chair.*

SYBIL Not quite, Auntie.

COMTESSE *(the mirror of la politesse)* Tell me all about Mr Shand. Was it here that he picked up the pin?

DAVID The pin?

COMTESSE As I have read, a self made man always begins by picking up a pin. After that, as the memoirs say, his rise was rapid.

DAVID, *however, is once more master of himself, and indeed has begun to tot up the cost of their garments.*

DAVID It wasn't a pin he picked up, my lady; it was £300.

ALICK *(who feels that* JOHN'S *greatness has been outside the conversation quite long enough)* And his rise wasn't so rapid, just at first, David!

---

[1] I hope that you – find – this – meeting – interesting?/You speak French? How charming! Let's see, let's chat a bit. Tell me everything about this great man, all the wonderful things he has done./I – I – I know –

DAVID He had his fight. His original intention was to become a minister; he's university educated, you know; he's not a workingman member.

ALICK *(with reverence)* He's an M.A. But while he was a student he got a place in an iron cementer's business.

COMTESSE *(now far out of her depths)* Iron cementer?

DAVID They scrape boilers.

COMTESSE I see. The fun men have, Sybil!

DAVID *(with some solemnity)* There have been millions made in scraping boilers. They say, father, he went into business so as to be able to pay off the £300.

alick *(slyly)* So I've heard.

COMTESSE Aha – it was a loan?

DAVID and ALICK are astride their great subject now.

DAVID No, a gift – of a sort – from some well-wishers. But they wouldn't hear of his paying it off, father!

ALICK Not them!

COMTESSE *(restraining an impulse to think of other things)* That was kind, charming.

ALICK *(with a look at DAVID)* Yes. Well, my lady, he developed a perfect genius for the iron cementing.

DAVID But his ambition wasn't satisfied. Soon he had public life in his eye. As a heckler he was something fearsome; they had to seat him on the platform for to keep him quiet. Next they had to let him into the Chair. After that he did all the speaking; he cleared al! roads before him like a fire engine; and when this vacancy occurred, you could hardly say it did occur, so quickly did he step into it. My lady, there are few more impressive sights in the world than a Scotsman on the make.

COMTESSE I can well believe it. And now he has said farewell to boilers?

DAVID *(impressively)* Not at all; the firm promised if he was elected for to make him their London manager at £800 a year.

COMTESSE There is a strong man for you, Sybil; but I believe you are asleep.

SYBIL *(stirring herself)* Honestly I'm not. *(Sweetly to the others.)* But would you mind finding out whether my brother is drawing to a close?

DAVID goes out, leaving poor ALICK marooned. The COMTESSE is kind to him.

COMTESSE Thank you very much. *(Which helps ALICK out.)* Don't you love a strong man, sleepy head?

SYBIL *(preening herself)* I never met one.

COMTESSE Neither have I. But if you did meet one, would he wake you up?

SYBIL I dare say he would find there were two of us.

COMTESSE *(considering her)* Yes, I think he would. Ever been in love, you cold thing?

SYBIL *(yawning)* I have never shot up in flame, Auntie.

COMTESSE Think you could manage it?

SYBIL If Mr Right came along.

COMTESSE As a girl of today it would be your duty to tame him.

SYBIL As a girl of today I would try to do my duty.

COMTESSE And if it turned out that he tamed you instead?

SYBIL He would have to do that if he were my Mr Right.

COMTESSE And then?

SYBIL Then, of course, I should adore him. Auntie, I think if I ever really love it will be like Mary Queen of Scots, who said of her Bothwell that she could follow him round the world in her nighty.

COMTESSE My petite!

SYBIL I believe I mean it.

COMTESSE Oh, it is quite my conception of your character. Do you know, I am rather sorry for this Mr John Shand.

SYBIL *(opening her fine eyes)* Why? He is quite a boor, is he not?

COMTESSE For that very reason. Because his great hour is already nearly sped. That wild bull manner that moves the multitude – they will laugh at it in your House of Commons.

SYBIL *(indifferent)* I suppose so.

COMTESSE Yet if he had education –

SYBIL Have we not been hearing how superbly he is educated?

COMTESSE It is such as you or me that he needs to educate him now. You could do it almost too well.

SYBIL *(with that pretty stretch of neck)* I am not sufficiently interested. I retire in your favour. How would you begin?

COMTESSE By asking him to drop in, about five, of course. By the way, I wonder is there a Mrs Shand?

SYBIL I have no idea. But they marry young.

COMTESSE If there is not, there is probably a lady waiting for him, somewhere in a boiler.

SYBIL I dare say.

MAGGIE *descends.*

MAGGIE Mr Shand will be down directly.

COMTESSE Thank you. Your brother has been giving us such an interesting account of his career. I forget, Sybil, whether he said that he was married.

MAGGIE No, he's not married; but he will be soon.

COMTESSE Ah! *(She is merely making conversation.)* A friend of yours?

MAGGIE *(now a scorner of herself)* I don't think much of her.

COMTESSE In that case, tell me all about her.

MAGGIE There's not much to tell. She's common, and stupid. One of those who go in for self culture; and then when the test comes they break down. *(With sinister enjoyment.)* She'll be the ruin of him.

COMTESSE But is not that sad! Figure to yourself how many men with greatness before them have been shipwrecked by marrying in the rank from which they sprang.

MAGGIE I've told her that.

COMTESSE But she will not give him up?

MAGGIE No.

SYBIL Why should she if he cares for her? What is her name?

MAGGIE It's – Maggie.

COMTESSE *(still uninterested)* Well, I am afraid that Maggie is to do for John. (JOHN *comes down.*) Ah, our hero!

JOHN Sorry I have kept you waiting. The Comtesse?

COMTESSE And my niece Lady Sybil Tenterden. (SYBIL'S *head inclines on its stem.)* She is not really all my niece; I mean I am only half of her aunt. What a triumph, Mr Shand!

JOHN Oh, pretty fair, pretty fair. Your brother has just finished addressing the crowd, Lady Sybil.

SYBIL Then we must not detain Mr Shand, Auntie.

COMTESSE *(who unless her heart is touched thinks insincerity charming)* Only one word. I heard you speak last night. Sublime! Just the sort of impassioned eloquence that your House of Commons loves.

JOHN It's very good of you to say so.

COMTESSE But we must run. Bon soir.

SYBIL *bows as to some one far away.*

JOHN Goodnight, Lady Sybil. I hear you think I'm vulgar.

Eyebrows are raised.

COMTESSE My dear Mr Shand, what absurd –

JOHN I was told she said that after hearing me speak.

COMTESSE Quite a mistake, I –

JOHN *(doggedly)* Is it not true?

SYBIL *('waking up')* You seem to know, Mr Shand; and as you press me so unnecessarily – well, yes, that is how you struck me.

COMTESSE My child!

SYBIL *(who is a little agitated)* He would have it.

JOHN *(perplexed)* What's the matter? I just wanted to know, because if it's true I must alter it.

COMTESSE There, Sybil, see how he values your good opinion.

SYBIL *(her svelte figure giving like a fly rod)* It is very nice of you to put it in that way, Mr Shand. Forgive me.

JOHN But I don't quite understand yet. Of course, it can't matter to me, Lady Sybil, what you think of me; what I mean is, that I mustn't be vulgar if it would be injurious to my career.

The fly rod regains its rigidity.

SYBIL I see. No, of course, I could not affect your career, Mr Shand.

JOHN *(who quite understands that he is being challenged)* That's so, Lady Sybil, meaning no offence.

SYBIL *(who has a naughty little impediment in her voice when she is most alluring)* Of course not. And we are friends again?

JOHN Certainly.

SYBIL Then I hope you will come to see me in London as I present no terrors.

JOHN *(he is a man, is* JOHN*)* I'll be very pleased.

SYBIL Any afternoon about five.

JOHN Much obliged. And you can teach me the things I don't know yet, if you'll be so kind.

SYBIL *(the impediment becoming more assertive)* If you wish it, I shall do my best.

JOHN Thank you, Lady Sybil. And who knows there may be one or two things I can teach you.

SYBIL *(it has now become an angel's hiccough)* Yes, we can help one another. Goodbye till then.

JOHN Goodbye. Maggie, the ladies are going. *(During this skirmish* MAGGIE *has stood apart. At the mention of her name they glance at one another.* JOHN *escorts* SYBIL, *but the* COMTESSE *turns back. She says:)*

'Are you, then, the Maggie? (MAGGIE *nods rather defiantly and the* COMTESSE *is distressed.)* But if I had known I would not have said those things. Please forgive an old woman.'

'It doesn't matter.'

'I – I dare say it will be all right. Mademoiselle, if I were you I would not encourage those tete-d-tetes with Lady Sybil. I am the rude one, but she is the dangerous one; and I am afraid his impudence has attracted her. Bon voyage, Miss Maggie.'

'Goodbye but I can speak French. Je parle français. Isn't that right?'

'But, yes, it is excellent. *(Making things easy for her.)* C'est très bien.'

'Je me suis embrouillée la dernière fois.'

'Good! Shall I speak more slowly?'

'No, no. Non, non, faster, faster.'

'J'admire votre courage!'[1]

'Je comprends chaque mot.'[1]

'Parfait! Bravo!'

'Voilà!'

'Superbe!'

---

[1] I speak French./That's very good./I got mixed up last time./I admire your courage.

The COMTESSE *goes, applauding; and* MAGGIE *has a moment of elation, which however has passed before* JOHN *returns for his hat.*

'Have you more speaking to do, John?' *(He is somehow in high good humour.)*

'I must run across and address the Cowcaddens Club. *(He sprays his throat with a hand spray.)* I wonder if I am vulgar, Maggie?'

'You are not, but I am.'

'Not that I can see.'

'Look how over dressed I am, John! I knew it was too showy when I ordered it, and yet I could not resist the thing. But I will tone down, I will. What did you think of Lady Sybil?'

'That young woman had better be careful. She's a bit of a beson,[2] Maggie.'

'She's beautiful, John.'

'She has a neat way of stretching herself. For playing with she would do as well as another.' *(*MAGGIE *looks at him wistfully.)*

'You couldn't stay and have a talk for a few minutes?'

'If you want me, Maggie. The longer you keep them waiting, the more they think of you.'

'When are you to announce that we're to be married, John?'

'I won't be long. You've waited a year more than you need have done, so I think it's your due I should hurry things now.'

'I think it's noble of you.'

'Not at all, Maggie; the nobleness has been yours in waiting so patiently. And your brothers would insist on it at any rate. They're watching me like cats with a mouse.'

'It's so little I've done to help.'

'Three hundred pounds.'

'I'm getting a thousand per cent for it.'

'And very pleased I am you should think so, Maggie.'

'Is it terrible hard to you, John?'

'It's not hard at all. I can say truthfully, Maggie, that all, or nearly all, I've seen of you in these six years has gone to increase my respect for you.'

'Respect!'

'And a bargain's a bargain.'

'If it wasn't that you're so glorious to me, John, I would let you off.'

(There is a gleam in his eye, but he puts it out.)

'In my opinion, Maggie, we'll be a very happy pair.'

(She accepts this eagerly.)

'We know each other so well, John? don't we?'

'I'm an extraordinary queer character, and I suppose nobody knows me well except myself; but I know you, Maggie, to the very roots of you.'

(She magnanimously lets this remark alone.)

'And it's not as if there was any other woman you – fancied more, John.'

'There's none whatever.'

'If there ever should be – oh, if there ever should be! Some woman with charm.'

'Maggie, you forget yourself. There couldn't be another woman once I was a married man.'

'One has heard of such things.'

'Not in Scotsmen, Maggie; not in Scotsmen.'

'I've sometimes thought, John, that the difference between us and the English is that the Scotch are hard in all other respects but soft with women, and the English are hard with women but soft in all other respects.'

'You've forgotten the grandest moral attribute of a Scotsman, Maggie, that he'll do nothing

---

[1] I understand each word.
[2] Witch.

which might damage his career.'

'Ah, but John, whatever you do, you do it so tremendously; and if you were to love, what a passion it would be.'

'There's something in that, I suppose.'

'And then, what could I do? For the desire of my life now, John, is to help you to get everything you want, except just that I want you to have me, too.'

'We'll get on fine, Maggie.'

'You're just making the best of it. They say that love is sympathy, and if that's so mine must be a great love for you, for I see all you are feeling this night and bravely hiding; I feel for you as if I was John Shand myself. (JOHN *sighs.*)

'I had best go to the meeting, Maggie.'

'Not yet. Can you look me in the face, John, and deny that there is surging within you a mighty desire to be free, to begin the new life untrammeled?'

'Leave such maggots alone, Maggie.'

'It's a shame of me not to give you up.'

'I would consider you a very foolish woman if you did.'

'If I were John Shand I would no more want to take Maggie Wylie with me through the beautiful door that has opened wide for you than I would want to take an old pair of shoon. Why don't you bang the door in my face, John?' *(A tremor runs through* JOHN.)

'A bargain's a bargain, Maggie.'

MAGGIE *moves about, an eerie figure, breaking into little cries. She flutters round him, threateningly.*

'Say one word about wanting to get out of it, and I'll put the lawyers on you.'

'Have I hinted at such a thing?'

'The document holds you hard and fast.'

'It does.'

(She gloats miserably.)

'The woman never rises with the man. I'll drag you down, John. I'll drag you down.'

'Have no fear of that, I won't let you. I'm too strong.'

'You'll miss the prettiest thing in the world, and all owing to me.'

'What's that?'

'Romance.'

'Poof.'

'All's cold and grey without it, John. They that have had it have slipped in and out of heaven.'

'You're exaggerating, Maggie.'

'You've worked so hard, you've had none of the fun that comes to most men long before they're your age.'

'I never was one for fun. I cannot call to mind, Maggie, ever having laughed in my life.'

'You have no sense of humour.'

'Not a spark.'

'I've sometimes thought that if you had, it might make you fonder of me. I think one needs a sense of humour to be fond of me.'

'I remember reading of some one that said it needed a surgical operation to get a joke into a Scotsman's head.'

'Yes, that's been said.'

'What beats me, Maggie, is how you could insert a joke with an operation.'

(He considers this and gives it up.)

'That's not the kind of fun I was thinking of. I mean fun with the lasses, John — gay, jolly, harmless fun. They could be impudent fashionable beauties now, stretching themselves to attract you, like that hiccoughing little devil, and running away from you, and crooking their fingers to you to run after them.'

(JOHN *draws a big breath.*)

'No, I never had that.'

'It's every man's birthright, and you would have it now but for me.'

'I can do without, Maggie.'

'It's like missing out all the Saturdays.'

'You feel sure, I suppose, that an older man wouldn't suit you better, Maggie?'

'I couldn't feel surer of anything. You're just my ideal.'

'Yes, yes. Well, that's as it should be.'

(She threatens him again.)

'David has the document. It's carefully locked away.'

'He would naturally take good care of it.'

(The pride of the Wylies deserts her.)

'John, I make you a solemn promise that, in consideration of the circumstances of our marriage, if you should ever fall in love I'll act differently from other wives.'

'There will be no occasion, Maggie.'

(Her voice becomes tremulous.)

'John, David doesn't have the document. He thinks he has, but I have it here.'

(Somewhat heavily JOHN surveys the fatal paper.)

'Well do I mind the look of it, Maggie. Yes, yes, that's it. Umpha.'

'You don't ask why I've brought it.'

'Why did you?'

'Because I thought I might perhaps have the courage and the womanliness to give it back to you. (JOHN *has a brief dream.*) Will you never hold it up against me in the future that I couldn't do that?'

'I promise you, Maggie, I never will.'

'To go back to the Pans and take up my old life there, when all these six years my eyes have been centred on this night! I've been waiting for this night as long as you have been; and now to go back there, and wizen and dry up, when I might be married to John Shand!'

'And you will be, Maggie. You have my word.'

'Never – never – never. *(She tears up the document. He remains seated immovable, but the gleam returns to his eye. She rages first at herself and then at him.)* I'm a fool, a fool, to let you go. I tell you, you'll rue this day, for you need me, you'll come to grief without me. There's nobody can help you as I could have helped you. I'm essential to your career, and you're blind not to see it.'

'What's that, Maggie? In no circumstances would I allow any meddling with my career.'

'You would never have known I was meddling with it. But that's over. Don't be in too great a hurry to marry, John. Have your fling with the beautiful dolls first. Get the whip hand of the haughty ones, John. Give them their licks. Every time they hiccough let them have an extra slap in memory of me. And be sure to remember this, my man, that the one who marries you will find you out.'

'Find me out?'

'However careful a man is, his wife always finds out his failings.'

'I don't know, Maggie, to what failings you refer.'

> The Cowcaddens Club has burst its walls, and is pouring this way to raise the new Member on its crest. The first wave hurls itself against the barber's shop with cries of 'Shand, Shand, Shand.' For a moment JOHN stems the torrent by planting his back against the door.

'You are acting under an impulse, Maggie, and I can't take advantage of it. Think the matter over, and we'll speak about it in the morning.'

'No, I can't go through it again. It ends tonight and now. Good luck, John.'

> She is immediately submerged in the sea that surges through the door, bringing much wreckage with it. In a moment the place is so full that another cupful could not find standing

room. Some slippery ones are squeezed upwards and remain aloft as warnings. JOHN *has jumped on to the stair, and harangues the flood vainly like another Canute. It is something about freedom and noble minds, and, though unheard, goes to all heads, including the speaker's. By the time he is audible sentiment has him for her own.*

'But, gentlemen, one may have too much even of freedom. *(No, no.)* Yes, Mr Adamson. One may want to be tied. *(Never, never.)* I say yes, Willie Cameron; and I have found a young lady who I am proud to say is willing to be tied to me. I'm to be married. *(Uproar.)* Her name is Miss Wylie. *(Transport.)* Quiet; she's here now. *(Frenzy.)* She was here! Where are you, Maggie?' *(A small voice –* 'I'm here.' *A hundred great voices –* 'Where where where?' *The small voice –* 'I'm so little none of you can see me.')

Three men, name of Wylie, buffet their way forward. Anon is heard the voice of DAVID.

'James, father, have you grip of her?'
'We've got her.'
'Then hoist her up.'

The queer little elated figure is raised aloft. With her fingers she can just touch the stars. Not unconscious of the nobility of his behaviour, the hero of the evening points an impressive finger at her.

'Gentlemen, the future Mrs John Shand!' ('Speech, speech.') 'No, no, being a lady she can't make a speech, but – '

(The heroine of the evening surprises him.)

'I can make a speech, and I will make a speech, and it's in two words, and they're these – *(holding out her arms to enfold all the members of the Cowcaddens Club) –* My Constituents!' *(Dementia.)*

ACT THREE

A few minutes ago the Comtesse de la Brière, who has not recently been in England, was shown into the London home of the Shands. Though not sufficiently interested to express her surprise in words, she raised her eyebrows on finding herself in a charming room; she had presumed that the Shand scheme of decoration would be as impossible as themselves.

It is the little room behind the dining room for which English architects have long been famous; 'Make something of this, and you will indeed be a clever one,' they seem to say to you as they unveil it. The Comtesse finds that John has undoubtedly made something of it. It is his 'study' (mon Dieu, the words these English use!) and there is nothing in it that offends; there is so much not in it too that might so easily have been there. It is not in the least ornate; there are no colours quarrelling with each other (unseen, unheard by the blissful occupant of the revolving chair); the Comtesse has not even the gentle satisfaction of noting a 'suite' in stained oak. Nature might have taken a share in the decorations, so restful are they to the eyes; it is the working room of a man of culture, probably lately down from Oxford; at a first meeting there is nothing in it that pretends to be what it is not. Our visitor is a little disappointed, but being fair minded blows her absent host a kiss for disappointing her.

He has even, she observes with a twinkle, made something of the most difficult of his possessions, the little wife. For Maggie, who is here receiving her, has been quite creditably toned down. He has put her into a little grey frock that not only deals gently with her personal defects, but is in harmony with the room. Evidently, however, she has not 'risen' with him, for she is as stupid as ever; the Comtesse, who remembers having liked her the better of the two, could shake her for being so stupid. For instance, why is she not asserting herself in that other apartment?

The other apartment is really a correctly solemn dining room, of which we have a glimpse through partly open folding doors. At this moment it is harbouring Mr Shand's ladies' committee, who sit with pens and foolscap round the large table, awaiting the advent of their leader. There are nobly wise ones and some foolish ones among them, for we are back in the strange days when it was considered 'unwomanly' for women to have minds. The Comtesse peeps at them with curiosity, as they arrange their papers or are ushered into the dining room through a door which we cannot see. To her frivolous ladyship they are a species of wild fowl, and she is specially amused to find her niece among them. She demands an explanation as soon as the communicating doors close.

'Tell me since when has my dear Sybil become one of these ladies? It is not like her.'

(MAGGIE *is obviously not clever enough to understand the woman question. Her eye rests longingly on a half finished stocking as she innocently but densely replies:)*

'I think it was about the time that my husband took up their cause.'

(The COMTESSE *has been hearing tales of* LADY SYBIL *and the barbarian; and after having the grace to hesitate, she speaks with the directness for which she is famed in Mayfair.)*

'Mrs Shand, excuse me for saying that if half of what I hear be true, your husband is seeing that lady a great deal too often. (MAGGIE *is expressionless; she reaches for her stocking, whereat her guest loses patience.)* Oh, mon Dieu, put that down; you can buy them at two francs the pair. Mrs Shand, why do not you compel yourself to take an intelligent interest in your husband's work?'

'I typewrite his speeches.'

'But do you know what they are about?'

'They are about various subjects.'

'Oh!'

(Did MAGGIE *give her an unseen quizzical glance before demurely resuming the knitting? One is not certain, as* JOHN *has come in, and this obliterates her. A 'Scotsman on the make', of whom* DAVID *has spoken reverently, is still to be read – a somewhat better bound volume – in* JOHN SHAND'S *person; but it is as doggedly honest a face as ever; and he champions women, not for personal ends, but because his blessed days of poverty gave him a light upon their needs. His self satisfaction. however, has increased, and he has pleasantly forgotten some things. For instance, he can now call out 'Porter' at railway stations without dropping his hands for the barrow.* MAGGIE *introduces the* COMTESSE, *and he is still undaunted.)*

'I remember you well – at Glasgow.'

'It must be quite two years ago, Mr Shand.'

*(*JOHN *has no objection to showing that he has had a classical education.)*

'Tempus fugit, Comtesse.'

'I have not been much in this country since then, and I return to find you a coming man.'

(Fortunately his learning is tempered with modesty.)

'Oh, I don't know, I don't know.'

'The Ladies' Champion.'

(His modesty is tempered with a respect for truth.)

'Well, well.'

'And you are about, as I understand, to introduce a bill to give women an equal right with men to grow beards *(which is all she knows about it.* JOHN *takes the remark literally.)*

'There's nothing about beards in it, Comtesse. *(She gives him time to cogitate, and is pleased to note that there is no result.)* Have you typed my speech, Maggie?'

'Yes; twenty-six pages.' *(She produces it from a drawer.)*

(Perhaps JOHN *wishes to impress the visitor.)*

'I'm to give the ladies' committee a general idea of it. Just see, Maggie, if I know the peroration. "In conclusion, Mr Speaker, these are the reasonable demands of every intelligent Englishwoman" – I had better say British woman – "and I am proud to nail them to my flag".' *(The visitor is properly impressed.)*

'Oho! defies his leaders!'

'"So long as I can do so without embarrassing the Government."'

'Ah, ah, Mr Shand!'

'. . . "I call upon the Front Bench, sir, loyally but firmly."'

'Firm again!'

'. . . "either to accept my Bill, or to promise without delay to bring in one of their own; and if they decline to do so I solemnly warn them that though I will not press the matter to a division just now –"'

'Ahem!'

'I will bring it forward again in the near future. And now, Comtesse, you know that I'm not going to divide – and not another soul knows it.'

'I am indeed flattered by your confidence.'

'I've only told you because I don't care who knows now.'

'Oh!'

(Somehow MAGGIE *seems to be dissatisfied.)*

'But why is that, John?'

'I daren't keep the Government in doubt any longer about what I mean to do. I'll show the whips the speech privately tonight.'

(But still MAGGIE *wants to know.)* 'But not to go to a division is hedging, isn't it? Is that strong?'

'To make the speech at all, Maggie, is stronger than most would dare. They would do for me if I went to a division.'

'Bark but not bite?'

'Now, now, Maggie, you're out of your depth.'

'I suppose that's it.' *(The* COMTESSE *remains in the shallows.)*

'But what will the ladies say, Mr Shand?'

'They won't like it, Comtesse, but they've got to lump it.'

(Here the MAID *appears with a card for* MAGGIE, *who considers it quietly.)*

'Any one of importance?'

'No.'

'Then I'm ready, Maggie.'

> *(This is evidently an intimation that she is to open the folding doors, and he makes an effective entrance into the dining room, his thumb in his waistcoat. There is a delicious clapping of hands from the committee, and the door closes. Not till then does* MAGGIE, *who has grown thoughtful, tell her maid to admit the visitor.)*

'Another lady, Mrs Shand?'

'The card says "Mr Charles Venables".'

(The COMTESSE *is really interested at last.)*

'Charles Venables! Do you know him?'

'I think I call to mind meeting one of that name at the Foreign Office party.'

'One of that name! He who is a Minister of your Cabinet. But as you know him so little why should he call on you?'

'I wonder.'

*(*MAGGIE'S *glance wanders to the drawer in which she has replaced* JOHN'S *speech.)*

'Well, well, I shall take care of you, petite.'

'Do you know him?'

'Do I know him! The last time I saw him he asked me to – to – hem! – ma cherie, it was thirty years ago.'

'Thirty years!'

'I was a pretty woman then. I dare say I shall detest him now; but if I find I do not – let us have a little plot – I shall drop this book; and then perhaps you will be so charming as – as not to be here for a little while?'

(MR VENABLES, who enters, is such a courtly seigneur that he seems to bring the eighteenth century with him; you feel that his sedan chair is at the door. He stoops over MAGGIE's plebeian hand.)

'I hope you will pardon my calling, Mrs Shand; we had such a pleasant talk the other evening.'

(MAGGIE, of course, is at once deceived by his gracious manner.)

'I think it's kind of you. Do you know each other? The Comtesse de la Brière.'

(He repeats the name with some emotion, and the COMTESSE half mischievously, half sadly, holds a hand before her face.)

'Comtesse.'

'Thirty years, Mr Venables.'

(He gallantly removes the hand that screens her face.)

'It does not seem so much.' *(She gives him a similar scrutiny.)*

'Mon Dieu, it seems all that.'

(They smile rather ruefully. MAGGIE like a kind hostess relieves the tension.)

'The Comtesse has taken a cottage in Surrey for the summer.'

'I am overjoyed.'

'No, Charles, you are not. You no longer care. Fickle one! And it is only thirty years.'

(He sinks into a chair beside her.)

'Those heavenly evenings, Comtesse, on the Bosphorus.'

'I refuse to talk of them. I hate you.'

(But she drops the book, and MAGGIE fades from the room. It is not a very clever departure, and the old diplomatist smiles. Then he sighs a beautiful sigh, for he does all things beautifully.)

'It is moonlight, Comtesse, on the Golden Horn.'

'Who are those two young things in a caïque?'

'Is he the brave Leander, Comtesse, and is she Hero of the Lamp?'

'No, she is the foolish wife of the French Ambassador, and he is a good-for-nothing British attaché trying to get her husband's secrets out of her.'

'Is it possible! They part at a certain garden gate.'

'Oh, Charles, Charles!'

'But you promised to come back; I waited there till dawn. Blanche, if you had come back – '

'How is Mrs Venables?'

'She is rather poorly. I think it's gout.'

'And you?'

'I creak a little in the mornings.'

'So do I. There is such a good man at Wiesbaden.'

'The Homburg fellow is better. The way he patched me up last summer – Oh, Lord, Lord!'

'Yes, Charles, the game is up; we are two old fogies. *(They groan in unison; then she raps him sharply on the knuckles.)* Tell me, sir, what are you doing here?'

'Merely a friendly call.'

'I do not believe it.'

'The same woman; the old delightful candour.'

'The same man; the old fibs. *(She sees that the door is asking a question.)* Yes, come, Mrs Shand, I have had quite enough of him; I warn you he is here for some crafty purpose.'

MAGGIE *(drawing back timidly)* Surely not?

VENABLES Really, Comtesse, you make conversation difficult. To show that my intentions are innocent, Mrs Shand, I propose that you choose the subject.

MAGGIE *(relieved)* There, Comtesse.

VENABLES I hope your husband is well

MAGGIE Yes, thank you. *(With a happy thought.)* I decide that we talk about him.

VENABLES If you wish it.

COMTESSE Be careful; he has chosen the subject.

MAGGIE I chose it, didn't I?

VENABLES You know you did.

MAGGIE *(appealingly)* You admire John?

VENABLE Very much. But he puzzles me a little. You Scots, Mrs Shand, are such a mixture of the practical and the emotional that you escape out of an Englishman's hand like a trout.

MAGGIE *(open-eyed)* Do we?

VENABLES Well, not you, but your husband. I have known few men make a worse beginning in the House. He had the most atrocious bowwow public park manner–

COMTESSE I remember that manner!

MAGGIE No, he hadn't.

VENABLES *(soothingly)* At first. But by his second session he had shed all that, and he is now a pleasure to listen to. By the way, Comtesse, have you found any dark intention in that?

COMTESSE You wanted to know whether he talks over these matters with his wife; and she has told you that he does not.

MAGGIE *(indignantly)* I haven't said a word about it, have I?

VENABLES Not a word. Then, again, I admire him for his impromptu speeches.

MAGGIE What is impromptu?

VENABLES Unprepared. They have contained some grave blunders, not so much of judgment as of taste–

MAGGIE *(hotly)* I don't think so.

VENABLES Pardon me. But he has righted himself subsequently in the neatest way. I have always found that the man whose second thoughts are good is worth watching. Well, Comtesse, I see you have something to say.

COMTESSE You are wondering whether she can tell you who gives him his second thoughts.

MAGGIE Gives them to John? I would like to see anybody try to give thoughts to John.

VENABLES Quite so.

COMTESSE Is there anything more that has roused your admiration, Charles?

VENABLES *(purring)* Let me see. Yes, we are all much edified by his humour.

COMTESSE *(surprised indeed)* His humour? That man!

MAGGIE *(with hauteur)* Why not?

VENABLES I assure you, Comtesse, some of the neat things in his speeches convulse the house. A word has even been coined for them – Shandisms.

COMTESSE *(slowly recovering from a blow)* Humour!

VENABLES In conversation, I admit, he strikes one as being – ah – somewhat lacking in humour.

COMTESSE *(pouncing)* You are wondering who supplies his speeches with the humour.

MAGGIE Supplies John?

VENABLES Now that you mention it, some of his Shandisms do have a curiously feminine quality.

COMTESSE You have thought it might be a woman.

VENABLES Really, Comtesse–

COMTESSE I see it all. Charles, you thought it might be the wife!

VENABLES *(flinging up his hands)* I own up.

MAGGIE *(bewildered)* Me?

VENABLES Forgive me, I see I was wrong.

MAGGIE *(alarmed)* Have I been doing John any harm?

VENABLES On the contrary, I am relieved to know that there are no hairpins in his speeches. If he is at home, Mrs Shand, may I see him? I am going to be rather charming to him.

MAGGIE *(drawn in two directions)* Yes, he is – oh yes – but –

VENABLES That is to say, Comtesse, if he proves himself the man I believe him to be.

> *This arrests* MAGGIE *almost as she has reached the dining room door.*

MAGGIE *(hesitating)* He is very busy just now.

VENABLES *(smiling)* I think he will see me.

MAGGIE Is it something about his speech?

VENABLES *(the smile hardening)* Well, yes, it is.

MAGGIE Then I dare say I could tell you what you want to know without troubling him, as I've been typing it.

VENABLES *(with a sigh)* I don't acquire information in that way.

COMTESSE I trust not.

MAGGIE There's no secret about it. He is to show it to the Whips tonight.

VENABLES *(sharply)* You are sure of that?

COMTESSE It is quite true, Charles. I heard him say so; and indeed he repeated what he called the 'peroration' before me.

MAGGIE I know it by heart. *(She plays a bold game.)* 'These are the demands of all intelligent British women, and I am proud to nail them to my flag'–

COMTESSE The very words, Mrs Shand.

MAGGIE *(looking at her imploringly)* 'And I don't care how they may embarrass the Government. *(The* COMTESSE *is bereft of speech, so suddenly has she been introduced to the real* MAGGIE SHAND.*)* If the right honourable gentleman will give us his pledge to introduce a similar bill this session I will willingly withdraw mine; but otherwise I solemnly warn him that I will press the matter now to a division.'

> *She turns her face from the great man; she has gone white.*

VENABLES *(after a pause)* Capital.

> *The blood returns to* MAGGIE'S *heart.*

COMTESSE *(who is beginning to enjoy herself very much)* Then you are pleased to know that he means to, as you say, go to a division?

VENABLES Delighted. The courage of it will be the making of him.

COMTESSE I see.

VENABLES Had he been to hedge we should have known that he was a pasteboard knight and have disregarded him.

COMTESSE I see.

> *She desires to catch the eye of* MAGGIE, *but it is carefully turned from her.*

VENABLES Mrs Shand, let us have him in at once.

COMTESSE Yes, yes, indeed.

> MAGGIE'S *anxiety returns, but she has to call* JOHN *in.*

JOHN *(impressed)* Mr Venables! This is an honour.

VENABLES How are you, Shand?

JOHN Sit down, sit down. *(Becoming himself again.)* I can guess what you have come about.

VENABLES Ah, you Scotsmen.

JOHN Of course I know I'm harassing the Government a good deal–

VENABLES *(blandly)* Not at all, Shand. The Government are very pleased.

JOHN You don't expect me to believe that.

VENABLES I called here to give you the proof of it. You may know that we are to have a big meeting at Leeds on the 24th, when two Ministers are to speak. There is room for a third speaker, and I am authorised to offer that place to you.

JOHN To me!

VENABLES Yes.

JOHN *(swelling)* It would be the Government taking me up.

VENABLES Don't make too much of it; it would be an acknowledgment that they look upon you as one of their likely young men.

MAGGIE John!

JOHN *(not found wanting in a trying hour)* It's a bribe. You are offering me this on condition that I don't make my speech. How can you think so meanly of me as to believe that I would play the women's cause false for the sake of my own advancement. I refuse your bribe.

VENABLES *(liking him for the first time)* Good. But you are wrong. There are no conditions, and we want you to make your speech. Now do you accept?

JOHN *(still suspicious)* If you make me the same offer after you have read it. I insist on your reading it first.

VENABLES *(sighing)* By all means. (MAGGIE *is in an agony as she sees* JOHN *hand the speech to his leader. On the other hand, the* COMTESSE *thrills.*) But I assure you we look on the speech as a small matter. The important thing is your intention of going to a division; and we agree to that also.

JOHN *(losing his head)* What's that?

VENABLES Yes, we agree.

JOHN But – but – why, you have been threatening to excommunicate me if I dared.

VENABLES All done to test you, Shand.

JOHN To test me?

VENABLES We know that a division on your Bill can have no serious significance; we shall see to that. And so the test was to be whether you had the pluck to divide the House. Had you been intending to talk big in this speech, and then hedge, through fear of the Government, they would have had no further use for you.

JOHN *(heavily)* I understand. *(But there is one thing he cannot understand, which is, why* VENABLES *should be so sure that he is not to hedge..)*

VENABLES *(turning over the pages carelessly)* Any of your good things in this, Shand?

JOHN *(whose one desire is to get the pages back)* No, I – no – it isn't necessary you should read it now.

VENABLES *(from politeness only)* Merely for my own pleasure. I shall look through it this evening. *(He rolls up the speech to put it in his pocket.* JOHN *turns despairingly to* MAGGIE, *though well aware that no help can come from her.*)

MAGGIE That's the only copy there is, John. *(To* VENABLES.*)* Let me make a fresh one, and send it to you in an hour or two.

VENABLES *(good naturedly)* I could not put you to that trouble, Mrs Shand. I will take good care of it.

MAGGIE If anything were to happen to you on the way home, wouldn't whatever is in your pocket be considered to be the property of your heirs?

VENABLES *(laughing)* Now there is forethought! Shand, I think that after that–! *(He returns the speech to* JOHN, WHOSE HAND SWALLOWS IT GREEDILY.*)* She is Scotch too, Comtesse.

COMTESSE *(delighted)* Yes, she is Scotch too.

VENABLES Though the only persons likely to do for me in the street, Shand, are your ladies' committee. Ever since they took the horse out of my brougham, I can scent them a mile away.

COMTESSE A mile? Charles, peep in there.

He softly turns the handle of the dining room door, and realises that his scent is not so good as he had thought it. He bids his hostess and the COMTESSE *goodbye in a burlesque whisper and tiptoes off to safer places.* JOHN *having gone out with him,* MAGGIE *can no longer avoid the* COMTESSE'S *reproachful eye. That much injured lady advances upon her with accusing finger.*

'So, madam!' (MAGGIE *is prepared for her.*)

'I don't know what you mean.'

'Yes, you do. I mean that there is some one who 'helps' our Mr Shand.'

'There's not.'

'And it is a woman, and it's you.'

'I help in the little things.'

'The little things! You are the pin he picked up and that is to make his fortune. And now what I want to know is whether your John is aware that you help at all.'

(JOHN *returns, and at once provides the answer.*)

'Maggie, Comtesse, I've done it again!'

'I'm so glad, John.' *(The* COMTESSE *is in an ecstasy.*)

'And all because you were not to hedge, Mr Shand.'

(His appeal to her with the wistfulness of a schoolboy makes him rather attractive.)

'You won't tell on me, Comtesse! *(He thinks it out.)* They had just guessed I would be firm because they know I'm a strong man. – You little saw, Maggie, what a good turn you were doing me when you said you wanted to make another copy of the speech.'

(She is dense.)

'How, John?'

'Because now I can alter the end.'

(She is enlightened.)

'So you can!'

'Here's another lucky thing, Maggie: I hadn't told the ladies' committee that I was to hedge, and so they need never know. Comtesse, I tell you there's a little cherub who sits up aloft and looks after the career of John Shand.'

(The COMTESSE *looks not aloft but toward the chair at present occupied by* MAGGIE.*)*

'Where does she sit, Mr Shand?'

(He knows that women are not well read.)

'It's just a figure of speech.'

(He returns airily to his committee room; and now again you may hear the click of MAGGIE'S *needles. They no longer annoy the* COMTESSE; *she is setting them to music.)*

'It is not down here she sits, Mrs Shand, knitting a stocking.'

'No, it isn't.'

'And when I came in I gave him credit for everything; even for the prettiness of the room!'

'He has beautiful taste.'

'Goodbye, Scotchy.'

'Goodbye, Comtesse, and thank you for coming.'

'Goodbye Miss Pin.'

(MAGGIE *rings genteelly.*)

'Goodbye.'

(The COMTESSE *is now lost in admiration of her.*)

'You divine little wife. He can't be worthy of it, no man could be worthy of it. Why do you do it? '

(MAGGIE *shivers a little.*)

'He loves to think he does it all himself; that's the way of men. I'm six years older than he is. I'm plain, and I have no charm. I shouldn't have let him marry me. I'm trying to make up for it.'

(The COMTESSE *kisses her and goes away.* MAGGIE, *somewhat foolishly, resumes her knitting.)*

Some days later this same room is listening – with the same inattention – to the outpouring of JOHN SHAND'S *love for the lady of the hiccoughs. We arrive – by arrangement – rather late; and thus we miss some of the most delightful of the pangs. One can see that these two are playing no game, or, if they are, that they little know it. The wonders of the world (so strange are the instruments chosen by Love) have been revealed to* JOHN *in hiccoughs; he shakes in* SYBIL'S *presence; never were more swimming eyes; he who has been of a wooden face till now, with ways to match, has gone on flame like a piece of paper; emotion is in flood in him. We may be almost fond of* JOHN *for being so worshipful of love. Much has come to him that we had almost despaired of his acquiring, including nearly all the divine attributes except that sense of humour. The beautiful* SYBIL *has always possessed but little of it also, and what she had has been struck from her by Cupid's flail. Naked of the saving grace, they face each other in awful rapture.*

'In a room, Sybil, I go to you as a cold man to a fire. You fill me like a peal of bells in an empty house.'

(She is being brutally treated by the dear impediment, for which hiccough is such an inadequate name that even to spell it is an abomination though a sign of ability. How to describe a sound that is noiseless? Let us put it thus, that when SYBIL *wants to say something very much there are little obstacles in her way; she falters, falls perhaps once, and then is over, the while her appealing orbs beg you not to be angry with her. We may express those sweet pauses in precious dots, which some clever person can afterwards string together and make a pearl necklace of them.)*

'I should not . . . let you say it, . . . but . . . you . . . say it so beautifully.'

'You must have guessed.'

'I dreamed . . . I feared . . . but you were . . . Scotch, and I didn't know what to think.'

'Do you know what first attracted me to you, Sybil? It was your insolence. I thought, "I'll break her insolence for her."'

'And I thought . . . "I'll break his str . . . ength!"'

'And now your cooing voice plays round me; the softness of you, Sybil, in your pretty clothes makes me think of young birds. *(The impediment is now insurmountable; she has to swim for it, she swims toward him.)* It is you who inspire my work.'

(He thrills to find that she can be touched without breaking.)

'I am so glad . . . so proud . . . '

'And others know it, Sybil, as well as I. Only yesterday the Comtesse said to me, "No man could get on so fast unaided. Cherchez la femme, Mr Shand."'

'Auntie said that!'

'I said "Find her yourself, Comtesse."'

'And she?'

'She said "I have found her," and I said in my blunt way, "You mean Lady Sybil," and she went away laughing.'

'Laughing?'

'I seem to amuse the woman.' (SYBIL *grows sad.*)

'If Mrs Shand – It is so cruel to her. Whom did you say she had gone to the station to meet?'

'Her father and brothers.'

'It is so cruel to them. We must think no more of this. It is mad . . . ness.'

'It's fate. Sybil, let us declare our love openly.'

'You can't ask that, now in the first moment that you tell me of it.'

'The one thing I won't do even for you is to live a life of underhand.'

'The . . . blow to her.'

'Yes. But at least she has always known that I never loved her.'

'It is asking me to give . . . up everything, every one, for you.

'It's too much.'

(JOHN *is humble at last.*)

'To a woman who truly loves, even that is not too much. Oh! it is not I who matter – it is you.'

'My dear, my dear.'

'So gladly would I do it to save you; but, oh, if it were to bring you down!'

'Nothing can keep me down if I have you to help me.'

'I am dazed, John, I . . . '

'My love, my love.'

'I . . . oh . . . here . . . '

'Be brave, Sybil, be brave.'

(In this bewilderment of pearls she melts into his arms. MAGGIE *happens to open the door just then; but neither fond heart hears her.)*

'I can't walk along the streets, Sybil, without looking in all the shop windows for what I think would become you best. *(As awkwardly as though his heart still beat against corduroy, he takes from his pocket a pendant and its chain. He is shy, and she drops pearls over the beauty of the ruby which is its only stone.)* It is a drop of my blood, Sybil.'

(Her lovely neck is outstretched, and he puts the chain round it. MAGGIE *withdraws as silently as she had come; but perhaps the door whispered 'd–n,' or (humourously) 'd . . . n' as it closed, for* SYBIL *wakes out of Paradise.)*

'I thought – Did the door shut?'

'It was shut already.'

(Perhaps it is only that SYBIL *is bewildered to find herself once again in a world that has doors.)*

'It seemed to me – '

'There was nothing, but I think I hear voices; they may have arrived.'

(Some pretty instinct makes SYBIL *go farther from him.* MAGGIE *kindly gives her time for this by speaking before opening the door.)*

'That will do perfectly, David. The maid knows where to put them. *(She comes in.)* They've come, John; they would help with the luggage. (JOHN *goes out.* MAGGIE *is agreeably surprised to find a visitor.)* How do you do, Lady Sybil? This is nice of you.'

'I was so sorry not to find you in, Mrs Shand.'

(The impediment has run away. It is only for those who love it.)

'Thank you. You'll sit down?'

'I think not; your relatives – '

'They will be so proud to see that you are my friend.'

(IF MAGGIE *were less simple her guest would feel more comfortable. She tries to make conversation.)*

'It is their first visit to London?'

(Instead of relieving her anxiety on this point, MAGGIE *has a long look at the gorgeous armful.)*

'I'm glad you are so beautiful, Lady Sybil.'

(The beautiful one is somehow not flattered. She pursues her investigations with growing uneasiness.)

'One of them is married now, isn't he? *(Still there is no answer;* MAGGIE *continues looking at her, and shivers slightly.)* Have they travelled from Scotland today? Mrs Shand, why do you look at me so? The door did open! (MAGGIE *nods.)* What are you to do?'

'That would be telling. Sit down, my pretty.'

As SYBIL *subsides into what the Wylies with one glance would call the best chair,* MAGGIE'S *menfolk are brought in by* JOHN, *all carrying silk hats and looking very active after their long rest in the train. They are gazing about them. They would like this lady, they would like* JOHN, *they would even like* MAGGIE *to go away for a little and leave them to examine the room. Is that linen on the walls, for instance, or just paper? Is the carpet as thick as it feels, or is there brown paper beneath it? Had* MAGGIE *got anything off that bookcase on account of the worm holes?* DAVID *even discovers that we were simpletons when we said there was nothing in the room that pretended to be what it was not. He taps the marble mantelpiece, and is favourably impressed by the tinny sound.*

DAVID Very fine imitation. It's a capital house, Maggie.

MAGGIE I'm so glad you like it. Do you know one another? This is my father and my brothers, Lady Sybil.

The lovely form inclines toward them. ALICK *and* JOHN *remain firm on their legs, but* JAMES *totters.*

JAMES A ladyship! Well done, Maggie.

ALICK *(sharply)* James! I remember you, my lady.

MAGGIE Sit down, father. This is the study.

JAMES *wanders round it inquisitively until called to order.*

SYBIL You must be tired after your long journey.

DAVID *(drawing the portraits of himself and partners in one lightning sketch)* Tired, your ladyship? We sat on cushioned seats the whole way.

JAMES *(looking about him for the chair you sit on)* Every seat in this room is cushioned.

MAGGIE You may say all my life is cushioned now, James, by this dear man of mine.

She gives JOHN'S *shoulder a loving pressure, which* SYBIL *feels is a telegraphic communication to herself in a cipher that she cannot read.* ALCIK *and the* BROTHERS *bask in the evidence of* MAGGIE'S *happiness.*

JOHN *(uncomfortably)* And is Elizabeth hearty, James?

JAMES *(looking down his nose in the manner proper to young husbands when addressed about their wives)* She's very well, I thank you kindly.

MAGGIE James is a married man now, Lady Sybil.

SYBIL *murmurs her congratulations.*

JAMES I thank you kindly. *(Courageously.)* Yes, I'm married. *(He looks at* DAVID *and* ALICK *to see if they are smiling; and they are.)* It wasn't a case of being catched; it was entirely of my own free will. *(He looks again and the mean fellows are smiling still.)* Is your ladyship married?

SYBIL Alas! no.

DAVID James! *(Politely.)* You will be yet, my lady.

SYBIL *indicates that he is kind indeed.*

JOHN Perhaps they would like you to show them their rooms, Maggie?

DAVID Fine would we like to see all the house as well as the sleeping accommodation. But first *(He gives his father the look with which chairmen call on the next speaker.)*

ALICK I take you, David. *(He produces a paper parcel from a roomy pocket.)* It wasn't likely, Mr Shand, that we would forget the day.

JOHN The day?

DAVID The second anniversary of your marriage. We came purposely for the day.

JAMES *(his fingers itching to take the parcel from his father)* It's a lace shawl, Maggie, from the three of us, a pure Tobermory; you would never dare wear it if you knew the cost. *(The shawl in its beauty is revealed, and* MAGGIE *hails it with little cries of joy. She rushes at the donors and kisses each of them just as if she were a pretty woman. They are much pleased and give expression to their pleasure in a not very dissimilar manner.)*

ALICK Havers.

DAVID Havers.

JAMES Havers.

JOHN It's a very fine shawl.

He should not have spoken, for he has set JAMES'S *volatile mind working.*

JAMES You may say so. What did you give her, Mr Shand?

JOHN *(suddenly deserted by God and man)* Me?
ALICK Yes, yes, let's see it.
JOHN Oh – I–

> *He is not deserted by* MAGGIE, *but she can think of no way out.*

SYBIL *(prompted by the impediment, which is in hiding, quite close)* Did he . . . forget?

> *There is more than a touch of malice in the question. It is a challenge, and the Wylies as a family are almost too quick to accept a challenge.*

MAGGIE *(lifting the gage of battle)* John forget? Never! it's a pendant, father.

> *The impediment bolts.* JOHN *rises.*

ALICK A pendant? One of those things on a chain? *He grins, remembering how once, about sixty years ago, he and a lady and a pendant – but we have no time for this.*
MAGGIE Yes.
DAVID *(who has felt the note of antagonism and is troubled)* You were slow in speaking of it, Mr Shand.
MAGGIE *(this is her fight)* He was shy, because he thought you might blame him for extravagance.
DAVID *(relieved)* Oh, that's it.
JAMES *(licking his lips)* Let's see it.
MAGGIE *(a daughter of the devil)* Where did you put it, John?

> JOHN'S *mouth opens but has nothing to contribute.*

SYBIL *(the impediment has stolen back again)* Perhaps it has been . . . mislaid.

> *The* BROTHERS *echo the word incredulously.*

MAGGIE Not it. I can't think where we laid it down, John. It's not on that table, is it, James? *(The Wylies turn to look, and* MAGGIE'S *hand goes out to* LADY SYBIL: JOHN SHAND, *witness. It is a very determined hand, and presently a pendant is placed in it.)* Here it is! (ALICK *and the* BROTHERS *cluster round it, weigh it and appraise it.)*
ALICK Preserve me. Is that stone real, Mr Shand?
JOHN *(who has begun to look his grimmest)* Yes.
MAGGIE *(who is now ready, if he wishes it, to take him on too)* John says it's a drop of his blood.
JOHN *(wishing it)* And so it is.
DAVID Well said, Mr Shand.
MAGGIE *(scared)* And now, if you'll all come with me, I think John has something he wants to talk over with Lady Sybil. *(Recovering and taking him on.)* Or would you prefer, John, to say it before us all?
SYBIL *(gasping)* No!
JOHN *(flinging back his head)* Yes, I prefer to say it before you all.
MAGGIE *(flinging back hers)* Then sit down again.

> *The Wylies wonderingly obey.*

SYBIL Mr Shand, Mr Shand!–
JOHN Maggie knows, and it was only for her I was troubled. Do you think I'm afraid of them? *(With mighty relief.)* Now we can be open.
DAVID *(lowering)* What is it? What's wrong, John Shand?
JOHN *(facing him squarely)* It was to Lady Sybil I gave the pendant, and all my love with it. *(Perhaps* JAMES *utters a cry, but the silence of* ALICK *and* DAVID *is more terrible.)*
SYBIL *(whose voice is smaller than we had thought)* What are you to do? *It is to* MAGGIE *she is speaking.*
DAVID She'll leave it for us to do.

JOHN That's what I want.

The lords of creation look at the ladies.

MAGGIE *(interpreting)* You and I are expected to retire, Lady Sybil, while the men decide our fate. (SYBIL *is ready to obey the law, but* MAGGIE *remains seated.)* Man's the oak, woman's the ivy. Which of us is it that's to cling to you, John?

With three stalwarts glaring at him, JOHN *rather grandly takes* SYBIL'S *hand. They are two against the world.*

SYBIL *(a heroine)* I hesitated, but I am afraid no longer; whatever he asks of me I will do. *(Evidently the first thing he asks of her is to await him in the dining room.)* It will mean surrendering everything for him. I am glad it means all that. *(She passes into the dining room looking as pretty as a kiss.)*

MAGGIE So that settles it.

ALICK I'm thinking that doesn't settle it.

DAVID No, by God! *(But his love for* MAGGIE *steadies him. There is even a note of entreaty in his voice.)* Have you nothing to say to her, man?

JOHN I have things to say to her, but not before you.

DAVID *(sternly)* Go away, Maggie. Leave him to us.

JAMES *(who thinks it is about time that he said something)* Yes, leave him to us.

MAGGIE No, David, I want to hear what is to become of me; I promise not to take any side.

And sitting by the fire she resumes her knitting. The four regard her as on an evening at The Pans a good many years ago.

DAVID *(barking)* How long has this been going on?

JOHN If you mean how long has that lady been the apple of my eye, I'm not sure; but I never told her of it until today.

MAGGIE *(thoughtfully and without dropping a stitch)* I think it wasn't till about six months ago, John, that she began to be very dear to you. At first you liked to bring in her name when talking to me, so that I could tell you of any little things I might have heard she was doing. But afterwards, as she became more and more to you, you avoided mentioning her name.

JOHN *(surprised)* Did you notice that?

MAGGIE *(in her old-fashioned way)* Yes.

JOHN I tried to be done with it for your sake. I've often had a sore heart for you, Maggie.

JAMES You're proving it!

MAGGIE Yes, James, he had. I've often seen him looking at me very sorrowfully of late because of what was in his mind; and many a kindly little thing he has done for me that he didn't used to do.

JOHN You noticed that too!

MAGGIE Yes.

DAVID *(controlling himself)* Well, we won't go into that; the thing to be thankful for is that it's ended.

ALICK *(who is looking very old)* Yes, yes, that's the great thing.

JOHN All useless, sir, it's not ended; it's to go on.

DAVID There's a devil in you, John Shand.

JOHN *(who is an unhappy man just now)* I dare say there is. But do you think he had a walk over, Mr David?

JAMES Man, I could knock you down!

MAGGIE There's not one of you could knock John down.

DAVID *(exasperated)* Quiet, Maggie. One would think you were taking his part.

MAGGIE Do you expect me to desert him at the very moment that he needs me most?

DAVID It's him that's deserting you.

JOHN Yes, Maggie, that's what it is.

ALCIK Where's your marriage vow? And your church attendances?

JAMES *(with terrible irony)* And your prize for moral philosophy?

JOHN *(recklessly)* All gone whistling down the wind.

DAVID I suppose you understand that you'll have to resign your seat.

JOHN *(his underlip much in evidence)* There are hundreds of seats, but there's only one John Shand.

MAGGIE *(but we don't hear her)* That's how I like to hear him speak.

DAVID *(the ablest person in the room)* Think, man, I'm old by you, and for long I've had a pride in you. It will be beginning the world again with more against you than there was eight years ago.

JOHN I have a better head to begin it with than I had eight years ago.

ALICK *(hoping this will bite)* She'll have her own money, David!

JOHN She is as poor as a mouse.

JAMES *(thinking possibly of his Elizabeth's mother)* We'll go to her friends, and tell them all. They'll stop it.

JOHN She's of age.

JAMES They'll take her far away.

JOHN I'll follow, and tear her from them.

ALICK Your career—

JOHN *(to his credit)* To hell with my career. Do you think I don't know I'm on the rocks. What can you, or you, or you, understand of the passions of a man! I've fought, and I've given in. When a ship founders, as I suppose I'm foundering, it's not a thing to yelp at. Peace all of you. *(He strides into the dining room, where we see him at times pacing the floor.)*

DAVID *(to JAMES, who gives signs of a desire to take off his coat)* Let him be. We can't budge him. *(With bitter wisdom.)* It's true what he says, true at any rate about me. What do I know of the passions of a man! I'm up against something I don't understand.

ALICK It's something wicked.

DAVID I dare say it is, but it's something big.

JAMES It's that damned charm.

MAGGIE *(still by the fire)* That's it. What was it that made you fancy Elizabeth, James?

JAMES *(sheepishly)* I can scarcely say.

MAGGIE It was her charm.

DAVID Her charm!

JAMES *(pugnaciously)* Yes, her charm.

MAGGIE She had charm for James.

> *This somehow breaks them up.* MAGGIE *goes from one to another with an odd little smile flickering on her face.*

DAVID Put on your things, Maggie, and we'll leave his house.

MAGGIE *(patting his kind head)* Not me, David.

> *This is a* MAGGIE *they have known but forgotten; all three brighten.*

DAVID You haven't given in!

> *The smile flickers and expires.*

MAGGIE I want you all to go upstairs, and let me have my try now.

JAMES Your try?

ALICK Maggie, you put new life into me.

JAMES And into me.

> DAVID *says nothing; the way he grips her shoulder says it for him.*

MAGGIE I'll save him, David, if I can.

DAVID Does he deserve to be saved after the way he has treated you?

MAGGIE You stupid David. What has that to do with it?

When they have gone, JOHN *comes to the door of the dining room. There is welling up in him a great pity for* MAGGIE, *but it has to subside a little when he sees that the knitting is still in her hand. No man likes to be so soon supplanted.* SYBIL *follows, and the two of them gaze at the active needles.*

MAGGIE *(perceiving that she has visitors)* Come in, John. Sit down, Lady Sybil, and make yourself comfortable. I'm afraid we've put you about.

She is, after all, only a few years older than they and scarcely looks her age; yet it must have been in some such way as this that the little old woman who lived in a shoe addressed her numerous progeny.

JOHN I'm mortal sorry, Maggie.

SYBIL *(who would be more courageous if she could hold his hand)* And I also.

MAGGIE *(soothingly)* I'm sure you are. But as it can't be helped I see no reason why we three shouldn't talk the matter over in a practical way.

SYBIL *looks doubtful, but* JOHN *hangs on desperately to the word practical.*

JOHN If you could understand, Maggie, what an inspiration she is to me and my work.

SYBIL Indeed, Mrs Shand, I think of nothing else.

MAGGIE That's fine. That's as it should be.

SYBIL *(talking too much)* Mrs Shand, I think you are very kind to take it so reasonably.

MAGGIE That's the Scotch way. When were you thinking of leaving me, John?

Perhaps this is the Scotch way also; but SYBIL *is English, and from the manner in which she starts you would say that something has fallen on her toes.*

JOHN *(who has heard nothing fall)* I think, now that it has come to a breach, the sooner the better. *(His tone becomes that of* JAMES *when asked after the health of his wife.)* So long as it is convenient to you, Maggie.

MAGGIE *(making a rapid calculation)* It couldn't well be before Wednesday. That's the day the laundry comes home.

SYBIL *has to draw in her toes again.*

JOHN And it's the day the House rises. *(Stifling a groan.)* It may be my last appearance in the House.

SYBIL *(her arms yearning for him)* No, no, please don't say that.

MAGGIE *(surveying them sympathetically)* You love the House, don't you, John, next to her? It's a pity you can't wait till after your speech at Leeds. Mr Venables won't let you speak at Leeds, I fear, if you leave me.

JOHN What a chance it would have been. But let it go.

MAGGIE The meeting is in less than a month. Could you not make it such a speech that they would be very loath to lose you?

JOHN *(swelling)* That's what was in my mind.

SYBIL *(with noble confidence)* And he could have done it.

MAGGIE Then we've come to something practical.

JOHN *(exercising his imagination with powerful effect)* No, it wouldn't be fair to you if I was to stay on now.

MAGGIE Do you think I'll let myself be considered when your career is at stake? A month will soon pass for me; I'll have a lot of packing to do.

JOHN It's noble of you, but I don't deserve it, and I can't take it from you.

MAGGIE Now's the time, Lady Sybil, for you to have one of your inspiring ideas.

SYBIL *(ever ready)* Yes, yes – but what?

> *It is odd that they should both turn to* MAGGIE *at the moment.*

MAGGIE *(who has already been saying it to herself)* What do you think of this: I can stay on here with my father and brothers; and you, John, can go away somewhere and devote yourself to your speech?

SYBIL Yes.

JOHN That might be. *(Considerately.)* Away from both of you. Where could I go?

SYBIL *(ever ready)* Where?

MAGGIE I know.

> *She has called up a number on the telephone before they have time to check her.*

JOHN *(on his dignity)* Don't be in such a hurry, Maggie.

MAGGIE Is this Lamb's Hotel? Put me on to the Comtesse de la Brière, please.

SYBIL *(with a sinking)* What do you want with Auntie?

MAGGIE Her cottage in the country would be the very place. She invited John and me.

JOHN Yes, but–

MAGGIE *(arguing)* And Mr Venables is to be there. Think of the impression you could make on him, seeing him daily for three weeks.

JOHN There's something in that.

MAGGIE Is it you, Comtesse? I'm Maggie Shand.

SYBIL You are not to tell her that–?

MAGGIE No. *(To the* COMTESSE.) Oh, I'm very well, never was better. Yes, yes; you see I can't, because my folk have never been in London before, and I must take them about and show them the sights. But John could come to you alone; why not?

JOHN *(with proper pride)* If she's not keen to have me, I won't go.

MAGGIE She's very keen. Comtesse, I could come for a day by and by to see how you are getting on. Yes – yes – certainly. *(To* JOHN.) She says she'll be delighted.

JOHN *(thoughtfully)* You're not doing this, Maggie, thinking that my being absent from Sybil for a few weeks can make any difference? Of course it's natural you should want us to keep apart, but–

MAGGIE *(grimly)* I'm founding no hope on keeping you apart, John.

JOHN It's what other wives would do.

MAGGIE I promised to be different.

JOHN *(his position as a strong man assured)* Then tell her I accept. *(He wanders back into the dining room.)*

SYBIL I think – *(she is not sure what she thinks)* – I think you are very wonderful.

MAGGIE Was that John calling to you?

SYBIL Was it? *(She is glad to join him in the dining room.)*

MAGGIE Comtesse, hold the line a minute. *(She is alone, and she has nearly reached the end of her self control. She shakes emotionally and utters painful little cries; there is something she wants to do, and she is loath to do it. But she does it.)* Are you there, Comtesse? There's one other thing, dear Comtesse; I want you to invite Lady Sybil also; yes, for the whole time that John is there. No, I'm not mad; as a great favour to me; yes, I have a very particular reason, but I won't tell you what it is; oh, call me Scotchy as much as you like, but consent; do, do, do. Thank you, thank you, goodbye.

> *She has control of herself now, and is determined not to let it slip from her again. When they reappear the stubborn one is writing a letter.*

JOHN I thought I heard the telephone again.

MAGGIE *(looking up from her labours)* It was the Comtesse; she says she's to invite Lady Sybil to the cottage at the same time.

SYBIL Me!

JOHN To invite Sybil? Then of course I won't go, Maggie.

MAGGIE *(wondering seemingly at these niceties)* What does it matter? Is anything to be
considered except the speech? *(It has been admitted that she was a little devil.)* And, with
Sybil on the spot, John, to help you and inspire you, what a speech it will be!

JOHN *(carried away)* Maggie, you really are a very generous woman.

SYBIL *(convinced at last)* She is indeed.

JOHN And you're queer too. How many women in the circumstances would sit down to
write a letter.

MAGGIE It's a letter to you, John.

JOHN To me?

MAGGIE I'll give it to you when it's finished, but I ask you not to open it till your visit to
the Comtesse ends.

JOHN What is it about?

MAGGIE It's practical.

SYBIL *(rather faintly)* Practical?

> *She has heard the word so frequently today that it is beginning to have a Scotch sound. She
> feels she ought to like* MAGGIE, *but that she would like her better if they were farther apart.
> She indicates that the doctors are troubled about her heart, and murmuring her adieu she goes.*
> JOHN, *who is accompanying her, pauses at the door.*

JOHN *(with a queer sort of admiration for his wife)* Maggie, I wish I was fond of you.

MAGGIE *(heartily)* I wish you were, John.

> *He goes, and she resumes her letter. The stocking is lying at hand, and she pushes it to the
> floor. She is done for a time with knitting.*

ACT FOUR

Man's greatest invention is the lawnmower. All the birds know this, and that is why, when it
is at rest, there is always at least one of them sitting on the handle with his head cocked,
wondering how the delicious whirring sound is made. When they find out, they will change
their note. As it is, you must sometimes have thought that you heard the mower very early in
the morning, and perhaps you peeped in negligee from your lattice window to see who was
up so early. It was really the birds trying to get the note.

On this broiling morning, however, we are at noon, and whoever looks will see that the
whirring is done by Mr Venables. He is in a linen suit with the coat discarded (the bird is
sitting on it), and he comes and goes across the Comtesse's lawns, pleasantly mopping his face.
We see him through a crooked bowed window generously open, roses intruding into it as if
to prevent its ever being closed at night; there are other roses in such armfuls on the tables that
one could not easily say where the room ends and the garden begins.

In the Comtesse's pretty comic drawing room (for she likes the comic touch when she is
in England) sits John Shand with his hostess, on chairs at a great distance from each other. No
linen garments for John, nor flannels, nor even knickerbockers; he envies the English way of
dressing for trees and lawns, but is too Scotch to be able to imitate it; he wears tweeds, just as
he would do in his native country where they would be in kilts. Like many another Scot, the
first time he ever saw a kilt was on a Sassenach; indeed kilts were only invented, like golf, to
draw the English north. John is doing nothing, which again is not a Scotch accomplishment,
and he looks rather miserable and dour. The Comtesse is already at her Patience cards, and
occasionally she smiles on him as if not displeased with his long silence. At last she speaks:

'I feel it rather a shame to detain you here on such a lovely day, Mr Shand, entertaining an
old woman.'

'I don't pretend to think I'm entertaining you, Comtesse.'

'But you are, you know.'

'I would be pleased to be told how?'

(She shrugs her impertinent shoulders, and presently there is another heavy sigh from JOHN.)

'Again! Why do not you go out on the river?'

'Yes, I can do that.' *(He rises.)*

'And take Sybil with you. *(He sits again.)* No?'

'I have been on the river with her twenty times.'

'Then take her for a long walk through the Fairloe woods.'

'We were there twice last week.'

'There is a romantically damp little arbour at the end of what the villagers call the Lovers' Lane.'

'One can't go there every day. I see nothing to laugh at.'

'Did I laugh? I must have been translating the situation into French.'

(Perhaps the music of the lawn mower is not to JOHN'S *mood, for he betakes himself to another room.* MR VENABLES *pauses in his labours to greet a lady who has appeared on the lawn, and who is* MAGGIE. *She is as neat as if she were one of the army of typists (who are quite the nicest kind of women), and carries a little bag. She comes in through the window, and puts her hands over the* COMTESSE'S *eyes. The* COMTESSE *says:)*

'They are a strong pair of hands, at any rate.'

'And not very white, and biggish for my size. Now guess.'

(The COMTESSE *guesses, and takes both the hands in hers as if she valued them. She pulls off* MAGGIE'S *hat as if to prevent her flying away.)*

'Dear abominable one, not to let me know you were coming.'

'It is just a surprise visit, Comtesse. I walked up from the station. *(For a moment* MAGGIE *seems to have borrowed* SYBIL'S *impediment.)* How is – everybody?'

'He is quite well. But, my child, he seems to me to be a most unhappy man.'

(This sad news does not seem to make a most unhappy woman of the child. The COMTESSE *is puzzled, as she knows nothing of the situation save what she has discovered for herself.)*

'Why should that please you, O heartless one?'

'I won't tell you.'

'I could take you and shake you, Maggie. Here have I put my house at your disposal for so many days for some sly Scotch purpose, and you will not tell me what it is.'

'No.'

'Very well then, but I have what you call a nasty one for you. *(The* COMTESSE *lures* MR VENABLES *into the room by holding up what might be a foaming glass of lemon squash.)* Alas, Charles, it is but a flower vase. I want you to tell Mrs Shand what you think of her husband's speech.'

*(*MR VENABLES *gives his hostess a reproachful look.)*

'Eh – ah Shand will prefer to do that himself. I promised the gardener – I must not disappoint him – excuse me – '

'You must tell her, Charles.'

'Please, Mr Venables, I should like to know.'

(He sits down with a sigh and obeys.)

'Your husband has been writing the speech here, and by his own wish he read it to me three days ago. The occasion is to be an important one; and, well, there are a dozen young men in the party at present, all capable of filling a certain small ministerial post. *(He looks longingly at the mower, but it sends no message to his aid.)* And as he is one of them I was anxious that he should show in this speech of what he is capable.'

'And hasn't he?'

(Not for the first time MR VENABLES *wishes that he was not in politics.)*

'I am afraid he has.'

'What is wrong with the speech, Charles?'

'Nothing – and he can still deliver it. It is a powerful, well-thought-out piece of work, such as only a very able man could produce. But it has no special quality of its own – none of the little touches that used to make an old stager like myself want to pat Shand on the shoulder. *(The* COMTESSE'S *mouth twitches, but* MAGGIE *declines to notice it.)* He pounds on manfully enough, but, if I may say so, with a wooden leg. It is as good, I dare say, as the rest of them could have done; but they start with such inherited advantages, Mrs Shand, that he had to do better.'

'Yes, I can understand that.'

'I am sorry, Mrs Shand, for he interested me. His career has set me wondering whether if *I* had begun as a railway porter I might not still be calling out, "By your leave."'

(MAGGIE *thinks it probable but not important.*)

'Mr Venables, now that I think of it, surely John wrote to me that you were dissatisfied with his first speech, and that he was writing another. *(The* COMTESSE'S *eyes open very wide indeed.)*

'I have heard nothing of that, Mrs Shand. (VENABLES *shakes his wise head.*) And in any case, I am afraid – ' *(He still hears the wooden leg.)*

'But you said yourself that his second thoughts were sometimes such an improvement on the first.'

(The COMTESSE *comes to the help of the baggage.)*

'I remember your saying that, Charles.'

'Yes, that has struck me. *(Politely.)* Well, if he has anything to show me in the mean time – '

(He regains the lawn, like one glad to escape attendance at JOHN'S *obsequies. The* COMTESSE *is brought back to speech by the sound of the mower – nothing wooden in it.)*

'What are you up to now, Miss Pin? You know as well as I do that there is no such speech.' (MAGGIE'S *mouth tightens.*)

'I do not.'

'It is a duel, is it, my friend?'

(The COMTESSE *rings the bell and* MAGGIE'S *guilty mind is agitated.*)

'What are you ringing for?'

'As the challenged one, Miss Pin, I have the choice of weapons. I am going to send for your husband to ask him if he has written such a speech. After which, I suppose, you will ask me to leave you while you and he write it together.' (MAGGIE *wrings her hands.*)

'You are wrong, Comtesse; but please don't do that.'

'You but make me more curious, and my doctor says that I must be told everything. *(The* COMTESSE *assumes the pose of her sex in melodrama.)* Put your cards on the table, Maggie Shand, or – *(she indicates that she always pinks her man.* MAGGIE *dolefully produces a roll of paper from her bag.)* What precisely is that?'

(The reply is little more than a squeak.)

'John's speech.'

'You have written it yourself!'

(MAGGIE *is naturally indignant.*)

'It's typed.'

'You guessed that the speech he wrote unaided would not satisfy, and you prepared this to take its place!'

'Not at all, Comtesse. It is the draft of his speech that he left at home. That's all.'

'With a few trivial alterations by yourself, I swear. Can you deny it?'

(No wonder that MAGGIE *is outraged. She replaces* JOHN'S *speech in the bag with becoming hauteur.)*

'Comtesse, these insinuations are unworthy of you. May I ask where is my husband?' *(The* COMTESSE *drops her a curtsy.)*

'I believe your Haughtiness may find him in the Dutch garden. Oh, I see through you. You are not to show him your speech. But you are to get him to write another one, and somehow all your additions will be in it. Think not, creature, that you can deceive one so old in iniquity as the Comtesse de la Briére.'

(There can be but one reply from a good wife to such a charge, and at once the COMTESSE *is left alone with her shame. Anon a footman appears. You know how they come and go.)*

'You rang, my lady?'

'Did I? Ah, yes, but why? *(He is but lately from the ploughshare and cannot help her. In this quandary her eyes alight upon the bag. She is unfortunately too abandoned to feel her shame: she still thinks that she has the choice of weapons. She takes the speech from the bag and bestows it on her servitor.)* Take this to Mr Venables, please, and say it is from Mr Shand. (THOMAS – *but in the end we shall probably call him* JOHN – *departs with the little explosive; and when* MAGGIE *return she finds that the* COMTESSE *is once more engaged on her interrupted game of Patience.)* You did not find him in?' *(All the bravery has dropped from* MAGGIE'S *face.)*

'I didn't see him, but I heard him. *She* is with him. I think they are coming here.'

(The COMTESSE *is suddenly kind again.)*

'Sybil? Shall I get rid of her?'

'No, I want her to be here, too. Now I shall know.'

(The COMTESSE *twists the little thing round.)*

'Know what?'

'As soon as I look into his face I shall know.' *(A delicious scent ushers in the fair* SYBIL, *who is as sweet as a milking stool. She greets* MRS SHAND *with some alarm.)*

MAGGIE How do you do, Lady Sybil? How pretty you look in that frock. (SYBIL *rustles uncomfortably.)* You are a feast to the eye.

SYBIL Please. I wish you would not.

Shall we describe SYBIL'S frock, in which she looks like a great strawberry that knows it ought to be plucked; or would it be easier to watch the coming of JOHN? Let us watch JOHN.

JOHN You, Maggie! You never wrote that you were coming.

No, let us watch MAGGIE. As soon as she looked into his face she was to know something of importance.

MAGGIE *(not dissatisfied with what she sees)* No, John, it's a surprise visit. I just ran down to say goodbye.

At this his face falls, which does not seem to pain her.

SYBIL *(foreseeing another horrible Scotch scene)* To say goodbye?

COMTESSE *(thrilling with expectation)* To whom, Maggie?

SYBIL *(deserted by the impediment, which is probably playing with rough boys in the Lovers' Lane)* Auntie, do leave us, won't you?

COMTESSE Not I. It is becoming far too interesting.

MAGGIE I suppose there's no reason the Comtesse shouldn't be told, as she will know so soon at any rate?

JOHN That's so. (SYBIL *sees with a sinking that he is to be practical also..)*

MAGGIE It's so simple. You see, Comtesse, John and Lady Sybil have fallen in love with one another, and they are to go off as soon as the meeting at Leeds has taken place.

The COMTESSE'S breast is too suddenly introduced to Caledonia and its varied charms.

COMTESSE Mon Dieu!

MAGGIE I think that's putting it correctly, John.

JOHN In a sense. But I'm not to attend the meeting at Leeds. My speech doesn't find favour. *(With a strange humility.)* There's something wrong with it.

COMTESSE I never expected to hear you say that, Mr Shand.

JOHN *(wondering also)* I never expected it myself. I meant to make it the speech of my career. But somehow my hand seems to have lost its cunning.

COMTESSE And you don't know how?

JOHN It's inexplicable. My brain was never clearer.

COMTESSE You might have helped him, Sybil.

SYBIL *(quite sulkily)* I did.

COMTESSE But I thought she was such an inspiration to you, Mr Shand.

JOHN *(going bravely to* SYBIL'S *side)* She slaved at it with me.

COMTESSE Strange. *(Wickedly becoming practical also.)* So now there is nothing to detain you. Shall I send for a fly?

SYBIL *(with a cry of the heart)* Auntie, do leave us.

COMTESSE I can understand your impatience to be gone, Mr Shand.

JOHN *(heavily)* I promised Maggie to wait till the 24th, and I'm a man of my word.

MAGGIE But I give you back your word, John. You can go now.

JOHN looks at SYBIL, and SYBIL looks at JOHN and the impediment arrives in time to take a peep at both of them.

SYBIL *(groping for the practical, to which we must all come in the end)* He must make satisfactory arrangements about you first. I insist on that.

MAGGIE *(with no more imagination than a hen)* Thank you, Lady Sybil, but I have made all my arrangements.

JOHN *(stung)* Maggie, that was my part.

MAGGIE *(the hens are saying it all the time)* You see, my brothers feel they can't be away from their business any longer; and so, if it would be convenient to you, John, I could travel north with them by the night train on Wednesday.

SYBIL I – I – The way you put things–!

JOHN This is just the 21st.

MAGGIE My things are all packed. I think you'll find the house in good order, Lady Sybil. I have had the vacuum cleaners in. I'll give you the keys of the linen and the silver plate; I have them in that bag. The carpet on the upper landing is a good deal frayed, but–

SYBIL Please, I don't want to hear any more.

MAGGIE The ceiling of the dining room would be the better of a new lick of paint–

SYBIL *(stamping her foot, small fours)* Can't you stop her?

JOHN *(soothingly)* She's meaning well. Maggie, I know it's natural to you to value those things, because your outlook on life is bounded by them; but all this jars on me.

MAGGIE Does it?

JOHN Why should you be so ready to go?

MAGGIE I promised not to stand in your way.

JOHN *(stoutly)* You needn't be in such a hurry. There are three days to run yet. *(The French are so different from us that we shall probably never be able to understand why the* COMTESSE *laughed aloud here.)* It's just a joke to the Comtesse.

COMTESSE It seems to be no joke to you, Mr Shand. Sybil, my pet, are you to let him off?

SYBIL *(flashing)* Let him off? If he wishes it. Do you?

JOHN *(manfully)* I want it to go on. *(Something seems to have caught in his throat: perhaps it is the impediment trying a temporary home.)* It's the one wish of my heart. If you come with me, Sybil, I'll do all in a man's power to make you never regret it. *(Triumph of the Vere de Veres.)*

MAGGIE *(bringing them back to earth with a dump)* And I can make my arrangements for Wednesday?

SYBIL *(seeking the* COMTESSE'S *protection)* No, you can't. Auntie, I am not going on with this. I'm very sorry for you, John, but I see now – I couldn't face it–

> She can't face anything at this moment except the sofa pillows.

COMTESEE *(noticing* JOHN'S *big sigh of relief)* So that is all right, Mr Shand!

MAGGIE Don't you love her any more, John? Be practical.

SYBIL *(to the pillows)* At any rate I have tired of him. Oh, best to tell the horrid truth. I am ashamed of myself. I have been crying my eyes out over it – I thought I was such a different kind of woman. But I am weary of him. I think him – oh, so dull.

JOHN *(his face lighting up)* Are you sure that is how you have come to think of me?

SYBIL I'm sorry; *(with all her soul)* but yes – yes – yes.

JOHN By God, it's more than I deserve.

COMTESSE Congratulations to you both.

> SYBIL *runs away; and in the fullness of time she married successfully in* Cloth of Silver, *which was afterwards turned into a bed spread.*

MAGGIE You haven't read my letter yet, John, have you?

JOHN No.

COMTESSE *(imploringly)* May I know to what darling letter you refer?

MAGGIE It's a letter I wrote to him before he left London. I gave it to him closed, not to be opened until his time here was ended.

JOHN *(as his hand strays to his pocket)* Am I to read it now?

MAGGIE Not before her. Please go away, Comtesse.

COMTESSE Every word you say makes me more determined to remain.

MAGGIE It will hurt you. *(Distressed.)* Don't read it, John; tear it up.

JOHN You make me very curious, Maggie. And yet I don't see what can be in it.

COMTESSE But you feel a little nervous? Give me the dagger.

MAGGIE *(quickly)* No. *(But the* COMTESSE *has already got it.)*

COMTESSE May I? *(She must have thought they said Yes, for she opens the letter. She shares its contents with them.)* 'Dearest John, It is at my request that the Comtesse is having Lady Sybil at the cottage at the same time as yourself.'

JOHN What?

COMTESSE Yes, she begged me to invite you together.

JOHN But why?

MAGGIE I promised you not to behave as other wives would do.

JOHN It's not understandable.

COMTESSE 'You may ask why I do this, John, and my reason is, I think that after a few weeks of Lady Sybil, every day, and all day, you will become sick to death of her. I am also giving her the chance to help you and inspire you with your work, so that you may both learn what her help and her inspiration amount to. Of course, if your love is the great strong passion you think it, then those weeks will make you love her more than ever and I can only say goodbye. But if, as I suspect, you don't even now know what true love is, then by the next time we meet, dear John, you will have had enough of her. – Your affectionate wife, Maggie.' Oh, why was not Sybil present at the reading of the will! And now, if you two will kindly excuse me, I think I must go and get that poor sufferer the eau de Cologne.

JOHN It's almost enough to make a man lose faith in himself.

COMTESSE Oh, don't say that, Mr Shand.

MAGGIE *(defending him)* You mustn't hurt him. If you haven't loved deep and true, that's just because you have never met a woman yet, John, capable of inspiring it.

COMTESSE *(putting her hand on* MAGGIE'S *shoulder)* Have you not, Mr Shand?

JOHN I see what you mean. But Maggie wouldn't think better of me for any false pretences. She knows my feelings for her now are neither more nor less than what they have always been.

MAGGIE *(who sees that he is looking at her as solemnly as a volume of sermons printed by request)* I think no one could be fond of me that can't laugh a little at me.

JOHN How could that help?

COMTESSE *(exasperated)* Mr Shand, I give you up.

MAGGIE I admire his honesty.

COMTESSE Oh, I give you up also. Arcades ambo. Scotchies both.

JOHN *(when she has gone)* But this letter, it's not like you. By Gosh, Maggie, you're no fool. *(She beams at this, as any wife would.)* But how could I have made such a mistake? It's not like a strong man. *(Evidently he has an inspiration.)*

MAGGIE What is it?

JOHN *(the inspiration)* Am I a strong man?

MAGGIE You? Of course you are. And self made. Has anybody ever helped you in the smallest way?

JOHN *(thinking it out again)* No, nobody.

MAGGIE Not even Lady Sybil?

JOHN I'm beginning to doubt it. It's very curious, though, Maggie, that this speech should be disappointing.

MAGGIE It's just that Mr Venables hasn't the brains to see how good it is.

JOHN That must be it. *(But he is too good a man to rest satisfied with this.)* No, Maggie, it's not. Somehow I seem to have lost my neat way of saying things.

MAGGIE *(almost cooing)* It will come back to you.

JOHN *(forlorn)* If you knew how I've tried.

MAGGIE *(cautiously)* Maybe if you were to try again; and I'll just come and sit beside you, and knit. I think the click of the needles sometimes put you in the mood.

JOHN Hardly that; and yet many a Shandism have I knocked off while you were sitting beside me knitting. I suppose it was the quietness.

MAGGIE Very likely.

JOHN *(with another inspiration)* Maggie!

MAGGIE *(again)* What is it, John?

JOHN What if it was you that put those queer ideas into my head!

MAGGIE Me?

JOHN Without your knowing it, I mean.

MAGGIE But how?

JOHN We used to talk bits over; and it may be that you dropped the seed, so to speak.

MAGGIE John, could it be this, that I sometimes had – the idea in a rough womanish sort of way and then you polished it up till it came out a Shandism?

JOHN *(slowly slapping his knee)* I believe you've hit it, Maggie: to think that you may have been helping me all the time and neither of us knew it.

> *He has so nearly reached a smile that no one can say what might have happened within the next moment if the* COMTESSE *had not reappeared.*

COMTESSE Mr Venables wishes to see you, Mr Shand.

JOHN *(lost, stolen, or strayed a smile in the making)* Hum.

COMTESSE He is coming now.

JOHN *(grumpy)* Indeed.

COMTESSE *(sweetly)* It is about your speech.

JOHN He has said all he need say on that subject, and more.

COMTESSE *(quaking a little)* I think it is about the second speech.

JOHN What second speech?

> MAGGIE *runs to her bag and opens it.*

MAGGIE *(horrified)* Comtesse, you have given it to him.

COMTESSE *(impudently)* Wasn't I meant to?

JOHN What is it? What second speech?

MAGGIE Cruel, cruel. *(Willing to go on her knees.)* You had left the first draft of your speech at home, John, and I brought it here with – with a few little things I've added myself.

JOHN *(a seven-footer)* What's that?

MAGGIE *(four foot ten at most)* Just trifles – things I was to suggest to you – while I was knitting – and then, if you liked any of them you could have polished them – and turned them into something good. John, John – and now she has shown it to Mr Venables.

JOHN *(thundering)* As my work, Comtesse? *(But the* COMTESSE *is not of the women who are afraid of thunder.)*

MAGGIE It is your work – nine-tenths of it.

JOHN *(in the black cap)* You presumed, Maggie Shand! Very well, then, here he comes, and now we'll see to what extent you've helped me.

VENABLES My dear fellow. My dear Shand, I congratulate you. Give me your hand.

JOHN The speech?

VENABLES You have improved it out of knowledge. It is the same speech, but those new touches make all the difference. (JOHN *sits down heavily.*) Mrs Shand, be proud of him.

MAGGIE I am. I am, John.

COMTESSE You always said that his second thoughts were best, Charles.

VENABLES (*pleased to be reminded of it*) Didn't I? didn't I? Those delicious little touches! How good that is, Shand, about the flowing tide.

COMTESSE The flowing tide?

VENABLES In the first speech it was something like this – 'Gentlemen, the Opposition are calling to you to vote for them and the flowing tide, but I solemnly warn you to beware lest the flowing tide does not engulf you.' The second way is much better.

COMTESSE What is the second way, Mr Shand?

JOHN does not tell her.

VENABLES This is how he puts it now. (JOHN *cannot help raising his head to listen.*) 'Gentlemen, the Opposition are calling to you to vote for them and the flowing tide, but I ask you cheerfully to vote for us and dam the flowing tide.'

VENABLES *and his old friend the* COMTESSE *laugh heartily, but for different reasons.*

COMTESSE It is better, Mr Shand.

MAGGIE I don't think so.

VENABLES Yes, yes, it's so virile. Excuse me, Comtesse, I'm off to read the whole thing again. (*For the first time he notices that* JOHN *is strangely quiet.*) I think this has rather bowled you over, Shand. (JOHN'S *head sinks lower.*) Well, well, good news doesn't kill.

MAGGIE (*counsel for the defence*) Surely the important thing about the speech is its strength and knowledge and eloquence, the things that were in the first speech as well as in the second.

VENABLES That of course is largely true. The wit would not be enough without them, just as they were not enough without the wit. It is the combination that is irresistible. (JOHN'S *head rises a little.*) Shand, you are our man, remember that, it is emphatically the best thing you have ever done. How this will go down at Leeds.

He returns gaily to his hammock; but lower sinks JOHN'S *head, and even the* COMTESSE *has the grace to take herself off.* MAGGIE'S *arms flutter near her husband, not daring to alight.*

'You heard what he said, John. It's the combination. Is it so terrible to you to find that my love for you had made me able to help you in the little things?'

'The little things! It seems strange to me to hear you call me by my name, Maggie. It's as if I looked on you for the first time.'

'Look at me, John, for the first time. What do you see?'

'I see a woman who has brought her husband low.'

'Only that?'

'I see the tragedy of a man who has found himself out. Eh, I can't live with you again, Maggie.' (*He shivers.*)

'Why did you shiver, John?'

'It was at myself for saying that I couldn't live with you again, when I should have been wondering how for so long you have lived with me. And I suppose you have forgiven me all the time. (*She nods.*) And forgive me still? (*She nods again.*) Dear God!'

'John, am I to go? or are you to keep me on? (*She is now a little bundle near his feet.*) I'm willing to stay because I'm useful to you, if it can't be for a better reason. (*His hand feels for her, and the bundle wriggles nearer.*) It's nothing unusual I've done, John. Every man who is high up loves to think that he has done it all himself; and the wife smiles, and lets it go at that. It's our only joke. Every woman knows that. (*He stares at her in hopeless perplexity.*) Oh, John, if only you could laugh at me.'

'I can't laugh, Maggie.'

But as he continues to stare at her a strange disorder appears in his face.
MAGGIE feels that it is to be now or never.

'Laugh, John, laugh. Watch me; see how easy it is.'

A terrible struggle is taking place within him. He creaks. Something that may be mirth forces
a passage, at first painfully, no more joy in it than in the discoloured water from a spring that
has long been dry. Soon, however, he laughs loud and long. The spring water is becoming
clear. MAGGIE claps her hands. He is saved.

Barbara's Wedding

The Colonel is in the sitting-room of his country cottage, staring through the open windows
at his pretty garden. He is a very old man, and is sometimes bewildered nowadays. You must
understand that at the beginning of the play he is just seeing visions of the past. No real people
come to him, though he thinks they do. He calls to Dering, the gardener, who is on a ladder,
pruning. Dering, who comes to him, is a rough, capable young fellow with fingers that are
already becoming stumpy because he so often uses his hands instead of a spade. This is a sign
that Dering will never get on in the world. His mind is in the same condition as his fingers,
working back to clods. He will get a rise of one and sixpence in a year or two, and marry on
it and become duller and heavier; and, in short, the clever ones could already write his
epitaph.

COLONEL A beautiful morning, Dering.
DERING Too much sun, sir. The roses be complaining, and, to make matters worse, Miss
Barbara has been watering of them – in the heat of the day.
COLONEL Has she? She means well. *(But that is not what is troubling him. He approaches the*
subject diffidently.) Dering, you heard it, didn't you? *(He is longing to be told that DERING*
heard it.)
DERING What was that, sir?
COLONEL The thunderstorm – early this morning.
DERING There was no thunderstorm, sir.
COLONEL *(dispirited)* That is what they all say. *(He is too courteous to contradict any one, but he*
tries again; there is about him the insistence of one who knows that he is right.) It was at four
o'clock. I got up and looked out at the window. The evening primroses were very
beautiful.
DERING *(equally dogged)* I don't hold much with evening primroses, sir, but I was out and
about at four; there was no thunderstorm.

The COLONEL still thinks that there was a thunderstorm, but he wants to placate DERING.

COLONEL I suppose I just thought there was one. Perhaps it was some thunderstorm of
long ago that I heard. They do come back, you know.
DERING *(heavily)* Do they, sir?
COLONEL I am glad to see you moving about in the garden, Dering, with everything just as
usual. *(There is a cautious slyness about this as if the COLONEL was fishing for information; but*
it is too clever for DERING, who is going with a 'Thank you sir.') No don't go. *(The old man*
lowers his voice and makes a confession reluctantly.) I am – a little troubled, Dering. *(DERING*
knows that his master has a wandering mind and he answers nicely.)
DERING Everything be all right, sir.
COLONEL *(with relief)* I'm glad of that. It is pleasant to see that you have come back, Dering.
Why did you go away for such a long time?

DERING Me, sir? *(He is a little aggrieved.)* I haven't had a day off since Christmas.

COLONEL Haven't you? I thought–

The COLONEL *tries to speak casually, but there is a trembling eagerness in his voice.*

COLONEL Is everything just as usual, Dering?

DERING Yes, sir. There never were a place as changes less than this.

COLONEL That's true. Thank you, Dering, for saying that. *(But next moment he has lowered his voice again.)* Dering, there is nothing wrong, is there? Is anything happening that I am not being told about?

DERING Not that I know of, sir.

COLONEL That is what they all say, but – I don't know. *(He stares at his old sword which is hanging on the wall.)* Where is every one?

DERING They're all about, sir. There is a cricket match on at the village green.

COLONEL Is there?

DERING If the wind had a bit of south in it you could hear their voices. You were a bit of a nailer at cricket yourself, sir.

The COLONEL *sees himself standing up to fast ones. He is gleeful over his reminiscences.*

COLONEL Ninety-nine against Mallowfield, and then bowled off my pads. Biggest score I ever made. Mallowfield wanted to add one to make it the hundred, but I wouldn't let them. I was pretty good at steering them through the slips, Dering! Do you remember my late cut? It didn't matter where point stood, I got past him. You used to stand at point, Dering.

DERING That was my grandfather, sir. If he was to be believed, he used to snap you regular at point.

The COLONEL *is crestfallen, but he has a disarming smile.*

COLONEL Did he? I dare say he did. I can't play now, but I like to watch it still. *(He becomes troubled again.)* Dering, there's no cricket on the green today. I have been down to look. I don't understand it, Dering. When I got there the green was all dotted with them. But as I watched them they began to go away, one and two at a time; they weren't given out, you know, they went as if they had been called away. Some of the little shavers stayed on – and then they went off, as if they had been called away too. The stumps were left lying about. Why is it?

DERING It's just fancy, sir. I saw Master Will oiling his bat yesterday.

COLONEL *(avidly)* Did you? I should have liked to see that. I have often oiled their bats for them. Careless lads, they always forget. Was that nice German boy with him?

DERING Mr Karl? Not far off, sir. He was sitting by the bank of the stream playing on his flute; and Miss Barbara, she had climbed one of my apple-trees – she says they are your trees. *(He lowers.)*

COLONEL *(meekly)* They are, you know, Dering.

DERING Yes, sir, in a sense, but I don't like any of you to meddle with them. And there she sat, pelting the two of them with green apples.

COLONEL How like her! *(He shakes his head indulgently.)* I don't know how we are to make a demure young lady of her.

DERING They say in the village, sir, that Master Will would like to try.

To the COLONEL *this is wit of a high order.*

COLONEL Ha! ha! he is just a colt himself. *(But the laughter breaks off. He seems to think that he will get the truth if* DERING *comes closer.)* Who are all here now, Dering; in the house, I mean? I sometimes forget. They grow old so quickly. They go out at one door in the bloom of youth, and come back by another, tired and grey. Haven't you noticed it?

DERING No, sir. The only visitors staying here are Miss Barbara and Mr Karl. There's just them and yourselves sir, you and the mistress and Master Will. That's all.

COLONEL Yes, that's all. Who is the soldier, Dering?

DERING Soldier, sir? There is no soldier here except yourself.

COLONEL Isn't there? There was a nurse with him. Who is ill?

DERING No one, sir. There's no nurse. *(He backs away from the old man.)* Would you like me to call the mistress, sir?

COLONEL No, she has gone down to the village. She told me why, but I forget. Miss Barbara is with her.

DERING Miss Barbara is down by the stream, sir.

COLONEL Is she? I think they said they were going to a wedding. *(With an old man's curiosity.)* Who is being married today, Dering?

DERING I have heard of no wedding, sir. But here is Miss Barbara. *(It is perhaps the first time that DERING has been glad to see MISS BARBARA, who romps in, a merry hoyden running over with animal spirits.)*

COLONEL *(gaily)* Here's the tomboy!

BARBARA *looks suspiciously from one to the other.*

BARBARA Dering, I believe you are complaining to the Colonel about my watering the flowers at the wrong time of day.

The COLONEL *thinks she is even wittier than* DERING *who is properly abashed.*

DERING I did just mention it, miss.

BARBARA You horrid! *(She shakes her mop of hair at the gardener.)* Dear, don't mind him. And every time he says they are his flowers and his apples, you tell me, and I shall say to his face that they are yours.

COLONEL The courage of those young things!

DERING'S *underlip becomes very pronounced but he goes off into the garden.* BARBARA *attempts to attend to the* COLONEL'S *needs.*

BARBARA Let me make you comfy – the way Granny does it.

She arranges his cushions clumsily.

COLONEL That is not quite the way she does it. Do you call her Granny, Barbara?

BARBARA She asked me to – for practice. Don't you remember why?

Of course the COLONEL *remembers.*

COLONEL I know! Billy Boy.

BARBARA You are quick today. Now, wait till I get your cane.

COLONEL I don't need my cane while I'm sitting.

BARBARA You look so beau'ful, sitting holding your cane. *(She knocks over his cushions.)* Oh dear! I am a clumsy.

COLONEL *(politely)* Not at all, but perhaps if I were to do it for myself. *(He makes himself comfortable.)* That's better. Thank you, Barbara, very much.

BARBARA I didn't do it. I'm all thumbs. What a ghastly nurse I should make.

COLONEL Nurse? *(The* COLONEL'S *troubles return to him.)* Who is she, Barbara?

BARBARA Who is who, dear?

COLONEL That nurse?

BARBARA There's no nurse here.

COLONEL Isn't there?

BARBARA *(feeling that she is of less use than ever today)* Where is granny?

COLONEL She has gone down to the village to a wedding.

BARBARA There's no wedding. Who could be being married?

COLONEL I think it's people I know, but I can't remember who they are. I thought you went too, Barbara.

BARBARA Not I. Catch me missing it if there had been a wedding!

COLONEL You and the nurse.

BARBARA Dear, you have just been imagining things again. Shall I play to you, or sing? *(She knocks over a chair.)* Oh dear, everything catches in me. Would you like me to sing 'Robin Adair', dear?

COLONEL *(polite, but firm)* No, thank you, Barbara. *(For a few moments he forgets her; his mind has gone wandering again.)* Barbara, the house seems so empty. Where are Billy and Karl?

BARBARA Billy is where Karl is, you may be sure.

COLONEL And where is Karl?

BARBARA He is where Billy boy is, you may be sure.

COLONEL And where are they both?

BARBARA Not far from where Barbara is, you bet. *(She flutters to the window and waves her hand.)* Do you hear Karl's flute? They have been down all the morning at the pool where the alder is, trying to catch that bull-trout.

COLONEL They didn't get him, I'll swear!

BARBARA You can ask them.

COLONEL I spent a lot of my youth trying to get that bull-trout. I tumbled in there sixty years ago.

BARBARA I tumbled in sixty minutes ago! It can't be the same trout, dear.

COLONEL Same old rascal!

> BILLY *and* KARL *come in by the window, leaving a fishing rod outside. They are gay, careless, attractive youths.*

BARBARA *(with her nose in the air)* You muddy things!

COLONEL *(gaily firing his dart)* Did you get the bull-trout, Billy boy?

BILLY He's a brute that.

COLONEL He is, you know.

BILLY He came up several times and had a look at my fly. Didn't flick it, or do anything as complimentary as that. Just yawned and went down.

COLONEL Yawned, did he? Used to wink in my time. Did you and Billy fish at Heidelberg, Karl?

KARL We were more worthily employed, sir, but we did unbend at times. Billy, do you remember– *(He begins a gay dance.)*

BILLY Not I. *(Then he joins in.)*

BARBARA Young gentlemen, how disgraceful! *(She joins in.)*

COLONEL Harum-scarums!

KARL Does he know about you two?

BILLY He often forgets. I'll tell him again. Grandfather, Barbara and I have something to say to you. It's this. *(He puts his arm round* BARBARA.)

COLONEL *(smiling)* I know – I know. There's nothing like it. I'm very glad, Barbara.

BARBARA You see, dear, I've loved Billy boy since the days when he tried to catch the bull-trout with a string and a bent pin, and I held on to his pinafore to prevent his tumbling in. We used to play at school at marrying and giving in marriage, and the girl who was my bridegroom had always to take the name of Billy. 'Do you, woman, take this man Billy' the clergyman in skirts began, and before I could answer diffidently, some other girl was sure to shout, 'I should rather think she does.'

COLONEL *(in high good humour)* Don't forget the ring, Billy. You know, when I was married I couldn't find the ring!

KARL Were you married here, sir?

COLONEL Yes, at the village church.

BILLY So were my father and mother.

COLONEL *(as his eyes wander to the garden)* I remember walking back with my wife and bringing her in here through the window. She kissed some of the furniture.

BILLY I suppose you would like a grander affair, Barbara?

BARBARA No, just the same.

BILLY I hoped you would say that.

BARBARA But, Billy, I'm to have such a dream of a wedding-gown. Granny is going with me to London to choose it *(laying her head on the* COLONEL'S *shoulder)* if you can do without her for a day, dear.

COLONEL *(gallantly)* I shall go with you. I couldn't trust you and granny to choose the gown.

KARL You must often be pretty lonely, sir, when we are all out and about enjoying ourselves.

COLONEL They all say that. But that is the time when I'm not lonely, Karl. It's then I see things most clearly – the past, I suppose. It all comes crowding back to me – India, the Crimea, India again – and it's so real, especially the people. They come and talk to me. I seem to see them; I don't know they haven't been here, Billy, till your granny tells me afterwards.

BILLY Yes I know. I wonder where granny is.

BARBARA It isn't often she leaves you for so long, dear.

COLONEL She told me she had to go out but I forget where. Oh yes, she has gone down to the village to a wedding.

BILLY A wedding?

BARBARA It's curious how he harps on that.

COLONEL She said to me to listen and I would hear the wedding-bells.

BARBARA Not today, dear.

BILLY Best not to worry him.

BARBARA But granny says we should try to make things clear to him.

BILLY Was any one with granny when she said she was going to a wedding?

COLONEL *(like one begging her to admit it)* You were there, Barbara.

BARBARA No, dear. He said that to me before. And something about a nurse.

COLONEL *(obstinately)* She was there, too.

BILLY Any one else?

COLONEL There was that soldier.

BARBARA A soldier also!

COLONEL Just those three.

BILLY But that makes four. Granny and Barbara and a nurse and a soldier.

COLONEL They were all there; but there were only three.

BILLY Odd.

BARBARA *(soothingly)* Never mind, dear. Granny will make it all right. She is the one for you.

COLONEL She is the one for me.

KARL If there had been a wedding, wouldn't she have taken the Colonel with her?

BARBARA Of course she would.

KARL You are not too old to have a kind eye for a wedding, sir.

COLONEL *(wagging his head)* Aha, aha! You know, if I had gone, very likely I should have kissed the bride. Brides look so pretty on their wedding day. They are often not pretty at other times, but they are all pretty on their wedding day.

KARL You have an eye for a pretty girl still, sir!

COLONEL Yes, I have; yes, I have!

BARBARA I do believe I see it all. Granny has been talking to you about Billy boy and me, and you haven't been able to wait; you have hurried on the wedding!

BILLY Bravo, Barbara, you've got it.

COLONEL *(doubtfully)* That may be it. Because I am sure you were to be there, Barbara.

BARBARA Our wedding, Billy!

KARL It doesn't explain those other people, though.

The COLONEL *moves about in agitation.*

BARBARA What is it, dear?

COLONEL I can't quite remember, but I think that is why she didn't take me. It is your wedding, Barbara, but I don't think Billy boy is to be there, my love.

BARBARA Not at my wedding!

BILLY Grandfather!

COLONEL There's something sad about it.

BARBARA There can't be anything sad about a wedding, dear. Granny didn't say it was a sad wedding, did she?

COLONEL She was smiling.

BARBARA Of course she was.

COLONEL But I think that was only to please the nurse.

BARBARA That nurse again! Dear, don't think any more about it. There's no wedding.

COLONEL *(gently, though he wanders why they can go on deceiving him)* Is there not? *(The village wedding-bells begin to ring. The* COLONEL *is triumphant.)* I told you! There is a wedding!

The bells ring on gaily. BILLY *and* BARBARA *take a step nearer to each other, but can go no closer. The bells ring on and the three young people fade from the scene. When they are gone and he is alone, the* COLONEL *still addresses them. Soon the bells stop. He knows that he is alone now, but he does not understand it. The sun is shining brightly, but he sits very cold in his chair. He shivers. From this point to the end of the play it is the real people he sees as they are now. He is very glad to see his wife coming to him through the open window. She is a dear old lady, and is dressed brightly, as becomes one who has been to a wedding. Her face beams to match her gown. She is really quite a happy woman again, for it is several years since any deep sorrow struck her; and that is a long time. No one, you know, understands the* COLONEL *as she does; no one can soothe him and bring him out of his imaginings as she can. He hastens to her. He is no longer cold. That is her great reward for all she does for him.*

ELLEN *(tranquilly)* I have come back, John. It hasn't seemed very long, has it?

COLONEL No, not long, Ellen. Had you a nice walk?

She continues to smile, but she is watching him closely.

ELLEN I haven't been for a walk. Don't you remember where I told you I was going, John?

COLONEL Yes, it was to a wedding.

ELLEN *(rather tremulously)* You haven't forgotten whose wedding, have you?

COLONEL Tell me, Ellen.

He is no longer troubled. He knows that ELLEN *will tell him.*

ELLEN I have been seeing Barbara married, John.

COLONEL Yes, it was Barbara's wedding. They wouldn't – Ellen, why wasn't I there?

ELLEN *(like one telling him amusing gossip)* I thought you might be a little troubled if you went, John. Sometimes your mind – not often, but sometimes if you are agitated – and then you think you see – people who aren't here any longer. Oh dear, oh dear, help me with these bonnet strings.

COLONEL Yes, I know. I'm all right when you are with me, Ellen. Funny, isn't it?

She raises her shoulders in a laugh.

ELLEN It is funny, John. I ran back to you. I thinking of you all the time, even more than of Billy boy.

The COLONEL *is very gay.*

COLONEL Tell me all about it, Ellen. Did Billy boy lose the ring? We always said he would lose the ring.

She looks straight into his eyes.

ELLEN You have forgotten again, John. Barbara isn't married to Billy boy.

He draws himself up.

COLONEL Not marry Billy? I'll see about that!

She presses him into his chair.

ELLEN Sit down, dear, and I'll tell you something again. It is nothing to trouble you, because your soldiering is done, John; and greatly done. My dear, there is war again, and our old land is in it. Such a war as my soldier never knew.

He rises. He is a stern old man.

COLONEL A war! That's it, is it? So now I know! Why wasn't I told? I'm not too old yet.

ELLEN Yes, John, you are too old, and all you can do now is to sit here and – and to take care of me. You knew all about it quite clearly this morning. We stood together upstairs by the window listening to the aircraft guns.

COLONEL I remember! I thought it was a thunderstorm. Dering told me he heard nothing.

ELLEN Dering?

COLONEL Our gardener, you know. *(His voice becomes husky.)* Haven't I been talking with him, Ellen?

ELLEN It is a long time since we had a gardener, John

COLONEL Is it? So it is! A war! That is why there is no more cricket on the green.

ELLEN They have all gone to the war, John.

COLONEL That's it; even the little shavers. *(He whispers.)* Why isn't Billy boy fighting, Ellen?

ELLEN Oh, John!

COLONEL Is Billy boy dead? *(She nods.)* Was he killed, in action? Tell me, tell me! *(She nods again.)* Good for Billy boy. I knew Billy boy was all right. Don't cry, Ellen I'll take care of you. All's well with Billy boy.

ELLEN Yes, I know, John.

He hesitates before speaking again.

COLONEL Ellen, who is the soldier? He comes here. He is a captain.

ELLEN He is a very gallant man, John. It is he who was married to Barbara today.

COLONEL *(bitterly)* She has soon forgotten.

ELLEN *(shaking her brave head)* She hasn't forgotten, dear. And it's nearly three years now since Billy died.

COLONEL So long! We have a medal he got, haven't we?

ELLEN No, John; he died before he could win any medals.

COLONEL Karl will be sorry. They were very fond of each other, those two boys, Ellen.

ELLEN Karl fought against us, dear. He died in the same engagement. They may even have killed each other.

COLONEL They hadn't known, Ellen.

ELLEN *(with thin lips)* I dare say they knew.

COLONEL Billy boy and Karl!

She tells him some more gossip.

ELLEN John, I had Barbara married from here because she has no people of her own. I think Billy would have liked it.

COLONEL That was the thing to do, Ellen. Nice of you. I remember everything now. It's Dering she has married. He was once my gardener!

ELLEN The world is all being re-made, dear. He is worthy of her.

He lets this pass. He is has remembered something almost as surprising.

COLONEL Ellen, is Barbara a nurse?

ELLEN Yes, John, and one of the staidest and most serene. Who would have thought it of the merry madcap of other days! They are coming here, John, to say goodbye to you. They have only a few days' leave. She is in France, too, you know. She was married in her nurse's uniform.

COLONEL Was she? She told me today that – no, it couldn't have been today.

ELLEN You have been fancying you saw them, I suppose. *(She grows tremulous again.)* You will be nice to them, John, won't you, and wish them luck? They have their trials before them.

COLONEL *(eagerly)* Tell me what to do, Ellen.

ELLEN Don't say anything about Billy boy, John.

COLONEL No no, let's pretend.

ELLEN And I wouldn't talk about the garden, John; just in case he is a little touchy about that.

COLONEL *(beginning to fancy himself as a tactician)* Not a word!

ELLEN *(who knows what is the best way to put him on his mettle)* You see, I'm sure I should make a mess of it, so I'm trusting to you, John.

COLONEL *(very pleased)* Leave it all to me, Ellen. I'll be frightfully sly. You just watch me.

She goes to the window and calls to the married couple. CAPTAIN DERING, *in khaki, is a fine soldierly figure.* BARBARA, *in her Red Cross uniform, is quiet and resourceful. An artful old boy greets them.*

COLONEL Congratulations, Barbara. No, no, none of your handshaking; you don't get past an old soldier in that way. Excuse me, young man. *(He kisses* BARBARA *and looks at his wife to make sure that she is admiring him.)* And to you, Captain Dering – you have won a prize.

DERING *(a gallant gentleman)* I know it. I'll try to show I know it.

COLONEL *(perturbed)* I haven't given Barbara a wedding present, Ellen. I should like–

BARBARA Indeed you have, dear, and a lovely one. You haven't forgotten?

Granny signs to the COLONEL *and he immediately says, with remarkable cunning:*

COLONEL Oh – that! I was just quizzing you, Barbara. I hope you will be as happy, dear, staid Barbara, as if you had married–

He sees that he has nearly given away the situation. He looks triumphantly at granny as much as to say, 'Observe me; I'm not going to say a word about him.' Granny comes to his aid.

ELLEN Perhaps Captain Dering has some little things to do: and you, too, Barbara. They are leaving in an hour, John.

For a moment the COLONEL *is again in danger.*

COLONEL If you would like to take Barbara into the garden, Captain Dering *(He recovers himself instantly.)* No, not the garden, you wouldn't know your way about in the garden.

DERING *(smiling)* Wouldn't I, Colonel?

COLONEL No, certainly not. I'll show it you some day. *(He makes gleeful signs to granny.)* But there is a nice meadow just beyond the shrubbery. Barbara knows the way; she often went there with– *(He checks himself. Granny signs to them to go and* BARBARA *kisses both the* COLONEL'S *hands.)* The Captain will be jealous, you know!

BARBARA Let me, dear *(arranging his cushions professionally.)*

ELLEN She's much better at it than I am now, John.

The COLONEL *has one last piece of advice to give.*

COLONEL I wouldn't go down by the stream, Barbara – not to the pool where the alder is. There's – there's not a good view there, sir; and a boy – a boy I knew, he often – nobody in particular – just a boy who used to come about the house – he is not here now – he is on duty. I don't think you should go to the alder pool, Barbara.

BARBARA We won't go there, dear.

She and her husband go out, and the COLONEL *scarcely misses them he is so eager to hear what his wife thinks of him.*

COLONEL Did I do all right, Ellen?

ELLEN Splendidly. I was proud of you.

COLONEL I put them completely off the scent! they haven't a notion! I can be very sly, you know, at times. Ellen, I think I should like to have that alder tree cut down. There is no boy now, you see.

ELLEN I would leave it alone, John. There will be boys again. Shall I read to you; you like that, don't you?

COLONEL Yes, read to me – something funny, if you please. About Sam Weller! No, I expect Sam has gone to the wars. Read about Mr Pickwick. He is very amusing. I feel sure that if he had tried to catch the bull-trout he would have fallen in. Just as Barbara did this morning.

ELLEN Barbara?

COLONEL She is down at the alder pool. Billy is there with that nice German boy. The noise they make, shouting and laughing!

She gets from its shelf the best book for war time.

ELLEN Which bit shall I read?

COLONEL About Mr Pickwick going into the lady's bedroom by mistake.

ELLEN Yes, dear, though you almost know it by heart. You see, you have begun to laugh already.

COLONEL You are laughing too, Ellen. I can't help it!

Samuel Crockett (1860 – 1914)

Like 'Ian Maclaren', (1850–1907, and thus represented in Vol. II) Crockett was a minister of the Scottish Free Church, and a noted writer of kailyard fiction. Crockett was also capable of a vigorous historical narrative (as in *The Raiders*, of 1894). His most famous kailyard work is probably the collection of sketches in The Stickit Minister (1893). His fine short story, 'The Last Anderson of Deeside', is an example of the genuine pathos the kailyarders were at times able to achieve.

The Last Anderson of Deeside

Pleasant is sunshine after rain,
Pleasant the sun;
To cheer the parched land again,
Pleasant the rain.

Sweetest is joyance after pain,
Sweetest is joy;
Yet sorest sorrow worketh gain,
Sorrow is gain.

          – As in the Days of Old

'Weel, he's won awa'.'

'Ay, ay, he is that.'

The minister's funeral was winding slowly out of the little manse loaning. The window-blinds were all down, and their bald whiteness, like sightless eyes looking out of the white-washed walls and the trampled snow, made the Free Church manse of Deeside no cheerful picture that wild New Year's Day. The green gate which had so long hung on one hinge, periodically mended ever since the minister's son broke the other swinging on it the summer of the dry year before he went to college, now swayed forward with a miserably forlorn lurch, as though it too had tried to follow the funeral procession of the man who had shut it carefully the last thing before he went to bed every night for forty years.

Andrew Malcolm, the Glencairn joiner, who was conducting the funeral – if, indeed, Scots funerals can ever be said to be conducted – had given it a too successful push to let the rickety hearse have plenty of sea room between the granite pillars. It was a long and straggling funeral, silent save for the words that stand at the opening of this tale, which ran up and down the long black files like the irregular fire of skirmishers.

'Ay, man, he's won awa'!'

'Ay, ay, he is that!'

This is the Scottish Lowland 'coronach,' characteristic and expressive as the wailing of the pipes to the Gael or the keening of women among the wild Eirionach.

'We are layin' the last o' the auld Andersons o' Deeside amang the mools[1] the day,' said Saunders M'Quhirr, the farmer of Drumquhat, to his friend Rob Adair of the Mains of Deeside, as they walked sedately together, neither swinging his arms as he would have done on an ordinary day. Saunders had come all the way over Dee Water to follow the far-noted man of God to his rest.

'There's no siccan men noo as the Andersons o' Deeside,' said Rob Adair, with a kind of pride and pleasure in his voice. 'I'm a dale aulder than you, Saunders, an' I mind weel o' the faither o' him that's gone.' (Rob had in full measure the curious South-country disinclination to speak directly of the dead.)

'Ay, an angry man he was that day in the '43 when him that's a cauld corp the day, left the kirk an' manse that his faither had pitten him intil only the year afore. for, of coorse, the lairds o' Deeside were the pawtrons o' the pairish; an' when the auld laird's yae son took it intil his head to be a minister, it was in the nature o' things that he should get the pairish.

'Weel, the laird didna speak to his son for the better part o' twa year; though mony a time he drave by to the Pairish Kirk when his son was haudin' an ootdoor service at the Auld Wa's where the three roads meet. For nae *sicht* could they get on a' Deeside for kirk or manse, because frae the Dullarg to Craig Ronald a' belanged to the laird. The minister sent the wife an' bairns to a sma' hoose in Cairn Edward, an' lodged himsel' amang sic o' the farmers as werena feared for his faither's factor. Na, an' speak to his son the auld man wadna, for the very dourness o' him. Ay, even though the minister wad say to his faither, "Faither, wull ye no' speak to yer ain son?" no' yae word wad he answer, but pass him as though he hadna seen him, as muckle as to say – "nae son o' mine!"

'But a week or twa after the minister had lost yon twa nice bairns wi' the scarlet fever, his faither an' him forgathered at the fishin' – whaur he had gane, thinkin' to jook the sair thochts that he carried aboot wi' him, puir man. They were baith keen fishers an' graun' at it. The minister was for liftin' his hat to his faither an' gaun by, but the auld man stood still in the middle o' the fit-pad wi' a gae queer look in his face. "Wattie!" he said, an' for yae blink the minister thocht that his faither was gaun to greet[2], a thing that he had never seen him do in all his life. But the auld man didna greet. "Wattie," says he to his son, "hae ye a huik?"

'Ay, Saunders, that was a' he said, an' the minister juist gied him the huik and some half-dizzen fine flees forbye, an' the twa o' them never said *Disruption* mair as lang as they leeved.'

---

[1] 'Molds' (dirt).
[2] Weep.

'"Ye had better see the factor aboot pittin' up a meetin'-hoose and a decent dwallin', gin ye hae left kirk and manse." That was a' that the auld laird ever said, as his son gaed up stream and he down.

'Ay, he's been a sair tried man in his time, your minister, but he's a' by wi't the day,' continued Saunders M'Quhirr, as they trudged behind the hearse.

'Did I ever tell ye, Rob, aboot seein' young Walter – his boy that gaed wrang, ye ken – when I was up in London the year afore last? Na? 'Deed, I told naebody bena the mistress. It was nae guid story to tell on Deeside!

'Weel, I was up, as ye ken, at Barnet Fair wi' some winter beasts, so I bade a day or twa in London, doin' what sma' business I had, an' seein' the sichts as weel, for it's no' ilka day that a Deeside body finds themsel's i' London.

'Yae nicht wha should come in but a Cairn Edward callant[1] that served his time wi' Maxwell in the *Advertiser* office. He had spoken to me at the show, pleased to see a Gallawa' face, nae doot. And he told me he was married an' workin' on the *Times*. An' amang ither things back an' forrit, he told me that the minister o' Deeside's son was here. "But," says he, "I'm feared that he's comin' to nae guid." I kenned that the laddie hadna been hame to his faither an' his mither for a maitter o' maybe ten year, so I thought that I wad like to see the lad for his faither's sake. So in a day or twa I got his address frae the reporter lad, an' fand him after a lang seek doon in a gye queer place no' far frae where Tammas Carlyle leeves near the waterside. I thocht that there was nae ill bits i' London but in the East-end; but I learned different.

'I gaed up the stair o' a wee brick hoose nearly tummlin' doon wi' its ain wecht – a perfect rickle o' brick – an chappit. A lass opened the door after a wee, no' that ill lookin', but toosy[2] aboot the heid an' unco shilpit[3] aboot the face.

'"What do you want?" says she, verra sharp an' clippit in her mainner o' speech.

'"Does Walter Anderson o' Deeside bide here?" I asked, gye an' plain, as ye ken a body has to speak to thae Englishers that barely can understand their ain language.

'"What may you want with him?" says she.

'"I come frae Deeside," says I – no' that I meaned to lichtly my ain pairish, but I thocht that the lassie micht no' be acquant wi' the name o' Whunnyliggate. "I come frae Deeside. an' I ken Walter Anderson's faither."

'"That's no recommend," says she. "The mair's the peety," says I, "for he's a daicent man."

'So she took ben my name, that I had nae cause to be ashamed o', an' syne she brocht word that I was to step in. So ben I gaed, an' it wasna a far step, eyther, for it was juist yae bit garret room; an' there on a bed in the corner was the minister's laddie, lookin' nae aulder than when he used to swing on the yett[4] an' chase the hens. At the verra first glint I gat o' him I saw that Death had come to him, and come to bide. His countenance was barely o' this earth – sair disjaskit[5] an' no' manlike ava' – mair like a lassie far gane in a decline; but raised-like too, an' wi' a kind o' defiance in it, as if he was darin' the Almichty to His face. O man, Rob, I hope I may never see the like again.'

'Ay, man, Saunders, ay, ay!' said Rob Adair, who, being a more demonstrative man than his friend, had been groping in the tail of his 'blacks' for the handkerchief that was in his hat. Then Rob forgot, in the pathos of the story, what he was searching for, and walked for a considerable distance with his hand deep in the pocket of his tailcoat.

The farmer of Drumquhat proceeded on his even way.

'The lassie that I took to be his wife (but I asked no questions) was awfu' different ben the room wi' him, frae what she was wi' me at the door – fleechin'[6] like wi' him to tak' a sup o'

---

[1] Young fellow.
[2] Untidy.
[3] Drawn, thin.
[4] Gate.
[5] Dejected.
[6] Cajoling, coaxing.

soup. An' when I gaed forrit to speak to him on the puir bit bed, she cam' by me like stour,[1] wi' the water happin' off her cheeks, like hail in a simmer thunder-shoo'er.'

'Puir bit lassockie!' muttered Rob Adair, who had three daughters of his own at home, as he made another absent-minded and unsuccessful search for his handkerchief.

'There's a smurr o' rain beginnin' to fa', I think,' he said, apologetically.

"An' ye're Sandy MacWhurr frae Drumquhat,' says the puir lad on the bed. 'Are your sugar-plums as guid as ever?'

'What a question to speer on a dying bed, Saunders!' said Rob.

'Deed, ye may say it. Weel, frae that he gaed on talkin' aboot hoo Fred Robson an' him stole the hale o' the Drumquhat plooms yae back-end, an' hoo they gat as far as the horse waterin'-place wi' them when the dogs gat after them. He threepit[2] that it was me that set the dogs on, but I never did that, though I didna conter him. He said that Fred an' him made for the seven-fit march dyke, but hadna time to mak' ower it. So there they had to sit on the tap o' a thorn bush in the meadow on their hunkers, wi' the dogs fair loupin' an' yowlin' to get haud o' them. Then I cum' doon mysel' an' garred them turn every pooch inside oot. He minded, too, that I was for hingin' them baith up by the heels, till what they had etten followed what had been in their pooches. A' this he telled juist as he did, when he used to come ower to hae a bar wi' the lassies, in the forenichts after he cam' hame frae the college the first year. But the lad was laughin' a' the time in a way I didna like. It wasna natural – something hard an' frae the teeth oot, as ye micht say – maist peetifu' in a callant like him, wi' the deid-licht shinin' already in the blue een o' him.'

'D've no' mind, Saunders, o' him comin' hame frae the college wi' a hantle o' medals an' prizes?' said Rob Adair, breaking in as if he felt that he must contribute his share to the memories which shortened, if they did not cheer, their road. 'His faither was rael prood o' him, though it wasna his way to say muckle. But his mither could talk aboot naething else, an' carriet his picture aboot wi' her a' ower the pairish in her wee black recktical basket. Fegs, a gypsy wife gat a saxpence juist for speerin' for a sicht o' it, and cryin', "Blessings on the laddie's bonny face!"'

'Weel,' continued Saunders, imperturbably taking up the thread of his narrative amid the blattering of the snow, 'I let the lad rin on i' this way for a while, an' then says I, 'Walter, ye dinna ask after yer faither!'

"No, I don't," says he, verra short. "Nell, gie me the draught." So wi' that the lassie gied her een a bit quick dab, syne cam' forrit, an' pittin' her airm aneath his heid she gied him a drink. Whatever it was, it quaitened him, an' he lay back tired like.

"Weel," said I, after a wee, "Walter, gin ye'll no' speer for yer faither, maybe ye'll speer for yer ain mither?"

'Walter Anderson turned his heid to the wa'. "Oh, my mither! my ain mither!" he said, but I could hardly hear him sayin' it. Then more fiercely than he had yet spoken he turned on me an' said, "Wha sent ye here to torment me before my time?"

'I saw young Walter juist yince mair in life. I stepped doon to see him the next mornin' when the end was near. He was catchin' an' twitchin' at the coverlet, liftin' up his hand an' lookin' at it as though it was somebody else's. It was a black fog outside, an' even in the garret it took him in his throat till he couldn't get breath.

'He motioned for me to sit doon beside him. There was nae chair, so I e'en gat doon on my knees. The lass stood white an' quaite at the far side o' the bed. He turned his een on me, blue an' bonnie as a bairn's; but wi' a licht in them that telled he had eaten o' the tree o' knowledge, and that no seldom.'

"O Sandy," he whispered, "what a mess I've made o't, haven't I? You'll see my mither when ye gang back to Deeside. Tell her it's no' been so bad as it has whiles lookit. Tell her I've aye loved her, even at the warst – an' – an' my faither too!" he said, with a kind o' grip

---

[1] Storm.
[2] Asserted argumentatively.

in his words.

'"Walter," says I, "I'll pit up a prayer, as I'm on my knees onyway." I'm no giftit like some, I ken; but, Robert, I prayed for that laddie gaun afore his Maker as I never prayed afore or since. And when I spak aboot the forgiein o' sin, the laddie juist steekit[1] his een an said "Amen!"

'That nicht as the clock was chappin twal the lassie cam to my door (an the landlady wasna that weel pleased at bein raised, eyther), an she askit me to come an see Walter, for there was naebody else that had kenned him in his guid days. So I took my stave an' my plaid an gaed my ways wi her intil the nicht – a' lichtit up wi lang raws o' gas-lamps, an awa doon by the water side whaur the tide sweels black aneath the brigs. Man, a big lichtit toun at nicht is far mair lanesome than the Dullarg muir when it's black as pit-mirk. When we got to the puir bit hoosie, we fand that the doctor was there afore us. I had gotten him brocht to Walter the nicht afore. But the lassie was nae sooner within the door than she gied an unco-like cry, an flang hersel distrackit on the bed. An there I saw, atween her white airms and her tangled yellow hair, the face o' Walter Anderson, the son o' the Manse o' Deeside, lyin on the pillow with the chin tied up in a napkin!'

'Never a sermon like that, Robert Adair!' said Saunders M'Quhirr solemnly, after he had paused a moment.

Saunders and Robert were now turning off the windswept muir-road into the sheltered little avenue which led up to the kirk above the white and icebound Dee Water. The aged gravedigger, bent nearly double, met them where the roads parted. A little further up the newly elected minister of the parish kirk stood at the manse door, in which Walter Anderson had turned the key forty years ago for conscience sake.

Very black and sombre looked the silent company of mourners who now drew together about the open grave – a fearsome gash on the white spread of the new-fallen snow.

There was no religious service at the minister's grave save that of the deepest silence. Ranked round the coffin, which lay on black bars over the grave-mouth, stood the elders, but no one of them ventured to take the posts of honour at the head and the foot. The minister had left not one of his blood with a right to these positions. He was the last Anderson of Deeside.

'Preserve us! wha's yon they're pittin' at the fit o' the grave? Wha can it be ava?' was whispered here and there back in the crowd. 'It's Jean Grier's boy, I declare – him that the minister took oot o' the puirhoose, and schuled and colleged baith. Weel, that cowes a'! Saw ye ever the like o' that?'

It was to Rob Adair that this good and worthy thought had come. In him more than in any of his fellow elders the dead man's spirit lived. He had sat under him all his life, and was sappy with his teaching. Some would have murmured had they had time to complain, but no one ventured to say nay to Rob Adair as he pushed the modest, clear-faced youth into the vacant place.

Still the space at the head of the grave was vacant, and for a long moment the ceremony halted as if waiting for a manifestation. With a swift, sudden startle the coil of black cord, always reserved for the chief mourner, slipped off the coffin-lid and fell heavily into the grave.

'He's there afore his faither,' said Saunders M'Quhirr.

So sudden and unexpected was the movement, that, though the fall of the cord was the simplest thing in the world, a visible quiver passed through the bowed ranks of the bearers. 'It was his ain boy Wattie come to lay his faither's heid i' the grave!' cried Daft Jess, the parish 'natural', in a loud sudden voice from the 'thruch' stone near the kirkyaird wall where she stood at gaze.

And there were many there who did not think it impossible.

As the mourners 'skailed' [scattered] slowly away from the kirkyaird in twos and threes, there was wonderment as to who should have the property, for which the late laird and

---

[1] Shut.

minister had cared so little. There were very various opinions; but one thing was quite universally admitted, that there would be no such easy terms in the matter of rent and arrears as there had been in the time of 'him that's awa'.' The snow swept down with a biting swirl as the groups scattered and the mourners vanished from each other's sight, diving singly into the eddying drifts as into a great tent of many flapping folds. Grave and quiet is the Scottish funeral, with a kind of simple manfulness as of men in the presence of the King of Terrors, but yet possessing that within them which enables every man of them to await without unworthy fear the Messenger who comes but once. On the whole, not so sad as many things that are called mirthful.

So the last Anderson of Deeside, and the best of all their ancient line, was gathered to his fathers in an equal sleep that snowy January morning. There were two inches of snow in the grave when they laid the coffin in. As Saunders said, 'Afore auld Elec could get him happit, his Maister had hidden him like Moses in a windin'-sheet o' His ain.' In the morning, when Elec went hirpling into the kirkyaird, he found at the gravehead a bare place which the snow had not covered. Then some remembered that, hurrying by in the rapidly darkening gloaming of the night after the funeral, they had seen some one standing immovable by the minister's grave in the thickly drifting snow. They had wondered why he should stand there on such a bitter night.

There were those who said that it was just the lad Archibald Grier, gone to stand a while by his benefactor's grave.

But Daft Jess was of another opinion.

Francis Lauderdale Adams (1862 – 1893)

William Wallace

(For the Ballarat Statue of Him)

This is Scotch William Wallace. It was he
Who in dark hours first raised his face to see:
Who watched the English tyrant nobles spurn,
Steel-clad, with iron hoofs the Scottish free:

Who armed and drilled the simple footman Kern,
Yea, bade in blood and rout the proud knight learn
His feudalism was dead, and Scotland stand
Dauntless to wait the day of Bannockburn.

O Wallace, peerless lover of thy land
We need thee still, thy moulding brain and hand.   10
For us, thy poor, again proud tyrants spurn,
The robber rich, a yet more hateful band.

To the Christians

Take, then, your paltry Christ,
Your gentleman God.
We want the carpenter's son,
With his saw and hod.

We want the man who loved
The poor and oppressed,
Who hated the rich man and king
And the scribe and the priest.

We want the Galilean
Who knew cross and rod.   10
It's your 'good taste' that prefers
A bastard God.

Violet Jacob (1863 – 1946)

The Wild Geese

'Oh, tell me what was on yer road, ye roarin' norlan' wind
As ye cam' blawin' frae the land that's niver frae my mind?
My feet they trayvel England, but I'm deein' for the north – '
'My man, I heard the siller tides rin up the Firth o' Forth.'

'Aye, Wind, I ken them well eneuch, and fine they fa' and rise,
And fain I'd feel the creepin' mist on yonder shore that lies,
But tell me, ere ye passed them by, what saw ye on the way?'
'My man, I rocked the rovin' gulls that sail abune the Tay.'

'But saw ye naethin', leein' Wind, afore ye cam' to Fife?
There's muckle lyin' yont★ the Tay that's mair to me nor life.' 10   beyond
'My man, I swept the Angus braes ye haena trod for years – '
'O Wind, forgie a hameless loon★ that canna see for tears! – '   fellow

'And far abone the Angus straths★ I saw the wild geese flee,   valleys
A lang, lang skein o' beatin' wings wi' their heids towards the sea,
And aye their cryin' voices trailed ahint them on the air – '
'O Wind, hae maircy, haud yer whisht★, for I daurna listen mair!'   be silent

Tam i' the Kirk

O Jean, my Jean, when the bell ca's the congregation
O'er valley an' hill wi' the ding frae its iron mou',
When a'body's thochts is set on their ain salvation,
Mine's set on you.

There's a reid rose lies on the Buik o' the Word afore ye   peep
That was growin' braw on its bush at the keek★ o' day,
But the lad that pu'd yon flower i' the mornin's glory –
He canna pray.

He canna pray, but there's nane i' the kirk will heed him
Whaur he sits sae still his lane¹ at the side o' the wa',   10
For nane but the reid rose kens what my lassie gied him –
It and us twa.

He canna sing for the sang that his ain he'rt raises,
He canna see for the mist that's afore his e'en,
And a voice drouns the hale o' the psalms an' the paraphrases,
Crying 'Jean! Jean! Jean!'

The Rowan

When the days were still as deith
And ye couldna see the kye
Though ye'd maybe hear their breith
I' the mist oot-by;
When I'd mind the lang grey een
O' the warlock by the hill
And sit fleggit★ like a wean★   afraid/child
Gin★ a whaup★ cried shrill;   if/curlew
Tho' the he'rt wad dee in me
At a fitstep on the floor,   10
There was aye the rowan tree
Wi' its airm across the door.

But that is far, far past
And a' thing's just the same,
There's whisper up the blast
O' a dreid I daurna name;
And the shilpit★ sun is thin,   weakened
Like auld men deein' slow,
And a shade comes creepin' in
When the fire is fa'in' low;   20
Then I feel thae lang een set
Like a doom upon ma heid,
For the warlock's livin' yet –
But the rowan's deid.

---

¹ 'His lane': by himself.

The Gowk

I see the Gowk an' the Gowk sees me
Beside a berry-bush by the aipple-tree. (Old Scots rhyme.)

Tib my auntie's a deil to wark,
Has me risin' a fore the sun;
Aince her heid is abune her sark
Then the clash o' her tongue's begun.
Warslin', steerin' wi' hens an' swine,
Naucht kens she o' a freend o' mine –
But the gowk★ that bides i' the woods o' Dun   cuckoo
He kens him fine.

Past the yaird an' ahint★ the stye,   beyond
Oh, the aipples grow bonnilie.   10
Tib, my auntie, she canna spy
Wha comes creepin' to kep★ wi' me.   meet
Aye, she'd sort him, for, dod, she's fell.
Whist now, Jimmie, an' hide yersel',
An' the wise-like bird i' the aipple-tree
He winna tell.

Aprile-month, or the aipples flower,
Tib, my auntie, will rage an' ca';
Jimmie lad, she may rin an' glower –
What care I? We'll be far awa'.   20
Let her seek me the leelang day,
Wha's to tell her the road we'll gae?
For the cannie gowk, tho' he kens it a',
He winna say.

The Field by the Lirk o' the Hill

Daytime and nicht,
Sun, wind an' rain,
The lang cauld licht
O' the spring months again;
The braird's a' weed
And the fairm's a' still –
Wha'll sow the seed
I' the field by the lirk★ o' the hill?   fold, crevice

Prood maun ye lie,
Prood did ye gang,   10
Auld, auld am I
And oh! life's lang!
Ghaists i' the air
Whaups'★ voices shrill,   sea birds
And you nae mair
I' the field by the lirk o' the hill –
Ay, bairn, nae mair, nae mair,
I' the field by the lirk o' the hill.

The Neep-Fields by the Sea

Ye'd wonder foo the seasons rin
This side o' Tweed an' Tyne;
The hairst's awa'; October month
Cam in a whilie syne,
But the stooks are oot in Scotland yet,
There's green upon the tree,
And oh, what grand's the smell ye'll get
Frae the neep*-fields by the sea.   *turnip*

The lang lift* lies abune the warld,   *sky*
On ilka windless day   10
The ships creep doon the ocean line
Sma' on the band o' grey;
And the lang sigh heaved upon the sand
Comes pechin'* up tae me'   *panting*
And speils the cliffs tae whaur ye stand
I' the neep-fields by the sea.

Oh, time's aye slow, though time gangs fast
When siller's a' tae mak',
An' deith, afore ma poke is fu'
May grip me i' the back;   20
But ye'll tak ma banes an' my Sawbath braws,
Gin deith's owe smairt for me,
And set them up amang the shaws*   *woods*
I' the lang rows plantit atween the wa's,
A tattie-dulie* for fleggin' craws   *scarecrow*
I' the neep fields by the sea.

The Baltic

'Whaur are ye gaen sae fast, my bairn,
It's no tae the schule ye'll win?'
'Doon tae the shore at the fit o' the toon
Tae bide till the brigs come in.'

'Awa' noo wi' ye and turn ye hame,
Ye'll no hae time tae bide;
It's twa lang months or the brigs come back
On the lift o' a risin' tide.'

'I'll sit me doon at the water's mou'
Till there's niver a blink o' licht,   10
For my feyther bad me tae tryst wi' him
In the dairkness o' yesternicht.'

'Rise ye an' rin tae the shore,' says he,
'At the cheep o' the waukin' bird,
And I'll bring ye a tale o' a foreign land
The like that ye niver heard.'

'Oh, haud yer havers ye feckless wean,
It was but a dream ye saw,
For he's far, far north wi' the Baltic men
I' the hurl o' the Baltic snaw;   20

And what did he ca' yon foreign land?'
'He tell'tna its name tae me,
But I doot it's no by the Baltic shore,
For he said there was nae mair sea.'

The Howe o' the Mearns

Laddie, my lad, when ye gang at the tail o' the plough
An' the days draw in,
When the burnin' yellow's awa' that was aince a-lowe
On the braes o' whin★,   gorse
Do ye mind o' me that's deaved★ wi' the wearyfu' south   deafened
An' its puir concairns★,   concerns
While the weepies fade on the knowes★ at the river's mouth   knolls
In the Howe★ o' the Mearns?   low valley

There was nae twa lads frae the Grampians doon to the Tay
That could best us twa;   10
At bothie★ or dance, or the field on a fitba' day   worker's cottage
We could sort them a';
An' at courtin'-time when the stars keeked★ doon on the glen   peeked
An' its theek★ o' fairns   thatch
It was you an' me got the pick o' the basket then
In the Howe o' the Mearns.

London is fine, an' for ilk o' the lasses at hame
There'll be saxty here,
But the springtime comes an' the hairst★ – an' its aye the same   harvest
Through the changefu' year.   20
Oh, a lad thinks lang o' hame ere he thinks his fill
As his breid he airns★ –   earns
An' they're threshin' noo at the white fairm up on the hill
In the Howe o' the Mearns.

Gin★ I mind mysel' an' toil for the lave★ o' my days   if/rest
While I've een to see,
When I'm auld an' dune wi' the fash★ o' their English ways   trouble
I'll come hame to dee;
For the lad dreams aye o' the prize that the man'll get,
But he lives an' lairns,   30
An' its far far ayont★ him still – but it's farther yet   beyond
To the Howe o' the Mearns.

Laddie, my lad, when the hair is white on your pow★   head
An' the wark's put past,
When your hand's ower auld an' heavy to haud the plough
I'll win★ hame at last,   go
An' we'll bide our time on the knowes whaur the broom stands braw
An' we played as bairns,
Till the last lang gloamin' shall creep on us baith an' fa'
On the Howe o' the Mearns.   40

A Change o' Deils

'A change o' deils is lichtsome.'
Scots Proverb

My Grannie spent a merry youth,
She niver wantit for a joe★,   sweetheart
An gin she tell't me aye the truth,
Richt little was't she kent na o'.
An' while afore she gae'd awa'
To bed her doon below the grass,
Says she, 'Guidmen I've kistit★ twa,   buried
But a change o' deils is lichtsome, lass!

Sae dinna think to maister me,
For Scotland's fu' o' brawlike chiels★,   10   fellows
And ablins★ ither folk ye'll see   perhaps
Are fine an' pleased to change their deils.

Aye, set yer bonnet on yer heid,
An' cock it up upon yer bree★,   brow
O' a' yer tricks ye'll hae some need
Afore ye get the best o' me!

Sma' wark to fill yer place I'd hae,
I'll seek a sweethe'rt i' the toon,
Or cast my he'rt across the Spey
An' tak' some pridefu' Hieland loon.   20

I ken a man has hoose an' land,
His arm is stoot, his een are blue,
A ring o' gowd is on his hand,
An' he's a bonnier man nor you!

But hoose an' gear an' land an' mair,
He'd gie them a' to get the preen★   pin
That preened the flowers in till my hair
Beside the may-bush yestere'en.'

Jist tak' you tent★, an' mind forbye,   care
The braw guid sense my Grannie had,   30
My Grannie's dochter's bairn am I,
An a change o' deils is lichtsome, lad!

Craigo Woods

Craigo Woods, wi' the splash o' the cauld rain beatin'
I' the back end o' the year,
When the clouds hang laigh wi' the weicht o' their load o' greetin'★   weeping
And the autumn wind's asteer;
Ye may stand like ghaists, ye may fa' i' the blast that's cleft ye
To rot i' the chilly dew,
But when will I mind on aucht since the day I left ye
Like I mind on you – on you?

Craigo Woods, i' the licht o' September sleepin'
And the saft mist o' the morn,   10
When the hairst★ climbs to yer feet, an' the sound o' reapin'   harvest
Comes up frae the stookit corn,
And the braw reid puddock-stules★ are like jewels blinkin'   toadstools
And the bramble haps★ ye baith,   clothes
O what do I see, i the lang nicht, lyin' an' thinkin'
As I see yer wraith – yer wraith?

There's a road to a far-aff land, an' the land is yonder
Whaur a' men's hopes are set;
We dinna ken foo★ lang we maun hae to wander,   how
But we'll a' win to it yet;   20
An' gin there's woods o' fir an' the licht atween them,
I winna speir★ its name,   ask
But I'll lay me doon by the puddock-stules when I've seen them,
An' I'll cry 'I'm hame – I'm hame!'

The Debatable Land

Of the birth and origin of Jessie-Mary no one in the parish knew anything definite. Those who passed up the unfrequented cart-road by her grandmother's thatched hovel used to see the shock-headed child among the gooseberry bushes of the old woman's garden, peering at them, like an animal, over the fence.

Whether she were really the granddaughter of the old beldame inside the mud walls no one knew, neither, for that matter, did anybody care. The hovel was the last remaining house of a little settlement which had disappeared from the side of the burn. Just where it stood, a shallow stream ran across the way and plunged into a wood in which Jessie-Mary had many a time feasted on the plentiful wild raspberries, and run, like a little squirrel, among the trees.

It was not until she was left alone in the world that much attention was paid to her existence, and then she presented herself to the parish as a problem; for her life was lived a full half-century before the all-powerful Board School arose to direct rustic parents and guardians, and she had received little education. She had grown into a sturdy girl of twenty, with brown hair which the sun had bleached to a dull yellow, twisted up at the back of her head and hanging heavily over her brows. She was a fierce looking lass, with her hot grey eyes. The parish turned its mind to the question of how she might earn a living and was presently relieved when Mrs Muirhead, who was looking for an able-bodied servant, hired her in that capacity. She was to have a somewhat meager wage and her clothes, and was to help her mistress in house and yard. When the matter was settled she packed her few possessions into a bundle and sauntered up the green loaning which ran between the hovel and Mrs Muirhead's decent roof, marking where one fir-wood ended and another began.

Mrs Muirhead was the widow of a joiner, and she inhabited a cottage standing just where the woods and the mouth of the loaning touched the high road that ran north to the hills. She was well to do, for a cottager, and her little yard, besides being stacked with planks which her son, Peter, sawed and planed as his father had done before him, contained a row of hen-coops and a sty enclosing a pig whose proportions waxed as autumn waned. When the laird trotted by, he cast a favorable eye on the place, which was as neat as it befitted the last house on a man's property to be. When he had passed on and was trotting alongside the farther wood he was no longer on his own ground, for the green, whin-choked loaning was debatable land lying between him and his neighbour.

As Jessie-Mary, with her bundle, came through the whins and opened the gate, Peter Muirhead, who was in the yard, heard the latch click and looked up from his work. At sight of the yellow head by the holly bushes he laid down the spokeshave he was using and came round to the front. The girl was looking at him with eyes whose directness a youth of his type is liable to misunderstand. He began to smile.

'Will Mistress Muirhead be ben?' said Jessie-Mary tentatively.

Peter did not answer, but approached, his smile taking meaning.

'Will Mistress Muirhead be ben the hoose?' she inquired, more loudly.

It occurred to her that he might not be in his right senses, for the mile or two of debatable track which separated her old home from her future one might as well have been ten, for all she had seen of the world at the other end of it. She knew very well that Muirhead the joiner had lived where she now stood, and she had seen the old man, but the shambling figure before her was entirely strange. Once, at the edge of the wood, she had listened to the whirr of sawing in the vicinity of the road and had gathered that the work went on, though Muirhead himself had departed.

'She's no here. Ye'll just hae to put up wi' me,' said Peter jocosely. His mother was in the house, but he saw no reason for divulging the fact.

Jessie-Mary stood silent, scarcely knowing what to say.

'Ye're a fine lassie,' observed Peter, still smiling alluringly.

She eyed him with distrust and her heavy brows lowered over her eyes; she began to walk towards the cottage. He sprang forward, as though to intercept her, and, as she knocked, he laid hold of her free hand. Mrs Muirhead, from within, opened the door just in time to see him drop it. She was a short, hard-featured woman, presenting an expanse of white apron to the world; a bunch of turkeys' feathers, in which to stick knitting needles, was secured between her person and the band of this garment, the points of the quills uppermost. She looked from one to the other, then drawing Jessie-Mary over the threshold, she slammed the door.

'Dinna think a didna see ye, ye limmer!' she exclaimed, taking the girl roughly by the shoulder.

And so Jessie-Mary's working life began.

The little room allotted to her, looking over the yard, was no smaller than the corner she had inhabited in the mud cottage, yet it had a stifling effect; and its paper, which bore a small lilac flower on a buff ground, dazzled her eyes and seemed to press on her from all sides. In the cracked looking-glass which hung on it she could see the disturbing background behind her head as she combed and flattened her thick hair in accordance with Mrs Muirhead's ideas. In leisure moments she hemmed at an apron which she was to wear when completed. Mrs Muirhead was annoyed at finding she could hardly use a needle; she was far from being an unkind woman, but her understanding stopped at the limits of her own requirements. Jessie-Mary's equally marked limitations struck her as the result of natural wickedness.

Wherever the yard was unoccupied by the planks or the pigsty, it was set about with hen-coops, whose inmates strayed at will from the enclosure to pervade the nearer parts of the wood in those eternal perambulations which occupy fowls. Just outside, where the trees began, was a pleasant strip of sandy soil in which the hens would settle themselves with much clucking and tail-shaking, to sit blinking, like so many vindictive dowagers, at their kind. Through this, the Dorking cock, self-conscious and gallant, would conduct the ladies of his family to scratch among the tree-roots; and the wood for about twenty yards from the house wore that peculiar scraped and befeathered look which announces the proximity of a hen-roost. At night the lower branches were alive with dark forms and the suppressed gurgling that would escape from them. It was part of Jessie-Mary's duty to attend to the wants of this rabble.

There were times when a longing for flight took the half-civilised girl. Life, for her, had always been a sort of inevitable accident, a state in whose ordering she had no part as a whole, however much choice she might have had in its details. But now there was little choice in these; Mrs Muirhead ordered her day and she tolerated it as best she could. She hardly knew what to do with her small wage when she got it, for the finery dear to the heart of the modern country lass was a thing of which she had no knowledge, and there was no dependent relative who might demand it of her.

The principal trouble of her life was Peter, whose occupations kept him of necessity at home, and whose presence grew more hateful as time went on. There was no peace for her within sight of his leering smile. There was only one day of the week that she was free of him; and on these Sunday afternoons, as he went up the road to join the loitering knot of horsemen from the nearest farm, she would thankfully watch him out of sight from the shelter of the loaning. She hated him with all her heart.

He would lurk about in the evenings, trying to waylay her amongst the trees as she went to gather in the fowls, and once, coming suddenly on her as she turned the corner of the house, he had put his arm about her neck. She had felt his hot breath on her ear, and, in her fury, pushed him from her with such violence that he staggered back against a weak place in the yard fence and fell through, cutting his elbow on a piece of broken glass.

She stood staring at him, half terrified at what she had done, but rejoicing to see the blood trickle down his sleeve. She would have liked to kill him. The dreadful combination of his instincts and his shamblingness was what physically revolted her, though she did not realise it; and his meanness had, more than once, got her into trouble with his mother. She had no consideration to expect from Mrs Muirhead, as she knew well. To a more complicated nature the position would have been unendurable, but Jessie-Mary endured stubbornly, vindictively, as an animal endures. She was in a cruel position and her only safeguard lay in the fact that Peter Muirhead was repulsive to her. But neither morality nor expediency nor the armed panoply of all the cardinal virtues have yet succeeded in inventing for a woman a safeguard so strong as her own taste.

It was on a Sunday afternoon towards the end of September that Peter emerged from the garden and strolled up the road. The sun was high above the woods, his rim as yet clear of the tree-tops, and the long shadow from the young man's feet lay in a dark strip between himself and the fence at his side. He wore his black Sunday suit and a tie bought from a travelling salesman who had visited Montrose fair the year before. In his best clothes he looked more ungainly than usual, and even the group of friends who watched his approach allowed themselves a joke at his expense as he neared them. He could hear their rough laughter, though he was far from guessing its cause. Nature had given him a good conceit of himself.

Jessie-Mary drew a breath of relief as his steps died away and she hailed the blessed time, granted to her but weekly, in which she might go about without risk of meeting him. Everything was quiet. Mrs Muirhead was sitting in the kitchen with her Bible; the door was ajar and the girl could just see a section of her skirt and the self-contained face of the cat which blinked on the hearth beside her. She had accompanied her mistress to the kirk that morning and had thought, as they returned decorously together, that she would go down the loaning again to see the thatched cottage by the burn – perhaps stray a little in the wood among the familiar raspberry-stalks. She had not seen these old haunts since she left them for Mrs Muirhead's service.

She took off her apron and went out bare-headed. On the outskirts of the trees the hens were rustling and fluttering in the dust; as she passed, they all arose and followed her. She had not remembered that their feeding-time was due in half an hour and for a moment she stood irresolute. If she were to go on her intended way there would be no one to give them their food. She determined to make and administer it at once; there would be plenty of time afterwards to do what she wished to do.

She was so little delayed that, when the pail was put away and the water poured into the tin dishes, there was still a long afternoon before her. She threaded her way slowly through the fir-stems, stopping to look at the rabbit-runs or to listen to the cooing of wood pigeons, her path fragrant with the scent of pine. After walking some way she struck across the far end of the loaning into the road which led to the mud hovel.

Autumn was approaching its very zenith, and the debatable land offered gorgeous tribute to the season. Like some outlandish savage ruler, it brought treasures unnumbered in the wealth of the more civilised earth. Here and there a branch of broom stood, like a scepter, among the black jewels of its hanging pods, and brambles, pushing through the whin-thickets like flames, hung in ragged splashes of carmine and orange and acid yellow. Bushes of that sweetbrier whose little ardent-coloured rose is one of the glories of eastern Scotland were dressed in the scarlet hips succeeding their bloom, and between them and the whin the thrifty spider had woven her net. Underfoot, bracken, escaping from the ditches, had invaded the loaning to clothe it in lemon and russet. Where the ground was marshy, patches of fine rush mixed with the small purple scabious which has its home in the vagabond corners of the land. As Jessie-Mary emerged from the trees her sun-bleached hair seemed the right culmination to this scale of natural colour; had it not been for the dark blue of her cotton gown she might as easily have become absorbed into her surroundings as the roe-deer, which is lost, a brown streak, in the labyrinth of trunks.

The air had the faint scent of coming decay which haunts even the earliest of autumn days, and the pale, high sky wore a blue suggestive of tears; the exhalations of earth were touched with the bitterness of lichen and fungus. Far away under the slope of the fields, and so hidden from sight, Montrose lay between the ocean and the estuary of the South Esk, with, beyond its spire, the sweep of the North Sea.

A few minutes later she found herself standing on the large, flat stone which bridged the burn where the footpath crossed it by her grandmother's hovel. She remained gazing at the walls rising from the unkempt tangle to which months of neglect were reducing the garden. The fence was broken in many places, and clumps of phlox, growing in a corner, had been trodden by the feet of strayed animals. Beneath her, the water sang with the same irresponsible babble which had once been the accompaniment to her life; she turned to follow it with her eyes as it dived under the matted grasses and disappeared into the wood.

All at once, from beyond the cottage, there rose a shout that made her heart jump, and she started to see two figures approaching through the field by the side of the burn; the blood left her face as she recognised one of them as Peter Muirhead. She sprang quickly from the stone and over the rail dividing the wood from the path; it was a foolish action and it produced its natural result. As she did so, a yell came from the field and she saw that Peter and his companion had begun to run.

Through the trees she fled, the derisive voices whooping behind her. She was terrified of her tormentor and the unreasoning animal fear of pursuit was upon her. As she heard the rail crack she knew that he had entered the wood, and instinct turned her towards the loaning, where the cover was thick and where she might turn aside in the tangle and be lost in some hidden nook while they passed her by. It was her best chance.

She plunged out from among the firs into the open track. For a hundred yards ahead the bushes were sparse and there was no obstacle to hinder her flight. She was swift of foot, and the damp earth flew beneath her. Through the whins beyond she went, scratching her hands on protruding brambles and stumbling among the roots. Once her dress caught on a stiff branch and she rent it away, tearing it from knee to hem. The voices behind her rose again and her breath was giving out.

Emerging from the thicket. she almost bounded into a little circle of fire, the smoke of which she had been too much excited to notice, though it was rising, blue and fine, from the clearing she had reached. A small tent was before her, made of tattered sail-cloth stretched over some dry branches, and beside it a light cart reposed, empty, upon its tailboard, the shafts to the sky.

In front of the tent stood a tall, lean man. His look was fixed upon her as she appeared and he had evidently been listening to the sound of her approaching feet. His face was as brown as the fir-stems that closed him in on either side of the loaning, and his eyes, brown also, had a peculiar, watchful light that was almost startling. He stood as still as though he were an image, and he wore a gold ring in either ear.

To Jessie-Mary, a living creature at this moment represented salvation, and before the man had time to turn his head she had leaped into the tent. Inside, by a little heap of brushwood, lay a tarpaulin, evidently used in wet weather to supplement its shelter, and she flung herself down on the ground and dragged the thing over her. The man stood immovable, looking fixedly at the bushes, from the other side of which came the noise of jeering voices.

As Peter Muirhead and his friend pushed into the open space, red and panting, they came upon the unexpected apparition with some astonishment. Tinkers and gypsies were far from uncommon in the debatable land, but the tall, still figure, with its intent eyes, brought them to a standstill. Peter mopped his forehead.

'Did ye see a lassie gae by yon way?' he inquired, halting disheveled from his race through the undergrowth, the sensational tie under one ear.

The brown man nodded, and, without a word, pointed his thumb over his shoulder in the direction in which they were going.

Peter and his companion glanced at each other; the former was rather blown, for he was not naturally active.

'Huts! a've had eneuch o' yon damned tawpie!' he exclaimed, throwing his cap on the ground.

The brown man looked him carefully over and smiled; there was a kind of primitive subtlety in his face.

Like many ill-favoured persons, Peter was vain and the look displeased him, for its faint ridicule was sharpened by the silence that accompanied it.

'A'll awa' to Montrose an' get the pollis tae ye the nicht,' he said, with as much superiority as he could muster; 'the like o' you's better oot o' this.'

'Ye'll no can rin sae far,' replied the other.

The answer was a mere burst of abuse.

'Come awa' noo, come awa',' said Peter's friend, scenting difficulties and unwilling to embroil himself.

But Peter was in a quarrelsome humor, and it was some time before the two young men disappeared down the track and Jessie-Mary could crawl from her hiding-place. She came out from under the sail-cloth, holding together the rent in her gown. The brown man smiled a different smile from the one with which he had regarded Peter; then he stepped up on a high tussock of rush to look after the pursuers.

'Are they awa'?' she asked, her eyes still dilated.

'Aye,' he replied. 'A didna tell on ye, ye see.'

'A'd like fine tae bide a bit,' said the girl nervously, 'they michtna be far yet.'

'Just sit ye doon there,' said he, pointing to his tattered apology for a dwelling.

She re-entered the tent and he seated himself before her on the threshold. For some minutes neither spoke and he considered her from head to foot. It was plain he was one chary of words. He took a short pipe from his pocket and, stuffing in some tobacco, lit it deliberately.

'A saw yon lad last time a was this way,' he said, jerking his head in the direction in which Peter had disappeared.

As she opened her mouth to reply the snort of a horse came through the bushes a few yards from where they sat. She started violently. There was a sudden gleam in his face which seemed to be his nearest approach to a laugh. 'Dod, ye needna be feared,' he said. 'Naebody'll touch ye wi' me.'

'A was fine an' glad tae see ye,' broke out the girl. 'Yon Muirhead's an ill lad tae hae i' the hoose a bide wi' his mither, ye ken.'

As she spoke the tears welled up in her eyes and rolled over. She was by no means given to weeping, but she was a good deal shaken by her flight, and it was months since she had spoken to anyone whose point of view could approach her own. Not that she had any conscious point of view, but in common with us all she had a subconscious one. She brushed her sleeve across her eyes.

He sat silent, pulling at his pipe. From the trees came the long-drawn note of a wood-pigeon.

'A'll need tae be awa' hame and see tae the hens,' said the girl, at last.

The man sat still as she rose, watching her till the whins closed behind her; then he got up slowly and went to water the pony which was hobbled a few yards off. When evening fell on the debatable land, it found him sitting at his transitory threshold, smoking as he mended the rabbit-snare in his hand.

For Jessie-Mary, the days that followed these events were troublous enough. The tear in her gown was badly mended, and Mrs Muirhead, who had provided the clothes her servant wore, scolded her angrily. Peter was sulky, and, though he left her alone, he vented his anger in small ways which made domestic life intolerable to the women. Added to this, the young Black Spanish hen was missing.

The search ranged far and near over the wood. The bird, an incorrigible strayer, had repaid previous effort by being found in some outlying tangle with a 'stolen nest' and an air of irritated surprise at interruption. But hens were not clucking at this season, and Mrs Muirhead, in the dusk of one evening, announced her certainty that some cat or trap had removed the truant from her reach for ever.

'There's mony wad put a lazy cutty like you oot o' the place for this!' she exclaimed, as she and Jessie-Mary met outside the yard after their fruitless search. 'A'm fair disgustit wi' ye. Awa' ye gang ben the hoose an' get the kitchen reddit up just awa in-by wi' ye, d'ye hear?'

Jessie-Mary obeyed sullenly. The kitchen window was half open and she paused beside it before beginning to clear the table and set out the evening meal. A cupboard close to her hand held the cheese and bannocks but she did not turn its key. Her listless look fell upon the planet that was coming out of the approaching twilight and taking definiteness above a mass of dark tree-tops framed in by the window sash. She had small conscious joy in such sights, for the pleasures given by these are the outcome of a higher civilisation than she had yet attained. But even to her, the point of serene silver, hung in the translucent field of sky, had a remote, wordless peace. She stood staring, her arms dropped at her sides.

The shrill tones of her mistress came to her ear; she was telling Peter, who stood outside, the history of her loss. Lamentation for the Black Spanish hen mingled with the recital of Jessie-Mary's carelessness, the villainy of serving-lasses as a body, the height in price of young poultry stock. Like many more valuable beings, the froward bird was assuming after death an importance she had never known in life.

A high-pitched exclamation came from Peter's lips.

'Ye needna speir owre muckle for her,' he said, 'she's roastit by this time. There's a lad doon the loan kens mair aboot her nor ony ither body!'

'Michty-me!' cried Mrs Muirhead.

'Aye, a'm tellin' ye,' continued he, 'the warst-lookin' great deevil that iver ye saw yet. He gie'd me impidence, aye did he, but a didna tak' muckle o' that. 'Anither word,' says I, 'an' ye'll get the best thrashin' that iver ye got.' He hadna vera muckle tae say after that, I warrant ye!'

Seldom had Mrs Muirhead been so much disturbed. Her voice rose to unusual heights as she discussed the matter; the local policeman must be fetched at once, she declared; and, as she adjured her son to start for his house without delay, Jessie-Mary could hear the young man's refusal to move a step before he had had his tea. She was recalled to her work by this and began hurriedly to set out the meal.

As she sat, a few minutes later, taking her own share at the farther end of the table, the subject was still uppermost, and by the time she rose mother and son were fiercely divided;

for Peter, who had taken off his boots and was comfortable, refused to stir till the following morning. The hen had been missing three days, he said, and the thief was still in his place; it was not likely he would run that night. And the constable's cottage was over a mile off. The household dispersed in wrath.

In the hour when midnight grew into morning, Jessie-Mary closed the cottage door behind her and stole out among the silent trees. The pine scent came up from under her feet as she trod and down from the blackness overhead. The moon, which had risen late, was near her setting, and the light of the little sickle just showed her the direction in which she should go. In and out of the shadows she went, her goal the clearing among the whins in the debatable land. As the steeple of distant Montrose, slumbering calmly between the marshes and the sea, rang one, she slipped out of the bushes and, going into the tent, awakened the sleeping man.

It was some time before the two came out of the shelter, and the first cock was crowing as the pony was roused and led from his tether under the tilted shafts. The sail-cloth was taken down and a medley of pots and pans and odd-looking implements thrown into the cart; the wheels were noiseless on the soft sod of the loaning as, by twists and turns, they thrust their way along the overgrown path.

Day broke on the figures of a man and woman who descended the slope of the fields towards the road. The man walked first.

And, in the debatable land among the brambles, a few black feathers blew on the morning wind.

Robert Murray (1863 – 1893)

Moonlight North and South

Love, we have heard together
The North Sea sing his tune,
And felt the wind's wild feather
Brush past our cheeks at noon,
And seen the cloudy weather
Made wondrous with the moon.

Where loveliness is rarest,
'Tis also prized the most;
The moonlight shone her fairest
Along that level coast   10
Where sands and dunes the barest,
Of beauty seldom boast.

Far from that bleak and rude land
An exile I remain,
Fixed in a fair and good land,
A valley and a plain
Rich in fat fields and woodland,
And watered well with rain.

Last night the full moon's splendor
Shone down on Taunton Dene;   20
And pasture fresh and tender,
And coppice dusky green,
The heavenly light did render
In one enchanted scene,

One fair unearthly vision.
Yet soon mine eyes were cloyed,
And found those fields Elysian
Too rich to be enjoyed.
Or was it our division
Made all my pleasure void?   30

Across the window glasses
The curtain then I drew,
And, as a sea-bird passes,
In sleep my spirit flew
To grey and windswept grasses
And moonlit sands – and you.

For Scotland

Oh, cruel off St Andrews Bay
The winds are wont to blow.
They either rest or gently play,
When there in dreams I go.

And there I wander, young again,
With limbs that do not tire,
Along the coast to Kittock's Den,
With whinbloom all afire.

I climb the Spindle Rock, and lie
And take my doubtful ease,   10
Between the ocean and the sky,
Derided by the breeze.

Where coloured mushrooms thickly grow,
Like flowers of brittle stalk,
To haunted Magus Muir I go,
By Lady Catherine's Walk.

In dreams the year I linger through,
In that familiar town,
Where all the youth I ever knew,
Burned up and flickered down.   20

There's not a rock that fronts the sea,
There's not an inland grove,
But has a tale to tell to me
Of friendship or of love.

And so I keep, and ever shall,
The best place in my heart for Scotland,
Scotland, Scotland,
The best place in my heart for Scotland.

After Many Days

The mist hangs round the College tower,
The ghostly street
Is silent at this midnight hour
Save for my feet.

With none to see, with none to hear,
Downward I go
To where beside the rugged pier
The sea sings low.

It sings a tune well loved and known
In days gone by   10
When often here, and not alone,
I watched the sky.

That was a barren time at best,
Its fruits were few;
But fruits and flowers had keener zest
And fresher hue.

Life has not since been wholly vain,
And now I bear
Of wisdom, plucked from joy and pain,
Some slender share.   20

But, howsoever rich the store,
I'd lay it down
To feel upon my back once more
The old red gown.

A December Day

Blue, blue is the sea today,
Warmly the light
Sleeps on St Andrews Bay –
Blue, fringed with white.
That's no December sky.
Surely 'tis June
Holds now her state on high,
Queen of the noon.

Only the tree-tops bare
Crowning the hill,   10
Clear-cut in perfect air,
Warn us that still

Winter, the aged chief,
Mighty in power,
Exiles the tender leaf,
Exiles the flower.

Is there a heart today,
A heart that grieves
For flowers that fade away,
For fallen leaves?   20

Oh, not in leaves or flowers
Endures the charm
That clothes those naked towers
With love-light warm.

O dear St Andrews Bay,
Winter or Spring
Gives not nor takes away
Memories that cling

All round thy girdling reefs,
That walk my shore,   30
Memories of joys and griefs
Ours evermore.

Mary Symon (1863 – 1938)

The Hedonist

(After Béranger)

I kent o' a king o' the Cabrach aince,
An' a gey bit kingie was he;
He had nae sowl, nae siller, nor sense,
But did fine withoot a' three.
For he sleepit, ochone! an' snored, ochone!
A' day in his beddie ba' –
Wi' a tosselled trok o' a nicht-kep on
An' his croon in the crap o' the wa'
        Ay, his bonnie croon,
            Wi' the roset foun',   10
        It lay in the crap o' the wa'.

He'd wauken fyles when the knock wad chap,
An' skirl fae the horn en':–
'Ye louts, ye loons, I've an awfu' yapp,
Fess plates an' trenchers ben;
An' dinna forget, I've a drooth* evenoo   *thirst*
That could drink the Deveron dry –
An' the mair o' guid ye pit into my mou',
The mair'll come oot, say I,
     Oh, better for you,   20
     A king half-fou,
     A hantle*, than ane that's dry.'   *great deal*

Weel suppered an' slockit, they'd saiddle him
On a shalt* as' sweer's* himsel'   *pony/lazy as*
An' he'd ride his realm fae the Rooster's rim
To the lythe o' the Balloch well;
A' his bodygaird was a fozelin'* tyke   *wheezing*
As ready to row's to run –
'I'm a king,' says he, 'I can dae as I like
An' I'm giein' my fowk their fun –   30
     'He gar't's a' laugh,'
     Is the epitaph,
     I wad like when I'm naith the grun'.'

When the kingie dee'd ae Lammas mirk,
His folk made muckle mane,
An' they happit him snod in Walla Kirk
Wi' this at his cauld head-stane:
'A cheery Craitur's lyin' here' –
An' they said baith gret an' sma',
'He never gar't ane o's shed a tear.   40
Except when he wore awa'.'

'Mang heather an' whaups, an' whins an' mist,
Oh, laughin, lonely hedonist,
I like to think of you.

The Wedding

By an Opposite Neighbour

'See, here's the bridegroom, Kirsty,
I ken him by his breeks,
His chumley-hat and dickey,
An' the way he bobs an' keeps
Like a hen that's heark'nin' thunner,
Or a corbie seekin' 's hole
He'll be mirkier at his burial
Tho' he winna look as drool.

I winner gin they're ready noo;
There's reek in ilka lum*,   10   chimney
An' there's the aul' vricht*, he's been in   carpenter
To set the table plumb.
Wheest! There's the quarter chappin',
They'll be a' here in a briest;
Is that the pock-faced lawyer
An' his mither? Ay, it's jist.

Humph! Some ane spak' o' gentry!
Guid saves gin they be a' –
Him stinkit up wi' hair-ile
That ye'd smell a mile awa',   20
An' her – a nochty craiter,
Choke-fu' o' fulsome wile –
But – ay, that's Willie Muncy,
I thocht I kent the tile:

An' that's his father's weskit,
I'll bet ye half-a-croon;
I min' his mither tellin' me
She thocht o' makin' 't doon.
An' there's the lassie Taylor –
Losh! foo they're steerin' in   30
They hinna missed a livin' sowl
Fae Badenoch to the Binn.

Fat wis't the wifie said yestreen
When spreadin' oot the braws?
I kent she'd something in her crap,
Wi' a' her hums an' haws;
That Annie's lad had cheated you!
She hadna't hardly oot
Afore I had her fite's her mutch,
An' mim's a chokit troot.   40

I tell ye I was in a pirr,
'Yon peesweep!' Syne I leugh,
An' when she speired me gin I thocht
Ae kebbuck* was eneuch.   cheese
It's growin' dark, come lass, an' edge
My chair a thochtie ben,
An' lift the screen – But fat's that noo,
Anither rosten hen?

That mak's a score. I wish I had
The feathers an' the banes;   50
But loshy, there's the bride an' groom
Jist jinkin' aff their lanes.
An' save us! foo he's kissin' her!
Hoots! dinna licht the licht,
It's mony a day sin' I hae seen
Half sic a humblin' sicht.

Oh, kiss awa', ere sax month's gane
Ye'll baith be tired o' that!
Faur are ye, Kirsty? Mercy on's,
That wasna you that grat?   60
It wasna. Weel, you're unco short,
Ye'll better mask the tay;
Ay, there's the bride an' groom: they'll get
The meen gaun owre the brae.'

Neil Munro (1864 – 1930)

Munro is known primarily as a novelist and short story writer. Especially successful are his historical romances, of which *John Splendid* (1898) may be his most notable. The historical novels are a striking mixture of poetic atmosphere, psychological realism and attention to historical detail. Perhaps his most popular works are the Para Handy tales, a series of humourous sketches about the crew of a Clyde steamer, *The Vital Spark*. Two of the Para Handy stories are represented here, along with 'Red Hand', a grim little masterpiece in Munro's historical/romantic manner.

Wild Geese

It was not any songster of the forest
That brought to me, yon night, unholy fears,
Thrush of the thicket nor the questioning owlet,
Though these knew all my deeds in those wild years;
It was the grey lag goose that comes to Barra,
That found me desolate and dry of tears.

I was alone within my winter dwelling,
My children gone, my peat-fire dead and grey,
Old and unable – I who once was tempest!
Shivering to hear the rattle of the spray,   10
When high above my chimney came the wild geese,
And brought my ghosts about me where I lay.

Ah! well I knew they came from gran'ries opened,
Where old mad joys and folly's crops are stored,
Grain o' the wild-oat, ready for the grind-stone,
To make the bitter bread of age abhorred.
My grief! they found me unprepared for pardon,
With all my youth of tumult undeplored!

I had forgot those ancient joys and sinnings,
And now was far too old for penitence.   20
From out the north, beyond the seven mountains,
Those grey birds of the evening had brought hence
My memories, but no remorse, through darkness,
The weeping night, lost fields of innocence.

Lament for Macleod of Raasay

Allan Ian Og Macleod of Raasay,
Treasure of mine, lies yonder dead in Loos,
His body unadorned by Highland raiment,
Trammeled, for glorious hours, in Saxon trews★.   trousers
Never man before of all his kindred
Went so appareled to the burial knowe★,   knoll
But with the pleated tartan for his shrouding,
The bonnet on his brow.

My grief, that Allan should depart so sadly,
When no wild mountain pipe his bosom wrung;   10
With no one of his race beside his shoulder,
Who knew his history and spoke his tongue.
Ah, lonely death and drear for darling Allan.
Before his ghost had taken wings and gone,
Loud would he cry in Gaelic to his gallants,
'Children of storm, press on!'

Beside him, when he fell there in his beauty,
Macleods of all the islands should have died;
Brave hearts his English! – but they could not fathom
To what old deeps the voice of Allan cried,   20
When in that strange French countryside, war-battered,
Far from the creeks of home and hills of heath,
A boy, he kept the old tryst of his people
With the dark girl Death.

O Allan Ian Og, O Allan aluinn!
Sore is my heart remembering the past,
And you of Raasay's ancient gentle children
The farthest-wandered, kindliest and last.
It should have been the brave dead of the islands
That heard ring o'er their tombs your battle-cry,   30
To shake them from their sleep again, and quicken
Peaks of Torridon and Skye.

Gone in the mist the brave Macleods of Raasay.
Far furth from fortune, sundered from their lands;
And now the last grey stone of Castle Raasay
Lies desolate and leveled with the sands;
But pluck the old isle from its roots deep planted
Where tides cry coronach round the Hebrides,
And it will bleed of the Macleods lamented,
Their loves and memories.   40

Hurricane Jack

I very often hear my friend the Captain speak of Hurricane Jack in terms of admiration and devotion, which would suggest that Jack is a sort of demigod. The Captain always refers to Hurricane Jack as the most experienced seaman of modern times, as the most fearless soul that ever wore oilskins, the handsomest man in Britain, so free with his money he would fling it at the birds, so generally accomplished that it would be a treat to be left a month on a desert island alone with him.

'Why is he called Hurricane Jack?' I asked the Captain once.

'What the duvvle else would you caal him?' asked Para Handy. 'Nobody ever caals him anything else than Hurricane Jeck.'

'Quite so, but why?' I persisted.

Para Handy scratched the back of his neck, made the usual gesture as if he were going to scratch his ear, and then checked himself in the usual way to survey his hand as if it were a beautiful example of Greek sculpture. His hand, I may say, is almost as large as a Belfast ham.

'What way wass he called Hurricane Jeck?' said he. 'Well, I'll soon tell you that. He wass not always known by that name; that wass a name he got for the time he stole the sheep.'

'Stole the sheep!' I said, a little bewildered, for I failed to see how an incident of that kind would give rise to such a name.

'Yes; what you might call stole,' said Para Handy hastily; 'but, och! it wass only wan smaal wee sheep he lifted on a man that never went to the church, and chust let him take it! Hurricane Jeck would not steal a fly – no, nor two flies, from a Chrustian; he's the perfect chentleman in that.'

'Tell me all about it,' I said.

'I'll soon do that,' said he, putting out his hand to admire it again, and in doing so upsetting his glass. 'Tut, tut!' he said. 'Look what I have done – knocked doon my gless; it wass a good thing there wass nothing in it.'

'Hurricane Jeck,' said the Captain, when I had taken the hint and put something in it, 'iss a man that can sail anything and go anywhere, and aalways be the perfect chentleman. A millionaire's yat or a washing-boyne – it's aal the same to Jeck; he would sail the wan chust as smert as the other, and land on the quay as spruce ass if he wass newly come from a baal. Oh, man! the cut of his jeckets! And never anything else but 'lastic-sided boots, even in the coorsest weather! If you would see him, you would see a man that's chust sublime, and that careful about his 'lastic sided boots he would never stand at the wheel unless there wass a bass[1] below his feet. He'll aye be oil-oiling at his hair, and buying hard hats for going ashore with: I never saw a man wi' a finer heid for the hat, and in some of the vessels he wass in he would have the full of a bunker of hats. Hurricane Jeck wass brought up in the China clipper tred, only he wassna called Hurricane Jeck then, for he hadna stole the sheep till efter that. He wass captain of the *Dora Young,* wan of them clippers; he's a hand on a gaabert the now, but aalways the perfect chentleman.'

'It seems a sad downcome for a man to be a gabbart hand after having commanded a China clipper,' I ventured to remark. 'What was the reason of his change?'

'Bad luck,' said Para Handy. 'Chust bad luck. The fellow never got fair play. He would aye be somewhere takin' a gless of something wi' somebody, for he's a fine big cheery chap. I mind splendid when he wass captain on the clipper, he had a fine hoose of three rooms and a big decanter, wi' hot and cold watter oot at Pollokshaws. When you went oot to the hoose to see Hurricane Jeck in them days, time slupped bye. But he wassna known as Hurricane Jeck then, for it wass before he stole the sheep.'

'You were just going to tell me something about that,' I said.

'Jeck iss wan man in a hundred, and ass good ass two if there wass anything in the way of

---

[1] A mat of straw or rushes.

trouble, for, man! he's strong, strong! He has a back on him like a shipping-box, and when he will come down Tarbert quay on a Friday night after a good fishing, and the trawlers are arguing, it's two yerds to the step with him and a bash in the side of his hat for fair defiance. But he never hit a man twice, for he's aye the perfect chentleman iss Hurricane Jeck. Of course, you must understand, he wass not known as Hurricane Jeck till the time I'm going to tell you of, when he stole the sheep.

'I have not treveled far mysel' yet, except Ullapool and the time I wass at Ireland; but Hurricane Jeck in his time has been at every place on the map, and some that's no'. Chust wan of Brutain's hardy sons – that's what he iss. As weel kent in Calcutta as if he wass in the Coocaddens, and he could taalk a dozen of their foreign kinds of languages if he cared to take the bother. When he would be leaving a port, there wassna a leddy in the place but what would be doon on the quay wi' her Sunday clothes on and a bunch o' floo'ers for his cabin. And when he would be sayin' goodbye to them from the brudge, he would chust take off his hat and give it a shoogle, and put it on again; his manners wass complete. The first thing he would do when he reached any place wass to go ashore and get his boots brushed, and then sing 'Rule Britannia' roond aboot the docks. It wass a sure way to get freend or foe aboot you, he said, and he wass aye as ready for the wan as for the other. Brutain's hardy son!

'He made the fastest passages in his time that wass ever made in the tea trade, and still and on he would meet you like a common working man. There wass no pride or nonsense of that sort aboot Hurricane Jeck; but, mind you, though I'm callin' him Hurricane Jeck, he wasna Hurricane Jeck till the time he stole the sheep.'

'I don't like to press you, Captain, but I'm anxious to hear about that sheep,' I said patiently.

'I'm comin' to't,' said Para Handy. 'Jeck had the duvvle's own bad luck; he couldna take a gless by-ordinar' but the ship went wrong on him, and he lost wan job efter the other, but he wass never anything else but the perfect chentleman. When he had not a penny in his pocket, he would borrow a shilling from you, and buy you a stick pipe for yourself chust for good nature – '

'A stick pipe?' I repeated interrogatively.

'Chust a stick pipe – or a wudden pipe, or whatever you like to call it. He had three medals and a clock that wouldna go for saving life at sea, but that wass before he wass Hurricane Jeck, mind you; for at that time he hadna stole the sheep.'

'I'm dying to hear about that sheep,' I said.

'I'll soon tell you about the sheep,' said Para Handy. 'It wass a thing that happened when him and me wass sailing on the *Elizabeth Ann, a* boat that belonged to Girvan, and a smert wan too, if she wass in any kind of trum at aal. We would be going here and there aboot the West Coast with wan thing and another, and not costing the owners mich for coals if coals wass our cargo. It wass wan Sunday we were passing Caticol in Arran, and in a place yonder where there wass not a hoose in sight we saw a herd of sheep eating gress near the shore. As luck would have it, there wass not a bit of butcher meat on board the *Elizabeth Ann* for the Sunday dinner, and Jeck cocked his eye at the sheep and says to me, 'Yonder's some sheep lost, poor things; what do you say to taking the punt and going ashore to see if there's anybody's address on them?'

'"Whatever you say yoursel',' I said to Jeck, and we stopped the vessel and went ashore, the two of us, and looked the sheep high and low, but there wass no address on them. "They're lost, sure enough," said Jeck, pulling some heather and putting it in his pocket – he wassna Hurricane Jeck then – "they're lost, sure enough, Peter. Here's a nice wee wan nobody would ever miss, that chust the very thing for a coal vessel," and before you could say "knife" he had it killed and carried to the punt. Oh, he iss a smert, smert fellow with his hands; he could do anything.

'We rowed ass caalm ass we could oot to the vessel and we had chust got the deid sheep on board when we heard a roarin' and whustling.

'"Taalk about Arran being releegious!" said Jeck. 'Who's that whustling on the Lord's day?'

'The man that wass whustling wass away up on the hill, and we could see him coming running doon the hill the same ass if he would break every leg he had on him.

'"I'll bate you he'll say it's his sheep," said Jeck. "Weel, we'll chust anchor the vessel here till we hear what he hass to say, for if we go away and never mind the cratur he'll find oot somewhere else it's the *Elizabeth Ann.*"

'When the fermer and two shepherds came oot to the *Elizabeth Ann* in a boat, she wass lying at anchor, and we were all on deck, every man wi' a piece o' heather in his jecket.

'"I saw you stealing my sheep," said the fermer coming on deck, furious. "I'll have every man of you jiled for this."

'"Iss the man oot of his wuts?" said Jeck. "Drink – chust drink! Nothing else but drink! If you were a sober Christian man, you would be in the church at this 'oor in Arran, and not oot on the hill recovering from last night's carry-on in Loch Ranza, and imagining you are seeing things that's not there at aal, at aal."

'"I saw you with my own eyes steal the sheep and take it on board," said the fermer, nearly choking with rage.

'"What you saw was my freend and me gathering a puckle heather for oor jeckets," said Jeck, "and if ye don't believe me you can search the ship from stem to stern."

'"I'll soon do that," said the fermer, and him and his shepherds went over every bit of the *Elizabeth Ann.* They never missed a corner you could hide a moose in, but there wass no sheep nor sign of sheep anywhere.

'"Look at that, Macalpine," said Jeck. "I have a good mind to have you up for inflammation of character. But what could you expect from a man that would be whustling on the hill like a peesweep on a Sabbath when he should be in the church. It iss a good thing for you, Macalpine, it iss a Sabbath, and I can keep my temper."

'"I could swear I saw you lift the sheep," said the fermer, quite vexed.

'"Saw your auntie! Drink; nothing but the cursed drink!" said Jeck, and the fermer and his shepherds went away with their tails behind their legs.

'We lay at anchor till it was getting dark, and then we lifted the anchor and took off the sheep that wass tied to it when we put it oot. "It's a good thing, salt mutton," said Hurricane Jeck as we sailed away from Caticol, and efter that the name he always got wass Hurricane Jeck.

'But why "Hurricane Jack"?' I asked, more bewildered than ever.

'Holy smoke! am I no' tellin' ye?' said Para Handy. 'It wass because he stole the sheep.'

But I don't understand it yet.

The Tar's Wedding

It was months after The Tar's consultation with Para Handy about a wife: The Tar seemed to have given up the idea of indulgence in any such extravagance, and Para Handy had ceased to recommend various 'smert, muddle-aged ones wi' a puckle[1] money' to the consideration of the young man, when the latter one day sheepishly approached him, spat awkwardly through the clefts of his teeth at a patch in the funnel of the *Vital Spark, a*nd remarked, 'I wass thinkin' to mysel' yonder, Captain, that if there wass nothing parteecular doing next Setturday, I would maybe get mairried.'

'Holy smoke!' said the Captain; 'you canna expect me to get a wife suitable for you in that time. It's no reasonable. Man, you're gettin' droll – chust droll!'

'Och, I needn't be puttin' you to any trouble' said The Tar, rubbing the back of his neck

---

[1] Little.

with a hand as rough as a rasp. 'I wass lookin' aboot mysel' and there's wan yonder in Campbeltown 'll have me. In fact, it's settled. I thocht that when we were in Campbeltown next Setturday, we could do the chob and be dune wi't. We were roared last Sunday – '

'Roared!' said the Captain. 'Iss it cried, you mean?'

'Yes, chust cried,' said The Tar, 'but the gyurl's kind of dull in the hearing, and it would likely need to be a roar. You'll maybe ken her – she's wan of the MacCallums.'

'A fine gyurl,' said the Captain, who had not the faintest idea of her identity, and had never set eyes on her, but could always be depended on for politeness. 'A fine gyurl! Truly sublime! I'm not askin' if there's any money; eh? – not a word! It's none of my business, but, tuts! what's the money anyway, when there's love?'

'Shut up aboot that!' said the scandalised Tar, getting very red. 'If you're goin' to speak aboot love, be dacent and speak aboot it in the Gaalic. But we're no' taalkin' aboot love; we're taalkin' aboot my merrage. Is it aal right for Setturday?'

'You're a cunning man to keep it dark till this,' said the Captain, 'but I'll put nothing in the way, seein' it's your first caper of the kind. We'll have high jeenks at Campbeltown.'

The marriage took place in the bride's mother's house, up a stair that was greatly impeded by festoons of fishing-nets, old oars, and net-bows on the walls, and the presence of six stalwart Tarbert trawlers, cousins of The Tar's, who were asked to the wedding, but were so large and had so many guernseys on, they would of themselves have filled the room in which the ceremony took place; so they had agreed, while the minister was there at all events, to take turn about of going in to countenance the proceedings. What space there was within was monopolised by the relatives of the bride, by Para Handy and Dougie, The Tar in a new slop-shop serge suit, apparently cut out by means of a hatchet, the bride – a good deal prettier than a Goth like The Tar deserved – and the minister. The wedding supper was laid out in a neighbour's house on the same stair landing.

A solemn hush marked the early part of the proceedings, marred only by the sound of something frying in the other house and the shouts of children crying for bowl-money in the street. The minister was a teetotaler, an unfortunate circumstance which the Captain had discovered very early, and he was very pleased with the decorum of the company. The MacCallums were not churchgoers in any satisfactory sense, but they and their company seemed to understand what was due to a Saturday night marriage and the presence of 'the cloth'. The clergyman had hardly finished the ceremony when the Captain began maneuvering for his removal. He had possessed himself of a bottle of ginger cordial and a plate of cake.

'You must drink the young couple's health, Mr Grant,' he said. 'We ken it's you that's the busy man on the Setturday night, and indeed it's a night for the whole of us goin' home early. I have a ship yonder, the *Fital Spark,* that I left in cherge of an enchineer by the name of Macphail, no' to be trusted with such a responsibility.'

The minister drank the cheerful potion, nibbled the corner of a piece of cake, and squeezed his way downstairs between the Tarbert trawlers.

'We're chust goin' away oorsel's in ten meenutes,' said the Captain after him.

'Noo that's aal right,' said Para Handy, who in virtue of his office had constituted himself master of ceremonies. 'He's a nice man, Mr Grant, but he's not strong, and it would be a peety to be keeping him late out of his bed on a Setturday night. I like, mysel', yon old-fashioned munisters that had nothing wrong wi' them, and took a Chrustian dram. Pass oot that bottle of chinger cordial to the laads from Tarbert and you'll see fine fun.'

He was the life and soul of the evening after that. It was he who pulled the corks, who cut the cold ham, who kissed the bride first, who sang the first song, and danced with the new mother-in-law.

'You're an aawful man, Captain Macfarlane,' she said in fits of laughter at his fun.

'Not me!' said he, lumberingly dragging her round in a polka to the strains of Dougie's trump. 'I'm a quate fellow, but when I'm in trum I like a high jeenk noo and then. Excuse my feet. It's no' every day we're merryin' The Tar. A fine, smert, handy fellow, Mrs MacCallum; you didn't make a bad bargain of it with your son-in-law. Excuse my feet. A sailor every inch of him, once you get him wakened. A pound a week of wages an' no incumbrance. My feet again, excuse them!'

'It's little enough for two,' said Mrs MacCallum; 'but a man's aye a man,' and she looked the Captain in the eye with disconcerting admiration.

'My Chove! she's a weedow wuman,' thought the Captain; 'I'll have to ca' canny, or I'll be in for an engagement.'

'I aye liked sailors,' said Mrs MacCallum; 'John – that's the depairted, I'm his relic – was wan.'

'A poor life, though,' said the Captain, 'especially on the steamers, like us. But your man, maybe, was sailin' foreign, an' made money? It's always a consuderation for a weedow.'

'Not a penny,' said the indiscreet Mrs MacCallum, as Para Handy wheeled her into a chair.

At eleven o'clock The Tar was missing. He had last been seen pulling off his new boots, which were too small for him, on the stair-head; and it was only after considerable searching the Captain and one of the Tarbert cousins found him sound asleep on the top of a chest in the neighbour's house.

'Colin,' said the Captain, shaking him awake, 'sit up and try and take something. See at the rest of us, as jovial as anything, and no' a man hit yet. Sit up and be smert for the credit of the *Fital Spark*.'

'Are you angry wi' me, Captain?' asked The Tar.

'Not a bit of it, Colin! But you have the corkscrew in your pocket. I'm no' caring myself, but the Tarbert gentlemen will take it amiss. Forbye, there's your wife; you'll maybe have mind of her – wan Lucy MacCallum? She's in yonder, fine and cheery, wi' two of your Tarbert cousins holding her hand.'

'Stop you! I'll hand them!' cried the exasperated bridegroom, and bounded into the presence of the marriage-party in the house opposite, with a demonstration that finally led to the breaking-up of the party.

Next day took place The Tar's curious kirking. The MacCallums, as has been said, were not very regular churchgoers; in fact, they had overlooked the ordinances since the departed John died, and forgot that the church bell rang for the Sabbath-school an hour before it rang for the ordinary forenoon service.

Campbeltown itself witnessed the bewildering spectacle of The Tar and his bride, followed by the mother and Para Handy, marching deliberately up the street and into the church among the children. Five minutes later they emerged, looking very red and ashamed of themselves.

'If I knew there wass so much bother to mind things I would never have got married at all,' said the bridegroom.

Red Hand

The smell of wet larch was in the air, and Glenaora was aburst to the coaxing of Spring. Paruig Dall the piper – son of the son of Iain Mor – filled his broad chest with two men's wind, and flung the drones over his shoulder. They dangled a little till the bag swelled out, and the first blast rang in the ear of the morning. Rough and noisy, the reeds cried each other down till a master's hand held them in check, and the long soft singing of the piobaireachd floated out among the tartan ribbons. The grey peak of Drimfern heard the music; the rock that wards the mouth of Carnus let it pass through the gap and over the hill and down to the isles below; Dun Corrbhile and Dunchuach, proud Kilmune, the Paps of Salachary, and a hundred other braes around, leaned over to listen to the vaunting notes that filled the valley. 'The Glen, the Glen is mine!' sang the blithe chanter; and, by Finne's sword, Macruimen himself could not have fingered it better.

It was before Paruig Dall left for Half Town; before the wars that scorched the glens; and Clan Campbell could cock its bonnet in the face of all Albainn. Paruig was old, and Paruig was blind, as the name of him tells, but he swung with a king's port up and down on the short grass, his foot firm to every beat of the tune, his kilt tossing from side to side like a bard's song, his sporran leaping gaily on his brown knees. Two score of lilting steps to the burnside, a slow wheel on a brogue-heel, and then back with the sun-glint on the buckles of his belt.

The men, tossing the caber and hurling the clachneart against the sun beyond the peat-bog, paused in their stride at the chanter's boast, jerked the tartan tight on their loins, and came over to listen; the women, posting blankets for the coming sheiling, stopped their splashing in the little linn,[1] and hummed in a dream; and men and women had mind of the days that were, when the Glen was soft with the blood of men, for the Stewarts were over the way from Appin.

'God's splendour, but he can play too,' said the piper's son, with his head areel to the fine tripling.

Then Paruig pushed the bag further into his oxter,[2] and the tune changed. He laid the ground of 'Bodaich nam Briogais,' and such as knew the story saw the 'carles with the breeks' broken and flying before Glenurchy's thirsty swords, far north of Morven, long days of weary march through spoiled glens.

'It's fine playing, I'll allow,' said the blind man's son, standing below a saugh-tree with the bag of his bannered pipes in the crook of his arm. He wore the dull tartan of the Diarmaids, and he had a sprig of gall in his bonnet, for he was in Black Duncan's tail.

'Son of Paruig Dall,' said the Chief seven years ago come Martinmas, 'if you're to play like your father, there's but Dunvegan for you, and the schooling of Patrick Macruimen.'

So Tearlach went to Skye — cold isle of knives and caves — and in the college of Macruimen he learned the piob-mhor. Morning and evening, and all day between, he fingered the feadan or the full set — gathering and march, massacre and moaning, and the stately salute. Where the lusty breeze comes in salt from Vaternish across Loch Vegan, and the purple loom of Uist breaks the sunset's golden bars, he stood on the braes over against Borearaig and charmed the grumbling tide. And there came a day that he played 'The Lament of the Harp Tree', with the old years of sturdy fight and strong men all in the strain of it, and Patrick Macruimen said, 'No more, lad; go home: Lochow never heard another like you.' As a cock with its comb uncut, came the stripling from Skye.

'Father,' he had said, 'you play not ill for a blind man, but you miss the look on the men's faces, and that's half the music. Forbye, you are old, and your fingers are slow on the grace notes. Here's your own flesh and blood can show you fingering there was never the like or anywhere east the Isles.'

The stepmother heard the brag.

'A pheasain,' she snapped, with hate in her peat-smoked face. 'Your father's a man, and you are but a boy with no heart for a long day. A place in Black Duncan's tail, with a gillie[3] to carry your pipes and knapsack, is not, mind ye, all that's to the making of a piper.'

Tearlach laughed in her face. 'Boy or man,' said he, 'look at me! north, east, south, and west, where is the one to beat me? Macruimen has the name, but there were pipers before Macruimen, and pipers will come after him.'

'It's maybe as you say,' said Paruig. 'The stuff's in you, and what is in must out; but give me cothrom na Feinne, and old as I am, with Finne's chance, and that's fair play, I can maybe make you crow less crouse.[4] Are ye for trying?'

'I am at the training of a new chanter-reed,' said Tearlach; 'but let it be when you will.'

They fixed a day, and went out to play against each other for glory, and so it befell that on

---

[1] Waterfall.
[2] Armpit.
[3] Retainer.
[4] Brave.

this day Paruig Dall was playing 'The Glen is Mine' and 'Bodaich nam Briogais' in a way to make stounding hearts.

Giorsal snapped her fingers in her stepson's face when her husband closed the crunluadh of his piobaireachd.

'Can you better it, bastard?' snarled she.

'Here goes for it, whatever,' said Tearlach, and over his back went the banner with its boar's head sewn on gold. A pretty lad, by the cross, clean-cut of limb and light of foot, supple of loin, with the toss of the shoulder that never a decent piper lacked. The women who had been at the linn leaned on each other all in the soft larch-scented day, and looked at him out of deep eyes; the men on the heather arose and stood nigher.

A little tuning, and then

'Is comadh leam's comadh leam, cogadh na sithe,
Marbhar 'sa chogadh na crochar 's an t-sith mi.'

'Peace or war!' cried Giorsal, choking in anger, to her man – 'peace or war! the black braggart! it's an asp ye have for a son, goodman!'

The lad's fingers danced merry on the chanter, and the shiver of something to come fell on all the folk around. The old hills sported with the prancing tune; Dun Corrbhile tossed it to Drimfern, and Drimfern sent it leaping across the flats of Kilmune to the green corries of Lecknamban. 'Love, love, the old tune; come and get flesh!' rasped a crow to his mate far off on misty Ben Bhreac, and the heavy black wings flapped east. The friendly wind forgot to dally with the pine-tuft and the twanging bog-myrtle, the plash of Aora in its brown linn was the tinkle of wine in a goblet.

'Peace or war, peace or war; come which will, we care not,' sang the pipe reeds, and there was the muster and the march, hot-foot rush over the rotting rain-wet moor, the jingle of iron, the dunt[1] of pike and targe, the choked roar of hate and hunger batter and slash and fall, and behind, the old, old feud with Appin.

Leaning forward, lost in a dream, stood the swank lads of Aora. They felt at their hips, where were only empty belts, and one said to his child, 'White love, get me yon long knife with the nicks on it, and the basket-hand, for I am sick of shepherding.' The bairn took a look at his face and went home crying.

And the music still poured on. 'Twas 'I got a Kiss o' the King's Hand' and 'The Pretty Dirk', and every air better than another. The fairy pipe of the Wee Folk's Knowe never made a sweeter fever of sound, yet it hurt the ears of the women, who had reason to know the payment of pipers' springs.

'Stop, stop, O Tearlach og,' they cried; 'enough of war: have ye not a reel in your budget?'

'There was never a reel in Boreraig,' said the lad, and he into 'Duniveg's Warning', the tune Coll Ciotach heard his piper play in the west on a day when a black bitch from Dunstaffnage lay panting for him, and his barge put nose about in time to save his skin.

'There's the very word itself in it,' said Paruig, forgetting the taunting of Giorsal and all but a father's pride.

'Twas in the middle of the 'Warning,' Black Duncan, his toe on the stirrup, came up from Castle Inneraora, with a gillie-wetfoot behind, on his way to Lochow.

'It's down yonder you should be, Sir Piper, and not blasting here for drink,' said he, switching his trews with his whip and scowling under black brows at the people. 'My wife is sick of the clarsach and wants the pipes.'

'I'm no woman's piper, Lochow; your wife can listen to the hum of her spinning wheel if she's weary of her harp,' said the lad; and away rode the Chief, and back to the limm went the women, and the men to the cabar and the stone, and Tearlach, with an extra feather in his bonnet, home to Inneraora, leaving a gibe as he went, for his father.

---

[1] Blow, pounding.

Paruig Dall cursed till the evening at the son he never saw, and his wife poisoned his mind.

'The Glen laughs at you, man, from Carnus to Croit-bhile. It's a black, burning day of shame for you, Paruig Dall.'

'Lord, it's a black enough day for me at the best,' said the blind man.

'It's disgraced by your own ill-got son you are, by a boy with no blood on his biodag, and the pride to crow over you.'

And Paruig cursed anew, by the Cross and the Dogs of Lorn, and the White Glaive of Light the giants wear, and the Seven Witches of Cothmar. He was bad though he was blind. and he went back to the start of time for his language.

'But Dhe! the boy can play!' he said at the last.

'Oh, amadain dhoill!' cried the woman; 'if it was I, a claw was off the cub before the mouth of day.'

'Witless woman, men have played the pipes before now, lacking a finger: look at Alasdair Corrag.'

'Allowing; but a hand's as easy to cut as a finger for a man who has gralloched deer with a keen sgian-dubh. Will ye do't or no'?'

Paruig would hearken no more, and took to his pillow.

Rain came with the gloaming. Aora, the splendid river, roared up the dark glen from the Salmon Leap; the hills gathered thick and heavy round about the scattered townships, the green new tips of fir and the copper leaves of the young oaks moaned in the wind. Then salt airs came tearing up from the sea, grinding branch on branch, and the whole land smoked with the drumming of rain that slanted on it hot and fast.

Giorsal arose, her clothes still on her, put a plaid on her black head, and the thick door banged back on the bed as she dived into the storm. Her heavy feet sogged through the boggy grass, the heather clutched at her draggled coat-tails to make her stay, but she filled her heart with one thought, and that was hate, and behold, she was on the slope of the Black Bull before her blind husband guessed her meaning. Castle Inneraora lay at the foot of the woody dun, dozing to the music of the salt loch that made tumult and spume north and south in the hollow of the mountains. Now and then the moon took a look at things, now and then a night-hag in the dripping wood hooted as the rain whipped her breast feathers; a roe leaped out of the gloom and into it with a feared hoof-plunge above Carlonan; a thunderbolt struck in the dark against the brow of Ben Ime and rocked the world.

In the cold hour before the mouth of day the woman was in the piper's room at the gate of Inneraora, where never a door was barred against the night while Strong Colin the warder could see from the Fort of Dunchuach to Cladich. Tearlach the piper lay on his back, with the glow of a half-dead peat on his face and hands.

'Paruig, Paruig!' said the woman to herself, as she softly tramped out the peat-fire and turned to the bed. And lo, it was over. Her husband's little black knife made a fast sweep on the sleeper's wrist, and her hand was drenched with the hot blood of her husband's son.

Tearlach leaped up with a roar in the dark and felt for his foe; but the house was empty, for Giorsal was running like a hind across the soaked stretch of Cairnban. The lightning struck at Glenaora in jagged fury and confusion; the thunder drummed hollow on Creag Dubh: in a turn of the pass at the Three Bridges the woman met her husband.

'Daughter of hell!' said he, 'is't done? and was't death?'

'Darling,' said she, with a fond laugh, ''twas only a brat's hand. You can give us "The Glen is Mine!" in the morning.'

Charles Murray (1864 – 1941)

Murray is one of the most important forces in the Scots revival of this century. His first important collection, *Hamewith*, appeared as early as 1900. He used the language of his native Aberdeenshire in a fresh (i.e., non-Burnsian), rather unsentimental way, and thus helped prepare for the MacDiarmid explosion which was to follow over twenty years later. 'The Whistle' is his most frequently reprinted poem, 'Dockens Afore His Peers' his most critically celebrated.

The Whistle

He cut a sappy sucker from the muckle rodden-tree
He trimmed it, an' he wet it, an' he thumped it on his knee;
He never heard the teuchat★ when the harrow broke her eggs,   lapwing
He missed the craggit heron nabbin' puddocks★ in the seggs,   frogs
He forgot to hound the collie at the cattle when they strayed,
But you should hae seen the whistle that the wee herd★ made!   shepherd

He wheepled on't at mornin' and he tweetled on't at nicht,
He puffed his freckled cheeks until his nose sank oot o sicht,
The kye were late for milkin' when he piped them up the closs,
The kitlin's got his supper syne, an' he was beddit boss★;   10   hungry
But he cared na doit nor docken what they did or thocht or said,
There was comfort in the whistle that the wee herd made.

For lyin' lang o' mornin's he had clawed★ the caup for weeks,   cleaned
But noo he had his bonnet on afore the lave★ had breeks;   rest
He was whistlin' to the porridge that were hott'rin on the fire;
He was whistlin' ower the travise to the baillie in the byre;
Nae a blackbird nor a mavis★ that hae pipin' for their trade   thrush
Was a marrow for the whistle that the wee herd made.

He played a march to battle, it cam' dirlin' through the mist,
Till the halflin★ squared his shoulders an' made up his mind to 'list;   apprentice
He tried a spring for wooers, though he wistna what it meant,   21
But the kitchen-lass was lauchin' an' he thocht she maybe kent;
He got ream★ an' buttered bannocks for the lovin' lilt he played;   cream
Wasna that a cheery whistle that the wee herd made?

He blew them rants sae lively, schottishes, reels an' jigs,
The foalie flang his muckle legs an' capered ower the rigs,
The grey-tailed futtrat★ bobbit oot to hear his ain strathspey,   weasel
The bawd★ cam' loupin' through the corn to 'Clean Pease Strae':   hare
The feet o' ilka man an' beast gat youkie★ when he played –   itchy
Hae ye ever heard o' whistle like the wee herd made?   30

But the snaw it stopped the herdin' an' the winter brocht him dool,
When in spite o' hacks an' chilblains he was shod again for school;
He couldna sough the catechis nor pipe the rule o' three,
He was keepit in an' lickit when the ither loons★ got free;   lads
But he aften played the truant – 'twas the only thing he played,
For the maister brunt the whistle that the wee herd made!

Jeames

It's but a fortnight since we laid him doon,
An' cut the sods to hap★ his narrow lair –   clothe
On Sunday still the grass was dry an' broon;
An' noo they're up again the kist★ is bare,   coffin
For Bell this day we e'en maun lay aboon,
An' face in fun'ral blacks the drift ance mair.

Twa Fiersdays back she seemed baith swak★ an' strang,   supple
A' day her clogs were clankin' roon' the closs★;   yard
An' tho' an income she'd complained o' lang,
It never kept her yet fae kirk or moss.   10
Wha would hae thocht she'd be the next to gang
That never grieved a grain at Jeames's loss?

It seemed richt unco – faith, 'twas hardly fair,
Just when he thocht to slip awa' at last
An' drap for aye the trams o' wardly care –
The muckle gates aboon were barely fast
Ere she was pechin' up the gowden stair,
An' fleechin' Peter till he let her past.

When Jeames – I'se warrant ye, wi' tremblin' shins –
Stands forrit, an' they tak' the muckle beuk   20
To reckon up his shortcomes, slips, an' sins,
She'll check the tally fae some canny neuk,
An' prod his memory when he begins
Should there be ony he would fain o'er leuk.

That Scuttrie Market when he was the waur –
He thocht the better – o' a drap o' yill,
An' fell at Muggart's door amo' the glaur★,   mud
Forgot the shaltie★ ower the hindmost gill★,   pony/ravine
Syne stoitered aff alone, he kent nae whaur,
An' sleepit wi' the sheep on Baadin's hill.   30

The Fast-day when he cawed an early load,
When craps were late an' weather byous saft,
Instead o' daund'rin' to the Hoose o' God
An' noddin' thro 'fourteenthly' in the laft;
Or how he banned★ the Laird upon the road –   cursed
His bawds★ an' birds that connached★ sae the craft.   hares/devoured

Nae chance for him to discount or excuse
The wee-est bit, wi' her there keen to tell
How a' was true; but yet, gin he should choose
To bid them look the credit side as well –   40
Ae conter claim they canna weel refuse –
The mony patient years he bore wi' Bell.

Dockens Afore His Peers

(Exemption Tribunal)

Nae sign o' thow yet. Ay, that's me, John Watt o' Dockenhill:
We've had the war throu' han' afore, at markets ower a gill.★   glass
O ay, I'll sit, birze ben a bit. Hae, Briggie, pass the snuff;
Ye winna hinner lang wi' me, an' speer★ a lot o' buff★,   ask/nonsense
For I've to see the saiddler yet, an' Watchie, honest stock,
To gar him sen' his 'prentice up to sort the muckle knock,
Syne cry upo' the banker's wife an' leave some settin' eggs,
An' tell the ferrier o' the quake that's vrang★ aboot the legs.   wrong
It's yafa wedder, Mains, for Mairch, wi' snaw an' frost an' win',
The ploos are roustin' i' the fur★, an' a' the wark's ahin'.   10   ground
Ye've grun yersel's an' ken the tyauve it is to wirk a ferm,
An' a' the fash★ we've had wi' fouk gyaun aff afore the term;   trouble
We've nane to spare for sojerin', that's nae oor wark ava',
We've rents to pey, an' beasts to feed, an' corn to sell an' saw;
Oonless we get the seed in seen, faur will we be for meal?
An' faur will London get the beef they leuk for aye at Yeel?
There's men aneuch in sooters' shops, an' chiels in masons' yards,
An' coonter-loupers, sklaters, vrichts, an' quarrymen, an' cyaurds,
To fill a reg'ment in a week, without gyaun very far,
Jist shove them in ahin' the pipes, an' tell them that it's 'War';   20
For gin aul' Scotland's at the bit, there's naethin' for't but 'list.
Some mayna like it very sair, but never heed, insist.

Bit, feich, I'm haverin' on like this, an' a' I need's a line
To say there's men that maun be left, an' ye've exemptit mine.
Fat said ye? Fatna fouk hae I enoo' at Dockenhill?
It's just a wastrie o' your time, to rin them throu', but still –
First there's the wife – 'Pass her,' ye say. Saul! had she been a lass
Ye hadna rappit oot sae quick, young laird, to lat her pass,
That may be hoo ye spak' the streen★, fan ye was playin' cairds,   yester'een
But seein' tenants tak' at times their menners fae their lairds,   30
I'll tell ye this, for sense an' thrift, for skeel wi' hens an' caur★,   calves
Gin ye'd her marrow for a wife, ye wouldna be the waur.

Our maiden's neist, ye've herd o' her, new hame fae buirdin' squeel,
Faur she saw mair o' beuks than broth, an' noo she's never weel,
But fan she's playin' ben the hoose, there's little wird o' dwaams★,   faints
For she's the rin o' a' the tunes, strathspeys, an' sangs, an' psalms;

O' 'Evan' an' 'Neander' baith, ye seen can hae aneuch,
But 'Hobble Jeanie' gars me loup, an' crack my thooms, an' hooch★.   shout
Weel, syne we hae the kitchie deem, that milks an' mak's the maet,
She disna aft haud doon the deese★, she's at it ear' an' late,   40   settle
She cairries seed, an' braks the muck, an' gies a han' to hyow,
An' churns, an' bakes, an' syes the so'ens, an' fyles there's peats to rowe.
An' fan the maiden's frien's cry in, she'll mak a cup o' tay,
An' butter scones, an dicht her face, an' cairry ben the tray,
She's big an' brosy★, reid and roch, an' swippert★ as she's stoot,   stout/nimble
Gie her a kilt instead o' cotts, an' thon's the gran' recruit.

There's Francie syne, oor auldest loon, we pat him on for grieve★, foreman
An', fegs, we would be in a soss, gin he should up an' leave;
He's eident★, an' has lots o' can, an' cheery wi' the man, eager
An' I'm sae muckle oot aboot wi' markets till aten'. 50
We've twa chaps syne to wirk the horse, as sweir★ as sweir can be, lazy
They fussle better than they ploo, they're aul' an' mairret tee,
An' baith hae hooses on the ferm, an' Francie never kens
Foo muckle corn gyangs hame at nicht, to fatten up their hens.
The baillie syne, a peer-house geet, nae better than a feel,
He sliwers, an' has sic a mant★, an' ae clog-fit as weel; stutter
He's barely sense to muck the byre, an' cairry in the scull,
An' park the kye, an' cogue the caur, an' scutter wi' the bull.

Weel, that's them a' – I didna hear – the laadie i' the gig?
That's Johnie, he's a littlan jist, for a' he leuks sae big. 60
Fy na, he isna twenty yet – ay weel, he's maybe near't;
Ower young to lippen★ wi' a gun, the crater would be fear't. trust
He's hardly throu' his squeelin' yet, an' noo we hae a plan
To lat him simmer i' the toon, an' learn to mizzer lan'.
Fat? Gar him 'list! Our laadie 'list? 'Twould kill his mither, that,
To think o' Johnnie in a trench awa' in fat-ye-ca't;
We would hae sic a miss at hame, gin he was hine awa',
We'd raither lat ye clean the toon o' ony ither twa;
Ay, tak' the wife, the dother, deem★, the baillie wi' the mant, girl
Tak' Francie, an' the mairret men, but John we canna want. 70
Fat does he dee? Ye micht as weel speir fat I dee mysel',
The things he hisna time to dee is easier to tell;
He dells the yard, an' wi' the scythe cuts tansies★ on the brae, weeds
An' fan a ruck gyangs throu' the mull, he's thrang at wispin' strae,
He sits aside me at the mart, an' fan a feeder's sell't
Tak's doon the wecht, an' leuks the beuk for fat it's worth fan fell't;
He helps me to redd up the dask, he tak's a han' at loo,
An' sorts the shalt, an' yokes the gig, an' drives me fan I'm fou.
Hoot, Mains, hae mind, I'm doon for you some sma' thing wi' the bank;
Aul' Larickleys, I saw you throu', an' this is a' my thank; 80
An' Gutteryloan, that time ye broke, to Dockenhill ye cam' –
'Total exemption.' Thank ye, sirs. Fat say ye till a dram?

The Hint o' Hairst

O for a day at the hint★ o' hairst★, end/harvest
With the craps weel in an' stackit,
When the farmer steps through the corn-yard,
An' counts a' the rucks he's thackit:

When the smith stirs up his fire again,
To sharpen the ploughman's coulter;
When the miller sets a new picked stane,
An' dreams o' a muckle moulter★: grinding

When cottars' kail★ get a touch o' frost, cabbage
That mak's them but taste the better, 10

An' through the neeps★ strides the leggined laird,   turnips
Wi' 's gun an' a draggled setter:

When the forester wi' axe an' keel
Is markin' the wind-blawn timmer★,   timber
An' there's truffs★ aneuch at the barn gale   peat
To reist a' the fires till simmer.

Syne O for a nicht, ae long forenicht,
Owre the dambrod★ spent or cairtin',   draught-board
Or keepin' tryst wi' a neebour's lass –
An' a mou' held up at pairtin'.   20

Gin I Was God

Gin I was God, sittin' up there abeen,
Weariet ne doot noo a' my darg★ was deen,   task
Deaved★ wi' the harps an' hymns oonendin' ringin',   deafened
Tired o' the flockin' angels hairse wi' singin',
To some clood-edge I'd daunder★ furth an', feth★,   saunter/faith
Look ower an' watch hoo things were gyaun aneth.
Syne, gin I saw hoo men I'd made mysel'
Had startit in to pooshan, sheet★ and fell,   shoot
To reive★ an' rape, an' fairly mak' a hell   thieve
O' my braw birlin'★ Earth – a hale week's wark –   10   whirling
I'd cast my coat again, rowe up my sark,
An', or★ they'd time to lench a second ark,   ere
Tak' back my word an' sen' anither spate,
Droon oot the hale hypothec, dicht★ the sklate,   erase
Own my mistak', an', aince I'd cleared the brod★,   board
Start a' thing owre again, gin I was God.

Douglas Ainslie (1865 – 1948)

The Stirrup Cup

*Lines Written on Meeting the Granddaughter of
Cameron of Lochiel*[1]

Lady whose ancestor
Fought for Prince Charlie,
Met once and never more,
No time for parley.

---

[1] See Thomas Campbell's 'Lochiel's Warning', (Vol. II, 504) for a famous study of this redoubtable Jacobite soldier.

Yet drink a glass with me
'Over the water.'
Memories pass to me,
Chieftain's granddaughter.

'Say, will he come again?'
Nay, Lady, never.   10
'Say, will he never reign?'
Ay, Lady, ever.

Ay, for the heart of us
Follows Prince Charlie;
There's not a part of us
Sways not as barley.

Under the breeze that blew
Up the Atlantic,
Wafting the one, the true
Prince, the romantic,   20

Back to his native land
Over the water;
Here's to Prince Charlie and
Lochiel's granddaughter.

Memory

See the leaves are falling faster,
Wet with rain from autumn trees,
All in brown and gold disaster –
Is your memory dead with these?

No, never dead, for every season
(We were lovers all a year)
Has for me a mystic reason,
Breathes her subtle atmosphere.

So in change of form and features
Seen in strangers leagues apart,   10
In the gambols of earth's creatures,
Strikes her memory to my heart.

When the world to ruin crashes,
Lying where all manhood must,
Dust myself, from other ashes
I shall know her delicate dust.

Nocturne

I walk upon the waves tonight,
The pathway of the moon
Leads straight unto the halls of light,
I shall be with thee soon.

And thou, my darling, open wide
Thy window on the sea.
Behold the stars, a-thousand-eyes;
I gaze with them on thee.

Hark to the rustling breeze among
The shadows of the grove: 10
'Tis I draw near to sing my song
Of immemorial love.

All other voices fade away,
All other wings are furled
Save mine: I come, we kiss, I stay;
Ours is the sleeping world.

The Last Wish

O let me not be buried deep
Beneath the mould:
O let me sleep out my last sleep,
Tinged with the gold
Of Sun and Moon and Galaxy,
The Heaven's flambeaux;
With all that lives escorting me,
Thus would I go.

Katherine Mann (dates unknown)

Chateau de Monthiers

*A Revived Impression on Receiving a Spray of
Lily of the Valley in Scotland*

I will go back –
I will go back to Monthiers.
None whom I knew will now be there,
But from the woods adown the dale
The scent will still be in the air
Of sweet, sweet lily of the vale.

It will come wafting dreamily
Through open lattice night and day,
Sifting its pollen o'er the sense,
After to flower in memory,   10
And fruitful to be stored long hence.

There will be lilac in the land,
White cherry boughs o'er green slopes spanned;
The road to Rheims will fall and rise,
A winding trail of dazzling sand,
Slim poplars casting shade slantwise.

I'll wander where the vine shoots grow,
Half weeded wilds of poppies too;
And sure, slow chipping with her hoe,
Some wrinkled dame, in apron blue,   20
Will smile: 'Bo'jour, ma'mselle, fait beau!'

G[eorge] Gregory Smith (1865 – 1932)

The Caledonian Antisyzygy

Along with Edwin Muir's 'Scottish Literature: Language', the following by G. Gregory Smith
is probably the most influential essay in Scottish literary criticism. Titled originally 'Two
Moods', it is the first in a book of ten related essays called *Scottish Literature: Character and
Influence*, published in 1919. Smith seems to have coined the now-famous phrase,
'Caledonian antisyzygy', which is here used as the essay's title, and to be more responsible
than any writer for pointing to the 'zigzag of contradictions' as a principle feature of Scottish
literature. MacDiarmid and many other Scottish writers have been influenced by Smith's
thesis (and of course by the tradition itself). Smith's numerous footnotes have been omitted.

It is never easy to describe national idiosyncrasy, but Englishmen think they know their Scot.
He has long been a very near neighbour, and every habit of his has become familiar. In his
literature, as in his other activities, he stands so self-confessed that any man of intelligence can
– as they phrase it in the high places of Jargon – 'discern the true Scottish note'. Yet one
sometimes wonders what these words are intended to mean, and whether they are not used,
in an offhand impressionist way, to turn the reader from stricter enquiry. For criticism has
learnt as much from that sacred bird the lapwing as from the sacred ostrich.

Many in the South have a ready touchstone for the detection of Scottish quality. By an
easy metaphor they transfer to Scottish literature the eccentricities which have vexed their five
senses in their dealings with the aggressive North. They think of the freakish colour schemes
of the tartans, of the skirl of the pipes, of the reek of haggis, of the flavour of John Barleycorn,
in one or more of his three disguises, of the rudeness of the thistle. They seem to see, hear,
and gust these glaring, noisy, redolent things at every turn in Northern art. They allow that
there are occasions when these qualities are proper and even pleasing, but on the whole these
are not comfortable virtues and they are sadly lacking in the finesse required of the superior
artist.

Others, declining this crude analogy, discover their Scot in quaint words and accent, in a certain whinstone jocularity, in a patriotism rampant as his lion and prickly as his motto, in an idealism tempered with kirk politics and a love of small change. To these, as to the tartan-and-haggis critics, it appears to be of little moment that they should show that the Scot thus gives himself away when he takes pen in hand, or that they should testify, on oath, that they have ever met such a guy in real life or reputable romance. The fiction is too useful when they are at a loss or have a crow to pluck with the North; and it at once assumes an air of truth when the Perfervids rush in with vulgar clamour against southern prejudice.

Generalities on the Scot himself or on national genius are here irrelevant. We are reminded how Sainte-Beuve dealt with Nisard's attempt to answer the question 'What is French genius?' He showed that the setting-up of a standard and the measuring of books and periods by it are always inadequate, even in classicist France; that the method does not allow for the variety of Nature's molds; and that there is no Genius which presides over a nation's literature with the authority of a Platonic archetype. The warning is not unnecessary here, for critics, Scottish as well as English, have approached northern work with strong prepossessions on what they choose to call the essential and abnormal in Scotticism, and have explained and judged both the whole literature and its parts in terms of a pattern which is imaginary, or, if it be framed, as it so often is, on their knowledge of Burns and Burns alone, is illusory.

In the second place, it is well to be on guard against concerning ourselves overmuch with externals, as if we must judge a man by his clothes. Though this counts for something in the pictorial or plastic medium — for when Rodin's Victor Hugo declines the tailor there is no telling whether he is a great poet or a marooned philosopher — it fails in the interpretation of literature. It should not confirm even the hastiest of critics in the heresy that Scotticism is only a matter of filibeg and muslin-kail.

Two considerations of contrary bearing present themselves at the outset. One is of encouragement; that the literature is the literature of a small country, that it runs a shorter course than others, and that there is no linguistic divorce between its earlier and later stages, as in southern English. In this shortness and cohesion the most favorable conditions seem to be offered for the making of a general estimate. But, on the other hand, we find at closer scanning that this cohesion, at least in formal expression and in choice of material, is only apparent, that the literature is remarkably varied, and that it becomes, under the stress of foreign influence and native division and reaction, almost a zigzag of contradictions. The antithesis need not, however, disconcert us. Perhaps in the very combination of opposites — what either of the two Sir Thomases, of Norwich and Cromarty, might have been willing to call 'the Caledonian antisyzygy' — we have a reflection of the contrasts which the Scot shows at every turn, in his political and ecclesiastical history, in his polemical restlessness, in his adaptability, which is another way of saying that he has made allowance for new conditions, in his practical judgement, which is the admission that two sides of the matter have been considered.

If therefore Scottish history and life are, as an old northern writer said of something else, 'varied with a clean contrair spirit,' we need not be surprised to find that in his literature the Scot presents two aspects which appear contradictory. Oxymoron was ever the bravest figure, and we must not forget that disorderly order is order after all. We can be indifferent to the disciples of De Quincey who will suspect us of making 'ambitious paradoxes' and 'false distinctions'. We may dwell on these incongruities, the better to explain their remarkable synthesis in Scottish literature; as we may, in a later chapter, on the breaks and thwarts, the better to show the continuity of a literary tradition.

One characteristic or mood stands out clearly, though it is not easily described in a word. We stumble over 'actuality', 'grip of fact', 'sense of detail', 'realism', yet with the conviction that we are proceeding in the right direction. We desire to express not merely the talent of close observation, but the power of producing, by a cumulation of touches, a quick and perfect image to the reader. What we are really thinking of is 'intimacy' of style. Scottish literature has no monopoly of this, which is to be found in the best work everywhere, and is indeed a first axiom of artistic method, no matter what processes of selection and recollection may follow; but in Scots the zest for handling a multitude of details rather than for seeking broad effects by suggestion is very persistent. When Allan Ramsay commended two of the authors represented in his Ever Green because they 'painted to the life', he might have said this of nearly all the writers in his collection. Everywhere it is the Dutch style – interiors, country folk and town 'bodies', farmyard and alehouse; everywhere a direct and convincing familiarity; little or nothing left out, and much almost pedantically accurate. 'Matter-of-fact' shall we say, befitting the practical genius of the Scot, and the seriousness which provoked Sydney Smith's taunt? Some would see in this gluttony of the particular the nemesis of the national earnestness, and conclude that in a literature so enmeshed there is no play for lighter qualities, that the writers must 'joke wi' difficulty' and be in no mood for fun or faery. Half truths make good theories.

In Scott, for example, we find that much of his success in description, whether of scene, or movement, or conversation, is achieved by the piling up of detail, and that in those passages which our impatient generation calls the duller, the failure, such as it is, is often due to extravagance in the use of material. There are many places, especially in the Waverley Novels, where the description leaves nothing to the imagination; which, if made the task of half a dozen artists, would painfully disabuse them of belief in their own originality. The reader will recall such passages as the account of the Green Room at the entry of Oldbuck and Lovel; or, in the same novel of the cave to which Lovel is taken by Edie or the parallel, yet fuller, sketch in *Ivanhoe* of the Black Knight's approach to the hermitage; or the picture of Old Mortality on his white pony, drawn to a 'hair tether', as no other nag, not even the palfrey of Chaucer's monk, or Rocinante, has been portrayed. There is nothing omitted for the illustrator who would venture. Perhaps it is because the 'instructions' are so absolute that Scott has escaped so well from foolish commentary in black and white. But it remains a question whether this revel in minutiae does not strain the art of descriptive prose which is something more than inventory: as we seem to see in an earlier novelist, also a Scot, whose persistency in piling up details does not always achieve the success of the opening scene of *Sir Launcelot Greaves*. Defoe, our master realist, does not so distrust his reader; and Fielding, who was realist enough, knew when to hold his hand.

In his verse, however, Scott's keen sense of movement, his greatest 'romantic' gift to his age, produces happier results. There – it may be because he is working with a different medium – the close succession of minute touches neither oppresses us nor distracts us in our enjoyment of the complete effect.

'Day set on Norham's castled steep,
And Tweed's fair river, broad and deep,
And Cheviot's mountains lone:
The battled towers, the donjon keep,
The loop-hole grates where captives weep,
The flanking walls that round it sweep,
In yellow lustre shone.
The warriors on the turrets high,
Moving athwart the evening sky,
Seem'd forms of giant height;
Their armour, as it caught the rays,
Flash'd back again the western blaze,
In lines of dazzling light.

St George's banner, broad and gay,
Now faded, as the fading ray
Less bright and less, was flung;
The evening gale had scarce the power
To wave it on the donjon tower,
So heavily it hung . . .'

Full as these lines from *Marmion* are, there is no overcrowding of detail. By the climax of individual touches, notwithstanding the aid of word and vowel ('So heavily it hung') and the canter of the rhyme, the pictorial success is achieved. But 'pictorial success' is, *pace* Pitt's compliment, a poor phrase for the poet's triumph in the trenches at Torres-Vedras, when soldiers under fire took courage from their captain's reading of the battle passage in the sixth canto of *The Lady of the Lake*.

In Burns the evidence is not less convincing; in the opening lines of *Tam o' Shanter* and in the central episode at Alloway Kirk, in the satire on Captain Grose and in the climax of Hornbook's delinquencies, and in the rush of *Hallowe'en*. As it is in Fergusson, and in Ramsay before him, and in yet earlier specimens of the intimate style, such as *Christis Kirk on the Green;* or in the anglicised Thomson, where this same evidence is the main excuse for certain hackneyed sayings about 'Scottish quality' and 'Scottish sense of colour.' As it is, too, in many passages in the older prose, such as Pitscottie's description of the royal banquet in Athole, or the pastoral monologue in the *Compilaynt of Scotlande* – each a crude endeavor after realism by a conglomerate of details.

Even the artificial verse of the Middle Scots Makars may be called to witness, however remote real life appears to be from the conventions of the Rose, the medieval litanies of love, or the formalities of fifteenth century court poets. We do not look for Nature's colours in the gold and enamel of their rhetorical verse, in rivers 'Of balmy liquour, cristallyne of hew,' or in nightingales, with 'angel feathers' shining as the peacock's, singing their 'sugared notes,' or in sunrise described as the 'upspringing' of

'the goldyn candill matutyne,
With clere depurit bemes cristallyne.'

Closer acquaintance, however, will correct this estimate.

It may seem strange that in Sir David Lyndsay, the last and most modern of the 'Middle' Scots, this quality of intimacy is less marked than in his predecessors. He is so conscious of the formalism of the Chaucerian tradition that he cannot avoid being formal; and so zealous in polemic and so ready to preach to a foolish generation that he gives himself few opportunities of free enjoyment, and, when he finds them, never uses them to the full. His best work *The Satyre of the Thrie Estaitis* supplies some hints of this intimate power; yet it is hard to recall in that long play, or in any of his poems, a single character or episode which is self-explained and real. The rough folk of the interludes are mere vulgar voices; and the description of 'Pedder Coffeis' (if it be his), which would have given Henryson or Dunbar his opportunity, is but a tattered sketch.

The medievalist Douglas is more generous. Such things as the tedious geography in the 'voyage' in the *Palice of Honour* are no more than the 'catalogue' pictures of earlier days, but there are suggestions of a crisper and more direct art, as in the passage describing the halt in the pleasant plain amid cedar trees at the foot of a green mountain, or in the Prologues to his *Virgil,* where he breaks away from his task in almost desperate contrariness to give a picture of a Lothian countryside in Spring or a winter day in old Edinburgh.

Take, for example, these lines –

'The dowy dichis war all donk and wait,
The law vaille flodderit all wyth spait,
The plane stretis and every hie way
Full of fluschis, doubbis, myre, and clay . . .
The wynd maid wayfe the reid weyd on the dyk,
Bedovin in donkis deyp was every syk;
Our craggis, and the front of rochis seyre,
Hang gret isch schoklis lang as ony spere;
The grund stude barrand, widderit, dosk, and grey . . .
Smal byrdis, flokand throw thik ronnis thrang,

In chyrmyng and with cheping changit thair sang,
Sekand hidlis and hirnys thaim to hyde
Fra feirful thudis of the tempestuus tyde.
The wattir lynnis routtis, and every lynde
Quhyslyt and brayt of the swouchand wynde' —

vivid in detail, even to the red weed swaying in the wind, and strong in their cumulative effect. As we read on, we see that this realism is neither woven in nor embroidered, but is the very warp of the literary fabric.

'Repaterit weill, and by the chymnay beykyt,
At evin be tyme dovne a bed I me streikit,
Warpit my heid, kest on claythis thrinfauld,
For till expell the perrellus peirsand cauld.
I crocit me, syne bownit for to sleip' —

but fitfully, with the moonlight streaming in, the screeching of an owl nearby, and the 'clacking' of wildgeese as they fly over the city. Later, he tells us —

'Fast by my chalmir, in heych wysnit treis,
The soir gled quhislis loud wyth mony ane pew,
Quhairby the day was dawin weil I knew;
Bad beit the fyire, and the candill alycht,
Syne blissit me, and, in my wedis dycht
Ane schot wyndo vnschet a lytill on char,
Persawit the morning bla, wan, and har,
Wyth cloudy gum and rak ourquhelmyt the air,
The soulye stythlie, hasart, rowch, and hair,
Branchis brattlyng, and blayknit schew the brays,
With hyrstis harsk of waggand wyndilstrays;
The dew droppis congelyt on stibyll and rynd,
And scharp hailstanis, mortfundit of kynd,
Hoppand on the thak and on the causay by.
The schot I clossit and drew inwart in hy,
Chiverand for cauld, the sessoun was so snell.'

Thus confined indoors, and taking thought of his unfinished translation, he sets to work on the seventh book; and the reader, 'repaterit weill' with this domestic realism, passes on to the high matters of Turnus and Aeneas. The interest of this Prologue lies not so much in the literary ingenuity as in the revelation of the intimate and simple in the solemn places of scholarship. The poet turns to a real world to refresh and steady his eye for his next flight. That 'indisputable air of truth' of which Carlyle speaks is so easily lost in the ceremonious tale of gods and heroes. If some of the other Prologues are critical or 'artificial', they too have a tonic purpose of contrast like those which are directly pictorial. We feel that we are as far from Troy when he gossips of Caxton or makes heavy 'sport' in his eighth Prologue, and that we are always within cry of the lodging of the garrulous Provost of St Giles.

Dunbar gives like testimony. Critics in calling him the 'Scottish Chaucer' and the 'Scottish Skelton' hint at his formal discipleship, in his Chaucerian allegory and language and his Skeltonic variety of verse, to the neglect of certain stronger likenesses in the directness or realistic fullness of their art. There are, of course, differences, always in favour of the 'maister dere,' but the intimacy is there, and it is the Scot's own. There is the tale of 'gay ladies in a grene arbeir,' where the persons and conversation are as real to us as to Dunbar's first readers, though in their truthfulness a little more scabrous to us than to that age. There is the *Flyting* with Kennedy, where by the sheer heaping up of personalities he achieves a portrait; and there are *The Tidings from the Session, The Dance of the Sevin Deidlie Synnis, The Turnament,* and others – all showing the same direct manner, and all working up the picture by a climax of detail. So persistent is this habit of imposing word upon word and epithet on epithet, that it appears even in the most artificial verse of Dunbar and his fellow poets. In such a piece as the following the recurrences and rhymes, though individually vague or even frivolous, win for the poem, by their united rush, some measure of respect.

> 'Haile, sterne superne! Haile in eterne,
> In Goddis sicht to schyne!
> Lucerne in derne, for to discerne
> Be glory and grace devyne;
> Hodiern, modern, sempitern,
> Angelicall regyne!
> Our tern inferne for to dispern,
> Helpe rialest rosyne.'

Should research discover that these lines, and others of similar structure, like Henryson's Prayer for the Pest, are a Scottish borrowing from some medieval Ave, we shall not be deprived of the interesting fact that in this form the Scot found something that suited his idiosyncrasy.

Still earlier, there is Henryson, the greatest of the Makars, and most truly the 'Scottish Chaucer', if the catch-title be worth the keeping; and before him, at the beginnings of Scottish literature, the Archdeacon of Aberdeen; and, between and after these, minors willing to add to the evidence. We must leave the *Fables,* with their *vie intime* of the Town Mouse and Chanticleer, and Sprutok and Pertok, and their picaresque tales of Reynard and Wolf Waitskaith, and the *Testament's* picture of the leper Cresseid, and the story of Orpheus's sad journey; and we must pass by the *Brus,* bringing with us the conviction that in the crowded movement of the poem – its processional of shining shields and basnets, 'browdyn baneris', 'pennons upon spears' – we have more than a hint of the art of the later poet of Scottish chivalry.

An exhaustive survey of all this material would show that the completed effect of the piling up of details is one of movement, suggesting the action of a concerted dance or the canter of a squadron. We have gone astray if we call this art merely meticulous, a pedant's or cataloguer's vanity in words, as some foolish persons have inclined to make charge against the 'antiquary' Scott. The whole is not always lost in the parts: it is not a compilation impressive only because it is greater than any of its contributing elements, but often single in result, and above all things lively. For which reason our earlier epithet of 'Dutch' must be understood 'with a difference', if we incline to think only of the careful brushwork of every tile and pot-lid in an interior. The verse forms of both popular and artificial Scots poetry aid this purpose of movement – in the stanzas of the *Cherrie and the Slae,* in *Philotus,* in some of Douglas's Prologues, in *Christis Kirk* and *Peblis to the Play,* in much of Burns. In the older popular verse, partly cast in the mould of the alliterative romance, as well as in the seventeenth- and eighteenth-century copies, the details catch each other up like dancers in a morris.

> 'Than thai come to the tounis end
> Withouttin moir delai,
> He befoir, and scho befoir,
> To see quha wes maist gay.
> All that lukit thame upon
> Leuche fast at thair array:
> Sum said that thay were mercat folk,
> Sum said the Quene of May
> Wes cumit
> To Peblis to the play.'

Thus in *Peblis to the Play;* so too in *Christis Kirk* –

'To dans thir damysellis thame dicht,
Thir lassis licht of laitis,
Thair gluvis wes of the raffel rycht,
Thair schone wes of the straitis;
Thair kirtillis wes of lynkome licht,
Weill prest with mony plaitis.
Thay wer so nys quhen men thame nicht,
Thay squeilit lyk ony gaitis
So lowd
At Chrystis Kirk of the Grene that day.'

There, surely, the swish of the skirt, the fling and bob of rustic festivity! Just as in one of the stanzas of the *Buke of the Howlat* the author suggests in his elaborate account of the four and twenty musical instruments an orchestral effect, dying away in the short lines of the finale. So, too, in the lively tale of *Sym and his Brudir* and in *Colkelbie's Sow* the appeal to the reader is in like terms – the familiar *crescendo* of frolic, rush, and noise. In the former, when the hubbub is over, the poet naively makes confession of his restless mood –

'He endis the story with harme forlorne;
The nolt begowth till skatter,
The ky ran startling to the corne.'

There is the same motive in the recital of the 'tocher-gud' in the *Wowing of Jok and Jynny,* and in the husbandman's long tale of woe in the *Wyf of Auchtirmuchty,* where the climax is aided, as more familiarly in the Ballads, by an ingenious repetition of phrase.

It is this sense of movement which has done something to save the Scot's zeal in observation from becoming merely antiquarian and tiresome. It achieves in some of the best examples that higher realism in which R. L. Stevenson found 'the sentiment assimilating the facts of natural congruity', not what is suggested only by the sheer force of numbers. The old saw comes to mind, 'An artist should learn his anatomy and forget it'; or as one has said, 'Anatomy, indispensable to the artist, becomes a source of all error if we forget that it is inertia.'

Criticism has concerned itself too exclusively with these inert elements in Scottish poetry. It has talked much of the 'sense of colour' and the 'feeling for nature', but has gone no further than to make an inventory of the references, or to theorise very airily on the Celtic origin of these likings, or, with Sydney Smith and Russell Lowell, to discover in this uncouth verse the early hints of what they might have agreed to call the tedious arithmetic of the Scottish mind.

The Scottish Muse has, however, another mood. Though she has loved reality, sometimes to maudlin affection for the commonplace, she has loved not less the airier pleasure to be found in the confusion of the senses, in the fun of things thrown topsy-turvy, in the horns of elfland and the voices of the mountains. It is a strange union of opposites, alien as Hotspur and Glendower; not to be explained as if this liking for 'skimble-skamble stuff' were derived from the very exuberance of the poets' realism by an inevitable reaction, or were a defect of its quality, or a sort of saturnalian indulgence to the slaves of observation. The opinion, so popular with Renan's and Matthew Arnold's generation, that this whimsical delight is a Celtic heritage may or may not be true, but the attempt to find a source is useful as a reminder that this characteristic is not a mere accident, or wantoning, no matter how much of its extravagance may be a direct protest against the prose of experience. It goes better with our knowledge of Scottish character and history to accept the antagonism as real and necessary. The Scot is not a quarrelsome man, but he has a fine sense of the value of provocation, and in the clash of things and words has often found a spiritual tonic.

Does any other man combine so strangely the severe and tender in his character, or forgo the victory of the most relentless logic at the sudden bidding of sentiment or superstition? Does literature anywhere, of this small compass, show such a mixture of contraries as his in outlook, subject, and method; real life and romance, everyday fact and the supernatural, things holy and things profane, gentle and simple, convention and 'cantrip', thistles and thistledown? We see this constitutional liking for contrasts in the old fun of the *flyting,* so popular in the North, in which the pitting of East against West, Angle against Gael, commended itself less for the roughness and obscenity which an obscene taste fostered than for the sheer exhilaration of conflict.

We are least concerned here with the plainest of all devices in contrariety, that of simply reversing experience, as when Swift and Voltaire make great things small and small things great; for once the convention is stated and understood, everything that follows is matter-of-fact. There is more in the Scottish antithesis of the real and fantastic than is to be explained by the familiar rules of rhetoric. The sudden jostling of contraries seems to preclude any relationship by literary suggestion. The one invades the other without warning. They are the 'polar twins' of the Scottish Muse.

We have a modern and familiar illustration of this bizarrerie in Byron's *Don Juan.* Everybody knows the hymn to Greek liberty, but not everybody, perhaps nowadays, its setting in the poem.

In the description of the poet in Juan's suite, we are told

'In France, for instance, he could write a chanson;
In England a six canto quarto tale;
In Spain, he'd make a ballad or romance on
The last war – much the same in Portugal;
In Germany, the Pegasus he'd prance on
Would be old Goethe's (see what says De Staël);
In Italy he'd ape the 'Trecentisti';
In Greece he'd sing some sort of hymn like this t'ye.'

On the heels of these gibes and the flippant 'this t'ye' follow the familiar lines on the Isles of Greece, till, at the height of patriotic fervour and lyrical beauty, which still count for something to Byron's faded reputation, the other Byron breaks in, in contrary mood –

'Thus sung, or would, or could, or should have sung
The modern Greek, in tolerable verse,' etc.

Let us avoid the irrelevance that Byron is here finding a place for a copy of verses, as Pope did for his 'Character of Addison'; or, as Jeffrey appears to have thought, that he is merely throwing his 'cold-blooded ribaldry' into stronger relief by his smooth heroics; or, with some solemn persons, that he is only showing us his poet's weakness and the degenerate taste he served. It is frivolous to look for a deep purpose in this conjunction of opposite moods, especially in a poet whom the critics have singled out as 'daemonic'. These moods are individual and alien, 'dremis or dotage in the monis cruik', which interrupt the prose of life as dreams will, in Puck's own way, and at his own time.

Historians and critics of Scottish literature have made scant allowance, if any, for these interruptions in the plain tale of experience, even though the poets themselves have given not a few hints of surprise at their own change of mood and have at times attempted an explanation. The author of Lichtounis *Dreme* ends his whimsical story by saying –

'As wiffis commandis, this dreme I will conclude;
God and the rude mot turn it all to gud!
Gar fill the cop, for thir auld carlingis clames
That gentill aill is oft the caus of dremes;'

just as Burns delicately ascribes Tam's adventure 'wi' warlocks in the mirk', or the picturesque harangue to Auld Cloots, to the machinations of the bourgeois fairy, John Barleycorn; or as Sir John Redgauntlet tells Steenie it were better to lay the 'haill dirdum' on 'Major Weir' and say nothing about the dream in the wood of Pitmurkie, as he 'had taken ower muckle brandy to be very certain about onything'.

We are dull indeed if we do not see in this reference to the contrast and in its explanation a quizzing of those prosaic and precise persons who must have that realism which resents everything as sober fact, within an ell of their noses. The poets seem to say: 'Here is fantasy strange enough; if you, drunkard of facts, must explain it, do so in the only way open to you, or to any 'auld carlin'. Be satisfied, if you think it is we who are drunk. As for us, let the contrast be unexplained, and let us make merry in this clash of strange worlds and moods.' It is beside the point to hint at or deny John Barleycorn's aid to the poetic imagination, and unnecessary to consider the ingenious view of a recent writer on Celtic literature, that bardic intemperance is not the satisfying of a sordid appetite but proof of the 'cravings for the illusion of an unreal world'.

We have probably lost much of the evidence of this delight in the grotesque and uncanny, for these things are not the decorous tasks of copyists or of poets printing for posterity. Yet enough remains. It is interesting, for example, to note that when each of the greater Middle Scots Makars doffs the ceremonial robes required by the courtly Muse and takes his ease in his own inn, he turns to alliterative burlesque and the wonderland of Gog Magog and the fairies. Lyndsay reminds us that he cheered his young master the prince, when he was 'sorye', with the prophecies of Thomas the Rhymer and Merlin and such 'pleasant stories' as the *Red Etin* and the *Gyre Carling* – the last sheer skimble-skamble, telling of Blasour's love for a witch who defied his army of moles and beat him badly, and, when the King of Faery with his elves and all the dogs from Dunbar to Dunblane and all the tykes of Tervey laid siege to her tower, changed herself into a sow and went 'gruntling our the Greik Sie'; of her marriage to Mahoun, and of Scotland's distress, so that the cocks of Cramond ceased to crow and the hens of Haddington to lay.

The tale of King Berdok is better nonsense. This 'great King of Babylon', who in summer dwelt on a 'bowkaill stock' (cabbage runt) and in winter retired for warmth to a cockleshell, had wooed for seven years Mayok, 'the golk of Maryland', who was 'but yeiris thre'. He set out to ravish this 'bony bird', who, though she had but one eye, was loved by him, 'for hir foirfute was langer than hir heill'. He found her milking her mother's cows, and cast her into a creel on his back. When he returned, his burden was but a 'howlat nest, full of skait birdis': so he wept, and ran back for his love. But in vain, for the King of Faery was out with his many, and Berdok hid himself within a kiln. On this refuge the King, with the aid of the Kings of the Picts and of Portugal, Naples, and Strathnaver, trained his guns and showered bullets of dough. Jupiter invoked father Saturn to save the amorous Berdok by transforming him to a toad, but Mercury gave him the shape of a bracken bush.

> 'And quhen thay saw the buss waig to and fra,
> Thay trowd it wes ane gaist, and thay to ga.'

Lichtoun, at one stage of his dream journey, sails in a barge of draff to Paradise, 'the place where Adam was', and, as he enters the port, sees Enoch and Eli

> 'Sittand, on Yule euin, in ane fresch grene schaw,
> Rostand straberries at ane fyre of snaw;'

and later, at the blowing of an 'elrich horne', beholds, besides other 'ferlies', three white whales, tied by grasshoppers' hairs in a meadow. Of the ghost of Lord Fergus, which another anonymous writer seeks to lay with extravagant ritual, it is said that –

'It stall Goddis quhittill;
It stall fra peteous Abrahame
Ane quhorle and ane quhum quhame;
It stall fra the carle of the mone
Ane pair of awld yrn schone;
It ran to Pencaitlane
And wirreit ane awld chaplane.'

In the *Littill Interlud,* ascribed to Dunbar, the dwarf sketches his giant grandsire Gog Magog, who, when he danced, made the world 'schog', and

'wald upoun his tais up stand
And tak the starnis doun with his hand,
And set thame in a gold garland
Aboif his wyvis hair.'

And in Dunbar's short fantasy of *Kynd Kittok* we have the story of a gay wife who, having died of thirst and taken the highway to heaven, wandered by an 'elriche well', where she met a newt riding on a snail,

'And cryit, 'Ourtane, fallow, haill!'
And raid ane inche behind the taill,
Till it wes neir evin;'

of the tedium of her heavenly task as Our Lady's henwife; and of her escape to enjoy once more the lower delights of inn-keeping. When the poet concludes, wantonly –

'Frendis, I pray you hertfully,
Git ye be thirsty or dry,
Drink with my guddame, as ye ga by,
Anys for my saik,'

we seem to catch the sentiment, even the turn of phrase, of Burns's *Address to the Deil*. Of 'ugsum horribilities' and of the doings of sprites like Inflar Tasy and Belly Bassy in *Sir John Rowll's Cursing,* there are examples enough; so too of that gentler topsy-turvy humour, with its nursery note, as in the 'Dreg-song' and 'When I was a wee thing' preserved for us in Herd's MS. With these and many other passages in mind, we see that the Scottish Muse, expert as she is in life's realities, has, like Burns's 'douce honest woman', her moments when she hears the rustling of strange things 'thro' the bourtrees comin''. 'The Lord guide us,' we may say with Mistress Baby in the *Pirate,* 'what kind of a country of guisards and gyre-carlines is this!'

The consideration of this second element and of its contrasted character has generally been narrowed down to argument about its Celtic origin. The problem does not press on us as it did upon Renan and Matthew Arnold, and the latter's plea for the Celt is, in spite of its abiding elegance of exposition, not so convincing as it was, even to the most partisan. While we are willing to make some allowance for the influence of locality and the mixing of races, and to find Scottish instance for the Irish commonplace about Norman settlers *ipsis Hibernis hiberniores,* we must take account of certain stubborn facts. In the first place, it is hard to find traces of this whimsical quality in the extant literature of the Scottish Gael, in the book of the Dean of Lismore, in the Ossianic *corpus,* or in the oral traditions collected by Campbell of Islay. There we have persistent evidence of a lively talent for observation and of some cunning in obtaining general effects by the device of massing details; and in many passages which cannot be so described – where the mists of Morven often descend most provokingly upon the poet – the characteristic Celtic touch is merely impressionist, not shirking the use of detail, either directly or fantastically, but omitting what is of lesser importance and leaving the reader to complete the picture. Here is a short Finn poem, for illustration –

'A tale here for you: oxen lowing, winter's snowing, summer's passing; wind from the North, high and cold, low the sun and short his course, wildly tossing the wave of the sea. The fern burns deep red. Men wrap themselves closely. The wild goose raises her wonted cry; cold seizes the wing of the bird; "tis the season of ice; sad my tale!'

In the second place, we must not forget that Old English literature, especially of the 'Riddle' kind, is streaked with this vein; and thirdly, that the long-continuing antagonism of racial elements and areas down to a late period makes against a theory of ready absorption, and more clearly in the North than in Wales. Even in the case of the latter we have grown suspicious of Arnold's conclusions. His argument means little more than this: given one quality which is to all appearance unlike another admittedly characteristic of a people, it may, must, and does come from an outside source; given a spiritual lightness and vivacity in the dull, heavy, practical genius of Teutonic England, it must have come from the Celts. We ask for proof; indeed, we decline to think it capable of proof, when we are told that the richest gifts are a sense of colour, an appreciation of natural effects, and other aptitudes, all of which are the ordinary talents and tools in the realist's workshop.

Were any distinctions in this general denial of Celtic indebtedness worth making in this connection, we might be tempted to say that the Welsh evidence, on which current opinion mainly rests, is less convincing than that of the Scottish Gaelic, and that the latter only commends itself when it shows some direct touch with Irish Gaelic. The plausible affiliation with Cymric fancy, as illustrated in the tale of *Kilhwch and Olwen* in the *Mabinogion,* discloses nothing more than the familiar device of hyperbole. Drem can see the gnat rising with the sun in far-off Cornwall and Clust hears the ant fifty miles off rustling from her nest. When the bard tells us that Gwevyl in his sad moods 'let one of his lips drop below his waist, while he turned up the other like a cap upon his head', and that Hornyhead was wont 'to go upon his head to save his feet', like 'a rolling stone upon the floor of the court', we smoke an old jest which involves no bardic mystery.

In such passages there is little, if any, parodic intention. In Irish, on the other hand, the evidence is not so negative, even if we have to confine ourselves to the rather exceptional *Vision of MacConglinne.* Description like that in the *Feast of Bricriu* of Cuchulainn's straining to heave the feast-house to its upright position is only hyperbolic. 'He tried to lift the house at a tug and failed. A distortion thereupon got hold of him, whilst a drop of blood was at the root of each single hair, and he absorbed his hair into his head, so that, looked on from above, his dark-yellow curls seemed as if they had been shorn by scissors: and, taking upon him the motion of a mill-stone, he strained himself till a warrior's foot could find room between each pair of ribs.' The fun of Guzzledom – of Fluxy, son of Elcab the Fearless, from the Fairy-knoll of Eating, and of Bacon-lad, son of Butter-lad, son of Lard, with his leggings of pot-meat and tunic of corned beef, and his steed of bacon with its four legs of custard – is nothing but a straightforward tale of Cockayne. Once the premises are admitted, we know what to expect. There is little or nothing of the wantonness of grotesque, the curious turns and contradictions and general chaos of sense, all expressed within narrow limits.

It has been pointed out, in reference to the Irish influence on Welsh story-telling, that the peculiar Celtic 'note' consists in the 'vivid contrast between the realism of the introductory framework' of certain pieces and the 'fantastic gorgeousness' of dream passages interpolated. When we turn to the tale which suggested this comment we find that it has no bearing on our present purpose. Rhonabwy falls asleep and dreams that 'he journeyed and heard a mighty noise, the like whereof heard he never before; and looking behind him, he beheld a youth with yellow curling hair, and with his beard newly trimmed, mounted on a chestnut horse, whereof the legs were grey from the top of the forelegs, and from the bend of the hind legs downwards. And the rider wore a coat of yellow satin sewn with green silk, and on his thigh was a gold-hilted sword, with a scabbard of new leather of Cordova, belted with the skin of the deer, and clasped with gold. And over this was a scarf of yellow satin wrought with green silk, the borders whereof were likewise green. And the green of the caparison of the horse, and of his rider, was as green as the leaves of the fir tree, and the yellow was as yellow as the blossom of the broom' – and so on, in sober recital of a thousand details. It is a very methodical knight this Rhonabwy, dreaming and waking; and we miss the promised contrasts, such as come to us in the Vision of a poet of a less golden age, when, sitting by the ingle-cheek, 'fill'd wi' hoast-provoking smeek', and hearing

'the restless rattons squeak
About the riggin,'

he saw the cottage door open to the 'outlandish hizzie' from dreamland.

It may be that the lowland Muse has learnt something from the Muse of Erscherie in her Galloway and Ayrshire haunts, as neighbours will; but, as neighbourhood often provokes criticism, it might not be too fantastic on our part, were the borrowing to be taken for granted, to see in the more complicated grotesques of the borrower an element of conscious parody rather than a family tradition. If it be hard to admit borrowing in the more patent habit of language, it becomes a hopeless task in the analysis of literary faculty. Even if any evidence were available to those on whom the onus of proof at present rests, we should be loath to surrender the opinion that opposites and contrasts in an individual or literature are, more often than not, original and constitutional in that individual or literature, and that neither of the contraries may be imposed from without. To separate the contrasts in character, as Scott, with the licence of the novelist and of his age, has done in his chapters on Saxon and Norman, or Arnold in his Essay, is to place the obverse of a coin in one bag and the reverse in another.

It may not appear unreasonable to lay this emphasis on the contrariety in northern literary mood, especially as certain conditions, or accidents, in the later national development, to be glanced at later, too readily obscure the second element and leave the Muse the narrower reputation of being painfully concerned with the Annals of the Five Senses. Even if it be said that much of this skimble-skamble is but the stuff of dreams which engages the irresponsible hours of the slowest minds, or if the humourous excuses of Lichtoun, and Burns himself, be taken literally, it would be worth noting that the Scot, the methodical, level-headed, self-conscious creature of popular tradition, has so far forgotten his conventional manner as to make confession of these disordered moments. For the 'douce' travesty which stands for the Scot with the general *never* says as much as he thinks: he is a mute philosopher on warlocks, and as calm as a country Sabbath morn on the cantrips of his mind. But he is not the Scot who steps forth self-confessed in the Makars old and new, despite the accidents or 'thwarts' of history which stayed, or appear to stay, the freer play of his fancy.

This mixing of contraries – 'intermingledons', to recall Burns's word – helps to explain the presence of certain qualities which have come to be considered as characteristic of Scottish literature. In the first place, it throws some light on that talent for the picturesque so generally allowed to northern writers. And what is the picturesque, in spite of the cheapening of the term in the marketplace, but the quality which, as Hazlitt tells us 'depends chiefly on the principle of discrimination and contrast' and 'runs imperceptibly into the fantastical and grotesque'? In other words, in its exercise and effect it does not show mere sensitiveness to fact, with or without the art of intensifying and completing the impression by the heaping-up of details.

Scottish literature is not so placid. If we neglect its more striking or astonishing extravagances, we have to account for that prevailing sense of movement, that energy and variety, call it what we like, that stirs even its most narrative mood. If a formula is to be found it must explain this strange combination of things unlike, of things seen in an everyday world and things which, like the elf-queen herself, neither earth or heaven will claim. This mingling, even of the most eccentric kind, is an indication to us that the Scot, in that medieval fashion which takes all things as granted, is at his ease in both 'rooms of life', and turns to fun, and even profanity, with no misgivings. For Scottish literature is more medieval in habit than criticism has suspected, and owes some part of its picturesque strength to this freedom in passing from one mood to another. It takes some people more time than they can spare to see the absolute propriety of a gargoyle's grinning at the elbow of a kneeling saint.

In the second place, the recognition of these opposites must modify some popular views, even among Scotsmen, about the element of humour in Scottish literature – humour in its most inclusive sense, not mere 'wut' (of the 'jocose' kind) or rough fun. We may assent to Lamb's tale of 'imperfect sympathy' with the Caledonian whose 'Minerva is born in panoply', whose ideas 'do not grow', who 'never hints or suggests anything, but unlades his stock of ideas in perfect order and completeness'.

We know that Scot as well as they did at the India House, though even he has been misjudged a little. We have met him in railway carriages and at foreign Universities, but rarely in northern writing, except in the polemical tracts of the seventeenth century or other documents as unliterary in pretence. In that Scot there is, in Lamb's phrase, 'no borderland within'. He dwells far from Huntlie Bank, where we shall find our poet, if *he* be not on seven years' leave in the land of mystery. If logic keeps this solemn person from being caught in the druid's mist, it denies him the secrets of humour and pathos, and an understanding companionship with the poets he is always ready to praise.

In the third place, we seem to find some connection between this double mood and the easy passing in Scottish literature between the natural and supernatural, as if in challenge to the traditional exclusiveness of certain subjects, each within its own caste. Here, again, we call to mind the preaching and arguing Scot of the seventeenth century, who placed impossible barriers to the poet's free passage from the one to the other; and the neo-classical Scot of the eighteenth century, who, while admitting that on occasion the supernatural and natural might have, as it were, a drawing-room introduction, had no desire to promote their closer acquaintance.

Neither of these attitudes represents the true feeling of Scottish literature, which at all periods has shown a readiness not only to accept the contrary moods more or less on equal terms, but to make the one blend imperceptibly into the other. Coleridge has shown this as convincingly as any English writer, not so much by direct critical argument as by the interwoven magic and reality of his verse. His gentle association of the two elements, so unlike the cumbrous coupling by many of his 'romantic' contemporaries, was one of his great aids to the poetic enlightenment of the nineteenth century.

We find a like quality in a northern poet of his time, the Ettrick Shepherd; but in him its interest is less individual. We strike, as it were, upon a vein, which had been worked before and would be later. Hogg, with pardonable egotism, when comparing himself with Scott, claimed that he was 'king of the mountain and fairy school', and we cannot, with the elfin music of *Kilmeny* in our ears, dispute the self-appreciation, even though compelled to admit that in the Shepherd's work there is so much of the local and of the earth earthy. That the Hogg of this verse, sticky with the mud of Mitchelslacks, the writer of veterinary prose on *Diseases of Sheep,* should be a Pilgrim to the Sun and hold fairyland in fee has almost turned some critics to a belief in miracles, to the forgetting of all the inspired moments which have come to simple folk from Caedmon's days to ours. The true miracle, if so must be the word, of the Shepherd's art is the way in which we pass without a hint of change from the land of real men and women to that other, as we might do from one parish to another on an afternoon's walk. His lost Kilmeny returns as unexpectedly, but as gently, as she went. Like his lark, she is of earth and sky. There is no wrench, no lumbering change of scenery when the stage harlequin has waved his wand.

'When many a day had come and fled,
When grief grew calm and hope was dead,
When mass for Kilmeny's soul had been sung,
When the beadsmen had prayed and the dead-bell rung,
Late, late in a gloamin, when all was still,
When the fringe was red on the westlin' hill,
The wood was sere, the moon i' the wane,

The reek o' the cot hung over the plain
Like a little wee cloud in the world its lane;
When the ingle lowed with an eiry leme,
Late, late in the gloamin Kilmeny came hame.'

The cottage calm is unbroken; there are no strange lights in the west at this home-coming. Kilmeny floats into her mother's ken; returns to her a real child, to be asked in natural and kindly curiosity about her truant doings and the gift of her skirt of lily sheen and her bonny snood. Again in the poem, after the tale of her fairy-life is told, and she has 'raiked' the lonely glen and tamed beast and bird by her beauty and innocence,

'There laid her down on the leaves so green,
And Kilmeny on earth was never mair seen!'

Hogg guides us back to *Tamlane,* once popular in his Ettrick Forest, and *Thomas Rymer,* and others, both Border ballad and Makars' verse. It is of no moment what any one of these may owe to predecessors, for the most deliberate *pastiche* is testimony to this sensitiveness to the twilight of earth and fairyland. Down to our own day there has been continuous witness, in all types of the literary Scot. We see the elements combined in the work of the greatest of the moderns, as humdrum Edinburgh lawyers saw it in their neighbour 'Sprite' and Samoans in their loved Tusitala. We see it in one who, though scholar, researcher, bibliographer – as pleased to be Gifford lecturer as Stevenson would have been to be Professor of Constitutional History – is remembered as our chief fairy-book maker.

Of him the creator of Peter Pan has said: 'Mr Lang was as Scotch as peat . . . He thought Mr Lang always puzzled the Sassenach a little. That was one of the duties of the Scot. He was so prodigal of his showers of gold and so wayward. There was a touch of the elf about him. A "touch" hardly seemed quite right, because one could never touch him – he was too elusive for that. The same could be said of Stevenson. No doubt if Scotland were searched long enough it would be found that there were others. It was perhaps a Scottish quality.' And what say the Auld Lichts to the capers of this Peter and his whimsical friends within hearing of the kirk-session of Thrums?

So it has fallen out with Scottish literature, as Burns tells us it fell out with his art, that it has been cared for by fairies, and brownies, and witches, and warlocks, and spunkies, and kelpies 'and other trumpery,' he adds, with a Scot's privilege and a Scottish meaning. So, too, this literature has satisfied that 'first condition of the poetic way of seeing and presenting things' which is, in Pater's phrase, 'particularisation' and 'the delight in concrete definition'. Contraries indeed, but as warp and woof.

Marion Angus (1866 – 1946)

Anemones

Anemones, they say, are out
By sheltered woodland streams,
With budding branches all about
Where Spring-time sunshine gleams;
Such are the haunts they love, but I
With swift remembrance see

Anemones beneath a sky
Of cold austerity –
Pale flowers too faint for winds so chill
And with too fair a name –   10
That day I lingered on a hill
For one who never came.

The Sang

The auld fouks praised his glancin' e'en,
Tae ilka★ bairn he was a frien',   every
A likelier lad ye wadna see
Bit – he was nae the lad fur me.

He brocht me troots frae lochans clear,
A skep o' bees, a skin o' deer,
There's nane s'uld tak' wha canna gie,
An' he was nae the lad fur me.

He luiket aince, he luiket lang,
He pit his hert-brak in a sang;   10
He heard the soondin' o' the sea,
An' a' wis bye wi' him an' me.

The tune gaed soughin' thro' the air,
The shepherds sang't at Lammas fair,
It ran ower a' the braes o' Dee,
The bonnie sang he made fur me.

Sae lang 'twill last as mithers croon
And sweethearts seek the simmer's moon;
Oh, I hae gi'en wha wadna gie,
For it s'all live when I maun dee.   20

Mary's Song

I wad ha'e gi'en him my lips tae kiss,
Had I been his, had I been his;
Barley breid and elder wine,
Had I been his as he is mine.

The wanderin' bee it seeks the rose;
Tae the lochan's★ bosom the burnie★ goes;   lake's/stream
The grey bird cries at evenin's fa',
'My luve, my fair one, come awa'.'

My beloved sall ha'e this he'rt tae break,
Reid, reid wine and the barley cake,   10
A he'rt tae break, and a mou' tae kiss,
Tho' he be nae mine, as I am his.

Winter

Down by the water-meadows
All on a winter's noon,
There was a naked thorn-bush
Sang a mournful rune;
She told the reeds a story
Of memories and sighs,
Of the robber bees' carousal
And the waft of butterflies.

All in a winter's gloaming
Down by the shingly shore,   10
There were two ancient sailormen
Outside a tavern door,
Complaining to each other
With lamentable lips
For the great dead captains,
And the old Sailing Ships.

Treasure-Trove

Do you mind* rinnin' barefit   remember
In the saft, summer mist,
Liltin' and linkin' on the steep hill-heids?
In below your tartan shawl, your hand wad aye twist
Your bonnie green beads.

Do you mind traivellin', traivellin'
Ower and ower the braes,
Reistlin' the heather, and keekin'* 'naith the weeds,   peeking
Seekin' and greetin'* in the cauld weet days   weeping
For yer tint* green beads?   10   lost

Whist! Dinna rouse him,
The auld sleepin' man –
Steek* the door; the mune-licht's on the lone hill-heids –   shut
Wee elfin craturs is delvin' in the sand,
They canna' miss the glimmer
O' yer auld green beads.

Here they come, the wee folk,
Speedin' fast and fleet –
There's a queer, low lauchin' on the grey hill-heids –
An' the bricht drops, glancin', following at their feet –   20
It's green, green beads –
The last ye'll ever see o' yer bonnie green beads.

Fairy Tales

Ye tell me o' the Guid Folk
Aneth the hills o' whin*,   furze
Wha ne'er hae grat* for sorrow   wept
Nor yet hae tasted sin;

Wi' een like lichted candles,
Ahint* their laigh doors   behind
Weavin' silken mantles
O' the rose and lily floors.

Strange folk and sorrowless
Their een as clear as glass –   10
But I hae seen a bonny licht
In the face o' a Gipsy lass,

As she slipit aff her shou'der
The plaid sae thin and auld
And hapt* it roond her nameless bairn dressed
Agin the winter's cauld.

Think Lang

Lassie, think lang, think lang,
Ere his step comes ower the hill.
Luve gi'es wi' a lauch* an' a sang,   laugh
An' whiles for nocht but ill.

Thir's weary time tae rue
In the lea-lang nicht yer lane[1]
The ghaist o' a kiss on yer mou'
An' sough o' win' in the rain.

Lassie, think lang, think lang,
The trees is clappin' their han's,   10
The burnie clatterin' wi' sang
Rins ower the blossomy lan's.

Luve gi'es wi' a lauch an' a sang,
His fit* fa's licht on the dew.   foot
Oh, lass, are ye thinkin' lang,
Star een an' honey mou'?

[1] 'Yer lane': alone.

The Lilt

Jean Gordon is weaving a' her lane
Twinin' the threid wi' a thocht o' her ain,
Hearin' the tune o' the bairns at play
That they're singin' amang them ilka day;
And saftly, saftly, ower the hill
Comes the sma', sma' rain.

Aye, she minds o' a simmer's nicht
Afore the waning o' the licht –
Bairnies chantin' in Lover's Lane
The sang that comes ower an' ower again,   10
And a young lass stealin' awa' to the hill,
In the sma', sma' rain.

Oh lass, your lips were flamin' reid,
An' cauld, mist drops lay on yer heid,
Ye didna gaither yon rose yer lane
And yer he'rt was singin' a sang o' its ain,
As ye slippit hameward, ower the hill,
In the sma', sma' rain.

Jean Gordon, she minds as she sits her lane,
O' a' the years that's bye and gane,   20
And naething gi'en and a'thing ta'en
But yon nicht o' nichts on the smoory★ hill   cloudy, very misty
In the sma', sma' rain –
And the bairns are singin' at their play
The lilt that they're liltin' ilka day.

Wee Jock Todd

The King cam' drivin' through the toon,
Slae and stately through the toon;
He bo'ed tae left, he bo'ed tae richt,
An' we bo'ed back as weel we micht;
But wee Jock Todd he couldna bide,
He was daft tae be doon at the waterside;
Sae he up an' waved his fishin' rod –
    Och, wee Jock Todd.

But in the quaiet hoor o' dreams,
The lang street streekit wi' pale moonbeams,   10
Wee Jock Todd cam' ridin' doon,
Slae an' solemn through the toon,
He bo'ed tae left, he bo'ed tae richt
(It maun ha'e been a bonnie sicht)
An' the King cam' runnin – he couldna bide –
He was mad tae be doon at the waterside;
Sae he up wi' his rod and gaed a nod
    Tae wee Jock Todd.

In a Little Old Town

The haar* creeps landward from the sea,   *mist*
The laigh sun's settin' reid.
Wha's are the bairns that dance fu' late
On the auld shore-heid?
Wi linkit hands and soople feet.
Slae turnin' in a ring,
Even on and even on
They sing and better sing.

'In gangs she' and 'Oot gangs she,'
Their steps noo lood, noo saft,   10
Witless words to an eerie tune,
Sae solemn and sae daft

And come they from the Windy Wynds
Or oot o' the years lang deid,
I harken wi' a stounin'* he'rt   *throbbing*
On the auld shore-heid.

The Ghost

The wind that brings
The twilight in
Is musky-scented,
Faint and thin,
When light as dew
On tender herb
A footstep falls
Across the curb.

Into the street
The children pack,   10
With, 'Here's the peddler-
Man come back!
The peddler with
The red balloons
And flutes that play
The dancing tunes.'

The wind that brings
The twilight home
Is frailer than
The drifted foam,   20
When light as vapour
On a glass
The footstep falls
Upon the grass.

O Mary, loose
Your cloudy wrap!
The gate is shut,
No timorous tap
Comes on the empty
Window-pane,   30
To wake your life
To joy again.

The old wife broods
Beside the fire.
No grief has she,
And no desire.
With puckered lips
And crooked smile
She mutters to
Herself the while.   40

'A year, or two –
Or maybe three –
And I the peddler-
Man shall be,
And I the baby
Soft and white
That Mary cries for
In the night,
And I the wind
So faint and thin,   50
The wind that blows
The twilight in.'

Ronald Macfie (1867 – 1931)

Ampelopsis

I flaunt no garden flowers,
Yet leafy thoughts in rhyme
Around thy spirit's towers
Like ampelopsis[1] climb;
And in Autumnal hours,
When all the buds are dead,
Will build thee flaming bowers
With hearts of vermeil red.

---

[1] Virginia Creeper.

Lilies

The solid world of sense dissolves away;
The forest swoons; the mountains swing and sway;
The sea becomes a blue amorphous mist,
Like vapours of a melted amethyst;
The whole round globe is as a bubble blown;
Nothing seems real save your soul alone.
For through your lucent eyes our dazzled sight
Espies the glimmer of immortal light;
And through your eyelid lilies sees enshrined
The deathless lilies of Eternal Mind,   10
And all things seem unreal and untrue
Beside the bright apocalypse of you.

The Dying-Day of Death

I, who had slept the dreamless sleep of Death
For aeons, wakened to a sense of pain,
Wrenched my stiff arms asunder, gasped for breath,
And was a man again.

The tatters of torn heaven overhead
Were swayed by hurrying wings and busy breath.
It was the resurrection of the dead,
The dying-day of Death.

The sun had halted half-way down the west;
But in the shadow of the pendant blue,   10
Patient and calm amid the world's unrest,
There shone a star or two.

Weird voices wailed about the vexed sea;
Cold corses* lay upon the yellow sands,   corpses
Panting themselves to life and painfully
Moving their ashen hands.

And in a valley a black cloud was lying,
Lifted by some great giant's morning breath.
I dared to ask, 'Is that old Thunder dying?'
One whispered – 'Nay, but Death.'   20

E'n where I stood I heard him moan and gasp;
Saw the cloud rising, falling like a sea;
And watched the hungry fingers pluck and grasp
The rocks deliriously.

Then moving onward for a little space,
I climbed a hill, and on the plain below
Behold astonièd the hollow face
Of man's relentless foe.

About his temples, sinuous serpent veins
Seemed writhing; and his lips were thin and starven;   30
While by the chisel of a myriad pains
His great brow-dome was carven.

A broken scythe had fallen on the grass;
I saw brown blood upon it from afar.
But one small corner was as bright as glass,
And had a mirrored star.

So huge the blade, it might have formed an arch
O'er Jordan; and the heavy handle leant
Its weight against a plumèd patriarch larch
Until it bowed and bent.   40

Lo, as I looked, Death's talon-fingers locked
Convulsively; his hands were heart-wards pressed:
The whole land on a sudden rolled and rocked,
Then lapsed into rest.

There lay God's grimmest, greatest servant, Death.
There lay the old inexorable reaper,
Moanless and motionless, devoid of breath,
A cloud-enfolded sleeper.

A Day in June

The sun was zenith high. A lifeless cloud
Lay in the west
Like a dead angel lying in a shroud,
With lilies on her breast.

O'erladen was the shimmering air with balm
And pollen-gold.
There reigned a perfect silence and a calm
O'er hill and wold;

Save for the wind gasping among the trees,
The gurgle of a spring,   10
The momentary sound of gossip-bees
Low murmuring;

Or crackle of the ripe broom's purple pod
Bursting apart,
Or song-bird palpitating up to God
Singing its heart.

With light and butterfly the world did seem
To flicker and flit
As though the Maker slept, and in a dream
Imagined it.   20

Caves

Caves are there, trodden by the sea alone,
With labyrinths and mazes – long ago
Silently sculptured by its secret flow –
Where crooked bones of uncouth beasts are strewn,
And hideous monsters lie and sleep, unknown
Even to the waves that wander to and fro
With eyes shut, fearing what their sight might show;
And trembling as they hear their echoed moan.

And every heart knows caves as dim and deep
Where moldy bones of uncouth sins decay,   10
With corners where old devils, half-asleep,
Wait only for a voice or step to say
'Awake!' And full of awe we blindly creep
From the deep darkness to the light of day.

A Proposal

Timed by the rhythm of a languid strain,
Leaning together in a waltz we turned;
And a pent passion in my being burned
Till dumb endurance grew a very pain.
Yet I was silent, deeming speech in vain:
Surely, as one in nether hell, I yearned –
Why should I climb to heaven to be spurned.
Why pray for what I never could attain?

The music throbbed. Across my lips there swept
A flame of hair. And then – I know not why –   10
But, seeing by her lashes that she wept,
I dared my hopeless love to testify.
O God! against my side her heart upleapt
In sudden, silent, passionate reply.

Loveland

Loveland, alas, has locusts,
Pestilence and pain,
Storms that lay the lilies,
Wind and rain,

Marshes without a moon,
Where black Death hangs and hovers,
Forests where bleach the bones
Of poor blind lovers.

★   ★   ★

– Nay, nay, the lilies in loveland
Never wither and die;   10
And locusts have never darkened
Its azure sky.

These were not bones of lovers
In yon dark dell:
Fool, you had lost your way;
And that was – hell.

David Rorie (1867 – 1946)

The Lum Hat Wantin' the Croon

The burn was bit wi' spate,
An' there cam' tum'lin doon
Tapsalteerie★ the half o' a gate,   upside down
Wi' an auld fish-hake an' a great muckle skate,
An' a lum-hat★ wantin' the croon.   top hat

The auld wife stood on the bank
As they gaed swirlin' roun',
She took a gude look an' syne says she:
'There's food an' there's firin' gaun to the sea,
An' a lum hat wantin' the croon.'   10

Sae she gruppit the branch o' a saugh★,   willow
An' she kickit aff ane o' her shoon,
An' she stuck oot her fit – but it caught in the gate,
An' awa she went wi' the great muckle skate,
An' the lum hat wantin' the croon.

She floatit fu' mony a mile,
Past cottage an' village an' toon,
She'd an awfu' time astride o' the gate,
Though it seemed to gree fine wi' the great muckle skate,
An' the lum hat wantin' the croon.   20

A fisher was walkin' the deck,
By the licht o' his pipe an' the mune,
When he sees an auld body astride o' a gate,
Come bobbin' alang in the waves wi' a skate,
An' a lum hat wantin' the croon.

'There's a man overboard!' cries he,
'Ye leear!' says she, 'I'll droon!
A man on a boord? It's a wife on a gate,
It's auld Mistress Mackintosh here wi' a skate,
An' a lum hat wantin' the croon.'   30

Was she nippit to death at the Pole?
Has India bakit her broon?
I canna tell that, but whatever her fate,
I'll wager ye'll find it was shared by a skate,
An' a lum hat wantin' the croon.

There's a moral attached to my sang,
On greed ye should aye gie a froon,
When ye think o' the wife that was lost for a gate,
An auld fish-hake an' a great muckle skate,
An' a lum hat wantin' a croon.   40

The Pawky Duke

There aince was a very pawky★ duke,   sly
Far kent for his joukery-pawkery,
Wha owned a hoose wi' a grand outlook,
A gairden and a rockery.
Hech mon! The pawky duke –
Hoot ay, an' a rockery!
For a bonnet-laird wi' a sma kailyard
Is naethin' but a mockery.

He lived far up a Heelant glen,
Where the foamin' flood an' the crag is,   10
An' he dined each day on the usquebae★   whisky
An' he washed it doon wi' haggis.
Hech mon! The pawky duke –
Hoot ay, an' a haggis!
For that's the way the Heelanters dae,
Where the foamin' flood an' the crag is.

He wore a sporran and a dirk
An' a beard like besom★ bristles,   broom
He was an elder o' the kirk
An' he hated kists o' whistles.[1]   20
Hech mon! The pawky duke –
An' doon on kists o' whistles.
They're a reid–heidit fowk up north
Wi' beards like besom bristles.

---

[1] 'A kist (chest) of whistles' is slang for a church organ.

Then ilka four hoors through the day
He took a muckle jorum★,   rowing song
An' when the gloamin' gathered grey
Got fou'★ with great decorum.   drunk
Hech mon! The pawky duke –
Blin' fou' wi' great decorum.   30
There ne'er were males among the Gaels
But loo'ed a muckle jorum.

His hair was reid as ony rose,
His legs were lang an' bony,
He keepit a hoast an' a rubbin'-post
An' a buskit★ cockernony★.   dressed/wig?
Hech mon! The pawky duke –
Wi' a buskit cockernony.
Ye ne'er will ken true Heelant men
Who'll own they hadna ony.   40

An' if he met a Sassenach★ loon★   English/fellow
Attour in Caledonia,
He garred him lilt in a cotton kilt
Till he had an acute pneumonia.
Hech mon! The pawky duke –
An' a Sassenach wi' pneumonia.
He lat him feel that the land o' the leal★   true
Is gey★ near Caledonia.   quite

He never went awa doon Sooth
To mell★ wi' legislation,   50   mix
For weel he kent sic things to be
Unfitted for his station.
Hech mon! The pawky duke –
An' weel he kent his station,
For dustmen noo we a' alloo
Are best at legislation.

Then aye afore he socht his bed,
He danced the Ghillie-Callum,
An' wi' Kilmarnock★ owre his neb★   nightcap, bonnet/nose
What evil could befall 'im?   60
Hech mon! The pawky duke –
What evil could befall 'im,
When he casts his buits and soupled his cuits★   ankles
With a gude-gaun Ghillie-Callum?

But they brocht ae day a muckle joke
For his ducal eedification,
An' they needit to trephine his heid,
An' he dee'd o' the operation.
Hech mon! The pawky duke –
Wae's me for the operation.   70
For weel I wot this typical Scot
Was a michty loss to the nation.

Ronald Ross (1867 – 1932)

Song of the Sun

From the thronged and thick world under
I arise with step of thunder.
Through the mantle of my fire,
Through my flaming locks of hair,
Glows the form that all desire,
But more bright than they can bear;
For although I make men see,
None can dare to gaze on me.
Whether I rise in fire or blood,
Mortals hail me lord or god.   10
Then, before my battling knees,
Bubbling boil the surging seas,
And the clouds are writhing brent
By my fiery chastisement.
With my right hand held on high,
I let Life, the Angel, fly;
With my left, I grip and quell
Death, the Old Man, dragged from hell.

But ye men, who bow so low
At my gorgeous orient, know   20
That for ever in chains I go.
I am lord, for I am slave;
Conqueror, because I save;
Master, for I must obey;
God, because I burn away.
Though my lordly planets pace,
Peers before my sovran face,
In them every grain of sand
Governs me with like command.
So within my empery,   30
Only he who serves is free
And shall win the victory.

Algernon Blackwood (1869 – 1951)

Born in England of Scottish ancestors, Blackwood was one of the giants of horror fiction during his career. He studied at Edinburgh University, made many trips throughout Scotland and seems to have had a great interest in the Old Country. A habitual traveller through his life, Blackwood spent much time in Canada and in the United States. 'The Wolves of God', set in the wild places of Canada, of Scotland, and of the human soul, is one of the finest of Scottish horror stories.

The Wolves of God

I

As the little steamer entered the bay of Kettletoft in the Orkneys the beach at Sanday appeared so low that the houses almost seemed to be standing in the water; and to the big, dark man leaning over the rail of the upper deck the sight of them came with a pang of mingled pain and pleasure. The scene, to his eyes, had not changed. The houses, the low shore, the flat treeless country beyond, the vast open sky, all looked exactly the same as when he left the island thirty years ago to work for the Hudson Bay Company in distant N.W. Canada. A lad of eighteen then, he was now a man of forty-eight, old for his years, and this was the home-coming he had so often dreamed about in the lonely wilderness of trees where he had spent his life. Yet his grim face wore an anxious rather than a tender expression. The return was perhaps not quite as he had pictured it.

Jim Peace had not done too badly, however, in the Company's service. For an islander, he would be a rich man now; he had not married, he had saved the greater part of his salary, and even in the far-away Post where he had spent so many years there had been occasional opportunities of the kind common to new, wild countries where life and law are in the making. He had not hesitated to take them. None of the big Company Posts, it was true, had come his way, nor had he risen very high in the service; in another two years his turn would have come, yet he had left of his own accord before those two years were up. His decision, judging by the strength in the features, was not due to impulse; the move had been deliberately weighed and calculated; he had renounced his opportunity after full reflection. A man with those steady eyes, with that square jaw and determined mouth, certainly did not act without good reason.

A curious expression now flickered over his weather-hardened face as he saw again his childhood's home, and the return, so often dreamed about, actually took place at last. An uneasy light flashed for a moment in the deep-set grey eyes, but was quickly gone again, and the tanned visage recovered its accustomed look of stern composure. His keen sight took in a dark knot of figures on the landing pier – his brother, he knew, among them. A wave of home-sickness swept over him. He longed to see his brother again, the old farm, the sweep of open country, the sand-dunes, and the breaking seas. The smell of long-forgotten days came to his nostrils with its sweet, painful pang of youthful memories.

How fine, he thought, to be back there in the old familiar fields of childhood, with sea and sand about him instead of the smother of endless woods that ran a thousand miles without a break. He was glad in particular that no trees were visible, and that rabbits scampering among the dunes were the only wild animals he need ever meet . . .

Those thirty years in the woods, it seemed, oppressed his mind; the forests, the countless multitudes of trees, had wearied him. His nerves, perhaps, had suffered finally. Snow, frost and sun, stars, and the wind had been his companions during the long days and endless nights in his lonely Post, but chiefly – trees. Trees, trees, trees! On the whole, he had preferred them in stormy weather, though, in another way, their rigid hosts, 'mid the deep silence of still days, had been equally oppressive. In the clear sunlight of a windless day they assumed a waiting, listening, watching aspect that had something spectral in it, but when in motion – well, he preferred a moving animal to one that stood stock-still and stared. Wind, moreover, in a million trees, even the lightest breeze, drowned all other sounds – the howling of the wolves, for instance, in winter, or the ceaseless harsh barking of the husky dogs he so disliked.

Even on this warm September afternoon a slight shiver ran over him as the background of dead years loomed up behind the present scene. He thrust the picture back, deep down inside himself. The self-control, the strong, even violent will that the face betrayed, came into operation instantly. The background was background; it belonged to what was past, and the past was over and done with. It was dead. Jim meant it to stay dead.

The figure waving to him from the pier was his brother. He knew Tom instantly; the years had dealt easily with him in this quiet island; there was no startling, no unkindly change, and a deep emotion, though unexpressed, rose in his heart. It was good to be home again, he realised, as he sat presently in the cart, Tom holding the reins, driving slowly back to the farm at the north end of the island. Everything he found familiar, yet at the same time strange. They passed the school where he used to go as a little bare-legged boy; other boys were now learning their lessons exactly as he used to do. Through the open window he could hear the droning voice of the schoolmaster, who, though invisible, wore the face of Mr Lovibond, his own teacher.

'Lovibond?' said Tom, in reply to his question. 'Oh, he's been dead these twenty years. He went south, you know – Glasgow, I think it was, or Edinburgh. He got typhoid.'

Stands of golden plover were to be seen as of old in the fields, or flashing overhead in swift flight with a whir of wings, wheeling and turning together like one huge bird. Down on the empty shore a curlew cried. Its piercing note rose clear above the noisy clamour of the gulls. The sun played softly on the quiet sea, the air was keen but pleasant, the tang of salt mixed sweetly with the clean smells of open country that he knew so well. Nothing of essentials had changed, even the low clouds beyond the heaving uplands were the clouds of childhood.

They came presently to the sand-dunes, where rabbits sat at their burrow-mouths, or ran helter-skelter across the road in front of the slow cart.

'They're safe till the colder weather comes and trapping begins,' he mentioned. It all came back to him in detail.

'And they know it, too – the canny little beggars,' replied Tom. 'Any rabbits out where you've been?' he asked casually.

'Not to hurt you,' returned his brother shortly.

Nothing seemed changed, although everything seemed different. He looked upon the old, familiar things, but with other eyes. There were, of course, changes, alterations, yet so slight, in a way so odd and curious, that they evaded him; not being of the physical order, they reported to his soul, not to his mind. But his soul, being troubled, sought to deny the changes; to admit them meant to admit a change in himself he had determined to conceal even if he could not entirely deny it.

'Same old place, Tom,' came one of his rare remarks. 'The years ain't done much to it.' He looked into his brother's face a moment squarely. 'Nor to you, either, Tom,' he added, affection and tenderness just touching his voice and breaking through a natural reserve that was almost taciturnity.

His brother returned the look; and something in that instant passed between the two men, something of understanding that no words had hinted at, much less expressed. The tie was real, they loved each other, they were loyal, true, steadfast fellows. In youth they had known no secrets. The shadow that now passed and vanished left a vague trouble in both hearts.

'The forests,' said Tom slowly, 'have made a silent man of you, Jim. You'll miss them here, I'm thinking.'

'Maybe,' was the curt reply, 'but I guess not.'

His lips snapped to as though they were of steel and could never open again, while the tone he used made Tom realise that the subject was not one his brother cared to talk about particularly. He was surprised, therefore, when, after a pause, Jim returned to it of his own accord. He was sitting a little sideways as he spoke, taking in the scene with hungry eyes. 'It's a queer thing,' he observed, 'to look round and see nothing but clean empty land, and not a single tree in sight. You see, it don't look natural quite.'

Again his brother was struck by the tone of voice, but this time by something else as well he could not name. Jim was excusing himself, explaining. The manner, too, arrested him. And thirty years disappeared as though they had not been, for it was thus Jim acted as a boy when there was something unpleasant he had to say and wished to get it over. The tone, the gesture, the manner, all were there. He was edging up to something he wished to say, yet dared not utter.

'You've had enough of trees then?' Tom said sympathetically, trying to help, 'and things?'

The instant the last two words were out he realised that they had been drawn from him instinctively, and that it was the anxiety of deep affection which had prompted them. He had guessed without knowing he had guessed, or rather, without intention or attempt to guess. Jim had a secret. Love's clairvoyance had discovered it, though not yet its hidden terms.

'I have – ' began the other, then paused, evidently to choose his words with care. 'I've had enough of trees.' He was about to speak of something that his brother had unwittingly touched upon in his chance phrase, but instead of finding the words he sought, he gave a sudden start, his breath caught sharply. 'What's that?' he exclaimed, jerking his body round so abruptly that Tom automatically pulled the reins. 'What is it?'

'A dog barking,' Tom answered, much surprised. 'A farm dog barking. Why? What did you think it was?' he asked, as he flicked the horse to go on again. 'You made me jump,' he added, with a laugh. 'You're used to huskies, ain't you?'

'It sounded so – not like a dog, I mean,' came the slow explanation. 'It's long since I heard a sheep-dog bark, I suppose it startled me.'

'Oh, it's a dog all right,' Tom assured him comfortingly, for his heart told him infallibly the kind of tone to use. And presently, too, he changed the subject in his blunt, honest fashion, knowing that, also, was the right and kindly thing to do. He pointed out the old farms as they drove along, his brother silent again, sitting stiff and rigid at his side. 'And it's good to have you back, Jim, from those outlandish places. There are not too many of the family left now – just you and I, as a matter of fact.'

'Just you and I,' the other repeated gruffly, but in a sweetened tone that proved he appreciated the ready sympathy and tact. 'We'll stick together, Tom, eh? Blood's thicker than water, ain't it? I've learnt that much, anyhow.'

The voice had something gentle and appealing in it, something his brother heard now for the first time. An elbow nudged into his side, and Tom knew the gesture was not solely a sign of affection, but grew partly also from the comfort born of physical contact when the heart is anxious. The touch, like the last words, conveyed an appeal for help. Tom was so surprised he couldn't believe it quite.

Scared! Jim scared! The thought puzzled and afflicted him who knew his brother's character inside out, his courage, his presence of mind in danger, his resolution. Jim frightened seemed an impossibility, a contradiction in terms; he was the kind of man who did not know the meaning of fear, who shrank from nothing, whose spirits rose highest when things appeared most hopeless. It must, indeed, be an uncommon, even a terrible danger that could shake such nerves; yet Tom saw the signs and read them clearly. Explain them he could not, nor did he try. All he knew with certainty was that his brother, sitting now beside him in the cart, hid a secret terror in his heart. Sooner or later, in his own good time, he would share it with him.

He ascribed it, this simple Orkney farmer, to those thirty years of loneliness and exile in wild desolate places, without companionship, without the society of women, with only Indians, husky dogs, a few trappers or fur-dealers like himself, but none of the wholesome, natural influences that sweeten life within reach. Thirty years was a long, long time. He began planning schemes to help. Jim must see people as much as possible, and his mind ran quickly over the men and women available. In women the neighbourhood was not rich, but there were several men of the right sort who might be useful, good fellows all. There was John Rossiter, another old Hudson Bay man, who had been factor at Cartwright, Labrador, for many years, and had returned long ago to spend his last days in civilisation. There was Sandy McKay, also back from a long spell of rubber planting in Malay . . . Tom was still busy making plans when they reached the old farm and presently sat down to their first meal together since that early breakfast thirty years ago before Jim caught the steamer that bore him off to exile – an exile that now returned him with nerves unstrung and a secret terror hidden in his heart.

'I'll ask no questions,' he decided. 'Jim will tell me in his own good time. And, meanwhile, I'll get him to see as many folks as possible.' He meant it too; yet not only for his brother's sake. Jim's terror was so vivid it had touched his own heart too.

'Ah, a man can open his lungs here and breathe!' exclaimed Jim, as the two came out after supper and stood before the house, gazing across the open country. He drew a deep breath as though to prove his assertion, exhaling with slow satisfaction again. 'It's good to see a clear horizon and to know there's all that water between – between me and where I've been.' He turned his face to watch the plover in the sky, then looked towards the distant shore-line where the sea was just visible in the long evening light. 'There can't be too much water for me,' he added, half to himself. 'I guess they can't cross water – not that much water at any rate.'

Tom stared, wondering uneasily what to make of it.

'At the trees again, Jim?' he said laughingly. He had overheard the last words, though spoken low, and thought it best not to ignore them altogether. To be natural was the right way, he believed, natural and cheery. To make a joke of anything unpleasant, he felt, was to make it less serious. 'I've never seen a tree come across the Atlantic yet, except as a mast – dead,' he added.

'I wasn't thinking of the trees just then,' was the blunt reply, 'but of – something else. The damned trees are nothing, though I hate the sight of 'em. Not of much account, anyway' – as though he compared them mentally with another thing. He puffed at his pipe a moment.

'They certainly can't move,' put in his brother, 'nor swim either.'

'Nor another thing,' said Jim, his voice thick suddenly, but not with smoke, and his speech confused, though the idea in his mind was certainly clear as daylight. 'Things can't hide behind 'em – can they?'

'Not much cover hereabouts, I admit,' laughed Tom, though the look in his brother's eyes made his laughter as short as it sounded unnatural.

'That's so,' agreed the other. 'But what I meant was' – he threw out his chest, looked about him with an air of intense relief, drew in another deep breath, and again exhaled with satisfaction – 'if there are no trees, there's no hiding.'

It was the expression on the rugged, weathered face that sent the blood in a sudden gulping rush from his brother's heart. He had seen men frightened, seen men afraid before they were actually frightened; he had also seen men stiff with terror in the face both of natural and so-called supernatural things; but never in his life before had he seen the look of unearthly dread that now turned his brother's face as white as chalk and yet put the glow of fire in two haunted burning eyes.

Across the darkening landscape the sound of distant barking had floated to them on the evening wind.

'It's only a farm-dog barking.' Yet it was Jim's deep, quiet voice that said it, one hand upon his brother's arm.

'That's all,' replied Tom, ashamed that he had betrayed himself, and realising with a shock of surprise that it was Jim who now played the role of comforter – a startling change in their relations. 'Why, what did you think it was?'

He tried hard to speak naturally and easily, but his voice shook. So deep was the brothers' love and intimacy that they could not help but share.

Jim lowered his great head. 'I thought,' he whispered, his grey beard touching the other's cheek, 'maybe it was the wolves' – an agony of terror made both voice and body tremble – 'the Wolves of God!'

II

The interval of thirty years had been bridged easily enough; it was the secret that left the open gap neither of them cared or dared to cross. Jim's reason for hesitation lay within reach of guesswork, but Tom's silence was more complicated.

With strong, simple men, strangers to affectation or pretense, reserve is a real, almost a sacred thing. Jim offered nothing more; Tom asked no single question. In the latter's mind lay, for one thing, a singular intuitive certainty: that if he knew the truth he would lose his brother. How, why, wherefore, he had no notion; whether by death, or because, having told an awful thing, Jim would hide – physically or mentally – he knew not, nor even asked himself. No subtlety lay in Tom, the Orkney farmer. He merely felt that a knowledge of the truth involved separation which was death.

Day and night, however, that extraordinary phrase which, at its first hearing, had frozen his blood, ran on beating in his mind. With it came always the original, nameless horror that had held him motionless where he stood, his brother's bearded lips against his ear: *The Wolves of God*. In some dim way, he sometimes felt – tried to persuade himself, rather – the horror did not belong to the phrase alone, but was a sympathetic echo of what Jim felt himself. It had entered his own mind and heart. They had always shared in this same strange, intimate way. The deep brotherly tie accounted for it. Of the possible transference of thought and emotion he knew nothing, but this was what he meant perhaps.

At the same time he fought and strove to keep it out, not because it brought uneasy and distressing feelings to him, but because he did not wish to pry, to ascertain, to discover his brother's secret as by some kind of subterfuge that seemed too near to eavesdropping almost. Also, he wished most earnestly to protect him. Meanwhile, in spite of himself, or perhaps because of himself, he watched his brother as a wild animal watches its young. Jim was the only tie he had on earth. He loved him with a brother's love, and Jim, similarly, he knew, loved him. His job was difficult. Love alone could guide him.

He gave openings, but he never questioned:

'Your letter did surprise me, Jim. I was never so delighted in my life. You had still two years to run.'

'I'd had enough,' was the short reply. 'God, man, it was good to get home again!'

This, and the blunt talk that followed their first meeting, was all Tom had to go upon, while those eyes that refused to shut watched ceaselessly always. There was improvement, unless, which never occurred to Tom, it was self-control; there was no more talk of trees and water, the barking of the dogs passed unnoticed, no reference to the loneliness of the backwoods life passed his lips; he spent his days fishing, shooting, helping with the work of the farm, his evenings smoking over a glass – he was more than temperate – and talking over the days of long ago.

The signs of uneasiness still were there, but they were negative, far more suggestive, therefore, than if open and direct. He desired no company, for instance – an unnatural thing, thought Tom, after so many years of loneliness.

It was this and the awkward fact that he had given up two years before his time was finished, renouncing, therefore, a comfortable pension – it was these two big details that stuck with such unkind persistence in his brother's thoughts. Behind both, moreover, ran ever the strange whispered phrase. What the words meant, or whence they were derived, Tom had no possible inkling. Like the wicked refrain of some forbidden song, they haunted him day and night, even his sleep was not free from them entirely. All of which, to the simple Orkney farmer, was so new an experience that he knew not how to deal with it at all. Too strong to be flustered, he was at any rate bewildered. And it was for Jim, his brother, he suffered most.

What perplexed him chiefly, however, was the attitude his brother showed towards old John Rossiter. He could almost have imagined that the two men had met and known each other out in Canada, though Rossiter showed him how impossible that was, both in point of time and of geography as well. He had brought them together within the first few days, and Jim, silent, gloomy, morose, even surly, had eyed him like an enemy. Old Rossiter, the milk of human kindness as thick in his veins as cream, had taken no offense. Grizzled veteran of the wilds, he had served his full term with the Company and now enjoyed his well-earned pension. He was full of stories, reminiscences, adventures of every sort and kind; he knew men and values, had seen strange things that only the true wilderness delivers, and he loved nothing better than to tell them over a glass. He talked with Jim so genially and affably that little response was called for luckily, for Jim was glum and unresponsive almost to rudeness. Old Rossiter noticed nothing. What Tom noticed was, chiefly perhaps, his brother's acute uneasiness. Between his desire to help his attachment to Rossiter, and his keen personal distress, he knew not what to do or say. The situation was becoming too much for him.

The two families, besides – Peace and Rossiter – had been neighbours for generations, had intermarried freely, and were related in various degrees. He was too fond of his brother to feel ashamed, but he was glad when the visit was over and they were out of their host's house. Jim had even declined to drink with him.

'They're good fellows on the island,' said Tom on their way home, 'but not specially entertaining, perhaps. We all stick together though. You can trust 'em mostly.'

'I never was a talker, Tom,' came the gruff reply. 'You know that.' And Tom, understanding more than he understood, accepted the apology and made generous allowances.

'John likes to talk,' he helped him. 'He appreciates a good listener.'

'It's the kind of talk I'm finished with,' was the rejoinder. 'The Company and their goings-on don't interest me any more. I've had enough.'

Tom noticed other things as well with those affectionate eyes of his that did not want to see yet would not close. As the days drew in, for instance, Jim seemed reluctant to leave the house towards evening. Once the full light of day had passed, he kept indoors. He was eager and ready enough to shoot in the early morning, no matter at what hour he had to get up, but he refused point blank to go with his brother to the lake for an evening flight. No excuse was offered; he simply declined to go.

The gap between them thus widened and deepened, while yet in another sense it grew less formidable. Both knew, that is, that a secret lay between them for the first time in their lives, yet both knew also that at the right and proper moment it would be revealed. Jim only waited till the proper moment came. And Tom understood. His deep, simple love was equal to all emergencies. He respected his brother's reserve. The obvious desire of John Rossiter to talk and ask questions, for instance, he resisted staunchly as far as he was able. Only when he could help and protect his brother did he yield a little. The talk was brief, even monosyllabic; neither the old Hudson Bay fellow nor the Orkney farmer ran to many words:

'He ain't right with himself,' offered John, taking his pipe out of his mouth and leaning forward. 'That's what I don't like to see.' He put a skinny hand on Tom's knee. and looked earnestly into his face as he said it.

'Jim!' replied the other. 'Jim ill, you mean!' It sounded ridiculous.

'His mind is sick.'

'I don't understand,' Tom said, though the truth bit like rough-edged steel into the brother's heart.

'His soul, then, if you like that better.'

Tom fought with himself a moment, then asked him to be more explicit.

'More'n I can say,' rejoined the laconic old backwoodsman. 'I don't know myself. The woods heal some men and make others sick.'

'Maybe, John, maybe.' Tom fought back his resentment. 'You've lived, like him, in lonely places. You ought to know.' His mouth shut with a snap, as though he had said too much. Loyalty to his suffering brother caught him strongly. Already his heart ached for Jim. He felt angry with Rossiter for his divination, but perceived, too, that the old fellow meant well and was trying to help him. If he lost Jim, he lost the world – his all.

A considerable pause followed, during which both men puffed their pipes with reckless energy. Both, that is, were a bit excited. Yet both had their code, a code they would not exceed for worlds.

'Jim,' added Tom presently, making an effort to meet the sympathy half way, 'ain't quite up to the mark, I'll admit that.'

There was another long pause, while Rossiter kept his eyes on his companion steadily, though without a trace of expression in them – a habit that the woods had taught him.

'Jim,' he said at length, with an obvious effort, 'is skeered. And it's the soul in him that's skeered.'

Tom wavered dreadfully then. He saw that old Rossiter, experienced backwoodsman and taught by the Company as he was, knew where the secret lay, if he did not yet know its exact terms. It was easy enough to put the question, yet he hesitated, because loyalty forbade.

'It's a dirty outfit somewheres,' the old man mumbled to himself.

Tom sprang to his feet. 'If you talk that way,' he exclaimed angrily, 'you're no friend of mine – or his.' His anger gained upon him as he said it. 'Say that again,' he cried, 'and I'll knock your teeth – '

He sat back, stunned a moment.

'Forgive me, John,' he faltered, shamed yet still angry. 'It's pain to me, it's pain. Jim,' he went on, after a long breath and a pull at his glass, 'Jim *is* scared, I know it.' He waited a moment, hunting for the words that he could use without disloyalty. 'But it's nothing he's done himself,' he said, 'nothing to his discredit. I know *that.*'

Old Rossiter looked up, a strange light in his eyes.

'No offense,' he said quietly.

'Tell me what you know,' cried Tom suddenly, standing up again.

The old factor met his eye squarely, steadfastly. He laid his pipe aside.

'D'ye really want to hear?' he asked in a lowered voice. 'Because, if you don't – why, say so right now. I'm all for justice,' he added, 'and always was.'

'Tell me,' said Tom, his heart in his mouth. 'Maybe, if I knew – I might help him.' The old man's words woke fear in him. He well knew his passionate, remorseless sense of justice.

'Help him,' repeated the other. 'For a man skeered in his soul there ain't no help. But – if you want to hear – I'll tell you.'

'Tell me,' cried Tom. 'I *will* help him,' while rising anger fought back rising fear.

John took another pull at his glass.

'Jest between you and me like.'

'Between you and me,' said Tom. 'Get on with it.'

There was a deep silence in the little room. Only the sound of the sea came in, the wind behind it.

'The Wolves,' whispered old Rossiter. 'The Wolves of God.'

Tom sat still in his chair, as though struck in the face. He shivered. He kept silent and the silence seemed to him long and curious. His heart was throbbing, the blood in his veins played strange tricks. All he remembered was that old Rossiter had gone on talking. The voice, however, sounded far away and distant. It was all unreal, he felt, as he went homewards across the bleak, wind-swept upland, the sound of the sea for ever in his ears . . .

Yes, old John Rossiter, damned be his soul, had gone on talking. He had said wild, incredible things. Damned be his soul! His teeth should be smashed for that. It was outrageous, it was cowardly, it was not true.

'Jim,' he thought, 'my brother, Jim!' as he plowed his way wearily against the wind. 'I'll teach him. I'll teach him to spread such wicked tales!' He referred to Rossiter. 'God blast these fellows! They come home from their outlandish places and think they can say anything! I'll knock his yellow dog's teeth . . .!'

While, inside, his heart went quailing, crying for help, afraid.

He tried hard to remember exactly what old John had said. Round Garden Lake – that's where Jim was located in his lonely Post – there was a tribe of Redskins. They were of unusual type. Malefactors among them – thieves, criminals, murderers – were not punished. They were merely turned out by the Tribe to die.

But how?

The Wolves of God took care of them. What were the Wolves of God?

A pack of wolves the Redskins held in awe, a sacred pack, a spirit pack – God curse the man! Absurd, outlandish nonsense! Superstitious humbug! A pack of wolves that punished malefactors, killing but never eating them. 'Torn but not eaten,' the words came back to him, 'white men as well as red. They could even cross the sea.'

'He ought to be strung up for telling such wild yarns. By God – I'll teach him!'

'Jim! My brother, Jim! It's monstrous!'

But the old man, in his passionate cold justice, had said a yet more terrible thing, a thing that Tom would never forget, as he never could forgive it: 'You mustn't keep him here; you must send him away. We cannot have him on the island.' And for that, though he could scarcely believe his ears, wondering afterwards whether he heard aright, for that, the proper answer to which was a blow in the mouth, Tom knew that his old friendship and affection had turned to bitter hatred.

'If I don't kill him, for that cursed lie, may God – and Jim – forgive me!'

III

It was a few days later that the storm caught the islands, making them tremble in their sea-born bed. The wind tearing over the treeless expanse was terrible, the lightning lit the skies. No such rain had ever been known. The building shook and trembled. It almost seemed the sea had burst her limits, and the waves poured in. Its fury and the noises that the wind made affected both the brothers, but Jim disliked the uproar most. It made him gloomy, silent, morose. It made him – Tom perceived it at once – uneasy. 'Scared in his soul' – the ugly phrase came back to him.

'God save anyone who's out tonight,' said Jim anxiously, as the old farm rattled about his head. Whereupon the door opened as of itself. There was no knock. It flew wide, as if the wind had burst it. Two drenched and beaten figures showed in the gap against the lurid sky – old John Rossiter and Sandy. They laid their fowling pieces down and took off their capes; they had been up at the lake for the evening flight and six birds were in the game bag. So suddenly had the storm come up that they had been caught before they could get home.

And, while Tom welcomed them, looked after their creature wants, and made them feel at home as in duty bound, no visit, he felt at the same time, could have been less opportune. Sandy did not matter – Sandy never did matter anywhere, his personality being negligible – but John Rossiter was the last man Tom wished to see just then. He hated the man; hated that sense of implacable justice that he knew was in him; with the slightest excuse he would have turned him out and sent him on to his own home, storm or no storm. But Rossiter provided no excuse; he was all gratitude and easy politeness, more pleasant and friendly to Jim even than to his brother. Tom set out the whisky and sugar, sliced the lemon, put the kettle on, and furnished dry coats while the soaked garments hung up before the roaring fire that Orkney makes customary even when days are warm.

'It might be the equinoctials,' observed Sandy, 'if it wasn't late October.' He shivered, for the tropics had thinned his blood.

'This ain't no ordinary storm,' put in Rossiter, drying his drenched boots. 'It reminds me a bit' – he jerked his head to the window that gave seawards, the rush of rain against the panes half drowning his voice – 'reminds me a bit of yonder.' He looked up, as though to find someone to agree with him, only one such person being in the room.

'Sure, it ain't,' agreed Jim at once, but speaking slowly, 'no ordinary storm.' His voice was quiet as a child's. Tom, stooping over the kettle, felt something cold go trickling down his back.

'It's from acrost the Atlantic too.'

'All our big storms come from the sea,' offered Sandy, saying just what Sandy was expected to say. His lank red hair lay matted on his forehead, making him look like an unhappy collie dog.

'There's no hospitality,' Rossiter changed the talk, 'like an islander's,' as Tom mixed and filled the glasses. 'He don't even ask "Say when?"' He chuckled in his beard and turned to Sandy, well pleased with the compliment to his host. 'Now, in Malay,' he added dryly, 'it's probably different, I guess.' And the two men, one from Labrador, the other from the tropics, fell to bantering one another with heavy humour, while Tom made things comfortable and Jim stood silent with his back to the fire. At each blow of the wind that shook the building, a suitable remark was made, generally by Sandy: 'Did you hear that now?' 'Ninety miles an hour at least!' 'Good thing you build solid in this country!' while Rossiter occasionally repeated that it was an 'uncommon storm' and that 'it reminded him' of northern tempests he had known 'out yonder.'

Tom said little, one thought and one thought only in his heart – the wish that the storm would abate and his guests depart. He felt uneasy about Jim. He hated Rossiter. In the kitchen he had steadied himself already with a good stiff drink, and was now half-way through a second; the feeling was in him that he would need their help before the evening was out. Jim, he noticed, had left his glass untouched. His attention, clearly, went to the wind and the outer night; he added little to the conversation.

'Hark!' cried Sandy's shrill voice. 'Did you hear that? That wasn't wind, I'll swear.' He sat up, looking for all the world like a dog pricking its ears to something no one else could hear.

'The sea coming over the dunes,' said Rossiter. 'There'll be an awful tide tonight and a terrible sea off the Swarf. Moon at the full, too.' He cocked his head sideways to listen. The roaring was tremendous, waves and wind combining with a result that almost shook the ground. Rain hit the glass with incessant volleys like duck shot.

It was then that Jim spoke, having said no word for a long time.

'It's good there's no trees,' he mentioned quietly. 'I'm glad of that.'

'There'd be fearful damage, wouldn't there?' remarked Sandy. 'They might fall on the house too.'

But it was the tone Jim used that made Rossiter turn stiffly in his chair, looking first at the speaker, then at his brother. Tom caught both glances and saw the hard keen glitter in the eyes. This kind of talk, he decided, had got to stop, yet how to stop it he hardly knew, for his were not subtle methods, and rudeness to his guests ran too strong against the island customs. He refilled the glasses, thinking in his blunt fashion how best to achieve his object, when Sandy helped the situation without knowing it.

'That's my first,' he observed, and all burst out laughing. For Sandy's tenth glass was equally his 'first,' and he absorbed his liquor like a sponge, yet showed no effects of it until the moment when he would suddenly collapse and sink helpless to the ground. The glass in question, however, was only his third, the final moment still far away.

'Three in one and one in three,' said Rossiter, amid the general laughter, while Sandy, grave as a judge, half emptied it at a single gulp. Good-natured, obtuse as a cart-horse, the tropics, it seemed, had first worn out his nerves, then removed them entirely from his body. 'That's Malay theology, I guess,' finished Rossiter. And the laugh broke out again. Whereupon, setting his glass down, Sandy offered his usual explanation that the hot lands had thinned his blood, that he felt the cold in these 'Arctic islands,' and that alcohol was a necessity of life with him. Tom, grateful for the unexpected help, encouraged him to talk, and Sandy accustomed to neglect as a rule, responded readily. Having saved the situation, however, he now unwittingly led it back into the danger zone.

'A night for tales, eh?' he remarked, as the wind came howling with a burst of strange noises against the house. 'Down there in the States,' he went on, 'they'd say the evil spirits were out. They're a superstitious crowd, the natives. I remember once – ' And he told a tale, half foolish, half interesting, of a mysterious track he had seen when following buffalo in the jungle. It ran close to the spoor of a wounded buffalo for miles, a track unlike that of any known animal, and the natives, though unable to name it, regarded it with awe. It was a good sign, a kill was certain. They said it was a spirit track.

'You got your buffalo?' asked Tom.

'Found him two miles away, lying dead. The mysterious spoor came to an end close beside the carcass. It didn't continue.'

'And that reminds me – ' began old Rossiter, ignoring Tom's attempt to introduce another subject. He told them of the haunted island at Eagle River, and a tale of the man who would not stay buried on another island off the coast. From that he went on to describe the strange man-beast that hides in the deep forests of Labrador, manifesting but rarely, and dangerous to men who stray too far from camp, men with a passion for wild life over strong in their blood – the great mythical Wendigo. And while he talked, Tom noticed that Sandy used each pause as a good moment for a drink, but that Jim's glass still remained untouched.

The atmosphere of incredible things, thus, grew in the little room, much as it gathers among the shadows round a forest campfire when men who have seen strange places of the world give tongue about them, knowing they will not be laughed at – an atmosphere, once established, it is vain to fight against. The ingrained superstition that hides in every mother's son comes up at such times to breathe. It came up now. Sandy, closer by several glasses to the moment, Tom saw, when he would be suddenly drunk, gave birth again, a tale this time of a Scottish planter who had brutally dismissed a native servant for no other reason than that he disliked him. The man disappeared completely, but the villagers hinted that he would – soon indeed that he had – come back, though 'not quite as he went'. The planter armed, knowing that vengeance might be violent. A black panther, meanwhile, was seen prowling about the bungalow. One night a noise outside his door on the verandah roused him. Just in time to see the black brute leaping over the railings into the compound, he fired, and the beast fell with a savage growl of pain. Help arrived and more shots were fired into the animal, as it lay, mortally wounded already, lashing its tail upon the grass. The lanterns, however, showed that instead of a panther, it was the servant they had shot to shreds.

Sandy told the story well, a certain odd conviction in his tone and manner, neither of them at all to the liking of his host. Uneasiness and annoyance had been growing in Tom for some time already, his inability to control the situation adding to his anger. Emotion was accumulating in him dangerously; it was directed chiefly against Rossiter, who, though saying nothing definite, somehow deliberately encouraged both talk and atmosphere. Given the conditions, it was natural enough the talk should take the turn it did take, but what made Tom more and more angry was that, if Rossiter had not been present, he could have stopped it easily enough. It was the presence of the old Hudson Bay man that prevented his taking decided action. He was afraid of Rossiter, afraid of putting his back up. That was the truth. His recognition of it made him furious.

'Tell us another, Sandy McKay,' said the veteran. 'There's a lot in such tales. They're found the world over – men turning into animals and the like.'

And Sandy, yet nearer to his moment of collapse, but still showing no effects, obeyed willingly. He noticed nothing; the whisky was good, his tales were appreciated, and that sufficed him. He thanked Tom, who just then refilled his glass, and went on with his tale. But Tom, hatred and fury in his heart, had reached the point where he could no longer contain himself, and Rossiter's last words inflamed him. He went over, under cover of a tremendous clap of wind, to fill the old man's glass. The latter refused, covering the tumbler with his big, lean hand. Tom stood over him a moment, lowering his face. 'You keep still,' he whispered ferociously, but so that no one else heard it. He glared into his eyes with an intensity that held danger, and Rossiter, without answering, flung back that glare with equal, but with a calmer, anger.

The wind, meanwhile, had a trick of veering, and each time it shifted, Jim shifted his seat too. Apparently, he preferred to face the sound, rather than have his back to it.

'Your turn now for a tale,' said Rossiter with purpose, when Sandy finished. He looked across at him, just as Jim, hearing the burst of wind at the walls behind him, was in the act of moving his chair again. The same moment the attack rattled the door and windows facing him. Jim, without answering, stood for a moment still as death, not knowing which way to turn.

'It's beatin' up from all sides,' remarked Rossiter, 'like it was goin' round the building.'

There was a moment's pause, the four men listening with awe to the roar and power of the terrific wind. Tom listened too, but at the same time watched, wondering vaguely why he didn't cross the room and crash his fist into the old man's chattering mouth. Jim put out his hand and took his glass, but did not raise it to his lips. And a lull came abruptly in the storm, the wind sinking into a moment's dreadful silence. Tom and Rossiter turned their heads in the same instant and stared into each other's eyes. For Tom the instant seemed enormously prolonged. He realised the challenge in the other and that his rudeness had roused it into action. It had become a contest of wills – Justice battling against Love.

Jim's glass had now reached his lips, and the chattering of his teeth against its rim was audible.

But the lull passed quickly and the wind began again, though so gently at first, it had the sound of innumerable swift footsteps treading lightly, of countless hands fingering the doors and windows, but then suddenly with a mighty shout as it swept against the walls, rushed across the roof and descended like a battering-ram against the farther side.

'God, did you hear that?' cried Sandy. 'It's trying to get in!' and having said it, he sank in a heap beside his chair, all of a sudden completely drunk. 'It's wolves or panthersh,' he mumbled in his stupor on the floor, 'but whatsh's happened to Malay?' It was the last thing he said before unconsciousness took him, and apparently he was insensible to the kick on the head from a heavy farmer's boot. For Jim's glass had fallen with a crash and the second kick was stopped midway. Tom stood spellbound, unable to move or speak, as he watched his brother suddenly cross the room and open a window into the very teeth of the gale.

'Let be! Let be!' came the voice of Rossiter, an authority in it, a curious gentleness too, both of them new. He had risen, his lips were still moving, but the words that issued from them were inaudible, as the wind and rain leaped with a galloping violence into the room, smashing the glass to atoms and dashing a dozen loose objects helter-skelter on to the floor.

'I saw it!' cried Jim, in a voice that rose above the din and clamor of the elements. He turned and faced the others, but it was at Rossiter he looked. 'I saw the leader.' He shouted to make himself heard, although the tone was quiet. 'A splash of white on his great chest. I saw them all!'

At the words, and at the expression in Jim's eyes, old Rossiter, white to the lips, dropped back into his chair as if a blow had struck him. Tom, petrified, felt his own heart stop. For through the broken window, above yet within the wind, came the sound of a wolf-pack running, howling in deep, full-throated chorus, mad for blood. It passed like a whirlwind and was gone. And, of the three men so close together, one sitting and two standing, Jim alone was in that terrible moment wholly master of himself.

Before the others could move or speak, he turned and looked full into the eyes of each in succession. His speech went back to his wilderness days.

'I done it,' he said calmly. 'I killed him — and I got ter go.'

With a look of mystical horror on his face, he took one stride, flung the door wide, and vanished into the darkness.

So quick were both words and action, that Tom's paralysis passed only as the draught from the broken window banged the door behind him. He seemed to leap across the room, old Rossiter, tears on his cheeks and his lips mumbling foolish words, so close upon his heels that the backward blow of fury Tom aimed at his face caught him only in the neck and sent him reeling sideways to the floor instead of flat upon his back.

'Murderer! My brother's death upon you!' he shouted as he tore the door open again and plunged out into the night.

And the odd thing that happened then, the thing that touched old John Rossiter's reason, leaving him from that moment till his death a foolish man of uncertain mind and memory, happened when he and the unconscious, drink-sodden Sandy lay alone together on the stone floor of that farm-house room.

Rossiter, dazed by the blow and his fall, but in full possession of his senses, and the anger gone out of him owing to what he brought about, this same John Rossiter sat up and saw Sandy sober as a judge, his eyes and speech both clear, even his face unflushed.

'John Rossiter,' he said, 'it was not God who appointed you executioner. It was the devil.' And his eyes, thought Rossiter, were like the eyes of an angel.

'Sandy McKay,' he stammered, his teeth chattering and breath failing him. 'Sandy McKay!' It was all the words that he could find. But Sandy, already sunk back into his stupor again, was stretched drunk and incapable upon the farm-house floor, and remained in that condition till the dawn.

Jim's body lay hidden among the dunes for many months and in spite of the most careful and prolonged searching. It was another storm that laid it bare. The sand had covered it. The clothes were gone, and the flesh, torn but not eaten, was naked to the December sun and wind.

Andrew Dodds (1872 – ?)

The Coo Park

I'm echty-five; and frae I was a bairn
I never mind the coo park 'neth the ploo;
And, when I saw the cou'ter tearin' 't thro',
Deep in my very hairt I felt the airn.

Gin the auld maister in his grave could lairn
O' this, he wad be mad. It never grew
But tails tae cattle beasts. And here it's noo –
They want a crap o' tatties oot the shairn*.   cow-dung

Ay, weel-a-wat, I've lived ayont my lease:
Auld days, auld ways, auld things are at an end.   10
The war has finished a'; and ne'er will peace
Bring back tae me the auld warld that I kenned.
Ay when that airman landed on the coo,
I jist said tae mysel', *We've come till't noo*.

John Ferguson (1873 – 1928)

The 'little theatre' movement which swept Europe following the revolutionary plays of Ibsen, Strindberg and the like reached Scotland, where it took root in the Glasgow Repertory Theatre (1909–1914). Most of the plays produced therein were English or Continental, but a few Scottish works appeared. One of these was a fine one-act tragedy, 'Campbell of Kilmohr' (1914). It is John Ferguson's only significant work.

    The play describes an incident in the pursuit of Bonnie Prince Charlie following the latter's 1746 defeat at Culloden. It is useful to remember that the Campbell clan had remained loyal to King George and thus stood to profit from the Jacobite loss, and that the then nearly incredible sum of thirty thousand pounds had been offered as a reward for Charles' capture.

Campbell of Kilmohr

Scene: Interior of a lonely cottage on the road from Struan to Rannoch, in North Perthshire.
Time: 1746, just after the collapse of the '45 Rebellion.

MORAG is restlessly moving backwards and forwards. The old woman is seated on a low stool beside the peat fire in the centre of the floor. The room is scantily furnished and the women are poorly clad. MORAG barefooted. At the back is the door that leads to the outside. On the left of the door is a small window. On the right side of the room there is a door that opens into a barn.

MORAG stands for a moment at the window, looking out.

MORAG It is the wild night outside.

MARY STEWART Is the snow still coming down?

MORAG It is that then – dancing and swirling with the wind too, and never stopping at all,
Aye, and so black I cannot see the other side of the road.

MARY STEWART That is good.

> MORAG *moves across the floor and stops irresolutely. She is restless, expectant.*

MORAG Will I be putting the light in the window?

MARY STEWART Why should you be doing that! You have not heard his call *(turns eagerly)*,
have you?

MORAG *(with sign of head)* No, but the light in the window would show him all is well.

MARY STEWART It would not then! The light was to be put there after we had heard the
signal.

MORAG But on a night like this he may have been calling for long and we never hear him.

MARY STEWART Do not be so anxious, Morag. Keep to what he says. Put more peat on the
fire now and sit down.

MORAG *(with increasing excitement)* I canna, I canna! There is that in me that tells me
something is going to befall us this night. Oh, that wind, hear to it, sobbing round the
house as if it brought some poor lost soul up to the door, and we refusing it shelter.

MARY STEWART Do not be fretting yourself like that. Do as I bid you. Put more peats to the
fire.

MORAG *(at the wicker peat-basket)* Never since I . . . What was that? *(Both listening for a
moment.)*

MARY STEWART It was just the wind; it is rising more. A sore night for them that are out in
the heather.

> MORAG *puts peat on the fire without speaking.*

MARY STEWART Did you notice were there many people going by today?

MORAG No. After daybreak the redcoats came by from Struan: and there was no more till
nine, when an old man like the Catechist from Killichonan passed. At four o'clock, just
when the dark was falling, a horseman with a lad holding to the stirrup, and running
fast, went by towards Rannoch.

MARY STEWART But no more redcoats?

MORAG *(shaking her head)* The road has been as quiet as the hills, and they as quiet as the
grave. Do you think he will come?

MARY STEWART Is it you think I have the gift, girl, that you ask me that? All I know is that
it is five days since he was here for meat and drink for himself and for the others – five
days and five nights, mind you; and little enough he took away; and those in hiding no'
used to sore lying I'll be thinking. He must try to get through tonight. But that
quietness, with no one to be seen from daylight till dark, I do not like it, Morag. They
must know something. They must be watching.

> A sound is heard by both women. They stand listening.

MARY STEWART Haste you with the light, Morag.

MORAG But it came from the back of the house – from the hillside.

MARY STEWART Do as I tell you. The other side may be watched.

> A candle is lit and placed in the window. GIRL goes hurrying to the door.

MARY STEWART Stop, stop! Would you be opening the door with a light like that shining
from the house? A man would be seen against it in the doorway for a mile. And who
knows what eyes may be watching? Put out the light now and cover the fire.

> Room is reduced to semi-darkness, and the door unbarred. Someone enters.

MORAG You are cold, Dugald!

> STEWART, *very exhausted, signs assent.*

MORAG And wet, oh, wet through and through!

STEWART Erricht Brig was guarded, well guarded. I had to win across the water.

> *The* OLD WOMAN *has now relit candle and taken away plaid from fire.*

MARY STEWART Erricht Brig – then –

STEWART *(nods)* Yes – in a corrie, on the far side of Dearig half-way up.

MARY STEWART Himself is there then?

STEWART Aye, and Keppoch as well, and another and a greater is with them.

MARY STEWART Wheest! *(Glances at Morag.)*

STEWART Mother, is it that you can°

MARY STEWART Yes, yes, Morag will bring out the food for ye to carry back. It is under the hay in the barn, well hid. Morag will bring it. Go, Morag, and bring it.

> MORAG *enters other room or barn which opens on right.*

STEWART Mother, I wonder at ye; Morag would never tell – never.

MARY STEWART Morag is only a lass yet. She has never been tried. And who knows what she might be made to tell.

STEWART Well, well, it is no matter, for I was telling you where I left them, but not where I am to find them.

MARY STEWART They are not where you said now?

STEWART No; they left the corrie last night, and I am to find them *(whispers)* in a quiet part on Rannoch Moor.

MARY STEWART It is well for a young lass not to be knowing. Do not tell her.

STEWART Well, well, I will not tell her. Then she cannot tell where they are even if she wanted to. *(He sits down at table; the* OLD WOMAN *ministers to his wants.)*

STEWART A fire is a merry thing on a night like this; and a roof over the head is a great comfort.

MARY STEWART Ye'll no can stop the night?

STEWART No. I must be many a mile from here before the day breaks on Ben Dearig.

> MORAG *re-enters.*

MORAG It was hard to get through, Dugald?

STEWART You may say that. I came down Erricht for three miles, and then when I reached low country I had to take to walking in the burns because of the snow that shows a man's steps and tells who he is to them that can read; and there's plenty can do that abroad, God knows.

MORAG But none spied ye?

STEWART Who can tell? Before dark came, from far up on the slopes of Dearig I saw soldiers down below; and away towards Rannoch Moor they were scattered all over the country like black flies on a white sheet. A wild-cat or anything that couldna fly could never have got through. And men at every brig and ford and pass! I had to strike away up across the slopes again; and even so as I turned round the bend beyond Kilrain I ran straight into a sentry sheltering behind a great rock. But after all that it was easy going.

MORAG How could that be?

STEWART Well, you see, I took the boots off him, and then I had no need to mind who might see my steps in the snow.

MORAG You took the boots off him!

STEWART *(laughing)* I did that same. Does that puzzle your bonny head? How does a lad take the boots off a redcoat? Find out the answer, my lass, while I will be finishing my meat.

MORAG Maybe he was asleep?

STEWART Asleep! Asleep! Well, well, he sleeps sound enough now, with the ten toes of him pointed to the sky.

The OLD WOMAN *has taken up dirk from table. She puts it down again.* MORAG *sees the action, and pushes dirk away so that it rolls off the table and drops to the floor. She hides her face in her hands.*

MARY STEWART Morag, bring in the kebbuck o' cheese. Now that all is well and safe it is we that will look after his comfort tonight. (MORAG *goes into barn.)* I mind well her mother saying to me – it was one day in the black winter that she died, when the frost took the land in its grip and the birds fell stiff from the trees, and the deer came down and put their noses to the door – I mind well her saying just before she died– *(Loud knocking at the door.)*

A VOICE In the King's name! *(Both rise, startled.)*

MARY STEWART *(recovering first)* The hay in the barn – quick my son. *(Knocking continues.)*

A VOICE Open in the King's name!

STEWART *snatches up such articles as would reveal his presence and hurries into barn. He overlooks dirk on floor. The* OLD WOMAN *goes towards door, slowly, to gain time.*

MARY STEWART Who is there? What do you want?

A VOICE Open, open.

MARY STEWART *opens door, and* CAMPBELL OF KILMOHR *follows* CAPTAIN SANDEMAN *into the house. Behind Kilmohr comes a man carrying a leather wallet,* JAMES MACKENZIE, *his clerk. The rear is brought up by soldiers carrying arms.*

SANDEMAN Ha, the bird has flown.

CAMPBELL *(who has struck dirk with his foot and picked it up)* But the nest is warm; look at this.

SANDEMAN It seems as if we had disturbed him at supper. Search the house, men.

MARY STEWART I'm just a lonely old woman. You have been misguided. I was getting through my supper.

CAMPBELL *(holding up dirk)* And this was your toothpick, eh? Na! na! We ken whaur we are, and wha we want, and, by Cruachan, I think we've got him.

Sounds are heard from barn, and soldiers return with MORAG. *She has stayed in hiding from fear, and she still holds the cheese in her hands.*

SANDEMAN What have we here!

CAMPBELL A lass!

MARY STEWART It's just my dead brother's daughter. She was getting me the cheese, as you can see.

CAMPBELL On men, again: the other turtle-doo will no be far away. *(Bantering, to the old woman.)* Tut, tut, Mistress Stewart, and do ye have her wait upon ye while your leddyship dines alane! A grand way to treat your dead brother's daughter; fie, fie upon ye!

SOLDIERS *reappear with Stewart, whose arms are pinioned.*

CAMPBELL Did I no' tell ye! And this, Mrs Stewart, will be your dead sister's son, I'm thinking; or aiblins your leddyship's butler! Weel, woman, I'll tell ye this: Pharaoh spared ae butler, but Erchie Campbell will no spare anither. Na! na! Pharaoh's case is no' to be taken as forming ony preceedent. And so if he doesna answer certain questions we have to speir at him, before morning he'll hang as high as Haman. (STEWART *is placed before the table at which Campbell has seated himself:* TWO SOLDIERS *guard Stewart. Another is behind Campbell's chair and another is by the door. The clerk,* MACKENZIE, *is seated at up corner of table.* SANDEMAN *stands by the fire.)*

CAMPBELL *(to Stewart)* Weel, sir, it is within the cognisance of the law that you have knowledge and information of the place of harbor and concealment used by certain persons who are in a state of proscription. Furthermore, it is known that four days ago certain other proscribed persons did join with these, and that they are banded together in an endeavor to secure the escape from these dominions of His Majesty, King George, of certain persons who by their crimes and treasons lie open to the capital charge. What say ye?

> STEWART *makes no reply.*

CAMPBELL Ye admit this then?

> STEWART *as before.*

CAMPBELL Come, come, my lad. Ye stand in great jeopardy. Great affairs of state lie behind this which are beyond your simple understanding. Speak up, and it will be the better for ye.

> STEWART *silent as before.*

CAMPBELL Look you. I'll be frank with you. No harm will befall you this night (and I wish all in this house to note my words) – no harm will befall you this night if you supply the information required.

> STEWART *as before.*

CAMPBELL *(with sudden passion)* Sandeman, put your sword to the carcass o' this muckle ass and see will it louse his tongue.

> SANDEMAN *does not move.*

STEWART It may be as well then, Mr Campbell, that I should say a word to save your breath. It is this: Till you talk Rannoch Loch to the top of Schiehallion ye'll no' talk me into a yea or nay.

CAMPBELL *(quietly)* Say ye so? Noo, I wadna be so very sure if I were you. I've had a lairge experience o' life and speaking out of it I would say that only fools and the dead never change their minds.

STEWART *(quietly too)* Then you'll be adding to your experience tonight, Mr Campbell, and you'll have something to put on the other side of it.

CAMPBELL *(tapping his snuff-box)* Very possibly, young sir, but what I would present for your consideration is this: While ye may be prepared to keep your mouth shut under the condition of a fool, are ye equally prepared to do so in the condition of a dead man?

> CAMPBELL *waits expectantly.* STEWART *silent as before.*

CAMPBELL Tut, tut, now if it's afraid ye are, my lad, with my hand on my heart and on my word as a gentleman . . .

STEWART Afraid! *(He spits in contempt towards Campbell.)*

CAMPBELL *(enraged)* Ye damned stubborn Hieland stot . . . *(To Sandeman.)* Have him taken out. We'll get it another way.

> CAMPBELL *rises.* STEWART *is moved into barn by soldiers, who remain with him.*

CAMPBELL *(walking)* Some puling eediots, Sandeman, would applaud this contumacy and call it constancy. Constancy! Now, I've had a lairge experience o' life, and I never saw yet a sensible man insensible to the touch of yellow metal. If there may be such a man, it is demonstrable that he is no sensible man. Fideelity! quotha, it's sheer obstinacy. They just see that ye want something oot o' them, and they're so damned selfish and thrawn[1] they winna pairt. And with the natural inabeelity o' their brains to hold mair

----

[1] Twisted, cantankerous.

than one idea at a time, they canna see that in return you could put something into their palms far more profitable. *(Sits again at table.)* Aweel, bring Mistress Stewart up.

OLD WOMAN *is placed before him where son had been.*

CAMPBELL *(more ingratiatingly)* Weel noo, Mistress Stewart, good woman, this is a sair predeecament for ye to be in. I would jist counsel ye to be candid. Doubtless yer mind is a' in a swirl. Ye kenna what way to turn. Maybe ye are like the Psalmist and say: 'I lookit this way and that, and there was no man to peety me, or to have compassion upon my fatherless children.' But, see now, ye would be wrong; and, if ye tell me a' ye ken, I'll stand freends wi' ye. Put your trust in Erchie Campbell.

MARY STEWART I trust no Campbell.

CAMPBELL Weel, weel, noo, I'm no' jist that set up wi' them myself. There's but ae Campbell that I care muckle aboot, after a'. But, good wife, it's no' the Campbells we're trying the noo; so, as time presses, we'll jist birze yont as they say themselves. Noo then, speak up.

MARY STEWART *is silent.*

CAMPBELL *(beginning grimly and, passing through astonishment, expostulation, and a feigned contempt for mother and pity for son to a pretense of sadness which, except at the end, makes his words come haltingly)* Ah! ye also. I suppose ye understand, woman, how it will go wi' your son? *(To his clerk.)* Here's a fine mother for ye, James! Would you believe it? She kens what would save her son – the very babe she nursed at her breast; but will she save him? Na! na! Sir, he may look after himself! A mother, a mother! Ha! ha! (CAMPBELL *laughs.* MACKENZIE *titters foolishly.* CAMPBELL *pauses to watch effect of his words.)* Aye, you would think, James, that she would remember the time when he was but little and afraid of all the terrors that walk in darkness, and how he looked up to her as to a tower of safety, and would run to her with outstretched hands, hiding his face from his fear, in her gown. The darkness! It is the dark night and a long journey before him now. *(He pauses again.)* You would think, James, that she would mind how she happit[1] him from the cold of winter and sheltered him from the summer heats, and, when he began to find his footing, how she had an eye on a' the beasts of the field, and on the water and the fire that were become her enemies. And to what purpose all this care? – tell me that, my man, to what good, if she is to leave him at the last to dangle from a tree at the end of a hempen rope – to see his flesh to be meat for the fowls of the air – her son, her little son!

MARY STEWART *(softly)* My son – my little son! . . . oh, *(more loudly)* but my son he has done no crime.

CAMPBELL Has he no'? Weel, mistress, as ye'll no' take my word for it, maybe ye'll list to Mr Mackenzie here. What say ye, James?

MACKENZIE He is guilty of aiding and abetting in the concealment of proscribed persons; likewise with being found in the possession of arms, contrary to statute, both very heinous crimes.

CAMPBELL Very well said, James! Forby, between ourselves, Mrs Stewart, the young man in my opeenion is guilty of another crime *(snuffs)* – he is guilty of the heinous crime of not knowing on which side his bread is buttered. Come now . . .

MARY STEWART Ye durst not lay a finger on the lad, ye durst not hang him.

MACKENZIE And why should the gentleman not hang him if it pleasure him?

CAMPBELL *taps snuff-box and takes pinch.*

MARY STEWART *(with intensity)* Campbell of Kilmohr, lay but one finger on Dugald Stewart

---

[1] Clothed, sheltered.

and the weight of Ben Cruachan will be light to the weight that will be laid on your soul. I will lay the curse of the seven rings upon your life. I will call up the fires of Ephron, the blue and the green and the grey fires, for the destruction of your soul. I will curse you in your homestead and in the wife it shelters, and in the children that will never bear your name. Yea and ye shall be cursed.

CAMPBELL *(startled, betrays agitation – the snuff is spilt from his trembling hand)* Hoot, toot, woman! ye're, ye're . . . *(Angrily.)* Ye auld beldame, to say such things to me! I'll have ye first whippit and syne droont for a witch. Damn thae stubborn and supersteetious cattle! *(To* SANDEMAN.) We should have come in here before him and listened in the barn, Sandeman!

SANDEMAN *(in quick staccato, always cool)* Ah, listen behind the door you mean! Now I never thought of that!

CAMPBELL Did ye not! Humph! Well, no doubt there are a good many things in the universe that yet wait for your thought upon them. What would be your objections, now?

SANDEMAN There are two objections, Kilmohr, that you would understand.

CAMPBELL Name them.

SANDEMAN Well, in the first place, we have not wings like crows to fly . . . and the footsteps on the snow . . . Second point: the woman would have told him we were there.

CAMPBELL Not if I told her I had the power to clap her in Inverness jail.

MARY STEWART *(in contempt)* Yes, even if ye had told me ye had power to clap me in hell, Mr Campbell.

CAMPBELL Lift me that screeching Jezebel oot o' here; Sandeman, we'll mak' a quick finish o' this. (SOLDIERS *take her towards barn.)* No, not there, pitch the old girzie into the snow.

MARY STEWART *(as she is led outside)* Ye'll never find him, Campbell, never, never!

CAMPBELL *(enraged)* Find him, aye, by God I'll find him, if I have to keek under every stone on the mountains from the Boar of Badenoch to the Sow of Athole. (OLD WOMAN *and* SOLDIERS *go outside, leaving only* CAMPBELL, MACKENZIE, SANDEMAN, *and* MORAG *in the room;* MORAG *huddled up on stool.)* And now, Captain Sandeman, you an' me must have a word or two. I noted your objection to listening ahint doors and so on. Now, I make a' necessary allowances for youth and the grand and magneeficent ideas commonly held, for a little while, in that period. I had them myself But, man, gin ye had trod the floor of the Parliament Hoose in Edinburry as long as I did, wi' a pair o' thin hands at the bottom o' toom[1] pockets, ye'd ha'e shed your fine notions, as I did. Noo, fine pernickety noansense will no' do in this business–

SANDEMAN Sir!

CAMPBELL Softly, softly, Captain Sandeman, and hear till what I have to say. I have noticed with regret several things in your remarks and bearing which are displeasing to me. I would say just one word in your ear; it is this: These things, Sandeman, are not conducive to advancement in His Majesty's service.

SANDEMAN *(after a brief pause in which the two eye each other)* Kilmohr, I am a soldier, and if I speak out my mind you must pardon me if my words are blunt: I do not like this work, but I loathe your methods.

CAMPBELL Mislike the methods you may, but the work ye must do! Methods are my business. Let me tell you the true position. In ae word it is no more and no less than this. You and me are baith here to carry out the proveesions of the Act for the Pacification of the Highlands. That means the cleaning up of a very big mess, Sandeman, a very big mess. Now, what is your special office in this work? I'll tell ye,

---

[1] Empty.

man; you and your men are just beesoms[1] in the hands of the law-officers of the Crown. In this district, I order and ye soop.[2] *(He indicates door of barn.)* Now soop, Captain Sandeman.

SANDEMAN What are you after? I would give something to see into your mind.

CAMPBELL Ne'er fash[3] aboot my mind: what has a soldier to do wi' ony mental operations? It's His Grace's orders that concerns you. Oot wi' your man and set him up against the wa'.

SANDEMAN Kilmohr, it is murder – murder, Kilmohr!

CAMPBELL Hoots awa', man, it's a thing o' nae special signeeficence.

SANDEMAN I must ask you for a warrant.

CAMPBELL Quick, then: Mackenzie will bring it out to you. (CLERK *begins writing as* SANDEMAN *goes and orders the soldiers to lead Stewart outside.* CAMPBELL *sits very still and thoughtful.* CLERK *finishes writing and places warrant before Campbell for his signature.)*

MACKENZIE At this place, sir.

CAMPBELL *(again alert)* Hoots, I was forgetting.

MACKENZIE It is a great power ye have in your hands, Kilmohr, to be able to send a man to death on the nod, as ye might say.

CAMPBELL *(sitting back, pen in hand)* Power! power say ye? Man, do ye no' see I've been beaten. Do ye no' see that? Archibald Campbell and a' his men and his money are less to them than the wind blowing in their faces.

MACKENZIE Well, it's a strange thing that.

CAMPBELL *(throwing down the pen and rising)* Aye, it's a strange thing that. It's a thing fit to sicken a man against the notion that there are probabilities on this earth . . . Ye see, James, beforehand I would have said nothing could be easier.

MACKENZIE Than to get them to tell?

CAMPBELL Aye, just that. But you heard what he said: 'You'll be adding to your experience this night, Mr Campbell, and you'll have something to put to the other side of it,' says he. *(Paces away, hands behind back.)* Aye, and I have added something to it, a thing I like but little. *(Turning to face Mackenzie with raised hand.)* Do you see what it is, James? A dream can be stronger than a strong man armed. Just a whispered word, a pointed finger even, would ha'e tell'd us a'. But no! no! And so I am powerless before the visions and dreams of an old woman and a half-grown lad.

MACKENZIE *(who now stands waiting for the warrant)* No' exactly powerless, Kilmohr, for if ye canna open his mouth ye can shut it; and there's some satisfaction in that.

CAMPBELL *(sitting down to sign warrant)* No' to me, man, no' to me. *(He hands the paper to Mackenzie, who goes out.)* For I've been beaten. Aye, the pair o' them have beat me, though it's only a matter o' seconds till one o' them be dead.

MORAG *(her voice coming quickly, in a sharp whisper, like an echo of Campbell's last word as she sits up to stare at him)* Dead!

CAMPBELL *(startled)* What is it?

MORAG *(slowly)* Is he dead?

CAMPBELL *(aloud)* Oh, it's you. I'd forgotten you were there.

MORAG *(in same tone)* Is he dead?

CAMPBELL *(grimly)* Not yet. But if ye'll look through this window presently ye'll see him gotten ready for death.

> He picks up hat, gloves, cloak, and is about to go out.

MORAG *(after a pause, very slowly and brokenly)* I – will – tell – you.

CAMPBELL *(astounded)* What!

---

[1] Brooms.
[2] Sweep.
[3] Trouble.

MORAG I will tell you all you are seeking to know.

CAMPBELL *(in a whisper, thunderstruck)* God, and to think, to think I was on the very
act . . . on the very act of . . . *(Recovering.)* Tell me – tell me at once.

MORAG You will promise that he will not be hanged?

CAMPBELL He will not. I swear it.

MORAG You will give him back to me?

CAMPBELL I will give him back – unhung.

MORAG Then (CAMPBELL *comes near*), in a corrie half-way up the far side of Dearig – God
save me!

CAMPBELL *(in exultation)* Dished after a'. I've clean dished them! Loard, Loard! *(With intense
solemnity clasping hands and looking upwards.)* Once more I can believe in the rationality
of thy world. *(Gathers up again his cloak, hat, etc.)* And to think . . . to think . . . I was on
the very act of going away like a beaten dog!

MORAG He is safe from hanging now?

CAMPBELL *(chuckles and looks out at window before replying, and is at door when he speaks)* Very
near it, very near it. Listen! *(He holds up his hand – a volley of musketry is heard.* KILMOHR
goes out, leaving door wide open. After a short interval of silence, the OLD WOMAN *enters and
advances a few steps towards the girl, who has sunk on her knees at the volley.)*

MARY STEWART Did you hear, Morag Cameron, did you hear?

The GIRL *is sobbing, her face covered by her hands.*

MARY STEWART Och! be quiet now. I would be listening till the last sound of it passes into
the great hills and over all the wide world . . . It is fitting for you to be crying, a child
that cannot understand, but water shall never wet eye of mine for Dugald Stewart. Last
night I was but the mother of a lad that herded sheep on the Athole hills: this morn it is
I that am the mother of a man who is among the great ones of the earth. All over the
land they will be telling of Dugald Stewart. Mothers will teach their children to be men
by him. High will his name be with the teller of fine tales . . . The great men came,
they came in their pride, terrible like the storm they were, and cunning with the words
of guile were they. Death was with them . . . He was but a lad, a young lad, with great
length of days before him, and the grandeur of the world. But he put it all from him.
'Speak,' said they, 'speak, and life and great riches will be for yourself.' But he said no
word at all! Loud was the swelling of their wrath! Let the heart of you rejoice, Morag
Cameron, for the snow is red with his blood. There are things greater than death. Let
them that are children shed the tears.

She comes forward and lays her hand on the girl's shoulder.

MARY STEWART Let us go and lift him into the house, and not be leaving him lie out there
alone.

Curtain.

Donald Mackenzie (1873 – 1936)

The Blue Men of the Minch

When the tide is at the turning and the wind is fast asleep,
And not a wave is curling on the wide, blue Deep,
O the waters will be churning on the stream that never smiles,
Where the Blue Men are splashing round the charmed isles.

As the summer wind goes droning o'er the sun-bright seas,
And the Minch is all a-dazzle to the Hebrides;
They will skim along like salmon – you can see their shoulders gleam,
And the flashing of their fingers in the Blue Men's Stream.

But when the blast is raving and the wild tide races,
The Blue Men are breast-high with foam-grey faces;   10
They'll plunge along with fury while they sweep the spray behind,
O, they'll bellow o'er the billows and wail upon the wind.

And if my boat be storm-tossed and beating for the bay,
They'll be howling and be growling as they drench it with their spray –
For they'd like to heel it over to their laughter when it lists,
Or crack the keel between them, or stave it with their fists.

O weary on the Blue Men, their anger and their wiles.
The whole day long, the whole night long, they're splashing round the isles;
They'll follow every fisher – ah, they'll haunt the fisher's dream –
When billows toss, O who would cross the Blue Men's Stream?   20

The Wee Folk

    In the knoll that is the greenest,
    And the grey cliff side,
    And on the lonely ben*-top   mountain
    The wee folk bide;
    They'll flit among the heather,
    And trip upon the brae –
    The wee folk, the green folk, the red folk and grey.

    As o'er the moor at midnight
    The wee folk pass,
    They whisper 'mong the rushes   10
    And o'er the green grass.
    All through the marshy places
    They glint and pass away –
    The light folk, the lone folk, the folk that will not stay.

O many a fairy milkmaid
With the one eye blind,
Is 'mid the lonely mountains
By the red deer hind.
Not one will wait to greet me,
For they have naught to say –   20
The hill folk, the still folk, the folk that flit away.

When the golden moon is glinting
In the deep, dim wood,
There's a fairy piper playing
To the elfin brood;
They dance and shout and turn about,
And laugh and swing and sway –
The droll folk, the knoll folk, the folk that dance alway.

O we that bless the wee folk
Have naught to fear,   30
And ne'er an elfin arrow
Will come us near;
For they'll give skill in music,
And every wish obey –
The wise folk, the peace folk, the folk that work and play.

They'll hasten here at harvest,
They will shear and bind;
They'll come with elfin music
On a western wind;
All night they'll sit among the sheaves,   40
Or herd the kine that stray –
The quick folk, the fine folk, the folk that ask no pay.

Betimes* they will be spinning   early
The while we sleep.
They'll clamber down the chimney,
Or through keyholes creep;
And when they come to borrow meal
We'll ne'er them send away –
The good folk, the honest folk, the folk that work alway.

O never wrong the wee folk –   50
The red folk and green,
Nor name them on the Fridays,
Or at Hallowe'en.
The helpless and unwary then
And bairns they lure away –
The fierce folk, the angry folk, the folk that steal and slay.

Robert Service (1874 – 1958)

Robert Service is sometimes treated as a Canadian poet, but he seems to have regarded himself as a citizen of the world, and of Scotland as much as any particular country. He was born in England, raised and educated in Scotland. As a young man he emigrated to Canada, where he wrote the Yukon ballads that made him famous. Thereafter, he spent most of his life in Europe, primarily in France, still writing poetry, though with steadily decreasing popular success. His ballads, not unlike the ones he encountered as a boy in Scotland, have narrative vigor, strong rhythm and a considerable degree of whimsy.

The Cremation of Sam McGee

There are strange things done in the midnight sun
By the men who moil for gold;
The Arctic trails have their secret tales
That would make your blood run cold.
The Northern Lights have seen queer sights,
But the queerest they ever did see
Was that night on the marge of Lake Lebarge
I cremated Sam McGee.

Now Sam McGee was from Tennessee, where the cotton blooms and blows.
Why he left his home in the South to roam 'round the Pole, God only knows.

10

He was always cold, but the land of gold seemed to hold him like a spell;
Though he'd often say in his homely way that 'he'd sooner live in hell.'

On a Christmas Day we were mushing our way over the Dawson trail.
Talk of your cold! through the parka's fold it stabbed like a driven nail,
If our eyes we'd close, then the lashes froze till sometimes we couldn't see;
It wasn't much fun, but the only one to whimper was Sam McGee.

And that very night, as we lay packed tight in our robes beneath the snow,
And the dogs were fed, and the stars o'er head were dancing heel and toe,
He turned to me, and 'Cap,' says he, 'I'll cash in this trip, I guess;
And if I do, I'm asking that you won't refuse my last request.'

20

Well, he seemed so low that I couldn't say no; then he says with a sort of moan:
'It's the cursed cold, and it's got right hold till I'm chilled clean through to the bone.
Yet 'tain't being dead – it's my awful dread of the icy grave that pains;
So I want you to swear that, foul or fair, you'll cremate my last remains.'

A pal's last need is a thing to heed, so I swore I would not fail,
And we started on at the streak of dawn; but God! he looked ghastly pale.
He crouched on the sleigh, and he raved all day of his home in Tennessee;
And before nightfall a corpse was all that was left of Sam McGee.

There wasn't a breath in that land of death, and I hurried, horror-driven,
With a corpse half hid that I couldn't get rid, because of a promise given,   30
It was lashed to the sleigh, and it seemed to say: 'You may tax your brawn and brains,
But you promised true, and it's up to you to cremate those last remains.'

Now a promise made is a debt unpaid, and the trail has its own stern code.
In the days to come, though my lips were dumb, in my heart how I cursed that load.
In the long, long night, by the lone firelight, while the huskies, round in a ring,
Howled out their woes to the homeless snows – O God! how I loathed the thing.

And every day that quiet clay seemed to heavy and heavier grow;
And on I went, though the dogs were spent and the grub was getting low:
The trail was bad, and I felt half mad, but I swore I would not give in;
An I'd often sing to the hateful thing, and it hearkened with a grin.   40

Till I came to the marge of Lake Lebarge, and a derelict there lay;
It was jammed in the ice, but I saw in a trice it was called the 'Alice May.'
And I looked at it, and I thought a bit, and I looked at my frozen chum;
Then 'Here,' said I, with a sudden cry, 'is my cre-ma-tor-eum.'

Some planks I tore from the cabin floor, and I lit the boiler fire;
Some coal I found that was lying around, and I heaped the fuel higher;
The flames just soared, and the furnace roared – such a blaze you seldom see;
And I burrowed a hole in the glowing coal, and I stuffed in Sam McGee.

Then I made a hike, for I didn't like to hear him sizzle so;
And the heavens scowled, and the huskies howled, and the wind began to blow.
                    50
It was icy cold, but the hot sweat rolled down my cheeks, and I don't know why;
And the greasy smoke in an inky cloak went streaking down the sky.

I do not know how long in the snow I wrestled with grisly fear;
But the stars came out and they danced about ere again I ventured near;
I was sick with dread, but I bravely said: 'I'll just take a peep inside.
I guess he's cooked, and it's time I looked'; . . . then the door I opened wide.

And there sat Sam, looking cool and calm, in the heart of the furnace roar;
And he wore a smile you could see a mile, and he said: 'Please close that door.
It's fine in here, but I greatly fear you'll let in the cold and storm –
Since I left Plumtree, down in Tennessee, it's the first time I've been warm.'   60

> There are strange things done in the midnight sun
> By the men who moil for gold;
> The Arctic trails have their secret tales
> That would make your blood run cold.
> The Northern Lights have seen queer sights,
> But the queerest they ever did see
> Was that night on the marge of Lake Lebarge
> I cremated Sam McGee.

The Haggis of Private McPhee

'Hae ye heard whit ma auld mither's postit tae me?
It fair maks me hamesick,' says Private McPhee.
'And whit did she send ye?' says Private McPhun,
As he cockit his rifle and bleezed at a Hun.
'A haggis! A Haggis!' says Private McPhee;
'The brawest big haggis I ever did see.
And think! it's the morn when fond memory turns
Tae haggis and whuskey – the Birthday o' Burns.
We maun find a dram; then we'll ca' in the rest
O' the lads, and we'll hae a Burns' Nicht wi' the best.' 10

'Be ready at sundoon,' snapped Sergeant McCole;
'I want you two men for the List'nin' Patrol.'
Then Private McPhee looked at Private McPhun:
'I'm thinkin', ma lad, we're confoundedly done.'
Then Private McPhun looked at Private McPhee:
'I'm thinkin' auld chap, it's a' aff wi' oor spree.'
But up spoke their crony, wee Wullie McNair;
'Just lea' yer braw haggis for me tae prepare;
And as for the dram, if I search the camp roun',
We maun hae a drappie tae jist haud it doon. 20
Sae rin, lads, and think, though the nicht it be black,
O' the haggis that's waitin' ye when ye get back.'

My! but it wis waesome on Naebuddy's Land,
And the deid they were rottin' on every hand.
And the rockets like corpse candles hauntit the sky,
And the winds o' destruction went shudderin' by.
There wis skelpin' o' bullets and skirlin' o' shells,
And breengin' o' bombs and a thoosand death-knells;
But cooryin' doon in a Jack Johnson hole
Little fashed★ the twa men o' the List'nin' Patrol.   bothered
For sweeter than honey and bricht as a gem
Wis the thocht o' the haggis that waitit for them. 30

Yet alas! in oor moments o' sunniest cheer
Calamity's aften maist cruelly near.
And while the twa talked o' their puddin' divine
The Boches★ below them were howkin'★ a mine.   Germans/digging
And while the twa cracked★ o' the feast they would hae,   chatted
The fuse it wis burnin' and burnin' away.
Then sudden a roar like the thunner o' doom,
A hell-leap o' flame . . . then the wheesht★ o' the tomb.   silence

'Haw, Jock! Are ye hurtit?' says Private McPhun.
'Ay, Geordie, they've got me: I'm fearin' I'm done. 40
It's ma leg, I'm jist thinkin' it's aff at the knee;
Ye'd best gang and leave me,' says Private McPhee.
'Oh leave ye I wunna,' says Private McPhun;
'And leave ye I canna, for though I micht run,
It's no faur I wud gang, it's no muckle I'd see:

I'm blindit, and that's whit's the maiter wi' me.'
Then Private McPhee sadly shakit his heid:
'If we bide here for lang, we'll be bidin' for deid.
And yet, Georgie lad, I could gang weel content
If I'd tasted that haggis ma auld mither sent.'   50
'That's droll,' says McPhun; 'ye've just speakit ma mind.
Oh I ken it's a terrible thing tae be blind;
And yet it's no that that embitters ma lot –
It's missin' that braw muckle haggis ye've got.'
For a while they were silent; then up once again
Spoke Private McPhee, though he whussilt wi' pain:
'And why should we miss it? Between you and me
We've legs for tae run; and we've eyes for tae see.
You lend me your shanks and I'll lend you ma sicht,
And we'll baith hae a kyte-fu' o' haggis the nicht.'   60

Oh the sky it wis dourlike and dreepin' a wee,
When Private McPhun gruppit Private McPhee.
Oh the glaur* it wis fylin' and crieshin' the grun',   mud
When Private McPhee guidit Private McPhun.
'Keep clear o' them corpses – they're maybe no deid!
Haud on! There's a big muckle crater aheid.
Look oot! There's a sap; we'll be haein' a coup.
A staur-shell! For Godsake! Doun, lad, on yer daup.
Bear aff tae yer richt . . . Aw yer jist daein' fine:
Before the nicht's feenished on haggis we'll dine.'   70

There wis death and destruction on every hand;
There wis havoc and horror on Naebuddy's Land.
And the shells bickered doun wi' a crump and a glare,
And the hameless wee bullets were dingin'* the air.   striking
Yet on they went staggerin', cooryin' doun
When the stutter and cluck o' a Maxim crept roun'.
And the legs o' McPhun they were sturdy and stout,
And McPhee on his back kept a bonnie look-oot.
'On, on, ma brave lad! We're no faur frae the goal;
I can hear the braw sweerin' o' Sergeant McCole.'   80

But strength has its leemit, and Private McPhun,
Wi' a sab and a curse fell his length on the grun'.
Then Private McPhee shoutit doon in his ear:
'Jist think o' the haggis! I smell it from here.
It's gushin' wi' juice, it's embaumin' the air;
It's steamin' for us, and we're – jist – aboot – there.'
Then Private McPhun answers: 'Dommit, auld chap!
For the sake o' that haggis I'll gang till I drap.'
And he gets on his feet wi' a heave and a strain,
And onward he staggers in passion and pain.   90
And the flare and the glare and the fury increase,
Till you'd think they'd just taken a' hell on a lease.
And on they go reelin' in peetifu' plight,
And someone is shoutin' away on their right;

And someone is runnin', and noo they can hear
A sound like a prayer and a sound like a cheer;
And swift through the crash and the flash and the din,
The lads o' the Hielands are bringin' them in.

'They're baith sairly woundit, but is it no droll
Hoo they rave aboot haggis?' says Sergeant McCole.   100
When hirplin⋆ alang comes wee Wullie McNair,   limping
And they a' wonnert whey he wis greetin'⋆ sae sair.   weeping
And he says: 'I'd just liftit it oot o' the pot,
And there it lay steamin' and savoury hot,
When sudden I dooked at the fleech o' a shell,
And it – *drapped on the haggis and dinged it tae hell.*'

And oh but the lads were fair taken aback:
Then sudden the order wis passed tae attack,
And up from the trenches like lions they leapt,
And on through the nicht like a torrent they swept.   110
On, on, wi' their bayonets thirstin' before!
On, on tae the foe wi' a rush and a roar!
And wild to the welkin⋆ their battle-cry rang,   sky
And doon on the Boches like tigers they sprang:
And there wisna a man but had death in his ee,
For he thocht o' the haggis o' Private McPhee.

Sheila

When I played my penny whistle on the braes above Lochgyle
The heather bloomed about us, and we heard the peewit call;
As you bent above your knitting something *fey* was in your smile,
And fine and soft and slow the rain made silver on your shawl.
Your cheeks were pink like painted cheeks, your eyes a pansy blue . . .
My heart was in my playing, but my music was for you.

And now I play the organ in this lordly London town;
I play the lovely organ with a thousand folk in view.
They're wearing silk and satin, but I see a woollen gown,
And my heart's not in my music, for I'm thinking, lass, of you;   10
When you listened to a barefoot boy, who piped of ancient pain,
And your ragged shawl was pearly in the sweet, shy rain.

I'll play them mighty music – O I'll make them stamp and cheer;
I'll give the best that's in me, but I'll give it all for you.
I'll put my whole heart in it, for I feel that you are near,
Not yonder, sleeping always, where the peat is white with dew.
But I'll never live the rapture of that shepherd boy the while
I trilled for you my whistle on the braes above Lochgyle.

Lewis Spence (1874 – 1955)

The Prows o' Reekie

O wad this braw hie-heapit toun
Sail aff like an enchanted ship,
Drift ower the warld's seas up and doun
And kiss wi' Venice lip tae lip,
Or anchor intae Naples Bay
A misty island far astray,
Or set her rock tae Athens' wa'
Pillar tae pillar, stane tae stane,
The cruiket spell o' her backbane,
Yon shadow-mile o' spire and vane,   10
Wad ding* them a', wad ding them a'.   beat
Cadiz wad tine* the admiralty   lose
O' yonder emerod-fair sea,
Gibraltar frown for frown exchange
Wi' Nigel's Crags at elbuck-range,
The rose-red banks o' Lisbon make
Mair room in Tagus for her sake.

A hoose is but a puppet-box
Tae keep life's images frae knocks,
But mannikins scrieve oot their sauls   20
Upon its craw-steps and its walls;
Where hae they writ them mair sublime
Than on yon gable-ends o' time?

Bride or Handmaiden?

Beauty ever was designed
To thrill the heart and not the mind,
To speak to the immediate blood,
But never to the pensive mood.
And when I hear one say that thought
Has been to him by Beauty brought
I know that Beauty in his house
Has dwelt as servant, not as spouse.

Great Tay of the Waves

O that yon river micht nae mair
Rin through the channels o' my sleep;
My bluid has felt its tides owre sair,
Its waves hae drooned my dreams owre deep.

O why should Tay be a' my day
And Buddon links be a' my nicht,
The warld o' a' my walks be grey
Wi' yon far sands' unwarldly licht?

As haars★ the windless waters find   mists
The unguarded instant falls a prey   10
To sakeless★ shadows o' the mind,   innocent
And a' my life rins back to Tay.

Deep in the saul the early scene –
Ah, let him play wi' suns wha can,
The cradle's pented on the een,
The native airt★ resolves the man.   quarter

The Stown Bairn

O dinna ye spy yon castel braw
Ayont★ the gress-green riggs★ o' sea,   beyond/ridges, crests
There's a tower intil't and a bower intil't
And a louping lion has power intil't
Rampin' amang the win's that thraw★   twist
Yon banner bousteouslie★.   boisterously
O whaten a castel is yon, ma minnie★,   mother
That harles the hert's bluid oot o' me
And beckons me owre a warld o' waters
To seek its weird★ or dee?   10   fate
Yon castel braw, ma bonny bit hinny,
It is the Scottis Glamourie★,   magic
There's a spell intil't and a well intil't
And the sang o' a siller bell intil't,
But the braes abune it are dowf★ and whinny,   barren
And the bracken buries the lea.
It's noo a ship wi' the haar for sail,
And syne a strength, as ye may see,
Forbye it's a hill wi' a hollow ha',
Whaur the fludes sough eerily.   20

O minnie, see yon mune-white steed
That sowms★ sae soople owre the sea;   swims
Wi' a horn on his heid, he mak's sic speed
As alanerlie★ the clan o' the deid,   solely
And I ken he's fain★ o' me.   fond
O whaur are ye, ma gentle bairn
This moment was upon ma knee?
I cuddled ye i' the cruik o' ma airm,
And noo ye're awa frae me!   30

Autumnal

I have loved Autumn as an amethyst
Set into cunning silver, and her mist
Dimming the golden trees to goblin treasure,
The exquisite slow measure
Of leaf-fall in her visionary rains,
Her brooks, those passionate veins
That rush like rapture in a poet's blood,
I have loved and understood.

What though the sheep upon the distant hills
The first white footfalls of the winter seem?   10
He lives, who feels this last irradiate gleam,
A thousand summers, and its magic stills
Winter for ever in his heart. I hear
The phoenix-fabled burning of the year,
And summer's soul, a rainbow-feathered ghost,
Soar to that secret coast
Where the unnumbered seasons have their sphere.

John Buchan (1875 – 1940)

Barrister, journalist, diplomat and government bureaucrat, Member of Parliament, and finally Governor-General of Canada, Buchan was also one of the most popular novelists of his day. Primarily a writer of action novels or 'thrillers,' he was particularly successful in the Richard Hannay series, notably *The Thirty-nine Steps* (1915). Buchan also wrote some fine historical fiction, one of the best being *Witch Wood* (1927). 'The Kings of Orion' is typical of his love of adventure and travel, and his emphasis upon the 'manly' virtues of courage, resolution, honour, straightforwardness. In recent years Buchan's type of fiction has been accused of jingoism, male chauvinism, or even racism. The reader may spot elements in 'The Kings of Orion' which can be viewed in this unpleasant light, but may also see a calculated moral ambiguity which examines these very issues. At least one observes a considerable narrative skill. In this story too is the theme of the Divided Self so prevalent in Scottish literature.

Home-Thoughts from Abroad

Aifter the war, says the papers, they'll no be content at hame,
The lads that hae feucht wi' death twae 'ear i' the mud and the rain and the snaw;
For aifter a sodger's life the shop will be unco★ tame;   very
They'll ettle★ at fortune and freedom in the new lands far awa'.   strive

No me!
By God! No me!
Aince we hae lickit oor faes
And aince I ger oot o' this hell,
For the rest o' my leevin' days
I'll mak a pet o' mysel'.   10

I'll haste me back wi' an eident★ fit   eager
And settle again in the same auld bit.
And oh! the comfort to snowk again
The reek o' my mither's but-and-ben★,   cottage
The wee box-bed and the ingle★ neuk   fireplace
And the kail-pat★ hung frae the chimley-heuk!   cabbage-pot
I'll gang back to the shop like a laddie to play,
Tak doun the shutters at skreigh o' day,
And weigh oot floor wi' a carefu' pride,
And hear the clash o' the countraside.   20
I'll wear for ordinar' a roond hard hat,
A collar and dicky and black cravat.
If the weather's wat I'll no stir ootbye
Wi'oot an umbrella to keep me dry.
I think I'd better no tak a wife –
I've had a' the adventure I want in life. –
But at nicht, when the doors are steeked★, I'll sit,   shut
While the bleeze loups high frae the aiken★ ruit,   oaken
And smoken my pipe aside the crook,
And read in some douce★ auld-farrant book; 30 decent
Or crack★ wi' Davie and mix a rummer,   chat
While the auld wife's pow★ nid-nods in slum'er;   head
And hark to the winds gaun tearin' bye
And thank the Lord I'm sae warm and dry.

When simmer brings the lang bricht e'en,
I'll daunder doun to the bowling-green,
Or delve my yaird and my roses tend
For the big floo'er-show in the next back-end.
Whiles★, when the sun blinks aifter rain,   sometimes
I'll tak my rod and gang up the glen;   40
Me and Davie, we ken the püles
Whaur the troot grow great in the howes★ o' the hills; hollows
And, wanderin' back when the gloamin' fa's
And the midges dance in the hazel shaws★,   woods
We'll stop at the yett★ ayond★ the hicht   gate/beyond
And drink great wauchts★ o' the scented nicht,   draughts
While the hoose lamps kin'le raw★ by raw   row
And a yellow star hings ower the Law.
Davie will lauch like a wean at a fair
And nip my airm to mak certain shüre   50
That we're back frae yon place o' dule and dreid,
To oor ain kind warld –
But Davie's deid!
Nae mair gude nor ill can betide him.
We happit★ him doun by Beaumont toun,   dressed (buried)
And the half o' my he'rt's in the mools★ aside him. earth

Fisher Jamie

Puir Jamie's killed. A better lad
Ye wadna find to busk★ a flee   dress
Or burn a püle or wield a gad
Frae Berwick to the Lints o' Dee.

And noo he's in a happier land. –
It's Gospel truith and Gospel law
That Heaven's yett★ maun open stand   gate
To folk that for their country fa'.

But Jamie will be ill to mate;
He lo'ed nae music, kenned nae tunes   10
Except the sang o' Tweed in spate,
Or Talla loupin' ower its linns★.   waterfalls

I sair misdoot that Jamie's heid
A croun a' gowd will never please;
He liked a kep o' dacent tweed
Whaur he could stick his casts o' flees.

If Heaven is a' that man can dream
And a' that honest herts can wish,
It maun provide some muirland stream,
For Jamie dreamed o' nocht but fish.   20

And weel I wot he'll up and speir★   ask
In his bit blate★ and canty★ way,   shy/pleasant
Wi' kind Apostles standin' near
Whae in their time were fishers tae.

He'll offer back his gowden croun
And in its place a rod he'll seek,
And bashfu'-like his herp lay doun
And speir a leister and a cleek.

For Jims had aye a poachin' whim;
He'll sune grow tired, wi' lawfu' flee   30
Made from the wings o' cherubim,
O' castin' ower the Crystal Sea . . .

I picter him at gloamin' tide
Steekin'★ the backdoor o' his hame   shutting
And hastin' to the waterside
To play again the auld auld game;

And syne wi' saumon on his back,
Catch't clean against the Heavenly law,
And Heavenly byliffs on his track,
Gaun linkin' doun some Heavenly shaw★.   40   wood

The Kings of Orion

'An ape and a lion lie side by side in the heart of a man.'
— Persian Proverb

Spring fishing in the North is a cold game for a man whose blood has become thin in gentler climates. All afternoon I had failed to stir a fish, and the wan streams of the Laver, swirling between bare grey banks, were as icy to the eye as the sharp gusts of hail from the northeast were to the fingers. I cast mechanically till I grew weary, and then with an empty creel and a villainous temper set myself to trudge the two miles of bent to the inn. Some distant ridges of hill stood out snow-clad against the dun sky, and half in anger, half in a dismal satisfaction, I told myself that fishing tomorrow would be as barren as today.

At the inn door a tall man was stamping his feet and watching a servant lifting rod cases from a dog-cart. Hooded and wrapped though he was, my friend Thirlstone was an unmistakable figure in any landscape. The long, haggard, brown face, with the skin drawn tightly over the cheek bones, the keen blue eyes finely wrinkled round the corners with staring at many suns, the scar which gave his mouth a humorous droop to the right, made up a whole which was not easily forgotten.

I had last seen him on the quay at Funchal bargaining with some rascally boatman to take him after mythical wild goats in the Desertas. Before that we had met at an embassy ball in Vienna, and still earlier at a hill station in Persia to which I had been sent post-haste by an anxious and embarrassed government. Also I had been at school with him, in those far-away days when we rode nine stone and dreamed of cricket averages. He was a soldier of note, who had taken part in two little wars and one big one; had himself conducted a political mission through a hard country with some success, and was habitually chosen by his superiors to keep his eyes open as a foreign attaché in our neighbours' wars.

But his fame as a hunter had gone abroad into places where even the name of the British army is unknown. He was the hungriest shikari I have ever seen, and I have seen many. If you are wise you will go forthwith to some library and procure a little hook entitled *Three Hunting Expeditions,* by A. W. T. It is a modest work, and the style is that of a leading article, but all the lore and passion of the Red Gods are in its pages.

The sitting-room at the inn is a place of comfort, and while Thirlstone warmed his long back at the fire I sank contentedly into one of the well-rubbed leather armchairs. The company of a friend made the weather and the scarcity of salmon less the intolerable grievance they had seemed an hour ago than a joke to be laughed at. The landlord came in with whisky, and banked up the peats till they glowed beneath a pall of blue smoke.

'I hope to goodness we are alone,' said Thirlstone, and he turned to the retreating landlord and asked the question.

'There's naebody bidin' the nicht forbye yoursels,' he said, 'but the morn there's a gentleman comin'. I got a letter frae him the day. Maister Wiston, they ca' him. Maybe ye ken him?'

I started at the name, which I knew very well. Thirlstone, who knew it better, stopped warming himself and walked to the window, where he stood pulling his mustache and staring at the snow. When the man had left the room, he turned to me with the face of one whose mind is made up on a course but uncertain of the best method.

'Do you know this sort of weather looks infernally unpromising? I've half a mind to chuck it and go back to town.'

I gave him no encouragement, finding amusement in his difficulties.

'Oh, it's not so bad,' I said, 'and it won't last. Tomorrow we may have the day of our lives.'

He was silent for a little, staring at the fire. 'Anyhow,' he said at last, 'we were fools to be so far up the valley. Why shouldn't we go down to the Forest Lodge? They'll take us in, and we should be deucedly comfortable, and the water's better.'

'There's not a pool on the river to touch the stretch here,' I said. 'I know, for I've fished every inch of it.'

He had no reply to this, so he lit a pipe and held his peace for a time. Then, with some embarrassment but the air of having made a discovery, he announced that his conscience was troubling him about his work, and he thought he ought to get back to it at once. 'There are several things I have forgotten to see to, and they're rather important. I feel a beast behaving like this, but you won't mind, will you?'

'My dear Thirlstone,' I said, 'what is the good of hedging? Why can't you say you won't meet Wiston?'

His face cleared. 'Well, that's the fact – I won't. It would be too infernally unpleasant. You see, I was once by way of being his friend, and he was in my regiment. I couldn't do it.'

The landlord came in at the moment with a basket of peats. 'How long is Capt – Mr Wiston staying here?' I asked.

'He's no bidin' ony time. He's just comin' here in the middle o' the day for his denner, and then drivin' up the water to Altbreac. He has the fishin' there.'

Thirlstone's face showed profound relief. 'Thank God!' I heard him mutter under his breath, and when the landlord had gone he fell to talking of salmon with enthusiasm. 'We must make a big day of it tomorrow, dark to dark, you know. Thank Heaven, our beat's downstream, too.' And thereafter he made frequent excursions to the door, and bulletins on the weather were issued regularly.

Dinner over, we drew our chairs to the hearth, and fell to talk and the slow consumption of tobacco. When two men from the ends of the earth meet by a winter fire, their thoughts are certain to drift overseas. We spoke of the racing tides off Vancouver, and the lonely pine-clad ridges running up to the snow peaks of the Selkirks, to which we had both travelled once upon a time in search of sport. Thirlstone on his own account had gone wandering to Alaska, and brought back some bear-skins and a frost-bitten toe as trophies, and from his tales had consorted with the finest band of rogues which survived unhanged on this planet.

Then some casual word took our thoughts to the south, and our memories dallied with Africa. Thirlstone had hunted in Somaliland and done mighty slaughter; while I had spent some never-to-be forgotten weeks long ago in the hinterland of Zanzibar, in the days before railways and game preserves. I had gone through life with a keen eye for the discovery of earthly paradises, to which I intend to retire when my work is over, and the fairest I thought I had found above the Rift valley, where you have a hundred miles of blue horizon and the weather of Scotland.

Thirlstone, not having been there, naturally differed, and urged the claim of a certain glen in Kashmir, where you may hunt two varieties of bear and three of buck in thickets of rhododendron, and see the mightiest mountain wall on earth from your tent door. The mention of the Indian frontier brought us back to our professions, and for a little we talked 'shop,' with the unblushing confidence of those who know each other's work and approve it.

As a very young soldier Thirlstone had gone shooting in the Pamirs, and had blundered into a Russian party of exploration which contained Kuropatkin. He had in consequence grossly outstayed his leave, having been detained for a fortnight by an arbitrary hospitality; but he had learned many things, and the experience had given him strong views on frontier questions. Half an hour was devoted to a masterly survey of the East, until a word pulled us up.

'I went there in '99,' Thirlstone was saying, '– the time Wiston and I were sent – ' and then he stopped, and his eager face clouded. Wiston's name cast a shadow over our reminiscences.

'What did he actually do?' I asked after a short silence.

'Pretty bad! He seemed a commonplace, good sort of fellow, popular, fairly competent, a little bad-tempered perhaps. And then suddenly he did something so extremely blackguardly that everything was at an end. It's no good repeating details, and I hate to think about it. We know little about our neighbours, and I'm not sure that we know much about ourselves. There may be appalling depths of iniquity in every one of us, only most people are fortunate enough to go through the world without meeting anything to wake the devil in them. I don't believe Wiston was bad in the ordinary sense. Only there was something else in him – *somebody else,* if you like – and in a moment it came uppermost, and he was a branded man. Ugh! it's a gruesome thought.'

Thirlstone had let his pipe go out, and was staring moodily into the fire. 'How do you explain things like that?' he asked. 'I have an idea of my own about them. We talk glibly of ourselves and our personality and our conscience, as if every man's nature were a smooth, round, white thing, like a chuckiestone. But I believe there are two men – perhaps more – in every one of us. There's our ordinary self, generally rather humdrum; and then there's a bit of something else, good, bad, but never indifferent – and it is that something else which may make a man a saint or a great villain.'

'"The Kings of Orion have come to earth",' I quoted.

Something in the words struck Thirlstone, and he asked me what was the yarn I spoke of.

'It's an old legend,' I explained. 'When the kings were driven out of Orion, they were sent to this planet and given each his habitation in some mortal soul. There were differences of character in that royal family, and so the *alter ego* which dwells alongside of us may be virtuous or very much the reverse. But the point is that he is always greater than ourselves, for he has been a king. It's a foolish story, but very widely believed. There is something of the sort in Celtic folklore, and there's a reference to it in Ausonius. Also the bandits in the Bakhtiari have a version of it in a very excellent ballad.'

'Kings of Orion,' said Thirlstone musingly. 'I like that idea. Good or bad, but always great! After all, we show a kind of belief in it in our daily practice. Every man is always making fancies about himself; but it is never his workaday self, but something else. The bank clerk who pictures himself as a financial Napoleon knows that his own thin little soul is incapable of it; but he knows, too, that it is possible enough for that other bigger thing which is not his soul, but yet in some odd way is bound up with it. I fancy myself a field-marshal in a European war; but I know perfectly well that if the job were offered me, I should realise my incompetence and decline. I expect you rather picture yourself now and then as a sort of Julius Caesar and empire-maker, and yet, with all respect, my dear chap, I think it would be rather too much for you.'

'There was once a man,' I said, 'an early Victorian Whig, whose chief ambitions were to reform the criminal law and abolish slavery. Well, this dull, estimable man in his leisure moments was Emperor of Byzantium. He fought great wars and built palaces, and then, when the time for fancy was past, went into the House of Commons and railed against militarism and Tory extravagance. That particular king from Orion had a rather odd sort of earthly tenement.'

Thirlstone was all interest. 'A philosophic Whig and the throne of Byzantium. A pretty rum mixture! And yet – yet,' and his eyes became abstracted. 'Did you ever know Tommy Lacelles?'

'The man who once governed Deira? Retired now, and lives somewhere in Kent? Yes, I've met him once or twice. But why?'

'Because,' said Thirlstone solemnly, 'unless I'm greatly mistaken, Tommy was another such case, though no man ever guessed it except myself. I don't mind telling you the story, now that he is retired and vegetating in his ancestral pastures. Besides, the facts are all to his credit, and the explanation is our own business . . .

'His wife was my cousin, and when she died Tommy was left a very withered, disconsolate man, with no particular object in life. We all thought he would give up the service, for he was hideously well off; and then one fine day, to our amazement, he was offered Deira, and accepted it. I was short of a job at the time, for my battalion was at home, and there was nothing going on anywhere, so I thought I should like to see what the East Coast of Africa was like, and wrote to Tommy about it. He jumped at me, cabled offering me what he called his Military Secretaryship, and I got seconded, and set off. I had never known him very well, but what I had seen I had liked; and I suppose he was glad to have one of Maggie's family with him, for he was still very low about her loss. I was in pretty good spirits, for it meant new experiences, and I had hopes of big game.

'You've never been to Deira? Well, there's no good trying to describe it, for it's the only place in the world like itself. God made it and left it to its own devices. The town is pretty enough, with its palms and green headland, and little scrubby islands in the river's mouth. It has the usual half-Arab, half-Portugee look – white green-shuttered houses, flat roofs, sallow little men in duck, and every type of nigger from the Somali to the Shangaan. There are some good buildings, and Government House was the mansion of some old Portugee seignior, and was built when people in Africa were not in such a hurry as today. Inland there's a rolling forest country, beginning with decent trees and ending in mimosa-thorn, when the land begins to rise to the stony hills of the interior; and that poisonous yellow river rolls through it all, with a denser native population along its banks than you will find anywhere else north of the Zambesi. For about two months in the year the climate is Paradise, and for the rest you live in a Turkish bath, with every known kind of fever hanging about. We cleaned out the town and improved the sanitation, so there were few epidemics, but there was enough ordinary malaria to sicken a crocodile.

'The place was no special use to us. It had been annexed in spite of a tremendous Radical outcry, and, upon my soul, it was one of the few cases where the Radicals had something to say for themselves. All we got by it was half a dozen of the nastiest problems an unfortunate governor can have to face. Ten years before it had been a decaying strip of coast, with a few trading firms in the town, and a small export of ivory and timber. But some years before Tommy took it up there had been a huge discovery of copper in the hills inland, a railway had been built, and there were several biggish mining settlements at the end of it. Deira itself was filled with offices of European firms, it had got a Stock Exchange of its own, and it was becoming the usual cosmopolitan playground.

'It had a knack, too, of getting the very worst breed of adventurer. I know something of your South African and Australian mining towns, and with all their faults they are run by white men. If they haven't much morals, they have a kind of decency which keeps them fairly straight. But for our sins we got a brand of Levantine Jew who was fit for nothing but making money and making trouble. They were always defying the law, and then, when they got into a hole, they squealed to Government for help, and started a racket in the home papers about the weakness of the Imperial power.

'The crux of the whole difficulty was the natives, who lived along the river and in the foothills. They were a hardy race of Kaffirs, sort of far-away cousins to the Zulu, and till the mines were opened they had behaved well enough. They had arms, which we had never dared to take away, but they kept quiet and paid their hut taxes like men. I got to know many of the chiefs, and liked them, for they were upstanding fellows to look at and heaven-born shikaris. However, when the Jews came along they wanted labour, and, since we did not see our way to allow them to add to the imported coolie population, they had to fall back upon the Labonga. At first things went smoothly. The chiefs were willing to let their men work for good wages, and for a time there was enough labor for everybody. But as the mines extended, and the natives, after making a few pounds, wanted to get back to their kraals, there came a shortage; and since the work could not be allowed to slacken, the owners tried other methods. They made promises which they never intended to keep, and they stood on the letter of a law which the natives did not understand, and they employed touts who were little better than slave-dealers. They got the labour, of course, but soon they had put the Labonga into a state of unrest which a very little would turn into a rising.

'Into this kettle of fish Tommy was pitchforked, and when I arrived he was just beginning to understand how unpleasant it was. As I said before, I did not know him very well, and I was amazed to find how bad he was at his job. A more curiously incompetent person I never met. He was a long, thin man, with a grizzled mustache, and a mild sleepy eye – not an impressive figure, except on a horse; and he had an odd lisp which made even a shrewd remark sound foolish. He was the most industrious creature in the world, and a model of official decorum. His papers were always in order, his dispatches always neat and correct, and I don't believe anyone ever caught him tripping in office work. But he had no more conception than a child of the kind of trouble that was brewing. He never knew an honest man from a rogue, and the result was that he received all unofficial communications with a polite disbelief. I used to force him to see people – miners, prospectors, traders, anyone who had something to say worth listening to, but it all glided smoothly off his mind. He was simply the most incompetent being ever created, living in the world as not being of it, or rather creating a little official world of his own, where all events happened on lines laid down by the Colonial Office, and men were like papers, to be rolled into packets and properly docketed.

'He had an Executive Council of people like himself, competent officials and blind bats at anything else. Then there was a precious Legislative Council, intended to represent the different classes of the population. There were several good men on it – one old trader called Mackay, for instance, who had been thirty years in the country – but most were nominees of the mining firms, and very seedy rascals at that. They were always talking about the rights of the white man, and demanding popular control of the government, and similar twaddle.

'The leader was a man who hailed from Hamburg, and called himself Le Foy – descended from a Crusader of the name of Levi – who was a jackal of one of the chief copper firms. He overflowed with Imperialist sentiment, and when he was not waving the flag he used to gush about the beauties of English country life and the grandeur of the English tradition. He hated me from the start, for when he talked of going "home" I thought he meant Hamburg, and said so; and then a thing happened which made him hate me worse. He was infernally rude to Tommy, who, like the dear sheep he was, never saw it, and, if he had, wouldn't have minded.

'But one day I chanced to overhear some of his impertinences, so I hunted out my biggest sjambok and lay in wait for Mr Le Foy. I told him that he was a representative of the sovereign people, that I was a member of an elite bureaucracy, and that it would be most painful if unpleasantness arose between us. But, I added, I was prepared, if necessary, to sacrifice my official career to my private feelings, and if he dared to use such language again to his Majesty's representative I would give him a hiding he would remember till he found himself in Abraham's bosom. Not liking my sjambok, he became soap and butter at once, and held his tongue for a month or two.

'But though Tommy was no good at his job, he was a tremendous swell at other things. He was an uncommonly good linguist, and had always about a dozen hobbies which he slaved at; and when he found himself at Deira with a good deal of leisure, he became a bigger crank than ever. He had a lot of books which used to follow him about the world in zinc-lined boxes – your big paper-backed German books which mean research – and he was a Fellow of the Royal Society, and corresponded with half a dozen foreign shows. India was his great subject, but he had been in the Sudan and knew a good deal about African races. When I went out to him, his pet hobby was the Bantu, and he had acquired an amazing amount of miscellaneous learning. He knew all about their immigration from the North, and the Arab and Phoenician trade routes, and the Portuguese occupation, and the rest of the history of that unpromising seaboard.

'The way he behaved in his researches showed the man. He worked hard at the Labonga language – which, I believe, is a linguistic curiosity of the first water – from missionary books and the conversation of tame Kaffirs. But he never thought of paying them a visit in their native haunts. I was constantly begging him to do it, but it was not Tommy's way. He did not care a straw about political expedience, and he liked to look at things through the medium of paper and ink. Then there were the Phoenician remains in the foothills where the copper was mined – old workings, and things which might have been forts or temples. He knew all that was to be known about them, but he had never seen them, and never wanted to. Once only he went to the hills, to open some new reservoirs and make the ordinary Governor's speech; but he went in a special train and stayed two hours, most of which was spent in lunching and being played to by brass bands.

'But, oddly enough, there was one thing which stirred him with an interest that was not academic. I discovered it by accident one day when I went into his study and found him struggling with a map of Central Asia. Instead of the mild, benevolent smile with which he usually greeted my interruptions, he looked positively furtive, and, I could have sworn, tried to shuffle the map under some papers. Now it happens that Central Asia is the part of the globe that I know better than most men, and I could not help picking up the map and looking at it. It was a wretched thing, and had got the Oxus two hundred miles out of its course. I pointed this out to Tommy, and to my amazement he became quite excited. "Nonsense," he said. "You don't mean to say it goes south of that desert. Why, I meant to—" and then he stammered and stopped. I wondered what on earth he had meant to do, but I merely observed that I had been there, and knew. That brought Tommy out of his chair in real excitement. "What!" he cried, "you! You never told me," and he started to fire off a round of questions, which showed that if he knew very little about the place, he had it a good deal in his mind. I drew some sketch-plans for him, and left him brooding over them.

'That was the first hint I got. The second was a few nights later, when we were smoking in the billiard-room. I had been reading Marco Polo, and the talk got on to Persia and drifted all over the north side of the Himalaya. Tommy, with an abstracted eye, talked of Alexander and Timour and Genghis Khan, and particularly of Prester John, who was a character that took his fancy. I had told him that the natives in the Pamirs were true Persian stock, and this interested him greatly.

'"Why was there never a great state built up in those valleys?" he asked. "You get nothing but a few wild conquerors rushing east and west, and then some squalid khanates. And yet all the materials were there — the stuff for a strong race, a rich land, the traditions of an old civilisation, and the natural barriers against invasion."

'"I suppose they never found the man," I said.

'He agreed. "Their princes were sots, or they were barbarians of genius who could devastate to the gates of Peking or Constantinople, but could never build. They did not recognise their limits, and so they went out in a whirlwind. But if there had been a man of solid genius he might have built up the strongest nation on the globe. In time he could have annexed Persia and nibbled at China. He would have been rich, for he could tap all the inland trade-routes of Asia. He would have had to be a conqueror, for his people would be a race of warriors, but first and foremost he must have been a statesman. Think of such a civilisation, *the* Asian civilisation, growing up mysteriously behind the deserts and the ranges! That's my idea of Prester John. Russia would have been confined to the line of the Urals. China would have been absorbed. There would have been no Japan. The whole history of the world for the last few hundred years would have been different. It is the greatest of all the lost chances in history." Tommy waxed pathetic over the loss.

'I was a little surprised at his eloquence, especially when he seemed to remember himself and stopped all of a sudden. But for the next week I got no peace with his questions. I told him all I knew of Bokhara, and Samarkand, and Tashkend, and Yarkand. I showed him the passes in the Pamirs and the Hindu Kush. I traced out the rivers, and I calculated distances; we talked over imaginary campaigns, and set up fanciful constitutions. It was a childish game, but I found it interesting enough. He spoke of it all with a curious personal tone which puzzled me, till one day when we were amusing ourselves with a fight on the Zarafshan, and I put in a modest claim to be allowed to win once in a while. For a second he looked at me in blank surprise. "You can't," he said; "I've got to enter Samarkand before I can" . . . and he stopped again, with a glimmering sense in his face that he was giving himself away. And then I knew that I had surprised Tommy's secret. While he was muddling his own job, he was salving his pride with fancies of some wild career in Asia, where Tommy, disguised as the lord knows what Mussulman grandee, was hammering the little states into an empire.

'I did not think then as I think now, and I was amused to find so odd a trait in a dull man. I had known something of the kind before. I had met fellows who after their tenth peg would begin to swagger about some ridiculous fancy of their own — their little private corner of soul showing for a moment when the drink had blown aside their common sense. True, I had never known the thing appear in cold blood and everyday life, but I assumed the case to be the same. I thought of it only as a harmless fancy, never imagining that it had anything to do with character. I put it down to that kindly imagination which is the old opiate for failures.

So I played up to Tommy with all my might, and though he became very discreet after the first betrayal, having hit upon the clue, I knew what to look for, and I found it. When I told him that the Labonga were in a devil of a mess, he would look at me with an empty face and change the subject; but once among the Turcomans his eye would kindle, and he would slave at his confounded folly with sufficient energy to reform the whole East Coast.

'It was the spark that kept the man alive. Otherwise he would have been as limp as a rag, but this craziness put life into him, and made him carry his head in the air and walk like a free man. I remember he was very keen about any kind of martial poetry. He used to go about crooning Scott and Macaulay to himself, and when we went for a walk or a ride he wouldn't speak for miles, but keep smiling to himself and humming bits of songs. I dare say he was very happy – far happier than your stolid, competent man, who sees only the one thing to do, and does it. Tommy was muddling his particular duty, but building glorious palaces in the air.

'One day Mackay, the old trader, came to me after a sitting of the precious Legislative Council. We were very friendly, and I had done all I could to get the Government to listen to his views. He was a dour, ill-tempered Scotsman, very anxious for the safety of his property, but perfectly careless about any danger to himself.

'"Captain Thirlstone," he said, "that Governor of yours is a damned fool."

'Of course I shut him up very brusquely, but he paid no attention. "He just sits and grins, and lets yon Pentecostal crowd we've gotten here as a judgment for our sins do what they like wi' him. God kens what'll happen. I would go home tomorrow, if I could realise without an immoderate loss. For the day of reckoning is at hand. Maark my words, Captain – at hand."

'I said I agreed with him about the approach of trouble, but that the Governor would rise to the occasion. I told him that people like Tommy were only seen at their best in a crisis, and that he might be perfectly confident that when it arrived he would get a new idea of the man. I said this, but of course I did not believe a word of it. I thought Tommy was only a dreamer, who had rotted any grit he ever possessed by his mental opiates. At that time I did not understand about the Kings from Orion.

'And then came the thing we had all been waiting for – a Labonga rising. A week before I had got leave and had gone up country, partly to shoot, but mainly to see for myself what trouble was brewing. I kept away from the river, and therefore missed the main native centers, but such kraals as I passed had a look I did not like. The chiefs were almost always invisible, and the young bloods were swaggering about and bukking to each other, while the women were grinding maize as if for some big festival. However, after a bit the country seemed to grow more normal, and I went into the foothills to shoot, fairly easy in my mind. I had got up to a place called Shimonwe, on the Pathi River, where I had ordered letters to be sent, and one night coming in from a hard day after kudu I found a post-runner half-dead of fatigue with a chit from Utterson, who commanded a police district twenty miles nearer the coast. It said simply that all the young men round about him had cleared out and appeared to be moving towards Deira, that he was in a devil of a quandary, and that, since the police were under the Governor, he would take his orders from me.

'It looked as if the heather were fairly on fire at last, so I set off early next morning to trek back. About midday I met Utterson, a very badly scared little man, who had come to look for me. It seemed that his policemen had bolted in the night and gone to join the rising, leaving him with two white sergeants, barely fifty rounds of ammunition, and no neighbour for a hundred miles. He said that the Labonga chiefs were not marching to the coast, as he had thought, but north along the eastern foothills in the direction of the mines. This was better news, for it meant that in all probability the railway would remain open. It was my business to get somehow to my chief, and I was in the deuce of a stew how to manage it. It was no good following the line of the natives' march, for they would have been between me and my goal, and the only way was to try and outflank them by going due east, in the Deira direction, and then turning north, so as to strike the railway about halfway to the mines. I told Utterson we had better scatter, otherwise we should have no chance of getting through a densely populated native country. So, about five in the afternoon, I set off with my chief shikari, who, by good luck, was not a Labonga, and dived into the jungly bush which skirts the hills.

'For three days I had a baddish time. We steered by the stars, travelling chiefly by night, and we showed extraordinary skill in missing the water holes. I had a touch of fever and got light-headed, and it was all I could do to struggle through the thick grass and wait-a-bit thorns. My clothes were torn to rags, and I grew so footsore that it was agony to move. All the same we travelled fast, and there was no chance of our missing the road, for any route due north was bound to cut the railway. I had the most sickening uncertainty about what was to come next. Hely, who was in command at Deira, was a good enough man, but he had only three companies of white troops, and the black troops were as likely as not to be on their way to join the rebels. It looked as if we should have a Cawnpore business on a small scale, though I thanked Heaven there were no women in the case. As for Tommy, he would probably be repeating platitudes in Deira and composing an intelligent dispatch on the whole subject.

'About four in the afternoon on the third day I struck the line near a little station called Palala. I saw by the look of the rails that trains were still running, and my hopes revived. At Palala there was a coolie stationmaster, who gave me a drink and a little food, after which I slept heavily in his office till wakened by the arrival of an up train. It contained one of the white companies and a man Davidson, of the 101st, who was Hely's second in command. From him I had news that took away my breath. The Governor had gone up the line two days before with an A.D.C. and old Mackay. "The sportsman has got a move on him at last," said Davidson, "but what he means to do Heaven only knows. The Labonga are at the mines, and a kind of mine guard has been formed for defense. The joke of it is that most of the magnates are treed up there, for the railway is cut and they can't get away. I don't envy your chief the job of schooling that nervous crowd."

'I went on with Davidson, and very early next morning we came to a broken culvert and had to stop. There we stuck for three hours till the down train arrived, and with it Hely. He was for ordinary a stolid soul, but I never saw a man in such a fever of excitement. He gripped me by the arm and fairly shook me. "That old man of yours is a hero," he cried. "The Lord forgive me! and I have always crabbed him."

'I implored him in Heaven's name to tell me what was up, but he would say nothing till he had had his pow-wow with Davidson. It seemed that he was bringing all his white troops up the line for some great demonstration that Tommy had conceived. Davidson went back to Deira, while we mended the culvert and got the men transferred to the other train. Then I screwed the truth out of Hely. Tommy had got up to the mines before the rebels arrived, and had found as fine a chaos as can be imagined.

'He did not seem to have had any doubts what to do. There were a certain number of white workmen, hard fellows from Cornwall mostly, with a few Australians, and these he got together with Mackay's help and organised into a pretty useful corps. He set them to guard the offices, and gave them strict orders to shoot at sight anyone attempting to leave. Then he collected the bosses and talked to them like a father. What he said Hely did not know, except that he had damned their eyes pretty heartily, and told them what a set of swine they were, making trouble which they had not the pluck to face. Whether from Mackay, or from his own intelligence, or from a memory of my neglected warnings, he seemed to have got a tight grip on the facts at last.

'Meanwhile, the Labonga were at the doors, chanting their battle-songs half a mile away, and shots were heard from the far pickets. If they had tried to rush the place then, all would have been over, but, luckily, that was never their way of fighting. They sat down in camp to make their sacrifices and consult their witch-doctors, and presently Hely arrived with the first troops, having come in on the northern flank when he found the line cut. He had been in time to hear the tail end of Tommy's final address to the mine owners. He told them, in words which Hely said he could never have imagined coming from his lips, that they would be well served if the Labonga cleaned the whole place out. Only, he said, that would be against the will of Britain, and it was his business, as a loyal servant, to prevent it. Then, after giving Hely his instructions, he had put on his uniform, gold lace and all, and every scrap of bunting he possessed – all the orders and "Golden Stars" of half a dozen Oriental States where he had served. He made Ashurst, the A.D.C., put on his best Hussar's kit, and Mackay rigged himself out in a frock coat and a topper; and the three set out on horseback for the Labonga. "I believe he'll bring it off," said Hely, with wild eyes, "and, by Heaven, if he does, it'll be the best thing since John Nicholson!"

'For the rest of the way I sat hugging myself with excitement. The miracle of miracles seemed to have come. The old, slack, incompetent soul in Tommy seemed to have been driven out by that other spirit, which had hitherto been content to dream of crazy victories on the Oxus. I cursed my folly in having missed it all, for I would have given my right hand to be with him among the Labonga. I envied that young fool Ashurst his luck in being present at that queer transformation scene. I had not a doubt that Tommy would bring it off all right. The Kings from Orion don't go into action without coming out on top. As we got near the mines I kept my ears open for the sound of shots; but all was still – not even the kind of hubbub a native force makes when it is on the move. Something had happened, but what it was no man could guess. When we got to where the line was up, we made very good time over the five miles to the mines. No one interfered with us, and the nearer we got the greater grew my certainty. Soon we were at the pickets, who had nothing to tell us; and then we were racing up the long sandy street to the offices, and there, sitting smoking on the doorstep of the hotel, surrounded by everybody who was not on duty, were Mackay and Ashurst.

'They were an odd pair. Ashurst still wore his uniform; but he seemed to have been rolling about in it on the ground; his sleek hair was wildly ruffled, and he was poking holes in the dust with his sword. Mackay had lost his topper, and wore a disreputable cap, his ancient frock coat was without buttons, and his tie had worked itself up behind his ears. They talked excitedly to each other, now and then vouchsafing a scrap of information to an equally excited audience. When they saw me they rose and rushed for me, and dragged me between them up the street, while the crowd tailed at our heels.

'"Ye're a true prophet, Captain Thirlstone," Mackay began, "and I ask your pardon for doubting you. Ye said the Governor only needed a crisis to behave like a man. Well, the crisis has come; and if there's a man alive in this sinful world, it's that chief o' yours." And then his emotion overcame him, and, hard-bitten devil as he was, he sat down on the ground and gasped with hysterical laughter, while Ashurst, with a very red face, kept putting the wrong end of a cigarette in his mouth and swearing profanely.

'I never remember a madder sight. There was the brassy blue sky and reddish granite rock and acres of thick red dust. The scrub had that metallic greenness which you find in all copper places. Pretty unwholesome it looked, and the crowd, which had got round us again, was more unwholesome still. Fat Jew boys, with diamond rings on dirty fingers and greasy linen cuffs, kept staring at us with twitching lips; and one or two smarter fellows in riding-breeches, mine managers and suchlike, tried to show their pluck by nervous jokes. And in the middle was Mackay, with his damaged frocker, drawling out his story in broad Scots.

'"He made this laddie put on his braws, and he commandeered this iniquitous garment for me. I've raxed its seams, and it'll never look again on the man that owns it. Syne he arrayed himself in purple and fine linen till he was like the king's daughter, all glorious without; and says he to me, 'Mackay,' he says, 'we'll go and talk to these uncovenanted deevils in their own tongue. We'll visit them at home, Mackay,' he says. 'They're none such bad fellows, but they want a little humoring from men like you and me.' So we got on our horses and started the procession – the Governor with his head in the air, and the laddie endeavoring to look calm and collected, and me praying to the God of Israel and trying to keep my breeks from working up above my knees. I've been in Kaffir wars afore, but I never thought I would ride without weapon of any kind into such a black Armageddon. I am a peaceable man for ordinair', and a canny one, but I wasna myself in that hour. Man, Thirlstone, I was that overcome by the spirit of your chief, that if he had bidden me gang alone on the same errand, I wouldn't say but what I would have gone.

'"We hadna ridden half a mile before we saw the indunas and their men, ten thousand if there was one, and terrible as an army with banners. I speak feeguratively, for they hadna the scrap of a flag among them. They were beating the war drums, and the young men were dancing with their big skin-shields and wagging their ostrich feathers, so I saw they were out for business. I'll no' say but what my blood ran cold, but the Governor's eye got brighter and his back stiffer. 'Kings may be blest,' I says to myself, 'but thou art glorious.'

"'We rode straight for the centre of the crowd, where the young men were thickest and the big war drums lay. As soon as they saw us a dozen lifted their spears and ran out to meet us. But they stopped after six steps. The sun glinted on the Governor's gold lace and my lum hat, and no doubt they thought we were heathen deities descended from the heavens. Down they went on their faces, and then back like rabbits lo the rest, while the drums stopped, and the whole body awaited our coming in a silence like the tomb.

"'Never a word we spoke, but just jogged on with our chins cocked up till we were forent the big drum, where yon old scoundrel Umgazi was standing with his young men looking as black as sin. For a moment their spears were shaking in their hands, and I heard the click of a breech-bolt. If we had winked an eye we would have become pincushions that instant. But some unearthly power upheld us. Even the laddie kept a stiff face, and for me I forgot my breeks in watching the Governor. He looked as solemn as an archangel, and comes to a halt oppositeUmgazi, where he glowers at the old man for maybe three minutes, while we formed up behind him. Their eyes fell before his, and by and by their spears dropped to their sides. 'The father has come to his children,' says he in their own tongue. 'What do the children seek from their fathers?'

"'Ye see the cleverness of the thing. The man's past folly came to help him. The natives had never seen the Governor before till they beheld him in gold lace and a cocked hat on a muckle horse, speaking their own tongue and looking like a destroying angel. I tell you the Labonga's knees were loosed under them. They durstna speak a word until the Governor repeated the question in the same quiet, steely voice. 'You seek something,' he said, 'else you had not come out to meet me in your numbers. The father waits to hear the children's desires.'

"'Then Umgazi found his tongue and began an uneasy speech. The mines, he said, truly enough, were the abode of devils, who compelled the people to work under the ground. The crops were unreaped and the buck went unspeared, because there were no young men left to him. Their father had been away or asleep, they thought, for no help had come from him; therefore it had seemed good to them, being freemen and warriors, to seek help for themselves.

"'The Governor listened to it all with a set face. Then he smiled at them with supernatural assurance. They were fools, he said, and people of little wit, and he flung the better part of the Book of Job at their heads. The Lord kens where the man got his uncanny knowledge of the Labonga. He had all their heathen customs by heart, and he played with them like a cat with a mouse. He told them they were damned rascals to make such a stramash, and damned fools to think they could frighten the white man by their demonstrations. There was no brag about his words, just a calm statement of fact. At the same time, he said, he had no mind to let anyone wrong his children, and if any wrong had been done it should be righted. It was not meet, he said, that the young men should be taken from the villages unless by their own consent, though it was his desire that such young men as could be spared should have a chance of earning an honest penny. And then he fired at them some stuff about the British Empire and the King, and you could see the Labonga imbibing it like water. The man in a cocked hat might have told them that the sky was yellow, and they would have swallowed it.

"''I have spoken,' he says at last, and there was a great shout from the young men, and old Umgazi looked pretty foolish. They were coming round our horses to touch our stirrups with their noses, but the Governor stopped them.

"''My children will pile their weapons in front of me,' says he, 'to show me how they have armed themselves, and likewise to prove that their folly is at an end. All except a dozen,' says he, 'whom I select as a bodyguard.' And there and then he picked twelve lusty savages for his guard, while the rest without a cheep stacked their spears and guns forent the big drum.

"'Then he turned to us and spoke in English. 'Get back to the mines hell-for-leather, and tell them what's happening, and see that you get up some kind of a show for tomorrow at noon. I will bring the chiefs, and we'll feast them. Get all the bands you can, and let them play me in. Tell the mines fellows to look active, for it's the chance of their lives.' Then he says to the Labonga, 'My men will return,' he says, 'but as for me I will spend the night with my children. Make ready food, but let no beer be made, for it is a solemn occasion.'

"'And so we left him. I will not describe how I spent last night mysel', but I have something to say about this remarkable phenomenon. I could enlarge on the triumph of mind over matter . . ."

'Mackay did not enlarge. He stopped, cocked his ears, and looked down the road, from which came the strains of *Annie Laurie,* played with much spirit but grievously out of tune. Followed *The British Grenadiers,* and then an attempt at *The March of the Priests.* Mackay rose in excitement and began to crane his disreputable neck, while the band – a fine scratch collection of instruments – took up their stand at the end of the street, flanked by a piper in khaki who performed when their breath failed. Mackay chuckled with satisfaction. "The deevils have entered into the spirit of my instructions," he said. "In a wee bit the place will be like Falkirk Tryst for din."

'Punctually at twelve there came a great hullabaloo up the road, the beating of drums and the yelling of natives, and presently the procession hove in sight. There was Tommy on his horse, and on each side of him six savages with feather head-dress, and shields and war paint complete. After him trooped about thirty of the great chiefs, walking two by two, for all the world like an Aldershot parade. They carried no arms, but the bodyguard shook their spears, and let yells out of them that would have scared Julius Caesar. Then the band started in, and the piper blew up, and the mines people commenced to cheer, and I thought the heavens would fall. Long before Tommy came abreast of me I knew what I should see. His uniform looked as if it had been slept in, and his orders were all awry. But he had his head flung back, and his eyes very bright and his jaw set square. He never looked to right or left, never recognised me or anybody, for he was seeing something quite different from the red road and the white shanties and the hot sky.'

The fire had almost died out. Thirlstone stooped for a moment and stirred the peats.

'Yes,' he said, 'I knew that in his fool's ear the trumpets of all Asia were ringing, and the King of Bokhara was entering Samarkand.'

The Herd of Standlan

When the wind is nigh and the moon is high
And the mist on the riverside,
Let such as fare have a very good care
Of the Folk who come to ride.
For they may meet with the riders fleet
Who fare from the place of dread;
And hard it is for a mortal man
To sort at ease with the Dead.
– THE BALLAD OF GREY WEATHER

When Standlan Burn leaves the mosses and hags which gave it birth, it tumbles over a succession of falls into a deep, precipitous glen, whence in time it issues into a land of level green meadows, and finally finds its rest in the Gled. Just at the opening of the ravine there is a pool shut in by high, dark cliffs, and black even on the most sunshiny day. The rocks are never dry but always black with damp and shadow. There is scarce any vegetation save stunted birks, juniper bushes, and draggled fern; and the hoot of owls and the croak of hooded crows is seldom absent from the spot. It is the famous Black Linn[1] where in winter sheep stray and are never more heard of, and where more than once an unwary shepherd has gone to his account. It is an Inferno on the brink of a Paradise, for not a stone's throw off is the green, lawn-like turf, the hazel thicket, and the broad, clear pools, by the edge of which on that July day the Herd of Standlan and I sat drowsily smoking and talking of fishing and the hills. There he told me this story, which I here set down as I remember it, and as it bears repetition.

'D'ye mind Airthur Morrant?' said the shepherd, suddenly.

I did remember Arthur Mordaunt. Ten years past he and I had been inseparables, despite some half-dozen summers' difference in age. We had fished and shot together, and together we had tramped every hill within thirty miles. He had come up from the South to try sheep-farming, and as he came of a great family and had no need to earn his bread, he found the profession pleasing. Then irresistible fate had swept me southward to college, and when after two years I came back to the place, his father was dead and he had come into his own. The next I heard of him was that in politics he was regarded as the most promising of the younger men, one of the staunchest and ablest upstays of the Constitution. His name was rapidly rising into prominence, for he seemed to exhibit that rare phenomenon of a man of birth and culture in direct sympathy with the wants of the people.

'You mean Lord Brodakers?' I said.

'Dinna call him by that name,' said the shepherd, darkly. 'I hae nae thocht o' him now. He's a disgrace to his country, servin' the Deil wi' baith hands. But nine year syne he was a bit innocent callant wi' nae Tory deevilry in his heid. Well, as I was sayin', Airthur Morrant has cause to mind that place till his dying day'; and he pointed his finger to the Black Linn.

I looked up the chasm. The treacherous water, so bright and joyful at our feet, was like ink in the great gorge. The swish and plunge of the cataract came like the regular beating of a clock, and though the weather was dry, streams of moisture seamed the perpendicular walls. It was a place eerie even on that bright summer's day.

'I don't think I ever heard the story,' I said casually.

'Maybe no,' said the shepherd. 'It's no yin I like to tell'; and he puffed sternly at his pipe, while I awaited the continuation.

'Ye see it was like this,' he said, after a while. 'It was just the beginning o' the back-end, and that year we had an awfu' spate o' rain. For near a week it poured hale water, and a' doon by Drumeller and the Mossfennan haughs was yae muckle loch. Then it stopped, and an awfu' heat came on. It dried the grund in nae time, but it hardly touched the burns; and it was rale queer to be pourin' wi' sweat and the grund aneath ye as dry as a potato-sack, and a' the time the water neither to haud nor bind. A' the waterside fields were clean stripped o' stooks, and a guid wheen[2] hay-ricks gaed doon tae Berwick, no to speak o' sheep and nowt[3] beast. But that's anither thing.

'Weel, ye'll mind that Airthur was terrible keen on fishing. He wad gang oot in a' weather, and he wasna feared for only mortal or naitural thing. Dod, I've seen him in Gled wi' the water rinnin' ower his shouthers yae cauld March day playin' a saumon. He kenned weel aboot the fishing, for he had traivelled in Norroway and siccan outlandish places, where there's a heap o' big fish. So that day – and it was a Setterday tae and far ower near the Sabbath – he maun gang awa' up Standlan Burn wi' his rod and creel to try his luck.

'I was bidin' at that time, as ye mind, in the wee cot-house at the back o' the faulds. I was alane, for it was three years afore I mairried Jess, and I wasna begun yet to the coortin'. I had been at Gledsmuir that day for some o' the new stuff for killing sheep-mawks, and I wasna very fresh on my legs when I gaed oot after my tea that night to hae a look at the hill-sheep. I had had a bad year on the hill. First the lambin'-time was snaw, snaw ilka day, and I lost mair than I wad like to tell. Syne the grass a' summer was so short wi' the drought that the puir

---

[1] Waterfall.
[2] Many.
[3] Cattle.

beasts could scarcely get a bite and were as thin as pipe-stapples. And then, to crown a', auld Will Broun, the man that helpit me, turned ill wi' his back, and had to bide at hame. So I had twae man's work on yae man's shouthers, and was nane so weel pleased.

'As I was saying, I gaed oot that nicht, and after lookin' a' the Dun Rig and the Yellow Mire and the back o' Cramalt Craig, I cam down the burn by the road frae the auld faulds. It was geyan dark, being about seven o'clock o' a September nicht, and I keepit weel back frae that wanchancy¹ hole o' a burn. Weel, I was comin' kind o' quick, thinkin' o' supper and a story-book that I was readin' at the time, when just abune that place there, at the foot o' the Linn, I saw a man fishing. I wondered what ony body in his senses could be daein' at that time o' nicht in sic a dangerous place, so I gae him a roar and bade him come back. He turned his face round and I saw in a jiffy that it was Mr Airthur.

'"O, sir," I cried, "What for are ye fishing there? The water's awfu' dangerous, and the rocks are far ower slid."

'"Never mind, Scott," he roars back cheery-like. "I'll take care o' mysel."

'I lookit at him for two-three meenutes, and then I saw by his rod he had yin on, and a big yin tae. He ran it up and doon the pool, and he had uncommon wark wi' 't, for it was strong and there was little licht. But bye and bye he got it almost tae his feet, and was just about to lift it oout when a maist awfu' thing happened. The tackets o' his boots maun hae slithered on the stane, for the next thing I saw was Mr Airthur in the muckle hungry water.

'I dinna exactly ken what happened after that, till I found myself on the very stone he had slipped off. I maun hae come doon the face o' the rocks, a thing I can scarcely believe when I look at them, and a thing no man ever did afore. At ony rate I ken I fell the last fifteen feet or sae, and lichted on my left airm, for I felt it crack like a rotten branch, and an awfu' sairness ran up it.

'Now, the pool is a whirlpool as ye ken, and if anything fa's in, the water first smashes it against the muckle rock at the foot, then it brings it round below the fall again, and syne at the second time it carries it doon the burn. Weel, that was what happened to Mr Airthur. I heard his heid gang dunt on the stane wi' a sound that made me sick. This must hae dung him clean senseless, and indeed it was a wonder it didna knock his brains oot. At ony rate there was nae mair word o' swimming, and he was whirled round below the fa' just like a corp.

'I kenned fine that nae time was to be lost, for if he once gaed doun the burn he wad be in Gled or ever I could say a word, and nae wad ever see him mair in life. So doon I got on my hunkers on the stane, and waited for the turnin'. Round he came, whirling in the foam, wi' a lang line o' blood across his brow where the stane had cut him. It was a terrible meenute. My heart fair stood still. I put out my airm, and as he passed I grippit him and wi' an awfu' pu' got him out o' the current into the side.

'But now I found that a waur thing still was on me. My left airm was broken, and my richt sae numbed and weak wi' my fall that, try as I micht, I couldnae raise him ony further. I thocht I wad burst a blood vessel i' my face and my muscles fair cracked wi' the strain, but I would make nothing o' 't. There he stuck wi' his heid and shouthers abune the water, pu'd close until the edge of a rock.

'What was I to dae? If I once let him slip he wad be into the stream and lost forever. But I couldna hang on here a' nicht, and as far as I could see there wad be naebody near till the mornin', when Ebie Blackstock passed frae the Head o' the Hope. I roared wi' a' my power; but I got nai answer, naething but the rummle o' the water and the whistling o' some whaups on the hill.

'Then I turned very sick wi' terror and pain and weakness and I kenna what. My broken airm seemed a great lump o' burnin' coal. I maun hae given it some extra wrench when I hauled him out, for it was sae sair now that I thocht I could scarcely thole² it. Forbye, pain and a', I could hae gone off to sleep wi' fair weariness. I had heard tell o' men sleepin' on

---

¹ Unlucky.
² Endure.

their feet, but I never felt it till then. Man, if I hadna warstled wi' myself, I wad hae dropped off as deid's a peery.

'There there was the awfu' strain o' keepin' Mr Airthur up. He was a great big man, twelve stone I'll warrant, and weighing a terrible lot mair wi' his fishing togs and things. If I had had the use o' my ither airm I micht hae taen off his jacket and creel and lichtened the burden, but I could do naething. I scarcely like to tell ye how I was tempted in that hour. Again and again I says to mysel, "Gidden Scott," say I, "what do ye care for this man? He's no a drap's bluid to you, and forbye ye'll never be able to save him. Ye micht as weel let him gang. Ye've dune a' ye could. Ye're a brave man, Gidden Scott, and ye've nae cause to be ashamed o' givin' up the fecht." But I says to mysel again: "Gidden Scott, ye're a coward. Wad ye let a man die, when there's a breath in your body? Think shame o' yoursel, man." So I aye kept haudin' on, although I was very near bye wi' 't. Whenever I lookit at Mr Airthur's face, as white's death and a' blood, and his een sae stelled-like, I got a kind o' groo and felt awfu' pitiful for the bit laddie. Then I thocht on his faither, the auld Lord, wha was sae built up in him, and I couldna bear to think o' his son droonin' in that awfu' hole. So I set myself to the wark o' keepin' him up a' nicht, though I had nae hope in the matter. It wasna what ye ca' bravery that made me dae't, for I had nae ither choice. It was just kind o' dourness that runs in my folk, and a kind o' vexedness for sae young a callant in sic an ill place.

'The nicht was hot and there was scarcely a sound o' wind. I felt the sweat standin' on my face like frost on tatties, and abune me the sky was a' misty and nae mune visible. I thocht very likely that it micht come a thunder-shower and I kind o' lookit forrit tae 't. For I was aye feared at lichtning, and if it came that nicht I was bound to get clean dazed and likely tummle in. I was a lonely man wi' nae kin to speak o', so it wouldna maitter muckle.

'But now I come to tell ye about the queer side o' that nicht's wark, while I never telled to nane but yoursel, though a' the folk about here ken the rest. I maun hae been geyan weak, for I got into a kind o' doze, no sleepin', ye understand, but awfu' like it. And then a' sort o' daft things began to dance afore my een. Witches and bogles and brownies and things oot o' the Bible, and leviathans and brazen bulls – a' cam fleerin' and flauntin' on the top o' the water straucht afore me. I didna pay muckle heed to them, for I half kenned it was a' nonsense, and syne they gaed awa'. Then an auld wife wi' a mutch[1] and a hale procession o' auld wives passed, and just about the last I saw yin I thocht I kenned.

'"Is that you, grannie?" says I.

'"Ay, it's me, Gidden," says she; and as shure as I'm a leevin' man, it was my auld grannie, whae had been deid thae sax year. She had on the same mutch as she aye wore, and the same auld black stickie in her hand, and, Dod, she had the same snuff-box I made for her out o' a sheep's horn when I first took to the herdin'. I thocht she was lookin' rale weel.

'"Losh, Grannie," says I, "Where in the warld hae ye come frae? It's no canny to see ye danderin' about there."

'"Ye've been badly brocht up," she says, "and ye ken nocht about it. Is't no a decent and comely thing that I should get a breath o' air yince in a while?"'

'"Deed," said I, "I had forgotten. Ye were sae like yoursel I never had a mind ye were deid. And how d' ye like the Guid Place?"

'"Wheesht, Gidden," says she, very solemn-like, "I'm no there."

'Now at this I was fair flabbergasted. Grannie had aye been a guid contentit auld wumman, and to think that they hadna let her intil Heeven made me think ill o' my ain chances.

'"Help us, ye dinna mean to tell me ye're in Hell?" I cries.

'"No exactly," says she, "But I'll trouble ye, Gidden, to speak mair respectfu' about holy things. That's a name ye uttered the noo whilk we dinna daur to mention."

'"I'm sorry, Grannie," says I, "but ye maun allow it's an astonishin' thing for me to hear. We aye counted ye shure, and ye died wi' the Buik in your hands."

---

[1] Kerchief.

"'Weel,'" she says, "it was like this. When I gaed up till the gate o' Heeven a man wi' a long white robe comes and says, 'Wha may ye be?' says I, 'I'm Elspeth Scott.' He gangs awa' and consults a wee and then he says, 'I think, Elspeth my wumman, ye'll hae to gang doon the brae a bit. Ye're no quite guid eneuch for this place, but ye'll get a very comfortable doonsittin' whaur I tell ye.' So off I gaed and cam' to a place whaur the air was like the inside of the glass-houses at the Lodge. They took me In wi'oot a word and I've been rale comfortable. Ye see they keep the bad part o' the Ill Place for the reg'lar bad folk, but they've a very nice half-way house where the likes o' me stop."

"'And what kind o' company hae ye?'"

"'No very select,'" says she. "There's maist o' the ministers o' the countryside and a pickle fairmers, tho' the maist o' them are further ben.[1] But there's my son Jock, your ain faither, Gidden, and a heap o' folk from the village, and oh, I'm nane sae bad.'"

"'Is there naething mair ye wad like then, Grannie?'"

"'Oh aye,'" says she, "we've each yae thing which we canna get. It's a' the punishment we hae. Mine's butter. I canna get fresh butter for my bread, for ye see it winna keep, it just melts. So I've to take jeely to ilka slice, whilk is rale sair on the teeth. Ye'll no hae ony wi' ye?'"

"'No,'" I says, "I've naething but some tobaccy. D' ye want it? Ye were aye fond o' 't.'"

"'Na, na,'" says she. "I get plenty o' tobaccy doon bye. The pipe's never out o' the folks' mouth there. But I'm no speakin' about yoursel, Gidden. Ye're in a geyan ticht place.'"

"'I'm a' that,'" I said. "Can ye no help me?'"

"'I micht try.'" And she raxes out her hand to grip mine. I put out mine to take it, never thinkin' that that wasna the richt side, and that if Grannie grippit it she wad pu' the broken airm and haul me into the water. Something touched my fingers like a hot poker; I gave a great yell; and ere ever I kenned I was awake, a' but off the rock, wi' my left airm aching like hell-fire. Mr Airthur I had let slunge ower the heid and my ain legs were in the water.

'I gae an awfu' whammle and edged my way back though it was near bye my strength. And now anither thing happened. For the cauld water roused Mr Airthur frae his dwam.[2] His een opened and he gave a wild look around him. "Where am I?" he cries, "Oh God!" and he gaed off intil anither faint.

'I can tell ye, sir, I never felt anything in this warld and I hope never to feel anything in anither sae bad as the next meenutes on that rock. I was fair sick wi' pain and weariness and a kind o' fever. The lip-lap o' the water, curling round Mr Airthur, and the great crush o' the Black Linn itsel dang me fair silly. Then there was my airm, which was bad eneuch, and abune a' I was gotten into sic a state that I was fleyed[3] at ilka shadow just like a bairn. I felt fine I was gaun daft, and if the thing had lasted anither score o' meenutes I wad be in a madhouse this day. But soon I felt the sleepiness comin' back, and I was off again dozin' and dreamin'.

'This time it was nae auld wumman but a muckle black-avised man that was standin' in the water glowrin' at me. I kenned him fine by the bandy-legs o' him and the broken nose (whilk I did mysel), for Dan Kyle the poacher deid thae twae year. He was a man, as I remembered him weel, wi' a great black beard and een that were stuck sae far in his heid that they looked like twae wull-cats keekin'[4] oot o' a hole. He stands and just stares at me, and never speaks a word.

"'What d'ye want?'" I yells, for by this time I had lost a' grip o' mysel. "Speak, man, and dinna stand there like a dummy.'"

"'I want naething,'" he says in a mournfu' sing-song voice, "I'm just thinkin'.'"

"'Whaur d' ye come frae?'" I asked, "and are ye keepin' weel?'"

"'Weel,'" he says bitterly. "In this warld I was ill to my wife, and two-three times I near killed a man, and I stole like a pyet, and I was never sober. How d'ye think I should be weel in the next?'"

---

[1] In.
[2] Swoon.
[3] Frightened.
[4] Peeping.

'I was sorry for the man. "D'ye ken I'm vexed for ye, Dan," says I; "I never likit ye when ye were here, but I'm wae to think ye're sae ill off yonder."

"'I'm no alane," he says. "There's Mistress Courhope o' the Big House, she's waur. Ye mind she was awfu' fond o' gum-flowers. Weel, she canna keep them Yonder, for they a' melt wi' the heat. She's in an ill way about it, puir body." Then he broke off. "Whae's that ye've got there? Is't Airthur Morrant?"

"'Ay, it's Airthur Morrant," I said.

"'His family's weel kent doon bye," says he. "We've maist o' his forebears, and we're expectin' the auld Lord every day. May be we'll sune get the lad himsel'."

"'That's a damned lee," says I, for I was angry at the man's presumption.

'Dan lookit at me sorrowfu'-like. "We'll be gettin' you tae, if ye swear that gate,"[1] says he, "and then ye'll ken what it's like."

'Of a sudden I fell into a great fear. "Dinna say that, Dan," I cried; "I'm better than ye think. I'm a deacon, and 'll maybe sune be an elder, and I never swear except at my dowg."

"'Tak care, Gidden," said the face afore me. "Where I am, a' things are taken into account."

"'Then they'll hae a gey big account for you," says I. "What-like do they treat you, may be?"

'The man groaned.

"'I'll tell ye what they dae to ye doon there," he said. "They put ye intil a place a' paved wi' stanes and wi' four square walls around. And there's naething in 't, nae grass, nae shadow. And abune you there's a sky like brass. And sune ye get terrible hot and thirsty, and your tongue sticks to your mouth, and your eyes get blind wi' lookin' on the white stane. Then ye gang clean fey, and dad your heid on the ground and the walls to try and kill yoursel. But though ye dae 't till a' eternity ye couldna feel pain. A' that ye feel is just the awfu' devourin' thirst, and the heat and the weariness. And if ye lie doon the ground burns ye and ye're fain to get up. And ye canna lean on the walls for the heat, and bye and bye when ye're fair perished wi' the thing, they tak ye out to try some ither ploy."

"'Nai mair," I cried, "nae mair, Dan!"

'But he went on malicious-like–

"'Na, na, Gidden, I'm no dune yet. Syne they tak you to a fine room but awfu' warm. And there's a big fire in the grate and thick woollen rugs on the floor. And in the corner there's a braw feather bed. And they lay ye down on 't, and then they pile on the tap o' ye mattresses and blankets and sacks and great rolls o' woolen stuff miles wide. And then ye see what they're after, tryin' to suffocate ye as they dae to folk that a mad dowg has bitten. And ye try to kick them off, but they're ower heavy, and ye canna move your feet nor your airms nor gee your heid. Then ye gang clean gyte[2] and skirl to yoursel, but your voice is choked and naebody is near. And the warst o' 't is that ye canna die and get it ower. It's like death a hundred times and yet ye're aye leevin'. Bye and bye when they think ye've got eneuch they tak you out and put ye somewhere else."

"'Oh," I cries, "stop, man, or you'll ding me silly."

'But he says never a word, just glowrin' at me.

"'Aye, Gidden, and waur than that. For they put ye in a great loch wi' big waves just like the sea at the Pier o' Leith. And there's nae chance o' soomin', for as sune as ye put out your airms a billow gulfs ye down. Then ye swallow water and your heid dozes round and ye're chokin'. But ye canna die, ye must just thole. And down ye gang, down, down, in the cruel deep, till your heid's like to burst and your een are fu' o' bluid. And there's a' kind o' fearfu' monsters about, muckle slimy things wi' blind een and white scales, that claw at ye wi' claws just like the paws o' a drooned dog. And ye canna get away though ye fecht and fleech, and bye and bye ye're fair mad wi' horror and choking and the feel o' thae awfu' things. Then–"

'But now I think something snapped in my heid, and I went daft in doonricht earnest.

---

[1] Way.
[2] Mad.

The man before me danced about like a lantern's shine on a windy nicht and then disappeared. And I woke yelling like a pig at a killing, fair wud wi' terror, and my skellochs made the rocks ring. I found mysel in the pool a' but yae airm – the broken yin – which had hankit in a crack o' rock. Nae wonder I had been dreaming o' deep waters among the torments o' the Ill Place, when I was in them mysel. The pain in my airm was sae fearsome and my heid was gaun round sae wi' horror that I just skirled on and on, shrieking and groaning wi'oot a thocht what I was daein'. I was as near death as ever I will be, and as for Mr Airthur he was on the very nick o' 't, for by this time he was a' in the water, though I still kept a grip o' him.

'When I think ower it often I wonder how it was possible that I could be here the day. But the Lord's very gracious, and he works in a queer way. For it so happened that Ebie Blackstock, whae had left Gledsmuir an hour afore me and whom I thocht by this time to be snorin' in his bed at the Head o' the Hope, had gone intil the herd's house at the Waterfit, and had got sae muckle drink there that he was sweered to start for hame till about half-past twal i' the night. Weel. he was comin' up the burnside, gae happy and contentit, for he had nae wife at hame to speir about his ongaeings, when, as he's telled me himsel, he heard sic an uproar doon by the Black Linn that made him turn pale and think that the Deil, whom he had long served, had gotten him at last.

'But he was a brave man, was Ebie, and he thinks to himsel that some fellow-creature micht be perishin'. So he gangs forrit wi' a' his pith, trying to think on the Lord's Prayer and last Sabbath's sermon. And, lookin' ower the edge, he saw naething for a while, naething but the black water wi' the awfu' yells coming out o' 't. Then he made out something like a heid near the side. So he rins doon by the road, no ower the rocks as I had come, but round by the burnside road, and soon he gets to the pool, where the crying was getting aye fainter and fainter. And then he saw me. And he grips me by the collar, for he was a sensible man, was Ebie, and hauls me oot. If he hadna been geyan strong he couldna hae dune it, for I was a deid wecht, forbye having a heavy man hanging on to me. When he got me up, what was his astonishment to find anither man at the end o' my airm, a man like a crop a' bloody about the heid. So he got us baith out, and we wae baith senseless; and he laid us in a safe bit back frae the water, and syne gaed off for help. So bye and bye we were baith got home, me to my house and Mr Airthur up to the Lodge.'

'And was that the end of it?' I asked.

'Na,' said the shepherd. 'I lay for twae month there raving wi' brain fever, and when I cam to my senses I was as weak as a bairn. It was many months ere I was mysel again, and my left airm to this day is stiff and no muckle to lippen to. But Mr Airthur was far waur, for the dad he had gotten on the rock was thocht to have broken his skull, and he lay long atween life and death. And the warst thing was that his faither was sae vexed about him that he never got ower the shock, but dee'd afore Airthur was out o' bed. And so when he cam out again he was My Lord, and a monstrously rich man.'

The shepherd puffed meditatively at his pipe for a few minutes.

'But that's no a' yet. For Mr Airthur wad take nae refusal but that I maun gang awa' doon wi' him to his braw house in England and be a land o' factor or steward or something like that. And I had a rale fine cottage a' to mysel, wi' a very bonny gairden and guid wages, so I stayed there maybe sax month and then I gaed up till him. "I canna bide nae longer," says I. "I canna stand this place. It's far ower laigh, and I'm fair sick to get hills to rest my een on. I'm awfu' grateful' to ye for your kindness, but I maun gie up my job." He was very sorry to lose me, and was for giein' me a present o' money or stockin' a fairm for me, because he said that it was to me he owed his life. But I wad hae nane o' his gifts. "It wad be a terrible thing," I says, "to take siller for daein' what ony body wad hae dune out o' pity." So I cam awa' back to Standlan, and I maun say I'm rale contentit here. Mr Airthur used whiles to write to me and ca' in and see me when he cam North for the shooting; but since he's gane sae far wrang wi' the Tories, I've had naething mair to dae wi' him.'

I made no answer, being busy pondering in my mind on the depth of the shepherd's political principles, before which the ties of friendship were as nothing.

'Aye,' said he, standing up, 'I did what I thocht my duty at the time and I was rale glad I saved the callant's life. But now, when I think on a' the ill he's daein' to the country and the Guid Cause, I whiles think I wad hae been daein' better if I had just drappit him in.

'But whae kens? It's a queer warld.' And the shepherd knocked the ashes out of his pipe.

Nannie Wells (1875 – ?)

A Prayer

God, give us the grace to hate
our unemancipated state,
and to wipe from Scotland's face
her intellectual disgrace.

The eye that peers forth cannily,
how can it reach the stars on high?
The ear that waits on market price
obeys the voice of cowardice.

The mouth that babbles out 'Ay, ay'
how shall it utter prophecy?   10
Who on self-interest spends his days
forgets the noble art of praise.

Free us from fear of other folk,
our minds from weight of foreign yoke;
teach us to take our true delight
in things that are our own by right.

The soil that nourished flesh and bones,
the chemistry of Scotland's stones,
in our bodily substance shout
what we ought to be about.   20

Unmistakable the note
the Northern Wind sings in its throat;
the Highland rivers' sudden rush
raises the authentic blush.

Our mountains that above us tower
alone can judge our 'finest hour';
to clear our word-beclouded minds
we need the Bible of the Winds.

The things for which we ought to die
are plainly written on the sky;   30
God, now to us the vision give
to know for what we ought to live.

Rachel Taylor (1876 – 1960)

Lord Roland

Lord Roland lay but half asleep
After his dreich★ lang ride,   tiring
When he was ware o' a gentle ghaist
Stood weeping by his side.

'Depart frae me, a weary man:
I sweir I ken ye not.
Depart frae me, ye burnin' wraith
Whose name I hae forgot.'

'I ken I smell o' cauld grave-mool★   mold
That washed in lavender.'   10
A stound★ garred★ a' his heart to fail   blow/made
As he stared straight at her.

'Oh, whatten a boon seek ye o' me,
Even if I mind your face?
Your time is ower. The quick and deid
Meet not in ony place.'

'I ken I'm changed that once was white
Wi' things o' Italy.'
'Frae Hell's red pit o Paradise,
Wha would ye now o' me?'   20

'I ken my tongue is eerie now
That sang the songs o' France.
Langsyne ye vowed I swayed to you
A lily in the dance.'

'May Marie, am I Lord or Deil
To holpen i' the mirk?
I saw you on a gowden bier
Outside the Lady-Kirk.'

'There is nae place in Paradise,
There is nae place in Hell,   30
Till seven kisses ransom me
That living kissed ye well.'

He's risen and stood afore her face,
And kissed her mou' o' ice.
'Will seven kisses buy your peace? –
It is a little price.'

'Seven little kisses buy a place
In Paradise or hell.' –
They bore him through the toon neist day
Wi' sounding sacring-bell.   40

They bore him through the thrawn★ grey day,   twisted
The gowd bier through the mirk:
And laid the bridegroom by the bride
Beside the Lady-Kirk.

The Preference

'I will give you a gay blue cloak
Soft with queen's miniver.'
'He will give me a shroud of flame
And I find it lovelier.'

'I will lap you in smooth white silk
In a carved-angel bed.'
'But he has doomed me to the stake,
And I have bowed my head.'

The Spiral Stair

In the carven House of the Spiral Stair
I met you startling and unaware.
We suddenly kissed and parted there.

On that surprising Spiral Stair
We may meet again. You shall not dare
To look in mine eyes, and I shall not care.

There are broidered blades on the Spiral Stair.
My delicate violent kiss and rare
You ravished once. And so, beware!

The Exile

The rains are sweeter in my ballad-land,
(So saith my heart, grown sick and feverish).
The very winds and waters understand.
Like golden apples on a silver dish,
The autumn days come smoothly to one's hand:
While, if you wander where the moor-paths wind,
The Earth herself is clean and kith and kind.

The folk are surer in my ballad-land:
They do not stretch the soul upon the rack:

Their honour is their holy deodand, –   10
They do not smile and stab you in the back
Where the great skies by peacock-plumes are fanned. –
My feet are leaden with the stranger's clay:
My heart is broken with the stranger's way.

Thy rains are purer, O my ballad-land,
But it is sad to come a beggar home.
Thy tragic moors and waters understand
What may befall thy fey frank fools that roam.
Even as thou givest they will render, and
Plead alien love for what is none of his,   20
Imploring sorry grace where no grace is.

(O Faëry Mother, touch me with thy wand,
Make me a sea-bird for thee, ballad-land!)

The Princess of Scotland

The following poem is the one by which this poet is best known.

'Who are you that so strangely woke,
And raised a fine hand?'
Poverty wears a scarlet cloak

                    In my land.

'Duchies of dreamland, emerald, rose
Lie at your command?'
Poverty like a princess goes

                    In my land.

'Wherefore the mask of silken lace
Tied with a golden band?'   10
Poverty walks with wanton grace

                    In my land.

'Why do you softly, richly speak
Rhythm so sweetly-scanned?'
Poverty hath the Gaelic and Greek

                    In my land.

'There's a far-off scent about you seems
Born in Samarkand.'
Poverty hath luxurious dreams

                    In my land.

'You have wounds that like passion-flowers you hide: 21
I cannot understand.'
Poverty hath one name with Pride

                    In my land.

'Oh, will you draw your last sad breath
'Mid bitter bent⋆ and sand?'   grass
Poverty begs from none but Death
                                                        In my land.

In Aberdeen

In Aberdeen, in years long perished,
The sunset-wings were gold and green.
What marvellous mad hopes were cherished
In Aberdeen.

Oh, that's a city to be born in.
The pure air kindles you, and witty
Your mind goes dancing. To learn scorn in,
Oh, that's a city.

Tha sea-birds cry wild things above, in
The tender and the stainless sky.   10
Oh, that's a city to learn love in,
Where sea-birds cry.

Under the Crown that dreams of Flodden
And Borgia, in scarlet gown
Youth lightly treads where Youth hath trodden
Under the Crown.

In Aberdeen, through years of spendour,
You may ride mailed in gold and green.
Ironic folk to Youth are tender
In Aberdeen.   20

Ecstasy

O ye that look on Ecstasy
The Dancer lone and white,
Cover your charmed eyes, for she
Is Death's own acolyte.
She dances on the moonstone floors
Against the jeweled peacock doors:
The roses flame in her gold hair,
The tired sad lids are overfair.
All ye that look on Ecstasy
The Dancer lone and white   10
Cover your dreaming eyes, lest she –
(Oh, softly, strangely –) float you through
These doors all bronze and green and blue
Into the Bourg of Night.

Robert Crawford (1877 – 1931)

I Took My Love

I took my love by a woodside
Which soft grass washes like a tide,
Where drunk bees stagger past the ear,
From inn to inn with sudden cheer.

To warm her love I wished her brought
Where the bee sings and time is nought,
And over Clyde's impassioned skies
The air breaks into butterflies.

I took her where the wanton flowers
Can keep the sunshine after hours,   10
And daisies' puritan-caress
Might teach the kiss of holiness;

And stayed while beams drew slant, too soon,
That soft glow makes an afternoon;
Then like a wild bird in her side,
Her heart sprang up at eventide.

Hawthorn-Time

O girls upon these Scottish roads,
By glen and tree,
In far-succeeding Junes whose buds
I will not see,
I loved your mothers, and (though sleep
Is on me) back my dreams will creep

To hedgerows white and hawthorn hours
In lanes where you
Take what the scented gloaming dowers,
(As we did too),   10
And will not know each happy breath
Stores up a sweet can conquer death.

For all my soul is scented soul
And wooing dew
From heavy windless dusks, that stole
Me through and through;
And thrills at hawthorn-time my clay
That's laid just off your evening way.

John Caie (1879 – 1949)

The Fiddler

Some say 'twas Priest Logie first learnt himn the knack,
An nae muckle winner★,   wonder
For files fin ye h'ard him ye'd sweer he could mak'
A saint o' a sinner.

But ither times, fegs, he wad play ye a spring
Wad set your bleed dirlin'★   tingling
Until ye gaed daft, an' yer bonnet ye'd fling
Oot ow'r the meen birlin'.

He'd sangs and laments, a reel, a strathspey,
Some tune that cam' greetin';   10
A rant that wad turn and aul' maid fairly fey,
Wi' he'rt wildly beatin'.

For young an' for aul', for blither an' for dour,
For dancers an' singers,
For a' that had lugs★, there was magical poo'r   ears
In's bow an' in's fingers.

But noo he's awa', an' his meesic nae mair
Comes lauchin' or sabbin',
Tae hiz onywye – although maybe up there,
As seen's they loot Rab in.   20

The Almichty wad say tae the angels a' roun'
His deece★ i' the middle,   settle
'Jist heely a meenit: your harps lay ye doon;
Rab, hae ye your fiddle?'

The Puddock

A puddock★ sat by the lochan's brim,   frog
An' he thocht there was never a puddock like him.
He sat on his hurdies, he waggled his legs,
An' cockit his heid as he glowered through the seggs★.   iris
The bigsy wee cratur' was feelin' that prood
He gapit his mou' an' he croakit oot lood:
'Gin ye'd a' like tae see a richt puddock,' quo' he,
'Ye'll never, I'll sweer, get a better nor me.
I've fem'lies an' wives an' a weel-plenished hame,
Wi' drink for my thrapple★ an' meat for my wame★.   10   throat/belly
The lasses aye thocht me a fine strappin' chiel★,   fellow
An' I ken I'm a rale bonny singer as weel.
I'm nae gaun tae blaw, but th' truth I maun tell –
I believe I'm the verra MacPuddock himsel'.'

A heron was hungry an' needin' tae sup,
Sae he nabbit th' puddock and gollup't him up;
Syne runkled his feathers: 'A peer thing,' quo' he,
'But – puddocks is nae fat they eesed tae be.'

Snaw

Snaw,
Dingin' on slaw,
Quait, quait, far nae win's blaw,
Haps up bonnily the frost-grippit lan'.
Quait, quait, the bare trees stan',
Raisin' caul' fingers tae the deid, leiden lift⋆,   sky
Keppin' a' they can as the flakes doon drift.
Still, still,
The glen an' the hill
Nae mair they echo the burnie's bit v'ice,   10
That's tint⋆, death-silent, awa' neth the ice.   gone, lost
Soun'less, the warl' is row'd up in sleep,
Dreamless an' deep,
Dreamless an' deep.
Niver a move but the saft doon–glidin'
O' wee, wee fairies on fite steeds ridin',
Ridin', ridin', the haill earth hidin',
Till a'thing's awa'
An' there's naething but snaw,
Snaw.   20

John Ferguson (1879 – 1928)

A Cock Crowing in a Poulterer's Shop

He will not see the East catch fire again,
Nor watch the darkening of the drowsy West,
Nor sniff the morning air with joyous zest,
Nor lead his wives along the grassy lane.

Cooped in a crate, he claps his wings in vain,
Then hangs his crimson head upon his breast;
Tomorrow's sun will see him plucked and dressed,
One of a ghastly row of feathered slain.

O chanticleer, I cannot bear it more;
That crow of anguish, pitiful and stark,   10
Makes my flesh quail at thy unhappy lot –
The self same cry with which thine ancestor
Emptied his soul into the tragic dark
The night that Peter said, 'I know Him not.'

Harold Monro (1879 – 1932)

Child of Dawn

O gentle vision in the dawn:
My spirit over faint cool water glides,
Child of the day,
To thee;
And thou art drawn
By a same impulse over silver tides
The dreamy way
To me.

I need thy hands, O gentle wonder-child,
For they are molded unto all repose;   10
Thy lips are frail,
And thou art cooler than an April rose;
White are thy words and mild:
Child of the morning, hail!

Breathe thus upon mine eyelids – Oh, we twain
Will build the day together out of dreams.
Life, with thy breath upon mine eyelids, seems
Exquisite to the utmost bounds of pain.
I cannot wish to live, except so far
As I may be compelled for love of thee.   20
O let us drift,
Frail as the floating silver of a star,
Or like the summer humming of a bee,
Or stream-reflected sunlight through a rift.

I will not hope, because I know, alas,
Morning will glide to noon, and then the night
Will take thee from me. Everything must pass
Swiftly – but nought so swift as dawn-delight.
If I could even make thee last till day,
Child of repose,   30
Were broad upon the lea,
What god can say,
What god or mortal knows,
What wonder might not happen unto me?

O gentle vision in the dawn:
My spirit over faint cool water glides,
Child of the day,
To thee;
And thou art drawn
By a same impulse over silver tides   40
The dreamy way
To me.

To the Desired

Love, I go with hopeless gaze
Searching all the torrid day
Which of earth's unnumbered ways
Thou art fled – Which way? Which way?

I have thought, where roadways meet
By some faint delicious stream,
Sometimes, thou hast left the sweet
Perfume of a passing dream.

Or upon a summer's hour,
In a garden by the sea,   10
Suddenly have seen a flower
With a wonder face, like thee.

Or have turned me, when a voice
Lifted at a village fair
Made my startled blood rejoice,
Quickly, and perceived thy hair.

Yea, some scent, or sound, or sight
Brings a moment swift to me
Of our single summer night –
But it never brings me thee.   20

Art thou with the summer dead?
Didst thou, as a butterfly,
Flash upon my vision, shed
One quick rapture, pass and die?

Or perchance, I often fear,
While I search the whole world wide,
Art thou hidden trembling near,
Almost at my very side?

Had I but the cunning gaze
Fixed upon events to be   30
To distinguish through the days
That which is the soul of thee!

Oh, alas, the fitful breath,
And the ever changing light,
And the mystery of death,
And the fleetness of delight!

Fear me not: I sometimes dread
Thou mayst hold thyself away
Hid as though among the dead
Out of innocent dismay.   40

Yet I love thee with the love
That was once revealed to me
Out of where the spirits move
In the light beyond the sea.

Love, I go with hopeless gaze
Searching all the torrid day
Which of earth's unnumbered ways
Thou art fled – Which way? Which way?

Lake Leman

It is the sacred hour: above the far
Low emerald hills that northward fold,
Calmly, upon the blue, the evening star
Floats, wreathed in dusky gold.
The winds have sung all day: but now they lie
Faint, sleeping; and the evening sounds awake.
The slow bell tolls across the water: I
Am haunted by the spirit of the lake.
It seems as though the sounding of the bell
Intoned the low song of the water-soul,   10
And at some moments I can hardly tell
The long-resounding echo from the toll.
The spirit of the water is awake:
O thou mysterious lake,
Thou art enchanted, and thy spell
Holds all who round thy fruitful margin dwell.
Oft have I seen home-going peasants' eyes
Lit with the peace that emanates from thee.
Those who among thy waters plunge, arise
Filled with new wisdom and serenity.   20
What knowledge, what remembrance can have thus
Set beauty for a token on thy brow?
Lake that I love, whence comest thou to us? –
So strange and wistful in our midst art thou.
Thy veins are in the mountains. I have heard,
Down-stretched beside thee at the silent noon,
With leaning head attentive to thy word,
A secret and delicious mountain-tune,
Proceeding as from many shadowed hours
In ancient forests carpeted with flowers,   30

And, father still, where trickling waters haunt
Between the crevices of white crags gaunt.
Ah, what repose at breathless noon to go,
Lean on thy bosom, hold thee with stretched hands,
And listen for the music of the snow!
But most, as now,
When harvest covers thy surrounding lands,
I love thee, with a coronal of sheaves
Crowned regent of the day;
And on the air thy placid breathing leaves   40
A scent of corn and hay.
For thou hast gathered (as a mother will
The sayings of her children in her heart),
The harvest-thoughts of reapers on the hill,
When the cool rose and honeysuckle fill
The air, and fruit is laden on the cart.
Thou breathest the delight
Of summer evening at the deep-roofed farm,
And meditation of the summer night,
When the enravished earth is lying warm   50
From recent kisses of the conquering sun.
Dwell as a spirit in me, O thou one
Sweet natural presence. In the years to be
When all the mortal loves perchance are done,
Them I will bid farewell, but, oh, not thee.
I love thee. When the youthful visions fade,
Fade thou not also in the hopeless past.
Be constant and delightful, as a maid
Sought over all the world, and found at last.

Pastoral

I found a place of olden trees
Beyond the glaring light of day,
And, following my reveries,
Along a grassy way
I went, in contemplation fond,
By flowery brake and leafy pond
Through forest glades, and out beyond,
Where pastures lay.

Between the tops of trees I saw,
High in the far primeval sky,   10
Swift inland from some ocean shore
The gleaming sea-gulls fly.
The shepherd's pipe, where sheep abound,
White-winged with still and silvery sound,
Rose from the nibbled pasture-ground,
Where shepherds lie.

Tall, gnarled and firm, the rugged oak,
Flushed with its youth the bramble too,
The flaring lowly flowers all spoke
A purpose that I knew;   20
And unto no desire inclined,
With cool and unexpectant mind,
Upon the pasture I reclined,
As shepherds do.

Then I was joined to sense and sound:
I grew within the growth of trees,
Oak-hearted from the placid ground;
I sang within the breeze.
I floated with the scent of flowers,
Moved with the living power of powers,   30
The spirit of the dreaming hours
Upon the leas.

I was unconscious of the pain
Of will and meditated plan,
And, at the heart of life again,
Forgot the life of man,
Time lingered at the fruitful height,
Unconscious of its own delight,
Unconscious of the coming night,
– But night began.   40

For suddenly the hour was ripe,
And all the fruit thereof was spent;
And suddenly the shepherd's pipe
Ceased, like a bow unbent.
The light upon the pasture ceased;
The beating of my heart increased;
My blood was suddenly released:
I rose, and went.

O shepherds of the verdant lea,
You are more fortunate than I,   50
Untroubled by the mystery
Of whither, whence, and why.
O shepherds of the pasture ground,
The mystery we all shall sound
Lies six feet buried in profound
Eternity.

The Cottage, Planned to Suit the British Mind

The cottage, planned to suit the British mind,
Is stationed high upon the English shore.
Outside, the rain is falling, and the wind
Shrieks at the corners, whistles at the door.

Within the cold damp parlor, to the light
Of one thin gas-flame, meager as his life,
The grocer has assembled towards night
His family of seven and his wife.

'Tis Sunday, and he talks about himself:
She tolerates his oft-repeated stock   10
With eyes uplifted to the mantleshelf,
Yawning toward the hideous gilded clock.

God, who ordained the British Sunday even
To most resemble his own placid life,
Looks, smiling out of comfortable Heaven,
Down on the British grocer and his wife.

Midnight Lamentation

When you and I go down
Breathless and cold,
Our faces both worn back
To earthly mould,
How lonely we shall be.
What shall we do,
You without me,
I without you?

I cannot bear the thought
You, first, may die,   10
Nor of how you will weep,
Should I.
We are too much alone;
What can we do?
To make our bodies one:
You, me; I, you?

We are most nearly born
Of one same kind;
We have the same delight,
The same true mind.   20
Must we then part, we part;
Is there no way
To keep a beating heart,
And light of day?

I could now rise and run
Through street on street
To where you are breathing – you,
That we might meet,
And that your living voice
Might sound above   30
Fear, and we two rejoice
Within our love.

How frail the body is,
And we are made
As only in decay
To lean and fade.
I think too much of death;
There is a gloom
When I can't hear your breath
Calm in some room.   40

O, but how suddenly
Either may droop;
Countenance be so white,
Body stoop.
Then there may be a place
Where fading flowers
Drop on a lifeless face
Through weeping hours.

Is then nothing safe?
Can we not find   50
Some everlasting life
In our one mind?
I feel it like disgrace
Only to understand
Your spirit through your word,
Or by your hand.

I cannot find a way
Through love and through;
I cannot reach beyond
Body, to you.   60
When you or I must go
Down evermore,
There'll be no more to say
– But a locked door.

Thistledown

This might have been a place for sleep
But, as from that small hollow there
Hosts of bright thistledown begin
Their dazzling journey through the air,
An idle man can only stare.

They grip their withered edge of stalk
In brief excitement for the wind;
They hold a breathless final talk,
And when their filmy cables part
One almost hears a little cry.   10

Some cling together while they wait
And droop and gaze and hesitate,
But others leap along the sky,
Or circle round and calmly choose
The gust they know they ought to use.

While some in loving pairs will glide,
Or watch the others as they pass,
Or rest on flowers in the grass,
Or circle through the shining day
Like silvery butterflies at play.   20

Some catch themselves to every mound,
Then lingeringly and slowly move
As if they knew the precious ground
Were opening for their fertile love:
They almost try to dig, they need
So much to plant their thistle-seed.

Strange Meetings

If suddenly a clod of earth should rise,
And walk about, and breathe, and speak, and love,
How one would tremble, and in what surprise
Gasp: 'Can you move?'

I see men walking, and I always feel:
'Earth, how have you done this? What can you be?'
I can't learn how to know men, or conceal
How strange they are to me.

J. E. Stewart (? – 1917)

Left Her Lane

Aiblins she thocht he'd hap her doon
In the auld kirk-yaird ayont the toon
Whaur the kirkspire shadows his father's stane –
But she maun tak that gait* her lane.   way

For at the mirk on yon hill-face
They dug for him a resting-place
Whaur the grass is wat wi' the red-warm rain –
And she maun tak her gait her lane.

John MacDougall Hay (1881 – 1919)

Hay is a distinguished novelist, whose masterpiece is the classic of grim realism, *Gillespie*, written in 1914. Relative to the fine poem below, the reader may bear in mind that the word 'Ichabod' means 'The glory is departed'. (1 Sam. 4.21; 14.3.)

Celtic Melancholy

It is not in the sorrow of the deep,
For sunset's magic turns to pearls her tears;
Nor in old forests stiff with frost that sleep
Bowed with the legend of her ghostly years;
Nor in the sombre grandeur of the hills,
Whose snows have cold communion with the skies;
Not in the mourning of the moor with rain,
Or solemn mist that spills
Its weariness of silence: or the cries
Of great winds wandering through the glens in pain.   10

Thou hadst no knowledge of the market-place
And cities white and glad with statuary;
The hiving ports of a far-travelled race,
Idols in gold and jeweled sacristy;
Men hot with story from the ends o' earth,
Plaudits in theatres; an eager fleet
Taking the tide, bound for the goodly wars.
Such stuff of song and mirth
Was never thine amidst the sleet
And noise of black whales spouting to the stars.   20

Thine is the heritage of wandering men
Whose deeds are fragments passing like the stream;
They build the tower; they forge the shield; and then
Their labours vanish like a fragrant dream.
Wistful and dim with sad magnificence
Ye are the men destined to doom and death.
A purpose ye could never realise;
And stable recompense
Of victory was fleeting as a breath.
Only the face of death is kind and wise.   30

Ye are the men of perished hopes, of things
Most dear that now are ever lost – home, name,
And country – song of triumph never brings
Like requiem the meaning that's in fame.
Slogan ne'er stirred the heart to dare and die
As coronach loud wailing in the glen.
Ah! aye for you the best's beneath the sod;
Over the sea to Skye;
All's over; falls the night on broken men,
Culloden's sword with blood writes Ichabod.   40

Alexander Gray (1882 – 1968)

Scotland

Here in the uplands
The soil is ungrateful;
The fields, red with sorrel,
Are stony and bare.
A few trees, wind-twisted –
Or are they but bushes? –
Stand stubbornly guarding
A home here and there.

Scooped out like a saucer,
The land lies before me;   10
The waters, once scattered,
Flow orderly now
Through fields where the ghosts
Of the marsh and the moorland
Still ride the old marches,
Despising the plough.

The marsh and the moorland
Are not to be banished;
The bracken and heather,
The glory of broom,   20
Usurp all the balks
And the fields' broken fringes,
And claim from the sower
Their portion of room.

This is my country,
The land that begat me.
These windy spaces
Are surely my own,
And those who here toil
In the sweat of their faces   30
Are flesh of my flesh,
And bone of my bone.

Hard is the day's task –
Scotland, stern Mother! –
Wherewith at all times
Thy sons have been faced –
Labour by day,
And scant rest in the gloaming,
With Want an attendant,   40
Not lightly outpaced.

Yet do thy children
Honour and love thee.
Harsh is thy schooling,
Yet great is the gain:
True hearts and strong limbs,
The beauty of faces,
Kissed by the wind
And caressed by the rain.

Grief

What ails you, you puir auld body?
What gars you greet sae sair?
Hae you tint the man that's been kind to you
This forty year and mair?

O, I didna greet when I tint him,
Nor yet on the burrel-day;
But though I saw to the hoose and the byre,
God kens that my hert was wae.

But this mornin' I cam on his bauchles★;   old boots
Wha cud I dae but greet?   10
For I mindit hoo hard he had wrocht for me,
Trauchlin'★ wi' sair feet.   working, worrying

Disquiet

Wahtever brocht me hame?
There's naething juist the same.
The trees are a' blawn doon
About the big fairm toon;
What ance was lown and fair
Is noo sae cauld and bare.
I wander a' my lane★   alone
Wi' tear begrutten★ een,   bewept
Up by the auld Kirkyaird,
And think hoo few are spared.   10
O, it is sair to tine★   lose
The friends o' auld lang syne.
The place is grown that sma',
The auld fowk are awa'.
There's naething juist the same,
I've been ower lang at hame.

The Deil o' Bogie

When I was young, and ower young,
I wad a deid-auld wife;
But ere three days had gane by,
Gi-Ga-Gane-by,
I rued the sturt★ and strife.   trouble

Sae to the kirkyaird furth I fared,
And to the deil I prayed:
'O, muckle deil o' bogie,
Bi-Ba-Bogie,
Come, tak the runkled jade.'   10

When I got haem, the soor auld bitch
Was deid, ay, deid eneugh.
I yokkit the mare to the dung cairt,
Ding-Dang-Dung-cairt,
And drove her furth – and leuch★.   laughed

And when I cam to the place o' peace,
The grave was howked★, and snod: dug up
'Gae canny wi' the corp, lads,
Ci-Ca-Corp, lads,
You'll wauk her up, by God!   20

Ram in, ram in the bonnie yird★   earth
Upon the ill-daein wife.
When she was hale and herty,
Hi-Ha-Herty,
She plagued me o' my life.'

But when I gat me hame again,
The hoose seemed toom★ and wide.   empty
For juist three days I waited,
Wit-Wat-Waited,
Syne took a braw young bride.   30

In three short days my braw young wife
Had ta'en to lounderin★ me.   beating
'Gie's back, dear deil o' bogie,
Bi-Ba-Bogie,
My auld calamitie.'

The Dancers

From where I sat, apart, unseen,
I saw the dancers pass below,
Like phantom figures on a screen,
Dreamily moving to and fro.

The music held me in its power
As long I watched, in that high hall,
Beauty unconscious of its hour,
And careless Youth that will have all.

And all within me rose to praise
And bless them in their revellings,   10
So heedless of Life's darkened ways,
So brave for Life's adventurings.

Then Envy came, with fingers cold,
And sudden in my heart there sprung
Madness and rage that I was old
And that I never had been young.

The Grave of Love

The auld sangs soored and cankered,
Ill dreams that kept me fleyed★, –   frightened
Let's get a michty coffin,
And stow them a' inside.

There's muckle I maun lay there,
Though what I daurna tell.
The coffin may be bigger
Than St Andrews' auld draw-well.

And bring a bier well-timbered,
O' brods★ baith lang and wide.   10   boards
Needs be they maun be longer
Than the auld brig ower the Clyde.

And bring me twal' great giants,
A' men o' muckle worth –
As strang as William Wallace
That looks across the Forth.

And they maun tak' the coffin
And sink it in the wave,
For sic a michty coffin
Maun hae a michty grave.   20

D'ye ken what way the coffin
Maun be sae great and strang?
It's my love I mean to lay there,
And the dule I've tholed★ so lang.   endured

(*Translated from Heine's 'Die Alten Bosen Lieder'.*)

The Kings from the East

There were three kings cam frae the East.
They speered* in ilka clachan*:   asked/village
'O, which is the way to Bethlehem,
My bairns, sae bonnily lachin'?'

O neither young nor auld could tell.
They trailed till their feet were weary.
They followed a bonny gowden starn,
That shone in the lift* sae cheery.   sky

The starn stude ower the ale-hoose byre*   animal barn
Whaur the stable gear was hingin'.   10
The owsen mooed, the bairnie grat*,   wept
The kings begoud* their singin'.   began

(Translated from Heine's 'Die Heil'gen Drei Kon'ge aus Morgenland'.)

The Auld Earl o' Huntly

(Translation of German Folk-song: 'Der Kurfurst von Hessen'.)

The auld Earl o' Huntly
Is a verra fine man;
For he cleiths a' his sodgers
As well as he can.

The auld Earl o' Huntly,
It's himsel' says it's true,
That a' the young callants*   fellows
Maun gae sodgerin' noo.

And he wales* them that's bonnie,   chooses
The strang and the swack*;   10 active
But the crupples and lammiters*,   lame
He turns them a' back.

O, ye puir hapless lassies!
And ye'll no think it richt,
When there's nane but the crupples
To daff* wi' at nicht.   fool

William Lorimer (1885 – 1967)

The familiar stories below are taken from Lorimer's monumental *The New Testament in Scots*. The reader may well assume the original Biblical texts have been roughened in his translation, but Lorimer's work has been praised as in many ways more faithful – than the standard English translations – to the style (and the variety of styles) of the source. The *Anthology* assumes that a familiarity with the King James or similar translation makes glosses unnecessary.

The Birth of the Christ Child (Luke 2)

About this time the Emperor Augustus pat furth an edick ordeinin at aa the fowk i the haill warld suid be registrate. This wis whan Quirinius wis Governor o Syria, an it wis the first time at siccan a thing hed been dune. Sae aabodie gaed tae be registrate, ilkane til his ain toun, Joseph amang the lave.

He belanged til the stock an faimlie o Dauvit, an sae it wis tae Dauvit's Toun, Bethlehem in Judaea, at he gaed doun frae Nazareth in Galilee for tae gae in his name, takkin Mary, at wis haundfastit til him, wi him. She wis boukin gin this; an whan they war in Bethlehem, she cam til her time an brocht hame her first-born son. She swealed the baim in a barrie an beddit him in a heck, sin there wis nae room for them intil the inn.

Nou, i that same pairt the' war a wheen herds bidin thereout on the hill an keepin gaird owre their hirsel at nicht. Suddent an angel o the Lord cam an stuid afore them, an the glorie o the Lord shined about them, an they war uncolie frichtit. But the angel said tae them: 'Binna nane afeared: I bring ye guid news o gryte blytheness for the haill fowk – this day in Dauvit's Toun a sauviour hes been born til ye, Christ, the Lord! This gate ye s' ken it is een as I say: ye will finnd a new-born bairn swealed in a barrie an liggin intil a heck.'

Syne in a gliff an unco thrang o the airmies o heiven kythed aside the angel, giein laud tae God an liltin:

'Glore tae God i the heicht o heiven,
an peace on the yird tae men he delytes in!'

Whan the angels quat them an gaed back til heiven, the herds said til ither, 'Come, lat us gang owre-bye tae Bethlehem an see this unco at the Lord hes made kent til us.' Sae they hied owre tae Bethlehem what they coud drive, an faund Mary an Joseph there wi the new-born babe liggin intil the heck; an whan they saw him, they loot fowk ken what hed been said tae them anent the bairn. Aabodie ferliet tae hear what the herds tauld them, but Mary keepit aa thir things lown an cuist them throu her mind her lane. Syne the herds gaed back tae their hirsel, praisin an ruisin God for aa at they hed hard an seen; aathing hed been een as they war tauld.

Whan the ouk wis gane by, an he wis tae be circumcised, they gied him the name Jesus, the same at the angel hed said afore his conception. Whan the time ordeined i the Law o Moses for their purification wis by, they tuik him doun tae Jerusalem tae present him tae the Lord (for sae it staunds i the Law: Ilka man-bairn at apens the wame sal be haudenfor dedicate tae the Lord), an tae offer the saicrifice laid doun i the Law o the Lord, a pair o cushats, or twa yung dous.

Nou, there wis wonnin in Jerusalem at that time a man o the name o Simeon. A weill-daein, strick, God-fearin man he wis, at leeved bidin on the day whan the Consolation o Israel wad kythe. He wis gey faur ben, an the Halie Spirit hed looten him ken at he wadna see deith afore his een hed behauden the Lord's Anointit. Sae nou, muived bi the Spirit, he hed come intil the Temple, an whan Jesus' faither an mither brocht him in for tae dae wi him what wis necessar bi law an custom, Simeon tuik the bairn in his oxter, an blissed God, an said:

'Maister, nou may thy servan,
lowsed frae thy service,
gang his waas in peace,
een as thou hecht him;
for my een hes seen thy salvation,
whilk thou hes made redd i the sicht
o aa the fowks o the yird,
tae be a licht tae enlichten the haithen
an a glorie til Israel thy fowk.'

His faither an mither ferliet sair at what wis said anent him.

Syne Simeon blissed the baith o them; an tae Mary, the wane's mither, he said, 'Tent my wurds: this bairn o yours is appointit tae cause the dounfaa o monie an the rise o monie in Israel, an tae be a sign frae God forbye at monie feck will speak again – ay, an throu your ain saul a swuird will gang – at the dern thochts o monie a hairt may kythe.'

The' wis forbye a prophetess, Anna, the dauchter o Phanuel, o Clan Asher. She wis a gey an eildit carlin, at hed mairriet in her quean-days, but hed tint her guidman efter seiven year an bidden a widow-wuman sinsyne. She wis nou nae less nor echtie-fowr year o age, an niver quat she the Temple, but wis ey there wurshippin God wi fastin an prayer. Juist at this maument she cam up an, efter giein thenks tae God, spak anent the bairn til aa them at wis bidin on the redemption o Jerusalem.

Whan they hed cairriet out aa at wis prescrived i the Law i the Lord, Joseph an Mary gaed back tae Galilee, til their ain toun o Nazareth. The bairn raxed up, growin ey the langer, the stranger, an getherin ay the mair wisdom; an the fauvour o God bade on him.

The Parable of the Talents (Matthew 25)

'Or again, it is like this. A man at wis gaein out o the kintra caa'd up his servans an haundit his haudin owre tae them tae gyde. He lippent ane wi five talents, anither wi twa, an a third wi ane – ilkane wi the soum confeirin til his capacitie. Syne he gaed his waas out o the kintra. The man at hed gotten the five talents gaed strecht awa an yuised them sae weill in tredd at he made ither five talents; an siclike him at hed gotten the twa talents wan ither twa talents. But him at hed gotten the ae talent gaed awa an howkit a hole i the grund an hade his maister's siller intil it.

'Efter a lang time, the maister o thae servans cam hame an huid a racknin wi them. Him at hed gotten the five talents cam forrit wi ither five talents forbye an said, "Maister, ye lippent me wi five talents: see, here's ither five talents I hae made."

'"Weill dune, guid an leal servan!" said his maister til him. "Ye hae been leal wi the gydin o little, I s' gie ye the gydin o muckle. Awa in tae your Maister's banqet!"

'Syne him at hed gotten the twa talents cam forrit an said, "Maister, ye lippent me wi twa talents: see, here's ither twa talents I hae made."

'"Weill dune, guid an leal servan!" said his maister. "Ye hae been leal wi the gydin o little, I s' gie ye the gydin o muckle. Awa' in tae vour Maister's banqet!"

'Lest, him at gat the ae talent cam forrit an said, "Maister, I kent ye for a dour man an a stour, at maws whaur he hesna sawn, an shears whaur he hesna seedit; sae I wis feared, an gaed awa an hade your talent i the grund: here it is back tae ye."

'"Ye sweird wratch o a servan!" said his maister. "Ye kent at I maw whaur I haena sawn, an shear whaur I haena seedit – ye kent that, na? A-weill, than, ye suid hae pitten my siller i the Bank, an syne I wad hae gotten it back wi annualrent at my hamecome. Tak his talent awa frae him, an gie it til him at hes the ten talents:

For til havers mair is gien,
till it faur outgangs their need:
frae not-havers is taen
een what they hae.

An cast yon wanwurdie servan intil the mirk outbye." It is there at the yaumer an the chirkin
o teeth will be!'

The Crucifixion (Mark 14)

It wantit but twa days or the Passowre an the Feast o Barmless Breid, an the Heid-Priests an
Doctors o the Law wis castin owre hou they micht git their haunds on Jesus bi some prat an
pit him tae deith. 'But no throu the Feast,' said they, 'or we'r like tae hae the fowk raisin a
stramash!'

Ae day, whan he wis lyin at the buird i the houss o Simon the Lipper at Bethanie, a
wuman cam in wi a stowp o dairthfu uilie o rael nard in her haund an, brakkin aff the tap o
the stowp, tuimed the uilie owre his heid.

Some o them at wis there wis sair ill-pleised an said til ither, 'What for's this waistrie o
guid nard? It micht hae been sauld for three hunder white shillins an mair, an the siller gien
tae the puir!' Syne they turned an yokit on the wuman.

But Jesus said, 'Lat her abee; what cause hae ye tae fash her? It wis braw an weill dune o
her, this at she hes dune for me. The puir ye hae ey wi ye, an ye can dae them kindness
whaniver ye will, but me ye s' no hae ey wi ye. She hes dune aa at wis in her pouer tae dae;
she hes anointit my bodie for my buiral afore the day. Atweill, I tell ye, whauriver the Gospel
is preached i the haill warld her storie will be tauld, sae as she s' ne'er be forgot.'

Syne Judas Iscariot, ane o the Twal, gaed awa til the Heid-Priests tae offer tae betray him
intil their haunds. Whan he tauld them what he hed comed for, they war fair liftit up an
shored him a soum o siller, an he begoud tae luik out for a guid opportunitie o betraym him.

On the first day o the Feast, whan the Jews wis in yuiss tae fell the Passowre Lamb, the
disciples speired at Jesus whaur it wis his will they suid ging an mak fore-redd for him tae ait
his Passowre. Sae he sent aff twa o them wi thir orders: 'Ging intil the toun,' he tauld them,
'an there ye'll forgether wi a man wi a watter-kit cairriein. Fallow him; an whan he gaes intil
a houss, say til the guidman o the same, 'The Maister baud us ax ye whaur is the chaumer
trystit for him an his disciples tae ait the Passowre in.' The man will tak ye up the stair an shaw
ye a muckle chaumer wi couches weill spreid up, an aathing in order. That is whaur ye ar tae
mak fore-redd for us.' Sae the twasome tuik the gate an cam intil the toun, whaur they faund
aathing as Jesus hed tauld them; an they made reddie for the Passowre.

Whan it wis weirin late, Jesus cam til the place wi the Twal. As they lay at the buird takkin
their sipper, he said, 'Atweill, I tell ye, ane o ye is tae betray me, ane o ye at is here *at the buird
wi me.*

Dule war they tae hear him, an they said til him, ane efter anither, 'No me, shairlie?'

'It is ane o the Twal,' qo he, 'ane at is dippin his piece i the bicker wi me. The Son o Man
maun een gae the gate at Scriptur foretells for him: but waesucks for the man at is tae betray
him! Better wad it been for that man, gin he hed ne'er been born.'

Whan they war ey at the buird, Jesus tuik a laif an, efter he hed axed a blissin, brak it an
gied it til them, sayin, 'Tak ye this, it is my bodie.'

Syne he tuik a caup, gae thenks tae God, an raxed it til them, an ilkane o them drank frae
it, an he said til them, 'This is my Bluid o the Covenant, whilk is skailed for monie. Atweill,
I tell ye, I winna lip the bree o the grape again or the day, whan I drink a new wine i the
Kingdom o God.'

Whan they hed sung the Passowre Psaum, they gaed out an awa' til the Hill o Olives. Belyve Jesus said tae them, 'Ye will aa turn fauss an faithless, for it is written in Scriptur:

'I will ding the herd,
an the hersel will be sparpelt abreid.'

But efter I hae risen frae the deid, I will ging on afore ye tae Galilee.'

Peter said til him, 'Lat ithers be fauss an faithless, Peter will ey haud leal an true!'

Jesus answert, 'Atweill, I tell ye, nae later nor this day's nicht, or the cock craws twice, ye will disavou me thrice.'

But Peter threapit the mair, 'Tho I buid die wi ye, I winnae disavou ye nane, at winna I!' An siclike said the haill o them.

Syne they cam til a dail caa'd Gethsemane, an he said til his disciples, 'Sit ye here, till I ging an pray.'

Sae they bade there, but he gaed on wi Peter and Jeames an John. An nou an unco dridder cam owre him, an he said til them, 'My saul is likin tae die for wae; bide ye here an haud ye wauken.'

Syne he gaed forrit a bittock an cuist himsel on the grund an prayed at, gin it coud be, the hour o dree micht ging by him. 'Abba, Faither,' he prayed, 'nocht is abuin thy pouer, hain me this caup: yit no as my will, but as thy will, is.'

Syne he cam back an faund them asleep, an he said til Peter, 'Asleep, Simon, asleep? Docht-ye-na bide waukin ae hour? Bide ye aa waukin, an haud at the prayin, at ye haena tae dree nae sair seyal. Tho the spirit be freck, the flesh is feckless.'

Again he gaed awa an prayed the same prayer as afore. Syne he cam back aince mair an faund them asleep, for their een wis hivvie wi tire; an they kentna what answer tae gie him.

Yit a third time he cam back, an nou he said til them, 'Ey sleepin? Ey takkin your rest? Lang eneuch hae ye sleepit. The hour is comed: see, the Son o Man is eenou tae be betrayed intil the haunds o sinners! Rise ye up, an lat us gae meet them: ay, here he comes, my betrayer.'

The wurds wisna aff his tung afore Judas – ane o the Twal! – cam up, an wi him a thrang o fowk airmed wi whingers an rungs, at hed been sent bi the Heid-Priests, Doctors o the Law, an Elders. The traitor hed gree'd a taiken wi them: 'Him at I kiss is the man ye'r seekin,' he hed sayen: 'grip him, an tak him awa under siccar gaird.' Sae, nou he wis at the bit, he gaed strecht up til him an caa'd him 'Maister' an kissed him; an than the ithers laid haunds on him an huid him siccar.

Ane o the staunders-by drew his whinger an lent the Heid-Priest's servan a straik at sneddit aff his lug. Jesus than tuik speech in haund: 'Am I some reiver,' qo he, 'at ye needs come out wi whingers an rungs for tae fang me? Day an dailie I wis in amang ye teachin i the Temple, an ye laidna a haund on me. But Scriptur buid be fulfilled, I trew.'

Syne the haill o his disciples forhoued him an scoured awa. The' war ae callan, tho, at ey huid efter Jesus. He wis cled in nocht but a linnen hap, an they claucht hauds o him. But he wan lowse o their grips, an awa he ran scuddie-bare, laein his hap i their haunds.

Syne they cairriet Jesus awa til the pailace o the Heid-Priest, whaur the haill o the Heid-Priests an Doctors o the Law an Elders convened. Peter fallowt him a lang gate ahent richt intil the pailace yaird, whaur he sat doun amang the servitors an beikit himsel at the ingle.

I the meantime the Heid-Priests an the haill Council wis seekin evidence on whilk they coud pit Jesus tae deith, but coudna finnd onie; for, tho monie-ane buir witness again him, their witness wis fauss, an their lies didna een compluther. Syne the' was some stuid up an buir fauss witness again him, sayin at hou they themsels hed hard him say, 'I will ding doun this Temple at haund o man biggit, an in three days' time I will raise up anither temple, biggit bi nae man's haund.' But no een thir witnesses' depositions compluthert.

Syne the Heid-Priest rase frae his sait an, comin forrit intil the bodie o the court, speired at Jesus, 'Answer ye nocht? What mak ye o this witness again ye?' But the ne'er a wurd spak he.

The Heid-Priest than pit anither queystin til him: 'Ar ye the Christ,' said he, 'the Son o the Blissit Ane?'

'I am,' qo Jesus, 'an, mairfortaiken, ye will see
the Son o Man
sittin on the richt haund o God Almichtie
an comin amang the clouds o the lift.'

Wi that the Heid-Priest rave his goun an said, 'What needs we seek mair witness? Ye hae hard his blasphemie yoursels: what, than, is your juidgement?'

Ane an aa they juidged him giltie o a capital crime. Syne some fell tae spittin on him, an they blinfauldit him an lent him ey the tither gowff, cryin at ilka flewit: 'Spae awa nou, Prophet!' An the servitors, tae, lent him monie a clink athort the haffits.

Aa this while, Peter wis doun ablo i the yaird. As he wis sittin there beikin himsel at the fire, ane o the Heid-Priest's servan-queans cam in an, seein him, tuik a guid luik o him an said, 'Ye war wi the man frae Nazareth, this Jesus, tae, I'm thinkin.'

But he wadna own wi it: 'I kenna buff nor sty what ye'r speakin o,' said he; an wi that he slippit out intil the fore-close.

The servan-lass saw him there an said tae the staunders-by, 'This chiel's ane o them': but aince mair he denied it.

Belyve the staunders-by cam back til it an said tae Peter: 'Deed, but ye ar sae ane o them; ye'r frae Galilee!'

At that he set tae the bannin an swuir at he kentna 'this man,' says he, 'at ye'r speakin o.' Nae shuner wis the wurds mout o his mou nor the cock crew the saicond time. Than Peter caa'd tae mind hou Jesus hed sayen til him, 'Afore the cock craw twice, ye will disavou me thrice.' An he banged out an fell agreitin.

Strecht awa at the first styme o daylicht the haill Council – Heid-Priests, Elders, an Doctors o the Law – tuik counsel thegither, efter whilk they caused binnd Jesus an cairriet him awa an haundit him owre tae Pilate.

'Prisoner at the bar, ar ye the King o Jews?' Pilate speired at him; an Jesus answert, 'Ye hae said it.'

Syne the Heid-Priests cam forrit wi monie chairges again him, an Pilate speired at him aince mair, 'Hae ye nocht ava tae say? Luik what monie chairges they hae again ye!' But Jesus wadna answer mae, sae at Pilate ferliet.

Ilka Passowre Pilate wis in yuiss tae set free onie ae prisoner at the fowk socht o him. Nou, at this time the man caa'd BarAbbas wis lyin in waird alang wi the reibels at hed committit murther i the Risin. Sae the croud gaed up tae Pilate an begoud tae seek o him what he wis in yuiss tae dae for them, an Pilate speired at them, 'Is it your will I suid liberate the King o Jews for ye?' Weill kent he at it wis for ill-will the Heid-Priests hed brocht Jesus up afore him. But the Heid-Priests eggit up the croud tae seek him tae lowse BarAbbas raither.

'Syne what will I dae,' answert Pilate again. 'wi him ye caa King o Jews?'

'Tae the cross wi him!' raired they again.

'But what ill hes he dune?' speired Pilate.

'Tae the cross wi him! Tae the cross wi him!' wis aa the answer he gat.

Nou, Pilate wis laith tae conter the croud, sae he loot them hae their will an set BarAbbas at libertie: Jesus he caused screinge an haundit owre tae the sodgers tae be crucified. Sae the sodgers cairriet him awa intil the Court, or Governor's Pailace, an whan they hed gethert the haill regiment in about, they reikit him out in purpie an crouned him wi a wreathe they hed plettit o thorn rysses. Syne they begoud tae hailse him wi 'Haill, King o Jews!' an they gaed on tae yether him owre the heid wi a wand an spat on him an kneeled on the grund afore him in fenyiet homage. An than, whan they war throu wi their jamphin-wark, they tirred the purpie aff him an cled him again in his ain claes.

Syne they led him awa tae crucifie him.

On the road they met in wi Simon frae Cyrene, the faither o Elshinder an Rufus, at wis comin in frae the kintra an wis ettlin tae ging by them, an gart him gae wi them an cadge his cross.

Sae they brocht Jesus til the place caa'd Golgotha, or the Hairn-Pan. Here they offert him a tass o droggit wine, but he wadna pree it.

Than they crucified him an *haufed his claes amang them, castin caivels,* ilkane for his skair. It wis the beginnin o the forenuin whan he wis crucified. A plaicard wis pitten abuin his heid shawin the chairge again him:

THE KING O JEWS

An alang wi him they crucified twa reivers, the tane on his richt haund, an the tither on his left.

Aa them at gaed by ill-tung'd him, *geckin their heids* an sayin, 'Hey! Ye at dings doun temples an biggs them up again in three days, come ye doun aff the cross an sauf yoursel!' Siclike the Heid-Priests an Doctors o the Law jeistit owre him amang themsels: 'He saufed ithers,' said they, 'but himsel he canna sauf. Lat this Christ, this King o Israel, come doun eenou aff the cross; we will believe whan we see that!' An een the twa at wis crucified wi him flytit on him.

At nuin mirk cam owre the haill kintra an bade till the mids o the efternuin. At that hour Jesus cried out wi a loud stevven, *'Eloi, Eloi, lema sabachthani?'* whilk means, *'My God, my God, what for hes thou forleitit me?'*

Some o the staunders-by hard him an said, 'Hairken, he's cryin Elijah!' At that someane ran an dippit a spunge in sour wine, set it on the end o a wand, an r*axed it up* til him *tae souk:* 'Lat us see,' said he, 'gin Elijah will come an tak him doun frae the cross!' But Jesus gied a loud cry, an wi that he wis by wi it. At the same maument the courtain o the Temple screidit atwa frae heid tae fit. Whan the centurion at wis staundin richt forenent the cross saw hou he died, he said, 'Atweill, that man wis a son o God!'

The' war some weimen there, tae, luikin on frae a guid gate aff. Amang them wis Mary o Magdala, Mary the mither o Jeames the Yunger an Joses, an Salome, at hed gane about wi him whan he wis in Galilee an tentit him; an the' war a fell wheen ithers forbye at hed comed doun wi him tae Jerusalem.

It was nou late owre i the eenin, an seein it wis the Preparation, or Fore-Sabbath, Joseph o Arimathaea, a sponsible councillor, at wis himsel bodin the Kingdom o God, gaed bauldlie inbye til Pilate an socht o him the bodie o Jesus. Pilate misdoutit he coudna be sae shune deid an sent for the centurion an speired at him gin he hed been lang deid, an whan he faund it wis een sae, he gae Joseph freedom tae tak awa Jesus' corp.

Joseph caft a piece o linnen claith an, takkin Jesus' bodie doun frae the cross, swealed it i the claith an laired it in a graff howkit out o the rock an syne rowed up a stane again the ingang. Mary o Magdala an Mary the mither o Joses wis luikin on an saw whaur he wis yirdit.

Whan the sabbath wis by, Mary o Magdala, Mary the mither o Jeames, an Salome bocht themsels spices, at they micht ging an anoint him; an gey an air on the first day o the ouk they war tae the gate an cam til the graff on the back o sunrise.

'Wha'll we git tae shift the muckle stane frae the in-gang?' they speired at ilk ither, for it wis a fell thing o a stane. But, whan they luikit up, they saw it hed been rowed awa else.

Sae they gaed intil the graff-chaumer, an there they saw a yung man sittin on their richt haund, cled in a side white goun, an they war uncolie frichent. But he said til them, 'Binna frichent. Ye will be seekin Jesus o Nazareth, him at wis crucified. He hes risen; he isna here. Luik, there is whaur they laid him . . .

'Gang your waas nou, an tell his disciples – an, mairfortaiken, Peter – at he is gaein afore ye tae Galilee, whaur ye will see him, as he tauld ye.'

At that they cam out o the graff-chaumer an screived awa' trimmlin an 'maist by themsels wi feirich an dreid. An they tauld naebodie naething, sae afeared war they.

Andrew Young (1885 – 1971)

This graceful poet has been somewhat neglected in Scotland, as both his style and subject matter were traditional and he lived most of his long life in England. The Scottish Renaissance passed him by entirely. Born, raised and educated in Scotland he became a minister of the Church of Scotland in 1912. In 1918 he moved to Sussex to take a position as minister of a Presbyterian Church, and in 1936 he converted to the Church of England, serving therein as curate, then vicar, in Sussex until he retired in 1959.

After the Funeral

Standing beneath the jewelled trees
That waved with slow mournful unease;
I lifted up my eyes to them –
The stars caught in the trees' dark stratagem.

But when I asked which is the wonder,
All stars above the earth and under
And in the vast hollow of space
Or the stern look on that defeated face;

I said, 'Not even the Milky Way
Shines like the golden streak of clay –   10
All, all of her that I could save –
My foot has gathered from her open grave.'

The Scarecrow

He strides across the grassy corn
That has not grown since it was born,
A piece of sacking on a pole,
A ghost, but nothing like a soul.

Why must this dead man haunt the spring
With arms anxiously beckoning?
Is spring not hard enough to bear
For one at autumn of his year?

Wiltshire Downs

The cuckoo's double note
Loosened like bubbles from a drowning throat
Floats through the air
In mockery of pipit, lark and stare.

The stable-boys thud by
Their horses slinging divots at the sky
And with bright hooves
Printing the sodden turf with lucky grooves.

As still as a windhover
A shepherd in his flapping coat leans over   10
His tall sheep-crook
And shearlings, tegs and yoes cons like a book.

And one tree-crowned long barrow
Stretched like a sow that has brought forth her farrow
Hides a king's bones
Lying like broken sticks among the stones.

The Falls of Glomach

Rain drifts forever in this place
Tossed from the long white lace
The Falls trail on the black rocks below,
And golden-rod and rose-root shake
In wind that they forever make;
So though they wear their own rainbow
It's not in hope, but just for show,
For rain and wind together
Here through the summer make a chill wet weather.

Culbin Sands

Here lay a fair fat land;
But now its townships, kirks, graveyards
Beneath bald hills of sand
Lie buried deep as Babylonian shards.

But gales may blow again;
And like a sand-glass turned about
The hills in a dry rain
Will flow away and the old land look out;

And where now hedgehog delves
And conies* hollow their long caves   10   rabbits
Houses will build themselves
And tombstones rewrite names on dead men's graves.

May Frost

It was the night May robbed September
Killing with frost the apple-bloom,
The sunset sunk to its last ember,
I climbed the dew-webbed combe;
There floating from the earth's round rim
I saw the red sun rise.
At first I only thought 'How soon,'
And then 'Surely I must be dying;
These are death's cobwebs on my eyes
That make the dawn so dim';   10
And yet my sight was lying:
The frost had set on fire the full-faced moon.

The Shepherd's Hut

The smear of blue peat smoke
That staggered on the wind and broke,
The only sign of life,
Where was the shepherd's wife,
Who left those flapping clothes to dry,

For Beauty thus not only glows
Within the wine-cup of the rose,
But like a hermit clad may be
In garment of austerity.

Spring

I never noticed, till I saw today
How budding birches stand in their green spray
And bracken like a snake from earth upheaves,
How many in this wood are last year's leaves.

The Moon

'What gars★ Garskadden luk sae gash★?'   makes/bad
Kilmardinny said to one,
While late into the early morn
They sat drinking on.

'Garskadden's been wi' his Maker
These twa hours,' said he;
'I saw him step awa, but, faith,
Why spoil gude company?'

The Sea

I ever feared the sea;
Ah, false and fawning even as he,
That Greek, who with his fishing-rod
And two cross-sticks makes a tripod;
Then waits till bass or ling too late
Finds the sly bait.

Now as I walk away,
Across the flats of Pevensey Bay,
My footsteps keep so harsh a speech
With these loose miles and miles of beach   10
I think that it is still the sea
That follows me.

Helen Cruickshank (1886 – 1975)

Overdue

O ragin' wind
An' cruel sea,
Ye put the fear
O' daith on me.
I canna sleep,
I canna pray,
But prowl aboot
The docks a' day,
An' pu' my plaid
Aboot me ticht.   10
'Nae news yet, mistress'
– Ae mair nicht!

The Gipsy Lass

The road I traivel's no for ye,
    Sandy, Sandy.
The weird★ that's mine ye maunna dree★,   fate/suffer
    Sandy dear my lad.
Ye maunna link yer life wi' shame
Nor think to tak' into yer hame
A gipsy lass without a name,
    Sandy dear my lad.

I never kent wha faithered me,
    Sandy, Sandy,   10
For mither's gane wi' twa or three,
    Sandy dear my lad.
The gipsy-he'rt maun ever range
An' so it's mebbe no that strange
That I, like her, am fond o' change,
    Sandy dear my lad.

I couldna thole★ a hoose o' stane,   endure
    Sandy, Sandy.
For me, the brackens up the lane,
    Sandy dear my lad.   20
Yer e'en sae bonny blue an' clear
Wad tine★ their cheery look, I fear,   lose
Afore we had been wed a year,
    Sandy dear my lad.

An' tho' I lo'e ye weel the noo,
    Sandy, Sandy,
I doot I'd gi'e ye cause tae rue,
    Sandy dear my lad.
Sae gang yer ways – they'll ne'er be mine,
For you an' me that kissed maun twine★.   30   separate
(But oh! I'm wae my lad tae tine,
    Sandy dear my lad!)

Lizzie

Bessie walked oot wi' Tam yestreen,
    Robin is coortin' Mary,
The halflin-laddie is unco★ keen   very
    On Kate doonbye at the dairy;
But naebody comes a-coortin' me –
    Me, that's bonnier nor the three.

Bess is a thowless shilpit★ quean★,   starved/wench
    Mary is mim★ an' primsy,   prissy
Kate has a tongue as sharp's a preen,
    Forbye, she's muckle★ an' clumsy.   10   big
It's queer they ha'e a' got lads but me –
    Me, that's cleverer nor the three.

Tam, he's lanky an' pirny-taed,
    Robin's owre fond o' siller★:   silver
As for Kate an' the halflin-lad,
    What can he see intil her?
In fac', it's clear – as clear's can be –
    There's nane o' them guid eneuch for me.

Kate, she leuch★ i' my face the day   laughed
An' sneered, the impident hizzie.   20
'Ye've muckle conceit o' yersel', ye ha'e,
But ye're green wi' envy, Lizzie.'
Envy? My wumman, juist bide a wee,
I'se warrant I wed the best o' the three.

I'm wastin' mysel' on this weary ferm,
My thochts to the toon are turnin'.
I'll tak' a place at the Marti'mas term
An' be dune wi' milkin' an' kirnin'.
An' Kate will see what she will see,
For mebbe a P'liceman will mairry me.   30

Background

Frost, I mind, an' snaw,
An' a bairn comin' hame frae the schule
Gretin'★, nearly, wi' cauld,   weeping
But seein', for a' that,
The icicles i' the ditch,
The snaw-ploo's marbled tracks,
An' the print o' the rabbits' feet
At the hole i' the wire.

'Bairn ye're blue wi' cauld!'
An apron warmed at the fire,   10
An' frostit fingers rubbed
Till they dirl★ wi' pain.
Buttered toast an' tea,
The yellow licht o' the lamp,
An' the cat on the clootie★ rug
Afore the fire.

Only Daughter

She mucks the byre★   animal barn
An' slices neeps★,   turnips
I' the frosty dark
While her father sleeps.
A' green wi' sharn★   dung, dirt
An' warped wi' weet
Man's buits are on
Her shauchlin'★ feet.   shuffling
Wi' hands a' grime
An' gnarled an' roch   10
She stirs the meat
I' the gussie's★ troch,   sow's

Till frae the door
A girnin'* man   grimacing
Cries 'Whaur's my parritch,
Maggie Ann?'

A couch of down,
A silk bedspread,
A tray of tea
Brought to her bed;   20
Red slippers for
Her dainty feet,
A maid to wait on
Marguerite.

The hands o' lovely
Lady Jane
Were aince nae safter
Than your ain.
They brushed an' dressed
Her hair sae fine,   30
But noo they ser'
The gutsy swine.
O' Fate had led ye
A bonny dance
Tae bring ye frae
Your place in France,
Tae toil an' moil
For a weedow-man,
O grey hard-workin'
Maggie Ann.   40

Spring in the Mearns

In Memoriam, Lewis Grassic Gibbon

Clouds of smoke on the hill
Where the whin* is burning,   furze
Staining the clear cold sky
As the sun goes down.
Brighter the fire leaps up
As night grows darker;
Wild and lovely the light
Of the flaming whin.

Blackened the stubborn bush;
No more the golden   10
Nut-sweet blossom shall lure
The wandering bee.
Twisted branches sink
To a sullen smoulder
Where the small stonechat clinked
Contentedly.

Come again, when the rains
Have carried the ashes
Into the hungry soil,
And lo, the green!   20
Earth that was seared by fire
Has now begotten
Tender herbage for tough,
Grain for whin.

Body of man to death,
Flesh to ashes,
Muscle and tissue and bone
To dust are come.
Ah, but the spirit leaps
From the cindered fibre,   30
Living, laughs at death,
That is but a name.

Life goes on for ever;
The body smoulders,
Dies in the heat of the pace,
Is laid in earth.
Life goes on; the spirit
Endures for ever,
Wresting from death itself
A brave new birth.   40

This man set the flame
Of his native genius
Under the cumbering whin
Of the untilled field;
Lit a fire in the Mearns
To illuminate Scotland,
Clearing the sullen soil
For a richer yield.

– Arbuthnott Churchyard, 23 February 1935

To an Aberdeen Poet Who Writes Solely in English

What ails ye at yer mither tongue?
Hae ye forgot the tang o' it?
The gurly guttrals, malmy soonds,
The dirly words, the sang o' it?
An wad ye cuist it a awa,
Like bauchles on a midden–heid?
Man, think agen afore ye sell
Yer saul tae saft–like English leid★.   speech

Wad ye forget the ballad-speik,
Melodeon's chord and fiddle's clink,   10
Forsweir yer grandad's weys o' life,

Swap uisge-beatha★ for Kola drink?   whisky
Say 'Shinty is too rough a game
And cricket's more my cup of tea.'
Weel, hyne awa fae Aiberdeen,
For feich, ye'e owre genteel for me!

Glenskenno Wood

Under an arch o' bramble
Saftly she goes,
Dark broon een like velvet,
Cheeks like the rose.

Ae lang branch o' the bramble
Dips ere she pass,
Tethers wi' thorns the hair
O' the little lass.

Ripe black fruit, an' blossom
White on the spray,   10
Leaves o' russet an' crimson,
What wad ye say?

What wad ye say to the bairn
That ye catch her snood★,   hair ribbon
Haudin' her there i' the hush
O' Glenskenno Wood?

What wad ye say? The autumn
O' life draws near.
Still she waits, an' listens,
But canna hear.

William Hamilton (1886 – ?)

The Spirit

The sunset speaks not, nor the woods;
Yet in their silence cries
The secret voice of olden moods
That deep within me rise.

It gives the silent fields a song,
Old tales to every stone,
And calls the bygone folk along
When I would walk alone.

Immortality

A trumpet cries under the still stars.
I know not whence its ring, nor whence in the deep of my heart
Rises an obstinate, froward longing to burst the bars
Of prudence and of right, and to bear a part
In all high lovely strife for hopes forlorn,
And perish utterly, utterly in the gates of morn.

I know not whence – for I hold convictions dear
(The wrong of slaughter, the might of lowly love)
'Gainst all gainsayers. Yet now I only hear
The blood shout in my bursting veins, above   10
All that Commanded Good that fools deride,
And I betray by impulse and by pride.

I will be gone before the break of day;
The lost cause calls me sooner than the true,
Far sooner than the safe. Perchance I obey
Some old religious rapture my forbears knew,
The problem unresolved but by this test –
'Whoever saves his life hath missed Life's best.'

To die for error . . . rather than, being right,
To rot or slumber or grow wise in my ease,   20
– False doctrine, doubtless; be it so. I fight,
And no reward but sacrifice would seize;
My one strange hope to swell some day the flying
Imperious call in that sad blown trumpet crying.

Edwin Muir (1887 – 1959)

As detailed in his *Autobiography* (1954), Muir's life was dominated by the shock of his removal at age 14 from the pastoral Orkney Islands to the teeming and chaotic city of Glasgow. This became in his poetry a central symbol: the Fall of Man. A long period of psychoanalysis helped to further his interest in the power of dreams and symbols, in the permanence of childhood influences and in time itself. Muir began to write poetry at a late age – in his forties – and achieved real success only a few years before his death. Notable features of his poems, beside the ones named, are craftsmanship of the very highest order, a tendency toward abstraction, and an apparent and powerful self-control which seems all the more remarkable given frequent suggestion of pressure from the maelstrom of the unconscious. 'The Horses' may be the most frequently anthologised of all twentieth century Scottish poems.

Muir's famous essay, 'Scottish Literature: Language' embroiled him in a bitter controversy with Hugh MacDiarmid, the leader of the Scottish Renaissance. Ever the gentleman, Muir did not respond to MacDiarmid's angry and personal attacks, but in effect allowed his essay to stand, where it remains a seminal position in a still ongoing argument – whether Scots has a place in the international creative marketplace.

Muir is somewhat underrepresented in this Anthology, as it was not possible to get permission to reprint the number of poems this fine poet deserves.

Scotland 1941

We were a tribe, a family, a people.
Wallace and Bruce guard now a painted field,
And all may read the folio of our fable,
Peruse the sword, the scepter and the shield.
A simple sky roofed in that rustic day,
The busy corn-fields and the haunted holms,[1]
The green road winding up the ferny brae.
But Knox and Melville clapped their preaching palms
And bundled all the harvesters away,
Hoodicrow[2] Peden in the blighted corn   10
Hacked with his rusty beak the starving haulms★.   holdings
Out of that desolation we were born.

Courage beyond the point and obdurate pride
Made us a nation, robbed us of a nation.
Defiance absolute and myriad-eyed
That could not pluck the palm plucked our damnation.
We with such courage and the bitter wit
To fell the ancient oak of loyalty,
And strip the peopled hill and the altar bare,
And crush the poet with an iron text,   20
How could we read our souls and learn to be?
Here a dull drove of faces harsh and vexed,
We watch our cities burning in their pit,
To salve our souls grinding dull lucre out,
We, fanatics of the frustrate and the half,
Who once set Purgatory Hill in doubt.
Now smoke and dearth and money everywhere,
Mean heirlooms of each fainter generation,
And mummied housegods in their musty niches,
Burns and Scott, sham bards of a sham nation,   30
And spiritual defeat wrapped warm in riches,
No pride but pride of pelf. Long since the young
Fought in great bloody battles to carve out
This towering pulpit of the Golden Calf,
Montrose, Mackail, Argyle, perverse and brave,
Twisted the stream, unhooped the ancestral hill.
Never had Dee or Don or Yarrow or Till
Huddled such thriftless honour in a grave.

Such wasted bravery idle as a song,
Such hard-won ill might prove Time's verdict wrong,   40
And melt to pity the annalist's iron tongue.

---

[1] 'Holms' are level areas beside a river.
[2] 'Hooded crow' or carrion eater.

In the following poem, the speaker is, of course, the great Scottish king and national hero. The man to whom he is speaking is James Douglas, his faithful supporter and military second in command who is said to have taken Bruce's heart on a pilgrimage to the Holy Land. The 'Comyn' referred to here was Bruce's political rival whom Bruce stabbed in a church, thus committing sacrilege, and precipitating the great war of rebellion against the English, so celebrated in history and legend.

Robert the Bruce

To Douglas in Dying:

'My life is done, yet all remains,
The breath has gone, the image not,
The furious shapes once forged in heat
Live on though now no longer hot.

'Steadily the shining swords
In order rise, in order fall,
In order on the beaten field
The faithful trumpets call.

'The women weeping for the dead
Are not sad now but dutiful,   10
The dead men stiffening in their place
Proclaim the ancient rule.

'Great Wallace's body hewn in four,
So altered, stays as it must be.
O Douglas do not leave me now,
For past your head I see

'My dagger sheathed in Comyn's heart
And nothing there to praise or blame,
Nothing but order which must be
Itself and still the same.   20

'But that Christ hung upon the Cross,
Comyn would rot until time's end
And bury my sin in boundless dust,
For there is no amend

'In order; yet in order run
All things by unreturning ways.
If Christ live not, nothing is there
For sorrow or for praise.'

So the King spoke to Douglas once
A little while before his death,   30
Having outfaced three English kings
And kept a people's faith.

The Castle

All through that summer at ease we lay,
And daily from the turret wall
We watched the mowers in the hay
And the enemy half a mile away.
They seemed no threat to us at all.

For what, we thought, had we to fear
With our arms and provender, load on load,
Our towering battlements, tier on tier,
And friendly allies drawing near
On every leafy summer road.   10

Our gates were strong, our walls were thick,
So smooth and high, no man could win
A foothold there, no clever trick
Could take us, have us dead or quick.
Only a bird could have got in.

What could they offer us for bait?
Our captain was brave and we were true . . .
There was a little private gate,
A little wicked wicket gate.
The wizened warder let them through.   20

Oh then our maze of tunneled stone
Grew thin and treacherous as air.
The cause was lost without a groan,
The famous citadel overthrown,
And all its secret galleries bare.

How can this shameful tale be told?
I will maintain until my death
We could do nothing, being sold;
Our only enemy was gold,
And we had no arms to fight it with.   30

The Combat

It was not meant for human eyes,
That combat on the shabby patch
Of clods and trampled turf that lies
Somewhere beneath the sodden skies
For eye of toad or adder to catch.

And having seen it I accuse
The crested animal in his pride,
Arrayed in all the royal hues
Which hide the claws he well can use
To tear the heart out of the side.   10

Body of leopard, eagle's head
And whetted beak, and lion's mane,
And frost-grey hedge of feathers spread
Behind – he seemed of all things bred.
I shall not see his like again.

As for his enemy, there came in
A soft round beast as brown as clay;
All rent and patched his wretched skin;
A battered bag he might have been,
Some old used thing to throw away.   20

Yet he awaited face to face
The furious beast and the swift attack.
Soon over and done. That was no place
Or time for chivalry or for grace.
The fury had him on his back.

And two small paws like hands flew out
To right and left as the trees stood by.
One would have said beyond a doubt
This was the very end of the bout,
But that the creature would not die.   30

For ere the death-stroke he was gone,
Writhed, whirled, huddled into his den,
Safe somehow there. The fight was done,
And he had lost who had all but won.
But oh his deadly fury then.

A while the place lay blank, forlorn,
Drowsing as in relief from pain.
The cricket chirped, the grating thorn
Stirred, and a little sound was born.
The champions took their posts again.   40

And all began. The stealthy paw
Slashed out and in. Could nothing save
These rags and tatters from the claw?
Nothing. And yet I never saw
A beast so helpless and so brave.

And now, while the trees stand watching, still
The unequal battle rages there.
The killing beast that cannot kill
Swells and swells in his fury till
You'd almost think it was despair.   50

The Return

I see myself sometimes, an old old man
Who has walked so long with time as time's true servant,
That he's grown strange to me – who was once myself –
Almost as strange as time, and yet familiar
With old man's staff and legendary cloak,
For see, it is I, it is I. And I return
So altered, so adopted, to the house
Of my own life. There all the doors stand open
Perpetually, and the rooms ring with sweet voices,
And there my long life's seasons sound their changes,   10
Childhood and youth and manhood all together,
And welcome waits, and not a room but is
My own, beloved and longed for. And the voices,
Sweeter than any sound dreamt of or known,
Call me, recall me. I draw near at last,
An old old man, and scan the ancient walls
Rounded and softened by the compassionate years,
The old and heavy and long-leaved trees that watch
This my inheritance in friendly darkness.
And yet I cannot enter, for all within   20
Rises before me there, rises against me,
A sweet and terrible labyrinth of longing,
So that I turn aside and take the road
That always, early or late, runs on before.

The Labyrinth

Since I emerged that day from the labyrinth,
Dazed with the tall and echoing passages,
The swift recoils, so many I almost feared
I'd meet myself returning at some smooth corner,
Myself or my ghost, for all there was unreal
After the straw ceased rustling and the bull
Lay dead upon the straw and I remained,
Blood-splashed, if dead or alive I could not tell
In the twilight nothingness (I might have been
A spirit seeking his body through the roads   10
Of intricate Hades) – ever since I came out
To the world, the still fields swift with flowers, the trees
All bright with blossom, the little green hills, the sea,
The sky and all in movement under it,
Shepherds and flocks and birds and the young and old,
(I stared in wonder at the young and the old,
For in the maze time had not been with me;
I had strayed, it seemed, past sun and season and change,
Past rest and motion, for I could not tell
At last if I moved or stayed; the maze itself   20
Revolved around me on its hidden axis
And swept me smoothly to its enemy,

The lovely world) – since I came out that day,
There have been times when I have heard my footsteps
Still echoing in the maze, and all the roads
That run through the noisy world, deceiving streets
That meet and part and meet, and rooms that open
Into each other – and never a final room –
Stairways and corridors and antechambers
That vacantly wait for some great audience,   30
The smooth sea-tracks that open and close again,
Tracks undiscoverable, indecipherable,
Paths on the earth and tunnels underground,
And bird-tracks in the air – all seemed a part
Of the great labyrinth. And then I'd stumble
In sudden blindness, hasten, almost run,
As if the maze itself were after me
And soon must catch me up. But taking thought,
I'd tell myself, 'You need not hurry. This
Is the firm good earth. All roads lie free before you.'   40
But my bad spirit would sneer, 'No, do not hurry.
No need to hurry. Haste and delay are equal
In this one world, for there's no exit, none,
No place to come to, and you'll end where you are,
Deep in the centre of the endless maze.'
I could not live if this were not illusion.
It is a world, perhaps; but there's another.
For once in a dream or trance I saw the gods
Each sitting on the top of his mountain-isle,
While down below the little ships sailed by,   50
Toy multitudes swarmed in the harbours, shepherds drove
Their tiny flocks to the pastures, marriage feasts
Went on below, small birthdays and holidays,
Ploughing and harvesting and life and death,
And all permissible, all acceptable,
Clear and secure as in a limpid dream.
But they, the gods, as large and bright as clouds,
Conversed across the sounds in tranquil voices
High in the sky above the untroubled sea,
And their eternal dialogue was peace   60
Where all these things were woven, and this our life
Was as a chord deep in that dialogue,
As easy utterance of harmonious words,
Spontaneous syllables bodying forth a world.

That was the real world; I have touched it once,
And now shall know it always. But the lie,
The maze, the wild-wood waste of falsehood, roads
That run and run and never reach an end,
Embowered in error – I'd be prisoned there
But that my soul has birdwings to fly free.

Oh these deceits are strong almost as life.   70
Last night I dreamt I was in the labyrinth,
And woke far on. I did not know the place.

The Horses

Barely a twelvemonth after
The seven days war that put the world to sleep,
Late in the evening the strange horses came.
By then we had made our covenant with silence,
But in the first few days it was so still
We listened to our breathing and were afraid.
On the second day
The radios failed; we turned the knobs; no answer.
On the third day a warship passed us, heading north,
Dead bodies piled on the deck. On the sixth day   10
A plane plunged over us into the sea. Thereafter
Nothing. The radios dumb;
And still they stand in corners of our kitchens,
And stand, perhaps, turned on, in a million rooms
All over the world. But now if they should speak,
If on a sudden they should speak again,
If on the stroke of noon a voice should speak,
We would not listen, we would not let it bring
That old bad world that swallowed its children quick★   alive
At one great gulp. We would not have it again.   20
Sometimes we think of the nations lying asleep,
Curled blindly in impenetrable sorrow,
And then the thought confounds us with its strangeness.

The tractors lie about our fields; at evening
They look like dank sea-monsters couched and waiting.
We leave them where they are and let them rust:
'They'll molder away and be like other loam.'
We make our oxen drag our rusty plows,
Long laid aside. We have gone back
Far past our fathers' land.
                              And then, that evening   30
Late in the summer the strange horses came.
We heard a distant tapping on the road,
A deepening drumming: it stopped, went on again
And at the corner changed to hollow thunder.
We saw the heads
Like a wild wave charging and were afraid.
We had sold our horses in our fathers' time
To buy new tractors. Now they were strange to us
As fabulous steeds set on an ancient shield
Or illustrations in a book of knights.   40
We did not dare go near them. Yet they waited,
Stubborn and shy, as if they had been sent
By an old command to find our whereabouts
And that long-lost archaic companionship.
In the first moment we had never a thought
That they were creatures to be owned and used.
Among them were some half a dozen colts
Dropped in some wilderness of the broken world,
Yet new as if they had come from their own Eden.

Since then they have pulled our plows and borne our loads,   50
But that free servitude still can pierce our hearts.
Our life is changed; their coming our beginning.

Scotland's Winter

Now the ice lays its smooth claws on the sill,
The sun looks from the hill
Helmed in his winter casket,
And sweeps his arctic sword across the sky.
The water at the mill
Sounds more hoarse and dull.
The miller's daughter walking by
With frozen fingers soldered to her basket
Seems to be knocking
Upon a hundred leagues of floor   10
With her light heels, and mocking
Percy and Douglas dead,[1]
And Bruce on his burial bed,
Where he lies white as may
With wars and leprosy,
And all the kings before
This land was kingless,
And all the singers before
This land was songless,
This land that with its dead and living waits the Judgment Day.
But they, the powerless dead,   21
Listening can hear no more
Than a hard tapping on the sounding floor
A little overhead
Of common heels that do not know
Whence they come or where they go
And are content
With their poor frozen life and shallow banishment.

Adam's Dream

They say the first dream Adam our father had
After his agelong daydream in the Garden
When heaven and sun woke in his wakening mind,
The earth with all its hills and woods and waters,
The friendly tribes of trees and animals,
And earth's last wonder Eve (the first great dream
Which is the ground of every dream since then) –
They say he dreamt lying on the naked ground,
The gates shut fast behind him as he lay
Fallen in Eve's fallen arms, his terror drowned   10

---

[1] The action described in the ballad 'The Battle of Otterbourne'.

In her engulfuing terror, in the abyss
Whence there's no further fall, and comfort is –
That he was standing on a rocky ledge
High on the mountainside, bare crag behind,
In front a plain as far as eye could reach,
And on the plain a few small figures running
That were like men and women, yet were so far away
He could not see their faces. On they ran,
And fell, and rose again, and ran, and fell,
And rising were the same yet not the same,   20
Identical or interchangeable,
Different in indifference. As he looked
Still there were more of them, the plain was filling
As by an alien arithmetical magic
Unknown in Eden, a mechanical
Addition without meaning, joining only
Number to number in no mode or order,
Weaving no pattern. for these creatures moved
Towards no fixed mark even when in growing bands
They clashed against each other and clashing fell   30
In mounds of bodies. For they rose again,
Identical or interchangeable,
And went their way that was not like a way;
Some back and forward, back and forward, some
In a closed circle, wide or narrow, others
In zigzags on the sand. Yet all were busy,
And tense with purpose as they cut the air
Which seemed to press them back. Sometimes they paused
While one stopped one – fortuitous assignations
In the disorder, whereafter two by two   40
They ran awhile,
Then parted and again were single. Some
Ran straight against the frontier of the plain
Till the horizon drove them back. A few
Stood still and ne'er moved. Then Adam cried
Out of his dream, 'What are you doing there?'
And the crag answered 'Are you doing there?'
'What are you doing there?' – 'you doing there?'
The animals had withdrawn and from the caves
And woods stared out in fear or condemnation,   50
Like outlaws or like judges. All at once
Dreaming or half-remembering, 'This is time',
Thought Adam in his dream, and time was strange
To one lately in Eden. 'I must see',
He cried, 'the faces. Where are the faces? Who
Are you all out there?' Then in his changing dream
He was a little nearer, and he saw
They were about some business strange to him
That had a form and sequence past their knowledge;
And that was why they ran so frenziedly.   60
Yet all, it seemed, made up a story, illustrated
By these the living, the unknowing, cast
Each singly for his part. But Adam longed
For more, not this mere moving pattern, not

This illustrated storybook of mankind
Always a-making, improvised on nothing.
At that he was among them, and saw each face
Was like his face, so that he would have hailed them
As sons of God but that something restrained him.
And he remembered all, Eden, the Fall,   70
The Promise, and his place, and took their hands
That were his hands, his and his children's hands,
Cried out and was at peace, and turned again
In love and grief in Eve's encircling arms.

The Brothers

Last night I watched my brothers play,
The gentle and the reckless one,
In a field two yards away.
For half a century they were gone
Beyond the other side of care
To be among the peaceful dead.
Even in a dream how could I dare
Interrogate that happiness
So wildly spent yet never less?
For still they raced about the green   10
And were like two revolving suns;
A brightness poured from head to head,
So strong I could not see their eyes
Or look into their paradise.
What were they doing, the happy ones?
Yet where I was they once had been.

I thought, How could I be so dull,
Twenty thousand days ago,
Not to see they were beautiful?
I asked them, Were you really so   20
As you are now, that other day?
And the dream was soon away.
For then we played for victory
And not to make each other glad.
A darkness covered every head,
Frowns twisted the original face,
And through that mask we could not see
The beauty and the buried grace.

I have observed in foolish awe
The dateless mid-days of the law   30
And seen indifferent justice done
By everyone on everyone.
And in a vision I have seen
My brothers playing on the green.

Scottish Literature: Language

Scottish literature, considered linguistically, may be divided into Early Scots, Middle Scots, and Anything At All. The first two periods exhibit a certain homogeneity of language and as a result of that a definite style; the third, which began tentatively with Knox (the first Scotsman to write good English prose), and definitely with the acceptance of the English translation of the Bible, signalises a disintegration of the language of Scottish literature and the disappearance of a distinctive Scottish style. Scotland continued to produce writers, but they wrote in a confusion of tongues ranging from orthodox English to the dialects of the various Scottish districts. The only speech which they did not continue to use was Scots, for that had disappeared. Consequently, since some time in the sixteenth century Scottish literature has been a literature without a language. Middle Scots survived Sir David Lyndsay for a while in the lyrics of Alexander Scott and Montgomery. But a little later Drummond of Hawthornden was already writing in pure English, and since then Scottish poetry has been written either in English, or in some local dialect, or in some form of synthetic Scots, such as Burns's, or Scott's, or Hugh M'Diarmid's. Scottish prose disappeared altogether, swept away by Knox's brilliant *History of the Reformation* and the Authorised Version of the Bible.

The reasons for this disintegration of the language of Scottish literature are controversial, and I have no space to enter into them here. But it is clear that the Reformation, the Union of the Crowns, and the Union of the Kingdoms had all a great deal to do with it. I must confine myself, however, to certain of its consequences. The prerequisite of an autonomous literature is a homogeneous language. If Shakespeare had written in the dialect of Warwickshire, Spenser in Cockney, Ralegh in the broad Western English speech which he used, the future of English literature must have been very different, for it would have lacked a common language where all the thoughts and feelings of the English people could come together, add lustre to one another, and serve as a standard for one another. A common language of this kind can only be conceived, it seems to me, as an achievement continuously created and preserved by the highest spiritual energy of a people: the nursing ground and guarantee of all that is best in its thought and imagination: and without it no people can have any standard of literature. For this homogeneous language is the only means yet discovered for expressing the response of a whole people, emotional and intellectual, to a specific body of experience peculiar to it alone, on all the levels of thought from discursive reason to poetry. And since some time in the sixteenth century Scotland has lacked such a language.

Every genuine literature, in other words, requires as its condition a means of expression capable of dealing with everything the mind can think or the imagination conceive. It must be a language for criticism as well as poetry, for abstract speculation as well as fact, and since we live in a scientific age, it must be a language for science as well. A language which can serve for one or two of those purposes but not for the others is, considered as a vehicle for literature, merely an anachronism.

Scots has survived to our time as a language for simple poetry and the simpler kind of short story, such as *Thrawn Janet*; all its other uses have lapsed, and it expresses therefore only a fragment of the Scottish mind. One can go further than this, however, and assert that its very use is a proof that the Scottish consciousness is divided. For, reduced to the its simplest terms, this linguistic division means that Scotsmen feel in one language and think in another; that their emotions turn to the Scottish tongue, with all its associations of local sentiment, and their minds to a standard English which for them is almost bare of associations other than those of the classroom. If Henryson and Dunbar had written prose they would have written in the same language as they used for poetry, for their minds were still whole; but Burns never thought of doing so, nor did Scott, nor did Stevenson, nor has any Scottish writer since.

In an organic literature poetry is always influencing prose, and prose poetry; and their interaction energises them both. Scottish poetry exists in a vacuum; it neither acts on the rest of literature nor reacts to it; and consequently it has shrunk to the level of anonymous folk-song.

Hugh M'Diarmid has recently tried to revive it by impregnating it with all the contemporary influences of Europe one after another, and thus galvanise it into life by a series of violent shocks. In carrying out this experiment he has written some remarkable poetry; but he has left Scottish verse very much where it was before. For the major forms of poetry rise from a collision between emotion and intellect on a plane where both meet on equal terms; and it can never come into existence where the poet feels in one language and thinks in another, even though he should subsequestly translate his thoughts into the language of his feelings. Scots poetry can only be revived, that is to say, when Scotsmen begin to think *naturally* in Scots. The curse of Scottish literature is the lack of a whole language, which finally means the lack of a whole mind.

This division in the Scottish consciousness is so far-reaching that if I were to enumerate all its consequences this chapter would go on to the end of the book. So I shall confine myself to some of its effects on poetry. I have often wondered why the Scots, who have shown themselves in the past to be a theological and speculative race, should have produced scarcely a single verse of good religious or metaphysical poetry. In the seventeenth century Scotland was steeped in theology far more thoroughly than England. Yet England produced the religious and metaphysical poetry of that time, and against Donne, Marvell, Traherne, Vaughan, Herbert and Crashaw, all that Scotland could show was a metrical version of the Psalms which is a curiosity.

Now it is clear that there are other reasons for this poverty of Scots poetry in the seventeenth century and since than the fact that Scotsmen already felt in one language and thought in another, and that there was no effective collaboration between their sensibility and their intellect. It will be best, therefore, to consider some of these reasons first. One of them was without doubt the strict Calvinism of the Scots, which was adverse both to the production of poetry, and to poetry itself. Another was the complete prohibition put upon poetic drama by the Reformers just when it seemed on the point of developing a prohibition which killed not only the drama itself, but also a great number of other forms of poetry which normally flow from it. This matter of dramatic poetry, indeed, or rather the lack of it, was probably crucial for Scottish literature; and if that is so, then the Reformation truly signalised the beginning of Scotland's decline as a civilised nation. For poetic drama occupies a central and decisive position in the development of the three literatures which I mentioned at the beginning of this essay. In all three, English, French and German, poetry and literature in general came to self-consciousness in a great burst of poetic drama, and this achievement of self-consciousness influenced all the poetry that followed, whether lyrical or dramatic: poetry was thenceforth more aware of itself and more capable of essaying the non-dramatic major forms. If one compares the lyrical poetry of England before Shakespeare, of France before Racine, and of Germany before Goethe, with the lyrical poetry after them, one can see quite clearly this difference in self consciousness. Before the change one finds the simple lyric with all its natural thoughtless grace; after it one finds a body of poetry lyrical in form, but expressing all the richness and complexity of experience as it is known to the self-perusing mind. To take a simple instance, the English metaphysical poetry of the sixteenth century with its 'dialogue of one' would be inconceivable without the rich dramatic 'dialogue of many' which preceded it or was contemporaneous with it.

The strict surveillance of Calvinism, then, and the consequent failure of Scotland to achieve poetic drama, may partly account for the fact that in her poetry since the sixteenth century she has failed to rise above the level of the simple lyric; why she has no Donne, no Baudelaire, no Holderlin; why she has no romantic poet even of the rank of Beddoes; and why the only poetry with which hers can be compared is early medieval poetry such as that of Walter von der Vogelweide, and the folk-song which belongs indiscriminately to all peoples.

Yet allowing for Calvinism and the failure to achieve poetic drama, we do not completely ac-count for the poverty and simplicity of Scottish poetry since the sixteenth century, for at the time when Scotland had a homogeneous literary language – when thought and feeling, in other words, could come to equal collision in the poet's mind, she did produce one major poem, Henryson's 'Testament of Cresseid', and a number of poems by such writers as Scott and Montgomery and the anonymous authors of the lyrics in the Bannatyne and Maitland collections, which in their intricacy of movement and fusion of feeling and thought foreshadowed the English metaphysicals. Take this verse from one of Alexander Scott's lyrics:

> Luve is ane fervent fire,
> Kendillit without desire:
> Short plesour, lang displesour,
> Repentance is the hire;
> Ane puir tressour without mesour:
> Luve is ane fervent fire.

Then take this from one of Burns's songs:

> But a' the pleasures e'er I saw,
> Tho' three times doubl'd fairly,
> That happy night was worth them a',
> Amang the rigs o' barley.

The first of these verses is written by a man who thinks and feels with equal intensity, on the same plane and in the same language, so that the thought heightens the feeling and the feeling the thought; while the second is a mere effusion of thoughtless emotion, with a commonplace judgment tagged on to it exalting feeling at the expense of everything else. If Burns had wished to express his real judgment on that night among the rigs of barley he would have turned to English, as he did in *Tam o' Shanter* in the one passage where he makes a serious reflection on life. Everybody knows it:

> But pleasures are like poppies spread,
> You seize the flow'r, its bloom is shed;
> Or like the snow falls in the river,
> A moment white – then melts for ever;
> Or like the Borealis race,
> That flit ere you can point their place;
> Or like the rainbow's lovely form
> Evanishing amid the storm.

I had often wondered why Burns suddenly dropped into English at this point, and for a long time I put down the whole passage as an unaccountable blemish, until I saw that it was the touch that made the poem perfect, the one serious reference that gave all the rest proportion. The point to be noticed, however, is that when Burns applied thought to his theme he turned to English. The reflection in this passage is neither deep nor original, but in the context it is quite adequate. And it is clear that Burns felt he could not express it in Scots, which was to him a language for sentiment but not for thought. He had no language which could serve him equally for both.

When emotion and thought are separated, emotion becomes irresponsible and thought arid. When they are separated so radically that they require two separate languages to express them, the first takes on very much the aspect of an indulgence and the second of disapproval. Scottish poetry is therefore largely emotion, and Scottish criticism has been until quite recent and degenerate times largely condemnation. They are alike in this, that they are equally without standards; for where poetry is written in a variety of dialects with no central language as a point of reference, it is impossible to evolve a criterion of style (there is no standard of Scots poetic style); and where criticism is divorced from sensibility, and consists in the mere elaboration or application of theories, it would in any case fail to judge poetry on genuine literary principles, even if such a criterion existed. Criticism, like poetry, requires a union of emotion and intellect, and where that union is broken criticism comes off as badly as poetry itself. So that in both provinces the division in the Scots mind and the Scots language has had disastrous effects. The worst thing that can be said about Scottish poetry and Scottish criticism is that they never come together, either in general or in the mind of the writer. And until Scotland has a common language for its prose and poetry, its thought and feeling, this evil must continue.

Janetta Murray (dates unknown)

Ultima Thule

She thought in Gaelic. All her English speech
Was slow and halting, with a sibilance
Of hiss on hiss. She spoke as through thick wool;
Stammering idly, like the lap of waves
You hearken after in some woodland pool
Mist-shrouded, hear at last beat faint and low.
She looked afar as though nought near could know
Eyes sick with longing for wild wind-swept space;
Looked till the dull look faded from her face
And, where her dreams danced, danced her pent soul too. 10
Stupid she seemed, and dour, and soft and still,
Moved by an alien, deep, instinctive will,
Having no words to tell her grief and pain,
Her horror of this town. She left her bed
One night unslept in, sought and found the quays,
A boat for Lewis, and sailed home again.

'James Bridie' (O[sborne] H. Mavor, 1888 – 1951)

Born in Glasgow, Bridie became a doctor and worked at that profession for nearly twenty years. Meanwhile, he wrote plays, the most important in the Scottish national theatre movement. Many of his plays were successes on the London stage as well. Only James Barrie has been more significant as a Scottish dramatist. A primary theme in James Bridie's plays is the ambiguity of good and evil (i.e., not simply the difficulty of choice, but the problem of definition). *The Anatomist*, a treatment of the notorious 'body-snatchers' Burke and Hare, and of the docotr who paid for the corpses, is one of his most thoughtful, puzzling dramas. The play is relentless in its exposure and condemnation of Victorian moral and dramamtic convention, but it does not replace those conventions with any twentieth century certainties. This refusal to commit has seemed to some viewers a trivialising of his great subject, a mere 'drawing room irreverence' *a la* Oscar Wilde. But in fact Bridie is a maddeningly orginal thinker, and a careful and skillful dramatist.

The Anatomist [1]

PERSONS IN THE PLAY

Miss Amelia Dishart.
Miss Mary Belle Dishart.
Walter Anderson, L.R.C.S., Edinburgh. A Demonstrator in Anatomy.
Jessie Ann. A Maid-servant.
Robert Knox, M.D. A Lecturer in Anatomy.
Augustus Raby. A Student of Anatomy.
The Landlord of the Three Tuns.
Mary Paterson. A Woman of the Town.
Janet. A Servant-girl.
Davie Paterson. Porter at Surgeons' Hall.
William Burke.
William Hare.
Sundry Students of Anatomy.

The scene is laid in Edinburgh, in 1828.

Act I: The Disharts' drawing-room.
Act II, Scene I: The Three Tuns Tavern. Scene II: The Lobby at Dr Knox's rooms,
    Surgeons' Square.
Act III: Same as Act I.

ACT I

The withdrawing-room at the DISHARTS'. MARY BELLE DISHART is at her piano. MISS AMELIA
DISHART, her elder, is embroidering by the dying light from the window. WALTER ANDERSON
is watching MARY and turning over her music. The time is autumn in 1828.

MARY   I attempt from love's sickness to fly in vain,
    Since I am myself my own fever and pain.
    No more now, fond heart, with pride shall we swell:
    Thou canst not raise forces enough to rebel.
    For love has more power and less mercy than fate
    To make me seek ruin and love those that hate.
    I attempt from love's sickness to fly in vain,
    Since I am myself my own fever and pain.
WALTER Thank you very much.
AMELIA I have heard you sing better, Mary Belle.
MARY   I know. I am in poor voice tonight. I don't know why.
WALTER I thought you sang it with great feeling and expression.
MARY   Oh, feeling! Yes.

She looks at her sister, who rises.

AMELIA The light is almost gone. How lovely and sad these autumn evenings are! We shall
    miss them when we go abroad next month.
WALTER Don't go abroad, Miss Amelia . . . I think the evenings are more beautiful in
    Scotland than anywhere else in the whole world.

---

[1] All rights in this play are strictly reserved and no performance may be given unless a license has been issued
by Lemon Unna & Durbridge Ltd, 24 Pottery Lane, Holland Park, London W11 4LZ.

AMELIA In the whole world, Walter? You must be the great traveller to pass your judgments on so wide an area.

WALTER Well, I have been to Calais and to Madeira.

MARY You are quite the Christopher Columbus.

WALTER And you are suddenly very waggish. I rejoice to see you have become sprightly again.

MARY I rejoice, sir, in your rejoicings.

WALTER Mary, I . . . Will you sing again?

MARY No, indeed I will not.

AMELIA Walter, I think you are a sufficiently old friend of the family to excuse my leaving you and my sister together for a few moments. We expect another guest tonight – a gentleman – and I have some instructions to give to Jessie Ann. We may overlook the proprieties for once in a way, may not we?

WALTER Of course, Miss Amelia. Permit me . . .

MARY We have pulled each other's hair and torn each other's clothes often enough in the past. Is it wise to leave us together?

AMELIA I cannot think why Walter comes here at all. You are making him blush with your coarseness. Don't mind her naughtiness, Walter. Her heart is in the right place.

WALTER I hope so, indeed, Miss Dishart. As a student of anatomy I hope so. It is tidier so.

AMELIA You are being indelicate now. I doubt I should not leave you after all.

MARY Do go away, Amelia. You are filling the room with a dreadful draught and poor Walter will be frozen to the door-handle, and what will your dear Mr Knox think?

WALTER Dr Knox? Is he coming tonight?

AMELIA Oh, yes. Poor soul, he is lonely! And he is so fond of female society. And he does love Mary Belle and me to accompany him with his flute. He plays shockingly, poor soul. And he has married, we are told, so unhappily. Mrs Knox cannot or will not go out with him. They say she is hardly presentable. He is so kind to her too.

MARY You are sorry for an Irish tinker in the street, but you do not ask him in to your with-drawing-room.

AMELIA Mary Belle, please do not talk in that way. Mr Knox is a most interesting man. Such a fund of information! And he is Walter's hero. You must not speak ill of Walter's hero.

MARY I cannot congratulate either Walter on his hero or you on your – on your protégé.

AMELIA Mary Belle dear, what has come over you tonight? You are quite unlike yourself.

MARY I am fey, I think. Amelia, your great bear of a surgeon will be upon us at any moment. And I will not be left alone with sulky Walter and ogreish Dr Knox. Do hurry, dearest.

AMELIA I shall be back presently. Be good.

She goes.

MARY Well, Walter?

WALTER Well?

MARY Amelia was right. I sing Purcell abominably.

WALTER Oh, no! I thought . . .

MARY Ah, 'with feeling and expression,' yes. With too much feeling. 'To make us seek ruin and love those that hate.'

WALTER If you are referring to me you are treating me most cruelly. You know and you know that I love you tenderly, devotedly.

MARY Perhaps.

WALTER What do you mean?

MARY You know very well what I mean.

WALTER On my honour I do not. Tell me.

MARY Your honour! It is a pretty honour that forces a lady to say what she never should say.

WALTER Oh, don't tell me it is the same old quarrel again. I hoped and believed that it was all done with.

MARY Why may we not marry?

WALTER But we shall marry, my heart's love! Only we must wait. Others can wait. Why should not we?

MARY Wait, wait, wait! I am sick of waiting. Three of my friends were married this summer. I shall have no bridesmaids left.

WALTER But you agreed . . . You said you would wait twenty years if need be.

MARY I know I did. Don't be so ungentlemanly as to cast it up to me. (MARY *picks up a skein of wool and twists it in her hands.*) How you humiliate me!

WALTER Mary . . .

MARY Uncle Matthew talked about it all this afternoon. He asked again whether you would accept the money he will lend you to commence practice in Fife. He says he can't understand why you won't take his offer. We could marry in spring, he says.

WALTER Mary, I explained to you why I could not commence practice in Fife. I thought you understood.

MARY Of course I understand. I understand only too well. You love your loathsome dissecting-rooms and your horrible Dr Knox better than you love me.

WALTER You know that's not true. And please don't speak in that way of Dr Knox.

MARY 'Don't speak in that way of Dr Knox?' It is how everyone speaks of Dr Knox. He *is* horrible. He is conceited. He is overdressed. He is ugly. He is pompous. He's rude. And they say worse things of him than that.

WALTER Who say so? What do they say?

MARY Never mind.

WALTER But I *do* mind. I insist upon knowing.

MARY You *insist*, Dr Anderson?

WALTER I do insist. Mary, you of all people must not have your judgment corrupted by malicious lies. It is intolerable that . . .

MARY Walter, please don't gesticulate. You will knock down the what-nots. Besides, I am in no mood to admire it. Pray sit down. Here. (*She gives him her wool to hold and begins to wind.*) Now you are bound. I wish I could gag you too.

WALTER Mary. Tell me. What lies have you heard against Dr Knox?

MARY They are not lies . . . Well, he is a married man and he is for ever dancing attendance on unmarried females.

WALTER Dr Knox's domestic life has been a tragedy.

MARY There is no compulsion upon him to transform it into a French farce . . . Besides . . .

WALTER Besides what?

MARY Well, besides, everybody knows that hand in glove with the sack-'em-up men.

WALTER With the *what*?

MARY With the sack-'em-up men. The body-snatchers. The resurrectionists. It is utterly dreadful to think . . .

WALTER It is dreadful. It is dreadful to hear you talking thieves' slang – worthy of the lips that invented the lie but unspeakably unworthy of yours.

MARY You can't deny it. *Do* hold my wool properly. Everyone says it . . . Walter, dear, I'm horribly unhappy.

WALTER Who has been filling your head with this? I can't bear to hear you talking of such things. Oh, put down that damned wool!

MARY Oh, Walter, you've fankled it all up. It will take hours to unravel.

WALTER Mary, if I went to Fife I should be profaning something – something greater than my love for you.

MARY Your own selfish personal inclinations.

WALTER No, no, no, no! I have to fight them. God knows how I have to fight them. They tell me to go to Fife. To marry you at once. I adore you. My whole soul aches for you.

MARY I see. Only it aches a little bit more for the great, one-eyed, bald-headed, nasty Dr Knox; and just a little bit more for your horrid dead people. You are like a cannibal. Oogh! I dreamed last night that you were a black, molting carrion crow, pecking, pecking – You come here reeking of mortality. It's disgusting.

WALTER It isn't disgusting. It's beautiful. Lovely, intricate human bodies. It teaches me to see God.

MARY That's blasphemous.

WALTER No, no, no. Mary, if only you . . . It's God's work. Anatomy is God's work. He made us and we ought to know how. It is as if they had taken the noblest of an atist's works and locked them in a dark gallery and barricaded the door. We are breaking down the barricade. We'll go on . . . We'll make the manifest God's work to man! We will! Oh, I can't express myself. Ask Knox. He'll tell you. He knows.

MARY God's work! God and Dr Knox! A singular association! Indeed I cannot think why my sister does not forbid him the house.

WALTER Forbid Dr Knox the house! Oh, very pleasant. Miss Dishart at least has some dim conception that his visits are an honour, ma'am, an honour!

MARY You dare to speak to me like that!

WALTER Listen to me. Knox will be remembered when Buonaparte and Wellington are forgotten. His work in the comparative anatomy of the eye . . .

MARY Dr Anderson, you are beside yourself. Please go away.

WALTER Forgive me, Mary.

MARY You are unpardonable.

WALTER You are right. I am not myself tonight.

MARY I think you are yourself tonight. I think I have never known your true self till tonight. I count myself fortunate to have discovered you – in time. Here is your ring.

WALTER I won t take it. This is a foolish quarrel.

MARY I am foolish, am I? I talk thieves' slang, do I? I am unladylike, am I?

WALTER I said no such thing. I said it was a foolish quarrel, and so it is.

MARY It is NOT. You must choose between me and Dr Knox.

WALTER I choose both. I will have both. I will make you see my point of view.

MARY You will never drag me so low as that. This is your last chance. I will share the affections of a gentleman with nobody. Which do you choose?

WALTER Oh, my God, what shall I do?

> MAID *knocks, and enters. Enter* DR. KNOX. *He carries a flute in its case. The room has darkened, and his presence appears to make it darker.*

MAID Dr Knox!

KNOX You rehearse some theatricals? I intrude, as usual.

MARY No, no, Dr Knox. We are very much obliged by your visit. We were expecting you. My sister will be here presently. Walter, do you light the candles, please. Be seated, sir.

KNOX I thank you, ma'am. Well, Mr Anderson, you tear yourself from your studies to sport with Amaryllis in the shade. I am interested to observe this in you, sir. Madam, do I interrupt your idyll?

MARY I don't know what you mean, sir. Jessie Ann, tell Miss Dishart that the Doctor is here.

> *The* MAID *goes out.*

KNOX I'll explain my meaning, if you are really an anxious inquirer. I take any amount of trouble with a truly anxious inquirer. I do, do I not, Mr Daphnis Anderson?

MARY You are facetious, Mr Knox.

KNOX Your only jig-maker.

MARY If you will excuse me, I shall go fetch my sister.

WALTER No.

MARY No? Let me pass, please, Mr Anderson.

WALTER Mary, We cannot leave things as they are. Listen. Dr Knox will speak for me. He'll tell you, Mary. Mary, do listen.

MARY I can't conceive what Mr Knox will think of you. Open the door, please.

She goes out.

KNOX *Une affaire des tendresses,* I perceive. You are a sad rogue, Anderson, I fear.

WALTER Sir, I –

KNOX Not a word, not a word. Keep your amours to yourself. I am not a good natural confidant. Besides, I wanted to talk to you about something. What was it, now? Eureka! I have it. Was it you who gave that dolt Raby a head to dissect?

WALTER Yes, sir. This morning.

KNOX And why, pray? Do you think that dissecting-room subjects are so easily come by that I can afford to have them mangled by that imbecile?

WALTER Well, sir, he hadn't yet dissected the head. He's a dull fellow, sir, but conscientious and anxious to learn.

KNOX *Ach, Gott!* Then he is a *rara avis.* But he may fly to the Himalayas and learn from the vultures who mutilate the liver of poor Prometheus by the most up-to-date Edinburgh methods. Or, better still, send him to my worthy and honoured colleague, the Professor of Anatomy. I won't have him in my rooms.

WALTER I think you do him an injustice, sir. There are many worse students than old Raby.

KNOX *C'est vrai. C'est juste.*[1] There are. Mr Anderson, when I survey the brutish faces of the youths ranged round my lecture room, I thank my Maker that I once studied the habits of the hyena. I presented a communication on them, sir, to the Royal Society. I have no doubt you are too occupied with petticoats to have read it, sir, but it is in the library.

WALTER I have read the paper, sir.

KNOX This is fame, sir. This is glory. It is worth all the labour of stuffing these Bartholomew pigs for the slaughter to have awakened a glimmer of interest in one of them. If you would follow my instructions without question, I should be better pleased. But that is too much to hope for.

WALTER Very well, sir. I shall make an arrangement with Raby.

KNOX Send him out to rob graveyards. It is all the ass is fit for.

WALTER If you are serious, sir, I must tell you that that is no part of my duty.

KNOX What, pray, is no part of your duty?

WALTER Arranging churchyard raids. I disapprove of them very strongly.

KNOX You do, do you? We will have you in the Militia, with a cocked hat and a blunderbuss. You are a prig, Mr Anderson.

WALTER You are not very kind to me, Dr Knox.

KNOX Would you like to weep on my bosom? You looked on the verge of tears when I arrived. You appear to be enjoying a merry evening.

WALTER Damnation! Tonight I meet the two people I most reverence in the world, and they make me a butt. I had better go home.

Enter AMELIA *and* MARY BELLE.

KNOX Mademoiselle, your humble servant. I have been annoying Mr Walter Anderson.

AMELIA Oh, you must not do that, Dr Knox. Mr Walter is under my especial protection.

KNOX He is indeed happy. How are you?

AMELIA I am very well indeed, thank you. Pray sit down and tell us the news. Walter has been very silent all evening. He is a poor gossip.

---

[1] 'That's true. That's quite right.'

KNOX In Mr Walter's trade and mine that is a high qualification.

AMELIA Oh, do you think so? I used to rely on old Dr Bell for all the crack[1] of the country-side. Mamma used to say he was better than a clergyman.

KNOX His scandal was more piquant, ma'am.

AMELIA Ah, I would not say that. What a pity Mr Sidney Smith went away. What a chatterbox! And a minister of the gospel, too. Mamma adored him.

KNOX He is a Canon now, I am told.

AMELIA And a very explosive one, too. Did you know him, Doctor?

KNOX No, ma'am.

AMELIA I did so admire his writing in the *Review.* So polished. So unlike those boors in *Maga.* Little Mr Macaulay is writing now in the *Review.*

KNOX Ah?

AMELIA Mary Belle, have you the latest number? Yes. On Machiavelli. He was here last night. Not Machiavelli – Mr Macaulay; and he told us. He was very proud. He is a chatterbox, if you like. Have you read his essay?

KNOX On Machiavelli?

AMELIA Yes.

KNOX I have no time for the follies of young scribblers. What does he say of Machiavelli?

AMELIA He makes some sort of a hero of him. I cannot think why. I myself think Machiavelli was a great rascal.

KNOX You are wrong, ma'am, you are wrong. He had the hall-mark of greatness upon him.

AMELIA And what is the hall-mark of greatness?

KNOX To be assailed by the mob.

MARY Mercy! When everyone is telling us that the voice of the people is the voice of God!

KNOX Ladies, I have, as you know, fought against the French at some personal danger. If there is such a thing as physical courage, I do not possess it; but I would give all I have for the proud and happy privilege of standing with my back to the wall and my pistols in my hand, with a thousand of the canaille before me, ravening for my blood.

AMELIA It is a strange wish. But your cause would, of course, be a good one?

KNOX What do I care for the cause? I have no opinions I would die for. But if I heard but once the noble patriotic cry, 'Crucify him!' I would know my cause was good.

AMELIA You are making yourself quite hot, Mr Knox.

WALTER But you have heard the cry already, Mr Knox. The University –

KNOW Want my blood. I was referring to the full-throated bellow of the mob. Not the squeak of vampire flittermice.

AMELIA You should go into Parliament, Mr Knox. How well you speak.

KNOX Miss Amelia, how beautifully and tenderly you make us ranting actors look absurd. Shall we practise on the flute? Miss Mary Belle, your harp has shed its garments and fallen from the willow. Shall we have a trio? What have you been playing? 'I attempt from love's sickness to fly . . . '

WALTER But, Mr Knox – do pardon me a moment – you say you have no opinions you would die for. But surely you must feel, must know you are right?

KNOX Right about what, my disciple?

WALTER Oh, everything. You stand up so boldly against the schools, and the clergy, and – and the talk of all the drawing-rooms. You preach a gospel. You *must* have confidence in it?

KNOX Only a fool is sure of himself until the mob denies him. The learned Regius Professor, Alexander Monro the Third, would think he was right, if he could think at all. But I am not such a dolt.

MARY You hear that?

---

[1] Chat, gossip.

KNOX Hoho!

AMELIA Let us have some music.

WALTER No, no. You don't know how important this is to me. If you are being witty, please tell me. I have no sense of humour.

MARY Walter, you must not.

WALTER Please, Mary. I am at my wits' end.

KNOX No very long journey. What is the matter with you?

WALTER Tonight I have been offered the choice between my dearest happiness and another year's work at anatomy. I risked my happiness – I may have lost it – to work with you. Am I in the right? Have I been a fool?

KNOX You are in the right. You have been a fool. Your are in the right to be a fool and a fool to be in the right.

MARY Mr Knox . . .

AMELIA Now, now, now, now, now, now. Dr Knox has come to practise on the flute and not to be deeved[1] with dull family matters.

KNOX Family matters are never dull, ma'am. That is a mistake you ladies make. Come. I shall be Judge in Chambers. What is the cause?

WALTER Sir, Miss Mary Belle Dishart says . . .

KNOX *I* don't want to hear what she says, sir. She will say it herself. What have you to say?

Enter the MAID.

MAID Please, Miss Amelia –

AMELIA What is it, Jessie Ann?

MAID Please ma'am, are you at home to a Mr Baby?

AMELIA Mister who, girl?

MAID Mr Baby. An English-spoken gentleman.

WALTER Oh pardon me, Miss Dishart. She means Mr Raby. I took the liberty of asking him to come. He is a medical student. He comes from Warwickshire, I think. He has very few friends in Edinburgh, and I thought to ask permission to present him. He is very well connected . . .

KNOX Ha! He is also most conscientious and anxious to learn. He ceased this evening, at my urgent request, to pursue his studies at Surgeons' Square, but I have no doubt his exclusiveness and genteel connections will appeal to other poor devils of Lecturers in Anatomy in this city.

AMELIA And he's kicking his heels downstairs all this time! Show the gentleman up, Jessie Ann.

Exit MAID.

AMELIA Why don't you simply say he is a friend of yours Walter? He is welcome if he is, and I'll soon get his biography out of him for myself.

KNOX And this cause these two people were about to bring before me?

AMELIA The cause can wait. It is a pack of nonsense, anyway.

Enter the MAID *and* RABY.

MAID Mr Baby.

AMELIA How do you do, Mr Raby? Will you present Mr Raby, Walter?

WALTER May I present Mr Adolphus Raby, Miss Dishart. Miss Mary Belle Dishart, Mr Raby. Dr Knox, I think you already know Mr Raby. He is a student of yours.

KNOX He was.

AMELIA Dr Knox has been speaking so kindly of you, Mr Raby. Do you sit down by me.

RABY Most happy.

---

[1] Deafened.

AMELIA Have you been long in Edinburgh, Mr Raby?

RABY Not very. No. Not very.

AMELIA We are enchanted that Walter should have asked you to come to see us. He is a
very old friend of ours, and his friends are very welcome. You are a native of England,
Mr Raby?

RABY Yes. Yes, ma'am.

AMELIA Where is your home?

RABY Oh, I lodge in the Canongate.

AMELIA No. I mean your real home. In England.

RABY Sutton Bottom.

AMELIA And where is that? In which county?

RABY Bucks.

AMELIA I have never been there, but I am told it is a very beautiful county.

RABY Oh, in parts. Parts are so-so.

AMELIA And parts are not so so-so. But that is like all other counties. Even our own
Midlothian. Do you like Edinburgh, Mr Raby?

RABY Yes.

AMELIA It is an interesting old city. Every stone speaks of history. Doesn't it?

RABY Yes. It does.

AMELIA Do you like negus?

RABY Oh, yes, ma'am.

AMELIA Mary Belle, will you prepare the negus and ask Jessie Ann to bring it up?

MARY Very well, Amelia.

She goes out.

AMELIA The nights are drawing in now. Walter, draw the curtains. You will find the
autumn nights shorter here than in England, Mr Raby?

RABY Yes, ma'am.

AMELIA What is your honest opinion of Scotland, Mr Raby? We Scots are always anxious
to know how 'ithers see us.'

RABY Pardon?

AMELIA You know our poet Burns has a couplet:
'O wad some poo'er the giftie gie us
To see oorsel's as ithers see us.'
But no doubt that sounds barbarous to you.

RABY Yes, ma'am. I mean, no, ma'am.

AMELIA Do you find the Scots tongue easy to understand?

RABY No, ma'am.

WALTER How is the reading getting on, Raby? Have you finished that text-book I lent
you?

RABY A bit slowly, sir. I am rather slow, sir, as you know. But I'm sticking to it. I'm
determined to get through, this time, sir. Oh, and I wanted to ask you, sir – you know
where it says that about the development of the spinal cord in the chick embryo . . .

WALTER Will you talk to me about it tomorrow? Oh – yes – I forgot . . . In any case, will
you see me at Surgeons' Hall tomorrow morning, early?

RABY Yes, sir. I will.

WALTER I have something to talk to you about.

RABY Yes.

AMELIA I am told you work very hard, Mr Raby.

RABY Oh, I don't know. So-so.

AMELIA Oh, you are too modest. Is he not, Doctor?

KNOX I have no means of judging. I have never had occasion to shock his modesty.

AMELIA But surely that is not the only way of appraising modesty, to shock it!

KNOX It is the only way I know, ma'am.

AMELIA Doctor, you are terrible. Are his lectures full of terrible things like that, Mr Raby?

RABY Oh, no, ma'am. Nothing of the sort. They're wonderful. About bones and joints and so forth . . . and bowels.

AMELIA And what?

RABY Oh, it doesn't matter really. What I mean is . . . Yes.

> *Re-enter* MARY *and* JESSIE ANN, *with a tray full of materials for negus.* JESSIE ANN *goes out, and during the ensuing conversation* MARY *prepares and hands round the negus, accepting* WALTER'S *help with a bad grace.*

KNOX He says that what I teach him doesn't matter. You hear that, Miss Amelia?

AMELIA No, I don't. I will not have Mr Raby teased. Walter, will you be so good as to hand me the album of Neapolitan 'Views?' I want to show them to Mr Raby. Are you fond of Naples, Mr Raby?

RABY Yes, ma'am. I like them very much.

> KNOX *snorts.*

AMELIA My sister and I visited Naples last year. This is Mount Vesuvius. At night, particularly, it is a very awe-inspiring sight.

RABY It must be, ma am.

AMELIA Have you been to Naples?

RABY No, ma'am.

AMELIA Tons of molten lava are thrown into the air.

RABY Yes, ma'am.

AMELIA This is the Bay. But no pictorial representation can give the remotest idea of the depth of azure presented by the still waters in the sunlight.

RABY No, ma'am. Very deep, I'm sure.

AMELIA Do have some negus.

RABY Thank you, ma'am.

AMELIA Do you like negus? No. I asked you that before.

KNOX With the deepest respect, Miss Amelia, may I draw your attention to this? However fascinating the lunge and riposte of your conversation with Mr Raby, it was not to listen to intellectual dialogue that I came here. I came here to play on the flute. It became clear that a domestic imbroglio made the atmosphere impossible for the flute until the tangle was resolved. I was about to resolve it when Mr Raby entered like a high wind from Mount Olympus. May we not proceed where we left off?

AMELIA Really, Mr Knox, I am very indulgent with you, but this is intolerable.

KNOX I find it so, ma'am. I shall go.

AMELIA You will do nothing of the sort. Sit down and behave yourself. I am very, very angry. Mr Raby, please don't mind him.

RABY I don't, ma'am. At least . . .

KNOX At least? Well? At least . . . ?

AMELIA Mister Knox! Well, perhaps Mr Raby will excuse us. I know it seems inhospitable, but –

RABY *(sitting tight)* Nothing to excuse, ma'am, really.

AMELIA We shall be charmed to see you any other evening you care to call, Mr Raby.

RABY *(sitting tight)* Very good of you, ma'am, I'm sure.

AMELIA *(going towards him)* So if you . . .

> RABY *gets up.*

KNOX Oh, let him stay. He might as well be a pig in an Irishman's cabin for all the notice he will take. I know. I have lectured to him. Let him be the jury. Sit down, you fool. Fifteen good asses and true concentrated and sublimated into one sublime and concentrated ass. Hold your tongue and listen. Miss Amelia, forgive me. I may not appear so, but I am a very sensitive man. I am conscious of a suppressed atmosphere of strife. If there is a battle, I insist on taking part. Now, Miss Mary Belle Dishart, let us have your story.

AMELIA I simply will not allow this sort of thing.

KNOX Why not, ma'am? Why not? We have a hidden abscess here, an impostume. Let us have incision. Let us imbrue.

AMELIA Mr Knox, you may mix metaphors till you are black in the face. I will not have it in my house.

KNOX You mean that you will not talk about it. You have it already, and in your house. Be a sensible woman.

AMELIA I never in all my life heard the like of this.

KNOX Then do not forgo a new experience. It is always a mistake to forgo a new experience. Miss Mary Belle, I am waiting.

MARY Waiting for what, sir?

KNOX For what you have to say.

MARY I doubt you will hardly be pleased with what I have to say.

KNOX Signorina, I do not solicit your compliments. I am unaccustomed to compliments. I ask you to add honesty to your natural beauty and wit, and to add dispatch to all three.

MARY Amelia!

AMELIA It is not the least use appealing to me.

MARY You asked this gentleman to our house.

AMELIA When I asked him, he gave no evidence of being lunatic.

WALTER Miss Amelia, pray listen. You misunderstand Mr Knox's eccentricity of manners. He . . .

KNOX *Dieu vous remercie, mon Prince.*[1]

WALTER This cannot go on. Mary and I are near breaking-point.

MARY We reached breaking-point half-an-hour ago.

WALTER This must be settled. Mr Knox can help us. Pray, pray don't anger him. Let him go his own way. Mary! My sweetheart! If ever you had any regard for me, tell Dr Knox our difficulty. If you will not, I don't know what I shall do.

AMELIA I think you had better, Mary Belle. More of this and we shall all be raving – except Mr Raby.

MARY Very well. What does it matter? . . . Mr Knox, Mr Anderson and I were affianced. We were to be married this year. Since you appointed him your assistant, he has altered his plans.

WALTER My darling, no. No, no, no!

KNOX You must not say 'My darling, no, no, no, no,' while the witness is giving evidence. Pray proceed, Signorina.

MARY My uncle, Sir Matthew Goudie, has offered him an advance of £1000 that he may commence medical practice in Fife. Now. At once. He has refused it.

KNOX Quite rightly. He is unfit to start practice. He is better than most, but he is not yet fit to be responsible for human lives.

MARY He is. He is. Or he never will be. Besides that was not his excuse for breaking his word to me.

KNOX And what was his excuse?

MARY He said he was doing God's work. He said he was engaged on an heroic task. He said if he went to Fife he would be – he would be profaning something holier than his – than his love for me.

KNOX He said all that, did he?

WALTER Yes; and I meant it.

---

[1] 'May God thank you, my Prince.'

KNOX No doubt you did. And you, my dear young lady, took all this play-acting *aux grands serieux?*

WALTER Mr Knox!

MARY It was. I knew it was. Play-acting! That's what it was.

KNOX Be calm. Be calm. Be calm. Ninety per cent of all the amatory game is play-acting. And by far the most delightful part. Compose yourself. I have no doubt he meant what he said. But he had a far better reason for breaking his engagement with you.

WALTER I did not break my engagement.

KNOX Hold your tongue, you. Miss Mary Belle, I can quite understand that the pursuit of science may appear mean and trivial to a young female brought up on Shakespeare, crewel-work and the use of the musical glasses. But life, my dear young lady, is not all assemblies and quadrilles, or even dressing, bathing and smacking babies.

MARY Don't you dare speak like that to me. I am not a child. If you had the least sensibility you would feel – as Walter *knows* – that if he had been a poet or a musician or – or inspired in any way, I would have followed him barefoot through the world, or waited for him to the end of time.

KNOX That would have been very foolish of you.

MARY What do I care for foolishness or wisdom? I know what is right. I know Walter.

KNOX He is better employed than in making foolish jingles or spoiling canvas in the attempt to copy what cannot be copied.

MARY Better employed! He is employed on work I abhor. He cuts up dead bodies. He does it because he likes it. He is mad. He is *infected,* as people are infected with typhoid fever. That is my opinion of your dissecting, if you would like to know.

KNOX What do I care for your opinions? I am a man of science. I want your reasons.

MARY You want me to argue. I can't argue. I won't argue.

KNOX You prefer to jump to conclusions.

MARY Of course I do. Every sensible person does. All women jump to conclusions, just as all men crawl on their hands and knees, looking for them, counting every cobble-stone and never arriving, or arriving at the wrong place.

   AMELIA *has taken up her sewing.* WALTER *is listening intently.* RABY *is looking foolish.*

KNOX But look at the trouble your leaping causes! Nam fuit ante Helenam, femina teterrima causa belli.

MARY I don't know Latin.

KNOX You should study the classics. I have quoted Horace to the effect that Helen was not the first female to raise a rumpus.

AMELIA Doctor, you are being very naughty. I do think you might help, instead of parading your classics. The poor young people are in sad trouble.

KNOX Trouble! They know nothing of trouble. Let them go, as I did, to the deserts of South Africa, and hunt carnivora across the wastes accompanied only by ape-like Caffres . . .

AMELIA Yes, yes. You have told us. You must have had a terrible time. But black men can't be any worse than black thoughts. And, besides, you said you could settle things.

KNOX I did. Come, my dear. We are straying from the point. Let us have your absurdities. I am all ears. Mr Raby, will you stop looking at me in that manner? I have only one eye. This patch covers an eyeless socket.

AMELIA Doctor!

KNOX Your pardon. Proceed, Miss Mary Belle.

MARY Dr Knox, you appear to find this situation humourous. I find it humiliating. Walter tells me that this occupation which keeps us apart is God's work. You tell me he is play-acting when he says so. You have answered my question with jeers. I don't understand. I *must* understand. Won't you tell me what you mean?

KNOX My dear, we all seek to explain ourselves in big words and windy notions. The wise disregard these things. Our friend Walter has a sacred thirst of which he is only half-conscious. The vulgarian, the quack and the theologian are confronted with the Universe. They at once begin to talk and talk and talk. They have no curiosity. They know all about it. They build a mean structure of foolish words and phrases, and say to us, 'This is the World.' The comparative anatomist *has* curiosity. He institutes a divine search for facts. He is unconcerned with explanations and theories. In time, when you and I are dead, his facts will be collected and their sum will be the Truth. Truth that will show the noblest thing in creation, how to live. Truth that will shatter the idol Mumbo Jumbo, before which man daily debases his magnificence. Truth . . .

MARY No doubt that is very fine. But it is all words, too.

KNOX It is a religion. It is a passion.

MARY It is a very horrid sort of religion.

KNOX My dear young lady, it is less horrid than the religions of most of mankind. It has its martyrs, it has its heresy-hunts, but its hands are clean of the blood of the innocent.

MARY Are they?

KNOX Of course they are.

MARY Do you call the hands of a resurrectionist clean.

KNOX Of the blood of the innocent.

MARY Grave-robbing is worse than murder.

KNOX Madam, with all respect, you are a pagan atheist to say so. If you believed in an immortal soul, why should you venerate the empty shell it has spurned in its upward flight? And with a false veneration, too. The anatomist alone has a true reverence for the human body. He loves it. He knows it.

MARY He pays ruffians to tear it from the grave where loving hands have laid it. Your friend Mr Liston, the surgeon, goes himself and beats the guardians, like the pot-house bully he is.

KNOX Bob Liston is no friend of mine. I abhor his methods.

MARY Where do *you* get your bodies from?

A pause.

KNOX How should I know? My duty is to teach.

MARY Ah!

KNOX My child . . . *(He tries to take her hands.)* You love my friend. To love is to understand. Try to understand that he is doing great things, of which not the least is to sacrifice a part of his happiness.

WALTER Mary . . .

MARY Mr Anderson, your presence here is inexpressibly painful to me. I am greatly obliged to Dr Knox for his attempt to put me in the wrong. But he has only convinced me how right I am. I cannot look at one of the three of you without a shudder. I feel as if you had lifted a lid and showed me a glimpse of unspeakable things. Will you excuse me? I'll retire.

AMELIA Oh, darling, darling!

WALTER Then that's the end. You can go to hell. If you want me you'll find me in the gutter!

He dashes rudely out.

KNOX Mr Raby, perhaps it would be well if you followed him to his gutter and exercised a restraining supervision on his wallowing.

RABY Eh? I don't quite follow, sir.

KNOX Go after him and see he comes to no harm. I cannot afford to lose a good assistant.

RABY Very well, sir. Goodnight, ma'am, and thank you very much for a pleasant evening. Goodnight, ma'am. Goodnight, sir.

He bows himself out.

KNOX And God's benison on you, sir . . .
'To arms! to arms!' the fierce virago cries,
And swift as lightning to the combat flies.
All side in parties, and begin the attack;
Fans clap, silks rustle, and tough whalebones crack.
Heroes' and Heroines' shouts confusedly rise,
And bass and treble voices strike the skies.
No common weapons in their hands . . .

MARY Mr Knox!

KNOX No common weapons . . .

MARY Mr Knox, it is the common talk of this town that you are generally admired by persons of our sex. And this in spite of your hideous face and cynical, filthy, scandalous tongue. There is one lady who does not share their admiration. She loathes and detests and abhors you and all your ways. And she wishes you a very goodnight.

Exit MARY.

KNOX Poor things. Poor hearts.

AMELIA Your sentiment rings abominably false, Dr Knox.

KNOX False, Miss Amelia! I have never in my life been accused . . . Well. perhaps it does. What does it matter?

AMELIA My sister's happiness matters to me a very great deal. And Walter's too.

KNOX I did my best, Miss Amelia. But we who are groping among the roots of life cannot be expected to take too seriously the whimsies of the creatures of the air. You are crying! You mustn't cry. It congests the conjunctival sac. Let us consult Schubert. Let us hear what Rossini has to say on the quarrels of lovers. Come.

AMELIA Ah, no. I couldn't play for you tonight, Doctor.

KNOX I insist. Look –
'I attempt from love's sickness to fly in vain.'
Strike up!

He begins to play, extremely badly, on his flute. MISS AMELIA *struggles helplessly with laughter, tears and his accompaniment.*

Curtain.

ACT II / SCENE I

A low dive in the Canongate of Edinburgh – 'The Three Tuns.' The only occupants are the LANDLORD, dozing behind his bar, and WALTER ANDERSON, drinking solus at a little table in the corner. He is drunk. (An hour or so has passed since Act I.)

WALTER Nebby.

LANDLORD Aye, Doctor?

WALTER Nebby, bring m'nother shot of gin.

LANDLORD Right you was, Professor. *(He brings it.)* Ye're out for a bit o' fun the nicht, Doctor?

WALTER Fun? Fine fun. Nebby, my girl has thrown me over. D'ye call that funny? Eh?

LANDLORD No. I wouldna just. Providential, maybe, but no' just funny.

WALTER If you had called that funny, I would have figged you. I would have tapped your claret.

LANDLORD Nae doubt. Nae doubt.

WALTER I would. You thinkawouldn't?

LANDLORD Oh, you re a braw lad wi the maulies, Mr Walter.

WALTER I see. You think I'm drunk. Well I don't care for your opinion. Nor for anybody's opinion. I do what I like. Y'understand?

LANDLORD Aye, aye.

WALTER I'm the only judge of what I do. I don't ask anybody's opinion.

LANDLORD Aye. You're fine upstanding lads, you o' the Surgeons' Hall.

WALTER You hold your mouth about the Surgeons' Hall.

LANDLORD Aye. We're well to hold our mouth aboot the Surgeons' Hall. There's owre mony Bow Street runners cam' to the toon the day . . . Was ye waiting for onybody?

WALTER May I ask whether that is any of your business?

LANDLORD There's nae harm in speirin'.[1] But Merryandrew, the Sack-'em-up man, was here and awa' hauf an hour bye; wi' a' his gang, Spune and Moudiewarp and Praying Howard. I'm feared ye're owre late. There was word o' a job out by Mid-Calder. But Dr Liston, he was in and awa wi them. Ye're owre late.

WALTER Blast your eyes, you ought to ken very well I've no truck with the resurrectionists. Nor me nor Dr Knox.

LANDLORD Aye, weel. No offence.

WALTER You'll take that back. No, not the gin. Bring another one . . . Damned ruffians! Moudiewarp, indeed!

LANDLORD (bringing gin) Oh, I kenned fine you werena' in the way of business wi' the Sack-'em-up boys. But I thocht maybe you was game for a ploy.

WALTER And so I am. But not with Bob Liston and his friend Spune. Not by a long, long, long, long way, Nebby. Discretion. That's what I believe in. Discretion. You think no anatomist has a conscience. Well, some have.

LANDLORD I can weel believe that.

WALTER Well, Miss Ma – I mean a certain young person does not believe it. You believe that?

LANDLORD Aye, aye. I believe that.

WALTER Well, if sh'can't believe that, I'm finished with her. Un'stand? Finished with her. I go my own way aft' this. Don't care whatappens. Aft'll got my own life to live. No woman can bully me. I'm going to have – (LANDLORD has returned to his bar.) – jolly good evening. Tha's what I'm going to have. Bring 'nother drink.

Enter MARY PATERSON *and* JANET. MARY *is a glorious-looking creature. It is not apparent till she speaks that she has been drinking. She has a loud, harsh voice and her dialect is sometimes mincing and affected and sometimes pure Calton gutter-talk. The contrast between her speech and her appearance is indescribable.* JANET *is a colourless, frightened wisp who has much earlier in the evening decided that a joke can be carried too far.*

MARY P Nebby.

LANDLORD Good-e'en to you, Mary.

MARY P My bonnie wee Nebby! Jennie, Nebbie's my only joe.[2] Nebby, this is Janet.

LANDLORD Good-e'en to you, mistress.

MARY P Jennie. is he no' bonnie? His neb is like a red, red rose that's newly sprung in June. If ye tak' him frae me, I'll kill ye.

LANDLORD Wheesht wheesht,[3] Mary.

MARY P I'll misguggle your thrapple.[4] I'll mashackerel ye to rights. And I'll no wheesht, Mr Nebby. Wheesht to a leddy, indeed! I'll wheesht ye.

JANET Wheesht, Mary. Come on awa' hame.

WALTER Nebby, introduce me to your lady friends.

------

[1] Asking.
[2] Sweetheart.
[3] Be quiet.
[4] Throat.

LANDLORD This is Mistress Mary Paterson and a freen' o' hers.

WALTER Your servant, ma'am; 'n yours, ma'am.

MARY P And what may your name be, sir?

LANDLORD He's Mr Wotherspoon, frae Dalkeith.

WALTER He is nothing of sort. Nothing of sort. I am Dr Walter Anderson – at your service . . . Don't you tell lies about me! D'you hear?

LANDLORD Aye. I hear.

WALTER May I beg f'you to join me in a glass of cordial?

MARY P With great pleesure. We are mich obleeged.

WALTER Pleasure's mine. What may I order for you?

LANDLORD I ken what Mistress Paterson takes. Awa' you, and sit doon. Ye'll mak' a better impression that way.

> *The party sit at* WALTER'S *table. The* LANDLORD *brings drinks. An air of tipsy gentility pervades the scene.* MARY *takes off her bonnet.*

MARY P The evenings is beginning to draw in.

WALTER Yesh. I think autumn evenings are more beautiful in Scotland than anywhere else in the whole . . . Oh, dear me! Dear me! *(He begins to weep.)*

MARY P Puir wee thing wi' your mouth a' treacle and your tail a' parritch and your heid a' wumps! What are ye greetin' for?

WALTER I – I said that before, tonight.

MARY P Tuts! I didnae hear ye. It's a' richt, my wee hen.

WALTER It's not that. I don't object to repeating myself. Now and again. But it reminded me – *(He weeps again.)*

MARY P Nownie! Nownie! Was it a lassie that was bad to ye?

WALTER How did you know?

MARY P Oh, I ken mair nor I let dab, as the man said. Nownie, nownie! Wha' ca'd ye partan[1]-face, my bonnie wee pet lamb?

WALTER You're very kind to me. You're as kind and good as you are bonnie. And you are bonnie! What m'nificent hair! Like polished copper.

MARY P Now, now, young man, none of that. That's not genteel. Dry your eyes on your mooshwar and sit up like a wee gentleman.

WALTER But honestly I mean it. I'll never forget your kindness to me. You'll never know what you've done for me. How can I repay you – ever?

MARY P Weel, if ye dinna let poor Jenny die of thirst.

JANET Nae mair, Mary. We've had plenty. Come on awa' hame.

WALTER A thousand pardons. Landlord, same again. Mary, your hair is like fallen beech leaves. 'N as shoft as shilk. It's beautiful hair.

> *As the* LANDLORD *is bringing the drinks, enter* DAVID PATERSON.

MARY P See! – stop it.

WALTER Davie! Dear old Davie! Davie, my long-lost brother. Come away in, Davie. We're having a party, Davie. Bring Davie's tipple, Nebby. Now comes in the sweet o' the night!

PATERSON Most kind of you, Dr Anderson, I'm sure. But I couldnae think o' presuming . . .

WALTER Not a word. Miss Mary, may've the honour t' present to you my friend 'n colleague, Davie Paterson. Lord High Seneschal to the Great Dr Knox. Same name, b' Jove – Paterson! Your Uncle Davie.

MARY P I'm sure he is no uncle of mine, Dr What's-your-name.

WALTER Oh, can't be sure. Can't be sure. These are naughty times, Miss Mary.

---

[1] Crab.

MARY P *(laughing uproariously)* Come on, then, Uncle. Your wee niece'll sit on your knee.

PATERSON I'm sure it's real kind of you, miss. If the doctor has no objection, begging his pardon.

WALTER Not least in world. Here's y' jolly good health. Interestin' reunion. Happy family gathering. Proudest moment of my life.

> *He falls on a seat, and would fall on the floor if* JANET *didn't catch him.*

MARY P Aw, the puir wee soul. They shouldnae tak' that amount of drink, Mr Paterson. See; we'll hap him up.

> WALTER *is stretched on a bench, and* MARY *puts her shawl over him.*

WALTER Chaos is come again.

PATERSON Are ye all richt, Doctor?

WALTER I'm all right, but the world's all wrong. It is spinning backwards through the constellations and the ether is full of thunder and lightning.

MARY P Is that not awful, now? Just you go to sleep for a wee, and it'll be all richt in a wee while.

WALTER Do you think I had better? Very well; I will.

> *He goes to sleep.*

PATERSON Well, ma'am, what's the clash o' the toon?

MARY P Sh! Sh!

PATERSON Faith, you'll no' wake him this side of tomorrow morning. The deil couldnae wauken him.

MARY P Weel, dinna you try.

PATERSON Och, ye're awfu' backsettin' the nicht.

MARY P Will you keep your hands off me, ye blasted crult? Sit down and be at peace, and tak' your dram, or tak' your mangy carcase out o' here.

PATERSON Och, I'm no' wantin' your conversation.

> *A silence.* MARY *smooths* WALTER'S *hair.*

MARY P Can ye sew cushions and can ye sew sheets,
And can ye sing Balaloo
When the bairnie greets?
Then ho and baw birdie
Then ho and baw lamb,
Then ho and baw birdie, my bonnie wee lamb.
Hey Oh, hyooch Oh, what'll 'a dae wi' ye?
Black's the life I lead wi' the hale o' ye –
Mony o' ye and little to gie ye.
Hey Oh, hyooch Oh, what'll I dae wi' ye?

> *She sings the refrain twice. After the first time she repeats the third last line wearily and bitterly to herself. Enter* BURKE *and* HARE. *They take a high-backed settle by the fireside.*

BURKE It's a fine night, Mister Nebby, glory be to God, an' I'm that dry that me throat feels the like of the insides of a lime-kiln. Will you give us a couple gills of malt? An' be quick about it.

NEBBY Hae you the siller to pay for it?

BURKE Silver is it? Holy St Joseph, will you listen to him, Bill! Silver is it? There's what's better than silver, a note. And you can take an' nail it to the counter, if you've a mind to, so long as we have drink for the worth of it.

NEBBY There's the stink of the mort-cloth on it, Mr Burke.

HARE Will you hould your prate. That's no way to speak to your betters. Stink indeed! It 'ud make a cat laugh to hear you talkin' of stinks an' you livin' in a moldy old shebeen the like of this.

BURKE Yes, an' you hold yours along with him, or I'll give you a puck in the gob that'll make ye. And as for you, Mister Nebby, it 'ud be far better for you to keep reddnin' that ugly nose of yours with your rotten rum than to be smellin' out stinks where there is none. Let you bring us our drinks and stop your blatherin'.

LANDLORD *retires.* PATERSON *comes over to* BURKE *and* HARE.

PATERSON Fine night.

HARE It is that.

PATERSON How's trade with ye?

HARE Oh, not so bad. I've seen it worse,

PATERSON Well?

BURKE Well what?

PATERSON Have ye the like of a shot for us the morn?

HARE Musha, they're not so easy come by as all that. Why, man alive, we brought you one last week.

PATERSON I know that. But Mr Knox is aye at me to get more. Ssht.

LANDLORD *brings drinks.*

HARE Give us a glass for Mr Paterson, will you, Mister Nebby. You'll have a drop with us, won't you?

PATERSON Nay, b' Heavens. I don't drink with you.

HARE Oh, glory be, you won't, won't ye. Well, that laves the more for us that will. Slainthe.

BURKE (*to* HARE) Here's lookin towards ye. (*Drinks.*) And it's what I'm tellin' you, Mr Paterson, it's no shot we have for you in the mornin'.

PATERSON Come along, Burke. You've aye served us well before at a pinch. The session's just started and they havenae the subjects tae gang round.

HARE Dear me, is that so? Now supposin', I say supposin', we did obleege the Doctor, what would he be willin' to give for it these bad times?

PATERSON Ye ken weel the price. Seven pounds. An' it's more than ye'd ever get from Lizars or even the Professor.

HARE Your sowl to glory. What's that? Seven pounds. An' we've got to get it in a hurry. It's crazy you are with your seven pounds. Think of the risk, man! Why, the last one we brought you paid us seven ten.

PATERSON A moldy ould body that dropped to bits when I took it out the tea-kist.

BURKE It's jokin' you are, Mr Paterson. Moldy indeed! A fine fresh body it was. I never handled better. An' the divil's own trouble we had gettin' it anyway. I know where there is a grand one we could get for ye quick, but it would cost you ten pounds. The Professor himself has offered us more. But I'm thinkin' we'd sooner a fine gentleman like Dr Knox 'ud have it. Not forgetting that honest man his janitor.

PATERSON I'll gie eight. I'll get me heid in me hands for it, but I'll gi'e ye eight.

BURKE (*to* HARE). Has Nellie been down to see your missus tonight?

HARE Musha! How would I know?

BURKE It's what I was thinkin', that if the four of us took a little jaunt as far as Portobello the salt say air would do us a power of good. I haven't been that way for a long time. What do ye say, Bill?

HARE There nothin' I'd like better this blessed minit and no mistake, than to be stravagin'[1] down to the say an' to be fillin' me lungs with the fine fresh air instead of sittin' here talkin' blather in a rotten stinkin' old den the like of this.

---

[1] Wandering.

BURKE Well, if we're goin', we better start early in the mornin'.

PATERSON But, Mr Burke . . .

BURKE Goodnight to you, Mr Paterson. Bill, you better slip down and borrow a loan of Grogan's ass-cart. He's got new tackling for the donkey. And I'll get Nellie. An' you can drive it round to my place shortly after five.

HARE *(rising)* I'll start this minit or he'll be off on his round with it. An' it's the fine time we'll have with the little birds fair burstin' themselves with song an' the sunlight fit to dazzle your eyes an' it shinin' on the say. And it's there you'll find cockles and periwinkles enough to feed an army.

BURKE And meself an' Nellie will be wadin' in the say. Hurry up now, will ye?

PATERSON Can't you wait a minit, Mr Burke? I'll make you a better offer. I'll give you two pounds now this minute, and seven more when you bring the shot. I canna say fairer than that, can I?

HARE An' what'll it come to altogether?

BURKE Nine pounds.

HARE Nine pounds is it? Well, I'd not say but that might be worth doin' somethin' for. You can lave it to us.

PATERSON Mind, if ye bring another auld rickle of bones you can just take it back where you found it, and never darken ma doors again. Now, mind. A guid fresh young juicy corp.

HARE You're the fine juicy one yourself and that no lie. Well, lave it to us; we'll find you one. Though the blessed St Patrick himself knows it's the divil's job to get them. What with sentries at the cemeteries and militia rampagin' the town, it's hard set a man is to earn an honest livin' be the sweat of his brow.

BURKE Come on with the money, for we have a night's work before us yet, if you want your shot in the morning.

PATERSON Mind, the same time as usual. And none of last month's capers, Hare comin' up the High Street drunk in the full light of day with a box on his back with a shot in it. Half-past four, mind you, and no later.

HARE We'll be there on time all right. So don't get flustered. And it's little light there be at that time to see whether it's drunk or sober I am. Won't you have a small one with us now, Mr Paterson, just to clinch the bargain?

PATERSON No. I've the young doctor owre by to see safe. And forbye, I've no notion to take a dram wi' you and wake up the morn on a marble table, wi' Dr Knox fumbling among my tripes. Eh? Ha, ha!

HARE Ha, ha, ha!

BURKE Ha!

RABY *appears at the door, questing.*

RABY Oh, hello, Paterson. And so on.

PATERSON Good evening to you, Mr Raby.

RABY I say, have you seen Dr Anderson, eh? The Chief told me to take charge of him, and I'm damned if I haven't lost him.

PATERSON There he is, over there, Mr Raby, sir. I must say he's in bonny-like hands. A wheen[1] o' Jezebels. I'll leave him to you, sir. If ye bring him up to the Square later, we'll play the pump on him. It's the best thing to do.

RABY Oh, right. Very good. Aye, aye, and all that sort of thing.

PATERSON Goodnight to you, sir. And, see here, sir. Dinna lose sight of him again.

RABY Oh, au revoir.

Exit PATERSON. RABY *goes over to* ANDERSON, *whose head is in the lap of the sleeping* MARY. *He shakes* ANDERSON's *shoulder.* ANDERSON *sits up abruptly without waking* MARY.

---

[1] Number, group.

RABY Now, sir. Now, Doctor. You must come home. Indeed you must.

WALTER Whassa? That you, Raby? You're good fellow, Raby. Goodnight.

MARY P *(waking up)* Eh! Deevil sain[1] us! What's this, now, the wind's blown in?

RABY It's all right, my good girl. I'm taking him home.

MARY P Who are you?

RABY It doesn't matter really.

MARY P I'll come wi ye.

RABY Oh. dear. no! You'll do nothing of the sort. Come along, Doctor, get up. Now you go to bye-byes again, like a good young lady, or I'll call a constable.

> *He gets his hand under* WALTER'S *armpit, and hoists him to his feet.*

MARY P You will, you tinker's messan! You will, you deil's brat! Awa' wi' you, you gentry pup! I ken the likes o' you. You call yoursel' a man? You wouldnae mak' a pair o' breeks for a man!

JANET Mary, Mary, come on.

WALTER Where's Mary?

MARY P *(attempting to get up, but restrained by Janet)* I'm here, my lamb.

WALTER Wan' speak to Mary. Oh, goo' Lor', I'm sleepy. Did you notice her hair, Raby? Beautiful!

RABY Come along, sir. Steady does it.

> *They go out.*

JANET Now, Mary Paterson, you'll just sit still. You'll just sit still, Mary Paterson. This is an awful-like place to bring a decent girl to. An awful-like place. You should think shame, Mary.

MARY P Och, sneck up!

> HARE *gets up and comes over, bowing politely as he approaches.*

HARE Good-evenin' to you, Miss.

MARY P And what is it your business to interfere and put your ugly phiz between me and me lady friend?

HARE Business is it? None at all. It's only I was wonderin' could it be yourself was singin' like an angel from heaven and I comin' in through the passage beyond.

MARY P Aye, maybe.

HARE I thought it might be, an' yet I wasn't sure. Then when I cem in an' seen you all dressed up so grand, says I to myself, a pretty girl that's all dolled up as fine as a peacock is hardly likely to have a voice like a weeshy little nightingale. But I was wrong, I see. So it was yourself I heard singin' so soft and low that it would melt the heart in a man to be listening to the like of it. Well now, wonders will never cease. Would you be vexed with me now if I asked you to let me oil that lovely throat of yours with a drop of Nebby's best?

MARY P It looks to me you've a hantle[2] ower muckle to say, Mr Man. But I'll drink wi' ye, for I've a gullet like a hearthstane in hell, this very nicht.

JANET Ach, Mary, come awa hame. I dinna like his looks, Mary. He's got a face like a warlock. I'm frichtit. Come awa hame.

MARY P Tyach. Haud your wheesht. He's a wee shilpit[3] cratur I could crack him like macaroni if I minded. And he's a nice weel-spoken chiel. It's the last time ever you come out wi' me, Mistress.

HARE You don't like me looks, don't you? Well, if you don't you can go and look at a picture. And who cares what you like anyway, so long as me little sweetheart here'll

---

[1] Bless.
[2] Lot.
[3] Stunted, weak.

have a drink with me?

MARY P Here's to your good health, Mister Irishman.

HARE *(to* JANET*)* Come along and let's be friends. Have a drop yourself.

JANET declines.

MARY P Aweel, we'll have your health again the two of us.

HARE And where does this one live now? *(to* JANET*).*

JANET I'll take her home with me. Come on, Mary. Come on awa' hame wi' me.

MARY P Hame wi' you, ye fushionles wee besom?[1] Hame wi' you, ye slut? 'Deed, and I'll no come hame wi' you.

JANET *(catching* BURKE'S *eye as he peers round the settle)* See here, I'm awa'.

MARY P Then awa' ye go.

HARE Don't you bother with her, sweetheart. Let her go her own way and be damned to her. Dirty little slut. Never heed her. Come over here till you meet me mate. It's he's the right playboy with the girls. Come on over and we'll have such a time that you'll feel like kickin' the stars.

JANET Mary!!

MARY P The deil harle ye through hell. Give ow're skirling like a pea-hen.

JANET Mary. I'll never see you again.

MARY *sits on* BURKE'S *knee and kisses his forelock.*

MARY P My heart! You're an ugly old dog. You're uglier than your black faced mate. I'd be blithe to see that ugly phiz grinning at the hangman. (JANET *steals out.)* 'Deed an' I will, ae day!

BURKE Be me sowl that's what you'll never see. It's courting and courting the two of us will be from now till the Judgment day. *(To* HARE.) What the hell are you gapin' at. you black-faced omadhaun. Away with ye and get me sweetheart another drink.

He kisses her. She strikes him and springs up.

MARY P You stop that. I'll take no familiarity from you or any man.

BURKE Aisy now. Aisy, alannah. I meant no harm. It's great strength you have in them pretty arms of yours. An' a figure that's fine enough to make Venus herself go back into the say. And it's great joy I'd have pullin' you to pieces the way I'd see if you're as beautiful inside as you are out.

MARY P I'm – I'm feelin' no weel. I'll awa' hame with me.

HARE Ye'll not stir a foot till you drink this. Go on now, it'll put new life into ye.

BURKE An' as for goin home you'll do nothin' of the kind. It's meself that will take you with me to the grand hotel I'm stoppin' at in West Port. There's beds there fit for a queen to be sleepin' in. An' you can sleep there quiet an' easy till the morning.

MARY P You're gey gentle to a puir orphan lassie.

BURKE Nebby, Nebby.

NEBBY Aye.

BURKE Will what's left of that note I gave ye pay for a demijohn?

NEBBY It will.

BURKE Then give it us quick. We want to be gettin' on to West Port.

HARE *gets the demijohn and the two of them help* MARY *up the steps.* NEBBY *polishes the bar with a dirty rag.*

HARE Easy now, me darlin'. We'll help you along. We'll take care of you. Don't you worry, you'll sleep sound this night.

Curtain.

---

[1] Witch.

SCENE II

DR KNOX'S *rooms at* 10, *Surgeons' Square. Four or five hours later. A door at either side and one at back to the right. One window with a broken blind. The grey light of morning is filtering in.*

PATERSON, *in a leather apron and a sailor's cap with a leather peak, is reading the Bible at a small table on which an oil lamp is set. His skinny arms are bare. He follows the print with his finger and reads aloud in a low, mumbling voice in which the nasal whine of the religious Scot is perceptible.*

PATERSON 'And if you despise my statutes, or if your soul abhors my judgments, so that ye will not do all my commandments, but that ye break my covenant: I also will do this unto you: I will even appoint over you terror, consumption and the burning ague that shall consume the eyes and cause sorrow of heart . . . ' Guid save us, that's an awfu' curse . . . 'and ye shall sow your seed in vain, for your enemies shall eat it. And I will set my face against you . . . ' (*A key turns in the lock.*) What's that?

KNOX *comes in.*

PATERSON *(rising)* Ye frichtit me, Dr Knox. You're early aboot the day.
KNOX Yes. (*He hangs his hat and cloak on a peg and takes off his gloves.*)
PATERSON I was expecting twa callants wi' a corpse.
KNOX Good.
PATERSON They was wantin' twelve pound for it, Doctor.
KNOX They were, were they?
PATERSON I'm feart we'll hae to pay.
KNOX Well, pay them, damn it.
PATERSON I havenae the siller by me.
KNOX You can get it from Dr Anderson or Dr Wharton Jones. Which is on duty tonight?
PATERSON Dr Jones is awa. I was expectin' Dr Anderson any minute.
KNOX Then what the devil do you mean by bothering me? What's that you're reading? (*Picking up the Bible.*)
PATERSON It's lonely for me here. I was readin' the Book. It's bread and meat to me is the Book.
KNOX You're a canting humbug, Paterson. There is poetry and Philosophy here, but what do you know of poetry and philosophy?
PATERSON There's God's Word in it, Doctor. There's religion.
KNOX If they could cut out the religion it would be a more useful book.

KNOX *goes out, R., slamming the door behind him.*

PATERSON Aye. Bang the door. Ye blasphemous bitch!

A knock.

PATERSON Wha's there? What's your wull?
WALTER *(outside)* It's all right, Davie. Open.

PATERSON *opens the door. Enter* WALTER *and* RABY. WALTER *is sober but haggard.*

PATERSON Oh, Dr Walter, I m richt glad to see ye. Are ye all richt noo, Doctor?
WALTER Oh, yes, I'm all right. Raby gave me a corpse-reviver at his lodging, and we walked to queens ferry and swam in the Forth. It washes the troubles off a man, the old Firth of Forth. Have you tried it, Davie?
PATERSON Watter on my skin aye gives me the bronchitis. But I'm real joco you're better.

The Chief was askin' for ye.

WALTER The Chief? What's he doing here at this hour?

PATERSON He would be on the randan too yestreen. He'll have his lectures to get ready. There's times in the early days he would go into the lecture-hall and gesture and rant to naebody but the auld skeleton in the cauld o' the morning. A gey queer thing yon.

WALTER *(sitting down)* Heavens, I'm tired. You tired, Raby?

RABY Oh, so-so.

WALTER You should go away home to your bed. Raby wants to see daybreak in the Chamber of horrors, David. He has a gruesome mind.

PATERSON The Chief's the only horror I ken here. Do ye ken what he said?

WALTER No. What did he say?

PATERSON Och, it's no' charity to repeat it. It was about the Book.

WALTER What book?

PATERSON The Book of Books. The very Word of the fairest amang the ten thousand of the altogether lovely.

RABY Who is she?

PATERSON She? Young man, take thought. It were more tolerable –

WALTER That's enough, Paterson.

PATERSON While I have a tongue, I will not cease to testify –

WALTER Yes, you will. I'm going to take a nap on the bench. Raby, you'll do so too if you take my advice.

RABY I couldn't sleep here, sir. It's – it's – I couldn't sleep here.

WALTER You're not feared, are you? You're here day after day.

RABY It's all right in the day time, and it might not be so bad in the night time, if you understand me; but it's this half way time is so uncanny.

PATERSON I've been here ten year wi' old Dr Barclay and two wi' Dr Knox, and I've never got ower the eerie feeling o' the half licht. It's as if the deid men stirred.

A knock.

RABY What's that?

PATERSON It's a richt, sir. It'll be a corp I was expectin'.

He opens the door.

HARE *(without)* Are ye there, janitor?

PATERSON Aye, I'm here. Hae ye got the parcel?

HARE *(to BURKE)* He's here. *(To PATERSON.)* We've got it.

PATERSON Bring it in then, and carry it ben.

BURKE *and* HARE, *drunk, stumble in with a large tea-chest carelessly roped. The drop it on the floor with a heavy thud, and stand near the door.*

WALTER What is your name, my man?

BURKE William Burke, your honour.

WALTER What do you work at?

BURKE I'm an ould soldier, your honour.

WALTER That's not work. What else do you do?

BURKE I'm a shoemaker, your honour.

WALTER I see. This is the body, I presume?

BURKE It is, your honour.

WALTER How did you come by the body?

BURKE It's a young woman, a cousin of Mrs Hare – this gentleman's good lady, your honour. She come over from Belfast three days back and was took badly in Hare's lodging.

WALTER Took badly with what?

BURKE Wid the colic, your honour.

WALTER What name?

BURKE The name of the young lady, sir?

WALTER Yes, yes.

BURKE Euphemia Brannigan, your worship – I mean, your honour.

WALTER You have been here before with subjects?

BURKE Sure, your honour, I have. Mr Paterson knows me well.

PATERSON I know him. A very honest man, Dr Anderson.

WALTER No doubt. Well, shift the box into the mortuary.

BURKE If you please, sir, we'd be afeared to go into a place the like of that. It's bad enough havin' to bring them here at all. And beggin' your pardon, will you give us our seven guineas and let us be gone out of this?

PATERSON Guineas! You Irish thief. Guinea! You cannae trust them, Dr Anderson, ye cannae really. Pounds it is, sir.

BURKE Holy St Patrick and all the Saints, will you listen to him? Did you ever hear the like of that, Hare?

HARE I can't believe me ears. Guineas you said, Mr Paterson. Seven guineas, them were your very words.

PATERSON Don't gie them a penny more than they bargained for, Dr Anderson. Seven pounds it was.

WALTER. Oh, damnation. Let them have their pieces of silver. Here's the seven guineas for you, Burke. *(Gives money.)*

BURKE May the Lord Almighty watch over you, sir, and keep you in the palm of his hand for your great kindness to honest hard-workin' poor people the like of ourselves.

WALTER *(to* HARE). Here, you. Move that box in there.

HARE In there, is it? Don't ask me to do it, sir. On me two bended knees I'll ask you. It 'ud frighten me out of me seven senses so it would, the Lord be between us and all harm. Come along, Will, we better lose no time or we'll be late for early Mass.

> *Exit* BURKE *and* HARE. PATERSON *is making an entry in his ledger.* WALTER
> *throws off his coat and, with* RABY, *lifts the box towards the door at the back.*

WALTER By George, it's heavy! Easy there. I can't compliment you on your friends, Davie.

PATERSON You should have had a keek at the corp before you paid them. And seven guineas! I never heard the like.

> RABY *and* WALTER *carry the box out of sight.*

WALTER Oh, it will be all right. They know which side their bread's buttered on, these hounds. *(From the room.)* Bring a tack-hammer, Davie; they've nailed down the lid.

PATERSON Verra weel, sir.

> *He goes out.* WALTER *leans on the door jamb, waiting for him*
> *and talking over his shoulder to* RABY.

WALTER Wait a minute, Raby. He's getting a hammer. Light a candle.

RABY They – they've nailed a lock of red hair between the lid and the sides.

WALTER Eh? What do you say? Lord, my head aches!

RABY They've nailed a lock of red hair between the lid and the sides. Six inches of it. It's very pretty hair.

WALTER It's nice to have an eye for the beautiful, Raby, even in Davie Paterson's dead-house.

RABY The – the lid's fairly loose. I – I think I could . . . Yes, that's it. The lid's off now, sir.

WALTER Oh! Davie, never mind the hammer. *(He goes into the mortuary.)* Bring that candle over here.

> *Enter* PATERSON, *with a hammer. A pause.*

WALTER *(screaming).* My God!

> *He rushes into the ante-room, white and shaking. He carries the candle.*
> RABY'S *scared face appears in the doorway.*

PATERSON God save us! What's the matter, Doctor?

WALTER Raby, did you see what I saw? Am I still drunk? Did you see that face?

RABY Yes.

WALTER Have you seen it before?

RABY I think I have.

WALTER You think? You think? Take the candle and go and look at it again.

RABY Not for a thousand pounds.

WALTER Did I see that girl last night?

PATERSON Hoots, toots, you were in nae condition to see anyone last night.

WALTER Damn you, be quiet, you! Raby, was that the girl I spoke to in the Three Tuns?

RABY Yes.

WALTER And she's dead! *(He sits down on the bench.)* She was so beautiful, a man's heart stopped when he looked at her . . .

RABY She looked in excellent health, I must say.

WALTER *(springing up)* There's been foul work here. Raby, Paterson, get after those men.

> *He rushes to the door and fumbles with the lock. Enter* KNOX.

KNOX May I ask what is all this?

WALTER Dr Knox, there's been murder done. *(He is on the edge of collapse.* RABY *catches him by the arm.)* Let go, Raby. Dr Knox, there's been murder done. We must get them. They can't be far off. They left a moment ago. Let go, Raby.

RABY You won't catch them now, sir. wait a bit. There's plenty of time.

KNOX Has Dr Anderson been drinking, Paterson?

PATERSON Weel, sir, as you might say . . .

WALTER I'm not drunk. I swear I'm not. Go in there, sir. Look for yourself. She's dead! She's dead!

KNOX You are a very foolish young man. You've been drinking spirits. You're reeking of stale spirits. Go home to your bed.

WALTER Dr Knox, a very few hours ago I was in conversation with a young woman in the Three Tuns public house. She was brought up here ten minutes ago by two Irish ruffians. Rigor mortis had set in, but the body was still warm. I believe to the bottom of my soul that she has had foul play.

KNOX Sit down. Give me the candle. Come with me, Paterson.

> *He goes into the mortuary.*

WALTER Oh, Raby, what shall I do? What shall I do? And this may not be the first time, either. You heard that man? They've brought bodies here before. I may have seen them. I forget . . . Mary! That was it. Mary Paterson. Her soft, cool hands on my head! . . .

RABY I shouldn't take it so much to heart. I expect it's all right, really.

WALTER All right! She was so full of life, and they've let the life out of her. Oh, the bloody murderers!

> *Re-enter* KNOX *and* PATERSON.

KNOX What are you raving about, man?

WALTER Dr Knox, don't you realise? That girl was murdered!

KNOX How the devil do you know? There isn't a mark of violence on her body.

WALTER She was murdered, I tell you!

KNOX Dear, dear, dear, dear, dear. What a pity. Murdered, eh? And suppose she were, Dr

Anderson? Do you imagine her life was so significant that we must grue[1] at her death? She looks to me to have been some common trull off the streets.

WALTER Don't you dare say that!

KNOX Sit down, sit down, sit down. I see. I understand you, my dear lad. *Et ego* in Arcadia. But it is past the hour for sentiment. At four in the morning cold common-sense creeps into the chamber, and it is now after half-past five. You must not sentimentalise, if you please, over my anatomy-room subjects. You owe them at least that respect.

RABY Sir, he thinks he recognises the girl.

WALTER Thinks!

KNOX Ah! . . . It will be perhaps a satisfaction to you to know that your friend will be improving the minds of the youth of the town in place of corrupting their morals . . . Come, my dear lad, I perceive you have had a shock. You must not mind my rough tongue. It is a defect in me as sentimentality is in you. The life of this poor wretch is ended. It is surely a better thing that her beauty of form should be at the service of divine science than at the service of any drunken buck with a crown in his pocket. Our emotions, Walter, are for ever tugging at our coat-tails lest at any time we should look the Truth in the face . . .

WALTER The truth is she was murdered. You know she was. You are as bad as a murderer yourself. Worse. You pay blood money!

KNOX You've been drinking.

WALTER This is what all your fine words come to! This is your passion! This is your religion! You hire murderers to choke the life out of poor, handsome girls! You pay blood money!

KNOX You paid the money, Mr Anderson, I think.

WALTER God help me, so I did!

KNOX That fact seems to me pertinent, if we are talking of blood money. Another point that may interest you is this: that if I did not think you a drunken young fool, in no way responsible for his words, I would call you out and shoot you like a dog at twenty paces.

WALTER You mean a duel?

KNOX You are very intelligent.

WALTER Then I'll fight you. You know to what address to send your friends. After I have reported this matter to the police I shall be at my lodging for the rest of the day.

KNOX Can you shoot the pips out of a cinq of hearts at forty paces? If you can, it is strange that I had not heard of your accomplishment. I can perform that feat. You are a good prosector in your sober moments. I have no wish to he compelled to maim you.

WALTER You are a coward and a murderer. Take that. *(He strikes at* KNOX, *who catches his wrist.)*

KNOX Mr Anderson, I shall not require your services this forenoon. In the afternoon you will present yourself at my private room and apologise to me. In the meantime you will go to bed. In the future I advise you to abstain from alcohol. Now take yourself off.

After a pause, WALTER *turns about and goes.*

RABY Would you like me to go down to the police station, sir? I know where it is.

KNOX You do, do you, you gaby? You poroncephalic monstrosity! You will keep quiet, imbecile! You will gabble of nothing you have seen or heard or thought this morning. You will forget with that Lethe-like forgetfulness you apply to your studies. Do you understand?

RABY I understand, sir.

KNOX Then go and help the janitor to prepare the subject. I shall demonstrate it to the class this afternoon.

RABY Very well, sir.

---

[1] Feel revulsion.

KNOX *throws a piercing glance at him, and goes out,* R. PATERSON *pulls up the blind.*
It is broad daylight.

PATERSON It's a nice morning, Mr Raby.
RABY Yes . . . I say, he's a cool fish, the Governor.
PATERSON Robert the Devil they call him.
RABY Deep, ain't he?
PATERSON As deep as the pit.
RABY What do you think? Does he think they knocked that girl on the head?
PATERSON His Maker only kens what yon man's thinking.

Curtain.

ACT III

The same scene as in act I. It is early afternoon on 28th January, 1829.

The DISHARTS *are from home and the furniture is covered with dust sheets; the curtain is drawn and the blinds are down.*

The key is heard turning in the door and enter JESSIE ANN, *the maid, precipitately. She is in outdoor dress and is obviously excited. She carries a taper and a basket.*

MAID Guid save us! A' the fiends of hell are louse the day!

She lights the fire and goes to the window, throwing off the dust sheets as she goes. She draws the curtain and pulls up the blind.

MAID Michty, what a day of days! And there's the chaise and me no ready!

A bell rings. She rushes out, grabbing some of the remaining dust sheets. After a pause the MAID *returns with the* MISSES DISHART, *who are in travelling dress. The* MAID *has taken off her bonnet and shawl.*

MAID If you'll come awa' in here Miss Dishart. I've just lit the fire.
AMELIA So I see, Jessie Ann. Just!
MAID Michty. this is a bonny like home-coming frae foreign parts. But it's a God's mercy you're safe. I'll hae a tassie o' tae ready for ye in a jiffy. It's on in the kitchen, and I brocht some griddle scones for ye, Miss Amy.
AMELIA But what possessed you to be so late? I told you to be here at six.
MAID Six! I was feart to cross ma Auntie's doorstep. Did ye no see the crood? Did ye no hear them?
AMELIA We heard a noise up at the road end. What is it? An election?
MAID An election! Did ye no ken they were hanging Burke the murderer this morning?
AMELIA Burke the murderer?
MAID Aye. Now, if I didna forget ye wouldna' hear tell!
MARY Oh, Amelia! The vinaigrette we thought we'd lost at Dover!
AMELIA You startled me. What about it?
MARY It's here! It's been standing here all the time!
AMELIA How odd, darling. – Jessie Ann, if they had been hanging the General Buonaparte it would be no excuse for being late.
MAID But it was the croods, Mem. A' the gangrel[1] buddies in the toun raging roun' the streets crying, 'Gie us Hare! Gie us Hare!'

----

[1] Vagrant, idle.

AMELIA Give us whose hair? Do compose yourself, Jessie Ann.

MARY *has taken off her travelling cloak and is tidying herself before the mirror.* RABY *appears at the door carrying a heavy cabin trunk. He stands gaping and breathing heavily.*

AMELIA Mr Raby, I am so sorry. You should not have brought that heavy case up here. Do put it down.

RABY Indeed, it is all right, ma'am. It's nothing. Nothing whatever.

MARY I'll help you, Mr Raby.

RABY Not at all. Not at all.

They lower the trunk between them.

MARY It is heavy! I believe Amelia has killed the courier and brought him home to stuff him. He was so fat and so funny with his beautiful moustachios. Is he in the box, Amelia?

Raby stares at her.

AMELIA Mary, how can you say such things?

MARY *completes the drawing of the blinds and curtains.*

AMELIA How ungrateful we are, Mr Raby! And it was so kind of you to meet us at the stage.

RABY *(staring after* MARY*)* What! Oh, I beg your pardon, ma'am. Yes. Oh, yes! It was nothing. Dr Anderson will be here presently. The new demonstrator has arrived, you know. Dr Anderson was showing him the – the ropes.

AMELIA What new demonstrator?

RABY Dr Anderson is leaving Edinburgh ma'am. Didn't you know?

AMELIA No. He has not written since we left Dover. Why is he leaving Edinburgh?

RABY Well – ah – perhaps you had better ask him yourself, ma'am. I mean, ma'am, he is sure to know, isn't he? I am no hand at explaining. He'll be here presently. He said he would. But he made a point of somebody meeting you. And I happened to be about.

AMELIA That was very thoughtful of Walter and very kind of you.

RABY Oh, not at all. Not at all. It's of no consequence. Only the streets are not over-safe today.

AMELIA Really? I didn't see anything to be alarmed about. Oh! what was that you were telling us, Jessie Ann? I am afraid I didn't listen very attentively.

MAID The riots, Mem. Ower the heid o' the hanging Burke, Mem. I saw them hang him wi' my own eyes, Mem. Fornenst my Auntie's hoose in the High Street. Faces on a' the causies and faces at a' the windies. And oh, ye should ha' seen him, Mem. He'd a naipkin ower his heid. And a big fellow in a black surtout took awa' what he was staunin' on, Mem. And he played paw paw for it wi' his feet and syne birled roond three times. And syne he gied a kin' o' a hunch wi' his shouthers and syne he hung still. And oh! I was feart, Mem!

AMELIA How perfectly horrible!

MAID He was drunk, they say, Miss, when they choked him. And then a' them that was there begood tae cry: 'Knox neist! Hang Knox.'

AMELIA Good God, girl, what you do mean?

MAID Knox, Mem, Dr Knox. *(Proudly.)* Our Dr Knox.

AMELIA *(sitting down)* Mary, what is all this about?

MARY I haven't the remotest notion. Dearest, you look ill. Take my smelling-salts.

MAID I've been telling you, Miss Mary Belle. They broke all his windows yestreen. He's in a ballant too. A'body's singing it:

'Up the close and doon the stair,
Ben the hoose wi' Burke and Hare.

Burke's the butcher, Hare's the thief,
Knox the boy who buys the beef.'
That's our Dr Knox, Miss Mary Belle.

AMELIA Mr Raby! What has happened? You never told us!

MARY We hadn't heard . . .

RABY Well, you see, of course, it was just after you sailed for Dieppe. It was all a frightful
scandal. And we've certainly not heard the last of it yet.

AMELIA But who is this Burke and what has he to do with Dr Knox?

RABY Well, you see it's this way . . .

AMELIA Is Dr Knox in danger?

RABY Well, yes, ma'am in a way. But you don't know Dr Knox. He can fight. They'll catch
a Tartar in Dr Knox.

MARY Can't you see you are upsetting my sister? What has happened, man?

RABY Well, ma'am, it's very difficult to explain. But it was this way. – Oh, thank God,
here's Dr Anderson.

Enter WALTER.

RABY Well, here you are, Dr Anderson. I met the ladies all right. Here they are all right.

WALTER Good-afternoon. You shouldn't have left the door open. Anybody might have
come in, and all the bad characters in the city are abroad today.

AMELIA Walter, what is all this about?

WALTER Hasn't Raby explained?

RABY Yes, Doctor, but they didn't seem to cotton on to what I was saying.

MARY Do tell us, Walter. Go away, Jessie Ann. Have you nothing at all to do?

The MAID *goes away reluctantly.*

AMELIA Sit down, Mr Raby.

WALTER You left to go on the Grand Tour on Hallowe'en?

AMELIA Yes, yes.

WALTER That night, an old vagrant Irishwoman was found murdered in Burke's lodging in
the West Port. This man Burke and his associate Hare had inveigled her into a trap and
smothered her in cold blood. An artisan called Gray gave the alarm.

AMELIA Go on. Where does Dr . . . ? Go on.

WALTER At the trial Hare turned King's evidence. And he told an appalling story.
November a year ago Burke and Hare sold the body of an old pensioner to the
anatomy-room to recoup themselves for his rent. They were paid five pounds ten. They
had some plausible cock-and-bull story. The rooms to which they took the body were
those of Dr Knox. Paterson, the janitor, and Wharton Jones bought the body. We – we
were very short of subjects at the time.

MARY Oh, Walter!

AMELIA Don't, Mary. Go on.

WALTER Their next lodger was a woman. She was an unconscionable time in dying, and
they – they put a pillow over her face. They sold her body to Paterson. They killed
about sixteen people – they are not quite certain of the numbers.

AMELIA What a dreadful thing! And Dr Knox . . . ?

WALTER (*rises*) Dr Knox never in his life set eyes on either of these men. I swear to that. He
left the supply of subjects to – others.

MARY To whom did he leave it?

WALTER Oh, to – to his assistants and his porter. He never – he never would deal with
known resurrectionists, and that made it difficult. He . . .

MARY Oh, Walter, did you buy bodies from these men?

WALTER Yes, I did.

Silence.

AMELIA Go on.

WALTER Burke was hanged this morning. There has been an outcry against Knox. They are preaching from every pulpit. Christopher North[1] is lashing him with lies in the Press. Every man's hand is against him. The other surgeons have deserted him. The mob is mad for his blood.

AMELIA But I thought – Surely he has fled the town?

WALTER No. He is facing it out.

AMELIA What is he doing?

WALTER He is delivering his lectures as if nothing had happened. He is too proud even to answer his persecutors. God knows I admired and loved him, but never so much as at this hour.

AMELIA Is he in danger?

WALTER They broke his windows last night and tried to set fire to his house. He came out and faced them with two pistols in his hands. The mob hadn't the courage to go on. He is a dead shot, you know.

AMELIA But the constables? Have they not given him a guard?

WALTER He won't have a guard.

RABY He's lectured every day since the trial. Nobody can stop him. We all carry life preservers and take turns to mount guard. He's afraid of nothing. He's a hero, that's what he is.

AMELIA Forgive me, Walter. Your news is a little overwhelming. I – I think I shall lie down for a little. I should like to see you before you go.

She goes out.

RABY Do you want me, Dr Anderson?

WALTER No . . . At least . . . Why do you ask?

RABY Dr Knox's lecture is in twenty minutes.

WALTER And do you want to miss it?

RABY I would rather die. Au revoir, Miss Mary Belle. I shall see you again, sir.

MARY Au revoir, Mr Raby. *(He goes.)* Mr Raby says that you are leaving Edinburgh, Walter.

WALTER Yes, I am leaving Edinburgh.

Pause.

MARY Amelia and I were surprised to see you today.

WALTER You were Scottish enough not to show it. In the circumstances I had to come. You see why I hesitated at first. *(Pause.)* I am glad I came.

MARY I am glad you came too, Walter . . . Walter!

WALTER Yes!

MARY It is nearly six months since we saw each other.

WALTER Six months. Yes.

MARY Six months is a long time.

WALTER I found it long, but you had new places and the stir of travel. Did you enjoy your journey?

MARY No. Oh, no, no! oh, it's no use pretending. I missed you dreadfully.

WALTER Did you? Oh, did you? Heavens, how I missed you too. There was never a time when I needed you more.

MARY Walter! Then why didn't you write? Were you too proud? Oh! I'm a beast. that night, that night, that night! I acted like a madwoman. I drove you into the street . . .

WALTER You? Oh, my beautiful, no, no! You were right. God knows how right you were . . . But something else happened that night. It shook me to the depths. I have the horror of it still in my bones.

---

[1] Pen name of John Wilson (1785–1854). See the introduction to his works in Vol. II. 580.

MARY Darling, you are ill and unhappy.

WALTER I suppose I am. What does unhappiness matter?

MARY It is terrible to see you unhappy. Darling, forgive me. We'll forget it all. We'll begin again.

WALTER Dearest, dearest, there is nothing to forgive.

MARY Then I'll wait for you for ever and ever. And you can stay in Edinburgh and help Dr Knox to fight it out. And everything will be as if it hadn't been.

WALTER I can't stay in Edinburgh. I can't stay in Scotland.

MARY But why? Dr Knox is in need of friends. I . . .

WALTER Dr Knox understands. I wanted to go before. But he persuaded me to stay. I must go to London now.

MARY Is there a better Anatomy School in London?

WALTER No. Not so good. Not nearly so good.

MARY Then I don't understand. Walter . . . you said something just now . . . about something horrible . . . that happened . . . What did you mean?

WALTER You mustn't ask what happened. That shadow mustn't fall on you, too my dearest one, my darling . . . You must trust me. I am taking this step because I must. There is no other way.

Pause.

MARY Very well, Walter.

WALTER You will marry me no matter what happened?

MARY It is nothing to me what happened. I love you. Oh, Walter, I thought of you every step of the tour.

WALTER Did you? Did you?

MARY I cried my eyes out at my cruelty to you.

WALTER Oh, you weren't cruel. You were just.

MARY I was cruel. It was because I loved you. All lovers are cruel. Kiss me again. Is the pain at your heart well again?

WALTER Almost well again.

MARY Walter, what happened on that night?

WALTER Mary Belle, I can never tell you that. You must help me to forget it.

MARY But how can I help you to forget it if I don't know what it is?

WALTER This way.

Enter AMELIA.

AMELIA Walter! Mary Belle!

MARY Oh, Amy!

AMELIA What has happened?

MARY Don't ask such silly questions.

WALTER Mary Belle is coming to London with me. She has forgiven me.

AMELIA I think you yourself have more to forgive, Walter.

MARY Yes, hasn't he? and he doesn't realise it. Isn't he a darling?

AMELIA You are both my darlings. What's that?

An approaching rumour of voices is heard. WALTER *goes to the window.*

WALTER Some of the rioters are coming this way. Keep back from the window.

MARY Are they after you? Is that your secret?

WALTER No, no. I am too small a fish. No. Hare and Knox will satisfy them . . . I can't see them yet. *(The voices are louder. Cries of 'Hang Knox' predominate.)* Here comes someone. He's walking briskly. Nearly a run. By Jove, it's the Chief. They're after him. I must let him in.

He rushes out. MARY *looks out of the window, biting her handkerchief.*

AMELIA Oh, where shall we hide him?

There is a roar as the mob rushes past. Enter KNOX. *He wears a military riding cloak, and a brace of pistols in a belt strapped round his middle. His bald head is bleeding from a slight graze.* WALTER *follows. The noise dies away.*

KNOX By Heaven, they stone me! They stone me! They stone me! Pigs! Offal! *Canaille!* Rot their souls! I'm no mealy-mouthed saint and martyr, as they shall very soon find. I'm not the sort of man to die in a night-shirt looking like an angel. Not I, by God! I'll break a few heads first.

AMELIA Doctor, don't. Stand back from the window. You are beside yourself.

KNOX Beside myself. Then, faith, I am in better company than I've been during the last five minutes . . . I beg your pardon, Miss Amelia. It is somewhat a heady business to be embroiled with a mob. I forgot my notoriously polite manners.

The noise dies away.

MARY *(at the window)* They have gone.

KNOX I have given them the slip, it appears. Good afternoon, Miss Dishart; your servant, Miss Mary Belle. You look both of you in excellent health. You have returned early. I expected to see your house still closed. I am glad it was not for more than one reason. I must hurry on now, or I shall be late for my lecture. I hope to pay my duty to you this evening – if I am still welcome.

AMELIA Doctor, your head is hurt. We must get bandages.

KNOX No, no. It's nothing.

AMELIA Is it safe for you to go out?

KNOX Safe? Oh, I think so.

AMELIA Don't show yourself at the window.

KNOX Ah! Someone has told you that I am unpopular? Never mind, they are more afraid of me than I am of them.

MARY Do sit down, Dr Knox, and rest yourself. You have been running.

KNOX I running? Nothing of the sort.

WALTER Dr Knox, I don't think it would be wise for you to go out again till nightfall.

KNOX I have said that I will lecture. It will take more than the riff-raff of Auld Reekie to prevent me.

WALTER The public dissection of Burke is going on now and the rioters are blockading Surgeons' Hall. It will be impossible for you to get near it.

KNOX I shall get through somehow.

WALTER Very well, sir. But you had better wait a moment or two. There are organised bands out after you. It is better to know beforehand how the enemy is disposed. Let me go and find out, sir. I shall only be a few minutes.

KNOX Very well.

AMELIA Is it safe?

WALTER Perfectly safe. I am not so kenspeckle[1] as Dr Knox, I am afraid.

AMELIA Then do be careful, dear Walter.

WALTER I shan't be long.

He goes.

AMELIA Do be seated, Dr Knox.

KNOX *takes off his cloak and sits down.*

KNOX Thank you, ma'am.

-----

[1] Conspicuous, well-known.

A silence. KNOX *looks at his watch.*

KNOX It is twenty minutes to the hour. I thought so. That is my only superstition, Miss Amelia.

AMELIA This is a terrible time, Dr Knox. My sister and I have just heard of the monstrous things that are being said against you. We are so sorry.

KNOX You waste your sympathy on me. I find all this inexpressibly exhilarating. It is like swimming in a storm.

MARY Dr Knox . . .

KNOX Signorina?

MARY No, it doesn't matter.

KNOX You were about to ask a question.

MARY Dr Knox, you and I have never been friends.

AMELIA Oh, Mary! Candid, rather quarrelsome friends, but still friends!

MARY No, not friends at all; but please believe that I and my sister will listen to nothing that anybody says – says against you in this frightful business.

KNOX I am sincerely grateful. I expected nothing less of you.

MARY Only . . .

KNOX You make a reservation?

MARY No, no. But . . . Doctor, why is Walter going to London?

KNOX I should say because of some essential and ineradicable strain of vulgarity in his nature. It is this that drives many of our most promising young men to these provincial towns. They shiver in the snell[1] east wind of Modern Athens. London! Pompous Ignorance sits enthroned there and welcomes Pretentious Mediocrity with flattery and gifts. Oh, dull and witless city! Very hell for the restless, inquiring, sensitive soul. Paradise for the snob, the parasite and the prig; the pimp, the placeman and the cheap-jack. The women chatter like parakeets, the men fawn like jackals. On my soul, vulgarity or no vulgarity, I cannot tell you why Walter Anderson is going there. Or what there is in London to awaken in a realist any feeling but loathing and contempt. Yet she entraps great men and sucks their blood. Her streets are littered with their bones.

MARY Dr Knox, six months ago, Walter left this house in a rage. You remember. He has not been back till today. Something happened that night. What was it?

KNOX My dear young lady, even if I ever knew, it is not likely I should remember.

MARY Whatever it was, it drove him from us and from Edinburgh. Our quarrel wouldn't have done it. We have quarrelled again and again. Tell me.

KNOX I know what you mean now. Yes. He was excited, poor boy. He felt you had treated him ill. His imagination was ready for all manner of phantasmagoria. A subject was brought into the anatomy rooms by some of our middlemen. He thought he recognised her – a girl, I think it was; I am nearly sure it was a girl – and would have it that she had been murdered.

AMELIA Murdered!

MARY But had she been?

KNOX How can I tell? I know enough now to be sure that I can trust nobody.

AMELIA Dr Knox, what did you do? What did he do?

KNOX If you want to know, he told me I had murdered her.

MARY What did you say to him?

KNOX I told him not to play the fool. If it was anybody's duty to probe into the source of our supply – and I stoutly deny that it was – the responsibility was his. He apologised to me that same afternoon for his wild words.

MARY And that was all?

---

[1] Fierce.

KNOX That was all.

MARY And he said he must leave Edinburgh?

KNOX Yes. something of the sort, I could nor possibly allow him to do so.

MARY Why not?

KNOX My dear young lady, do you realise the pains and patience I had spent in making Mr Anderson into some semblance of an anatomist? Do you realise that I have a class of 400 students to whom my honour compels me to do my duty? Do you realise that Mr Anderson was my demonstrator? I simply could not spare him. I have another demonstrator now and Walter can go to London or Jericho if he likes. If he remembers a tenth of what I have taught him he will be a great man there in a twelvemonth.

MARY I understand. Dr Knox, will you excuse me?

KNOX Certainly, my dear. You should marry him after all. They will make him a knight. You see if they don't. You will be Lady Anderson and drive in your carriage to visit fat duchesses.

MARY I intend to marry him, Dr Knox.

MARY goes out.

KNOX *(to* AMELIA*)* You see I am the same as ever. Adversity has not taught me to bridle my unfortunate tongue. I had better go.

He rises and puts on his cloak.

AMELIA You must wait for Walter to return, Doctor.

KNOX He is taking a very long time. Miss Amelia, I cannot help this jeering vein of talk. But it is a poor reward for loyalty.

AMELIA My sister needs no rewards to be loyal to you, Dr Knox.

KNOX And you?

AMELIA I think you need hardly ask.

Pause.

KNOX Miss Amelia, in this quiet house I have known the only happiness I have ever known. You will never know what you have done for me.

AMELIA Your visits have been a great happiness to us. We are proud of your friendship.

Pause.

KNOX You understand me so well, so well. You see the little pink shivering boy crouching within this grotesque, this grisly shell of a body. You are sunshine to me, Amelia. You are safe harbourage in storms. I love you. You are everything to me. I love you.

AMELIA Doctor, you mustn't –

KNOX Say only the word and I'll strike my flag. In the light of your presence I see this battle as so much foolish bombast and vanity. Come with me to Italy. Will you come? We'll forget this squalid, torturing farce. We can only live once. Come with me. I love you.

AMELIA And how is Mrs Knox? These times must be very trying for her.

KNOX Oh, how can you! Mrs Knox, madam, enjoys her usual ill-health.

AMELIA I am sorry she keeps so poorly. I have so looked forward to meeting her some day.

KNOX God forbid that you should.

AMELIA You can hardly expect me to go to Italy with you without having the benefit of Mrs Knox's advice. It would be most valuable.

KNOX Woman, have you no heart? Have you no manners? You must know that no real lady would make her lover talk about his wife. It embarrasses him beyond bearing.

AMELIA I know that. *(A knock.)* Ah, here is Jessie Ann with the tea. Come in.

KNOX I shall not drink tea with you.

Enter JESSIE ANN *with tea-things.*

AMELIA Sit down. Take off your cloak. I feel very much inclined to whip you. That will do, Jessie Ann. *(The* MAID *goes out.)* Now try to be a man and not a barn-storming tenor.

KNOX I will try.

AMELIA Do you take sugar? How absurd of me to forget.

KNOX No.

AMELIA No what?

KNOX No, thank you.

AMELIA That is better. Would you like one of Jessie Ann's griddle scones?

KNOX No, thank you. One thing and another have impaired my appetite.

AMELIA But Jessie Ann will be very disappointed. She was so proud when you used to commend her griddle scones. For Jessie Ann's sake. Please.

KNOX A hundred thousand devils take Jessie Ann and her griddle scones; and with the deepest regret you also, madam.

AMELIA Doctor, you are becoming quite heated again. You must . . . Oh, what a callous wretch I am! Your poor head. Does it hurt? It must be bandaged.

She rings the bell.

KNOX No, no, it is nothing. A glancing blow from a stone.

Enter JESSIE ANN.

AMELIA Jessie Ann, have you been listening at the door?

MAID No, no, Mem, honestly, Mem.

AMELIA Go and get some bandages and hot water, and be quick.

MAID Yes, Mem.

She goes.

AMELIA *(at the window)* I do hope nothing has happened to Walter.

KNOX I think it unlikely. He is an active fellow, and the mob are cowards to a man.

AMELIA Their hatred is a dreadful thing.

KNOX Dreadful? It is the only compliment they can pay me.

AMELIA You will stay in Edinburgh?

KNOX Yes, ma'am. No man shall threaten or bully or talk me out of Edinburgh. I do my little dog's tricks for you, ma'am. I love soft voices and sugar, but I do not brook the whip.

AMELIA You will talk yourself out of Edinburgh. You are a very injudicious man.

KNOX That's as may be, ma'am. I shall do what I believe to be right, as I have always done.

AMELIA As you have always done?

KNOX What do you mean?

Re-enter MAID *with a bowl and some bandages.*

AMELIA Thank you. Put them down there. Now you may take the tea-things. I shall not need you after that. You have brought the lint. Ah, yes, here it is. *(Exit* MAID *with tea-things.)* Now let us have a look at the wound. Am I hurting you?

KNOX Not at this moment, ma'am. But you have the capacity to hurt me.

AMELIA It is not very deep. Am I not the clever surgeon? Why don't you let the ladies be surgeons, Dr Knox? Are you afraid of them?

KNOX I am afraid of them. Miss Amelia . . . I find myself at a loss . . . Do you think that I am a murderer?

AMELIA Heavens! what a question! Keep still.

KNOX I must know what is in your mind.

AMELIA Keep quite still. Doctor, it is terrible that put in this position. I think of you galloping on a crusade with your eyes to the front, fixed on your goal. How could you know that your horses' hoofs were trampling poor crushed human bodies? You don't realise it yet.

KNOX Good God, ma'am, do you think that of me! Do you think because I strut and rant and put on a bold face that my soul isn't sick within me at the horror of what I have done? What *I* have done. Do you hear?

AMELIA No, no, you didn't mean to . . .

KNOX Didn't mean to? What a beast's excuse. Do me the justice to believe that I would never make that excuse even to myself. No, I carry the deaths of these poor wretches round my neck till I die. And perhaps after that. Perhaps after that . . . But I tell you this, that the cause is between Robert Knox and Almighty God. I shall answer to no one else. As for the world, I shall face it. I shall play out the play till the final curtain.

AMELIA Doctor. Oh, poor Doctor! What will you do?

KNOX That is easy. I have acquired certain knowledge of benefit to mankind. It is my duty to pass that knowledge on. I shall lecture at Surgeons' Square as long as I have strength. And nobody on earth shall prevent me. That is clear. That is simple. The .things that will trouble me in the night are not so simple.

AMELIA Is the bandage comfortable?

KNOX I thank you, it is.

AMELIA *(suddenly kissing him)* Oh, Robert, you are not the only one who has to fight battles.

KNOX kisses her hand silently. Enter MARY.

MARY Amelia, Walter has not come back yet.

KNOX I will go and find him.

MARY You are sure your value to Science is not too great for you to hazard yourself so?

KNOX Miss Mary Belle, you may use me as you like. I am not the monstrous fine fellow I thought I was half an hour ago.

MARY You are not a monstrous fine fellow at all.

KNOX Oh! . . . You think I am a murderer, do you? A murderer! Or worse than that, a sneaking *souteneur* of assassins – too great a coward to strike the blow? You think well of me, by Heaven!

MARY I think you are a vain, hysterical, talented, stupid man. I think that you are wickedly blind and careless when your mind is fixed on something. But all men are like that. There is nothing very uncommon about you, Dr Knox.

KNOX Indeed, ma'am I shall leave posterity to judge of that.

MARY Posterity will have to be very clever to judge you justly.

KNOX At least it will have the facts before it.

MARY But the excuses will be hard to find.

KNOX I make no excuses. You will do me the justice to say that.

MARY You are too pig-headed.

AMELIA Mary Belle!

KNOX I shall take my leave of you.

MARY You are sulking now.

KNOX *(to* AMELIA*)* Madam, have I your permission to withdraw?

AMELIA Nothing of the sort. You will stay here till Walter comes back.

KNOX Ladies, I will not consent to be treated like a naughty schoolboy. Do you know who I am? Do you know that I am the apostolic successor of Cuvier, the great naturalist? Do you know that, although I am a comparatively young man, much of my work is already immortal? Do you know that I brush aside that snarling pack of curs, strong in the knowledge that the name of Knox will resound throughout the ages . . .

MARY Yes, for bullying and blustering at poor Mary of Scots. Don't be absurd, Dr Knox.

She goes to the window.

KNOX Absurd! I congratulate you on your sense of humour.

MARY Oh, if you prefer to be sinister, you are welcome . . . Oh I thank God, there is Walter at last!

AMELIA Doctor, you must not mind her. She is naturally very – very discomposed. She does not mean half she says.

KNOX I see, she is merely making conversation. To put me at my ease . . . Have I shrunk visibly, Miss Dishart?

AMELIA What do you mean?

KNOX I feel as if I were two feet high and still dwindling. I never felt so small in my life.

AMELIA It will do you good. It must be so dull always to be a giant.

Enter WALTER.

MARY *(running to him)* Walter!

WALTER My love, mt darling! *(Embrace.)*

AMELIA Mary Belle, darling.

KNOX You have settled your difficulties then?

WALTER What difficulties? . . . Oh, Dr Knox, I had almost forgotten. It isn't safe for you to go out yet. There is a crowd two thousand strong outside the Surgeons' Hall. I couldn't get through, sir, but I saw Raby, and he said he'd try. They have broken the windows and are very threatening. There are patrols all over the town, too. One of them is doubling back on the trail. Someone may have seen you come in, sir.

KNOX Then they will break your windows too, Miss Amelia. I had better go.

AMELIA But they will kill you.

KNOX What will that matter? I am a nobody.

AMELIA Oh no, no, Doctor. I am sure you are a very good anatomist. Isn't he, Walter?

WALTER He is a great anatomist.

MARY We are not discussing Dr Knox's proficiency, but his immediate safety. Will they be watching the back of the house?

WALTER I don't know. It is probable. The lane opens into the main street.

MARY If he went that way now . . .

KNOX Do you still take sufficient interest in this vain, careless, stupid person to . . .

MARY For God's sake don't be a fool. I'll give you an old gown and shawl and a market basket. We could go out like mistress and maid going shopping.

KNOX Or you could carry me out in the buck basket buried in dirty linen. No, thank you, ma'am. I have my pistols and I will fight if necessary.

AMELIA You are gesturing again, Dr Knox. I thought we had cured you of that . . . Hush! *(An approaching rumour of voices is heard.)* Here they come.

KNOX I'll go to meet them. *(He assumes his cloak.)*

The two women throw themselves at him.

MARY No, Dr Knox.

AMELIA You must stay here.

The din becomes louder. A hunting horn is heard.

KNOX Ladies, ladies! Don't you realise? There may be bloodshed. I could never forgive myself if . . .

MARY It will be all right. They may not know you are here.

WALTER I do think you had better stay, sir.

Crash at the door. Enter the MAID *as if shot from a gun.*

MAID Oh, Miss Amelia, Miss Amelia!

AMELIA Compose yourself, Jessie Ann.

MAID A wheen o' ruffians at the door. They want Dr Knox to hang him.

KNOX throws back the flaps of his cloak and looks to the priming of his pistols. A stone crashes through the window. Someone in the street calls for a battering ram.

MARY Dr Knox, you must come upstairs to my room. You can escape along the roof.

AMELIA Yes, do, Dr Knox.

The hunting horn sounds again. WALTER *takes up a poker.*

WALTER There isn't much time. Give me one of your pistols, and I'll hold them at bay from the steps.

KNOX I'll speak to them myself. I'll tell them what I think of mobs.

WALTER No, no, sir.

KNOX fires a pistol through the window. A loud crash is heard. The voices become louder. They've broken down the door.

MAID They're in the house. Oh, mercy me, they're in the house.

KNOX Get behind me everyone. Do you hear me?

He sweeps the women behind him, and stands facing the door. WALTER, *with his back to the windows, stands on guard with the poker. After a short pause* RABY *rushes in. His clothes are torn. With one hand he holds a handkerchief to a bleeding nose, and with the other a bludgeon. A dozen or more* STUDENTS, *variously armed and battered, follow him.*

KNOX Stand back, you! . . . Oh, it's you, is it?

RABY Are you all right, Dr Knox? Are you all right, sir?

KNOX Yes, I am all right. What has happened?

RABY We heard they were after you. We came down, hell for leather. They had the door down before we reached 'em. We gave them hell, sir. *(To his bodyguard.)* He's all right, Knoxites. Three cheers for Dr Dox. Hip, hip, hip . . .

STUDENTS Hooray, hooray, hooray!

RABY *(to AMELIA)* Oh, I beg your pardon, ba'ab. Knoxities, three cheers for Biss Dishart. Hip, hip, hip . . .

STUDENTS Hooray, hooray, hooray!

RABY It's all right now, sir. You're quite safe now. We gave them hell, sir, – beg pardon, Miss Dishart, I'b sure. You can't see the seats of their small-clothes for dust. I'b sorry about by dose, Miss Dishart. A great heavy cad got it a clout with his bludgeon. I settled his hash. You're all right now, sir.

KNOX Well then, gentlemen, if you are ready, I shall lead you to Surgeons' Square.

STUDENTS But it can't be done, sir.

RABY We'll never bake our way through that mob, sir, not without cannon, sir.

KNOX Well. What the devil does it matter where we lecture? I'll lecture in the Grassmarket. I'll lecture on the Calton Hill. I'll lecture on the steps of St Giles.

WALTER *(aside to AMELIA)* For God's sake don't let him go. He'll be killed.

More STUDENTS *have drifted in. The room is full.*

AMELIA Dr Knox, if it doesn't matter where you lecture, why not lecture here?

KNOX Here, ma'am?

AMELIA Why not?

KNOX The place is unsuitable, ma'am.

AMELIA For lectures, Doctor? You have given so many here.

RABY Why not give the lecture here, sir? It's past the time for starting anyhow.

AMELIA Oh, do, Dr Knox. And may we listen? It is on a subject to which ladies may listen?

KNOX Eminently so, madam. It is on the Heart.

AMELIA How charming! Do say you will.

KNOX *(looking hard at MARY)* Very well.

The STUDENTS, *chattering loudly, begin to arrange the room as a lecture theatre. The travelling trunk is used as a rostrum for* KNOX. *The ladies are accommodated with chairs in front. The* STUDENTS *keep asking* KNOX *for instruction.* WALTER, *a little distrait, wanders to the spinet and keeps gazing at* MARY BELLE, *who is giving instructions to the* STUDENTS.

RABY Shall we shift the spinet out of the way, sir?
WALTER Eh . . . Oh, yes, I suppose.

They bring the spinet down stage.

KNOX No, no, you fool! I want the rostrum over there. No. Over there.

During the bustle and noise, WALTER, *still standing, picks out* MARY PATERSON'S *lullaby with one finger on the spinet. The verse portion is only heard vaguely through the noise. When the theatre is ready there is a silence.* WALTER, *miles away, plays the refrain.*

KNOX Mr Anderson, when you have completed your overture I will commence my lecture.

Laughter.

WALTER I am dreadfully sorry, Dr Knox. My mind was wandering.
KNOX You compose a love lyric?
WALTER No. It is an air that came into my head. I can't remember what it is.

He drifts to the window.

KNOX *(wagging his head at* MARY BELLE*)* Ah, Cyprian, thou who makest strong men mad.

MARY BELLE *bridles.* WALTER *looks at* RABY. *They both recognise the tune.* WALTER *buries his face in his hands.*

KNOX And now, gentlemen, I should say ladies and gentlemen, I am humbly obliged to you. You are well aware that every sneaking scribbler in this intellectual Gomorrah who can smudge an ungrammatical sentence employs his miserable talent to scratch venom on the public news-sheets; that, for the benefit of those worthy citizens who are unable to read, gap toothed mountebanks scream and splutter at every street corner. And I, gentlemen, I am the unworthy occasion of all this. I have argued with the great Cuvier in the Academies of Paris. I shall not profane the sacred gift of human speech by replying to these people in any other language than that of the cudgel. With you I shall take the liberty of discussing a weightier matter . . . 'The Heart of the Rhinoceros'. This mighty organ, gentlemen, weighs full twenty-five pounds, a fitting fountain-head for the tumultuous stream that surges through the arteries of that prodigious monster. Clad in proof gentlemen, and terribly armed as to his snout, the rhinoceros buffets his way through the tangled verdure engirdling his tropical habitat. Such dreadful vigour, gentlemen such ineluctable energy requires to be sustained by no ordinary forces of nutrition . . .

While he is speaking the curtain slowly falls. The students are listening with a passionate intentness which will, it is hoped, communicate itself to the audience.

The end of the play.

Muriel Stuart (1889 – 1967)

The Seed-Shop

Here in a quiet and dusty room they lie,
Faded as crumbled stone or shifting sand,
Forlorn as ashes, shriveled, scentless, dry –
Meadows and gardens running through my hand.

Dead that shall quicken at the call of Spring,
Sleepers to stir beneath June's magic kiss,
Though birds pass over, unremembering,
And no bee seek here roses that were his.

In this brown husk a dale of hawthorn dreams;
A cedar in this narrow cell is thrust   10
That will drink deeply of a century's streams.
These lilies shall make Summer on my dust.

Here in their safe and simple house of death,
Sealed in their shells a million roses leap;
Here I can blow a garden with my breath,
And in my hand a forest lies asleep.

Revenant

'It is cold in the room, lamp's out, the moon is late,
Something cried out just now as in great fear! . . .
Ghost that I knew, what brings you suddenly near?'
'You said you would come to me if I would wait . . . '
'But you died long ago, poor foolish dear!

'And dead and living cannot mix or meet,
You to the dark, and I to love must go.'
'Last night but not tonight?' 'What can you do
To hinder me from one who is as sweey
As you were once? You're dead . . . ' 'But
You're dead too.'

The Harebell

You give no portent of impermanence
Though before sun goes you are long gone hence,
Your bright, inherited crown
Withered and fallen down.

It seems that your blue immobility
Has been for ever, and must for ever be.
Man seems te unstable thing,
Fevered and hurrying,

So free of joy, so prodigal of tears;
Yet he can hold his fevers seventy years,   10
Out-wear sun, rain and frost
By which you are soon lost.

Turn Again . . .

Do not take me, Stranger,
I am not free.
The old gods of the mountains
Have a lien on me.

And when your mates ask you,
Will you dare say,
'The sons of Cytherea
Have stolen her away?'

For when on Dion's mountain
The first hound calls   10
There'll be no keeping me
In these four walls.

The Cloudberry

Give me no coil of daemon flowers –
Pale Messalines that faint and brood
Through the spent secret twilight hours
On their strange feasts of blood.

.Give me wild things of moss and peat –
The gypsy flower that bravely goes,
The heather's little hard, brown feet,
And the black eyes of sloes.
But most of all the cloudberry
The offers in her clean, white cup   10
The melting snows – the cloudberry!
Where the great winds go up

To the hushed peak whose shadow fills
The air with silence calm and wide –
She lives, the Dian of the hills,
And the streams course beside.

Common Fires

The fern and flame had fought and died together,
From fading frond the falling smoke crept grey,
The heath drew close her old brown shawl of heather,
And turned her face away.

Today the bee no bell of honey misses,
The birds are nesting where the bracken lies
Green, tranquil, deep, quiet as dreams or kisses
On weary lips and eyes.

The heath has drawn the blackened threads together;
My heart has closed her lips upon old pain;   10
But somewhere in my heart and in the heather,
No bud shall grow again.

Neil Gunn (1891 – 1973)

Neil Gunn is generally recognised as the finest of modern Scottish novelists, especially esteemed for his evocative pictures of Highland life, and his constant emphasis upon the influence of nature. Restricting himself to non-sentimental Scottish backgrounds, Gunn has been almost indifferent to international popularity, and has to a considerable extent paid the price for his choice. He is little known outside his native country and many of his fine novels are now hard to obtain. He is represented here by a fairly typical short story, 'The Moor,' and by two of the sketches from his collection, *Highland Pack*.

The Moor

A few miles back it had looked like a sea-anemone on a vast tidal ledge, but now, at hand, it rose out of the moor's breast like a monstrous nipple. The scarred rock, heather tufted, threw a shadow to his aching feet, and because he was young enough to love enchantment in words, he savoured slowly, 'like the shadow of a great rock in a weary land'. With a nameless shudder of longing he passed his tongue between his sticky lips. The wide Sutherland moor under the August sun was silent as a desert.

At a little pool by the rock-base he drank and then dipped his face.

From the top of the rocky outcrop the rest of his tramp unrolled before him like a painted map. The earth fell away to the far sea, with cottages set here and there upon it like toys, and little cultivated strips, green and brown, and serpentine dark hollows.

He kept gazing until the sandwich in his mouth would not get wet enough to swallow. Then his eyes rested on the nearest cottage of all.

The loneliness of that cottage was a thing to catch the heart. Its green croft was snared in the moor's outflung hand. In the green stood a red cow. Creaming in upon his mind stole the seductive thought of milk. Tasting it made a clacking sound in his mouth and he stopped eating.

As he neared the cottage the red cow stared at him, unmoving save for the lifeless switch of her tail. The cottage itself, with its grey curved thatch and pale gable-end, made no move. The moor's last knuckle shut off the world.

The heather had not yet stirred into bloom and, far as the eye could see, lay dark under the white sun. He listened for a sound . . . and in that moment of suspense it came upon him that the place was bewitched.

A dog barked and every sense leapt. The tawny brute came out at the front door, showing half-laughing teeth, twisting and twining, and in no time was at his back. He turned round, but still kept moving towards the door, very careful not to lift his eyes from those eyes, so that he nearly tumbled backwards over the doorstep . . . and was aware, with the beginnings of apologetic laughter, that he was in the presence of a woman. When he looked up, however, the laugh died.

Her eyes were gipsy dark. Perhaps she was twenty. Sunk in the darkness of her eyes were golden sun motes. Madonna of the adder-haunted moor. His confusion stared speechless. A tingling trepidation beset his skin. A tight drawn bodice just covered and repressed her breasts. Her beauty held the still, deep mesmerism of places at the back of beyond. She was shy, yet gazed at him.

The dry cup of his flesh filled with wine. Then his eyes flickered, shifted quickly; he veiled them, smiling, as though the rudeness of his bared emotion had gone forth unpardonably and touched her skin.

To his stammered request for milk, she smiled faintly, almost automatically, and disappeared.

Then he heard the beating of his heart. Through the warmth of his tired body swept a distinct heat. Excitement broke in spindrift. He smiled secretly to himself, absorbed.

When he caught himself listening at the door, however, he immediately bespoke the dog, inviting its approach with such a sudden snapping hand that the brute leapt back, surprised into a short growl. He awaited her appearance so alive and happy that he was poised in apprehension.

She brought the milk in a coarse tumbler. He barely looked at her face, as if good manners could not trust his instinct; but the last grain of thanks he concentrated in a glance, a word or two, a smile breaking into a laugh. She had covered somewhat the wide V gleam of her breast, had swept back her hair; but the rents, the burst seam under an arm, the whole covering for her rich young body was ragged as ever, ragged and extraordinarily potent, as if it sheathed the red pulse at white beauty's core. He said he would drink the milk sitting outside if she didn't mind. She murmured, smiled, withdrew.

He ate his lunch excitedly, nibbling at the sandwiches to make them last, throwing crusts to the dog. His mind moved in its bewilderment as in coloured spindrift, but underneath were eyes avid for the image of her body, only he would not let their stare fix. Not yet. Not now . . . Living here at the back of beyond . . . this secret moor . . . Extraordinary! The wave burst in happy excited spindrift . . . But underneath he felt her like a pulse and saw her like a flame – a flame going to waste – in the dark of the moor, this hidden moor. Attraction and denial became a tension of exquisite doubt, of possible cunning, of pain, of desire. His soul wavered like a golden jet.

As the last drop of the milk slid over, he heard a sound and turned – and stared.

A withered woman was looking at him, eyes veiled in knowingness. She said, 'It's a fine day that's in it.'

'Yes, isn't it!' He got to his feet.

She slyly looked away from him to the moor, the better to commune with her subtle thought. A wisp of grey hair fell over an ear. Her neck was sinewy and stretched, her chin tilted level from the stoop of her shoulders. The corners of her eyes returned to him. Just then the girl came to the door.

'It's waiting here, Mother.' Through a veiled anxiety quietly, compellingly, she eyed the old woman.

'Are ye telling me?'

'Come on in.'

'Oh, I'm coming.' She turned to the young man and gave a little husky laugh, insanely knowing. The daughter followed her within, and he found himself with the thick glass in his hand staring at the empty doorway. 'She leuch' rose a ballad echo, like a sunless shudder. A sudden desire to tiptoe away from that place seized him. My God! he thought. The blue of heaven trembled.

But he went to the door and knocked.

'This is the glass – ' he began.

She smiled shyly, politely, and, taking the glass from his outstretched hand, smoothly withdrew.

His hand fell to his side. He turned away, going quietly.

Down between the cottages, the little cultivated strips green and brown, the serpentine dark hollows, he went jerkily, as though the whole place were indeed not earth, but a painted map, and he himself a human toy worked by one spring. Only it was a magic spring that never got unwound. Even in the hotel that overlorded the final cluster of cottages, the spring seemed wound up tighter than ever.

For privacy he went up and sat on his bed. 'Lord, I cannot get over it!' he cried silently. He got off his bed and walked about the floor. This was the most extraordinary thing that had ever happened to him . . . without, as it were, quite happening to him.

Inspiration had hitherto thrilled from within. This was from without, and so vast were its implictions that he could not feel them all at once in a single spasm of creation. He got lost in them and wandered back to his bed, whereon he lay full length, gazing so steadily that he sank through his body into a profound sleep.

He awoke to a stillness in his room so intense that he held his breath, listening. His eyes slowly turned to the window where the daylight was not so much fading as changing into a glimmer full of a moth-pale life, invisible and watchful. Upon his taut ear the silence began to vibrate with the sound of a small tuning fork struck at an immense distance.

His staring eyes, aware of a veiled face . . . focused the face of the girl on the moor. The appeal of her sombre regard was so great that he began to tremble; yet far back in him cunningly he willed body and mind to an absolute suspense so that the moment might remain transfixed. Footsteps on the corridor outside smashed it, and all at once he was listening acutely to perfectly normal voices.

'Well, Mr Morrison – you here? What's up now?'

'Nothing much. The old woman up at Albain – been certified.'

'So I heard. Poor old woman. When are you lifting her?'

'Tomorrow.'

'There's no doubt, of course, she is . . . ay, ay, very sad.'

'Yes. There's the girl, too – her daughter. You'll know her?'

'Well – yes. But she's right enough. I mean there's nothing – there. A bit shy, maybe . . . like the heather. You know.'

'I was wondering what could be done for her.'

'Oh, the neighbours will look after her, I'm sure. She'll just have to go into service. We're fixed up for the season here now, or I . . . '

The footsteps died away, and the light in the bedroom withdrew itself still more, like a woman withdrawing her dress, her eyes, but on a lingering watchfulness more critical than ever, and now faintly ironic.

His body snapped into action and began restlessly pacing the floor, irony flickering over the face. Suddenly he paused . . . and breathed aloud – 'The auld mither!' His eyes gleamed in a profound humour.

The exclamation made him walk as it were more carefully, and presently he came to the surface of himself some distance from the hotel and realised where he was going.

But now he cunningly avoided the other cottages and in a roundabout way came in over the knuckle of moor in the deepening dusk. The cow was gone and the cottage seemed more lonely than ever. Indeed, it crouched to the earth with rounded shoulders drawing its grey thatch about its awful secret. Only the pale gable-end gloomed in furtive watchfulness.

Grey-green oasis, dark moor, and huddled cottage were privy to the tragedy of their human children, and, he felt, inimical to any interference from without. Never before had he caught this living secretive intensity of background, although, as a young painter believing in vision, it had been his business to exploit backgrounds of all sorts.

The girl herself walked out from the end of the house, carrying two empty pitchers. On the soft turf her feet made no sound. Unlike her background she was not inimical but detached. And, as her slave, her background spread itself in quiet ecstasy under her feet.

By the time he joined her at the well she had her buckets full, and as he offered to carry them she lifted one in each hand. He pursued his offer, stooping to take them. The little operation brought their bodies into contact and their hands, so that there was a laughing tremble in his voice as he walked beside her, carrying the water. But at the doorway, which was reached in a moment, he set down the buckets and raised his cap.

As he went on into the moor, still smiling warmly as though she were beside him, he kept saying to himself that to have dallied or hesitated would have been unpardonable . . . yet not quite believing it . . . yet knowing it to be true.

He sat down on the moor, his heart aflame. The moor lost its hostility and became friendly. Night drew about them her dim purple skin. Silence wavered like the evening smoke of a prehistoric fire. The sense of translation grew in him . . . until the girl and himself went walking on the moor, on the purple, the rippled skin, their faces set to mountain crests and far dawns.

He tore his vision with a slow humour and, getting to his feet, shivered. As he returned by the cottage he saw her coming out of the byre-door and on a blind impulse went up to her and asked:

'Are you not lonely here?'

'No,' she answered, with a smile that scarcely touched her still expression.

'Well – it does seem lonely – doesn't it?'

Her eyes turned to the moor and only by a luminous troubling of their deeps could he see that his words were difficult. She simply did not speak, and for several seconds they stood perfectly silent.

'I can understand,' he broke through, 'that it's not lonely either.' But his awkwardness rose up and clutched him. If the thickening dusk saved his colour, it heightened her beauty in a necromantic way. Mistrust had not touched her, if tragedy had. A watchfulness, a profound instinct young and artless – yet very old.

The front door opened and her mother came peering on to the doorstep. In low quick tones he said:

'I'll come – tomorrow evening.'

Her eyes turned upon his with a faint fear, but found a light deeper than sympathy.

By the time he got back to the hotel, his companion, Douglas Cunningham, had arrived, round about, with the motor-cycle combination.

'Sorry I'm so late. The beastly clutch kept slipping. I had the devil's own time of it.'

'Had you?'

'Yes. We'll have to get down to it tomorrow . . . What happened?' Douglas looked at Evan shrewdly. 'Seems to have lit you up a bit, anyhow!'

'Does it?'

Then Evan told him.

Douglas met his look steadily.

'You can't see?' probed Evan, finally. 'The moor, the lonely cottage, the mad mother, and the daughter . . . My God, what a grouping! Can't you see – that it transcends chance? It has overwhelmed me.'

'My dear chap, if you'd been in the ditch with a burst clutch and umpteen miles from nowhere you would have been, by analogy, completely pulverized.'

Their friendly arguments frequently gathered a mocking hostility.

'You show me the clutch of your tinny motor bike,' thrust Evan. 'I show you the clutch of eternal or infernal life. I'm not proving or improving anything: I'm only showing you. But you can't see. Lord, you are blind. Mechanism, clutch, motor bike . . . these are the planets wheeling about your Cyclops glassy eye. You are the darling of evolution, the hope of your country, the proud son of your race. You are the thing we have arrived at! . . . By the great Cuchulain, is it any wonder that your old mother is being taken to a mad-house?'

'By which I gather that you have found the daughter's mechanism – fool-proof?'

Evan took a slow turn about the floor, then with hands in pockets stood glooming satanically. 'I suppose,' he said, 'we have sunk as low as that.'

Douglas eyed him warningly.

'Easy, Evan.'

Evan nodded. 'Whatever I do I must not go in off the deep end!' He suddenly sat down and over his closed fist on the table looked Douglas in the face. 'Why shouldn't I go in off the deep end?'

Douglas turned from the drawn lips and kicked off his boots.

'You can go in off any damned end you like,' he said.

And in bed, Evan could not sleep. To the pulse of his excitement parable and symbol danced with exquisite rhythm and to a pattern set upon the grey-green oasis of the croft, centring in the cottage . . . fertile matrix of the dark moor.

Vision grew and soon wholly obsessed him. He found in it a reality at once intoxicating and finally illuminating. A pagan freedom and loveliness, a rejuvenation, an immense hope . . . and, following after, the moods of reflection, of beauty, of race . . . to go into the moor not merely to find our souls but to find life itself – and to find it more abundantly.

But the following evening the little cottage presented quite another appearance. He came under its influence at the very first glance from the near moor crest. It had the desolate air of having had its heart torn out, of having been raped. A spiritless shell, its dark-red door pushed back in an imbecile gape. One could hear the wind in its emptiness. A sheer sense of its desolation overcame him. He could not take his eyes off it.

And presently an elderly woman came to the door, followed by the girl herself. They stood on the doorstep for a long time, then began slowly to walk up to the ridge beyond which lay the neighbours' cottages. But before they reached the ridge they stopped and again for a long time stood in talk. At last the elderly woman put out her hand and caught the girl's arm. But the girl would not go with her. She released herself and stepped back a pace, her body bending and swaying sensitively. The elderly woman stood still and straight, making her last appeal. The girl swayed away from that appeal also, turned and retreated. With hooded shawl her elder remained looking after her a moment, then like a woman out of the ages went up over the crest of the moor.

From his lair in the heather, Evan saw the door close, heard, so still the evening was, the clash and rattle of the latch. And with the door closed and the girl inside, the house huddled emptier than ever. His heart listened so intently that it caught the dry sound of desolate thought . . . she was not weeping . . . her arms hung so bare that her empty hands kept plucking down her sleeves . . .

She came at his knock. The pallor of her face deepened the dark of her eyes. Their expressionlessness was troubled and she stood aside to let him in. Only when they were by the fire in the gloom of the small-windowed kitchen did she realise what had happened.

But Evan did not feel awkward. He knew what he had to do like a man who might have imaginatively prepared himself for the test. He placed her chair at the other side of the fire but did not ask her to sit down. He sat down himself, however, and looking into the fire began to speak.

Sometimes he half turned with a smile, but for the most part kept his eyes on the burning peat, with odd silences that were pauses in his thought. He was not eager nor hurried; yet his gentleness had something fatal in it like the darkness of her mood. Sensitiveness that was as exquisite as pain transmuted pain to a haunted monotone.

She stood so still on the kitchen floor that in the end he dared not look at her. Nor did his immobility break when he heard her quietly sit down in the opposite chair, though the core of the fire quickened before his gaze.

Without moving, he started talking again. He did not use words that might appeal to a primitive intelligence. He spoke in the highest – the simplest – way he could to himself.

He looked at himself as a painter desiring to paint the moor. Why? He found himself dividing the world into spirit and mechanism. Both might be necessary, but spirit must be supreme. Why? Even if from no other point than this that it afforded the more exquisite delight. And the more one cultivated it the more varied and interesting life became, the deeper, the more charming, and yes, the more tragical. Yes, the more tragical, thereby drawing spirit to spirit in a communion that was the only known warmth in all the coldness of space. And we needed that particular warmth; at moments one needed it more than anything else. Man's mechanism was a tiny flawed toy in the vast flawless mechanism of the universe. But this warmth of his was a thing unique; it was his own special creation . . . and in a way – who could say? – perhaps a more significant, more fertile, thing than even the creation of the whole mechanical universe . . .

As he thought over this idea for a time, he felt her eyes on his face. The supreme test of spirit would be that while not knowing his words it would yet understand him perfectly – *if it was there.*

'I do not know,' he said at last, and repeated it monotonously. 'Coming in over the moor there I saw you and the woman. Then there was the moor itself. And you in the cottage. I wish I could understand that. But I cannot understand it, any more than you – or the woman. Yet we understand it, too. And the woman could have helped you. Only you didn't want to be helped in her way yet.' He paused, then went on slowly: 'I can see that. It's when I go beyond that to my sitting here that it becomes difficult. For what I see is you who are the moor, and myself with the moor about me, and in us there is dawn, and out of the moor comes more of us . . . That sounds strange, but perhaps it is truer than if I said it more directly. For you and I know that we cannot speak to each other yet – face to face.'

Then he turned his face and looked at her.

Her dark eyes were alight with tears that trickled in slow beads down her cheeks.

He gave his face to the fire again. It was there.

Quietly he got to his feet. 'I'll make a cup of tea.'

She also arose. 'I'll make it.'

It had grown quite dark in the kitchen. They stood very still facing the unexpected darkness. Caught by something in the heart of it, they instinctively drew together. He turned her face from it.

In the morning Douglas arrived at the cottage on the heels of the woman with the shawl. The woman had tried the door and found it locked. But her quick consternation lessened when she found the key under the thatch.

Douglas, grown oddly curious, waited for her to come out. She came, with a face as grey as the wall.

'She hasn't slept in her bed at all.'

'Oh!' His lips closed.

The woman looked at him.

'Do you know . . . ?'

'Not a thing,' said Douglas. 'Must have gone over the hills and far away. They've got a fine morning for it.' And he turned and left her, his scoffing sanity sticking in his throat like a dry pellet.

Mountain Calendar

There is a knoll on the moor beyond the crofting land that we sometimes visit. It is not conspicuous in any way except for its four standing stones. Obviously it was an important spot in prehistoric days, and we never fail to be impressed by the nature and the vast extent of the view obtained from its gentle summit. For it not only takes in great mountain ranges, but overlooks the fertile valleys on their way to the sea. Chance led me on the shortest day of the year to stand amid the four stones as the sun was setting, and suddenly it came upon me how easy it would be for the simplest shepherd of prehistoric times to tell fairly accurately from the setting sun the time of the year. The sun was going down on a mountain that was higher than any to the south of it. Farther south than that summit the sun never sets. My eye could stare without much discomfort at the round molten ball with its flickering black shadow. From now onwards the sun will set farther west. The peaks that stretch in an arc through west to north-west, where the sun sets in the height of summer, could readily be used as a sort of notch-board, and certainly one not likely to be mislaid. It may be interesting to watch for the months from the standing stones.

A wise divine, whom I asked about these stones, told me that they were known to old Gaelic inhabitants as Na Daoine Gorach, meaning The Foolish Men. From his smile I understood his hidden meaning, for we have occasionally discussed antiquities and place-names. The early Christians had undoubtedly an understanding of the human mind in fellowship that went very deep. Whatever the original form of worship or rite at the standing stones, the men of the new faith did not as a rule attack it with brutal intolerance in an effort at utter annihilation. Sometimes they simply put a cross on the stone, or reared a new stone in the shape of a cross. But in any case, and in the new light, these old stones were just foolish stones. Indeed they do rather look today like four old foolish men or bodachs. And once you have seen them like that, fellowship is not lost, it is deepened. We are one with them. What is lost is animosity.

'Ah,' says the cattleman as we leaned on the gate, 'how times have changed! In my young days we would be preparing for a whole week for the New Year. What fun there would be! Now no one is preparing. It's nothing.'

Some think that we are entering upon a new period of the dark ages. Once again groups may form, little isolated groups, to take delight in the stars, in sunlight, in various arts, in religious experience, in birds, in trees, in darkness, in things made by man's hand, in flowers, and above all in the simple goodness of fellowship.

Meantime the gardener reports that the green shoots of her snowdrops, crocuses, scillas, and hyacinths are well above the grey frost, confident of the sun that will blow them into blossom. And how certain it is that the sun, whom the folk of the standing stones may have worshipped, will not betray their confidence.

Death of the Lamb

As he approached the solitary elm in the upland pasture field of the large glen farm, his eye was caught by the flight of a grey crow from its upper branches. His mind quickened sharply for he did not like the bird; his eyes narrowed as they followed the watchful sideways flight, the careless haphazard onflying that was always so sinister; then they dropped to search around and saw the full-grown lamb in the long grass of the ditch.

He came within a few feet of it and stopped. A round hole over two inches deep and about an inch across had been eaten out of its right flank. The hole was red but no blood flowed from it. The lamb swayed very slightly on its legs, its eyes were inclined to close and its ears to droop.

The man was seized with a strong revulsion of feeling, with a hatred of the loathsome grey-black bird, with anger, and also with a desire to walk away, for he could do nothing. There was no one anywhere to be seen; no one who had seen him. Even the crow had vanished. He took a few steps downward and paused, for as surely as he went on would the crow return and continue its ghastly meal. The earth around him caught the dark silence of a battlefield.

He went back to the lamb and stared at it, stooped to stare into the red hole, at the intermittent quiver that went over the flesh, at the half-closed eyes, at the head drooping towards fatal sleep. It seemed quite unaware of him. Death wasn't far off – yet the brute was still on its legs, might endure like this for hours, perhaps a whole night, and its eyelids would continue to flicker down to defeat the beak that liked to peck the eyeball as a titbit.

He glanced about the grass, looking for a stone or a stick. There was neither. One sharp blow on the forehead and all would be over. But it was not his lamb. There was nothing he could properly do about it except walk away and report the matter to the shepherd should he happen to come across him. So he set off, leaving the lamb swaying in the tall grass, lifting an eye to watch for the crow, with bitter anger in his mind and a queer undefined hatred. Once he cleared his throat and spat, but that did not cleanse his mouth.

Soon he felt he must find the shepherd, and when he saw the farm workers harvesting a field, he went through the wire fence and strolled over towards them. Yes, there was the shepherd helping with the stooking,[1] and he knew at once a sharp sense of relief. When he had told the shepherd, his responsibility would end.

'Come to give us a hand?' the shepherd greeted him cheerfully.

The man returned the sally, and after they had chatted about the good crop said: 'By the way, there's a lamb of yours up there on its last legs. A crow was pecking a hole in its flank. It's still standing.'

'Oh,' said the shepherd, and looked at him.

'I didn't know what to do about it, so thought I'd come and tell you.'

'I see,' said the shepherd, looking away. Then he picked up a couple of sheaves and set them leaning against each other. 'It seems he's done for in that case.'

'Yes.'

The shepherd picked up another couple of sheaves, and then paused. There obviously wasn't much that he could do about it. He seemed reluctant to leave the field. 'I had one that went like that last week.' He walked away a few paces and came back with another two sheaves.

'I felt like putting it out of its misery, but I didn't know what to do, so I thought I'd tell you,' said the man, looking at the other workers.

When the shepherd had completed his stook of eight sheaves, he paused again. 'Is it far up?'

'Not very. Just up at the elm tree. I don't suppose there's much you can do for it.'

'No,' said the shepherd in a flat voice; then he began to move over to his black jacket which lay against a stook. When the shepherd had his jacket on, they started walking across to the fence. The shepherd took out his pipe and paused to light its already half-consumed tobacco. 'When they get that trouble on them, there's nothing can be done.'

He felt that the shepherd now had a grudge against him, and this embarrassed him. There was nothing a man could do. He should have left the shepherd alone, instead of coming like a sensitive woman to tell what he had seen. But he answered in his normal voice, and the shepherd spoke calmly. Yes, there were showers, but the wind soon dried everything up. It was good enough harvest weather.

As they approached the elm-tree, two crows got up and flapped away. 'Ugly brutes,' said the shepherd, and then, going forward, he stood before the lamb.

It was still on its legs, swaying very slightly, shivering now and then, its eye-lids half-

---

[1] Collecting into 'stooks' or shocks of ten or so sheaves to dry in a field.

closed, its head drooping. The shepherd squatted down and peered at the bloody hole; then remained squatting for a long time, apparently lost in contemplation of the lamb.

He got up with an odd and distant air. In a voice dry and practical, he said: 'No, there's nothing can be done now, nothing but the one thing.' He looked at the tree and abroad over the bare upland pasture. 'You need a license to kill a beast these days,' he said with a humour in which there was no stress. Then he took out his pocket-knife and opened the big blade.

'Well,' he greeted the lamb, patting it gently on the back. 'It will be all right now, all right.' He got his left hand across the throat. The lamb struggled. 'It's all right,' murmured the shepherd soothingly, 'all right,' as if talking to a fevered child, and now with all his strength he was getting at the bone. The vertebrae snapped, and the shepherd severed the spinal cord which then showed between the bone joints like two frilled ends of white tape. He dropped the lamb. The body continued to jerk convulsively.

The shepherd cleaned the blade of his knife by stabbing it in the grass. Then he gave it a final wipe against his trousers.

'It's a job I hate,' he said in his calm voice as he clicked the blade shut.

'Well, I'm glad it's out of its misery, anyway,' said the man as lightly as he could.

They returned, as they had come up, talking in even, friendly tones, but when the shepherd left him the man felt that in some way he had been a soft fool. Also there was somehow in the air a feeling of misery, of guilt. The shadow of the whole business had not only come between the shepherd and himself, but between himself and everything. It attached itself to his clothes and to the trees, and the grey crows flew through it.

William Ogilvie (1891 – 1939)

My Mither's Aunt

I see the livin' an' the deid
Sittin' thegither plain as day,
Crackin'* in a frien'ly way.   chatting

Noo I'm in an empty hoose,
Gangin my lane frae room tae room;
An' a' the wa's are strippit bare,
An' a' the presses toom*.   empty
The flair boards fu' o' dusty cracks
An' bits o' claith an' rusty tacks;
An' whaur a picter used tae hing,   10
A shadow, frae a shadow string,
Glowerin' like nae livin' thing.

Somebody's opened the entry door,
I heard it gi'e a click the noo;
I feel the cauld wind in my hair,
I feel the cauld wind on my broo.
That wee bit waxclaith on the flair
Lifted wi' a breath the noo.

Was that a rat, or was it rain?
Was that the door shut to again?   20
I haud the banister for breath,
An' a'thing hings as still as death.

A bed an' on't a strippit tyke★,   mattress cover
A bed an' on't some dirty cloots;
An' on the flair I see a pair
O' auld elastic-sided boots.
An auld black bag wi' twa brass clips,
A tumbler an' some orange pips;
An' naething else I see ava',
Save a hantle★ o' cloots agin the wa'   30   clump, few
An' a dirty bedspread flung ower a'.

I turn it doon an' there I see
My mither's aunt as plain can be,
The twa een bulgin' frae the croon,
The twa lids blinkin' up an' doon.
'They've gane an' left me by mysel','
Quo' my mither's aunt tae me.
'O dinna leave me by mysel'!
O dinna leave me here tae dee!'
An' fine I ken tho' she speak and see,   40
Tho' the tears rin doon frae the bulgin' e'e,
That she's as deid as deid can be.

I lift her syne on til my back,
The stiffent body gied a crack;
I feel my way along the wa',
I grip the banister an' a',
An' at the turn I let her fa'.

I hear the thud upon the stair,
I hear her greetin'★, greetin' sair −   weeping
The wheelin' steps, the rail, the stair,   50
An' a'thing else is made o' air.

Somebody's opened the entry door,
Shairly the flittin'★ men are there,   removal
Lightin' their pipes at the fit o' the stair.
I hear them laugh, an' spit, an' swear,
I hear them ropin' up the gear,
I hear the horses paw the stane,
I hear the door shut to again.

I stan' my lane at the turn o' the stair,
I hear the wifie greetin' sair;   60
I peer i' the mirk but naething see,
Save the tears that rin frae the bulgin' e'e.
I try, but I canna speak at a';
I try, but I canna find the wa';
An' thro the hoose I hear the mane
O' the wind, an' the blatterin' o' the rain.

'Hugh MacDiarmid' (Christopher Grieve, 1892 – 1978)

MacDiarmid is the most influential of twentieth-century Scottish writers, both through his own work as a splendid writer of verse in Scots, and by his incessant propagandising for Scotland, and the Scots language. He was the major force behind what is sometimes called the Scottish Renaissance. He has written some of the finest lyrics of our age and one very long poem, *A Drunk Man Looks at the Thistle*, which is usually cited as the masterwork of modern Scottish poetry. He is a controversial figure on many counts – he was a socialist, then a communist, a supporter of Scottish nationalism – but perhaps most for his insistence upon using Scots in verse – a stand which became rather confused later in his life when he himself began writing mostly in English – though he attacked Edwin Muir, the other internationally recognised modern Scottish poet, for his insistence upon standard English. MacDiarmid wished to create a diction which would be totally responsive to the full range of twentieth-century intellectual and cultural experience, as he conceived the language of the Makars had been to their own age. He was not impressed by the conventional diction of nineteenth-century Scottish poets. He therefore ransacked Scottish dictionaries and older works of Scottish literature to increase his word hoard. One result, of course, is that, for all his reputation, and his great gifts, MacDiarmid is not really much read outside of Scotland, even by those who love poetry.

Later, when MacDiarmid turned to writing primarily in English, the general critical estimate was that the new poems showed serious decline, but some critics have commended them, and a few regard one long work, 'On a Raised Beach', as a masterpiece, fit to rank with his best work in Scots.

The Bonnie Broukit Bairn

For Peggy

Mars is braw★ in crammasy★,   handsome/crimson
Venus in a green silk goun,
The auld mune shak's her gowden feathers,
Their starry talk's a wheen o' blethers★,
Nane for thee a thochtie sparin',
Earth, thou bonnie broukit bairn!
 – *But greet★, an' in your tears ye'll droun*   weep
 The haill clanjamfrie★!   motley bunch

The Watergaw

Ae weet forenicht i' the yow-trummle[1]
I saw yon antrin★ thing,   strange
A watergaw★ wi' its chitterin'★ licht rainbow/shivering
Ayont★ the on-ding★;   beyond/storm
An' I thocht o' the last wild look ye gied
Afore ye deed!

There was nae reek★ i' the laverock's ★ hoose smoke/lark's
That nicht – an' nane i' mine;
But I hae thocht o' that foolish licht

---

[1] 'Ewe-tremble' (shearing time).

Ever sin' syne;   10
An' I think that mebbe at last I ken
What your look meant then.

Crowdieknowe

Oh to be at Crowdieknowe
When the last trumpet blaws,
An' see the deid come loupin' owre
The auld grey wa's.

Muckle men wi' tousled beards,
I grat★ at as a bairn   wept
'll scramble frae the croodit★ clay   crowded
Wi' feck★ o' swearin'.   plenty

An' glower at God an' a' his gang
O' angels i' the lift★   10   sky
– Thae trashy bleezin' French-like folk
Wha gar'd★ them shift!   made

Fain the weemun-folk'll seek
To mak' them haud their row
– *Fegs, God's no blate★ gin he stirs up*   shy
The men o' Crowdieknowe!

The Innumerable Christ

Other stars may have their Bethlehem, and their Calvary too.
– PROFESSOR J. Y. SIMPSON

Wha kens on whatna Bethlehems
Earth twinkles like a star the nicht,
An' whatna shepherds lift their heids
   In its unearthly licht?

'Yont a' the stars oor een can see
An' farther than their lichts can fly,
I' mony an unco★ warl' the nicht   strange
   The fatefu' bairnies cry.

I' mony an unco warl' the nicht
The lift gaes black as pitch at noon,   10
An' sideways on their chests the heids
   O' endless Christs rool doon.

An' when the earth's as cauld's the mune
An' a' its folk are lang syne deid,
On coontless stars the Babe maun★ cry   must
   An' the Crucified maun bleed.

Wheesht, Wheesht

Wheesht, wheesht, my foolish hert,
For weel ye ken
I widna ha'e ye stert
Auld ploys again.

It's guid to see her lie
Sae snod★, an' cool,   neat
A' lust o' lovin' by –
Wheest, wheest, ye fule!

Empty Vessel

I met ayont★ the cairney★   beyond/cairn
A lass wi' tousie★ hair   dishevelled
Singin' till★ a bairnie   to
That was nae langer there.

Wunds wi' warlds to swing
Dinna sing sae sweet,
The licht that bends owre a' thing★   everything
Is less ta'en up wi't.

Scunner

Your body derns★   hides
In its graces again
As dreich grun' does
In the gowden grain,
And oot o' the daith
O' pride you rise
Wi' beauty yet
For a hauf-disguise.

The skinklan' stars
Are but distant dirt.   10
Tho' fer owre near
You are still – whiles – girt
Wi' the bonnie licht
You bood ha'e tint★   lost
– And I lo'e a Love
Wi' a scunner★ in't.   disgust, blemish

A Drunk Man Looks at the Thistle

This long poem, MacDiarmid's masterpiece, is the most important work of Scottish verse in our century. David Daiches, perhaps the best known modern Scottish critic, calls *A Drunk Man* 'the greatest long poem in Scottish literature and one of the greatest in any literature.'[1] MacDiarmid was well read in the traditions of both Scottish and world letters, and the *Thistle* is a tissue of literary references. The narrator's drunkenness, for example, is akin to the dream-vision of medieval poetry and to the prophetic mysticism of the romantics, such as Blake or Shelley. The thistle the drunk man confronts represents Scotland itself, of course, and as such is in a constant state of change. In the poem Scotland becomes ultimately the centre of the world and the riddle of its identity represents as well the unresolved puzzle of existence and man's place in the universe.

The range of styles is wide, but artfully complementary. The simplicity of the basic form – the dramatic monologue – and the basic rhythm and verse structure – the ballad – is a necessary counterpoint to the philosophical complexity and the endless shifts in moods and perspectives. Similarly, the almost homespun circumstances – the stereotypical Scottish drunk, his colloquial outbursts, the thistle itself, the many easily-remembered lines from Burns – give us islands of familiarity amid a sea of strange words and literary references.

T. S. Eliot's multi-cultured epic of modern fragmented life, *The Waste Land,* had been published four years before, in 1922, and made a considerable impact upon MacDiarmid, who refers to Eliot several times in *A Drunk Man*. The Scottish poem reflects Eliot's sense of contemporary spiritual emptiness, his quest motif, and his all-encompassing literary and historical range. To emphasise both the universality of his theme, and his conviction that modern Scots and modern Scotland must become thoroughly European, MacDiarmid utilises sizable whole passages (placed in italics) he derived from a number of modern poets: the Russians, Alexander Blok and Zinaida Hippius, the German Else Lasker-Schüler, the Belgian, George Ramaeker, and the Frenchman, Edmond Rocher – this besides countless other literary echoes. *A Drunk Man* has been much studied. Recommended as a particularly sensible and clear short analysis of the poem and its sources is the chapter, 'Sic a Nicht,' in Alan Bold's *MacDiarmid: A Critical Biography* (1988).

I amna' fou'★ sae muckle as tired – deid dune.	full (drunk)
It's gey and hard wark' coupin' gless for gless	
Wi' Cruivie and Gilsanquhar and the like,	
And I'm no' juist as bauld as aince I wes.	
The elbuck★ fankles★ in the coorse o' time,	elbow/weakens
The sheckle's no' sae souple, and the thrapple★	throat
Grows deef and dour: nae langer up and doun	
Gleg★ as a squirrel speils★ the Adam's apple.	agile/climbs
Forbye, the stuffie's no' the real Mackay,	
The sun's sel' aince, as sune as ye began it,	10
Riz in your vera saul: but what keeks in	
Noo is in truth the vilest 'saxpenny planet.'	
And as the worth's gane doun the cost has risen.	
Yin canna throw the cockles o' yin's hert	
Wi'oot ha'en' cauld feet noo, jalousin'★ what	suspecting
The wife'll say (I dinna blame her fur't).	

---

[1] 'Hugh MacDiarmid's Early Poetry', *Hugh MacDiarmid: A Critical Survey* (1972).

It's robbin' Peter to pey Paul at least...
And a' that's Scotch aboot it is the name,
Like a' thing else ca'd Scottish nooadays
– A' destitute o' speerit juist the same.   20

(To prove my saul is Scots I maun begin
Wi' what's still deemed Scots and the folk expect,
And spire up syne by visible degrees
To heichts whereo' the fules ha'e never recked.

But aince I get them there I'll whummle★ them   overturn
And souse the craturs in the nether deeps,
– For it's nae choice, and ony man s'ud wish
To dree★ the goat's weird★ tae as weel's the sheep's!)   suffer/fate

Heifetz in tartan, and Sir Harry Lauder!
Whaur's Isadora Duncan dancin' noo?   30
Is Mary Garden in Chicago still
And Duncan Grant in Paris – and me fou'?

Sic transit gloria Scotia – a' the floo'ers
O' the Forest are wede awa'. (A blin' bird's nest
Is aiblins biggin' in the thistle tho'? . . .
And better blin' if'ts brood is like the rest!)

You canna gang to a Burns supper even
Wi'oot some wizened scrunt o' a knock-knee
Chinee turns roon to say, 'Him Haggis – velly goot!'
And ten to wan the piper is a Cockney.   40

No' wan in fifty kens a wurd Burns wrote
But misapplied is a'body's property,
And gin there was his like alive the day
They'd be the last a kennin' haund to gie –

Croose★ London Scotties wi' their braw shirt fronts   proud
And a' their fancy freen's, rejoicin'
That similah gatherings in Timbuctoo,
Bagdad – and Hell, nae doot – are voicin'

Burns' sentiments o' universal love,
In pidgin' English or in wild-fowl Scots,   50
And toastin' ane wha's nocht to them but an
Excuse for faitherin' Genius wi' *their* thochts.

A' *they've* to say was aften said afore
A lad was born in Kyle to blaw aboot.
What unco★ fate mak's him the dumpin'-grun'   strange
For a' the sloppy rubbish they jaw oot?

Mair nonsense has been uttered in his name
Than in ony's barrin' liberty and Christ.
If this keeps spreedin' as the drink declines,
Syne turns to tea, wae's me for the *Zeitgeist!*   60

Rabbie, wad'st thou wert here – the warld hath need,
And Scotland mair sae, o' the likes o' thee!
The whisky that aince moved your lyre's become
A laxative for a' loquacity.

O gin they'd stegh★ their guts and haud their wheesht   stuff
I'd thole★ it, for 'a man's a man,' I ken,   endure
But though the feck ha'e plenty o' the 'a' that,'   talking nonsense
They're nocht but zoologically men.

I'm haverin'★, Rabbie, but ye understaun'
It gets my dander up to see your star   70
A bauble in Babel, banged like a saxpence
'Twixt Burbank's Baedeker and Bleistein's cigar.

There's nane sae ignorant but think they can
Expatiate on you, if on nae ither.
The sumphs ha'e ta'en you at your wurd, and, fegs!
The foziest o' them claims to be a – Brither!

Syne 'Here's the cheenge' – the star o' Rabbie Burns.
Sma' cheenge, 'Twinkle, Twinkle.' The memory slips
As G. K. Chesterton heaves up to gi'e
'The Immortal Memory' in a huge eclipse,   80

Or somebody else as famous if less fat.
You left the like in Embro' in a scunner★   disgust
To booze wi' thieveless★ cronies sic as me.   feeble
I'se warrant you'd shy clear o' a' the hunner

Odd Burns' Clubs tae, or ninety-nine o' them,
And haud your birthday in a different kip★   joint, brothel
Whaur your name isna' ta'en in vain – as Christ
Gied a' Jerusalem's Pharisees the slip,

– Christ wha'd ha'e been Chief Rabbi gin he'd lik't! –
Wi' publicans and sinners to foregather,   90
But, losh! the publicans noo are Pharisees,
And I'm no' shair o' maist the sinners either.

But that's aside the point! I've got fair waun'ert.
It's no' that I'm sae fou' as juist deid dune,
And dinna ken as muckle's whaur I am
Or hoo I've come to sprawl here 'neth the mune.

That's it! It isna me that's fou' at a',
But the fu' mune, the doited jade, that's led
Me fer agley, or 'mogrified the warld.
– For a' I ken I'm safe in my ain bed.   100

Jean! Jean! Gin she's no' here it's no' oor bed,
Or else I'm dreamin' deep and canna wauken,
But it's a fell queer dream if this is no'
A real hillside – and thae things thistles and bracken!

It's hard wark haud'n by a thocht worth ha'en'
And harder speakin't, and no' for ilka man;
Maist Thocht's like whisky – a thoosan' under proof,
And a sair price is pitten on't even than.

As Kirks wi' Christianity ha'e dune,
Burns' Clubs wi' Burns – wi' a'thing it's the same,   110
The core o' ocht is only for the few,
Scorned by the mony, thrang★ wi'ts empty name.   busy

And a' the names in History mean nocht
To maist folk but★ 'ideas o' their ain,)   without
The vera opposite o' onything
The Deid 'ud awn gin they cam' back again.

A greater Christ, a greater Burns, may come.
The maist they'll dae is to gi'e bigger pegs
To folly and conceit to hank their rubbish on.
They'll cheenge folks' talk but no their natures, fegs!   120

I maun feed frae the common trough ana'
Whaur a' the lees o' hope are jumbled up;
While centuries like pigs are slorpin' owre't
Sall my wee 'oor be cryin': 'Let pass this cup'?

In wi' your gruntle then, puir wheengin' saul,
Lap up the ugsome aidle wi' the lave★,   rest
What gin it's your ain vomit that you swill
And frae Life's gantin' and unfaddomed grave?

I doot I'm geylies mixed, like Life itsel',
But I was never ane that thocht to pit   130
An ocean in a mutchkin. As the haill's
Mair than the pairt sae I than reason yet.

I dinna haud the warld's end in my heid
As maist folk think they dae; nor filter truth
In fishy gills through which its tides may poor
For ony animalculae forsooth.

I lauch to see my crazy little brain
– And ither folks' – tak'n itsel' seriously,
And in a sudden lowe o' fun my saul
Blinks dozent★ as the owl I ken't to be.   140   stupid

I'll ha'e nae hauf-way hoose, but aye be whaur
Extremes meet – it's the only way I ken
To dodge the curst conceit o' bein' richt
That damns the vast majority o' men.

I'll bury nae heid like an ostrich's,
Nor yet believe my een and naething else.
My senses may advise me, but I'll be
Mysel' nae maitter what they tell's . . .

I ha'e nae doot some foreign philosopher
Has wrocht a system oot to justify   150
A' this: but I'm a Scot wha blin'ly follows
Auld Scottish instincts, and I winna try.

For I've nae faith in ocht I can explain,
And stert whaur the philosophers leave aff,
Content to glimpse its loops I dinna ettle★   struggle
To land the sea serpent's sel' wi' ony gaff.

Like staundin' water in a pocket o'
Impervious clay I pray I'll never be,
Cut aff and self-sufficient, but let reenge
Heichts o' the lift and benmaist deeps o' sea.   160

Water! Water! There was owre muckle o't
In yonder whisky, sae I'm in deep water
(And gin I could wun hame I'd be in het,
For even Jean maun natter, natter, natter) . . .

And in the toon that I belang tae
– What tho'ts Montrose or Nazareth? –
Helplessly the folk continue
To lead their livin' death! . . .

¹*At darknin' hings abune the howff*★   tavern
A weet and wild and eisenin'★ *air.*   170   lustful
Spring's spirit wi' its waesome sough
Rules owre the drucken stramash★ *there.*   commotion

And heich abune the vennel's★ *pokiness,*   lane's
Whaur a' the white-weshed cottons lie;
The Inn's sign blinters★ *in the mochiness,*   gleams
And lood and shrill the bairnies cry.

The hauflins 'yont the burgh boonds
Gang ilka nicht, and a' the same,
Their bonnets cocked; their bluid that stounds
Is playin' at a fine auld game.   180

And on the lochan there, hauf-herted
Wee screams and creakin' oar-locks soon',
And in the lift, heich, hauf-averted,
The mune looks owre the yirdly★ *roon'.*   earthly

And ilka★ *evenin', derf*★ *and serious*   every/secret, quiet
(Jean ettles nocht o' this, puir lass),
In liquor, raw yet still mysterious,
A'e freend's aye mirrored in my glass.

---

¹ From Alexander Blok, 'The Stranger'.

Ahint★ the sheenin' coonter gruff   behind
Thrang barmen ding the tumblers doun   190
'In vino veritas' cry rough
And reid-een'd fules that in it droon.

But ilka evenin' fey★ and fremt★   strange/quiet
(Is it a dream nae wauk'nin' proves?)
As to a trystin'-place undreamt,
A silken leddy darkly moves.

Slow gangs she by the drunken anes,
And lanely by the winnock sits;
Frae'r robes, atour★ the sunken anes,   around
A rooky dwamin'★ perfume flits.   200   swooning,
                                                                    dreaming

Her gleamin' silks, the taperin'
O' her ringed fingers, and her feathers
Move dimly like a dream wi'in,
While endless faith aboot them gethers.

I seek, in this captivity,
To pierce the veils that darklin' fa'
— See white clints★ slidin' to the sea,   cliffs
And hear the horns o' Elfland blaw.

I ha'e dark secrets' turns and twists,
A sun is gi'en to me to haud,   210
The whisky in my bluid insists,
And spiers★ my benmaist history, lad.   asks

And owre my brain the flitterin'
O' the dim feathers gangs aince mair,
And, faddomless, the dark blue glitterin'
O' twa een in the ocean there.

My soul stores up this wealth unspent,
The key is safe and nane's but mine.
You're richt, auld drunk impenitent,
I ken it tae — the truth's in wine!   220

The munelicht's like a lookin'-glass,
The thistle's like mysel',
But whaur ye've gane, my bonnie lass,
Is mair than I can tell.

Were you a vision o' mysel',
Transmuted by the mellow liquor?
Neist time I glisk★ you in a glass,   glimpse
I'se warrant I'll mak' siccar.

A man's a clean contrairy sicht
Turned this way in-ootside,   230
And, fegs, I feel like Dr Jekyll
Tak'n guid tent★ o Mr Hyde . . .   care, heed

Gurly thistle – hic – you canna
Daunton★ me wi’ your shaggy mien,   frighten
I’m sair – hic – needin’ a shave,
That’s plainly to be seen.

But what aboot it – hic – aboot it?
Mony a man’s been that afore.
It’s no’ a fact that in his lugs★   ears
A wund like this need roar! . . .   240

¹*I hae forekent ye! O I hae forekent.*
The years forecast your face afore they went.
A licht I canna thole is in the lift.
I bide in silence your slow-comin’ pace.
The ends o’ space are bricht: at last – oh swift!
While terror clings to me – an unkent★ face!   unknown

Ill-faith stirs in me as she comes at last,
The features lang forekent . . . are unforecast.
O it gangs hard wi’ me, I am forespent.
Deid dreams ha’e beaten me and a face unkent 250
And generations that I thocht unborn
Hail the strange Goddess frae my hert’s-hert torn! . . .

Or dost thou mak’ a thistle o’ me, wumman? But for thee
I were as happy as the munelicht, withoot care,
But thocht o’ thee – o’ thy contempt and ire –
Turns hauf the warld into the youky★ thistle there, itchy

Feedin’ on the munelicht and transformin’ it
To this wanrestfu’ growth that winna let me be.
The munelicht is the freedom that I’d ha’e
But for this cursed Conscience thou hast set in me. 260

It is morality, the knowledge o’ Guid and Ill,
Fear, shame, pity, like a will and wilyart★ growth, unsure
That kills a’ else wi’in its reach and craves
Nae less at last than a’ the warld to gi’e it scouth★. scope

The need to wark, the need to think, the need to be,
And a’ thing that twists Life into a certain shape
And interferes wi’ perfect liberty –
These feed this Frankenstein that nae man can escape.

For ilka thing a man can be or think or dae
Aye leaves a million mair unbeen, unthocht, undune, 270
Till his puir warped performance is,
To a’ that micht ha’ been, a thistle to the mune.

---

¹ From Alexander Blok, ‘The Unknown Woman’.

It is Mortality itsel' – the mortal coil,
Mockin' Perfection, Man afore the Throne o' God
He yet has bigged himsel', Man torn in twa
And glorious in the lift★ and grisly on the sod! . . .   sky

There's nocht sae sober as a man blin' drunk.
I maun ha'e got an unco bellyfu'
To jaw like this – and yet what I am sayin'
Is a' the apter, aiblins, to be true.   280

This munelicht's fell like whisky noo I see't
– Am I a thingum mebbe that is kept
Preserved in spirits in a muckle bottle
Lang centuries efter sin' wi' Jean I slept?

– Mounted on a hillside, wi' the thistles
And bracken for verisimilitude,
Like a stuffed bird on metal like a brainch,
Or a seal on a stump o' rock-like wood?

Or am I juist a figure in a scene
O' Scottish life a.d. one-nine-two-five?   290
The haill thing kelters★ like a theatre claith   ripples
Till I micht fancy that I was alive!

I dinna ken and nae man ever can.
I micht be in my ain bed efter a'.
The haill damned thing's a dream for ocht we ken,
– The Warld and Life and Daith, Heaven, Hell ana'.

We maun juist tak' things as we find them then,
And mak' a kirk or mill o' them as we can,
– And yet I feel this muckle thistle's staun'in'
Atween me and the mune as pairt o' a Plan.   300

It isna there – nor me – by accident.
We're brocht thegither for a certain reason,
Ev'n gin it's naething mair than juist to gi'e
My jaded soul a necessary *frisson*.

I never saw afore a thistle quite
Sae intimately, or at sic an 'oor.
There's something in the fickle licht that gi'es
A different life to't and an unco poo'er.

¹ '*Rootit on gressless peaks, whaur its erect
And jaggy leafs, austerly cauld and dumb,*   310
Haud the slow scaly serpent in respect,
The Gothic thistle, whaur the insect's hum
Soon's fer aff; lifts abune the rock it scorns

---

¹ The source for this passage is 'The Thistle', identified in line 339 and elsewhere as by the Belgian poet,
George Ramaekers.

Its rigid virtue for the Heavens to see.
The too'ering boulders gaird it. And the bee
Mak's honey frae the roses on its thorns.'

But that's a Belgian refugee, of coorse.
This Freudian complex has somehoo slunken
Frae Scotland's soul – the Scots aboulia –
Whilst a' its *terra nullius*[1] is *betrunken*★.   320   intoxicated

And a' the country roon' aboot it noo
Lies clapt and shrunken syne like somebody wha
Has lang o' seven devils been possessed;
Then when he turns a corner tines★ them a',   loses

Or like a body that has tint★ its soul,   lost
Perched like a monkey on its heedless kist★,   chest
Or like a sea that peacefu' fa's again
When frae its deeps an octopus is fished.

I canna feel it has to dae wi' me
Mair than a composite diagram o'   330
Cross-sections o' my forbears' organs
– And mine – 'ud bring a kind o' freen'ly glow.

And yet like bindweed through my clay it's run,
And a' my folks' – it's queer to see't unroll.
My ain soul looks me in the face, as 'twere,
And mair than my ain soul – my nation's soul!

And sall a Belgian pit it into words
And sing a sang to't syne, and no' a Scot?
Oors is a wilder thistle, and Ramaekers
Canna bear aff the gree★ – avaunt the thocht!   340   prize

To meddle wi' the thistle and to pluck
The figs frae't is my metier, I think.
Awak', my muse, and gin you're in puir fettle,
We aye can blame it on th' inferior drink.

T. S. Eliot – it's a Scottish name –
Afore he wrote 'The Waste Land' s'ud ha'e come
To Scotland here. He wad ha'e written
A better poem syne – like this, by gum!

Type o' the Wissenschaftsfeindlichkeit,
Begriffsmüdigkeit that has gar't★   350   made
Men try Morphologies der Weltgeschichte,
And mad Expressionismus syne in Art.

---

[1] No man's land.

¹A shameless thing, for ilka vileness able,
¹*A shameless thing, for ilka vileness able,*
It is deid grey as dust, the dust o' a man.
I perish o' a nearness I canna win awa' frae,
Its deidly coils aboot my buik are thrawn.

A shaggy poulp, embracin' me and stingin',
And as a serpent cauld agen' my hert.
Its scales are poisoned shafts that jag me to the quick
— And waur than them's my scunner's fearfu' smert!   360

O that its prickles were a knife indeed,
But it is thowless, flabby, dowf*; and numb.   dull, inert
Sae sluggishly it drains my benmaist* life   inmost
A dozent dragon, dreidfu', deef, and dumb.

In mum obscurity it twines its obstinate rings
And hings caressin'ly, its purpose whole;
And this deid thing, whale-white obscenity,
This horror that I writhe in — is my soul!

Is it the munelicht or a leprosy
That spreids aboot me; and a thistle   370
Or my ain skeleton through wha's bare banes
A fiendish wund's begood to whistle?

The devil's lauchter has a *hwll* like this.
My face has flown open like a lid
— And gibberin' on the hillside there
Is a' humanity sae lang has hid! . . .

My harns* are seaweed — when the tide is in   brains
They swall like blethers and in comfort float,
But when the tide is oot they lie like gealed
And runkled* auld bluid-vessels in a knot!   380   wrinkled

The munelicht ebbs and flows and wi't my thocht,
Noo' movin' mellow and noo lourd* and rough.   heavy
I ken what I am like in Life and Daith,
But Life and Daith for nae man are enough . . .

And O! to think that there are members o'
St Andrew's Societies sleepin' soon',
Wha to the papers wrote afore they bedded
On regimental buttons or buckled shoon,

Or use o' England whaur the U.K.'s meent,
Or this or that anent the Blue Saltire,   390
Recruitin', pedigrees, and Gude kens what,
Filled wi' a proper patriotic fire!

---

¹ From Zinaida Hippius, 'Psyche'.

Wad I were them – they've chosen a better pairt,
The couthie★ craturs, than the ane I've ta'en,   smug
Tyauvin'★ wi' this root-hewn Scottis soul;   struggling
A fer, fer better pairt – except for men.

Nae doot they're sober, as a Scot ne'er was,
Each tethered to a punctual-snorin' missus,
Whilst I, puir fule, owre continents unkent
And wine-dark oceans waunder like Ulysses . . .   400

¹The Mune sits on my bed the nicht unsocht,
And mak's my soul obedient to her will;
And in the dumbdeid★, still as dreams are still   middle-night
Her pupils narraw to bricht threids that thrill
Aboot the sensuous windin's o' her thocht.

But ilka windin' has its coonter-pairt
– The opposite 'thoot which it couldna be –
In some wild kink or queer perversity
O' this great thistle, green wi' jealousy,
That breenges 'Twixt the munelicht and my hert . . .   410

Plant, what are you then? Your leafs
Mind me o' the pipes' lood drone
– And a' your purple tops
Are the pirly-wirly notes
That gang staggerin' owre them as they groan.

Or your leafs are alligators
That ha'e gobbled owre a haill
Company o' Heilant sodgers,
And left naethin' but the toories
O' their Balmoral bonnets to tell the tale.   420

Or a muckle bellows blawin'
Wi' the sperks a' whizzin' oot;
Or green tides sweeshin'
'Neth heich-skeich stars,
Or centuries fleein' doun a water-chute.

Grinnin' gargoyle by a saint,
Mephistopheles in Heaven,
Skeleton at a tea-meetin',
Missin' link – or creakin'
Hinge atween the deid and livin' . . .   430

(I kent a Terrier★ in a sham fecht aince,   Territorial
Wha louped a dyke and landed on a thistle.
He'd naething on ava aneth his kilt.
Schonberg has nae notation for his whistle.) . . .

----

¹ From Else Lasker-Schuler, 'Sphynx'.

(Gin you're surprised a village drunk
Foreign references s'ud fool in,
You ha'ena the respect you s'ud
For oor guid Scottish schoolin'.

For we've the maist unlikely folk
Aye braggin' o' oor lear★, 440 learning
And, tho' I'm drunk, for Scotland's sake
I tak my barrowsteel here!

Yet Europe's faur eneuch for me,
Puir fule, when bairns ken mair
O' th' ither warld than I o' this
– But that's no' here nor there!) . . .

Guid sakes, I'm in a dreidfu' state.
I'll ha'e nae inklin' sune
Gin I'm the drinker or the drink,
The thistle or the mune. 450

I'm geylies feart I couldna tell
Gin I su'd lay me doon
The difference betwixt the warld
And my ain heid gaen' roon'! . . .

Drums in the Walligate, pipes in the air,
Come and hear the cryin' o' the Fair.

A' as it used to be, when I was a loon★ lad
On Common-Ridin' Day in the Muckle Toon.

The bearer twirls the Bannock-and-Saut-Herrin',
The Croon o' Roses through the lift is farin', 460

The aucht-fit thistle wallops on hie;
In heather besoms★ a' the hills gang by. brooms

But noo it's a' the fish o' the sea
Nailed on the roond o' the Earth to me.

Beauty and Love that are bobbin' there;
Syne the breengin' growth that alane I bear;

And Scotland followin' on ahint
For threepenny bits spleet-new frae the mint.

Drums in the Walligate, pipes in the air,
The wallopin'★ thistle is ill to bear. 470 dancing

But I'll dance the nicht wi' the stars o' Heaven
In the Mairket Place as shair's I'm livin'.

Easy to carry roses or herrin',
And the lave may weel their threepenny bits earn.

Devil the star! It's Jean I'll ha'e
Again as she was on her weddin' day . . .

Nerves in stounds o' delight,
Muscles in pride o' power,
Bluid as wi' roses dight
Life's toppin' pinnacles owre,   480
The thistle yet'll unite
Man and the Infinite!

Swippert★ and swith★ wi' virr   active/quick
In the howes★ o' man's hert   hollows
Forever its muckle roots stir
Like a Leviathan astert,
Till'ts coils like a thistle's leafs
Sweep space wi' levin★ sheafs.   lightning

Frae laichest★ deeps o' the ocean   lowest
It rises in flight upon flight,   490
And 'yont its uttermaist motion
Can still set roses alight,
As else unreachable height
Fa's under its triumphin' sight.

Here is the root that feeds
The shank wi' the blindin' wings
Dwinin' abuneheid to gleids
Like stars in their keethin' rings,
And blooms in sunrise and sunset
Inowre★ Eternity's yett★.   500   over/gate

Lay haud o' my hert and feel
Fountains ootloupin' the starns
Or see the Universe reel
Set gaen' by my eident★ harns,   diligent
Or test the strength o' my spauld★   shoulder
The wecht o' a' thing to hauld!

– The howes o' Man's hert are bare,
The Dragon's left them for good,
There's nocht but naethingness there,
The hole whaur the Thistle stood,   510
That rootless and radiant flies
A Phoenix in Paradise! . . .

Masoch and Sade
Turned into ane
Havoc ha'e made
O' my a'e brain.

Weel, gin it's Sade
Let it be said
They've made me mad
– That'll da'e instead.   520

But it's no' instead
In Scots, but insteed.
– The life they've led
In my puir heid.

But aince I've seen
In the thistle here
A' that they've been
I'll aiblins wun clear.

Thistleless fule,
You'll ha'e nocht left   530
But the hole frae which
Life's struggle is reft! . . .

Reason ser's nae end but pleasure,
Truth's no' an end but a means
To a wider knowledge o' life
And a keener interest in't.

We wha are poets and artists
Move frae inklin' to inklin',
And live for oor antrin★ lichtnin's   rare
In the haingles★ atweenwhiles,   540   dullness

Laich★ as the feck★ o' mankind   low/mass
Whence we breenge in unkennable shapes
– *Crockats up, hair kaimed to the lift,*
And no' to cree legs wi'! . . .

We're ootward boond frae Scotland.
Guid-bye, fare-ye-weel; guid-bye, fare-ye-weel.
– A' the Scots that ever wur
Gang ootward in a creel.

We're ootward boond frae Scotland.
Guid-bye, fare-ye-weel; guid-bye, fare-ye-weel.   550
The cross-tap is a monkey-tree
That nane o' us can spiel★.   climb

We've never seen the Captain,
But the first mate is a Jew.
We've shipped aboord Eternity.
Adieu, kind freends, adieu! . . .

In the creel or on the gell★   go
O' oor coutribat★ and ganien★.   struggle/boast
What gin ithers see or hear
Naething but a gowkstorm?   560

Gin you stop the galliard
To teach them hoo to dance,
There comes in Corbaudie★   difficulty
And turns their gammons★ up! . . .   hooves

You vegetable cat's melody!
Your *Concert Miaulant*★ is   'Concert of Meows'
A triumph o' discord shairly,
And suits my fancy fairly
– I'm shair that Scott'll agree
He canna vie wi' this . . .   570

Said my body to my mind,
'I've been startled whiles to find,
When Jean has been in bed wi' me,
A kind o' Christianity!'

To my body said my mind,
'But your benmaist thocht you'll find
Was 'Bother what I think I feel
– Jean kens the set o' my bluid owre weel,
And lauchs to see me in the creel
O' my courage-bag confined.' . . .   580

I wish I kent the physical basis
O' a' life's seemin' airs and graces.

It's queer the thochts a kittled cull★   testicle
Can lowse★ or splairgin'★ glit annul.   loose/splattering

Man's spreit is wi' his ingangs twined
In ways that he can ne'er unwind.

A wumman whiles a bawaw★ gi'es   sneer
That clean abaws him gin he sees.

Or wi' a movement o' a leg
Shows'm his mind is juist a geg★.   590   deception

I'se warrant Jean 'ud no' be lang
In findin' whence this thistle sprang.

Mebbe it's juist because I'm no'
Beddit wi' her that gars it grow! . . .

A luvin' wumman is a licht
That shows a man his waefu' plicht,
Bleezin' steady on ilka bane,
Wrigglin' sinnen★ an' twinin' vein,   sinews
Or fleerin'★ quick an' gane again,   flaring
And the mair scunnersome the sicht   600
The mair for love and licht he's fain
Till clear and chitterin'★ and nesh★   shivering/alert
Move a' the miseries o' his flesh . . .

O lass, wha see'est me
As I daur hardly see,
I marvel that your bonny een
Are as they hadna' seen.

Through a' my self-respect
They see the truth abject
– *Gin you could pierce their blindin' licht*   610
You'd see a fouler sicht! . . .

O wha's the bride that cairries the bunch
O' thistles blinterin' white?
Her cuckold bridegroom little dreids
What he sall ken this nicht.

For closer than gudeman can come
And closer to'r than hersel',
Wha didna need her maidenheid
Has wrocht his purpose fell.

O wha's been here afore me, lass,   620
And hoo did he get in?
– *A man that deed or I was born*
This evil thing has din.

And left, as it were on a corpse,
Your maidenheid to me?
– *Nae lass, gudeman, sin' Time began*
's hed ony mair to gi'e.

But I can gi'e ye kindness, lad,
And a pair o' willin' hands,
And you sall ha'e my briests like stars,   630
My limbs like willow wands,

And on my lips ye'll heed nae mair,
And in my hair forget,
The seed o' a' the men that in
My virgin womb ha'e met . . .

Millions o' wimmen bring forth in pain
Millions o' bairns that are no' worth ha'en.

Wull ever a wumman be big again
Wi's muckle's a Christ? Yech, there's nae sayin'.

Gin that's the best that you ha'e comin',   640
Fegs but I'm sorry for you, wumman!

Yet a'e thing's certain. – Your faith is great.
Whatever happens, you'll no' be blate⋆! . . .   shy

Mary lay in jizzen⋆   childbirth
As it were claith o' gowd,
But it's in orra⋆ duds   off-hand, shabby
Ilka ither bairntime's row'd.

Christ had never toothick,
Christ was never seeck,
But Man's a fiky★ bairn   650   troublesome
Wi' bellythraw, ripples, and worm–i'–the–cheek! . . .

Dae what ye wull ye canna parry
This skeleton–at–the–feast that through the starry
Maze o' the warld's intoxicatin' soiree
Claughts★ ye, as micht at an affrontit quean   clutches
A bastard wean!

Prood mune, ye needna thring your shouder there,
And at your puir get like a snawstorm stare,
It's yours – there's nae denyin't – and I'm shair
You'd no' enjoy the evenin' much the less   660
Gin you'd but openly confess!

Dod! It's an eaten and a spewed–like thing,
Fell like a little–bodie's changeling,
And it's nae credit t'ye that you s'ud bring
The like to life – yet, gi'en a mither's love,
– Hee, hee! – wha kens hoo't micht improve? . . .

Or is this Heaven, this yalla licht,
And I the aft'rins o' the Earth,
Or sic's in this wanchancy★ time   unfortunate
May weel fin' sudden birth?   670

The roots that wi' the worms compete
Hauf–publish me upon the air.
The struggle that divides me still
Is seen fu' plainly there.

The thistle's shank scarce holes the grun',
My grave'll spare nae mair I doot.
– The crack's fu' wide; the shank's fu' strang;
A' that I was is oot.

My knots o' nerves that struggled sair
Are weel reflected in the herb;   680
My crookit instincts were like this,
As sterile and acerb.

My self–tormented spirit took
The shape repeated in the thistle;
Sma' beauty jouked★ my rawny★ banes   avoided/prominent
And maze o' gristle.

I seek nae peety, Paraclete,
And, fegs, I think the joke is rich
– Pairt soul, pairt skeleton's come up;
They kentna which was which! . . .   690

Thou Daith in which my life
Sae vain a thing can seem,
Frae whatna source d'ye borrow
Your devastatin' gleam?

Nae doot that hidden sun
'Ud look fu' wae ana',
Gin I could see it in the licht
That frae the Earth you draw! . . .

Shudderin' thistle, gi'e owre, gi'e owre!
A'body's gi'en in to the facts o' life;   700
The impossible truth'll triumph at last,
And mock your strife.

Your sallow leafs can never thraw,
Wi' a' their oorie* shakin',   unusual
Ae doot into the hert o' life
That it may be mistak'n . . .

O Scotland is
THE barren fig.
Up, carles, up*   peasants, fellows
And roond it jig.   710

Auld Moses took
A dry stick and
Instantly it
Floo'ered in his hand.

Pu' Scotland up,
And wha can say
It winna bud
And blossom tae.

A miracle's
Oor only chance.   720
Up, carles, up
And let us dance!

Puir Burns, wha's bouquet like a shot kail* blaws   cabbage
– Will this rouch sicht no' gi'e the orchids pause?
The Gairdens o' the Muses may be braw,
But nane like oors can breenge and eat ana'!

And owre the kailyaird-wa' Dunbar they've flung,
And a' their countrymen that e'er ha'e sung
For ither than ploomen's lugs or to enrichen
Plots on Parnassus set apairt for kitchen.   730

Ploomen and ploomen's wives – shades o' the Manse
May weel be at the heid o' sic a dance,
As through the polish't ha's o' Europe leads
The rout o' bagpipes, haggis, and sheep's heids!

The vandal Scot! Frae Branksome's deidly barrow
I struggle yet to free a'e winsome marrow,
To show what Scotland micht ha'e hed instead
O' this preposterous Presbyterian breed.

(Gin Glesca folk are tired o' Hengler,
And still need breid and circuses, there's Spengler,   740
Or gin ye s'ud need mair than ane to teach ye,
Then learn frae Dostoevski and frae Nietzsche.

And let the lesson be – to be yersel's,
Ye needna fash★ gin it's to be ocht else.   trouble
To be yersel's – and to mak' that worth bein',
Nae harder job to mortals has been gi'en.

To save your souls fu' mony o' ye are fain,
But de'il a dizzen to mak' it worth the daein'.
I widna gi'e five meenits wi' Dunbar
For a' the millions o' ye as ye are).   750

I micht ha'e been contentit wi' the Rose[1]
Gin I'd had ony reason to suppose
That what the English dae can e'er mak' guid
For what Scots dinna – and first and foremaist should.

I micht ha'e been contentit – gin the feck
O' my ain folk had groveled wi' less respec',
But their obsequious devotion
Made it for me a criminal emotion.

I micht ha'e been contentit – ere I saw
That there were fields on which it couldna draw,   760
(While strang-er roots ran under't) and a'e threid
O't drew frae Scotland a' that it could need,

And left the maist o' Scotland fallow
(Save for the patch on which the kail-blades wallow),
And saw hoo ither countries' genius drew
Elements like mine that in a rose ne'er grew . . .

Gin the threid haud'n us to the rose were snapt
There's no' a'e petal o't that 'ud be clapt.
A' Scotland gi'es gangs but to jags or stalk,
The bloom is English – and 'ud ken nae lack! . . .   770

O drumlie★ clood o' crudity and cant,   dreary
Obliteratin' as the Easter rouk★   mist
That rows up frae the howes and droons the heichs,
And turns the country to a faceless spook.

---

[1] Of course, the emblem of England, but the symbol is used in many other ways as the poem goes on.

Like blurry shapes o' landmarks in the haar★   mist
The bonny idiosyncratic place-names loom,
Clues to the vieve★ and maikless life that's lain   vivid
Happit for centuries in an alien gloom . . .

Eneuch! For noo I'm in the mood,
Scotland, responsive to my thoughts,   780
Lichts mile by mile, as my ain nerves
Frae Maidenkirk to John o' Groats!

What are prophets and priests and kings,
What's ocht to the people o' Scotland?
Speak – and Cruivie'll goam★ at you,   gape
Gilsanquhar jalouse you're dottlin!

And Edinburgh and Glasgow
Are like ploomen in a pub.
They want to hear o' naething
But their ain foul hubbub . . .   790

The fules are richt; an extra thocht
Is neither here nor there.
Oor lives may differ as they like
– The self-same fate we share.

And whiles I wish I'd nae mair sense
Than Cruivie and Gilsanquhar,
And envy their rude health and curse
My gnawin' canker.

Guid sakes, ye dinna need to pass
Ony exam. to dee   800
– Daith canna tell a common flech
Frae a performin' flea! . . .

It sets you weel to slaver
To let sic gaadies fa'
– *The mune's the muckle white whale*
I seek in vain to kaa!

The Earth's my mastless samyn★,   deck
The thistle my ruined sail.
– Le'e go as you maun in the end,
And droon in your plumm o' ale! . . .   810

Clear keltie★ aff an' fill again   bumper
Withoot corneigh★ bein' cryit,   that's enough
The drink's aye best that follows a drink.
Clear keltie aff and try it.

Be't whisky gill or penny wheep★,   light beer
Or ony ither lotion,
We 'bood to ha'e a thimblefu' first,
And syne we'll toom★ an ocean! . . .   empty

'To Luna at the Craidle-and-Coffin
To sof'n her hert if owt can sof'n: —   820

Auld bag o' tricks, ye needna come
And think to stap me in your womb.

You needna fash to rax★ and strain.   stretch
Carline, I'll *no* be born again

In ony brat you can produce.
Carline, gi'e owre — O what's the use?

You pay nae heed but plop me in,
Syne shove me oot, and winna be din,

— Owre and owre, the same auld trick,
Cratur withoot climacteric! . . .   830

'Noo Cutty Sark's tint that ana,
And dances in her skin — Ha! Ha!

I canna ride awa' like Tam,
But e'en maun bide juist whaur I am.

I canna ride — and gin I could,
I'd sune be sorry I hedna stood,

For less than a' there is to see
'll never be owre muckle for me.

Cutty, gin you've mair to strip,
Aff wi't, lass — and let it rip!' . . .   840

Ilka pleesure I can ha'e
Ends like a dram ta'en yesterday.

And tho' to ha'e it I am lorn
— What better 'ud I be the morn? . . .

My belly on the gantrees★ there,   barrel-stand
The spigot frae my cullage★,   genitals
And wow but how the fizzin' yill★   ale
In spilth increased the ullage!

I was an anxious barrel, lad,
When first they tapped my bung.   850
They whistled me up, yet thro' the lift
My freaths★ like rainbows swung.   foam

Waesucks★, a pride for ony bar,   alas
The boast o' barleyhood,
Like Noah's Ark abune the faem
Maun float, a gantin'★ cude,   gaping

For I was thrawn fu' cock owre sune,
And wi' a single jaw★   spurt
I made the pub a blindin' swelth★,   whirlpool
And how'd★ the warld awa'! . . .   860   washed

What forest worn to the back-hauf's this,
What Eden brocht doon to a bean-swaup?
The thistle's to earth as the man
In the mune's to the mune, puir chap.

The haill warld's barkin' and fleein',
And this is its echo and aiker★,   ripple
A soond that arrears in my lug
Herrin'-banein' back to its maker,

A swaw★ like a flaw in a jewel   ripple
Or Nadryv★ jaloused in a man,   870   tragic flaw
Or Creation unbiggit again
To the draucht wi' which it began . . .

Abordage★ o' this toom houk's nae mowse★.   embarking/joke
It munks★ and's ill to lay haud o',   shies
As gin a man ettled to ride
On the shouders o' his ain shadow.

I canna biel't★; tho' steekin' an e'e   tie it
Tither's munkie★ wi' munebeam for knool★ in't,   noose/peg
For there's nae sta'-tree★ and the brute's awa'   tether
Wi' me kinkin'★ like foudrie★ ahint . . .   880   twisting/
                                                        lightning

Sae Eternity'll buff nor stye
For Time, and shies at a touch, man;
Yet aye in a belth★ o' Thocht   spurt
Comes alist like the Fleein' Dutchman . . .

As the worms'll breed in my corpe until
It's like a rice-puddin', the thistle
Has made an eel-ark o' the lift
Whaur elvers★ like skirl-in-the-pansizzle,   young eels

Like a thunder-plump on the sunlicht,
Or the slounge o' daith on my dreams,   890
Or as to a fair forfochen★ man   exhausted
A breedin' wife's beddiness seems,

Saragossa Sea, St Vitus' Dance,
A cafard in a brain's despite,
Or lunacy that thinks a' else
Is loony – and is dootless richt! . . .

Gin my thochts that circle like hobby-horses
'Udna loosen to nightmares I'd sleep;
For nocht but a chowed core's left whaur Jerusalem lay
Like aipples in a heap! . . .   900

It's a queer thing to tryst wi' a wumman
When the boss o' her body's gane,
And her banes in the wund as she comes
Dirl★ like a raff o' rain.   rattle

It's a queer thing to tryst wi' a wumman
When her ghaist frae abuneheid keeks★,   peeps
And you see in the licht o't that a'
You ha'e o'r's the cleiks★ . . .   shadow

What forest worn to the backhauf's this,
What Eden brocht doon to a beanswaup?   910
– A' the ferlies★ o' natur' spring frae the earth,   marvels
And into't again maun drap.

Animals, vegetables, what are they a'
But as thochts that a man has ha'en?
And Earth sall be like a toom skull syne.
– Whaur'll its thochts be then? . . .

The munelicht is my knowledge o' mysel',
Mysel' the thistle in the munelicht seen,
And hauf my shape has fund itsel' in thee
And hauf my knowledge in your piercin' een.   920

E'en as the munelicht's borrowed frae the sun
I ha'e my knowledge o' mysel' frae thee,
And much that nane but thee can e'er mak' clear,
Save my licht's frae the source, is dark to me.

Your acid tongue, vieve★ lauchter, and hawk's een,   vivid
And bluid that drobs like hail to quicken me,
Can turn the mid-day black or midnicht bricht,
Lowse me frae licht or eke frae darkness free.

Bite into me forever mair and lift
Me clear o' chaos in a great relief   930
Till, like this thistle in the munelicht growin',
I brak in roses owre a hedge o' grief . . .

I am like Burns, and ony wench
Can ser' me for a time.
Licht's in them a' – in some a sun,
In some the merest skime★.   flicker

I'm no' like Burns, and weel I ken,
Tho' ony wench can ser',
It's no' through mony but through yin
That ony man wuns fer . . .   940

I weddit thee frae fause love, lass,
To free thee and to free mysel';
But man and wumman tied for life
True can be and truth can tell.

Pit ony couple in a knot
They canna lowse and needna try,
And mair o' love at last they'll ken
– If ocht! – than joy'll alane descry.

For them as for the beasts, my wife,   950
A's fer frae dune when pleesure's owre,
And coontless difficulties gar
Ilk hert discover a' its power.

I dinna say that bairns alane
Are true love's task – a sairer task
Is aiblins to create oorsels
As we can be – it's that I ask.

Create oorsels, syne bairns, syne race.
Sae on the cod★ I see't in you   pillow
Wi' Maidenkirk to John o' Groats
The bosom that you draw me to.   960

And nae Scot wi' a wumman lies,
But I am he and ken as 'twere
A stage I've passed as he maun pass't,
Gin he grows up, his way wi' her! . . .

A'thing wi' which a man
Can intromit's★ a wumman,   mix with
And can, and s'ud, become
As intimate and human.

And Jean's nae mair my wife
Than whisky is at times,   970
Or munelicht or a thistle
Or kittle★ thochts or rhymes.   exciting

He's no' a man ava',
And lacks a proper pride,
Gin less than a' the warld
Can ser' him for a bride! . . .

Use, then, my lust for whisky and for thee,
Your function but to be and let me be
And see and let me see.

If in a lesser licht I grope my way,   980
Or use't for ends that need your different ray
Whelm't in superior day.

Then aye increase and ne'er withdraw your licht.
– Gin it shows either o's in hideous plicht,
What gain to turn't to nicht?

Whisky mak's Heaven or Hell and whiles mells* baith,   mixes
Disease is but the privy torch o' Daith,
– But sex reveals life, faith!

I need them a' and maun be aye at strife.
Daith and ayont are nocht but pairts o' life.   990
– Then be life's licht, my wife! . . .

Love often wuns free
In lust to be strangled,
Or love, o' lust free,
In law's sairly tangled.

And it's ill to tell whether
Law or lust is to blame
When love's chokit up
– It comes a' to the same.

In this sorry growth   1000
Whatna beauty is tint
That freed o't micht find
A waur fate than is in't? . . .

Yank oot your orra* boughs, my hert!   worthless

God gied man speech and speech created thocht,
He gied man speech but to the Scots gied nocht
Barrin' this clytach* that they've never brocht   nonsense
To onything but sic a Blottie O
As some bairn's copybook micht show,

A spook o' soond that frae the unkent grave   1010
In which oor nation lies loups up to wave
Sic leprous chuns* as tatties have   sprouts
That cellar-boond send spindles gropin'
Towards ony hole that's open,

Like waesome fingers in the dark that think
They still may widen the ane and only chink
That e'er has gi'en mankind a blink
O' Hope – tho' ev'n in that puir licht
They s'ud ha'e seen their hopeless plicht.

This puir relation o' my topplin' mood,   1020
This country cousin, streak o' churl-bluid,
This hopeless airgh* 'twixt a' we can and should,   gap
This Past that like Astarte's sting I feel,
This arrow in Achilles' heel.

Yank oot your orra boughs, my hert!

Mebbe we're in a vicious circle cast,
Mebbe there's limits we can ne'er get past,
Mebbe we're sentrices★ that at the last   scaffolding
Are flung aside, and no' the pillars and props
O' Heaven foraye as in oor hopes.   1030

Oor growth at least nae steady progress shows,
Genius in mankind like an antrin★ rose   rare
Abune a jungly waste o' effort grows,
But to Man's purpose it mak's little odds,
And seems irrelevant to God's . . .

Eneuch? Then here you are. Here's the haill story.
Life's connached★ shapes too'er up in croons o' glory,   spoiled
Perpetuatin', natheless, in their gory
Colour the endless sacrifice and pain
That to their makin's gane.   1040

The roses like the saints in Heaven treid
Triumphant owre the agonies o' their breed,
And wag fu' mony a celestial heid
Abune the thorter-ills o' leaf and prick
In which they ken the feck maun stick.

Yank oot your orra boughs, my hert!

A mongrel growth, jumble o' disproportions,
Whirlin' in its incredible contortions,
Or wad-be client that an auld whore shuns,
Wardin' her wizened orange o' a bosom   1050
Frae importunities sae gruesome,

Or new diversion o' the hormones
Mair fond o' procreation than the Mormons,
And fetchin' like a devastatin' storm on's
A' the uncouth dilemmas o' oor natur'
Objectified in vegetable maitter.

Yank oot your orra boughs, my hert!

And heed nae mair the foolish cries that beg
You slice nae mair to aff or pu' to leg,
You skitin★' duffer that gars a'body fleg★,   1060   dancing/fear
– What tho' you ding the haill warld oot o' joint
Wi' a skier to cover-point!

Yank oot your orra boughs, my hert!

There was a danger – and it's weel I see't –
Had brocht ye like Mallarmé to defeat: –
'Mon doute, amas de nuit ancienne s'achève

En maint rameau subtil, qui, demeuré les vrais
Bois mêmes, prouve, hélas! que bien seul je m'offrais
Pour triomphe la faute idéale de roses.'[1]

Yank oot your orra boughs, my hert! . . .   1070

I love to muse upon the skill that gangs
To mak' the simplest thing that Earth displays,
The eident life that ilka atom thrangs★,   crowds
And uses it in the appointit ways,
And a' the endless brain that nocht escapes
That myriad moves them to inimitable shapes.

Nor to their customed form or ony ither
New to Creation, by man's cleverest mind,
A' needfu' particles first brocht thegither,
Could they wi' timeless labour be combined.   1080
There's nocht that Science yet's begood to see
In hauf its deemless detail or its destiny.

Oor een gi'e answers based on pairt-seen facts
That beg a' questions, to ebb minds' content,
But hoo a'e feature or the neist attracts,
Wi' millions mair unseen, wha kens what's meant
By human brains and to what ends may tell
– For naething's seen or kent that's near a thing itsel'!

Let whasae vaunts his knowledge then and syne
Sets up a God and kens *His* purpose tae   1090
Tell me what's gart a'e strain o' maitter twine
In sic an extraordinary way,
And what God's purpose wi' the Thistle is
– I'll aiblins ken what he and his God's worth by this.

I've watched it lang and hard until I ha'e
A certain symp'thy wi' its orra★ ways   offhand
And pride in its success, as weel I may,
In growin' exactly as its instinct says,
Save in sae fer as thwarts o' weather or grun'
Or man or ither foes ha'e'ts aims perchance fordone.   1100

But I can form nae notion o' the spirit
That gars it tak' the difficult shape it does,
Nor judge the merit yet or the demerit
O' this detail or that sae fer as it goes
T' advance the cause that gied it sic a guise
As maun ha'e pleased its Maker wi' a gey surprise.

----

[1] Stéphane Mallarmé, 'L'après-midi d'un faune'. My doubt, star cluster of an ancient night, is drawing to an end in many a subtle branch, which, remaining (as) the true and very woods, proves, alas, that quite alone I was offering myself as a triumph: the ideal fault of the roses.

The craft that hit upon the reishlin' stalk,
Wi'ts gausty leafs and a' its datchie★ jags,   sly
And spired it syne in seely flooers to brak
Like sudden lauchter owre its fousome★ rags   1110   disgusting
Jouks me, sardonic lover, in the routh★   plentitude
O' contrairies that jostle in this dumfoondrin' growth.

What strength 't'ud need to pit its roses oot,
Or double them in number or in size,
He canna tell wha canna plumb the root,
And learn what's gar't its present state arise,
And what the limits are that ha'e been put
To change in thistles, and why – and what a change 'ud boot . . .

I saw a rose come loupin' oot
Frae a camsteerie★ plant.   1120   crooked
O wha'd ha'e thocht yon puir stock had
Sic an inhabitant?

For centuries it ran to waste,
Wi' pin-heid flooers at times.
O'ts hidden hert o' beauty they
Were but the merest skimes.

Yet while it ran to wud and thorns,
The feckless growth was seekin'
Some airt★ to cheenge its life until   direction
A' in a rose was beekin'.   1130

'Is there nae way in which my life
Can mair to flooerin' come,
And bring its waste on shank and jags
Doon to a minimum?

'It's hard to struggle as I maun
For scrunts★ o' blooms like mine,   stunted growths
While blossom covers ither plants
As by a knack divine.

'What hinders me unless I lack
Some needfu' discipline?   1140
– I wis I'll bring my orra life
To beauty or★ I'm din!'   ere

Sae ran the thocht that hid ahint
The thistle's ugsome guise,
'I'll brak' the habit o' my life
A worthier to devise.

'My nobler instincts sall nae mair
This contrair shape be gi'en.
I sall nae mair consent to live
A life no' fit to be seen.'   1150

Sae ran the thocht that hid ahint
The thistle's ugsome guise,
Till a' at aince a rose loupt oot
– I watched it wi' surprise.

A rose loupt oot and grew, until
It was ten times the size
O' ony rose the thistle afore
Hed heistit to the skies.

And still it grew till a' the buss
Was hidden in its flame.   1160
I never saw sae braw a floo'er
As yon thrawn★ stock became.   twisted

And still it grew until it seemed
The haill braid earth had turned
A reid reid rose that in the lift
Like a ball o' fire burned.

The waefu' clay was fire aince mair,
As Earth had been resumed
Into God's mind, frae which sae lang
To grugous★ state 'twas doomed.   1170   ugly

Syne the rose shriveled suddenly
As a balloon is burst;
The thistle was a ghaistly stick,
As gin it had been curst.

Was it the ancient vicious sway
Imposed itsel' again,
Or nerve owre weak for new emprise
That made the effort vain,

A coward strain in that lorn growth
That wrocht the sorry trick?   1180
– The thistle like a rocket soared
And cam' doon like the stick.

Like grieshuckle★ the roses glint,   embers
The leafs like farles★ hing,   ash
As roond a hopeless sacrifice
Earth draws its barren ring.

The dream o' beauty's dernin'★ yet   hiding
Ahint the ugsome shape.
– Vain dream that in a pinheid here
And there can e'er escape!   1190

The vices that defeat the dream
Are in the plant itsel',
And till they're purged its virtues maun
In pain and misery dwell.

Let Deils rejoice to see the waste,
The fond hope brocht to nocht.
The thistle in their een is as
A favourite lust they've wrocht.

The orderin' o' the thistle means
Nae richtin' o't to them.   1200
Its loss they ca' a law, its thorns
A fule's fit diadem.

And still the idiot nails itsel'
To its ain crucifix,
While here a rose and there a rose
Jaups oot abune the pricks.

Like connoisseurs the Deils gang roond
And praise its attitude,
Till on the Cross the silly Christ
To fidge★ fu' fain's begood!   1210   fidgit

Like connoisseurs the Deils gang roond
Wi' ready platitude.
It's no' sae dear as vinegar,
And every bit as good!

The bitter taste is on my tongue,
I chowl my chafts★, and pray   jaws
'Let God forsake me noo and no'
Staund connoisseur-like tae!' . . .

The language that but sparely flooers
And maistly gangs to weed;   1220
The thocht o' Christ and Calvary
Aye liddenin'★ in my heid;   jerking about
And a' the dour provincial thocht

That merks the Scottish breed
– These are the thistle's characters,
To argie there's nae need.
Hoo weel my verse embodies
The thistle you can read!
– But will a Scotsman never
Frae this vile growth be freed? . . .   1230

O ilka man alive is like
A quart that's squeezed into a pint
(A maist unScottish-like affair!)
Or like the little maid that showed
Me into a still sma'er room.

What use to let a sunrise fade
To ha'e anither like't the morn,
Or let a generation pass
That ane nae better may succeed,

Or wi' a' Time's machinery   1240
Keep naething new aneth the sun,
Or change things oot o' kennin' that
They may be a' the mair the same?

The thistle in the wund dissolves
In lichtnin's as shook foil gi'es way
In sudden splendors, or the flesh
As Daith lets slip the infinite soul;
And syne it's like a sunrise tint
In grey o' day, or love and life,
That in a cloody blash o' sperm   1250
Undae the warld to big't again,
Or like a pickled foetus that
Nae man feels ocht in common wi'
– But micht as easily ha' been!
Or like a corpse a soul set free
Scunners★ to think it tenanted   feels disgust
– And little recks that but for it
It never micht ha' been at a',
Like love frae lust and God frae man!

The wasted seam that dries like stairch   1260
And pooders aff, that micht ha' been
A warld o' men and syne o' Gods;
The grey that haunts the vievest green;
The wrang side o' the noblest scene
We ne'er can whummle to oor een,
As 'twere the hinderpairts o' God
His face aye turned the opposite road,
Or's neth the flooers the drumlie clods
Frae which they come at sicna odds,
As a' Earth's magic frae a spirt,   1270
In shame and secrecy, o' dirt!

Then shak' nae mair in silly life,
Nor stand impossible as Daith,
Incredible as a'thing is
Inside or oot owre closely scanned.
As mithers aften think the warld
O' bairns that ha'e nae end or object,
Or lovers think their sweethearts made
Yince-yirn★ – wha haena waled the lave,   unique
Maikless – when they are naebody,   1280
Or men o' ilka sort and kind
Are prood o' thochts they ca' their ain,
That nameless millions had afore
And nameless millions yet'll ha'e,
And that were never worth the ha'en,
Or Cruivie's 'latest' story or
Gilsanquhar's vows to sign the pledge,
Or's if I thocht maist whisky was,
Or failed to coont the cheenge I got,

Sae wad I be gin I rejoiced,   1290
Or didna ken my place, in thee.

O stranglin' rictus, sterile spasm,
Thou stricture in the groins o' licht,
Thou ootrie gangrel frae the wilds
O' chaos fenced frae Eden yet
By the unsplinterable wa'
O' munebeams like a bleeze o' swords!

Nae chance lunge cuts the Gordion knot,
Nor sall the belly find relief
In wha's entangled moniplies   1300
Creation like a stoppage jams,
Or in whose loins the mapamound★   world
Runkles in strawns o' bubos★ whaur   swellings
The generations gravel★.   combine
The soond o' water winnin' free,
The sicht o' licht that braks the rouk★,   mist
The thocht o' every thwart owrecome
Are in my ears and een and brain,
In whom the bluid is spilt in stour★,   struggle
In whom a' licht in darkness fails,   1310
In whom the mystery o' life
Is to a wretched weed bewrayed.

But let my soul increase in me,
God dwarfed to enter my puir thocht
Expand to his true size again,
And protoplasm's look befit
The nature o' its destiny,
And seed and sequence be nae mair
Incongruous to ane anither,
And liquor packed impossibly★   1320
Mak' pint-pot an eternal well,
And art be relevant to life,
And poets mair than dominies yet,
And ends nae langer tint in means,
Nor forests hidden by their trees,
Nor men be sacrificed alive
In foonds★ o' fates designed for them,   foundations
Nor mansions o' the soul stand toom
Their owners in their cellars trapped,
Nor a' a people's genius be   1330
A rumple★-fyke in Heaven's doup★.   anus/rear end
While Calvinism uses her
To breed a minister or twa!

A black leaf owre a white leaf twirls,
A grey leaf flauchters in atween,
Sae ply my thochts aboot the stem
O' loppert★ slime frae which they spring.   coagulated

The thistle like a snawstorm drives,
Or like a flicht o' swallows lifts,
Or like a swarm o' midges hings, 1340
A plague o' moths, a starry sky,
But's naething but a thistle yet,
And still the puzzle stands unsolved.
Beauty and ugliness alike,
And life and daith and God and man,
Are aspects o't but nane can tell
The secret that I'd fain find oot
O' this bricht hive, this sorry weed,
The tree that fills the universe,
Or like a reistit herrin' crines★. 1350 shrivels

Gin I was sober I micht think
It was like something drunk men see!

The necromancy in my bluid
Through a' the gamut cheenges me
O' dwarf and giant, foul and fair,
But winna let me be mysel'
– My mither's womb that reins me still
Until I tae can prick the witch
And 'Wumman' cry wi' Christ at last,
'Then what hast thou to do wi' me?' 1360

The tug-o'-war is in me still,
The dog-hank o' the flesh and soul,
Faither in Heaven, what gar'd ye tak'
A village slut to mither me,
Your mongrel o' the fire and clay?
The trollop and the Deity share
My writhen form as tho' I were
A picture o' the time they had
When Licht rejoiced to file itsel'
And Earth upshuddered like a star. 1370

A drucken hizzie gane to bed
Wi' three-in-ane and ane-in-three.

O fain I'd drink until I saw
Scotland a ferlie o' delicht,
And fain bide drunk nor ha'e't recede
Into a shriveled thistle syne,
As when a sperklin' tide rins oot,
And leaves a wreath o' rubbish there!

Wull a' the seas gang dry at last
(As dry as I am gettin' noo), 1380
Or wull they aye come back again,
Seilfu' as my neist drink to me,

Or as the sunlicht to the mune,
Or as the bonny sangs o' men,
Wha're but puir craturs in themsels,
And save when genius mak's them drunk,
As donnert★ as their audiences,   dull
— As dreams that mak' a tramp a king,
A madman sane to his ain mind,
Or what a Scotsman thinks himsel',   1390
Tho' naethin' but a thistle kyths★.   appears

The mair I drink the thirstier yet,
And whiles when I'm alowe★ wi' booze,   ablaze
I'm like God's sel' and clad in fire,
And ha'e a Pentecost like this.
O wad that I could aye be fou',
And no' come back as aye I maun
To naething but a fule that nane
'Ud credit wi' sic thochts as thae,
A fule that kens they're empty dreams!   1400

Yet but fer drink and drink's effects,
The yeast o' God that barms★ in us,   ferments
We micht as weel no' be alive.
It maitters not what drink is ta'en,
The barley bree, ambition, love,
Or Guid or Evil workin' in's,
Sae lang's we feel like souls set free
Frae mortal coils and speak in tongues
We dinna ken and never wull,
And find a merit in oorsels,   1410
In Cruivies and Gilsanqullars tae,
And see the thistle as ocht but that!

For wha o's ha'e the thistle's poo'er
To see we're worthless and believe 't?

A'thing that ony man can be's
A mockery o' his soul at last.
The mair it shows't the better, and
I'd suner be a tramp than king,
Lest in the pride o' place and poo'er
I e'er forgot my waesomeness.   1420
Sae to debauchery and dirt,
And to disease and daith I turn,
Sin' otherwise my seemin' worth
'Ud block my view o' what is what,
And blin' me to the irony
O' bein a grocer 'neth the sun,
A lawyer gin Justice ope'd her een,
A pedant like an ant promoted,
A parson buttonholin' God,
Or ony cratur o' the Earth   1430
Sma'-bookt to John Smith, High Street, Perth,
Or sic like vulgar gaffe o' life

Sub speciem aeternitatis[1] −
Nae void can fleg★ me hauf as much   frighten
As bein' mysel', whate'er I am,
Or, waur, bein' onybody else.

The nervous thistle's shiverin' like
A horse's skin aneth a cleg★,   horse fly
Or Northern Lichts or lustres o'
A soul that Daith has fastened on,   1440
Or mornin' efter the nicht afore.

Shudderin' thistle, gi'e owre, gi'e owre . . .

Grey sand is churnin' in my lugs
The munelicht flets, and gantin'★ there   gaping
The grave o' a' mankind's laid bare
− On Hell itsel' the drawback rugs!

Nae man can ken his hert until
The tide o' life uncovers it,
And horror-struck he sees a pit
Returnin' life can never fill! . . .   1450

Thou art the facts in ilka airt
That breenge into infinity,
Criss-crossed wi' coontless ither facts
Nae man can follow, and o' which
He is himsel' a helpless pairt,
Held in their tangle as he were
A stick-nest in Ygdrasil![2]

The less man sees the mair he is
Content wi't, but the mair he sees
The mair he kens hoo little o'   1460
A' that there is he'll ever see,
And hoo it mak's confusion aye
The waur confoondit till at last
His brain inside his heid is like
Ariadne wi' an empty pirn★,   bobbin
Or like a birlin'★ reel frae which   whirling
A whale has rived the line awa'.

What better's a forhooied★ nest   abandoned
Than skasloch★ scattered owre the grun'?   straw

O hard it is for man to ken   1470
He's no creation's goal nor yet
A benefitter by't at last −
A means to ends he'll never ken,
And as to michtier elements

---

[1] Viewed from the point of view of eternity.
[2] A figure from Norse mythology, and defined in line 1349 as 'The tree that fills the universe'.

The slaughtered brutes he eats to him
Or forms o' life owre sma to see
Wi' which his heedless body swarms,
And a' man's thocht nae mair to them
Than ony moosewob★ to a man,   spider-web
His Heaven to them the blinterin'★ o'   1480   glittering
A snail-trail on their closet wa'!

For what's an atom o' a twig
That tak's a billion to an inch
To a' the routh o' shoots that mak'
The bygrowth o' the Earth aboot
The michty trunk o' Space that spreids
Ramel★ o' licht that ha'e nae end,   branches
– The trunk wi' centuries for rings,
Comets for fruit, November shooers
For leafs that in its Autumns fa'   1490
– And Man at maist o' sic a twig
Ane o' the coontless atoms is!

My sinnens and my veins are but
As muckle o' a single shoot
Wha's fibre I can ne'er unwaft
O' my wife's flesh and mither's flesh
And a' the flesh o' humankind,
And reveled thrums★ o' beasts and plants   threads
As gangs to mak' twixt birth and daith
A'e sliver for a microscope;   1500
And a' the life o' Earth to be
Can never lift frae underneath
The shank o' which oor destiny's pairt
As heich's to stand forenenst★ the trunk   next to
Stupendous as a windlestrae★!   straw

I'm under nae delusions, fegs!
The whuppin' sooker★ at wha's tip   sucker
Oor little point o' view appears,
A midget coom★ o' continents   comb
Wi' blebs o' oceans set, sends up   1510
The braith o' daith as weel as life,
And we maun braird★ anither tip   sprout
Oot owre us ere we wither tae,
And join the sentrice★ skeleton   scaffold
As coral insects big★ their reefs.   build

What is the tree? As fer as Man's
Concerned it disna maitter
Gin but a giant thistle 'tis
That spreids eternal mischief there,
As I'm inclined to think.   1520
Ruthless it sends its solid growth
Through mair than he can e'er conceive,
And braks his warlds abreid and rives
His Heavens to tatters on its horns.

The nature or the purpose o't
He needna fash to spier, for he
Is destined to be sune owre grown
And hidden wi' the parent wud
The spreidin' boughs in darkness hap,
And a' its future life'll be   1530
Ootwith'm as he's ootwith his banes.

Juist as man's skeleton has left
Its ancient ape-like shape ahint,
Sae states o' mind in turn gi'e way
To different states, and quickly seem
Impossible to later men,
And Man's mind in its final shape,
Or lang'll seem a monkey's spook,
And, strewth, to me the vera thocht
O' Thocht already's fell like that!   1540
Yet still the cracklin' thorns persist
In fitba' match and peepy show,
To antic hay a dog-fecht's mair
Than Jacob v. the Angel
And through a cylinder o' wombs,
A star reflected in a dub★,   puddle
I see as 'twere my ain wild harns
The ripple o' Eve's moniplies★.   intestines
And faith! yestreen in Cruivie's een
Life rocked at midnicht in a tree,   1550
And in Gilsanquhar's glower I saw
The taps o' waves 'neth which the warld
Ga'ed rowin' like a jeelyfish,
And whiles★ I canna look at Jean   sometimes
For fear I'd seen the sunlicht turn
Worm-like into the glaur★ again!   mud, ooze

A black leaf owre a white leaf twirls,
My liver's shadow on my soul,
And clots o' bluid loup oot frae stems
That back into the jungle rin,   1560
Or in the waters underneath
Kelter★ like seaweed, while I hear   ripple
Abune the thunder o' the flood,
The voice that aince commanded licht
Sing 'Scots Wha Ha'e' and hyne awa'
Like Cruivie up a different glen,
And leave me like a mixture o'
A wee Scotch nicht and Judgment Day,
The bile, the Bible, and the *Scotsman*,
Poetry and pigs – Infernal Thistle,   1570
Damnition haggis I've spewed up,
And syne return to like twa dogs!
Blin' Proteus wi' leafs or hands
Or flippers ditherin' in the lift
– Thou Samson in a warld that has
Nae pillars but your cheengin' shapes

That dung doon, rise in ither airts
Like windblawn reek frae smoo'drin' ess*!   *ash*
– Hoo lang maun I gi'e aff your forms
O' plants and beasts and men and Gods   1580
And like a doited* Atlas bear   *crazed*
This steeple o' fish, this eemis* warld,   *unsteady*
Or, maniac heid wi' snakes for hair,
A Maenad, ape Aphrodite,
And scunner the Eternal sea?
Man needna fash and even noo
The cells that mak' a'e sliver wi'm,
The threidy knit he's woven wi',
'Ud fain destroy what sicht he has
O' this puir transitory stage,   1590
Yet tho' he kens the fragment is
O' little worth he e'er can view,
Jalousin' it's a cheatrie weed,
He tyauves* wi' a' his micht and main   *struggles*
To keep his sicht despite his kind
Conspirin' as their nature is
'Gainst ocht wi' better sicht than theirs.

What gars him strive? He canna tell –
It may be nocht but cussedness.
– At best he hopes for little mair   1600
Than his suspicions to confirm,
To mock the sicht he hains* sae weel   *preserves*
At last wi' a' he sees wi' it,
Yet, thistle or no' whate'er its end,
Aiblins the force that mak's it grow
And lets him see a kennin' mair
Than ither folk and fend his sicht
Agen their jealous plots awhile
'll use the poo'ers it seems to waste,
This purpose ser'd, in ither ways,   1610
That may be better worth the bein'
– Or sae he dreams, syne mocks his dream
Till Life grows sheer awa' frae him,
And bratts* o' darkness plug his een.   *scum*

It may be nocht but cussedness,
But I'm content gin a' my thocht
Can dae nae mair than let me see,
Free frae desire o' happiness,
The foolish faiths o' ither men
In breedin', industry, and War,   1620
Religion, Science, or ocht else
Gang smash – when I ha'e nane mysel',
Or better gin I share them tae,
Or mind at least a time I did!

Aye, this is Calvary – to bear
Your Cross wi'in you frae the seed,
And feel it grow by slow degrees
Until it rends your flesh apairt,
And turn, and see your fellow-men
In similar case but sufferin' less   1630
Thro' bein' mair wudden frae the stert! . . .

I'm fu' o' a stickit⋆ God.   frustrated, shut out
THAT'S what's the maitter wi' me,
Jean has stuck sic a fork in the wa'
That I row in agonie.

Mary never let dab⋆.   be known
SHE was a canny wumman.
She hedna a gaw⋆ in Joseph at a'   hold
But, wow; this secund comin'! . . .

Narodbogonosets⋆ are my folk tae,   1640   God-holders
But in a sma' way nooadays –
A faitherly God wi' a lang white beard,
Or painted Jesus in a haze
O' blue and gowd, a gird aboot his heid
Or some sic thing. It's been a sair come-doon,
And the trade's nocht to what it was.
Unnatural practices are the cause.
Baith bairns and God'll be obsolete soon
(The twaesome gang thegither), and forsooth
Scotland turn Eliot's waste – the Land o' Drouth.   1650

But even as the stane the builders rejec'
Becomes the corner-stane, the time may be
When Scotland sall find oot its destiny,
And yield the *vse-chelovek⋆*.   all-human
– At a' events, owre Europe flaught⋆ atween,   abased
My whim (and mair than whim) it pleases
To seek the haund o' Russia as a freen'
In workin' oot mankind's great synthesis . . .

Melville (a Scot) kent weel hoo Christ's
Corrupted into creeds malign,   1660
Begotten strife's pernicious brood
That claims for patron Him Divine.
(The Kirk in Scotland still I cry
Crooks whaur it canna crucify!)

Christ, bleedin' like the thistle's roses,
He saw – as I in similar case –
Maistly, in beauty and in fear,
'Ud 'paralyze the nobler race,
Smite or suspend, perplex, deter,
And, tortured, prove the torturer.'   1670

And never mair a Scot sall tryst,
Abies* on Calvary, wi' Christ,   except
Unless, mebbe, a poem like this'll
Exteriorise things in a thistle,
And gi'e him in this form forlorn
What Melville socht in vain frae Hawthorne . . .

Spirit o' strife, destroy in turn
Syne this fule's Paradise, syne that;
In thee's in Calvaries that owrecome
Daith efter Daith let me be caught,   1680

Or in the human form that hauds
Us in its ignominious thrall,
While on brute needs oor souls attend
Until disease and daith end all,

Or in the grey deluded brain,
Reflectin' in anither field
The torments o' its parent flesh
In thocht-preventin' thocht concealed,

Or still in curst impossible mould,
Last thistle-shape men think to tak',   1690
The soul, frae flesh and thocht set free,
On Heaven's strait if unseen rack.

There may be heicher forms in which
We can nae mair oor plicht define,
Because the agonies involved
'll bring us their ain anodyne.

Yet still we suffer and still sall,
Altho', puir fules, we mayna ken 't
As lang as like the thistle we
In coil and in recoil are pent.   1700

And ferrer than mankind can look
Ghast shapes that free but to transfix
Twine rose-crooned in their agonies,
And strive agen the endless pricks.

The dooble play that bigs and braks
In endless victory and defeat
Is in your spikes and roses shown,
And a' my soul is haggar'd wi't . . .

Be like the thistle, O my soul,
Heedless o' praise and quick to tak' affront,   1710
And growin' like a mockery o' a'
Maist life can want or thole,
And manifest forevermair
Contempt o' ilka goal.

O' ilka goal – save ane alane;
To be yoursel', whatever that may be,
And as contemptuous o' that,
Kennin' nocht's worth the ha'en,
But certainty that nocht can be,
And hoo that certainty to gain.   1720

For this you still maun grow and grope
In the abyss wi' ever-deepenin' roots
That croon your scunner wi' the grue★   revulsion
O' hopeless hope
– And gin the abyss is bottomless,
Your growth'll never stop! . . .

What earthquake chitters★ oot   trembles
In the Thistle's oorie shape,
What gleids o' central fire
In its reid heids escape,   1730
And whatna coonter forces
In growth and ingrowth graip
In an eternal clinch
In this ootcuissen★ form   outcast
That winna be outcast,
But triumphs at the last
(Owre a' abies itsel'
As fer as we can tell,
Sin' frae the Eden o' the world
Ilka man in turn is hurled,   1740
And ilka gairden rins to waste
That was ever to his taste?)

O keep the Thistle 'yont the wa'
Owre which your skeletons you'll thraw.

I, in the Thistle's land,
As you in Russia where
Struggle in giant form
Proceeds for evermair,
In my sma' measure 'bood★   intend to
Address a similar task,   1750
And for a share o' your
Appallin' genius ask.

Wha built in revelations
What maist men in reserves
(And only men confound!)
A better gift deserves
Frae ane wha like hissel
(As ant-heap unto mountain)
Needs big his life upon
The everloupin' fountain   1760

That frae the Dark ascends
Whaur Life begins, Thocht ends
– A better gift deserves
Than thae wheen★ yatterin' nerves!   few

For mine's the clearest insicht
O' man's facility
For constant self-deception,
And hoo his mind can be
But as a floatin' iceberg
That hides aneth the sea   1770
Its bulk: and hoo frae depths
O' an unfaddomed flood
Tensions o' nerves arise
And humours o' the blood
– Keethin's★ nane can trace   appearances
To their original place.

Hoo mony men to mak' a man
It tak's he kens wha kens Life's plan.

But there are flegsome★ deeps   frightening
Whaur the soul o' Scotland sleeps   1780
That I to bottom need
To wauk Guid kens what deid,
Play at stertle-a-stobie,
Wi' nation's dust for hobby,
Or wi' God's sel' commerce
For the makin' o' a verse.

'Melville, sea-compelling man,
Before whose wand Leviathan
Rose hoary-white upon the Deep,'[1]
What thou hast sown I fain 'ud reap   *1790*
O' knowledge 'yont the human mind
In keepin' wi' oor Scottish kind,
And, thanks to thee, may aiblins reach
To what this Russian has to teach,
Closer than ony ither Scot,
Closer to me than my ain thocht,
Closer than my ain braith to me,
As close as to the Deity
Approachable in whom appears
This Christ o' the neist thoosand years.   1800

As frae your baggit★ wife   big-bellied
You turned whenever able,
And often when you werena,
Unto the gamin' table,
And opened wide to ruin
Your benmaist hert, aye brewin'

---

[1] Robert Buchanan.

A horror o' whatever
Seemed likely to deliver
You frae the senseless strife
In which alane is life,   1810
– As Burns in Edinburgh
Breenged arse-owre-heid thoro'
A' it could be the spur o'
To pleuch his sauted★ furrow,   salted
And turned frae a' men honour
To what could only scunner
Wha thinks that common-sense
Can e'er be but a fence
To keep a soul worth ha'en
Frae what it s'ud be daein'   1820
– Sae I in turn maun gie
My soul to misery,
Daidle★ disease   dandle
Upon my knees,
And welcome madness
Wi' exceedin' gladness
– Aye, open wide my hert
To a' the thistle's smert.

And a' the hopes o' men
Sall be like wiles then   1830
To gar my soul betray
Its only richtfu' way,
Or as a couthie★ wife   comfortable
That seeks nae mair frae life
Than domesticity
E'en wi' the likes o' me –
As gin I could be carin'
For her or for her bairn
When on my road I'm farin'
– O I can spend a nicht   1840
In ony man's Delicht
Or wi' ony wumman born
– But aye be aff the morn!

In a' the inklin's cryptic,
Then, o' an epileptic,
I ha'e been stood in you
And droukit★ in their grue★   drenched/revulsion
Till I can see richt through
Ilk weakness o' my frame
And ilka dernin'★ shame,   1850   hiding
And can employ the same
To jouk★ the curse o' fame,   avoid
Lowsed★ frae the dominion   loosed (freed)
O' popular opinion,
And risen at last abune
The thistle like a mune
That looks serenely doon

On what queer things there are
In an inferior star
That couldna be, or see,   1860
Themsel's, except in me.

Wi' burnt-oot hert and poxy face
I sall illumine a' the place,
And there is ne'er a fount o' grace
That isna in a similar case.

Let a' the thistle's growth
Be as a process, then,
My spirit's gane richt through,
And needna threid again,
Tho' in it sall be haud'n   1870
For aye the feck o' men
Wha's queer contortions there
As memories I ken,
As memories o' my ain
O' mony an ancient pain.
But sin' wha'll e'er wun free
Maun tak' like coorse to me,
A fillip I wad gi'e
Their eccentricity,
And leave the lave to dree   1880
Their weirdless destiny.

It's no' withoot regret
That I maun follow yet
The road that led me past
Humanity sae fast,
Yet scarce can gi'e a fate
That is at last mair fit
To them wha tak' that gait
Than theirs wha winna ha'e't,
Seein' that nae man can get   1890
By ony airt or wile,
A destiny quite worth while
As fer as he can tell
– Or even you yoursel'!

And O! I canna thole
Aye yabblin' o' my soul,
And fain I wad be free
O' my eternal me,
Nor fare mysel' alane
– Withoot that tae be gane,   1900
And this, I ha'e nae doot,
This road'll bring aboot.

The munelicht that owre clear defines
The thistle's shrill cantankerous lines
E'en noo whiles insubstantialises
Its grisly form and 'stead devises
A maze o' licht, a siller-frame,
As 'twere God's dream frae which it came,
Ne'er into bein' coorsened yet,
The essence lowin'★ pure in it,   1910   blazing
As tho' the fire owrecam' the clay,
And left its wraith in endless day.

These are the moments when a' sense
Like mist is vanished and intense,
Magic emerges frae the dense
Body o' bein' and beeks★ immense   appears
As, like a ghinn oot o' a bottle,
Daith rises frae's when oor lives crottle★.   crumble

These are the moments when my sang
Clears its white feet frae oot amang   1920
My broken thocht, and moves as free
As souls frae bodies when they dee.
There's naething left o' me ava'
Save a' I'd hoped micht whiles befa'.

Sic sang to men is little worth.
It has nae message for the earth.
Men see their warld turned tapsalteerie,
Drookit★ in a licht owre eerie,   drenched
Or sent birlin'★ like a peerie★ –   whirling/top
Syne it turns a' they've kent till then   1930
To shapes they can nae langer ken.

Men canna look on nakit licht.
It flings them back wi' darkened sicht,
And een that canna look at it,
Maun draw earth closer roond them yet
Or, their sicht tint, find nocht instead
That answers to their waefu' need.

And yet this essence frae the clay
In dooble form aye braks away,
For, in addition to the licht,   1940
There is an e'er-increasin' nicht,
A nicht that is the bigger, and
Gangs roond licht like an airn band
That noo and then mair tichtly grips,
And snuffs it in a black eclipse,
But rings it maistly as a brough★   halo
The mune, till it's juist bricht enough –
O wull I never lowse a licht
I canna dowse again in spite,
Or dull to haud within my sicht?   1950

The thistle canna vanish quite.
Inside a' licht its shape maun glint,
A spirit wi' a skeleton in't.

The world, the flesh, 'll bide in us
As in the fire the unburnt buss,
Or as frae sire to son we gang
And coontless corpses in us thrang.

And e'en the glory that descends
I kenna whence on me depends,
And shapes itsel' to what is left   1960
Whaur I o' me ha'e me bereft,
And still the form is mine, altho'
A force to which I ne'er could grow
Is movin' in't as 'twere a sea
That lang syne drooned the last o' me
– That drooned afore the warld began
A' that could ever come frae Man.

And as at sicna times am I,
I wad ha'e Scotland to my eye
Until I saw a timeless flame   1970
Tak' Auchtermuchty for a name,
And kent that Ecclefechan stood
As pairt o' an eternal mood.

Ahint the glory comes the nicht
As Maori to London's ruins,
And I'm amused to see the plicht
O' Licht as't in the black tide droons,
Yet even in the brain o' Chaos
For Scotland I wad hain a place,
And let Tighnabruaich still   1980
Be pairt and paircel o' its will,
And Culloden, black as Hell,
A knowledge it has o' itsel'.

Thou, Dostoevski, understood,
Wha had your ain land in your bluid,
And into it as in a mould
The passion o' your bein' rolled,
Inherited in turn frae Heaven
Or sources fer abune it even.

Sae God retracts in endless stage   1990
Through angel, devil, age on age,
Until at last his infinite natur'
Walks on earth a human cratur'
(Or less than human as to my een
The people are in Aiberdeen);
Sae man returns in endless growth
Till God in him again has scouth★.   scope

For sic a loup towards widsom's croon
Hoo fer a man maun base him doon,
Hoo plunge aboot in Chaos ere   2000
He finds his needfu' fittin' there,
The matrix oot o' which sublime
Serenity sall soar in time!

Ha'e I the cruelty I need,
Contempt and syne contempt o' that,
And still contempt in endless meed
That I may never yet be caught
In ony satisfaction, or
Bird–lime that winna let me soar?

Is Scotland big enough to be   2010
A symbol o' that force in me,
In wha's divine inebriety
A sicht abune contempt I'll see?

For a' that's Scottish is in me,
As a' things Russian were in thee,
And I in turn 'ud be an action
To pit in a concrete abstraction
My country's contrair qualities,
And mak' a unity o' these
Till my love owre its history dwells,   2020
As owretone to a peal o' bells.

And in this heicher stratosphere
As bairn at giant at thee I peer . . .

O Jean, in whom my spirit sees,
Clearer than through whisky or disease,
Its dernin' nature, wad the searchin' licht
Oor union raises poor'd owre me the nicht.

I'm faced wi' aspects o' mysel'
At last wha's portent nocht can tell,
Save that sheer licht o' life that when we're joint   2030
Loups through me like a fire a' else t' aroint★.   expel

Clear my lourd★ flesh, and let me move   heavy
In the peculiar licht o' love,
As aiblins in Eternity men may
When their swack★ souls nae mair are clogged wi' clay.   supple

Be thou the licht in which I stand
Entire, in thistle-shape, as planned,
And no' hauf-hidden and hauf-seen as here
In munelicht, whisky, and in fleshly fear,

In fear to look owre closely at 2040
The grisly form in which I'm caught,
In sic a reelin' and imperfect licht
Sprung frae incongruous elements the nicht!

But wer't by thou they were shone on,
Then wad I ha'e nae dreid to con
The ugsome problems shapin' in my soul,
Or gin I hed – certes, nae fear you'd thole!

Be in this fibre like an eye,
And ilka turn and twist descry,
Hoo here a leaf, a spine, a rose – or as 2050
The purpose o' the poo'er that bringst to pass.

Syne liberate me frae this tree,
As wha had there imprisoned me,
The end achieved – or show me at the least
Mair meanin' in't, and hope o' bein' released.

I tae ha'e heard Eternity drip water
(Aye water, water!), drap by drap
On the a'e nerve, like lichtnin', I've become,
And heard God passin' wi' a bobby's feet
Ootby in the lang coffin o' the street 2060
– Seen stang by chitterin' knottit stang loup oot
Uncrushed by th' echoes o' the thunderin' boot,
Till a' the dizzy lint-white lines o' torture made
A monstrous thistle in the space aboot me,
A symbol o' the puzzle o' man's soul
– And in my agony been pridefu' I could still
Tine nae least quiver or twist, watch ilka point
Like a white-het bodkin ripe my inmaist hert,
And aye wi' clearer pain that brocht nae anodyne,
But rose for ever to a fer crescendo 2070
Like eagles that ootsoar wi' skinklan'* wings   shining
The thieveless* sun they blin'   dull
        – And pridefu' still
That 'yont the sherp wings o' the eagles fleein'
Aboot the dowless* pole o' Space,   unfathomable
Like leafs aboot a thistle-shank, my bluid
Could still thraw roses up
        – And up!

O rootless thistle through the warld that's pairt o' you,
Gin you'd withstand the agonies still to come, 2080
You maun send roots doon to the deeps unkent,
Fer deeper than it's possible for ocht to gang,
Savin' the human soul,
Deeper than God himsel' has knowledge o',
Whaur lichtnin's canna probe that cleave the warld,
Whaur only in the entire dark there's founts o' strength
Eternity's poisoned draps can never file,
And muckle roots thicken, deef to bobbies' feet.

A mony-brainchin' candelabra fills
The lift and's lowin' wi' the stars;   2090
The Octopus Creation is wallopin'
In coontless faddoms o' a nameless sea.
I am the candelabra, and burn
My endless candles to an Unkent God.
I am the mind and meanin' o' the octopus
That thraws its empty airms through a' th' Inane.

And a' the bizzin' suns ha'e bigged
Their kaims* upon the surface o' the sea.   (honey)combs
My lips may feast for ever, but my guts
Ken naething o' the Food o' Gods.   2100

'Let there be Licht,' said God, and there was
A little: but He lacked the poo'er
To licht up mair than pairt o' space at aince,
And there is lots o' darkness that's the same
As gin He'd never spoken
– Mair darkness than there's licht,
And dwarfin't to a candle-flame,
A spalin'* candle that'll sune gang oot.   fragmenting
– Darkness comes closer to us than the licht,
And is oor natural element. We peer oot frae't   2110
Like cat's een bleezin' in a goustrous* nicht   frightening
(Whaur there is nocht to find but stars
That look like ither cats' een),
Like cat's een, and there is nocht to find
Savin' we turn them in upon oorsels;
Cats canna.

Darkness is wi' us a' the time, and Licht
But veesits pairt o' us, the wee-est pairt
Frae time to time on a short day atween twa nichts.
Nae licht is thrawn on *them* by ony licht.   2120
Licht throws nae licht upon itsel';
But in the darkness them wha's een
Nae fleetin' lichts ha'e dazzled and deceived
Find qualities o' licht, keener than ony licht,
Keen and abidin'
That show the nicht unto itsel',
And syne the licht,
That queer extension o' the dark,
That seems a separate and a different thing,
And, seemin' sae, has lang confused the dark,   2130
And set it at cross-purposes wi' itsel'.

              O little Life
In which Daith guises and deceives itsel',
Joy that mak's Grief a Janus,
Hope that is Despair's fause-face,
And Guid and ill that are the same,
Save as the chance licht fa's!

And yet the licht is there,
Whether frae within or frae withoot.
The conscious Dark can use it, dazzled nor deceived.   2140
The licht is there, and th' instinct for it,
Pairt o' the Dark and o' the need to guise,
To deceive and be deceived,
But let us then be undeceived
When we deceive,
When we deceive oorsels.
Let us enjoy deceit, this instinct in us.
Licht cheenges naething,
And gin there is a God wha made the licht
We are adapted to receive,   2150
He cheenged naething.
And hesna kythed★ Hissel!   revealed
Save in this licht that fa's whaur the Auld Nicht was,

Showin' naething that the Darkness didna hide,
And gin it shows a pairt o' that
Confoondin' mair than it confides
Ev'n in that.

The epileptic thistle twitches
(A trick o' wund or mune or een – or whisky).
A brain laid bare,   2160
A nervous system,
The skeleton wi' which men labour
And bring to life in Daith
– I, risen frae the deid, ha'e seen
My deid man's eunuch offspring.
– The licht frae bare banes whiteening evermair,
Frae twitchin' nerves thrawn aff,
Frae nakit thocht,
Works in the Darkness like a fell disease,
A hungry acid and a cancer,   2170
Disease o' Daith-in-Life and Life-in-Daith.

O for a root in some untroubled soil,
Some cauld soil 'yont this fevered warld,
That 'ud draw darkness frae a virgin source,
And send it slow and easefu' through my veins,
Release the tension o' my grisly leafs,
Withdraw my endless spikes,
Move coonter to the force in me that hauds
Me raxed and rigid and ridiculous
          – And let my roses drap   2180
          Like punctured ba's that at a Fair
          Fa' frae the loupin' jet!
          – Water again! . . .

Omsk and the Calton turn again to dust,
The suns and stars fizz out with little fuss,
The bobby booms away and seems to bust,
And leaves the world to darkness and to us.

The circles of our hungry thought
Swing savagely from pole to pole.
Death and the Raven drift above   2190
The graves of Sweeney's body and soul.

My name is Norval. On the Grampian Hills
It is forgotten, and deserves to be.
So are the Grampian Hills and all the people
Who ever heard of either them or me.

What's in a name? From pole to pole
Our interlinked mentality spins.
I know that you are Deosil, and suppose
That therefore I am Widdershins.

Do you reverse? Shall us? Then let's.   2200
Cyclone and Anti? – how absurd!
She should know better at her age.
Auntie's an ass, upon my word.

This is the sort of thing they teach
The Scottish children in the school.
Poetry, patriotism, manners –
No wonder I am such a fool . . .

Hoo can I graipple wi' the thistle syne,
Be intricate as it and up to a' its moves?
A' airts its sheenin' points are loupin' 'yont me,   2210
Quhile still the firmament it proves.

And syne it's like a wab in which the warld
Squats like a spider, quhile the mune and me
Are taigled in an endless corner o't
Tyauvin'* fecklessly . . .   struggling

The wan leafs shak' atour us like the snaw.
Here is the cavaburd* in which Earth's tint.   snowstorm
There's naebody but Òblivion and us,
Puir gangrel* buddies, waunderin' hameless in't.   wandering

The stars are larochs* o' auld cottages,   2220   ruins
And a' Time's glen is fu' o' blinnin' stew*.   dust
Nae freen'ly lozen* skimmers: and the wund   window
Rises and separates even me and you.

I ken nae Russian and you ken nae Scots.
We canna tell oor voices frae the wund.
The snaw is seekin' everywhere: oor herts
At last like roofless ingles it has f'und,

And gethers there in drift on endless drift,
Oor broken herts that it can never fill;
And still – its leafs like snaw, its growth like wund –   2230
The thistle rises and forever will! . . .

The thistle rises and forever will,
Getherin' the generations under't.
This is the monument o' a' they were,
And a' they hoped and wondered.

The barren tree, dry leafs and cracklin' thorns,
This is the mind o' a' humanity,
– The empty intellect that left to grow
'll let nocht ither be.

Lo! It has choked the sunlicht's gowden grain,   2240
And strangled syne the white hairst★ o' the mune.   harvest
Thocht that mak's a' the food o' nocht but Thocht
Is reishlin'★ grey abune . . .   rustling

O fitly frae oor cancerous soil
May this heraldic horror rise!
The Presbyterian thistle flourishes,
And its ain roses crucifies . . .

No' Edinburgh Castle or the fields
O' Bannockburn or Flodden
Are dernin' wi' the miskent soul   2250
Scotland sae lang has hod'n★.   hidden

It hauds nae pew in ony kirk,
The soul Christ cam' to save;
Nae R.S.A.'s ha'e pentit it,
F.S.A.'s fund its grave.

Is it alive or deid? I show
My hert – wha will can see.
The secret clyre★ in Scotland's life   tumour
Has brust and reams through me,

A whummlin' sea in which is heard   2260
The clunk o' nameless banes;
A grisly thistle dirlin'★ shrill   vibrating
Abune the broken stanes.

Westminster Abbey nor the Fleet,
Nor England's Constitution, but
In a' the michty city there,
You mind a'e fleggit★ slut,   frightened

As Tolstoi o' Lucerne alane
Minded a'e beggar minstrel seen!
The woundit side draws a' the warld.   2270
Barbarians ha'e lizards' een.

Glesca's a gless whaur Magdalene's
Discovered in a million crimes.
Christ comes again – wheesht, whatna bairn
In backlands cries betimes?

Hard faces prate o' their success,
And pickle-makers awn the hills.
There is nae life in a' the land
But this infernal Thistle kills . . .

    Nae mair I see   2280
    As aince I saw
    Mysel' in the thistle
    Harth★ and haw★!   lean/hollow

Nel suo profondo vidi che s'interna
Legato con amore in un volume
(Or else by Hate, fu' aft the better Love)
Ciò che per l'universo si squaderna.

Sustanzia ed accidenti, e lor costume,
Quasi conflati insieme per tal modo.
(The michty thistle in wha's boonds I rove)   2290
Ché cio ch'io dico è un semplice lume.[1]

And kent and was creation
In a' its coontless forms,
Or glitterin' in raw sunlicht,
Or dark wi' hurrying storms.

But what's the voice
That sings in me noo?
– A'e hauf o' me tellin'
The tither it's fou!

It's the voice o' the Sooth   2300
That's held owre lang
My Viking North
Wi' its siren sang . . .

Fier comme un Ecossais★.   'proud as a Scot'

If a' that I can be's nae mair
Than what mankind's been yet, I'll no'
Begink★ the instincts thistlewise   deceive
That dern★ – and canna show.   hide

Damned threids and thrums and skinny shapes
O' a' that micht, and su'd, ha' been   2310
– Life onyhow at ony price! –
In sic I'll no' be seen!

Fier comme un Ecossais.

---

[1] Dante. *Paradiso*. xxxiii. 85–90. Deep inside it [the divine light] I saw the leaves which are separate in this world bound together in one volume by love. Substance and accidents virtually fused together in such a [marvellous] way that what I say is only a weak hint of it.

The wee reliefs we ha'e in booze,
Or wun at times in carnal states,
May hide frae us but canna cheenge
The silly horrors o' oor fates.

Fier – comme un Ecossais!

There's muckle in the root,
That never can wun oot,   2320
Or't owre what is 'ud sweep
Like a thunderstorm owre sheep.

But shadows whiles upcreep,
And heavy tremors leap . . .
C'wa', Daith, again, send Life's vain shoot,
And your ain coonsel keep! . . .

Time like a bien★ wife,   snug, comfortable
Truth like a dog's gane –
The bien wife's gane to the aumrie★   cupboard
To get the puir dog a bane.   2330

Opens the aumrie door,
And lo! the skeleton's there,
And the gude dog, Truth, has gotten
Banes for evermair . . .

Maun I tae perish in the keel o' Heaven,
And is this fratt★ upon the air the ply   fretwork
O' cross-brath'd cordage that in gloffs★ and gowls★   light/dark
Brak's up the vision o' the warld's bricht gy★?   show

Ship's tackle and an eemis★ cairn o' fraucht   unsteady
Darker than clamourin' veins are roond me yet,   2340
A plait o' shadows thicker than the flesh,
A fank★ o' tows★ that binds me hand and fit.   coil/rope

What gin the gorded★ fullyery★ on hie   frosted/foliage
And a' the fanerels★ o' the michty ship   scattered objects
Gi'e back mair licht than fa's upon them ev'n
Gin sic black ingangs haud us in their grip?

Grugous★ thistle, to my een   ugly
Your widdifow★ ramel evince,   perverse
Sibness to snakes wha's coils
Rin coonter airts at yince,   2350
And fain I'd follow each
Gin you the trick'll teach.

Blin' root to bleezin' rose,
Through a' the whirligig
O' shanks and leafs and jags
What sends ye sic a rig?
Bramble yokin' earth and heaven,
Till they're baith stramulyert★ driven!   horrified

Roses to lure the lift
And roots to wile the clay   2360
And wuppit* brainches syne   binding
To claught them 'midyards tae
Till you've the precious pair
Like hang'd men dancin' there,

Wi' mony a seely* prickle   happy
You'll fleg a sunburst oot,
Or kittle* earthquakes up   tickle
Wi' an amusin' root,
While, kilted in your tippet*,   noose
They still can mak' their rippit* . . .   2370   fuss

And let me pit in guid set terms
My quarrel wi' th' owre sonsy* rose,   smug
That roond aboot its devotees
A fair fat cast o' aureole throws
That blinds them, in its mirlygoes*,   dazzle
To the necessity o' foes.

Upon their King and System I
Glower as on things that whiles in pairt
I may admire (at least for them),
But wi' nae claim upon my hert,   2380
While a' their pleasure and their pride
Ootside me lies – and there maun bide.

Ootside me lies – and mair than that,
For I stand still for forces which
Were subjugated to mak' way
For England's poo'er, and to enrich
The kinds o' English, and o' Scots,
The least congenial to my thoughts.

Hauf his soul a Scot maun use
Indulgin' in illusions,   2390
And hauf in gettin rid o' them
And comin' to conclusions
Wi' the demoralisin' dearth
O' onything worth while on Earth . . .

I'm weary o' the rose as o' my brain,
And for a deeper knowledge I am fain
Than frae this noddin' object I can gain.

Beauty is a'e thing, but it tines anither
(For, fegs, they never can be f'und thegither),
And 'twixt the twa it's no' for me to swither*.   2400   hesitate

As frae the grun' sae thocht frae men springs oot,
A ferlie that tells little o' its source, I doot,
And has nae vera fundamental root.

And cauld agen my hert are laid
The words o' Plato when he said,
'God o' geometry is made.'

Frae my ain mind I fa' away,
That never yet was feared to say
What turned the souls o' men to clay,

Nor cared gin truth frae me ootsprung   2410
In ne'er a leed* o' ony tongue   language
That ever in a heid was hung.

I ken hoo much oor life is fated
Aince its first cell is animated,
The fount frae which the flesh is jetted.

I ken hoo lourd* the body lies   heavy
Upon the spirit when it flies
And fain abune its stars 'ud rise.

And see I noo a great wheel move,
And a' the notions that I love   2420
Drap into stented* groove and groove?   set, kept in place

It maitters not my mind the day,
Nocht maitters that I strive to dae,
– For the wheel moves on in its ain way.

I sall be moved as it decides
To look at Life frae ither sides;
Rejoice, rebel, its turn abides.

And as I see the great wheel spin
There flees a licht frae't lang and thin
That Earth is like a snaw-ba' in.   2430

(To the uncanny thocht I clutch
– The nature o' man's soul is such
That it can ne'er wi' life tine touch.

Man's mind is in God's image made,
And in its wildest dreams arrayed
In pairt o' Truth is still displayed.)

Then suddenly I see as weel
As me spun roon' within the wheel,
The helpless forms o' God and Deil.

And on a birlin'* edge I see   2440   whirling
Wee Scotland squattin' like a flea,
And dizzy wi' the speed, and me!

I've often thrawn the warld frae me,
Into the Pool o' Space, to see
The Circles o' Infinity.

Or like a flat stone gar'd it skite,
A Morse code message writ in licht
That yet I couldna read aricht

The skippin' sparks, the ripples, rit★   scrape
Like skritches o' a grain o' grit   2450
'Neth Juggernaut in which I sit.

Twenty-six thoosand years it tak's
Afore a'e single roond it mak's,
And syne it melts as it were wax.

The Phoenix guise 'tll rise in syne
Is mair than Euclid or Einstein
Can dream o' or's in dreams o' mine.

Upon the huge circumference are
As neebor points the Heavenly War
That dung doun Lucifer sae far,   2460

And that upheaval in which I
Sodgered 'neth the Grecian sky
And in Italy and Marseilles,

And there isna room for men
Wha the haill o' history ken
To pit a pin twixt then and then.

Whaur are Bannockburn and Flodden?
– O' a'e grain like facets hod'n,
Little wars (twixt that which God in

Focht and won, and that which He   2470
Took baith sides in hopelessly),
Less than God or I can see.

By whatna cry o' mine oot-topped
Sall be a' men ha'e sung and hoped
When to a'e note they're telescoped?

And Jesus and a nameless ape
Collide and share the selfsame shape
That nocht terrestrial can escape?

But less than this nae man need try.
He'd better be content to eye   2480
The wheel in silence whirlin' by.

Nae verse is worth a ha'et* until   trifle
It can join issue wi' the Will
That raised the Wheel and spins it still,

But a' the music that mankind
'S made yet is to the Earth confined,
Poo'erless to reach the general mind,

Poo'erless to reach the neist star e'en,
That as a pairt o'ts sel' is seen,
And only men can tell between.   2490

Yet I exult oor sang has yet
To grow wings that'll cairry it
Ayont its native speck o' grit,

And I exult to find in me
The thocht that this can ever be,
A hope still for humanity.

For gin the sun and mune at last
Are as a neebor's lintel passed,
The wheel'll tine its stature fast,

And birl in time inside oor heids   2500
Till we can thraw oot conscious gleids*   gleams
That draw an answer to oor needs,

Or if nae answer still we find
Brichten till a' thing is defined
In the huge licht-beams o' oor kind,

And if we still can find nae trace
Ahint the Wheel o' ony Face,
There'll be a glory in the place,

And we may aiblins swing content
Upon the wheel in which we're pent   2510
In adequate enlightenment.

Nae ither thocht can mitigate
The horror o' the endless Fate
A'thing 's whirled in predestinate.

O whiles I'd fain be blin' to it,
As men wha through the ages sit,
And never move frae aff the bit*,   one's original
                                                                    position
Wha hear a Burns or Shakespeare sing,
Yet still their ain bit jingles string,
As they were worth the fashioning.   2520

Whatever Scotland is to me,
Be it aye pairt o' a' men see
O' Earth and o' Eternity

Wha winna hide their heids in't till
It seems the haill o' Space to fill,
As t'were an unsurmounted hill.

He canna Scotland see wha yet
Canna see the Infinite,
And Scotland in true scale to it.

Nor blame I muckle, wham atour   2530
Earth's countries blaw, a pickle★ stour★,   little/dust storm
To sort wha's grains they ha'e nae poo'er.

E'en stars are seen thegither in
A'e skime o' licht as grey as tin
Flyin' on the wheel as t'were a pin.

Syne ither systems ray on ray
Skinkle★ past in quick array   twinkle
While it is still the self-same day,

A'e day o' a' the million days
Through which the soul o' man can gaze   2540
Upon the wheel's incessant blaze,

Upon the wheel's incessant blaze
As it were on a single place
That twinklin' filled the howe o' space.

A'e point is a' that it can be,
I wis nae man 'll ever see
The rest o' the rotundity.

Impersonality sall blaw
Through me as 'twere a bluffert o snaw
To scour me o' my sense o' awe,   2550

A bluffert o' snaw, the licht that flees
Within the Wheel, and Freedom gi'es
Frae Dust and Daith and a' Disease,

– The drumlie doom that only weighs
On them wha ha'ena seen their place
Yet in creation's lichtnin' race,

In the movement that includes
As a tide's resistless floods
A' their movements and their moods, –

Until disinterested we,   2560
O' a' oor auld delusions free,
Lowe★ in the wheel's serenity   flame

As conscious items in the licht,
And keen to keep it clear and bricht
In which the haill machine is dight,

The licht nae man has ever seen
Till he has felt that he's been gi'en
The stars themsels insteed o' een,

And often wi' the sun has glowered
At the white mune until it cowered,   2570
As when by new thocht auld's o'erpowered.

Oor universe is like an e'e
Turned in, man's benmaist hert to see,
And swamped in subjectivity.

But whether it can use its sicht
To bring what lies withoot to licht
To answer's still ayont my micht.

But when that inturned look has brocht
To licht what still in vain it's socht
Ootward maun be the bent o' thocht.   2580

And organs may develop syne
Responsive to the need divine
O' single-minded humankin'.

The function, as it seems to me,
O' Poetry is to bring to be
At lang, lang last that unity . . .

But wae's me on the weary wheel!
Higgledy-piggledy in't we reel,
And little it cares hoo we may feel.

Twenty-six thoosand years 'tll tak'   2590
For it to threid the Zodiac
— A single roond o' the wheel to mak'!

Lately it turned — I saw mysel'
In sic a company doomed to mell★.   mix
I micht ha'e been in Dante's Hell.

It shows hoo little the best o' men
E'en o' themsels at times can ken,
— I sune saw *that* when I gaed ben.

The lesser wheel within the big
That moves as merry as a grig★,   2600   child
Wi' mankind in its whirligig

And hasna turned a'e circle yet
Tho' as it turns we slide in it,
And needs maun tak' the place we get,

I felt it turn, and syne I saw
John Knox and Clavers in my raw,
And Mary Queen o' Scots ana',

And Rabbie Burns and Weelum Wallace,
And Carlyle lookin' unco gallus★,   reckless
And Harry Lauder (to enthrall us).   2610

And as I looked I saw them a',
A' the Scots baith big and sma',
That e'er the braith o' life did draw.

'Mercy o' Gode, I canna thole
Wi' sic an orra mob to roll.'
– 'Wheesht! It's for the guid o' your soul.'

'But what's the meanin', what's the sense?'
– 'Men shift but by experience.
'Twixt Scots there is nae difference.

They canna learn, sae canna move,   2620
But stick for aye to their auld groove
– The only race in History who've

Bidden in the same category
Frae stert to present o' their story,
And deem their ignorance their glory.

The mair they differ, mair the same.
The wheel can whummle a' but them,
– They ca' their obstinacy "Hame",

And "Puir Auld Scotland" bleat wi' pride,
And wi' their minds made up to bide   2630
A thorn in a' the wide world's side.

There ha'e been Scots wha ha'e ha'en thochts,
They're strewn through maist o' the various lots
– Sic traitors are nae langer Scots!'

'But in this huge ineducable
Heterogeneous hotch and rabble,
Why am I condemned to squabble?'

'A Scottish poet maun assume
The burden o' his people's doom,
And dee to brak' their livin' tomb.   2640

Mony ha'e tried, but a' ha'e failed.
Their sacrifice has nocht availed.
Upon the thistle they're impaled.

You maun choose but gin ye'd see
Anither category ye
Maun tine your nationality.'

And I look at a' the random
Band the wheel leaves whaur it fand 'em.
        'Auch to Hell,
I'll tak' it to avizandum.' . . .   2650

O wae's me on the weary wheel,
And fain I'd understand them!
And blessin' on the weary wheel
Whaurever it may land them! . . .

But aince Jean kens what I've been through
The nicht, I dinna doot it,
She'll ope her airms in welcome true,
And clack nae mair aboot it . . .

            ★   ★   ★   ★   ★

The stars like thistle's roses floo'er
The sterile growth o' Space ootour,   2660
That clad in bitter blasts spreids oot
Frae me, the sustenance o' its root.

O fain I'd keep my hert entire,
Fain hain★ the licht o' my desire,   preserve
But ech! the shinin' streams ascend,
And leave me empty at the end.

For aince it's toomed my hert and brain,
The thistle needs maun fa' again.
– But a' its growth 'll never fill
The hole it's turned my life intill! . . .   2670

Yet ha'e I Silence left, the croon o' a'.

No' her, wha on the hills langsyne I saw
Liftin' a foreheid o' perpetual snaw.

No' her, wha in the how-dumb-deid★ o' nicht   midnight
Kyths★, like Eternity in Time's despite.   appears

No' her, withooten shape, wha's name is Daith,
No' Him, unkennable abies★ to faith   except

– God whom, gin e'er He saw a man, 'ud be
E'en mair dumfooner'd at the sicht than he.

– But Him, whom nocht in man or Deity,   2680
Or Daith or Dreid or Laneliness can touch,
Wha's deed owre often and has seen owre much.

O I ha'e Silence left,
                     – 'And weel ye micht,'
Sae Jean'll say, 'efter sic a nicht!'

*   *   *   *   *

Milk-Wort and Bog-Cotton

To Seumas O'Sullivan

Cwa' een like milk-wort and bog-cotton hair!
I love you, earth, in this mood best o' a'
When the shy spirit like a laich wind moves
And frae the lift★ nae shadow can fa'   sky
Since there's nocht left to thraw a shadow there
Owre een like milk-wort and milk-white cotton hair.

Wad that nae leaf upon anither wheeled
A shadow either and nae root need dern★   hide
In sacrifice to let sic beauty be!
But deep surroondin' darkness I discern   10
Is aye the price o' licht. Wad licht revealed
Naething but you and nicht nocht else concealed.

A Daughter of the Sea

A wumman cam' up frae the blae deeps o' the sea
And 'I'm Jeannie MacQueen,' she said, lauchin', to me.

But it's 'Gi way wi' your oyster-shine, lassie, gi way'
– For she'd a different colour in the nail o' each tae.

Towards a New Scotland

I

In these lane voes whaur the airms o' bare land
Lie on the grey waters like shadows oor boat
Seems to haud a' the life that there is – there's nae need
To rin a line oot; there's nae fish to be got
     – Yet aye there's a cry, 'I see white in the lum'
     And up on the line coontles ferlies* come.   *wonders*

Toom* tho' the waters may look, useless oor quest,   *empty*
We find on ilka hook a yield 'yont* a' hope   *beyond*
– a scallop, a hoo*, a sea-sponge, and syne   *dog fish*
A halibut big as a table-top   10
     – Never say die, tho' auld Scotland seems bare
     Oot wi' your line; there's prodigies there.

II

As the hills o' Morven were hills afore
The Himalayas or Alps were born
And established through a' geological time,
Can look at sic muckle ephemera wi' scorn

Sayin': 'We saw you come and we'll see you gang
Nae maitter hoo you may too'er the day,'
Sae a' the giantisms o' England and Empire
Auld Scotland can dismiss in the self-same way.   20

III

Was it for little Belgium's sake
Sae mony thoosand Scotsmen dee'd?
And never ane for Scotland fegs
Wi' twenty thoosand times mair need!

IV

I wad dae onything for you, Scotland, save
– Even tho' your true line should be wi' such –
Become like ninety per cent o' Scots;
That 'ud be askin' faur owre much!

V

Ah, Scotland, you ken best. Why should I complain
That my poo'ers tae canna redound to you,   30
But micht hae been jewels elsewhere if I'd foreseen
     An' been to you a kennin' mair untrue?

Why should I complain when for centuries back
You've cast sae muckle aside that maist men deem
The best you bred – maist fit to serve and honour you,
     And elsewhere these worthless glories gleam?

Why I should complain wha least o' a' men rate
What you rejected as foreigners and renegades rate,
But at whatever cost approve your barrenness
     Faur abune a' their meretricious state?   40

The time isna ripe yet and in vain I hae tried
To separate the base elements you ne'er could accept
Frae sic faint forerinners o' your comin' dawn
     As whiles I thocht within me leapt.

Ah, Scotland, you ken best. I've been hailly wrang,
Mist'aen bog-fires for your true licht at last.
Yet gladly I rejected ither literatures for yours,
     Nor covet them noo you've ootcast!

And sae my failure suddenly reveals itsel'
A pairt – a strengthenin' – o' your reserved intent;   50
Harder the task, greater the triumph; I'm prood to be
     Failin' the latter wi' the former blent.

Ah, Scotland, you ken best. Why should I complain
That my poo'ers tae canna redound to you;
They couldna been jewels elsewhere; I couldna been
     To you ony mair – or less–untrue!

          VI
My dreams for you, Scotland, no' till I heard
Them repeated on ither folks' lips did I ken
Their utter inadequacy to your need
And rejoice in your steadfast sterility again.   60

My dreams for you, Scotland, they flamed in me
To a monstrous height while I dreamed them alane;
I kent they were better than ocht that opposed
Save you – and you hadna spoken to me then.

My dreams for you, Scotland, as soon as I heard
Ithers cry I was right and repeat what I'd said
I kent I was hopelessly wrang and was glad
O' the light sic fools inadvertently shed!

          VII
Let nae man think he can serve you, Scotland,
Withoot muckle trial and trouble to himsel'.   70
The slightest service to you compares
Wi' fetchin' a bit o' Heaven doon into Hell.

Let wha wad serve you reflect for a minute
On a' the thoosands that seemed to and failed to
– Ony service demands heich qualities then
These coontless thoosands ne'er scaled to.

And even at the best hoo mony folk coont
O' the least consequence to you since Time began.
Lightly to fancy he's o' the favoured few
Nearly aye disposes o' the claims o' a man.   80

Nay, fegs, it's wi' you as wi' a lion-cub
A man may fetch hame and can play wi' at first,
But if he has it lang, it grows up an syne
– Suddenly his fool's paradise is burst!

    VIII
Surely the weediest of all the sons of Mars,
    The final shakings of his poke,
A pimply-faced Cockney soldier in Edinburgh Castle
    I saw, and thus he spoke.

Looking down upon the heaving city there
    As o'er the precipice he spat: 90
'Gor-blimey, we've made Scotland wot she is;
    Wot would she be wivaht?'

Cattle Shaw

I shall go among red faces and virile voices,
See stylish sheep, with fine heads and well-wooled,
And great bulls mellow to the touch,
Brood mares of marvelous approach, and geldings
With sharp and flinty bones and silken hair.

And through th' enclosure draped in red and gold
I shall pass on to spheres more vivid yet
Where countesses' coque feathers gleam and glow
And, swathed in silks, the painted ladies are
Whose laughter plays like summer lightning there.   10

The Storm-Cock's Song

My song today is the storm-cock's song.
When the cold winds blow and the driving snow
Hides the tree-tops, only his song rings out
In the lulls in the storm. so let mine go!

On the topmost twig of a leafless ash
He sits bolt upright against the sky
Surveying the white fields and the leafless woods
And distant red in the East with his buoyant eye.

Surely he has little enough cause to sing
When even the hedgerow berries are already pulped by the frost   10
Or eaten by other birds – yet alone and aloft
To another hungry day his greeting is tossed.

Blessed are those who have songs to sing
When others are silent; poor song though it be,
Just a message to the silence that someone is still
Alive and glad, though on a naked tree.

What if it is only a few churning notes
Flung out in a loud and artless way?
His 'Will I do it? Do it I will!' is worth a lot
When the rest have nothing at all to say.   20

Ewart MacKintosh (1893 – 1917)

Cha Till MacCruimein

Departure of the 4th Camerons

The pipes in the street were playing bravely,
The marching lads went by,
With merry hearts and voices singing
My friends marched out to die;
But I was hearing a lonely pibroch
Out of an older war,
'Farewell, farewell, farewell, MacCrimmon,
MacCrimmon comes no more.'

And every lad in his heart was dreaming
Of honour and wealth to come,   10
And honour and noble pride were calling
To the tune of the pipes and drum;
But I was hearing a woman singing
On dark Dunvegan shore,
'In battle or peace, with wealth or honour,
MacCrimmon comes no more.'

And there in front of the men were marching,
With feet that made no mark,
The grey old ghosts of the ancient fighters
Come back again from the dark;   20
And in front of them all MacCrimmon piping
A weary tune and sore,
'On the gathering day, for ever and ever,
MacCrimmon comes no more.'

– Bedford, 1915

Joe Corrie (1894 – 1968)

Scottish Pride

It's fine when ye stand in a queue
at the door o' the 'Dole'
on a snawy day,
To ken that ye leive in the bonniest
land in the world,
The bravest, tae.

It's fine when you're in a pickle
Whether or no'
you'll get your 'dough,'
To sing a wee bit sang   10
o' the heather hills,
And the glens below.

It's fine when the clerk says,
'Nae "dole" here for you!'
To proodly turn,
and think o' the bluidy slashin'
the English got
at Bannockburn.

The Lover

Here in the guts of the earth –
In my father's tomb;
In the forests of aeons past;
In the gas and the gloom;
Naked, and blind with sweat,
I strive and I strain;
Helpless, and racked to the heart
With hate and pain.

But home, I will wash me clean,
And over the hill,   10
To the glen of their fair primrose,
And the daffodil;
And there I will sing of my Love
So tenderly,
That even the love-lorn gods
Will envy me.

The Pithead Lass

I watch you passing down the street
These grey days;
Grey houses, grey skies, and the pit-smoke's
Grey haze.

Jauntily humming an April air;
And the morning sun
Floods with its gold an ancient street
In Babylon.

And Thisbe, robed in virgin white,
Gaily doth pass,   10
Innocent of the tragic eyes
Of Pyramus.

I watch you passing down the street
These grey days;
And, thinking of your mother's fate,
My heart prays.

Guttin' Herrin'

Guttin' herrin' in the rain,
Och! my heart is sad and sore,
And it canna sing again,
Till I see my Love once more.

Round my head the seagulls fly,
Screechin', screechin' all the day,
How they keep tormenting me,
Now my Love is far away.

White the mist comes down, and cold,
Never was this Isle so drear,   10
Yet the sun would shine, I know,
If I saw my own Love here.

Speed his boat, ye winds that blow,
Guide him safely home to Skye,
Tell him he is all my joy,
And without him I would die.

Guttin' herrin' in the rain.

Hewers of Coal

Corrie had been a miner himself and his subject was always the working classes. *Hewers of Coal* was hugely popular among the amateur drama groups that provided a strong populist alternative to the mainstream theatres of Glasgow and Edinburgh. The printed source for this play (*Joe Corrie*. Edinburgh: 7:84 Publications, 1985) contains a number of typographical eccentricities. Some have been silently regularised; the others remain as indicative of Corrie's style.

CHARACTERS

SANDY   A Miner of middle age
WILLIE   A boy
PETER   A pit handyman, 50 years of age
NED   A Miner of middle age
BOB   An underground gaffer about 50 years old

SCENE 1

A 'headin' underground. It is a narrowly-confined place about five feet six inches high, hewn out of the solid rock with the exception of a narrow strip of coal which is seen at the bottom of the back wall. Against the back wall there may be a prop, on which hangs a miner's jacket on a nail.

The only entrance is in the right wall (spectator's). This has a prop at each side and one across, an opening of about four and a half feet high and three and a half feet wide. Over this opening there hangs a coarse canvas 'screen'. This is one of the pit precautions for a better air current. A few old hutch road sleepers lie here and there on which the men sit when they are taking their meal.

When the curtain rises sandy sits in the centre of the stage eating bread and cheese from a 'piece tin' and drinking from a tea flask. At his side there is a larger flask for the holding of water. At the right willie sits also at his meal. They have had three hours work in the pit and their faces are black. Both have donned their jackets as is the custom with miners when they are having their meal. Their safety lamps are beside them. But there should be an added dim blue light for stage purposes.

> WILLIE *with his mouth full, puts his 'piece tin' together with a snap, and pushes it in his jacket pocket as much as to say 'Weel, that's that.'* SANDY *still taking his meal, looks at* WILLIE.

SANDY Is that you finished wi' your piece already, Wullie?

WILLIE *(still chewing)* Imph!

SANDY Ye shouldna eat sae quick – it's no' guid for the stomach.

WILLIE Ach, I have a stomach that can digest nails . . . What's wrang that Peter's no' in for his ham and eggs?

SANDY There was a smash up o' hutches doon your brae, did ye no' ken that.

WILLIE Oh. Was that the way the haulage was stopped?

SANDY Ay, it was a big smash, I believe.

WILLIE What happened?

SANDY I dinna ken. I just came up for my piece when the haulage stopped.

> WILLIE, *not so keenly interested, is looking rather enviously at* SANDY'S *piece tin.*

WILLIE Is that scone ye have on your piece the-day, SANDY?

SANDY Ay. *(Smiling.)* Would ye like a bit?

> WILLIE *needs no second bidding, he is at* SANDY'S *side immediately.* SANDY, *still smiling, hands him a piece of the scone.* WILLIE *takes a bite.*

WILLIE Thanks – a million.

He returns to his former seat enjoying the scone to the full.

SANDY You're a great wee lad for scone, Wullie.

WILLIE I could eat till it was comin' oot o' my ears. Sandy – It was a bad day for me when my mither died – *(Sighs.)* She used to bake every day.

SANDY Does your sister no' bake for ye?

WILLIE *(full of scorn)* Her! She hasna time to bake for pooderin' her face and wavin' her hair. Pictures and dancin', that's a' she can think aboot. Daft to get a man, Sandy, and when she does get yin she'll poison him wi' tinned meat. I've got a new name for her noo.

SANDY *(with a smile)* Oh, what d'ye ca' her, Wullie?

WILLIE *(very definitely as if with great satisfaction)* Tin-opener Teenie! By gee! she's an expert at it. Would ye believe it, Sandy, the back o' oor hoose is like a muni-tion work wi' empty tins.

SANDY *(still amused)* They tell me she's a champion dancer, Willie.

WILLIE That's right – but it's no' roon a girdle. *(Pause.)* This scone's just great, Sandy. Ye must be prood o' your wife?

SANDY (suddenly thoughtful) Ay – but no' as prood as I micht be, Willie. The miner is a thouchtless kind o' chap. He goes hame on pay day wi' aboot forty shillin's, hands it ower to his wife like a hero, and forgets that even the Chancellor o' the Exchequer would have to throw in the sponge if he had to feed a man, a wife, and fower weans on it. Hoo the damn they manage is a mystery to me. *(Looking at* WILLIE.*)* And yet they have the he'rt to laugh and sing, tae.

WILLIE Ay, my mither was aye singin', Sandy – aye singin'. *(Pause. Downcast eyes.)* By gee! I DAE miss her.

SANDY Hoo's your faither keepin' noo?

WILLIE Ach! some days he's up, Sandy, and ither days he's doon. I don't think he'll ever be much better noo.

SANDY You've had a rotten time o' it, Wullie?

WILLIE Ay. Still it's a guid job that I'M workin', Sandy. I dinna get that much in the pit, but it keeps us gaun in the hoose.

SANDY It must be a struggle for ye.

WILLIE As lang as I keep my job, Sandy, we'll no' be sae bad.

SANDY *(thoughtfully)* Ay – a JOB? – The hale world whiles goes roon' on a job . . . Nae job, nae breid, and nae breid nae laughter. It's a queer wey o' runnin' a world in my opinion.

There is a slight pause then a pony is heard neighing off: WILLIE *looks at* SANDY *quite tragically.*

WILLIE Aw! listen to Danny . . . I forgot to keep him a bit o' my piece.

SANDY *(lightly)* But he has plenty o' corn, Willie.

WILLIE Mebbe, but he looks furrit to gettin' a bit o' my piece and a drink o' my tea. *(Pony neighs again.)* D'ye hear him, Sandy. *(Pause.)* Him and me are great pals noo, Sandy . . . If ever I win a big coupon, I'll buy him frae the company and tak' him up to the green fields.

SANDY D've like workin' doon the pit, Wullie?

WILLIE No' bad. But it's just because I drive that wee pownie. *(Pause. Sadly.)* I wish I had minded to keep him a bit o' my piece.

SANDY *holds out the last piece of scone he has left.*

SANDY Here, take this oot to him.

WILLIE *jumps to it.*

WILLIE You're public hero number one, SANDY.

He goes towards exit.

SANDY Lift that screen, Wullie, and gi'e us a breath o' air.

While WILLIE *is doing this, hanging it at left on a nail, the pony neighs again.*

WILLIE *(loudly)* I'm comin', Danny . . . I'm comin'!

He hurries out. SANDY *smiles and shakes his head. He puts his flask and piece tin in his pockets.* PETER *enters. He is in his shirt sleeves. He puffs and blows and is wiping his brow with a red and white spotted hankerchief:* SANDY *is conscious of* PETER'S *entrance but doesn't look at him.* PETER *is speaking on his entry, and goes directly to his jacket hanging on nail.*

PETER The things that happen doon this pit would break the he'rt o' a saint.

Takes his flask and piece-tin from pockets of his coat. SANDY *looks up at him unpleasantly.*

SANDY What's wrang wi' ye noo?

PETER Did ye no' see that smash-up at the bottom o' the brae? A race o' hutches ran awa' frae the top, and they were jammed richt to the roof. Where's Wullie?

He looks round for him.

SANDY What d'ye want wi' him?

PETER The gaffer's comin' up to tell him something. He put a twisted couplin' on that race o' hutches, that's what caused the run-awa'. I wouldna be surprised if he gets the sack for it – Robert's in a fine rage.

SANDY And hoo did Robert ken it was a twisted couplin' that caused the smash?

PETER I tellt him.

SANDY *(getting angry)* And hoo did YOU ken?

PETER It was the only way it COULD come off.

PETER sits at left to take his meal.

SANDY You're damned quick in spoutin' things like that to the gaffer, Peter. D'ye believe he thinks ony mair o' ye for it?

PETER What are ye barkin' at?

SANDY You! The boy wouldna put on a twisted couplin' intentionally. Mistakes WILL happen. Have you never made yin?

PETER If ye saw the mess that I had to clear up doon there you would talk different.

SANDY Isn't it your job in this pit to clear up messes? And you're weel suited to the job, if ye get what I mean.

PETER Look here, Sandy, if there's ony mair o' this at piecetime I'm seein' the gaffer aboot it. I'm no' standin' this talk off you.

SANDY If Wullie gets the sack because o' this you'll have to stand mair than talk off me.

PETER It's nane o' your business, anyway.

SANDY I'm makin' it my business. That laddie canna afford to lose his job. Ye micht have made shair o' your facts before ye tellt the gaffer.

PETER If I had kept the blame off Wullie it micht ha' fa'n on me.

SANDY Ay, and that would have been a hell o' a tragedy, wouldn't it? You're damned selfish, Peter.

PETER If a body doesna look after themsel's in this world there's naebody else will.

SANDY *(scornfully)* And is that YOUR ootlook on life?

PETER It is.

SANDY There micht come a day when you're dependin' on the help o' somebody. What'll ye dae then?

PETER That day'll never come, Sandy – never.

SANDY Better men than you have needed help, and have been damned glad to take it when it DID come.

PETER Weel, there's YIN thing ye can be shair o', Sandy – It'll be a bad day for me when I'm lookin' for help frae you.

SANDY Dinna craw, Peter. This is a gey queer world, remember, and some queer things happen in it.

PETER Maybe, but that's yin thing that'll NEVER happen. (WILLIE *returns. He immediately sniffs and looks at* PETER *who is now well on with his meal*).

WILLIE Great smell o' ham an' eggs in here.

SANDY Nae bairns, Wullie, and lots o' extra shifts.

PETER *(to* WILLIE*)* Did you see the gaffer when ye were oot there?

WILLIE *(showing signs of fear)* No – what is it?

SANDY You're gettin' the blame o' that smash doon the brae, Wullie.

WILLIE Me!

PETER You put a twisted couplin' on that race o' hutches and it came off gaun ower the snap. (WILLIE *is silent.*)

WILLIE *(to* SANDY*)* Does that mean that I'll get the sack, Sandy?

SANDY If you have to go up the pit the-day, Wullie, you'll no' be the only yin. *(Pause.)* Does Ned ken that it's piece time?

WILLIE *(still suffering from the shock)* I couldna say, Sandy. He didna leave his jacket here, this mornin'. I saw him takin' it into the coal face when he went in.

SANDY *(looking round)* Oh, I didna notice that . . . Gi'e him a shout onywey. (WILLIE *goes off giving* PETER *a nasty look as he goes*).

SANDY *(to* PETER*)* Wullie's faither's badly – ye ken that.

PETER Weel?

SANDY They're gey hard up at hame.

PETER And what has that to do wi' me?

SANDY Ye micht gi'e Wullie the benefit o' the doot. Tell the gaffer ye found a broken link on the brae and it caused the smash.

PETER I'm dain' naething o' the kind. If it was found oot I micht get the sack mysel'. (SANDY *adopts a threatening attitude.*)

SANDY Peter! if that boy get's the sack because o' this I'll . . . I'll . . .

> BOB *enters. He is the gaffer. A tall man, wearing a blue flannel shirt with long sleeves, and short leggings. He hangs his lamp on his belt.*

BOB Peter, there's a loose strand in that rope doon there. Get your splicin' tools and put it richt before the haulage starts.

> PETER *closes his piece tin immediately, lays it down beside him, then rises quickly, and obediently.*

PETER Very guid, Robert, very guid. I'll no' be a minute.

> PETER *hurries off.* BOB *takes a pocket note book from his pocket and writes down something on it.*

BOB If it's no' yin thing doon here it's anither. That's half an 'oor lost this mornin'.

SANDY Ay, but a pit's no' a biscuit factory, Bob, where everything goes like clock-work.

BOB There's too much carelessness. I'll have to make an example. Where's that pownie driver.

SANDY Awa' into the coal face to see Ned Marshall.

BOB Weel, tell him no' to start work until I see him.

SANDY You're no' thinkin' o' sackin' him, are ye?

BOB That smash was HIS faut.

SANDY Ye have nae proof o' that – just Peter's word. But mistakes can happen wi' us a'.

BOB Ay, but we canna afford them to happen.

SANDY *(sarcastically)* WE! When did you get a share in the coal company, Bob.

BOB *looks at him quickly.*

BOB What d'ye mean?

SANDY You said WE canna afford to make mistakes. I suppose you've made them yoursel' before ye were sae perfect.

BOB Look here, I want nae sarcasm. And mind your ain business or you'll be gettin' mair fresh air than is guid for ye.

SANDY So ye DAE ken what fresh air is, then?

BOB What d'ye mean by that?

SANDY We could be dain' wi' mair o' it doon here.

BOB You have a damned sicht mair than your share. Close that screen. There are ither folk in the pit needin' air as weel as you.

SANDY *does it, letting the screen fall angrily.*

SANDY It would be fine if everything could be put richt as easy, Bob.

BOB What are ye drivin' at?

SANDY Have ye got that fa' redd-up in the main aircourse yet?

BOB *(sarcastically)* And what'll happen to me if it's no'?

SANDY It's no' what micht happen to you, it's what micht happen to us a'. *(Significantly.)* There's gas doon this pit, remember.

BOB *(with a sarcastic smile)* Oh, is there? Thanks for the information. *(A bit sinisterly.)* Ye had better come into my office when ye get to the surface. I'll have a talk wi' ye there.

PETER *enters carrying his splicing tools.*

PETER I'm ready noo, Robert.

BOB *makes to go off. He turns and looks at* SANDY *before going.*

BOB Gas in the pit, is there? And a fa' in the main aircourse. And you'd like the inspector to ken eh? There's ways and means o' dealin' wi' your kind, Sandy – Mind that!

BOB *goes off followed by* PETER, *at his heels.* SANDY *is troubled.* WILLIE *enters.*

WILLIE What's the gaffer angry aboot, SANDY?

SANDY I've just been gi'in' him the hint aboot that fa' in the air-course! and remindin' him that it's healthier and safer to let the gas go up to the sky.

WILLIE Is he gaun to sack me?

SANDY If he sacks you the-day, Wullie, he'll ha'e me to reckon wi'. Is Ned comin' in for his piece?

WILLIE He's had his piece, SANDY, he took it at the coal-face. *(Troubled.)* Sandy, I hope I dinna get the sack the noo, it takes a' the money we can get to keep the hoose gaun.

SANDY *(patting* WILLIE *on the shoulder kindly)* You keep your mind easy, son.

NED *enters. He looks ill, and enters coughing.*

SANDY That's a bad cough you've got, Ned?

NED *(with a struggle)* Ay – it's stayin' ower long on me this time. The air doon here's no' helpin' it ony either.

NED *sits in centre exhausted.*

SANDY What did you take your piece at the face for?

NED I . . . I took it a wee bit early.

SANDY Why?

NED The . . . the roof has been workin' a' mornin'. There's mair gas in my place, tae.

SANDY What we should dae, Ned, is blacklist this section.

NED *(with a faint smile)* And ye ken what that would mean, Sandy – we'd get oor books. And I dinna want mine the noo.

SANDY *(slowly)* Ay – oor books. So we've just got to take the risk.

SANDY *catches a glimpse of* NED *looking at* PETER'S *piece-tin.*

SANDY *(deliberately)* Here! have ye HAD a piece this mornin'?
NED *(greatly embarrassed)* Ay . . . I . . . I . . .
SANDY *(angry)* What's the guid o' tellin' a lie! It's nae crime to come withoot a piece to the pit when there's a wife and weans to come first. *(Regretting his tone.)* I'm sorry, Ned.

There is a slight pause.

WILLIE I wish I had kent, Ned, you could have had a share o' mine.

SANDY *glances at* PETER'S *tin, then exchanges glances with* WILLIE.

SANDY *(to* WILLIE*)* Peter left the rest o' his piece for the pownie, didn't he?
WILLIE *(puzzled)*. Eh . . . What's that, Sandy?
SANDY *(nodding his head secretly that* WILLIE *will agree)* I'm sayin' that Peter left the rest o' his piece for the pownie.
WILLIE *(understanding)* Ay, that's what he said before he went oot, Sandy.
SANDY Weel, the pownie has plenty o' corn. (SANDY *opens* PETER'S *piece-tin, takes the bread from it, and hands it to* NED.) Here ye are, Ned. There seems to be ham and egg on it, tae.
NED *(as if shrinking from it)* No, Sandy! If Peter was to ken I got it he would talk aboot it a' through the pit.
SANDY *(forcing it on him)* Take it, and don't be a damned fule. I'll explain to Peter, and he'll keep it quiet.

NED *takes the bread reluctantly, hanging his head, and nearly breaking down.*

SANDY *(seeing* NED'S *predicament)* If ye dinna want to take it here, Ned, go into your place wi' it.

NED *looks at* SANDY *in a hopeless manner.*

NED Sandy, I'm tired . . . I'm no' fit to be workin' doon here, but I've got to do it to keep my wife and weans respectable. *(Hopelessly.)* Ach! there's whiles I wish the roof would come doon on top o' me, and end it . . . Mary would get compensation, and her worries would be a' by . . . I was just thinkin' this mornin' that . . .
SANDY *(interrupting)* Noo, noo, Ned, nane o' thae ideas! Awa' and eat that piece – you'll feel the better o' it. (NED *rises.*)
NED *(humbly)* You can thank Peter frae me, Sandy.
SANDY That's a' richt, Ned.

NED *goes off coughing.*

SANDY Ned's just aboot a waster I think.
WILLIE By gee? Peter'll be angry when he misses his piece.
SANDY *(with a smile)* We'll blame the rats for it, Wullie. He has as much ham and egg in him as dae him for the rest o' the shift, onywey.

SANDY *is having a quiet chuckle to himself when* PETER *enters.*

PETER *(entering)* Nae wonder my meals never dae me ony guid. I never get peace to sit doon to them.

PETER *sits down to have the rest of his meal.* SANDY *looks at* WILLIE *and smiles.* WILLIE *is deeply interested in* PETER'S *face.* PETER *opens his box and gets a shock.*

PETER Here! what has happened to my piece!
SANDY A couple o' rats came in and took it awa'.

PETER *(sarcastically)* Oh, did they. And opened the tin and shut it after them, I suppose.

SANDY You're a guid guesser, Peter.

PETER *(rising. Angrily.)* Where's my piece!

SANDY *(to* WILLIE) He doesna believe me, Wullie. (WILLIE *enjoys this scene.)*

PETER *(threateningly)* Are ye gaun to gi'e me back my piece!

SANDY You're ower late, Peter. It's awa' ta-ta!

PETER Where is it?

SANDY Peter . . . Ned Marshall came in here and I found oot that he didna have a crust oot to the pit wi' him. So I thoucht ye wouldna mind me gi'en him what you had left.

PETER Eh! You ga'e my piece to HIM! And what am I gaun to do?

SANDY You've had no' a bad breakfast, Peter.

PETER *(madly)* Ye swine! *(He lifts one of his splicing tools in his rage and is about to attack* SANDY). I'll teach ye to gi'e awa' MY piece! (SANDY *rises hurriedly to defend himself:* BOB *enters).*

BOB Here? What's the maitter here?

PETER *(piteously)* Robert! This yin has stolen my piece.

BOB *(puzzled)* Stolen your piece?

PETER *(almost in tears)* Ay, and gi'en' it to that Ned Marshall.

BOB *(to* SANDY) Is this true?

SANDY Ned came in here starvin', so I thoucht that Peter would be only too pleased to do a guid turn for yince in his life.

PETER *(still whining)* He didna even ask me for it, Robert. And here I am, left withoot onything noo.

BOB Look here, Sandy, the best thing you can dae is get up the pit. *(To* WILLIE.) And you dae the same.

SANDY Right o! Bob. But before I go I'm gaun to gi'e this greedy swine the bonniest pair o' black e'en that he has ever had in his life.

> SANDY *is taking off his coat angrily.* WILLIE *cowers in corner at right front.*

BOB *(concerned)* Sandy! Ye ken what it means to strike a man doon a pit?

SANDY Ay, it means sixty days in jile, but it'll be worth it!

> PETER *has retreated to left back.* SANDY *looks at him.* BOB *goes in front of* SANDY *to hold him back. But* SANDY *gradually gets nearer to* PETER. *He is near enough him to strike, and raise his hand. Then there is heard a terrific roar, like thunder. Immediately they all look right. The quarrel is forgotten.* WILLIE *runs to the shelter of* SANDY, *holding on to him with a childish fear The noise gets louder and more terrible. They stand helplessly, all gradually retreating to the left wall. There is a pause in the action. Then* NED *staggers in.*

NED We're trapped – trapped!

> The noise is now horrible, and the sound of crashing debris can be heard. A stone, accompanied by a cloud of dust, falls on the scene. A loud crash is heard at the opening. The noise gradually fades, like thunder amongst the hills. For a few seconds there is a pause. Then quietness, but for the echoing noise of falls in other parts of the pit. SANDY *slowly goes to the opening and lifts the screen. He starts backwards with a shock, for the way out is closed by fallen rock.* SANDY *turns and looks at the stricken men.*

SANDY God! . . . we're entombed!

> *A slow curtain.*

SCENE 2

> *Shortly after the close of the curtain the voice of a wireless announcer is heard.*

ANNOUNCER This is the National Programme. The deathroll in the Glendinning pit disaster has now reached 42. Another two bodies having been found this morning. For the past five days the rescue parties have worked in relays, day and night. They're endeavouring now to reach the Hard Coal Heading, where it is hoped, some of the men may have succeeded in reaching. Little hope, however, is being held on eventually bringing them to safety. Messages of condolence have been received from His Majesty the King, the Prime Minister, the Minister for Mines, and from the Archbishop of Canterbury . . . A relief fund has been opened for the bereaved relatives, and contributions will be gratefully received at the office of the Miners' Federation, or may be sent to the Provost of Glendinning . . . In the South Wales coalfield another strike has broken out. It is entirely unofficial, and . . .

The last few words fade out as the curtain slowly opens. The scene is the old Hard Coal Heading. It is on a slope, rising from right to left. This can be done by using a slope platform, a sloped frontpiece rising from about 1 foot at right to 3 feet at left. A black curtain can be lowered from the top, also at a corresponding slope. There is a small opening at right, but only an opening. There is no outlet to the world. There is only one lamp alight, hanging near SANDY, *who sits in the centre.* BOB *is at right putting up a silent prayer.*

WILLIE *lies to left of* SANDY; *asleep, too* PETER *is at extreme left. They all wear jackets. All the men are nearly done. It is the hope of* SANDY *that has kept them alive. On the back wall are five chalked strokes. The water can is beside* SANDY.

BOB *(just a faint whisper)* Amen.

There is a dead pause for a moment or two then BOB *looks at* SANDY *pleadingly.*

BOB Can I have a few drops o' water, Sandy?
SANDY *(lifting the water can and shaking it at his ear)* It can only be a drop or twa, Bob.
BOB I ken.
SANDY The-day'll finish it.

He hands the can to BOB. PETER *rises to his knees looking on the scene with staring eyes. While* BOB *sips* PETER *crawls forward.* SANDY *watches him closely.* BOB *hands the can back to* SANDY.

PETER Can I wet my tongue, tae, Sandy?
SANDY *(after looking at Ned)* I think we'll have to keep the rest for Ned . . . I'm worried aboot him noo – he looks done.
PETER *(piteously)* Oh! just twa drops, Sandy – for God's sake! *(SANDY looks at him).*
SANDY Very weel, then, but it'll have to be the last.
PETER Ay.

SANDY *gives him the water can but holds on to it. He pulls it away from* PETER *when he thinks he has had enough.* PETER *returns to his former position. There is a pause.* BOB *goes to* SANDY *and clasps his hand.*

BOB Sandy – before it's ower late – thanks for a' you have done for us. It was your pluck that got us here – oor yin and only hope – if it has failed.
SANDY Life is sweet, Bob. Yet it micht have been better if we had gane wi' the ithers . . . Still, we ken each ither better noo – and that's something.
BOB Ay, but it's a pity we dinna ken o' the guid things in life till it's ower late.

BOB *returns to his former position. There is a pause.*

BOB *(hopelessly)* No' a soon'.

SANDY Listen!

SANDY, PETER and BOB are all attention.

SANDY *(hopelessly)* No.

BOB No.

PETER No.

BOB It's queer that the HUNGER has passed awa' frae us, Sandy?

SANDY Ay. It was hellish while it lasted, but there's nae cravin' noo for food – only water.

PETER *(in a sudden outburst)* I'm burnin' inside like a fire! – roastin'! *(He makes a quick attempt to get the water can. SANDY and BOB both defend the water can). (Hysterically).* Gi'e me that water! . . . Gi'e me that water, or I'll kill ye!

BOB *(lifting a stone from the floor)* Touch that water and it'll be your last.

SANDY *(who really is master without force)* Bob! nae temper. *(PETER goes back to his place).*

PETER *(going)* Oh! this is unbearable – unbearable! *(When he does reach his seat he has a wild outburst of despair.)* Help! . . . Help! . . . Help!

SANDY *(angrily)* Here! cut that oot! D'ye want to wauken Wullie?

PETER is shamed and hides his face. BOB and SANDY look at the sleeping boy.

BOB Puir wee sowl . . . Hasn't he been plucky, Sandy?

SANDY By God he has.

PETER *(very slowly)* Oh, this waitin' . . . waitin' on something that'll never happen . . . Oh!

SANDY *(quickly)* Listen! *(They rise to sudden attention. There is a pause).*

SANDY *(hoarsely)* No.

BOB *(very tired)* Just imagination . . . I wonder what has been happenin'? Hoo mony have lost their lives? *(Hysterically.)* And I'll be gettin' the blame – me! They'll be blamin' me!

PETER *(also hysterically)* Ay, YOU were to blame! The air course was NEVER kept clear.

SANDY *(to PETER)* That'll dae. We were a' to blame for something or ither. If it wasna greed and selfishness, it was fear and cowardice . . . Thinkin' only o' oorsel's, and the rest could go to hell . . . But what has it been worth the-day, Bob?

BOB If ever I leive to come through this, Sandy, I'll be a different man.

SANDY I'm thinkin' we'll a' be different men.

There is a silence. Then NED begins to rave in his delirium.

NED Three hunner pounds! . . . She'll get three hunner pounds! . . . Mary! tell the bairns that you'll get three hunner pounds!

NED laughs very weakly. The others look at him with suspense and fear.

BOB *(in a whisper)* He's started again.

SANDY *(suddenly realising the danger)* What'll happen if he should go mad?

PETER *(hysterically)* Mad! . . . We'd have to finish him!

SANDY Peter, ha'e ye no' YIN kind thoucht in that miserable he'rt o' yours. In a short time we'll a' be knockin' at the door o' Kingdom Come. Let's go wi' clean hands and he'rt.

NED Three hunner pounds o' compensation! Three hunner pounds and a corpse! Ha! ha!

PETER I canna stand this! . . . I canna stand it!

PETER beats his hands against the stone wall of his prison. Then he gives it up in despair. There is another silence. BOB and SANDY listen, but only sigh hopelessly. WILLIE begins to talk in his sleep. BOB and SANDY look down at him.

WILLIE Mither! . . . Mither! . . . Sandy says that I have been brave . . . You ay tellt me to be a man . . . Sandy says I've been great. *(SANDY smiles, but it is sadly.)* But wee Danny will be deid, Mither . . . my wee pownie . . . Him and me were great pals.

SANDY Plucky wee chap.

NED And Peter grudged me his bite o' breid *(PETER rises as if his conscience was tormenting*

JOE CORRIE ~ 399

him.) And, oh! I was hungry, Mary, hungry . . . Three hunner pounds!

PETER *(piteously)* Sandy, I DIDNA grudge him my piece, did I?

SANDY No, Peter, it was a' a mistake. You were angry because I didna ask it frae ye. Forget aboot it.

NED Three hunner pounds! . . . And a' you had before was a man that was never weel . . . Mary, ye can start a wee shop noo, and be happy for the rest o' your days . . . But you'll look weel after the weans . . . You'll tell them whiles aboot their daddy?

> NED *tries to sing a verse o' 'The Auld Hoose', but only gets a few faint notes when he stops,*
> *exhausted.*

BOB *(quietly)* The sun! . . . Just to look up again at the blue sky! . . . To walk amang the trees! . . . To climb the hills! . . . To lie doon and drink the clear, cauld water. *(This makes* PETER *rise again and cast an envious eye on the water-can.* SANDY *guards it.)* Five days in Hell! . . . And every day an eternity!

SANDY Bob, gi'e me your book and pencil. I'm gaun to write to Jean again. (BOB *hands over his book and pencil.)*

SANDY *(slowly, as he writes, after counting the chalk marks)* Friday – the fifth day. Water is finished – keeping the rest for Ned – he is still raving – Willie sleeps a lot – tell his father that he was plucky. Hope you're not worrying too much – We still keep hoping. – Good night, Jean – God bless ye. – Give the bairns a kiss from me. *(Overcome.)* Oh! merciful Christ. *(He buries his head in his hands.* BOB *goes to him quickly).*

BOB *(quickly)* Sandy! for heaven's sake dinna let yoursel' go like that? You've been oor biggest hope a' the time. Dinna let us doon noo. (SANDY *raises his head slowly.)*

SANDY I'm sorry, Bob . . . It was the thoucht o' the bairns.

> *He tears the leaf from the book, kisses it then puts it in his pocket.* BOB *takes the book and pencil and begins writing his letter.* NED *opens his eyes and stares blankly round the cavern. Gradually he realises where he is.*

NED Sandy – can I have a wee sip o' water?

SANDY Sure. *(Going to him with a can.)* Have ye had a wee sleep?

> NED *tries to put his hand to his head but is too weak.*

NED Ay – I think – I have.

> SANDY *holds the water can to* NED's *lips.* PETER *keeps looking on in an attitude of fear.*
> SANDY *lets* NED *empty the flask, all but a drip or two which he must keep for* WILLIE. *He shakes the can at his ear and wonders whether he should give* NED *still another half dozen drops. But he looks at* WILLIE, *and puts the can down.* NED *looks at* PETER.

NED Peter – I didna EAT your piece. (BOB *and* SANDY *are surprised at this.)* I put it in my pocket to tak' hame to the bairns, and – it was buried in the fa' – buried! *(He laughs very weakly, then looks up at* SANDY *helplessly).* Sandy, I doot I'm done for.

SANDY No' a bit o' it, Ned. You'll leive to play dominoes wi' me yet – eh?

NED You were ay left wi' the double six – what we used to ca' the big pay.

SANDY You werena easy beat, Ned. (NED *laughs very weakly.)* The big pay! . . . Breid and margarine!

PETER *(hysterically)* I didna grudge ye my piece, Ned. I didna!

NED Oh! . . . I'm cauld.

> PETER, *to the surprise of* BOB *and* SANDY, *feels* NED's *hand.*

PETER *(very softly)* Cauld!

> *He takes off his jacket and puts it over* NED. SANDY *nods his head to* BOB *in a happy manner. There is a short pause after* PETER *returns to his former position.* SANDY *looks at the lamp.*

SANDY This lamp canna last much langer. We should put it oot and save it.

BOB No! no! let it bide in, Sandy. It's the only hope we ha'e.

PETER If ye put it oot it micht no' licht again!

SANDY Right o! but when it DOES go oot – that'll be the end. *(There is silence.* WILLIE *rises up, opening his eyes).*

WILLIE *(full of joy)* Oh! *(Then he realises where he is and begins to weep in despair.)*

SANDY *(comforting him)* Noo, noo, Willie, ye tellt your mither that you had been a man.

WILLIE *gradually stops sobbing.*

WILLIE I'm sorry, Sandy – I couldna help it when I saw where I was.

SANDY Good old sodger! I kept the last o' the water for ye. Will ye tak' it the noo?

WILLIE Ay. (SANDY *lets him empty the can.)* Has naebody been here yet, Sandy?

SANDY They canna be far awa' noo, son.

BOB Hoo are ye feelin', Wullie?

WILLIE Fine, Bob.

BOB You're a great wee chap.

WILLIE You'll no' gi'e me the sack noo, Bob?

We see that all his fear of BOB *has gone.*

BOB *(putting his arm round the boy)* No, son, I'll never gi'e onybody the sack after this. I'm finished wi' gafferin'.

WILLIE *looks up at the lamp.*

WILLIE Sandy! – that lamp's gaun doon.

It does flicker slightly. The others stare at it tragically. There is a profound silence.

NED *(in delirium)* Three hunner pounds! – And I never thoucht I was worth ony mair than a wheen shillin's.

He tries to laugh but is far too weak. WILLIE *stares at him in fear.*

WILLIE What's wrang wi' Ned, Sandy?

SANDY It's a' richt, Wullie, he's just dreamin'.

WILLIE But his e'en are open – look!

SANDY *(to take* WILLIE's *attention from* NED) Come on. we'll have anither wee sing-song Wullie. What'll we sing this time – oor favourite? – You start up, Bob?

BOB Let me off this time, SANDY.

SANDY You and me then, Wullie.

SANDY *starts the song.* WILLIE *joins in.*

Speed bonnie boat like a bird on the wing,
Onward the sailors cry,
Carry the lad that's born to be king,
Over the sea to Skye.

They all join in with the exception of NED *who now closes his eyes.*

SANDY *(wisely)* I think we'll just let him sleep, Bob.

SANDY *slowly doffs his cap.* BOB *follows suit. Then* PETER. WILLIE, *still wondering, does likewise.* SANDY *is the first to bow his head. The others follow. The lamp flickers and is gradually going down. Through the silence we can hear the tapping of the rescuers, and the song still far away. A very slow curtain.*

The end.

Charles Sorley (1895 – 1915)

Sorley, killed in battle during the First World War when just out of his teens, wrote on a variety of subjects, but is almost entirely known for his poems on the War. 'All the Hills and Vales Along' is his most frequently anthologised work.

All the Hills and Vales Along

All the hills and vales along
Earth is bursting into song,
And the singers are the chaps
Who are going to die perhaps.
    O sing, marching men,
    Till the valleys ring again.
    Give your gladness to earth's keeping,
    So be glad, when you are sleeping.

Cast away regret and rue,
Think what you are marching to.   10
Little live, great pass.
Jesus Christ and Barabbas
Were found the same day.
This died, that went his way.
    So sing with joyful breath.
    For why, you are going to death.
    Teeming earth will surely store
    All the gladness that you pour.

Earth that never doubts nor fears,
Earth that knows of death, not tears,
Earth that bore with joyful ease
Hemlock for Socrates,   20
Earth that blossomed and was glad
'Neath the cross that Christ had,
Shall rejoice and blossom too
When the bullet reaches you.
    Wherefore, men marching
    On the road to death, sing!
    Pour your gladness on earth's head,
    So be merry, so be dead.

From the hills and valleys earth
Shouts back the sound of mirth, 30
Tramp of feet and lilt of song
Ringing all the road along
All the music of their going,
Ringing swinging glad song-throwing,
Earth will echo still, when foot
Lies numb and voice mute.
    On marching men, on
    To the gates of death with song.
    Sow your gladness for earth's reaping,
    So you may be glad, though sleeping. 40
    Strew your gladness on earth's bed,
    So be merry, so be dead.

When You See Millions of the Mouthless Dead

When you see millions of the mouthless dead
Across your dreams in pale battalions go,
Say not soft things as other men have said,
That you'll remember. For you need not so.
Give them not praise. For, deaf, how should they know
It is not curses heaped on each gashed head?
Nor tears. Their blind eyes see not your tears flow.
Nor honour. It is easy to be dead.
Say only this, 'They are dead.' Then add thereto,
'Yet many a better one has died before.' 10
Then, scanning all the o'ercrowded mass, should you
Perceive one face that you loved heretofore,
It is a spook. None wears the face you knew.
Great death has made all his for evermore.

Rooks

There where the rusty iron lies,
The rooks are cawing all the day.
Perhaps no man, until he dies,
Will understand them what they say.

The evening makes the sky like clay.
The slow wind waits for night to rise.
The world is half content. But they
Still trouble all the trees with cries,
That know, and cannot put away,
The yearning to the soul that flies 10
From day to night, from night to day.

William Jeffrey (1896 – 1946)

The Mechanical Age

'Twas six upon the farm-house clock,
And almost dark outside.
'What is that noise?' 'It is the winds
That whinny as they ride.'

''Tis not the winds that whinny so,
Thou man of volt and steel!
It is a herd of ghostly horse
That once sped plough and wheel.

'They wander through the autumn night,
And soon each tree they knew,   10
For their great sorrow, shall appear
Clad in their life-blood's hue.'

Angus Remembers

The years are crowding on me
With press and reach of hands,
With sudden rasp of footsteps
And shout of age that brands,
And 'midst them in my dreaming
No April-tide I see
Blazing the Earth with red buds
And eyes of greenery.

'Tis fog of dreich November
That clips my day's breath now;   10
The suns of youth have vanished,
And winter's near my brow.
Yet would I, in this season,
Ere brain and heart be null,
Leave work and board and lodging
And walk by Lorne and Mull.

For there, at sup of evening,
When prime stars pour the wine
Of darkness from their bright spouts
I've seen the crushed sea shine   20
With love-light round the beaches
And skerries of the isles,
And lone birds planing homeward
From salt Atlantic miles.

And there in old inn parlours
I've heard the glasses clink
And tongues hoist sail with friendship,
Afloat on golden drink;
And if I go there, hobbling,
Some lass – who knows, who knows?   30
Shall look with kindness on me
And seed my heart with rose.

The Hollow Bone

Beating a hollow bone
Across his scraggy knee,
A toothless Ancient sits
Under a dark pine tree.

Above him bright clouds move,
And past him people flee,
Yet graven to the earth
He sits, and beats his knee.

He lifts the fleshless bone
And beats a hollow knee,   10
While endless ages come
And flicker past the tree.

Seaweed

A myriad tides have foamed
And myriad moons been lit
While this brown weed was made
And sea-stones clothed in it.

All time, and this vast world's
Strong tides, sun, moon, and air
Have laboured to display
Eternal autumn there.

She's a Fey Young Thing
A Tree Song

She's a fey young thing
When the lips o' spring
Dispute with the winds to love her;

She's a douce★ wise lass   sober, serious
While the lang days pass
And the sun's in power above her;

She's a gossip good
That's proud o' her brood
Till goud★ o' the hairst surround her.   gold

She's a carline★ auld   10   old woman
When the black north's cauld
Is wrapt like a shroud around her.

Walking One Winter Midnight

Walking one winter midnight through the cold
And velvet darkness of the wartime street
I saw the walls and chimneys of my house
Upsurge and move stupendous – like great bergs
That crowd towards a ship in Arctic seas –
Until they cut the firmament in two,
Removing half the hesitating stars from view.

I shuddered at the fierce primordial scene –
The universe reduced to hollow dark
And pale steel-shafted keenness of cold light.   10
Within the house my wife and children lay
In sleep's oblivion or garth★ of dreams,   garden
Yet at that hour nor house nor life seemed there,
Only a toppling void and whirling of cold air.

That flick of nescience passed. Again I saw
The massive form of my reposing roof
Uplift its black horizon to the stars,
While over it the great Orion swung,
Superb in star-extended majesty,
Impartial watcher of the human host,   20
Empowered not to dismember sleeping thorpe or coast.

That night a score of airmen dropped like stone
On rolling Flanders and on Rhineland hills;
That night, from cuckoo glens and woods of roe
Exiled and in arms, a thousand fell,
A thousand Scots, upon dynastic sands;
That night the liberators of the Don
Undying died, and calm and free the Volga shone.

That night beneath the constellation's fire
The race of Heine went the tumbril way,   30
The Chosen by the Chosen put to shame
In acts of twisted bestiality;
That night the cellars woke in Europe's towns,
And footfalls scurried, and the patriot's hand
Shed Nazi blood upon the sea-cleansed Lowland sand.

What images of violence trod the air,
Upcast from these distended agonies!
I saw them with the mind's eye hurtling past –
Cannon and bomb, eruptions of man's hate,
And claw and fang, aggressions of the brute –   40
I heard their horrid silence: skirl and drone
Such as the climber hears from fall of mountain stone.

O that some convulsion in the loins
Of vast Orion might outflare (I said)
And instantaneous, o'erleaping light,
Engulf these images and change this world,
A new creation in the heart of man
Implanting, so his destiny advance,
His speech transpose to flower and song, his eyes to dance.

What joy to hear the children then with high   50
Glad voice salute the newly minted earth.
An orchard windfall had they never seen
Without reflection there of plunging bomb,
Or twilight seen without enfolding fear.
Now grace of nature should command their minds,
Their heaven and earth be breathed upon by sunny winds.

I gaze upon the stars: remote and cold,
Emblems of blank indifference. No change
Within their keeping or in mine remains.
Awaits the slow-evolving cirque of time   60
Denouement of this clash of bestial will.
And so in my brief hour perforce I'll rest
Content that patterns fill the mind and hope the breast.

My shoes now ceased to echo in the street.
I stood beneath the frontage of my house
That rose and spanned the sky from pole to pole,
And seemed prepared for motion with the stars.
A feathered calm prevailed, enfolding all
In transient semblance of stability,
And midnight passed with undisturbed tranquillity.   70

Gude Sakes

Gude sakes! It were a glammer'd* thing,   eerie, magical
Seein' a star frae wast gang east,
Or at the beddin' o' the sun
Seein' the licht o' day increased.

And yet, lass, at an antrin* time   strange
We've seen the god wi' flichtert* hair   fluttering
Mak sic a love-lowe* in the nicht,   flame
We thocht eternal noon stood there.

When Shepherds Lace Their Boots

When shepherds lace their boots at dawn
And dogs stretch for the hill,
The lark within his globe of song
Thinks all things mark his skill.

But through the dark and stubborn clay
A worm churns in its slime
And sees not wing by quivering wing
Uphold the living chime.

For him, since Adam spat on hand,
The first spade trenched the soil,   10
Lark-song and soar have been a vain
Expenditure of toil.

Our age has shown little interest in religious verse, but the poem which follows, often considered
Jeffrey's finest, is sometimes cited as among the best modern poems of faith.

Stones

The stones in Jordan's stream
Perceived the dove descend
In its lily of light:
That glory entered
Their interminable dream.
The stones in Edom's wilderness
Observed the fiend
Take five of their number
And build a cairn thereof,
And beckoning to Jesus   10
He pointed to the stones and said:
Make bread.
But because of his great love
For the uniqueness of created things,
The confraternity in disparity
Of plant and rock, of flesh and wings,
Jesus would not translate the stones
Out of their immobile immortality
Into that dynasty of death,
Decaying bread: 20

The stones upon Golgotha's hill
Took the shadow of the cross
Upon them like the scorch of ice:
And they felt the flick of dice
And Jesus' blood mingling with his mother's tears;
And these made indelible stains;
And some of them were taken up

And with curses thrown
At that rejected throne,
And others felt the clamorous butts of Roman spears: 30
And the pity, horror, and love within them pent
Welled out and shook the earth.
And the veil was rent.

The great stones of the tomb
Enfolded Jesus' body
In silence and deep gloom.
They had him to themselves alone,
That shard of him, sinew and bone,
Transient dust on their immortality.
And now their inanimate heart   40
Yearned over that shrouded form:
And while three midnights passed
They made of that tomb
A womb:

The fragile bones renewed their strength,
The flesh trembled and moved,
The glory of the dove
Re-descended from above
And with the break of day
The door was rolled away:
The function of the stones was done: 50
His second birth
Achieved on earth,
Jesus walked into the sun.

Edward Gaitens (1897 – 1966)

A native of the Glasgow working-class district called The Gorbals, Gaitens is known entirely for his realistic stories of life in that slum area. His first collection, *Growing Up and Other Stories* (1942) he augmented and reorganised into a novel of sorts, *Dance of the Apprentices* (1948). The individual chapters of the latter are largely self contained. 'The Minodge' is one of them.

The Minodge

Among Glasgow housewives, the 'Minodge' is a very important institution that provides them with frequent opportunities to call on each other for a gossip and a dram and supplies them with footwear, hats, clothes, furniture, household ornaments or utensils for a few coppers or a shilling or so per week. Anyone, either the most improvident poor or thriftiest well-to-do, can 'haud a minodge'.

The phrases, MENAGES SUPPLIED, ONLY FINEST GOODS, BEST

COMMISSION GIVEN, can be seen on the windows of small shops in dark back-streets and big stores in the main thoroughfares. The organiser of this easy-payments club receives a small commission from the shop at which each member in turn, according to the number on her ticket, is obliged to cash a voucher for a stipulated amount of goods.

Mrs Macdonnel was preparing to 'draw a minodge' one winter afternoon in her little kitchen that glowed in firelight like an old Dutch painting. Her range, famous in the tenement, sparkled with immaculate steel and glistening tiles and a riotous fire bellowed up the draught as if it meant to hurl itself into the darkness outside. It flickered a pool of light on new linoleum and illumined the coal-bunker in the dresser opposite. Everything bright in the kitchen – the new bedspread, the dazzling rubber tablecloth and the dishes on the shelves above the dresser – got a blink from the terrific blaze and returned it cheerfully.

Mrs Macdonnel sat a little away from the fire, musingly cutting minute slips of paper from a page torn out of a penny cash-book, and thinking it was time to be lighting the gas. The snips fluttered into her lap; she stopped cutting and slowly counted twelve pieces, three times to make sure, then rose and placed them in a saucer in the table and dropped the book into a dresser drawer. As she lit the gas her eyes roved over her new belongings, shining with especial pleasure at the gaudy pattern of the linoleum and the expensive, greenish globe around the incandescent gas-mantle, and she foresaw the surprise of the women who were coming to join her minodge. 'Goash, they'll be gey envious!' she reflected, smiling, as she opened the stairhead door in answer to a timid knock and admitted a red-headed girl of twelve, home from school, her face and hands pink with cold.

'Oh, it's cauld, maw!' exclaimed the girl timidly – for she was never sure of her mother's temper – throwing down her ragged satchel and putting her hands to the heat.

'Ah want ye tae write oot they minodge tickets,' said her mother, pointing to the saucerful of slips, 'hae ye goat a pencil?' and she looked expectantly at her daughter. The child searched hurriedly in her satchel and said: 'Och, maw, Ah had a pencil an' it's drapped through a hole in me school-bag!'

'We'll need tae hurry!' said her mother, 'they'll be here the noo.' They both began an agitated search in holes and corners till they unearthed a two-inch pencil-stub from a dusty tangle of string, thread, wool, buttons and pins at the bottom of a big brass vase on the mantelshelf. 'It needs shairpnin'!' complained Mrs Macdonnel, slicing the stub unskilfully with a long bread-knife. The girl began writing numbers on the slips of paper with the reduced pencil, then ceased in a moment, crying: 'Och, maw, Ah canny write! Ma fingers are that stiff!'

'Come here an' warm thim.' Mrs Macdonnel sat back in her chair and received the small hands in her own. The girl smiled gratefully for the embrace and winced at the pain of quickening blood. 'Ma fingers are tinglin'!' she laughed.

'Whaur's yer wee gloves?' asked her mother. The child answered in a frighted voice: 'Oh, maw, Ah've loast thim! They were ta'en fae ma desk this moarnin'!' and Mrs Macdonnel echoed: 'My, it's an awfu' school, that Saint Peter's! The wee yins are aye stealin'!' Then she said, thinking of her commission: 'Never mind! Ah'll buy ye a nice new pair fae the minodge money,' and the girl smiled with relief.

'Ma ain pet! Ma ain wee lassie!' Mrs Macdonnel murmured, as she drew her daughter's red head to her breast and bent her own greying, red head to it. 'Ah wonder whaur Jimmy is the night? Ma brave wee son! Mibbe he's lyin' oan a big field in yon Mespotamy wi' nae yin near him, cryin' fur me!' She began weeping easily and the girl drew away her head, scared by the gloomy vision. 'Naw he isnae, maw!' she cried. 'Naw he isnae! He'll come hame when the war's done. He's no deid!' There was a knock at the stairhead door. Mrs Macdonnel quickly wiped her own and the girl's eyes with her apron. 'See wha 'tis,' she urged, hastily tidying her hair. 'Mibbe it's Missis Glynn,' said the girl, 'she aye comes first. It's like her chap.' But Mrs Macdonnel, who, like all tenement housewives, knew the individual peculiarities of the knocks of her friends and neighbours, said with absolute certainty: 'Naw it isnae. It's wee Minnie Milligan. Ah ken fine her sleekit wee chap!' and she laughed slyly.

It was Mrs Milligan, who slipped in past the heavy girl after saying: 'Is yer mither in,

Mary?' and greeted Mrs Macdonnel with a shivering reference to the weather. She sat down with her fawn-coloured shawl tightly hugged to her breast and was not tempted to loosen it by the warmth of the kitchen.

There was no admixture of Irish in Mrs Milligan. She was a genuine Glaswegian, a small dark woman with a little canny voice, which, in its flat cautiousness, suggested the futility of all earthly doings and which, when she felt lively, was high-pitched and skirled like the bagpipes. 'My it's an awfu' war!' she remarked; then con-tinued, pronouncing the word like tush: 'They say the Alleys are goin' tae give a Big Push next week. Ah hear the Kaiser's done a bunk an' oor boays'll soon be dancin' through the streets o' Berlin!' – and she laughed a dim, asthmatic laugh, like the rustling of dry reeds.

Young Mary, who had resumed scribbling the minodge tickets at a corner of the table, swung her stolid face round in a look of annoyance at the visitor. She disliked Mrs Milligan, who was always talking about the War and making her mother cry about Jimmy. She was at it again!

'Hiv ye heard ony mair aboot yer son, Mrs Macdonnel?' the little woman was saying: 'yer puir hert must be gey heavy an' ye'll be thinkin' the postman's brocht ye bad news every time he knoaks. Ay, it's a sad time!' Mrs Macdonnel, who loved a 'good cry' and always seized on the slightest excuse to indulge her weakness, hid her eyes in her apron, and the girl, fearing her mother was going to be maudlin again, hurriedly exclaimed: 'The tickets are ready, maw!' But Mrs Macdonnel's mind was preoccupied with her minodge; she dropped her apron, deciding she had shown sufficient grief, and told her daughter to come and stand by her chair at the fire.

Mrs Milligan eyed inquisitively the saucerful of slips and announced: 'Ah see ye're haudin' a minodge. Hoo minny are jinin'?'

'Twelve,' said Mrs Macdonnel, laconic and aloof. She was alarmed by Mrs Milligan's manner and her pinched, worried look. Her neighbour always hugged her-self tightly in her shawl and looked like that when she had come to borrow money, and Mrs Macdonnel was determined not to lend her a farthing. It would be unlucky to begin a minodge by lending money, and anyway she hadn't got it, and besides Mrs Milligan always took a long time to pay back! All these negative reasons flashed through her mind as she looked meaningly at the clock and hinted: 'Yer man'll shin be hame fur his tea, Missis Milligan.' Looking more pinched and worried, Mrs Milligan immediately poured out a sad, desperate story about pawning the trousers of her man's best suit which she would have to redeem this very night because her husband was to be a very important delegate at a big trade-union meeting in the morning. Could Mrs Macdonnel lend her five shillings to get them out of pawn?

Mrs Macdonnel set her face and flatly refused to lend her anything. She nodded secretly and significantly at her daughter. She had guessed right!

Mrs Milligan rose at once, saying she would have to get the money from somebody, pulled her shawl yet closer to herself and with an offended look went out, closing the stairhead door rather ungently. But she had hardly been gone five minutes when Mrs Macdonnel, touched by the vision of Mr Milligan facing his colleagues without his best trousers, sent her girl to inform the inveterate little borrower that she would give her the loan as soon as the minodge money was paid in; then she opened the door to admit the first arrivals for her club, two ladies oddly dissimilar – Mrs Laurie, a raw-boned woman six feet tall, and Mrs Kelly, a lady with abnormally small, screwed-up features, who barely reached five feet.

Mrs Macdonnel's delight increased as the members of her minodge steadily arrived, for it sometimes happened that one or two would exercise inconveniently the feminine right to change their minds and, notifying their decision at the eleventh hour, leave her with unwanted tickets on her hands. She was holding a 'three pound minodge' in which the twelve members would pay her five shillings weekly for twelve weeks and purchase their goods in the first or twelfth week, according to the luck of the draw. Her minodges were popular. Women could trust her to pay in their contributions and knew they would not meet with the awful experience of having their vouchers rejected when they went to cash them at warehouse or shop. Though she could drink away her family's wages during periods of moral weakness, she had a respectable horror of even the smallest debt and prided herself on owing no woman any-thing.

She smiled as she thought of the three pounds that would be paid in. She loved handling money and she greeted all comers with lively pleasure, delighted by their glances of surprise at her new belongings. Her kitchen was soon crowded with a mere knot of nine ladies. 'It's like 'Maggie Murphy's Home'!' laughed Aunt Kate, who arrived last, her vitality heightened by a short dillydally with the bottle. They all talked about the War. Two of them had lost husbands and three given sons and they were all disgusted at the measly pensions they were receiving for the sacrifice of their dear ones – pensions which were small enough at the beginning (God knows!), they said, and which the Government had so often reduced it was now hardly worth the bother of going to the post office to draw them!

'Oi hear the Pope's thryin' to stop the War,' said Mrs Glynn, a dark little Irish woman with rosy cheeks and a squint. 'Shure His Holiness must be worn out intirely wid prayin' all the hours of the day an' noight for Payce! He would have to be stayin' till eternity on his bended knees to turn the heart of a man loike that Koiser!' A mutter that sounded like 'To Hell wi' the Pope!' was heard from the corner between the dresser and the window. Aunt Kate jumped to her feet and glared fanatically at the black head of Mrs McCleery, a stout Ulsterwoman who was whispering closely with a grey-haired elderly lady. 'Tae hell wi' the Pope, is it?' she cried, 'an' what wid ye be doin' without the Cathlic boys in the War? Heh!' Her voice rose as she rolled up the sleeves of her blue, print blouse and smacked her fists to her hips. 'Heh!' She tossed her raven head and her side-combs with the sham pearls glittered. 'Shure there's more Cathlics in the War than Prodesans! Shure isn't ma two big Cathlic sons fightin' fur King an' Country?' Then she began snuffling in her handkerchief. 'Ma wee Josie an' Peter! Ye'll no' come back again!'

Mrs Macdonnel, fearing her minodge was about to open with a battle, led her sister back to her chair, with furtive, annoyed glances at her and Mrs McCleery, whose face was inflamed with Protestant loyalty. 'Och, come oan, Katey!' she said, 'naebuddy's said onything. Haud yer wheesht an' Ah'll get ye a wee hauf!' The tension was eased and Mrs McCleery, apparently at peace with the Pope and all his flock, went on talking to the elderly lady.

Mrs Macpherson, a stout Highland woman with a large kind face and a small, soft voice, said gently: 'Och, what's the use of fighting about religion? Shure we all go to the same place, Catholic and Protestant, and God's the Father of us all!'

'Begob, ye're roight, Annie!' agreed Mrs Glynn, the innocent introducer of His Holiness, comfortably tucking folded arms within her shawl. 'Shure it's ayquil we'll all be before the Trone of The Almoighty God!' But the champions of Popery and Protestantism had only put their opinions aside for the time and at the rear of their minds were each firmly convinced that Hell was the destination of the other's soul.

Mrs Macpherson felt extremely pleased with her successful peacemaking. She was regarded as a simple body by her neighbours, who talked and smiled condescendingly about her. She loved cats, dogs and mice, and kept her working-man's Dining Rooms in Calder Street in such a profusion of cats that 'Macpherson's Eating House' was equally famous in the neighbourhood as 'The Cats' Home' because everyone swore that more cats than customers patronised her shop. She hadn't the heart to chase them and they knew it. Feline ladies and gentlemen of every class and colour walked in whenever they pleased and sat at her door licking their whiskers after the theft and digestion of a tasty bite, or walked forth calm and unhurried for an after-dinner stroll. It was said that the 'Sanitary Man' had called many times without result to complain about her four-legged lodgers, who rubbed against his legs and jumped on his shoulders while he put the case for the Corporation Cleansing Department, and it was common report that mice brought forth whole families and dined in leisure at her feet while a dozen cats sat on the big hob and talked to her as she lifted lids and stirred and tasted the contents of a dozen big iron pots.

Once a week, Mrs Macpherson cooked a fruit dumpling the size of a prize pumpkin which she retailed from her window at fourpence a pound. On the day it came from the pot to repose between a plate of salt ling and a trencher of houghs, two cats sat on either side the platter, staring in insolent ease into the street while steam billowed from the dumpling. Dogs were affected by this anarchy, admitted the cats' right to live, and simply didn't bother to fulfil their terrorist function.

'Ye hivnae broaght ony cats wi' ye the day, Annie!' cried Aunt Kate, 'shair the puir things'll be that lonely wi'oot ye!' and Mrs Macdonnel almost doubled up with laughter as she added: 'Weel, ye ken, Katey, she's left thim warrm an' comfortable oan yon hob! There's nae cat need want fur bite or sup while Annie Macpherson's alive!' A laugh went round, and Mrs McCleery cried: 'Goad, ye're right, Mary! Annie's goat a hert o' gold an' widnae herm a flea! The cats oaght tae gie her a Benefit Coancert!' Mrs Macpherson laughed so vigorously at their fun that the two large black birds which dashed at each other's beaks across the front of her hat seemed to fly up and down to the tune of her laugh.

The arrival of two children, whom busy mothers had sent to draw their tickets, caused a pause in the chaff. They were an extremely small, bright girl and a small boy with a persistently wet nose, both painfully shy, the boy covering his embarrassment by repeatedly applying his sleeve to his nostrils. The women greeted them as 'puir wee lambs' and they looked grateful for their welcome into the warmth. 'It's wee Billy Quinn an' Maggie Magonigle,' explained Mrs Macdonnel; 'their mithers aye send them tae draw because they're luckier than theirsel's.' 'Ay, the wee yins are gey lucky,' agreed a toothless middle-aged lady whose wide mouth seemed to be the only mobile part of her enormous red face. She had a habit of champing her lips while she sat silent and resembled a cogitating ventriloquist's dummy; her lips snapped on her remark and disappeared entirely as she went on chewing, like a cow mouthing the cud.

Aunt Kate, with put-on sternness, ordered the boy, who was still engaged with his nose, to produce a handkerchief. 'Och, ye're no' a gaintleman tae come oot wi'oot a hanky!' she said, with a smiling frown. 'Look at wee Maggie's nose! There's a nice leddy's nose for ye!' The boy looked tearful at the women's laughter, and Mrs Macpherson fumbled in her handbag and produced a handkerchief so small that it tickled them all to further laughter; Mrs Macpherson's ladyish ways were always a source of fun. The boy promptly pocketed the dainty rag and used his sleeve as Aunt Kate embraced him and gave him a penny for sweeties.

A thin, nervous little woman, who was regarded as peculiar because she always sat silent in company with trembling hands on shaking knees, whispered anxiously to Mrs Macdonnel her desire to get home before her man returned from work, the agitation of her limbs increasing as she spoke. Mrs McCleery tittered to the grey lady beside her, and Aunt Kate remarked: 'Ye're gey nervous the day, Missis McGovern.' The thin woman gave a melancholy smile, while her knees clapped like castanets and Mrs Macdonnel opened the draw, taking up the saucerful of slips and asking who would like to take it round.

A drymannered little woman, impatient to be going, nodded her shawled head sharply and suggested drawing the tickets from Mrs Macdonnel's apron, but Mrs McCleery and Aunt Kate demanded that Mrs Macpherson should draw them from her bonny hat. 'Come awa, Annie!' they cried 'turn yer wee burds upside-doon!'

Though its style was antique, Mrs Macpherson prized her hat as a marriage gift from her dead husband. She was the only one present with costume and hat and made an odd figure among the shawl-clad women. She unfastened her hat reluctantly by drawing out three blackheaded pins of fearsome length, which Mrs Macdonnel placed on the mantelshelf. The slips of paper were crushed into pellets and dropped in the hat, then Mrs Macdonnel shook it vigorously and put her hand inside and stirred the tickets round. 'That's roight, give thim a good sthirrin' an' ye'll have no complaints!' cried Mrs Glynn. 'Ay, steer the parritch weel an' ye'll hae nae lumps!' added the impatient woman, who regarded everyone and all the proceedings with suspicion.

Mrs Macdonnel returned the hat to its owner, saying the 'unlucky yins' wouldn't blame her if Mrs Macpherson took it round. Mrs Macpherson presented her hat to each member in turn, beginning with the children. As each one dipped out and read her ticket her expression betrayed her luck. The red-faced lady champed more excitedly; Mrs McCleery exclaimed 'Humph!' and threw the paper pellet on the floor as if it was some nasty insect; Mrs Glynn announced: 'Begod, the oul' man'll get his new boots next month!'; the dry woman's suspicion increased as she remarked:

'Ah've goat number eleeven, whit hae you drawn?' to her companion with the trembling knees, who complained in a husky, spectral voice: 'Och, Ah never hae ony luck! Ah've goat number ten!' while her hands danced on her lap; the boy had drawn number twelve and began to wail that his mother would beat him if he returned with such ill luck.

It was Mrs Macpherson's turn to pick, but ticket number one, the only number not yet drawn, had vanished. Mrs Macdonnel accused her daughter of forgetting to write it out; young Mary asserted that she hadn't and joined the boy in crying; Mrs Macdonnel reddened with embarrassment, and the suspicious lady looked as if she was smelling out foul play; then Mrs Macpherson, after a deal of flushed fumbling, extracted the ticket from the ancient lining of her hat; she then said she was in no hurry for her goods and generously gave the boy her 'turn' for his; he paid his mother's five shillings and went home happily with the girl, who had also picked well for her mother.

Mrs Macdonnel produced a small bottle of whisky to wet the first week's contributions; the nervous lady and her suspicious friend, who had hung on hoping for a drink, drank their deoch-andoris simultaneously, gathered in their shawls and departed with sharp nods. Mrs Macdonnel then told the remaining women, whose laughter skirled through the kitchen like screams of tropic birds, the story of Minnie Milligan and her man's best trousers, which she knew fine Minnie had pawned to bet unsuccessfully on a horse. She had a talent for telling a funny story, and, with the Glaswegian's habit of exaggeration, she larded the little punter's plight with fanciful details; her features wrinkled up like the face of a happy cat, her eyes closed tightly and she flushed an apoplectic red as her choking laughter interrupted her story. 'Goad, Mary, Minnie'll be sennin' her aul' man tae work wi'oot his troosers yin o' these moarnin's!' shrieked her sister. 'Ay, and thair she is, runnin' roon like a madwumman, fair distractit fur that five sheelin's!' concluded Mrs Macdonnel, who had enjoyed the story more than the audience.

Suddenly all their laughter was silenced by the postman's knock. Mrs Macdonnel's face went dead white, she clutched at her breast and her eyes stared like the eyes of a woman waking from a swoon. 'It's aboot James!' she cried. 'He's deid! Ah ken it! He's deid! Don't answer, Mary! Don't go!' but her girl had opened the stairhead door and taken the letter from the hand that pushed in. She rushed forward, crying: 'Oh maw, it's aboot James!' and stood before her mother weeping, with the letter trembling in her hand.

Mrs Macdonnel completely buried her head in her apron and rocked to and fro in her chair wailing: 'Ma wee son, ma firstboarn!'; Aunt Kate embraced her and they keened loudly together with the girl crying violently by their side, still holding the letter. All the women stood and hovered round them, but no one thought of opening the buff envelope. Its message was taken for granted. Mrs Macdonnel had been expecting for many months the news of her son's death since he had been posted as 'missing'. Mrs Macpherson took the letter from the girl's hand; Mrs McCleery whispered: 'Dinny show it her, Annie! Puir saul, she's gey upset!'; the red faced woman ceased champing her lips and stared as if hypnotised; and Mrs Glynn began to relate how long she herself had sorrowed when they brought her son home dead, from an accident in the shipyards.

Mrs Macdonnel pushed her sister away, sprang up and seized the letter. 'Let me see it!' she cried; 'Whit dae they say aboot ma son? Ma wee Jimmy!' She tore open the envelope and tried to read the form, then thrust it weakly at her sister: 'You read it, Katey! Ah canny see!' Her sister puzzled over it, then handed it to Mrs Macpherson, who read out that 'No. 2044, Private James Macdonnel, The First Battalion, The 7th Cameronian Scottish Rifles,' had been 'Killed On Active Service.'

'But he's no deid! He'll come hame!' moaned Mrs Macdonnel, pointing dramatically at the set-in bed. 'Every night Ah lie there an' hear 'im runnin' up the stairs! He chaps at the door an' fa's in ma airms!' She turned and held out her hands to a framed enlargement of a photograph of her dead son which occupied the place of honour, facing everyone who entered the kitchen. One day a Jewish gentleman had called, canvassing for orders for enlargements of photographs – 'in goylt frames, lady; ver' cheap!' – and had later returned with a bad copy of the excellent original. Jimmy looked into the bright room, neat and upright in a mercantile petty officer's uniform, a jaunty, foolish smile on his face, while his mother cried to him: 'Jimmy, can ye hear me awa oot there? Ah'll show ye the way hame, son! Ah'll show ye the way hame!' She stepped on a chair and took down the picture, hugging it to her breast, crooning over it. Her sister took it from her. 'Och, steedy yersel', Mary. Ye mustnae gie way. It's Goad's Wull! Mabbe he's at peace noo, lying in the airms o' the Blessed Virgin. Ah'll say a wee prayer fur 'im!' She rehung the picture and knelt at the bed, straining her hands to the nickel crucifix on the wall. 'Sacred Heart o' Jesus,' she prayed, 'watch ower Jimmy this night an' guide 'im tae Thy breist!' Mrs Glynn knelt near her, agitatedly repeating the sign of the cross, and Mrs McCleery, having for-gotten her hatred of the Pope, stood weeping behind them.

Mrs Macdonnel started at the sound of a beggar singing in the back-court, saying the man was singing a favourite song of Jimmy's. She gave one of the women her purse to throw the busker a copper, then continued mourning, loving her dead son and hating her husband who had been hard on Jimmy. Mr Macdonnel, the petty, righteous man, had always been enraged at Jimmy's indulgence in drink, his own greatest weakness. Mrs Macdonnel remembered her son's first night of drunkenness and the savage fight between him and her husband that had sown undying hatred. Jimmy was throwing himself at the door, which had been locked against him, when her husband, with planned malice, had suddenly thrown it open and caused Jimmy to hurtle through and smash his forehead against the door-knob. When the house was asleep she had slipped Jimmy in and bathed his wounds.

All the women were now in tears, repeating after each other: 'Ay, it's Goad's Wull. He's at peace noo. He canny suffer nae mair. Goad's just!' Mrs McCleery recalled what great pals Jimmy and her son had been; Mrs Glynn remembered him as 'a broth of a boy' when he ran about the back-courts in his schooldays; and Aunt Kate said: 'Shure, Mary, minny's the time Ah've nursed 'im in these airms fur ye when ye warnae weel. He'll no furget his aunty up in Heevin!'; and everyone chorused: 'Ay, it's Goad's Wull!'

Aunt Kate put Mrs Macdonnel's shawl around her and they all urged her to come out. She must have 'a wee hauf' and try and forget, they said. They were thoroughly enjoying themselves.

They trailed out. Young Mary tugged at her mother's shawl, pleading: 'Ye won't drink a loat, will ye maw? Will Ah make ma da's tea?' Her mother pushed her aside. 'Dinny bother me! Ma hert's broken. Tae hell wi' yer da! He wisnae kind tae ma Jimmy!'; then she paused in the doorway and shrieked into the kitchen: 'Curse the bloody War! Whit right had they tae take ma son fae me? Ay, ma boay Eddy wis right tae be a coanshense objaictor!' Her sister and Mrs Macpherson put their arms round her and gently led her out, and the child shut the door on her voice echoing inanely on the stairs: 'A coanshense objaictor! Ay, a coanshense objaictor!'

Young Mary paused in the lobby with her ear against the crack of the door, then she opened it and stood on the stairhead leaning over the rusty iron banister listening to the women's voices as they stopped to argue and talk in the close. When they had moved into the street and she could hear them no longer, she returned to the kitchen and began making slices of toast and covering them with pieces of cheese which she melted before the fierce fire on the steel plate-rack fixed to the grate. The appetising odour filled the room as her Uncle Wullie came in from his evening round of lamp-lighting. He sniffed and grinned. 'Toastit cheese! Och, my, that's champion. Jist whit ye want oan a cauld night like this,' then he sat by the fire and rubbed his long hands close to it, cracking his bony fingers. He was feeling proud and pleased because he had been accepted at last by the Army, after being rejected. He had to report in a week's time to be drafted to a Labour Battalion for training. The promise of any kind of change after his long years of running up and down tenement stairs with his ladder and lamp, attracted him strongly. He began to cough harshly, gripping his weak chest and his dull complexion reddened. Young Mary, forgetting his deafness, said quietly while he coughed, 'James has been killed, Wullie.'

He held his head down to her, his palm curved round his ear. 'Whit?' he said.

The girl shouted tremulously, with tears starting to her eyes, 'James has been killed.'

He stared at her silently while sorrow at her news worked in his face.

'Hoo d'ye know?' he said.

'Me maw goat a letter fae the Govermint,' she said.

'Whaur is it?' said her uncle.

'She's ta'en it oot wi' her,' said the girl.

Uncle Wullie sat at the table and stared awhile with open mouth in depressed silence.

'Yer tea's ready,' said the girl, placing before him a plate of toasted bread and cheese and filling his cup. He stirred his tea slowly, then he said, 'Aw, poor James! it's a peety he wisnae a prisoner,' and he began wondering what would be his fate, his expectation of change and adventure darkened by dread. He took a few coppers from his waistcoat pocket and sent the girl to the corner bakery for some penny cakes. She returned along with the youngest son of the family, a pale, quiet boy of fifteen, home from his apprentice work at a jeweller's in Renfield Street. He had been ridiculously christened 'Egbert' because of his mother's affection for a venerable English priest of that name among the priests of Saint Peter's chapel. The name was ill-suited to him and he hated it because his schoolmates had nicknamed him 'Egg' and 'Ham and Egg.' Young Mary addressed him as 'Aigburt' and asked him if he wanted his tea. He went to the end of the table, facing his Uncle and pushed the door to with his behind as he sat down.

'Hiv ye heard aboot poor James?' said Uncle Wullie.

'Ay,' said the boy, his eyes fixed expressionless on the laid table.

'D'ye mind the wee parakeet he broaght hame fae sea yon time? My, yon was a rare wee burrd!' Uncle Wullie said laughing at the memory of the long-dead pet. 'D'ye mind hoo it used tae scrape at the door wi' its beak, tae get in? Och, it was gie'in it too much breed soaked in tea an' sugar that killed it. Wee Polly goat too fond o' that. She wid have lived longer wi' the right kind o' food.'

The children laughed with him. 'Ay, she wis a rare wee burrd!' said Egbert, his eyes shining as he remembered his dead brother's generosity when he came home from sea with pocketsful of money. He munched several mouthfuls, then said, 'Mibbe James is alive somewhere wi' a loast memory.'

'Ach, Ah doan't believe he's deid!' said Uncle Wullie, trying to make his voice sound hearty to cheer up himself and them.

Young Mary went to answer a timid knock at the door and Wee Minnie Milligan flustered in, saying, 'Goad, Mary, is yer maw no' in? She proamised tae sen' me that five sheelin's! If Ah dinnae get it soon the pawn'll be shut!' She nodded to Uncle Wullie. 'Yon was a bad tip ye gie'd me!' she said, shaking her fist at him with feigned annoyance.

Uncle Wullie leant across the table with his hand to his ear, his lower lip stupidly hanging. Minnie Milligan shouted, he nodded, smiled and seemed ashamed. 'Ay, Ah backed it masel',' he said. 'It wis a good hoarse but it didnae run up tae form.'

Minnie Milligan's feckless face looked silly with apprehension as she asked Mary where her mother could be.

'Mibbe she's over at The Shielin',' said the girl, 'an' if she's no' there, she'll be in The Clachan, but mibbe ye'll find her in the Rob Roy Arms.'

In desperation Mrs Milligan rushed away to thrust her head in at the swing doors of those public houses in search of the only woman who would lend her anything. As she went out, Uncle Wullie was frowning and pointing at the penny tin of pepper standing beside the sugar-basin. Egbert passed him the bottle of worcester sauce, then the salt at which Uncle Wullie frowned irritably and shook his head, then Egbert handed him the pepper. He grinned and nodded and began shaking it on his toasted cheese.

John Milne (1897 – 1962)

The Proposal

Ye'll get hens that'll keckle a' winter,
Birns o' reid-kamed cocks,
Hame-ower turkeys that gobble,
And reid-luggit bubbly-jocks★;   turkeys

Rich ream-bannocks and butter,
Sweet-milk kebbucks★ o' cheese,   slices
And honey as clear as yer een, lass,
Fae three muckle skeps★ o' bees;   gleanings

The best biggit hoosie in Buchan
That sits on the tap o' the brae,   10
And sheets o' my mither's great-granny's –
Od, lassie, fut mair wad ye hae!

Jean Calder

Fin first I sa' Jean Calder
A winsome lass was she,
Walkin doon the Spital
Wi' a lad I wished was me.

Fin neist I sa' Jean Calder
Wow, she lookit grim
Wi' twenty years o' teachin'
And drivin learnin in.

Fin last I sa' Jean Calder
She'd squandered breath and brain   10
On mony a hunner littlins,
And deil the ane her ain.

Havers!

As I gaed doon by dark Loch A'an,
I thocht I sa' – but havers★ man!   nonsense ('shucks')
'Twas jist a wisp o' grey mist blawn!

As I cam roon yon corrie wa'
I thocht I heard – but havers na!
'Twas jist the on-ding o' the snaw!

As I gaed owre the Derry Glen,
'Twas aye I lookit but and ben,
For, havers man, ye nivver ken!

The Ghaist

In the deid o' nicht fin bleed rins sweir
The ghaist o' my mither cam' ben* the fleer.   in

'O faur's* my laddie, ye carle grey,   where is
Wi' yer bleery lids and looks sae blae?

'O faur's my laddie, ye doitet* loon,   foolish
Wi' yer wrinkled face and aul' grey croon?

'His hair wis black as the raven's wing,
And the licht o' his een wis a winnerfu' thing!'

Quo I, 'Nae laddie, as faur's I ken,
Is here i' the hoose nor but nor ben!'   10

Quo I, 'Nae laddie, as faur's I min',
Has been i' the hoose sin' gey lang syne!'

'Nae laddie!' quo she. Quo I nae mair.
And the ghaist o' my mither gaed doon the stair.

Discipline!

As I gaed doon by kirk and toun
I heard the larkies singin,
And ilka burnie treetlin doon,
And wid* and welkin* ringin.   wood/sky

As I gaed doon by kirk and toun,
Quo I, 'A skweel*, gweed feth!'   school
And there I heard nae sang nor soun',
But bairns quaet as death!

Buchan, 1917

Buchan! Ye're bare an' bleak an' cauld like the coast around ye,
Wi' its auld grey rocks.
Nae a tree or a burn or a hull or a buss tae hap* ye   clothe, protect
Fae the winter's shocks!

But ye're nae sae bare an' bleak an' cauld as the plain o' Flanders,
Wi' its shell-scarred skull.
And och! I wad rise and rin te whaur the fish-wife wanders,
And the hungry gull.

Faithlie Toon

O Tam gie me auld Faithlie toon
Whaur trees are scrunts* for miles aroon   blasted, stunted
And nae a burn wad slake or droon
A drunken miller;
But sands and bents* that wear a croon   grasses, fields
O' gowd and siller.

Naomi Mitchison (1897 – 1999)

Mitchison has been a remarkably fertile writer, especially of novels reflecting her mythological, anthropological and historical interests. She writes poetry and short stories as well, as the selections below illustrate.

The House of the Hare

At the time I was four years old
I went to glean with the women,
Working the way they told;
My eyes were blue like blue-bells,
Lighter than oats my hair;
I came from the house of the Haldanes
Of work and thinking and prayer
To the God who is crowned with thorn,
The friend of the Boar and the Bear,
But oh when I went from there,   10
In the corn, in the corn, in the corn,
I was married young to a hare!
We went to kirk on the Sunday
And the Haldanes did not see
That a Haldane had been born
To run from the Boar and the Bear,
And the thing had happened to me
The day that I went with the gleaners,
The day that I built the corn-house,
That is not built with prayer.   20
For oh I was clean set free,
In the corn, in the corn, in the corn,
I had lived three days with the hare.

Five Men and a Swan

The boys were all sitting round the table in the cabin of the *Highland Mary*. They had their cups of tea and the thick pieces with red jam, the pips of the rasps gritting on their teeth and the tea strong and sweet. They were talking about women. The engineer, who had been in a collier, was telling them about yon place in Cardiff; but they had heard it before. Black Rob was telling about a girl at one of the bars a wee bit up from the Broomielaw and the man she was with said that was all right, but he had been frightened to do much. You never knew with the Glasgow girls; or maybe you did, and that was the worst.

Willie the cook was not listening. He was reading a piece about the Rangers on the bit newspaper there was on the table. It was an old paper and there were jam stains on it here and there; he could read through them. If he could ever get over to Glasgow on a Friday then he would get to one of the big matches on the Saturday afternoon.

But Black Rob, Johnnie the Ghost and Alec the engineer, who was mostly called Alec Shop, the way his father used to keep the shop at the crossroads after he left the fishing, all went on talking about women, though it was little enough they knew when it came to the bit, and less they had done. For they were mostly all shy in the big towns where people spoke differently, and perhaps it would be an English girl talking quick and rough, and they would not understand her at all, for all they might let on that they did. Johnnie the Ghost had got married to Effie MacDonald in August, and time too; he was not saying much for himself, in case the boys would be laughing at him, and Effie expecting her bairn a while before the New Year. But indeed she was a nice enough girl, though a wee bit homely.

Outside it was rough late afternoon, and the light beginning to go. In another half hour they would need to be starting. The *Highland Mary* had not been a lucky boat at all these last weeks. There had been little herring in it, and the one time they had a good shot, the net had torn below on a reef, and their neighbour boat saying it was their fault. Their neighbour was the *Annie MacQueen;* she had been a Tarbert boat to start with, named after a Tarbert skipper's wife, a fine red haired woman that had eight bairns and all the boys brought up to the fishing.

The skipper of the *Highland Mary*, who was mostly called Hat, just sat at the end of the table, and first he ate a good lot of bread and butter and jam, and then he told Willie to get the cheese and he ate a good lot of that, and he put four spoonfuls of sugar in his tea, for all this happened a few years back, before the war, and he swilled it round. But he said nothing for a bit. He was a big man and when he left off shaving for a day or two you could see it was a red beard he had on him. All of a sudden he said 'Stop it, boys!' And they thought that was queer, for Hat was not one to get annoyed with this kind of talk, except it would be a Sunday, which it was not.

So Johnnie the Ghost asked what was the matter, and Hat let out with a great deep groan, the way he might have had a knock on the head. And he put his hand in his pocket and he took out a stiff white feather and laid it down on the table between the jam jar and the cheese. Now the boys all looked at the feather, and it was clear it was a swan's feather, the like of those you might find on the edge of the West Loch when the swans are in. But there was something queer about it, for each one of them had a quick feeling as though what they had been saying was just bairns' talk and blethers and the truth away brighter and bonnier, and nothing at all to do with the girls that could be dirty girls in the bars by the Broomielaw. And even wee Willie the cook stopped his reading and listened, and all believed in the thing Hat told them he had done.

For it seemed he was walking along by the point one night in the warm weather near two months back; he was coming home from seeing a man that had a cousin in Gourock with a winch he was wanting to sell. The two of them had been late talking, but there was a full moon in it, and Hat was walking back slow looking at the bonny sight the moon made playing on the water, and a sweet south wind coming in gusts now and then and ruffling the tops of the waves the way they would be catching the light. And then in the moon track he caught sight of a girl swimming and it was the long hair she had on her, the kind you are not seeing much these days, and this long shining hair was not shut in a bathing cap, but hanging loose into the water. And as he watched her, he saw she had no bathing dress on her at all and she was playing about in the water, rising her long white arms out of it, the like of a bird.

So first he thought she must be one of the summer visitors and he looked for a rock to hide behind, the way he could watch her closer when she came out. There was a rock and he knelt down, but as he knelt he put his hand onto a thing that was warm and soft, and he thought ah, it was the clothes of her he had and maybe he could be tricking her a wee bit. But when he held them up in the moonlight to look at, he saw it was no woman's dress, but the feathers of a white swan, a woman's shape of feathers.

Now, Hat was a man that took things as they came, and he had been a skipper fifteen years, and his wife died a while back, leaving him with one lassie that was away training to be a nurse and another lassie at school yet; but the school lassie would be asleep in the back room now. So Hat took up the swan's dress and away with it to his house, and when he looked over his shoulder, there, as he had thought, was the Swan herself coming up out of the water wet and white, and her black hair dripping behind her, and cried on him to drop her dress.

There are plenty men who would have found that an awesome thing, and so it seemed to the boys round the cabin table; and plenty would have dropped the shape of feathers there and then, and run for it. But not Hat.

He took a tight grip of the feathers and walked on, and every time he looked back the Swan herself was nearer and calling to him, and oh it was a bonny sweet voice she had. And when he was at his own door she was just by him, and he tucked the feathers under his arm and opened the door with one hand and pulled her in after him with the other.

He laid the feathers down on the bed and he lighted the lamp and held it up and looked close at the Swan. She was in every way like a young girl, he told them, but only this, that where women mostly all have hair growing on them she had the wee white feathers. And when you put your fingers on them one way they were smooth and cool, but when you ran your fingers under they were warm and soft the way swansdown is. She was dry now and she kept looking at the feather dress and asking for it back in thon sweet voice that almost melted the heart in him, for she seemed as young as his own lassie, younger than his wife had been at the time they were courting and away bonnier. And indeed, said Hat, he had only meant to keep the Swan a short, short time to look fully at her and maybe to have her on his knee for a while, but not to be spoiling her. But when he had got her on his knee right, he needed to be holding her there, and one thing led to another and he went just a hairsbreadth too far with the Swan. And the third time he went too far with the Swan that night, he was that sleepy afterwards, and when he woke the Swan was away and her dress with her and it was cold morning.

But the Swan had told him that once a month on the Saturday of full moon she was under a necessity to swim in the water off the point, and she must leave her feather dress among the rocks. So he knew he was bound to go back for her in a month's time.

The skipper stopped speaking then, and Black Rob asked quick had he done that, and Hat said Aye, he had gone, but this was the way of it. He had gone down that Saturday night to the point and he had heard her laughing and he had smelt the smell of her that was partly the smell of a woman's body and breath, and partly the oily queer smell of a swan, and maybe that sounded not just right, yet it was a thing that had stayed in his nostrils ever since. But he had seen neither her nor her dress, and it was borne in upon him that he would never see her again.

Then Black Rob said: 'It will be time again in three days.' For it was near the October moon. And he looked at the skipper and his tongue licked at his lips.

'It is not myself will stop you from going,' said Hat, 'but it is no luck she has brought me.' And that was true enough surely, since it was in these last weeks that the *Highland Mary* and the *Annie MacQueen* had been getting the bad fishings when other pairs were doing well enough. And Hat said low to the rest of his crew that it was because he could not think right now. Any time when he should be looking at the land for the marks, or asking himself was it a right bottom where they were, there would come a thing like the flap of a swan's wing across his mind, and he would be left all in a maze and not able to act quick as a skipper should.

By now it was dusk. Alec Shop went off to start up the diesel; wee Willie got the tea things washed and redded up in the cabin. Behind the grey of the low clouds the moon was after rising. Dougie shouted over from their neighbour boat where the engine was starting up too. But on the *Highland Mary* the boys were all thinking of thon woman with the wee white feathers on her, except for Willie the cook, and he was thinking that it could not be fair how they worked the football pools, for he had been going in for them these three years back and never once got anything out of them, and if you added up the sixpenny postal orders he had sent off it was fair staggering.

Again that night they had poor fishings and so for the rest of the week. If they had a ring at all there would only be a scatter of fish in it, and the herring boat giving them bottom prices, so that there were only shillings to share out at the end of the week. But Black Rob was caring little. He washed and shaved and put a bit brilliantine on his hair that was wavy like a black retriever dog's, and he put on a clean white shirt and his best Sunday suit, and off he went on the Saturday night to the point and whatever was there for him.

There she was, sure enough, and there behind a rock was the shape of feathers, and the October moon white on it, and Black Rob warmed his hands in it, and it was more than his hands were warming, and when the Swan came up out of the water Black Rob caught hold of her, for he was never one for beds and houses when there was bracken on the braeside. And the more the Swan cried out, the more Rob was not caring at all what he did with her. And he made her promise he would see her again at the next full moon.

Not one of them said a thing on Sunday and who would be asking Black Rob what kind of thoughts he was having at sermon time. But on the Monday they all asked him, and he said Aye, it was so, and laughed a bit. But Hat was angry all the week, and an angry skipper makes poor fishing, forby a white wing blinding his mind at the time he needs his judgment quickest.

So another month went by, and in November Black Rob put on his best suit again and off to the point. And he saw the Swan indeed by frosty moonlight. But that was all there was to it. For he could not anyway lay hands on her feather dress. Black Rob came home with his good coat torn and himself cut and bruised, the way he was running about and bashing himself against the rocks, and that Sunday he was not at the morning service nor yet the evening.

Now it was mostly Rob who was at the wire in the *Highland Mary,* and he had a quick and certain feel of it, but now it seemed he had lost that altogether, and though they might be ringing, it was for nothing but a scatter of herring or a ball of mackerel, and the rest swearing at Black Rob and he swearing back at them. And the noise they made would be skipping across the water until one of the Lamlash skippers who was a gey religious man, bid them be quiet for fear a vengeance would come on the whole fleet.

But when it came on to December, Alec Shop had a thought of all this. He said: 'You will all be taking her the wrong way. How were you not saying you would marry her? It is this marrying that the lasses are always after.'

'Who would be marrying a swan?' says Black Rob. 'It is eggs she would be laying on you!' And that was not all he said, for he had a great hatred and anger at the Swan for the trick she had played on him.

But Alec wiped his hands that were all filed with the diesel oil, 'I would be marrying her,' says he, 'for I am thinking breakfast would be easy come by with only the bacon to be got!' And then he says: 'The first time I was after seeing yon feather it came in my mind to marry the lass, and I will have my witnesses waiting, and I am telling you this, Black Rob, she will be keeping my house for me and never a thought in the head of her but for the way she will be pleasing me best. And I am telling you another thing, it is not you will be speaking to my wife of anything that may have passed!'

Now Black Rob made an answer to that, and it was none of the best, and Alec gave him as good as he got, for he had found the trick of it, working in the south. And the skipper laughed, for he was cold angry at Rob over what had happened, though he was not saying it, being an older man. But Black Rob answered again, and Alec caught up a spanner, and there were the two of them fighting. And before the rest could get them out of it, they were cut and sore, and Alec had his shoulder knocked against the corner of the wheel house, so that he could hardly get lifting his arm for four days afterwards, and Black Rob's hair full of blood from the spanner. And Hat was going from one to the other saying he would need to give them their books if they could not be behaving themselves.

But the way it worked out just before the full moon, the engine had a breakdown and, Swan or no Swan, Alec needed to stay by the boat and work on her, all the more because Dougie and the rest of the boys on the *Annie MacQueen* were not pleased at all with the way things had been going, and indeed there was talk of them looking for another neighbour. So Alec was cursing and swearing, but stay he must, and wee Willie the cook stayed with him to help work on the engine. But he had a packet of Wild Wests with him, for next to football what Willie liked best was a book with six-shooters and all that in it.

Effie MacDonald was near her time, and there was her mother and her aunties for ever in and out the house, and it was no place at all for Johnnie the Ghost and they casting their looks at him. So the night of the full moon he slipped out, but before he went he took a wee nip, and after he got clear of the houses he took another. For he was a man that had a trick of seeing some kind of frightening appearances, and that was the way he got his by-name.

When he was half way to the point he took another nip, for he was feeling the wee-est bit shoogly about the knees, and by the time he was there he had all the courage in the world and had forgotten there was ever such a girl as Effie MacDonald. And he seemed to have everything right clear and arguable in his head and shooting up from one moment to the next the same as a fountain. And he was asking himself how could the Swan not be saying sweet words to a man as personable and noble as himself? But what at all happened when he saw the Swan and what he was doing to her, were not clear any longer, and there was a blackness cutting into his mind, and there was a screeching and groaning that first seemed to be the Swan and then all of a sudden was his wife Effie with her time come on her, and he standing in the door of his own house looking over at the bed. And as he stood he grew cold and vomited, and Effie's mother gave him one push out that landed him in a rosebush, and when it was morning and Effie's bairn come into the world, he found himself covered with scratches and vomit and ashamed to go into his own house and wash.

So he went to the spring behind and took his coat off and washed. And there were white feathers and swansdown in under his shirt and every place, and whenever he saw a bit of it a deep sadness came on him and he took the bottle out of his pocket and drank again, the way he could forget that he had forgotten all he needed so sore to re-member. He was not back on the boat that week, and he was not sober one day of it. And that was the hardest for Effie, and there are plenty skippers would never have taken him back at all, but Hat knew fine what had come to him, and at the end of the week Johnnie went back. But he was an ill man to have to do with for long enough af-ter that, and Effie was right glad always when he went off on the Monday.

Then it was New Year, and those were the days that folk kept it as it should be kept. And after New Year Alec Shop began to make his plans. He lived in the shed at the back of his mother's house, where she and his aunties were; and he asked his two witnesses to be at the shed that Saturday night. The one of them was his own brother and the other was his skipper, for Hat was thinking that they needed to deal with the Swan some way, or there would never be any luck at all for the *Highland Mary,* and if this was to be the way of it and Alec to be the man, well then, he would rather be helping than hindering, and maybe when the Swan was another man's wife he would be able to give over thinking of her and could turn his mind to the fishing again.

Alec got in a cake and a bottle of sweet port wine, the kind that they were telling him the ladies would like, and he put a new red cloth with fringes on the table and a mug with some snowdrops, and he put his budgie cage into the window, with the two budgies that his aunties looked after for him during the week. And he redded up everything in the shed, and he got sweeping up the cigarette ends and throwing them on the back of the fire, and forby that he took out the dirty photos that he had got in the south and that he had in the foot of one of his old sea boots so that his aunties would not get seeing them, and he threw them onto the fire without so much as looking at them again. He was doing all this in a regular and quiet kind of way, the way an engi-neer would be getting on with a job, and then it got to be evening, and he polished up the lamp and put a new wick in it: and he had bought a pink shade for it with kind of lacey trimming, the way he thought a woman would have her eye pleasantly caught by it.

And then he started to wash and he whistling to himself, and the budgies chirping and rustling. And then all of a sudden he caught sight of himself in the bit looking glass over the basin. And he fell to wondering what will the Swan say to me, and will the Swan have me at all? And he had never ever thought of it that way in all his life, for the girls in Cardiff or Glasgow are taking a man's money even if the man is dead ugly, and the dirty photos will look back at you the same way whoever you are, and when it comes to a dance you are mostly all thinking more of the music and of the dancing itself than of your partner, anyway in the hard dances and those were the kind Alec liked best himself.

But now he stared hard at the face in the looking glass and thought what is this odd face I have on me that I have never studied it at all? And he could not tell what a woman would be thinking of it, nor whether a woman would like the colour of his eyes that were grey blue with a darker ring round them, and he wished now he had his teeth white and not all stained with the smoking. And he thought maybe she will not have me in marriage at all, maybe there is only one thing to be done with the Swan and that is what Hat and Black Rob and Johnnie the Ghost have done, and it is not a lucky thing at all, but if it is bad luck she is bringing on us, then that is the luck we must take. And yet, he thought, the way I am thinking on the Swan now, it is not that way I want her, but somehow else. And he fell to studying how it would make all the difference if he and the Swan were married, but he could not see right yet how it was, and his heart beating at full speed with the difficult thoughts he had.

But while he was on that, and putting the comb through his hair so it would stay flat down, in came his brother and his skipper. His brother was wearing his kilt, for he was in the Gaelic choir, and the skipper was in his best suit, with the hat he had for weddings and funerals, and a Bible in his hand. So Alec said: 'You will wait in the back room until the time I am calling for you,' and he set candles for them there.

Then he put on his coat and he was shaking a bit, and Hat looked him over and then took up some few of the snowdrops and put them in his button hole. And by now the moon was risen, so he went on his way to the point.

For a little he had the feeling that there was no truth at all in any of this, that there would be nothing at the point but air and moonshine and the cold beating of waves. And he wished he had a bottle with him, for he was dead sober and shivering. But then he came to the rocks and looked out, and his heart turned over on him, for there she was, and in a little he came on the shape of feathers, and he took it up and began to walk back, looking over his shoulder for her to follow. And follow she must, wet and shining and sweet voiced, and he saw it was all true, and for a short time he felt himself near to doing what Black Rob had done, for she was so bonny, and he needed to touch her and have her, the same way a sad man might be needing the whisky, for it would mean the breaking of a black and hard and terrible thing in himself. It would mean light and life and an escaping. But he walked on and she at his elbow, and he trying not to look at her too often, and she asking, asking for her feathers back. So he said: 'Marry me, lassie, and you shall have your dress again.'

And she said: 'Much good it would be to you, Alec, to have a wife only at the full moon!'

And he said: 'I would rather a night of you, lassie, than four weeks of any other woman in the whole of Scotland!' And then he said: 'It is only week ends I am home, anyway, so I would be seeing you one time in four, and maybe,' he went on, 'if we were up north at Mallaig or Castlebay itself, or on the East Coast, you would be coming to me on your wings?'

'You would need to keep your faith to me, Alec,' says the Swan, 'and never ever to lay hands on me to be hurting me, for indeed I have been sore hurt the way it was with the rest of your crew, and I will tell you, Alec, what it was your skipper did to me, forby Black Rob and Johnnie – '

'You will not be telling me!' says Alec quick and hard. 'For I could not bear it at all. And indeed and indeed, lassie, you will keep yourself quiet and you will not be looking at me too much until after we are married, for I cannot know what I will do and you are over bonny for the like of me or for any of us poor souls, but if you will have me I will do anything in the wide world for you.' And a great shame came over Alec, thinking how they were only poor fishermen, with no education beyond the age of fourteen and no chances at all, and some years there would be little herring in it and if any pair did well then the rest would be angry at them and jealous, and if at any time there was plenty of herring, then the buyers would get together and force the prices down, or maybe they would be needing to dump their catch at Ayr, and there was no way out of it at all for the fishermen, and what kind of a man was he to think he could be marrying such a bonny one as the Swan? And he wiped his sleeve across his eyes because of the shame he was in, and the tears that had come on him so sudden, and there was the Swan with her arms round him and her long wet hair and her cheeks yet cold from the sea, but softer and kinder than anything Alec had ever known. But he sprang away from her, for he saw the light of the lamp in the window of his shed, and he was remembering the clean cloth and the cake that had not been cut and the glasses that were dry and polished and the bed that had not been rumpled; and when he came to the door he shut his eyes and he lifted the Swan in over the threshold and took his hands from her quick. Then he said: 'I will call my witnesses and we will be married now at once, and later on I will be going to the Sheriff's Court to pay the fine on it, but all the same this will be as lawful a marriage as any in Scotland.'

And she smiled at him and said: 'Are your witnesses to see your wife naked, Alec?'

And he said: 'I would not like that at all, but if I give you the feathers back, you will not fly away on me, lassie? For if you did that I am thinking I would lie down and die.'

And she did not answer, but she smiled at Alec again. And it went dancing through him like an electric current running through wires when the starter makes its contact, and he gave her the feathers without a word and she held them to her, and she began to change into a bird, and he cried at her: 'Stop, stop, lassie!'

And she stopped, the way her face and hands were clear of the feathers and as for the rest of her, there was a kind of swaying in that room, so that sometimes she was a bird with the high cold breast of a swan, and the great wings starting back, and sometimes she was a woman in a white shining wedding dress. And Alec called in his witnesses and took her hand and said aloud before his brother and his skipper that they were man and wife. And the Swan was saying the same in thon sweet and bonny voice she had.

There was a kind of daze and enchantment on them all, and Hat was standing stiff and staring at the Swan, with a tight grip on his Bible; and Alec's brother was looking on the floor where the lamp light was running shadows in the cracks between the boards, and his hands fidgeting at the chain of his sporran and a singing in his ears. And then Alec and the Swan had their hands together on the knife, cutting the cake, and Hat opened the bottle of port wine, and for a little there was the circle of lamp light on cake and glasses and hands, and the white clean feathers reaching up the back of a girl's fingers, the way a long sleeve would, and moving with her. And then Alec said low to the witnesses that they could be going and he would surely see them in the morning on their way to the kirk, and he with his wife on his arm. And they went out and they said nothing to one another, but Hat could not get seeing in his mind at all how yon swan winged and snowy woman could be walking the kirk road with Alec, and all the old wives staring at her.

But Alec turned to take the Swan in his arms, now they were married and alone, and there was a fire and a hurry in him, and his hands were seeking for the flesh of her under the feathers. But it was not a right woman's shape he was holding to, and as he caught at her she swept out with an arm or a wing and the lamp went over. He jumped at it and threw the rug on the burning oil and tramped on the flames and had it out before it had set the shed on fire. And then he pulled the curtains back and the moonlight came lapping in. And then he saw that the feather shape had closed over the face and hands of the Swan, and it was a great bird he had with him and no woman at all.

Then Alec let out a great screech and seized hold of the bird, and the long supple neck of it came down beside his own as it might have been her arm round his neck when he had wept coming back from the point, and he knew fine it was her somewhere and he cried out: 'Lassie, lassie, where are you at all?'

And he battered with his face and fingers against the bird as though it were some-thing between him and his lassie. And it seemed to him as though she must be within the feather shape, and all at once he pulled out his knife and opened it with one hand and his teeth, holding all the time with the other hand onto the bird's wing where it joined the shoulder, and he struck with the knife to open a hole in the feather dress and tear it away from her. But when he struck, a terrible skirl came from the Swan and the wings beat at his head and knocked him clean over, and he was left on the floor in a flurry of feathers and blows and broken glass where at last the Swan had burst her way through the window and out.

All night Alec lay there on the floor and the fire died on the hearth and in the early morning rain blew in through the broken window, and he turned about and moaned and opened his eyes in the dark, and he was alone and hurt. And when it was right light he sat up, and there was the open knife and blood on it. And Alec went to the table with the cut cake and the glasses and he leaned his forehead on it and he wept, and there he was when Hat came back and knocked on the door of the shed.

Alec told Hat the way things had been, and old Hat nodded and said he had best be taking a good dram, even if it was Sunday morning. But Alec said no. no. And then he said he must look for another berth and maybe not in a fishing boat at all and not among the kindly folk of the West coast, but on the East or maybe in England itself.

Hat said would he not wait for the next full moon, but Alec said: 'No. I have broken my promise to the Swan and I cannot see how she will ever forgive me, and maybe I have killed her, and there is no good in me at all.'

'There is not that much good in any of us,' said Hat, 'and I will be sorry to lose you, Alec, and I wish I had never set eyes or hands on this damned woman or bird, for she has brought bad luck on every man of us!'

'She is my wife,' Alec said, 'and I do not even know what name she has. I was thinking to find all that out after we had been to bed.' And he fell to shivering, and his head ached from the blow he had got from her.

So on Monday Alec went off to Greenock to find a new berth, and Hat was needing to see about a new engineer for the *Highland Mary,* and it was a heavy heart he had on him. The fishing was no better at all, and Dougie on the *Annie MacQueen* saying he would try to get another neighbour. None of the boys said a word in front of the new engineer, and when it got round to full moon again, none of them said a word either, and it was a wild night that was in it that Saturday, and Johnnie the Ghost and Black Rob went off in the bus to the pictures and the whisky, though it was little enough they had got on the shareout, and Johnnie should have been letting Effie have the lot of it, for she was needing to get credit at the shop and that is not the best for a woman with a wee bairn. And Hat sat at home with his school lassie and she learning off her psalm and he reading in the Book of Revelations to try and take his mind off what it was for ever on.

Then on the Monday afternoon the new engineer was down the hatch oiling the engine and wee Willie was making the tea for the rest, and when they were all sitting to, Willie says: 'I saw the Swan on Saturday.'

'You!' says the lot of them.

'And what for no?' says Willie.

'Well,' says the skipper at last, 'how did it go, Willie?'

'It went fine,' he said.

'How?' says Black Rob and Johnnie together, and their voices snapped like two dogs wanting to fight.

'Well,' says Willie, 'I met her down on the shore the way all the boys did, and I went off home with her coat and she after me as bare as a plucked hen.'

'And so?' says Black Rob.

'She asked me what it was I wanted of her,' Willie says and goes to fill up the tea pot.

Just then the new engineer came down and Hat began quick speaking with him about the weather and the way the herring were shifting their ground, and the other two were eating their pieces and glaring at wee Willie. He stood up with the kettle in his hand. 'I told her I was after filling in the names of the football pool,' says he, 'and would she get helping me – for I thought maybe she might have some kind of knowledge and would be bringing me luck, and at least she could not be bringing me worse luck than I have been having, and she said Aye she would tell me the right names to put down. So that was the way the two of us were spending our time.'

'Are you telling me the whole of it?' says Black Rob low.

'Aye, surely,' says Willie, 'and it took us all of two hours what with the information she was giving me about the teams and indeed I am thinking she knows more than the newspapers themselves. And I have the forms in the post now!'

The new engineer said women were no good on football though he had known some could pick a horse. But it worked out the way wee Willie had said, and it was five hundred pounds he got out of the pools, and his photo in the paper grinning, because the Swan had given him all the names right. And Hat said this had changed the luck and he was praising up wee Willie. And indeed things went better for the *Highland Mary* for the few weeks that were left in the season.

But it was not that good for Willie himself. His father took the half of the money and had it invested the way Willie could not get touching it; but with the rest he took to the betting. Maybe the Swan could have guided him right there too, but he had no skill in it himself, and he was off at Glasgow the next full moon. Then he started to lose the money and the next thing was he was away spending what was left of it all April when the boats were lying up, and he got into bad company. And if it had not been for him losing the money so quick he would have ended up in the jail. But he came back to the *Highland Mary* the next season and there was no more talk of the Swan one way or the other.

So a year and a day went by, and months and weeks, and Alec wrote home to his mother and his aunties, and sometimes he would be one place and sometimes another, but never coming back. And the truth was he was homesick enough; he did not like the food or the weather in the south; there seemed to him to be neither seriousness in the folk nor yet a right gaiety. But he could not come back, because it was not in him to forget the Swan and, whatever way you looked at it, he was married to her by Scots law, and both his brother and his skipper agreed to that. And if he went with a woman now, he could not do it sober, and there was little pleasure he got out of it, and nothing but shame and sorrow on him afterwards.

But at home the fishing would be worse and then it would be better, and then came the war. Wee Willie was the first to register, and then the new engineer who was a young chap. Then the *Highland Mary* was requisitioned and Black Rob and Johnnie needing to get berths where they could until the time came for them to register. But Alec volunteered as an engineer, and he was put into an east coast patrol boat. He liked it well enough, better than he had done anything for all this last while. They were mostly all English and Irish in that boat, but there were two Scots forby himself, and the pay was good enough, and he had his photo taken in his uniform to send home. But one of his aunties was dead by then. And it was new budgies they had in his old cage.

Then, on a clear day and out of the eye of the sun, a bomber came down on them. Alec was below most of the time and it sounded the way hell sounds. Then a bomb came through one of the hatches and there was Alec trying to do a dozen things at the once, and in the middle of it he saw his overalls were on fire, and he beat them out, and someone shouted to him to come up, and he saw that his right hand was bleeding all over the iron rungs of the ladder though he could feel nothing at all in it yet, and first he was in a boat and then after the next explosion he was in the sea and swimming, but he did not think he would be able to keep it up for long, the way he was.

And then there was something under him, holding him up so he could rest him-self from swimming, and he seemed to let go, and life went dark on him for awhile. Then he woke clear up, and he was in pain, but most of all he wondered where he was, for he was not lying on any plank or raft or hard thing. And he put his left hand down to feel, and it was feathers was in it, and he knew he was on the back of a swan. And after a bit he said: 'Are you not wearied, my darling?'

'Aye,' said the Swan, 'but we are near land, Alec.'

And soon enough they were in shallow water and a sandy bottom, and he waded to shore, steadying himself by the Swan's lifted wing. But when they had made their way beyond high tide mark, Alec shook at the knees and he could not get any further, but he lay down on the sand and said to the Swan that it was dying he was.

'It is only cold you are and hurt and hungry,' said the Swan. 'But take you off your wet clothes, Alec, and let them dry.'

So Alec sat up and began to strip off his things, and his hands and everything covered with oil and blood; and he saw that the bonny whiteness of the Swan was smeared here and there with it, and he said: 'I have dirtied you, my dearie.'

But the Swan said – and oh, the sweet gentle voice she had on her and not like an English voice at all: 'You are my man, Alec. I am thinking nothing of it. And do you not be so shy to be taking off your things in front of me, Alec, for we are married by Scots law and there is no getting out of it.'

So Alec said: 'My darling, did I hurt you that time?'

'Aye,' said she, 'I bear the mark of it yet.'

By now the Swan was beside him on that English beach, and she brooding over him and he burrowing with his hands and face under the smooth top feathers of her and into the warm down that kept the sand and the hard English air out of the hurts on him. 'I did that to you,' he said, 'and I was not faithful to you. I broke my promise all round and every way.'

'Aye,' said she, 'but it is over and I am your wife, Alec.'

So they lay quiet for a time and he half asleep and happy the way he had forgotten one could be happy. Then the Swan said to him: 'I am hearing the Home Guards up in the dunes, Alec, and I must be leaving you.'

'No!' he said, and held onto her.

'You will get six weeks' leave out of this, Alec,' said she, 'and there will be two full moons in it.'

'And after that?' said Alec.

'Ach,' said she, 'it is the war now and which one of us can see more than the two moons ahead?' And with that she rose out of his arms, and a few minutes later the Home Guards came running, and one of them asking Alec had he seen a parachute, for they had seen some great white thing flapping in the sky and were minded to shoot at it. But Alec laughed a bit and said: No, no, and then he said to the man that was helping him: 'How much leave will I get out of this?'

'You will get six weeks easy,' the man said. And Alec laughed again, and they all thinking that the Scots were a queer lot entirely and no one in the south could ever see what they would be after at all.

William Soutar (1898 – 1943)

Soutar may be cited as an example of a Scottish writer whose work was galvanised by his conversion to Scots as a poetic medium. His English poems are not very interesting. The poems in Scots are among the best of his age. A half dozen are little miracles in which a colloquial directness and vigor are wedded to a lyrical inevitability and classical economy of phrase equalled only by MacDiarmid himself. Soutar was a victim of a rare disease, spondylitis, which affected most of his adult life. By 1930, he had become permanently bedridden. Among his achievements is the *Diaries of a Dying Man*, which he kept late in his life.

Scotland

Atween the world o' licht
And the world that is to be
A man wi' unco★ sicht   uncanny
Sees whaur he canna see:

Gangs whaur he canna walk:
Recks whaur he canna read:
Hauds what he canna tak:
Mells★ wi' the unborn dead.   mixes

Atween the world o' licht
And the world that is to be   10
A man wi' unco sicht
Monie a saul maun see:

Sauls that are stark and nesh★:   fine
Sauls that wud dree the day:
Souls that are fain for flesh
But canna win the wey.

Hae ye the unco sicht
That sees atween and atween
This world that lowes in licht:
Yon world that hasna been?   20

It is owre late for fear,
Owre early for disclaim;
Whan ye come hameless here
And ken ye are at hame.

The Tryst

O luely, luely, cam she in
and luely she lay doun:
I kent her be her caller★ lips   fresh
and her breists sae smaa and roun.

A' throu the nicht we spak nae word
nor sindered bane frae bane:
aa throu the nicht I heard her hert
gang soundin wi my ain.

It was about the waukrif hour
whan cocks begin to craw   10
that she smooled★ saftly throu the mirk   glided
afore the day wad daw.

Sea luely, luely, cam she in
sae luely was she gane
and wi her aa my simmer★ days   summer
like they had never been.

The Thocht

Young Janie was a strappin' lass
Wha deed in jizzen★-bed,   childbirth
And monie a thocht her lover thocht
Lang aftir she was dead:

But aye, wi' a' he brocht to mind
O' misery and wrang,
There was a gledness gathered in
Like the owrecome o' a sang:

And, gin the deid are naethingness
Or★ they be minded on.   10   unless
As hinny★ to a hungry ghaist   honey
Maun be a thocht like yon.

The Minister

As the minister prayed wi' hands in air
He had the dreid thocht that he was bare:
That his goun and a' his ither claes
Were huggerin doun ablow his knees.

But he wudna daur unsteek his e'en
To see what mebbe his fowk had seen –
That, waur nor John Baptist frae the waist,
He stude mither-naked like a beast.

Sae ablow the prayer that soundit abune
He slippit in twa, three words o' his ain –   10
That heids were doun, and e'en were ticht,
And afore he was dune a' wud be richt.

Wi' as guid a grace as he cud fend
He brocht his petition to its end:
Gowkit to see gin he was douce★ –   presentable
And, the Lord be thankit, sae he was.

The Guns

Now, on the moors where the guns bring down
The predestinated birds,
Shrill, wavering cries pass
Like the words of an international peace;
And I would that these cries were heard in every town,
Astounding the roar of the wheel
And the lying mouth of the news:
And I would that these cries might more and more increase
Until the machine stood still;
And men, despairing in the deathly queues,   10
Heard their own heart-beats
Shouting aloud, in the silence of the streets:
'Are we not also hand-fed in a wilderness:
What are we waiting for?'

Song

Whaur yon broken brig★ hings owre;   bridge
Whaur yon water maks nae soun';
Babylon blaws by in stour★:   storm, dust
Gang doun wi' a sang, gang doun.

Deep, owre deep, for onie drouth★:   thirst
Wan enouch an ye wud droun:
Saut, or seelfu'★, for the mouth;   sweet
Gang doun wi' a sang, gang doun.

Babylon blaws by in stour
Whaur yon water maks nae soun':   10
Darkness is your only door;
Gang doun wi' a sang, gang doun.

The Makar

Nae man wha loves the lawland tongue
but warstles wi the thocht –
there are mair sangs that bide unsung
nor aa that hae been wrocht.

Ablow the wastery o the years,
the thorter★ o himsel,   frustration
deep buried in his bluid he hears
a music that is leal★.   true

And wi this lealness gangs his ain;
and there's nae ither gait   10
though aa his feres★ were fremmit★ men   companions/foreign
wha cry: Owre late, *owre late*.

The Lanely Mune

Saftly, saftly, through the mirk
the mune walks a' hersel:
ayont★ the brae; abune the kirk;   beyond
and owre the dunnlin bell.
I wudna be the mune at nicht
for a' her gowd and a' her licht.

The Auld House

There's a puckle★ lairds in the auld house   few
wha haud the waas thegither:
there's no muckle graith★ in the auld house   furniture
nor smeddum★ aither.   nerve

It was aince a braw and bauld house
and guid for onie weather:
kings and lords thranged in the auld house
or★ it gaed a'smither★.   ere/to bits

There were kings and lords in the auld house
and birds o monie a feather: 10
there were sangs and swords in the auld house
that rattled ane anither.

It was aince a braw and bauld house
and guid for onie weather:
but it's noo★ a scruntit★ and cauld house   now/stunted
whaur lairdies forgaither.

Lat's caa in the folk to the auld house,
the puir folk aa thegither:
it's sunkit on rock is the auld house,
and the rock's their brither.   20

It was aince a braw and bauld house
and guid for onie weather:
but the fok maun funder★ the auld house   root up
and bigg up anither.

The Gowk

Half doun the hill, whaur fa's the linn★   waterfall
Far frae the flaught o' fowk,
I saw upon a lanely whin★   stone
A lanely singin' gowk:
Cuckoo, cuckoo;
And at my back
The howie hill stude up and spak:
Cuckoo, cuckoo.

There was nae soun'; the loupin' linn
Hung frostit in its fa':   10
Nae bird was on the lanely whin
Sae white wi' fleurs o' snaw:
Cuckoo, cuckoo;
I stude stane still;
And saftly spak the howie hill:
Cuckoo, cuckoo.

The following work, one of Soutar's finest achievements, is a tribute in both style and subject to Hugh
MacDiarmid's *A Drunk Man Looks at the Thistle*, which had been published some five years before.

The Auld Tree
(For Hugh McDiarmid)

There's monie a sicht we dinna see
Wi' oniething ye'd ca' an e'e:
There's monie a march o' fantoun grund
The forret★ fit has never fund: forward
And gin we tak nae yirdlin★ road   earthly
Our body, halflins corp and clod,
Sits steerless as a man o' stane
Unwarly that it is alane.
'Twas sic a body I had kent
Ae simmer mornin' whaur the bent★   10   grass, field
I ligg'd on, flichter'd a' its fleurs

Up to the lift*: hours upon hours   sky
My thowless banes fu' streekit were
Like ane unhappit frae his lair.
I heard nae mair the laverock's chitter
Nor crawin' corbie* wi' a flitter   crow
Gae up frae howkin': a' my sicht
Was rinnin' thru the reemlin' licht
And whitter'd yont* that fleury brae   beyond
Without a sidlins gliff*: a' day   20   movement
My body ligg'd and but a breath
Hingin' atween itsel' and death.
It's no for makars* to upvant*   poets/boast
Themsel's; lat mummers mak a mant
O' a' their makins: what's to tell
Is mair nor oniebody's sel':
Is mair nor is the word that tells it;
And mair nor is the mind that spells it.
There is a tree that lifts its hands
Owre a' the worlds: and though it stands   30
Aye green abune* the heids o' men   above
Afttimes it's lang afore we ken
That it is there. Auld, auld, is it;
And was a tree or onie fit,
Nor God's, daunner'd* in its saft schaw*:   wandered/grove
Nor sall it be a runt* though the ca'   dry stalk
O' times hinnermaist sea dees doun
Intill a naething wi' nae soun'.
It's thramml'd deeper nor the pit
O' space, and a' our planets sit   40
As toad-stools crinin'* whaur the rit   shrinking
Raxes* into the licht: owreheid   reaches
The heichest stern*, like to a gleed   star
Blawn up, hings waukrifelie* and waif   wakefully
Nor lunts* upon the laichest leaf.   burns
Aye, monie a sicht we canna see
Wi' oniething ye'd ca' an e'e:
Yet maun the makar carry back
A ferlie* that the e'en can tak;   wonder
And busk* his roun-tree on the hill   50   dress
In shape o' haly Yggdrasil.[1]
There was a carl*; it's lang sin he   fellow, peasant
Gowkit upon this eldren tree
Whaur thru the mornin' haar* it boo'd   mist
A rung owre earth's green solitude:
And there, ablow the sanctit schaw,
Baith bird and beastie and the sma'
Flitterin' fikies o' the air
Heez'd at a ca' – and they were there.
That's lang, lang syne; but at the yett*   60   gate
O' yon saft gairthen still is set

---

[1] In Norse mythology, the great tree whose roots stretch around the world. It figures prominently in MacDiarmid's *Drunk Man*.

The challance o' the singin' word
That whunners like a lowin'* sword.   flaming
Strauchtly I lookit, whaur the kennin'
O' that auld prophet aince was wennin,
And in ablow the haly tree
Noo sat, in crouse* clanjampherie*,   merry/hodge-podge
A' the leal* makars o' the world.   loyal, true
Up through the leaves their claivers skirl'd
The hale o' the day; nae rung but dirl'd*   70   tingled,
Wi' sang, or lauchter, or the diddle   reverberated
O' flochtersome fife, and flute, and fiddle.
Some gate I slippit in mysel',
But ask na how – I canna tell,
And sittin' cheek-for-chow wi' Rab¹
I hearkint while he eas'd his gab
On him wha screed the *Sang to Davy*.
'Aye:' Rab was sayin': 'monie a shavie
Time ploys on man: just tak a gliff
Richt round – wha's here that seem'd nae cüfe*   80   fool
In ither days: it maks a body
Nicher, like onie traikit cuddie,
To ken he's hame in spite o' a'
Was thocht his folly and his fa'.
Man, wha o' us, on lookin' back,
Sees ocht misgoggl'd, or wud tak
Ill-will at oniebody's flyte;
Nae doot the maist o' us gaed gyte*,   mad
But mebbe gyteness is the sweek
O' makin'. Hae anither keek*   90   peek
At a' our cronnies plankit saft
Ablow this tree: a hantle's* daft   few are
Just like yoursel', and hardly ane
Hadna a wuddrum i' the bane.
I ken, I ken it's mair nor airms
And legs, or puckle harns* and thairms   brains
That maks a man: and weel I ken
Aft, or a man may win richt ben
To screenge* his sel's sel', doun he snools   search
To death – but nane liggs in the mools*:   100   molds (earth)
Na, na; it's up and buskit and awa,
The earth's aye whummlin', aye the ca'
O' water jowin' to the müne:
The lang day's darg* is never düne.   work
But aften times it's sair to dree*   endure
The fa'in o' braw fullyery
And the wagaein o' the bird:
What gin the hert ken, frae the yird,
Anither tree sall rax itsel'
And ither sangsters flee and mell*   110   mix
Intill its airms: what gin the hert
Ken weel the auld tree is a pairt

---

¹ Robert Burns.

O' a' to come: time brocht its fa'
And, yonder, time maun rin awa.
O Scotland, whatna thistle rits
Into the mools; what bird noo sits
Whaur lang, lang syne there was a tree,
Younglin' and braw wi' fullyery,
Booin' its green and sternie croun
Abune Dunbar and Henrysoun.   120
And I mysel' hae set a fit
Ablow a tree that rov'd its rit
Doun to the deid runt o' the auld;
But whatna rung noo lifts to fauld
The warblin' bird; what spatrels★ rin   musical notes
Out on the four wings o' the win'.
Ah shairly, gin nae makar's breath
Blaw sune thru Scotland, doun to death
She'll gang and canker a' the world.
Owre lang her bastard sons hae skirl'd   130
Around the reid rose; wha sall name
The wild, sma' white-rose¹ o' our hame.
Gin love were routh★ whaur nae hert socht;   abundant
Gin rhyme were fund whaur nae mind wrocht;
Gie me but ane frae oot this howff★   haunt, dwelling
And I'd wauk Scotland frae her souff.
O' wha wi' onie styme★ o' sang   spark
Wud con her story and be lang
In liltin'; were it but to tell
It owre again to his ain sel'.'   140

                    ★ ★ ★ ★

Noo, as I harkint, I was waur
O' a lang stillness: and a haar
Cam owre me and nae mair I heard
O' sang, or minstrelsy, or word:
My mind churn'd round like murlin' stanes
And a cauld sough gaed thru my banes.
Mair snell★ it blew and riv'd awa   fierce
The haar afore my e'en; but a'
That erlish gairthen had gaen by
And in a lanely place was I;   150
Whaur naething sounded but the whins
Clawn up to gansh★ the wheeplin' win's.   snap at
I glour'd a' round like ane afaird
O' his ain schedaw; nocht I heard
Till richt afore my e'en upstude
A harnest★ body bleach'd o' bluid: armoured
I kent, or he had spak a word,
This deid man wi' the muckle sword.
Liftin' his airm he swung it roun'
And I cud see that on a croun   160

---

¹ The Jacobite emblem.

O' a bare hill I'd taen my stand
Wi' a like hill on ilka hand.
'Here are the Eildons:' Wallace said;
Then louted dounward wi' his blade:
'And yonder in the green kirk-shot
Ligg Merlin and the warlock Scot:
And yonder the guid Douglas fand
The marches o' his promised land
Whaur Bruce's hert, gin it cud stound,
Wud wauken Scotland frae her swound.'   170

He turn'd him then and in a stride
Had taen me round the bare hillside
Whaur derk against the lift upstude
The Eildon tree: about its wud
(Deathly as ivy on an aik)
Was wuppit a twa-heided snake.
Bare, bare, the boughs aince bricht as beryl
Whaur sang the mavis and the merle,
And whaur True Thomas' fairy feir★   fere (comrade)
Won him away for seven year: 180
Ah! cud he busk his banes, and dree
Yon burn o' bluid, this dowie★ tree   sad
Wud flichter wi' braw fullyery.
But noo the nicht was comin' owre;
The lither★ lift began to lour;   undulating
As yont the hill the floichans★ flew   snowflakes
Mair snell the yammerin' blufferts blew;
Nae bleat was there o' beast or bird:
I wud hae spak but had nae word.
The Wallace stude like he was stane   190
His cauld lips wordless as my ain,
But saftly on the mirken'd sicht
His muckle blade, wi' an eerie licht,
Glister'd; and in his e'en the poo'r
Low'd up to thraw this weirded hour.
'Twas then I spak: but no my ain
Spirit, in anguishment, alane,
But Scotland's sel', wi' thorter'd★ pride,   thwarted
Cried oot upon that cauld hillside:
And her ain name was a' she cried.   200
Wi' that the Wallace rax't his hicht
Like he wud rive the sternless nicht;
And as his wuntlin' blade cam doun
The snell wind, wi' a wheemerin' soun',
Gaed owre me; and my spirit heard
The challance o' yon singin' word
That whunners like a lowin' sword.
Nae mair nor thrice the Wallace straik;
And first he sklent the heided snake:
He sklent it strauchtly into twa   210
And kelterin' they skail'd awa;
The ane haud'n southard to his hame,
The ither wast owre Irish faem★.   foam

The neist straik, wi' a sklinterin' dird,
Lowden'd the auld tree to the yird
And a' the seepin' sap, like bluid,
Pirr'd saftly frae the cankert wud:
A sough gaed by me, laich★ and lang,   low
Like the owrecome o' an auld-world sang.
The hinmaist straik deep doun was driven   220
(As it had been a flaucht★ o' levin★)   flash/lightning
And riv'd by runt, and craig, until
A muckle slap thraw'd thru the hill
Shawin' the auld tree's wizzen'd rit
A' tangl'd owre that reekin' pit
That gaes richt doun, frae ilka airt,
To the livenin' lowe★ at the world's hert.   hollow
Like ane wha at the deid o' nicht
Is wander'd on a haarie hicht,
And wi' a switherin' breath stands still   230
Kennin' that at his fit the hill
Hings owre into the mirk o' space,
Sae stude I be that antrin★ place.   strange
And first cam up frae oot the pit
A souff★; and on the wings o' it   sigh
A laich and lanely maunner cam
Like an awaukenin' frae a dwalm★:   dream
Sae wunner'd was I and afaird
I kent na a' the sounds I heard
But they were rowth – o' reeshlin' banes,   240
And sklinterin' rocks, and brakin' chains,
And wails o' women in their thraws,
And the rummlin' march o' harnest raws.
Then maisterin' my mauchless★ wit   spiritless
I glour'd richt doun the drumlie★ pit   gloomy
And far awa the flichterin' lowe★   flame
Gather'd itsel' and, wi' a sough,
Cam loupin'; flaucht on flaucht o' flame
That beller'd owre in fiery faem
And wi' a crack, like the levin's whup,   250
Flirn'd and flisk'd and fluther'd up.
I wud hae riv'd mysel' awa
But cudna; and the breeshilin'★ ca'   rushing
Jow'd on until its spindrift brunt
The auld tree's wizzen'd rit and runt:
I goup't upon the glisterin' sicht
My twa e'en blinded wi' the licht
And a' my senses, ane be ane,
Fluff't oot like they had never been;
Yet, far ben★ in the breist o' me,   260   inwards
I heard the soundin o' the sea.

                    ★ ★ ★ ★

Whan I cam roun' the lowe was gaen
And I was standin' a' alane;
But whaur the slap had gaunted wide

And whaur, abune the bare hillside,
The auld tree crin'd; deep in the yird
Wallace had sheuch'd★ his muckle sword.   furrowed
And noo the yirlich★ steer★ was düne   eerie/commotion
And up the lowdenin' lift the müne
Cam saftly till her cannie licht   270
Kyth'd on the cauld hill and made bricht
The caulder sword's begesserant★ rime   sparkling
That braidly skinkl'd, styme on styme.
But wha on onie frostit fale
Saw cranreuch★ bleezin' like a bale,   frost
As in this lifted leam I saw
The hale blade rax itsel' and thraw,
Ryce★ upon ryce like it had been   branch
A fiery cross a' growin' green
In its ain loupin' leure★ o' wud;   280   blaze
Till deein' doun – a thistle stude
Whaur aince had dwin'd the Eildon tree.
There was nae soun': it seem'd to me
On that bare hill nae soun' wud be
For evermair; nor birth, nor death,
As God were haudin' in His breath:
The müne, far in the midmaist lift,
Ligg'd like a stane nae hand cud shift,
And strauchtly on the thistle's croun
Its lipper★ licht cam spinnerin' doun.   290   rippling
But a' that stillness, in a crack,
Was by and düne whan at my back
I heard a fitterin' fit; and turn'd
And saw a man wha's twa e'en burn'd
Wi' byspale glamer like he sklent
On routhie years time yet maun tent.
Word-drucken★ was he, but his words   drunken, soaked
As the rambusteous lilt o' birds
Wauken'd the thistle; and for lang
I harkint while he sang his sang: 300
But wi' his words I winna mell
Sin he has screed them a' himsel'.[1]
Aye richt owreheid the müne ligg'd still
And lows'd her cauld licht on the hill;
But noo she was nae mair alane,
In the lirk o' the lift, for ane be ane
The sma' sternes soom'd frae oot the slack
O' space that gaed awa far back
Ahint the müne; and as they cam
The müne hersel' dreng'd★ frae her dwalm★   310   rallied/swoon
And cannily began to steer
Yont her lang nicht o' seven year.
Wi' that the drucken man upstüde
And shog'd the muckle thistle's wud
Until the flounrie draff like snaw

---

[1] *A Drunk Man Looks at the Thistle* by Hugh MacDiarmid (WS).

Flew up, and owre, and far awa:
And weel I kent, as it gaed by,
That on a guidly hill was I;
And that there breer'd, at ilka hand,
The braid shires o' a promised land.   320
Noo, as the day began to daw,
The thistle wi' a warstlin' thraw
Rax't out its airms — and was a tree
Younglin' and green wi' fullyery;
And as the licht low'd in its hert
The flichterin' birds, frae ilka airt,
Cam hameart to their norlan nest
In the saft bieldin★ o' its breist.   shelter
Richt in the rowsan★ sin the wud   rousing
O' this green tree sae leamin' stüde   330
Like it had been a buss o' fire;
And as it stude the warblin' choir
O' birds were singin' o' their hame:
But what they sang I canna name
Though I was singin' wi' the birds
In my ain countrie's lawland words.
Lang, lang, I stude upon that hicht
And aye it was in louthe★ o' licht;   abundance
And aye the birds sang owre their sang;
And aye the growthy tree outflang   340
Its fullyery afore the sin:
'Daw★ on o' day that winna düne:'   dawn
I sang: 'or Scotland stands abune
Her ain deid sel'; and sterkly steers
Into the bairn-time o' her years.'

I wauken'd; and my hert was licht
(Though owre my ain hill cam the nicht)
For aye yon antrin hill I saw
Wi' its green tree in the gowdan daw:
And, as I swaver'd doun the slack,   350
I heard, aye branglant★ at my back,   brandishing
The challance o' the singin' word
That whunners like a lowin' sword.

Eric Linklater (1899 – 1974)

Born in South Wales, Linklater spent most of his youth in Scotland, especially in the Orkney Islands, with which area he is especially associated. His first novel, still as fine as any he has written, *White Maa's Saga* (1929), was set there. Later he wrote novels on a wide variety of subjects and in many styles, especially satiric. The short story printed here, 'The Goose Girl', is a nice blend of fantasy and realism. It has become a classic of modern Scottish literature.

The Goose Girl

When I woke among the currant-bushes I saw her coming out of the cottage door with her fist round the gander's neck. I heard them too, for she was yelling and the gander was beating the doorposts and beating her thighs with his great creaking wings. Like a windmill in the distance, like the slap of a rising swan's black feet on the water, like clothes on the line thrashing in a breeze: the gander was making nearly as much noise as she was, and she was shouting her head off. There was no leaping tune in her voice that morning. It was just the air in her lungs being driven through the funnel of her throat like steam from a well-fired boiler; and some of the words she was using were no prettier than what goes on in any stoker's mind. I wasn't listening so much as looking. I had heard those words before, but I had never seen a woman's body like hers, so firm and long of limb, like a young reed in firmness and round as an apple where it should be, and white as a pearl. Against the gander's wings, which were a cold white like snow, her pallor was warm and glowing. Not reflecting light, but glowing with it. She was naked as the sky, and the sky, at four o'clock in the morning, was bare of cloud except for a little twist of wool low down in the west.

Now she gripped the gander's neck with both her hands, and even her hands weren't red like any other country girl's, but small and white. They were strong though, and I could see the hardness of her forearms. She was throttling the bird, and its beak was wide open, a gaping stretch of yellow skin, the upper mandible at right angles to the lower. Its eyes were hidden in the ruffling of its little head-feathers. She dragged it through the door, gave a great heave, and threw it with a noise of breaking stalks into some overgrown rhubarb. A splash of dewdrops rose from the leaves and caught the light. For a moment she stood looking at the bird, her arms a little bent and her hair dishevelled, her mouth open, and her breast rising and falling. Then abruptly, she turned and went back into the cottage, slamming the door behind her. I listened, I remember, for the sound of a key turning or a bolt going home; but in this part of the country they never lock their doors. It was lack of custom, not lack of feeling, that prevented her from giving this final emphasis to her act of expulsion.

The gander shook himself, hissing loudly, and broke more stalks of rhubarb as he made his way to a narrow path of little sea-shore pebbles. I had seen him before, half a dozen times with the girl, and always marveled at the size of him, but now, from where I lay among the currantbushes, he looked bigger than ever and his ruffled headfeathers stood out like a crown. His neck was as stiff as a broom-handle but twice as thick, and he turned his head this way and that with a twitch of the bill, an angry snap. His little black eyes were swollen and bright, and the broad webs of his feet fell on the path with the heavy tread of German infantry. He stopped when he saw me and stood for a little while, hissing like a burst tyre; but not in the way of an ordinary gander, with its neck low to the ground and its beak reaching forward. He stood upright, his head swaying back as if to look at me from a greater height, and when he had done with hissing he turned his back on me and went tramping through some rows of cabbage-plants to a gap in the low garden wall where the old turf-dyke on which it was built had collapsed and brought down the stone. It was a plain little garden with no colour in it except some yellow daisies under the cottage windows and a thin growth of honeysuckle beside the door. There was a fuchsia hedge on one side, not in flower yet, and gooseberries and blackcurrant bushes along the other walls, with a clump of greybarked elder-trees in the corner. On one side of the dividing pebble-path rhubarb and spring onions, early potatoes and cabbage on the other: that was all. And the gander, marching like a Prussian, flattened the cabbages under his broad splayed feet as if there had been the weight of a man in him. Perhaps there was. He was no ordinary bird, that was certain.

I got up and followed him, cautiously, as he disappeared, and watched him swimming down the little stream that runs behind the cottage to the big loch a quarter of a mile away. I saw his head, still ruffled, still indignantly twitching, behind a bank of meadowsweet; and then he vanished.

I leant against the wall of a cartshed, thinking. The air was still, and the country looked as though no one had ever touched it. The day before had been wet and ugly, and I remembered with a kind of shame how unhappy I had been; and how clumsily I had behaved, getting drunk so that I could tell the truth. But now I felt uncommonly well – and I had done my duty. There's nothing like sleeping in the open air to prevent a hangover, and I had, after long delay, disburdened my mind. The evening before I had gone to see John Norquoy to tell him how his young brother had been killed on the shore of Lake Commachio.

We had been together for a long time, Jim Norquoy and I, in the Seaforths to begin with and then in the Commando, and between Primo Sole in Sicily and that great cold lagoon of Commachio, mud and water and a dancing mirage, we had had our fill of fighting. Jim was hit in shallow water, wading ashore after our boats had grounded on a mudbank just as the sun came up, and I carried him in. But he died on the edge of the land, and his last words were, 'You'll find it difficult to go back too, after all this.'

That was an understatement. I found it impossible to go back to the life I had known before, and when I came north to the islands, to tell his people about Jim and give him what immortality I could, by feeding their pride in him, I was looking for something for myself as well. No more school teaching for me. I was never meant to be a teacher anyway, either by Providence or my parents. I had only wanted to live – I mean to live in such a way that life came in through my eyes and I could feel it on my skin – but never had I known how to go about it till the war came. And now, when the war was over, I was more at a loss than ever. I couldn't go back to an elementary school in Falkirk, and teach little boys the parts of speech and the more blatant pieces of history, for fear that one of them, some day, might ask me, 'What's it all for? What are we going to say when we've learnt the parts of speech; and if we learn all the history in the world, what would it mean?'

I was no coward, not in the physical sense, and I had been a good soldier – not as good as Jim, though I earned my pay – but when I looked at those questions in the solitude of my mind I knew that I couldn't face them in public. Nor did I want to. I wanted to live, but not to set myself up as a preceptor of living. As a small boy I had gone about in a state of perpetual astonishment; a book or a feather, a mouse or a fish or the dining-room table had all seemed equally miraculous, and I lacked the ordinary confidence in my own reality. I never went to bed without wondering what new shape I might inhabit by the morning. Almost from the beginning I was a disappointment to my parents. They had a position to keep up, and were ambitious too. They took it very badly when I was expelled from the school where my elder brother had been Head of his House and Captain of Cricket.

Now, after six years in the Army, I felt that I had served my apprenticeship to war, but I was still a novice in peace. So I couldn't, in honesty, set up as a teacher, and I had been looking for something else to do. I hadn't much to guide me except negatives. I didn't want to live in a town, for one thing, because I felt, at that time, the need to think; and peace to think, in my view of it, required the open sky.

I started badly, for after I had seen John Norquoy at a cattle market one day, I couldn't bring myself to go and tell him about Jim. I had wanted to make him, and all his friends, so proud of Jim that he would live for ever in their minds like a lighted lamp, to which their love would be as moths, gathering to his memory and beating its wings in the glow of him. Jim was my friend, and even the Seaforth Highlanders had never known a better man.

But when I first saw John Norquoy I realised wasn't going to be easy to talk about pride to him, for he knew enough al-ready. That was evident, though it was quite an ordinary occasion. He was looking at a thin-faced cattle dealer pulling the loose black skin on the rump of a two-year-old heifer. There was nothing of the braggart in him, nothing loud or boastful, but he had the same build as Jim, the same sort of head ten years older, the look of a man who knew what he was after and what it was worth. He was smiling, and there was the same irony in his smile, though he was only selling a beast, as I had seen in Jim's face, grey with the strain of battle, when we had to withdraw from the Primo Sole bridge because our ammunition was spent, and the in-fantry who should have relieved us hadn't been able to get forward in time. There was nothing I could tell John Norquoy about pride, and when I realised that I put off going to see him. I put it off for about three weeks.

I stayed with the village schoolmaster, a good man who had fought in the last war. I told him about my other difficulty, and he thought I could teach with safety in a country school. 'The children here,' he said, 'wouldn't worry you with awkward questions. They don't grow up with doubt in their minds. Life for them means birth and marriage and death, and they're all natural things. It means hard work and hard weather, and what amusement they and their neighbours can make for themselves. It means dancing and making love when they're young, and breeding a good beast and gossiping when they're older. And if, from time to time, they're troubled about the deeper significance of life, they keep their trouble to themselves. They know that it's an old trouble, and it wouldn't occur to them that you could cure it.'

But I didn't want to teach, either in country or town, so I spent my three weeks in idleness, but kept my eyes open. I had an open mind too, and no accomplishments. I was ready for suggestions; but not for going to see John Norquoy. I met Lydia one day, and talked to her for a quarter of an hour till her mother came out and called her in. The next time I saw her she had the gander with her, and she wasn't so friendly. I felt hurt and disappointed and a little angry, though I didn't realize then what she was really like. We pay too much attention to clothes, and hers were the sort you don't see in a town unless a strayed gipsy has come in. She had a small, beautifully shaped head, but her hair was tangled by the wind and greasy, and her features were so regular that I didn't notice, to begin with, how good they were. Her throat was lovely, long and as white as milk, but her neck was dirty, and when I saw her for the second time it was the same dirt, I'm fairly sure, that still darkened her skin. And yet I felt hurt when she wouldn't stay and talk to me.

I asked the schoolmaster about her, and he told me she was illegitimate, a state of being that's not extraordinary in country districts. Her mother was a grim old woman named Thomasina Manson, a crofter's only child, unpopular as a girl, who had lived a lonely and blameless life till she was about thirty-five, when she had gone to Edinburgh, and what she did there, except get herself into trouble, no one ever knew. It was generally supposed that she had been in domestic service, and when her baby was born, about three months after she came home, she told the doctor that its father came of the gentry. But that's all she told, and her father and mother, who had married late in life, never recovered from the shock. They were Plymouth Brethren, said the schoolmaster, sternly pious and pitiably dependent on their respectability. They died, one after the other, within a couple of years of Lydia's birth, and Thomasina was left alone to work the croft and bring up the child.

How, I asked, did she come to give it a name like Lydia?

The schoolmaster showed me a register of the village children. About half of them had been christened simply enough: Thomas and James and Mary, Ellen and Jean and William and David, and a few of the girls had clumsy feminine transforma-tions of masculine names such as Williamina and Davidina and – like Lydia's mother – Thomasina. But the rest were a fancy array of Corals and Dereks, Stellas and Audreys, and so forth. 'Their mothers take a fancy to names they've seen on the films or in a magazine,' he said. 'They don't suit our island surnames, but they produce, I suppose, the same effect in the house as a piece of new wallpaper or a set of new cur-tains. They seem bright and cheerful.'

A moment later he said, 'When are you going to see the Norquoys? They know who you are, and they're expecting you. But they won't ask you to come, they'll just wait.'

'It's not easy,' I said.

'It won't be as difficult as you think. They won't show any emotion, you needn't be afraid of that.'

'I'm thinking of myself,' I answered.

I waited another ten days; and then, one Saturday morning, I went to town – four thousand inhabitants and a little red cathedral – and managed to get a bottle of whisky. I arrived at the Norquoys' about six o'clock, and though I hadn't told them I was coming, they seemed to be expecting me. News travels quickly here, and even a man's intentions become public property as soon as he has realised them himself, and sometimes before. So I sat down to a mighty farmhouse tea in the kitchen, and no one said a word about Jim. They asked me what I thought of the islands, and where I belonged to, and if my parents were still alive, and they all laughed when I mistook a young sister of John Norquoy's wife for one of his daughters. There were ten or a dozen people at table, and I had to be told very carefully who they all were, and they thought it a great joke when I couldn't remember. But no one mentioned Jim.

After tea John Norquoy took me out to see the animals. He had a couple of fine young Clydesdales, a small herd of black-polled cattle, a great surly white boar, and a few score of sheep on hill pasture. We walked in his fields for a couple of hours, and still no word of Jim. But when we came back to the farm he led me into the ben-room; a peat fire had been lighted in it, and going through the passage where I had hung my waterproof I took my bottle out of the pocket. Norquoy paid no attention to it when I set it down, but went to a little table in the window where another bottle, the same brand as my own, stood on a tray with glasses and a jug of water. He poured a couple of deep drams and said, 'It was very good of you to write about Jim in the way you did. We're most grateful to you, and we're glad to see you here. If you're thinking of stay-ing, there's a bed for you whenever you want it.'

I took my drink before I answered, and then, slowly and little by little I told him about Jim, and about the war, and what it means to go through five or six battles with the same friend beside you, and then to lose him in the last one. I realised, in an hour or two, that I was playing the bereaved brother myself, but I couldn't help it by then. Mrs Norquoy came in, and their eldest boy, and her sister that I had taken for Norquoy's daughter, and then two or three neighbours. I went on talking, and they listened. I got most of the load off my mind, and if they didn't realise, by the end of it all, that Jim had been a soldier, well, it wasn't my fault. And every word I spoke was the simple truth. But when I got up to go Mrs Norquoy said, 'We're peaceful folk here, Mr Tyndall, and Jim was one of us. How he endured all that fighting I just can't understand.' It wasn't till a few days later, when I remembered her words, that I began to realise how much they had disliked what I had been telling them. They were peaceful folk, and they didn't approve of war.

But at the time I wasn't in the mood to catch a fine shade of meaning. Both bottles were empty, and I had had a lot more than my share. John Norquoy drank moderately and showed no sign of having drunk at all. He had listened carefully, with little change of expression, and the questions he asked showed that he was following and remembering all I said. But he made no comments on my story. One of the neighbours liked his whisky well enough, but carried it as solemnly as a cask. I was the only one who seemed to have taken any benefit from what we had been doing, and Norquoy insisted on coming with me as far as the main road. I was walking well enough, but talking too much by then, and I told him – without difficulty – what I had been waiting for the strength to tell. I got rid of the guilt on my mind.

For a black minute or two, splashing through the shallows of Commachio, I had been glad when Jim was killed. Glad it was he and not I whom death had taken, for we knew, both of us, that our luck was too good to last, and one or the other must go before the end. And when I saw it was Jim I was glad, and the guilt of it had lain on me ever since. Norquoy said nothing that I can remember, though I think he tried to comfort me and I know that he wanted to take me home. But I wouldn't let him.

Soon after we had said good-night it came into my head that I would like to take a look at the goose girl's house. Lydia's, I mean. The last time I had seen her she had been driving her whole flock, fifteen or sixteen of them with the great gander in front like a drum-major, past a big shallow pool in the stream, where the cattle came to drink, and the whole procession had been reflected in the calm water as if to make a picture. To see her like that, in a picture, had made her more real – or am I talking nonsense? Ideal may be the word, not real. Anyone who's fit to be a teacher could tell you, and tell you the difference between them, but I'm not sure myself. But whatever the word should be, I looked at her on the other bank of the stream, she was wearing an old yellow jersey and a dirty white skirt and her legs were bare among the meadowsweet, and I looked at her reflection in the picture, and that night I dreamt of her, and in my dream she was trying to tell me something, but I couldn't hear her.

So I turned off the main road towards her mother's house, and before I got there I realised how drunk I was. I'm not trying to excuse myself, but the whisky had been mixed with a lot of emotion, and as the result of one coming in and the other going out my knees were beginning to buckle, and when I came to the cottage I had one hunger only, and that was for sleep. There was a south-easterly breeze blowing, chill in the middle of the night, and to get into shelter I clambered over the garden wall, and the softness of the dug soil on the other side seemed very comfortable. I fell asleep under the currant bushes, and what woke me was Lydia's screaming and the clattering of the gander's wings as she threw it out of the house.

Well, after I'd seen the bird go marching off, and disappear downstream, I went round, as I said before, to the lee-side of the cartshed and smoked a cigarette. I had been lying on the packet and they were pretty flat, but I rolled one into shape again, and while I smoked I thought. and came to a conclusion.

I fingered my chin and it was smooth enough. I had shaved about five o'clock the afternoon before. I felt fresh and well. Sleeping on the ground had done me no harm, for I had grown used to that, and the night had been mild. My clothes were damp with dew and soiled with earth, but I took off my coat and shook it, and cleaned myself fairly well with some cut grass. Then I went down to the stream, and kneeling on the bank I washed my face and rinsed my mouth, and drank a few handfuls of water.

The door, the unlocked door, opened easily enough and I made no noise going in. I stood in a little passage with some old coats hanging on the opposite wall, and an uncarpeted wooden stair before me that led to a loft. To the right there was a door into the kitchen, where the old woman slept in a box-bed, and to the left was the ben-room with a closet on the inner side where Lydia slept. The ben-room door was closed with a latch, or a sneck, as they call it here, and my hand was steady. I opened the door without a sound, but only two or three inches, and looked in.

Lydia had put on a long white nightgown, an old-fashioned garment with coarse lace at the neck, and she was sitting at the north window, the one that opens into the yard. She held a looking-glass in both hands, and was staring at her reflection. Her right cheek – the one I could see – was pink.

She jumped up with a gasp of fear, a hoarse little noise, when I went in, and faced me with the looking-glass held to her breast like a shield. 'What do you want?' she asked, but her voice was quiet.

I closed the door behind me and said, 'If you had asked me that a week ago, I couldn't have answered you. I might have said Everything or Nothing. I didn't know. But that was a week ago.'

'What does that matter to me?' she asked. 'Why have you come here?'

'Because now,' I said, 'I do know.'

'You have no right to come into my room,' she whispered.

'I want you to marry me,' I said. 'I want a wife.'

She flushed and asked me, 'Why do you think you can find one here?'

Then I told her, or tried to tell her, that nothing had any force or weight in my mind, after seeing her as I had seen her that morning, but to live with her in the love of a man for his wife, in the love of possession without term or hindrance. She turned pale, then red again, when I said that I had seen her wrestling with the gander, and tried to push me out. But I caught her by the wrists, and spoke as a man will when he is wooing, in fumbling and broken words, of her beauty and the worship I would give her. Fiercely, but in a voice as low as a whisper still, she cried, 'I want no one's worship!'

'Last night,' I said, as urgently but as softly as she spoke herself – for the old woman was sleeping only a few yards away – 'Last night my mind was full of bitterness and grief. There had been little else in it for a year or more. But I emptied it, last night, and this morning you came into its emptiness and took possession. And I'm not going to live again like a man who's haunted. I'm not going to live with a ghost in my mind, with a ghost walking on my nerves as if they were a tight-rope, a ghost outside the window of my eyes and just beyond my fingers! I want reality. I want you, in my arms as well as in my mind, and I want the Church and the Law to seal you there.'

She answered nothing to that, and I went on talking, but I don't think she listened very closely, for presently she interrupted and asked me, 'Where did the gander go?'

'Down the burn towards the loch,' I told her.

'That's where he came from. He came here about a month ago, and killed the old one. The gander we had before, I mean.'

'He won't come back,' I said. 'He's had enough of you, after the way you handled him.'

She turned to the window, the one that opens into the yard, and looked out, saying nothing. I went behind her and put my arms round her. She tried to push me away, but with no determination in her movement, and I talked some more. She listened to me now, and presently turned and faced me, and said yes.

The next morning I began my new life of work and responsibility. I bought a boat, a heavily built, round bellied dinghy, ten-and-a-half-foot keel and in need of paint, for £18. 10s. Two days later I took a summer visitor out fishing, and made fifteen shillings for six hours' easy work. It was a good fishing loch, and there were visitors in the islands again for the first time since 1939. I could look forward to three or four days' work a week, and as trout were selling for 2s. 9d. a pound I sent home for my own rod and tackle, and did quite well on my unemployed days in addition to enjoying them. I could have done still better with night-lines and an otter at dusk and a little caution, but I like fishing too much to cheat at it.

I was still living with the schoolmaster, for £2. 10s. a week, but our relations became a little cooler when his wife discovered that I was sleeping out. That didn't worry me, however, for my happiness that summer was like the moon and the stars, shining and beyond the reach of malice.

It puzzled me a little that I couldn't persuade Lydia to settle a date for the wedding, as I thought there might be a proper reason for it before long, but when I once spoke of it more seriously than usual, she said, 'We're perfectly happy as we are. I don't see why we should bother. Not yet, at any rate. And I'll have to explain to mother, and she's difficult sometimes.'

'I'll do any explaining that's necessary.'

'No, no! You must leave that to me. You won't say anything to her, will you?'

I said I wouldn't. She asked very little of me – she never has asked much – and neither then nor now could I refuse her anything. She had made a good pretence of surrendering, but my surrender went deeper. I had become the roof and the walls within which she lived, but she was the soul of the house. I thought of Jim whenever I looked up at the Kirk hill and saw Norquoy's farm on the slope of it, but to think of him didn't make me feel guilty now. I was no longer obsessed by him, and if a new obsession had taken his place, I had no cause to grumble against it. So June and July went quickly by in that happiness and in good weather, though not settled weather, for the island skies are always changeable, till one day in mid-August, when I came ashore in a rising wind, colder than it had been for weeks, the old woman met me and without a word of greeting said, 'You'd better come home to your tea.'

'That's very kind of you,' I said, and pulled the boat up and took out the two trout which were all I had caught.

'Would you like these?' I asked.

'It's a poor return for a day's work,' she said, though they were good fish, the better one a little over the pound, and slipped them into the pockets of the old rain-coat she was wearing without a word of thanks. She had a man's cap on her head, and boots like a ploughman's. We walked along the road together, not saying much, and tea was a silent meal but a good one. She or Lydia had newly baked bere bannocks and white bannocks, there was sweet butter and salt butter, and I ate a duck's egg and the half of a stewed cockchicken. Then when we had finished, she said, 'Lydia tells me that you're wanting to be married.'

'It's what I've been wanting for the last two months and more,' I told her.

'She couldn't agree, and you wouldn't expect her to, until she'd spoken to her mother about it,' said the old woman grimly. 'She's a good girl, and it's a treasure that you're getting.'

I told her, humbly, that I was well aware of that.

'You've been a soldier, she says?'

'For six years I was.'

'I'm glad of that,' she cried, nodding her head. 'It's an ill world we live in and there's times when the soldiers are all we can depend on, though it's a fool's trade if you look at it squarely.'

I had nothing to say to that, and she went on briskly: 'Well, if you're going to be married you'll be married in a decent manner, with the neighbours there to see it, and something good enough for them to remember too.'

'A wedding,' I said, 'is a woman's affair. I'm willing to be married in any way that suits Lydia. If she wants a big wedding, we'll have it. I've got about a hundred and sixty pounds in the bank . . . '

'We're not asking you for money,' said the old woman. 'It's not a pauper you're marrying, no, faith! nor anything like poverty neither.'

She went to an old black wooden desk that stood in a corner of the kitchen, with a calendar pinned above it, and took a bank pass-book from a pigeon-hole stuffed with papers. 'Look at that,' she said, and held it open in front of me.

I was flabbergasted. It had never occurred to me that they could have any money at all, but the pass-book showed a credit of £1,207.

'Eight hundred and fifteen pounds of that is Lydia's own money,' said the old woman. 'Five hundred pounds came to her when she was born, and the rest is the interest which I've never touched and never shall. Her money will be hers to spend as she wants when she's of age – you've got three years to wait, so you needn't go to market yet – and the wedding I'll pay for out of my own.'

She gave me a dram then, and took one herself. Just the one each: it was the first time I had tasted whisky since that night at the Norquoys' – and then she put the bottle away in a cupboard with some fancy tumblers and glass dishes. She went out to the byre after that, to milk their two cows, and left Lydia and me together. Lydia had hardly spoken a word since I came in.

The following Sunday the banns were read in the Parish Church, and a few days later the old woman showed me the invitation cards she had had printed for the wedding. She hadn't done it cheaply, that was clear. They were a good thick board with gilt edges, and they read:

Miss Thomasina Manson

requests the pleasure of your company
at the wedding of her daughter
Lydia
to Mr Robert Lacey Tyndall
in the Ladyfirth Parish Hall
at 6 p.m. on Wednesday, September 6th
R.S.V.P.   Dancing

I said they had a very dignified appearance, and so they had if you weren't so hide-bound by convention as to be startled by the prefix to the mother's name. The old woman was very proud of them, and propped one up on the chimneypiece. Then Lydia and I sat down at the kitchen table and began to write in names and address envelopes. The old woman had prepared a list, and there were two hundred and eighteen names on it. But by then I was beyond surprise.

I had no difficulty in dissuading my own parents from coming. I had always been the unwanted member of my family, and I had disillusioned them so often that they could guess the disappointment they would find in my wedding. They had grown accustomed to my disappointing them. I had never enjoyed teaching in an elementary school in Falkirk – that was due to my falling in love, at the age of nineteen, with a female Socialist with red hair and the sort of figure that, in a jersey, is like an incitement to riot – but they were shocked by my choice of a profession. They were less perturbed when, later, I went to sea as a deck-hand on a tramp steamer. They didn't like that, but they regarded it as an escapade. In comparison with the rest of the family I was, of course, an utter failure, for both my brothers had gone to

Oxford and done well there, and my sister had married the junior partner in a highly regarded firm of stockbrokers. When Archie, my elder brother, was given an O.B.E. my father was much better pleased than when I got my D.C.M. Neither he nor my mother made any serious offer to come to the wedding. I used to get drunk, when I was younger, and once or twice I had caused them serious embarrassment, so I suppose they thought I should get high, loud and truculent, and make a spectacle of myself. My father sent Lydia a dressing-case, for which she could discover no purpose at all, and me a cheque for £25. But he missed something by not coming himself.

The old woman wore a black dress that had belonged to her mother, and a man's cap. Not the old ragged tweed one she usually wore, but a new black one such as coun-trymen sometimes wear at a funeral. She sat in a high-backed chair beside the band, and it was easy enough to guess her thoughts. 'I bore my child without benefit of clergy or the neighbours' good-will,' she was thinking, 'but my child, by God! will have all the favour and fair wishes that money can buy. My child will be wedded as well as bedded, and no one will forget it.'

And no one who saw her will forget Lydia that night. I realised that I still had things to learn, for though I had doted on her beauty, now I was humbled by it. By her beauty and her dignity. I stood beside her, while the Minister was reading the service, and felt like a Crusader keeping his vigil. The schoolmaster was my best man, though his wife hadn't wanted him to be, and I could hear him breathing, hoarsely, as if in perplexity. He ate little more than I did at supper, and I could eat nothing. I danced twice with Lydia, and the rest of the time stood like a mooncalf while people talked to me. But Lydia was never off the floor, and all night her mother, in the high-backed chair beside the band, sat with a look that was simultaneously grim and gloating.

There was a great crowd there, the fiddlers were kept hard at it, and the wedding was well spoken of. Nearly everyone who had been invited had come, and thirty or forty more as well. All the Norquoys were there, but John and his wife left about two o'clock. Before he went he said to me, 'I'm very glad that you've become one of us, and I hope you'll settle down happily here. You were a good friend to Jim, and if I can help you in any way, be sure and tell me.'

'There's no one can help me more,' I told him, 'than by wishing that as I am tonight, so I may continue.'

Lydia came to say goodbye to them while we were speaking, and after they had gone she said, 'Jim Norquoy was always my mother's favourite among the boys in the parish. She used to tell him that he mustn't be in a hurry to get married, but wait till I grew up and see what he thought of me before going farther afield.'

The schoolmaster came and asked her to dance and I went outside. The hall was hot and men's faces shone as if they had been oiled, but the night air was cool. There was no wind and the sky was a veiled purple with a little haze round the moon. I could hear the slow boom and dulled thunder of the Atlantic on the west cliffs, four miles away. West of the cliffs there was no land nearer than Labrador, and for a few minutes I felt dizzy, as if I hung in space over a gulf as great as that. The old woman had meant to marry her to Jim, but Jim had died, and I had fallen heir to his portion. 'You won't find it easy to go back,' he had said, as if he knew that another fate would claim me. Nor had I gone back to my own country, but come instead to his, to do what I had to do.

I remember sailing once, near Oban, in a little yacht I had hired, and getting into a strong tide and being carried swiftly past a rocky shore though the wind had fallen and the sail hung loose. The moon was pulling the tide to sea, and I was going with it. I was helpless in the grip of the moon, and I felt the excitement of its power. – The sensation came back to me as I stood outside the hall where the band was playing, and listened to the Atlantic waves, driven by the wind of invisible distant clouds to march against our cliffs. I was moon-drawn again, though I could not see my star. But I knew then that I had come north to the islands, though innocent of any purpose, to take Jim's place, who should have married her but had been killed instead. That was my doom; and I wanted no other. In a little while I went in again and saw the old woman. She was satisfied.

It was nearly seven in the morning when the wedding finished, with the drink done, the band exhausted, and the guests hearing in their imagination the lowing of their cows waiting to be milked. Lydia and her mother and I walked home together, and as soon as we arrived the two of them changed into old clothes and went out to the byre.

Her wedding, however, wasn't the only time when I saw Lydia well-dressed. She had gone to the town day after day, and bought clothes in plenty. Her more ancient garments were thrown away, and her everyday appearance was now smart enough by country standards. She told me one night that it was her mother who had insisted on her dressing like a scarecrow, and of-ten enough wouldn't even let her wash her face for fear of bringing men about the house.

The weeks passed with nothing to spoil our happiness, and I got a job under the County Council, driving a lorry. The mornings and the evenings grew darker, and after a great gale had blown for three days from the north-west the winter came. It was cold and stormy, but after the wildest days the sky might suddenly clear for an evening of enormous calm with a lemon-coloured sky in the west and little tranquil clouds high in the zenith. After the harvest had been gathered and the cattle brought in, the country became strangely empty and its colours were dim. But I liked it. Wherever you stood you had a long view of land and water, and though the sky might be violent, the lines of the hills were gentle.

When I came home one evening about the middle of November, the old woman told me that Lydia wasn't well. There was nothing seriously wrong, but she would have to stay in bed for a few weeks, and she wanted her – the old woman – to make up a bed for herself in the ben-room. I would have to sleep in the loft.

'The doctor has seen her?' I asked.

'No,' said the old woman. 'I don't believe in doctors.'

I had a general knowledge that accidents might occur in pregnancy, but no precise information, and I couldn't make a physiological picture in my mind. I thought of blood and mortality, and the old woman saw that I was frightened.

'Don't fret yourself,' she said. 'She's not going to die yet, nor for many a long year to come. She'll be a brisk stirring woman long after you're in the kirkyard.'

'Is it only rest that she needs?' I asked then, thinking vaguely of some anatomi-cal bolt or washer that might have shaken loose, and needed immobility to re-establish itself.

'Rest,' said the old woman, 'a long rest and a lot of patience. Now go in and see her, but don't worry her with questions.'

Lydia was pale and she had been crying, but when I knelt beside the bed she put her arms round my neck and told me, as her mother had done, that I mustn't worry. And I didn't worry long. Two or three days, I suppose, and then it began to seem natural that she should have to stay in bed. I took to reading to her when I came home from work. My mother had sent a lot of things that belonged to me, including a box of books. I never had many books, I can't remember having had much time for reading when I was younger, but there were some good stories of adventure that I had enjoyed: *Typhoon* and *The Nigger of the Narcissus, Kim,* and *The White Company,* and Trelawny's *Adventures of a Younger Son, Kidnapped,* and *The Forest Lovers,* and *Revolt in the Desert,* and so on. I've read them all to Lydia at one time or another, and she seemed to enjoy them. I liked reading them again. It was Conrad who was responsible for my going to sea after I had had a year of teaching in Falkirk, and couldn't stand it any longer. I made three or four trips to the Baltic and the Mediterranean in tramp steamers, and a voyage to Australia as a steward in a Blue Funnel boat. But when the war began I had had enough of the sea, so I joined the Army. Lawrence of Arabia may have had something to do with that, or it may have been Kipling.

Only one thing happened to annoy me in the next two or three months, and that occurred one morning when I was tak-ing a load of road-metal to a secondary road we were patching, and drove past the old woman's cottage. It was a dark day, as dark as gun-metal, and the rain was blowing across country in blustering squalls. As I came near the cottage I saw Lydia crossing the road, leaning against the wind with a half-buttoned waterproof flapping round her, and a zinc pail on her arm. I pulled up hard and jumped out.

'Are you trying to kill yourself?' I shouted. 'You're supposed to be in bed, aren't you?'

For the first time since the morning when I'd seen her throwing the gander out of doors, she was angry. Her face seemed to grow narrower than usual, and her lips as hard as marble. She stared straight at me – her eyes are grey, with sometimes a flash of blue in them – and said fiercely, 'I can look after myself. You go about your business, and I'll take care of mine.'

'You're supposed to be in bed,' I said again, stupidly and sullenly. There were some eggs in her pail. They had a hen-house across the road, and she had been feeding the hens and gathering what eggs the draggled birds had the strength to lay in that weather. 'It's madness for you to be stooping and bending and carrying buckets of meal,' I said.

'I wanted some fresh air,' she said. 'I can't stay in bed for ever.'

'Your mother ought to know better, even if you don't. I'm going in to see her,' I said.

'You'll do no such thing!' she cried. 'You leave Mother and me to manage our own affairs. Don't you interfere, or you'll be sorry for it. And now go! Go, I tell you. You've got work to do, haven't you? Well, go and do it!'

She was ten years younger than I and a good head shorter, but her words came like the smack of an open hand on my face, palm and knuckles, this way and that, and I stepped back, muttering some limp excuse, and got into my lorry again.

I brought her some oranges at night, that I'd bought from a sailor, and we said no more about it. But two or three days passed before she asked me to read to her again, and then for another six or seven weeks we were calm and happy, though the loft was a cold place to sleep in, and sometimes when the moon shone through the sky-light I woke up to see the rafters and their black shadows, and thought for a moment or two that I was still in the Army, making the best of it in a deserted farm-house, and once I stretched out my arm to feel if Jim was beside me.

About the middle of February I began to worry about arrangements for her lying-in. Or, to put it more accurately, to worry because no arrangements had been made. I talked with the old woman, who wouldn't listen to me, or wouldn't listen seriously, but I didn't say anything to Lydia in case I should upset her again. And then, before we had come to any decision, I got a telegram from Edinburgh to say that my father had had a stroke, and would I come at once. Archie, my elder brother, was with some Government commission in Washington, and Alastair, the younger, was still in the Army in Rangoon. I didn't want to go, I had never got on well with my father, but the old woman said that if he died without seeing me I would be saddled with regret, like a heavy curse on me, for all the days of my life, and Lydia was plainly shocked, as if by the sight of some fearful wickedness, when I said that he could die as happily by himself as with me holding his hand.

So, after a day of argument, I went to Edinburgh, and for a week my mother and I were uncomfortable in each other's presence, and my father slowly recovered. I had been wrong when I said that he wouldn't want to hold my hand. He did. I sat by his bedside for two or three hours every day, and sometimes, with a lot of difficulty, he managed to speak a few words. I was glad, then, that I had done what Lydia wanted. One day my mother told me that he meant to give me a present, and when I went upstairs he smiled and pointed to a leather case that lay on a chair beside him. It was his favourite gun, a fine piece by Holland, far too good for a man who lived in a cottage and drove a lorry for the County Council.

I said goodbye to them in a hurry when a letter came from Lydia to say that she had given birth to a daughter the day after I left her. 'I am very well and so is she,' she wrote, 'and I didn't want to disturb you with my news when you had so much to harass you already. But now, if your father is no longer in danger, I hope you will be able to come home again.'

I said goodbye, but I didn't leave them for another fortnight. My father had a second stroke, and while I was sitting in the train and waiting for it to start, my sister came running along the platform, looking for me, to tell me I mustn't go. He lived for more than a week, but never regained proper consciousness, and then I waited for the funeral. I read Lydia's letter again and again, and two others that she wrote, both of which were full of news about the child. 'I think she may be the most beautiful baby in the world,' she said.

In my mind, when I saw her, there was no doubt at all. She had the perfection of a doll that some dead sculptor – a sculptor too great to be alive in this world – had carved in love from a rosy-veined alabaster. She was very small, and perfect. She was sleeping, and I had a monstrous fear that she might never wake. I put out my hand to touch her, but Lydia caught my wrist and shook her head. 'Let her sleep.'

I made no mention of something I found, a day or so after my return, for I couldn't be certain, then, that there was any meaning in it, and if there was I didn't want to think about it. The sight of it, in the grass, struck deep into my mind like a forester's wedge that splits the fibres of a tree, and for a minute or two I stood trembling. But there was no sense in it, and I didn't want to curse myself with a madman's doubt. I wanted to be at peace, and dote upon the child, so I denied the meaning of it and let it drown in the daily ebb and flow, the tidal waters of common life. It sank into the darker parts of my mind like a body into the deep sea with a sack of coal lashed to its ankles, as I had seen a sailor buried once. Committed to the deep, as they said.

The child grew quickly, and at six months she was like an Italian picture of a cherub, her head covered with small tight curls, paler than gold, and eyes the colour of a harebell. The old woman said she could understand already every word we said, and neither Lydia nor I was very serious about contradicting her. For we all thought of her in a way that I suppose is unusual even in the fondest of parents. It wasn't only with pride of possession and a flood of affection whenever we looked at her, but with a kind of glee that never grew stale or sour in the remembrance of its excess.

In May I gave up my job but told the Road Surveyor that I should be glad to have it again in October. He wasn't too favourably disposed to my plans at first, but I had served him well, he was a fisherman himself and knew the compulsion of it, so after a little argument he agreed to let me go and take me back again when autumn came. I painted my boat, put my rod together, and had a week's fine sport before the first of the summer visitors arrived. Then, for three or four days a week till September, I watched my patrons fish, and calculated by the end of September that my own average, on the intervening days, was about as good as the best of theirs. But I fished longer hours than they did, and the price of trout was still high.

Sometimes I used to wake up at night, with Lydia beside me, and see the darkness about us like the mouth of a huge engulfing fear. I had no right to be so happy. No one had such a right. It was like oil on the top step, it was like a German white flag with a sniper lying beside it, it was like a spider telegraphing Walk-into-my parlour over his lethal gossamer. I would lie in the darkness, open-eyed, for perhaps an hour, drenched in fear, but in the morning, waking and turning to Lydia, and then playing with the child for half an hour, my happiness would come back like the returning tide. I couldn't help it. They were both so beautiful.

Once when the child was about fifteen months old, I woke in the first phase of one of my frightened moods, and saw her standing up at the end of her crib. She had taken off her nightgown and she was poised with her head tilted up, her arms out and her hands resting on the side-rails of the crib as if she were addressing a public meeting; or facing her judges, unafraid. There was a late moon that night, and though the window was small there was light in the room. But that wasn't the light that irradiated the child. Her light, unless I'm the simple victim of some cuckoo-born delusion, came from within. Now Lydia's body, on that first morning when I saw her throwing the gander out of doors, was gleaming like mother-of-pearl, or a pearl on velvet, with a light of its own; but never since then had I seen her better than a milky white. – As white as milk and as smooth as curds but not with that radiance. – Yet now the child, naked in the darkness was gleaming with such a light. It was no brighter than the moonlight dimmed by white curtains, but it wasn't in the overflow of moonlight she was shining. It was in a light of her own.

I slipped out of bed, quietly so as not to waken Lydia, and said to the child, 'You'll catch cold, standing up like that. You ought to be asleep.' She looked at me for a moment, as if surprised to see me there, and then twined her arms round my neck and kissed me. I put on her nightgown and obediently she slid down between the blankets.

A year went by and part of another. I came, I suppose, to take my good fortune for granted, and my happiness perhaps lost something of its fine edge and became a rounder contentment. Time, when I look back, seems to have gone very quickly and as smoothly as the water curving over a weir in a polished flow without break or interruption. We were on friendly terms with our neighbours, I saw the Norquoys and the schoolmaster every week or two, and gradually I came to think of the islands as my own place, my proper environment in which I had become an accepted part. But my real life was lived on the old woman's croft, at home. My senses were livelier there, my feelings more profound, my consciousness of life more widely awake.

The old woman could work as well as a man. She could plough and harrow, and between us, when harvest came, we cut and bound and stacked four acres of oats. Lydia looked after the poultry, and singled turnips, took her fork to hayfield and harvest, as well as doing housework and tending the child. We were rarely idle and often our work was hard, though I don't remember that we found it unduly hard because we did it all in our own time, and we had no master to drive us or reprove us or thank us. I couldn't spend so much time fishing as I had done when I first lived there, but I enjoyed working on the land so long as it wasn't continual work.

In the winter months, when I drove a lorry again, I used to read in the evenings. Both Lydia and her mother liked the tales of adventure best. I had some other books, by Jane Austen and Dickens and Galsworthy, that I had never read myself, but we didn't care for them. It was a tale of far-off lands, with the noise of a dangerously running sea, or the thud of a sword going stiffly home, the crack of a rifle, that the women liked. There was something fierce in them, an appetite for deeds, that couldn't show itself in their ordinary life, but there all the time and came out of hiding a little when I read to them. But domestic scenes, and comedy and conversation, bored them.

Well, this good easy life continued – it wasn't physical ease that characterized it, not in those northern winters, but we were all contented – till the child was in her third year, and then one summer day when there fell a flat calm and the loch lay like a mirror, pocked with rising trout, but not one that would look at a fly, I came ashore at midday and on the road a little way past the house I saw five carts standing, three of them loaded with peat and two empty. The loaded ones, coming home from the hill, were John Norquoy's, and the horses between their shafts stood motionless with drooping heads, their shoulders dark with sweat. The empty carts belonged to a neighbour of his who had started earlier and was on his way back to the hill for a second load. His horses were restless, tossing their heads and pecking at the road with steel-shod hooves. But their drivers paid no attention to them. John Norquoy and two others were squatting on their heels, on the road, and two were leaning against the nearest cart, and in the midst of them, her hands behind her back like a girl reciting poetry at a village prizegiving, was the child. She was talking, and they were listening.

I waited for a little while, some forty yards away, but none of them turned a head in my direction, and when I went up and spoke to them some looked sheepish and embarrassed, but John Norquoy, still on his heels, said to me, 'I could wish you had stayed away and not interrupted us. It's a real diversion, listening to her.'

I picked the child up and asked her, 'What were you talking about?'

'I was telling them a story,' she said, and when I set her on my shoulder she turned and cried to them, 'Good-bye now!'

I don't fully know why, but this small incident annoyed me at the time of it and worried me later. I told Lydia and her mother what I had seen, and said they would have to take better care of the child, for I wasn't going to have her grow up to believe she must always be the centre of attention. I didn't like to see a child showing-off, I said. 'Perhaps,' I went on, 'we ourselves are to blame, for we've always made much of her – too much, I dare say – and let her see that we're proud of her. But we'll have to change our ways if they're going to have a bad effect.'

'We could change our ways a dozen times without changing her,' said Lydia.

'That's nonsense,' I said. 'A child is the product, very largely, of what she's taught. I used to be a teacher myself . . .'

The old woman interrupted me with a cackle of laughter. 'It would take more than you,' she said, 'to make an ordinary bairn out of that one.'

Then I lost my temper, and for the first time we had a proper quarrel. We had had differences of opinion before, and sometimes grown hot about them, but this was different. Now we grew bitter and said things to each other that were meant to hurt, and did. The argument didn't last long, but at night, when Lydia and I were alone, it flared up again. It was she who began it, this time, and when I saw that she was bent on making trouble, her face to put on its fierce and narrow look, her lips were hard – I smacked her soundly on the side of her head, and before she could recover I hid her across my knee and gave her an oldfashioned beating with a slipper.

A week or two passed before she forgave me. Or, perhaps, before she openly forgave me. I knew her fairly well by that time, and I don't think she bore a grudge against me for the beating, but because she didn't want to admit defeat she maintained an appearance of hostility till the affair could be regarded as a drawn battle. Then for a week or two we were in love again with a new fervour.

It was towards the end of February, a few days before the child's third birthday, that the gander came back, and I realised that fear of his return, an unregarded but persistent fear, like the white wound-scar on my leg that I never thought of unless I was tired or there came a hard frost, had always been with me.

There had been heavy snow, piled into great drifts by a strong wind, and for a few days work on the roads came to a stop and I had a winter holiday. The sun came out, the sky cleared to a thin bright blue, and the land lay still as death under a flawless white surface that gave to every little hill and hollow the suavity of ancient sculpture. The loch within a fringe of crackling ice, a darker blue than the sky, was framed in white, and a few swans like small ice-floes swam in a narrow bay. On land there was nothing stirring and the smoke rose straight from the chimneys of diminished houses.

I had gone out with my gun – the fine piece by Holland – to try and shoot a late hare, and after following tracks in the snow for an hour or two I had got a couple. I was on my way home again when I saw, by the burnside a few hundred yards from the house, the child in her blue cap and her little blue coat. The burn, bank-high, was running strongly, and I hurried towards her with a sudden feeling, as of a man caught among thorns, of nervousness and annoyance that she should be there with no one to look after her.

She stood with her back to me, in her favourite position, her hands clasped behind her, and not until I had come within a few yards of her did I see the gander. He was afloat in a little smooth backwater of the burn, but as soon as he caught sight of me he came ashore, his broad feet ungainly on the snow but moving fast, and I thought he was going to attack me. The child turned and I called to her: 'Come here, Nell! Come here at once!'

But she stayed where she was and the gander came up behind her and opened his wings so that she stood by his breast within a screen of feathers as hard as iron and as white as the snow beyond them. It must have been the whiteness of the fields, with the bright haze of the sun upon them, that dazzled me and deluded me into thinking that the gander had grown to three times or four times his proper size. His neck seemed a column of marble against the sky, his beak was bronze, and his black eyes reflected the sun like shafts from a burning-glass. A low rumbling noise, like the far-off surge of the sea on a pebble-beach, came from his swollen throat.

I'm not a coward and I couldn't have been frightened of a bird. It was snow-sickness, I suppose, that set my brain swimming and undid the strength of my knees, so that I thought I was going to faint. I remember seeing the same sort of thing happen to a soldier in Italy, in the mountains in winter-time. He was a friend of my own, a big fellow as tall as myself. He stumbled and fell, and the strength went out of him. We thought he had gone blind, but after we got him into a house and had given him some brandy, he was all right.

When I came to myself and knew what I was doing, I was on my hands and knees, crawling, and my hands were on fire with the friction of the snow. I had to crawl another twenty or thirty yards before I felt fit to stand up, and then I staggered and stumbled as if I were drunk. I wasn't far from home by then, and I rested for a while in the barn.

When I felt better I went into the kitchen. The child was there already, and as soon as I came in she ran towards me, and pushing me into a chair climbed on to my knee. She began to pat my face and play with my hair, as if trying to comfort me.

Presently I went out again, and found my gun and the two hares where I had dropped them. There was no sign of the gander. They were big hares, both of them, and I took them into the back-kitchen and got a basin, and cleaned and skinned them. But all the time I was thinking: Well, this is the end of pretence. There's no point or purpose in denial now. But what am I going to do?

The women were on the other side, so I couldn't talk to them. Lydia was in love with me, as I with her – there was no doubt about that – and the old woman liked me well enough; but now I knew the dividing-line between us, and I couldn't cross it. But I had to talk to someone.

John Norquoy wouldn't do. I had made a confession to him before, and it was too soon to make another. Nor would he believe me if I did. I had no great faith in the schoolmaster either, but I had to do something, say something to someone, and after tea I set out for his house, walking heavily through the snow, and if he was surprised to see me he didn't show it, but made me welcome. He had spent three or four idle days, with only a dozen children able to come to school, and in his own way he too may have been glad of a chance to talk for a while. His wife left us to ourselves.

I didn't know how to begin, but he helped me. He had been reading a book whose author was trying to prove that modern war was the result of conflicting demands for oil; and he, full of brand-new information, was ready to argue that war had always had economic causes, and no other causes. I didn't believe him, and said so. It was ideas that made war, I said. If an economist went to war, with material gains in view, it was because he was a bad economist, a quack and a charlatan; for any practical economist knows that war is likely to waste far more than it can win. 'But if men believe in ideas, of power and glory, or religious ideas, or even social ideas,' I went on, 'they may go to war for the simple reason that idealists don't count the cost of what they want. They go to war, that is, in despite of the economic arguments against it. And they're always against it.'

We talked away on those lines, getting warmer all the time, and the schoolmaster, really enjoying himself now, went back into history, back and back, till he had proved to his own satisfaction that the Peloponnesian War was due entirely to the imperialism of Athens, and the determination of the Athenians to brook no interference with their mercantile marine.

'And did Agamemnon and Menelaus,' I asked him, 'go to war to win the right of exploiting mineral resources in the windy plains of Troy?'

'If we really knew anything about the Trojan War,' he said, 'we should probably have to admit that that indeed was the cause of it; or something very like that.'

'It's not the generally accepted cause,' I said.

'According to the fable,' he answered, 'the purpose of the war was to recover, from the person who had carried her off, the erring wife of Menelaus. And who was she? Zeus, who never existed, is said to have visited a fictitious character called Leda in the guise of a swan and the result of their impossible union was a legendary egg out of which a fabulous being named Helen was incredibly hatched. Helen, says the story, grew to miraculous beauty, married Menelaus, and ran away with Paris. You can't seriously regard a woman who wasn't even a woman, but only a myth, as the cause of a war.'

'It lasted for ten years,' I said.

'I've been talking history,' he said. 'You really shouldn't try to answer me with mythology.'

'How does a myth begin?' I asked.

'How does a novelist go to work?' he demanded.

'By drawing on his experience, I suppose.'

He got up impatiently and fetched a bottle of whisky and two glasses from the sideboard. Then he went out for a jug of water, and when he came back I said, 'What's worrying me is this. If a man discovers something within the scope of his own life that will eventually be a cause of war between nations, what can he do about it?'

'What could such a thing be?' he asked.

'I can't explain.'

'But it's impossible,' he said. 'War hasn't a simple origin or a single cause that you can take in your hand like a trophy to be fought for in a tournament. You have to consider the whole economy of the rival countries, their geographical situation, the growth of their population – '

'And their ideas,' I said. 'Their leaders' desire for power, or a new religion, or a woman.'

'You're going back to your myth,' he said.

'You fought in one war, I fought in another. My experience of war is that you fight for five years, and at the end of it you see your best friend killed beside you, and you're glad – you're glad, by God! – that it's he who's dead, and not you. I don't want another war.'

'Well,' he said, 'whatever starts the next war, it won't be a woman. You can put that fear out of your head.'

'I'm not so sure,' I said.

The argument went on for a long time, and gave me no satisfaction. But talking did me good, and we drank a lot of whisky. When I got home I felt calmer, but very old, as if I were a character in a Greek play who saw the enormous tragedy that was coming, and could do nothing but wait for it, and then abide it.

Lydia and her mother were in bed, and I got a lantern from the back-kitchen. I lighted it and went to the stable. Meg, the old black mare, was twenty-seven or twenty-eight, and we dared not let her lie down in her stall for fear she could never get up again, so every night I put a broad canvas sling under her belly, to take the weight off her legs, and she slept standing. She woke as I went in, whinnying softly, and turned her head to watch me.

I stood on a wheelbarrow in the empty stall beside her, and reaching to the top of the wall, where the rafters go in, took down what I had hidden there, and never looked at since, nearly three years before. I had made a parcel of it, with string and brown paper, and now it was covered with thick cobweb. I brushed off the web and cut the string. For a moment or two I held in my hands the cigarette-box – covered with a fine Florentine leather stamped in gold, that I had taken from one of those little shops on the Ponte Vecchio – and then I opened it. Inside lay the broken shell of a big white egg. I fitted the larger fragments together, and judged it to have been about seven inches long and rather more than four inches in diameter at the widest part.

That was what I had picked up, after coming home from my father's funeral, in the long grass under the ben-room window. It may seem funny to you, but you're not

William Montgomerie (1904 – 1994)

Glasgow Street

Out of this ugliness may come,
Some day, so beautiful a flower,
That men will wonder at that hour,
Remembering smoke and flowerless slum,
And ask – glimpsing the agony
Of the slaves who wrestle to be free –
'But why were all the poets dumb?'

Epitaph

(for 2nd Officer James S. Montgomerie of the S. S. Carsbreck,
torpedoed off Gibraltar, 24 October 1941)

My brother is skull and skeleton now
Empty of mind behind the brow
In ribs and pelvis empty space
Bone-naked, without a face.

On a draughty beach drifting sand
Clawed by a dry skeleton hand
Sifts in the hourglass of his head
Time, useless to bones of the dead.

Sleeping Beauty

A blade of grass curved over,
Yellow and sharp,
To touch your lips,
Forbidden me.

Had I leaned over,
I would have laid my lips
Upon your brow,
To tell my meaning better.

Instead,
I dreamed of her   10
Who made herself a nun,
Because they said
That her betrothed had died in war,
And how her lover was not dead.

Coming home
He built himself a tower above the river,
Only to look at her
Upon the island where she sang
Among the nuns,
Morning by morning till the day of death.   20

Daft Jenny

David walked up Dalmarnock Street in a very stilted manner, head down, left foot in a space, right foot on a line, left foot in a space, right foot on a line, saying the rhyme over and over to himself under his breath, emphasising the accents:

> Fraser's sausages are the best,
> In your belly they do rest;
> Simpson's sausages are the worst,
> In your belly they do burst.

He knew that if he could say the rhyme five times before reaching the draper's shop at the corner he would be lucky, and if he could reach it before the tramcar coming up the road stopped at the tramstop he would be doubly so. The tramcar unluckily stopped just as he reached the factor's office, but he was able to say the lines seven times and a half.

Then he ran round the corner to Fraser's ham-shop in Great Eastern Road. Daft Jenny was already in the shop, waiting patiently three yards away from the counter, holding her infant in a green plaid wrapped also round herself, as if the small sleeping face were another pale bud on the same green stem. The boy gazed at them intently, puzzled by a mother and child without a father.

Three weeks ago he had passed Jenny. She was walking along the pavement near the tenement wall, as if afraid of leaving the shadow of it. There was no infant then, but the same green plaid sheathed her forehead and cheeks, crossed below her chin, and was clutched in both her hidden hands. Underneath her shapeless grey skirt she walked on the outsides of her feet, so worn were the heels of her black boots. David had called after her:

'Jenny! Jenny! Jenny!'

But when she turned slowly round and looked at him the sadness in her dark eyes had made him ashamed, so that when he heard other boys calling after her he repeated to them his mother's words.

'Leave her alone! She's harmless.'

The manager of the shop, a stout man in white overalls, served him first, pulling the heavy round of bacon from the row of hams on the shelf at the back of the window. David liked to watch him unspike the bacon from its handled board, remove the enamelled price ticket and the label with 'Delicious' in black letters; to listen to the wheepwheep of the broad hamknife on the whetting steel hanging, when not in use, from the man's belt, and the hiss of its edge keenly cutting the thin slices that fell one by one on the grease proof paper. The man's eyes rested once or twice on Daft Jenny. He lifted a hambone from the counter, wrapped it up in paper, and laid it without a word beside the quarter pound of funeral ham his girl assistant was preparing for Jenny. The girl nodded slightly, and placed the two packages together on the front of the counter.

Then she walked round the end of the counter and raised the edge of the plaid from the infant's forehead. The other girl followed her, and the two of them peered together at the sleeping child.

'I wonder where you come from?' said the second girl. It was a rhetorical question, and she expected no answer.

'Ah dinny ken,' said Daft Jenny.

The manager began to cough, and coughed so long that he recovered only when Jenny had put out her white hand with the blue veins and clutched the two packages from the girl who had picked them off the counter, withdrawn her hand under the plaid like a small carnivorous animal retreating into its burrow, and left the shop.

David saw that the man's face was wet with tears, yet he was laughing.

'Ah dinny ken,' said the man.

'It's a crying shame,' said the girl who had wrapped up Jenny's ham, and she was smiling.

'I'm crying,' said the manager, wiping his eyes with his wrist, for his fingers were greasy from the bacon slices he arranged neatly on the paper. Then he pushed the paper package across the counter, and dropped David's half-crown into the till.

'He should get ten years,' said the other girl.

'He should be made to marry her,' said the first one.

'A life sentence,' said the manager, spiking the boiled bacon on its board, and sticking on a new word 'Superfine' instead of the one he had taken off.

'Up ye go!' he said, heaving the heavy board up to the gap in the row of hams in the window.

'I wonder who he is,' said one girl, as if she were trying to identify the accused in a line of men stretching from the door of the shop to the end counter.

'*Ah* dinny ken,' said the manager, emphasising the first word. Then he looked at David who was still standing there.

'What do you want, sonny?' The three of them looked at the boy, as if he had overheard something he shouldn't have heard.

'You've forgotten my change,' said David.

'So I have,' said the man, finding it on the edge of the counter.

David told the story to nobody, but turned it over and over in his mind. He felt that he had learned something new about adult life, but was not quite sure how much.

'Daft Jenny's got a baby,' said his mother to his father a few days later, and his father said the same thing as the girl in Fraser's.

'I wonder who he is.'

He said it in the same tone as the girl in the hamshop, and very slowly, as if he were looking into his mind at all the men in the district.

'I can't understand some men,' said his mother, and then his father looked at his mother, and nodded slightly in David's direction. They changed the subject.

This knowledge that there were things they did not tell him, nor even discuss in his presence, planted in the boy's mind one very curious illusion which, because of the limitation of his experience, he could neither prove nor disprove.

'Suppose my father and mother are German spies. They wouldn't tell me. Suppose my father is a German spy. Maybe he wouldn't tell even my mother.'

He couldn't ask them, because they would either refuse to tell him or, if they were not German spies, they would only laugh at his silly notions. The boy could think of no way out of the suspicion, except by watching them very carefully in case they would give themselves away by some chance remark, but they never did.

When David met Jenny next she had no infant, and no green plaid. Her arms were folded under her breast as if she did not know what else to do with them. She was walking along close to the tenement wall, and anyone looking out from behind the lace curtains of the ground-floor windows of the tenements would not have seen her eyes, nor did she look into the face of anyone who passed. Perhaps her head was a little more bowed than usual as though she were looking for something on the ground or at the bottom of her own mind.

David's mother heard in the grocer's that detectives had called at Jenny's house and questioned her about her baby, but all she had answered had been:

'Ah dinny ken.'

'It wiz better deed onywey,' was the general verdict.

Daft Rab brought the news that they were dragging the river, 'wi' boats, an' ropes, an' a'thing.' He stopped everyone he knew, or half-recognised, and told them in broken phrases that were always difficult to understand. David heard the rumour, and went down in the evening to the River Clyde, past the place where the gambling school met on the coup near the fever hospital. There was a boat he had never seen before, moored across the river to a new post. He looked into the water as if he might see something where the police had failed.

A young man, wearing a brown muffler, came along the path at the top of the high riverbank, carrying a young white dog. He laid it down on the greasy grass very carefully, and when David looked at the animal he saw that its hind legs were broken. Then the man took a brick from under his oxter, and a hank of string from a pocket of his blue serge suit, tied the string twice round the brick with a firm knot, and twice round the dog's neck. He looked at David and said:

'Ah canny dae onythin' else wi' him. Can ah?' He stroked the animal's head, and it licked his hand. Very gently he picked up the dog and the brick together, and threw them into the air. They swung round each other as they rose, and fell to strike the water together. The brick sank fast and dragged the white terrier head first to the bottom, where it swayed like a pale green weed anchored to the ground, its broken hind legs pointing upward to the light and air, its forefeet pawing blindly down.

Norman Cameron (1905 – 1953)

Fight with a Water-Spirit

Though many men had passed the ford, not one
Had ever seen that jeering water-ghost
Denying their true conquest of the stream.
But I, who saw him smile behind a stone,
Stopped, challenged him to justify his boast.
Then came the fight, exhausting as a dream,
With stuff not quite impalpable. He sank,
Sighing, at last, in a small shrinking pile.
But my victorious paean changed to fright
To see once more the pale curve of his flank   10
There in the water, and his endless smile
Broaden behind the stone. No use to fight.
Better to give the place a holy name,
Go on with less ambition than I came.

The Wanton's Death

She, wild with wantonness, to her two suitors,
A merman and a landman, gave this challenge:
'To prove his love the sturdier, each abandon
The element in which his suit was fostered
And undergo this test of transmutation,
Merman ashore, landman beyond the breakers.'
The two obeyed, in fear and pride and passion.
One gasped and writhed, the other choked and floundered;
She, to both quarters native, found them sporting.
At length each suitor found a spacious refuge,   10
Merman a pool, landman a reefy foothold,
Both claiming still the guerdon of achievement.
And, when she mocked their lie, each vowed in anger

His new-adapted element more kindly
Than the fair promiser who brought him thither . . .
Her relics rot on the sea-wasted foreshore,
Half-wooed, half-spurned by the land-tainted spindrift.

'That Wierd Sall Never Daunton Me' [1]

('Syne he hath kissed her rosy lips
All underneath the Eildon tree')

Aye, marry, will she, boastful Scot.
A kiss is not the fee
Will gar★ a wierd come share your lot   make
Like any other she.

Yet 'tis a she, whate'er may come,
With woman's round, fierce eyes.
She hath a womb, and ilka★ womb   every
Doth teem with greed and lies.

She'll daunton thee and drag thee down
In worship and despair,   10
In sorry self-negation
Hating thyself in her.

If thou a wierd wilt rightly woo,
Kiss not, and hush thy mirth,
For firstly must thou undergo
The pangs of a new birth.

Thy resurrection then is hers;
She showeth another face,
A woman still, but unawares,
And dowered with faery grace;   20

And thou canst woo her not afear'd –
Or poets thus do say.
But ah! what suitor of a wierd
Hath lived to tell the day?

---

[1] The title quotation is from the folk poem *Thomas of Erceldoun*. 'Wierd' usually means fate. Here it seems to
be taken as referring to that poem's fairy queen, or witch, who placed Thomas the Rhymer under a spell.
It is worth noting that Thomas, like Cameron, was a poet.

Dwellers in the Sea

My soul is some leviathan in vague distress
That travels up great slopes of hills beneath the sea.
Up from the darkness and the heaviness
Into a slowly gathering radiancy.
But wiser now, alas! to plunge and swim away;
For if he burst upon that mystic light of day,
Leviathan must gasp in lack of breath
And find what dwellers in the sea call death.
We hapless dwellers in the sea cannot be told,
No brave leviathan has ever back returned   10
To tell us how stupendous mountains rolled
Like porpoises, beneath a sky that burned,
How unimaginable light along his scales
Changed colour, till Leviathan was mailed in glory.
We have but rumours, unsubstantial tales;
And who would give his life up for a story?

Ian Macpherson (1905 – 1943)

Alive-oh!

He was proud of his name. When he was a child and his namesake's story was read to him he used to send himself to sleep saying 'David Livingstone, David Livingstone' over and over until the sweet pleasure of the sound blurred into the sweeter confusion of sleep and dreams.

As he grew from childhood his father's small business dwindled, and when the old man died it died too. The boy found himself in the world, and all he preserved of his childhood was a very clear picture of his mother ironing, and himself watching her, his small hands level with his face on the edge of the table where she ironed, while she told the often-told story of his namesake.

It made him happy, even now he was grown to manhood, to remember the happiness which filled him then. He had renounced many things. He had closed the doors of his mind against romantic imaginings, he would not go into unknown countries even in fancy, but he could never forget that recollection of his childhood.

His mother did not outlive his father many years, and he found himself alone when she was dead. The pride he took in being wage-earner for them both, eking out the few pounds his father left, evaporated before his mother's death. But he was far from discontented with his clerk's wages, and his unexciting occupation. He was nineteen when she died.

At the back of his mind he was still proud of his name. He was unaware of his pride, for he was humble by nature, and if he had dreamt that he still took honour because he was named after a famous man, he would have been at pains to exorcise his pride. But he was still hero-worshipper in his heart. He gave up the Church after his mother's death. He became infected with a zeal for change. He was gifted with a sardonic wit: he developed an intense zeal for the removal of institutions which had weathered so many years that their utility was not glaringly apparent, and their picturesque air gave them the appearance of ornament, not of use. The Church was chief of such institutions, he despised it, and all its functions, and all its officers. He had a passion for new things, whose purpose shone through them. Sometimes when he met acquaintances, or gathered with his companions in the office by a window overlooking the busy street, he grew eloquent, and sweeping the churches with their spires, the conglomerate mass of ill-planned city, and all the scene with its hidden misery and squalor, into the dust-bin of time, he built new cities for men.

And he was fond of writing his name. In spite of his societies, his earnest young men who listened as if he was a prophet, in spite of the baser sort who enjoyed his wit and drew him on to hear what he would say next, what ancient foundation he would demolish – in spite of his occupations he was lonely. He read with avidity. He lived very simply, in a poor quarter of the town, for as he preached, so he must act, but he spent the money he saved on comfort, buying books.

There was no sweeter moment in his day than the time when, his tea over, his cigarette smoked, his office clothes put off and older clothes put on, he washed his hands and undid the string and brown paper which held his treasures. It was a ritual whose every action was significant. The fair white fly-leaves were like an enchantment. His pen, his ink, were ennobled at this moment, while he wrote his name in tiny perfect letters. And then he slipped from the country of enchantment back to his threadbare restless talkative present as easily as a child ceases to be king when it is called to dinner.

It was childish, and he was a child. The dapper little clerk was more than a little clerk: he had simplicity of heart which made him as great, and as full of promise for the future, as a child. He was small and dark and neat like a thing not meant for use. His complexion was fairer than a woman's and drew many a woman's pitying regard for what it betokened. He knew that he had the seeds of death in him. Had the hectic beauty of his cheeks not warned him, it was plain in his parents' death certificates. But though he knew his disease he did not know how death shone in his face, he did not know why all women were gentle when he was near, and even his harridan of a landlady kept her ill-nature in leash when she spoke to him. Perhaps the simplicity which looked from his clerk's eyes with most unclerkly greatness was not the simplicity of the child which remained alive in him, but of that older inhabitant, who sat with him daily on an office stool, and when he ate his meals, made each meal a communion, and turned the bread and the water into the body of death.

No one was very angry with him when he preached revolution. His boss's large face beamed affectionately at him, like sun through the morning fog of his city, even when he heard his clerk calling down fire to destroy all bosses. One could not be angry with the fragile mite whose eyes' brown gentleness spoke louder than his tongue. The slums of his city and evils of the world had defeated him before he was born.

To himself his disease was not a grief. It belonged somehow to the world's distress, not to himself. Like dirt, and poverty, and all that afflicted men, it was a trouble to the flesh, not grievous to the spirit, for those things had an end. It brought home to him the imperfection of a world where some were rich and some poor, some healthy, some born with death in their bosoms, feeding there. What was wrong could be remedied, his trouble was a part of mankind's, it never came home to himself until one bright April morning he found his pillow bloody, and his mouth salt.

Perhaps because he was so lonely, he cried a long time, but tears, which once could end sorrow, get him kindness and help, would not wipe out this stain. He was not without courage, although life had until now denied him opportunity to show it. When he had cried, he washed himself and suffered the pains as well as the fear of death. By the time he was ready to go to his office, he was prepared. He had died in his heart, the pain was past, he could wait now for the end of his life. If he had not grown up in loneliness he might not have suffered so much at once; he would not have suffered so finally, but now with no intercessor and no friend he met the angel of death, and was defeated, and rose, captive, submissive to his victor's will.

By the time he composed himself it was nine o'clock, and he should have been already in his office. The tremendous thing that had happened came home to him when he looked at his watch, for until now, without fail, he had been in the office by this time. He gathered his coat and hat and put them on. When he saw himself distorted in his shaving mirror he murmured 'Poor David Livingstone' to his image.

A knock sounded on his door and a breathless voice called 'Are you in?'

'Come in, Beldy,' he said. A girl opened the door and slipped into the room. Words tumbled from her.

'You're late. Did you not know you were late? Did you sleep in?'

He nodded his head.

'I slept in,' he agreed.

'Hurry!' she said. 'Ma left your breakfast – it's cold. She's out.'

They looked with understanding at each other, knowing his landlady, and the girl smiled.

He thought it strange that she should smile so happily. He had never noticed until now that her body, set though she was not yet fifteen, and her shrewd old face, had youth in them. He glanced from her face to his hands, and from his hands to his own face in the mirror. The new thing he saw in her was in himself also. His eyes hurried round the room, and everything he saw was new. He seemed to see things as if a glass screen had been taken from before his eyes.

The girl shook his arm impatiently.

'You'd better hurry,' she said, and then 'You ill?'

He shook his head.

'Oh!' she exclaimed, looking at his pillow.

'A tooth,' he explained, 'tooth come out, Beldy.' He had never realised how alive she was. She held the door open for him.

'I'll fix it all right,' she said casually. 'Best not let Ma see. Best not say a lot, eh?'

His go-to-work habit sent him over the street to a tram-standard. The streets were empty of the children he usually saw going to school. He looked a little for them before he realised what was missing. The conductor on his tram was one of his acquaintances. Forbes heard all the gossip of the town and retailed it above the noise of the tram to friends. His news was often useful to such small revolutionaries as Livingstone; in an argument the clerk often made use of the stories of rent-racking and sharp practice which Forbes had told him in the morning. David Livingstone was not proud of the source of his knowledge, he did not like Forbes's leer when he spoke of business men and their love affairs, but he consoled himself and rebuked himself with the thought that it was all for the good Cause. In spite of that he did not like the man, and he did not like to be singled out, to have scandal hurled at him across a line of stout old ladies, and to be made into a red revolutionary to the horror of passengers, to the tune of a clacking ticket-punch.

But this morning he did not shrink when Forbes hailed him. He had the lower deck to himself, and sat white and small and forlorn in a corner while the conductor rushed upstairs. The curious nakedness with which his room, and Beldy, appeared to him, was general. He felt elated. He felt as if he was deeply alive inside, and he saw the livingness of the scene with a feeling almost of ecstasy, as if he was alive outside himself as well as in, and the crowds, the morning air as yet uncontaminated by smoke, and he himself, had a communion which was unknown until now. The street was almost terrifying to his sharpened senses. He was for the first time in his life deeply aware of the life around him. He saw an old woman walk slowly down the gutter, between the throng of people and a stream of cars. She was tall, and the baskets she carried in either hand did not make her stoop. She sauntered down the gutter crying in a loud clear voice 'Caller Dulse! Caller Dulse!' Her cry, the dignity of the old woman, moved him.

Forbes tumbled down the stair in his hurry to meet his friend. 'A bit late old boy, what?' he cried, ringing the bell twice to restart the tram. 'Easy now, madam,' he urged an old lady who clambered aboard. He rushed her into the seat beside Livingstone and sat down opposite them.

'You're looking white about the gills, boy,' he said. 'Out on the binge, now?' His head shook reproving his own levity.

'No, I know,' he went on in less sprightly tones. 'Needing a rest, needing a holiday. "What a hope," sez you! Fat chance of holidays for the likes of us working blokes. If we was rich men's sons now – d'you hear 'bout young Frazer?'

He rambled on. To Livingstone his talk was vague, and yet important. Names, names, and every name a living soul; what living things there were in the world, how queer the gift of life, a little proud thing wrapped in clay; everything that was a name a living thing. It looked through their eyes, it was in their flesh, their voices, how strange and terrible it was to be alive.

Forbes checked his oratory.

'Your stop, old man, your stop. See you later, cheero.'

When David recalled this morning, and it came often into his mind during the month that followed, he thought wistfully of his own strange adventure. He did not go to the office, but led by random impulses, now by the sight of men working, now in pursuit of that goal to which a stream of people seemed to have their faces set, he walked along busy quays, down muddy lanes between shipyards, and from the point of masonry where the harbour ended and rock began, he weaved his way inland, by suburban streets, to a little hill on the country's outskirts. The country stretched before him.

Everything he saw excited him. Like a thread of scarlet silk his path wound through the city, and everything he saw was lovely, even when it frightened him; long weeks afterwards he traced his path through the city, and wondered why the morning ended.

In the afternoon he went to the office. He was tired out. Bobby roared and back-slapped his way through a story of the streets, an encounter, and the bawdy conclusion. The office laughed, dutifully, for Bobby was the boss's nephew.

The day was over and it left him nothing but a tired body and an almost insufferable feeling of futility. He was so tired that he could not stand by a tram station, in the home-going rush; he began to walk towards his lodgings, and reached them, almost collapsing.

His landlady was still out. Beldy set his tea, brought hot water for his face and hands, and helped him off with his coat. She brought his kipper in, and sat over from his table, with sewing in her lap. He ate by force of will, and drank four cups of tea. The girl bit a thread through, and with one end still in her mouth she mumbled: 'You gotta get out of here, Dave. You gotta go to the country.'

He shook his head.

Suddenly her head dropped in her hands and she began to sob, crying, 'Dave, you're gonna die and leave me. For God's sake don't leave me.'

He leaned over her, patting her shoulder. 'Don't, Beldy,' he said in a shaking voice. 'Please don't.'

'Don't!' she flared. 'How can I? You've gotta get out of here.'

'I can't,' he said. 'You know I can't.'

'Oh me, oh me,' she went on, not heeding him, 'what'll I do, whatever'll I do?'

She looked at him and tried to smile.

'Sorry, Dave,' she said. 'I'm no damn good.'

'Yes you are,' he murmured. 'You're very good to me.'

'Am I, Dave?' she demanded. 'Am I really?' She shook her head. 'You're just saying that,' she said.

'No, Beldy, it's true. You know I wouldn't tell you lies.'

'Why'd you say it was your tooth then?' she cried. 'Why'd you say that, Dave?'

'Oh, Beldy, I'm so tired,' he said.

'Poor Dave,' she murmured, laying her hands on his shoulders and drawing him down until he was kneeling beside her. She drew his face close to her heart. 'Poor Dave,' she said; 'rest now, boy.'

In the month that followed he thought more and more of the morning he spent walking through the streets of his city, and the old occupations of his mind gradually slipped away. He was always on the alert, eager to recapture that morning's vision, and although it eluded him, there were instants when he waited on the brink of a revelation, and once or twice he saw common drudgery in that morning's light.

He searched for what he had found and lost; he rose in the bright May mornings and followed that morning's way through the empty streets, ending always on the hill which had the city before it, and the country reaching out on the other side.

Although he saw the light which illumined that morning only in glimpses, he began to find solace, instead of ecstasy. He found two easeful things. One was Beldy. The other was the country, from whose edge he no longer looked back upon the city. Instead he watched rooks in the woods which lay like smoke in the valley.

He went at last secretly to a doctor and had the term of his life told him. From the doctor's he went to draw his small savings from the post-office. And one morning in the merry month of May he walked with Beldy along the familiar way until they came to the hill he had found. They looked for the last time at the city, where he had put his name on books. It was grey in the morning sunshine; its dust had killed him, but he saw a vision in it. Then, poor city fools, they turned their backs on it, and walked down to the valley, sitting often to rest because a little exertion tired him; they never turned their heads to look at what was everything. The Dark Continent waited for his coming.

Robert McLellan (1907 – 1985)

McLellan was born in Linmill, Kirkfieldbank, in Lanarkshire; his upbringing there is celebrated in his several 'Linmill Stories,' as narrated by a boy. He was better known in his lifetime as a dramatist, whose major work is the historical character study, *Jamie the Saxt* (1937). Both the Linmill stories and the plays are generally written in a rich Scots. *The Carlin Moth* (1947), given here, is a verse 'fairy tale' written for radio. It may be McLellan's most polished drama.

Sang

There's a reid lowe* in yer cheek,		flame
Mither, and a licht in yer ee,		
And ye sing like the shuilfie in the slae,		
But no for me.		

The man that cam the day,
Mither, that ye ran to meet,
He drapt his gun and fondlet ye
And I was left to greit*.   weep

Ye served him kail frae the pat,
Mither, and meat frae the bane.   10
Ye brocht him cherries frae the gean*,   bush
And I gat hardly ane.

And nou he lies in yer bed,
Mither, and the licht growes dim,
And the sang ye sing as ye hap me ower
Is meant for him.

The Carlin Moth

An Island Fairy Tale in Four Scenes

SCENE I

Upstage, the window and door of a white-washed cottage. Left, a fishing-net draped over a frame, the posts of which have pegs for other gear. Beside the frame a bench and a small herring barrel. Centre and downstage right, the foliage of bushes and trees. The sun is setting. The CARLIN MOTH, invisible to the audience, breaks into a dance, the shadows she casts resembling those of a fluttering moth.

THE MOTH *(pausing in her dance, her shadow visible among the foliage downstage right)*

The gowden lowe★ that warms the shimmerin sea	flame
Flees as the bleize o the reid sinkin sun	
Dees in the lift★ ahint the faurmaist isles.	sky
Blae mirk steals ower the ripple, and eerie gloamin	
Abune the daurklin hills brings oot the staurs.	

(Her shadow flutters beyond the foliage in the centre of the stage.)

The quait reid deer wind doun frae stanie scaurs		
To seek the green blade in the corrie bield★,		shelter
And muckle troots slip frae their hidie-holes		
To lowp across the pules at deein flees,		
And though the merle quaitens in the trees	10	
And wi the mavis and the reid-breist sleeps,		
The ghaistly houlet hovers ower the neeps		
Seekin the squeekin mouss aneth the shaw,		
And whaur the rabbits courie by the kail		
The sleekit weasel threids the dry-stane waa.		

(Her shadow flutters beyond the fishing-net.)

Nicht has its life, baith guid and ill, and I,		
For guid or ill, wauk wi the brichtenin mune,		
And sune, whan the wearie fisher lifts his line,		
And coonts his catch, and pous him to the shore,		
His lamp will leme★ ayont the winnock there,	20	gleam
And it will draw me in.		

Her shadow flutters back across the stage, to still again beyond the foliage downstage right. A homely crofter LASS enters left, agitated.

THE LASS Come mither, hurry.

THE MOTHER *(following slowly, out of breath)*
　　Lassie, dinna be in sic a flurry;
　　The lad's no in yet, and the tide's at ebb.
　　He'll hae to draw his boat abune the wrack.

THE LASS Mither, let's gang back. Were he to come
　　Afore we'd left the hoose and won the loanin
　　I ken I couldna face him.

THE MOTHER There's time, I tell ye.

Dinna be sae blate★. The lad's a neibor	30	shy
Wi nane to lift a haund aboot his hoose,		
Sae wha can say, gin we redd★ ower his flair.		put in order

And mak his bed, and set his supper ready,
That there was thocht o ocht but kindliness
For the lad in his laneliness.
THE LASS Na, mither, he'll jalouse★.   suspect
He'll ken I want him.
THE MOTHER He'll think ye micht, ye fule,
And whaur's the ill? His pulse will quicken
To think a lass has thocht to comfort him.   40
THE LASS Watch for me weill, then. Tell me whan he comes.

She enters the cottage. Her MOTHER *keeps watch left. The* CARLIN MOTH'S *shadow flutters
again across the stage, to still beyond the fishing-net. The* LASS *reappears at the door.*

THE LASS Whaur is he nou?
THE MOTHER He's drawin in his oars.
He'll be a while yet.
THE LASS Mither, it's daurk inside.
THE MOTHER Then licht the lamp.

The CARLIN MOTH'S *shadow flickers momentarily.*

THE LASS The lamp. He'll see the lowe.
THE MOTHER No till he's on the brae.
THE LASS Then warn me airily.
THE MOTHER Ay ay, awa, wark fast.   50

She moves offstage left as the LASS *goes back into the cottage.*

THE MOTH *(her shadow suddenly changing its orientation as the lamp is lit)*
Nou comes the hour
Whan mair than mortal craiturs are asteer,
Born amang mortal thochts to fill the daurk
Nae mortal ee can pierce. Up in the hills
The banie witch gangs bizzin like a bee,
Behunkert ower her besom★. The awesome kelpie★   broom/water
                                                                              monster

Deep in his black den in the fernie gill,
Chinners and graens abune the splashie din
O tummlin watter. Roun the muckle stanes
That staun in broken rings aboot the muirs   60
The peerie craiturs frae the chaumert★ cairns   chambered
Fling taes heid heich in skirlin fowersome reels,
Drunk wi the heather yill★. And in the still   ale
Lown loanins by the byres the hornie kye
Staun slaiverin wi fricht, for fairy fingers
Rise frae amang the ferns to draw their milk.
I tae maun to my wark. I tae am born
Whan mortal thochts rax★ oot into the mirk.   reach
And roun the leme that lichts the room inbye
The lanely fisher dreams I wait for him.   70

She is seen in silhouette entering the cottage swiftly.

THE MOTHER *(appearing suddenly left)*
He's comin nou. Mak haste.

The light from both door and window is momentarily dimmed. There is a scream.

THE LASS *(coming from the cottage in a panic)*
    Oh mither, a ghaist
    Flew bye me as I spread the claith, and laid
    A daurk haund on the lamp and dimmed the lowe.
THE MOTHER *(scornfully)* Havers★, ye tawpie. It was a jennie-meggie.   nonsense
    Whaur had ye gotten?
THE LASS The dishes were to lay.
THE MOTHER Then lay them. Quick.
THE LASS I canna gang. I'm feart.
THE MOTHER Then bide ye here and watch. I'll gang mysell.   80
THE LASS Na, dinna leave me.
THE MOTHER Look to the brae, my dawtie★.   pet
    The lad's in sicht and ye hae nocht to fear.
(She enters the cottage, but reappears immediately, shaken.)
    That's queer. Ye said the dishes were to lay?
THE LASS I hadna stertit to them.
THE MOTHER *(drawing the* LASS *to the door, and pointing)*
    Look. They're laid.
THE LASS The kettle. I left it on the fender last
    And nou it's on the swee. And look. It moves!
(She flees in terror.)
THE MOTHER Oh dinna leave me. Wait.

       She follows. The CARLIN MOTH *moves in the cottage making shadows in the window. A crofter* LAD *enters left with bass and scull, which he drops beside the bench. He moves towards the cottage, but suddenly pauses, startled.*

THE LAD Wha's in the hoose?   90
    Come oot and name yersell.

       The CARLIN MOTH, *now a crofter lass idealised, appears carrying a storm lantern.*

THE CARLIN *(hanging the lantern on a post beside the bench)*
    There. Sit ye doun.
    And set yer line to dry, and clean the fish.
THE LAD *(amazed)* Hou cam ye here?
THE CARLIN Ye brocht me here yersell,
    For ye hae wished me here. Ay, mony a day
    Whan ye hae sawn yer corn in the broun yirth★,   earth
    Or cut yer hey, or sailed alang the rocks
    To troll for gowden lythe abune the weed,
    Yer thochts hae dwalt aboot the steadin★ here   100   farm,
                                                holding

    Whaur nae haund caaed the kirn or gethert cream,
    And mony an ein, whan ye hae gaen inbye
    To rest yer banes aside a fire lang deid,
    Yer thochts hae dwalt upon yer lanely bed,
    And ye hae wearied sair, and wished for me.
THE LAD *(afraid)* I dinna ken ye. Neir in aa my days,
    Ower aa the isle, hae I set een on ye.
THE CARLIN And yet ye ken me weill, for ye yersell
    Hae fashioned me to meet yer hairt's desire.
    Is there a crofter lass in ony clachan★,   110   village
    Or smeekit★ tinker bissom in a tent,   stinking
    That has sic gentle haunds, sae snawie white?

Yet I hae soopit oot the hoose inbye,
And made the fire, and laid the table for ye.

THE LAD *(seizing her extended hands and drawing her to the light)*
    Ye maun be mortal, for I can feel yer haunds,
    And they are warm. And yet I ken fou★ weill   full
    Ye are nae neibor lass. Whaur is yer hame?
    Whaur hae ye been eir nou?

THE CARLIN *(stepping back from the light)*
    My hame is here,
    And I hae been a moth.   120

THE LAD A moth!

THE CARLIN A moth,
    And in the sair bricht glare o sunny day
    I sleepit aye upon a nettle leaf
    Aneth the elder by the gairden waa,
    Safe in the shade. I waukent in the mirk
    Whaneir a lamp was lichtit and I flew
    Abune the roses and the grozet busses
    Whaureir there was a leme, but whan I socht
    This ein the lowe abune the wick inbye   130
    I bleized and shrivelt. Nou I am a queyn★.   girl

THE LAD A witch, I caa ye!

THE CARLIN *(stepping farther back into the darknest, her voice harshening)*
    I am as ye wad hae me.
    Caa me witch and ye shall see my een
    Bleize in my runklet★ face like fiery coals;   wrinkled
    My banie neb★ shall curl like a heuk   beak
    Abune my tuithless mou, and muckle warts
    Shall spread aboot my chin and sprout lang hairs
    As teuch as bristles on an auld boar's back.

THE LAD Come back into the licht!   140

THE CARLIN *(returning into the light unchanged, and smiling provokingly)*
    Noo caa me witch.

THE LAD Na na, bide as ye are.

THE CARLIN Then mak me a promise.

THE LAD I promise what ye will.

THE CARLIN This is my will:
    That gin I bide wi ye frae this day on
    And dae aa wifely darg★ aboot the hoose,   work
    And milk the kye and mend the nets for ye,
    And ower the fender sit wi ye at ein,
    Or at the faa o nicht lie by yer side,   150
    Ye shall say nocht to ony. Speak ae word
    And I maun tak my former shape again
    And flutter in the mirk abune the flouers
    Or sleep by day aneth the elder tree.

THE LAD *(in a hoarse whisper)* Na, bide like this.

THE CARLIN Then sweir ye winna talk.

THE LAD I sweir, and gin I say a mortal word
    May I be lanely till I end my days.

            She advances to him. They embrace.

SCENE II

The same. A few days later. Forenoon. The MOTHER is nodding on the bench downstage left. The CARLIN MOTH, in her human form, appears with a cogie¹ from the trees right, sees the MOTHER, places the cogie out of sight behind the trees, creeps stealthily to the window, looks in, becomes alarmed, and retires swiftly into the trees again. The LASS comes from the cottage and walks to her MOTHER at the bench, seemingly dispirited. She sits beside her MOTHER and sighs. Her MOTHER raises her head and opens her eyes.

THE MOTHER Weill, hae ye dune?
THE LASS Ay, aa there was to dae.   160
THE MOTHER I neir kent sic a lad. He maun be thrang★   busy
    Afore the cock craws at the hen-hoose door.
    The pipe-cley curliewurlies roun his flair
    Are aye as clean as milk, and aa his linen
    As sweet as myrtle and as fresh as air.
    Keek★ in his jeelie-pan. Ye'll see yer face   peek
    As clear as in a gless. Its hardly cannie.
THE LASS There's ae thing clear. He daesna need a wife.
THE MOTHER A wife's mair nor a dish-clout. Dinna haver★.   talk nonsence
THE LASS He daesna seem to want ane.   170
THE MOTHER Hou dae ye ken?
THE LASS He passed me on the brae the ither day
    Whan he cam aff the hill. His collie dug
    Cam slinkin at my heel and frichtent me.
    He haurdly turnt his heid, the hairtless deil.
THE MOTHER Ye didna mention it.
THE LASS I was sae shamed.
THE MOTHER He haurdly turnt his heid?
THE LASS Haurdly at aa.   180
    A jerk it was, to caa the collie in.
THE MOTHER Mebbe he's shy.
THE LASS Oh mither, it micht be sae,
    And yet I dout it. He didna look awa,
    Or at his taes, but socht aa ower the brae,
    His een aye gleg★, as if he had nae thocht   sharp
    Save for a taiglet yowe amang the slaes,
    Or a puir wanert lammie in the bracken
    Wantin its mither's milk. He wasna shy.
THE MOTHER I canna mak it oot. He canna think
    That aa thae tuithsome pancakes I hae bakit   190
    And left upon his dresser ilka day
    Hae drappit through his celin frae the lift.
THE LASS Or aa the bonnie flouers that I hae gathert
    And left in watter by the winnock for him.
    He canna think they grew there wantin rutes.
    He's no sae glaikit★.   foolish
THE MOTHER Na, there's something wrang.
THE LASS (dejected) He daesna like me.
THE MOTHER (preoccupied) Hoots, he daesna ken ye.
THE LASS He's seen me.   200

---

¹ Pail.

THE MOTHER Haurdly at aa.

THE LASS Oh I can thole★ it.   endure

    He's seen me and he daesna like my face.

    He hates my fernie-tickles. Ay, that's it.

    It canna be ocht else. My middle's jimp★,   slender

    My breists are shapely and my hips are smaa,

    And shairly my legs are braw? Oh dinna lee.

    Mither, my legs are braw?

THE MOTHER *(mildly scandalised)* Oh haud yer tongue.

THE LASS I ken it's naething else. He hates my face.   210

    Yet morn and ein through ilka weary day

    I lave it weill wi meal and butter-milk.

    A wee roun box o pouther frae a toun

    To mak my reuchent★ skin as saft as silk   roughened

    He'd loe me then. But there, ye winna listen.

THE MOTHER I'm thinkin.

THE LASS What aboot?

THE MOTHER The hoose inbye.

THE LASS And what aboot it?

THE MOTHER Lassie, there's someane else.   220

       The CARLIN MOTH *can be seen listening from the trees right.*

THE LASS Oh mither na! Whiles I hae wonert that.

THE MOTHER Ye silly queyn, we canna be shair he loes her,

    But this bye-ordinar polishin and scrubbin

    Is nae mere man's wark. Someane else

    Caas like yersell ilk day to dae his reddin

    And she wins aa the credit.

THE LASS Ay, but mither,

    We haena seen a body aa the week.

THE MOTHER That's what I dinna like. She canna be

    Some puir auld manless craitur frae the clachan   230

    That daes the wark for siller. Sic a ane

    Wad gang aboot the brae afore oor een

    And whan we caaed wad aye be thrang inbye.

THE LASS Wha can she be?

THE MOTHER Some ither stricken queyn.

    That daes her wark in secret like yersell.

THE LASS But wha?

THE MOTHER I canna think.

THE LASS Nae mair can I.

    Pause. The CARLIN MOTH *moves quietly and swiftly behind the fishing-net.*

THE MOTHER It canna be that hissie frae the castle fairm?   240

THE LASS But she's aye keepit thrang amang the kye

    And bides ower faur awa to caa sae aften.

THE MOTHER I dinna ken. The auld road through the wuid

    And ower the balloch★ on the castle brae   pass

    Wad fetch her here wi nae great waste o time.

    And she could caa efter she lowsed★ at ein,   loosed

    Juist whan the brae was quait.

THE LASS Ay ay, but mither,

    She's sic a muckle lump to tak that gait★.   way

The castle brae's sae stey★, and she's sae creishie★,   250   steep/fat
  She'd melt afore she won the auld mairch dyke,
  And tell me if I'm wrang, but shairly, mither,
  The lad wad scunner★ at sae coorse a tyke?   feel disgust
THE MOTHER She likes her parritch. That I dinna dout.
THE LASS Shairly it canna be. *(Pause.)* And yet it micht.
THE MOTHER It micht.
THE LASS I dout it, though.
THE MOTHER Oh ay, it micht.
THE LASS There's ae thing clear. She hasna won her wey.
  We haena seen the lad and her thegither.   260
THE MOTHER *(pointedly)* We haena been here at nicht.
THE LASS Oh mither,
  Ye dinna think he's daein ocht he suldna
  Wi sic a laithly pudden-poke as that?
  Oh I wad hate him.
THE MOTHER Dinna think the warst
  Afore the warst is kent.
THE LASS *(scornfully)* Whan will we ken?
THE MOTHER We'll ken this very nicht.
THE LASS Ye wadna spy!   270
THE MOTHER Na, na, but if ye could forget the fricht
  The bogle gied ye here the ither ein
  We could come daunrin ower again the nicht
  Wi mebbe a muckle scone straucht aff the girdle,
  Or mebbe some cruds and whey. We needna be late,
  But juist in time to catch him comin in
  As we were comin oot. It's nae great sin
  To spare a thocht whiles for a lanely neibor.
  He couldna tak it ill. Ye needna be blate.
THE LASS But what if she was here?   280
THE MOTHER We'd ken the warst,
  And if she wasna, dinna ye see, ye silly,
  He'd learn the truith aboot the wark inbye
  That till this day he hasna kent was oors.
  Whan will he leave the clippin to come hame?
THE LASS I dinna care. I winna come. I couldna.
THE MOTHER Oh ay, ye'll come.
THE LASS Mither, ye couldna coax me
  Gin ye tried aa day. Hou could I thole
  To walk in there and fin that brosie★ queyn   290   bloated
  Clumpin aboot his hoose in muckle buits
  For aa the warld as if she were its mistress?
  What could I say to her? What wad she think?
  She'd mak me oot as shameless as hersell.
  And if I saw her in his airms . . . Oh mither,
  I grue★ ein at the thocht.   shudder
THE MOTHER Keep cuil, ye fule,
  Come hame and think the matter ower in peace.
THE LASS I needna. I ken my mind. Frae this day on
  I dinna set a fute inside his door.   300
  Or wait, I'll hae the flouers I brocht the day.
  What wey suld she hae credit for my flouers?
THE MOTHER Hear me, ye tawpie. Bide.

The LASS *goes quickly into the cottage. Her* MOTHER *follows to the door and waits. Pause.*
The LASS *returns slowly, carrying a bunch of flowers at which she gazes tragically.*

THE LASS Oh but they're bonnie,
    And I was blye whan I was pouin them.
    Mither, my hairt's like leid.
THE MOTHER Yer heid's like feathers.
THE LASS *(moving slowly right)* Ye dinna understaun.
THE MOTHER Whaur are ye gaun?
THE LASS *(bursting into tears)* To droun mysell.   310
THE MOTHER *(seizing her by the arm and dragging her left)*
    Come hame, ye senseless limmer★,   fool
    And let me splairge★ a pail o watter ower ye.   splatter
THE LASS *(listlessly)* Oh lowse me. Let me gang.
THE MOTHER Na na, come hame.

    She drags the LASS *off left. Pause. The* CARLIN MOTH *emerges from the net, goes to the trees*
    right, lifts her cogie and enters the cottage briskly, shutting the door with an impatient bang.

SCENE III

The same. Evening of the same day. The CARLIN MOTH, still in her human form, enters
furtively and breathlessly right, crosses to the left, looks beyond, and enters the cottage swiftly.
Pause. The LASS enters swiftly left, looks towards the cottage, goes to the trees right and looks
beyond. Her MOTHER enters left also, carrying some scones wrapped in a cloth. She goes to
the window of the cottage and looks in.

THE MOTHER Whaur has he gotten nou?
THE LASS I canna see.
    He maun be in the glen amang the birks★   birches
    Crossin the watter at the steppin stanes.
THE MOTHER We're weill on time, and aa seems quait inbye.
THE LASS Mither, I'm gled I cam. Oor thochts this morn   320
    That gart me greit sae sair seem silly nou.
    Look at me weill and tell me: Am I braw?
THE MOTHER Ay ay, ye'll dae, but mind what I hae telt ye.
    Whaneir he passes through the rick-yaird whirlie
    And crosses to the stable wi his collie
    Tak ye the scones inbye. I'll sit me doun
    And wait aside the nets to greet him first.
THE LASS *(taking the scones)* And I shall bide inbye until ye caa.
    I ken my pairt. Mither, my silly breists
    Will burst my bodice, for they rise and faa   330
    Like a wee shuilfie scuddie's beatin hairt.
    Think ye he'll notice? I wad feel sic shame.
THE MOTHER Ye laced yer bodice laich yersell, ye limmer.
    Gang ower and watch the brae. He'll be in sicht.

    The LASS *moves right, to the trees, and looks beyond.*
    Her MOTHER *remains on the bench. The sun is setting.*

THE LASS *(worried)* Mither, I canna see him on the brae.
THE MOTHER *(rising and moving right)*
    He suld be this side o the glen by nou.
THE LASS He's naewhaur to be seen. I hear his whistle!

He's aff the muir and doun amang the corn,
Herdin his collie at the yearlin quey.
THE MOTHER The yearlin quey suld be amang the rashes.   340
THE LASS It's in the corn.
THE MOTHER Wha left the yett*, I woner.   gate
It couldna weill hae been the lad himsell,
For he's been aa day clippin, and at nune
The quey was in the rashes wi the tups.
Someane's been bye that wey. I woner wha.
(Light appears in the cottage window.)
Lassie, look roun.
THE LASS *(startled)* Mither, the ghaist again.
THE MOTHER The ither queyn.
THE LASS She wad hae heard us, shairly,   350
And come oot, or else she wad hae hidden
And left the hoose in daurkness till we gaed.
THE MOTHER I woner.
THE LASS Mither, come awa.
THE MOTHER Na na.
We'll hae to settle this. Ye hae the scones.
Gang forrit to the door and gie a chap.
THE LASS I canna. Gang yersell.
THE MOTHER Then bide ahint me
Dinna gang awa.   360

> The LASS *stands by the trees fearfully. Her* MOTHER *goes to the cottage door and knocks.*
> *The door is suddenly opened and the* CARLIN MOTH *appears, transformed into a fat, ugly*
> *farm girl, and weirdly lit by a ray of light from the setting sun.*

THE CARLIN *(coarsely)* Weill, what's yer will?
THE MOTHER *(taken aback)* We cam to see the lad. We brocht some scones.
We thocht he was at hame.
THE CARLIN He's on the hill.
And I can mak him aa the scones he wants.
THE MOTHER *(recovering herself)*
Ye shameless tink,[1] what brings ye here at nicht?
THE CARLIN *(leering)* What dae ye think?
(She slams the door.)
THE LASS Mither, it's as we thocht.
THE MOTHER Ay lass, I dout sae.
THE LASS I canna credit it.   370
That ugly puddock.
THE MOTHER Weill we ken the warst.
THE LASS Hurry, afore he comes.
THE MOTHER Gang ye yersell.I'll bide and face the blaggard.
THE LASS Na, come hame. Mither I hear him whistle in his collie.
THE MOTHER Haste ye awa, then. I maun hae my say.
THE LASS Nocht ye can say will mend my broken hairt,
And ocht ye say will fling it in his face.   380
Think o my pride.
THE MOTHER I hear him comin nou.
THE LASS Oh mither, dinna bide.

---

[1] 'Tinker', gypsy, low-class peddler. A general term of abuse.

THE MOTHER Awa and leave me.

The LASS *hurries out left. The* LAD *enters right whistling to announce his arrival to the girl inside the house. He halts abruptly on seeing the* MOTHER.

Guid ein, my lad. Ye hae a cheerie whistle.
THE LAD *(apprehensively)* What brings ye here?
THE MOTHER I cam like ony neibor
　　Thinkin to mak a lanely lad his supper,
　　And brocht some girdle scones.
THE LAD *(suspiciously)* I dinna see them.　　　　　　　　　390
THE MOTHER My dochter had them, but she's gaen awa.
THE LAD What gart ye bide yersell? Ye arena wantit.

A narrow slit of light shows at the cottage door.

THE MOTHER I ken it weill.
THE LAD What dae ye ken? Speak oot.
THE MOTHER I ken ye werena caaed three times in kirk,
　　Ye and that sou-faced slut ye keep inbye.
THE LAD *(hoarsely)* I'll cut yer tongue oot at the rute, ye beldam.
　　Ye haena seen the lass.
THE MOTHER The lass, forsooth.
　　She's like a tattie bogle.　　　　　　　　　　　　400
THE LAD Ye lee, I tell ye.
　　She wadna show hersell. Ye haena seen her.
THE MOTHER The shameless queyn cam flauntin to the door
　　Whaneir I gied a chap. Ay, ye may gowp.

The CARLIN MOTH *has opened the door fully and stands silhouetted against the light from within but beyond reach of the dying ray of sunlight.*

THE CARLIN *(coarsely)* Send the auld hag awa and come inbye.
THE MOTHER *(indignantly)* Nae dout I'm auld and mebbe no weill-faured,
　　But gin I could be aulder than the hills,
　　I wadna growe to fricht the very staurlins,
　　As ye dae whan ye gie the hens their mash.
THE LAD Auld wife, ye're daft. The lass is like a flouer.　　410
THE MOTHER Lad, she's bewitched ye.
THE LAD *(startle)* Bewitched!
THE MOTHER Ay, she's bewitched ye.
　　A fozie⋆ neep beglaubert in the rain,　　　　　　　spongy
　　Hauf eaten by a tup⋆, and fou o snails,　　　　　　ram
　　Wad put her face to shame, she's sic a sicht.
THE LAD Ye're blin, ye houlet.
THE MOTHER Look at the muckle trollop.
(To the CARLIN MOTH.*)*
　　Come forrit to the licht and let him see ye.
THE CARLIN Send her awa.　　　　　　　　　　　　420
THE MOTHER She kens hersell I'm richt.
THE LAD *(afraid)* Lassie, what's wrang? Come forrit to the licht.
　　Prove that she lees, the ill-tongued wurricraw⋆.　　demon

(The ray of sunlight flickers and dies. The shadows weaken. The CARLIN MOTH *is seen dimly in the twilight. She is grotesque.)*

Ye witch!

THE MOTHER I telt ye sae. Juist look at that.
    Hoo ye could stamack it I dinna ken.
THE LAD *(trembling)* Cannie, auld wife. The craitur isna mortal.
THE MOTHER Hae ye gaen gyte★? Shairly ye ken the queyn?   mad
She mucks the byre doun at the castle fairm.

       The CARLIN MOTH *backs slowly into the cottage.*

THE LAD Yer een hae leed. I tell ye she's a witch.   430
    I fand her warkin here aboot the hoose
    Ae nicht whan I cam lanely frae the shore.
    She was as fair a lass as ony rose,
    In aa her weys as dentie as a deer,
    And whan she promised she wad be my bride
    Gin I said nocht in ony mortal ear
    I took her to my breist and gart her bide,
    I couldna thole to pairt wi sic a prize.
(The light in the cottage dims momentarily.)
    What hae I said? Deil tak my tongue, she's lost.
THE MOTHER Ye glaikit sumph★. She's solid as a stot★.   441

                                               simpleton/
                                             bullock

      The shadow of the CARLIN MOTH *flutters in the cottage window.*

THE LAD She's lost, I tell ye. Seek inbye and see.
    Save for a moth that flutters roun the lamp
    Ye'll fin nae craitur there.
THE MOTHER A moth?
THE LAD Ay, look!

    The shadow of the CARLIN MOTH *flutters for a second beyond the nets then disappears.*

THE MOTHER *(trembling with fear and clutching the* LAD *by the arm)*
    God save us baith.

SCENE IV

The same. Several months later. Moonlight. A storm lamp hangs from the post of the net-frame. By its light the LAD is hanging a splash-net to dry stretching it backwards and forwards across the frame as the LASS feeds it to him from the coil on the ground. They finish.

THE LASS There nou, I maun gang hame. It's growing late.
THE LAD Sit doun a wee and rest.
THE LASS I daurna bide.
    I'm shair my mither saw us leave the shore.   450
    She'll ken I'm here wi ye.
THE LAD She lat ye come
    And spend the haill ein on the watter wi me.
    She canna think I mean ye ony hairm.
THE LASS We were in sicht whan we were on the watter.
THE LAD That may be sae, but shairly she winna fret.
    She kens I hae the net to spread to dry
    Afore I tak ye hame.
THE LASS The haill net's spread.
THE LAD Ye dinna want to bide. Ye dinna trust me.   460

THE LASS It wad be wrang to bide.

THE LAD *(curtly)* Then ye can gang. *(He sits.)*

THE LASS I canna gang mysell. It's efter daurk,
    And sune the mune will drap ahint the hill,
    And there's the burn to cross, and there are trees:
    It's black amang the trees ein wi the mune.

THE LAD Then tak the lamp.

THE LASS Oh, ye're a hairtless deil.
    Ye ken I hae the auld kirk ruin to pass.
    The leme aboot the waas wad draw the bats,   470
    And they wad flee at me.

THE LAD Then bide a wee.

THE LASS *(sitting)* I canna dae ocht else. *(He moves towards her.)*
    Dinna come near.

THE LAD Lassie, I loe ye. Dinna be sae cauld.

THE LASS Gin ye were eident★ ye wad tak me hame.   diligent

THE LAD *(moving closer)* I winna hairm ye, but the mune's sae bricht
    And the quait sea sae siller in its licht
    And aa the hills sae still, I canna thole
    To let ye gang and leave me aa my lane.   480

THE LASS I canna help but think that in the simmer
    Ye sat oot here and made the same sheep's een
    At yon big randy castle milk-hoose limmer.

THE LAD I sweir I didna. She was nocht to me.

THE LASS She maun hae come gey aften to the hoose,
    For aye whan I caaed ower here wi my mither
    The haill day's darg was dune, and aa thing ready
    To greet ye comin aff the hill at ein.
    Shairly ye kent she cam? Nou dinna lee.

THE LAD I didna ken wha cam until the day   490
    I left the clippin at the corrie burn
    To fin her here inbye. Shairly yer mither
    Has telt ye that the queyn dumfounert me?

THE LASS My mither's queer. She speaks aye in yer favour.

THE LAD She canna dae ocht else. She kens the truith.
    And shairly, lass, ye dinna think I'm blin?
    Ye canna think I could hae gien a thocht
    To sic a muckle fat monstrosity?

THE LASS I thocht ye mebbe likt sonsie★ craiturs,   plump, buxom
    For some men dae, ye ken.   500

THE LAD She wasna sonsie.
    She was as braid as ony gable end.

THE LASS Her een were black as slaes.

THE LAD I hate black een.

THE LASS She had the daurkest brous that I hae seen.

THE LAD I hate dark brous. They mak a lass look hard.

THE LASS She wasna bonnie. Was she?

THE LAD Dinna haver.
    She was as ugly as a dune auld sou.

THE LASS She was. I think she was.   510

THE LAD She gart me grue.

THE LASS Oh I'm sae gled. Ye wadna lee to me?
    For whan the craitur cam there to the door
    She tried to hint that ye and she were jos★.   sweethearts

THE LAD I didna ken she eir cam near the hoose.
    I wad hae chased her doun the brae. I sweir it.
THE LASS Sweir that ye haena ance gien her a thocht.
THE LAD Lassie, we're wastin time. It's growin late.
THE LASS Havers, the nicht's young yet. Look at the mune.
    It winna drap ahint the hill for hours.   520
Blaw oot the lamp and sit up close to me.
THE LAD I'd leifer leave the lamp. I like to see ye.
THE LASS The munelicht flaitters mair, and I'm sae plain.
THE LAD Lassie, ye arena plain. Nae burnett rose
    Blumes eir sae bonnily aneth the sun
    As ye dae wi the lamplicht on yer face.
THE LASS *(lowering her head to his breast)*
    The mune's gaen to my heid. Be cannie, lad.

      She lets her head fall into the crook of his arm waiting to be kissed. The shadow of the
CARLIN MOTH *flutters for a second among the trees right. The* LAD *starts visibly and stiffens.*
                 The LASS *waits in vain for her kiss.*

THE LASS What's wrang wi ye? Ye're like a lump o leid.
THE LAD *(gathering his wits awkwardly)*
    My haunds. I had forgotten. They stink o fish.
THE LASS *(offended)* Ye mean mine stink o fish?   530
THE LAD I mean my ain.
THE LASS Ye ken ye dinna.
THE LAD I sweir I mean my ain.
THE LASS Yer ain were roun my waist, oot o yer thochts,
    And mine were on yer shouthers, *(she sniffs at her hands)* but they're clean
    Save for the sautie tang o the wat net.
    Was it my braith that gart ye draw awa?
THE LAD I sweir it was my haunds.
THE LASS Oh dinna lee.
THE LAD *(exasperated)* Deil tak ye, then, ye jaud, it was yer braith.
THE LASS Ye hairtless deil, that ye suld tell me sae.   541
THE LAD I didna tell ye till ye forced me to.
THE LASS A lad wi ony mainners wad hae leed.
    And wha are ye to be pernicketty
    Whan yer ain haunds are fyled wi finnock guts
    And aa yer guernsey clartie* wi their scales?   besmeared
    I woner I could thole to hae ye close.
    I'd suner hae a drukken tinker maul me.
THE LAD He'd hae to be gey fou to think o it.
THE LASS Oh ye're a blaggard. Gin I had the pouer   550
    I'd pyke yer een oot like a corbie craw,
    Or scart yer skin aff like a heilan cat.
THE LAD *(losing his patience completely)*
    Ye jezebel. Awa afore I fell ye.
THE LASS *(retreating from him)*
    God keep me safe. There's murder in yer een.
THE LAD Awa, I say, afore I dae ye ill.
(She flees. Pause. He sits and turns to where he last saw the CARLIN MOTH.*)*
    Oh, carlin moth, what gart ye flutter sae
    Whan ye were lang forgotten, and I was fain
    To tak the mortal lassie in my airms?

THE MOTH *(invisible)* Nae mortal lass shall hae what ance was mine.

THE LAD Then flee ance mair into the lamp-wick's lowe
    And be a comely queyn again, and bide   561
    By day and nicht again my dearest jo.

THE MOTH That canna be, for I can tak but ance
    The form a mortal fashions in his dreams,
    And whan I rase the first time frae the lowe
    Ye didna haud me to yer ain conceit
    But lat the mortals roun ye smittle★ ye   stain
    Wi ugly thochts born o their jealousy,
    And whan I grew sae monstrous that ye grued
    Ye wished that I suld be a moth again.   570

THE LAD And nou I wish ye were my queyn again.

THE MOTH It canna be.

THE LAD It shall.

THE MOTH It canna be.

THE LAD It shall, or I will kaim the fullyery
    And fin the ae green leaf whauron ye lie,
    And I will kep ye in my cuppit haunds
    And tak ye to the fire that burns inbye
    And cast ye helpless in its lowin hairt,
    And aither ye will rise a queyn again   580
    Or shrivel into nocht and be nae mair.

THE MOTH Ye shanna fin me though ye seek for me
    On ilka leaf that growes on ilka tree,
    For I am free to flutter in the air.
    Her shudow flutters across the foliage, away from him. He follows.

THE LAD Gang whaur ye will. I'll follow till ye tire.

        He follows her offstage. The LASS *returns suddenly, distraught.*

THE LASS Oh lad, whaur are ye? Hae ye gaen inbye?
(She goes to the cottage door, opens it, and looks fearfully in dark interior.)
    Lad, are ye there? God keep me safe frae hairm.
    I'll hae the lamp.

    She goes to the net-frame and takes the lamp from the post. The shadow of the CARLIN
        MOTH *reappears and plays around her. She screams and runs off.*

THE MOTH *(from beyond the fishing-net, her shadow motionless against the cottage wall)*
    The antlert stag aneth the corrie gills
    May roar his challenge wi his hinds at heel,   590
    The jealous tup amang the benty★ knowes   grassy
    Herd wi his curly horns his skeerie★ yowes,   skittish
    But while the lass rins lost aboot the loan
    The lad seeks shaddas in the birken shaw★,   wood
    And gin they chance to tak ilk ither's airt
    I'll skeer the lass, or draw the lad awa.
(She dances, her shadow moving to the foliage in the centre of the stage.)
    Doun in the sea the restless saumon speed
    To fin the burns whaur they were born langsyne,
    And though there may be slack daurk pules aheid
    Whaur they maun lie in autumn's drouth and pine   600
    For winter's spate to gie their fins the pouer
    To cairry them abune the craigie linns★,   waterfalls

Yet whan they win the shallas on the muirs
And rowe abune the graivel redds in pairs
And toom* their heavy wames*, their journey dune,   empty/stomachs
They canna set against the bliss they fin
A lang held dream o ecstasy sae sweet
That aa their bliss is dule, their journey vain.
(She dances, her shadow moving among the foliage downstage right.)
The pouer to bigg a braw warld in his brain
Marks man the only craitur that can greit*.   610   weep

(She dances off.)

Curtain.

The Cat

There were three grocers' shops in Kirkfieldbank, but I was best acquaint wi Mistress Yuill's. It had been a guid shop at ae time, clean as a new preen[1] and weill stockit, and when I was a laddie haurdly auld eneuch for the schule I could hae thocht o naething better than the chance o cawin in wi a bawbee.[2] It wasna juist for what ye could buy, but for the sicht and smell o it. She selt gey nearly everything ye could think o, frae paraffin and cheese to weekly papers and tacketty buits, and ye could hae spent a haill efteernune peerin into aw the odd neuks at the faur end o the coonter, sniffin yer fill.

As time gaed bye, though, Mistress Yuill grew less able, and syne began to turn blin, and the last time I had cawed in the shop had been a fair disgrace, though the puir auld craitur couldna help it, nae dout. My first look at the winnock had gart me woner, for at ae end there was an auld grey cat sittin on a box o kippers, and at the tither a wheen[3] sticks a gundie that the sun had meltit into ae big stickie mess.

I had come that day to Linmill for my simmer holiday, though, and Mistress Yuill's had aye been pairt o it, sae I didna let the winnock keep me oot. I liftit the sneck[4] and pusht the door open.

The bell didna ping, and that was new tae. It gied a clatter like a pat lid. It was lood eneuch, for aw that, to hae brocht her forrit, but for a while there was nae sign o her, and I had rowth[5] o time to hae a guid look roun.

It wasna plaisint. The flair was dirty and the coonter a fair clutter. Naething was fresh. The butter stank and the cheese was mouldie, and there was an auld ham-end aside the scales sae thick wi big blue flees that ye could haurdly see it. The papers, weeks auld by the look o them, were aw markit. At first I thocht the cat had dune it, and the marks o its pads were on them shair eneuch, but on a closer look I foun finger-marks, hunders o them; and no juist on the papers. Aw over the coonter, aw ower the haill shop, there were fingermarks, creeshie,[6] flourie and aw sorts; and there was a look aboot them that wasna cannie.

---

[1] Pin.
[2] A small coin.
[3] Few.
[4] Latch.
[5] Plenty.
[6] Greasy.

The auld grey cat rase aff the kippers and cam in frae the winnock, slinkin alang wi its tail up, rubbin its backside on everything it passed and purrin like a kettle on the beyl. I followed its een and a cauld shiver cam ower me. Mistress Yuill had come forrit, hoo I dinna ken, and was feelin her wey alang the coonter, layin her hands on this and that, sweeties, puddens, papers and aw, and her blank blae een were like the shutters o a toom[1] hoose.

I stude like a gommeril.[2] I could think o naething to ask for. The cat pat its back up and spat in my face

'Ay?'

'A pair o whangs.'[3]

It was aw I could think that wadna be foustie. They wad dae for my grandfaither.

The whangs were hinging frae a nail on a post that took the wecht o the upstairs flair. She felt alang the coonter for her knife, pawin the papers, and syne for the post, pawin the sweeties and puddens again. She ran her fingers ower the whangs to fin the ends o them. She cut aff twa.

'A penny.'

I pat the penny on the coonter and turnt to rin.

'Haud on,' she said.

She fingert the penny and let it drap on the coonter, listenin for the ring. It was a guid ane, nearly new. She felt for it, foun it, and haundit me the whangs.

'What is it?'

I couldna speak. Her een didna alter, but she soundit gey bitter.

'Ye're gey blate[4] the day, Rab. Did ye think I wadna ken ye?'

Still I could say naething.

'Whan did ye stert usin whangs?'

'They're for my grandfaither.'

'Ay ay. Ye arena the first o the laddies to stop buyin sweeties.'

I backit and fell ower a pail. The cat lowpit doun aff the coonter and spat in my face again. I ran for the door.

I gied her shop the bye frae that day on, though whan my grandfaither drave me to Kirkfieldbank I couldna help but pass it, and ilka time I spied the winnock I grued[5] at the sicht o the cat.

It was aboot twa months efter, whan the strawberries were bye and the blae plooms were turnin ripe, that I drave wi my grandfaither to Lanark to the Cattle Show. On oor wey through Kirkfieldbank he lat me haud the reyns, sae I didna look roun muckle except mebbe to see if the folk were watchin me, but as we passed Mistress Yuill's I gied a keek for the cat, for I couldna get it oot o my mind. I lay wauken aw nicht, whiles, thinkin o it, and aye whaun I foun mysell alane in the daurk I could see the wee nerra slits o its glintin green een.

The cat wasna there, or if it was it couldna be seen, for the shop was shuttert.

'Is it the hauf day, grandfaither?'

'Na.'

'Mistress Yuill's shop's shut.'

'Ay.'

'Is she no weill?'

'That's richt.'

'What's wrang wi her?'

'Naething.'

'There maun be something wrang if she's no weill.'

'Ay, there's something.'

---

[1] Empty.
[2] Fool.
[3] Shoe-laces.
[4] Shy.
[5] Shuddered.

'What is it?'

'She's deid, but dinna speak aboot it.'

'What wey that?'

'Dinna heed. Keep yer ee on the horse or I'll hae to tak the reyns mysell.'

That was eneuch. I didna press him. But the neist day, whan I was doun at the fute o the bottom orchard haein a look at the blae plooms, I met my kizzen Jockie, and he telt me his wey o it.

Aboot a fortnicht syne Mistress Yuill had grown sae desperate that she had peyed a laddie to come in and help her. I kent the laddie weill, for his mither had poued strawberries at Linmill. She didna pey him muckle, Mistress Yuill, but aw he had to dae was soop the flair and redd things up, and watch that naebody gied her a penny for a hauf-croun. He ran errands, tae, but there couldna hae been mony, for up to that she had sent oot the messages by a laddie frae the schule, efter fower o'clock.

Noo this laddie, Will MacPherson was his name, had watchit Mistress Yuill, day in day oot, till he foun oot whaur she hid the till key. She didna tak it hame, for she had a son bidin wi' her, a deil for drink.

Then, ae daurk wat windy nicht, whan the Kirkfieldbank folk were sleepin, and there was nae soun bune the blatter o the wind and rain and the swish o Clyde watter, he had creepit roun to the shop back and sclimmed up on to a shed there. Frae the shed rufe he was able to wriggle up the sclaits o the shop itsell, and in the end he won to the skylicht abune the flair upstairs. There was a gey drap doun, but he maun hae managed it, for he foun the till key and filled his pooches wi siller, as muckle as there was, and syne wi cigarettes and sweeties, though hoo he could hae stamacked the sweeties I dinna ken. Then he tried to fin his wey oot.

The skylicht was ower heich to grip frae the flair, sae he stude a chair aneth it and sclimmed up on to that. Still he couldna grip it, it seems, and he sclimmed up on to the chair back. It fell whan he tried that, as ye wad hae thocht, but it maun hae served his turn, for he was able to pou himsell pairtly through. That was as faur as he gat, for to mak room for himsell he had putten the skylicht richt back on the sclaits, whaur it couldna be fastened.

The wind brocht it bash ower his heid.

The neist mornin Mistress Yuill gaed alang to the shop, and likely she missed him, and whether she gaed up the stair for something she keepit there, or whether she had second sicht like the lave o blin folk, naebody could say, but up the stair she gaed. She couldna hae seen the laddie, that was certain, sae she maun hae felt him wi her haunds.

He was hingin by the chin frae the skylicht, wi his airms stickin up oot through it.

She didna gang hame that nicht at her richt time, and her son didna bother, but a neibor that aye had her kettle beylin gat worrit, and gaed alang to the shop. The meenit she opened the door the cat flew at her. She gat aff wi a scart or twa and gaed for Galbraith, the polis. They had to throw a tattie bag ower it afore they could win in, and whan they gaed upstairs they foun Will MacPherson, wi Mistress Yuill on the flair at his feet. The shock had been ower muckle for her.

That was the story I heard frae my kizzen Jockie, but it wasna the trith. He hadna been telt richt himsell.

I gat the trith frae my faither, whan I was aulder, at Tam Baxter's funeral. Tam Baxter had been ane o the men to gang in wi Galbraith.

The laddie hadna filled his pooches wi siller at aw. He hadna haen the chance. Whan they had foun him hingin they had haurdly kent him. His claes were aw bluid and his face was like butcher-meat.

The cat had gaen for him the meenit he had landit on the flair.

J[ames] K. Annand (1908 – 1993)

Arctic Convoy

Intil the pit-mirk nicht we northwart sail
Facin the bleffarts and the gurly★ seas   angry
That ser' out muckle skaith★ to mortal men.   harm
Whummlin about like a waukrife★ feverit bairn   sleepless
The gude ship snowks★ the waters o a wave,   noses
Swithers, syne pokes her neb★ intil the air,   nose
Hings for a wee thing, dinnlin, on the crest,
And clatters in the trouch wi sic a dunt★   blow
As gey near rives the platin frae her ribs
And flypes the tripes o unsuspectin man.   10
Northwart, aye northwart, in the pit-mirk nicht.
A nirlin★ wind comes blawin frae the ice,   freezing
Plays dirdum★ throu the rails and shrouds and riggin,   havoc
Ruggin at bodies clawin at the life-lines.
There's sic a rowth★ o air that neb and lungs   mass
Juist canna cope wi sic a dirlin onding★.   on-coming
Caulder the air becomes, and snell★ the wind,   fierce
The waters, splairgin★ as she dunts her boo,   splattering
Blads★ in a blatter o hailstanes on the brig   pounds
And geals on guns and turrets, masts and spars,   20
Cleedin the iron and steel wi coat o ice.

Northwart, aye northwart, in the pit-mirk nicht.
The nirlin wind has gane, a lown★-ness comes;   calm
The lang slaw swall still minds us o the gale.
Restin aff-watch, a-sweein in our hammocks,
We watch our sleepin messmates' fozy★ braith   hoary
Transmogrify to ice upon the skin
That growes aye thicker on the ship-side plates.
Nae mair we hear the lipper o the water,
Only the dunsh o ice-floes scruntin by,   30
Floes that in the noonday gloamin licht
Are lily-leafs upon a lochan dubh★.   black
But nae bricht lily-flouer delytes the ee,
Nae divin bird diverts amang the leafs,
Nae sea-bird to convoy us on our gait.
In ilka deidlown airt smools★ Davy Jones,   glides
Ice-tangle marline spikes o fingers gleg★   quick
To claught the bodies o unwary sailors
And hike them doun to stap intil his kist★.   chest
Whiles 'Arctic reek' taks on the orra★ shapes   40   odd
O ghaistly ships-o-war athort our gait,
Garrin us rin ram-stam to action stations
Syne see them melt awa intil the air.
Owre lang this trauchle lasts throu seas o daith
Wi neer a sign o welcome at the port,
Nae 'Libertymen fall in!' to cheer our herts
But sullen sentries at the jetty-heid
And leesome lanesome waitin at our birth.

At length we turn about and sail for hame
Back throu rouch seas, throu ice and snaw and sleet,   50
Hirdin the draigelt remnants o our flock
Bieldin★ them weel frae skaith o enemie.   sheltering
But southwart noo we airt intil the licht
Leavin the perils o the Arctic nicht.

Purple Saxifrage

Aneath a hap★ of snaw it derns★   clothing/hides
Deep in a dwam★ for maist the year   dream, swoon
To burst throu in a bleeze o starns★   stars
Syne skail★ its flourish on the stour★.   scatter/dust

Gif I had ae short simmer o sang
Wi hauf the beauty o thon flouer
In the snaw o eild★ I'd hap my tongue   age
And haud my wheest★ for evermair.   silence

Hunter Diack (1908 – 1974)

The Croft

Sy Elrick worked this place for fifty year,
Sy and his wife Kirstin. Ye'll mind on Sy?
Six foot of bone and muscle and black beard,
A crooked leg his mare rolled over on,
And strings of oaths when one alone would do.
That weathered stone you scratched your match upon
To light your pipe – Sy's muscles set in there.
He made this dyke, where all along you see
Knuckles of braken thrust between the stones;
And, look, through all the land where Sy cropped oats   10
Bracken uncurls among the bloom of furze.

Down there Sy had his house. The gable stands,
And the stone cheese-press with the rusted screw –
Kirstin's strong arms could never twist it now –
She made grand cheese; at least you'd say she did
When you came in from giving Sy a hand.
Her flowering currant keeps its load of bloom –
Gardens she liked; go down there and you'll see
Primrose she planted, lupin-flowers,
And two-three berry bushes gone to wood –   20
Some were dug out to give that pylon room.

This was the place Sy worked for fifty year,
Sy and his wife Kirstin. – I'd have them back?
Well, no. They've lived their lives. Only I'd like –
When he saw land that he'd left in good heart
Smothered in bracken, and his house roof-fallen,
A pylon set in Kirstin's plot of ground –
I'd like to hear, what I have missed at times,
The black oaths that would rumble through Sy's beard.

Trawler

Curious to call this boat *Ulysses*,
But there it was – the rusty hulk,
And mess of scaly fishing-nets on deck
All tangled up like sea-weed, and the chains
Half-gnawed by the wet tooth of sea air,
The donkey engine coughing as she strained
Her iron heart against the bollard ropes
And slewed the boat towards the harbour mouth.

The siren rolled the echoes up the town
Shaking a fist at sun that would not stir   10
From warm side of his wet grey blanket,
Scaring the gull on wheelhouse, as the shouts
Of Vikings scared them from the beaked prows
Of long-boats in the days when steam was free
As clouds or wandering sea-winds . . .

               Now she bent
Her steam-chest energies to the outward thrust
And even with swan-like motion drove her way
Past the *Junge Jorge* in from Rotterdam
And Chian *Thermopylae* with her name   20
Lettered in Greek upon her heavy bows,
And a trim, white motor-boat from the Puddefiord.

She did not traipse the seas, the *Ulysses*,
Yet she had shot her nets on Dogger Bank
And trawled the dawn up from a heavy sea
Beyond Thorshavn in the Faroe Isles.

Soon, twisting water to a pole of force,
She pushed the land into the back horizon,
Where the Cairngorms grind their stumps of teeth
Pulp-wards upon the stubborn bone of weather.   30

Three days she drove about the northern grounds
Trailing her tarry fingers in the sea,
While patient winds rode high above the world
Shooting by day their white cloud-nets to catch,
When darkness came, the bright shoals of the stars,
And for three days and nights the hardened crew

Toiled at the nets between snatched food and rest,
Joking at times – for the catch was good –
And thinking silently what they would do
When they came back to port on Saturday: 40
Celtic they'd see play Aberdeen, and then
With wife to pictures or with girl to dance,
But first of all since salt brings thirst to men
They'd wet their whistles in the Wallace Tower
Where laughter breezes over tankards foaming –
All that they thought to do, yet never did.

Massed the storm-squadrons, and swift blades of wind
Leapt from the icy scabbard of the north;
Sword-blade or whip-thong flayed the sleek sea-skin,
Gouged out dark troughs, raised livid weals of foam,   50
And hail stones spat with bite and sting of fire.
Down in the spoke-hole arms of muscled steel
Teased into fury the red reeling coals
And forced the fevered needle to the danger line
While the screw lashed in onward-thrusting gyres.

Six hours she rode the anger of the waves,
Running for shelter; then a hatch was smashed
And the shipped water poured into the hold
Turning her fires into useless steam, while night
More furious still came swallowing sea and sky   60
And deadlier heaved the bludgeons of the waves.

So when the sun again with sinewed light
Drove towards the west the shadow of the earth,
He flicked with light the tossing spars of wood;
Then quietly went to seek those valleys out
Where men tend flocks behind the western hills.

And yet on Saturday the home team won,
Bright laughter splashed about the Wallace Tower,
Screen-shadows told their tales of high romance,
And in the dance-hall by the silent wharf   70
Gay couples wheeled in the old dance of life.

Kathleen Raine (1908 –)

Born in London, with roots in Northumberland, Scottish on her mother's side, Kathleen Raine is usually considered an English poet, but she has maintained a number of Scottish connections and, as the following attest, a frequently Scottish flavour. Also, she tends to identify her mother, and thus her Scottishness, with her own poetic, natural or mythic side. Lyric, intellectual, often philosophical, sometimes feminist, hers is a remarkable talent.

Bheinn Noamh

To Mary and John-Donald Macleod

1 SUN

Sun
Flashed from blades of salix of chitin of stone
Quiver of light on heather on hill on wings
Trembling makes one dazzling noon
Mirrored in rings of light that pulse in the burn
Glowing in eyes, throbbing in dust
Of butterflies dark as peat-pool brown
Endured in nerve, in ganglion in vein,
Budding of wings, leafing of lives
Myriadfold poised fragile on dark world lit with sight   10
Streaming undimmed, we suffer your joy
Poured down, down on in dark pools under
Overshadow of alder in undoing water.

2 GOLDEN FLOWERS

I have travelled so fast that I have come to the waterfall of Sgriol:
Curtain of mist, of netted leaves, inviolate leafy vale,
Fragrant veil of green-gold birch and song of the green-gold linnet
A shadow withdrawn I enter for ever the sun-filled gloaming of Sgriol.

Light you have travelled so far out of the boundless void
From beyond the Isle of Skye over the sound of Sleat
You have laid a path of wonder over the bright sea   20
And touched with your finger the golden summit of Sgriol.

Water you have gathered in mist high over ben Sgriol,
So fast your drifting curtain of rain has fallen
That the noise of the sun-brown burn is filling the glen of Sgriol.

Seed you have grown so fast from the mould of the dead
You have unfolded a hundred flowers with golden petals,
The hundred-petalled golden flowers are filled with light
And leaves are moist with the life-giving waters of the burn of Sgriol.

Oh sun and water and green-gold flowers, I was here and now in the glen of Sgriol.

Light how fast you have travelled on into the abyss   30
And into ocean the burn that played in the sunlit fern of Sgriol.

Seed of miraculous flowers lies cold in the bog,
Sun sets in the beautiful land of the dead beyond the Isle of Skye.

3 THE LOCH

High, high and still
Pale water mirrors
Thin air and still the high
Summit at rest in white
Water-spaces empty as thought.
The reeds wait
For ripple to trouble   40
Unsleeping gaze.
Nothing below it knows
But gathers the waters
That overflow
From the brim of reflection
Not all falls,
Soul remains
High and lonely
While blood runs
Down by the easy   50
Ways of sorrow.

4 THE SUMMIT

Farther than I have been
All is changed: no water for moist souls,
Wind and stone is the world of the summit, stone and rain,
Stone wind and cold, only the oldest things remain,
And wind unceasing has blown,
Without beginning or ending the wind has blown.

Noise of wind on rock cries to the soul 'Away,
Away, what wilt thou do?' The butterfly

Blown up against the summit meets the snow.   60
Those who rise there endure
Dragon of stone and dragon of air; by wind irresistible
Hurled, or still as stone, the long way
A dream while the wing of a bird
Brushes a grain of quartz from the unmoved hill.

5 MAN

Man on the mountain listens to star and stone:
Memory of earth and heaven
Lies open on the hill; sun moon and blood tell all.
The lonely voice that cried in the beginning
Calls in the belling of deer
And over the frozen lock unearthly music of the swan.   70
Thoughts of the dead are never silent
By the green mounds where houses stood,
Love and sorrow to come makes the air tremble.
Close as heartbeat is the word of the mountain,
Unsleeping the sky whose sight embraces all.

Heirloom

She gave me childhood's flowers,
Heather and wild thyme,
Eyebright and tormentil,
Lichen's mealy cup
Dry on wind-scored stone,
The corbies on the rock,
The rowan by the burn.

Sea-marvels a child beheld
Out in the fisherman's boat,
Fringed pulsing violet   10
Medusa, sea-gooseberries,
Starfish on the sea-floor,
Cowries and rainbow-shells
From pools on a rocky shore,

Gave me her memories,
But kept her last treasure:
'When I was a lass,' she said,
'Sitting among the heather,
Suddenly I saw
That all the moor was alive!   20
I have told no one before.'

That was my mother's tale.
Seventy years had gone
Since she saw the living skein
Of which the world is woven,
And having seen, knew all;
Through long indifferent years
Treasuring the priceless pearl.

The Return

I have come back to ancient shores where it is always now.
The beautiful troubled waters breaking over the skerry
On the wind in spindrift blown like lifting hair,
Clouds gathering over the summits of Rhum in the clear blue
Are as they were
When long ago I went my way in sorrow.
Time, measure of absence, is not here –
In the wide present of the sky
Fleet the broadcast light is already returning, while we,
Who tell the hours and days by the beat of a heart   10
Can only depart
After a vanishing radiance dragging mortal feet.
But joy outspeeds light's wheel, the moments in their flight
Stays, here where in patterned strands the weed holds fast to the shore,
Falls and lifts from ebb to flow
Of the unceasing tide that makes all things new,
And the curlew with immortal voices cry.

Eileann Chanaidh

To Margaret and John Lorne Campbell of Canna

1 THE ANCIENT SPEECH
A Gaelic bard they praise who in fourteen adjectives
Named the one indivisible soul of his glen;
For what are the bens and the glens but manifold qualities,
Immeasurable complexities of soul?
What are these isles but a song sung by island voices?
The herdsman sings ancestral memories
And the song makes the singer wise,
But only while he sings
Songs that were old when the old themselves were young,
Songs of these hills only, and of no isles but these.   10
For other hills and isles this language has no words.

The mountains are like manna, for one day given,
To each his own:
Strangers have crossed the sound, but not the sound of the dark oarsmen
Or the golden-haired sons of kings,
Strangers whose thought is not formed to the cadence of waves,
Rhythm of the sickle, oar and milking-pail,
Whose words make loved things strange and small,
Emptied of all that made them heart-felt or bright.

Our words keep no faith with the soul of the world.   20

2 HIGHLAND GRAVEYARD
Today a fine old face has gone under the soil;
For generations past women hereabouts have borne
Her same name and stamp of feature.
Her brief identity was not her own
But theirs who formed and sent her out
To wear the proud bones of her clan, and live its story,
Who now receive back into the ground
Worn features of ancestral mould.

A dry-stone wall bounds off the dislimned clay
Of many an old face forgotten and young face gone   30
From boundless nature, sea and sky.
A wind-withered escalonia like a song
Of ancient tenderness lives on
Some woman's living fingers set as shelter for the dead, to tell
In evergreen unwritten leaves,
In scent of leaves in western rain
That one remembered who is herself forgotten.

Many songs they knew who now are silent.
Into their memories the dead are gone
Who haunt the living in an ancient tongue   40
Sung by old voices to the young,
Telling of sea and isles, of boat and byre and glen;
And from their music the living are reborn

Into a remembered land,
To call ancestral memories home
And all that ancient grief and love our own.

3 THE ISLAND CROSS

Memories few and deep-grained
Simple and certain mark this Celtic stone
Cross eroded by wind and rain.
All but effaced the riding men, the strange beast,   50
Yet clear in their signature the ancient soul
Where these were native as to their hunting-hill.

Against grain of granite
Hardness of crystalline rock-form mineral
Form spiritual is countergrained, against nature traced
Man's memories of Paradise and hope of Heaven.
More complex than Patrick's emblem green trifoliate
Patterning the tree soul's windings interlace
Intricate without end its labyrinth.

Their features wind-worn and rain-wasted the man and woman
Stand, their rude mere selves   61
Exposed to the summers and winters of a thousand years.
The god on the cross is man of the same rude race,
By the same hand made from the enduring stone;
And all the winds and waves have not effaced
The vision by Adam seen, those forms of wisdom
From memory of mankind ineffaceable.

4 NAMELESS ISLETS

Who dreams these isles,
Image bright in eyes
Of sea-birds circling rocky shores   70
Where waves beat upon rock, or rock-face smiles
Winter and summer, storm and fair?
In eyes of eider clear under ever-moving ripples the dart and tremor of life;
Bent-grass and wind-dried heather is a curlew's thought,
Gull gazes into being white and shell-strewn sands.

Joy harsh and strange traced in the dawn
A faint and far mirage; to souls archaic and cold
Sun-warmed stones and fish-giving sea were mother stern,
Stone omphalos, birth-caves dark, lost beyond recall.
Home is an image written in the soul,   80
To each its own: the new-born home to a memory,

Bird-souls, sea-souls, and with them bring anew
The isles that formed the souls, and souls the isles
Are ever building, shell by painted shell
And stone by glittering stone.
The isles are at rest in vision secret and wild,
And high the cliffs in eagle heart exult,
And warm the brown sea-wrack to the seals,
And lichened rocks grey in the buzzard's eye.

5 STONE ON HIGH CRAG

Still stone   90
In heart of hill
Here alone
Hoodie and buzzard
By ways of air
Circling come.
From far shine
On wind-worn pinnacle
Star and moon
And sun, sun,
Wings bright in sun   100
Turn and return.

Centre of wing-spanned
Wheeling ways
Older than menhir
Lichen-roughened
Granite-grained
Rock-red
Rain-pocketed
Wind-buffeted
Heat-holding   110
Bird-whitened
Beak-worn
Insect-labyrinthine
Turf-embedded
Night-during
Race-remembered
Stands the known.

6 SHADOW

Because I see these mountains they are brought low,
Because I drink these waters they are bitter,
Because I tread these black rocks they are barren,   120
Because I have found these islands they are lost;
Upon seal and seabird dreaming their innocent world
My shadow has fallen.

Seen from the Window of a Railway-Carriage

They arise, approach, majestic shapes, their aspects change, and pass,
Each mountain a memory the slow hills rise,
Pure forms of light, divine body in repose,
In frowning stone of northern corries rifts of snow,
Summits of peace of the alone with the alone
Approach majestic, turn in grandeur, slowly go.

Green bosom of the hills my childhood knew,
Grass of Parnassus, golden asphodel –
But I cannot leave the speeding train that carries me on
Into an older land where memories not mine   10
Of ancestors long dead lift to their hills mine eyes
As they approach majestic, turn in grandeur, change and pass.

My mother a life far other than Scotland's songs and stories tell
Lived in an alien place among trivial things
Disdaining to behold what was not of the dream
Of tenderness and pride her ancestors lived by
Till the misty shapes grew dim in memory
That now again in grandeur in their abiding places rise.

I would give back to the host whose lost world I inherit
Rising from shrouded hearts, their longed-for land,   20
To my mother her girlhood's high heather moor,
To hers, the ferny linn*, to my grandfather his salmon-river,   waterfall
The substance of their dream, the wanting of their woe
Whose multitude in me clamours for their own
Ancestral hills that turn majestic their sunlit faces of enduring stone.

On an Ancient Isle

So like, they seem the same,
The young shoots of the yellow iris sheathed leaf through leaf,
Lit green of glittering blades and shadows quivering on the sanded turf
Where limpet shells are strewn among the celandine
And driftwood from the surf.
So like they seem, almost I to my own memories had come home.
Never green leaf nor golden flower again;
Yet from the one immaculate root spring after spring
Upon this farthest Western shore the one Paradise,
Earth sea and sky patterned with the one dream,   10
Traced on the wild that legendary land
More ancient than song or story or carved stone
My mother and her mother's mother knew: the green ways,
Clear wells, stones of power, presences
In hoodie's shape, high distant summits, hosts in the wind.
Signs in a language more heartfelt than holy book, or rune,
Each hill and hollow, each moving wing or shadow, means.
'Memory pours through the womb and lives in the air,'
And childhood with new eyes sees the for ever known:
The words by heart, we live the story as we will.   20

As I came over the hill to an unvisited shore
I seemed, though old, at the untold beginning of a familiar tale.

George Bruce (1909 –)

Like many poets, Bruce has been somewhat pigeon-holed by his first productions. *Sea Talk*, published in 1944, was a remarkable collection of spare, chiselled verses about the rugged coastal area of North-east Scotland. Though a prolific author who has lived long and written much since, he is still seen as the poet of cliffs and seascapes. He has not written extensively in Scots (though he has some Scots poems), nor connected himself with the MacDiarmid group of poets. Thus he has seemed at times out of the main stream. Nonetheless, George Bruce is one of Scotland's finest modern poets, a true craftsman whose understated style disguises art of a high order. Bruce has been a producer with the BBC, a critic, and one of the first creative-writing teachers in Scotland.

My House

My house
Is granite
It fronts
North,

Where the Firth flows,
East the sea.
My room
Holds the first

Blow from the North,
The first from the East,   10
Salt upon
The pane.

In the dark
I, a child,
Did not know
The consuming night

And heard
The wind,
Unworried and
Warm – secure.   20

Inheritance

This which I write now
Was written years ago
Before my birth
In the features of my father.

It was stamped
In the rock formations
West of my home town.
Not I write,

But, perhaps, William Bruce,
Cooper.   10
Perhaps here his hand
Well articled in his trade.

Then though my words
Hit out
An ebullition from   eruption
City or flower,

There not my faith,
These the paint
Smeared upon
The inarticulate,   20

The salt-crusted sea-boot,
The red-eyed mackerel,
The plate shining with herring,
And many men,

Seamen and craftsmen and curers,
And behind them
The protest of hundreds of years,
The sea obstinate against the land.

Kinnaird Head

I go North to cold, to home, to Kinnaird,
Fit monument for our time.

This is the outermost edge of Buchan.
Inland the sea birds range,
The tree's leaf has salt upon it,
The tree turns to the low stone wall.
And here a promontory rises towards Norway.
Irregular to the top of thin grey grass
Where the spindrift in storm lays it beads.
The water plugs in the cliff sides,   10
The gull cries from the clouds
This is the consummation of the plain.

O impregnable and very ancient rock,
Rejecting the violence of water,
Ignoring its accumulations and strategy,
You yield to history nothing.

The Fisherman

As he comes from one of those small houses
Set within the curve of the low cliff
For a moment he pauses
Foot on step at the low lintel
Before fronting wind and sun.
He carries out from within something of the dark
Concealed by heavy curtain,
Or held within the ship under hatches.

Yet with what assurance
The compact body moves,   10
Head pressed to wind,
His being at an angle
As to anticipate the lurch of earth.

Who is he to contain night
And still walk stubborn
Holding the ground with light feet
And with a careless gait?

Perhaps a cataract of light floods,
Perhaps the apostolic flame.
Whatever it may be   20
The road takes him from us.
Now the pier is his, now the tide.

Tom Alone on the Beach

With bent back, world's curve on it
I brood over my pretty pool
And hunt the pale, flat, sand-coloured
Fish, with cupped hands, in the cold.

Ah, but my warm heart, with hope
Wrapped in it in the bright afternoon
Feet glittering in the sand,
Eyes on my pale prey, was sure.

Suns have passed, suns have passed,
Skies purple now above the thin sand.   10
With bent back brooding on the round
World, over my shoulder

I feel the touch of future
In the cold. The little fish
Come not near me, cleaving
To their element and flattening on the sand.

How many years since with sure heart
And prophecy of success
Warmed in it
Did I look with delight on the little fish,   20

Start with happiness, the warm sun on me?
Now the waters spread horizonwards,
Great skies meet them,
I brood upon incompleted tasks.

Houses

1 Suddenly our house went up in the air.
The slates, rafters, chimneypots, masonry
burst out like a gust of starlings
and stopped 30 feet up.
They then decided to come down again.

That was 1941.
I believed my mother was inside.

2 In Edinburgh houses come down.
Without giving notice the cement balcony
of a council tenement left its assigned   10
position
and made a new map on the pavement.

3 Our house is different; it is very old
it creaks a bit in the wind,
is water-tight now and then,
comfortable for mice with good runways:
it should do my time.

Reflections at Sixty

Thunder knocks about the house,
tries doors and windows.
Night. I listen in bed.

Somewhere around
there's a birth going on
that concerns me.

At Bridlington Spa
my wax mustachioed purple uncle
used to sway in the salted breeze.

'Give it up,' he said,   10
'All this bother about meaning.
Douse lights and out.'

Old Man and Sea

Nightfall – was it still out there?

The rusty, white iron gate trembled
as it opened to the path to the sea
down by the ramblers, unseen,
no scent, for the salt had taken over.
With all my fearing childhood in it
I hear it growling in the dark. Ahead
from where the marram grass meets sand,
between me and the slapping water – a figure:
he stands square-shouldered staring   10
into that nothing.
              How many mornings
when the silvered horizon promised,
giving hope for that day
or when the mist stood impenetrable,
or when the sky burst and the sea met it,
I thought, he waited, thought I knew him,
might approach, touch him, claim him for kin,
he who stood his ground for us all,
but there is no reckoning in this matter.
Square-shouldered I stood looking into that nothing.   20

Sea Men

I
'God in the wave!' Joe bawled as it rose
and shut out the sky. How! How? –
when the swing took the boat to his death.
No words in that waste. Black she foundered.
The Lily, her curt moment stretched out in
wind-wail, sea-moan and a wrecked moon.
The cliff house waits in the long dark;
nothing given away about the life,
that must have been, must be there
still in the dark that moved   10
while the wind blurted about
the stone corners that stood on stone.
Inside the place awaiting return
her world stops, blazes and cries.

II
Spewed out of the sea we crawled in the dark.
Hung nets enmeshed, creosote in cans, tarred
ropes coiled – we smelled our way like animals.
At dawn we struggled to the door and saw
the long, low light greying the horizon.
Salt tingled our eyes to life. Our soft   20

bodies felt again the rocks that bled us.
Set this down in a hand that shakes.
Each knowledge requires respect –
Smell tar, creosote, wood and salt air.

Honeysuckle

Honeysuckle grew at the back door
of the house sheltered from the salt
wind by the granite wall. Girls came
to kiss there by the washing green
and the honeysuckle blossoming
while the sky was falling into night.

Under an impeccable noon sky
father left by the front door,
shoes shining, moustache bristling,
navy suit without a spot,   10
to do business, with a view to
profit, to keep the house upright.

At the back door the stars
reeled about in a purple sky,
drunk on honeysuckle dew.
Into a night of small noises,
voices one to another – lovers.
The back door squeaks shut.

Sea-Town Genesis

This orb – a sea moon –
was the brazen gong
that hurled our young
to love on the sandhills
that faced the sea:
on the lea side
the wind sifts the sand
between the iron railings
that enclose the flat
tombs of their fathers.   10

G. B. on the Rocks

The facts of time sit on my balding head,
while the permutations of water affront the rock,
water day and night on it. Speculation will not
alter its longevity, nor mine. I consult my drying skin.
Curious that in these circumstances we sing,
while fate drowns the precious young,
trips up old friends, damages the innocent.

Boy and Cod's Head

The grammar lesson. Macbeth as specimen.
'There is no speculation in those eyes.'
The line jumps from the page: gets lost.
Lines are for peerie fish, podlies, codlins.
Macbeth – a play. I play football. Sand blows
through the grasses of the football pitch
by the sea, the cemetery on the other side.
The fog settles down – sea smell, sea sound.
On the spit of sand, bleached white, a skull,
rabbit's, sand sifting through the cavities,   10
the bone structure a palace for life once,
where the dance began, the leap, the twist,
the scuttle to be safe, now safe in sea's cycle
with thin fan shells, buckies, whorls,
and the pink dried back shuffled off the crab.
At my feet a cod's head chopped off
its fish body, cast overboard, spewed out
with guts, entrails blood, reject of man
and sea, a violation of nature.
'There is no speculation in those eyes.'   20

Elizabeth Polishing an Agate

My love, you are pulled into a stone.
The skies run into night,
The stone stars are there.
In this lost momentary world
you treasure stone under your hand,
seek out what is most unlike,
smoothing stone like glass
till its fixed hair lines,
finer than Leonardo's line,
mirror stone's permanence.   10
There are no seasons in a stone.
Lode star it draws you,
you giving your brief warmth
to stone.
Gone, it stays cold.

Odd Goings-on in Dunfermline Toun

In yon gusty toun on the slope, folk
slip aff it, disappear,
gang in an oot o' doors
fast, like in auld films,
uphill thin man roon corner,
doonhill fat man intae shop,
lassies intae trees,
auld men intae ruins,
rinnin boys intae the grun,
auld wife gangs heilster gowdie   10
wi a puckle leaves,
is blawn richt ower the kirk steeple.
John Bell walks straucht through
the shut gates o' Pittendreigh Park,
never heard tell again an naebody speirs why?

Scots Bard

He wis taakin his breeks aff
when the thocht cam
in til's heid he
wad scrieve
a beeootiful pome

in English o' coorse.

Craftsman

His being is at the pace
given by stone, wood, clay
to wrists, hands and fingers,
nor may be moved from this.

The world blazes and cries,
is shattered. He puts his hand
on clay, stone, wood,
or writes words to stay,

while the stone stars stay.

Laotian Peasant Shot

He ran in the living air,
exultation in his heels.

a gust of wind will erect
a twisting tower of dried leaves
that will collapse when
the breath is withdrawn.

He turned momentarily,
his eyes looking into his fear,
seeking himself.

When he fell the dust   10
hung in the air
like an empty container
of him.

Olive Fraser (1909 – 1977)

A Gossip Silenced
The Thrush and the Eagle

'I keep the machair★ where   coastal land
The burnies gae.'
'I keep the mountain, bare
O' a' but snae.'

'I see the rush steikin'★   piercing
My bonny nest.'
'I see the ray seekin'
The amethyst.'

'I have a muckle pea
Inside my crap.'   10
'I hae two maukins★ wi'   maggots
A grouse on tap.'

'I hear the worms below
The mole's bings★.'   buildings
'I hear the whisprin' o'
The aungels' wings.'

'I sit wi' merles a' day,
An' crack★, an' a'.'   chat
'I sit wi' cloods and say
Naethin' ava.'   20

'I coont the lasses in
The simmer leas.'
'I ken the Lord coontin'
The centuries.'

Benighted in the Foothills of the Cairngorms: January

Cauld, cauld is Alnack . . .
Cauld is the snaw wind and sweet.
The maukin o' Creagan Alnack
Has snaw for meat.

Nae fit gangs ayont* Caiplich   beyond
Nae herd in the cranreuch* bricht.   hoarfrost
The troot* o' the water o' Caiplich   trout
Dwells deep the nicht.

On a' the screes, by ilk cairn
In the silence nae grouse is heard,   10
But the eagle abune Geal Charn
Hings like a swerd.

Yon's nae wife's hoose ayont A'an
In the green lift* ava   sky
Yon's the cauld lums* o' Ben A'an   chimneys
Wha's smeek* is sna.   latch

A' the lang mountains are silent
Alane doth wild Alnack sing.
The hern, the curlew are silent.
Silent a' thing.   20

Requiem for Dives

Sae routh*, routh was your table   rich, plentiful
Ahint* its yallow blinds.   behind
Your guests in gowd and sable
Ne'er saw the lyart* wynds,   grey

Where your bairn watched hungert and nameless.
The sna' o' winter skies
Wither your sawle that, hameless,
Glowers into Paradise.

'Robert Garioch' (Robert Garioch Sutherland, 1909 – 1981)

One of the most respected Scots poets of his time, Garioch is perhaps best known for his satiric view of Edinburgh life and of our modern age generally, especially as expressed in the famous 'Embro to the Ploy'. As an urban satirist in Scots he was much influenced by the great 18th-century Edinburgh poet Robert Fergusson, a debt he readily acknowledged. However, Garioch, who was a prisoner of war from 1942–1945, may have left as his finest memorial his harrowing account of that imprisonment, 'The Wire', and his most stringent comment upon modern society the symbolic inference therefrom.

At Robert Fergusson's Grave, October 1962

Canogait kirkyaird in the failing year
is auld and grey, the wee roseirs* are bare,   rose bushes
five gulls leam* white agen the dirty air: gleam
why are they here? There's naething for them here.

Why are we here coursels? We gaither near
the grave. Fergusons mainly, quite a fair
turn-out, respectfu, ill at ease, we stare
at daith – there's an address – I canna hear.

Aweill, we staund bareheidit in the haar*,   mist
murning a man that gaed back til the pool   10
twa hunner-year afore our time. The glaur*   mud

that haps* his banes glowres back. Strang present dool* clothes/dole
ruggs at my hairt. Lichtlie* this gin* ye daur: scorn/if
here Robert Burns knelt and kissed the mool*.   mold (earth)

Elegy

They are lang deid, folk that I used to ken,
their firm-set lips aa mowdert and agley,
sherp-tempert een rusting amang the cley:
they are baith deid, thae wycelife, bienlie* men,   snug

heidmaisters, that had been in poure for ten
or twenty year afore fate's taiglie* wey   entangling
brocht me, a young, weill-harnit*, blate* and fey smart/shy
new-fledgit dominie, intill their den.

Ane tellt me it was time I learnt to write,
roun-haun, he meant, and saw about my hair: 10
I mind of him, beld-heidit, wi a kyte*.   paunch

Ane sneerit quarterly (I cudna square
my saving-bank) and sniftert in his spite.
Weill, gin they arena deid, it's time they were.

Embro to the Ploy[1]

In simmer, whan aa sorts foregether
in Embro to the ploy,
folk seek out friens to hae a blether,
or faes they'd fain annoy;
smorit wi British Railways' reek
frae Glasca or Glen Roy
or Wick, they come to hae a week
of cultivated joy
          or three,
in Embro to the ploy.   10

Americans wi routh★ of dollars,   heaps
wha drink our whisky neat,
wi Susunachs★ and Oxford Scholars   English
are eydent★ for the treat   eager
of music sedulously high-tie
at thirty-bob a seat;
Wop opera performed in Eyetie
to them's richt up their street,
          they say,
in Embro to the ploy.   20

Furthgangan Embro folk come hame
for three weeks in the year,
and find Auld Reekie no the same,
fu sturrit in a steir★.   storm, confusion
The stane-faced biggins★ whaur they froze   buildings
and suppit puirshous★ lear★   poorhouse/learning
of cultural cauld-kale★ and brose   cabbage soup
see cantraips★ unco queer   tricks
          thae days
in Embro to the ploy.   30

The tartan tred wad gar★ ye lauch;   make
nae problem is owre teuch.
Your surname needna end in -och;
they'll cleik★ ye up the cleuch★.   lead/rock
a puckle★ dollar bills will aye   few
preive Hiram Teufelsdrockh
a septary of Clan McKay,
it's maybe richt eneuch,
          verfluch!
in Embro to the ploy.   40

The auld High Schule, whaur monie a skelp
of triple-tonguit tawse★   strap
has gien a heist-up and a help
towards Doctorates of Laws,

---

[1] The world-famous Edinburgh Festival, held usually for three weeks in August. It is an international showcase for music and drama.

nou hears, for Ramsay's cantie★ rhyme,   merry
loud pawmies★ of applause   palm-blows
frae fok that pey a pund a time
to sit on wudden raws
                                                gey hard
in Embro to the ploy.   50

The haly kirk's Assembly-haa
nou fairly coups★ the creel   upsets
wi Lindsay's Three Estaitis, braw
devices of the Deil.
About our heids the satire stots
like hailstanes till we reel;
the bawrs★ are in auld-farrant★ Scots,   jokes/old fashioned
it's maybe jist as weill,
                                          imphm,
in Embro to the ploy.   60

The Epworth Haa wi wonder did
behold a pipers' bicker;
wi *hadarid* and *hindarid*
the air gat thick and thicker.
Cumha na Cloinna pleyed on strings
torments a piper quicker
to get his dander up, by jings,
than thirty u.p. liquor,
                                     hooch aye!
in Embro to the ploy.   70

The Northern British Embro Whigs
that stayed in Charlotte Square,
they fairly wad hae tined★ their wigs   lost
to see the Stuarts there,
the bleeding Earl of Moray and aa
weill-pentit and gey bare;
Our Queen and Princess, buskit★ braw,   dressed
enjoyed the hale affair
                                   (see Press)
in Embro to the ploy.   80

Whan day's anomalies are cled
in decent shades of nicht,
the Castle is transmogrified
by braw electric licht.
The toure that bields★ the Bruce's croun   shelters
presents an unco sicht
mair sib to Wardour Street[1] nor Scone,
wae's me for Scotland's micht,
                                     says I
in Embro to the ploy.   90

---

[1] A somewhat raffish entertainment district in London.

A happening, incident, or splore
affrontit them that saw
a thing they'd never seen afore –
in the McEwan Haa:
a lassie in a wheelie-chair
wi naething on at aa;
jist like my luck! I wasna there,
it's no the thing ava,
                          tut-tut,
in Embro to the ploy.   100

The Cafe Royal and Abbotsford
are filled wi orra★ folk   strange
whas stock-in-trade's the scrievit word,
or twicet-scrievit joke.
Brains, weak or strang, in heavy beer,
or ordinary, soak.
Quo yin: This yill is aafie★ dear,   awful
I hae nae clinks in poke,
                          nor fauldan-money,
in Embro to the ploy.   110

The auld Assembly-rooms, whaur Scott
foregethert wi his fiers★,   brothers, peers
nou see a gey kenspeckle★ lot   famous
ablow the chandeliers.
Til Embro drouths★ the Festival Club   thirsts
a richt godsend appears;
it's something new to find a pub
that gaes on serving beers
                          eftir hours
in Embro to the ploy.   120

Jist pitten-out the drucken mobs
frae howffs in Potterraw,
fleean, to hob-nob wi the Nobs,
ran to this Music Haa,
Register Rachel, Cougait Kate,
nae-neb Nellie and aa
stauchert★ about amang the Great,   stumbled
what fun! I never saw
                          the like,
in Embro to the ploy.   130

They todle hame doun lit-up streets
filled wi synthetic joy;
aweill, the year brings few sic treats
and muckle to annoy.
There's monie hartsom braw high-jinks
mixed up in this alloy
in simmer, whan aa sorts foregether
in Embro to the ploy.

Yes, Yes, I Know Him, That Lean Fellow

The author's Scots version of this poem follows.

Yes, yes, I know him, that lean fellow,
but not the working, only the answer.
By God, an honest man. How I dislike
that leathery chamelion face.
I like a man with some expression about him,
somebody I can trust, of medium honesty,
whose mind works by knowable processes,
not this clicking perfection of a man
without a middle to his syllogism.
Lachie of Edenshaugh was such a one;   10
I read him 'like a book,' he talked me out
of fifty pounds before I broke with him.
I liked his brosy face, the expression of his moustache,
we were rare friends,
I am so much the better for knowing him.
But this gaunt granite man who does me favours
for no reason that I can ever discover,
this inexplicable honest man,
how can I get rid of his company?

Aye, Aye, A Ken Him, Thon Jimp Cratur

Aye, aye, A ken him, thon jimp cratur,
but no the workin, jist the answer.
By gode! a decent man. Hoo he scunners me!
Thon chameleon mou!
I like a chiel wi a legible physnomy,
yin A can trust, o medium honesty,
whaes mind warks bi kennable processes,
no this clickin perfection o a man
withoot a middle tae his syllogism.
Lachie o Edenhaugh was sik a yin.   10
I read him 'like a buik,' he did me oot
o fifty pun or A fell oot wi him.
I liked his brosy face, the expression o his whiskers,
we were graund cronies,
A'm that muckle better o kennin him.
But yon dour granite man whaw does me favours
fir nae reason that A ken o,
yon inexplicable honest man,
Yech, bit A'd fain be rid o him!

To Robert Fergusson

Fergusson, tho twa-hunder year
awa, your image is mair clear
nor monie things that nou appear
in braid daylicht.
What gars perspective turn sae queer?
What ails my sicht?

Pairtlie, nae dout, because your een
gey★ clearlie saw the Embro scene   very
in times when Embro was a quean
sae weill worth seein   10
that life wi her still had a wheen★   few
guid things worth preein.

A hameil★, Scottish place eneuch   homely
whas life was steiran★, het and reuch   stirring
whilst yet the fairmer wi his pleuch
turned owre the sod
whar classie Queen Street and Drumsheugh
nou stand sae snod★.   proper

But what a pairtner for your life!
Gey like a weill-bred, cantie★ wife   20   cheerful
wha wears an apron, no cauldrife
Wi fause gentilitie,
wi mind keen-edgit as a knife,
used wi civility.

In ae gret tenement or land,
a muckle rubble biggin★, planned   building
to hain★ grund-rent, folk wad be fand   save
aa mixter-maxter —
lordies and lawyers, no owre grand
to ken a baxter★   30   baker

or Ramsay wi his curlin-tangs,
guid makar baith of wigs and sangs,
or, Fergusson, yoursel; sae lang's
ye werena blate★,   shy
they were your friens, whatever bangs
were sair'd by fate.

Altho to tred a lawyer's hack
peyed by the bodle or the plack
for scrievin till your wrist wad crack,
baith ear and late,   40
yet of guid friens ye had nae lack
in ilk estait.

The 'Cape's'[1] self-knichted cavaliers
'Sir Scrape-Greystiel' and siclike fiers,
they waled★ ye weill abune their peers   *chose*
for cannie capers
whan ye'd got throu, wi nae arrears,
your stent of papers.

Hou gleglie★ they'd kick owre the traces   *quickly*
in the Daft Days[2] or at Leith Races,   50
wi trips to Fife or siccan places
to stech★ their leisor   *cram*
wi drouthie★ ploys, while plookie faces   *drunken*
birslit★ wi pleisor.   *warmed*

And what a knack ye had of scrievin
in caller★ verse yon rowth★ of levin,   *fresh/abundance*
your wee stane warld, fechtin, thievin,
drinkin and swinkin,
wi muckle fun and puckle grievin
and fowth★ of thinkin.   60   *plenty*

In praise of Wilkie ye declared
his verses wad be aye revered
while slaw-gaun owsen turned the swaird;
nou ither factors
hae shown the doctor gey ill-sair'd –
we dae't wi tractors.

But this I'll say: while there's a still
in Scotland, or a pint of yill,
houever washie, fit to swill
atween the tide   70
at Leith Port and the Blackford Hill,
your fame sall byde.

Whan Daith raxed★ out his airm and cleikit   *reached*
Ramsay, folk thocht the yett★ was steekit★,   *gate/shut*
yet sune your makar's burgess-ticket
gied ye the freedom
of Scottish verse, in whilk were eikit★   *joined*
baith hert and smeddum★.   *gumption*

For ye had at your fingernebbs
real levan words to weave your webs   80
of sound and sense, of smiles and slebs★,   *scowls*
whilst Embro callants
ne'er thocht to runkle up their nebs★   *noses*
at guid braid Lallans.

---

[1] The Edinburgh men's club to which Fergusson belonged.
[2] Christmas/New Year's holidays.

And yet, owre surelie did ye ken
guid Scots wad mak bad Englishmen
whan owre faur South they keekit★ ben★   peeked/in
and sune were smitten,
tho barelie three-score years and ten
had seen Great Britain.   90

South-keekan Scots gaed skellie-ee'd
and tuke it in their tawpie★-heid   foolish
to hae their bairns anglified
and gar their stiff tongues
transmogrifie their Lallan leid★   speech
frae vowels to diphthongs.

Of Heriot's or Watson's ghaist
or yours, I wonder whilk is maist
dumbfounert, dozent and bumbazed
wi indignation to see our modern Embro taste   100
in education.

We may jalouse★ George Watson's banes   suspect
will gowl the maist wi grieslie maens
nou that his schule for puirtith's weans,
foundit sae weill,
chairges sic fees and taks sic pains
to be genteel.

No that I'd hae a body think
our toun's the waur of bein perjink★   neat
in some weys; Embro's famous stink   110
is banish'd nou;
gane are the shouts, that garred ye jink,
of 'Gardyloo!'[1]

Our fulyie's★ pusionit the Firth   filth's
and caused, I dout, an unco dearth
of thae Pandores of muckle girth
ye thocht sae fair;
what wad ye think our gain was worth?
I'm no that shair.

Auld Reekie's bigger, nou, what's mair,   120
and folk wha hae the greater share
of warldlie gear may tak the air
in Morningside,
and needna sclim★ the turnpike stair   climb
whar ye wad byde.

But truth it is, our couthie★ city   snug
has cruddit in twa pairts a bittie
and speaks twa tongues, ane coorse and grittie,

---

[1] Roughly, 'watch out!', the warning call that refuse was to be thrown into the street.

heard in the Cougait,
the tither copied, mair's the pitie,   130
frae Wast of Newgate.

Whilk is the crudd and whilk the whey
I wad be kinna sweirt* to say,   driven
but this I ken, that of the twae
the corrupt twang
of Cougait is the nearer tae
the leid ye sang.

Thir days, whan cities seem unreal
to makars, inwit* gars us feel   conscience
fause as the hauf-inch marble peel   140
in Princes Street
whaur new shop-fronts wad shame the Deil
wi their deceit.

A conter, we've some rotten riggin
of ratton-eaten Cougait biggin
that heard langsyne the skeelie jiggin
of your new verse.
Hard-pressed, I wale yon airt to dig in
and micht dae worse.

Our life's a bogle-hauntit dream   150
owre thrang wi wirrikows* to seem   frights
quite real; our fun a fireflaucht-gleam
whang'd throu a nicht
of gurliewhirkies huge and breme,
loppert* wi fricht.   clotted

Ye gaed about in guid braid claith
Wi fient* a thocht of want or skaith,   scarcely
in howffs at hy-jinks never laith
to blaw your chanter,
syne in cursed Darien's bedlam, Daith   160
wrocht your mishanter.

What gart ye break throu reason's ice?
Compared wi ye, we're no sae wyce.
Maybe we're yaised wi madness; vice
and lust for pouer
bring furth some hellish new device
ilk ither hour.

Was it the dreidit mental state
in whilk things yerdlie*, smaa and great,   earthly
become irrelevant, and Fate   170
dauntin the Kirk,
glowres at a man frae ben Hell's gate
throu endless mirk?

Syne even poetrie becomes
a naething, an affair of thrums
of words, words, a noise that jumms
wi leean★ skreed,   lying
the purport tint, man's sperit numbs –
as weill be deid.

The flicker-pictur on the screen   180
bursts as by boomb-blast, and is gane;
What was sae firm and good yestreen
seems foul indeed.
Syne a man brenns his buiks bedeen,
afore he's deid.

Ye didna hae to fash★ your thoombs   bother
wi hydrogen or atom boombs,
nor monie a nesty thocht that soums★   swims
aye in our heid
and flegs★ us in our flimsie rooms,   scares
and yet, ye're deid.   190

Aweill, ye're deid, gey lang sinsyne –
the Scottish elegiac line
I'll spare ye, tho, as ye ken fine,
ye scrievit monie
crouse★ stanzas whan ye'd cam to tine★   bold/lose
some decent cronie.

My ain toun's makar, monie an airt
formed us in common, faur apairt
in time, but fell alike in hert;
I whiles forget   200
that ye ligg there ablow the clart★   mud
of Canogait.

Like me, nae dout, wi muckle darin,
ye pree'd grim joys at Muschat's cairn
and grugous★ thochts of Effie's bairn,   gruesome
or, as a laddie,
ye skliddert doun, for scarts no caring,
the Guttit Haddie.

The auld High Schule (gane Royal syne)
your Alma Mater was and mine,   210
and whar ye construed, line by line,
the Gallic Weirs
we ken the airt, doun by the Wynd
of the Black Friars.

The wind that blaws frae Nor to South,
skirlan frae ilka close's mouth,
has nithert baith o's in our youth
and coupt us, whiles,
as we gaed hame wi slockent drouth★   thirst
doun by Sanct Giles'.   220

But aye we'd rise wi little hairm
and cleik ilk ither by the airm,
singan in unison to chairm
awa the skaith,
syne seek some cantraip★, harum-skarum   gambol
and naething laith.

Ye stickit★ minister, young Rab,   unfinished, unhired
ye wadnae hain★ your giff-gaff gab   save
frae me, a dominie or crab
aye stickan it,   230
nor gruch★ your brain, nor cry me scab   begrudge
for pickin it.

To World's End Close frae Ramsay Lane
we'd ding Auld Reekie's black rigg-bane.
Whan Ne'er-gate's ten-hour bell had gane
that wadnae daunt us;
I'd gie scotch-convoy back again
to Dawnie Douglas.

Ye'd quote frae Ramsay, I frae Grieve;
wi Happy Days your wame I'd steeve★   240   fill
and aye the mair ye'd hae me prieve
your aqua vitae,
syne we wad rair out sangs to deave★   deafen
the swuffan citie.

Up gaed ilk sash wi feck of skriekan,
frae the wee windaes heids were keekan;
the Embro folk gied owre their gleekin
for very joy;
in ae bricht lowe★ we aa were beekan –   flame
wow! what a ploy!   250

But ach! the nippie-tongue of morn
pits aa sic glaumerie to scorn;
I stand here, glaikit★ and forlorn   foolish
in Canogait,
ettlesome★, yet feart to sorn★   determined/beg
on your estait.

Robert, fareweill; I maun awa.
My gait is stey★, no wyce ava,   steep
by Jacob's Ladder, Burns's smaa
Greek pepperpat,   260
Sanct Andrew's Hous an' aa an' aa –
nae mair of that!

Pechan★, I turn, whilst aye your leid   panting
of lowan Scots sounds in my heid
Wi levan braith, tho ye ligg deid;
I glowre faur doun
and see the waesome wrak outspreid
of your auld toun.

Syne trauchlan up the brae yince mair,
frae Canogait, I leave ye there,   270
whar wee white roses scent the air
about your grave,
and til some suburb new and bare
gang wi the lave★.   rest

I Was Fair Beat

I spent a nicht amang the cognoscenti,
a hie-brou clan, ilk wi a beard on him
like Mark Twain's miners, due to hae a trim.
their years on aiverage roun three-and-twenty.

Of poetry and music we had plenty,
owre muckle, but ye maun be in the swim:
Kurt Schwitters' Ur-sonata that gaes 'Grimm
glimm gnimm bimmbimm,' it fairly wad hae sent ye

daft, if ye'd been there; modern jazz wi juicy
snell wud-wind chords, three new anes, I heard say   10
by thaim that ken't, new, that is, sen Debussy.

Man, it was awfie. I wad raither hae
a serenata sung by randy pussy,
and what a time a reel of tape can play!

The Wire

This day I saw ane endless muir
wi sad horizon, like the sea
around some uncouth landless globe
whaur waters flauchter endlessly.

Heather bell and blaeberry
grow on this muir; reid burns rin
in clear daylicht; the luift★ is free   sky
frae haar★, and yet there is nae sun.   mist

Gossamers glint in aa the airts★,   quarters
criss-cross about the lang flure-heids   10
of girss★ and thristles here, and there   grass
amang the purpie willow-weeds.

Bog-myrtle scent is in the air
heavy wi hinnie-sap and peat
whiles mellit★ like uneasy thochts   mingled
wi something human, shairn or sweit.

Nou guns gaun off, and pouther-reik
and yappin packs of foetid dugs,
and blobs of cramosie★, like blebs   crimson
of bluid squeezed frae vanilla bugs   20

pash suddenlike intill the licht
that dings on this unshadowed muir
fra ilka airt, and syne are gane
like tourbillions of twisted stour★.   dust

The criss-cross gossamers, the while,
twang owre the heather, ticht and real;
I ken, houever jimp they seem,
that they are spun frae strands of steel.

And they are barbed wi twisted spikes
wi scant a handsbreidth space atween,   30
and reinforced wi airn rods
and hung about wi bits of tin

that hing in pairs alang the Wire,
ilkane three-cornered like a fang:
clashin thegither at a touch
they break aukwart the lairick's★ sang.   lark's

Heich in their sentry-posts, the guairds
wha daurna sleep, on pain of daith,
watch throu the graticules of guns,
cruel and persecuted, baith.   40

This endless muir is thrang wi folk
that hirple★ aye aa airts at aince   limp
wi neither purport nor content
nor rest, in fidgan impotence.

They gae in danger of the Wire
but staucher on anither mile
frae line to line of spider steel
to loup anither deidlie stile.

A man trips up; the Wire gaes ding,
tins clash, the guaird lifts up his heid;   50
fu slaw he traverses his gun
and blatters at him till he's deid.

The dugs loup on him, reivan flesh,
crunchin the bane as they were wud★;   crazed
swith★ they come and swith are gane,   quickly
syne nocht is left but pools of bluid.

Bluid dreipan doun amang the roots
is soukit up the vampire stem
and suin the gaudy felloun flures
begowk the man that nourished them.   60

Some pairts the Wires close in and leave
smaa space whaur men may freely gang,
and ilka step is taen in dreid;
there flures and men maist thickly thrang.

A man gets taiglit on a barb,
endlang his wame★ the cauld fear creeps;   stomach
he daurna muve, the hert beats hard,
but beats awa. The sentry sleeps.

Aye! his virr comes back in spate,
as some auld trout this man is slee;   70
he hauds himsel still as a stane,
back comes his ain self-maistery.

Cannily he sets to wark,
warp by warp his sleeve is free,
it hings nou by a single threid:
loud clash the tins and bullets flee.

Forrit and back and in and out
they darn in waesome figure-dance;
bydin still they canna thole★   endure
and ilk man warks his ain mischance.   80

They see the Wire, and weill they ken
whilk wey it warks. In middle-air
the glintan guns are clear in sicht,
tho nae man kens wha set them there.

Impersonal in uniform,
the guairds are neither friens nor faes;
nane ettles★ to propitiate   struggles
nor fashes★ them wi bribes or praise.   troubles

Efficient and predictable,
they cairry out their orders stricht;   90
here naething happens unforeseen;
it is jist sae, no wrang nor richt.

On this dour mechanistic muir
wi nae land's end, and endless day,
whaur nae thing thraws a shadow, here
the truth is clear, and it is wae.

The crouds that thrang the danger-spots
weill ken what wey their warld's wrocht,
but aye the mair they pauchle★ on   shuffle
to win release frae nigglin thocht.   100

Some pairts the pattern of the Wire
leaves clear for fifty yairds and mair
whaur soil has crined to desert stuir★   dust
wi scroggie bussels★ puir and bare.   undergrown bushes

Here some folk wycer nor the lave★   rest
or maybe suiner gien to skar
tether theirsels wi chains to stakes,
sae they may gang, but no owr far.

Birlan in wretchedness aroun
their safe lives' centre, they maun dree★   110   suffer
temptation sair to break their chains
for aye they ettle to gang free.

Some stark an strang stravaig★ their yird   roam
like shelties that hae never taen
the bit; mere smeddum★ drives them on,   nerve
their lives are short, but are their ain.

A wheen★ in orra★ ill-faur'd airts   few/odd
on barren streitches of the muir
gae whaur nae bluid is ever shed
to drouk the dreich unslockent stour.   120

Within a pentagon of wire
they gang alane, or twae by twae,
thole★ the condition of their life   suffer
and dree the weird★ as best they may.   fate

Alane in thon hale fremmit★ globe   strange
thae slaw-gaun folk hae in their een
some sapience, as gin their looks
refleckit ferlies★ they hae seen   wonders
in their ain thochts, the nucleus
of man himsel is keethit there.   130
Expressed in terms of happiness
are premises of pure despair.

Thae guidlie folk are nae great men;
the best of men are unco smaa
whan in the autumn of despair
irrelevance has dwined awa.

Their syllogisms widdershins[1]
wither the petal; syne the leaf
and stem crine★ in as life gaes doun   shrink
intill a corm of prime belief.   140

Wi utmaist pouer of forcy thocht
they crine their life within its core,
and what they ken wi certainty
is kent inby the bracken-spore.

And aye alane or twae by twae
they gang unhurt amang the noy
of thon fell planet, and their een
lowe★ wi the licht of inwart joy.   gleam

---

[1] In magic rituals, performed obliquely to the direction of the sun.

Outwartly they seem at rest,
binna the glint of hidden fires.   150
Their warld shaks, but they bide still
as nodal points on dirlan* wires.   tingling

In ither airts, whaur folk are thrang,
the Wire vibrates, clash gae the tins,
flures blume frae bluidie marl, dugs
yowl throu the blatter of the guns.

I saw thon planet slawlie birl*;   whirl
I saw it as ane endless muir
in daylicht, and I saw a few
guid men bide still amang the stour.   160

George Friel (1910 – 1975)

Friel is one of the most important early Scottish realists. Like most of them, he is
from Glasgow. Again like most of the Glasgow school, he is at home with slums and
working-class characters, but his most respected novel is probably *Mr Alfred M. A.*
(1972), a decidedly sombre treatment of a schoolteacher's life.

Blackleg

Mr Bulloch, a Corporation tram-driver, was so big and stout that they called him 'Bullock'
in the depot. His wife was a massive woman, and his two sons were big and fat. There was an
atmosphere of stolid strength, of aloofness and security, about the family. When they were
twelve, the two boys went to a higher grade school, and their mother talked like a west-end
lady. She meant them to go to the university after that and become engineers or doctors or
schoolmasters, and with that high ambition she didn't like them to play with the other
children who would leave school at fourteen and become errand boys.

In the back-court, the elder of the two boys was feared for his height and strength, and
he always got his own way without having to do much bullying. But one evening in the
spring his domineering interference provoked one of the fighting Plottels to oppose him, and
he so thoroughly buffeted the foolhardy boy that the others, jostling round the fight, began
to murmur against his cold-blooded brutality. Cornered and in tears, Plottel punched
ineffectively up at the looming bulk of his enemy.

'Away and fight somebody your own size!' shouted a girl righteously from the back of the
hostile throng.

'I'll fight who I like,' retorted Bulloch, and turning again he hit Plottel hard on the ear
with a large rough-skinned fist.

His sight blurred by tears and his head ringing with that blow, Plottel wriggled out of the
corner and stood tremblingly clear.

'I'll fight your young brother if I can't fight you,' he cried. 'He's my age. You're not.'

'Come on, James,' said the elder Bulloch magnanimously, gesturing his brother from the
fringe to the ring. 'You give him the same as you saw me do.'

Red-faced, drawing back and muttering something indistinctly, the younger Bulloch refused. And from that evening the strength of the brothers was no longer respected. Without an opponent to match against the elder Bulloch, the boys jeered at him safely from a distance, calling him Big Chief Sitting Bull, and the younger one shared his elder's disgrace.

Then, in the summer, the hostility and mockery that had arisen against the family in the squabbles of schoolboys spread to it on the adult level. The General Strike was declared, and the city was disorganised and excited. When it was seen that Mr Bulloch went on driving a tram, the whole street murmured against him.

'Imagine him, born and reared in the Butney, helping a gang of students to break the Strike!' said Mrs Reid in anger. 'Maybe he thinks he's a toff because he's got two boys at the high school. I know what I'd like to tell him!'

'Ach, and his wife's not much better,' said Mrs Farquhar. 'Her and her fine airs and her Kelvinside voice! I knew her before she came here, before she was ever married, and believe you me, she wasn't far from the gutter when she was born.'

'Deserting his own class like that!' said Mrs Houston. 'He should be ashamed of himself.'

In those sunlit mornings of May, the trams, driven by university students enjoying their voluntary task as an exciting adventure, were half empty, while the pavements were crowded with office girls, shop girls, clerks and message boys, righteously walking to their work.

Without newspapers, the city was full of fears and rumours. For the first time, politics had become something important to the women and girls in the conglomeration of back-streets and the two-roomed tenements of the main roads. They were hysterical when they talked of the Strike, loud-voiced in a determination to support it to the end, proclaiming that at last there was an open fight between the callous rich and the long-suffering poor.

'Class against class, that's what it is,' said Mrs Houston to Mrs Higney. 'Those communist fellows are not so very far wrong when you think of it. It's up to us to stick together.'

'Aye, with traitors like Bulloch in this very street,' scoffed Mrs Higney. 'And the Lord knows what's happening elsewhere! Ach, what's the use? It'll all come to nothing, and we won't be one bit better off, you'll see! So long as there's men like Bulloch . . . '

'What does one man matter?' demanded Mrs Houston.

'How do we know how many more there are?' retorted Mrs Higney.

All over the city the housewives of the tenements jabbered belligerently, while their menfolk stood at the street-corners sullen and afraid. But when the first excitement faded and a housewife here and there began to wonder if the Strike was a wise thing, the husband briefly scorned her nagging worries about his job and the children and food. Determination fluctuated. The same worker would speak of the Strike in the evening as a fight that was bound to end in a quick success, and see it in the morning as a foolish struggle that would break down in total defeat. Every day it was declared that one trade union or another had decided to call its members to return to work, and every day it was rumoured that the Army were to be called out to patrol the streets.

Amid the succession of transient rumours, there came one that persisted with a vague authentication, asserting that a student driving a tram had been stopped by a gang of pickets and assaulted, and then when he was running away someone had thrown a stone at him, hitting him on the head. The student had fallen on the cobble-stones and died from a fractured skull. The wives of the strikers heard of it with a grim satisfaction.

'Serves them right for interfering in something they don't understand,' they said; 'something they know nothing about. This is a fight. And they try to make a joke of it. Maybe that'll learn the others!'

'Them and their plus-fours,' jeered Mrs Houston. 'They needn't try to come out to us again on a Charities Day!'

But Mr Bulloch, portly in his green uniform and fur gloves, went on driving a tram, with a student as his conductor. They worked the Kelvinside to Parkhead route together, the student joyful and garrulous and Mr Bulloch silent and uncertain of what would happen next. It was all right in the west-end, going along the Great Western Road, but once they had left the centre of the city and turned eastward he was afraid. The only thing that kept him going was his belief that the Strike would be over in a couple of days, and that those who were booing him would lose their jobs for good then.

On the fourth day of the Strike Mr Hannah, secretary of the local branch of the Transport Workers' Union, decided it was time to attend to him. He had already stopped a handful of doubtful cases, and the case of Mr Bulloch was to him like a blot on his own honour. With two lieutenants, Mr Todd and Mr Porter, he called at the Bullochs' house in the evening, when he knew that Mr Bulloch was off duty.

He rang the door-bell imperiously, and, gesturing to the others to imitate his example, he straightened himself to his full height and put on a stern expression. He was a small man, slightly knock-kneed. Mrs Bulloch opened the door a little and went red in the face when she saw him.

'We want to see your man,' said Mr Hannah. 'Right now!'

'He's not in,' enunciated Mrs Bulloch with an aloof dignity, and tried to close the door.

But Mr Hannah had already got one foot over the threshold, and with a determined shove he pushed her and the door back.

'We'll soon see,' he declared, and entered the house followed silently by Mr Todd and Mr Porter.

Mr Bulloch had gone to bed after a small meal. He was finding that he could not eat, and, exhausted with the strain of the last three days, he had thought he needed a good night's rest. But he could not sleep, and when he saw the deputation come into the room he sat up panic-stricken, clutching the blankets up to his chin.

'What do you want?' he asked, and his voice emerged with an incongruous littleness from his embedded bulk. 'Who asked you to come here?'

'Nobody,' said Mr Hannah. 'We just came. We want to see you.'

'What do you want to see me for?' demanded Mr Bulloch, looking for support to his wife, who stood frightenedly at the door of the room. 'I've nothing to say to you. I want nothing to do with you!'

'Oh, but we've plenty to say to you,' responded Mr Hannah, calmly.

'You've no right to come breaking into people's house like this!' cried Mrs Bulloch, near to hysteria. 'I'll fetch the police, that's what I'll do. I'll get a policeman to you!'

'Aye, get the Army too,' jeered Mr Hannah, and bending over Mr Bulloch he jerked the blankets down to his waist. 'Come on, you scab! What've you got to say for yourself?'

Big-chested in his thick pyjama jacket, Mr Bulloch reached frantically down and tried to gather up the blankets again to cover himself, looking as if he felt indecently exposed.

'You get out of here!' he cried in a high-pitched tremor that was trying to be a frightening roar. 'Get out of here before I get up and put you out!'

'You're getting up all right,' declared Mr Hannah, pulling the blankets away from his outstretched hands and scattering them off the bed altogether. 'You're getting up and coming with us, that's what you're doing!'

'You can't order him about like that!' exclaimed Mrs Bulloch, moving determinedly forward a step and then stopping indecisively, her hand fluttering over her large bosom.

Silently, with a grim directness, Mr Todd stepped forward and grasped Mr Bulloch's ankle to haul the tram-driver half out of bed.

'Did you join our union or did you not?' he demanded.

To save himself from falling on his back, Mr Bulloch grasped the edge of the bed and got on his feet on the carpet beside it.

'What if I did?' he panted. 'You can't force me into anything, you can't keep me from my job. I've a wife and family to keep!'

'And that's why you're blacklegging other men with a wife and family, eh?' scoffed Mr Porter.

'You miserable traitor,' said Mr Todd, with cold venom. 'The whole working class is solid in this fight, except for a few scabs like you. Well, you're chucking it, do you hear? You're chucking it!'

'I've a wife and family to keep,' repeated Mr Bulloch, looking jerkily from one to the other of them as if he were wondering which one he should throw out first and then deciding to attack none of them.

'Aye, so have we,' said Mr Porter. 'But we're not stabbing our fellow workers in the back like you!'

'Do you know what you're going to do?' said Mr Hannah, sticking up his small thin face aggressively into Mr Bulloch's fat and florid one. 'You're coming out with us, and we'll take you to the Labour Hall and give you a picketing job for the morrow at the depot. You'll get your badge and your instructions.'

'I'm not, I'm not going!' cried Mr Bulloch.

'Get a hold of him, boys; we'll show him!' shouted Mr Hannah.

'Here you, what are you doing? Stop that! I'll get a policeman!' screamed Mrs Bulloch, taking another two steps determinedly forward before she halted again in alarm.

Grabbing Mr Bulloch round the waist, Mr Hannah tried to force him on his back on the bed.

'Get his trousers,' he panted. 'Not his uniform, his other trousers. We'll show him!'

But he could not shift the tram-driver's enormous bulk, even when assisted by Mr Todd and Mr Porter, and, struggling amid them, Mr Bulloch cowered in terror. In despair of carrying out his intention, Mr Hannah released his grasp and pushed him contemptuously on the chest with both hands. Mr Bulloch swayed and sagged backwards against Mr Todd. As if contaminated, Mr Todd pushed him forward again, and he fell at Mr Hannah's feet in a faint.

Erect around him, the deputation gaped, and screaming for the police Mrs Bulloch ran to her husband and knelt sobbingly beside him, rubbing his cheeks.

'So help me God!' said Mr Hannah, slowly. 'A man of his size, passing out like a lassie!'

He turned irresolutely, followed by the others, and with backward glances they sidled to the door.

'Murderers! slum hooligans!' screamed Mrs Bulloch. 'Oh, Andrew, Andrew! are you all right? Andrew, speak to me! I'll get you for this, Hannah! I'll make a police case out of it, I'll charge you! I'll get you; you wait. Bullies and ruffians! Oh, Andrew, are you all right?'

'Ach, shut your face!' retorted Mr Hannah. 'There's nothing up with the yellow-livered scab. Maybe you'd better keep him away from the depot now, or he might get worse.'

'Here, boys, get his uniform!' said Mr Todd. 'That'll keep him in!'

Hastening back into the room, they gathered up his uniform between them and marched out, their heads high, their conscience clear, and their faces slightly red.

The next morning the story of the assault and Mr Bulloch's collapse was all over the street.

'They put the fear of death in him,' said Mrs Houston, exultantly. 'He'll keep to his bed now, the scab! No more blacklegging for him for a while!'

But there was nothing more for Mr Bulloch at any time. He died in a fortnight. The doctor said it was heart trouble, and, callously scoffing, the gossips said it was just a weak heart. By that time the Strike was over, political uninterest had fallen again on the briefly disturbed city, and the only ones vocal were those saying: 'I told you so!' When the city's newspapers refused to take back the compositors who had joined the Strike, the once belligerent workers asserted to each other in gloomy agreement: 'We should never have done it. We should have made sure of our jobs first. I knew this would happen. They just made a fool of us. Leaders be damned! What do they care about the working-class? It's up to us to look after ourselves. Jobs aren't so easy come by these days.'

In the city's returned pessimism, amid the job-worrying of the tenements, the two Bulloch boys left the high school and went to work to keep their widowed mother. One became a van-boy and the other a public-house waiter.

Massive in her grief, alien to her neighbours in a bitter loneliness, Mrs Bulloch looked a meaningless megalith. She saw her sons grow up into rough-spoken young men who dressed like corner-boys and worked irregularly at blind-alley jobs. She strove to rule them and guide them, worrying about their future for them, and her ladylike voice chiding her fatherless family to its old pretence of breeding moved irrelevantly over a shattered security.

Norman MacCaig (1910 – 1996)

MacCaig ranks with Edwin Muir as the leading 'English' poet in modern Scotland. A versatile writer in subject matter and technique, his elegant, unforced style combines a restless, metaphysical wit, and a deep awareness of nature, together with the love of language and artistic form that one expects of a poet among poets. Though for years a close friend of those great and committed Scots writers Hugh MacDiarmid and Sydney Smith, MacCaig seems never to have felt pressure to write in other than his quietly classic English diction.

Summer Farm

Straws like tame lightnings lie about the grass
And hang zigzag on hedges. Green as glass
The water in the horse-trough shines.
Nine ducks go wobbling by in two straight lines.

A hen stares at nothing with one eye,
Then picks it up. Out of an empty sky
A swallow falls and, flickering through
The barn, dives up again into the dizzy blue.

I lie, not thinking, in the cool, soft grass,
Afraid of where a thought might take me – as   10
This grasshopper with plated face
Unfolds his legs and finds himself in space.

Self under self, a pile of selves I stand
Threaded on time, and with metaphysic hand
Lift the farm like a lid and see
Farm within farm, and in the centre, me.

You Went Away

Suddenly, in my world of you,
You created time.
I walked about in its bitter lanes
Looking for whom I'd lost, afraid to go home.

You stole yourself and gave me this
Torturer for my friend
Who shows me gardens rotting in air
And tells me what I no longer understand.

The birds sing still in the apple trees,
But not in mine. I hear   10
Only the clock whose wintry strokes
Say, 'Now is now,' that foul truth, over and over.

If I could kill this poem, sticking
My thin pen through its throat,
It would stand silent by your bed
And haunt your cruelty every empty night.

Wreck

The hulk stranded in Scalpay bay,
Hung like a hall with seaweed, stuck
Its long snout through my holiday.
It lay foundered on its own bad luck.

Twice every day it took aboard
A cargo of the tide; its crew
Flitted with fins. And sand explored
Whatever cranny it came to.

It should have carried deaths to give
To me stumbling across the stones;   10
It never spoke of what could live.
I saw no ghost between its bones.

It had not learned that it had failed;
Its voyages would not let it be.
More slow than glacier it sailed
Into the bottom of the sea.

High Street, Edinburgh

Here's where to make a winter fire of stories
And burn dead heroes to keep your shinbones warm,
Bracing the door against the jackboot storm
With an old king or two, stuffing the glories
Of rancid martyrs with their flesh on fire
Into the broken pane that looks beyond Fife
Where Alexander died and a vain desire,
Hatched in Macbeth, sat whittling at his life.

Across this gulf where skeins of duck once clattered
Round the black Rock and now a tall ghost wails   10
Over a shuddering train, how many tales
Have come from the hungry North of armies shattered,
An ill cause won, a useless battle lost,
A head rolled like an apple on the ground;
And Spanish warships staggering west and tossed
On frothing skerries; and a king come to be crowned.

Look out into this brown November night
That smells of herrings from the Forth and frost;
The voices humming in the air have crossed
More than the Grampians; East and West unite,   20
In dragonish swirlings over the city park,
Their tales of deaths and treacheries, and where
A tall dissolving ghost shrieks in the dark
Old history greets you with a Bedlam stare.

He talks more tongues than English now. He fetches
The unimagined corners of the world
To ride this smoky sky, and in the curled
Autumnal fog his phantoms move. He stretches
His frozen arm across three continents
To blur this window. Look out from it. Look out   30
From your November. Tombs and monuments
Pile in the air and invisible armies shout.

November Night, Edinburgh

The night tinkles like ice in glasses.
Leaves are glued to the pavement with frost.
The brown air fumes at the shop windows,
Tries the doors, and sidles past.

I gulp down winter raw. The heady
Darkness swirls with tenements.
In a brown fuzz of cottonwool
Lamps fade up crags, die into pits.

Frost in my lungs is harsh as leaves
Scraped up on paths. – I look up, there,   10
A high roof sails, at the mast-head
Fluttering a grey and ragged star.

The world's a bear shrugged in his den.
It's snug and close in the snoring night.
And outside like chrysanthemums
The fog unfolds its bitter scent.

Spate in Winter Midnight

The streams fall down and through the darkness bear
Such wild and shaking hair,
Such looks beyond a cool surmise,
Such lamentable uproar from night skies
As turn the owl from honey of blood and make
Great stags stand still to hear the darkness shake.

Through Troys of bracken and Babel towers of rocks
Shrinks now the looting fox,
Fearful to touch the thudding ground
And flattened to it by the mastering sound.   10
And roebuck stilt and leap sideways; their skin
Twitches like water on the fear within.

Black hills are slashed white with this falling grace
Whose violence buckles space
To a sheet-iron thunder. This
Is noise made universe, whose still centre is
Where the cold adder sleeps in his small bed,
Curled neatly round his neat and evil head.

Crofter's Kitchen, Evening

A man's-boots with a woman in them
Clatter across the floor. A hand
Long careless of the lives it kills
Comes down and thwacks on newspapers
A long black fish with bloody gills.

The kettle's at her singsong – minor
Prophetess in her sooty cave.
A kitten climbs the bundled net
On the bench and, curled up like a cowpat,
Purrs on the *Stornoway Gazette*.   10

The six hooks of a Mackerel Dandy
Climb their thin rope – an exclamation
By the curled question of a gaff.
Three rubber eels cling like a crayfish
On top of an old photograph.

Peats fur themselves in grey. The door
Bursts open, chairs creak, a hand reaches out
For spectacles, a lamp flares high . . .
The collie underneath the table
Slumps with a world-rejecting sigh.   20

Translations of Innocence

Small girls on bibles sailed away
Through pinks and whites and curly clouds
And boys hung through a black Nor'easter,
Gallant upon the rattling shrouds.

They used to. But the heavenly shores
Are empty round the sea of glass
And oilwells gush on tropic islands
Gunboats scarcely dare to pass.

Yet restless in their present tense,
The little siblings, scarcely born,   10
Jostle around the same old places,
The gates of ivory and horn.[1]

And paradisal images
Of pride and babies, blood and fear,
Obscure with trailing fumes of glory
The dreadful fact of being here.

And each one gulps his apple down
Under the dark forbidden tree.
Who would be angel now and notice
What's mirrored in the crystal sea?   20

Explorer

Trampling new seas with filthy timbers, he
Jotted down headlands, speculated on
Vestigial civilisations, ate strange fruits
And called his officers Mister. When sails were gone

Bundling and tumbling down the shrieking dark,
He trailed the Bible as sea-anchor; when
Reefs shaved the barnacles from the keel, he took
His gentlemanly snuff. Each night at ten,

Under the lamp from which his cabin swung,
He logged the latest, drank his grog and spread,   10
With only one uncomprehending sigh,
His wild uncharted world upon his bed.

Sleet

The first snow was sleet. It swirled heavily
Out of a cloud black enough to hold snow.
It was fine in the wind, but couldn't bear to touch
Anything solid. It died a pauper's death.

Now snow – it grins like a maniac in the moon.
It puts a glove on your face. It stops gaps.
It catches your eye and your breath. It settles down
Ponderously crushing trees with its airy ounces.

But today it was sleet, dissolving spiders on cheekbones,
Being melting spit on the glass, smudging the mind   10
That humped itself by the fire, turning away
From the ill wind, the sky filthily weeping.

---

[1] In Greek mythology, the portals for false and true dreams, respectively.

Struck by Lightning

The tall transformer stood
Biblically glorified, and then turned blue.
Space split. The earth tossed twelve hens in the air.
The landscape's hair stood up. The collie flew,
Or near it, back to the house and vanished there.

Roofed by a gravel pit,
I, in a safe place, as I always am,
Was, as I always am, observer only
– Nor cared. Why should I? The belief's a sham
That shared danger or escape cures being lonely.   10

Yet when I reached the croft
They excluded me by telling me. As they talked
Across my failure, I turned away to see
Hills spouting white and a huge cloud that walked
With a million million legs on to the sea.

Old Poet

The alder tree
shrivelled by the salt wind
has lived so long
it has carried and sheltered
its own weight
of nests.

Aunt Julia

Aunt Julia spoke Gaelic
very loud and very fast.
I could not answer her –
I could not understand her.

She wore men's boots
when she wore any.
– I can see her strong foot,
stained with peat,
paddling with the treadle of the spinningwheel
while her right hand drew yarn   10
marvellously out of the air.

Hers was the only house
where I've lain at night
in the absolute darkness
of a box bed, listening to
crickets being friendly.

She was buckets
and water flouncing into them.
She was winds pouring wetly
round house-ends.   20
She was brown eggs, black skirts
and a keeper of threepennybits
in a teapot.

Aunt Julie spoke Gaelic
very loud and very fast.
By the time I had learned
a little, she lay
silenced in the absolute black
of a sandy grave
at Luskentyre.   30

But I hear her still, welcoming me
with a seagull's voice
across a hundred yards
of peatscrapes and lazybeds
and getting angry, getting angry
with so many questions
unanswered.

Intrusion

We sat by a Scottish stream
in Massachusetts.
A groundhog observed us,
its whiskered face peering
from a hole in the ground
like a cartoon from World War I
and through the still, bright air
flew birds whose names
I did not know.

Suddenly, in front of us,   10
thirty yards away,
a twenty foot limb
crashed from an elm tree.

Now, three weeks later,
in a Scottish house in Scotland,
I tell myself
it was one of a million
dramatic acts
in the world of nature's
perpetually symbolic play   20
that, if we had not been there,
would have taken place anyway.

But it disturbs me. I try
to see it as no other than
the Scottish water crimpling away
through America and
the watchful face peering
from its dugout across
the No Man's Land that lies
between me and everything.   30

Old Edinburgh

Down the Canongate
down the Cowgate
go vermilion dreams
snake's tongues of bannerets
trumpets with words from their mouths
saying *Praise me, praise me.*

Up the Cowgate
up the Canongate
lice on the march
tar on the amputated stump   10
Hell speaking with the tongue of Heaven
a woman tied to the tail of a cart.

And history leans by a dark entry
with words from his mouth
that say *Pity me, pity me*
but never forgive.

So Many Summers

Beside one loch, a hind's neat skeleton,
Beside another, a boat pulled high and dry:
Two neat geometries drawn in the weather:
Two things already dead and still to die.

I passed them every summer, rod in hand,
Skirting the bright blue or the spitting grey,
And, every summer, saw how the bleached timbers
Gaped wider and the neat ribs fell away.

Time adds one malice to another one –
Now you'd look very close before you knew   10
If it's the boat that ran, the hind went sailing,
So many summers, and I have lived them too.

Stars and Planets

Trees are cages for them: water holds its breath
To balance them without smudging on its delicate meniscus.
Children watch them playing in their heavenly playground;
Men use them to lug ships across oceans, through firths.

They seem so twinkle-still, but they never cease
Inventing new spaces and huge explosions
And migrating in mathematical tribes over
The steppes of space at their outrageous ease.

It's hard to think that the earth is one –
This poor sad bearer of wars and disasters   10
Rolls-Roycing round the sun with its load of gangsters,
Attended only by the loveless moon.

The following is one of the most praised elegies in modern Scottish literature.

Poems for Angus
Notes on a winter journey, and a footnote

1
The snow's almost faultless. It bounces back
the sun's light but can do nothing with
those two stags, their cold noses, their yellow teeth.

2
On the loch's eye a cataract is forming.
Fistfuls of white make the telephone wires
loop after loop of snow buntings.

3
So few cars, they leave the snow snow.
I think of the horrible marzipan
in the streets of Edinburgh.

4
The hotel at Ullapool, that should be a bang of light,   10
is crepuscular. The bar is fireflied
with whisky glasses.

5
At Inchnadamph snow is falling. The windscreen wipers
squeak and I stare through
a segment of a circle. What more do I ever do? . . .

6

(Seventeen miles to go. I didn't know it, but when
I got there a death waited for me – that segment
shut its fan: and a blinding winter closed in.)

A. K. MacLeod

I went to the landscape I love best
and the man who was its meaning and added to it   20
met me at Ullapool.

The beautiful landscape was under snow
and was beautiful in a new way.

Next morning, the man who had greeted me
with the pleasure of pleasure
vomited blood
and died.

Crofters and fishermen and womenfolk, unable
to say any more, said,
'It's a grand day, it's a beautiful day.'   30

And I thought, 'Yes, it is.'
And I thought of him lying there,
the dead centre of it all.

Highland funeral

Over the dead man's house, over his landscape
the frozen air was a scrawny psalm
I believed in because it was pagan
as he was.

Into it the minister's voice
spread a pollution of bad beliefs.
The sanctimonious voice dwindled away   40
over the boring, beautiful sea.

The sea was boring as grief is,
but beautiful, as grief is not.
Through grief's dark ugliness I saw that beauty
because he would have.

And that darkened the ugliness . . . Can the dead
help? I say so. Because, a year later,
that sanctimonious voice is silent and the pagan
landscape is sacred in a new way.

A month after his death

An accordion and a fiddle   50
fit nimbly together their different natures
with such bouncing wit it makes small
the darkness outside that goes straight up

for ever and ever.
Out there are the dregs of history. Out there
mindlessness lashes the sea against the sea-wall:
and a bird flies screaming over the roof.

We laugh and we sing, but we all know we're thinking
of the one who isn't here.

The laughter and the singing are paper flowers   60
laid on a wet grave in a empty darkness.
For we all know we're thinking
of the one who can't be here,
not even as a ghost smiling through the black window.

Triple burden

I know I had my death in me
from the moment I yelled upside-down
in the world.

Now I have another death in me: yours.
Each is the image of the other.

To carry two deaths   70
is a burden for any man:
and it's a heavy knowledge that tells me
only the death I was born with
will destroy the other.

For a boat has sailed into
the sea of unknowing;
you are on board.

And somewhere another boat
rocks
by another pier.   80

It's waiting to take me
where I'll never know you again –
a voyage
beyond knowledge, beyond memory.

Comforter

Thank God you don't tell me
to stop thinking of him –
that I'm grieving, not for him,

but for my loss
– for, though that's true,
my grief is also   90
his celebration of me.

Praise of a man

He went through a company like a lamplighter –
see the dull minds, one after another,
begin to glow, to shed
a beneficent light.

He went through a company like
a knifegrinder – see the dull minds
scattering sparks of themselves,
becoming razory, becoming useful.

He went through a company   100
as himself. But now he's one
of the multitudinous company of the dead
where are no individuals.

The beneficent lights dim
but don't vanish. The razory edges
dull, but still cut. He's gone: but you can see
his tracks still, in the snow of the world.

From his house door

I say to myself, How he enriched my life.
And I say to myself, More than he have died,
he's not the only one.   110

I look at the estuary and see
a gravel bank and a glitter going through it
and the stealthy tide, black-masked,
drowning stone after stone.

Angus's dog

Black collie, do you remember yourself?

Do you remember your name was Mephistopheles,
though (as if you were only a little devil)
everyone called you Meph?

You'd chase everything – sea gulls, motor cars,
jet planes. (It's said you once set off   120
after a lightning flash.) Half over a rock,
you followed the salmon fly arcing
through the bronze water. You loved everything
except rabbits – though
you grinned away under the bed
when your master came home
drink taken. How you'd lay your head

on a visitor's knee and look up, so soulfully,
like George Eliot playing Sarah Bernhardt.

. . . Black Meph, how can you remember yourself   130
in that blank no-time, no-place where
you can't even greet your master
though he's there too?

Dead friend

How do I meet
a man who's no longer there?
How can I lament the loss
of a man who won't go away?
How can I be changed
by changelessness?

I stand in my gloomy field   140
like a Pictish carving
that keeps its meaning but is, too, weathered
into another one.

In memoriam

On that stormy night
a top branch broke off
on the biggest tree in my garden.

It's still up there. Though its leaves
are withered black among the green
the living branches
won't let it fall.   150

Defeat

What I think of him,
what I remember of him
are gifts I can't give
to anyone.
For all I can say of him
is no more
than a scribble in the margin
of a lost manuscript.

Old Sarah

What could she live on when her husband died?

He had spent most of his last summers
lying on his elbow on a green knowe, looking
for the black-sailed ship to come into the bay.
But death put no words in his mouth – he spoke only
kindnesses and small jokes. They squeezed past
the permanent pipe in his mouth.

So what could she live on when her world dwindled to
a leaking cottage with five hens
to cluck by the rickety door? She drew   10
her black memories around her,
her life savings. And fed the hens.
And smoothed the blankets
in the huge dark space of the box bed.

Highland Games

They sit on the heather slopes
and stand six deep round the rope ring.
Keepers and shepherds in their best plus-fours
who live mountains apart
exchange gossip and tall stories.
Women hand out sandwiches,
rock prams and exchange
small stories and gossip.
The Chieftain leans his English accent
on a five-foot crook and feels   10
one of the natives.

The rope ring is full
of strenuous metaphors.
Eight runners shoulder each other
eight times round it – a mile
against the clock that will kill them.
Little girls breasted only with medals translate
a tune that will outlast them
with formalised legs and
antler arms. High jumpers   20
come down to earth and,
in the centre
a waddling 'heavy' tries to throw
the tree of life in one straight line.

Thank God for the bar, thank God
for the Games Night Dance – even though they end
in the long walk home
with people no longer here – with exiles and deaths –
your nearest companions.

The Way It Goes

Reality isn't what it used to be,
I mutter gloomily
when I feel like Cortez on his peak in Darien
and then remember it wasn't Cortez at all
and feel more like him than ever.

Summer Idyll

Under a ferocious snowfall
of gulls and fulmars
a corner of the bay is simmering
with herring fry.

Into them slice
Assyrian hosts
of mackerel.

Sweet day, so cool, so calm, so bright . . . [1]

Three porpoises pronounce
three puffs and cavalry charge   10
into the Assyrians.

Clouds lisp across the sky in a trance of silence.

Farther out, a commando of killer whales
grin and leap.
They're setting their ambush
for the cavalry.

And in the gentle West
a ladylike sunset
swoons
on the chaise-lounge   20
of the Hebrides.

Old Highland Woman

She sits all day by the fire.
How long is it since she opened the door
and stepped outside, confusing
the scuffling hens and the collie
dreaming of sheep?
Her walking days are over.

---

[1] The first line of George Herbert's poem 'Virtue' (pub. 1633). The last line of Herbert's stanza is 'For thou must die.'

She has come here through centuries
of Gaelic labour and loves
and rainy funerals. Her people
are assembled in her bones.   10
She's their summation. *Before her time*
has almost no meaning.

When neighbours call
she laughs a wicked cackle
with love in it, as she listens
to the sly bristle of gossip,
relishing the life in it,
relishing the malice, with her hands
lying in her lap like holy psalms
that once had a meaning for her, that once   20
were noble with tunes
she used to sing long ago.

Still is the Night

I'm sleepless. I lie trying to hear
the house breathing, wondering
why the curtain trembles, wondering
what cracked a knuckle outside the door.

Still is the night? Not ever. Its creatures
scuttle and pounce and die.
A tree whispers to the window
and footsteps go by; there's a man on them.

Impossible to think of canoes paddling
on tropical lagoons or caravans   10
winding over mountain passes.
The night is nearness, it presses down on me.

A godlike car passes in a golden shower:
it throws a handful in through the window.
– Too much is going on. I think uneasily
of a hand twitching the bedclothes.

In a Snug Room

He sips from his glass, thinking complacently
of the events of the day:
a flattering reference to him in the morning papers,
lunch with his cronies, a profitable deal
signed on the dotted line, a donation sent

to his favourite charity.
And he smiles,
thinking of the taxi coming
with his true love in it.

Everything's fine.   10

And Nemesis slips two bullets
into her gun
in case she misses with the first one.

London to Edinburgh

I'm waiting for the moment
when the train crosses the Border
and home creeps closer
at seventy miles an hour.

I dismiss the last four days
and their friendly strangers
into the past
that grows bigger every minute.

The train sounds urgent as I am,
it says home and home and home.   10
I light a cigarette
and sit smiling in the corner.

Scotland, I rush towards you
into my future that,
every minute,
grows smaller and smaller.

J[ames] F[indlay] Hendry (1912 – 1986)

Tir-nan-Og

A man is born, a man dies,
And in between are miseries.

In between he is alive
But cannot be allowed to live

Since, body's hunger never fed,
The mind is never satisfied

And hands and feet and head and eyes
Are hourly humbled to the knees.

A man dies, a man is born,
And in between a burden borne.   10

In between, by force of love,
A grief in life is made alive

Whose mind is more than satisfied
And body's hunger always fed,

Whose hands rise up from feet and knees,
Encircle head and rub the eyes.

The Constant North

Encompass me, my lover,
With your eyes' wide calm.
Though noonday shadows are assembling doom,
The sun remains when I remember them;
And death, if it should come,
Must fall like quiet snow from such clear skies.

Minutes we snatched from the unkind winds
Are grown into daffodils by the sea's
Edge, mocking its green miseries;
Yet I seek you hourly still, over   10
A new Atlantis loneliness, blind
As a restless needle held by the constant north we always have in mind.

The Dead Larch

A wild wind, exulting, loud in violence
Uprooting earthly happiness, laid low
My larch whose every living hesitancy
Has vanished from its leaves.
Hoarse and dry they break, like tinder,
And wander where the wind wanders.

Blind were the roots that fondled earth
And bland as beggar sightlessness the path
Tapped out, until rigidity told their touch
Upon a stone. Then, barred was the search of each   10
Slow tendril for invisible water
And dim, diamond minerals that lit their night.

No sunken stars restored them heaven.
They sank upon that barrier in vain.
Older trees and dead had withered underground

Whose blind reef, stoned in fossil, slew the blind
Root in earth as sun-heat slew the living
Leaflight in the air above.

The Living Larch

Day's blind winds may roar
Upon you, like the sea
Against a stubborn pier.
They rouse you but to ecstasy,
A river of light leaves, hoar
Within your quivering walls,
A fountain that never falls.

Night shall still these storm-amassing
Winds and force their cloudy armies
In a slow rout through space.   10
I see your outstretched boughs
Thrown over us, dark with blessing,
And know their returning peace
Can never, never cease.

I Listen Where the Oceans

I listen where the oceans of the air
Rustle upon a world.
They beat upon the ear as on a shore.

She whispers out of these hushed voices
Large invisible seas
Falling on us white as innocence.

In waves there leap upon her pallid eyes
Loud, loud shapes of cloud.
This is the entrance of great silences.

Beyond the body of alabaster   10
Over cliffsman death, white shrouds
In a great fleet shine forth freedom in her majesty.

A bird's wing is broken into their current.
Across cerulean heights
Starring the dark and fivefold continent

The infinite allotropy of her spirit
Eludes me still. Her voice
Wanders on the wind with no wit in it.

Speak! Speak to me, o aerophyte!

So I Saw Her Soul

So I saw her soul the other night,
Like some fountain playing bright
Upon the spine and through the mind.
O be gentle to us, wind!
Scatter not its drops like spray
But wave its feathers; let it play
There in the clearing, between the trees,
Over the lovers and on to the frieze.
Let it forever flower there
Free and fertile as the air,   10
Hushing into silence sweet
Doubt that she and I shall meet.
Fountain, lodestone, mine and ore,
Source of earth and this heart's core.

Though the Fountain Freezes

Though the fountain freezes into a sword
Absolute in the hands of the Lord,
The armoured man at the side of the rose
Slays love's enemy with its snows.
Death is a wreath upon the sea
A mist of pearl where dawn walks free,
Scattering years upon the grass
Illumining lover and his lass,
Expanding like a purple flower
Imperceptibly every hour   10
It suddenly advances through the air
Dazzling a thousand trumpets where
Noon's unparalleled panoply of pride
Unravels needles in its tide.

In Remnants the Light is Hunted

In remnants the light is hunted.
O Diana dark is come.
From the day, a shattered drum,
Lost in the travel of wide cloud,
Smoke ascends in one great shroud,
And yet the night is haunted.

Sunk deep on the bed of night
Even the stars are stones.
Sun, splintered into cones,
Flees consciousness for crystal beauty   10
Gathering life in glittering roots,
And only the moon breaks rout.

Bent, it still is steel.
There is no blood upon its horn.
Now it is a sickle drawn
At the dark throat tilting universal history,
Crescent of ice and harbinger of glory,
Aura and scimitar of will.

Robin Jenkins (1912 –)

Jenkins, along with Neil Gunn and Muriel Spark, is one of the most important Scottish novelists of our century. A prolific writer, he has produced many books set in Scotland, and many set in Asia. A late Scottish work, *Fergus Lamont* (1979), is perhaps his most respected, along with an earlier Scottish novel, *The Cone-gatherers* (1955). He has written few short stories. The one which follows is the title story from his only collection, *A Far Cry from Bowmore* (1973).

A Far Cry from Bowmore

Macpherson wished the Reverend Donald Dougary would take his hand off his: not because it was clammy and feeble, or because in the big airport hall small brown-skinned men were showing their gold teeth in impertinent goodwill at such a show in public of affection between one white tuan and another, but simply because it confused and sullied his reactions to what the old minister was saying, or dribbling rather, for out of the corner of his wrinkled tired mouth saliva kept trickling.

'You could do it, Hugh. I've no doubt of that. You've got a natural piety. You were brought up to it: on that Skye croft long ago. It's still marked on your face. Isn't that so, Mary?'

Mary Macpherson, also uneasy about that old sweaty hand – it had tried to hold hers in the car, for no reason she could think of – nodded and tried to smile. She knew how offended Hugh would be by that much too intimate gesture. Though proud of her husband's solid Presbyterian worth in this hot lush land of dissipated expatriates, simple-minded pagans, and sinisterly successful Roman Catholic missionaries, she knew he had weaknesses; these she tried harder than he to remedy, since she suffered from them more than he did.

With his other hand the old clergyman took a sip of the sweet locally made orange that only increased his thirst. He wished it was time to go on the plane. At his home in Singapore, a thousand miles away over the South China Sea, he would have drunk refreshing beer. Here, in Kalimantan, on his annual visit to perform christenings and give communion, he had had to be very careful not to offend his hosts, the Macphersons, who allowed no alcohol into their house, far less their mouths. In a hot thirsty land such self-denial was undoubtedly Christian, but, alas, also in this day and age a bit priggish. The truth unfortunately was that Hugh Macpherson, gaunt in the face as his native Coolins, was a good man and an expert engineer, but as diligent a prig as Mr Dougary had ever met. His affections, even for his wife and children, were never warm, or at any rate warmly expressed. Moral calculations entered into everything he did and said.

What they were now talking about, in the airport hall, his holding weekly religious meetings in his house, was really Macpherson's own suggestion, but since it was his habit to avoid giving himself credit for anything, preferring to let others do it, he had wanted Mr Dougary to put it forward as his idea. The effort to humour so humourless a man was making the old minister sweat, more than the heat.

Macpherson laughed. 'I wouldn't want to make too much of it,' he said. 'Just an extension of Mary's Sunday school.'

'Exactly.' The old man longed for the announcement that would release him. He had a headache. During the past three days he had been obliged to discuss man's religious duties more deeply than he cared nowadays to do. He was far too old for talk: he just wanted to lie and float on faith, like the children he'd seen yesterday on a lilo in the warm sea.

'All the same,' said Macpherson, 'if I did it I'd have to take it seriously.'

'Of course, Hugh. But don't forget there's joy in Christ too.'

A plane came roaring in to land, with a roar. The old minister, with a secret smile, imagined it was the Lord angry at being saddled with so many conscientious fools, like Hugh Macpherson.

'That's true,' said Macpherson. 'But you should know, Mr Dougary, a country like this gives opportunity to so many empty pleasures it can rot a man's soul. I've seen it happen in a dozen cases.'

'I'm sure you're right, Hugh.'

'Don't misunderstand me. I'm not saying it's wrong to enjoy yourself.'

You are, but you shouldn't, thought the old minister who'd seen the Macpherson's launch, their big white car, their beautifully appointed house, their three servants, their gold Rolex watches, and their well-stocked table. By comparison he himself, with his congregation of two hundred prudish, abstemious Chinese, lived like an ascetic, despite his beers. His wife too, poor Peggy, however she tried, and no woman had tried harder, had never been in pew or bed the pleasure that Mrs Macpherson with her fair hair, ample breasts, and sonsy buttocks must be. Had King David got his eyes on a woman like her, messengers would have been sent in the night.

Over the loudspeaker came some blurred Chinese English.

Mr Dougary rose. 'What's she saying?' he cried.

'It's not for you,' said Mrs Macpherson. 'She was just saying the plane from Keningau has arrived.'

He sat down again. 'Keningau? Where's that?'

'In the interior. No road into it, so you've to fly, or go by river. It's on the Pensiangan.'

'I hope you won't mind, Mr Dougary,' said Macpherson, 'if I write to you now and then for advice.'

'By no means. I should be only too pleased to help, if I can.'

Inwardly the old minister asked himself why a man in confident charge of over a hundred natives should make so much fuss about weekly prayer meetings with no more than half a dozen present, if he was lucky. Taking a charitable view, it must be because Macpherson, accustomed to making certain that the bridges he built from one bank of a river to the other were strong, was similarly thorough about bridges intended to carry a man's soul to God. Mr Dougary himself nowadays was inclined to risk it with any old frayed rope he could lay hands on.

Passengers off the Keningau plane were now passing through the hall. Some were natives, in coloured robes. One was a brisk spectacled Englishman, dapper in a white cotton suit; he carried a black suitcase.

He hesitated and then stopped at their table.

'Hello, Macpherson,' he said. 'The very man I wanted to see. How extraordinarily convenient. How are you, Mrs Macpherson?'

She smiled. 'This is Mr Dougary, from Singapore. Mr Dougary, meet Dr Willard of Api hospital. He operated on Morag when she had appendicitis.'

The doctor smiled: an Anglican himself, with a cathedral in the town to go to if he wished, he found amusing this once-a-year service of the dour Scotch Presbyterians.

'I'm just back from Keningau,' he said. 'With a message for you, Macpherson, as a matter of fact.'

'For me?'

'Yes. Sent on by a colleague of mine, Dr Lall, an Indian, attached to Keningau hospital.'

'Can't say I know him, doctor.'

'And he doesn't know you. Lall goes out on up-river calls. He's just back from one, and he brought this message: from a fellow countryman of yours, a planter at Pensiangan, called McArthur.'

'McArthur? I don't know any McArthurs here.'

'Well, he thinks he knows you. His description was accurate enough: divisional engineer, PWD Api, Scotsman, tall, lean, called Macpherson, with a fair-haired wife.'

'That's you all right, Hugh,' said the fair-haired wife.

Macpherson frowned and shook his head.

'According to Lall,' said the doctor, 'he's a man of substance. Beautiful house. Owns the estate, as well as manages it. Well, his wife does. She's a Dusun, daughter of the chief that owned the whole territory. They've got a couple of children.'

Macpherson went on frowning. It was none of his business, but he did not like white men marrying native women, amahs or princesses, and having half-breed children. Others did not like it either; but his reasons were religious. Instructed by Christ as well as by Jehovah, he knew that compassion must be shown in addition to disapproval.

'He's dying,' said Dr Willard, quietly. 'Of cancer. In considerable pain, I'm afraid.'

Mrs Macpherson gasped with pity. 'Poor man,' she whispered.

'He wants to see you, Macpherson. He asked Lall to pass on the message.'

'Me? But I don't know him. I've never set eyes on the man.'

'He must have heard of you; must have been impressed. You should be flattered. That was three days ago. Lall thought he had a week at most left. You'd have to hurry to get there in time.'

'I assure you,' said Macpherson, 'he's made a mistake. Perhaps he was delirious.'

'No. According to Lall he's remarkably clear-headed, considering. Perhaps because you're a Scotsman too?'

'There are at least a dozen Scotsmen in Kalimantan.'

'Well, you're the one he's asked for. Whether or not you go is up to you. I've done my bit; passed on the baton, so to speak. Cheerio. Glad to have met you, Mr Dougary. Hope you have a pleasant flight.'

They watched him stride through the crowd in the hall. At the exit he stopped, turned, hesitated, and came back.

'Sorry,' he said. 'Just remembered. This damned climate rots the memory. It seems McArthur was born in Islay, one of the Hebrides. So were you, weren't you, Macpherson?'

'I was born in Skye.'

'Well, isn't that next door as islands go?'

'Far from it. They're hundreds of miles apart.'

'We went on holiday to Islay about five or six years ago,' said Mrs Macpherson.

'Perhaps you met him there then?'

'No. No, we didn't. Do you remember, Hugh?'

'We met nobody from Kalimantan there.'

'That can't be it then,' said the doctor. 'The mystery remains. Well, goodbye again.'

Again they watched him go.

If he had turned a second time he would have seen Macpherson snapping his fingers in triumph.

'Got it,' cried Macpherson. 'My memory's usually good. Years ago, in the Sports Club. Some of us were chatting about unusual churches we'd seen. I mentioned the Round Kirk at Bowmore, in Islay. This man was sitting at the bar. He must have been listening. He was pretty drunk, if I remember. He got up and came over.

'I was born in Bowmore,' he said. That was all. Then he went. I said nothing. I hardly got a good look at him. None of us knew who he was, but somebody at the bar called over that he was a planter from Pensiangan. I can't even remember what he looked like. Can you, Mary?'

'I didn't even notice him, Hugh.'

'Well,' murmured Mr Dougary, 'whatever he looked like then, he looks different now, poor soul.'

Then came the announcement they were waiting for. Passengers for Singapore were to go to the departure gate.

The Macphersons escorted the old man. He quavered thanks for their hospitality: perhaps they would see him again next year, if he was spared. Then at the very last moment he muttered, 'Go and comfort that poor man.'

Macpherson had no time to reply. He gazed after the old dotard in astonishment.

'Did you hear that?' he asked. 'Did he say I should go to Pensiangan?'

'That's what he said, Hugh.'

'I thought so.' Still astonished, Macpherson watched the old man staggering across the hot bright runway; a hostess helped him up the steps into the plane. He had been too long in the tropics, thought Macpherson: he had lost that fair but tight grip on essentials which every effective Christian must have.

'I'm afraid he's past it,' he said, as they made for their car.

'He does his best, Hugh.'

'Yes, but half the time he's not listening to what you're saying. Then out of the blue to say a thing like that!'

He shook his head, still astonished: she kept hers very still; what astonished her was his astonishment.

II

For the rest of that day Macpherson never once thought of Mr Dougary or of McArthur. Until five o'clock he was much too busy with his work where, indeed, his Christian forbearance was put at strain. This wasn't because the Chinese drivers of the big earth-moving machines, or the numerous native labourers, some of them women, provoked him with laziness and inefficiency. On the contrary, they all worked with their usual honesty and diligence, almost as if, he had often remarked to Mary, they were doing it, not for money – not that they got much – but for pride in themselves. Pagans or Buddhists of a peculiar sort, they gave many Christians a showing up.

No, what vexed him that day was what had been vexing him for weeks: this was the stupid stubbornness of an old native whose miserable ramshackle hovel happened to be right in the path of the new double carriage-way. Other much better houses had already been bull-dozed out of the way, their owners having eagerly accepted compensation. This old nuisance had refused. Work would soon be held up. The trouble was, owing to the political situation in the country, not long after Merdeka or freedom from British rule, with each of the three parties aspiring to be the champion of the aboriginal natives, compulsion was not to be used. Moreover, though the road would be to the whole country's benefit, those native politicians, with childish perversity, seemed to enjoy watching the mighty white tuans of the PWD being thwarted by one old man with a face like a coconut. When it suited them they would very quickly throw the old fool aside, and reduce his compensation for having made a pest of himself.

In the meantime, however, work would soon be halted.

As an engineer, Macpherson had hitherto left the negotiations to the PWD administrators; but that day, accompanied by his assistant Jock Neilson, he went to the house and tried to persuade the old man to give up. Obstructive senile obduracy, exhibited with imbecilic cackles, is never easy to oppose with patience or reasonableness or Christian tolerance. Macpherson tried hard, standing in that stinking little house with flies on his lips; but when he looked out of the window and saw not far off the great orange hungry machines that in a day or two would be baulked by this small, brown, skinny, 'ragged-arsed', to use Jock's word, semiimbecilic native, he had the greatest difficulty in reminding himself that in spite of everything this was a human being, a soul capable of worshipping God, and not a decrepit animal to be kicked out of the way. He had been harsher than he should.

When he got home he said nothing to Mary about his failure. As much as possible he liked to protect her from his professional troubles. After a shower and a cup of tea, he took the two children, Donald aged seven and a half and Morag aged nine, a stroll along the beach near their house. Soon the sky, and sea, and the sand, and their faces grew pink with the usual magnificent sunset. Better still, their young souls were peaceful with it.

An observant onlooker, such as his wife from her verandah, would have noticed that though he was obviously proud and fond of his children, and they of him, still there appeared to be a strangeness or awkwardness between them. Mary of course was most keenly aware of it. She knew it was because of his own upbringing, when affection might have been felt but never was spontaneously shown: as a result his had grown stiff and awkward.

More intimately still, she knew that he made love as though there was something impure in it; it made no difference that they had God's permission, having been married by a Church of Scotland minister in one of the best churches in Glasgow. With a similar puritanic upbringing, she had started out with the same foolish feeling of guilt, but she could easily have overcome it if Hugh just once had given joy full rein. Instead he had curbed it resolutely. Their love-making was always done in the dark, even the moon being shut out; and there were no preliminaries of affectionate nonsense. When he was finished he went to sleep as fast as he could, as if fleeing from something.

Often she lay in the bed next to his wondering what she could do to save him, though she could not name what it was he needed saving from.

That night, after Mr Dougary's departure, suddenly reckless, for the first time in her marital life, before he had time to escape into sleep, she said: 'Hugh, that poor man in Pensiangan, who's dying of cancer, who asked you to go and see him, don't you think you should, as Mr Dougary said?'

He said nothing, did not move. She was sure he was only pretending to be asleep. She did not have the necessary courage or vindictiveness or hope to say it twice. After four or five minutes of increasing disappointment she sighed, and prepared herself for sleep.

Suddenly he heaved round to face her.

'Did I hear right?' he asked. 'Did you say I should go to Pensiangan?'

'Yes, Hugh, I did.'

'To see a man I wouldn't even recognise?'

'Is that so important? He's dying.'

'Mary, this is Asia. There are millions dying.'

'But he's one of us, Hugh, a Scotsman.'

'Does that mean he's any better than all those millions of others?'

'No, but it makes him closer to us.'

He shook his head. 'Let's get this clear, Mary. I'm as sorry for him as you are. But pity's cheap, too cheap. We've got to keep up standards. Pity can lower them, you know. You're speaking as if he was alone. He's married, isn't he? He's got his wife to comfort him. Whose fault is it she's a native? He's got children, and in-laws. He's far from being alone. He made his choice. Good luck to him. But why should we lower our standards to accommodate him, or anyone else?'

She did not understand. His anger was as unintelligible as his meaning. He had no imagination. She had little, he had none. She remembered his mother, the devout Skye woman, telling her that proudly: her Hugh always gave things their true value.

'This is something that goes beyond nationality or even principle,' he said.

'Yes, Hugh. I'm sorry. Goodnight.'

'Goodnight.'

He was asleep inside five minutes. She lay awake for much longer, tears in her eyes, only now and then thinking of the unhappy man at Pensiangan.

Next morning Macpherson had forgotten their post-coital disagreement and the man who had caused it. He was very patient with the children at breakfast. Usually they were noisy and talkative, asking each other and their parents half a dozen shrill questions a minute, without waiting for answers. Previously their father, when asked something had insisted on answering and on being listened to. Recently though he had decided it was a mistake to attempt to discipline his children as rigorously as he had been disciplined at their age. Without anyone telling him, he had become aware that perhaps he was too slow and awkward at expressing his feelings. He must not imprison his children's feelings in the same long enforced silences.

Therefore this morning, when he was in the midst of an explanation as to why chichaks were able to walk on ceilings, he just smiled and shook his head when the children began to chatter about school.

He did not find it easy to see as harmless childish illogicality what he thought was downright impudence. He still rebuked them, but not as sternly as before. Morag seldom wept now when he scolded her. She kissed him goodnight more fondly.

He was on his way down to the car when the telephone rang. Mary answered it.

'It's for you,' she called down. 'Dave Sloan.'

He came hurrying up. Sloan was his boss, the Director of the PWD. About to retire in less than a year, he had more or less promised to recommend Macpherson as his successor. His qualifications as an engineer were not as good as Macpherson's.

'Hello, Dave. An early call surely. You just about missed me.'

'Sorry, Hugh. Something's come up. Another of these damned conferences. I just heard about it ten minutes ago, by phone. What you have to expect now that Jack's the master. I expect you know I was going to Keningau today, to consult with the Aussies about that damned village they want to knock down.'

At Keningau the Australian army, as a Commonwealth gesture, was building a road to open up part of the interior. A village stood in their way: they wanted to knock it down and build a better one a hundred yards or so away. The trouble was some holy trees would have to be chopped down too, and this the villagers objected to. Pagans though they were, Macpherson was inclined to sympathise with them: men willing to forego new houses for the sake of ancestral gods however heathenish were, in his view, to be complimented in an age so greedy for material benefits.

'Could you go in my place, Hugh? It's very short notice, I know, but it's really an engineering problem. You know more about building roads than I do.'

'Pleased to go, Dave. No bother.'

'I don't want to influence your decision, but the word is here at the Secretariat that the Aussies are to have their way.'

'I must say I've got a lot more sympathy for these villagers than for that old fellow that's holding up my own road.'

'Sure. Well, the plane's at ten. Your ticket will be waiting for you, and you can have my room at the Rest House. All right?'

'All right, Dave.'

Macpherson put the telephone down. He felt pleased. It certainly looked as if the succession was his. Being Director for a few years would make a big difference to his pension.

'What did Dave want?' asked Mary.

He told her, and was puzzled by the way she put her hand to her mouth as if to stifle a cry of amazement.

'I'll be back tomorrow,' he said, smiling.

'It's not that. I just thought, how funny. First you happened to be at the airport when Dr Willard arrived, and now you've been asked to go to Keningau.'

Having again forgotten McArthur, he saw no connection. 'What's funny about that?'

She saw that he was genuinely puzzled. 'Nothing. I'm being silly. I'd better get your bag packed.'

There were tears in her eyes again. He thought it was because he would be away from home for a night. He was touched, yet puzzled. She had never been a woman given to easy tears. He would never have married her if she had. It must be that her period was due. Perhaps that was the reason why last night she had behaved so oddly. Her nails had dug into his back. He had had to tell her not to.

Two hours later, flying high above the Pensiangan valley, with the jungle below like a vast garden of curly kale, he thought about McArthur. To die in that land of thick jungle, primitive villages, and hot, steamy climate was sad for any white man but especially so for one born in Islay, that island of delightful breezes, invigorating sea, and fresh green hills. Still, what difference did it make where a man died? One place was as near to God as another. For a few minutes of luxurious supposing, Macpherson pretended it was him dying in the Pensiangan jungle, far from Mary and the children. Thank God they were safe home in Scotland. He hoped he would not be sorry for himself: he would not make appeals to strangers. If he was too weak to read his Bible he would recite passages learnt in childhood and never forgotten. He would be an example to the heathens watching him die: they would talk about his Christian fortitude afterwards for years, and to that degree at least would be converted.

Just before they were over Keningau the plane lurched and dropped suddenly: a box fell off a shelf. Some of the other passengers, natives, looked as apprehensive as their dark thick faces could. Macpherson knew there was no danger, it had been only a freak current of air; already the plane was steady again. But for a second or two he, like the rest, had tasted the possibility of imminent death, and had been, for that fraction of time, terrified: Christian consolation had not been quite so swift as terror. This happened in his mind so quickly, and was over so soon, that he was never fully aware of it. He did not either notice any contrast between his moment of real panic and his long, slow, patient, faithful, agonised, pretended dying in McArthur's place.

Before the plane landed on the grassy runway he had assumed the role of deputy of the Director, first in command in that area. In this capacity he greeted Phil Barnes, Superintendent at Keningau, who was waiting with a Land Rover. On the way into town he asked what arrangements had been made.

Barnes was a quiet red-haired man with an enormous number of freckles on his brow and his knees. He was known to enjoy conviviality. The coming of the drouthy Australians had been a godsend to him. He did not like Macpherson, but thought he concealed it very well. An honest man, he could not help feeling a little embarrassed as he remembered how, last night in the soldiers' mess, exuberant on whisky and Foster's beer, he had described the divisional engineer as 'good at his job, better than anybody else to be sure, and a dour hater of strong drink.' He had said it in a Scotch accent, which he could imitate very well.

'We're meeting the Aussies at two at the village,' he said.

'What's your own opinion?'

'They're lucky to get offered a new village. The present one's filthy and falling to bits.'

'It's the trees they're worried about. They're sacred.'

'As I was saying, why can't they carry their ancestors' spirits with them, and install them in new trees?'

'It's not funny to them, Phil.'

Barnes replied in a high-pitched sing-song querulous voice: 'To chop down their trees will be sacrilege, no less.'

'Who's that supposed to be? Not Maluku?'

'No. A doctor at the hospital, Lall, an Indian. Passionate little character, especially after a couple of pints.'

'I thought Indians didn't touch alcohol.'

'He does. He thinks it shows he's a man of the world.'

The name Lall had meant nothing to Macpherson. 'Shows he's a fool, more like,' he said. 'What business is it of his?'

'None. One dark skin supporting other dark skins against white skins. He's a lot darker than they are, almost black.'

'His colour doesn't matter. But we can ignore him. What about Maluku the assembly-man?'

'Sniffing around for baksheesh.'

'A bribe, do you mean?'

'Sure. Mind you, what he gets for being an assembly-man wouldn't keep you in beer.'

'Very little would keep me in beer.'

'Sorry. You know what I mean. So he thinks he's got a right to add to it any chance he gets.'

'Well, he'll find this is no chance.'

'All the same, in these parts a little baksheesh can make things go a lot more smoothly.'

'I don't believe in bribes.'

'Oh well, if you call it bribes.'

'What else is it?'

Macpherson did not approve of bribes because, as he had more than once explained to Mary, when he was offered one himself he felt insulted; and, as he also explained to her, not noticing her slight incredulity, he always applied to other people, whatever their colour or station in life, the same standards by which he judged himself.

One bribe offered him had taken the form of a headman's barebosomed daughter with lice in her hair. She had been sent to his bed in the guest hut. He had received her courteously and asked her to get rid of some of the cockroaches with which the place was infested. She had done so, picking them up in her hands and throwing them out of the door. Then, with her hands unwashed, she had slipped off her one garment and lain down on the thin mat that was his bed. He had had difficulty in making her go. She could not understand, just as her old father hadn't understood why Macpherson had refused to take any tapai or rice beer. Even if she had been beautiful and clean he would have sent her away. When he saw her next morning, looking dejected, he had been surprised at the feeling of disgust that had surged up in him. He had hated her very nipples.

At the conference held that afternoon in the village under sentence he took an instant aversion to Maluku, who kept on talking with all the nasty ingratiation of the brown man in power jealous of the white man his servant but also overwhelmingly his superior. The villagers, on the other hand, won his sympathy. They were not only humble and respectful, they were also genuinely concerned about their sacred trees: if these were cut down they believed their own souls would be snatched away. Macpherson reassured them this was not so. He tried gently to remove their heathenish fears. He praised the trees as magnificent.

In the end of course he had to agree with the Australian engineers that to make the necessary detour would involve too much delay and extra work. He broke the bad news to the villagers as humanely as he could. He pointed out that the new village which would be built for them – it would take the sappers a couple of days – would be clean, free from the filth of generations which had brought so much disease. (Too many were consumptive and syphilitic.)

It would have been too much to expect them to be convinced, but they were obviously grateful to him for the trouble he had taken to make the position clear. It was him they kept clamouring round. When they asked him what would happen to them if they did not consent to their homes and their shrines being demolished he had to answer truthfully and regretfully that they would be shifted by force. Progress could not be held up by stupid or superstitious people. He took trouble to explain to them what progress meant.

To the whining Maluku he was outwardly most affable. As a person the man was a sneaky self-seeker, deserving contempt; but as an assemblyman and therefore a representative of the country he deserved respect. Macpherson did not hesitate to show it. The way to the Directorship was lined with Malukus.

He would have been angry but not ashamed if he had been in the Australians' mess that evening and heard Barnes mocking the diplomatic way he had spoken to Maluku. He would have reminded Barnes that in the UK he, who had only a mechanic's qualifications, would be lucky to be foreman of a garage.

However, since he declined the invitation to the mess, and never for a moment suspected he would be the subject there of drunken and ribald mockery, he felt content with himself in the Rest House that evening. He had it to himself, which pleased him. The last time he had been there two educationists, one Canadian and one from New Zealand, were his fellow guests. They were on an inspection tour of interior schools. Not only had they drunk too much whisky, they had also gone out on the prowl for whores. At breakfast they had expected him to laugh at their exploits.

Though the chef was Chinese, noted for his bamboo shoots, Macpherson asked for a plain meal of tomato soup, steak, and cherry pie. After eating he read an adventure story while waiting for his call to Api.

The line was bad. It blurred Mary's voice and gave the absurd impression she was reluctant to talk. He mentioned this to her.

'You sound cheery enough,' she said.

'Well, I've got reason to be. I think I handled it well. I'll be back tomorrow.'

'So you're not going to Pensiangan?'

He did not know what she meant. He had forgotten McArthur. 'I said nothing about going to Pensiangan.'

'I thought you might have changed your mind.'

'It never was on my mind. What are you talking about?'

'I'm talking about Mr McArthur, that's dying.'

He remembered at once. 'I thought I'd explained that.'

'I haven't been able to get him out of my mind.'

She seemed to be weeping.

Trying to be fair to her, he forced himself to think again about McArthur, and assess his own responsibility. He could not understand how his own wife, who knew how conscientious he was, could ever expect him to drop his work and go off into the wilds to see a man he'd never even spoken to.

'He's a Scotsman, Hugh. He was born in Bowmore. Remember you said you might retire to Islay? You could never be happy there if you turned your back on him.'

Yes, she was weeping.

Compassion for her, and anger against her, grew in him equally. He loved her for her kind heart but resented her hypocrisy. He had seen her in India in tears of vexation because some maimed and blind beggars wouldn't give her peace. For the past eight years she had lived in Api in great comfort, oblivious to the hungry, dying millions of Asia.

He let her weep. She struggled to subdue it. He loved her and was proud of her. At bottom she was a sensible, loyal, trustworthy woman. She was now honestly realizing that the emotion she had just shown was extravagant and, in the circumstances, more of a hindrance than a help.

'Never mind,' she said, dully. 'I'm sorry I spoke. You'll be home tomorrow then?'

'Yes. The plane's in about ten. Will you be there?'

'Yes, I'll be there. Goodnight.'

Surprised, and rather hurt, by the abruptness with which she had ended the conversation, he went into the big dimly lit lounge that hummed with mosquitoes, and found there, waiting for him, a small fat bald very black Indian with a smell fragrant but nasty. He bounced up, hand held out, and announced himself, almost ecstatically, to be Dr Lall.

'And you are Mr Macpherson, of the PWD, Api. Tall, lean, with a hard face, and a soft fair-haired wife: just as poor McArthur described you. Pity the said wife is unfortunately absent. How do you do, Mr Macpherson? You are a kind man, a stern man as I can see but also a kind one. So my good friend Dr Willard conveyed to you my message, and here you are, en route to Pensiangan. How wonderful is humanity.'

'Just a minute, Dr Lall. You've got it wrong, I'm afraid. I'm here in Keningau on PWD business. Tomorrow I return to Api. I'm going nowhere near Pensiangan.'

Lall, an exaggerating fellow if ever there was one shrank back as if a cobra had just struck at him.

'For God's sake, man,' he cried, 'you must go to Pensiangan. A hand has been held out, you must take it.'

'Mr McArthur seems to have made a mistake. I don't know him.'

Lall had been drinking: as well as that unpleasant perfume, there was a stink of beer off him. The tears that now came into his brown bloodshot eyes were beery. He was trying to make a tragedy out of what was an unhappy but very frequent occurrence, a man dying in pain. It was a fault of his race. Small wonder a handful of level-headed British had held countless millions of them in subjection for over a hundred years.

'He has his wife and family with him,' he said, reasonably. 'And all his wife's relations. I should think strangers wouldn't be welcome at such a time.'

Lall rose on his toes; even so he hardly came up to Macpherson's chin.

'Mr Macpherson,' he said solemnly, 'you are a man without vision.'

Macpherson took no offence. It would have been ridiculous letting himself be provoked by a fat half-drunk overheated Indian doctor with pretensions to be a poet or prophet. India, after all, was the land of fakirs.

'I see what's there,' he said. 'That's vision enough.'

'If you do not go to hold that dying man's hand, do you know what you will have done? You will have stopped the stars in their courses.'

Macpherson grinned. 'I'll take that risk.'

'You make us all take that risk. Imagine, please, it is your brother who is dying yonder in the jungle.'

'As I said, Dr Lall, I only see what's there. He isn't my brother.'

'Is not every man your brother?'

Macpherson shook his head. He was not to be enticed by that nonsense.

He had too often been in companies in Scotland when that brotherhood of man had been proclaimed with far more passionate tears than this little black man was capable of. Next day he had seen those fervent proclaimers of 'a man's a man for a' that', sober again, with dry eyes and a hard-faced acceptance of man's selfishness and the limitations it would impose forever.

'That's too easy to say,' he said.

'Forgive me,' whispered Lall. 'I see now you are a most unhappy man. You are a desert, not a green field. You, not Mr McArthur, is to be pitied. He has been very happy in his day. If I was a man of religion, sir, if I believed in God, I would pray to Him for you; but since I do not, since I believe that man must achieve his own destiny, all I can offer you is my pity.'

Then out he walked, or rather waddled: his very gait showed up his words as ludicrous.

From the verandah Macpherson watched and listened. The stars were bright and normal. The cicadas' hum was very loud. It appeared that the odd little man was either talking to himself or weeping. Once again it became obvious why the British, with so many Scots among them, had been able to conquer India and hold it so long.

Perhaps it was because this superiority of the Scot over the Indian was in his mind, as he was cleaning his teeth and looking at his face in the bathroom mirror, that the resolution, though it was nothing so dramatic at first, occurred to him. He was not merely cleaning his teeth, he was also saying his prayers. This he had done all his life. As a boy in Skye he had knelt on the cold waxcloth and shut his eyes tightly, but since then, when he could please himself, he had sat on the edge of his bed, or stood in front of the bathroom mirror as at present, or even, with no sense of impropriety, perched on the lavatory. In Skye too there had been a fixed form of words, to be spoken aloud, with grim humility. This also had changed. Adult prayer was best silent: nothing now about sins repented or favors begged; only a flicker or two of gratitude for another day safely and prosperously fulfilled. At some times the gratitude was warmer and more spontaneous than at others.

Suddenly then, with the toothbrush arrested, into his mind to join the thankfulness came the suggestion, the proposal, the challenge. It was not in any way inspired or provoked by Mary or by Dr Lall, for he hadn't been thinking of them at all. It simply rose out of the depths of his prayerful mind.

He found himself asking why not go to Pensiangan and see McArthur. It would be against his nature, against his common-sense, against his lifelong habit of avoiding extravagance in spending and living; and therefore it would be proved a mistake, in some way he could not foresee. His objections would be vindicated, Mary would have to admit his judgment was better than hers.

Next morning, when he awoke, he was rather surprised to find that what after all had been only a vote of self-confidence had, during sleep, hardened into a determination. If anyone had suggested the Lord had been at work in him he would not have denied it, though he might have tried to describe the process in more modern phraseology, for what had been adequate in Skye forty years ago would not quite do nowadays.

Before breakfast he telephoned Barnes and astonished him by saying he wanted to use the PWD launch to go up river to Pensiangan.

'What have we got going up there?' asked Barnes.

'This is private. I want to visit a planter called McArthur. He's dying.'

'I didn't know you knew him. You never mentioned him.'

'I don't know him. For some reason he sent a message through Lall that he wanted to see me.'

'My God! I mean, why? – if you don't know him.'

It was clear that Barnes, who seemed to know McArthur, could see little in common between him and Macpherson. Macpherson felt vindicated already.

'I don't know why. Perhaps I'll find out. Do you know him?'

'I've had a drink with him once or twice here at the club. I've been in his house. Look, Macpherson, would you like me to go with you? I'd like to see him, before he pushes off.'

'If you don't mind, I think I'd rather go myself. It's a kind of personal thing.'

'Please yourself. I wouldn't have thought Mac was your sort.'

'What's my sort?'

'Well, you don't drink, to begin with; and he does. You don't care much for coloured people; he married one. He's always been a great man for the women.'

Macpherson was angry at being accused of not caring much for coloured people. It was unfair and untrue. He had spoken to the villagers yesterday far more sympathetically than Barnes had done.

'I'd be obliged if you could have the boat at the quay by ten,' he said.

'It'll be there,' replied Barnes, after a long pause. He had been tempted to say it was under repair. Why should poor McArthur be plagued on his death-bed by this arrogant pussy-foot?

'Since this isn't PWD business I'll pay for the petrol and the men's wages.'

'No need for that.'

'I prefer it.'

'Suit yourself. You'll not manage back today, you know. Mac will put you up. He's got a beautiful house, and his wife's a charmer. Give them my regards.'

It was nearer eleven before the launch set out. Macpherson had been delayed trying to get through to Mary in Api to tell of his change of plan.

Her exclamations of joy, and of pride in him, had been strangely excessive, and there had been an element of forgiveness in them. He had been curter than he should in reminding her that all he was doing was travelling sixty miles or so up a tedious but not dangerous river, in a fairly comfortable launch, to humour a man either delirious or dead. There was nothing heroic or big-hearted in that. Lall did it fairly often, sometimes with an additional trek through sweltering jungle; and Lall, whom he'd met, was fat and conceited, nobody's idea of a hero.

She could not be dissuaded from her praises. She had even wept. Her present state must be menopausal. Yet she was only forty-two.

From early childhood Macpherson had been conditioned to look upon all of life as a duty, even the parts he enjoyed. Mary once, in the early days of their marriage, in half-humourous half-frightened expostulation, had accused him of making love dutifully. He had rather huffishly denied it, but later, after some private rumination, he had seen that she was right. He had not been ashamed as she seemed to think he should. On the contrary, he felt pleased and relieved, that even his sexual instincts were under the authority of the Lord.

Most men would have looked on that trip up the river as an adventure, a holiday not only from work, but also from home and family; especially those who, like him, were fond of boats. Macpherson could never feel like that: responsibility was closer to him than his shadow, for this in the dark when he was asleep took time off.

The two native boatmen, on the other hand, always felt on holiday. Dressed in the briefest shorts, and with coloured rags round their foreheads, they had squat-nosed piratical faces. As they gazed ahead, on the look-out for logs or crocodiles or, as they said gleefully, drowned women, or as they frowned at the wall of jungle on either side, they looked very like their great-grandfathers not so long ago as these raided villages along this river, raping, burning, killing, and hacking off heads.

Whenever they caught Macpherson's eye they would instantly grin in acceptance of their role as menial hirelings of the PWD, but when they didn't know he was looking at them they played at pirates. In their belts were knives, and razor-sharp parangs were to hand, to chop away obstructing branches or slaughter imaginary foes.

Now and then, for the first hour or so, he would call out something to them, harshly, to remind them of their true position.

For a few miles the river was the colour of cocoa made with milk, then it grew as green as crocodiles' backs, then suddenly blue in open spaces, and once as clear as a Skye burn. Crocodiles slept on banks. A python lay on sand, guarding its eggs. Monkeys swore from the tops of trees. Butterflies as big as birds, and birds as brightly coloured as butterflies, flew past. Sometimes jungle gave way to plantations of sago palms, and villages would be seen, with bamboo stairs leading down to the water's edge. Bare-breasted women washed clothes, or themselves; they waved to the boatmen. Big-bellied children slept on their feet.

The constant heat, the hypnotic swish of the water, the glimpses of people as remote as the stone age, the dazzle of sun seen through millions of leaves, all combined to give Macpherson the feeling that he was in the midst of a dream, especially as his purpose had become no more urgent or comprehensible, but less and less meaningful. He felt that this journey would never end, but would keep going round bends of the river and of time for all eternity.

He even wondered if he was ill, if the sweat pouring off him was that of fever. He had already taken the day's dose of anti-malaria tablets, and was too characteristically cautious to take more than was stated on the box.

He only noticed the quay ahead when one of the boatmen shouted and pointed to it. It was like a dream to see there, after so much jungle, a substantial pier, with sheds, and boats, and men dressed in shirts and shorts, and a Land Rover. Beyond were many thousands of rubber trees, healthy and well-kept. Among the trunks could be glimpsed tappers as devoted as priests in a huge pillared church.

On the quay was a small dapper Malay wearing a wide-brimmed white hat. He introduced himself, in prim self-satisfied English, as Razak the under-manager. He explained that Mr Barnes had sent a message by radio telephone. So Mr McArthur was expecting him.

'Is he well enough to expect anybody?' asked Macpherson. 'I was told he is dying.'

'Please listen.'

Macpherson now heard, some distance off, the sound of gongs, not beaten merrily as at a wedding, but slowly and sonorously.

'They are frightening off the evil spirits,' said Razak, with a Muslim's smile. 'They believe that these spirits gather round to snatch the soul as it leaves the body and carry it off to the mountain. Therefore they must be scared off.'

'Who believes such nonsense?' asked Macpherson, with a Christian's frown. 'Surely not McArthur?'

'Indeed, not. His wife's people. They are all pagans.'

'Why does he allow it? It would get on my nerves.'

'Mr McArthur says he has the tolerance of the man who believes in no-one's god.'

'That isn't tolerance,' said Macpherson. He was about to add that it was arrogance, but remembered in time he was speaking to a brown man.

They climbed into the Land Rover. The driver was told to take it easy. Even so, they had to hold on for the road was rough. Macpherson could smell its coral foundation. A lot of money and labour had been spent on this estate.

'I understand the estate belongs to McArthur,' said Macpherson.

'More properly to his wife. According to the law only natives can own land. Mrs McArthur is the daughter of the king of all this district.'

'You mean she's a kind of princess?'

'That is so.'

Not that she would look like a princess. None of the native women were beautiful. Their lips thick, their noses flat, their bellies big, and their legs lumpy.

'I've been told the house is beautiful,' he said.

'See for yourself.'

There it was, in a vast clearing, high, round, and made of wood. The roof was conical; on the point sat a great carved bird with wings outspread. The house itself was built of teak and ebony and other handsome woods. Surrounded by flowering trees and bushes, it too was like a tree, gigantic and glorious. Macpherson was astounded. In front of it was the most magnificent frangipani he had ever seen. The grass beneath was white with blossom. He was reminded of foam, and of the great strand at Laggan in Islay, near Bowmore, where it had been blown across the sand like white balls.

Here, though, was no sea breeze. It was very hot and still. No birds chirped. The gongs, louder now, emphasised the stillness.

Macpherson felt dirty and hot. He resented too an enticement he could not understand.

In the shade of a majestic tree, with white flowers that reminded him of the horse chestnuts of home, except that these were larger and heavily perfumed, was waiting a woman, his hostess, mistress of this extraordinary house, McArthur's wife, the princess. As he had thought, she was stout and heavy, both in the face and body. But even at rest she had what he was forced to acknowledge as dignity. She wore a native dress of black, red, and gold, with a head-band to match.

His Mary was considered to be a fine-looking woman. So she was, but she did not have anything of this woman's impressive presence. The admission shook the very foundations of his soul.

He began to feel a strange deep sadness. Here, in this marvellous place, in this house which had so much character, McArthur, the man from far-off Bowmore, must have lived a happy life. Into the sadness that Macpherson felt came pity, not only for McArthur, soon to be cut off from this happiness, but also somehow for himself, although his wife was waiting for him in Api and they would live together for many more years.

It was as though his mind, with its ballast of principles and beliefs, had broken loose and was beginning to drift.

The Land Rover with Razak in it drove away. The little Malay had been very respectful towards her.

Macpherson greeted her. His mind drifted still further from the shore of lifelong habit. He had thought that when he met McArthur's native wife he would naturally be sorry for her because her husband was dying, and because too she was a native woman. He had taken for granted that she would be protected from grief by the animal-like stoicism peculiar to primitives. After all, her ancestors less than fifty years ago had hunted for heads, and had been hunted for their own heads. Sudden bloody death must have been a commonplace for hundreds of years. The inhabitants must therefore have acquired a protective thickness or soul

How wrong he had been. Here she was greeting him with a dignity that the Governor's wife, in the British days, would have been proud of. She shed no tears, but no one, not even Macpherson with his prejudices loose within him, could have doubted that her husband was dying and she loved him.

She thanked him for coming and said her husband was expecting him; but first he must wash and rest and refresh himself.

The outside of the house had impressed him, the inside had him gaping in wonder and admiration. The great round room was like a church, paneled and floored with exotic woods. He had never been in a house that smelled so pleasantly. Everywhere were delicate green plants, and bright flowers. All round the wall was carved a frieze of leaves. There was a profusion of carvings, the largest and most astonishing being two life-sized figures, in a shining wood, one male and the other female, as naked as Adam and Eve, and looking, as Macpherson had to admit, just as innocent, though their private parts were boldly and meticulously fashioned.

Someone – could it have been a man from Bowmore? – had made beautiful and inspiring use of primitive skills.

Through a doorway came, like a creature in his dream, a young girl, a servant, feet and bosom bare; in her black hair was frangipani. If she had dropped her bright red sarong she could have been mistaken for the life-size statue.

In other expatriate houses Macpherson had seen amahs much too comely for mere dishwashing. They had evidently slept with their masters. He had been disgusted. This girl, though, lacked utterly that smugness which in a coloured woman indicated sexual claim on a white man. When she smiled, showing beautiful teeth, she meant only friendliness. It was a part of the welcome and the delight of that house.

Anxiously he warned himself not to exaggerate. McArthur had a large estate, a magnificent unusual house, a dignified native wife, and servants who knew their place. That was a great deal, worthy of wonder; but did it justify this feeling of light-headedness, worse of light-heartedness, that kept growing in him? He had always believed that his life of duty, obedience to God, thrift and caution had been leading towards some revelation. Could this be it? This was not his triumph, but McArthur's. He remembered that McArthur was dying.

He followed the girl up a staircase with a balustrade that deserved hours of study, so numerous and exquisite were its carvings of faces, birds, flowers, and fish. Under the thin red cloth the girl's buttocks were plump: sweat glistened faintly on her smooth back. For a moment or two he let himself imagine that this was his house, and this girl was his wife: they were going up to bed. He felt he knew her more intimately than he had ever known poor Mary.

She showed him into a bedroom with open French windows and a view of red and orange flowers. She opened a door and showed him a bathroom. Everything was ready. He felt deeply moved. A man in mortal pain, whom he did not know, was treating him with flawless consideration.

He had asked Mrs McArthur how her husband was. With a smile that not even he could have misinterpreted as congenital callousness, she had shaken her head. He was asleep, she said. Macpherson knew she meant drugged, deliberately no doubt to escape pain. She said there was no hurry. After he had washed and rested and refreshed himself, he would be taken to see her husband.

The gongs were still sounding. He could also hear the humming of a big generator.

He asked the girl where the children were. At their grandfather's house in the village, she replied.

Before taking a bath, he stood on the terrace gazing down at the garden and smelling its many perfumes. He was curiously conscious of the great bird on the roof above, though he could not see it from there. He wondered again why McArthur had asked to see him. Previously he had thought of the planter as living in squalid conditions with his native wife and children; therefore his asking Macpherson to come had been a kind of whine for help. Now he saw he had been honored. Whatever he had McArthur did not need it. Why then had he been asked to come?

About two hours later – it was now after six and almost dark – he went downstairs, much refreshed. The house was lit by electricity. In the large round room he studied the carvings more carefully. On a shelf were several dancing figures, about a foot high, in the shape of headhunters, each with a severed head clutched to his breast. He had heard that this taking of heads had been part of their religion: their gods could only be propitiated by such offerings. He had been disgusted. Now he gazed in uneasy wonder at the expression of fierce rapture depicted on all of these faces. He was still horrified, but he looked more deeply, and more humbly, at his horror.

Dimly he perceived that there were aspects and areas of faith that he had not known existed.

Mrs McArthur appeared. She looked tired. She wore the same dress. He thought she had been watching by her husband's bed.

'Can I see him now?' he asked.

'He is still asleep. Perhaps you would like to eat now?'

Coming up in the launch, he had swallowed two Enterovioform tablets. He always did this when in danger of having to accept native food. But in the dining-room he found prepared for him a meal he could have ordered in any good Scottish hotel: chilled pineapple juice, fish, gammon steak with peas, brussels sprouts and potatoes, and for dessert ice-cream with tinned pears. He was able to eat the lot with enjoyment and without a qualm. Again he felt grateful to McArthur who, in spite of his severe pain, had taken thought to what his guest would like.

The girl with the frangipani in her hair served him. She wore a red blouse. He was asked if he wanted wine or beer. His preference for water caused no surprise.

He was just finished, drinking his coffee, when his hostess appeared at the door. She was as calm as ever.

'He is awake now,' she said. 'He wants to see you.'

He noticed that, though she did not seem to hurry, she went quickly. As he followed her the thought that came into his mind, not altogether incongruously, was that he had never shown his love for Mary as he should.

The bedroom into which he was led was almost in darkness: the only light was a small lamp with a red shade. McArthur lay facing the door. He opened his eyes with a great effort as Macpherson came in, smiled very faintly, and closed them again. Macpherson had no recollection of what the man from Bowmore had looked like in the Sports Club: he had not looked at him attentively, or interestedly, enough. But he knew that in this dying man a terrible change had taken place. The face was hollow, the neck thin, the hair grey and wet.

Mrs McArthur wiped the sick man's face and head with a damp cloth. She bent low and whispered to him in her own language. He replied with hoarse painful slowness.

On a table was a tray with the means of keeping him drugged, safe from pain.

The gongs still sounded, louder now that it was dark outside. In Macpherson's hip pocket was the small New Testament he always carried with him on his travels. He had thought that even if he did not read from it or even take it out of his pocket, its presence would comfort the dying man. Now he saw that it was to him what the gongs were to the natives. He felt for them a respect he had never been capable of before, and for himself a pity that he had never thought he needed.

'You will pardon him if he cannot talk to you,' Mrs McArthur whispered. 'Perhaps a word or two. He wants you to talk about the place where he was born.'

'Of course.' Macpherson wished Mary was with him. She was so much better at finding something to talk about, and she had got to know more Islay folk than he during their holiday.

'I must tell you,' whispered Mrs McArthur. 'He may die at any moment.'

'Yes.' But he did not think he would notice any difference. Poor McArthur already looked dead.

'Only five minutes,' she said, with a glance at the syringe on the table.

'I understand.'

Despite his stillness the agonies were again gathering in the sick man.

In any case, thought Macpherson, five minutes would be as long as he could stand. Again he wished Mary was there.

Mrs McArthur went out. He sat down by the bed. For over half a minute, listening to the gongs and to McArthur's faint breathing, he could think of nothing to say.

'Well,' he said at last, 'this is a far cry from Bowmore.'

McArthur's hand moved an inch closer. Macpherson put his on it, lightly. Its touch reminded him of old Mr Dougary's, and he realised that the reason why the old minister was so often lost in thought and didn't listen was because he too was in pain.

'When my family and I were on holiday in Bowmore, five or six years ago, we went to the Round Kirk twice. It's a very bonny little church.'

It wasn't what he wanted to say, and he hadn't said it as he had wanted to say it. He had been too stiff, too formal, too much himself.

McArthur seemed to be trying to say something. Macpherson bent down and listened. But, after almost a minute, nothing was said.

'We took a car with us,' he went on, 'so we explored pretty nearly the whole island. I thought I wouldn't mind retiring to Islay. It's milder than Skye, where I was born. My wife liked Port Charlotte: all the white houses.'

Furtively he glanced at his watch. Three minutes had passed already.

'We went to a ceilidh in the Masonic Hall,' he said. 'Songs in Gaelic. We enjoyed it, though we hardly understood a word. I used to know it, but I let it go. Mary, that's my wife, said it would soon come back, if I was prepared to make the effort. There was one old man who'd been singing Gaelic songs for forty years, they said. Perhaps you'd have known him. But I forget his name.'

Again McArthur tried to speak, and again failed.

'Our children, one was about three and the other five at the time, liked the beaches best. Marvellous beaches. Particularly Laggan. We used to watch the planes coming in. A Land Rover drove the sheep off the runways.'

The thumb moved against his hand, with the force of a butterfly; yet it was trying to say something. What, Macpherson had no idea. It might have to do with why he had been asked to come.

Then words at last, one at a time. The eyes stayed closed. The fingers tensed and formed a claw. He should not have been speaking. It was too great an effort: it could kill him.

Macpherson had to put his ear close.

'Your . . . wife's . . . a . . . bonny . . . woman.'

At least that was what it sounded like. Macpherson could hardly ask for it to be said again. He felt dismayed, and yet happier than he had ever been in his life before.

McArthur was now tense all over and shaking; and whimpering.

Mrs McArthur came in, impassive as ever.

Macpherson got up. She nodded, and he went out, tears in his eyes. He felt a great need for Mary, and a great fear that he might never see her again; but above all he felt a great pride that she was his. McArthur had sent for him because of her; and there had been many previous unacknowledged occasions when he had been welcomed, accepted, tolerated, or even liked, for her sake.

If he had gone to his room he could not have rested; so he went downstairs, where he found Razak seated in a chair, his hat on his lap.

He got to his feet when he saw Macpherson.

'How is he?' he asked, in Malay.

He spoke defensively, as if he believed that Macpherson disapproved of him; and so Macpherson had, that afternoon, for no reason except that his way of life, his appearance, his religion, his people, his food, were different from Macpherson's. Mary, had she seen, would have said nothing, out of loyalty, but she would have been hurt.

He had a great longing to tell Razak about her.

'Very ill, I'm afraid,' he answered, also in Malay. 'I don't think Mrs McArthur expects him to last the night.'

'She will miss him very much. They are very devoted to each other.'

Could a man who thought his Mary bonny think Mrs McArthur bonny too? Yes, yes, he could.

'How long have you been here, Mr Razak?' he asked.

'Three years.'

'You must know them very well then.'

The little brown man nodded, and then hung his head. As if it was a signal the gongs began to sound much more loudly and wildly; those striking them seemed to have gone mad. Almost at the same time from upstairs, from McArthur's room, came a curiously deliberate shrieking; and from somewhere else in the house it was echoed.

'He is dead,' whispered Razak. 'They think the evil spirits are very close.'

But how had those beating the gongs known that McArthur was dead?

Macpherson touched his New Testament, not to counteract the pagan shrieks and gongs, but to assist them.

Sydney Tremayne (1912 – 1986)

The Swans of Berwick

Swans, like a yacht race in a heavy sea,
Scudding for Berwick under a dark sky,
Come like creation, wake the world alive,
Confer malevolence on the dead wave,
Storm into harbour in a tight array.

Sealed in a senseless cold of troubled mind,
A split-off deadness, deadness walking round,
I, greyness locked in absence, saw them come
Sudden as joy to focus present time,
And was awake and trod on real ground.   10

Life in foreboding cities drowns in talk.
The mind pulled from its senses hides to seek
The clear sight that it had, an active sight:
No sharper sight than this, no deeper night
Than dead wits walking where the dead seas quake.

Out of the mists of Berwick drive the swans,
Great, powerful birds intent on wild concerns
And making haste before the rising squall.
The slicing wave rolls over the sea wall.
The swans plunge through; the cloud follows and rains. 20

Earth Spirits

The leveret in the leaves
Eating forget-me-nots freshly in bloom,
Pulling the heads off and reversing them
Fastidiously, thrives.
Also the weasel thrives, the sleek rat thrives
In this great time of plenty that arrives.

The world of the young hare
Is hairy as his milky mother's teat
Who suckles him and rolls him off his feet,
Licks him with rapid care,   10
Then leaves him with a leap to his own care,
Among forget-me-nots to sit and stare.

Staring through sunlit hours
As in a dream, his harebrained vision flies
Over the fields, alert how the land lies
Outside the bed of flowers.
Not to be found but find, for instance, flowers
Is fortune in this Eden set with snares.

Colour of earth, alone
Almost from birth, hares when they reach full size   20
Leer out of landscapes like sardonic spies,
Hares that are closer kin
To tuft and stone than to their nearest kin,
And hold their ground by knowing where to run.

The Hare

In the split woods a broken sapling,
Cold catkins that I stoop below.
Explosion of a black bird's wings
Kicks up exclamatory snow.

Silence, the burden of the song,
Resumes where winds have blasted through.
The white fields swell to the dark sky,
The matrix they are frozen to.

Stopped in my fiftieth winter's track
I see the maze a March hare ran.   10
This wilderness supports a hare;
It also may support a man.

Outpost in Winter

Mist lines the ground, a tracing of fine snow.
The field's unsettled as a sea
Through which the moles like whales come up to blow.
The tree that swims in grey might be
A spineless weed buoyed up to reach the air.
Silence is deep. Night shrinks. There is no star.

We two adrift in winter share with birds
Confinement of the dark, that comes,
Silence banked upon silence, stranding words.
Outside, unsleeping stillness thrums   10
To our intensive listening like a heart
Echoing back from depths not on the chart.

Something that needs a refuge scrapes the eaves,
Birdfoot or ratfoot stirs the straw.
There is no wind to move the fallen leaves
For we should hear it softly draw
Ripples along the darkness: nothing at all
Except what seeks the shelter of a wall.

This is the arc of winter bending through
Its longest circuit from the light,   20
And we among the creatures, few,
That have a stake here, riding out the night
Feel the slow shift of time like a great strength
Reaching us up against our tether's length.

Moses

Head in a cloud Moses stands
Beckoning with explosive hands,
Threatening unpromised lands.

Tutmouse the Pharaoh rather bored
Hears the wind harp through his beard.
His heart is hardened by the Lord.

Superior persons tend to miss
Unreasoning people's deadliness.
Pharaoh is sunk because of this.

Pillar of cloud, pillar of fire,   10
Songs and timbrels fill the air.
Logic never led so far.

Moses harder than a stone
With the Laws engraved thereon
Knocks the gods and Pharaoh down.

In the desert, furious,
Rules with God's and Pharaoh's voice,
For the chosen have no choice.

Janet Caird (1913 – 1992)

The Quilt

A girl, she began the quilt,
dove-tailing the colours
into a kaleidoscope.
They said: It's a waste of time.
What you want, they said,
is stuff to boil and wash
and hang on the line
and use again and again.
But she finished the quilt
and laid it away in the drawer.   10
Came age;
went house, possessions, all;
came the high iron bed,
came kindly alien care.
The old woman took out her quilt.
Her hands moved over it
reading the textures,
the silk, the velvet, the mourning serge, the taffeta.
She draped it round her shoulders
and sat in peace.   20
But time's rag-picker fingers
found her quilt,
loosened the stitches,
undid the seams,
scattered the pieces on the bed-spread
and left her shivering.

Let the Snow Cover Her

Let the snow cover her.
She is too old to follow the sledge
and her fingers too stiff
to hold the bone-needle and stitch
the silk-soft sealskin.
It is years and years since she bore her children
in the warm snow-house on the ice-floe.
Here in the hollow
the down of the snow-drift
the silence and cold   10
will lull her to sleep.
Let the snow cover her.

Fossils

The shabby bull-nosed Morris Cowley turned from the main road on to the narrow track that led to Steadens. From the back seat Robert could see the house standing up against the skyline, square and bleak, and beside it the black farm buildings. He wriggled restlessly, uncomfortable in his best clothes – flannel suit, a clean white shirt, tie. Even with the air rushing past the open car, he was hot under the August sun; and if he put his hand on the mock-leather upholstery it felt burning hot. He glanced at his cousin Catherine beside him, envying her her loose white dress and the white sandals she wore. She had taken off her hat, tired of holding it on, and her fair hair was blowing back from her face. She didn't look as if she was hot and prickly, but he could see she was in a bad mood. So he said nothing. She could be very snappy when she was in a bad mood. All the same, having her to share the holiday had been, on the whole, agreeable. She was old of course – past sixteen – and he was only ten, but nevertheless they were friends; went walks together, shared the chores such as gathering eggs and feeding the hens; poled the leaky old punt on the river; swam in the murky water. And he had learned to keep out of her way when she turned moody and lay in the house reading.

She broke her sulky silence.

'Is that the house?'

'Yes.'

'What will we do there?'

'Well, we'll have tea. Mrs Wilkie always gives us a very good tea, with cream puffs and plums and junket and cream.'

'You're a greedy boy, Robert. Is that all we do?'

'We'll probably play a game with Mr Wilkie – a kind of billiards.'

'Don't they have children?'

'No.'

'Will there be any young people there?'

'No. Just us.'

'It sounds awful. I wish I wasn't going – '

Robert's mother, in the front seat, overheard her niece and said over her shoulder:

'It's very kind of Mrs Wilkie to ask us. She does it every summer. She and Mr Wilkie are fond of young people and you're to behave and not sulk.'

Her other aunt Jean who was driving said:

'You'll quite enjoy it Catherine. Robert doesn't mind it, do you Robert? And if you ask Mr Wilkie, he'll show you his fossils.'

'Fossils?'

Catherine looked at Robert.

'Mr Wilkie has boxes of fossils he's found around here. Fossils,' said Robert importantly, 'are animals that lived thousands of years ago and died and turned into stone.'

'I know what fossils are, silly.' She dropped her voice to a whisper. 'It's people like me I want to see, not fossils – or little boys.' She made a face at Robert which he ignored.

They were now drawing up at the garden gate and Mrs Wilkie was coming down the path to greet them. Robert braced himself for an ordeal to come. Mrs Wilkie would, he knew, kiss him in greeting, as she kissed his mother and aunt and doubtless would Catherine also. Perhaps if he stretched his arm out at full length and turned his head and hung back – but it was no use. Mrs Wilkie pulled him firmly on to her unyielding bosom and kissed him heartily.

'What a big boy you've grown, Robert!'

Well, if he was a big boy, she should know better than to kiss him. Kissing was for little boys – very little boys. He gave her a less than cordial look, caught his mother's eye and managed a reluctant smile. He saw Catherine was laughing at him and almost put his tongue out at her.

They moved into the garden. This was part of the ritual: a walk round the garden, then tea, then the game, then the fossils. Catherine and Robert lingered behind the three ladies and walked sedately up the brick-laid path. It was a very neat garden, divided into rectangles, each with its vegetables – peas, scarlet runners, cabbages, cauliflower; very different from the garden at aunt Jean's farm where the flowers and vegetables were not always separate and the net over the strawberries had holes that let in the blackbirds.

They were beside a plum tree trained against the garden wall, and hung with ripe Victoria plums. Catherine stretched up and plucked one.

'Don't.' Robert was alarmed.

'Why not?'

'It's . . . We're not allowed to.'

'Who said so?'

She picked another one and offered it to him. He took it of course, enjoying both its juicy savour and the guilt. Catherine took another for herself and said:

'You didn't tell me Mrs Wilkie was very old-fashioned.'

'Old-fashioned?'

'Oh you wouldn't notice, being just a little boy. Look how she's dressed.'

Robert looked. Mrs Wilkie's dress was different from his mother's and aunt's. Her skirts were longer, much longer, and her dress had a funny high lace collar that came right up under her chin. Her hair was different too – piled up in a big knob on the very top of her head.

'Well?' said Catherine.

'I see her dress is different. And her hair . . . '

'She's wearing it the way aunt Jean has hers in her wedding photo. If you ask me, Mrs Wilkie has got frozen in time.'

Robert did not understand this. A voice behind them saved him from having to admit it.

'Hullo Robert,' said Mr Wilkie. 'I'm glad to see you. Is this young lady your cousin Catherine? How do-you-do.'

As they shook hands he said:

'I see you've found the plum tree. Take as many as you like.'

'There,' said Catherine, 'I knew it would be all right about the plums. Mr Wilkie's nice. He's much younger than Mrs Wilkie. Or didn't you notice that either?'

'I didn't need to notice. I knew.'

'How?'

'How what?'

'How did you know? That Mrs Wilkie was older than Mr Wilkie?'

'I heard them' (he nodded towards his mother and aunt) 'talking.' He was smarting under her air of superiority. 'You don't know everything. I know a lot about the Wilkies.'

'Tell me.'

'Why should I? You're always sneering at me.'

'No I'm not. Do tell me. I won't be cross ever again.'

He knew this was a blatant lie, but when Catherine was nice and her voice was soft and gentle, he liked her very much. So he said:

'Well, Mr Wilkie's mother didn't want him to be a farmer, so he went to London to learn to be a draper. But Mr Wilkie hated it and turned ill and came back. But when he was in London he married the lady where he lodged. That's Mrs Wilkie and she's fifteen years older than he is.'

'She must be *ancient*,' said Catherine. 'Poor Mr Wilkie.'

'Why "poor Mr Wilkie"?'

'Well, she looks staid and dull. I bet she never laughs or goes on picnics, or – or – '

'They say she keeps house beautifully. And that's true. It's the cleanest house I've ever been in. But she takes nothing to do with the farm – not even the hens. She's a super baker – she makes lovely cream puffs.'

'There's more to life than cream puffs, only you're so greedy I don't suppose you understand that.'

Robert didn't answer. So much for promises never to be cross again!

The others had turned and were moving towards them. Soon they were all entering the house, into the dark cool hall, all the darker for the dazzle of sun outside. Robert's eyes soon cleared and yet once more he was struck by the rigid orderliness. The polished floor gleamed, every rug was straight; on one side a door opened to the dining-room, on the other side to the sitting-room which Mrs Wilkie called the drawing-room. On either side of these doors stood upright chairs with circular seats and long narrow tapering backs all covered with squiggly designs of flowers and fruit. Robert had been told they were 'poker-work' and had been done by Mrs Wilkie's mother when she 'was only twelve.' Mrs Wilkie saw Catherine looking at them and said:

'My mother did that poker-work when she was only twelve. I'm sure you couldn't do that could you?'

She turned to answer a remark of Robert's mother; so only he heard Catherine mutter:

'I shouldn't try. They're hideous.'

They sat in the sitting-room while Mrs Wilkie made tea. It was like no other room Catherine had ever seen. Everything that could be polished shone; the mirror was spotless; the hanging crystal ornaments on the mantelpiece sparkled like newly formed icicles. The pink of the velvet upholstery and fat satin cushions of the settee and chairs were repeated in the pink roses of the carpet. On little tables scattered round the room was a variety of ornaments – a blue glass box, frilly china figures, little jugs. On the walls were pictures in narrow gilt frames – ladies in crinolines looking out of a window, a Venetian scene with a gondola, a bluebell wood of beeches. The room's immaculate neatness made her feel ill at ease and when Robert whispered:

'Did you ever see such a tidy room?' she hissed hack:

'It's horrid. It's all Mrs Wilkie. You would never guess there was a Mr Wilkie from this room. I thought you said he had fossils?'

'He has. But they're kept in the wash-house.'

They moved into the dining-room, also gleaming and polished, but somberly functional, with a long solid table, mahogany chairs with green leather seats. The clock was black marble and on the mantel-piece were little statues of rearing bronze horses. The carpet was red, the paper midgreen. In this subdued setting the tea-table was an oasis of lightness: rosebud china on a starched damask cloth; a silver tea-kettle poised above a little blue flame; a huge velvet cover over a large silver tea-pot, plates of thin bread and butter; crystal jam dishes shining like jewels; jam sponges; plumcake, and huge cream-puffs.

Mrs Wilkie made her usual little joke; 'We'll let the men sit together' and Robert was placed beside Mr Wilkie, at an agreeable distance from his mother so that he could enjoy unchecked the good things with which Mr Wilkie plied his plate. The meal was rounded off with bottled plums, junket and cream. Mrs Wilkie might be older than Mr Wilkie, thought Robert, but she could make a jolly good tea. And what was all the fuss about age anyway?

After the table had been cleared, a green baize cloth was laid on it and the board for the game produced. It was a kind of miniature billiards. There was a special 'lady's cue' with a little wooden block on the end. Robert was flattered by having to share the 'gentleman's cue' with Mr Wilkie. The older women played for politeness' sake, with stiff awkward gestures, sitting down between their turns, but Catherine was good at games, and now, darting round the table, her white dress lighting up the sombre room, she played her strokes as skillfully as she could, eager to win even this ridiculous game. It developed into a duel between her and Mr Wilkie, but in the end she won, and went back to the sitting-room in a little glow of triumph.

But in the absence of Mr Wilkie, who was putting away the game, and as the ladies settled down to discuss recipes, boredom struck again. She nudged Robert and whispered:

'Fossils.'

So when Mr Wilkie came back, Robert said politely:

'May we look at the fossils, please?'

Mr Wilkie looked at his wife.

'If you spread a newspaper on the carpet, you may look at them in the dining-room.' She turned to Catherine. 'Mr Wilkie keeps his fossils in the wash-house. But this is a special occasion and I know Robert likes to see them. Your aunts and I will have a nice talk here.'

Mr Wilkie found an old newspaper and while Catherine spread it on the carpet in the dining-room, Robert helped Mr Wilkie carry through the fossils, jumbled up in wooden boxes. Robert began showing off as he lifted them out, for he had, from repeated visits, learned the names.

'Good boy,' said Mr Wilkie. 'I'm glad to see you have remembered things.'

'I'd like you to tell me about the fossils,' said Catherine. 'You would do it much better than Robert.'

So Mr Wilkie brought from the glass-fronted bookcase two volumes full of pictures of fossils and what they had been when alive. He began showing the illustrations to Catherine and identifying the fossils in his box, which were mostly of small fishy creatures. Robert who knew it all already became absorbed in the second volume, largely devoted to satisfyingly monstrous dinosaurs, and stopped listening to Mr Wilkie's gentle voice.

Catherine showed much interest and Tom Wilkie lost his stiffness, talking of belemnites and ammonites. Enthusiasm lit up his face, made him young, and Catherine gave him a smile as he dropped a sea-urchin into her waiting hands She turned the fossil over with careful fingers, scarcely hearing what he said, thinking it was sad that he should be tied to that starchy creature his wife. How could it have happened? She put down the sea-urchin and interrupted his description of a nautiloid.

'What made you begin collecting fossils?'

Tom Wilkie was silent for a moment.

'I don't really know.'

'You must know. To collect all these . . . You must know.'

He groped for words, unused to talk on this level.

'I saw fossils in a museum in London. And then one day I found one in the quarry, and in a field. I bought this book, and discovered there were lots of fossils round here.' He glanced at her searching for any sign of derision or contempt. But no, her eyes were serious and attentive. He went on:

'And they're wonderful I think. To have endured so long . . . And then, to think this was once the sea – the water and tides washing over where we are now, and these creatures – that urchin you're holding in your hand being alive in the water . . . '

'That's like poetry,' said Catherine.

Tom looked sharply at her. No, she was not mocking him. He remembered from long ago a sneering voice 'Quite the poet aren't we?' and felt again the stab. Into the silence came Robert's voice:

'I wish you could find a bit of a dinosaur, Mr Wilkie. They're more interesting than little fishes.'

Tom smiled, relieved and yet sorry at the interruption. 'I don't think that's likely, Robert. You'll have to go to London to see dinosaurs; in the Natural History Museum.'

Catherine began arranging the fossils in groups on the newspaper.

'They look nice like that, all in order. Couldn't you get a place with shelves where you could lay them out for people to see, not have them all mixed up in a box?'

'Mrs Wilkie doesn't like them in the house. They collect dust. They're lumps of stone you know.'

'They're not,' cried Robert. 'They're special, because they were once alive. Haven't you told Mrs Wilkie?'

He stopped. Mr Wilkie's face was flushing and Robert felt himself grow hot. He had said something wrong. But Catherine saved him.

'The fossils are very interesting and I'd like to find one. Could you show us where to look, Mr Wilkie?'

'If you and Robert like to come out with me tomorrow evening we could look.'

'That would be lovely, wouldn't it Robert? Now we must help Mr Wilkie to put the fossils away.'

She began carefully laying the belemnites in the bottom of a box, covered them with paper and then laid the sea-urchins and so on till all was neatly arranged. Then Mr Wilkie and Robert carried them back to the wash-house. When they came back to the dining-room Catherine had moved into the sunlight shining through the window and her body was a dark shape under her loose white dress. Mr Wilkie stopped so abruptly that Robert bumped into him. Catherine moved into the shade and said:

'I think the others are getting ready to go.' It was agreed that at the following evening Mr Wilkie, Catherine and Robert would meet at the quarry; and there he was waiting for them carrying a geologist's hammer and with a bag over his shoulder. He warned them they must not be too hopeful of finding anything in the chalk-pit, locally known as the quarry, which he had pretty well explored, but the field above had been recently ploughed and there might be something there.

It was a sultry evening of stillness and sunlight. The furrows were dusty and hard to walk on. It was not what Catherine had imagined fossil-hunting would be. She looked at her companions. Robert, head down, now and then stooping to pick up something and then discard it, was clearly absorbed. Mr Wilkie, also walking with head bowed seemed equally absorbed. Catherine began to feel bored and cross.

But Tom Wilkie was totally unaware of his surroundings, momentarily even unaware of the girl tramping the furrows so close to him. He was years away, back in that disastrous time in London when Gertrude's sympathy and kindness had been the only good things in life. She had welcomed him back in the evening, drawn him out, listened to his account of the dreary day's doings. She had been like a kind aunt. Then one night she had come to his bed. The next day he found himself engaged to be married. The wedding took place shortly after. He had been trapped, of course. Gertrude was a dutiful wife; kept the house beautifully; 'looked after him.' She hated the farm and all that went with it. They shared no interests. It was life in a well-organised ice-box.

But not until yesterday, and Catherine kneeling by his fossils, Catherine in the sunlight from the window, had he known how bleak, how chill, the ice-box was.

There was a shout from Robert. He had found something – a fossil shell. What was it? Tom identified it as a nautiloid. Now that they had found something, did they want to go on?

Robert did, but Catherine insisted on going back to the quarry. Here it was hot, the level evening sunlight bouncing off the chalk. Sitting on the turf at the top, Robert watched Catherine scrambling about. He thought she was being silly; he knew she was sure-footed as a deer, yet she kept saying she was slipping and asking Mr Wilkie to give her a hand. But she did spy a sea-urchin in the chalk, and with cries that she must get it herself, and balancing on a tangle of fallen turf and brambles she chipped round it. But as she reached up and grasped it, she slipped and would have fallen on her back, if Mr Wilkie had not caught her. He put her down very quickly – he probably thinks she's being silly too, thought Robert – then the two of them joined Robert. Catherine had brought apples, and as they sat and munched them, Robert chattered on about fossils.

'I wish we could find a bit of a dinosaur. Or supposing a fossil came alive. Supposing a pterodactyl came flying from the trees – or – or a brontosaurus came barging through the wood – or if even my little shell came alive . . . '

'Don't be silly,' said Catherine tartly, clearly not interested in fantasy. But Mr Wilkie in his kind way answered seriously:

'I don't think a fossil would be happy coming back to life. Everything would be completely strange and different and frightening. It would probably just die.'

'I suppose so,' said Robert. 'Anyway, I'm going to look for more shells.'

He jumped up and went back to the ploughed land. Halfway across the field he found another shell and hurried back to the quarry to show his prize. He was ready to shout his triumph as soon as the others came in sight. But the words died in his mouth.

Mr Wilkie had Catherine in his arms and was kissing her – kissing her with short jerky movements of his head – on her lips; her cheeks, her throat – he even buried his face in her hair. And leaning back on her elbows she was accepting it all, though he was almost on top of her. Then as the boy watched in bewildered astonishment, Tom Wilkie suddenly dropped the girl, snatched his bag and hammer and ran along the edge of the field to Steadens.

Robert came slowly down the slope to Catherine and stood staring at her. She was still leaning on her elbows, flushed, biting her lip. She didn't look at him for a moment or two. Then she snapped:

'Why are you looking at me like that?'

'You – Mr Wilkie! He was kissing you.'

'Yes. I made him kiss me.'

'You made him?' His voice rose to a squeak of surprise.

She looked up. To his deeper bewilderment, it seemed as she might be going to cry. Instead she jumped to her feet.

'I made a fossil come alive.'

She almost spat the words at him. And she was away, running down the field towards home.

He caught up with her at the farmyard gate. He was shaking, half-crying, aware that something important had happened not knowing what, her last words to him making him feel implicated.

Catherine caught his arm and squeezed it.

'You must never, ever, tell a living soul what you saw. Swear?'

He was only too ready. 'I swear.'

The post-girl brought the news next morning. There had been an accident. Mr Wilkie had been found with gun-shot wounds beside a stile leading to a spinney where he often went to shoot rabbits. He must have tripped crossing the stile and the gun had gone off. Mr Wilkie was dead.

Catherine and Robert slipped away unheeded from the babble of exclamations and distress down to the river that flowed past the garden. Catherine put her hand into the pocket of her dress and drew out the sea-urchin she had found in the quarry. She flung it into the dark water and it sank into the silt and was lost once more. And in time their guilt sank too, silted over, and became no more than a little nodule of unease and shame.

'David Toulmin' (John Reid, 1913 – 1998)

Toulmin was a farm servant in Aberdeenshire for most of his life. His tales often have little narrative impetus, but are marked by a powerful descriptive talent. 'Hardwood!' tells more of a story than most.

Hardwood!

The fog being down on the countraside when you couldna see a stirk in your ain parks in broad daylight was the time that Hardwood Harry choose to disappear. Harry Hernie was an old widower who had lived with his twin son and dother on the fairm of Clayfoons since his wife died, which was as many years back that younger folks couldna mind on't. Harry had been a joiner and undertaker in his younger day, before he took over the fairm from his father, and when his own turn came for growing old he handed over the lease to his unmarried twins, Wattie and Bannie Hernie, who had been born at Clayfoons and lived and worked there all their days, and were well on in middle-age when their father handed over the place to them.

But when the old man retired he had a hankering to go back to his joinery, or maybe it was just that he couldna rest and content himself in idleness, and there wasn't all that wark for him on a pair place of sixty acres, for Wattie and Bannie did most of it, so he started making barrows for the farming folk round about Clayfoons, lightsome kind of wark making box-barrows for mucking out their byres and stables, and lighter, flat-leaf barrows for wheeling out their peat in summer, peat barrows with a broader wheel for the soft lairs. Hardwood became a dab hand at the barrows, and they were that well made with good seasoned wood and lasted such a long time that they carried his name all over the district, and if you didn't have a Hardwood barrow sitting on your midden[1] plank you just wasn't worth speaking to.

Hardwood had built a fairly big shed at the gable of the steading,[2] near the peat stack, and set up a bench in it with a vice, and a rack along the wall for all the hand tools he needed for making and repairing barrows, besides a small circular base outside where he heated the iron rings when he fitted them on the wheels, kindling a fire with peat like the blacksmith did with the heavier cart wheels. The box-barrows he painted blue, with red inside and wheel, the peat barrows a dull brown, so they had a fine smell of fresh paint about them when you went in by with a horse cart for one of Hardwood's barrows.

Trade was brisk, because there was a lot of knacky work in making a farm barrow, and there weren't many joiners who took the trouble, so Hardwood got steady work to meet the demand for barrows. By and by he was earning more bawbees from his barrow making than his son was doing on the farm, so that a bit of jealousy sprang up between Wattie and his father, and even Bannie took sides with her brother against the old man, which wasn't surprising maybe them being twins. And sometimes Bannie kept the money when honest folk came to pay their accounts and there was a fair din about the place when the old man found her out. Hardwood would charge the customer a second time and when the body told him he had already paid his dother at the back kitchie door the old man was dumfoonert that his ain flesh and bleed could treat him like this. So he kept the books himself and told his customers to pay him in the shed, 'to keep things right,' as he said, though folk kent fine what Bannie was up to, and they thought it a right shame to swick the old man.

But he ups and gives Bannie and Wattie a right tinking with his sharp tongue and says they wouldna have done that gin their mother had been alive, pour soul, for it was enough to make her topple the stone that held her down in the kirkyard at the Bogside, and them huggin' and kissin' at one another, what would she think of that? Oh aye, he'd seen them at it he said, he wasn't blind or very deaf, and it wasn't a way for a brother and sister to be carrying on, even though they were twins. And what did they want with his money anyway? Wouldn't they get it all when he was dead and away, and they already had the lease of the place; but if they didn't mend their ways he would wipe them out of his will and leave every penny to others more deserving that he could think of.

But this outburst had little effect on the twins, in fact it made them worse when they knew that their relationship had been discovered; so they plotted and planned between them to make the old man's life a misery. So Bannie scrimps her old father at the table and treats him like a tike at the door, so that he could hardly light his pipe in the kitchen, living on kale brose like a caterpillar on a cabbage runt. So the old man took to sleeping on a couch in his joinery shed, covered up with rugs and old jackets, and kept himself warm with a bit peek of a stove that he burned with wood shavings and sawdust and broken peat, till he was nearly smoared with the reek, and his old brown eyes like to run out of his head, and when customers found him like this the twins at Clayfoons became the claik of the Buchan howes.

Folk that were ill-mannered and spied in at the windows after dark said that Wattie Hernie and his sister both slept in the same bed, and that they kissed and cuddled at each other like they were man and wife, and were likely to be doing most other things besides, though nothing had come of it and maybe they were just lucky. And they said that this annoyed the

---

[1] Trash.
[2] Farm, holding.

old man more than his ill-usage or taking his money, for he knew fine what was going on and that was why he had taken to sleeping on his couch in the joinery shed, maybe to spite them and set the neighbours talking, which might arouse a little sympathy for himself or bring the twins to their senses. But there were others who said plainly that the twins had shut their old father out of the farmhouse so that he couldn't spy on their courting, and that it was what the old fool deserved for giving them the farm in the first place.

Och but they said everything but their prayers in the Bogside, and Bannie Hernie didn't seem to care all that much what they said, or maybe she just got used to their wagging tongues; so the old man lay on his couch till his hurdies[1] were sore and the rheumatism stiffened him, and what with the want of proper food for his belly he became as thin and unwashed as a starved tink and fit to scare the craws from your tattie dreels. Fell crabbit he was too in his old age and like to bite off your lug[2] of a morning when you went in by with a barrow wheel that needed to be fitted with a new iron ring on it for a tyre. And if you hadn't given it a dabble in the mill-dam to wash off all the sharn[3] you heard about it from old Hardwood, which was odd you thought when he was sorer in need of a scrub himself, and folk thought he was getting a bit dottled in his old age, though he still had a waspish tongue.

But he wasn't as dottled as they thought the stock, for after his day at the barrow-making old Hardwood began working at something in the evening, so that if you went past Clayfoons in the dark on your bicycle you'd see a light in the far end of Hardwood's shed and the old man plaining and chiseling or spoke-shaving at something in the lamplight, so that though you got off your bike and went to the window for a peep you still couldn't make out what he was working at; maybe just another barrow you thought, and that he couldn't cope with the demand, and though you made an errand in by in daylight he always had the thing covered up, longish in shape it was, like a boat, though you didn't like to ask lest he told you to mind your own business, for he could be snappish at times.

Then Hardwood locked his shed and disappeared into the fog that had been hanging about for days on the hairst parks, so that you couldn't see the lads at stook parade, and the fog-horn at the Battery Head moaning all day and a cow foonert at the calving. When her father didn't go in for breakfast Bannie went over to the shed to waken him. She tried the lock and hammered on the door but when there was no response to her knocking she looked in the window. He wasn't in his couch either so she went to the far end and looked in the other window. The light was coming in slowly but she saw the naked coffin on its trestles, uncovered now for anyone who cared to look at it, and Bannie got a sore fright, for there it stood in polished oak, with brass handles on the ends and black cords and toshels draped along its sides, with a lid on top. Bannie couldn't think of anyone who had ordered a coffin from her father, nor could she mind of a new death in the Bogside, or anybody like to die that would be needing one, and it was the first coffin she had seen the old man make in his retirement, though she knew he had been an undertaker in his younger day.

Bannie tried the door again but it wouldn't budge, so she walked round the shed and came back to the window where the coffin was, staring in at it until she had a daft idea that her father must have made it for himself, that he would be lying in there now, and she rapped on the window with her knuckles, hoping to waken him up, half expecting the lid to be raised and the old man look out at her in his working clothes, reminding her of her ill-treatment and making her promise to mend her ways with her twin brother. Guilt began to rankle in Bannie's mind and she promised herself that though the old man was only playing a joke on her she would mend her ways, and the hot tears came into her eyes and she hammered on the window till it shook and cried out 'Father, oh father, speak to me. I promise father, I promise . . . ' and the greet grew loud in her throat, until you could hear it across the road, and the tears ran down her face and the dog came barking round and then Wattie to see what ailed his sister, thinking maybe that somebody had ravished her at the back of the shed.

---

[1] Buttocks.
[2] Ear.
[3] Dung.

Wattie took Bannie in his oxter[1] but she thrust him aside, pointing at the coffin through the window. 'Father's missing,' she cried, 'and I'll swear he's in there now, waiting for us to promise something. All the time we've been wicked he's been watching and this is our last chance. We must promise never to do it again Wattie!'

She was sobbing hard and Wattie said 'promise nothing' and pressed his nose against the glass, shading the growing light with his open hands against his cheeks, and when he saw the gleaming coffin on its trestles he was sore taken aback. 'So that was what he was hammerin'' at in the evenin's. It's a pity Bannie that we didna take a look over to see what he was at. I juist thocht it was anither barra.'

'I'll go to the hoose and see if I can find anither key,' Bannie said, a bit calmed down since Wattie came round, but she could find no other key to the shed. Wattie shook the door by the knob but it wouldn't move, so he threw his weight against it and burst it open, near going head first after it into the shed. Bannie followed him past the couch and the bench, the floor deep in wood shavings and a fine smell of wood and rosin and paint, with half-finished barrows propped against the walls and wheels on the floor, bits of sawn wood, sawdust and nails, and the coffin at the far end. The twins stood beside it, afraid to open the lid, like bairns with a Jack-in-the-Box, afraid that when they opened the lid their father would leap up in their faces and cry 'Bah!' A sudden frightening shout that would scare them to fits; or he would be lying in there asleep or dead, white and cold as snow and would never speak to them again in this world.

'You open it Bannie. I did my bit bursting the door.'

'No I couldna, and what if he is in there listening to us arguing aboot wha will open his coffin lid.' And Bannie was near to tears again.

Wattie plucked up courage and prised his thick thumbs under the heavy lid, until he got his hand under it and lifted it up on its edge, holding it there, wide open, while the two of them stared into the empty coffin, lined with white cotton, and Bannie couldn't think where her father had gotten all this stuff, unless he had ordered it through the post.

But the old man was not in the coffin, nor hiding in the shed, or anywhere about the steading or the farmhouse, for they had searched high and low for him, though Bannie was sure the coffin was a sign or a warning that they would find him dead somewhere. So they searched all the burns and hedges on Clayfoons and crawled under all the stooks on the hairst rigs looking for him, or simply threw them down in despair, hoping that they would find their father asleep somewhere and nobody would know about his disappearance, and they would be kinder to him after this scare, for he had certainly given them a lesson and they wouldn't forget it.

But no old man leapt out at them from any stook and he had disappeared at a time that would give them plenty to think about, this misty season in the middle o' hairst[2] when he would be ill to find, and when most other folks would have other things on their minds, what with their uncut corn drooping and weeping in the seep of the rain and the stubble as wet you could hardly set a stook on it, the burns all in spate and the snipes wheebling in the segs, though you couldna see them for the fog.

Before the day was out Bannie had to run up to Whistlebrae and tell them what had happened, and would they telephone the bobbies to come and help them look for her father. A sore disgrace it would be to the pair of them, but things had reached a stage when they felt they would be worse guilty if they didn't report it.

For two whole days half the countraside searched for the missing joiner, in the burns and hedges, in the segs and on the braes, among the whin and broom around the quarries, and up among the fir trees on the Spionkop, the highest hill in the Bogside. Folk even drained their mill-dams, thinking old Hardwood would stick in the sluice or go down the lade, but there was never a sign of him, not even in the miller's dam. The polis looked everywhere they could think of, and even the school bairns were told to look out for the old man when they went

[1] Armpit.
[2] Harvest.

over the moors and through the woods.

The stone quarry at Spionkop was a deep hole of water on the face of the brae, and the polis got a fire engine out of the toon with long hoses that went over the grass from the road and sucked the quarry dry, but the firemen shook their helmeted heads when they came upon all the rubbish at the bottom of the quarry but no sign of Hardwood. Folk wondered about the moss pots filled with brown peaty water that had no bottom to them, where a body might sink far enough and never be seen again, and they shuddered at the thought. Lads on stook parade in the hairst parks expected to find old Hardwood in every stook they shifted, and when you thought of all the multitude of corn and barley stooks in the Laich o' Buchan where an old body could hide you knew fine the old man wasn't a dottard; that he had chosen the right time to keep folk on the move, especially the twins at Clayfoons, for they hadna stickit an eye since he went missing.

Now you couldn't see the hill of the Spionkop from Clayfoons, though it was but two miles as the crow flies. You couldn't see it for the strip of wood on the Berry-hill, even though the cottars had thinned it with their axes over the years; beyond was the moss and the segs and the grass parks that lay on the shin of the Spionkop. It was an unco[1] name to give a bit hill and you thought maybe it was that if you went up there on a fine day you could spy on the folk in the howe; but it took its name from the farm toon high on its slopes, where a Dutch chiel[2] from South Africa had bought the place, and being homesick he changed the name from Fellrigs to Spionkop, and some said he was a Boer, seeing his name was Vanderskelp or something. But since he came to live there on the face of the brae they called it the Spionkop, which well-read folk told you was somewhere in Natal, and had something to do with a battle that the British had out there with the Boers, those ill-mannered chiels that were but farming folk and shot at the British like they were hares in the parks. But maybe the Vanderskelp chiel meant no harm, because the Boers got a thrashing at the Spionkop, and yon General Buller had to run with his breeks down, so maybe the lad was giving you credit naming your Buchan hill after a Boer defeat. Anyway the fuskered postie said that was the new address, and when you thought of other places in Buchan with foreign names like Waterloo, Pisgah and Jericho you wasn't surprised. And the postie said the Boer was a right civil chiel to speak to and that he didn't have a barking dog that would tear the arse out of your breeks like some he knew in the Bogside.

You had gone up on the Spionkop yourself in your time, looking for a Druids' Circle in such a likely place, but not a lintel stone did you find there from the olden days, nor any sign of a fort, for the Buchan Howes had small protection from the Vikings when the horned chiels came over in their long-boats from the Norse Lands, though King Malcolm had licked the Danes at Cruden Bay, and you could still see the cairns that marked their graves at Cairncatto, and such a song of the curlew there it was like an eternal requiem for the dead in their long forgotten burrows.

But down at the foot of the Spionkop lived Maggie Lawrence in her thachet biggin', where the fuschias hung their ruby bells over the stone dyke the long summer through, and the dog-rose clung to the walls, while the smell of dewy honeysuckle on an evening clear would nearly sicken you with pleasure, like you had drunk too much wine for your stomach's sake. Maggie was an old toothless body that could neither read nor write, and she lived there alone but for the rats that fed with her at table, and if you looked through her peep-hole windows with the little lace curtains you'd see old Maggie with her pets, and if any one of the creatures was impatient enough to snatch a morsel from Maggie she would give it a right quick smack with her hazel stick and cry out: 'Get doon ye Ted!' And the long-tailed rat would slink away to the other end of the table, with great respect for Maggie when her ire was up. When Maggie died your grandfather had to sit up with her corpse at night to keep the rats away from her coffin, and right glad he was when the funeral was over because he was afraid of the brutes.

---

[1] Strange.
[2] Fellow.

But meanwhile Maggie was still very much alive, smoking her clay pipe and gathering whin sticks on the brae for her fire, and any of the divots that she could rive from the heather. She carried her water from a wee well on the edge of a grass park just beyond her door, and Maggie would put on her bit plaid of red tartan with the tassled edges and a yoke on her shoulders, with two galvanised pails hanging from it, her clay pipe in her mouth, the blue reek[1] taking over her canty shoulder, away to the well for her drop water.

It was but two or three feet deep Maggie's well, a tender spring out of the sand with a trout in it to keep the water clean, and sometimes a frog that lept in to keep him company, and whiles a shrew-mouse that fell in by mistake, swam itself to exhaustion and drowned, and was thrown out by Maggie when she caught it in her pail. Maggie spoke to her trout like he was a human body, and they said he cocked an eye at her when her reflection hit the water. So it was a great surprise to her that day when she found this great big trout in her well, soon as she opened the gate that was for keeping out the cattle beasts, for here was this man standing in her well up to his thighs, his back bent level with the ground, his white head jammed into the water so that he couldn't fall over, his body supported by the rim of the wall. Old Hardwood at last, where nobody thought to look for him, drowned in Maggie's well. She dropped her pails and took the wooden yoke from her neck, stuck her bit pipe in the pocket of her apron and wondered where she would go for help. But first she went a bit closer to the human statue, crouched with its feet and hands in the well, bent in supplication the creature seemed, praying for death with its mouth in the water. Maggie went down the step and put her hand on the cold stiff shoulder, like a stuffed thing, swelling inside the damp clothing. She knew he was dead but she wasn't afraid of the poor old man, just wondered how he came to be there, and how she would ever have the heart again to drink the crystal clear water from her wallie. A pity she couldna see his face to see who he might be, for she knew nothing of Hardwood's disappearance, though she kenned that sic a body lived in the Bogside.

His jacket pockets were bulging in the water and Maggie lifted the sodden flap to see what might be in there, thinking maybe it was bawbees, though it didn't seem likely when he had done away with himself, or so she supposed, for nobody could put an old man into a well like that without a struggle, and he was as composed and peaceful as a sleeping lamb; not a speck of blood on him, nor a tare in his jacket, not a hair of his head ravelled and nothing in the well, nothing but the trootie, straight as an eel in the bottom. His jacket pockets were stuffed with coiryarn, coconut-hair rope that the farmer chiels were using nowadays to hold down their rucks and strae-soos, instead of straw rape, and Maggie thought the poor creature had been fell determined to put an end to himself, and that if the drowning failed he would hang himself from a fir tree on the Spionkop.

The fog had cleared and Maggie warsled away up the hill to Mr Vanderskelp, who was kind of a landlord to her, 'cause her clay biggin' was on his grun, though he never charged her any rent for the sagging roofed venel that she lived in, little more than a cairn of stones and clay with one lum[2] and an earthen floor, a hallan that some crofter chiel had biggit for his family a hunder years agone, with stones gathered on the hillside.

Mr Vanderskelp heard Maggie's story and said he had been through the park counting his cattle that very morning but never thought of looking in the well. It seemed impossible that anyone could drown himself in such a shallow trough. Maggie would have called it a wee skite of water, but never mind, she knew fine what he meant and she agreed with her laird. Mr Vanderskelp then telephoned the bobby and told him to get the doctor, and they came and lifted the dripping Hardwood out of Maggie's well and laid him on the yird, all but his false teeth that they found later and Maggie hadn't seen, and maybe just as well, for it might have scunnered[3] her completely from taking water there.

Two of Mr Vanderskelp's men lifted the corps on to a spring-cart and took him to Clayfoons, the water still dripping out of the cart, and followed by the school bairns that were

---

[1] Smoke.
[2] Chimney.
[3] Disgusted.

on their way home at the time. So the undertaker came in his black coat and stretched out Hardwood on a board and shaved him and laid him in his homemade coffin in the ben room. And Bannie bibbled and grat over him like a long lost bairn and would hardly bide in the hoose without a neighbour woman for company or the funeral was by. And such a trail of a funeral that the likes of it had never been seen in the Bogside, the road fair jammed with phaetons and gigs and Governess cars with their shelts and ponies and a motor car or twa, and the kirkyard black with folk, like the craws after a thrashin' mull, and Wattie Hernie by the gate when they left, shakin' as mony hands ye would have thought he was ca'in' a pump, with saut tears hingin' at his mouser.

So that was Hardwood and his barrows, and they survived him for mony a year and day, keeping his memory green in the Bogside, green as the sod where he lay with his wife at the gable o' the kirk yonder. But the twins didn't stay long in the fairm after this, maybe because they had a guilty conscience, though the neighbours gave them no cause to feel it. They had a roup the two of them the next May and sold nearly everything but the furniture and the grandfather clock. Everything else went: horse, nowt, pigs and poultry; pleuchs, harrows, grubber and rollers; binder, mower, scythes and horse-rake, all the hand tools and two or three of Hardwood's barrows and wheels that gave a stunning price. Sic a steer there was and a day or two after this the twins got a stem-waggon and lifted all their gear and set sail out of the Bogside and that was the last you ever heard of them.

Douglas Young (1913 – 1973)

Last Lauch

The Minister said it wald dee,
the cypress buss I plantit.
But the buss grew til a tree,
naething dauntid.

Hit's growan, stark and heich,
derk and straucht and sinister,
kirkyairdie-like and dreich★.   dull
But whaur's the Minister?

For a Wife in Jizzen[1]

Lassie, can ye say whaur ye hae been,
whaur ye hae come frae,
whatna ferlies★ seen?   wonders
Efir the bluid and swyte,
the warsslin o yestreen,
ye ligg forfochten★, whyte,   exhausted
prouder nor onie queen.
Albeid ye hardly see me

---

[1] Childbirth.

I read it i your een,   10
sae saft blue and dreamy,
mindan whaur ye've been.
Anerly★ wives ken   *only*
the ruits o joy and tene★,   *suffering*
the mairch o daith and birth,
the tryst o luve and strife
i the howedumbdied★-sunsheen,   *midnight*
fire, air, water, yirth
mellan★ tae mak new life,   *mixing*
lauchan and greetan, feiman★ and serene.   20   *foaming*
Dern★ frae aa men   *hide*
the ferlies ye has seen.

For the Old Highlands

That old lonely lovely way of living
in Highland places, – twenty years a-growing,
twenty years flowering, twenty years declining, –
father to son, mother to daughter giving
ripe tradition; peaceful bounty flowing;
one harmony all tones of life combining, –
Old wise ways, passed like the dust blowing.
That harmony of folk and land is shattered, –
the yearly rhythm of things, the social graces,   10
peat-fire and music, candle-light and kindness.
Now they are gone it seems they never mattered,
much, to the world, those proud and violent races,
clansmen, and chiefs whose passioned greed and blindness
made desolate these lovely lonely places.

The Twenty-third Psalm o King Davit

Composed on St Andrew's Day, 1942,
in Edinburgh Prison

The Lord's my herd, I sall nocht want.
Whaur green the gresses grow
sall be my fauld. He caas★ me aye   *drives*
whaur fresh sweet burnies rowe.

He gars★ my saul be blyth aince mair   *makes*
that wandert was frae hame,
and leads me on the straucht smaa gait
for sake o His ain name.

Tho I suld gang the glen o mirk
I'ld grue★ for nae mischance,   10   *fear*
Thou bydes wi me, Thy kent★ and cruik   *pole, rod*
maks aye my sustenance.

Thou spreids ane brod and gies me meat
whaur aa my faes may view,
Thou sains* my heid wi ulyie owre   blesses
and pours my cogie* fou.   basket

Nou seil* and kindliness sall gae   blessing
throu aa my days wi me,
and I sall wone* in God's ain hous   dwell
at hame eternallie.

Note: Young was a conscientious objector during the Second World War.

Ruthven Todd (1914 – 1978)

In September, 1937

Coming in September, through the thin streets,
I thought back to another year I knew,
Autumn, lifting potatoes and stacking peats
On Mull, while the Atlantic's murky blue
Swung sluggishly in past Jura, and the hills
Were brown lions, crouched to meet the autumn gales.

In the hard rain and the rip of thunder,
I remember the haze coming in from the sea
And the clatter of Gaelic voices by the breakwater,
Or in the fields as the reapers took their tea;   10
I remembered the cast foal lying where it died,
Which we buried, one evening, above high tide:

And the three rams that smashed the fank*-gate,   sheepfold
Running loose for five days on the moor
Before we could catch them – far too late
To prevent an early lambing the next year.
But these seemed out of place beside the chip-shop
And the cockney voices grumbling in the pub.

In September, I saw the drab newsposters
Telling of wars, in Spain and in the East,   20
And wished I'd stayed on Mull, their gestures
Frightened me and made me feel the unwanted guest,
The burden on the house who having taken salt
Could never be ejected, however grave his fault.

In September, we lit the fire and talked together,
Discussing the trivialities of a spent day
And what we would eat. I forgot the weather
And the dull streets and the sun on Islay,
And all my fear. I lost my carefully-kept count
Of the ticks to death, and, in September, was content.   30

The Explorer

I am an intruder in these regions
Where the snow burns a clear flame;
I am a traveller from temperate zones
Who is to a strange country come.

I did not know of this red valley
Where the moon lies for half the year,
Its silver bowl tended by the osprey.
Being civilised I am full of fear.

I had not heard of the whirlpool
That engulfs the sea in winter-time,   10
Or of the winds that regularly unroll
The ice as carpet to the earth's frame.

I shall not stay here long, I think,
But having learned a little will return.
That I am either raving mad or drunk
Will be proclaimed by those who scorn

The explorers who stumble on the truth.
It would be better to deny with gentle grace
The rumours that precede me of my finds.
But I know now I cannot hold my peace.   20

Recapitulation

To walk in the remembered places
Is to stir memories, to try to catch
The worn past and the rainbow faces
In the short flare of a lighted match.
But these things have long been altered
And recollection has grown as hard

As any lime-dripped image in the caves
Where water turns all flesh to stone;
So that the thin past only lives
In the false emotions, joy and pain.   10

Walking once more upon the ancient roads
I hope that I may meet my dream
As solid-fleshed as the famous gods
Who owned the moor behind my home.
However, the statue silent in the square
Presents the only known face there.

A Temporary Resurrection

There was a cold wind coming from the east
Scattering the leaves and papers in the gardens,
Weaving memories by ponds, sharpening the ice-crust
And disturbing the heart's etiolate wardens.

And I who had been dead for a very long time
Rose from my sofa on the blanching earth,
Tied my bones with tendons, scattering the worms,
And walked anew the ways that lead to birth.

Impotence was there in the fresh spring winds
And gripped the wiry hairs and the hollow bones,   10
Held them underground with its clammy hands
Mating the rising body with the cold limestone.

As doubt claws holes in the indelible brain,
Enclosed and ill-protected by the mortifying skull,
The mind gains harmony with the falling rain,
And the eyes' serrated sockets drink their fill.

G[eorge] S[Sutherland] Fraser (1915 – 1980)

Lean Street

Here where the baby paddles in the gutter,
Here in the slaty greyness and the gas,
Here where the women wear dark shawls and mutter
A hasty word as other women pass,

Telling the secret, telling, clucking and tutting,
Sighing, or saying that it served her right,
The bitch! – the words and weather both are cutting
In Causewayend, on this November night.

At pavement's end and in the slaty weather
I stare with glazing eyes at meager stone,   10
Rain and the gas are sputtering together
A dreary tune! O leave my heart alone,

O leave my heart alone, I tell my sorrows,
For I will soothe you in a softer bed
And I will numb your grief with fat to-morrows
Who break your milk teeth on this stony bread!

They do not hear. Thought stings me like an adder,
A doorway's sagging plumb-line squints at me,
The fat sky gurgles like a swollen bladder
With the foul rain that rains on poverty.   20

Meditation of a Patriot

The posters show my country blonde and green,
Like some sweet siren, but the travellers know
How dull the shale sky is, the airs how keen,
And how our boorish manners freeze like snow.
Romantic Scotland was an emigrant,
Half-blooded, and escaped from sullen weather.
Here, we toss off a dram to drown a cough
And whisky has the trade-mark of the heather.
My heart yearns southwards as the shadows slant,
I wish I were an exile and I rave: 10
    With Byron and with Lermontov
    Romantic Scotland's in the grave.

In Glasgow, that damned sprawling evil town,
I interview a vulgar editor,
Who, brawny, self-made, looks me up and down
And seems to wonder what my sort is for.
Do I write verse? Ah, man, but that is bad . . .
And, too polite, I fawn upon this tough,
But when I leave him, O my heart is sad.
He sings alone who in this province sings.   20
I kick a lamp-post, and in drink I rave:
    With Byron and with Lermontov
    Romantic Scotland's in the grave.

In the far islands to the north and west
Mackenzie and MacDiarmid have their peace.
St Andrews soothes that critic at her breast
Whose polished verse ne'er gave his soul release.
I have no islands and no ancient stone,
Only the sugary granite glittering crisp
Pleases the eye, but turns affection off,   30
Hard rhetoric, that never learned to lisp.
This town has beauty, but I walk alone
And to the flat and sallow sands I rave:
    With Byron and with Lermontov
    Romantic Scotland's in the grave.

Poem

Now cry your heart out if you can,
Cry for many a simple man.
I would weep, too, for my part,
But too soon I drained my heart,
Seeing only beauty could
Rouse or touch my tender blood,
Seeing that my coward will
Kept me far from beauty still
And my awkward limbs and tongue
Were not framed to charm the young;   10
Seeing all that beauty had
Time and circumstance forbade
Me to touch or me to taste,
Seeing all my youth ran waste.
Many a fool as dull as I
Now must rouse himself to die,
Now must seek a colder bed
Than the loneliest he had,
Now must learn to lie alone
In the nakedness of bone,   20
Or through nights of terror wake
When harder things than hearts can break;
When the inventive eye and head
Yield to duller lumps of lead,
When snaffling hand, and lying tongue,
And labyrinth gut, and bellows lung,
About the inhuman landscape spread
A natural history of the dead.

Christmas Letter Home

(To my sister in Aberdeen)

Drifting and innocent and like snow,
Now memories tease me, wherever I go,
And I think of the glitter of granite and distances
And against the blue air the lovely and bare trees,
And slippery pavements spangled with delight
Under the needles of a winter's night,
And I remember the dances, with scarf and cane,
Strolling home in the cold with the silly refrain
Of a tune by Cole Porter or Irving Berlin
Warming a naughty memory up like gin,   10
And Bunny and Sheila and Joyce and Rosemary
Chattering on sofas or preparing tea,
With their delicate voices and their small white hands
This is the sorrow everyone understands.
More than Rostov's artillery, more than the planes
Skirting the cyclonic islands, this remains,
The little, lovely taste of youth we had:

The guns and not our silliness were mad,
All the unloved and ugly seeking power
Were mad, and not our trivial evening hour   20
Of swirling taffetas and muslin girls,
Oh, not their hands, their profiles, or their curls,
Oh, not the evenings of coffee and sherry and snow,
Oh, not the music. Let us rise and go –
But then the months and oceans lie between,
And once again the dust of spring, the green
Bright beaks of buds upon the poplar trees,
And summer's strawberries, and autumn's ease,
And all the marble gestures of the dead,
Before my eyes caress again your head,   30
Your tiny strawberry mouth, your bell of hair,
Your blue eyes with their deep and shallow stare,
Before your hand upon my arm can still
The nerves that everything but home makes ill:
In this historic poster-world I move,
Noise, movement, emptiness, but never love.
Yet all this grief we had to have my dear,
And most who grieve have never known, I fear,
The lucky streak for which we die and live,
And to the luckless must the lucky give   40
All trust, all energy, whatever lies
Under the anger of democracies:
Whatever strikes the towering torturer down,
Whatever can outface the bully's frown,
Talk to the stammerer, spare a cigarette
For tramps at midnight . . . oh, defend it yet!
Some Christmas I shall meet you. Oh, and then
Though all the boys you used to like are men,
Though all my girls are married, though my verse
Has pretty steadily been growing worse,   50
We shall be happy: we shall smile and say,
'These years! It only seems like yesterday
I saw you sitting in that very chair.'
'You have not changed the way you do your hair.'
'These years ere painful, then?' 'I hardly know.
Something lies gently over them, like snow,
A sort of numbing white forgetfulness . . . '

And so, goodnight, this Christmas, and god bless!

To a Scottish Poet

Goddess or ghost, you say, by shuddering,
And ominous of evil to our land,
Twisting to ugliness the mouths that sing,
Parching the lover's moist and balmy hand.

Goddess or ghost, you say, by silence known,
The silence ticking in the rotten wood
Like our numb pain, that can no longer groan:
A grief so old, it gives the mind no food.

I also on bleak nights in Causewayend
Where the slate sky distorts the slaty stone   10
And the shawled women to their burrows wend,
Have felt my country suffering alone.

The slate sea splashes on the slaty pier
In lost St Andrews, where no poets now
Defy the crocodile to shed its tear
Or take what time the bitter years allow.

And the same sea is loud in Aberdeen:
Passing the gas-works and the fish-and-chips
One comes in summer on the radiant scene,
The golden beach, the girls with golden hips,   20

The sun that cooks and savours all their sex:
Then I have thought my country might arise
Like these half-sleeping girls with tawny necks
And summer's sensual softness in their eyes.

These skies bled warmth: and while my blood stays young,
That starving peace, or this protracted war,
Vows broken, or friends lost, or songs unsung
Shall leave no permanent and vexing scar.

Goddess or ghost, you say, by shuddering,
And ominous of evil to our land . . .   30
I say, defy her, while our blood can sing;
While we stand insolent, as poets stand.

For Tilly, Sick, with Love

People don't give such parties now. The young men are old.
You would curl on the carpet. Your thin pretty fingers unrolled,
Pulling pins out, your coils. They came down, a straight weir of green gold . . .

People don't give such parties now. The young men are old,
Busy with social do-gooding or class self-importance:
More on the make than we were, if all were told.

So little we had, and so gay, it is something to ponder:
Fringes and dirndls; guts twisted by weak, wersh* beer,   flat, insipid
Salami, Algerian wine-cup, hard cider, and spam.

And the talk going on till the man in the flat downstairs   10
(Who knew you at Oxford) comes up with his baby and swears
And out to the hot smoky London night we scram.

It rolled down your waist, little mermaid. The clever young men
Would leave their tall talk about Sartre, and come to you then,
As I came, old precious, as never I did not come –

I know what Time brings: I dance slow, to a Noh-play drum! –

All a-goggle. Oh what, the young men would say, could you be,
With your sweet puppy face, light blue eyes that seemed hardly to see,
Long sweet legs, a child's body? Oh, Goddess of Liberty,

You seemed all men's and no man's. Sweet child, in the mist of your stare
I am lost (you lie ill now) in love and not in despair: 21
I am lost in the green-gold cascade of your merciful hair

Drowning the knowledge, more deep, of how deep now your pain.
I would put out my hand in the dark to hold your hand.
I would bear your pain, if I could, in the waking night.

All I can say, sweet, is perhaps not just this land
Makes and destroys the image of delight.
Had a gay Muse ever so pure a brow?

God considers conditions. We shall meet for a drink again.
Is our love round you? People don't give such parties now.

University Road Graveyard

Across the road from the university buildings,
Behind trees, gravestones stand
And forgotten respectable Edwardian citizens
Possess this land.

There beneath the gritty grass sleep the prosperous
Of a humdrum age,
Each with his name and date in large letters
On a stone page.

There they laid to rest the small knitwear fortunes
And the glacier mints;   10
On polished granite mixed light industry
Glitters and glints.

And the young Turks in the Senior Common Room
With each sip they sup
From a cup of coffee wait very eagerly
To plough that up.

On the turf-covered crushed bones they hope to see arising
New Attenborough Towers
And longer echoing chambers for the noise of their
Own mortal hours.

George Campbell Hay (1915 – 1984)

Edinburgh

A windy toon o cloods an' sunny glints;
pinnacled, turreted, stey an' steep grey toon;
her soughin' gables sing their norlan' rants
tae saut an' caller★ blufferts on her croon.   fresh

Steeple an' toor an' battlement stand bauld,
an' gaze ootowre the kindly lands o Forth
tae the braid seaward lift★, far, clear an' cauld,   sky
an' front her airt★, the stern, abidin' north.   direction

Oh, I hae seen her leamin'★ frae afar,   gleaming
bricht thro the fleetin' blatter o the rain,   10
an' happed★ and' hidden, rowed in norsea haar★,   dressed/mist
secret an' dour, loom grandly, prood an' lane★.   lone

Tae stand an' watch frae oot the wooded west
the heich ranks o her dignity gang by,
an' see it surgein' seaward, crest on crest,
her lang swell merchin' ridged against the sky.

Looking Out from Kintyre

Rest on the hill and look beyond the sea.
Eastward the smoke hangs over Clyde and Ayr.
Yonder is all that Britain is, will be;
the blossoming of years is garnered there.

Look from this widowed land, wed to the deer,
and see uprise the incense offering,
the smoky mist that chokes the stars, and hear
the thunder of toom★ barrels rattling.   empty

Here is regret, and memory and song;
the long hills lie indifferent and smile.   10
Yonder the heirs of all their eras throng
their hives, with their inheritance of bile.

Had all our past and all our future, both,
to go like spindrift when the great wind blows;
had our green shoot to shrivel for the growth
of this gaunt sprawling weed that is their rose:

They sing no song. They see nor sun nor earth.
All are gone crazed with babbling. All shape ill.
Where is there mark for reverence, where is worth?
Where is the word that hand should yield to still?　　20

There is no robe we should give back before,
no honour that should walk the causey's crown.
Had this to be – that we should come once more
to iron counsels, long thought cassen down?

This is the end of precedent and gown,
of court, debate, procession, learning prim –
each will be quick to strike his striker down,
and he that bars the way, be hard with him.

Song

Day will rise and the sun from eastward,
the mist in his rays from marsh and plain,
the dew will rise from the bending branches –
och, when will my own heart rise again?
For a treasure shines on the head that haunts me,
like old kings' vaults or the spoils of Spain,
gold hair falling about her shoulders,
the red gold pouring like burning rain.

Her mouth is the sun through red wine shining,
lips that are tender and fine with pride,　　10
white is the neck where the ringlets cluster,
like a white stone under the running tide,
like a burst of sun on broken water
when the mad wind scatters the spindrift wide,
or the drifting snow that the wind is blowing,
whispering, cold on the bare hillside.

By night I travelled rough lonely places,
and down by Garvalt I took my way,
till I reached at dawning the rocky summit,
above the toun where my darling lay;　　20
the stars were fading, the sky was paling,
the cock told loud in her home of day,
I saw the smoke from her hearthstone rising,
I wept, and sighing I turned away.

From showery meadows the wind comes softly
with a scent of blossoms and tender grass;
heartsome the breezes from narrow valleys,
myrtle and heather they breathe, and pass;
but the south wind singing, that comes to lull us,
from sleepy hillsides and seas of glass,　　30
brings to me thoughts of care and sorrow
out of the airt* where dwells my lass.　　　　　　　　　　direction

Still Gyte, Man?

'Still gyte★, man? Stude I in yere claes   mad
I'd thole★ nae beggar's nichts an' days,   endure
chap-chappan, whideeran★ like a moose,   rushing about
at ae same cauld an' steekit★ hoose?   shut

'What stane has she tae draw yere een?
What gars ye, syne she aye has been
as toom★ an' hertless as a hoor,   empty
gang sornan★ kindness at her dure?'   begging

'Though ye should talk a hunner year,
the windblawn wave will seek the shore,   10
the muirlan watter seek the sea.
Then, wheesht★ man. Sae it is wi me.'   be quiet

Neil Paterson (1915 – 1996)

My Friend Joseph

1

FIRST: HOW I MET HIM

I had gone to Manchester to see my father. To ask my father for money. I wanted the money so that I could marry Lizzie and save her from a fate worse than death. Yes, that was how I thought of it. I was twenty-one.

'Tell me about her, then,' my father said, sitting stiff-backed behind his desk.

'How old is she, and what about her family?'

He had me there of course.

'She's nearly eighteen,' I said.

'And her family?'

'She can't help her family. And anyway, they're mostly dead.'

'What does she do?'

'Well,' I said, 'she's a sort of a kind of a maid. To Jacobus. Jacobus, the boxing manager, and Mrs Stevens. Mrs Stevens is his housekeeper.' I knew how it sounded. It sounded terrible. 'But you don't understand,' I said. 'She's different. Really she is, Dad. She's a wonderful girl.'

'Son,' my father said, 'the world is full of wonderful girls, especially the first one.' As he spoke he placed his hand on a sheaf of papers, raised his first two fingers, and drummed *con spirito*, as we said at home. I knew what this meant. It meant that the subject was closed.

'Then you won't help me?'

'No, son,' my father said.

I went out and walked the streets. I walked for a long time, along streets that I did not know and would not know again, and finally I walked into a fairground. I saw the notice that said MURPHY'S FAMOUS BOXING BOOTH, and I paid my sixpence and walked under the notice into the tent. I stood on my toes and, looking down an avenue of cloth caps, saw a large ugly white man hit a large ugly black man on the chin. It was a notable punch. It travelled only a few inches, but it wrenched the Negro's chin up from his chest, spun him half around, and sent him crashing like timber.

Gus, my boss in Sports, once told me always look at their heels, so I looked then at the Negro's heels, and saw that they were flat on the boards and that his toes were up. 'If their heels are flat,' Gus said, 'that's that.' And so it was of course.

'The Pole the winner!' the referee said. 'The killer diller!'

The crowd did not like it. They had paid for ten rounds and got only one. They thought they had been cheated and they said so, with emphasis. They were still booing when the Negro was carried from the ring, and they saved a special raspberry for the winner as he ducked through the ropes and, grinning, nodding, and shaking hands with himself, made for the canvas flap marked *Dressing-room*. He appeared to be pleased with his reception. He actually seemed to think that he was popular. I watched him till he disappeared from sight, and then, smelling a story, I elbowed across the tent to the partitioned-off section, raised the canvas flap, and peered into the Dressing-room.

The Negro lay almost at my feet. Two men in sweaters were working on him, slapping his face and hands, while a third sluiced him with water from a bucket. The Pole was over in the corner farthest from me. He was surrounded by a jostling mill of small men of the kind you always find around a boxing booth, and he was busy lifting these spivs two at a time and banging their heads together.

It was hard to know just what was going on. Everybody, except the Negro, was shouting at the top of his voice, and everybody, especially the Pole, was in a very bad temper. The little rat-faced referee had a restraining hand on the elastic waistband of the Pole's pants, but that wasn't stopping the Pole. When he saw me he dropped his victims and came at me, and there was no time for me to go. He came the direct way, stepping over the Negro's torso, and he came fast.

'You see William?' he demanded.

'I don't understand.'

'William is his bird,' Ratface said. 'His magpie.'

'You see her?' the Pole said, grabbing my coat lapels.

'No,' I said.

'For the love of God,' Ratface said to the roof. 'Sweet God, will somebody please find William!'

Well, that was the first time I met the Pole.

When I got back to London there was a dearth of news, and I slapped out a bit about Murphy's Famous Boxing Booth. Gus let the stuff through, and I had two small pars in each of the evening editions and one in the morning paper.

Next day I had a phone call from Jacobus.

'Hullo,' I said. 'Hullo, Mr Jacobus.' I cleared my throat to catch hold of my voice and waited. I was thoroughly scared. I thought of course that he had found out about Lizzie and me. I thought he knew it was me who had kept her out late the night before.

'Listen,' Jacobus said. 'Somebody in your paper wrote about a Pole. What I want to know is this. Is he good, this Pole? I mean, *good*.'

'He's wonderful,' I said. 'He's sensational, Mr Jacobus.' Now I did not think that the Pole was so very good. When I spoke I did not think of the Pole at all. I thought only of keeping Jacobus sweet, and I just opened my mouth and said what I knew he would like best to hear.

'You think he's worth looking at, boysie?'

'I certainly do, Mr Jacobus,' I said.

And that was how Jacobus came to sign up the Pole. That was the start of it all.

2

I went along to the Gym (Jacobus's Boxing Academy) the day after the Pole arrived. I went in the hope of catching a glimpse of Lizzie, but I let it be known that I had come to see the Pole. I stood and watched him at the heavy bag for a few minutes, then I stepped across to the plywood office to pay my respects to Jacobus.

'Well, how do you like him, Mr Jacobus?' I asked.

'All right,' Jacobus said. 'But he don't talk. I paid good money for him, and what I say is I got the right to have him talk to me. You tell him that, boysie. Tell him he's got to behave hisself when he's here and talk when he's talked at. So far he don't talk to nobody at all, not even the boys, but you tell him that, like I said, boysie. Maybe he'll listen to you.'

So I talked to the Pole.

'Hullo,' I said. 'How are you getting on?'

The Pole scowled and hit the bag with a double left hook.

'You like it here?' I asked.

The Pole hit the bag again, one-one-two, and he hit to hurt.

'How's William?' I said.

The Pole stepped back and looked at me. He had stopped scowling, and was wearing what I took to be an eager and a friendly look, but it hadn't done his face any good at all. I don't know if there are words to fit the Pole's face. It was very big and very, very ugly. When you first looked at it you got the impression that it had more bones in it than necessary, that these bones were bigger than human bones, and that they were not in the places where they ought to be. But after a bit you got accustomed to the idea of the Pole's face, and when you looked at it you didn't see it. You saw only his eyes. His eyes were okay. They were no different from anybody else's eyes, and I think they were brown.

'You know William?' he said.

'Not exactly,' I said. 'But I know about him. Did you ever find him?'

'No,' the Pole said.

That was the sum total of words spoken. I did not think that I had done very well, but Jacobus was impressed. 'You made a hit,' he said. And later, when he had thought it over, he called me into the office. 'Listen, boysie,' he said, 'do me a favour. You come and talk to him as often as you can, and some night you take him out. Will you do that for old Jacobus? There's no one else can start him talking, and it gets you down, that frozen puss – just take a look at it – my God, I seen ugly pans, but I never seen the like a that; you're his friend, you come along and take him out some night, make him laugh. Will you do that, boysie? I'll pay expenses.'

'I'll be glad to oblige you, Mr Jacobus,' I said. I always said yes to Jacobus. I knew that he was harmless. I knew that he was cheap and crooked and contemptible, and I used often to lie in bed at night and work out the way I would treat him the next time we met. The way I would treat him would be like dirt. I decided on it definitely, yet when I got face to face with him I always remembered that he was Lizzie's guardian and that he had Rags Gorman behind him (that especially) and I always got a tight feeling in my stomach and I always went out of my way to be very polite and agreeable, and I nodded my head and said yes, Mr Jacobus, no matter what Jacobus said. 'Certainly, I'll take him out, Mr Jacobus,' I said. 'What's his name?'

'God knows,' Jacobus said. 'I ain't thought one up yet. Now you take him to a cinema, see. Nothing flashy. And, boysie, no eats. He gets that at his place. Board and lodgings. Comprehensive. Good solid food. I got that all fixed. Just some little cinema place.'

I called for the Pole at the Gym at six the following evening.

Lizzie knew that I was due, and came down the stairs with something for the garbage tin, but Jacobus was there, and she would not look at me although she waggled her skirt, meaning affection. I was ashamed to walk with the Pole because of the way everyone stared, and I was angry with Lizzie for not having looked me once in the eyes. I didn't say a word, and I thumbed the Pole into the first cinema I saw. The main film was a marriage comedy with Melvyn Douglas and a blonde, I don't remember her name. It was a very funny film in parts, and I had to laugh, and when I laughed the Pole laughed too. He had a terrible laugh, like something in an opera.

When it was all over I walked the Pole home. I tried to make conversation in basic English and the Pole listened gravely, saying 'Please?' and 'Yes, thank you,' these at the wrong times, and precious little else. We finished the last half-mile in silence, and I was mighty relieved when we came to his lodgings. I thumbed out the door to him in case he hadn't the sense to know where he lived.

'Well, so long,' I said.

The Pole took my hand, shook it hard, and bowed.

'Thank you, pet,' he said.

I didn't have to think that out. It was straight from the film. Melvyn to his wife.

Thank you, pet. It certainly rocked me back on my heels. I could not think of an appropriate reply, and I was determined not to laugh. I merely said, 'So long, then,' and turned away. I looked back from the street corner and saw that the Pole was still standing at the door. When he saw me looking, he raised his hat and bowed again, and I giggled and shot quickly round the corner.

Thank you, pet!

That big gorilla.

Oh, it amused me. It gave me a fine laugh, but it also made me realise that the Pole was a human being, and now, when I look back at it, it does not seem at all funny. It seems sad.

3

The Pole, registered as Joseph Hamilton (Hamilton was Mrs Stevens's middle name: Mrs Stevens was Jacobus's housekeeper), K.O.'d his first two opponents in the third and first rounds respectively, and Jacobus, who believed a pound in the hand was worth ten in the offing, rushed him into a match with Al Kid Williams of Cardiff, who was good. I didn't like it at all. I had grown fond of Joseph. I had started him off on night classes, taken him twice to Bertram Mills, walked him interminably round the Zoo. I had got used to the big cuss, and I didn't want to see him cut to ribbons. I knew that this so-called fight could only be a massacre, and I would have stopped it if I could. But I couldn't. The contract was signed and the bills were up before I even learned of it. AL KID WILLIAMS v. BIG JOE HAMILTON. It was to be a ten-round supporting bout at Blackfriars, and the Pole was given what Jacobus described as 'an extensive preparation'. This included beef tea twice daily and a punch-drunk sparring partner. Joseph, reeking of embrocation, showed me his muscles and his secret left jab. He seemed perfectly content with his new existence, and I was fool enough to think that he was settling down.

Then, six days before the fight, he disappeared.

I met Lizzie on the evening of that day in the Public Library where we had a standing date, Wednesdays, and she told me about it out of the corner of her mouth. Joseph had not turned up at the Gym that morning, his bed had not been slept in, his landlady had not seen him since the previous day. The boys were all out searching. They were combing the parks and the river banks. They had divided the city into sectors, and in their various sectors they were taking in all the pubs, the police offices, the hospitals and the mortuaries. Jacobus was up to high doh, and when last seen was sitting purple at the telephone, working through the Directory. Lizzie wanted me to think where Joseph could be, but I could not think, and I did not want to waste our precious time together. I jockeyed her round to the Archaeology Stall.

Nine days out of ten we could count on getting the Archaeology Stall to ourselves, but this had to be one of the tenth days. An old man in a black reefer coat was seated on the ladder stool taking notes. Lizzie and I pretended to look at the books. We brushed hands and exchanged glances. We waited for a long time for the old man to move, but the old man sat on like a fixture, and at last Lizzie said desperately with her eyes that she had to go.

'Not unless,' I said.

'But him.'

'Him or no him,' I whispered. 'I mean it.'

Lizzie bit her lip, considering this. 'All right,' she said at last.

So I kissed her.

That was the first time we ever kissed in public. The old man was not watching us, and maybe it is not strictly correct to speak of a single unmindful old man as public, but that was how I thought of him. I thought, 'This is the first time I have ever kissed her in public,' and because of that thought that kiss became a very special one, and even now, after an interval of more than ten years, I exactly remember it. Lizzie was wearing a new and unfamiliar perfume, and I have no doubt that it was a very cheap perfume, that she had too much of it on, and that it smelled terrible, but it smelled like a million dollars to me, and it still does. Just before she slipped out of my arms she jerked in closer than she had ever been before, holding very tightly, and when she did so her breasts jellied and took up a new position against my chest. It was a moment of excruciating beauty.

She pushed me away very soon, but I caught at her hand and would not let her go. I had a question to ask her. It was a very important question, and I asked it every time I saw her.

'Lizzie!' I whispered. 'What about Rags Gorman?'

'What about him?'

'You know, Lizzie. Has he been at you again?'

'He hasn't been near the house for a week.'

'Truly?'

'Cross my heart.'

'Thank God,' I said. I was mightily pleased. I was lightheaded with relief. I felt as brisk and jaunty as a bee, and for the time being I forgot all about Joseph and Joseph's strange disappearance.

Next morning Jacobus was in the office at 9.30 a.m. Later, when Joseph was winning fights, he was Jacobus's boy, now he was my thattaty-that Pole. Jacobus was very high. He was talking in terms of the front page. He wanted posters and photographs and headlines, and he wanted them NOW. This was not my class of business, so I took him to Gus. I doubt if it was Gus's class of business either, but Jacobus could never have guessed that. Gus picked a cigarette off the back of his ear, lighted it carefully, put his hands on his stomach, and listened. Gus was fat and old and cynical, and nobody ever would stampede Gus.

'Is this the gorilla you told me about?' Gus said to me. 'This Pole?'

'Yes, Gus.'

'Well, we'll do what we can, Mr Jacobus,' Gus said.

That wasn't enough for Jacobus, though. Jacobus wanted a nation-wide search for the Pole. He wanted sandwich-men. He wanted front-page photographs and finger-size headlines. Jacobus wanted the moon. He talked quick and fast and very big, and as Gus did not interrupt him he got louder and bigger and more and more important. He got so important that he quite forgot himself and even went so far as to say that he would offer a reward.

'How much?' Gus snapped, quick as a ferret.

Jacobus shut his mouth with a click and subsided to his usual size. 'How much?' he said warily. 'How *much?* Well, just say a reward. You don't have to mention the exact cash. Leave that to me. Say, you boys don't mebbe think I'm a piker, do you? I'm no piker. No, sirs!' And he snatched a wad of greasy notes from his pocket and slapped it on the desk. 'Money's no object with Jacobus,' he said. 'Just take a look at that.' But we had time only to catch a glimpse of the wad before he swooped on it, two-handed, and thrust it back into his pocket.

Well, we put a photograph of Joseph in the Sports page and ran a feature story, MISSING HEAVYWEIGHT, and one or two of the other papers carried a similar story, but nothing came of any of them, nobody wrote or rang Jacobus to say that they had seen the Pole, and so one day passed and half of another; then, on the evening of the next day, Saturday that was, I walked out of the office door right into Joseph's arms. (Harry the doorkeeper told me afterwards that he had been hanging around for hours.) When I say that I walked into Joseph's arms I mean just that. He picked me up nose-high, shook me till I rattled, and shouted gleefully across the inch that separated our faces.

'Come home,' he said, grinning. 'Home with me.'

I tried to question him, but it was no good. Joseph had room for only one idea at a time, and when it was an urgent idea like this one he just plugged it, and kept on plugging it.

'Home,' he shouted, giving me another playful shake. 'Home. See John!'

So I went home with him. So I saw John.

John was seated in a cardboard box in the middle of the Pole's bed. John was a bird. I learned afterwards that he was a Blue Abyssinian Duck and extremely valuable, but I did not know that at the time. He was a medium-sized greyish bird with bright blue wings and a white diamond patch on his head, and he squawked like a goose. When I took a couple of steps into the room, he stood up and beat his wings at me. The Pole chk-chkd at him, lifted him and put him on his shoulder, and John sat quiet.

I stared at them and they stared back at me, unblinking, and I swear they both had wide grins on their incredible faces. I gave up, and sat down on the bed.

Jacobus said he had always suspected that the Pole was mad. Now he knew for certain. 'After the Williams fight I'll throw the big ape out on his ear,' he said. He did not say this to me. He said it to Mrs Stevens in Lizzie's presence, and Lizzie told me. 'But meantime I got to keep him from getting lost again, and the only way to make sure of that is to have him here in the house with us.'

'Sleeping?' Mrs Stevens said.

'Sleeping,' Jacobus said.

'And the bird?' Mrs Stevens enquired.

'The bird, too, I suppose. It's only till the fight. Only for a couple of days.'

'I'll have you know, Mr Jacobus,' Mrs Stevens said, 'that I'll have no bloody bird in my house. And that, Mr Jacobus, is final.' Mrs Stevens always called Jacobus Mr, and Jacobus had to call her Mrs too, even in bed. That was the sort of woman Mrs Stevens was. Exceedingly proper. Jacobus had taken her on as housekeeper in Lizzie's mother's place when Lizzie's mother died, and Mrs Stevens had never forgiven Lizzie, and never would, for being the daughter of her predecessor. She had so strong a sense of propriety that she even thought it indecent that Lizzie and she should be sleeping under the same roof, and she said so several times a day.

She was a big red-haired woman, handsome enough, I suppose, with an outstanding bosom and a wide muscular mouth which she used from morning to night, mostly on Lizzie. She was at pains to tell everyone that she did not wish Lizzie any harm. All she wished was that Lizzie was dead or settled in an institution or teamed up with Rags Gorman. Rags Gorman the bookie, who, only a few years ago, had been hawking rags in the streets and who mow wore a coat with an astrakhan collar and financed all the racketeers in the district, Jacobus included. It was Mrs Stevens, not Jacobus, who kept throwing Lizzie at Rags Gorman's head. It was Mrs Stevens who had first got the idea that Rags needed a 'housekeeper' and that Lizzie was just the girl for the job.

Give Jacobus his due, he didn't much like this idea. He never actually got the length of opposing it, he was too scared of Rags Gorman, and I guess he was scared of Mrs Stevens too, but he played for time, he said, 'Wait till she's eighteen,' and he came right out in the open over the new clothes that Mrs Sevens wanted to buy Lizzie for bait. He argued for a week, and in the end he said, 'All right. The costume. But not the fancy underclothes.'

Mrs Stevens said the underclothes were the most important of all.

She kept on at him about it, and each day when I saw Lizzie she told me how it was going; it was like a running commentary on a fight, with Jacobus always backing away ducking and weaving and Mrs Stevens chasing him all round the ring but unable to land a decisive blow. Lizzie wanted the underclothes, of course, but I didn't want her to have them. I couldn't sleep at nights and I prayed like I never prayed for or against any other thing that Lizzie wouldn't get those underclothes, and she didn't. Jacobus finally stood his ground. He said No. Every now and again when he got really cornered he said no to Mrs Stevens, but for every time he said no he said yes a hundred times or more, and even when he insisted on getting is own way he made a point of giving Mrs Stevens a bit of her own way too, to keep her sweet. Like over Joseph and the bird, for instance.

Joseph was duly installed in the spare bedroom (Jacobus). The bird was locked in the loft over the Gym (Mrs Stevens).

The day before the Williams fight Gus called me to his desk and put his finger on a paragraph in *The Evening News*. This paragraph stated that a bird, a valuable Blue Abyssinian Duck, had disappeared from St James's Park.

"'Any person having any information," Gus said, reading, "'please communicate with the Keeper of St James's Park or with any police station." That person, my boy, is you.'

It always was me when there was trouble and the Pole was in it. Well, I waited till after the fight. It was this fight which put the Pole on the map, because to everyone's amazement (especially, Jacobus's) he won in the fifth round, knocking out Al Kid Williams with as vicious a left uppercut as even Gus had ever seen. I waited till the morning after the fight, and then I tackled Joseph about the Blue Abyssinian Duck.

I was very severe. I gave him a long lecture, in the course of which I told him in a dozen different ways that it was wrong to steal. I kept it very simple. I said that John was not Joseph's bird: John was the public's bird. And so on. 'So you've got to take him back to where you found him,' I said finally.

'Why?' Joseph said.

I began all over again. I took it in steps. Each short sentence was a step, and at the end of each step I said, 'Do you understand?' and each time Joseph said, 'Yes,' so I worked up to the climax and said firmly, 'So there it is. You have to take him back to the Park, Joseph.'

Joseph fidgeted and hung his head.

'Why?' Joseph said.

This might have gone on for a long time if I had not hit on a simplification.

'Joseph,' I said, 'I think you know about the King, don't you?'

'Yes,' Joseph said, bowing.

'Well,' I said, 'John belongs to the King.'

'God Save the King,' Joseph said.

There was no more argument. That same night Joseph and I took a ride up West to St James's Park, and some time around midnight the King got back his duck.

4

Joseph's next escapade was far more serious.

It took place in September, after Joseph had beaten Tiger O'Malley and Vince Hammett, and while Jacobus was busy edging him into line for a crack at the British title. I was mixed up in all his troubles, but unfortunately I did not take them seriously. I had my own troubles at the time. Rags Gorman was beginning to put the screw on Lizzie, and I was half-crazed with worry; I was sleeping only an hour or two a night, and I was negotiating desperately for a job on a Union paper. If I got a job on a Union paper they would have to pay me a living wage and I could marry Lizzie then and cock a snook at Jacobus, and Rags Gorman too. I thought endlessly of ways and means to land this job, I just hadn't time to waste on Joseph, and I have to admit that I never really bothered about him or his affairs until after the killing, and then it was too late, of course, nobody could do anything for him then.

When Jacobus told me about Joseph's new pet I flatly disbelieved him. I thought he had been drinking.

'You're joking, Mr Jacobus,' I said. 'Surely you must be joking!'

'Do I look like I'm joking?' Jacobus said.

He didn't. He looked like a man who is having trouble with his blood pressure. His face was purple, there were veins throbbing on his forehead, and his lips hacked and sawed at each other.

'He's got a lion all right,' he said, nodding. He was making a great effort at self-control. He spoke with only a small part of his voice and dropped each word separately, like a penny in a slot. 'A live lion,' he said. 'And what's more, he's got it in my loft, and he's up there with it now.'

I saw that I was expected to say something, perhaps even to do something. I said helplessly, 'Where did he get it, Mr Jacobus?'

'He says he found it.'

'Where?'

'I think,' Jacobus said, showing his teeth like a rat, 'that he found it on a bus.'

That was Joseph's story, and he stuck to it. I tried him hard, but he would tell no other. He was scared, but resolute. I talked to him like a Dutch uncle. I told him he could not possibly keep a lion, and I told him why. Joseph fixed his eyes on a spot several feet above my shoulder and shook his head at it. 'This lion is a dog,' he said.

I consulted Jacobus. 'He says it's a dog,' I told him.

'He's a liar,' Jacobus said. 'It's a lion and nothing but a lion. You see it.'

So I saw the animal. It was a lion all right. I don't know a lot about lions, and I was content to see this one briefly through a chink in the loft door, but at a guess I would say it was about a year-old lion. It hadn't quite filled out; nevertheless, it was an ugly customer. It was the size of a big Alsatian dog and certainly lion enough to do damage.

I talked to Joseph till I ran short of saliva. He listened politely, and when I had finished he said, as far as I could make out, that he would do anything on earth for me, yea gladly, anything else, but he would not give up the lion.

'I love this lion,' he said.

That was probably true. I knew by this time that Joseph had a great capacity for loving all God's creatures, and I had to admit that it was possible that Joseph really did love this lion, as much perhaps as I loved Lizzie, although in a different way of course. I did not know what to say, and, not knowing, I got angry and argued. I should have known better than try to argue with Joseph. 'You can't possibly love a lion. Be sensible,' I said. 'The lion is one of the fiercest of all the beasts. It's a man-eating carnivore. It eats human beings. Do you understand that?' I made the motions with my mouth. 'Eats them.'

'This lion has a soft mouth,' Joseph said.

'No lion has a soft mouth,' I said. 'Think of the danger, man.' I thought of it myself. 'My God,' I said.

'This lion has a soft mouth and there is no danger,' Joseph said.

I pointed out in elaborate detail just how much danger there was.

'Not with this lion, Robert,' Joseph said. 'And this lion's nice soft mouth.'

I got mad then, and I spoke in a way that I had never spoken to him before. I spoke to hurt, and I did hurt him. I was savage and sarcastic. I really let myself go, and for good measure I threw in a home truth or two that was not strictly to the point. Joseph hung his head and trembled like a monstrous, miserable child. I couldn't go on shouting at him. I checked myself and clapped him on the arm. 'Now, Joseph,' I said gently, 'be sensible.'

He raised his head and looked at me, and his eyes were like a whipped dog's.

'You'll get over it, Joseph,' I said.

He shook his head. He sagged.

And then the idea hit him. It hit him quite visibly, like a kidney punch. He straightened up, his face jerked to life, and he thrust his hand to his mouth and pulled out his new plate of artificial dentures, a legacy from the O'Malley fight. 'See, Robert,' he said, brandishing this plate at me. 'No danger with my lion. My lion has false teeth, like me!'

There wasn't much you could do with a clown like that.

I went down to the Gymnasium and told Jacobus what the Pole had told me. Jacobus didn't think it funny. He threw a newly lighted cigarette to the floor and screwed it into shreds with the heel of his patent-leather shoe. 'I'll fix him,' he said, simmering. He lifted his foot and looked at the remains of the cigarette in a sudden new passion. 'The big suching so-and-so,' he said. 'I'll fix him see if I don't.'

Jacobus did not fix the Pole, however. At least not immediately.

The truth is, Jacobus was afraid of the Pole. The Pole never spoke to Jacobus, and when he looked at Jacobus he scowled. I didn't blame Jacobus for being scared. If the Pole had scowled every time he looked at me I would have been scared too.

Well, Jacobus waited.

He had good reason to wait, because just at this time he was engaged in a very delicate piece of fiddling. The British Board of Boxing Control was about to examine the question of Joseph's nationality and had summoned Joseph and Jacobus to appear before it at the end of the month. Jacobus had got documents from Rags Gorman's lawyer which purported to prove that Joseph was British, but all the documents in the world would not be enough if Joseph himself chose to be awkward. *(Unco-operative* was the word the lawyer used.)

Now Jacobus knew perfectly well that if he took Joseph's lion away from Joseph the odds were that Joseph would be extremely unco-operative. The result would be unfortunate. The Board would decide that Joseph was not eligible to fight for the British title and he, Jacobus, would lose a nice fat purse. In the circumstances he could not afford to be on worse than scowling terms with Joseph. He therefore decided, according to Lizzie, to sit tight and do nothing at all about the lion – *meantime.* He merely bought Mrs Stevens a fur cape, presented the Pole with a reinforced bar and padlock for the loft door, and settled down to wait till the British Boxing Board of Control gave their decision. 'By the Lord God,' he swore, 'I'll fix him then.'

'What's he going to do?' I asked.

'Tell the police,' Lizzie said.

The Board met on the last day of September. The stewards asked Joseph questions on which Joseph had not been primed, and Joseph could not answer these questions.

'Although he's pure British,' Jacobus said, 'the truth is, he don't understand English so good.'

After discussion the stewards decided to examine Joseph with the aid of an interpreter, and the meeting was duly adjourned for three weeks. During these three weeks Jacobus signed a contract (provisional on the Board's decision) for a twelve-round championship elimination fight at Harringay between Joseph and Jackie Wilson, the official contender; and some time also during these three weeks Joseph, spruced and nervous, came to the office to consult me on a personal matter of great importance.

We talked in the corridor outside the Reporters' Room.

'I have troubles,' Joseph said.

Joseph's troubles were small beer compared with those of everyone around him. Joseph's troubles were purely financial. He wanted more money for the coming fight. He told me this in a very roundabout way, and while he spoke he jigged from one leg to the other and raised his eyes only as far as my knees.

'I want a lot of money,' he said.

'How much?' I asked.

'Twenty pounds.'

'Let's get this straight,' I said. 'Do you want twenty pounds more than you've been getting or twenty pounds in all?'

'All of twenty pounds,' Joseph said. 'In my hand.'

His eyes crept up and touched me warily in the face. 'Is it reasonable, Robert?'

He was perfectly serious. I took a deep breath and let it out slowly. I asked him what money he had been getting from Jacobus.

'A five pound,' Joseph said. 'Each fight a five pound. I want twenty. Is it reasonable?'

'My God,' I said. I just couldn't believe that even Jacobus was as mean as that. I stared helplessly at the Pole, and he fidgeted and dropped his eyes back where they had come from. I realised that he was waiting for me to tell him whether his request for twenty pounds was reasonable, and I realised also that I had not yet heard the whole of this story. 'What do you want the twenty pounds for?' I asked.

'To buy a cow.'

'A what?'

'A cow,' Joseph said. 'The butcher says I give twenty pounds I get a cow. A whole cow. Dead.'

'You mean a carcass?' I said. I began to understand then. 'The body of a cow. You want to buy the body of a cow for your lion, is that it?'

'The body of a whole cow,' Joseph said. 'For twenty pounds. Therefore I want twenty pounds. Is it reasonable?'

'It is reasonable,' I had to say.

'Then you come with me,' Joseph said, 'and speak also to Jacobus, if you please.'

So I went with him.

When Jacobus heard what Joseph had to say his eyes got very shifty and he said, 'Yes, yes, yes. All right, I said yes, didn't I?'

'I put the rest into gilt-edged for him,' he said to me. 'He wouldn't know what to do with it, so I save it for him. I put the whole lot into gilt-edged.' He was still off balance, for he actually brought out his case and offered me a cigarette. 'But boysie,' he said. 'That's not for printing in your paper.'

I had the guts of a cockroach.

'No, no, of course not, Mr Jacobus,' I said.

5

I left Joseph at the Gym and boarded a number 13 bus at the corner of the street. I was about to go upstairs when I heard Lizzie's voice and, looking round, I saw her racing across the road from the Gymnasium. She ran like a little girl in a hurry, using the whole width of her skirt, her legs showing high-up, and her unbuttoned raincoat streaming from her shoulders.

The bus was already under way.

'Hey, Mac!' I said to the conductor. 'Just a minute, please.' I grabbed Lizzie by the elbow and hoisted her on to the platform, and Lizzie said, 'Phew! Thought I'd missed you,' and leaned for a moment, panting on my chest.

The people in the downstairs were staring, so we went up top. It was quiet up top, and we had the back of the bus to ourselves. 'I phoned,' Lizzie said. 'But they said you weren't at the office. I had to see you.'

'Something's happened!' I said, bracing myself.

'Certainly has,' Lizzie said. 'You'll never guess either. Something pretty terrible. Rags Gorman came last night and they left me alone with him and I had one bit of a time, I can tell you.'

I had a landslide in my stomach, and I guess something must also have happened in my face.

'Keep your shirt on,' Lizzie said. 'I didn't let him get his hands on me, if that's what you're thinking. No, Robert, it was worse than that.'

'Worse,' I said. *'Worse!'*

'Worse,' Lizzie said, nodding. 'He actually wants to marry me! It's not just a line either. He really and seriously wants to marry me. He said it in front of Jacobus and Mrs Stevens before they left us alone. He said he would come back tomorrow night for his answer, and they've both of them been at me ever since. Jacobus is mad at me for still calling him Mr Gorman to his face, he's all for it now that Rags is talking marriage, and Mrs Stevens, you know what she's like; it's been nag, nag, nag, Rags this, Rags that, nothing but Rags all day long, what a gent he is and what a compliment it is to have a really important kind of gent like Rags actually wanting to marry me. In church too, Mrs Stevens says. Rags never said nothing about church to me, but Mrs Stevens swears he said it to her. "Your own mother never had a wedding in her life," Mrs Stevens said. You know her. You know how she goes on about that. "And you – your own mother's daughter . . ." *etcetera* – all that dirt she rakes up – "here's you with an offer from the richest man in the district, a real gentleman, a bookmaker, and not only he wants to marry you but in a church too, and look at the house you'll have, and the money, and the respect, folks touching their caps to you in the streets and nobody'll dare not to; my God, it makes me certainly wonder. You bitch," Mrs Stevens said, "you don't deserve it."'

Lizzie stopped for breath, let her head fall limply on my shoulder, and said, 'Oh, Robert dearie, I've had a terrible, hell of a day!'

We sat on the top of that bus for a long time. We went all the way to the terminus, and half of the way back, and we talked continuously, but I don't know that we said very much. I remember I was all for getting married straight away. I said we had to, now. Lizzie said how could we, would I just please kindly tell her how we possibly could when I wasn't even able to keep myself in cigarettes. It was an old argument, and it went on and on. Lizzie was the practical one, and when she was being most practical I always saw a deep strain of idealism in her, deeper than any I possessed, and I always loved her very dearly. I was willing, no, eager, to take a chance on the gutter. But Lizzie wasn't. She knew it too well. She knew what the gutter did to you, and she wasn't going to let it do that dirty thing to me or to the nice clean feeling we had between us.

I tried to be masterful.

I told her that I wasn't going to stand for any more nonsense. I had made up my mind what we were going to do. We were going to get married.

Yes, *married*.

After we were married I would take her up north to my home, and she would live with my father and mother till I could afford to send for her. I said that once my mother got to know her she would love her, and I said that I knew Lizzie would love my mother too, and I made it all sound very convincing, so much so that I almost believed it myself. But Lizzie didn't. She gave me a calm, wise, female smile and shook her head.

She said decisively, 'The only thing to do is to tell them to their faces that I'm in love with you. They'll leave me alone then. I'll just tell them the truth, and if they don't like it they can go jump in the river.'

We finally agreed on that.

'After all,' Lizzie said, 'all they can do is get mad at me.'

This was not strictly correct. They could, and certainly would, try to prevent her from seeing me again, and they might also bring pressure to bear on me. I reckoned that henceforth I would be a marked man. I would have to watch my step, keep to the lighted streets. I had no illusions about Rags Gorman. I feared him almost as much as I hated him, and I had a great respect for what I thought to be his methods.

I put my arm round Lizzie's shoulders and held her very tight. 'Don't worry,' I said, lying. 'There's really nothing to worry about.' She felt extra small and brittle, and I loved her unbearably. 'Darling,' I said. 'Oh, darling, I'll make this up to you some day, I swear I will.'

'It's okay,' Lizzie said. 'Really it is. All this is much worse for you, Robert, than it is for me.' And she raised her face to mine and gave me a smile that hit me in the chest and hurt. She was magnificent.

'*I'm* not worrying,' she said.

6

The next day was the longest I have ever lived through. Lizzie was to phone in the evening. She was to slip out and ring me whenever she got rid of Rags Gorman, and I sat waiting by the office phone for three interminable hours, from 8 till 11 p.m. A crowd of the boys came in then and sat down at the long reporters' table, and I just couldn't take their bright talk. I sat for a little with my arms on the table and my face hidden in my arms, but I couldn't help raising my head each time the phone rang and the boys guessed that I had a date and started ribbing me, and I felt some sort of wild hysteria coming on. I had to get out. I had to get to Lizzie. I left the office at a run, jumped a number 13 at the traffic lights, and got off just opposite Jacobus's Gymnasium some fifteen minutes later.

It was then exactly twenty-two minutes past eleven, and there was nobody about.

I climbed the yard gate and, keeping to the shadow of the house wall, tiptoed up the flight of stone stairs that led to the kitchen door. I don't know exactly what I meant to do. I hoped to see Lizzie, but if I did not see Lizzie I think I meant to hammer on the door and ask to see Joseph. If Joseph was not in I would ask for Jacobus. Somehow or other I would get into that house, and, once in the house, I would find out what had happened to Lizzie.

I peered through the glass panel in the kitchen door. A glimmer of light came from the fire in the range, and I saw that the room was empty.

I tried the door.

The door opened, and I stepped inside.

The kitchen led into a narrow hall, flanked with doors. I had never been in the house before, but I knew something of its arrangements from Lizzie. I held my breath deep inside me, and edged across to the room which I thought to be the parlour. As I reached it another door was flung open, Jacobus's voice rattled out into the hall, and a broad band of light slid across the wall and exposed me. I closed my eyes in a kind of convulsion. When I opened them I saw Lizzie standing there in front of me, her hand on her throat. I breathed again and took a step towards her, and as I did so she wheeled round and jerked shut the door of the lighted room, grabbed my sleeve, pulled me a few paces down the corridor, opened another door, and thrust me in.

'Are you crazy?' she said in the dark. She sounded angry.

'I don't know,' I said. 'I suppose I am. Lizzie, are you all right?'

'Of course I'm all right. Why shouldn't I be all right? What's the matter with you?'

'Rags Gorman?' I whispered.

'He's been and gone.' She giggled, and I knew then that she wasn't angry: she was just strung-up, like me. 'You'll never believe it. Joseph . . . listen, Robert I . . . Joseph threw him downstairs.'

'Joseph what!'

'Threw Rags downstairs,' she said. 'Yes, he did, and broke his wrist for him too. So now Joseph's gone of course, bag and baggage. And the lion's gone too. You know about the Board, don't you?'

'The Board?' I said, dazed.

'The Boxing Board.'

'Oh, was that today?' I said. 'I'd forgotten. Today's been such a crazy day. No, I don't know. What happened, Lizzie?'

'They decided Joseph was a foreigner of unknown nationality and they said he couldn't fight for the title. Jacobus was raving mad about it. He was fair hopping. He said Joseph botched the whole thing, and when he came home he phoned the police about the lion and a special truck came up from the Zoo and they took the lion away. Joseph didn't know about it. He was at his elocution class, and when he came home Rags Gorman was here, he had just arrived. We were in the parlour, Rags and me, and we heard Jacobus screaming. You should of heard him, something terrible, he was screaming his head off, and Rags and me went out on to the landing to see what was wrong, and the Pole had Jacobus by the throat, up this high, his feet off the ground, and he threw Jacobus right down the stairs, and then he picked up Rags and shook him like a rat and threw him down the stairs too, and when he threw *him* down the stairs he broke his wrist for him.'

I felt the firm rim of an object behind my knees and sat down. It was the bed. I had a hold of Lizzie's hand, and when I sat down she had to sit down too. If I had realised it was Lizzie's bed I probably would not have sat down on it, but I don't know, I might have, I was in a flat spin and capable of almost anything.

'Old Joseph!' I said.

'Shht!' Lizzie whispered, tensing up suddenly and digging her nails into my wrist. 'Listen! What's that?'

I listened for noises in the house, but all I heard was the loud beating of my heart and a soft friction sound that seemed to come-from Lizzie's knees.

'It's only your stockings rubbing together,' I said.

'It must be the way my toes are,' Lizzie said, 'on the floor.' She rearranged her legs, but they didn't stop shaking. I sat holding her hand. I could feel the beat of the blood in her finger tips, and I was very conscious of her trembling legs. After a little I began to tremble too.

'You oughtn't to have come, Robert,' Lizzie said softly.

'I had to,' I said. 'I had to see that you were all right. Thank God you are all right, Lizzie. You must have had an awful time.'

'Oh, that,' Lizzie said. 'You don't know the half of it yet. You see, I told Rags Gorman I couldn't ever marry him. I said I was in love with somebody else, and when he pestered me to say who it was, do you know who I said? I said Joseph. I knew that Rags and Jacobus were so mad at Joseph over the Boxing Board that they just couldn't get any madder, and so I said it was Joseph I was in love with.' And she giggled happily. 'What do you think of that? Wasn't that clever of me, sugar?'

'Wonderful,' I said. I felt a great surge of relief and an even greater surge of love. I pulled Lizzie to me – she came very easily – and we lost our sitting balance and toppled full length on the bed. It was a very beautiful and terrible moment, and when I kissed her it was even more so.

I took a grip of myself. I put my hands flat on the bed and took the weight of my body on my arms. 'I'll have to go,' I said.

Lizzie didn't say anything. She just breathed on me.

'Lizzie!' I whispered.

'U-huh?'

'What if somebody comes in, Lizzie?'

'Nobody'll come in,' Lizzie said.

'Are you sure?'

'Quite sure,' Lizzie said. 'So long as you're here you're safe, It's when you try to leave that they might catch you. Now that you *are* here you'll just have to stay, that's all. I mean till they go to bed.'

'But, Lizzie,' I said. 'Do you think it's proper?'

Lizzie put her arms up and folded them firmly round my neck. 'Don't be silly,' she said.

So I stayed.

I stayed for a long time, because, as Lizzie said, we might as well be hung for a sheep as a lamb, and there just wasn't any sense in waiting for Jacobus and Mrs S. to go to bed if we didn't also wait until they went to sleep.

It was some time around 5 a.m. when Lizzie let me out at the kitchen door.

I walked all the way home, and I guess I walked with a swagger. I waved a good morning to the bakers and the milkmen. I whistled. Sometimes I even sang. All my troubles were miraculously gone, puffed away like dust in the high October wind that swirled my coat around me. For the first time in months I was happy. I hadn't a care in the world.

It was almost daylight when I reached my digs.

My digs were on the second floor of a tenement building. At one time or another there had been a lot of girls in the flats – my own landlady had had four daughters and the steps were neatly hollowed out in the places where the girls, over many generations, had sat canoodling with their boys. There was an especially comfortable big dent in the top stair but one, and when I reached the bend in the landing I saw that this dent was occupied.

'Robert?' a voice said in the gloom.

'Well, well. Joseph!' I said.

He came bounding down the stairs to meet me. A cone of light fell on to the landing from the 40-watt on the floor above, and we were caught in this light like flies in an upturned wineglass. I saw every jutting bone in his face, and I saw his eyes.

'Robert,' he said. 'They took my lion.'

'I know, I know, Joseph,' I said. I had my first pang of conscience then, for I owed my happiness to Joseph, and I had not thought of Joseph or Joseph's troubles for a long, long time. 'Never mind,' I said, 'you'll get another pet. I know what, Joseph. I'll buy you a dog. A fine, big Alsatian dog. A dog is a much better pet than a lion.'

'I don't want a dog,' Joseph said. 'I am unhappy about my lion, but I came to tell you about another thing. I am very happy about this other thing. It is beautiful and a surprise. Lizzie loves me. Jacobus's Lizzie. She loves me, Robert!'

I stared at him and he stared back at me, grinning, nodding violently, mouthing his words like an apoplectic ape. 'Yes, hahaha, yes, yes, yes,' he said, stuttering. 'She loves me.'

I saw him briefly as Jacobus must have seen him, not as a human being at all, but as a Thing – a monstrous and a crazy Thing. I loathed him then, and I wanted him to know it. I thrust my face at him, hating him. 'Don't be a fool,' I said. 'You crazy deformed fool,' I said. 'Who do you think *you* are for Lizzie to love?'

He didn't understand.

'She loves me, Robert,' he said doggedly. 'She said so.'

'She said so,' I said, speaking very coldly and deliberately, 'only in order to get rid of Rags Gorman who wanted to marry her. Do you understand that? She wanted to get rid of Rags Gorman, and the only way she could get rid of him was by saying that she loved somebody else, and when she was asked who it was that she loved she had a particular reason for not telling the truth, and so she just said the first name that came into her head and it happened to be yours. In point of fact,' I said, 'she is in love with me.' And I jabbed my thumb into my chest. 'Me. Do you understand that?'

He understood all right.

I wish now that he had not understood so well and that I had not seen his face in that moment of his understanding. His face was piteous. He stood stock-still, searching my eyes, and then, sucking his breath into his teeth, he swung away and bolted in a wild, animal-like clatter down the stairs.

When I heard the door slam below I came to my senses. I flung myself at the banister rail and shouted after him. 'Joseph,' I shouted, 'I didn't mean it, not like that.'

'Joseph!' I shouted. 'Come back!'

But I don't suppose he even heard me.

7

Well, I searched for Joseph everywhere. Everywhere I could think of. The public parks, the Embankment, Rowton House, the Salvation Army Hostels. I searched in all the likely places, and I went on searching day after day, but I did not find Joseph nor anyone who had seen him. Lizzie had the bright idea that he might go to the Zoo to be near his lion, but when we made enquiries at the Zoo they told us the lion was not there. The clerk whom we saw said he thought that some menagerie had claimed the lion. He could not tell us the name of the menagerie, but he seemed anxious to oblige, and he said if it was important I could leave my name and address and he would find out and send me a postcard.

'Will you *really?*' Lizzie said.

'Really,' the clerk said. 'Glad to.' He was a tall thin man of about thirty, with very light blue eyes and a nervous tic at one corner of his mouth. He had four beautifully sharpened pencils in his breast pocket, and he looked to be the sort of man you could rely on, not in a crisis, maybe, but in the little things of life. Only, he wasn't. He never sent the postcard, and the result was that I did not learn where Joseph's lion was until three weeks later, when I also learned where Joseph was.

Joseph was in jail.

I read about it in the noon edition of my own paper.

BRUTAL MENAGERIE MURDER, my paper said.

KEEPER KILLED

Tragedy struck Harrap's Menagerie in broad daylight yesterday afternoon, when, as reported fully in our earlier editions, a man gained entry to the lions' cage and was driven into the eating corner by one of the young male lions.

George Gavin Gould, the deceased, a keeper at Harrap's Menagerie, entered the cage and shot the lion through the back of the head. It is alleged that the man then attacked the keeper, raising him above his head and throwing him against the bars of the cage, and that as a result of this attack the keeper sustained injuries which proved fatal.

According to the reports of eye-witnesses, the man made repeated attempts to revive the dead lion. He refused to leave the cage even under the threat of fire-arms, and tear gas had eventually to be used. He then collapsed on the lion's body, and the police, who made the arrest, were unable to disengage his arms from the lion's neck. It is reported that it was necessary to drag both man and lion from the cage and to summon medical assistance to prise loose the man's grip.

This tragic incident took place at three o'clock in the afternoon, and was witnessed by a large crowd of holiday-makers, including many children.

SEE STOP PRESS

The STOP PRESS read:

SEQUEL TO MENAGERIE MURDER

Sequel to the tragedy at Harrap's Menagerie took place in Marylebone Police Court this morning, when a man was charged with the willful murder of George Gavin Gould. He gave his name as Joseph Hamilton, age unknown, professional boxer, of no fixed abode, and when asked if he wished to make a statement he said, 'He killed my lion.'

How I felt is not of much importance to anyone except myself, but I would like to say it, just once, and leave it at that. I felt terrible.

I went to see Joseph in Pentonville as soon as the authorization came through. They sat me down at one end of a long deal table, and after a little they brought Joseph in and sat him down at the other end. We were asked kindly to keep our hands on the table, and the warder who asked us this sat down midway between us.

I had got so used to Joseph's face that I hardly ever noticed it. Now I took a good look at it. I looked at it as I thought a juryman would, and I was appalled by what I saw.

It was a horrible face.

The forehead was low and ape-like. The eyes were obscured by monumental, fist-scarred cheek-bones. The nose had been broken at the bridge and punched right back into its base; the nostrils were upturned like a syphilitic's. The mouth was squint and puffy, and the jaw aggressive and immense. Each feature, taken separately, was sub-human, and the combination of these sub-human features was something that had to be seen to be believed. It was a brutal and degenerate face. It was undoubtedly the face of a murderer.

Joseph saw me staring and put his hand up to his throat. They had taken away his collar and tie, and he thought this was what I was looking at. He told me they had done this for fear he might hang himself.

'They think I'm criminal,' he said. His eyes were dark and distressed, the pupils dilated, and they took a hold of mine and clung tight, like lover's eyes. 'Me,' he said. 'Criminal!'

'Nobody could think that who knows you,' I said. I talked louder than natural, because I had been thinking precisely this myself, because I was embarrassed and unhappy, and determined to be very much at ease. 'Nobody could ever think that, Joseph,' I said emphatically. 'I have a message from Lizzie. Lizzie sends her love. All your friends are thinking about you. We're all standing by you, Joseph.'

'I have no friends,' Joseph said.

That was true, of course.

'Except you,' Joseph said. 'Only you, Robert. The rest is not my friends at all. They say that keeping-man was a good man and I am bad, but he was a bad man and he did a bad thing. You know what he did, Robert? He killed my lion.'

'I know, Joseph,' I said. 'I know. But, Joseph, the lion was going to kill you. He saved your life.'

'He killed my lion's life,' Joseph said.

'But Joseph . . . '

'No,' Joseph said. 'Listen, Robert. He killed my. lion's life. That was a very bad thing he did.'

What could I say? I looked at my hands. I folded up my fingers and stared at the nails.

'Nobody understands. But you will understand. Will you please understand, Robert?'

You should have seen his face then.

'Please, Robert.'

'All right,' I said. I'd have said anything. 'All right, Joseph. I'll understand. I promise.'

'This then,' Joseph said. 'A lion is different.' He wanted to get it right. There were just certain words that would carry the idea, and he wanted desperately to find those words. He thought very hard. He tested phrases soundlessly on his lips. He stared right into me, scowling, while little beads of sweat gathered on his brow and the big wall clock, inscribed JOYNER EIGHT DAY, ticked our precious seconds away. It was several minutes before he spoke, and then he said something like this.

'They took my lion away. The lion does not understand this. The lion does not know that anything happens except what happens to the lion. The lion does not know that there is anywhere at all except where the lion is. The lion does not know that it has been taken away from me. It thinks that I have been taken away from it. When my lion sees me again it thinks it has found me. It pushes me into a corner. It does not push me into a corner because it wishes to savage at me, but because it wishes to keep me safe. My lion was keeping me safe because it loved me, and the man came and shot into it and killed it. Do you understand, Robert?'

'I think I do, Joseph,' I said. 'It's a matter of psychology the way you put it. Animal psychology. But you killed the man.'

'I threw him away,' Joseph said. 'I was angry, and I did not know if he was going to shoot into my lion again, or into me perhaps. I was very angry.'

'But you didn't mean to kill him, did you?'

'No,' Joseph said.

I thought I had got something there. I saw Joseph's point of view perfectly. It was all a matter of interpretation. To you and to me and to George Gavin Gould that lion was a savage lion, about to do murder: to Joseph it was just his own friendly lion, about to lick his face. I put myself in Joseph's place and I thought with Joseph's mind (or tried to), and it all seemed perfectly reasonable, even the murder, which was no murder at all, but an act of self-defence or, at worst, of provoked assault

I thought I had got hold of something important from a legal angle, and I tried hard, but without success, to get it over on the lawyers. The solicitor was old and tired and the barrister was young and cold. They were not impressionable men and I did not impress them. I could not get them to see the importance of this psychological point.

'Might conceivably be of use,' the barrister said to the solicitor, 'to supplement an insanity plea.'

'But,' I said, 'Joseph's not mad.'

They ignored me.

'I doubt – I very much doubt,' the solicitor said, 'if you could make such insanity as the fellow exhibits into a valid exculpatory plea.'

'But I'm telling you,' I said, 'Joseph's not mad.'

'I quite agree,' the barrister said, speaking only to the solicitor. 'The fellow is undoubtedly a lunatic, but if I am to bring his mental condition sub judice I shall clearly have the greatest difficulty in persuading them that he is a King's pleasure Lunatic.'

'But,' I said. I kept butting.

'Young man,' the young barrister said, speaking directly to me for the first time, 'are you trying to teach me the Law?'

'No, sir,' I said.

It was hopeless.

I had been banking on that visit to the lawyers. So had Lizzie. When I told her what had happened, she broke down and cried openly in my arms. 'It's all my fault,' she said. 'None of this would have happened if it hadn't been for me.'

Lizzie was having a bad time. Ever since the night she had told the lie about being in love with the Pole they had been at her incessantly. Not Rags Gorman, of course. Rags Gorman was out of it. But Jacobus and Mrs Stevens. Nag, nag, nag. It was worse than ever now, because now they really had something on her. Mrs Stevens gave her no peace. I could have killed that woman. She would even force her way into Lizzie's bedroom during the night just to tell Lizzie all over again precisely what she thought of her. And Lizzie couldn't take it. She was getting thinner and whiter every day; she had violet smudges, like shiners, under her eyes; and her skin was so fine you could see through it. She was beginning to have a dangerously delicate look, and I did not like it at all. 'Everything they say about me is true,' she said. 'I spoil everything for everybody, and this is all my fault.'

I held her very tight and scratched her head and babied her. I told her it was crazy to worry; what had happened wasn't her fault, wasn't even her business. I told her that she was making a great fuss about nothing. Oh, I said all the reassuring things. I even said that Joseph would get off.

'Do you think he will, Robert?'

'Course he will,' I said, my mouth in her hair.

'Do you *really* think so?'

'I'm certain of it,' I said.

But I wasn't certain, of course. At best, I was hopeful. I hoped that they would amend the charge to manslaughter.

Gus gave me time off for the duration of the trial, and I was first in the gallery queue both days and got the end seat by the dock. This was the best seat in the Court, and the one nearest to Joseph.

Joseph pleaded Not Guilty, but there was no argument as to the facts. Joseph had assaulted George Gavin Gould. He had picked him up and thrown him against the bars of the cage, and as a result of this violence George Gavin Gould had died. The Defence called witnesses to prove that the deceased had been suffering from a disease called cardiac something, and the inference was that he had not taken a lot of killing. They put Joseph in the Box and asked him simple questions. They asked, 'Did you wish to kill this man? Did you mean to kill this man? Did you know that you had killed this man?' And each time Joseph said, 'No.' The counsel for the Defence was not the one I had seen in the Solicitor's Chambers; the one I had seen then was only the Junior, this one was a middle-aged man; he looked a distinguished and capable lawyer and I think he was; he made it quite clear to me, and I hoped he had also made it clear to the Jury, that Joseph's action was unpremeditated, and that he had never had the slightest intention of killing.

'This is a case of manslaughter,' he said. 'And manslaughter only.'

The question of Joseph's sanity was debated at length. Two alienists were called. One was on Joseph's side and one wasn't. The one who wasn't said that Joseph was suffering from a disease called 'systematised ambitious paranoia,' and that this meant that he was mad. The friendly one disagreed. He admitted that Joseph had a paranoiac mental constitution, but he said that this was a common mental state, many sane people had it, and that all one could say about such people was that they showed a tendency to develop a systematized delusional insanity. 'Compare this man's mental state to a soil,' he said. 'It is a soil which is prone to grow a particular weed, but I have found no sign that the weed has in fact grown in it.'

The Judge was a little, birdlike man, and he thrust his face over the Bench and pecked impatiently at this alienist. 'Your metaphors would no doubt be of interest to a Horticultural Society,' he said. 'But let us have the blunt facts in this Court. Is he responsible for his actions?'

'Yes, my lord.'

'Then that is all we want to know,' the Judge said. 'He is sane.'

It was all over by the forenoon of the second day. The jury, after retiring for only eleven minutes, returned a verdict of guilty of murder, with a recommendation for mercy; and the Judge, on passing sentence, declared that owing to the precarious state of the deceased's health he approved and endorsed the jury's recommendation, but was himself unable to give it effect.

'I sentence you, Joseph Hamilton,' he said, 'to be hanged by the neck until you are dead.'

Joseph swallowed and leaned forward towards me. He opened his mouth, closed it again, and shook his head.

The policemen turned him unobtrusively and led him down the steps.

I watched the back of Joseph's head for what seemed a very long time, and when at last it disappeared from sight, I put my arms on the gallery rail and hid my face in my arms, and cried.

Afterwards, I went to Jacobus's place. I had promised Lizzie that I would come straight to her with the verdict. I whistled at the foot of the backstairs, and Lizzie came down at a run.

Wiping her hands on her apron, her eyes hooked into mine.

'Well?' she said.

'Not so good, Lizzie,' I said. I cleared my throat.

'Go on. Tell me,' she said.

'They found him guilty.'

She made a small noise inside her shut mouth.

'But they'll never hang him,' I said. 'The jury recommended mercy and the Judge did too. They say he'll only get a few years.'

'Stop crying, Lizzie,' I said. 'There's nothing to cry about. Darling,' I said. 'Darling, don't. It's not your fault. It's not anybody's fault. Joseph'll be all right.'

She was crying terribly.

I took her in my arms. I didn't care if Jacobus or Mrs Stevens saw. I didn't care for anybody. 'It's all right, darling,' I said. 'You mustn't take it like this. Be reasonable, sweetheart. This is not your affair. Why should *you* blame yourself?'

'Why?' Lizzie said, tearing herself free. 'Because I love him, that's why. You fool,' Lizzie said ferociously. 'I *love* him.'

I knew immediately that it was true, but my voice went on in spite of me. 'But you couldn't,' my voice said. And it picked on the least of a thousand good reasons. 'You just couldn't, Lizzie. He's so ugly.'

'Beautiful,' she said, almost screaming. 'He's got the most beautiful body in the world, and I love him, do you hear!' And she began to cry again, differently – quietly and hopelessly – her hands flat on her face. 'He's so sweet,' she said. 'Oh, God. Oh, Joseph. I love him. I didn't know it, but I know now. Ah, Joseph.'

I just stood there and looked at her. I couldn't say anything. There wasn't a single thing left for me to say.

'I'm sorry, Robert,' Lizzie said.

★　　★　　★　　★　　★

Well, that's about all.

The following week Joseph's sentence was commuted to penal servitude for life, i.e., fifteen years, and a day or two later I got word from the Record Office that they at last had a vacancy in the Sub-Editors' Room. They offered me the job at seven-ten a week, which was – or, rather, would have been – quite enough for us to get married on.

I think it only fair to say that there is probably not a great deal of truth in this account of Joseph and Lizzie and Jacobus and Mrs Stevens and Rags Gorman. I have told the truth as I saw it at twenty-one, but the truth as you see it at twenty-one is not the whole truth by a long chalk, and I suspect now that I was not a very intelligent twenty-one. I saw only a little of what was going on, and I understood only a little of what I saw. I had a melodramatic mind. I saw villainy where none existed, and it wouldn't surprise me to learn that Jacobus is really a nice little man, that Rags Gorman is an honest and enterprising bookmaker, and that even Mrs Stevens has her good points. I am painfully aware that people are not so easy to understand as I once thought they were.

Take Lizzie, for instance.

Lizzie married Rags Gorman. Yes, she finally married Rags Gorman after all. I didn't believe it at first, but there can be no argument about it. They live in a big house out Esher way and have two fine boys. Lizzie does her shopping in a Daimler. I have seen her once or twice, though not to speak to, and I must say that she looks well. She is getting slightly plump, but it suits her. She is as pretty as ever, and in addition she has an amiable and contented look. I am sure she has no regrets.

And Joseph.

I am allowed to visit Joseph once a year and do so religiously. He has settled down to prison life. He is 'on the land,' as they say inside, and it is just the job for him. He has charge of two fine Suffolk mares, shares the responsibility for the pigs, and is hoping for the milk cows. He thinks there is a very good chance that he will get the milk cows when the cowman is discharged next year. He is still fond of birds and has a wide range of bird friends. It has become my duty to send him a sack of birdseed each month, and in return for this small service he has called his favourite raven Robert.

I couldn't ever bring myself to tell Joseph that Lizzie had married Rags Gorman. I was under the impression that Joseph thought that Lizzie was waiting for him and that the news would be a great shock to him, but I was as mistaken about this as I was about everything else, for I learned recently that the Gormans have been visiting Joseph each year since their marriage and that Rags has even promised to find him a job when he comes out.

I find it all very hard to understand.

Sydney Goodsir Smith (1915 – 1975)

Only Hugh MacDiarmid has written more impressive poetry in Scots than his friend Sydney Smith, though the latter was in fact born in New Zealand and had to learn Scots as a foreign language. His achievement in Scots is simply astonishing, given its extraordinary sense of natural speech and metaphor was in fact generated in part by a learned ransacking from older literature. Exuberance, wit, variety and a charismatic speaking voice combine to make one of the best arguments for the modern viability of Scots. His *Under the Eildon Tree* (1948) is one of the major achievements in modern poetry.

Epistle to John Guthrie

*(who had blamed the poet for writing in
Scots 'which no one speaks')*

We've come intil a gey queer time
Whan scrievin Scots is near a crime,
'There's no one speaks like that,' they fleer*, — sneer
– But wha the deil spoke like King Lear?

And onyweys doon Canongate
I'll tak ye slorpin pints till late,
Ye'll hear Scots there as raff* and slee – — rife
– It's no the point, sae that'll dae.

Ye'll fin the leid*, praps no the fowth*, — tongue/whole
The words're there, praps no the ferlie*; — well-phrased
For he wha'ld rant wi Rabbie's[1] mouth
Maun leave his play-pen unco erlie.

Nane cud talk lik Gawen Douglas writes,
He hanna the vocablerie,
Nor cud he flyte* as Dunbar flytes – — scold
Yir argy-bargy's tapsalteerie*! — upside-down

---

[1] Robert Burns's.

Did Johnnie Keats when he was drouth
Ask 'A beaker full o the warm South'?
Fegs no, he leaned across the bar
An called for 'A point o bitter, Ma!'   20

But the Suddron's* noo a sick man's leid,   southern (English)
Along the flattest plains it stots*;   staggers
Tae reach the hills his fantice* needs   fantasy
This bard maun tak the wings o Scots.

And so, dear John, ye just maun dree*   endure
My Scots; for English, man's near deid,
See the weeshy-washy Londer bree*   brew
An tell me then whaes bluid is reid!

But mind, nae poet eer writes 'common speech,'
Ye'll fin eneuch o yon in prose;   30
His realm is heich abune its reach –
Jeez! wha'ld use ale for Athol Brose?

Sang: Ma Moujik Lass

Ma hert is lowpan owre the trees
An fleein wi the wund –
Ma lips're weet wi barley bree,
Ma hurdies* hug the grund.   buttocks

The lass I loo has turned awa,
Tae me thon hert's a stane –
But fain I'd hae her flint an aa
Than bidan here alane.

Some airt* the linties maun be singan   quarter
Here the wuds are toom* –   10   empty
And aye the rain is dingan*, dingan,   pounding
Dingan on the toun.

O fain I'd loo ma moujik lass,
O fain I'd haud her breist –
I've nocht tae haud but a whusky glass,
A gey* wanchancy* feast.   very/unlucky

O dreich's* the exile here I sing,   dull's
The lyft* is mirk aroun,   sky
And aye I hear the raindraps ding,
Aye dingan on the toun.   20

Largo

Ae boat anerlie* nou   alone
Fishes frae this shore,
Ae black drifter lane
Riggs the cramasie* daw   crimson
– Aince was a fleet, but nou
Ae boat alane goes out.

War ir peace, the trawlers win
An the youth turns awa
Bricht wi baubles nou
And thirled* tae factory or store;   10   tied
Their faithers fished their ain,
Unmaistered; – ane ramains.

And never the clock rins back,
The free days are owre;
The warld shrinks, we luik
Mair t'our maisters ilka* hour –   every
Whan yon lane boat I see
Daith and rebellion blind ma ee.

Under the Eildon Tree

This great poem is a collection of love stories, some describing the fabled romances of yore, and others the poet's own experiences. It is Smith's masterpiece, and one of the major works in Scots from our century. The Eildon Hills are a range of three promontories just south of Melrose. They have many literary associations, but probably the most important is that of Thomas of Ercildoune (Thomas the Rhymer), the medieval poet who was said to have fallen in with the Queen of Fairy here, and to have been carried off to live with her for seven years. When Thomas returned he had the gift of prophecy. (See the Introduction to 'Thomas of Erceldoun' in Vol. I, page 36, and the ballad 'Thomas Rhymer' on page 475 of the same volume. There we are told Thomas saw the Queen of Elfland 'Come riding down by the Eildon Tree'.) Thus, the Eildon Hills are an emblem for the mystical experiences of both love and poetry.

As the *Collected Works* have allowed a number of errors to creep in, the poem below is reproduced from the first edition, published by Serif Books in 1948.

'Your sweet mirthis are mixt with bitterness;
Quhat is your drearie game? a merry pain;
Your wark unthrift, your quiet is restless,
Your lust liking in languor to remain,
Friendschip torment, your traist is but ane trane:
O luve, quhidder art thou joy or fulishness,
That makis folk sa glaid of thair distress.'

                        – Douglas. *Eneados. Prol. IV.*

I Bards Hae Sung

Bards hae sung o lesser luves
    Than I o thee,
Oh my great follie and my granderie★,   *arrogance*
That nane kens but anerlie thee.

Aa the haars★ that hap★ the yerth   *mists/clothe*
    In jizzen★ aince again,   *childbirth*
      Swirlan owre the warld
O' the centuries' great poesie,
    Can smore★ the names of aa,   *smother*
      Aa memories –   10
But yours, Ward o black-maned Artemis,
The Huntress, Slayer, White Unmortal Queyne,
    That aye sall byde undeean
    In this the final testament
    Infrangible as adamant –
      O' this dune bard afore
      His music turns to sleep, and
The endmaist ultimate white silence faas
Frae whilk for bards is nae retour.

II There's Monie Anither

i

There's monie anither bard alive the day   20
    In Scotland and the Isles
Maist kenspeckle★ and renouned,   *conspicuous*
Far-famed i their maisterie,
Aa maist dexterous and wurdie o makars –
    But anerlie I, my queyne,
Coud ever scrieve★ this leid★ o thee   *write/poem*
For anerlie I, excessive in aathing,
      Wad eer commit
    The follie o loein ye
Til siccan a daft extremitie.   30

ii

Forbye theres feck o bonnie and cruel wemen i the land
    Maist perfit o God's craturies in fairheid,
    Haean ilka grace and attribute praise-wurdie
    By a bard
      – whas names I sallna name,
Bean skeerie o their jalousie – or yours –
    That I coud mak immortal wi a verse
    – But nane o thae
      Wad tent compairisoun wi ye:
For aa their whiteness is as pitch aside your snaw,   40
Their hair but towe aside the raven wing,
Their een as flints til your bricht emerants,

Their mous as brick aside your lips o gean★,   cherry
Their lyre★ but hame-spun by your velvous schene,   skin
Their hands as but a hind's are til a Queen's,
Their thies but sticks aside your floueran dunes,
Their breists auld bitches' dugs til your white domes
    O hinnie-dew –
Ah, my black swan, maikless★ are ye,   matchless
    The Koh-i-Noor★ and A-per-se★   50   without peer
    O' womanheid.

iii

Forbye theres ither subjecks for a makar's pen
    Maist wechtie and profund indeed,
Maitters o war and peace and dour debate
O' foreign levie and domestic malice,
As the preachers say
      – But no for me!
As weill gie me the wale★ o skillie★ or drambuie!   choice/soup
As scrieve a leid o politics or thee!
You are my subjeck anerlie, there is nae ither   60
    Fills my musardrie★,   thought
Nae word but your name in my dictionarie,
The heidlines i the news mean nocht til me
    For your name isna there,
    The faces i the streets
Micht aa be walkan neeps★ or tattie-bogles★,   turnips/scarecrows
Or aiblins★ a new race descendit frae the mune,   perhaps
    I kenna, carena, for I see but you.
    And scrievin sangs o ye
    Is aa my haill activitie,   70
The occupation o my waukan days,
    The dwaums★ that thrang my restless nichts,   dreams
    The bouk in clouds,
    The figures i the reik★,   smoke
    The ferlies★ i the gleid   wonders
And i the trunks of auldern treen
    Is aye the face
    O' my dear lass.

iv

You alane, the minion o the race, and I,
Made great by my afflictioun that is you,   80
Are here rancountered at this flude o time
To raise this monument – and cease.
Biggit wi bluid and greit★   tears
      – and your damned flichterie!

v

You and I for wham the centuries hae conspired
Are melled thegither here like twa elements
    O' air and fire
Whas happie confluence in some divine laboratorie
    Concocts a new untolerable catalyst
    Whas pouer and potencie   90

For sel-destructioun, ruin, hell,
    Like a bombardment o the saul's uranium,
Owergangs and stachers aa 'foregaean computatiouns'
(– Sae that e'en the experts are bumbazed and speakless
                    For the first time on record.)
Insulate by the gods frae ither mortals –
Whan thegither, whiles, a skimmeran licht,
    Men say, plays round our heids,
Our hands become electric til the touch
And the causie brunt and smouchteran ahint our feet.   100
    A divinitie doth hedge a king
But our aureolie is surelie frae the pit;
Weirdit, we are set apert for ruin
    – And weill I ken that this fey exstacie
    Is nocht but Luve's Hiróshima.

vi

The gods hae laid their plans throu a billion aeons
    O' the menseless birlan★ universe   spinning
    At length to venge their enmitie on man
    (That put them on their seats to comfort him,
    Tochered★ them wi pouer unprincipled   110   dowered
    And syne forgot them utterlie.)
Nou they wad ding for aye the treisured name o Luve
    That is their anerlie rival on the yerth
    Wi this last cataclysm here –
Whar-in I helpless burn and you
        Gang no unskaitht.

We are the sport of the gods, my luve, to gie
    Gigmanitie for godlike ends
    A Spectacle o Follie!
                        – And they've gotten it!   120
    This our testament.

III *We Hae Loed Muckle*

We hae loed muckle, follie mine,
But gane is aa wi the wind,
    Here is endin, here the end,
    The ultlmate great sang
    Rounds aff the lustrum.
The sevin-pinioned bird is turnan,
    Nou in wide forfochen★ sweeps   exhausting
Intil its silence on the muir o winds

Whar nocht but words hert-lucken ring   130
    Again i the doitit★ lugs   crazed
O' thae that saw their Tir-nan-Og★   heaven
Within the raxin★ o hands, bricht   stretching
    On the haaf's grey brink

At sun's first dwynin,
Far i the Wast ayont the watergaw★   rainbow
    Bouled hiech in hevin's pend
Athort the weet Atlantic haar . . .

When the seas' brash on kelp-green skairs★   rocks
And the banshee-schriech o the outruggan swaw★   140   wave
    Throu a myriad glentan stanner,
    Sang wi the music o the spheres

    And i the morn
Saw nocht but fraith, the tuim★ spase★,   empty/sea
    Heard nocht
    But the drear sea-birds' mae.

IV I, Luve-Doitit Bard

I, luve-doited bard o the Westren Warld,
    That saw but coudna win
The fortunate Isles ayont★ the Westren Sun   beyond
    Forge this last testament to stand   150
Heroic wi the tale o Helen, Cleopatra, Lesbia.
    Wi Morfydd, Dido, Heloise,
    And Mary o the whitest blee,
    As Rab his Mary, Hugh his Jean,
Sae I nou sing o thee,
My ain Perdita, Phryne, Cynthia.
    Aa yon bonnie cruel thrang
    O' wemen lit unmortal luve
For bards to fleer the gods wi pride
And tak the lowes★ o hell for cauldrife comfortin!   160   fires
    Sae I here enumerate
    In yon fell companie for thee,
    My torment and my exstasie,
    Whas like disdain teuk me,
Held me and gied me Paradise enow
For aa the gowden green Hesperides were mine
    – For nocht but fulerie.

    Och weill, it was your richt, I ken,
    To gie, syne to withhaud again,
    My grail I got and it was taen   170
    Was it no yours til tak again?

Enumerate amang the legion o the damned I tak
My leave here in this endmaist coronach –
    Salud!
    Fareweill!
And syne the sleepless, waukless, dawless nicht
    O' life in daith
    And daith in daith.
(Chiche!

Echo answers Clichy!   180
  Whar the debtors went in gay Paree!
  O God!
      O Montrachet!
             O Arthur's Seat!)

But Daith!

V Slugabed

Here I ligg, Sydney Slugabed Godless Smith.
The Smith, the Faber, ποιητησ and Makar,
And Oblomov has nocht til lear⋆ me,   teach
Auld Oblomov has nocht on me,
Liggan my lane in bed at nune,   190
Gantan at grey, December haar,
A cauld, scummie, hauf-drunk cup o tea
  At my bed-side,
    Luntan⋆ Virginian fags   smoking
− The New Warld thus I haud in fief
And levie kindlie tribute. Black men slave
Aneth a distant sun to mak for me
Cheroots at hauf-a-croun the box.
  Wi ase on the sheets, ase on the cod,
And crumbs o toast under my bum,   200
Scrievan the last great coronach
O' the Westren flickeran bourgeois warld.
Eheu fugaces![1]
Lacrimae rerum![2]
Nil nisi[3] *et cetera ex cathedra,*
Requiescat up your jumper.

Oh michtie Stalin i the Aist!
Coud ye but see me nou,
The type, endpynt and final blume
O' decadent capitalistical thirldom⋆   210   serfdom
  − It teuk five hunder year to produce me −
Och, coud ye but see me nou
What a sermon coud ye gie
  Furth frae the Hailie Kremlin
Bummlan and thunderan owre the Steppes,
Athort the mountains o Europe humman
Till Swack! at my front door, the great Schloss Schmidt,
That's Numero Cinquante *(piat' desiat,*[4] ye ken)
I' the umquhile⋆ park o Craigmillar House   former
Whar Mary Stewart o the snawie blee   220

---

[1] 'Eheu fugaces' [Postume, Postume,/ labuntur anni]. 'Alas, O Postumus, Postumus, the years go swiftly by'.
Horace, *Odes* 2:14:1.
[2] 'Lacrimae rerum': tears caused by things [that happen]. *Aeneid* 1:462.
[3] 'Nil nisi' [cruce]: no dependence [or reliance] but on the cross.
[4] 'Fifty'. (SGS.)

Aince* plantit ane o a thousand treen.   once
  Losh, what a sermon yon wad be!
For Knox has nocht on Uncle Joe
And Oblomov has nocht on Smith
    And sae we come by a route maist devious
    Til the far-famed Aist-West Synthesis!
    Beluved by Hugh that's beluved by me
And the baith o us loe the barley-bree –
But wha can afford til drink the stuff?
    Certes no auld Oblomov!   230
      – And yet he does! Whiles!
    But no as muckle as Uncle Joe – I've smaa dout!
Na zdorovye[1] then, auld Muscovite!

Thus are the michtie faaen,
Thus the end o a michtie line,
Dunbar til Smith the Slugabed
Whas luve burns brichter nor them aa
And whas dounfaain is nae less,
  Deid for a ducat deid
By the crueltie o his ain maistress.   240

VI *What Wey Suld I*

i

    What wey suld I, my hert's luve,
      Scrieve ye mair?
    Hae ye no had a thrave o sangs
      Frae me ere nou?
    – And ye wad answer:
      Why indeed?
    Hae ye no had a haill beuk-fu
      O' sangs frae me?
      What need is there
      For scrievin mair?   250
    – And ye wad answer:
      What indeed?

ii

And trulie there are maitters o great moment
    Abraid the day.
Aa the great michtie
In their great seats are warslan
  For anither cushion maybe
    Or mair licht,
      Or the table
A wee thing nearer til the great hand,
    Or mair cigars, or better anes,
      Brandie, usquebae   260
      Or what hae ye.

---

[1] 'Good Health'. (SGS.)

And, tae, theres ithers maist important questions
    For a bard –
  'The Antenna o the Race,'
  'The Unacknowledged Legislators,'
  'Sperits o the Time,' and sae furth,
As some enthusiasts hae observed
Frae time til time in moments o exaltatioun
    Or euphoria
Sequant til the drinkin o wine maistlikelie   270

And the saft hand o a suppositatit virgin
    (Government Guarantee for Foreign Envoys)
Caller★ on their fevered powes★   fresh/heads
Wi promises o yet further exaltatiouns
Likelie til accume gif but they play
Their stack o aces eydentlie –
En effet, maist serious maitters
O' great argument til consider maist earnestlie
    And seriouslie.

This is nae time for lassies' fykes!★   280   whims
  I'm sure ye'll gree.
And Echo dulie answers:
    Gree!

    iii
And truth it is
There was a day I micht
Hae thocht there micht
Be sunkots★ intil't.   something
But nou a lassie's flegmageeries★   whims
And my ain tae, admittedlie,
Tak aa my time, aa thocht,   290
Aa dwaums and aa activitie.

For I was born excessive, Scorpio,
In aathing and in luve;
Eneuch's no near as guid's a feast til me,
The middle airt★, the Gowden Mean,   quarter
Has little recommandan hit
As far as I can see,
And i the hert's affectioun
I find nae exceptioun.

The warld and aa its ills   300
Are, certes, unco eerie,
But the nou til me theyre nil
Forenent a lassie's flegmageerie.
Tho Scotland's saul is brairan
As the saul o Europe dwynes★   wastes away
And tho I dout theres neer a Czar
Can ding us doun for aye –
Yet aa sic speculatiouns flee
Intil the mirkest airts

O' a zero o ariditie   310
Gin the blind bairn jags my hert
    By nicht and day
Wi a lassie's whims and whams,
    A lassie's yea and nay.

            (A maist reprehensible estate
            O' affairs, I maun admit.)

VII My Luve, My Luve

My luve, my luve,
Wad ye were here
By me i the touslit bed,
Or wad I had met ye never a day   320
Or wad ye were aye by me –
Theres nae hauf gaits in luve, ye ken.

My luve, my luve,
I wonder wad ye care
To be here by me
I' the Nirvana Oblomovian
Whar is nor nicht nor day
Nor day-o-the-week or year,

Whar nae rain faas,
Sunsheen or sleet or snaw,   330
Nor ocht but an antran tear
In a menner maist Tir-nan-Ogian⋆   heavenly
Frae the bardic ee
Acause ye arena here.

My luve, my luve,
What havers⋆ is this   nonsense
Gin ye didna ken
And you anerlie
That ahint the bravadie
This hert is near spent.   340

            (The sheer brass neck o the man!)

VIII New Hyne

I had a luve walked by the sea,
The waterfront at eenin,
Sol was a gowden pennie at our side
A bare league awa.
A wee boat wi a broun sail
Left the pier juist at our feet
And sailed awa intil the sunset

Silentlie, the water like a keekin-glass.
We spak nae word ava.   350
My luve turned til me wi her een
Owre-rin wi greit, and mine
Were weet wi the like mysterie.
We stude by the Pharos there
A lang while or the sun dwyned doun
And the grey-green simmer humin
Closed about the hyne★.   harbour
Syne it grew cauld, and in my airms
I felt her trummlan
Wi the like undeemous★ mysterie did steek★   incomprehensible/shut
My craig★, sae that I coudna speak.   361   throat

IX Hou Can We Hae Pitie?

Hou can we hae pitie, mercie, here
Liggan our lane on the gerss
    And Cynthia smilan abune
    Mercuric and sillerie
    I' the lythe★ simmer nicht,   calm
Hae pitie, ruth, for the misfortunate
That trachle, bleed and dee
On the warld's reid battlefronts,
Or the weak and seik,   370
    The faimished,
    And thae that wauk
By the beds o ailan weans
    And deean kin?

Hou can we think on thir, and mair,
    Black Swan?
My white lass wi the een o a fawn,
Straucht here by me on the gerss
Whar aa the warld is skrunken
    Till this wee gair★   380   grass patch
Mune-shadawed by a runkled tree
    In Cynthia's nicht
    O' siller glamerie –
Your hair a midnicht forest
    Thrang
        Wi the greitan dirl,
The schere sang-spate o rossignels★ –   nightingales
    While the great gowden ernes
    That rule my saul
    Like princes o the bluid   390
Scove★ throu the thrawan harns   glide
On what fell errand I ken nocht
    Nor you, my ain, my sleepan,
        Saft, born-skaithit★ hert.   injured

Here aa the warld is this wee gair
We hap nou wi our bodies' length
Thegither as we were but ane
– 'The twa-backit beast'! I ken –
  – But mair is twafauld nor the beast:
The Beautie that the Beast maun bed   400
Is twafauld here, the Fairheid
  O' our luve, and twafauld tae
  Is aa that ee can see;
The yerth is us, the lift*, the mune,   sky
Aa couplit in our couplin here,
And there is nocht but our twa sels,
Our passion's gleid, our herts, our sauls,
Ablow, aben, ayont, abune –
My luve that aince I had – and tint*.   lost

– As sayis the auntient Catechist: 410
'Luve is the great Solipsist.'

              (Verb. Sap.)

X Hieland Mary[1]

    i

I strak her doun, mine was the hand,
The dirk's bluid reid on my nieve.
Greitan I strak her doun, til the knees
– Thae gowden locks about her face,
Mistraucht een, the sabs, the wreithan palms!
The galley at the pier o Leith
Sails swault wi the Aist Wind blawan
Me til the Indies. 'Fredome
  Is ane nobil thing . . . !'   420
  Exile, chains and slaverie!
  – Och, what the hell!!

'Ye banks and braes and streams around
The Castle o Montgomerie . . . '
– Its aa i the texts, the gifts were gien,
The gifts were taen. The glune,
The Bible, bluid – . Aa this is kent.
The pacts and kisses and fareweills
– And I richt back til bonnie Jean!
Naxos for Ithaca – What then!   430

---

[1] The speaker here is Robert Burns. 'Highland Mary' is the name given to Mary Campbell, one of Burns' enamorata.

Ah, but the guilt, the ower-impendant wings,
Bluid-wyte★ at the hert like leed   punishments
   – What then, indeed?
The Channeran Worm doth chide
And aye sel-kennin brings
Hert-thraw – and the guilt again.
   Aye the tint luve leams
Mair brichter for its bein tint.
Distance, ye ken, enchantment . . . et cetera.

– Thus the philosophers!   440
     My fuit!
Nyaffs the haill clanjamphrie★!   crowd
What ken they o the hert,
O' bluid, o passion and the gleid
That blinds een, harns, mense★, mynd,   honour
Ay, and the saul itsel in its reid
Lowe wi the bleezan brazen seed?

     ii
Nou goave★ they ower documents,   pore
Auld screeds thocht tint for aye,
Nou they 'investigate,' 'collate,'   450
  – Guidsakes! – *collate!*
And pruve me nou that Mary Campbell
('Lingering star!' 'My white rose Mary!')
Was nae luve o mines ava,
A freat, sirs, o my ower-heatit fancie
In a time o tribulatioun;
   – Ye ken the leid★!   language

And why? And wharfae?
   – Juist acause
She was a wee thing flichterie. Thats aa!   460

     iii
   . . . And sae . . .
Let her name be expunged frae the records,
Her images dung doun
   And her temples and consecratit groves
Desecrate, razed, deracinate!
And the ase and grieshoch skailit
   Till the fowr airts!
   That the bardic guid-fame may,
   In some meisure, be restorit!
And her memorie nocht but a poetic fiction!   470

    Weill, let it be, what maitter
     Nou gin they disclose
      The suner or the later,
       The true, the fause,
       The former, latter,
    Cauk or kebbuk★ or guid cauf's-fuit?   cheese
    Theres me kens

And Mary kens
And aabodie ither will sune be deid –
Sae set the bottle rattlan, John,   480
    See us a gless thats full,
Set the bottle rattlan, John,
    And never fash★ your skull!   trouble
      For Mary kens
      And I kens.

XI *Moriturus Te Saluto*

Tell me, philosopher, hou can he tell
    Whas hert was made owre big,
By God creatit wi a hert
    Owre bruckle til the derts
O' yon wee loun★ wi wings and bow,   490   fellow, rascal
Blind loun that warks sic tragedie,
    Hou can he tell whats wrang, whats richt,
      And whilk the airt
Is his by richt
      And whilk by micht
O' the borneheid★ and eisenan★ hert?   headlong/aching

The question damns!
  – Guilty, m'lud!
    – Thoums doun!
      – Tak ower, centurion!   500
Moriturus te saluto![1]
    Poppeia nods sleepilie,
    Een blacked wi kohl
    The lids wi emerant green
    I' the Egyptian menner,
    Hair black and sleek as Isis.
The portes gant★. Their chafts outbock . . .   yawn
Lions? Wolves? It maitters nocht.
  – Rive him apert!
    – Hurroo!   510
      – Yippee!
The mob rairs like a sea.

Ay, ay, its aa weillkent attestit historie.
Wreist aa his ingyne wi your sapient
    And slee dexteritie, great gods, –
But his ript hert preserve,
    For demonstration purposes,
    And for his ain torment,
Fou, fouthie★, raff and rank wi bluid and greit,   rich
Aa puffed and adipose wi lust and pride,   520

---

[1] I who am to die salute you [a change from the usual third-person plural associated with gladiatorial contests: 'We who . . . '].

Oedematous wi luve's reid granderie!
       – There is your panel, *Advocatus Mei!*[1]
Dae what ye will, ye'll neer sain★ nou   bless
Whats lang been thrawen★ on a turnan wheel.   twisting

– O exquisite and souple, divine white chirurgeon,
Masquit and gauntelate as gin for barrace!
Madam, I ken ye fine. I'm pleased to meet ye,
   My maistress wi the satin smile,
     My dumb and dizzy blonde,
       O Mors![2]

XII Orpheus

   i

Wi sang aa birds and beasts coud I owrecome,   530
Aa men and wemen o the mapamound★ subdue,   world
   The flouers o the fields,
Rocks and trees, boued doun til hear my leid,
Gurlie★ waters rase upo the land to mak   stormy
   A throwgang for my feet.
I was the potent prince o ballatrie,
My clarsach★ opened portes whareer I thocht to gang,   harp
   My fleean sangs mair ramsh★ nor wine   spirits
At Beltane, Yule or Hogmanay
   Made wud★ the clans o men –   540   mad
There wasna my maik★ upo the yerth   equal
   (Why suld I no admit the fack?)
A hero, demi-god, my kinrik★ was the hert,   kingdom
   The passions and the saul,
Sic was my pouer.
– Anerlie my ain sel I coudna bend.

   'He was his ain warst enemie,'
     As the auld untentit bodachs★ say –   old men
     My hert, a leopard, ruthless, breme★,   ardent
     Gilravaged★ far and near   550   rioted
Seekan sensatiouns, passions that wad wauken
   My Muse whan she was lollish.
No seendil the hert was kinnelt like a forest-bleeze . . .
I was nae maister o my ain but thirlit
   Serf til his ramskeerie★ wants   lustful
   – And yet I hained★ but ane i the hert's deepest hert. cherished

   She, maist leefou, leesome leddy
   – Ochone, ochone, Euridicie –
Was aye the queen of Orpheus' hert, as I kent weill,
   And wantan her my life was feckless drinkin,   560

---

[1] Advocate of me.
[2] O Death.

Weirdless, thieveless dancin,
    Singin, gangrellin.
        – And nou she's gane.

ii

The jalous gods sae cast my weird* that she   fate
Was reift intil the Shades throu my negleck.
  I, daffan* i the groves and pools   fooling
    Wi the water-lassies,
      Riggish, ree*, and aye as fain   lecherous
  For lemanrie* as Orpheus was,   womanising
I never kent o her stravaigin*,   570   wandering
    Lane and dowie* i the fields;   sad
Nor that yon Aristaeus loed my queyne.
    It was fleean him she deed
But yet was my negleck that did the deed;
Neither was I by her to proteck
    Frae the dernit*-serpent's bane   hidden
Green and secret i the raff gerss liggan
– I was her daith as she was life til me,
    Tho I was feckless born and lemanous
Yet she was mair nor aa the daft ree nymphs   580
    O' wuid and burn til me
      – Yet it was I
That flung Euridicie
The aipple o my bruckle ee
    Til yon far bourne
Frae whilk, they said, theres can be nae retourn.
      'Quhair art thow gane, my luve euridicess?'

iii

Ye ken the tale, hou, wi my lute
  I doungaed amang the Shades
(Grey mauchie Hades, lichtless airt)   590
And Pluto and the damned stude round
  And grat, hearan my sang;
Hou, haean wan her manumissioun
Frae the Profund Magnifico,
I, cryan her name, socht and fand my luve
  Amang thae wearie shadaws,
  Yet tint her i the end.
    For her a second daith,
    For me a second shame,

        (The sycophantic gods, ulyied and curlit   600
        Reclynan i the bar on bricht Olympus.
        Soupan their meridian, outbocked
        Their lauchter like a tourbilloun*   hurricane
        At this the latest ploy o Zeus
        The Caird, the Conjuror, the aye-bydan
        Favourite and darlin o them aa,
        The Wide Boy – *ex officio!*
                – the Charlatan!)

She stummelt on a bourach★, outcried 'Orpheus!'   pile of stones
– Een, what wey were ye no blind?   610
– Lugs★, what wey were ye no deif?   ears
– Hert, what wey were ye no cauld as ice?
– Limbs, what wey were ye no pouerless?
– Harns★, what wey did ye no haud the owerance?   brains

       (And Jupiter, in order til extraict
       The maist exquisite quintessence
       O' the succulence o his wee ploy
       And wi his infantile perfectit sense
       O' the dramatic, kept this impeccabil
       And maikless agonie,   620
       As a *bonne-bouche*★, til the end.)   'dainty morsel'

We werena ten yairds frae the bank o Styx
The ferryin o whilk was luve and libertie
   – No ten yairds awa!
Our braith was hechlan★ and our een   harsh, panting
   Glaizie-glentit wi the joy
   Of our twa-fauld deliverance –
And than Jove strak wi serpent subtletie.
     Euridicie stummelt.

     (Lauchter cracked abune. Jupiter leuch!
     – And richtlie sae!   630
     Och, gie the gods their due
     They ken what theyre about.
     – The sleekans!)

She stummelt. I heard her cry. And hert ruled heid again.
– What hert coud eer refuse, then, siccan a plea?
   I turned –
       And wi neer a word,
          In silence,
Her een yet bricht wi the joy o resurrectioun,
She soomed★ awa afore my een intil a skimmeran wraith 640   swam
And for a second and last time was tint for aye
   Amang the gloams and haars o Hell
   – Throu my ain twafauld treacherie!

      'Quhair art thou gane, my luve euridicess?'

  iv
Sinsyne I haena plucked a note
   Nor made a word o a sang,
The clarsach, and the lyre, the lute,
   'The aitan reed,'
Byde untuned in a yerdit★ kist★.   650   buried/chest
My taiblets aa are broke, my pens brunt,
   The howff★ sees me nocht   tavern
   Nor the lassies i the glen.
   The hert in my bosom's deid
     For Euridicie is deid

And it was I that did the double deed,
    Twice-cursit Orpheus!

I gang til jyne her i the skuggie* airt,   shadowy
A convene fou o dreid for Orpheus' hert.

    Aa this will happen aa again,   660
    Monie and monie a time again.

                          (Explicit Orpheus.)

XIII The Black Bull o Norroway

i

I got her i the Black Bull
    (The Black Bull o Norroway),
Gin I mynd richt, in Leith Street,
Doun the stair at the corner forenent
The Fun Fair and Museum o Monstrosities,
    The Tyke-faced Loun, the Cunyiars* Den   coiner's
       And siclike.
I tine her name the nou, and cognomen for that –   670
Aiblins it was Deirdre, Ariadne, Calliope,
Gaby, Jacquette, Katerina, Sandra,
    Or sunkots; exotic, I expeck.
A wee bit piece
    O' what our faithers maist unaptlie
    But romanticallie designatit 'Fluff.'
My certie! Nae muckle o Fluff
    About the hures o Reekie!
Dour as stane, the like stane
As biggit the unconquerable citie   680
Whar they pullulate,
               Infestan
The wynds and closes, squares
And public promenads
       – The bonnie craturies!
              – But til our winter's tale.

ii

Fou as a puggie*, I, the bardic ee   monkey, pig
In a fine frenzie rollan,
Drunk as a fish wi sevin tails,
Purpie as Tiberio wi bad rum and beerio,   690
      (Io! Io! Iacche! Iacche, Io!)[1]
– Sevin nichts and sevin days
        (A modest bout whan aa's dune,
        Maist scriptural, in fack)
Was the Makar on his junketins

---

[1] Traditional shouts of the worshippers of Dionysus. *Io* is an exclamation used in addressing the god. *Iacchus* is one of his many names.

    (On this perticular occasioun
    O' the whilk we tell the nou
    Here i the records, for the benefit
    O' future putative historians) . . .
Wi sindrie cronies throu the wastage-land   700
O' howffs and dancins, stews
And houses o assignatioun
I' the auntient capital.

– Ah, she was a bonnie cou!
Ilka pennie I had she teuk,
Scoffed the halicarnassus lot,
As is the custom, due
And meet and mensefu⋆,   honourable, decent
Proper and proprietous,
    Drinkan hersel to catch up wi me   710
    That had a sevin-day stert on her
      – O' the whilk conditioun
Nae smaa braggandie was made at the time
Here and yont about the metropolis –
    And mysel drinkan me sober again
For reasouns ower obvious
Til needcessitate descriptioun,
              Explanatioun,
                  Or ither.

Nou, ye canna ging lang at yon game   720
And the hour cam on at length
That the Cup-bearer did refuse
The provision of further refreshment
– Rochlie, I mynd, and in a menner
Wi the whilk I amna uised,
    Uncomformable wi my lordlie spreit,
    A menner unseemlie, unbefittan
The speakin-til or interlocutioun
O' a Bard and Shennachie⋆,   poet
    Far less a Maister o Arts,   730
    – The whilk rank and statioun I haud
    In consequence and by vertue
    O' unremittan and pertinacious
    Applicatioun til the bottle
    Ower a period no exceedan
    Fowr year and sax munce or moneths
(The latter bean a *hiatus* or *caesura*
– or the purposes o rusticatioun
Or *villeggiatura* 'at my place in the country'):
    Aa the whilk was made sufficient plain   740
Til the Cup-bearer at the time –
    Losh me, what a collieshangie!
Ye'd hae thocht the man affrontit
    Deeplie, maist mortallie
        And til the hert.
Ay, and I cried him Ganymede,
    Wi the whilk address or pronomen

He grew incensed.
'Run, Ganymede!' quo I,
   'Stay me wi flagons!'   750
      (Or maybe tappit-hens★)   three-pint measure
– But I digress.
It was rum, I mynd the nou, rum was the bree,
Rum and draucht Bass.
           – Sheer *hara-kiri!*

iii

– Ah, she was a bonnie cou!
Saxteen, maybe sevinteen, nae mair,
Her mither in attendance, *comme il faut*
Pour *les jeunes filles bien élevées,*[1]
    Drinkan like a bluidie whaul tae!   760
Wee breists, round and ticht and fou
Like sweet Pomona i the oranger grove
Her shanks were lang, but no ower lang, and plump,
    A lassie's shanks,
Wi the meisurance o Venus –
   Achteen inch the hoch★ frae heuchle-bane til knap★,   thigh/knee
   Achteen inch the cauf frae knap til cuit★   ankle
As is the true perfercton calculate
By the Auntients efter due regaird
For this and that,   770
        The true meisurance
   O' the Venus dei Medici,
   The Aphrodite Anadyomene
And aa the goddesses o hie antiquitie –
   Siclike were the shanks and hochs
O' Sandra the cou o the auld Black Bull.
   Her een were, naiturallie, expressionless,
Blank as chuckie-stanes, like the bits
O' blae-green gless ye find by the sea.
        – Nostalgia! Ah, sweet regrets! –   780
   Her blee was yon o sweet sexteen,
Her lyre as white as Dian's chastitie
   In yon fyle, fousome, clartie slum.
Sound the tocsin, sound the drum!
The Haas o Balclutha ring wi revelrie!
The Prince sall dine at Hailie Rude the nicht!

iv

   The lums★ o the reikan toun   chimneys
   Spreid aa ablow, and round
   As far as ye coud leuk
   The yalla squares o winnocks★   790   windows
   Lit ilkane by a nakit yalla sterne
   Blenkan, aff, syne on again,
   Out and in and out again
   As the thrang mercat throve,
      The haill toun at it

---

[1] 'As is necessary for well brought up young ladies.'

Aa the lichts pip–poppan
In and out and in again
I' the buts and bens
And single ends,
The banks and braes   800
O' the toueran cliffs o lands,

Haill tenements, wards and burghs, counties.
Regalities and jurisdictiouns,
Continents and empires
Gien ower entire
Til the joukerie-poukerie!
Hech, sirs, whatna feck of fockerie!
Shades o Knox, the hochmagandie!★   fornication
My bonie Edinburrie,
Auld Skulduggerie!   810
Flat on her back sevin nichts o the week,
Earnan her breid wi her hurdies'★ sweit.   buttocks'

– And Dian's siller chastitie
Muved owre the reikan lums,
Biggan a ferlie toun o jet and ivorie
That was but blackened stane
Whar Bothwell rade and Huntly
And fair Montrose and aa the lave
Wi silken leddies doun til the grave.
– The hoofs strak siller on the causie!   820
And I mysel in cramasie★!   crimson, silk

v

There Sandra sleepan, like a doe shot
I the midnicht wuid, wee paps
Like munes, mune-aipples gaithert
I' the Isles o Youth,
Her flung straucht limbs
A paradisal archipelagie
Inhaudan divers bays, lagoons,
Great carses, strands and sounds,
Islands and straits, peninsulies,   830
Whar traders, navigators,
Odyssean gangrels★, gubernators,   wanderers
Mutineers and maister-marineers,
And aa sic outland chiels micht utilise wi ease
Cheap floured claiths and beads,
Gawds, wire and sheenan nails
And siclike flichtmafletherie★   trifles
In fair and just excambion
For aa the ferlies o the southren seas
That chirm in thy deep-dernit creeks,   840
– My Helen douce★ as aipplejack   sweet
That cack't★ the bed in exstasie!   shat
Ah, belle nostalgie de la boue![1]

---

[1] 'Ah, the fine nostalgia of the gutter!'

– Sandra, princess-leman o a nicht o lust,
    That girdelt the fishie seas
    Frae Leith til Honolulu,
Maistress o the white mune Cytherean,
    Tak this bardic tribute nou!
Immortalitie sall croun thy heid wi bays,
    Laurel and rosemarie and rue!   850
You that spierit me nae questions,
    Spierit at me nocht,
      Acceptit me and teuk me in
      A guest o the house, nae less;
Teuk aa there was to gie
    (And yon was peerie★ worth),   little
Gied what ye didna loss –
    A bien and dernit fleeman's-firth★   hideout
    And bodie's easement
    And saft encomfortin!   860
O Manon! Marguerite! Camille!
      And maybe tae the pox –
          Ach, weill!

XIV O Wha Can Flee?

    i
    O wha can flee his ain luve? No me!
My Cynthia, mune o the nicht, my saul's fever!
Tho I a skalrag★ crossed the seas   vagabond
And continents a lane fugee★,   refugee
Back-come Macbeth-like til the inventor is the bane,
Here it dirls nou, in this breist here.
    The deeper doun I dug intil the deeps o luve   870
(Yon principalitie o jungle-land and ice) –
    The further I stravaigit –
    The hiecher I piled the chirls★ o phonie passions –   coals
      Bricht
    And brichter blawed
    The lowe that I wad dowse!

I teuk the Syrens til Calypso's Isle for companie
And swacked my wey throu aa the Cyclades,
    Was pitten out frae Tara Haas
And tummlit flouerie Capri i the sea;   880
The tapless touers o Ilium we burned again,
And Camelot hapt aa her virgins under key,
We leuch, and Bulls of Bashan coudna droun
Our maist mellifluous cacophonie – !
    – And muckle mair i the like strain
    Wi the whilk I winna deave★ ye nou.   deafen

And thus it was I thocht to smore,
Luve, your daithless passion-flouer.

ii

– The haill thing was miscalculate.
Cuif I eer to consider – far less act upon –   890
Siccan a hauf-baked air-drawn phantasie,
   As gin I didna ken
The febrid lends★ held nocht auctoritie   loins
And cullage-bag nocht but a base mechanical . . . !
   The lowe, the damned, the bricht, aye-burnan,
     Inextinguishable lowe
Was citadelled, of course, i the hert.
   There, was its keep and donjon dour,
   Its battlementit waas, its oubliettes,
   Its dernit vennels★, drawbrig and the lave!   narrow passageways
– The hert!   901
      – The bruckle pith o hit!
– As I kent aa the while!

And sae I mak capitulatioun, Cynthia,
Aince mair devou★ til dimpled Aphrodite,   bow
Helen, Fann, and wanton Lesbia
   – That aye maun rule me.

And nocht to shaw for aa the darg★   labour
But a lordlie, nay, *Krugerische*[1] debt,
The ruin o haill sakless★ faimilies, nae dout,   910   innocent

– And a fell bumbazed curmurrin o the guts.

XV Cuchulainn[2]

A man atween twa lassies,
Ane like a field o simmer corn,
Ane like the raven's wing,
Neth a yew tree at the shoreheid
   Speakless standan
   On Baile's Strand.

Then: –
      'Thinkan ye coud ganecome
Juist as it pleisured ye,   920
Your pentit Jezebel on your airm,
– Hou thocht ye to find me then?
   Onwytan, wae, begrutten,
   Bydan expectant, blythe til see ye?

---

[1] *Landlordly.* Kruger: publican.
[2] Cuchulain is the great Irish hero, of whom many stories are told. The background to this section: Manannan Mac Lir is the Celtic sea god, married to Fand (Fann in this poem). Fand and Manannan quarrel and demons attack her kingdom. Cuchulain destroys the demons and becomes Fand's lover. Emer, Cuchulain's wife, comes to slay Cuchulain but is mollified when Manannan takes Fand back. Cuchulain gets a forgetting drink to ease his pain. The story is told in 'The Wasting Sickness of Cuchulain'.

Och, hou coud ye dae't, Cuchulainn?
Whar lernit ye sic traitorie;
Me unhonouran in face of aa!
Guid Grief! I coud greit like a wean – !
. . . And yet its truth I want ye back.'
Thus Eimhir;   930
              And he his heid
Dounhingan nae word spak.

And Fann stude speakless by his side,
Her een yet mirk and loweran wi a month
O' memories,
     – Saw the fairheid
O' his queen Cuchulainn left
At her luve-biddin frae the Blythefou Fields –
              But nocht she said.

He turned, and leukt aince mair   940
Upo the raven glamerie o the hure.
'. . . Ah Fann!'
                      And likeweys in his een
The weeks o wine and bed in her far isle
Ayont the watergaw i the Westren Spase
     Whar moth nor rust corrupts
     Nor ever a hair comes grey
     And claret lilts frae ilka spring
In yon countrie
And aye it is hie simmer by the sea.   950

And sae he turned til Eimhir at the end
And Fann wi Manannan backwent.

XVI Dido

He upped his anchors and a wind
Frae the deep south gousteran blawed out –
The swaulit sails o gowden silk,
The reid, the black, the purpie sails and white
Of aa the graithit⋆ ships o his great fleet –   outfitted, ready
'. . . And I, O fause Æenee, left wi a hert no mine,
The hert I tint til ye lang syne
Efter the great chase and the storm   960
That skail't⋆ the galand hunt   scattered
And us in dern sent secret and our lane
Storm-driven til the airms o luve . . .
     O blackest day that dawed for me,
     O traistless luve, ye messan⋆ fause Æenee!'   cur-like

On the siller shore she stude, a simmer sea,
The lippers curdlan cream at her sandalled feet,
The sun like a titan's gong raired i the emperean,
Lowed on the gowden sail of the furthest ship of aa
Nou hauf out athort the bay, onheidan the fleean fleet   970
Like an emperor erne abune his reivan kin –
    The gowden sheet like a sheet o hammered, new-mined ore
Bare aff the fause Ænee wi Dido's faithfu hert . . .
And never aince he leukt ahint,
For fear, and traitorie, and shame at last.

. . . The wind that drave his ships, rank on rank o them,
Sun on the flichteran-featherie oars, the faem,
Spindrift, spume, landbrist★ and speed,   surf
Sea-gaean wolves, a pack, wild geese owre the emerant spase
Their pennands bricht like tongues i the wind, swan-wings spreid,
The greinan★ outraxed craigs o swans   981   yearning
    Drinkan the wind for Italie,
                    Æneas' fleet
Speedan awa frae Carthagie and Afric's burnan queen
Wi a lassie's broken hert and een owre-rin wi greit.
And the like wind that teuk her fause man aff
Streamed throu her sable hair outblawn
Schere-black as Ethiop nicht, wild her raven glorie
Streamed i the wind, the speed-flung mane
O' a meir o Arabie hinnyan i the race   990
Owre siller sand – bluid cast til the wrack for libertie!
The unpenned cloud o midnicht streamed i the dry simoon
Sheenan like jet in sol's orsplendant nune.

The queen, fair Dido stude
And saw the ships far out on the spase,
At the heid o yon fause fleet the fause and gowden sail
O' her fause luve Ænee.
        – 'Oh, black, perjurit hert,
Sae brawlie dicht wi claith-o-gowd,
That leas me nou my lane that isna me   1000
For he bears aff my hert and aa that Dido was, leas
But a cokkil, a tuim husk that made a Trojan gallantrie,
Fause, black Æneas that I natheless loe!'

Far out on the Mediterranie blue,
Blue as the lift abune and the sea-blue een o water-maids,
The fleet becomes a toy, the ships as wee as laddies' boats . . .
Awa, awa, and nou but mirlie★ specks   mottled
Upo the deepest farrest blue, the haaf★, til ae   sea
Bricht leam alane is left til kep the ee
    – The gowd-bricht sail o Dido's fause Ænee,   1010
Gane for aatime . . . wi the hert
O' Carthage' queen a stane in Dido's breist.

    She grat. And greitan turned, her wemen
Round her speakless, aa the midnicht glorie o her hair
About her face hung doun like wedow's weeds,

Back til the tuim palace, tuim the great haas
Whar Æneas walked, whar Æneas drank and leuch,
Whar Æneas tellt his silken leman's talk,
Whar Æneas teuk her bodie and her hert,
Teuk aa her luve and gied back bonnie aiths and vous,   1020
Tuim tae the chaumer and the bed o luve,
    Tuim Dido's hert of aa but wanhowp's★ plenishins.   despair's
    Yon nicht the lift owre Carthage bleezed
And Dian's siller disc was dim
As Dido and her palace burned,
The oranger, scarlet, gowden lowes
Her ae wild protest til the centuries.

Queen Dido burned and burnan tashed★   soiled
Æneas' name for aye wi scleratrie.   1030

XVII The Faut Was Mine

The faut was mine, I admit.
It was I abandoned ye; its true.
    – And syne ye teuk me back
Wi a maist leefu leddy's gentrice, I admit.
    And syne aince mair
I, fickle, bruckle termagant,
Ramskeerit throu the nichtit streets,
    Negleckit ye,
        But yet
Nae word ye spak agin me.

                (Theres ithers gied ye ample consolation   1040
                        I've nae dout.)

– Sae we'd be friens! Friens! We!
    Baith kent and kens
This maist unpossible equivocatioun
    Coudna be.
    Baith kent and kens
Its aa or nocht – and maun be aa –
Theres fient★ a gowden mediatioun   scarcely
In this luve's damned, compound equatioun.

I ken, I ken, nane better kens nor I,   1050
There is nae rivalrie for us to square
    Atween Calypso and Penelope,
Theres nocht is gien til ane
    Thats frae the tither taen,
Nae peerie pickle★, jot or ocht –   trifle
    Heres me ettlan★ to find reasoun,   striving
    Fule, confrontit wi a wudness.

But, lass, ye hae the raxed mynd teeteran,
    And gin ye'se no receive the Fanns,

The Maries and the lassies o the grove and burn,   1060
    Or gin ye'se no accomodate
The Eimhirs, Jeans, Didos, Euridicies
I' the vast pantheon o passion –
The membrane rips! I cry Pax! Barla-fummil*!   'I surrender'

    – And here the gowden ernes
O' this reithe* hert like eastren khanns   passionate
Sweep doun the avalanches o the winds
    Gurlie and scriechan owre
    The saul's mune-fiefit fields
And brash the mynd promethean   1070
Till thocht nor will nor e'en desire
Can raise this foetus-huddert me
    Frae his numb bield
O' stachert murken lethargie.

            *   *   *   *   *

Nae settlement and nae escape . . .
Aff put the evil day and faa asleep.
Whar I nou blythelie byde, the burden aff
– Nae daemons rive the hert o Oblomov.

    And sae for lang I haena seen
    My leman wi the midnicht een.   1080

XVIII Strumpet Daith

Wearie wearie nou I dwyne,
I' the westren pend my starne declynes;
Aince enfieft theres nae release
Frae Luve but Strumpet Daith's embrace
    – And I maun seek her sune
    Gin my luve winna hae me mair.

I hae seen yon Messaline,
– Fata Morgana, to be complimentarie –
Gouned in royal cramasie, wi
Teats o pitch and yalla een   1090
Burnan and burstan, leonine,
Wi a reid wab o veins,
Settan whar the roads cross
Slummocked on her creishie hochs,
A vast Leviathan o Letcherie
Swaulit like a luver's hert
Wi eisenin and an ower-spicie dietarie
    (Hiech-livin and laich-thinkin,
        As sayis the diagnostician)
Aye-bydan sans impatience or concern   1100
The weirdit and current aipple o her ee.

Nane ever flees her, nane
   Escapes, no ever ane.
And she can byde, byde three
   Score year and ten
   And mair gif need be –
I' the end we aa gae doun
   The bricht and fleeran anes,
   The runklit and forworn,
Aa i the end maun gratifie   1110
Her deidlie aye-unstecht desire,
Clipped til her pyson-drappan paps
   O' cauld, cauld alabaister.

– And nou me-ward I see her leer,
        The hure!

XIX Nicht Lowers Fast

   i

Nicht lowers fast
The storms beat up,
Spring nae dout's on winter's traces,
But theres nae muckle glisk⋆ o it saefar.   glimpse
Ayont the hiechest hills   1120
The gods are seik til daith
– The ploy's gane wersh⋆ on them at length   sour
And aa will sune be endit
        And asleep.

Black Dian, raven Artemis,
Queen o the pitch and velvous nicht,
Whan yon tempest cracks I sweir
Come nicht or day,
Hevin or hell or purgatrie,
Brunstane or hie water, yet,   1130
Can maitter nocht til me
For, gin the spaedoms⋆ are propitious   prognostications
   And the gods willan,
I hae a godlike consolatioun
Left til me; that I hae set
   Wi thir her elegies
Perdurable the starne o my dark luve,
   My exstasie and torment,
Hiech i the unsleepan constellatiouns
     O' the North.   1140

   There she bydes nou,
My follie fair, my divine discontent,
   A goddess mang the wale
   O' wemen ever cut
A hert til flinders⋆ wi perversitie.   splinters

And sae I tak
My final bou.

ii
– But ere I gang –
Forgie me, sweet Dian,
In my maist fell adversitie,   1150
Dian, Iseult, Venus, hear
A bard struck doun wi a hail
O' derts frae Cupid's slee artillerie
– Wi fou and hert-felt consciousness that nou
By richts I suld be aff – Sweet Fann,
My sabil Cynthia, my white lass, grant til me
This boon . . . I'se never spier ye mair . . .
Ae wee boon til the last great
Shennachie o the Westren Warld
   Thats newlie pit   1160
A new sterne i the hevins the-nicht
And nou speaks but wi dwynan braith
Wi his sair skaith near until daith:
Mak saft the hert o Cressid aince again!

Roun★ til her o this my coronach,   whisper
Smoothe her wi clash o immortalitie,
Of honour, fame,
      . . . And streams o press-photographeers!
Flechter★ the woman,   flatter
         Play on her vanitie!   1170
Great Pluto, div I need to *tell* ye
   What to dae?

Juist aince, white Cynthia!
Dido, aid my plea! Juist aince!
   – The-nicht!

And I whan I come til the street I ken
Grant me a licht i the winnock leaman
   And the door ajee . . .
         And nae damned fulerie aben!
Juist aince again, afore, aye worshippan thee,   1180
   My sperit flee.

iii
Aince. aince! Tell me whan aince was eer eneuch!
. . . Til thine ain sel be true and
It maun follow as the nicht . . . I ken, I ken.
– And neither is twice eneuch or twentie,
Neither a million million times and ten!
   Eneuch is juist as lang as mynd can think;
And wha can think ayont a month or sae?
   He that says he can's   1190
   Nocht but the doitit fule
O' his puir forkit-radish follie.

... But let's no argie-bargie* nou wi bagatelles   split hairs
    For truth to tell
  At the moment ae nicht hence
Is juist my limit o belief in Providence.

    iv
  I mock, I mock, and speak o daith
  But aye you ken, my tyger luve,
  The hert can dee and nane
  Ken but its murtherer.

Sae sall we mock baith luve and daith,   1200
Trepann the idle gods wi hert's last braith
And brak the hert o the warld wi mockerie;
    – But lea me come til ye
    Or come ye, Iseult, til me.

XX Tristram

Sae it has come til this i the end –
A barren strand, a skaith, a man bydan at dayligaun
Wi's hert in targats*, onwytan a boat's retour;   tatters
Aa his dwynan ingyne bund up and concentrate
Aince mair on the outcome o a deean chance,
    (Deean in ilka sense o the word!)   1210
– Iseult, Iseult! Name that in my lugs
For a man's life o days and nichts,
The life o bard and warrior, no wi the custom
O' bydan hame o nichts or keepan house by day,
– For him yon name has meant aa that he kens o life,
Iseult that has meant aa life and licht, aa sun or storm,
    Howp, wanhowp, hell, but seendil hevin,
    Life, and nou but daith –
Sae nou as for the hauflin* chiel in Joyous Gard, lang syne,   youthful
Aince mair a boat hauds all o Tristram's weird.   1220
    Swallow at first and Swan at endin . . .
Swan, whan will ye come til me? White Swan! My Iseult!

– Ah, but i the days o the Swallow I was young and maister
    O' the keys o life (or sae I thocht),
Then, there was howp, and gifna howp then life at least . . .
Nou, the howp is smaa and anerlie daith at back o it;
    Neither nae maister I, seik and skaithit dour,
    Dependand on ithers' een, on ithers' hands –
And yet is but the same, for Iseult as aye his weird
                Can mak or mar.   1230

Ay, daith is on me, her cauldrife hand has strak at my hoch
Wi the horn o a muckle hart, lord o the wuids,
    A noble daith at least or sae they say.
But what til me's nobilitie? Daith is daith.

And life is daith wantan the anerlie life I want,
　　– Iseult, my hert's hert . . .
　　　　　　　　Sae what's the odds?

A hart has skaithit me:
　　Will the hart bring me my hert　　　　　　　　　1240
　　Here at the endin o a waefu tale?
　　　　– Theres a conundrum, Merlin!
It suld be sae, certes, by aa the laws o invocatioun,
Nominomancie, incitement, coincidence and exhortatioun,
　　But will't be sae?
– Ay, and heres anither: It was i the chase
My hert first brairit wi the dragon hervest o this luve!
Anither echo! The oracles are guid indeed!

Hou I mynd her yon bricht morn! – Siller and gowd!
– Siller on her bridle and her paufrie's graithin,
– Gowden the chain that held her siller horn,　　　　1250
– Siller her lauch amang the great bucks,
– Her hair that streamed like a gowden linn* adoun her back　　　waterfall
　　Bedimmed the gowden band that circelt it,
– And the wind was siller lauchin i the sun's great gowden face!
But bluid-reid was the spate that raired rambaleuch throu my hert
And dirled* intil my finger-tips like needles laced wi fire.　　　pierced
　　Gin she wad come!
　　　　　　　　The time is short eneuch.
Swan, my Swan, spreid your white wings and bear
My fair Iseult acrost the spase!　　　　　　　　　1260
　　　　　　　　But mak despatch.
Morgana's an impatient fey.

I coud hae taen her tae. She wad hae come wi me
Til the warld's end.
Lord Christ, what's aa the chivalrous laws o courtesie
Til twa herts reift apert for aye?
Twa herts as sacrifice til an auld lyart's* honour!　　　greybeard's
Honour! Vanitie, nae mair.
The follie, follie o't! Knichtlie troth . . . !
And this the fell fairin.　　　　　　　　　　1270

Och, I wad liefer be a schawaldour*, kennan nocht o this,　　wood-ranger
And deean blythe wi his ain clartie* maistress by his side　　filthy
As be thirlit til sic chivalrie, casquit and plumed,
　　　　Til wanhowp, dule,
And, i the end, a bier unsainit wi a leman's greit . . .
　　Syne sail owre the endmaist seas
Avont the sunset til the last lang hame o Avalon
Wi a luve yet in my breist like a stanchless chaudron o desire –
Never nae mair to find
　　　　　　　　Rest and hert's easement,　　　　1280
　　– Iseult! Iseult, haste ye! O my fair!

XXI I Heard a Lassie

I heard a lassie at the winnock sing
And aa her sang was o her luve,
And I bypassan i the causie leukit up
For aa the greit in her wae leid
Was aa the greit in my dowf hert
Sae that she sang for me, it seemed.
    Our een met on the instant –
       Deep, deep intil hers
I leukt and saw the hert was broken there,
And saw that she saw in my een   1290
The follie and the wilderness was there,
    And for neither tane nor tither
Was there sainin or a cure,
And, tho strangers baith, we kent ilk ither then
    For the 'Moment o Eternitie.'

Syne she smiled, and I at her
– O ilka luver kens a luver's grame★! –   torment
And aa the fever that I had drapt aa awa frae me
    On the hie road til Damascus.
She smiled and turned aside,   1300
    And I passed on intil the toun.

'O luve, quhidder art thou joy or fulishness
That makis fowk sa glaid of thair distress?'

XXII Thus Spak Antony

    i
      Thus spak Antony frae the stage of Kings:
Albeid the precipitate of our twa luves commelled★   mingled
Lowsit a combustioun whas Vesuvian spate
    Outran itsel
And thriftless waurit aa its heaped-up thesauries
Doundingan ten Pompeiis o the saul   1310
Til bourach, skau★, distractioun o the mense   ruin
    – And braggandie,
Yet aye amang the acres o the smouchteran grieshoch★   embers
    Blae gleids★ lowp here, there, ayont,   flames
An endemic flauchteran dispeace,
Reid-wud yet meaninless unhinged til its desire,
    Unpossible to dowse; destructioun,
    Ruin, wanhowp, exstasie? despair:
– The fey-bricht een o the addict's dwaum,
    Uncurable, unlownable★, unstawable, insane,   1320   unquietable
And nou at end as cynical as his ain turpitude.

ii

Then did waif Ængus mak respond:
And what the prophets tell i the warld o men
May yet be richt for aa we outlands ken
And the haill globe be hapt in nicht — and sune,
   And the silence may come swith★ on me   at once
   And the wild leid nae mair tak wing
   (For bards are subjeck til sic haps)
And yon means nae mair sangs for thee,
Black swan o the hert's dour maladie.

(But, in my hert, hou can there be   1330
An end o scrievin sangs o thee)

Yet, sae is whance and why and wharfae, 'cruel fair,'
As my last act in our lang drama, I
Nou scrieve this coronach to stand for aye
Uncassable★ by Time and Change, Decay   unbreakable
Or the Jurmumblement o baith the hemispheres
In a holocaust o scientific glamer
— As a monument and warnin til the fules coman after.   1340

iii

For I ken weill, as ilka luver kens,
That e'en i the abysses o the thirldom
Sune to be born —
            Yon bairn yet will haud
His regalitie and pouer — yon blind wee loun
Wi wings and bow and quiverfu o derts,
   There is your Tyrant and Czar Ultimate!
     That's sairlie strucken me
       And caad me doun
Intil the Chasm o Forgotten Things   1350
    Whar yet I dree★   endure
This damned dementit follie-weird o thee
   And neither wadna change my fell
For pavilions and the peacocks o Assam
    Or the Lordship o the Damned

— Or the poppy-peace o Hailisted★ itsel.   Heaven
      Yon's the bonnie mockerie!

Ay, I'se warand e'en i the netherst pit
      Yon fat loun sways
His ain involved and vast imperium —   1360
  For wha sae bauld as set a bund
    Til Luve's arcane delirium
Whas victims ken nor whance, whartil nor why
They dree sic trepidatiouns, dules and waes,
Sic joys unspeakabil, sic ill and weill . . . ?
               Nae mair div I!
               (Rhetoric!
               Juist sheer damned
               Rhetoric!)

XXIII *The Time Is Come*

The time is come, my luve,
 My luve, whan I maun gae –   1370
The sevin-pinioned bird is gyran
 Intil the muir o winds;
Aneth the hills the gigants turn
 In their ayebydan dwaum –
Finn under Nevis, the great King
Under Arthur's Seat, True Tammas
 Neth the Eildons steers again;
As the sand rins i the gless, aince mair
 Tannhauser, wersh and wan as sin,
 As I, deperts frae Horselberg,   1380
Lane and weirdless; nou aince mair
Ulysses bids his Calypso fareweill . . .
Fareweill!

Defeatit by his ain back-slitherin,
Efter lang strachle wi the serpent slee,
Lea him at least outgang wi mockerie,
 The Makar macironical!
 A sang on his perjurit lips
 And naething i the pouch
   – Or i the hert, for that!   1390
    Music maestro!

Bring on the Dancing Girls!
Vauntie i the muslins o Cos,
Wreathit wi hibiscus and bearan
Amphoræ o the richt Falernian!
– O let there be nae girnin at the Bar!
    Chi ha vessuto per amore
    Per amore si mori.[1]

XXIV *Fareweill*

Goddess, hae I wranged ye?
Hae my libatiouns been deficient?   1400
Did I negleck some peerie but maist needfu
 Detail o the ritual?
Aiblins hae I been ower sanguine i the maitter
 O' the deificatioun o my beluvit?
  For, Goddess, I dwyne,
  Wantan a sicht o her.
The door was steekit, neither was there answer
  Til my urgent summons,
  There was nae licht i the house,
  Tuim it was, fremmit and desertit.   1410

---

[1] Who has lived by love should die by love.

Dowilie★ I turnit back the road I'd come . . .   sadly
And syne sat doun and made this nobil leid
    O' the spulyies★ o luve.   spoils

Gin my luve eer suld see it, Cynthia,
And suld she comprehend her bard,
    Her hert, as she did aince,
        (Albeid I end thus in mockerie
        In sheer sel-defence
        Agin the jalous gods' decreets)
Afore, 'wan wi luve's sufferance,'   1420
    I turn my face until the waa,
  Gar my white lass in memorie
    Of our great days
Greit ae bricht tear for me, let faa
    Ae tear alane
           . . . and it sall be
For me an ocean o the fairest wine
    To slocken aye my drouth★   thirst
For aa the lang eternities I'm due in hell
Mang ither bonnie victims   1430
        O' a daithless luve!

        And sae fareweill!

Til you I kiss my hand, black Artemis,
  Nae wreathes required –
Theres be ample roses on my road.
  Aphrodite, Brigit!
Our immortalitie is in sauf keep.
  Guidnicht, leddies!

    ★   ★   ★   ★   ★

  Syne the hill opened
And the licht o the sun beglamert   1440
The een like the leam o virgin snaw,
  And the derkenin and the dawin
    Were the sevinth year.

        A lustrum endit.
Bards hae sung o lesser luves
  Than I o thee,
Oh my great follie and my granderie.

      Quod S. G. S., *Makar*,
        Embro toun, Dec. 1946 – Feb. 1947.

Leander Stormbound

The auld mune on her back
In a black luift* o rags   sky
That the wind pell-mell
Ryves wi a banshee yell
And a blaff of hail . . .

Out throu her eldritch* rags   unearthly
The auld mune-hag
Looks on the bylan seas
Whar sleek as backs o seals
Curls ilka* sweel,   10   every

And looks on the tuim* promenade,   empty
The folk all abed
On this daft nicht, but me
That looks on the stairvan sea
Wantan ye.

And awa ayont* the faem*   beyond/foam
And the black storm, at hame
Ye're sleepan peacefullie –
Or maybe hear the thunderan sea
. . . Wantan me.   20

Cokkils

Doun throu the sea
Continuallie
A rain o cokkils, shells
Rains doun
Frae the ceaseless on–ding
O' the reefs abune
Continuallie.

Slawlie throu millenia
Biggan* on the ocean bed   building
Their ain subaqueous Himalaya   10
Wi a fine white rain o shells
Faa' an continuallie
Wi nae devall*.   cease

Sae, in my heid as birdsang
Faas throu simmer treen
Is the thocht o my luve
Like the continual rain
O' cokkils throu the middle seas
Wi nae devall –
The thocht o my true-luve   20
Continuallie.

The Grace of God and the Meth Drinker

There ye gang, ye daft
And doitit dotterel, ye saft
Crazed outland skalrag★ saul   *tramp*
In your bits and end o winnockie duds
Your fyled★ and fozie-fousome★ clouts   *soiled/disgusting*
As fou's a fish, crackt and craftie-drunk
Wi bleerit reid-rimmed
Ee and slaveran crozie★ mou   *whining*
Dwaiblan owre the causie★ like a ship   *street*
Storm-toss't i' the Bay of Biscay O   10
At-sea indeed and hauf-seas-owre
Up-til-the-thrapple's-pap
Or up-til-the-crosstrees-sunk –
    Wha kens? Wha racks?
Hidderie-hetterie stouteran in a dozie dwaum★   *dazed and stumbling*
O'ramsh reid-biddie – Christ!
    The stink
O' jake ahint him, a mephitic
Rouk o miserie, like some unco exotic
Perfume o the Orient no juist sae easilie tholit★   20   *suffered*
By the bleak barbarians o the Wast
But subtil, acrid, jaggan the nebstrous★   *nostrils*
Wi'n owrehailan ugsome guff, maist delicat,
Like in scent til the streel★ o a randie gib★ . . .   *urine/tom-cat*
    O-hone-a-ree!

His toothless gums, his lips, bricht cramasie★   *crimson*
A schere-bricht slash o bluid
A schene like the leaman★ gleid o rubies   *gleaming*
Throu the grey-white stibble
O' his blank unrazit chafts★, a hangman's   30   *jaws*
Heid, droolie wi gob, the bricht een
Sichtless, cannie, blythe, and slee –
Unkennan.

Ay,
    Puir gangrel★!   *wanderer, vagrant*
        There
– But for the undeemous★ glorie and grace   *undying*
O' a mercifu omnipotent majestic God
Superne eterne and sceptred in the firmament
Whartil the praises o the leal rise   40
Like incense aye about Your throne,
Ayebydan, thochtless, and eternallie hauf-drunk
Wi nectar, Athole-brose, ambrosia – nae jake for
    You –
        God there! –
But for the 'bunesaid unsocht grace, unprayed-for,
Undeserved
  Gangs,
    Unregenerate,
        Me.   50

There is a Tide

There is a tide in luve's affair
Nae poem e'er was made –
The hairt hings like a gull in air
For★ aa the words are said.   before

Nou in this saagin★-tide we swey   slack-water
While the world wags and empires faa:
But we that burned high Ilium
What can we rack that ken it aa?

T. S. Law (1916 – 1997)

Law was an unabashedly populist writer, with a vigorous, colloquial, town-meeting
style, and an agenda of national and working-class causes.

The Free Nation

Preeve you tae me thare's natiounhood,
and I sall preeve thare's nane;
an that's as gyte★ as your belief   mad
that needs nae pruif tae ken.
And I can preeve ayont★ belief,   beyond
ayont corollarie,
no dae the-noo★ means never dae   now
an Scotland never free.

Preeve you tae me thare's natiouns nane,
and I shall preeve thare's yin★,   10   one
for that belief bydes ben belief
lik marra ben the baen.
And I can preeve ayont belief,
ayont corollarie,
gif we dae noo an dae nae mair,
then Scotland will be free.

Sae let the unthinkable be thocht
lik a fire-flaucht★ thru the haerns,   lightning
that the unsayable be said
lik thunder tae the bairns;   20
an let the unwurkable be wrocht
lik a spaein★ ben the speirin,   prophecy
that the unmakkable be made
lik het and hammered airn;

an let the unseeable be seen
lik the endmaist revelatioun,
then the undaeable will be duin
an Scotland made the natioun.

Seasoun in Hell

We had it aa gaun for us, but it gaed that fast
we never jaloused* we'd had it till the last: suspected
as the fuhll o oor een wi thon snawbaa bree in Hell[1]
gaes bye in soochin steam, and us harasst
for coolth, the het-faced wheesht we byde can tell
hoo we hae sellt oor caller* lown* for skelps*.   fresh/shelter/blows
Birthricht has gane; Gode's beild* has gane an aa.   building, shelter
Gode gied. We gied awo. Speir nane His help.
    Deil! Gie us snaw! Cauld's it can blaw!

Bye Auldgaet Kirk

Dae ye ken oor Wallace cleir,
        Graham, lad?
Heard ye tell o'm fae a leear,
        Graham, Graham?
They hauf-hingit him perqueir*,   perfectly
syne him grallocht* lyke a deer,   disembowelled
and him libbit* lyke a steer,   castrated
        Graham, lad.

Fae Westminster tae the Tooer,
        Graham, lad,   10
bluidie wi Imperial pooer,
        Graham, Graham,
syne bye Auldgaet in the stoor
tae the Elmes at Smithfield doore
thare tae thole thon deidlie cloore,
        Graham, lad.

Fae the Tooer bye Auldgaet Kirk,
        Graham, lad,
aa the wy bye that same kirk,
        Graham, Graham,   20
aa the wy bye Auldgaet Kirk
tae the hemp, the fire, the dirk,
aix an cleaver thrang* at wirk,   busy
        Graham, lad.

---

[1] Note: the common speak that something is 'No wurth the fuhll o ma erse bylt snaw', as weel as 'I'll gie ye the fuhll o yer een', meanin aither a pair o keekers, or een fou o tears, or baith. (TL.)

Mynd, gaun bye the Auldgaet Kirk,
  Graham, lad,
Wallace gaed bye that same kirk,
  Graham, Graham,
Wallace gaed bye Auldgaet Kirk,
daurklins tae the dowie⋆ mirk   30   sad, grey
saw him butchert lyke a stirk⋆,   bullock
  Graham, lad.

Draggit on at horses' heels,
  Graham, lad,
Lyke thur fousome midden⋆ creels,   dunghill
  Graham, Graham,
aa the wy tae thon Smithfield,
killt bi hemp an fire an steel
for the sake o Scotland's weal,
  Graham, lad.   40

Yince he had a freen at hame,
  Graham, lad,
Guid Sir John the Graham, the same,
  Graham, Graham,
focht and deed in Faakirk fame.
Mynd you hae the samin name.
Edwart never cood thaem tame,
  Graham, lad.

Renewal

Tae destroy us as Scots
hoo lang has it taen?
As lang as it taks
tae mak Scotsmen again.

Och, it's angersome butt,
an gy fashiouslyke ben
sic a weed in the hert
maks cankerous men.

Till the waather weares roon
we maun thole the auld pain   10
as the weerd o the year
drees the wuin an the rain.

Whitlikken a kinna
thing's that for tae hain⋆?   protect, preserve
Tae say it's tae ken it.
An that's whit we're sayin.

Syne, mair lyker oorsels,
an that wy remain
nae better nor ithers,
but Scotsmen again.   20

Importance

He daesnae juist drap a name
or set it up an say grace tae't,
he lays it oot on his haun
an hits ye richt in the face wi't.

Generous, tho, tae a faut,
Ay, no a ticht man, no mean wi't.
Gie him anither chance,
And he'll hit ye atween the een wi't.

W[illiam] S[ydney] Graham (1918 – 1986)

Falling into the Sea

Breathing water is easy
If you put your mind to it.
The little difficulty
Of the first breath
Is soon got over. You
Will find everything right.

Keep your eyes open
As you go fighting down
But try to keep it easy
As you meet the green   10
Skylight rising up
Dying to let you through.

Then you will seem to want
To stand like a sea-horse
In the new suspension.
Don't be frightened. Breathe
Deeply and you will go down
Blowing your silver worlds.

Now you go down turning
Slowly over from fathom   20
To fathom even remembering
Unexpected small
Corners of the dream
You have been in. Now
What has happened to you?

You have arrived on the sea
Floor and a lady comes out
From the Great Kelp Wood
And gives you scones and a cup
Of tea and asks you   30
If you come here often.

Malcolm Mooney's Land[1]

1

Today, Tuesday, I decided to move on
Although the wind was veering. Better to move
Than have them at my heels, poor friends
I buried earlier under the printed snow.
From wherever it is I urge these words
To find their subtle vents, the northern dazzle
Of silence cranes to watch. Footprint on foot
Print, word on word and each on a fool's errand.
Malcolm Mooney's Land. Elizabeth
Was in my thoughts all morning and the boy.   10
Wherever I speak from or in what particular
Voice, this is always a record of me in you.
I can record at least out there to the west
The grinding bergs and, listen, further off
Where we are going, the glacier calves
Making its sudden momentary thunder.
This is as good a night, a place as any.

2

From the rimed bag of sleep, Wednesday,
My words crackle in the early air.
Thistles of ice about my chin,   20
My dreams, my breath a ruff of crystals.
The new ice falls from canvas walls.
O benign creature with the small ear-hole,
Submerger under silence, lead
Me where the unblubbered monster goes
Listening and makes his play.
Make my impediment mean no ill
And be itself a way.
A fox was here last night (Maybe Nansen's,
Reading my instruments.) the prints   30
All round the tent and not a sound.
Not that I'd have him call my name.
Anyhow how should he know? Enough
Voices are with me here and more
The further I go. Yesterday
I heard the telephone ringing deep
Down in a blue crevasse.
I did not answer it and could
Hardly bear to pass.

---

[1] 'Malcolm Mooney' appears in several of Graham's poems, and serves, apparently, as the author's alter ego.

Landlice, always my good bedfellows,   40
Ride with me in my sweaty seams.
Come bonny friendly beasts, brother
To the grammarsow and the word-louse,
Bite me your presence, keep me awake
In the cold with work to do, to remember
To put down something to take back.
I have reached the edge of earshot here
And by the laws of distance
My words go through the smoking air
Changing their tune on silence.   50

   3

My friend who loves owls
Has been with me all day
Walking at my ear
And speaking of old summers
When to speak was easy.
His eyes are almost gone
Which made him hear well.
Under our feet the great
Glacier drove its keel.
What is to read there   60
Scored out in the dark?
Later the north-west distance
Thickened towards us.
The blizzard grew and proved
Too filled with other voices
High and desperate
For me to hear him more.
I turned to see him go
Becoming shapeless into
The shrill swerving snow.   70

   4

Today, Friday, holds the white
Paper up too close to see
Me here in a white-out in this tent of a place
And why is it there has to be
Some place to find, however momentarily
To speak from, some distance to listen to?
Out at the far-off edge I hear
Colliding voices, drifted, yes
To find me through the slowly opening leads.
Tomorrow I'll try the rafted ice.   80
Have I not been trying to use the obstacle
Of language well? It freezes round us all.

   5

Why did you choose this place
For us to meet? Sit
With me between this word
And this, my furry queen.

Yet not mistake this
For the real thing. Here
In Malcolm Mooney's Land
I have heard many   90
Approachers in the distance
Shouting. Early hunters
Skittering across the ice
Full of enthusiasm
And making fly and,
Within the ear, the yelling
Spear steepening to
The real prey, the right
Prey of the moment.
The honking choir in fear   100
Leave the tilting floe
And enter the sliding water.
Above the bergs the foolish
Voices are lighting lamps
And all their sounds make
This diary of a place
Writing us both in.

Come and sit. Or is
It right to stay here
While, outside the tent   110
The bearded blinded go
Calming their children
Into the ovens of frost?
And what's the news? What
Brought you here through
The spring leads opening?

Elizabeth, you and the boy
Have been with me often
Especially on those last
Stages. Tell him a story.   120
Tell him I came across
An old sulfur bear
Sawing his log of sleep
Loud beneath the snow.
He puffed the powdered light
Up on to this page
And here his reek fell
In splinters among
These words. He snored well.
Elizabeth, my furry   130
Pelted queen of Malcolm
Mooney's Land, I made
You here beside me
For a moment out
Of the correct fatigue.

I have made myself alone now.
Outside the tent endless
Drifting hummock crests.
Words drifting on words.
The real unabstract snow.   140

The Night City

Unmet at Euston in a dream
Of London under Turner's steam
Misting the iron gantries, I
Found myself running away
From Scotland into the golden city.

I ran down Gray's Inn Road and ran
Till I was under a black bridge.
This was me at nineteen
Late at night arriving between
The buildings of the City of London.   10

And then I (O I have fallen down)
Fell in my dream beside the Bank
Of England's wall to bed, me
With my money belt of Northern ice.
I found Eliot and he said yes

And sprang into a Holmes cab.
Boswell passed me in the fog
Going to visit Whistler who
Was with John Donne who had just seen
Paul Potts shouting on Soho Green.   20

Midnight. I hear the moon
Light chiming on St Paul's.

The City is empty. Night
Watchmen are drinking their tea.

The Fire had burnt out.
The Plague's pits had closed
And gone into literature.

Between the big buildings
I sat like a flea crouched
In the stopped works of a watch.   30

To My Wife at Midnight

1

Are you to say goodnight
And turn away under
The blanket of your delight?

Are you to let me go
Alone to sleep beside you
Into the drifting snow?

Where we each reach,
Sleeping alone together,
Nobody can touch.

Is the cat's window open?   10
Shall I turn into your back?
And what is to happen?

What is to happen to us
And what is to happen to each
Of us asleep in our places?

2

I mean us both going
Into sleep at our ages
To sleep and get our fairing.

They have all gone home.
Night beasts are coming out.   20
The black wood of Madron

Is just waking up.
I hear the rain outside
To help me to go to sleep.

Nessie, don't let my soul
Skip and miss a beat
And cause me to fall.

3

Are you asleep I say
Into the back of your neck
For you not to hear me.   30

Are you asleep? I hear
Your heart under the pillow
Saying my dear my dear

My dear for all it's worth.
Where is the dun's moor
Which began your breath?

4

Ness, to tell you the truth
I am drifting away
Down to fish for the saithe.

Is the cat's window open?   40
The weather is on my shoulder
And I am drifting down

Into O can you hear me
Among your Dunsmuir Clan?
Are you coming out to play?

5

Did I behave badly
On the field at Culloden?
I lie sore wounded now.

By all activities, and
The terrible acts of my time   50
Are only a distant sound.

With responsibility
I am drifting off
Breathing regularly

Into my younger days
To play the games of Greenock
Beside the sugar-house quays.

6

Nessie Dunsmuir, I say
Wheesht wheesht to myself
To help me now to go   60

Under into somewhere
In the redcoat rain
Buckle me for the war.

Are you to say goodnight
And kiss me and fasten
My drowsy armour tight?

My dear camp-follower,
Hap the blanket round me
And tuck in a flower.

Maybe from my sleep   70
In the stoure* at Culloden   dust, storm
I'll see you here asleep

In your lonely place.

To Alexander Graham

Lying asleep walking
Last night I met my father
Who seemed pleased to see me.
He wanted to speak. I saw
His mouth saying something
But the dream had no sound.

We were surrounded by
Laid-up paddle steamers
In The Old Quay in Greenock.
I smelt the tar and the ropes.   10

It seemed that I was standing
Beside the big iron cannon
The tugs used to tie up to
When I was a boy. I turned
To see Dad standing just
Across the causeway under
That one lamp they keep on.

He recognised me immediately.
I could see that. He was
The handsome, same age   20
With his good brows as when
He would take me on Sundays
Saying we'll go for a walk.

Dad, what am I doing here?
What is it I am doing now?
Are you proud of me?
Going away, I knew
You wanted to tell me something.

You stopped and almost turned back
To say something. My father,   30
I try to be the best
In you you give me always.

Lying asleep turning
Round in the quay-lit dark
It was my father standing
As real as life. I smelt
The quay's tar and the ropes.

I think he wanted to speak.
But the dream had no sound.
I think I must have loved him.   40

The Lost Miss Conn

To set the scene. The kirk
Helpers and two elders
Are clearing up from the fête.
Wasps are at the jam.
Miss Conn is going home.

She scorns young MacIvor
And trips into the wood.
Hazel and oak and rowan.
It is not a dark wood
Like the Black Wood of Madron.   10

Yellow-beak and the jay
Make a happy noise round
Where she treads. She treads
Her way budding gently
Unhappy for MacIvor.

So she was seen to enter
The wood with her young skirt
Flashing. Mr & Mrs
Conn never received her.
Hazel and oak and rowan.   20

To set the scene. The kirk
Helpers and two elders
Are clearing up from the fête.
Wasps are at the jam.
Miss Conn is going home.

Maurice Lindsay (1918 –)

Like his friend, George Bruce, Lindsay is a tireless Man of Letters, who wrote largely in English, stayed outside the MacDiarmid-MacCaig-Sydney Smith group of poets and has been unfairly neglected in recent years. Lindsay has written a great deal of poetry, and has published rough work along with finished work. But he has much first-rate verse, as the poems below attest. The judgement here is that his finest production is his 1000-line autobiographical poem, *A Net to Catch the Wind*, a vigorous, honest, iconoclastic summing-up of a long career as writer, critic and Scotsman. Few have done so much to advance the cause of Scottish literature. Among his many editions, anthologies and critical studies, *A History of Scottish Literature* (1977, rev. 1991) is especially notable.

Jock, the Laird's Brother

Strutting across the red moors of his memory, Jock, the Laird's brother,
tingling, tweedy bagpipe trousers, whisky map-veined face,
under his arm a leering gun, the image of his father,
the skirling tradition of fishes and pheasants, the ownership of space;

the purple, peopleless moors of Scotland where poverty seeds in the ground,
and love turns grey as the ashy, prickled, bleak-burned skeletoned heather,
where sleek guns splutter their patter in August, and gasping grouse are found
on the noses of snuffling dogs, and the hills are always the talk of weather.

Once, he was keeper of animals claimed from God to be owned by a Scottish lord;
once, he patrolled the edges of forests, a poacher's pleasure his full despair;
now, he is grown the villagers' measure with his regular walks, an old man, absurd,
with the look of one who's been left behind by thoughts that were never there.

Summer Daybreak, Innellan

Drowsily a cock climbs through the first grey
streak that cracks the shapelessness of night;
settles upon a hayrick, claps his wings
and brazenly bugles up another day.
Small creatures furred with darkness slide from sight
as dandily the cock crows, till he springs
the sun from under the hill, aroused to sound
a warmth of waking through the steaming ground.

The sea's the sounding-board for the sun's strings,
tuning the air with trembled chords of light.   10
Hidden in boughs, unnumbered dew-drenched throats
pour out their diapason of delight
in spraying trills, in tumbling, tendrilled notes,
till every height and fluted hollow sings
the moist new joy of morning, while the sky
makes silence hear and distance magnify.

Highland Shooting Lodge

Crouched up beneath a crowd of Grampian hills,
this old house waits to hear the report of guns
crisping the Autumn air, for its rooms again
to warm to the jokes of August-trampling men
roughed by the grasp and snap of salmon gills,
the twisted necks of grouse. But nobody comes.

Only, at times, a shapeless horde of cloud
that shifts about the rocky peaks, creeps down
to lick at gutters soured with rotting leaves,
or rub a shapeless back against cold eaves,   10
then vanish, thin as breath; the drifting shroud
of everything that men once thought they owned.

Farm Woman

She left the warmth of her body tucked round her man
before first light, for the byre, where mist and the moist
hot breath of the beasts half-hid the electric veins
of the milking machines. Later, she'd help to hoist
the heavy can for the tractor to trundle down
to the farm-road end, while her raw hands scoured the dairy.
By seven o'clock, she'd have breakfast on the table,
her kitchen bright as her apron pin, the whole house airy.
The men-folk out in the fields, the children off to school,
she'd busy herself with the house and the hens. No reasons   10
clouded the other side of the way she brought
to her man the generous amplitude of the seasons.

Not much of a life, they'd whisper at church soirées
as they watched her chat, her round face buttered with content,
unable to understand that for her each moment
rubbed out the one before, and simply lent
nothing for words of theirs to touch to argument.

Farm Widow

She moved among the sour smell of her hens' droppings,
her cheeks rubbed to a polish, her skirts bustled
with decent pride; alone since the day the tractor
hauled itself up the field on the hill and toppled

her man away from her. Around her feet
her daughter played, the face of innocence puckered
with the solemn self-importance of being alone
in a grown-up world; her friends, the hens that speckled

her mother's allotment. Some of the weekly folk
who came to buy their eggs, had watched her counting   10
their change from the money smooth in her purse, and given her
silent pity, then sensed that she wasn't wanting

in anything they could offer; that she seemed
like one whom life had used too soon for writing
some sort of purpose with, her gestures economies
spelling completeness; gone beyond our waiting

for times and places to happen, beyond the will,
to where time and place lie colourless and still.

At Hans Christian Andersen's Birthplace, Odense, Denmark

Sunlight folds back pages of quiet shadows
against the whitewashed walls of his birthplace. Tourists move
through crowded antiseptic rooms and ponder
what row after row of glass-cased papers ought to prove.

Somehow the long-nosed gangling boy who was only
at home in fairyland, has left no clues.
The tinder-box of Time we rub
answers us each the way we choose.

For kings have now no daughters left for prizes.
Swineherds must remain swineherds; and no spell   10
can make the good man prince; psychiatrists
have dredged up wonder from the wishing well.

The whole of his terrible, tiny world might be
dismissed as a beautiful madman's dream, but that each of us knows
whenever we move out from the warmth of our loneliness
we may be wearing the Emperor's new clothes.

At the Mouth of the Ardyne

The water rubs against itself,
glancing many faces at me.
One winces as the dropped fly
tears its tension. Then it heals.

Being torn doesn't matter.
The water just goes on saying
all that water has to say,
what the dead come back to.

Then a scar opens.
Something of water is ripped out,   10
a struggle with swung air.
I batter it on a loaf of stone.

The water turns passing faces,
innumerable pieces of silver.
I wash my hands, pack up, and
go home wishing I hadn't come.

Later, I eat my guilt.

Stones in Sky and Water

Under the lap of water sunken stones change
their indefinable shapes. A dazzle gleams
from the roof-tops of ripples. Summer's brightness peoples the loch with moveless stir that seems
to mingle height and distance. Clouds free-range,
trailing their aimless shadows. Water's peace
gets rubbed against by winds that peel off light.
But the smooth-bending forms the stones release
float upwards like cast images, to exchange
the appearance for reality and spring   10
fresh impulses, the flux of all delight
a moment in eternity can bring
when stones in sky and water silently sing.

Speaking of Scotland

What do you mean when you speak of Scotland?
The grey defeats that are dead and gone
behind the legends each generation
savours afresh, yet can't live on?

Lowland farms with their broad acres
peopling crops? The colder earth
of the North East? Or Highland mountains
shouldering up their rocky dearth?

Inheritance of guilt that our country
has never stood where we feel she should?   10
A nagging threat of unfinished struggle
somehow forever lost in the blood?

Scotland's a sense of change, an endless
becoming for which there was never a kind
of wholeness or ultimate category.
Scotland's an attitude of mind.

Anon

They are excavating the mound at the foot of the village,
young men with gentle eyes and curious beards,
and names like Brown and Soutar, and soft-breasted girls
on whom they'll one day stamp their borrowed image,
name upon name. What else have they to preserve?

They are digging for signs. How like were the other Browns
and Soutars, ripening out of the blameless soil,
and having to leave their names when it took them under?
Turning over the freshly wounded earth,
only Anon stares out from whitened bone.   10

Dusk in a Glasgow Square

Darkness obliterates. Round arcs of light
the street lamps probe dried leaves. Their naked rustle
edges decay against the smell of night.
Kerbing low-geared, a cruise of cars hustle
each other round an empty office block
to pull up when the flash of booted thighs
flickers. A shadow peels out from the flock
leaning her whispered offer. The driver buys,
and revs off to the nearest parking lot.
Crouched in the crumpled scuffle of a seat,   10
he satisfies the need he thinks he's bought,
then runs her freshly back to her old beat.
Some father re-adjusts the suit of his disguises;
some daughter finds again that men hold no surprises.

Das Lied von der Erde

Roses have fallen, the flesh has lost its tune,
the sound of flutes silvers a chilling moon;
the glint of wine has soured upon the tongue;
riderless now the horsing seasons come;
gone are the firm of limb whose laughter kissed
the morning air with hope, the longing dusk
with traced desires. Now, as the scent of musk
fingers old graveyards, moulders thought from books,
and breathes its doubt on well-remembered looks,
Ewig . . . the music sighs, and brings us near   10
the silence those it folds on never hear.

Scotland the What?

Six men out of seven who applied to us for executive jobs withdrew
their application when they learned that the job was in Scotland.
Report by a firm of Management Consultants,
quoted in 'The Glasgow Herald'

Scotland's image? You must be joking!
The less said about that, the better.
Bagpipes and haggis; tourist-broking
half-rainbow framed. A dead letter
dropped out of Europe's circulation.
Rounds of soliciting applause
for each enticed investing nation.
Ragbag of pound notes, ancient laws
and sour religion. Land whose thrust
once fashioned factories and ships   10
that shaped a reputation's trust.
A past that's locked by tightened lips
relaxing sentimental farce.
History's biggest little thinkers;
adjusting deferential blinkers
where politics and patronage speak
louder than risk or principle.
Quick takers-on of petty pique
reason proves unconvincible.
Proud worshippers of the dull and thick   20
confusing numbers with perception.
Romanticists whose ultimate trick
is swallowing their self-deception.
Scotland's image? The hell with it!
I love; I hate; I curse; I care
that we should let ourselves submit
might be to *what we think we were.*

Nocturne

In the middle of the night, the footless hours,
my fears take courage, crowd about my bed.
Leaning over me, the false breath
of their alarm chokes me. I rehearse
    the gasp of my own death.

In the morning, in the blood's awakening,
whey-faced, they slink away. A sunned-out moon
circles my living's dark side. Man again,
I wonder what it is they want of me:
    Or rather, how, and when?   10

An Elegy

A launch holds briskly out from the loch shore,
arrowing ripples. From a slowed-down turn,
a woman at the prow leans out to pour
ashes out of a silver funeral urn,
then, white and red, throws after, heads of roses
that float upon the patch of greyish rust;
hunched in the frozen posture grief imposes,
head bowed before the thinned dispersing dust.
Snorting, the boat churns up its normal pace
and chugs back where it started from, its wake   10
rocking the roses as a foam of lace
widens a trailing V astern, to take
roses and dust, so late the cause of weeping
into the water's wide anonymous keeping.

Tom Scott (1918 – 1995)

'Brand the Builder' is one of the sketches from a larger work with the same title. The entire work is sometimes considered Scott's major achievement – though perhaps his allegory, *The Ship*, has a better claim. Scott, whose close study of the middle Scots poets had surely affected his own Scots diction, was particularly given to work in very long forms, especially the epic, scientific treatise, 'The Tree'.

Brand the Builder

On winter days, aboot the gloamin hour,
When the nock on the college touer
Is chappan lowsin-time,
And ilka mason packs his mell* and tools awa   mallet
Under his banker*, and bien forenenst the waa   bench
The labourer haps the lave* o the lime   remainder
Wi soppan sacks, to keep it frae a frost, or faa

O suddent snaw
Duran the nicht;
When scrawnie craws flap in the shell-green licht   10
Towards yon bane-bare rickle o trees
That heeze*   raise
Up on the knowe abuin the toun,
And the red goun
Is happan mony a student frae the snell* nor'easter,   fierce
Malcolm Brand, the maister,
Seean the last hand through the yett*   gate
Afore he bars and padlocks it,
Taks yae look aroond his stourie* yaird   dusty
Whaur chunks o stane are liggin   20

Like the ruins o some auld-farrant★ biggin★; fashioned/building
Picks a skelf oot o his baerd,
Scliffs his tacketty buits, and syne
Clunters hamelins doun the wyn'.

Doun by the sea
Murns the white swaw★ owre the wrack ayebydanlie. wave

The main street echoes back his fuitfaas
Frae its waas
Whaur owre the kerb and causeys, yellow licht
Presses back the mirk nicht 30
As shop fronts flude the pavin-stanes in places
Like the pentit faces whures pit on, or actresses,
To please their different customers.

Aye the nordren nicht, cauld as rumour
Taks command,
Chills the toun wi his militarie humour,
And plots his map o starns★ wi felloun hand. stars

Alang the shore
The greinan white sea-stallions champ and snore.

Stoopin through the anvil pend 40
Gaes Brand,
And owre the coort wi the twa-three partan★-creels, crab
The birss air fu
O the smell o the sea, and fish, and meltit glue;
Draws up at his door, and syne
Hawkan his craig★ afore he gangs in ben, throat
Gies a bit scart at the grater wi his heels.

The kail-pat on the hob is hotteran fu
Wi the usual hash o Irish stew,
And by the grate, a red-haired beauty frettit thin, 50
His wife is kaain a spurtle★ roond. spatula
He swaps his buits for his baffies but★ a soond. without

The twa-three bairns ken to mak nae din
When faither's in,
And sit on creepies★ roond aboot. low stools
Brand gies a muckle yawn
And howks his paper oot.
Tither side the fire
The kettle hums and mews like a telephone wire.

'Lord, for what we are about to receive 60
Help us to be truly thankful – Aimen;
Woman ye've pit ingans★ in't again!' onions

'Gae wa, ye coorse auld hypocrite,
Thank the Lord for your meat syne grue★ at it!' feel disgust

Wi chowks drawn ticht in a speakless sconner★   disgust
He glowers on her,
Syne on the quate and strecht-faced bairns:
Faulds his paper doun aside his eatin-airns
And, til the loud tick-tockin o the nock
Sups, and reads wi nae other word nor look.   70

The warld ootside
Like a lug★-held seashell, sings wi the rinnan tide.   ear

The supper owre, Brand redds★ up for the nicht,   readies, straightens
Aiblins★ there's a schedule for to price   perhaps
Or somethin nice
On at the picters – secont hoose –
Or some poleetical meetin wants his licht,
Or aiblins, wi him t-total aa his life
And no able to seek a pub for relief frae the wife,
Daunders oot the West Sands 'on the loose.'   80
Whitever tis,
The waater slorps frae his elbucks as he synds★ his phiz.   washes

And this is aa the life he kens there is?

The Ship

This is perhaps Tom Scott's major work, and one of the most impressive poems in
Scots in this century. The ship of state has always been a favourite metaphor of writers.
In the poem, Scott uses as his emblem the death of the *Titanic*, the giant 'unsinkable'
British liner that went down after striking an iceberg on its maiden voyage in April,
1912, with the loss of more than 1500 lives out of about 2200 persons on board. The
details of 'The Ship's' sinking mirror those of the actual *Titanic* fairly closely. Scott's
ambitious, imaginative, and complex work employs the ship for many levels of meaning.

I
Sicna Ship the warld had never seen.
To link the Auld Warld til the brairdan★ New   burgeoning
We biggit up a hail pelagian toun,
And spared nor men nor lands in makin her.
I cannae tell hou mony thousant year,
Hou mony million fingers, wrocht at her,
Hou mony harns★ were, o their kennin, ryped –   brains
As bees' bykes★ o their hinney – or we gat   hives
This macro-microcosm afloat: say
Aa Europe like a lemon we squeezed out,   10
And frae her gleggest★, clearest sprietal juice,   sharpest
Distilled the purest essence for the boat.
Scarce a land nor man but peyed their fee
Til this gret darg★ o shouders. airms and harns.   task
We thocht we'd end Poseidon's timeless reign
And mak the ayebydan ocean aa wir ain.

We took our toll frae Sumer and frae Crete,
And pickit the banes o Babylon and Thebes.
No content, we reived* aa we could scran   stole
Frae Corinth, Sparta, Athens, Judah, Rome.   20
Troy and Carthage gied her maist of aa,
For their aa wes whit we gart them gie.
Marathon and Mylae laid her keel,
The gairnert wealth o Persia backed the ploy,
And Vulcan's smiddy raered baith nicht and day
To smelt the double templates for her sides,
And aa the engine-gear to drive her on
Owre the owre-maistered sea. The gods
Theirsels left aff their loves and feasts and fechts
To come and lend their mair-nor-human pouers   30
In biggin her, the goddesses pit bye
Their jealousies, to lend her grace and bewtie
And Orpheus left his waement and his lyre,
Forgot his tint* Eurydikee awhile   lost
To lend her frae his rowth o harmonie.
Suin she seemed a gret conspiracie
O men and lesser deities agin
Nature, and her Lord, the God o gods
And His creation dwined awa til nocht
Abees* whit godlins, heroes, men, had wrocht.   40   beside

Aeskhylus and Sophokles were baith
Conscriptit for the stagin o the Ship.
Sokrates and Plato peered throu time
To see her form eternal in God's mind,
And Alexander, Aristotle's pupil,
Trampt the Himalayan winepress out
To leave her his aa-India-jewelled pride –
A cairgae weyghs owre sair on ships at sea.
Sulla and Caesar syne took up the ploy
And strechtent out some fankles* in the plan   50   tangles
That Perikles, in thirty marble years,
Had gien its finest form afore their time,
And syne their heir Octavius, canny chiel,
Polished up the details till they shone,
And wi the rod o empire skelpt her on.

Frae deserts round about the Daed Sea cam
Baith help and hendrance for the darg afuit,
For there sublimest Ikhnaton had fund
The God o gods encirclit in the sun
And persecutit ilka* god but Him,   60   every
Leavan ahent his dogma o the Ane,
Whit tho war's priests huntit his exiled saul
Owre daeth's ayebydan, boundless wilderness.
This Ae God Nile-born Moses fund
Hidden in a buss* that lowed* and spoke   bush/burned
His egoistic name – I-am-that-I-am –
And spoke again wi Sinai's rumblan voice
His ten rules for the passengers and crew:

Rules o love, that werena to be borne
By worshippers o war in Thebes or Rome.   70
He raised an issue's never yet been settlet –
Are rules made for men, or men for rules?
And wes the Ship made for its passengers,
Or they juist human cairgae for the Ship?
Throu yon prophetic years the steir* gaed on,   storm
And mony a bell-tongued voice in warnin clanged
To mind us we are nocht but dust o God.
To cap it aa, a Man-God cam Himsel,
A lion – to be nailed on Caesar's tree:
A lamb – to burst frae Caesar's tomb.   80
He re-affirmed the broken rule o love
Embodied in the bluid and glaur o men –
Destroyit nocht, but lived the rulan Word
That wantin, our darg wad be in vain.
He preached. We heard. They answered. He wes slain.

Round about Provence grew up a tribe
O bards wha larnt the workers hou to sing
And helpt the Arno Eagle throu the deeps
Til whaur he saw a different Ship frae ours,
The Argo o God's face, pass owre his heid.   90
The banks o Florence, and Venetian trade,
Gangstered out a faus economie
Whase unreal values were to play, it proved,
Nae walk-on pairt in the drama o the Ship,
And croudit out the Muse's darlin's hell.
But God! the labour tae they aa pit in
Decoratan aa the Ship saloons!
Donatello's fire that rivalled Vulcan's:
Buonarotti's fingers tipped wi steel.
Angelico and Raphael walked thir streets   100
That reek the day wi the burnan words and flesh
O fierce Savonarola. Deck on deck
Maugre* the wars amang the labourers,   in spite of
The titan rose, the steel Leviathan
Hammered out by our Promethean thocht –
By vulture-riven liver sairly bocht.

By this time, tho, the bicker and the strife
There aye had been amang the labourers
Turned open wars. Byler-makars
Focht engineers, and they focht riveteers: 110
Painters focht wi plaisterers. Suin
The leaders and the shepherds o the flock
Began to quarrel owre the very plans,
For they, it seems, were fell ambiguous
And ilkan ego worthy o the name
Wes suir that he wes richt, aa ithers wrang.
They wrangled owre procedures, weys o daein,
And hou fowk suld live that wrocht the Ship,
Whit claes they'd wear, and whit they'd eat,
Until it seemed – seemed? na, till they *did*   120

Fair forget their duties til the Boat.
Luther, Calvin, Zwingli and their ilk
Were like yon sodgers sat ablow the Cross
Playan dice for their Redeemer's rags,
Dividan them amang them in the end.
Til clearer een they brocht the Ship til scorn.
Union wes broken, and unionism born.
In sicna warld the Ship cam til completion:
Aa real values tint in ostentation.
Food wes brunt to keep the prices up   130
While famine wastit million o the fowk.
Gowt and rickets were a twin disease
Rackt the dividit bodie o mankind.
Countries dee'd at some financier's whim:
'Economie' threw faimilies in the street,
And 'policie' pit millions out o darg.
War becam a politeecian's game
For thinnin out the numbers o the fowk
And findin mercats for the grub and gear
It didnae pey sae weel to sell at hame.   140
The 'times' indeed were fairly out o jynt,
But syne the 'times' aye were, aye are, aye will be,
At least until mankint has larnt to see
The human race as yae communitie.

Never wes kennin gretter, ignorance waur.
We set a cut-purse God owre Calvarie,
Worshipt the god o liars and o cheats,
Made banks temples til the king o hell,
Robbery and murder our religion,
And sanctifeed them wi the name o 'Freedom.'   150
In sicna warld we feenished aff the Ship,
And as the Bairns ance, Moses absent, danced
Around the Cauf, round the Ship we pranced.

II
Never had the warld seen sicna Ship.
Her length wes even langer nor the langest:
Her breadth wes even braeder nor the braedest:
Her hicht wes even heicher nor the heichest:
Her wecht wes even haevier nor the haeviest.
She had mair decks nor a skyscraper fluirs,
And she displaced a quarter o the sea.   160
Her screws were giant wind-mills at the stem,
Her cylinders as big as reservoirs,
And her turbines could hae driven earth itsel.
The haill warld's horse coudna hae matched her pouer,
And as for speed, nae cheetah could outrun her.
Double-waaed, she had for her defence
Twa-three bottoms decked in her forbye.
She'd steam to gar Vesuvius erupt,
And furnaces could keep it aye on fire.
Her hawsers could hae hauled Atlantis up,   170
Her valves supply the hert o Sol himsel:

Never had sic flanges duin sic couplin:
Never sic rods sic connections made:
Never sic heids crossed on sicna gibs:
Never bolts sae followed, pumps sae fed,
Sic spindles guidit, never cranks sae shaftit,
Never siccan heids wi siccan links,
Thraws sae threw, nor sniftered siccan rods.
The fittin-out gaed on for scores o years,
Her trials took some decades and a bit.   180
But finallie the thing wes fit to sail,
And she wes dubbed THE SHIP THAT CANNA SINK
By aa the bally-hooers o the press,
And selt as sich til mankind's stoundit een.
The like o sicna Ship wes never seen.

We crewed it wi the best men in the trade,
Skipper, officers, and men – a crew
Infallible as wes the Ship itsel –
Syne took on juist as flawless passengers.
Mr and Mrs Warld-Steel were there: 190
Sir James and Lady Banking and Finance,
Universal Metals and her son:
Lord and Lady Africa with dogs:
Miss Jo Berg the Rand, without her sire,
The son of Persian Oil with his new fwend:
Miss Dian Alaska and her aunt:
Cowl and Light and Housing too were theah.
Transcontinental Railways strode the decks,
And half the tea in China, hand in hand
Wi positively *aa* the grapes in Spain,   200
Hob nobbed wi twa-fifths Pacific Soap
And melled★ thegither on the upper decks   mixed
Wi umpteen dukes and duchesses o Land –
Totallan aa Europe's Revenue
In ony echteen month afore the war.
In fact, as mony interests were there
As whures were at the Ball o Kirriemuir.
Ablow the first-class sauls on the upper deck.
The middle-decks were filled wi middle fowk,
Maistlins weill-peyed stooges o the tap –   210
Lawyers that could pit throu shady deals:
Doctors that could chairge gret muckle fees
For kiddin the rich their ills were physical:
Accountants expert cookan up the books:
And whitna ither dow★ and worthless crooks.   dreary

The steerage held the laichest★ fowk in Europe.   lowest
Them that were no nae banker-bandits,
Capitalist robbers, usurous swindlers, nor
Even grabbers o land, and kent nae wey
Better to serve God and their fellae-men   220
Nor by tillan the soil, producan food,
Biggan houses, organizan sewage,
Transport, water supplies, beddin and cleddin,

Gettan bairns to replace them when they dee,
And whitna ither merely uisfu darg –
Sic as givan up their earnins til the rich.
They were faur the biggest class o fowk,
But unco different reasons brocht them there.
Whauras the tap were there on pleisure bent,
Business, visits, fashion, or to say   230
They had duin the first jaunt wi the Ship,
And the middle-class gaed juist til ape the tap,
Or for a rest, or to dodge the law awhile,
The bottom-class o third and fowrth-rate sauls
Were there because they ettlet★ til escape   intended
The hell for them the upper decks had made.
Frae rapit Ireland some were on the run,
Ithers to forget a Yorkshire slum;
A few frae Glesca★, brandit in the mind   Glasgow
Wi scabbit, raggit bairns in butcher-shops   240
Speiran★ for a pennyworth o scraps: asking
Some to solve some ghetto's ingrown cramps –
Ithers to gie their secret police the slip,
And mony dreamed that owre the baptist sea
They'd find a land whaur life wes *really* free.

As for the crew, they maistlins were the best
Authoritie could find for sicna Ship.
Some were there for their abilitie:
Some because nae better could be got:
And some because, in mony years at sea,   250
They'd been befreendit by the kind o fowk
That ken they can demand, and easy get
Whit staff they want – ay, even on the Ship –
Because their money rules whit rules the sea.
Some were Calvinistic engineers
That saw the kosmos in a gret machine
And theirsels, like God, the lord in the machine.
Ithers ettlet★ juist to dae a job,   struggled
Whit tho it peyed nae tax til mysticism,
Scrubban decks, or scouran lavatories.   260
Ithers were the servants o the rich,
A race that toadied for its vera life,
Helpan the rich stray further frae the Real
Nameless and unkennan murderers –
Makers o cream-puffs, sugar-cakes,
Born to kiss the buits they had to bleck,
Fashion's fuitstools, saffron taintit mirrors,
Fit for nocht but furtherin o vice.
Naethin like the best, nor yet the warst,
They lived and dee'd juist middlc-men o God.   270
Let not perdition damn their useless toil:
Poodles til Nature are as guid as men,
Whiles preferred til men – ay, mair,
The spirochete preferred til Baudelaire.

Bylins she wes set and outward bund,
The brawest Ship our lot had ever manned,
A thing to mak the Sea itsel look wee.
No even Noae roamed owre siccan decks,
And the Neptune stoundan Argo never cuist
Sae gleg and vast a sheddae owre the swaw★.   280   wave
Ahab never stumpt on sicna brig,
Nor temptit God by siccan arrogance
To demonstrate the pouer o HIS machine
Owre aucht His sillie vassal eer could mak,
And that, whitever worth a guest may boast,
He daurna uis it til insult the Host.
The passengers had never kent sic ease:
Ankle-deep in carpets in the First:
The Sacont in the airms o strumpet chairs:
And even the Inferiors in the Third,   290
Like Conrad's Chinee cairgae in the hold,
Had never kent sic space and luxurie
Even in the heyday o the Kirk.
The tap decks lounged and played the days awa.
Breakfast til deck-tennis, on til lunch,
Wi teas and coffees served at ony time,
Drink galore – syne, dressed to kill,
They snobbed it at the eenin denner tables,
Talked, and gushed, and walked the starlit decks,
Played at cairts, or roulette, and in wine   300
Forgot thon ither drink – the bitter brine.

The bitter brine itsel forgot to mind
Whit due respect the warld maun pey the rich,
The gret lords o the dollar and the pound:
Forgot to bou til arrogance and wealth,
Or to petie thir puir craturs o a day
Victimized by mere time and place.
They couldna see the stars for electric bulbs.
They couldna see the sea for Persian rugs.
They couldna see the ice for seean froth.   310
They couldna feel the cauld for feelan heat.
The brine gied nae thocht til priceless dogs,
Jewels, furs, braw nichtgouns, nor boxes
Filled wi stocks and shares and bonds and aa
The business o the rulers o the earth.
It petiedna my leddie's diamant rings,
Her therty trunks, big as the Ship's ain bylers,
That held whit claes she needit for the week,
Nor even Omar's priceless poetrie
That shared the hold wi sic vulgaritie.   320
The bitter, bitter brine forgot to mind,
And like some vicious baest frae Neptune's den,
It crouched, pounced, and wi its cruel claws
On a nicht as lown★ and douce★ as God's douce mercie   calm/sweet
Ripped a daeth-wound in her scrawny side –
Or the sea-god struck his trident throu her hide.

Whit wes she daean there amang the ice?
Water's ill to navigate when frozen.
Wes she drawn on by some magnetic weird★?   *fate*
Did her ain magnetism draw the ice?   330
Wes there nae warnan cry to ward it aff?
Wes God determined to destroy our darg
As Babel wes destroyed, Gomorrah, Sodom,
As the chariots o Pharaoh were engulfed,
Ay, as earth itsel gaed doun ablow the fluid?
It wesna God: it wes oursels
Gane owre faur astray frae the minimum
Observance o the real that sailin needs,
Holed her; as a drunk drives his car
Agin some unoffendan tree, and dees.   340
We were owre keen to hear the latest news
Frae Wall Street and the Bourse to gie a thocht
Til onythin sae profitless as ice.
Aiblins★ conscience engineered her doom,   *perhaps*
I dinna ken, but ken the double waas
We biggit up to spell Poseidon's daeth,
Poseidon's trident grallocht★ in a braeth.   *disembowelled*

The fowk on board at first kent little o't,
A brush agin some landin quay, thocht ane –
But how, when out some hunder mile frae land?   350
Like bumpin ower chuckies★, ithers thocht,   *pebbles*
Or did a giant finger stroke the Ship?
Nane kent a greislie surgeon wes at wark,
Scoran a wound nae medicine wad heal
And nearlins hauf as large as her ain keel.

The slain bull, wi steel deep throu his hert,
May staund fair stotious★ for whit seems an age   *paralysed*
Afore he slawlie sinks doun on his knees,
And slawlier still, keels owre – sae the Ship,
Slain by an ayebydan matador,   360
Stopped in its trecks afore it settled doun.
For lang there wesna ane had ony notion
That the house that we had biggit on the sea
Could nae mair staund. Some on the deck
Stravaiged★, vaguely speiran★. Some   *strolled/asking*
Lay in bed awake. A few
Noticed some tell-tale detail telt nae tale –
The mattresses nae langer shoogled★ wi the Ship: *shook*
The raw o ballroom gouns nae langer danced:
The wind nae langer seuched the porthole throu: 370
Shelfs o broken ice fell til the fluir.
Some fowk thocht it wes a 'jolly rag'
And snawbaaed wi the daeth they were to dee.
Ithers crouched in terror in their bunks –
Intuitives wha felt the lethal ice
Aaraedie freezan up their herts and thairms★   *guts*
Even afore they kent the Ship had struck.
A few got quately dressed in waarmest claes

To fecht for life agin the kosmic cauld,
While some gat word direct o whit wes whit   380
By uninvitit visits frae the sea.
The baggage suin wes sooman in the hold,
The post-room floatit unforewarnan★ letters.   unwarning
Furnace-men raked out the byler fires
And clampit dampers on the double-ends,
As gin by an ill-disponit fae, informed
By his fifth-column in the sleepan Ship
Exactly whaur her ilka weakness lay,
The sea filled water-ticht compairtments up
Wi anaesthetic ocean that, as a puma   390
On a bison neck, wad pu her doun,
And aa our aeons' darg wad senseless droun.

The maister, and her last chief architect
Gaed glegly owre the Ship, and frae their notes
Wrocht out the facts that rammed their simple faith
And sank it – as the iceberg did the Ship.
The Ship that wes unsinkable wes sunk,
As a peace that is unbreakable gets broken,
Wars that are unlosable are tint★,   lost
Wisdom that is fule proof aye is fuled.   400
The reason that wes 'sound' wad sound the abyss.
The truth that wes unfautable wes faus.
The house sae stably foundit nou wes foundert.
Aa the darg o countless thousant years
Had come til this; Moses and Alexander,
Jesus and Caesar, Plato's ideal form
Wrecked on icy appearance, the noble dream
Luther and Knox midwived, o democratic
Christian socialism, wrecked on the bourgeois
Oligarchie o wealth and usurie.   410
Aa the money saved in aa the banks
Wes uisless nou, aa capital in vain
To wring a haet★ o profit frae this loss.   jot
Even a Rothschild had nae pouer nou
To save the Interest that rain had tint,
Nor bran new sauls til issue frae the Mint.
The boats, of course, could tak aff only hauf
The total complement o sauls on board.
Whit anes there were were juist as ornaments,
Or juist to keep up aabodie's morale,   420
Like gasmasks in lethal aerial war.

A Ship that canna sink suld need nae boats.
The passengers were telt to come on deck,
A mere formalitie, and to get the rich
Wemen and bairns intil whit boats there were –
Just until the Ship wes 'sound' again –
A nuisance, true, but just for safetie's sake,
To please *me*, dahling – well, the children, then –
An awful bore, my deah, of course, I know,
But then, the Regulations have it so!   430

Madam, pit aathin on that ye can wear –
The mirk nicht ye gang out intil is cauld,
And caulder still the water ye may end in.
Naethin ye could buy in Montparnasse
Wes fashioned quite for this, sae wear the lot,
Your shifts and knickers, petticoats and steys,
And gin ye hae a coat o polar bear
Pit that on tap, for little less'll dae
In this coorse airt. And wap up weel
The bairns – nane o them hae been   440
Conditioned for a nicht out on the seas
In temperature o twenty-echt degrees.

Forget your jewels and sic fripperies.
Ye'll no be needin them whaur you'll be gauin.
Aa that's precious nou is life itsel
And life for aa the fowk are dear til ye.
Leave that box alane, sir, wi its bonds
And stocks and shares, whit tho there be
A billion dollars wapped up in the lot –
Whit maitters nou's the flesh that haps your banes.   450
Davie Jones' locker'll staw your gains.

Lat aa your treisures gaing, whiteer they be.
There's room for nocht but life in thir wee boats,
And they hae no hauf room eneuch for that.
The Purser hes nae time to taigle★ wi   bother
Your gew-gaws, and your trinkets, and *your* 'ice'.
Pit doun your cairts, pit bye your chess:
Lock up the pantry, lock up the mess:
The bar abandon, and the lounge –
Never mind whit ye can scrounge,   460
For aa ye'se ever get for aa ye gave
Is freedom o the seas, a staneless grave.

Bylins, ae first rocket streaks the lift
Til hevin aspiran: slaws:
Falters: stops: and syne it fails
And bursts in a spray o Icarian lichts
That tells aa whit naebody believed –
Her maiden goal's a grave. In earnest
Fowk lookt nou til the boats, tho numb and loath.
Gie up a palace to gang in an open boat?   470
Is that no daft? Go in a boat?
It isn't done, my deah – have you,
Has anybody, ever heard of boating
But at Henley? Wouldn't one lose caste?
Let the third class go! – Na,
The yetts★ are lockt atween them and the boats,   gates
They cannae gang, the boats are for the few
Fittest, meant by Nature to survive –
And hae nae fear, the rabble'll no rebel
Agin their maisters. Some'll slip throu,   480
The gleg self-preservers, some prevail

Agin Authoritie's reluctant serfs
And chivalrie, a former code, will save
A handfu o the wemen and their brats,
But haill faimlies by God's decree'll droun,
The lesser orders. The boats, madam,
Are only for you and your bairns, and, gin there's room,
Your husbands and your dogs. No leave'm?
Leddy, Love itsel cannae save him nou,
Nor you, nor only gript in this Machine   490
Law o Nature. God made it, true,
But cannae renegue it, even for me and you.

Goodbye, dahling, I'll be coming soon!
Ae fond kiss, alas, indeed forever!
Bid your son fareweel, leddy, and sir,
Your darlin blue eed dochter gie a hug,
For them ye'se see nae mair, I dout,
For them ye'se see nae mair.
And you, my bonie, days-lang bride, fareweel.
Fareweel the dawn-roused cuddles in the bed,   500
The kisses that hae brunt intil my saul
As Psyche's oil in Eros' shouder brunt.
At least my daeth this consolation hes
That I'd as weel be daed as pairt frae thee –
Lassie, neer love anither as ye did me!

The Moses ben Jehovahs made a steir
That nae survivor's likely to forget.
This auld descendant o the desert god
Wha damned aa gods and goddesses but Himsel,
Jibbed at boardin the boat they led him til   510
But like a man, wad bide wi the ither men.
At this his wife, aaready aboard the boat,
Cam out again, and nocht short o force
Wad make her leave again her husband's side.
To share his ayebidan bed, they lat her bide.
But she wes no the only woman, tho,
That wadnae gang. Some were owre feart
And simply wadnae believe the Ship wes a grave.
Put to sea? In that! My deah, you're mad!
Ae bewtie wadna leave without her love   520
And in the queen o cabins, as I hope,
Met her final climax under him.
A girl gaed rinnan back, to miss the boat,
Because she'd left the photae o her lad
And wadnae gang without it, giean Love
The simple, saikless tribute o her life.
Petie the man duin out o sic a wife!

Yet mony's the man wad sneak in, gin he could,
And did, and even rushed the hendmaist boats,
Driven by the imperious will o Pan.   530
Husband begged for saik o pregnant wife
And wife implored – but implored in vain

The Regulation juist said 'men', and 'men',
Faithers, husbands, boys, are aa the same.
Some bit lads got by Authoritie,
The martinet that classed them aa as 'men',
But only at surrender o their sex
In wemen's claes — no juist laddies
Either, but the very 'owner' o the Ship.
He'd tak a chance, like ony profiteer: 540
But couardice peyed clearly better here.

Besides God's chosen Anglo-Saxon race
A feck inferi-oreigners were there.
Finns and Swedes, Italian, Spanish, French,
And laichest* o the laich of course, the Erse,   lowest
Wha spurned the honour they were duin —
To pass as honorary Englishmen.
The cream-puff-makers never got awa,
For they were neither passengers nor crew,
And furriners forby, fit only for   550
The kitchen jobs beneath a saxon's pride.
But in the engine-room the engineers
Never thocht to gang, but gied their lives
To lessen the catastrophe for some
Few, wha micht hae some wee chance
Gin there were nae explosions as the Ship
Upendit for her final, dounwart trip.

But wes there no nae ither ship nearbye
To succour ours and save a few mair sauls?
Ten mile awa there lay anither boat   560
Sensibly feart to sail amang the ice,
And as our guid Ship sank, she watcht the scene
Wi England's Nelson ee, watcht the rockets
Streak the pit-mirk nicht, idly amused
At the jollifications on the Unsinkable Ship.
The captain slept, and the wireless operator.
Ilka sign and signal frae our coffin
Aabody on board this boat misread,
As gin some ill Ingyne had decreeit
That nae intelligence should turn aside   570
The weird that It intendit us to dree*   suffer
Til aa its will wes wrocht upon our kind:
Till twa-thirds o our number had gane doun
To feed the crabs — a meal as rare
As caviar til the Glesca Gorbals puir.

Left on board, a silence fell owre aa,
The boats gane, binna the twa were stuck,
And nocht could keep the mind frae seein nou
The gret grave creepan up to tak
Baith Ship and fowk intil its hellish maw,   580
As gin a whale should swallow doun a flee,
And fowk as helpless as Giovanni in
The grip that dragged him screaman doun til hell,

Or Faust dragged doun by Mephistopheles
Or Milton's Satan cuist doun the abyss.
Nou's the time when aabody sees clear
Hou helpless is a nakit man agin
The infinite and man-ignoran kosmos
God sae set in motion sae lang syne.
Aa arrogance and earthly riches vain   590
Pride o gear, genius, wit, or wealth.
Walkin amang thir michty mills o God,
Man, by God's ain will, learns their laws
In labour and in pain, and learns to uis
The laws for his ain ends, mills o his ain,
And smites his chest, and says 'Behold whit I,
Man, the unconquered overlord o fate,
By my unaided effort have achieved!'
And aa the mills o God grind slawly on,
Indifferent til his boasts as til his weird,   600
Until ae day he slips, the fates conspire
Agin him, aa the mony things that micht
Hae come to save him never come, and he
Faas, and his machines wi him faa,
And merciless Realitie grinds wee,
And tho it seems, as nou, malignant fate
Had planned it aa to bring pretension laich,
In truth the kosmos bears nae mair ill-will
Til man nor ony ither intricate machine
That helps him live, sae langs he minds its laws,   610
But mangles careless bodies in its jaws.

Nou there's time to realise, at last,
That daeth's a sentence that hes nae reprieve:
That aa the chances nou hae near rin out:
That aabody's hauf-conscious belief
In his ain somehou survival, hes played faus:
That daeth. the ayebydan ocean, sall prevaill.
Some pit on their eening uniform,
Determined to gang doun like gentlemen.
Bairns are dazed, or whimper, wemen greit★   620   weep
Or get hysterical, distraucht, or mad.
Men prepare theirsels to fecht it out
Until the last tormentit gasp o time,
Gettan intil life-belts, warmer claes,
Or gettan rid a sick impediments
To risk aa on a fast swim til some boat.
Some sit smokin, some sit playan cairts.
A few cheat fate by forms o suicide.
The band aye plays its rag-time on the deck
Agin the kosmic symphonie o God   630
Til emphasise the aff-beat time o men.

Members o the crew work to try and get
The last two boats awa, some o them
Giean up their place in ither boats.
A single woman paced about the deck

Eftir giean ane wi bairns her place,
Bydan to pey the debt o heroism.
Nou there cam in droves up frae the depths
The Third-class sauls, the aye-to-be-wi-us puir.
The aye-expendable, aye unlucky puir –   640
Nou that there were nae mair lifeboats there.

Near the end, the jazzy music stopt:
Diviner harmonies were struck up syne,
As, eftir rebellious bairns hae run frae hame,
Hunger drives them back again for tea.
It's no nae ragtime rhythm rules the sea.

Byde nae langer, sir, the Ship's a tomb.
And as til Tiber ance Horatius trustit
Roman life and airms, sae maun ye
Trust Munitions Inc. intil the sea.   650
Jump faur out owre the side – O God!
A thousant knives stab through your ilka pore,
The hert is stoundit, braeth bereft. Skin
Utterly outraged, and the fleggit testes
Swarm up in the pelvis, and the brain
Warstles to recover frae the shock.
Strike out, strike out – No til the Ship!
As faur's ye can frae her – yon boat!
Christ, the cat-o-nine-tails o this cauld
Weakens the ablest bicep, and the hert   660
Is thrangan★ like a doctor danged til daeth   struck
Amang the casualties o Ypres or Mons.
Never hae men, even in France's glaur,
Dree'd sae muckle frae greed and *laissez-fair*.

Like gaean doun a lift-shaft, syne she sank,
And Nature took owre ance again frae Man.
As seamaws clek and clamour round a sewer,
Sae the nicht wes scarred by cries o fowk.
Hauf-filled boats plied on and left them there,
Feart lest rescue-wark sould cowp★ the boat.   670   overturn
Sae Christ wes tint for Darwin, in the end,
For only yae boat took on aa it could.
The broken unitie o Man and God,
The tint Communitie o the human race
That nicht reaped a Nemesis o daeth.
The jungle law killed human dignitie
And raw Nature took us owre again –
Nae ither life sae sacred as your ain.

Some dee'd by the water's first assault.
Ithers lingered on for near an hour.   680
Twa or three survived. Booze
Kept some alive, and baccy kept ithers
To thole★ the frozen aeons in the boats.   endure
And some gaed mad, or rang alarms,
Or raged and rantit at their fellae-fowk

As gin the wreck had been the Ship o Fools.
Some played Captain Oates, and swam awa
To dee whaur they wad least afflict their freends,
While some dragged ither sauls doun wi their ain.
Maist were deid lang or the hour wes up,   690
For ance mankind is peeled o aa its culture
And its art, the kosmic cauld suin kills.
Thae that had some bits o wuid and tar
To keep them frae Dame Nature's lethal kiss
Could sit and thole the cross o Nature's cauld
As best they could, or labour at oars, or ither
Hert-revivan service til their brither.

Them in the boats were bylins pickit up
And sailed on ither decks til ither warlds,
Leavan ahent, as faur's it can be left,   700
A warld that dee'd in facile optimism,
In creature irreligion til the Real.
If there'd been boats eneuch for aa the fowk . . .
If we'd but listened til the prophecies . . .
If we'd gane a wee thing further south . . .
If that bit of ice had no been there . . .
If the Rules had been mair up til date . . .
If a better look-out had been keepit . . .
If ithers had gotten there on time . . .
Ay, *if* we'd made her iceberg-proof as weill!   710
If this, if that, if yon, or yon, or yon –
But no – intil the kosmic machine
We fell, and nane cam to pu us out until
Mair nor hauf our complement wes deid.
We sawed the arctic waters wi our seed.

The Third-class bairns o workers dree'd the warst,
Their mithers neist, and syne their faithers third.
Neist cam Sacont-class weans, wemen, men
And last the First men, weans, wemen.
Aa revealan Nature's descendan stair,   720
(Binna for a few that broke her laws
Giean up, by Grace, their naitral richts,
The captain leadan – whit else could he dae?
Even a Hitler gangs doun wi his ship,)
Her laws o 'initiative,' pouer, and drive
By which the anti-social may survive.

III

Whaur will it end, afore it end us aa?
Wi juist as muckle pride, irreverence,
And want o sense and harmonie wi God,
The ancient 'fear o the Lord' that means 'respect   730
For aa the operations o the Real
Throu aa His kosmic infinite machine,'
We follaed up the Ship wi ae gret war,
Refused to change, sae anither follaed that,
And refusan to change, a cauld war follaed that,

And we stand the-day like a scorpion ringed wi fire,
Ready to sting our racial sel til daeth
Raither nor brek throu the bourgeois creed
That God and wise men clearly hae condemned
As utterly unreal and moribund.   740
Ither Ships we're biggan til the stars
Afore we've learned the lesson o the first
Ettlan to mak a mercat* o the kosmos,   market
Ruled by the Usurer and the Profiteer.
'Freedom' they shout, but slaverie they mean,
No juist for the mony that's exploitit,
But even for the damned exploitan few,
As ony psycho-analyst can tell ye,
Enslaved til neurotic illusion. 'Christ,'
They shout, and lucky it is for them that Yeshu   750
Isna by wi scourge in hand til answer.
They talk about a 'wey o life,' and aa
Historie echoes 'daeth, daeth, daeth.'
They rant o 'values' wha nae value ken
That cash registers arena fit to meisure.
They talk o 'morals,' and gaing on as afore
Corruptan generations, and their ain bleck sauls.
Pouer concentrates in fewer hands,
Fascism lost the war and won the peace,
The liberal lee rules the deludit West   760
And hands us owre to fascist generals . . .
Hou lang, hou lang, O Lord, sall we hae to dree
Helpless slaves in siccan miserie?

Sea-Dirge: A Mither's Keenin

I found him drowned on the rock that night
And the wind high; moonlight it was
And the hungry sucking of the sea
At my feet, stretching away in front of me.
Never a lover was laid on the braes that night
Nor any living soul I'm thinking, unless they were mad
And drawn to the moon. I found him there
In the rocks that night and the wind was high;
Bare he was as the sea and the rock, on either side,
With a rag of silk in his hand   10
And sand in his nose; moonlight it was
And the sea before me: my hair dragged at my eyes.

I couldn't see, but a hand of ice was plunged
Deep in my womb, I found him lying
Drowned on the rock that night and
The wind was high; moonlight it was
And the sea sucked at my feet.
Then I heard from the cave behind
The skirl of the piper who died on rocks,
The wail of the pipes and then the cry of his soul.

I upped and screamed at the wind and the sea,
I stripped my forsaken breasts to the moon   20
And I kissed the frost of his mouth and the sand.
I found him drowned on the rock that night
And the wind high; moonlight it was
And the hungry sucking of the sea
At my feet and his clammy head in my breasts
That were bare as the rock and the sea and the sand.

Elspeth Davie (1919 – 1995)

The Foothold

'Yes, you'll need to get every one of those boots and shoes back in their boxes before you've another on your hands,' said the manageress, who had come down to find the havoc on the ground floor and to hear the reason for it. 'That was the sort who doesn't know his own mind, never will know it, and wouldn't buy a shoelace even if he did. Turning up at closing-time and expecting all heaven and earth!'

The young man, Thomas, still new to the job, stared at a floor littered with shoes – shoes with their heels together and wide-open feet, boots flung in a Cossack dance of inturned toes and parted heels, some drawn up stiffly in pairs as if on parade, and all the rest stranded, the one from the other, in distant corners or washed up on their sides in waves of blue and white tissue paper. This was the way his customer had abandoned them, mixing wildness with neatness, satisfied with none – as utterly unsatisfied as it was possible for a man to be with a shoe.

Thomas picked them all up, put them in their boxes and piled them on the shelves. He straightened the chairs and stools, replaced the footmeasures and the shelf ladders. His own feelings were mixed. The man had been more than restless. He'd had the look of one who would always be desperate to be off, no matter where or how, with new shoes on his feet or without. It corresponded more or less to his own view of things. To Thomas no part of the present could ever be right. He looked ahead. Along with the annoyance went a touch of fellow-feeling for his customer.

'It puts people off to see the place like a jumble sale,' said Miss Borthwick. 'Naturally I have to remind you of certain things if I'm to go off on holiday knowing the place is all right. I want to enjoy myself. I want to have peace of mind!'

'But I hope you do,' said Thomas. Everyone hoped the manageress would find peace of mind and that some residue of it would penetrate the place from top to bottom on her return.

On Thursday she left. Holidays had already taken one man from the place. Thomas had now sole charge of the men's shoes, while a Mrs Kirk and the young girl, Julia, dealt with the women and children on the floor above. Thomas enjoyed the new freedom in the place. He was interested in every person who came in and had been from the start.

'That's only because you don't intend to stay,' said Mrs Kirk, 'filling in time until better turns up. If you had to do it month after month, year after year, it would be different. You can afford to be interested.'

This question was often discussed in a friendly enough way – how the restless or the lucky ones moved on. How others got stuck for life. Thomas gave every sign of being restless. Even when putting back shoes, he had a way of looking into the empty spaces between boxes as though they were so many escape holes through which one of these days he might easily pass. In the opinion of the others he hadn't the staying power for the job. He was knocked out by a heavy day. When it came to the bit, all he had was a good ear.

It was true that Thomas had his own peculiar kind of patience, and perhaps be-cause he meant to be off so soon, he listened well. He listened as though each particular shoe was on his own foot: the walking shoe, for instance, which – with a mere stroll to the door and back – began to press upon a toe with all the fiery hell that leather could exact from flesh, or the fashionable boot which let the toes spread and relax while raising instant, scorching blisters at the heel. He had to show that never-theless he liked shoes himself, and that his faith in a happy future life for feet could endure through all the cruel ordeals of fitting.

This particular afternoon in late autumn was no exception. He was busy for twenty minutes before closing-time and during the last hour he had listened to the longest stories of the day. The last man out claimed to have climbed all the mountains of the northwest in a pair of old plimsolls until the arches of his feet had fallen utterly and finally. He not only wanted support for his arches; he also demanded moral sup-port for the worthiness of the plimsoll venture. Thomas was condemned for refusing this and loudly cursed for offering advice in its stead.

Not long before him, a courteous old man had come in looking for slippers to re-place the pair that had gone with him into hospital. One slipper had dropped off while he was being trundled along between wards and – though every lift and corridor was searched – was never seen again. He was home now with three gallstones in a pillbox and one soft slipper and he wanted, if possible, an identical pair, to have three handy in case of other accidents. He found it unbelievable that five minutes later, here, in the last shop of all, identical slippers were found, and found to fit.

A lull came after five o'clock, not only inside the shop itself, but along the few yards of pavement outside and even in the air directly over it, as though a gap had opened at that spot in preparation for a new idea – the idea of night. Yet in some re-spects it was still the busiest time of the day. Some distance away on the north-south motorway, the subdued but steady roll of lorries could be heard. On the other side of the street, last-minute shoppers were crowding out of a butcher's shop, and further up on the same side the home-bound bus queue was growing longer every second. But now, here and there over the whole town, the gaps of night were opening.

Thomas went into the small room at the end of his department and plugged in an electric kettle. It was not much more than a curtained-off partition, but it had a small table, a chair called easy in relation to the hard ones outside, and in the corner a washbasin with a roller towel and a sliver of cracked soap. Old shoe shelves belonging to a former shop were still here, but someone had now put bowls of bulbs on them, a teapot and some cups. There were also a shabby manual of First Aid, a couple of paperback thrillers and the first volume of an Encyclopedia, A–Bamboccio.

Thomas switched off the kettle and heard, through a declining sigh of bubbling water, the bell of the outside door. He parted the curtains and looked out. The line of back-to-back chairs was empty, but over in the far corner, scanning the shelves, was a young man. There was no mistaking the long, narrow back in the brown jacket. At once Thomas recognised his customer who, a few days before, had been prepared to discard shoes by the dozen. He was not only scanning boxes. Sometimes as he moved quickly along he would touch one, even shift it a little to look behind.

'Can I help?' said Thomas loudly from between the curtains. It was a phrase which never failed to irritate independent searchers for shoes. Thomas himself had a dislike for it. He seldom uttered it. Yet it had its uses. This particular customer however either missed the ironic note or was stubborn to a degree. 'Can I help?' said Thomas again, coming quickly forward through the shop, for several boxes now had their lids off. The young man turned without hurry, quietly bringing his hands down to his sides. For the second time that week they faced one another. Again Thomas saw the oval head, the pale, Modigliani face, egg-shaped, above the long neck. A blue shirt opened back from collarbones as sharp as winter twigs. The wrists were long, the ankles thin – Thomas remembered for he had seen these ankles. The pale brown hair was smooth as a cap and, either combed or blown that way, it formed a sleek little cone on top of his head. His look was neither hostile nor friendly. He waited. If Thomas had felt sympathy before, this time his heart sank. A second time round could bring more awkward things to light. It was nothing about the man, he told himself – simply that it was late. Time to be home.

'Can you – *can* you help?' said the young man suddenly. The trite phrase was echoed with such deadly seriousness that Thomas was silent for a moment while a pair of intent eyes searched his own.

'I can simply show you, more or less, what I showed you last time,' he said. 'You weren't, if you remember, very pleased with our stock. But I can bring them all out again, and one or two more if that's what you want to see.' The man moved to a chair and quickly untied the laces of his shoes. Thomas went to the shelves and began to look for the eights in walking shoes. He knew, as he shifted boxes and opened lids, that this was simply a repeat of the time before. He was certain the outcome would be the same. The difference lay in himself. He had long ago made up his mind that at five-thirty on the dot the place would be shut, the CLOSED placard hung on the door.

'But we measured you last time,' he said when he'd climbed down, his arms full of shoes, to find the young man with his foot already on the slanted board and sliding the rule towards his big toe.

'To make sure,' murmured the other. He took one shoe from the pair Thomas offered and examined it carefully, turning it over to look at the sole and sliding his hand inside before trying it on. But almost before his heel was in he shook his head.

'But tie it up first!' said Thomas. More vigorously the customer shook his head, returning it to the floor with one sharp kick of his foot. He tried the buckled shoes after the laced ones, the plastic shoes after the expensive leather, the black and tan suedes and the brown pigskin. All these he rejected.

It was two minutes past the half-hour. Mrs Kirk and Julia had come down together from the floor above and were now standing at the door looking out into the street. They were not worried about locking up. This they shared with Thomas on alternate nights. They were discussing whether it was worth putting up umbrellas for the first few drops of rain. Mrs Kirk with a hairset to preserve decided for it. Thomas watched them making for the bus stop, now separated from one another by deep, transparent umbrellas which came down almost to their waists. He missed their com-pany. Usually all three would stand and talk at the door. Tonight they had not given even one backward glance down the long shop.

'You tried those buckled ones before. They were too large,' said Thomas, 'but the first pair looked good. The fit was right. Try them again. I've got them in black as well, with a slightly built-up heel. Or if you'd care to try . . .'

'Oh, it is not the shape, the cut, the colour!' cried the young man. 'It is ease, *ease* I'm after!' Taken aback, Thomas stared down at him. Yet what was unnerving about this cry? Much the same plea could be heard a dozen, dozen times a day in the place. The brand-names of shoes spelt ease. The posters promised it. Day in, day out, the problem of comfort was thrashed out between these walls, moving from ardent will-to-believe to downright scepticism. Yet how different was this cry – wrung from a heart and not a foot! Its force was such that Thomas exclaimed with feeling: 'You'll get it. I can promise you that.'

'Don't think I'll give up, for I will not,' answered the young man. 'Oh, I *will not!*'

Thomas took a step back, breathing quickly. Quickly he resumed the salesman role. 'Then try other places,' he said. 'You've seen all our stuff and we can't help you. You'll find other shoes, no doubt – other shoes for your walks.'

'Walks!' cried his customer instantly. 'Do you call it that? This never-ending, never-resting plod. This ceaseless, useless search!' He had the loose, buckled shoe on one foot and leaning forward, he kicked it off with such violence that it flew up toward the far corner and landed soft as a cat on the rug at the foot of the stairs. 'Walks!' he exclaimed again with quieter scorn.

Thomas had not turned round. He sat forward, elbow on knee, his chin in his hand. A passer-by seeing them might imagine they had a problem to solve. A chess-board would have seemed more fitting between them than the footrest. It was very still inside the shop, but now and then there came a tentative needle-prick of rain at the windows.

'I am closing the shop now,' said Thomas quietly, making no move but looking obliquely past the feet of his customer. 'Don't, please, come back. There's nothing for you here. If it's shoes you want they'd better be made to measure. Go to someone who'll help – someone who knows the problem.'

'*You* will help,' said the young man, bending close. '*You* know the problem. You too are restless. Rootless. You are unfixed. Footloose you call it. Already malcontent.' A grimace drew the mouth down. 'You long to be, perhaps – a free spirit!'

Thomas sprang to his feet and went quickly to the shelves, grabbing up shoe boxes on the way. He pitched them in wherever there were spaces. Sizes and colours went by the board. He was noisy about it as he dragged the short ladder round with him, but he spoke only once to the figure in the centre of the room. 'No, no, I am not restless, not discontented,' he said as he crossed to the opposite wall. Again he climbed and searched for spaces, peering, tapping and leveling off boxes with the palm of his hand. This anxious search had changed his appearance. For the moment confidence had gone. At last he hurried to the room at the back and came out with a card on a string. 'Closed!' he shouted as he reached the outer door and threw it wide. The room, as if sealed for decades, burst open with noise. A long vehicle was going slowly past with a deck of cars, rattling and straining in their chains. In front was a lorry-load of beer barrels, and behind three motor cyclists had come to a shattering halt at the lights. This sudden bombardment swallowed up any sound that might have been made by the one late customer of the shoe shop as he brushed past Thomas in the doorway.

Thomas didn't wait to see more. He hung up the sign inside, then went quickly back to the small, inner room and drew the curtains. Tonight he was conscious that this dingy place with its bulb-bowls and cake-tins had an almost homely atmosphere compared to the outer room. It had the dusty smell of safety. He reminded himself that like everyone else he had ties he could break or renew, a home from which he could escape or return. But he was formidably tired. He sat on. It was long after six when he finally left the place and locked the shop behind him for the night.

Ten days later he was inclined to laugh at the idea of being put out, even in the smallest degree, by any customer – let alone one who had never bought shoes. Since then a crowd of people had passed through his hands. Some had been every bit as demanding as the young man. All of them had talked more. There were restless ones amongst them. It was not uncommon to hear how they too had walked and searched and longed for something or other, if not shoes then some other article. Or a room, a job, a person. There was nothing strange about this endless search, though it was true each story started in much the same way with feet. But the discomforts of feet quickly led to discomforts of the heart – how someone had walked in shoes, grown savagely tight, from street to street, directed by inquisitive landladies, looking for friend or lover who'd left no hint of an address. One young man complained bitterly of his cheap slippers with their uneven heels. He had fallen down and slid on his bottom in a dance. Made to feel clumsy as hell in front of someone who hated . . . who couldn't stand the idea of anyone . . .

'I see,' Thomas had said, '. . . anyone who's not absolutely sure on his feet . . . not footloose.' Yet 'footloose' missed the mark. He was uneasy as soon as it was out of his mouth, remembering how and when the word had been last spoken, on a day he'd taken pains to forget. He listened to all these stories, long and short. Yet why, he asked himself, give a patient ear to these young men and not to the other?

'Some people,' he said to Mrs Kirk as they locked up after a busy day, 'are never, never satisfied. I can understand that. I can cope with it. What I can't take are the desperate ones.'

'Desperate?' she replied. 'Well, I can't say I come across many like that. We've had the violent ones, of course. Don't let them get a foot in the door. Once they've a foot in they'll be back and back. They see your comings and goings. They know when you're alone. But desperate – no. I can't say that would bother me too much.' She paused and thought about it. 'You think I'm hard?'

'No – very sensible,' said Thomas.

She accepted this compliment without enthusiasm. 'Anyway,' she remarked briskly as she went out, 'Miss Borthwick won't find much to complain about when she gets back. Everything's gone smoothly, very, very smoothly indeed.'

'Has everything gone smoothly, Julia?' Thomas asked the girl as she came downstairs.

'Oh, like a swim round a whirlpool!' But there was sympathy in her glance. The manageress might or might not come back with peace of mind, but she knew it was something this young man had lost. Whether he'd ever had it she couldn't tell. It was not in him now.

September was nearly over. Within two or three days people had changed from cotton into wool and back again to cotton. Still in summer sandals, they brooded over fleece-lined boots. Yet suddenly the sun, hotter than ever, would come back to ripen more fruit on the allotments and lift the battered heads of chrysanthemums from garden fences. In a day or two it was the wind again, an early darkness and floods of rain. Thomas's restlessness came back with a vengeance. His moods changed. On good days distance meant nothing. The ends of the earth could be reached. He would then become so tired, imagining himself where he was not, that sometimes he'd have to leave the outer shop and go back for a few minutes to the room behind the curtains. There he would sit taking great breaths of the stuffy air, his head spinning. But on dark days, silent and inturned, he looked at distances inside himself far more disturbing, more alien, than a mere traveller's view.

'Never mind,' said Julia, who sensed a change in him, 'no doubt you'll be leaving us soon. Moving on as you've always meant to. Lucky you have the chance.'

'It's not so easy – not as easy as you think,' said Thomas who had grown silent in the last days.

'Brooding,' said Mrs Kirk to Julia later on, 'because he's had no holiday. But what does he expect? He made it clear he wouldn't stay. He needs the break, of course. You've only to look at him compared to one month back. He has rather a wintry face.'

On Tuesday – the last day of the month and two days before Miss Borthwick was due to return – it was already dark at three-thirty. The lights went on in the shop. At four when it brightened they were turned off, and went on again at five. The streets were already lit. In the west the black spires and chimneys lay against a gash in the sky which was rapidly closing into one narrow slit of brilliant light.

'I smell water,' said a late customer as, watched by his wife, he bent to lace his shoes. 'There'll be a downpour before night.' He was a keen fisher, he told Thomas. He knew about weather. 'Do you ever think, in your job, of all the sayings connected with feet?' he said as he stood up to test the shoes.

'"Putting one's foot in it",' said his wife.

'"Standing on one's own feet", "Having both feet on the ground",' said the fisherman. 'That's the one for me when I'm up to my thighs in the current and there's a whacking great fish on the line . . . '

'Oh, these great fish . . . ' murmured his wife.

'And you?' said the man with a shrewd glance at Thomas. 'It's not your favourite, I daresay – not those two feet firmly planted.'

'Why should it be?' said his wife. 'He's far too young for that.'

'What's age to do with it? It's a matter of common sense, of not being swayed.'

'He has lots of time.'

'Has he? Not like me you mean, with my one foot in the grave. No no, these ones aren't comfortable, I'm afraid.'

'They're soft,' said Thomas, 'and your foot could work into them.'

But the man was not the sort to be budged, no matter what currents flowed around. They were the last to leave from the men's department. Three women came down from the upper floor with their shoes in green and white carrier bags, and one child in new, red sandals whose eyes never left her feet as she went down. Mrs Kirk would now be clearing the long room above. At the far end Julia would be looking over the day's accounts. It was their turn to lock up.

The gap in the day came at five-fifteen. Thomas went softly round the walls putting in boxes here and there, and very quietly – not to disturb the unexpected calm – lifted the stools and chairs into place. It was so silent that at twenty-five past, Mrs Kirk came down a few stairs and looked over the banister. 'Why Thomas, for a moment I thought you were away!' she exclaimed.

'Not yet,' said Thomas.

'It's very nearly the half-hour.'

'Soon,' said Thomas. 'Don't hurry me. I've still got things to do.'

'I'm *not* hurrying you, Thomas. Just reminding you of the time.' She disappeared up the few stairs.

Thomas went through to the room at the back. This evening he prepared for his departure with particular care. He washed his hands with the new piece of lemon soap which the manageress kept for her own use, and dried them on a clean towel he found in the table drawer. As he combed his hair he examined himself critically in the mirror. He expected to look tired, but tonight he saw it had gone further than that. This was bone-tiredness. This was the kind that scarred the face and laid a purple shadow in the socket of the eye. Thomas took his jacket from its hook, but before putting it on, he sat down and reached for the first book on the pile beside him. Years ago someone had swotted up South America, and further on – though less industriously – the Atom, for the Encyclopedia opened easily on both sections. He turned in a desultory way from one to the other, reading a sentence or two from each. A page on the Amazon had been well thumbed. In spite of tiredness his interest quickened. From descriptions of the great river he ran forwards through a spinning universe of electrons, extricated himself, and turned back again to steer down river amongst rimmed, polished leaves large as floating platforms. There was no sound but a regular drip-drip of water falling from dense curtains of trees and plants which shut out the burning tropical sun on either side.

Thomas raised his head and stared straight through the slit in the curtains, through the shop, and out between a couple of window posters proclaiming: 'New styles in Freedom and Comfort.' Outside on the pavement, his head bisected by a poster, stood a customer. The half-face, touching the glass, stared in at him. Thomas moved back an inch. He held the book in his hands, still with his head bent absorbedly over it. But his hearing had sharpened dramatically. His room was not silent. It held his breathing and his heart-beat. It had a ticking watch and a dripping tap, and once, from the shelves overhead, came the light, familiar snapping of old wood fractured by decades of traffic. He heard the bell of the opening door and he heard the door pressed shut. There was a pause, and then a soft tread through the shop. The curtains parted.

The young customer stood quietly looking down. There was no change in his outward appearance. He wore the brown jacket and the blue shirt, still open-necked in spite of colder days. The wind had not touched his hair, for it was still in its smooth cone on top of his head. Yet in other ways he was greatly changed. There was no hint of the man who'd kicked up havoc amongst shoes. He showed no sign of impatience but stood smiling, holding the folds of cloth behind him with both hands like a confident actor appearing before the curtain long after it has gone down. His steady eyes held Thomas. If need be, he could wait forever.

'Oh – you are not after *shoes!*' murmured Thomas, leaning back.

'Company,' replied the other softly, 'company in my search!'

'What search?' said Thomas, raising an arm across his face. 'What is it you want?'

'A foothold,' replied the young man, letting go of the curtain and stepping inside. 'A life for a life cut short. I am looking for it. For lost years. A foothold is all I ask. And company – yes, company in my search!'

Thomas sprang through the curtains with a loud cry and ran through the shop. There was the sound of a stool clattering over, a rustling of paper, and one minute later the two women had run the full length of the floor above and were down the stairs on one another's heels.

Thomas lay at the bottom on his side, one arm across his eyes, the other laid on the wall with the hand outspread. Mrs Kirk, detaching this hand, found it cold. There was a small draught coming from behind and she took off her outdoor coat and put it over him. All they could see of his face were the pale, tight lips stubbornly set against all the calling and coaxing in the world. Yet as the girl ran to the phone he suddenly raised his head.

'Oh, Thomas – for a moment I thought you were away!' cried Mrs Kirk for the second time within the hour.

'Not yet,' said Thomas. 'Don't hurry me.'

'Don't joke about it, Thomas! You frightened us.'

'Soon. But not yet,' said Thomas again. 'Don't hurry me.'

Five minutes later, refusing all help from the two women, he stood up on his feet. Their advice was not welcome and his indifference alarmed them. They had almost ceased to exist. Mrs Kirk doubted whether he remembered the dragged curtain or the upset stool. For him, her coat lying below the stairs might have been some old, cast-off rug. They watched silently as he walked to the door and opened it. But from the threshold he looked back. *'Not yet, not yet!'* shouted Thomas through the shop. *'I have still got things to do!'* Gaping at his sudden harangue, the women watched him step out on to the pavement and stagger as the wind caught him. For a moment, before locking up, they waited in the doorway, then discreetly, at some distance, followed on down the street.

For a while the lights of cars, stopping and starting, swept the empty room. White boxes on the ends of shelves were highlighted, a foot-mirror flashed, and from time to time the headlamps of a late lorry would slowly circle the room from floor to ceiling with a bold, yellow glare. But gradually, as the night went on, fewer and fewer cars passed the windows of the shop. Between three o'clock and five there were none, and no pedestrian went by. The wind died down. The litter of the streets settled again, and there was a total silence along the pavements. Yet here and there on the floor of the shoe-shop small scraps of blue and white tissue paper were uneasily stirring, caught in a thin, persistent draught from the back.

Hamish Henderson (1919 – 2002)

Henderson served in North Africa during World War II. His only book of verse, *Elegies for the Dead in Cyrenaica* (1948), is based on this experience. It is surely one of the finest war poems in English. The author published a fairly extensive set of notes for the volume. All the notes here given with the *Elegies* are by Henderson.

The *Elegies* are sometimes difficult, because Henderson has used a wealth of literary or historical allusions – many associated with the North African locale – to comment on the cyclical nature of war and man's folly. Perhaps the poet's intentions can best be summed up by quoting two of his own lines:

'I will bear witness.' (l. 58)
'It had all happened before.' (l. 464)

Elegies for the Dead in Cyrenaica

Prologue
(for John Speirs)
Obliterating face and hands
The dumb-bell guns of violence

Show up our godhead for a sham.
Against the armour of the storm
I'll hold my human barrier,
Maintain my fragile irony.
I've walked this brazen clanging path
In flesh's brittle arrogance
To chance the simple hazard, death.
Regretting only this, my rash   10
Ambitious wish in verse to write
A true and valued testament.

Let my words knit what now we lack
The demon and the heritage
And fancy strapped to logic's rock.
A chastened wantonness, a bit
That sets on song a discipline,
A sensuous austerity.

PART ONE

Alles geben Gotter, die unendlichen,
Ihren Lieblingen ganz.
Alle Freuden, die unendlichen,
Alle Schmerzen, die unendlichen, ganz.
— GOETHE[1]

First Elegy

End of a Campaign

There are many dead in the brutish desert,
      who lie uneasy   20
among the scrub in this landscape of half-wit
stunted ill-will. For the dead land is insatiate
and necrophilous. The sand is blowing about still.
Many who for various reasons, or because
      of mere unanswerable compulsion, came here
and fought among the clutching gravestones,
shivered and sweated,
cried out, suffered thirst, were stoically silent, cursed
the spittering machine-guns, were homesick for Europe
and fast embedded in quicksand of Africa   30
      agonised and died.
And sleep now. Sleep here the sleep of the dust.

---

[1] Goethe's quatrain was frequently included in small anthologies 'for the Front' carried by German soldiers in the field – and indeed its thought lies very near the mood of many of them. One might translate it as follows:
    'The gods, the unending, give all things without stint to their beloved: all pleasures, the unending – and all pains, the unending, without stint.'

There were our own, there were the others.
Their deaths were like their lives, human and animal.
There were no gods and precious few heroes.
What they regretted when they died had nothing to do with
          race and leader, realm indivisible,
laboured Augustan speeches or vague imperial heritage.
(They saw through that guff before the axe fell.)
           Their longing turned to   40
the lost world glimpsed in the memory of letters:
an evening at the pictures in the friendly dark,
two knowing conspirators smiling and whispering secrets;
      or else
a family gathering in the homely kitchen
with Mum so proud of her boys in uniform:
           their thoughts trembled
between moments of estrangement, and ecstatic moments
of reconciliation: and their desire
crucified itself against the unutterable shadow of someone   50
whose photo was in their wallets.
Then death made his incision.

There were our own, there were the others.
Therefore, minding the great word of Glencoe's
son, that we should not disfigure ourselves
with villainy of hatred; and seeing that all
have gone down like curs into anonymous silence,
I will bear witness for I knew the others.
Seeing that littoral and interior are alike indifferent
and the birds are drawn again to our welcoming north   60
why should I not sing *them*, the dead, the innocent?

Second Elegy

Halfaya
(For Luigi Castigliano)

At dawn, under the concise razor-edge
of the escarpment, the laager sleeps. No petrol fires yet
blow flame for brew-up. Up on the pass a sentry
inhales his Nazionale. Horse-shoe curve of the bay
grows visible beneath him. He smokes and yawns.
Ooo-augh,
        and the limitless
shabby lion-pelt of the desert completes and rounds
his limitless ennui.   70

At dawn, in the gathering impetus of day, the laager sleeps.
Some restless princes dream: first light denies them
the luxury of nothing. But others their mates more lucky
drown in the lightless grottoes. (Companionable death has lent
them his ease for a moment).
        The dreamers remember
a departure like a migration. They recall a landscape

associated with warmth and veils and pantomime
but never focused exactly. The flopping curtain
reveals scene-shifters running with freshly painted   80
incongruous sets. Here childhood's prairie garden
looms like a pampas, where grown-ups stalk (gross outlaws)
on legs of tree trunk:recedes: and the strepitant jungle
dwindles to scruff of shrubs on a docile common,
all but real for a moment, then gone.

The sleepers turn
gone but still no nothing laves them.
O misery, desire, desire, tautening cords of the bedrack!
Eros, in the teeth of Yahveh and his tight-lipped sect
confound the deniers of their youth! Let war lie wounded!   90
Eros, grant forgiveness and release
and return – against which they erect it,
the cairn of patience. *No dear, won't be long now*
keep fingers crossed, chin up, keep smiling darling
be seeing you soon.

On the horizon fires fluff now,
further than they seem.

      Sollum and Halfaya
a while yet before we leave you in quiet
and our needle swings north.   100

      The sleepers toss
and turn before waking: they feel through their blankets
the cold of the malevolent bomb-thumped desert,
impartial
hostile to both.

The laager is one.
Friends and enemies, haters and lovers
both sleep and dream.

Third Elegy [1]

Leaving the City

Morning after. Get moving. Cheerio. Be seeing you
when this party's over. Right, driver, get weaving.

The truck pulls out
along the corniche. We dismiss with the terseness   110
of a newsreel the casino and the column,
the scrofulous sellers of obscenity,
the garries, the girls and the preposterous skyline.

---

[1] The quotations in this poem are from 'The God Leaves Anthony' by the Greek Alexandrian poet,
C.P. Cavafy (1868–1933). In Cavafy's poem, Alexandria is a symbol of life itself.

Leave them. And out past the stinking tanneries,
the maritime Greek cafes, the wogs and the nets
drying among seaweed. Through the periphery of the city
itching under flagrant sunshine. Faster. We are nearing
the stretch leading to the salt-lake Mareotis.
Sand now, and dust-choked fig-trees. This is the road
where convoys are ordered to act in case of ambush.   120
A straight run through now to the coastal sector.
One sudden thought wounds: it's a half-hour or over
since we saw the last skirt. And for a moment we regret
the women, and the harbour with a curve so perfect
it seems it was drawn with the mouseion's protractor.

Past red-rimmed eye of the salt-lake. So long then,
holy filth of the living. We are going to the familiar
filth of your negation, to rejoin the proletariat
of levelling death. Stripes are shed and ranks levelled
in death's proletariat. There the Colonel of Hussars,   130
the keen Sapper Subaltern with a first in economics
and the sergeant well known in international football
crouch with Jock and Jame in their holes like helots.
Distinctions become vain, and former privileges quite pointless
in that new situation. See our own and the opponents
advance, meet and merge: the commingled columns
lock, strain, disengage and join issue with the dust.

Do not regret
that we have still in history to suffer
or comrade that we are the agents   140
of a dialectic that can destroy us
but like a man prepared, like a brave man
bid farewell to the city, and quickly
move forward on the road leading west by the salt-lake.
Like a man for long prepared, like a brave man,
like to the man who was worthy of such a city
be glad that the case admits no other solution,
acknowledge with pride the clear imperative of action
and bid farewell to her, to Alexandria, whom you are losing.

And these, advancing from the direction of Sollum,   150
swaddies in tropical kit, lifted in familiar vehicles
are they mirage – ourselves out of a mirror?
No, they too, leaving the plateau of Marmarica
for the serpentine of the pass, they advancing towards us
along the coast road, are the others, the brothers
in death's proletariat, they are our victims and betrayers
advancing by the sea-shore to the same assignation.
We send them our greetings out of the mirror.

Fourth Elegy

El Adem

Sow cold wind of the desert. Embittered
reflections on discomfort and protracted absence.   160
Cold, and resentment stirred at this seeming
winter, most cruel reversal of seasons.
The weather clogs thought: we give way to griping
and malicious ill-turns, or instinctive actions
appearing without rhyme or reason. The landsknechte
read mail, play scat, lie mute under greatcoats.
We know that our minds are as slack and rootless
as the tent-pegs driven into cracks of limestone,
and we feel the harm of inaction's erosion.
We're uneasy, knowing ourselves to be nomads,   170
impermanent guests on this bleak moon-surface
of dents and ridges, craters and depressions.
Yet they make us theirs: we know it, and abhor them,
vile three in one of the heretic desert,
sand rock and sky . . . And the sow wind, whipping
the face of a working (or a dying) unit
who shoulders his shovel with corpse obedience.

The sons of man
grow and go down in pain: they kneel for the load
and bow like brutes, in patience accepting the burden,
the pain fort and dour . . . Out of shuttered Europe   180
not even a shriek or a howl for its doomed children
is heard through the nihilist windvoice. Tomorrow's victors
survey with grief too profound for mere lamentation
their own approaching defeat: while even the defeated
await dry-eyed their ineluctable triumph.
Cages are crammed: on guard crouch the fearful oppressors
and wait for their judgment day.
        Therefore recollecting
the ice-bound paths, and now this gap in the minefields
through which (from one side or the other) all must pass   190
shall I not speak and condemn?

Or must it always
seem premature: the moment always at hand,
and never arriving, to use
our rebellious anger for breaking
the vicious fetters that bind us?

Endure, endure. There is as yet no solution
and no short cut, no escape and no remedy
but our human iron.
        And this Egypt teaches us   200
that mankind, put to the torment, can bear
on their breast the stone tomb of immolation
for millennia. The wind. We can build our cairn.

Fifth Elegy

Highland Jebel

(for John Lorne Campbell)

Was ist es, das an die alten seligen Kusten mich
fesselt, dass ich sie mehr liebe als mein eigenes Land?
— HOELDERLIN

Our eyes, fatigued by the unsearchable desert's
moron monotony, lifted to the hills.

Strong-winged
our homing memory held us
on an unerring course: soared, leaving behind it
in an instant camp, coast-line and city,
sea, imbecile wasteland and the black sierras   210
for a well-known house.
        It found the treeless machair,
took in bay and snub headland, circled kirkyard and valley
and described once again our love's perfect circuit
till, flying to its own,
it dashed itself against the unresponsive windows.

So we waited
and lifted our eyes to
the hills, whence comes aid.

In our ears a murmur   220
of wind-borne battle. Herons stalk
over the blood-stained flats. Burning byres
come to my mind. Distance blurs
motive and aim. Dark moorland bleeding
for wrong or right.
Sons of the hounds
Come here and get flesh. Search, bite!

In what deep antre
of death is there refuge
from this living rock?   230

Beyond the gate of the pass
are a high and a low road: but neither
is the road back. No, laochain,[1] they must lead us
to the hauteur of battle. Must array, enroll us
among listening cohorts. Where both vaunting and atonement
remain muffled for ever. The caverns will number
our momentary cries among the stounds and echoes
of this highland's millennial conflict.
Another falls for Hector.[2]

---

[1] Literally means 'little hero'. Familiar term of endearment for a young lad in Gaelic.
[2] Patroclus: I was thinking also of the war cry of the Macleans who died in defence of their chief at
Inverkeithing: *Fear eile airson Eachainn* (Another for Hector).

Again there!
                          Aye, in spite of   240
the houses lying cold, and the hatred that engendered
the vileness that you know, we'll keep our assignation
with the Grecian Gael. (And those others). Then foregather
in a gorge of the cloudy jebel
older than Agamemnon.

Travelling light, and making the most of
the early coolness, we'll come before morning
to the raw uplands, and then by evening greet you
in the wilderness of your white corries, Kythairon.   250

INTERLUDE

Opening of an Offensive

   (a) the waiting

Armour has foregathered, snuffling
through tourbillions of fine dust.
The crews don't speak much. They've had
last brew-up before battle. The tawny
deadland lies in a silence
not yet smashed by salvoes.
No sound reaches us
from the African constellations.
The low ridge too is quiet.
But no fear we're sleeping,   260
no need to remind us
that the nervous fingers of the searchlights
are nearly meeting and time is flickering
and this I think in a few minutes
while the whole power crouches for the spring.
X – 20 in thirty seconds. Then begin

   (b) the barrage

Let loose (rounds)
the exultant bounding hell-harrowing of sound.
Break the batteries. Confound
the damnable domination. Slake   270
the crashing breakers-húrled rúbble of the guns.
Dithering darkness, we'll wake you! Hell's bell's
blind you. Be broken, bleed
deathshead blackness!
         The thongs of the livid
firelights lick you
        jagg'd splinters rend you
                    underground
we'll bomb you, doom you, tomb you into grave's mound

(c) the Jocks

They move forward into no man's land, a vibrant sounding board.
       As they advance   281
the guns push further murderous music.
Is this all they will hear, this raucous apocalypse?
The spheres knocking in the night of Heaven?
The drummeling of overwhelming niagara?
No! For I can hear it! Or is it? . . . tell
me that I can hear it! Now – listen!

       Yes, hill and shieling
sea-loch and island, hear it, the yell
of your war-pipes, scaling sound's mountains   290
guns thunder drowning in their soaring swell!
– The barrage gulfs them: they're gulfed in the clumbering guns,
gulfed in gloom, gloom. Dumb in the blunderbuss black –
lost – gone in the anonymous cataract of noise.
Now again! The shrill war-song: it flaunts
aggression to the sullen desert. It mounts. Its scream
tops the valkyrie, tops the colossal
        artillery.

Meaning that many
German Fascists will not be going home   300
meaning that many
will die, doomed in their false dream
We'll mak siccar![1]
Against the bashing cudgel
against the contemptuous triumphs of the big battalions
mak siccar against the monkish adepts
of total war against the oppressed oppressors
mak siccar against the leaching lies
against the worked out systems of sick perversion
mak siccar   310
        against the executioner
against the tyrannous myth and the real terror
mak siccar

---

[1] Mak siccar (make sure). One of the famous phrases of mediaeval Scottish history. After Bruce had stabbed the Red Comyn in Dumfries Kirk he was found outside the building by Lindsay and Kirkpatrick. Lindsay asked if Comyn were dead. Bruce replied that he didn't know. 'Aweel,' said Kirkpatrick, 'I'll mak siccar.'

PART TWO

'Na shuidhe marbh an 'Glaic a' Bhàis'
fo Dhruim Ruidhìseit,
gille òg 's a logan sìos m' a ghruaidh
's a thuar grìsionn.

Smaoinich mi air a' chòir 's an àgh,
a fhuair e bho Fhurair,
bhith tuiteam ann an raon an àir
gun éirigh tuilleadh

Ge b'e a dheòin-san no a chàs,
a neo-chiontas no mhìorun,
cha do nochd e toileachadh 'na bhàs
fo Dhruim Ruidhìseit.
— SOMHAIRLE MAC GHILL-EATHAIN[1]

Sixth Elegy

Acroma

Planning and execution
recede: the preliminary inertia,
the expectation, the lull, the relaxing and the encounter's
suddenness recede, become history:
                          thrusts, sieges and feints
that still blood maps with arrows
and left dead like refuse, these are the basis   320
of battle studies. And we're no better. The lying films
contain greater truth than most of our memories.

And the participants? — Staff Officers consider,
discuss and record their provisional verdicts.
These were go-getters, professional outflankers,
capable assault troops, or specialists in night warfare;
while those others had guts and lacked training, yet put up
a decent enough show at Himeimat or Munassib.
Occasionally there are doubts, dispute becomes acrimonious,
the case is not proven, judgment must be deferred.   330
On one point however there is unanimity: their sacrifice
though hard and heroic was on the whole 'necessary.'
I too have acquiesced
in this evasion: that the unlucky
or the destined must inevitably fall
and be impaled on the basalt pinnacles of darkness.

---

[1] The sceptical ironic spirit of a Gaelic poet who fought in the desert and was wounded at El Alamein. Sorley MacLean translates his own poem thus:
    'Sitting dead in 'Death Valley' below the Ruweisat Ridge, a boy with his forelock down about his cheek and his face slate-grey. I thought of the right and joy he had from his Fuehrer, of falling in the field of slaughter to rise no more . . . Whatever his desire or mishap, his innocence or malignance, he showed no pleasure in his death below the Ruweisat Ridge.'

Yet how can I shame them, saying that they
have died for us: that it was expedient
a generation should die for the people?

To justify them, what byways must I follow?   340
Into what inaccessible sierras
of naked acceptance, where mere reason cannot live,
where love shines like a glacier. Could I ever attain it?
Neither by dope of reportage, nor by anodyne of statistics
is *their* lot made easier: laughing couples at the tea-dance
ignore their memory, the memoirs almost slight them
and the queue forming up to see Rangers play Celtic
forms up without thought to those dead. – O, to right them
what requiem can I sing in the ears of the living?

No blah about their sacrifice: rather tears or reviling   350
of the time that took them, than an insult so outrageous.
All barriers are down: in the criss-crossed enclosures
where most lie now assembled in their aching solitude
those others lie too – who were also the sacrificed
of history's great rains, of the destructive transitions.
This one beach where high seas have disgorged them like flotsam
reveals in its nakedness their ultimate alliance.

So the words that I have looked for, and must go on looking for,
are words of whole love, which can slowly gain the power
to reconcile and heal. Other words would be pointless.   360

Seventh Elegy

Seven Good Germans

The track running between Mekili and Tmimi was at one time a kind of no-man's-land. British patrolling was energetic, and there were numerous brushes with German and Italian elements. El Eleba lies about half-way along this track.

> Of the swaddies
who came to the desert with Rommel
there were few who had heard (or would hear) of El Eleba.
They recce'd,
> or acted as medical orderlies
or patched up their tanks in the camouflaged workshops
and never gave a thought to a place like El Eleba.

To get there, you drive into the blue, take a bearing
and head for damn-all. Then you're there. And where are you?

– Still, of some few who did cross our path at El Eleba   370
there are seven who bide under their standing crosses.

The first a Lieutenant.
When the medicos passed him
for service overseas, he had jotted in a note-book
to the day and the hour keep me steadfast. There is only the
decision and the will

                  the rest has no importance

The second a Corporal.
          He had been in the Legion
and had got one more chance to redeem his lost honour.   380
What he said was
Listen here, I'm fed up with your griping –
If you want extra rations, go get 'em from Tommy!
You're green, that's your trouble. Dodge the column, pass the buck
and scrounge all you can – that's our law in the Legion.
You know Tommy's got 'em . . . He's got mineral waters,
and beer, and fresh fruit in that white crinkly paper
and God knows what all! Well, what's holding you back?
Are you windy or what?
                  Christ, you 'old Afrikaners!'   390
If you're wanting the eats, go and get 'em from Tommy!

The third had been a farm-hand in the March of Silesia
and had come to the desert as fresh fodder for machine guns.
His dates are inscribed on the files, and on the cross-piece.

The fourth was a lance-jack.
                He had trusted in Adolf
while working as a chemist in the suburb of Spandau.
His loves were his 'cello, and the woman who had borne him
two daughters and a son. He had faith in the Endsieg.
THAT THE NEW REICH MAY LIVE prayed the flyleaf of his Bible.

The fifth a mechanic.   401
               All the honour and glory,
the siege of Tobruk and the conquest of Cairo
meant as much to that Boche as the Synod of Whitby.
Being wise to all this, he had one single headache,
which was, how to get back to his sweetheart (called Ilse).
– He had said
          Can't the Tommy wake up and get weaving?
If he tried, he could put our whole Corps in the bag.
May God damn this Libya and both of its palm-trees!   410

The sixth was a Pole
                  – or to you, a Volksdeutscher –
who had put off his nation to serve in the Wehrmacht.
He siegheiled, and talked of 'the dirty Polacken,'
and said what he'd do if let loose among Russkis.
His mates thought that, though 'just a polnische Schweinhund,'
he was not a bad bloke.

On the morning concerned
he was driving a truck with mail, petrol and rations.
The M.P. on duty shouted five words of warning.   420
He nodded
            laughed
                        revved
                                    and drove straight for El Eleba
not having quite got the chap's Styrian lingo.

The seventh a young swaddy.
                                Riding cramped in a lorry
to death along the road which winds eastward to Halfaya
he had written three verses in appeal against his sentence
which soften for an hour the anger of Lenin.   430

                    Seven poor bastards
                    dead in African deadland
            (tawny tousled hair under the issue blanket)
                    wie einst Lili
            dead in African deadland
                                    einst Lili Marlene

Eighth Elegy

Karnak

Er lachelt uher die ganze Welt hinaus

Surely it is a holiday
or a day of national thanksgiving – Observe the King
as he offers up the spoils of Syria to Osiris.
No doubt he is acknowledging   440
the conclusion of some war to preserve civilisation.

Insolence of this civilisation,
to counterfeit with such assurance the eternal!

Yes, here among the shambles of Karnak
is Vollendung unknown to the restless Greeks.
Here, not in Elis and Olympia
are edle Einfalt und stille Grosse.
They bore many children
but their triumphal barque of civilisation
was weighed down with a heavy ballast   450
of magnetic death.
There is the Schwerpunkt, not here,
There across the river that made it all possible
the dead were taken across death
(listen to the waves of the flowing symbol,
lisping death) were taken to temporary slumber
and were introduced with courtesy to Osiris
and the immortal macabre company

But the envious desert
held at arm's length for millennia   460
had its own way at last –
        in the name of Mohammed
the nomads conquered:

        though not for the first time.
It had all happened before, as is the confounding way of history:
when the shepherd kings, Yaakeb and Yusuf,
heavy breathing with their hairy gutturals,
stood incredulously in the courts of Amun.
They looked down their noses at the phallic Min
and took up stones against impassive Osiris.   470
(Not of them hawk Horus, or the clerkish Thoth,
not of them the complacence on the lips of Pharaoh
not of them the capitals of lotus and papyrus).

Those who go a-whoring after death
will assuredly find it. Will be sealed in, confined
to their waste palaces. And Karnak the temple
be 'stalls for the nomads.'

        Puff of dust
on the blurred horizon means the imminent approach
of the solution, of subjection-deliverance.   480
These horsemen are merciful, they bring
the craved annihilation.
These are 'my servants, the Assyrians,'
        these the necessary antithesis,
these the standard-bearers of the superb blasphemy,
felling gods, levelling cities,
death-life grappling with life-death, severing
the umbilical cord of history.
These are the trampling migrations of peoples,
the horsemen of Amr, the 'barbarians' of Cavafy   490
and Rommel before the gates of Alexandria.

But still, in utter silence, from bas-relief and painted tomb
this civilisation asserts
its stylised timeless effrontery.

Synthesis is implicit
in Rilke's single column, (*die eine*)
denying fate, the stone mask of Vollendung.
(Deaf to tarbushed dragoman
who deep-throatedly extols it).

Yes, pinned with paint to walls, deep in stone carved, they cannot
resent the usurper. They fix and hold motionless   501
a protracted moment of time, a transitory eon.

The sun-boat travels through the hours of darkness
and Ra mounts heavenwards his chosen path.

What will happen during this day?
                                Will the King's Vizier
find time to be present at his public function?
Will silly girls fight among the stooks: will a sailor
be beaten for insubordination?

Is the harvest home yet: will stewards be computing   510
in the household office the extent of their surplus?
Will patient labourers work the shadouf?
Is fruit on the branch: and will ripe pomegranates
be shipped down to Thebes? Will rough Greeks land on Pharos?
Will prisoners of war drive the shaft for a tomb?

Is scaffolding up? Will the subsidised craftsmen
work diligently still on their couple of colossi,
all masters of the chisel, its calculated cutting?
Are Bedouin herds moving up from the South?

Will it be a feast-day: will the smooth priests   520
in bell-bottomed robes process between the sphinxes?
Detesters of the disk, possessors of the mystery,
shrewd guardians of the vested interests of Amun!
Where will the King be? Out boating for his pleasure;
while his boat shears through the Nile reeds
he aims at wild fowl with a boomerang –
Can he be sure of bringing home a bag?
                No doubt the court
will see to it, being solicitous.

In the evening he will return to Thebes, in his state   530
chariot, with the music of many instruments.
To his fellaheen a vision of flower strewn godhead
the scourge and the crook, under the sycamore leaves of life

            of life
            o unheeding
            the long ambiguous shadow
            thrown on overweening temple
            by the Other, the recurrent
            the bearded
            the killer in the rhythmical tragedy   540
            the heir   the stranger

Welcome O Hussein
When you enter Karbala

Ninth Elegy

Fort Capuzzo

For there will come a day
when the Lord will say
— Close Order!

One evening, breaking a jeep journey at Capuzzo
I noticed a soldier as he entered the cemetery
and stood looking at the grave of a fallen enemy.
Then I understood the meaning of the hard word 'pietas'
(a word unfamiliar to the newsreel commentator
as well as to the pimp, the informer and the traitor).   549

His thought was like this. — Here's another 'Good Jerry'!
Poor mucker. Just eighteen. Must be hard-up for man-power.
Or else he volunteered, silly bastard. That's the fatal.
the — fatal — mistake. Never volunteer for nothing.
I wonder how he died? — Just as well it was him, though,
and not one our chaps . . . Yes, the only good Jerry,
as they say, is your sort, chum.
              Cheerio, you poor bastard.
Don't be late on parade when the Lord calls 'Close Order.'
Keep waiting for the angels. Keep listening for Reveille.

Tenth Elegy

The Frontier

One must die because one knows them, die
of their smile's ineffable blossom, die
of their light hands

But dust blowing round them   560
has stopped up their ears
                              o for ever
not sleeping but dead

The airliner's passengers,
crossing without effort the confines
of wired-off Libya, remember
little, regret less. If they idly
inspect from their windows the ennui
of limestone desert
                              — and beneath them   570
their skimming shadow —
                              they'll be certain
they've seen it, they've seen all

(Seen all, maybe, including
the lunar qattaras, the wadis like family trees,
the frontier passes with their toyshop spirals –
seen nothing, and seen all

And the scene yields them? Nothing)

Yet that coast-line
could yield much: there were recces and sorties,   580
drumfire and sieges. The outposts
lay here: there ran the supply route.
Forgotten.
                        By that bend of Halfaya
the convoys used to stick raw meat for the Jabos.

And here, the bay's horseshoe:
how nobly it clanged through laconic communiqués!

Still, how should this interest the airborne travellers,
being less real to them than the Trojan defence-works
and touching them as little as the Achaean strategies?   590
Useless to deny. The memorial's obsequious
falsehoods are irrelevant. It has little to arrest them,
survivors by accident
                          that dried blood in the sangars.

So I turn aside in the benighted deadland
to perform a duty, noting an outlying
grave, or restoring a fallen cross-piece.
Remembrancer.
                       And shall sing them who amnestied
escaped from the tumult to stumble across sand-dunes   600
and darken their waves in the sea, the deliverer.

Run, stumble and fall in their instant of agony
past burnt-out brennpunkt, along hangdog dannert.
Here gutted, or stuck through the throat like Buonconte,
or charred to grey ash, they are caught in one corral.
We fly from their scorn, but they close all the passes:
their sleep's our unrest, we lie bound in their inferno –
this alliance must be vaunted and affirmed, lest they condemn us!

Lean seedlings of lament spring like swordsmen around us;
the coronach scales white arêtes. Bitter keening   610
of women goes up by the solitary column.
Denounce and condemn! Either build for the living
love, patience and power to absolve these tormented,
or else choke in the folds of their black-edged vendetta!
Run, stumble and fall in our desert of failure,
impaled, unappeased. And inhabit that desert
of canyon and dream – till we carry to the living
blood, fire and red flambeaux of death's proletariat.
Take iron in your arms! At last, spanning this history's
apollyon chasm, proclaim them the reconciled.   620

Heroic Song for the Runners of Cyrene

(to Gregorio Prieto)

> *Without suffering and death one learns nothing.*
> *We should not know the difference between the visions*
> *of the intellect and the facts.*
> *Only those ideas are acceptable that hold through*
> *suffering and death . . .*
> *Life is that which leaps.*
>   – DENIS SAURAT
>   'Death and the Dreamer'

I

The runners who would challenge
        the rough bounds of the desert
and strip for the test
        on this barbarous arena
must have sinews like hounds
        and be cunning as jerboas.

Rooting crowds'll not hail them
        in boisterous circus
nor sleek fame crown their exploit
        with triumph and obelisk.   630
Sun beats their path
        down the hours of blank silence:
each knows that in the end
        he'll be lucky to have respite.

Freely they'll run
        to the chosen assignation;
ineluctable role,
        and they ready to accept it!
Going with élan of pride
        to the furious onset   640
they'll reclaim the dead land
        for their city of Cyrene.

Sun beats their path:
        this no course measured plainly
between markers on the beach,
        no event for the novice.
The gates open: are closed.
        And the track leads them forward
hard by salt-lake and standing stone
        blind as the cyclops.   650

While keeping the same pace
        neither slower nor faster
but as yet out of sight
        behind plateau and escarpment
is history the doppelganger
        running to meet them.

II

Stroke of the sun means the hour that's to lay them
is present once more on the dust-blurred horizon.
They start, and awake from their stupor of rhythm –
and think, as they catch glimpse of sea beyond watch-tower   660
they cannot be far from . . . a place they'd forgotten.

At last it is sure. O, they know that they'll never
be hesitant feet on the marches of darkness
or humped epigonoi, outliving the Fians.[1]

No matter what hand stirs the dust, questions gently
with curious touch the grazed stones of the city
yon stroke of the sun vaunts their exploit for ever.

They quicken their pace. (And those others too.) Faster,
and livelier now than at jousts of the Toppo.[2]
The goal is in sight. Simultaneous the onrush,   670
the clash close at hand, o incarnate dialectic!
The runners gain speed. As they hail their opponents
they can hear in the air the strum of loud arrows
which predestined sing to their point of intersection.
Blaze of harsh day stuns their human defiance;
steel beats their path with its pendulum brilliance.

Sun's thong is lifted. And history the other
emerges at last from the heat's trembling mirror.

III

       Their ruin upon them
they've entered the lip of the burning enclosure.   680
Each runs to achieve, without pause or evasion
       his instant of nothing

       they look for an opening
grip, grapple, jerk, sway
and fall locking like lovers

down the thunderous cataract of day.

Cyrene, 1942 –
Carradale, Argyll, 1947

---

[1] *Oisein an deigh na Feinne* (Ossian after the Fians) is a Gaelic proverbial expression. Ossian is reputed to have outlived his compeers, the Fingalian heroes.
[2] Dante. *Inferno* xiii. 118-21. The fugitives in the Wood of the Suicides.

The Flyting o' Life and Daith

Quo life, the warld is mine
The floo'ers and trees, they're a' my ain.
I am the day, and the sunshine
Quo life, the warld is mine.

Quo daith, the warld is mine
Your lugs★ are deef, your een are blin   ears
Your floo'ers maun dwine★ in my bitter win'.   dwindle
Quo daith, the warld is mine.

Quo life, the warld is mine.
I hae saft win's, and healin' rain.   10
Aipples I hae, an' breid an' wine
Quo life, the warld is mine.

Quo daith, the warld is mine
Whit sterts in dreid, gangs doon in pain.
Bairns wantin' breid are makin' mane.
Quo daith, the warld is mine.

Quo life, the warld is mine.
Your deidly wark, I ken it fine
There's maet on earth for ilka wean.
Quo life, the warld is mine.   20

Quo daith, the warld is mine.
Your silly sheaves crine★ in my fire   shrivel
My worm keeks★ in your barn and byre.   peeps
Quo daith, the warld is mine.

Quo life, the warld is mine
Dule on your een!★ Ae galliard hert   damn your eyes!
Can ban tae hell your blackest airt.
Quo life, the warld is mine.

Quo daith, the warld is mine
Your rantin' hert, in duddies braw,   30
He winna lowp my preeson wa'.
Quo daith, the warld is mine.

Quo life, the warld is mine
Though ye bigg preesons o' marble stane
Hert's luve ye cannae preeson in
Quo life, the warld is mine.

Quo daith, the warld is mine.
I hae dug a grave, I hae dug it deep,
For war an' the pest will gar ye sleep.
Quo daith, the warld is mine.   40

Edwin Morgan (1920 –   )

Every generation produces a 'poet's poet', a writer whose originality and technical command of his craft give him more influence over his peers than anyone else. Edwin Morgan is perhaps the poet's poet for our time. He is everywhere the assured artist. The variety of his achievement is tremendous; the most experimental of major contemporary versifiers – more than any poet since MacDiarmid – he has made the point that the poet's range of style and subject may be and perhaps should be unlimited. Through his works, he has shown consistently that the modern poet is alive to the events and the changes in his age – as much as any writer of prose. Among his earlier poems especially are many which are colloquial in diction, working-class in milieu, and part of the social protest stream one associates with the 'Glasgow School'. In the end, Morgan may be most remembered for these verses – the 'Glasgow Poems'. But one finds as well – everywhere – a rich vein of humorous verse, as in 'The Starlings in George Square', and a strong interest in fantasy and in science and technology – combined in his science fiction poems, such as 'From the Domain of Arnheim'. And there are many experiments in verse form, for example, concrete poetry. For many years a teacher at Glasgow University, he is also a major critic and translator.

In the Snack-Bar

A cup capsizes along the formica,
slithering with a dull clatter.
A few heads turn in the crowded evening snack-bar.
An old man is trying to get to his feet
from the low round stool fixed to the floor.
Slowly he levers himself up, his hands have no power.
He is up as far as he can get. The dismal hump
looming over him forces his head down.
He stands in his stained beltless gabardine
like a monstrous animal caught in a tent   10
in some story. He sways slightly,
the face not seen, bent down
in shadow under his cap.
Even on his feet he is staring at the floor
or would be, if he could see.
I notice now his stick, once painted white
but scuffed and muddy, hanging from his right arm.
Long blind, hunchback born, half paralyzed
he stands   20
fumbling with the stick
and speaks:
'I want – to go to the – toilet.'

It is down two flights of stairs, but we go.
I take his arm. 'Give me – your arm – it's better,' he says.
Inch by inch we drift towards the stairs.
A few yards of floor are like a landscape
to be negotiated, in the slow setting out
time has almost stopped. I concentrate
my life to his: crunch of spilt sugar,   30

slidy puddle from the night's umbrellas,
table edges, people's feet,
hiss of the coffee-machine, voices and laughter,
smell of a cigar, hamburgers, wet coats steaming,
and the slow dangerous inches to the stairs.
I put his right hand on the rail
and take his stick. He clings to me. The stick
is in his left hand, probing the treads.
I guide his arm and tell him the steps.
And slowly we go down. And slowly we go down.   40
White tiles and mirrors at last. He shambles
uncouth into the clinical gleam.
I set him in position, stand behind him
and wait with his stick.
His brooding reflection darkens the mirror
but the trickle of his water is thin and slow,
an old man's apology for living.
Painful ages to close his trousers and coat –
I do up the last buttons for him.
He asks doubtfully, 'Can I – wash my hands?'   50
I fill the basin, clasp his soft fingers round the soap.
He washes, feebly, patiently. There is no towel.
I press the pedal of the drier, draw his hands
gently into the roar of the hot air.
But he cannot rub them together,
drags out a handkerchief to finish.
He is glad to leave the contraption, and face the stairs.
He climbs, and steadily enough.
He climbs, we climb. He climbs
with many pauses but with that one   60
persisting patience of the undefeated
which is the nature of man when all is said.
And slowly we go up. And slowly we go up.
The faltering, unfaltering steps
take him at last to the door
across that endless, yet not endless waste of floor.
I watch him helped on a bus. It shudders off in the rain.
The conductor bends to hear where he wants to go.
Wherever he could go it would be dark
and yet he must trust men.   70
Without embarrassment or shame
he must announce his most pitiful needs
in a public place. No one sees his face.
Does he know how frightening he is in his strangeness
under his mountainous coat, his hands like wet leaves
stuck to the half-white stick?
His life depends on many who would evade him.
But he cannot reckon up the chances,
having one thing to do,
to haul his blind hump through these rains of August.   80
Dear Christ, to be born for this!

Good Friday

Three o'clock. The bus lurches
round into the sun. 'D's this go – '
he flops beside me – 'right along Bath Street?
 – Oh tha's, tha's all right, see I've
got to get some Easter eggs for the kiddies.
I've had a wee drink, ye understand –
ye'll maybe think it's a – funny day
to be celebrating – well, no, but ye see
I wasny working, and I like to celebrate
when I'm no working – I don't say it's right   10
I'm no saying it's right, ye understand – ye understand?
But anyway that's the way I look at it –
I'm no boring you, eh? – ye see today,
take today, I don't know what today's in aid of,
whether Christ was – crucified or was he –
rose fae the dead like, see what I mean?
You're an educatit man, you can tell me –
 – Aye, well. There ye are. It's been seen
time and again, the working man
has nae education, he jist canny – jist   20
hasny got it, know what I mean,
he's jist bliddy ignorant – Christ aye,
bliddy ignorant. Well – ' The bus brakes violently,
he lunges for the stair, swings down – off,
into the sun for his Easter eggs,
on very

        nearly
        steady
        legs.

The Dog

    A dog on a grave in autumn,
    perhaps with the obscure sense
    of death, but of solitude
    it is certain. And to defend
    the dead old man below
    if he could still be hurt.
    The gravediggers shrug, leave,
    respecting the snarl as much
    as any grief under black,
    though the dog is black, and naturally   10
    makes the shadow of a headstone
    still to be, as he stretches
    along the crumbled earth
    with his muzzle on his paws
    and the afternoon darkens
    till at last no one would see
    what was watching or waiting.

The Starlings in George Square

I

Sundown on the high stonefields!
The darkening roofscape stirs –
thick – alive with starlings
gathered singing in the square –
like a shower of arrows they cross
the flash of a western window,
they bead the wires with jet,
they nestle preening by the lamps
and shine, sidling by the lamps
and sing, shining, they stir   10
the homeward hurrying crowds.
A man looks up and points
smiling to his son beside him
wide-eyed at the clamour on those cliffs –
it sinks, shrills out in waves,
levels to a happy murmur,
scatters in swooping arcs,
a stab of confused sweetness
that pierces the boy like a story,
a story more than a song.   20
He will never forget that evening,
the silhouette of the roofs,
the starlings by the lamps.

II

The City Chambers are hopping mad.
Councillors with rubber plugs in their ears!
Secretaries closing windows!
Window-cleaners want protection and danger money.
The Lord Provost can't hear herself think, man.
What's that?
Lord Provost, can't hear herself think.   30
At the General Post Office
the clerks write Three Pounds Starling in the savings-books.
Each telephone-booth is like an aviary.
I tried to send a parcel to County Kerry but –
The cables to Cairo got fankled*, sir.   tangled
What's that?
I said the cables to Cairo got fankled.

And as for the City Information Bureau –
I'm sorry I can't quite chirrup did you twit –
No I wanted to twee but perhaps you can't cheep –   40
Would you try once again, that's better, I – sweet –
When's the last boat to Milngavie? Tweet?
What's that?
I said when's the last boat to Milngavie?

III

There is nothing for it now but scaffolding:
clamp it together, send for the bird-men,
Scarecrow Strip for the window-ledge landings,
Cameron's Repellent on the overhead wires.
Armour our pediments against eavesdroppers.
This is a human outpost. Save our statues.   50
Send back the jungle. And think of the joke:
as it says in the papers, It is very comical
to watch them alight on the plastic rollers
and take a tumble. So it doesn't kill them?
All right, so who's complaining? This isn't Peking
where they shoot the sparrows for hygiene and cash.
So we're all humanitarians, locked in our cliff-dwellings
encased in our repellent, guano-free and guilt-free.
The Lord Provost sings in her marble hacienda.
The Postmaster-General licks an audible stamp.   60
Sir Walter is vexed that his column's deserted.
I wonder if we really deserve starlings?
There is something to be said for these joyous messengers
that we repel in our indignant orderliness.
They lift up the eyes, they lighten the heart,
and some day we'll decipher that sweet frenzied whistling
as they wheel and settle along our hard roofs
and take those grey buttresses for home.
One thing we know they say, after their fashion.
They like the warm cliffs of man.   70

Glasgow Sonnets

i

A mean wind wanders through the backcourt trash.
Hackles on puddles rise, old mattresses
puff briefly and subside. Play-fortresses
of brick and bric-a-brac spill out some ash.
Four storeys have no windows left to smash,
but in the fifth a chipped sill buttresses
mother and daughter the last mistresses
of that black block condemned to stand, not crash.
Around them the cracks deepen, the rats crawl.
The kettle whimpers on a crazy hob.   10
Roses of mould grow from ceiling to wall.
The man lies late since he has lost his job,
smokes on one elbow, letting his coughs fall
thinly into an air too poor to rob.

ii

A shilpit* dog fucks grimly by the close.   scrawny
Late shadows lengthen slowly, slogans fade.
The YY PARTICK TOI grins from its shade
like the last strains of some lost *libera nos
a malo*. No deliverer ever rose

from these stone tombs to get the hell they made
unmade. The same weans never make the grade.
The same grey street sends back the ball it throws.
Under the darkness of a twisted pram
a cat's eyes glitter. Glittering stars press 10
between the silent chimney-cowls and cram
the higher spaces with their SOS.
Don't shine a torch on the ragwoman's dram.
Coats keep the evil cold out less and less.

iii

'See a tenement due for demolition?
I can get ye rooms in it, two, okay?
Seven hundred and nothin legal to pay
for it's no legal, see? That's my proposition,
ye can take it or leave it but. The position
is simple, you want a hoose, I say
for eight hundred pound it's yours.' And they,
trailing five bairns, accepted his omission
of the foul crumbling stairwell, windows wired
not glazed, the damp from the canal, the cooker 10
without pipes, packs of rats that never tired –
any more than the vandals bored with snooker
who stripped the neighbouring houses, howled, and fired
their aerosols of squeaking 'Filthy lucre!'

iv

Down by the brickworks you get warm at least.
Surely soup-kitchens have gone out. It's not
the thirties now. Hugh MacDiarmid forgot
in 'Glasgow 1960' that the feast
of reason and the flow of soul has ceased
to matter to the long unfinished plot
of heating frozen hands. We never got
an abstruse song that charmed the raging beast.
So you have nothing to lose but your chains,
dear Seventies. Dalmarnock, Maryhill, 10
Blackhill and Govan, better sticks and stanes
should break your banes, for poets' words are ill
to hurt ye. On the wrecker's ball the rains
of greeting★ cities drop and drink their fill.   weeping

v

'Let them eat cake' made no bones about it.
But we say let them eat the hope deferred
and that will sicken them. We have preferred
silent slipways to the riveters' wit.
And don't deny it – that's the ugly bit.
Ministers' tears might well have launched a herd
of bucking tankers if they'd been transferred
from Whitehall to the Clyde. And smiles don't fit
either. 'There'll be no bevvying' said Reid
at the work-in. But all the dignity you muster 10
can only give you back a mouth to feed

and rent to pay if what you lose in bluster
is no more than win patience with 'I need'
while distant blackboards use you as their duster.

vi

The North Sea oil-strike tilts east Scotland up,
and the great sick Clyde shivers in its bed.
But elegists can't hang themselves on fled-
from trees or poison a recycled cup –
If only a less faint, shaky sunup
glimmered through the skeletal shop and shed
and men washed round the piers like gold and spread
golder in soul than Mitsubishi or Krupp –
The images are ageless but the thing
is now. Without my images the men   10
ration their cigarettes, their children cling
to broken toys, their women wonder when
the doors will bang on laughter and a wing
over the firth be simply joy again.

vii

Environmentalists, ecologists
and conservationists are fine no doubt.
Pedestrianization will come out
fighting, riverside walks march off the lists,
pigeons and starlings be somnambulists
in far-off suburbs, the sandblaster's grout
multiply pink piebald facades to pout
at sticky-fingered mock-Venetianists.
Prop up's the motto. Splint the dying age.
Never displease the watchers from the grave.   10
Great when fake architecture was the rage,
but greater still to see what you can save.
The gutted double fake meets the adage:
a wig's the thing to beat both beard and shave.

viii

Meanwhile the flyovers breed loops of light
in curves that would have ravished tragic Toshy –
clean and unpompous, nothing wishy-washy.
Vistas swim out from the bulldozer's bite
by day, and banks of earthbound stars at night
begin. In Madame Emé's Sauchie Haugh, she
could never gain in leaves or larks or sploshy
lanes what's lost in a dead boarded site –
the life that overspill is overkill to.
Less is not more, and garden cities are   10
the flimsiest oxymoron to distill to.
And who wants to distill? Let bus and car
and hurrying umbrellas keep their skill to
feed ukiyo-e beyond Lochnagar.

ix

It groans and shakes, contracts and grows again.
Its giant broken shoulders shrug off rain.
It digs its pits to a shauchling★ refrain.   twisting
Roadworks and graveyards like their gallus★ men.   bold
It fattens fires and murders in a pen
and lets them out in flaps and squalls of pain.
It sometimes tears its smoky counterpane
to hoist a bleary fist at nothing, then
at everything, you never know. The west
could still be laid with no one's tears like dust   10
and barricaded windows be the best
to see from till the shops, the ships, the trust
return like thunder. Give the Clyde the rest.
Man and the sea make cities as they must.

x

From thirtieth floor windows at Red Road
he can see choughs and samphires, dreadful trade –
the schoolboy reading *Lear* has that scene made.
A multi is a sonnet stretched to ode
and some say that's no joke. The gentle load
of souls in clouds, vertiginously stayed
above the windy courts, is probed and weighed.
Each monolith stands patient, ah'd and oh'd.
And stalled lifts generating high-rise blues
can be set loose. But stalled lives never budge.   10
They linger in the single-ends that use
their spirit to the bone, and when they trudge
From closemouth to laundrette their steady shoes
carry a world that weighs us like a judge.

From the Domain of Arnheim

And so that all these ages, these years
we cast behind us, like the smoke-clouds
dragged back into vacancy when the rocket springs –

The domain of Arnheim was all snow, but we were there.
We saw a yellow light thrown on the icefield
from the huts by the pines, and laughter came up
floating from a white corrie
miles away, clearly.
We moved on down, arm in arm.   10
I know you would have thought it was a dream
but we were there. And those were trumpets –
tremendous round the rocks –
while they were burning fires of trash and mammoths' bones.
They sang naked, and kissed in the smoke.
A child, or one of their animals, was crying.
Young men blew the ice crystals off their drums.
We came down among them, but of course

they could see nothing, on their time-scale.
Yet they sensed us, stopped, looked up – even into our eyes. 20
To them we were a displacement of the air,
a sudden chill, yet we had no power
over their fear. If one of them had been dying
he would have died. The crying
came from one just born: that was the cause
of the song. We saw it now. What had we stopped
but joy?
I know you felt
the same dismay, you gripped my arm, they were waiting
for what they knew of us to pass.   30
A sweating trumpeter took
a brand from the fire with a shout and threw it
where our bodies would have been –
we felt nothing but his courage.
And so they would deal with every imagined power
seen or unseen.
There are no gods in the domain of Arnheim.

We signaled to the ship; got back;
our lives and days returned to us, but
haunted by deeper souvenirs than any rocks or seeds.   40
From time the souvenirs are deeds.

The Poet

The poet shrieks getting
waiting out of his system
when the little wringing hands
of a valetudinary muse
fuse to one white claw.
He shivers as he bleeds.
Eagle country, winds
and pines, the lower air
thick with dying leaves,
a gleam of flooded fields.   10
Whatever it is that will
not wait, he still half waits
to find, half sees, feels
wholly as the unrelenting
hook hangs him higher
and higher and something like
wings or the single wing
of a great craft shadows
and flashes alternately past
the sun of that country.   20
At the right moment the claw
retracts, and his one clear cry
falls to the earth before him,
winding down like a song.

New Year Sonnets

1

Soaring, straining, craning, flying, dying,
courted by hope, gun-butted back to sorrow,
spoon-fed with salves of gall, well-sweetened sorrow,
spun in the finest icing of a dying,
raised beyond measure by those also dying,
clapping the fashion of a shroud of sorrow,
stopping the grave at last for others' sorrow,
leaving the living busy with their dying,
you have the child that plays about your feet,
you have the blackbirds listening in the dusk,   10
you have the light that shows above the door,
those gentle and those unreturning feet,
that dark wing fading back into the dusk,
that blank unvisited remorseless door.

2

One times one times one times one is one.
The adder is the one that gets it two.
One two's two ones, though, and a single two
would be a fabulously merry one.
What is the great unhappiness of one,
that there should seem such bundled grace in two?
It is the hardihood of truth to two
that truth should seem a luxury in one.
We scarcely dare to breathe the charms of three,
they blow and twine like clematis. For four,   10
we'd have a glade of square cool box, with five
a quincunx of the thymy paths. As three
begin to breast the life to come, as four
stand round the table of bread, a star is five.

3

Satan was squatting with his lurid tuba,
potting a blackly incandescent coda.
Hell is improvisatory, a coda
blurted in continents from an old tuba.
No god aborts that bitter-titted tuba
or docks its mortally transfixing coda.
The universe itself spills like a coda
to hear the hellish spell; it buys that tuba.
 − Somewhere in Lyra there began a silence
that spread along the stars like patient music.   10
It moved and wrapped the rocks in a white quiet.
If it should ever come to hell, that silence,
will there be space in Satan's rooky music
to drop between those blasts one rest of quiet?

4

I love that endless roll of city wheels
below the surging formless northern clouds.
It is the interchange: the wheeling clouds,
the winter sleet that blurs the cloudy wheels.
Deep in the sun a dying grindstone wheels,
and seas are heavy with unparted clouds.
There is no reason to be loving clouds
in chiding any captaincy of wheels.
Only, we love each as we love them both,
and brooding across city roofs we're joined   10
by drifts and troops come curiously together
steadily, stealthy and unsteady both
from the forge where all energy is joined
poised, and then we cross the world together.

5

Was it the proud full verse of his great sail
that gave America Columbus minds?
Martian badlands are the west for minds
that cannot rest in watching schooners sail
beyond the Golden Gate. The Gate's a sail
suspended in its arches like the minds
stretched under listening dishes to hear minds
unknown that might make men and gods set sail
for life. By interstellar mulls and voes
they dream of starships shuddering to shore.   10
Microminiaturized, their corded bales.
They hear and bear a poetry of voes
and mulls that pounds and champs and strains; their shore
is all lean-tos, goodbyes, slipways, and bales.

6

'I want to see a sonnet with a rose.'
'After Stein that is impossible.'
'I believe few things are impossible.'
'But if a rose is a rose is a rose,
metaphor goes. Nothing's left but the rose.'
'Get on with it. It's the impossible
that you are there to break.' 'Impossible
the rose: love is not like it; the white rose
does not break the heart; the rose and the fire
are not one. It withers quickly, draws blood,   10
has scents most people like. Its dried and crushed
petals are ghosts for years in bowls.' 'The fire
shows. A ghost you call it? It's in your blood.
Is a crushed rose a crushed rose, is it crushed?'

7

The sick man saw the waves turning to grass.
A wheatfield swayed where there had once been sea.
His cabin juddered as it ploughed a sea
of bracken; gulls were larks; then feather-grass,
a smudge of harvesters and smocks, the grass
an ancient rolling peace. He slept. The sea
was there as grey and cold as ever sea
was, and the doctor sponged his brow. Grass
clung to the sweat in his dream. How he'd rave
of a poor steading, of a collie, straw,   10
an autumn chimney and a chestnut-fall:
and there was nothing but to let him rave,
and to restrain him in his bunk of straw.
The sea gaped for the sheeted clod to fall.

8

The happy lid of tins was ringing blue.
The carpet biscuits cowered weakly grey.
Their tipsy guest breathed all the mirrors grey,
searching for proof they'd take his eyes were blue.
'The tinsel on the tree is nearly blue,'
said Jan, but Martin shook his head. 'It's grey;
what's silver but a nervous grey?' And grey
drove from the winter room the ghost of blue.
– Curtains are drawn; coal glows and sparks up red;
the table lamp jumps softly out, purrs gold;   10
a rug lies panting flecks of ragged flame.
'See – steady up – your eye is really red,'
Jan tells the mirror man. He coughs. The gold
swims on her sea-horse pendant – his old flame.

9

'In eating dandelions it is the flavour
you must savour as it lingers on the finger.
Press the cut stem down smartly on your finger,
and lick the nippy milky ring of flavour.'
'What if I grow besotted with that flavour,
hallucinating an ambrosial finger
tip to tip with my own milky finger
creating charges of supernal flavour?'
'The lamb shall lie down with the dandelion,
the tiger shall go mad on tansy wine,   10
the bear shall snort himself asleep in combs.
Eat up, and tumble with the dandelion;
crown yourself with tansy, dive in wine;
burrow into the dripping gorgeous combs.'

10

I know you love me. Love is not the rhyme.
The figure in the pattern may be free.
Mine is the love you need. I leave you free.
I bind you only in this iron rhyme
where love is hidden, shifting, and the rhyme
is like a lock but the treasure moves free
beneath it. To be vulnerably free
is still the pain of love; only in rhyme
we breathe together like a wedded pair
whose union is the sweetness of a line   10
closed cleanly, not like that, but pausing, this.
The only ark is words, where pair and pair
might even there go tremblingly in line,
fearing what lies beyond the end of this –

The Coals

Before my mother's hysterectomy
she cried, and told me she must never bring
coals in from the cellar outside the house,
someone must do it for her. The thing itself
I knew was nothing, it was the thought
of that dependence. Her tears shocked me
like a blow. As once she had been taught,
I was taught self-reliance, discipline,
which is both good and bad. You get things done,
you feel you keep the waste and darkness back   10
by acts and acts and acts and acts and acts,
bridling if someone tells you this is vain,
learning at last in pain. Hardest of all
is to forgive yourself for things undone,
guilt that can poison life – away with it,
you say, and it is loath to go away.
I learned both love and joy in a hard school
and treasure them like the fierce salvage of
some wreck that has been built to look like stone
and stand, though it did not, a thousand years.   20

In Argyll
For A. R.

We found the poet's skull on the machair.
It must have bobbed ashore from that shipwreck
where the winged men went down in rolling dreck
of icebound webs, oars, oaths, armour, blind air.
It watches westward still; dry, white as chalk,
perfect at last, in silence and at rest.
Far off, he sang of Nineveh the blest,

incised his tablets, stalked the dhow-bright dock.
Now he needs neither claws nor tongue to tell
of things undying. Hebridean light   10
fills the translucent bone-domes. Nothing brings
the savage brain back to its empty shell,
distracted by the shouts, the reefs, the night,
fighting sleet to fix the tilt of its wings.

The Coin

We brushed the dirt off, held it to the light.
The obverse showed us *Scotland*, and the head
of a red deer; the antler-glint had fled
but the fine cut could still be felt. All right:
we turned it over, read easily *One Pound*,
but then the shock of Latin, like a gloss,
Respublica Scotorum, sent across
such ages as we guessed but never found
at the worn edge where once the date had been
and where as many fingers had gripped hard   10
as hopes their silent race had lost or gained.
The marshy scurf crept up to our machine,
sucked at our boots. Yet nothing seemed ill-starred.
And least of all the realm the coin contained.

Alexander Scott (1920 – 1989)

Calvinist Sang

A hunder pipers canna blaw
Our trauchled times awa,
Drams canna droun them out, nor sang
Hap* their scarecraw heids for lang.   clothe

Gin aa the warld was bleezan fou*,   full (drunk)
Wh'at gowk* wald steer the plou?   fool
Gin cheils* were cowpan quines* aa day,   men/girls
They'd mak, (but fail to gaither), hay.

Pit by yir bagpipes, brak yir gless,
Wi quines, keep aff the gress,   10
The* day ye need a hert and harns*   in this/brains
Dour as the diamant, cauld as the starns.

Coronach

*For the deid o the 5th/7th Battalion,
The Gordon Highlanders*

Waement* the deid   pity
I never did,
Owre gled I was ane o the lave*   rest
That somewey baid alive

To trauchle my thowless* hert   spiritless
Wi ithers' hurt.

But nou that I'm far
Frae the fechtin's fear,
Nou I hae won awa frae aa thon pain
Back til my beuks and my pen,   10
They croud aroun me out o the grave
Whaur love and langourie* sae lanesome grieve.   longing

Cryan the cauld words:
'We hae dree'd* our weirds*,   endured/fates
But you that byde ahin,
Ayont our awesome hyne*,   haven
You are the flesh we aince had been,
We that are bruckle brokken bane.'

Cryan a drumlie* speak: dull, grey
'You hae the words we spak,   20
You hae the sang
We canna sing,
Sen death maun skail*   scatter
The makar's skill.

'Makar, frae nou ye maun
Be singan for us deid men,
Sing til the warld we loo'd
(For aa that its brichtness lee'd)
And tell hou the sudden nicht
Cam doun and made us nocht.'   30

Waement the deid
I never did,
But nou I am safe awa
I hear their wae
Greetan* greetan dark and daw*,   weeping/dawn
Their death the-streen my darg* the-day.   task

Continent o Venus

She lies ablow my body's lust and love,
A country dearly-kent and yet sae fremd★   foreign
That she's at aince thon Tir-nan-Og★ I've dreamed,   a Gaelic paradise
The airt★ I've lived in, whar I mean tae live,   quarter
And mair, much mair, a mixter-maxter world
Whar fact and dream are taigled up and snorled.

I ken ilk bay o aa her body's strand,
Yet ken them new ilk time I come to shore,
For she's the uncharted sea whar I maun fare
To find anither undiscovered land,   10

To find it fremd, and yet to find it dear,
To seek it aye, and aye be bydan there.

Senses

The beast in its earth ablow me,
The bird i the lift★ abune,   sky
Hae aa their senses lively
To watch the warld gae roun.

But here I walk atween them
Wi dazzle-darkened een
And lugs★ that the rair o the city   ears
Has deaved★ to simple soun.   deafened

I walked in a warld atween them
Wi theirs outside my ken,   10
A kind o stravaigan★ statue   meandering
Wi harns★ in a heid o stane.   brains

Heart of Stone
(A Poem on Aberdeen)

The sea-maw spires i the stane-grey lift
Owre sworlan swaws★ o the stane-grey sea,   waves
Flaffers her wings – a flash o faem-white feathers –
And warssles awa i the wake o the trauchled trawler
That hirples★ hame hauf-drouned wi the weicht o herrin.   limps

Heich owre the gantan★ mouth o the hairbour,   yawning
The lichthous heists a stick o chalk
To scrieve on the sclate air the message 'Safety',
The trawler taks the road the tounsmen wrocht
For watter to walk in and tent★ the toun,   10   watch over, heed
Its tides the bluid that beats her sea-grey hert.

The sea-grey toun, the stane-grey sea,
The cushat's croudle mells★ wi the sea-maw's skirl   mixes
Whaur baith gae skaichan★ fish-guts doun the quays   scavenging
Or scrannan★ crumbs in cracks o the thrang★ causeys,   hunting/busy
A lichthous plays the lamp-post owre a close,
The traffic clappers through a fishers' clachan★   village
Whaur aa the vennels spulyie★ names frae the sea,   pillage
And kirks and crans clanjamfrie★,   crowd
Heaven and haven mixter-maxtered heave   20
To the sweel o the same saut tide
Whaur aa the airts★ o the ocean anchor,   quarters, directions
Ships frae the Baltic, ships frae Brazil,
Archangel ships wi a flag that dings archangels,
Coals frae Newcastle to thowe the cauldrife granite,
Planks that were aince an acre o Swedish wuids,
Esparto gress that greened in Spain,
And aye the sea's ain hairst★ o skinklan siller,   harvest
Haill flaughtered★ fleets o fish,   flickered
The sea-maws scraichan triumph owre their wreckage.   30
Nae wreckage haudden in hemmeran yairds
Whaur ships tak shape for the showdan shift o the sea,
Their cleedin steel, their steekin reid-het rivets,
They'll sclim★ frae their iron cradles   climb
To fecht wi the iron faem and the stanie swaws,
Their strenthie★ sides as teuch as the sea-grey toun.   strong
A teuch toun, whaur even the strand maks siller,
A roch Riveera gleys★ at the granite sea,   squints
Wi a fun-fair squatteran roun the Muckle Dipper,
A sprauchle a stalls for sweeties and ice-a-da-cream   40
To fleech til the tongues o bairns o a fause simmer
And cant o the sun til bonnie bare-buff quines
On a bourached★ beach whaur crouds find crouseness★ in crouds,   crowded/bravery
Cantie★ to keek at the quines –   pleasant
A blae Blackpool, but owre ayont it
A mile o naukit sand whaur nets for salmon
Gae wydan out waist-deep, and in ahint them
The links are streekit lang for the lane gowfer
To clour his clypie★ baa wi nane to claik   tell-tale
But sea-maws habblan aside the ae bit★ hous   50   wee
In aa thon gant★ o green,   yawn
The ae bit hous the salmon-fishers' howff★   tavern
They plenish wi gear for wark whaur ithers play.

A weicht o wark aa weys, by land and watter!
Ablow the brig, 'Balgownie brig's black waa,'
The river rins romantic eneuch for Byron,
But 'by yon bonnie banks and by yon bonnie braes'
A paper mill on the t'ae brae
Looks owre at a woollen mill on the t'ither bank,
The Don atween them dargan★ nicht and day,   60   labouring
For ilka lynn★ that steers the stream to snaw   waterfall
Comes doun frae a dam that steers the stream to labour,
To plowter and plash i the fank★ o a factory lade.   enclosure

And richt by the factory waa, the first ferm,
The couthie country fat and fou o ferms
As far as the legend-land o Foggieloan,
Ayont the trees whas line alang the lift★   *sky*
Aince gart a bairn believe the mairch o the warld
Fand endin thonder, aye the warld gaes yokan★,   *beginning to work*
Wi park on park for the plou,   70
Park on park for the paidle,
Parks for the beasts and parks for the barley
(The meat and the meal and the bree o the barley –
Aye, aye, the haill hypothec),
And aa for the mercat, aa for the Friday mart,
The fermers fat as their ferms,
Braid as their beasts and bauld as their barley-bree,
Come traikan intil the toun to swap their trauchle★,   *drudgery*
To niffer★ for nowt★ at the unco unction,   *bargain/cattle*
Yarkan their bids at the yammeran unctioneer,   80
And syne frae the pens til the pubs whaur business is pleisure,
To slocken the stour★ frae thrang thrapples★   *dust/throats*
In whacks o whisky and lochans o lowse★ ale   *loose*
Whaur aa the clash o the country roun gaes sooman★, *swimming*
Skyrie★ wi mauts and skinklan-bricht wi beers   *bright*
That wash the langour awa frae the landwart week,
Their trinkle the toun's freedom for ilka fermer.
This toun is free til aa that live by the land
And aa that live by the sea, for fermers' faces
And fishermen's faces, strang to thole and strauchle,   90
To rive frae the sweirt★ rock and the ruggan swaw   *reluctant*
A rowth★ o smeddum★, thae are the same   *plenty/gumption*
As mak weel-faur'd (or ill) the fowk o the toun,
Sen aa are bairns o the bairns o fishers and fermers,
They weir their faces eftir their grandshers' fashion,
Thae faces callered by country winds
Or stobbed★ by the stang o saut in wallochan★ watters *jabbed/wallowing*
Look frae ahint a counter or owre a bar,
Frae a fitbaa croud or a queue at the pictur-palace,
Frae factory-yetts at yokan-time or at lowsan,   100
Or cleekit in Sabbath braws as the kirk skails,
Sic faces, fit to daur the dunt o storms
Frae clintie★ seas or bens as coorse as brine,   *rocky*
Mak city streets a warld o wild stramash★   *tumult*
Whaur bonnie fechters bolden at ilka ferlie★.   *wonder*

The tapmaist ferlie aye the toun itsel,
Graithed intil granite, stanced in stalliard★ stane,   *stately*
A hard hauld, a sterk steid,
A breem bield★ o stieve biggins★,   *shelter/buildings*
Riven frae raw rock, and rockie-rooted,   110
She bares her brou til the bite o the brashy gale
Or stares back straucht at the skimmeran scaud o the sun,
Fowr-square til aa the elements, fine or foul,
Heedless o rain and reek
(Sen rain can only wash the reek awa),
For nocht can fyle★ her adamant face,   *defile*

Itsel an armour proof til ilka onding.

But geyan★ gash★ she lours in a gurlie★ gloamin   quite/ghastly/roaring
Whan seipan★ swaws are graveyaird grey on the strand,   oozing
The hills as dreich as deid lichen,   120
The dowie★ rivers drounan the dark lift,   gloomy
The toun a cauldrife cairn o tauchie rock
Mair steel nor stane, the streets in snell★ canyons   fierce
Trenchan through craigie★ scaurs that sklaff★ the sun,   cliff-like/slap
A wersh warld, its colours aa wan-blae,
Whaur lugs★ are deaved★ by the drantan dirge o the sea   ears/deafened
And een blunted on grumlie★ blads o granite.   grim

Bonnieness-blind, thae fowk, for aa their birr!
Wha else, i the stanie straucht o Union Street,
Wi only the ae brig til open space,   130
Wad block thon brichtness out wi shargar★ shoppies?   starveling
What ither toun can blaw its blastie tooter
For siccan a rowth o temples til the Muses
(A pictur-hous for ilk ten thousand heid)?

Whaur else are fowk sae daft on 'the modern drama'
That time-woorn Hamlet plays til a toom★ haa   empty
While even courtan couples howder★ in queues   huddle
Gin X sud mark the spot – and X aye marks it –
For spang-new Nocht-Nocht-Seeven?
Whaur else wad Wallace pynt the finger o scorn   140
At a theatre thrang wi a clyter★ o Scoatch coamics,   mess
Kilted tenors, and cantrips★ frae Agatha Christie?   tricks
Whaur else wad Gordon tak sic a hint frae the toun
And turn til the Art Gall'ry a gallus★ back?   brave
Whaur else wad Burns far leifer glower at's gowan
Nor look his brither Scots i the ee – and lauch?
Na, na, he's nae amused – like vogie★ Victoria,   vaunting
The cross queen stuid standan at Queen's Cross,
And even she, her face til the fike o Balmoral,
Feels mair at hame in an artless airt nor Burns.   150

Ahint his back auld men find shool-the-board
A cantier ploy nor onie poetry clavers,
And neives★ that aince had haudden cleek★ or spad   fists/salmon-gaff
Are grippit nou for a game
In a green howe★ at the hert o the granite toun,   valley
Nae mair nor a sclim★ o steps frae the stane centre   climb
Whaur business breeds in banks its paper bairns
And hous-insurance biggs its hames in haas
Abune the heids o leddies wi smaa leisure
(And smaa-er cheenge) that jink★ frae shop til store   160   dodge
In het pursuit o twa for the price o the t'ane,
Their ae fond dwaum★ the mak o a braw bargain,   dream
Bonnier far nor a ballant threepit by Burns,
Thon daisy-daffer, deid in a thratch★ o debt.   death-throes

Gin onie debt be here, it's haudden dern★,   secret
Happed ahin stanes that sclent★ the speak o siller   sparkle
Frae raw on hauchty raw o terraced houses
Whiter nor whited sepulchres daur decore,
Their snawie fronts as clean as a banker's credit
And cauld as his arctic hert, a cranreuch★ beauty 170 frostly
Born frae the frore skinkle o iceberg stane,
The rock itsel (far mair nor the men that wrocht it),
The rock steekan its ain sterk style
On fowk whas foremaist fancy was biggan cheap
In hame-owre stane that speired the least o siller
To howk frae a hole out-by and bike★ in bields,   assemble
Syne fand themsels a fowk whas granite een
Were claucht in an icy wab o granite graithing★, clothing, equipment
A cauldrife charm they never meant to mak
But hytered★ on by chance, the luck o the land. 180 stumbled

Yet syne they socht to suit thon chancy charm
Til notions stown frae beuks on 'aht end beauteh' –
Save us, a bonnie soss★! Our sins in stane,   mess
The graveyairds sprauchle gantan★, their granite teeth yawning
Asclent wi a deid skinkle, a gless girn★   grimace
At nichtgouned angels far owre lourd★ to flie,   heavy
And nappied cherubs far owre cauld to flichter★,   fly
And whim-wham scrolls, and whigmaleerie★ urns, fantastic, useless
The haill jing-bang bumbazed★ in a sacred scutter confounded
To fleg★ the deid wi a fate that's waur nor death. 190 frighten

But fient★ the fate has pouer to ding sic fauters★, scarcely/offends
In life they looked wi never a blink o the ee
At horror mair profane nor the pynes o hell,
Thon maister-monsterpiece the Marischal College,
A Gothic nichtmare, granite steered like glaur★   mud
Til ferlie frills and fancy flichtmaflethers,
Stookie★ insteid o stane,   stucco
Whaur sterkness, strength, the granite's only graces,
Are raxed★ and rived til pranksome prettifications, stretched
The fraiky★ shots at grace o a graceless fowk. 200 freakish

Nae grace ava i the howder★ o growsome houses huddle
Biggit as bargains – and ilkane bad –
Whan Sassenach★ brick and Swedish timmer★, English/timber
Bocht for a groatsworth less nor the sillerie stane,
Got pride o place and connached★ pride o place destroyed
Wi street eftir street o the same subtopian slaur★, mud
Less fit to stand by granite's stey★ gramultion★ steep/common sense
Nor fremmit mountain-dew by the real Mackay,
A wersh bourach★ o bawbee braws, huddle
A clyter o menseless★ clart★. ill-mannered/dirt

But neither auld mistaks nor new mishanters 211
Can steerach the fine fettle o ferlie stane,
The adamant face that nocht can fyle,
Nae rain, nae reek,

Fowr-square til aa the elements, fine or foul,
She stares back straucht at the skimmeran scaud o the sun
Or bares her brou til the bite o the brashy gale,
Riven frae raw rock, and rockie-rooted,
A breem* bield o steive biggins,   *fierce*
A hard hauld, a sterk steid   220
Whaur bonnie fechters bolden at ilka ferlie,
The city streets a warld o wild stramash*   *tumult*
Frae clintie* seas and bens as coorse as brine   *rocky*
For fowk sae fit to daur the dunt* o storms   *pounding*
Wi faces stobbed by the stang o saut
Or callered* by country winds   *freshened*
In a teuch toun whaur even the strand maks siller,
Rugged frae the iron faem and the stanie swaws
As the sweel o the same saut tide
Clanjamfries crans and kirks by thrang causeys   230
Whaur cushat's croudle mells wi sea-maw's skirl,
And hirplan hame hauf-drouned wi the weicht o herrin
The trauchled trawler waffs in her wake
A flaffer o wings – a flash o faem-white feathers –
As the sea-maw spires i the stane-grey lift

Owre sworlan swaws o the stane-grey sea
And sclents til the sea-grey toun, the hert o stane.

Makars Meet

(To Helen B. Cruickshank)

The auld wife sings
At the kirkyaird waa,
And the middle-aged makar*   *poet*
Maun listen til aa,
Maun hear it sae young,
The lilt o her cry,
In spite o the years
And the love lang by,
The hopes that crottled*,   *crumbled*
The dwaums* that smoored*,   10
dreams/'smothered'
The freinds that connached*,   *destroyed*
The faiths that hured*,   *whored*
In spite o the hairsts*   *harvests*
That rain dinged doun,
Nae storm can winter
The spring o her tune –

But the middle-aged makar,
For aa the bricht air,
Kens ice in his hert
And snaw on his hair.   20

Scotched

Scotch God
Kent His
Faither.

Scotch Religion
Damn
Aa.

Scotch Education
I tellt ye
I tellt ye.

Scotch Queers   10
Wha peys wha
– For what?

Scotch Prostitution
Dear,
Dear.

Scotch Presbyterianism
Blue
Do.

Scotch Glasgow-Irish
God   20
Weirs a green jersey.

Scotch Orangemen
Bully
For Billy.

Scotch Liberty
Agree
Wi me.

Scotch Equality
Kaa the feet frae
Thon big bastard.   30

Scotch Fraternity
Our mob uses
The same razor.

Scotch Optimism
Through a gless,
Darkly.

Scotch Pessimism
Nae
Gless.

Scotch Modernity
Auld
Lang syne.

Scotch Initiative
Eftir
You.

Scotch Generosity
Eftir
Me.

Scotch Co-operation
Pou thegither
– My wey.

Scotch Geniuses
Deid
– Or damned.

Scotch Sex
In atween
Drinks.

Scotch Passion
Forgot
Mysel.

Scotch Love
Barely
A bargain.

Scotch Free-Love
Canna be
Worth much.

Scotch Lovebirds
Cheap
Cheap.

Scotch Fractions
A hauf
'n' hauf.

Scotch Troubles
Monie a pickle
Maks a puckle★.

Scotch Political-Parties
Monie a puckle
Maks a pickle.

40

50

60

70

few

Scotch Gaeldom
Up the
Erse.

80

Scotch Astronomy
Keek at
Uranus.

Scotch Astrology
Omen
In the gloamin.

Scotch Soccer
Robbery
Wi violence.

90

Scotch Waverley-Novels
Tales anent
Trains.

Scotch Exiles
Love ye
Further.

Scotch Charity
Ends
At hame.

Scotch Self-Sacrifice
Saxpence
– On Sundays.

100

Scotch Unionism
Wallace bled but
Here's their transfusion.

Scotch Socialism
Reid
– Indeed?

Scotch Liberalism
Pink
Kink.

110

Scotch Nationalism
Tartan
Scartan★.

scratching

Scotch Conservatism
Lowse★
Grouse.

loose

Scotch Labour
Nine months
Hard.   120

Scotch England
Dam'
Nation!

Scotch Afternoon-Tea
Masked
Pot.

Scotch Drink
Nip
Trip.

Scotch Poets   130
Wha's the
T'ithr?

Cauld Glory

The lift★ blae, the laich sun   sky
a louran★ bluidshot ee,   sullen
the cranreuch★ poutheran perished grun   frost
and sclentan frae ilka tree
in winternichts o steely starns★   stars
that stound★ the harns★.   pound/brains

The girss weirs icy threids,
its flouers hae frost as seeds,
ilk leaf gane bare and broun
til scartan★ Time   scratching,
                                                          weathering

is glenteran white as a bride's goun,   11
sae wapped in a rauchen★ o rime.   mantle

George Mackay Brown (1921 – 1996)

Brown, a major Scottish poet, short-story writer and novelist, was born in Stromness, in the Orkney Islands (just north of the mainland), where he lived most of his life. Orkney was a dominant influence upon Brown, and he set most of his works there, including *Greenvoe* (1972), Brown's first novel, and perhaps still his best. His works celebrate Orkney itself, the simple lives of its fishing communities, the influence of the past (especially the Vikings) upon the islands and the collective memories of its people, and finally a number of Christian themes – the triumph of faith and love, the value of suffering, the connection between faith and the rhythms of nature and the seasons. A convert to Catholicism, he may in fact be labelled a religious writer.

His technique, in both poetry and prose, utilises an apparent simplicity of statement with a complexity of symbolic references and frequent experiments with literary form, point of view and, especially, movements in time – since to Brown, the Great Truths are eternal (and thus cyclical). There is a constant interweaving of Orkney's history with its present. In this respect, he is a quintessential Scottish writer.

'Celia', realistic in mode, is one of the finest of modern Scottish short stories. 'Brig-o-Dread', a fantasy and an allegory, is a better example of Brown's overall work, in its combination of piety, thematic complexity and deceptive straightforwardness of style.

The Exile

So, blinded with Love
He tried to blunder

Out of that field
Of floods and thunder.

The frontiers were closed.
At every gate
The sworded pitiless
Angels wait.

There's no retreat.
The path mounts higher   10
And every summit
Fringed with fire.

The night is blind,
Dark winds, dark rains:
But now his blood
Pours through his veins,

His hammer heart
Thuds in his breast
'What Love devises,
That is best,'   20

And he would not turn,
Though the further side
Dowered his days
With fame and pride.

What though his feet
Are hurt and bare?
Love walks with him
In the menacing air.

The frontiers sealed;
His foot on the stone;   30
And low in the East
The gash of dawn.

The Old Women

Go sad or sweet or riotous with beer
Past the old women gossiping by the hour,
They'll fix on you from every close and pier
An acid look to make your veins run sour.

'No help,' they say, 'his grandfather that's dead
Was troubled with the same dry-throated curse,
And many a night he made the ditch his bed.
This blood comes welling from the same cracked source.'

On every kind of merriment they frown.
But I have known a grey-eyed sober boy   10
Sail to the lobsters in a storm, and drown.
Over his body dripping on the stones
Those same old hags would weave into their moans
An undersong of terrible holy joy.

The Lodging

The stones of the desert town
Flush; and, a star-filled wave,
Night steeples down.

From a pub door here and there
A random ribald song
Leaks on the air.

The Roman in a strange land
Broods, wearily leaning
His lance in the sand.

The innkeeper over the fire   10
Counting his haul, hears not
The cry from the byre★;   animal barn

But rummaging in the till
Grumbles at the drunken shepherds
Dancing on the hill;

And wonders, pale and grudging,
If the queer pair below
Will pay their lodging.

Unlucky Boat

That boat has killed three people. Building her
Sib drove a nail through his thumb. He died in his croft
Bunged to the eyes with rust and penicillin.
One evening when the Flow was a bar of silver
Under the moon, and Mansie and Tom, with wands
Were putting a spell on cuithes★, she dipped a bow   coal fish
And ushered Mansie, his pipe still in his teeth,
To meet the cold green angels. They hauled her up
Among the rocks, right in the path of Angus,
Whose neck, rigid with pints from the Dounby Market,   10
Snapped like a barley stalk . . . There she lies,
A leprous unlucky bitch, in the quarry of Moan.

Tinkers, going past, make the sign of the cross.

Fiddler's Song

The storm is over, lady.
The sea makes no more sound.
What do you wait for, lady?
His yellow hair is drowned.

The waves go quiet, lady,
Like sheep into the fold.
What do you wait for, lady?
His kissing mouth is cold.

Culloden: The Last Battle

The black cloud crumbled.
    My plaid that Morag wove
In Drumnakeil, three months before the eagle
Fell in the west, curled like the grey sea hag
Around my blood.
    We crouched on the long moor
And broke our last round bannock.
    Fergus Mor
Was praying to every crossed and beaded saint
That swung Iona, like the keel of Scotland,   10
Into the wrecking European wave.
Gow shook his flask. Alastair sang out
They would be drunker yet on German blood

Before the hawk was up. For 'Look,' cried he,
'At all the hogsheads waiting to be tapped
Among the rocks . . . '
    Old iron-mouth spilled his brimstone,
Nodded and roared. Then all were at their thunders,
And Fergus fell, and Donald gave a cry
Like a wounded stag, and raised his steel and ran   20
Into the pack.
    But we were hunters too,
All smoking tongues. I picked my chosen quarry
Between the squares. Morag at her wheel
Turning the fog of wool to a thin swift line
Of August light, drew me to love no surer
Than that red man to war. And his cold stance
Seemed to expect my coming. We had hastened
Faithful as brothers from the sixth cry of God
To play this game of ghost on the long moor.   30
His eyes were hard as dice, his cheek was cropped
For the far tryst, his Saxon bayonet
Bright as a wolf's tooth. Our wild paths raced together,
Locked in the heather, faltered by the white stone,
Then mine went on alone.
    'Come back, come back,'
Alastair cried.
    I turned.
        Three piercing shapes
Drifted about me in the drifting smoke.   40
We crossed like dreams.
    This was the last battle.
We had not turned before.
    The eagle was up
And away to the Isles.
    That night we lay
Far in the west. Alastair died in the straw.
We travelled homeward, on the old lost roads,
Twilight by twilight, clachan★ by weeping sheepfold.   village

My three wounds were heavy and round as medals   50
Till Morag broke them with her long fingers.

Weaving, she sings of the beauty of defeat.

The Poet

    Therefore he no more troubled the pool of silence.
    But put on mask and cloak,
    Strung a guitar
    And moved among the folk.
    Dancing they cried,
    'Ah, how our sober islands
    Are gay again, since this blind lyrical tramp
    Invaded the Fair!'

Under the last dead lamp
When all the dancers and masks had gone inside   10
His cold stare
Returned to its true task, interrogation of silence.

Trout Fisher

Semphill, his hat stuck full of hooks
   Sits drinking ale
     Among the English fishing visitors,
    Probes in detail
       Their faults in casting, reeling, selection of flies.
'Never, he urges, do what it says in the books.'
     Then they, obscurely wise,
      Abandon by the loch their dripping oars
And hang their throttled tarnish on the scale.

'Forgive me, every speckled trout,'   10
   Says Semphill then,
     'And every swan and eider on these waters.
    Certain strange men
      Taking advantage of my poverty
Have wheedled all my subtle loch-craft out
     So that their butchery
      Seem fine technique in the ear of wives and daughters.
And I betray the loch for a white coin.'

Old Fisherman with Guitar

A formal exercise for withered fingers.
   The head is bent,
     The eyes half closed, the tune
Lingers
    And beats, a gentle wing the west had thrown
Against his breakwater wall with salt savage lament.

So fierce and sweet the song on the plucked string,
   Know now for truth
     Those hands have cut from the net
The strong   10
    Crab-eaten corpse of Jock washed from a boat
One old winter, and gathered the mouth of Thora to his mouth.

Witch

Three horsemen rode between the hills
And they dismounted at Greenhill.
Tall they stooped in at the door.
No long time then
Till Wilma came out among them, laughing.
The fishless fishermen watched from the shore.
She sat behind the second dark rider.
They left the valley at noon.
And Wilma did not come back that day
Nor the next day   10
Nor any day at all that week.
And the dog barked lonely at Greenhill
And the girls took turns at milking her cow.
(One took the froth from her vat.)
The laird sent word
At the end of winter, to James of Reumin
That on Candlemas Friday
He should sail his dinghy to Kirkwall.
He sailed the *Lupin* to the red church.
And there at a steep place, Gallowsha,   20
Among tilted bottles, fists, faces
– A cold drunken wheel –
James saw the hangman put the red shirt on Wilma.
He sailed back smouldering
From the fire, the rum, the reproaches.
The dog of Greenhill
Barked in the throat of the valley.
And next morning
They launched their boat at the dawn with a wild shout,
The three unlucky fishermen.   30

Taxman

Seven scythes leaned at the wall.
Beard upon golden beard
The last barley load
Swayed through the yard.
The girls uncorked the ale.
Fiddle and feet moved together.
Then between stubble and heather
A horseman rode.

Buonaparte, the Laird and the Volunteers

I, Harry Cruickshank, laird in Hoy
Being by your lordships bidden
To supply from my lands in Rackwick, Hoy,
For His Majesty's ships-of-war
Seven hale hearty willing seamen
Upon payment of the agreed bounty, two guineas,
Did thereupon name
    John Stewart at Greenhill, fisherman,
    James Stewart at Greenhill, crofter,
    William Mowat at Bunertoon, fisherman,   10
    Andrew Sinclair at Mucklehouse, fisherman,
    Thomas Thomson at Crowsnest, fisherman,
    James Robb at Scar, fisherman,
    James Leask at Reumin, crofter and fisherman,
All unmarried, save for Wm Mowat,
Who got wife and cow from Graemsay at the fall of the year
And James Robb, a widower –
The rest all young men in their strength.
I duly rode with officers to the valley
To give notice of impressment to the said men   20
But found them removed
And the old people dumb and cold as stones.
One said, they were gone fishing, very far out –
Faroe, Rockall, Sulisker.
Another, to the horse-market in Caithness.
Another, 'the trows were taen them aneath the hill' . . .
Upon the Sabbath following
I came to the kirk of Hoy secretly with four officers
Between the sermon and the last psalm.
We took John and James Stewart in the kirk door.   30
They were quiet enough after the minister spoke with them.
(By this, they will be in Portsmouth.)
It is certain, my lords,
Robb and Thomson are in the caves.
Andrew Sinclair, fisherman, Mucklehouse
Listed in Hamnavoe for the Davis Straits
On the whaler *Tavistock*
(We found his mark and name in the agent's book).
And Mowat ferried himself to Graemsay
With wife and cow   40
And there hacked three fingers from his right hand
And stifled the ruin with tar.
As for Leask, he is broken with troll-music.
He lies day-long in the back of the bed,
Dark hollows about his skull.
The old woman says, 'in a decline, consumption.'
She stitches away at a shroud.
But like enough, the guns being silent
And Buonaparte down,
He will make his customary furrows along the hill.   50

A dozen old men are left in the valley.
Last week, your lordships,
I observed two women rowing to the lobsters.
Ploughmen next April will have shrill voices.

Ikey on the People of Hellya

Rognvald who stalks round Corse with his stick
I do not love.
His dog has a loud sharp mouth.
The wood of his door is very hard.
Once, tangled in his barbed wire
(I was paying respects to his hens, stroking a wing)
He laid his stick on me.
That was out of a hard forest also.

Mansie at Quoy is a biddable man.
Ask for water, he gives you rum.   10
I strip his scarecrow April by April.
Ask for a scattering of straw in his byre
He lays you down
Under a quilt as long and light as heaven.
Then only his raging woman spoils our peace.

Gray the fisherman is no trouble now
Who quoted me the vagrancy laws
In a voice slippery as seaweed under the kirkyard.
I rigged his boat with the seven curses.
Occasionally still, for encouragement,   20
I put the knife in his net.

Though she has black peats and a yellow hill
And fifty silken cattle
I do not go near Merran and her cats.
Rather break a crust on a tombstone.
Her great-great-grandmother
Wore the red coat at Gallowsha.[1]

The thousand rabbits of Hollandsay
Keep Simpson's corn short,
Whereby comes much cruelty, gas and gunshot.   30
Tonight I have lit a small fire.
I have stained my knife red.
I have peeled a round turnip,
And I pray the Lord
To preserve those nine hundred and ninety-nine innocents.

---

[1] Was burned as a witch.

Finally in Folscroft lives Jeems,
Tailor and undertaker, a crosser of limbs,
One tape for the living and the dead.
He brings a needle to my rags in winter,
And he guards, against my stillness,   40
The seven white boards
I got from the Danish wreck one winter.

Hamnavoe Market

They drove to the Market with ringing pockets.

Folster found a girl
Who put wounds on his face and throat,
Small diagonal wounds like red doves.

Johnstone stood beside the barrel.
All day he stood there.
He woke in a ditch, his mouth full of ashes.

Grieve bought a balloon and a goldfish.
He swung through the air.
He fired shotguns, rolled pennies, ate sweet fog from a stick.

Heddle was at the Market also.   11
I know nothing of his activities.
He is and always was a quiet man.

Garson fought three rounds with a Negro boxer
And received thirty shillings,
Much applause, and an eye loaded with thunder.

Where did they find Flett?
They found him in a brazen ring
Of blood and fire, a new Salvationist.

A gypsy saw in the hand of Halcro   20
Great strolling herds, harvests, a proud woman.
He wintered in the poorhouse.

They drove home from the Market, under the stars,
Except for Johnstone
Who lay in a ditch, his mouth full of dying fires.

Celia

ONE

The Norwegian whaler *Erika* tied up at the pier in the middle of Monday afternoon, and when the pubs opened at five o'clock all six of the crew went into the Hamnavoe Bar. Per Bjorling the skipper was with them, but about seven o'clock he bought a full bottle of vodka and left them drinking their whiskies and lagers and went outside. It was getting dark. He walked along the street till he came to an opening that descended step by step to a small pier with a house on it. From inside the house came the thwack of a hammer driving nails into leather. One room of the house had a lamp burning in the window but the other room next the sea was dark. Per Bjorling was about to knock at the door when it was opened from inside. He smiled and raised his sailor's cap and went in.

'What kind of a man is it this time?' shouted a voice from the lighted room. 'Is it that bloody foreigner? . . .' All the people in the neighbouring houses could hear what was being said. Maisie Ness came to the end of her pier and stood listening, her head cocked to one side.

The hammer smacked on leather, a rapid tattoo.

The seaward room remained dark; or rather, the window flushed a little as if a poker had suddenly woken flames from the coal.

'Yes,' yelled the shoemaker, 'a bloody drunken foreign sailor.'

Then silence returned to the piers and one by one the lights went on in all the houses round about.

TWO

The *Erika* and three other Norwegian whalers caught the morning tide on Tuesday and it was quiet again in the harbour. In the house on the small pier the shoe-repairing began early, the leisurely smack of the hammer on the moulded leather in between periods of quiet stitching. At ten o'clock Maisie Ness from the next close came with a pair of shoes to be soled. She walked straight in through the open door and turned into the room on the left next the street. The shoemaker sat on his stool, his mouth full of tacks. Maisie laid her shoes on the bench, soles upward.

'Celia isn't up yet, surely. I don't hear her,' she said.

'Celia's a good girl,' said the shoemaker.

'I don't believe you've had your breakfast,' cried Maisie Ness, 'and it's past ten o'clock. You need your food, or you'll be ill same as you were in the winter-time.'

'I'll get my breakfast,' said the shoemaker. 'Just leave the shoes on the bench. All they need is rubber soles and a protector or two in the right heel to keep it level. You're an impudent woman. Ignorant too. Could you read the deep books that Celia reads? I don't believe you can sign your name. I'll get my breakfast all right. Celia's a good girl. Just keep your tongue off her.'

Maisie Ness went up the steps of the pier shaking her head. She managed to look pleased and outraged at the same time.

'Celia,' the shoemaker called out, 'I'll make you a cup of tea. Just you lie in bed for an hour or two yet.'

THREE

It was early spring. Darkness was still long but the light was slowly encroaching and the days grew colder. The last of the snow still scarred the Orphir hills. One sensed a latent fertility; under the hard earth the seeds were awake and astir; their long journey to blossom and ripeness was beginning. But in Hamnavoe, the fishermen's town, the lamps still had to be lit early.

On Tuesday night every week Mr Spence the jeweler paid his visit. He would hesitate at the head of the close, look swiftly right and left along the street, then quickly descend the steps.

The shoemaker heard his precise footsteps on the flagstones outside and immediately took down from the shelf the draught-board and the set of draughtsmen. He had the pieces arranged on the board before Mr Spence was at the threshold.

'Come in, Mr Spence,' he shouted, 'come in. I heard your feet.'

And Mr Spence, without a single glance at the dark seaward window, went straight into the work-room on the left, bending his head under the lintel and smiling in the lamplight. 'Well, Thomas,' he said.

They always played for about an hour, best of three games. Mr Spence generally lost. Perhaps he was a poor player; perhaps he was nervous (he shuffled and blinked and cleared his throat a good deal); perhaps he genuinely liked to give the shoemaker the pleasure of winning; perhaps he was anxious to get this empty ritual over with. They played this night without speaking, the old man in his leather apron and the middle-aged bachelor in his smart serge tailor-made suit. The shoemaker won two games right away, inside half an hour, so that there was no need that night to play a decider.

'You put up a very poor show tonight,' said the shoemaker.

'I'm not in the same class as you, Thomas,' said Mr Spence.

He went over to his coat hanging on a peg and brought a half-bottle of whisky out of the pocket. 'Perhaps, Thomas,' he said, 'you'd care for a drink.'

'You know fine,' said the shoemaker, 'I never drink that filthy trash. The poison!'

'Then,' said Mr Spence, 'perhaps I'll go and see if Miss Celia would care to have a little drink. A toddy, seeing it's a cold night.'

'No,' said the shoemaker anxiously, 'I don't think you should do that. Or if you do, only a very small drop.'

But Mr Spence was already tiptoeing along the lobby towards the dark room, carrying the half-bottle in his hand. He tapped on the door, and opened it gently. The girl was bending over the black range, stabbing the coal with a poker. At once the ribs were thronged with red and yellow flames, and the shadow of the girl leapt over him before she herself turned slowly to the voice in the doorway.

'My dear,' said Mr Spence.

FOUR

'How are you, Thomas?' said Dr Wilson on the Wednesday morning, sitting down on the bench among bits and scrapings of leather.

'I'm fine,' said the shoemaker.

'The chest all right?'

'I still get a bit of a wheeze when the wind's easterly,' said the shoemaker, 'but I'm not complaining.'

There was silence in the room for a half-minute.

'And Celia?' said Dr Wilson.

'Celia's fine,' said the shoemaker. 'I wish she would eat more and get more exercise. I'm a nuisance to her, I keep her tied to the house. But she keeps her health. She's fine.'

'I'm glad to hear it,' said Dr Wilson.

'Celia's a good girl,' said the shoemaker.

'I know she's a good girl,' said Dr Wilson. Then his voice dropped a tone. 'Thomas,' he said, 'I don't want to worry you, but there are complaints in the town.'

'She's a good girl,' said the old man, 'a very good girl to me.'

'Complaints,' said Dr Wilson quietly, 'that this is a house of bad repute. I'm not saying it, for I know you're both good people, you and Celia. But the scandal-mongers are saying it along the street. You know the way it is. I've heard it twenty times this past week if I've heard it once. That all kinds of men come here, at all hours of the night, and there's drinking and carrying-on. I don't want to annoy you, Thomas, but I think it's right you should know what they're saying in the public, Maisie Ness and the other women. All this worry is not good for your lungs.'

'*I* don't drink,' said the shoemaker. 'How do I know who comes and goes in the night? That Maisie Ness should have her tongue cut out. Celia has a sweetheart, Ronald Leask of Clett, and she's applied to be a member of the Kirk. The minister's coming to see her Friday evening. She's a good girl.'

'Perhaps I could see Celia for a minute?' said Dr Wilson and got to his feet.

'No,' said the shoemaker, 'she's sleeping. She needs her rest. She's sleeping late. Celia is a very good girl to me. If it wasn't for Celia I know I'd have died in the winter-time.'

'Good morning, Thomas,' said Dr Wilson. 'I'll be back next Wednesday. You have plenty of tablets to be getting on with. Tell Celia I'm asking for her. Send for me if you need me, any time.'

FIVE

'Go away,' said the shoemaker to Mr William Snoddy the builder's clerk. 'Just you go away from this house and never come back, never so much as darken the door again. I know what you're after. I'm not a fool exactly.'

'I want you to make me a pair of light shoes for the summer,' said Mr Snoddy. 'That's all I want.'

'Is it?' said the shoemaker. 'Then you can go some other place, for I have no intention of doing the job for you.'

They were standing at the door of the house on the pier. It was Wednesday evening and the lamp was burning in the work-room but the room next the sea was in darkness.

'Last Saturday,' said Mr Snoddy, 'at the pier-head, you promised to make me a pair of light shoes for the summer.'

'I didn't know then,' said the shoemaker, 'what I know now. You and your fancy-women. Think shame of yourself. You have a wife and three bairns waiting for you in your house at the South End. And all you can do is run after other women here, there and everywhere. I'm making no shoes for whore-mastering expeditions. You can take that for sure and certain.'

'You've been listening,' said Mr Snoddy, 'to cruel groundless gossip.'

'And I believe the gossip,' said the shoemaker. 'I don't usually believe gossip but I believe this particular piece of gossip. You're an immoral man.'

'There's such a thing as a court of law,' said Mr Snoddy, 'and if ever I hear of these slanders being repeated again, I'll take steps to silence the slanderers.'

'You'll have your work cut out,' said the shoemaker, 'because you've been seen going to this house and that house when the men have been away at the fishing. I've seen you with my own two eyes. And if you want names I'll supply them to you with pleasure.'

'Let's go inside,' said Mr Snoddy in a suddenly pleasant voice, 'and we'll talk about something else. We'll have a game of draughts.'

The shoemaker stretched out foot and arm and blocked the door.

'Stay where you are,' he said. 'Just bide where you are. What's that you've got in the inside pocket of your coat, eh?'

'It's my wallet,' said Mr Snoddy, touching the bulge at his chest.

'It's drink,' said the shoemaker, 'it's spirits. I'm not exactly so blind or so stupid that I can't recognise the shape of a half-bottle of whisky. I allow no drink into this house. Understand that.'

'Please, Thomas,' said Mr Snoddy. 'It's a cold night.'

'Forby being a whore-master,' said the shoemaker, 'you're a drunkard. Never a day passed that you aren't three or four times in the pub. Just look in the mirror when you get home and see how red your nose is getting. I'm sorry for your wife and children.'

'I mind my own business,' said Mr Snoddy.

'That's fine,' said the shoemaker. 'That's very good. Just mind your own business and don't come bothering this house. There's one thing I have to tell you before you go.'

'What's that?' said Mr Snoddy.

'Celia is not at home,' shouted the old man. He suddenly stepped back into the lobby and slammed the door shut. Mr Snoddy stood alone in the darkness, his mouth twitching. Then he turned and began to walk up the pier slowly.

From inside the house came the sound of steel protectors being hammered violently into shoes.

Mr Snoddy's foot was on the first step leading up to the street when a hand tugged at his sleeve. He turned round. It was Celia. She had a grey shawl over her head and her hair was tucked into it. Her face in the darkness was an oval oblique shadow.

'Celia,' said Mr Snoddy in a shaking voice.

'Where are you off to so soon, Billy boy?' said Celia. 'Won't you stop and speak for a minute to a poor lonely girl?'

Mr Snoddy put his hands round her shoulders. She pushed him away gently.

'Billy,' she said, 'if you have a little drink on you I could be doing with it.'

The loud hammering went on inside the house.

Mr Snoddy took the flask from his inside pocket. 'I think, dear,' he said, 'where we're standing we're a bit in the public eye. People passing in the street. Maybe if we move into that corner . . . '

Together they moved to the wall of the watchmaker's house, into a segment of deeper darkness.

'Dear Celia,' muttered Mr Snoddy.

'Just one little mouthful,' said Celia. 'I believe it's gin you've gone and bought.'

SIX

Ronald Leask closed the door of the tractor shed. The whole field on the south side of the hill was ploughed now, a good day's work. He looked round him, stretched his aching arms, and walked slowly a hundred yards down to the beach. The boat was secure. There had been south-westerly winds and high seas for two days, but during that afternoon the wind had veered further west and dropped. He thought he would be able to set his lobster-creels the next morning, Friday, under the Hoy crags. The *Celia* rocked gently at the pier like a furled sea bird.

Ronald went back towards his house. He filled a bucket with water from the rain barrel at the corner. He stripped off his soiled jersey and shirt and vest and washed quickly, shuddering and gasping as the cold water slapped into his shoulders and chest. He carried the pail inside and kicked off his boots and trousers and finished his washing. Then he dried himself at the dead hearth and put on his best clothes – the white shirt and tartan tie, the dark Sunday suit, the pigskin shoes. He combed his wet fair hair till it clung to both sides of his head like bronze wings. His face looked back at him from the square tarnished mirror on the mantelpiece, red and complacent and healthy. He put on his beret and pulled it a little to one side.

Ronald wheeled his bicycle out of the lobby on to the road, mounted, and cycled towards Hamnavoe.

He passed three cars and a county council lorry and a young couple out walking. It was too dark to see their faces. As he freewheeled down into the town there were lights here and there in the houses. It would be a dark night, with no moon.

Ronald Leask left his bicycle at the head of the shoemaker's close and walked down the steps to the house. The lamp was lit in the old man's window but Celia's room, as usual, was dark. He knocked at the outer door. The clob-clob-clobbering of hammer against leather stopped.

'Who's that?' cried the old man sharply.

'It's me, Ronald.'

'Ronald,' said the shoemaker. 'Come in, Ronald.' He appeared at the door. 'I'm glad to see thee, Ronald.' He took Ronald's arm and guided him into the workroom. 'Come in, boy, and sit down.'

'How are you keeping, Thomas?' said Ronald.

'I'm fine, Ronald,' said the shoemaker, and coughed.

'And Celia?' said Ronald.

'Celia's fine,' said the shoemaker. 'She's wanting to see thee, I know that. It's not much of a life for a girl, looking after a poor old thing like me. She'll be glad of your company.'

'Last time I came, last Thursday, I didn't get much of a reception,' said Ronald.

'Celia wasn't well that day,' said the shoemaker. 'She likes thee more than anybody, I can assure thee for that.' He went over to the door and opened it and shouted across the lobby, 'Celia, Ronald's here.'

There was no answer from the other room.

'She's maybe sleeping,' said the shoemaker. 'Poor Celia, she works too hard, looking after me. What she needs is a long holiday. We'll go and see her.'

The old man crossed the lobby on tiptoe and opened the door of Celia's room gently. 'Celia,' he said, 'are you all right?'

'Yes,' said Celia's voice from inside.

'Ronald's here,' said the shoemaker.

'I know,' said Celia. 'I heard him.'

'Well,' said the shoemaker sharply, 'he wants to speak to you. And I'm taking him in now, whether you want it or not. And I'm coming in too for a minute.'

The two men went into the room. They could just make out the girl's outline against the banked-up glow of the fire. They groped towards chairs and sat down.

'Celia,' said the shoemaker, 'light your lamp.'

'No,' said Celia, 'I like it best this way, in the darkness. Besides, I have no money for paraffin. I don't get many shillings from you to keep the house going, and bread and coal and paraffin cost dear.'

'Speak to her, Ronald,' said the shoemaker.

'I can't be bothered to listen to him,' said Celia. 'I'm not well.'

'What ails you?' said the shoemaker.

'I don't know,' said Celia. 'I'm just not well.'

'Celia,' said Ronald earnestly, 'there's an understanding between us. You know it and I know it and the whole of Hamnavoe knows it. Why are you behaving this way to me?'

'That's true,' said the shoemaker. 'You're betrothed to one another.'

'Not this again,' said Celia, 'when I'm sick.' Then she said in a low voice, 'I need something to drink.'

'Drink!' said the old man angrily. 'That's all your mind runs on, drink. Just you listen to Ronald when he's speaking to you.'

'Celia,' said Ronald, 'it's a year come April since I buried my mother and the croft of Clett has stood there vacant ever since, except for me and the dog.'

'And a fine croft it is,' said the shoemaker. 'Good sandy soil and a tractor in the shed and a first-rate boat in the bay.'

'I'm not listening,' said Celia.

'It needs a woman about the place,' said Ronald. 'I can manage the farm work and the fishing. But inside the house things are going to wrack and ruin. That's the truth. Celia, you promised six months ago to come to Clett.'

'So that's all you want, is it?' said Celia. 'A housekeeper.'

'No,' said Ronald, 'I want you for my wife. I love you.'

'He does love you,' said the shoemaker. 'And he's a good man. And he has money put by. And he works well at the farming and the fishing. He's a fellow any girl would be proud to have for a man.'

'I'm not well tonight,' said Celia. 'I would be the better of a glass of brandy.'

'And what's more,' said the shoemaker, 'you love him, because you told me with your own lips not a fortnight ago.'

'I do not,' said Celia.

Ronald turned to the shoemaker and whispered to him and put something in his hand. The shoemaker rose up at once and went out. He banged the outer door shut behind him.

'Celia,' said Ronald.

'Leave me alone,' said Celia.

They sat in the growing darkness. The only light in the room was the dull glow from the range. Ronald could see the dark outline of the girl beside the fire. For ten minutes they neither moved nor spoke.

At last the door opened again and the old man came back. He groped his way to the table and put a bottle down on it. 'That's it,' he said to Ronald and laid down some loose coins beside the bottle. 'And that's the change.'

'Celia,' said Ronald, 'I'm sorry to hear you aren't well. I've got something here that'll maybe help you. A little brandy.'

'That's kind of you,' said Celia.

She picked up the poker and drove it into the black coal on top of the range. The room flared wildly with lights and shadows. The three dark figures were suddenly sitting in a warm rosy flickering world.

Celia took two cups from the cupboard and set them on the table and poured brandy into them.

'That's enough for me,' said Ronald, and put his hand over the cup next to him.

Celia filled the other cup to the top. Then she lifted it to her mouth with both hands and gulped it like water.

'Good health,' said the shoemaker. 'I'm saying that and I mean it though I'm not a drinking man myself. The very best of luck to you both.'

Ronald raised his cup and drank meagerly from it and put it down again on the table. 'Cheers,' he said.

Celia took another mouthful and set down her empty cup beside the bottle.

'Are you feeling better now, Celia?' said the shoemaker.

'A wee bit,' said Celia. She filled up her cup again. 'I'm very glad to see you,' she said to Ronald.

'That's better,' said the shoemaker, 'that's the way to speak.'

Celia took a drink and said, 'Ronald, supposing I come to live at Clett what's going to become of Thomas?'

'I'll be all right,' said the shoemaker, 'don't worry about me. I'll manage fine.'

'He'll come and live with us,' said Ronald. 'There's plenty of room.'

'No,' said Celia, 'but who's going to walk a mile and more to Clett to get their boots mended? We must think of that. He'll lose trade.'

'Don't drink so fast,' said the shoemaker.

'And besides that,' said Celia, 'he'll miss his friends, all the ones that come and visit him here and play draughts with him. What would he do without his game of draughts? Clett's a long distance away. I'm very pleased, Ronald, that you've come to see me.'

'I'm pleased to be here,' said Ronald.

'Light the lamp,' said the shoemaker happily.

'I love you both very much,' said Celia. 'You're the two people that I love most in the whole world.'

Celia filled up her cup again. This time half the brandy spilled over the table.

'I don't know whether I'll come to Clett or not,' said Celia. 'I'll have to think about it. I have responsibilities here. That's what makes me feel ill, being torn this way and that. I can't be in two places, can I? I love you both very much. I want you to know that, whatever happens.'

She suddenly started to cry. She put her hands over her face and her whole body shook with grief. She sat down in her chair beside the fire and sobbed long and bitterly.

The two men looked at each other, awed and awkward.

'I'll put a match to the lamp,' said the shoemaker. 'Then we'll see what's what.'

Celia stopped crying for a moment and said, 'Leave the bloody lamp alone.' Then she started to sob again, louder than ever.

Ronald got to his feet and went over to Celia. He put his arm across her shoulder.

'Poor Celia,' he said, 'tell me what way I can help thee?'

Celia rose to her feet and screamed at him. 'You go away from here, you bastard,' she shouted. 'Just go away! I want never to see you again! Clear off!'

'Celia,' pleaded the old man.

'If that's what you want, Celia,' said Ronald. He picked up his beret from the chair and stood with his back to the cupboard. 'Good night, Thomas,' he said.

'Come back, Ronald,' said the shoemaker. 'Celia isn't herself tonight. She doesn't mean a word of what she says.'

The flames were dying down in the range. Celia and Ronald and the shoemaker moved about in the room, three unquiet shadows.

'Good night, Celia,' said Ronald from the door.

'I hate you, you bastard,' she shrieked at him.

The last flame died. In the seething darkness the girl and the old man heard the bang of the outer door closing. Celia sat down in her chair and began to cry again, a slow gentle wailing.

Half-way up the steps of the close the shoemaker caught up with Ronald. 'This is the worst she's ever been,' he said. 'You know the way it is with her – she drinks heavily for a week or so, anything she can get, and then for a month or six weeks after that she's as peaceable as a dove. But this is the worst she's ever been. God knows what will come of her.'

'God knows,' said Ronald.

'It started on Monday night,' said the shoemaker. 'That Norsky was here with foreign hooch.'

'Don't worry, Thomas,' said Ronald. 'It'll turn out all right, like you say.'

'She'll be fine next time you come back,' said the shoemaker. 'Just you wait and see.'

Ronald got on to his bicycle at the head of the close.

The shoemaker went back slowly into the house. As he opened the door Celia's low voice came out of the darkness. 'God forgive me,' she was saying gently and hopelessly, 'O God forgive me.'

SEVEN

'No,' said Celia to the minister, 'I don't believe in your God. It's no good. You're wasting your time. What the Hamnavoe folk are saying is true, I'm a bad woman. I drink. Men come about the place all hours of the night. It isn't that I want them fumbling at me with their mouths and their hands. That sickens me. I put up with it for the drink they have in their pockets. I must drink.

'You're not a drinking man, Mr Blackie. I know that. I *had* to buy this bottle of wine from the licensed grocer's. It gives me courage to speak to you. Try to understand that. And we're sitting here in the half darkness because I can speak to you better in this secrecy. Faces tell lies to one another. You know the way it is. The truth gets buried under smiles.

'I drink because I'm frightened. I'm so desperately involved with all the weak things, lonely things, suffering things I see about me. I can't bear the pity I feel for them, not being able to help them at all. There's blood everywhere. The world's a torture chamber, just a sewer of pain. That frightens me.

'Yesterday it was a gull and a water rat. They met at the end of this pier. I was pinning washing to the line when I saw it. The gull came down on the rat and swallowed it whole the way it would gulp a crust of bread, then with one flap of its wing it was out over the sea again. I could see the shape of the rat in the blackback's throat, a kind of fierce twist and thrust. The bird broke up in the air. It screamed. Blood and feathers showered out of it. The dead gull and the living rat made separate splashes in the water.

'It seems most folk can live with that kind of thing. Not me – I get all caught up in it . . . '

Stars slowly thickened and brightened in the window that looked over the harbour. The rising tide began to lap against the gable ends of the houses.

'Mr Blackie,' said Celia, 'an earthquake ruined a town in Serbia last week. The ground just opened and swallowed half the folk. Did your God in his mercy think up that too? The country folk in Vietnam, what kind of vice is it they're gripped in, guns and lies and anger on both sides of them, a slowly tightening agony? Is your God looking after them? They never harmed anybody, but the water in the rice fields is red now all the time. Black men and white men hate each other in Chicago and Cape Town. God rules everything. He knew what was going to happen before the world was made. So we're told. If that's goodness, I have another name for it. Not the worst human being that ever lived would do the things God does. Tell me this, was God in the Warsaw ghetto too? I just want to know. I was reading about it last week in a book I got out of the Library.

'I know you don't like this darkness and the sound of wine being poured in the glass. It's the only way I can speak to you and be honest . . .

'I remember my mother and my father. They were like two rocks in the sea. Life might be smooth or rough for me – there was hunger every now and then when the fishing was poor – but the two rocks were always there. I knew every ledge and cranny. I flew between them like a young bird.

'We were poor, but closer together because of that. We gave each other small gifts. I would take shells and seapinks into the house for them. My father always had a special fish for me when he came in from the west, a codling or a flounder as small as my hand. Then my mother would bake a small bannock for me to eat with it at teatime, when I was home from school.

'I was twelve years old. One morning when I got up for school my mother was standing in the door looking out over the harbour. The fire was dead. She told me in a flat voice I wasn't to go to school that day, I was to go back to my room and draw the curtain and stay there till she called me. An hour later I heard feet on the pier. I looked through the edge of the curtain. Four fishermen were carrying something from the boat into the house. The thing was covered with a piece of sail and there was a trail of drops behind it. My father was in from his creels for the last time.

'We knew what real poverty was after that. My mother was too proud to take anything from the Poor Fund. "Of course not," she said, "my grandfather was schoolmaster in Hoy." . . . But in the middle of February she swallowed her pride and went to the Poor Inspector. One night I woke up and heard voices and came downstairs and I saw Thomas Linklater the shoemaker having supper beside the fire. A month after that my mother married him in the registry office. He came and sat in my father's chair and slept in my father's bed. He carried a new smell into our house, leather and rosin, like an animal of a different species.

'I hated him. Of course I smiled and spoke. But in my room, in the darkness, I hated the stranger.

'Three years went past. Then it was my mother's turn. I watched her changing slowly. I didn't know what the change was, nor why Dr Wilson should trouble to come so often. Then I heard Maisie Ness saying 'cancer' to the watchmaker's wife at the end of the close. My mother was a good-looking woman. She was a bit vain and she'd often look long in the mirror, putting her hair to rights and smiling to her reflection. The change went on in her all that summer. She looked in the mirror less and less. Every day though she did her housework. The room had to be swept and the dishes put away before Dr Wilson called. Half a ghost, she knelt at the unlit fire and struck a match. That last morning she laid three bowls of porridge on the table. She looked at her withered face in the mirror. Then she groped for her chair and sank into it. She was dead before I could put down my spoon. The shoemaker hurried away to find Dr Wilson. The body slowly turned cold in the deep straw chair.

'I heard the shoemaker crying in his room the day before the funeral.

'"Blessed are the dead which die in the Lord" – that's what you said at the graveside. It was a poor way to die. It was ugly and degrading and unblessed, if anything ever was.

'We were alone in the house together then, a girl and an old cobbler. It was the beginning of winter. We spoke to each other only when it was needful. He gave me the housekeeping money every Friday and it was never enough. "There'll be more soon," he would say, "It's hard times, a depression all over the country. So-and-so owes five pounds for two pairs of shoes and I had a bill from the wholesale leather merchant for twenty pounds odds." . . . I wanted cakes on the table at the week-end but there was never anything but the usual bread and oatcakes and margarine.

'Christmas came. I wanted a few decorations about the house, a tree, paper bells, some tinsel, a dozen cards to send to my special friends – you know the way it is with young girls. "We can't afford nonsense like that," the shoemaker said. "We should be thankful to God for a roof over our heads." . . . And so the walls remained bare.

'That Christmas I hated him worse than ever.

'"Celia," he said at Hogmanay, just before it struck midnight, "I'm not a drinking man. But it's bad luck not to drink a health to the house at this time of year. We'll take one small dram together."

'He brought a half-bottle of whisky out of the cupboard.

'The clock struck twelve. We touched glasses. I shuddered as the whisky went down. It burned my mouth and my stomach and it took tears to my eyes. "He's doing this deliberately to hurt me," I thought. My eyes were still wet when the door opened and Mr Spence the jeweller came in. He had a bottle of whisky in his hand to wish us a good New Year. He poured three glasses and we toasted each other. The cobbler merely wet his lips. I drank my whisky down quickly to get it over with.

'It's hard to explain what happened next. I knew who I was before I took that drink – a poor girl in an ordinary house on a fisherman's pier. I stood there holding an empty glass in my hand. A door was opening deep inside me and I looked through it into another country. I stood between the two places, confused and happy and excited. I still wore Celia's clothes but the clothes were all a disguise, bits of fancy dress, a masquerade. You know the ballad about the Scottish King who went out in the streets of Edinburgh in bonnet and tradesman's apron? I wore the clothes of a poor girl but I was wise, rich, great, gentle, good.

> Then doon he let his duddies fa',
> And doon he let them fa'
> And he glittered a' in gold
> Far abune them a'.

The world was all mine and I longed to share it with everybody. Celia was a princess in her little house on the pier. She pretended to be poor but she had endless treasures in her keeping, and it was all a secret, nobody knew about it but Celia. A wild happiness filled the house.

'I bent down and kissed the old shoemaker.

'Mr Spence, I remember, was pouring another whisky into my glass. The confusion and the happiness increased. I felt very tired then, I remember. I went to bed wrapped in silks and swan's feathers.

'It was Celia the poor girl who woke up next morning. There was a hard grey blanket up at her face. She had a mouth like ashes. The wireless when she switched it on downstairs told of people dying of hunger in the streets of Calcutta, drifting about like wraiths and lying down on the burning pavements. And a plane had fallen from the sky in Kansas and forty people were dead on a hillside.

'She cried, the poor princess, beside the dead fire.

'The next Friday out of the housekeeping money I bought a bottle of cheap wine.

'That's all there is to tell, really. You've heard the confession of an alcoholic, or part of it, for the bad fairy tale isn't over yet.

'Once a month, maybe every six weeks, the fisher girl craves for news of the lost country, the real world, what she calls her kingdom. For a week or more I enchant myself away from the town and the pier and the sound of cobbling. When I have no more money left I encourage men to come here with drink. I'm shameless about it now. Everybody who has a bottle is welcome, even Mr Snoddy. At the end of every bout I'm in deeper exile than the time before. Every debauch kills a piece of Celia − I almost said, kills a part of her soul, but of course I don't believe in that kind of thing any more.

'And so the bad fairy tale goes on and the fisher girl who thinks that somehow she's a princess is slowly fitted with the cold blood and leathery skin and the terrible glittering eye of a toad.

'This kingdom I've had a glimpse of, though − what about that? It *seemed* real and precious. It seemed like an inheritance we're all born for, something that belongs to us by right.

'If that's true, it should be as much *there* as this pier is in the first light of morning. Why do we have to struggle towards it through fogs of drink? What's the good of all this mystery? The vision should be like a loaf or a fish, simple and real, something given to nourish the whole world.

'I blame God for that too.'

There was no sound for a while but the lapping of harbour water against stone as the tide rose slowly among the piers and slipways. The huge chaotic ordered wheel of stars tilted a little westward on its axis.

'The bottle's nearly empty,' said Celia, 'and I haven't said what I meant to say at all. I wonder if the licensed grocer would sell me another bottle? No, it's too late. And besides, I don't think I have enough money in my purse. And besides, you don't want to listen to much more of this bad talk.

'All the same, you can see now why I could never be a member of your church. All I could bring to it is this guilt, shame, grief for things that happen, a little pity, a sure knowledge of exile.'

'Will Christ accept that?'

There was another longer silence in the room.

'Celia,' said the Reverend Andrew Blackie, a little hopelessly, 'you must try to have faith.'

The girl's window was full of stars. The sky was so bright that the outlines of bed and chair and cupboard could be dimly seen, and the shapes of an empty bottle and a glass on the table.

'I want to have faith,' said Celia. 'I want that more than anything in the world.'

EIGHT

Ronald Leask worked his creels with Jock Henryson all that Saturday afternoon along the west coast. They hauled eighty creels under Marwick Head and Yesnaby. In the late afternoon the wind shifted round to the north-west and strengthened and brought occasional squalls of rain. They decided to leave their remaining score of creels under the Black Crag till morning and make for home before it got dark. They had a box of lobsters and half a basket of crabs, a fair day's work. As Ronald turned the *Celia* into Hoy Sound he saw three Norwegian whalers racing for the shelter of Hamnavoe on the last of the flood tide. Another squall of rain hit them. Ronald put on his sou'wester and buttoned his black oilskin up to the chin. Jock Henryson was at the wheel now, in the shelter of the cabin.

'It's going to be a dirty night,' said Jock.

They delivered their lobsters and crabs at the Fishermen's Society pier. Then Jock said he must go home for his supper. 'You come too,' he said to Ronald. 'The wife'll have something in the pot.'

'No,' said Ronald, 'I think I'll go along for a drink.'

It was raining all the time now. The flagstones of the street shone. Ronald stopped for a few seconds at the head of the shoemaker's close, then he walked on more quickly until he came to the lighted window of the Hamnavoe Bar. He pushed open the door. Bill MacIsaac the boatbuilder was at the bar drinking beer with Thorfinn Vik the farmer from Helliar. Sammy Flett the drunk was in too – he was half stewed and he was pestering the barman to give him a pint, and Drew the barman was refusing him patiently but firmly. A half-empty bottle of cheap wine stuck out of Sammy Flett's pocket.

'Here's Ronald Leask, a good man,' said Sammy Flett, going up to Ronald unsteadily. 'Ronald, you're a good friend of mine and I ask you to accept a cigarette out of my packet, and I'm very glad of your offer to furnish me with a glass of beer for old time's sake.'

'A glass of whisky,' said Ronald to Drew the barman.

'Absolutely delighted, old friend,' said Sammy Flett.

'It's not for you,' said Drew the barman to Sammy Flett. 'You're getting nothing, not a drop. The police sergeant was here this morning and your father with him and I know all about the trouble you're causing at home, smashing the chairs and nearly setting fire to the bed at the week-end. This place is out of bounds to you, sonny boy. I promised the sergeant and your old man. You can push off any time you like.'

'That's all lies,' said Sammy Flett. 'Just give me one pint of ordinary beer. That's not much for a man to ask.'

'No,' said Drew the barman.

'I demand to see the manager,' said Sammy Flett.

Ronald Leask drank his whisky at one go and put down his empty glass and nodded to Drew. The barman filled it up again.

'No water?' said Bill MacIsaac the boatbuilder, smiling across at Ronald.

'No,' said Ronald, 'no water.'

'Men in love,' said Thorfinn Vik of Helliar, 'don't need water in their drink.' Vik was in one of his dangerous insulting moods.

Sammy Flett went into the toilet. They heard the glug-glug of wine being drunk, then a long sigh.

The door opened and Mr William Snoddy the builder's clerk came in out of the rain. He looked round the bar nervously. 'A small whisky,' he said to Drew the barman, 'and put a little soda in it, not too much, and a bottle of export, if you please.' He wiped his spectacles with his handkerchief and owled the bar with bulging naked eyes and put his spectacles on again. Then he recognised the man he was standing beside.

'Why, Ronald,' he said. 'It isn't often we see you in the bar. It's a poor night, isn't it?'

Ronald stared straight ahead at the rank of bottles under the bar clock. He put back his head and drank the remains of his second glass of whisky.

'Ronald, have a glass of whisky with me,' said Mr Snoddy, taking his wallet out of his inside pocket. 'It'll be a pleasure.'

'Same again,' said Ronald to the barman. 'And I'll pay for my own drink with my own money.'

Mr Snoddy flushed till his brow was almost as pink as his nose. Then he put his wallet back in his inside pocket.

Sammy Flett emerged from the toilet, smiling.

Bill MacIsaac and Thorfinn Vik began to play darts at the lower end of the bar.

'Oh well,' said Mr Snoddy, 'I don't suppose you can force a person to speak to you if he doesn't want to.' He drank his whisky down quickly and took a sip of beer.

Suddenly Sammy Flett came up behind Mr Snoddy and threw his arm round his neck. 'If it isn't my dear friend Mr Snoddy,' said Sammy Flett. 'Mr Snoddy, accept a cigarette, with my compliments.'

'Go away,' cried Mr Snoddy. 'Go away. Just leave me alone.'

'Mr Snoddy,' said Sammy Flett, 'I'll take the whisky that Mr Leask refused to accept for reasons best known to himself.'

'I come in here for a quiet drink,' said Mr Snoddy to the barman, trying to disengage his neck from Sammy Flett's arm.

'And you shall have it, dear Mr Snoddy,' said Sammy Flett. 'Accompany me to the gentleman's toilet. We shall have a drink of wine together. Mr Snoddy is always welcome to have a drink from Sammy.'

'Leave Mr Snoddy alone,' said Drew the barman.

The door opened and six Norwegian fishermen came in. 'Six double scotches, six Danish lagers,' Per Bjorling said to the barman. The Norwegians shook the rain from their coats and leaned against the bar counter. A row of six blond heads shone with wetness under the lamps.

'I know what they're saying about you, Mr Snoddy,' said Sammy Flett. 'They say you're going with other women. They say you're unfaithful to Mrs Snoddy. It's an evil world and they'll say anything but their prayers. But I don't believe that, Mr Snoddy. You and me, we're old friends, and I wouldn't believe such a thing about you. Not Sammy. Never.'

Mr Snoddy looked about him, angry and confused. He left his half-empty glass standing on the counter and went out quickly, clashing the door behind him.

'Mr Snoddy is a very fine man,' said Sammy Flett to the Norwegians.

'Is so?' said one of the Norwegians, smiling.

'Yes,' said Sammy Flett, 'and he's a very clever man too.'

'Interesting,' said another Norwegian.

'I'm no fool myself,' said Sammy Flett. 'I didn't sail up Hoy Sound yesterday in a banana skin. Sammy knows a thing or two.'

Dod Isbister the plumber came in and Jimmy Gold the postman and Andrew Thomson the crofter from Knowe. They went to the upper-end of the bar and ordered beer. They emptied a box of dominoes on the counter and began to play.

The dart players finished their game and stuck their darts in the cork rim of the board. Thorfinn Vik was a bit drunk. He came over and stood beside Ronald Leask and began to sing:

I was dancing with my darling at the Tennessee waltz
When an old friend I happened to see,
Introduced him to my sweetheart and while they were dancing
My friend stole my sweetheart from me.

'No singing,' said Drew the barman sternly. 'No singing in this bar. There's guests in the lounge upstairs.'

Thorfinn Vik turned to Ronald Leask. 'That's a song that you'll appreciate, Mr Leask,' he said. 'I sang it specially for you. A song about disappointed love.'

'Same again,' said Ronald Leask to the barman.

'A beautiful song,' said Sammy Flett from the middle of the Norwegian group. He had a glass of whisky in one hand and a glass of lager in the other that one of the whalers had bought for him. 'Very delightfully sung. Have you got songs in Norway as good as that? I daresay you have. Silence now for a Norwegian love song.'

'No singing,' said Drew.

'We sing only on our boat,' said Per Bjorling. 'We respect your rules. Please to give us seven double scotches and seven Danish lagers.' . . . To Sammy Flett he said, 'There will be singings later on the *Erika* – how you say? – a sing-song.'

'You are the true descendants of Vikings,' said Sammy Flett.

'No,' said a young Norwegian, 'they were cruel men. It is best to forget such people, no? We are peaceable fishermen.'

'Such is truthfully what we are,' said another Norwegian.

The door opened quietly and Mr Spence the jeweler tiptoed in. He shook his umbrella close and went up to the bar. 'One half-bottle of the best whisky, to carry out,' he murmured to Drew the barman. He laid two pound notes discreetly on the counter.

'Mr Spence,' cried Sammy Flett from the centre of the Norwegian group. 'My dear friend.'

'Leave Mr Spence alone,' said Drew. 'He doesn't want anything about you.'

'I am content where I am,' said Sammy Flett, 'in the midst of our Scandinavian cousins. But there's nothing wrong in greeting my old friend Mr Spence.'

Mr Spence smiled and picked up his change and slid the half-bottle into his coat pocket.

'I think I know where you're off to with that,' said Sammy Flett, wagging a finger at him.

Mr Spence smiled again and went out as quietly and quickly as he had come in.

'Yes,' said Thorfin Vik of Helliar, 'we all know where he's going . . .' He winked across at the domino players. 'Mr Leask knows too.'

'I want no trouble in here,' said Drew the barman.

'Same again,' said Ronald Leask and pushed his empty glass at the barman. His face was very red.

'Is clock right?' said Per Bjorling.

'Five minutes fast,' said Drew. 'It's twenty minutes to ten.'

Sammy Flett drank first his whisky and then his lager very quickly. The huge adams-apple above his dirty collar wobbled two or three times. He sighed and said, 'Sammy is happy now. Sammy asks nothing from life but a wee drink now and then.'

'I am happy for you,' said the Norwegian boy. 'I will now buy you other drink.'

'No,' said Sammy Flett, 'not unless you all promise to partake of a little wine with me later in the gentlemen's toilet. At closing time Sammy will show you the pleasures of Hamnavoe. Sammy knows all the places.'

'Here is pleasures enough,' said the oldest Norwegian, 'in the pub.'

'No,' said Sammy, 'but I will take you to girls.'

'Girls,' said the old man. 'Oh, no, no. I am grandfather.'

'I have little sweetheart outside of Hammerfest,' said the boy. 'Gerd. She is milking the cattles and makes butter, also cheese from goats.'

'Also I am married,' said another Norwegian, 'and also is Paal and Magnus and Henrik. No girls. All are committed among us but Per.'

'Is true,' said Per Bjorling gravely.

'Per is liberty to find a girl where he likes,' said the old man. 'Per is good-looking, is handsome, there is no trouble that Per our skipper will find a beautiful girl.'

The other Norwegians laughed.

'He's like a film star,' said Sammy Flett. 'Thank you most kindly, I'll have a glass of whisky and a bottle of beer. No offence. Per has a profile like a Greek hero.'

'Has found a beautiful girl already,' said the boy, smiling, 'in Hamnavoe.'

'One bottle of vodka,' said Per Bjorling to Drew, 'for outside drinking.'

Drew the barman took down a bottle of vodka from the shelf and called out, 'Last orders, gentlemen.'

'Double whisky,' said Ronald Leask.

Sammy Flett said to Per Bjorling, 'Are you going to visit this young lady now with your bottle of vodka?'

'A gift to her,' said Per Bjorling. 'Is a good girl. Is kind. Is understanding, intelligent. I like her very much.'

'What is the name of this fortunate young lady, if I might make so bold as to ask?' said Sammy Flett. 'Listen, Ronald. Per Bjorling is just going to tell us the name of his Hamnavoe sweetheart.'

Per Bjorling said, 'Celia.'

For about five seconds there was no sound in the bar but the click of dominoes on the counter.

Then Ronald Leask turned and hit Per Bjorling with his fist on the side of the head. The lager glass fell from Per Bjorling's hand and smashed on the floor. The force of the blow sent him back against the wall, his hands up at his face. He turned to Ronald Leask and said, 'Is not my wish to cause offence to any man present.'

'Cut it out,' cried Drew the barman. 'That's enough now.'

Ronald Leask stepped forward and hit Per Bjorling again, on the mouth. A little blood ran down Per Bjorling's jaw and his cap fell on the floor. He turned and hit Ronald Leask in the stomach and Ronald Leask flapped against the counter like a shiny black puppet. A score of glasses fell and smashed and a rapid pool of whisky and beer formed on the floor. Ronald Leask and Per Bjorling splintered and splashed through it, wrestling with each other. Ronald Leask clubbed down his fist on Per Bjorling's eye and Per Bjorling thrashed him across the jaw with the back of his hand. Ronald Leask went down on all fours among the beer and the broken glass.

'I am sorry for this,' said Per Bjorling and held out his hand.

Ronald Leask got slowly to his feet. His trouser knees were sopping wet and the palms of his hands cut and bleeding. A small bubble of blood grew and burst at his right nostril.

'Get out of here,' said Drew the barman, taking Ronald Leask by the sleeve of his oilskin, 'and never come back again. That applies to you too,' he said to Per Bjorling.

'So this is your Scotch hospitality,' said the Norwegian called Paal, 'to strike a man without reason. This we will not forget.'

'Remember this too,' said Thorfinn Vik, and struck Paal on the ear. 'This is our bar where we come to enjoy ourselves and this is our town and our women live in it.'

Drew picked up the telephone and his forefinger juggled in the dial.

'This is cowardice,' said the Norwegian boy. He stepped forward and took Thorfinn Vik by the throat. They lurched violently, locked together, between the seats and the bar counter. Half a dozen more glasses went over and smashed. Bill MacIsaac the boatbuilder tried to prise Thorfinn Vik and the young Norwegian apart. Andrew Thomson of Knowe put down his dominoes and began to take off his jacket slowly. 'I don't like fighting,' he said, 'but I'll fight if there's fighting to be done.'

'Gentlemen, gentlemen,' piped Sammy Flett from the fringe of the fight. Then he noticed an unattended glass of whisky on the bar counter and made for it. He was hidden behind a welter of heaving backs.

'You are bad man,' said the old Norwegian to Ronald Leask and slapped him magisterially across the face.

'Enough,' cried Per Bjorling.

Two policemen stood in the door.

Dod Isbister with a bottle in his hand and the Norwegian called Magnus with a glass in his hand were circling each other at the top end of the bar. Ronald Leask lashed out at Paal with his foot and missed and kicked Henrik on the elbow. Thorfinn Vik and the young Norwegian went over on the floor with a thud that made the bottles reel and rattle and clink. Dod Isbister threw the bottle he was holding and it missed Magnus's head and smashed into the lamp bulb. The light went out. The pub was a twilight full of grunting, breathing, slithering, cursing shadows.

'All right, gentlemen,' said the voice of Drew the barman, 'you can break it up. The law is here.'

The two policemen beamed their torches slowly over the wreckage. The fighters disengaged themselves. One by one they got to their feet.

'So this is the way it is,' said the sergeant, 'You'll have to come along to the station. We have accommodation for gentry like you. You haven't heard the last of this, I'm afraid. The sheriff will be wanting to see you all next Tuesday.'

'Not me, sergeant,' said Sammy Flett. 'Sammy never laid a finger on anybody.'

'You too,' said the sergeant. 'I wouldn't be surprised if you weren't at the bottom of this, Flett.'

Later, in the Black Maria going to the police station, Sammy Flett said, 'That was the best fight since the Kirkwall men threw Clarence Shaw into the harbour last carnival week.'

'Shut up, drunkard,' said Thorfinn Vik sleepily from the corner of the van.

'No, Thorfinn,' said Sammy Flett, 'but I want to reassure everyone, especially our

Norwegian guests. The beds in the lock-up are very comfortable. The sergeant's wife will give us a cup of tea and toast in the morning. I know, because I've had bed and breakfast at Her Majesty's expense on twenty-two occasions – no, this makes it twenty-three. Everybody is very nice.'

'The little Gerd,' said the young Norwegian miserably. 'I am thinking of her so very much.'

The Black Maria jolted to a stop. They had arrived.

NINE

In the shoemaker's room the lamp was turned down low. It threw a feeble pool of light in one corner. The shoemaker was in his iron bed; he leaned back on three pillows and struggled for breath. Every inhalation was hard-won and shallow; the slack strings of his throat grew taut to force a passage for it, and his whole torso laboured to expel it again. His breathing slowly thickened and roughened, came in a quick spasm, and then he turned over on the pillows in a storm of feeble importunate coughing.

Celia came quickly through from the other room. She sat down on the edge of the bed and took the shoemaker's damp hand in both hers. 'You'll be all right,' she said. 'Just take it easy.'

The coughing stopped and the old man lay back on his pillows with his mouth open. Celia wiped his face with her apron. Then she lifted a small brown bottle from the table and shook a tablet out and poured some water in a cup. 'You've to take a tablet every four hours, Dr Wilson says,' she said. 'It stops the coughing.' She put the tablet in his mouth and raised his head and gave him a sip of water.

'If only I could sleep,' whispered the shoemaker. He lay back on the pillows with his eyes shut. 'I'm a very poor old sick man.'

'I won't leave you,' said Celia.

'Tell me one thing,' said the shoemaker, 'then maybe I can get to sleep. Is there any man or drink in the room next door?'

'No,' said Celia.

'Tell me the truth,' he whispered sternly. 'The truth, mind. I heard someone at the door.'

'Snoddy came at half-past eight,' said Celia. 'I sent him away. I told him you were ill. What's more, I told him I didn't want his drink.'

'Till the next time,' said the shoemaker.

'I suppose so,' said Celia.

The shoemaker's breath slowly roughened as new threads of phlegm spun themselves into a thick cord in his chest. Then suddenly he was possessed by spasm after spasm of futile coughing. He drew himself up in the bed and Celia put her arms round his thin body and held him close to her until the tough cord of phlegm broke and the coughing stopped. She took a bowl from the bedside chair and he managed to spit into it. The effort exhausted him. Celia laid him back on his pillows. Then she wiped his face in her apron.

'If only I could sleep,' said the shoemaker. 'I was dropping off to sleep an hour and more ago and then I was wakened first by Snoddy and then by a terrible noise along the street.'

'There was fighting in the Hamnavoe Bar,' said Celia. 'So Snoddy said. That's what you heard. Drew had to get the police.'

'It sounded like an earthquake,' said the shoemaker.

Celia stroked his chest outside his grey flannel shirt. 'Try to sleep now,' she said. 'I'll stay beside you till you go to sleep.' . . . After a time she felt his chest grow quiet under her hand. His eyes were shut and his breath came deep and even through slightly parted lips. Celia knew that he wasn't asleep, but he was pretending to sleep so that she could get back to her bed.

Outside the rain slanted darkly. A sudden gust of wind caught the downpour and threw it against the window till all the panes surged and throbbed. Through the onset Celia heard a discreet tapping at the outside door.

'Don't let him in,' said the shoemaker, opening his eyes.

It was Mr Spence the jeweller. 'Celia,' he said.

'The old man isn't well,' said Celia in a low voice. 'The doctor was here in the afternoon. I'll have to be up with him all night.'

'Perhaps if I could just come in,' said Mr Spence.

'No,' said Celia.

'I'm very wet, my dear,' said Mr Spence.

'Please go home,' said Celia, 'Please.'

Mr Spence took the flask of whisky from his coat pocket.

'We will just have one little toddy,' he said. 'Thomas won't mind me being in the house. He tells me I can come whenever I like. You know that. A little dram for a damp night, eh?'

'Not tonight,' said Celia, 'I'm sorry.'

The rain slanted all about Mr Spence, a diagonal bright-dark nagging susurration on the flagstones of the pier. The gutters bubbled. Celia could smell the wetness from his clothes.

'Celia,' said Mr Spence in a hurt voice, 'I am a very lonely man.'

'Everyone is lonely,' said Celia gently. 'We're all prisoners. We must try to find out a way to be pardoned.'

She shut the door and drew the bar across it. She was just about to turn into her own seaward room when she heard the shoemaker speaking aloud to himself in the room with the dim light and the noise of rain in it. She stood in the lobby and listened.

'And so it'll be all right once we're settled in Clett. Ronald has a small room I can bide in. It doesn't matter about me. I won't live that long. But Celia, she'll be happy at last. She'll soon learn to look after the cow and the few hens, yes, he'll get a pot of soup when he comes in cold from the fishing. She'll be a good wife to Ronald. And I tell you this, Ronald won't allow all them bottles in his cupboard, no, and no bloody foreigners'll get within a stone's throw of the place, and as for Snoddy, the dog of Clett'll tear the arse off the likes of him. Mr Spence, he can come as usual twice a week for a game of draughts, I'm sure Ronald won't object to that. We'll be fine once we're settled in Clett. Not that Ronald Leask's conferring any favour on Celia, not a bit of it, he's a lucky chap to be getting the likes of Celia for a wife. She can cook and sew and wash as well as any woman in Hamnavoe. I'll maybe be a burden to them for a winter or two, but Ronald said I could come, and by that time they'll likely have another burden, a bairn in the cradle, but a sweet burden, not an old done man. Once Celia's settled in Clett she'll have a new life entirely, there'll be no more drink and no more poverty and no more stray men in the night. An end to this darkness.'

Celia went softly into the room. The shoemaker closed his eyes quickly and pretended to be asleep. But another rope of phlegm was beginning to rasp in his chest. There was a smell too, all about the bed. Celia sat beside him and wiped his face with her apron. He opened his eyes and said, 'I'm sorry. I think I've messed the bed up.' He was ashamed and his eyes were wet.

'I know,' said Celia. 'Don't worry. I'll get you cleaned up before anything else. There's a kettle of hot water on the range. Plenty of clean sheets in the cupboard.'

She opened the window to let the smell out. Rain and wind swirled in and the shoemaker began to cough. She closed the window again quickly.

For the next twenty minutes Celia washed the old man and dried him and put a clean shirt on him and stripped the bed and put clean sheets on it and set the soiled stinking sheets in a tub of disinfected water in the lobby.

'You'll feel better now,' said Celia. 'I'm going to make a cup of tea for the two of us.'

The shoemaker was racked with a violent spasm of coughing. She held him till the tough cord of phlegm shore in his throat and he spat it out. She laid him back exhausted on the pillows.

'Fighting along the street a while ago,' said the shoemaker wearily. 'It's always them foreigners.'

'It's all quiet now,' said Celia. 'Time you had another tablet though.'

She took a yellow tablet out of the bottle on to her hand and put it on his tongue. She laid her arm round his shoulders and raised him and put the cup of water to his mouth.

'They don't seem to help me, them tablets,' said the shoemaker.

'They will,' said Celia. 'Give them time. Dr Wilson's tablets always work, you know that.'

'Maybe I'll get a sleep now,' said the shoemaker.

'Try,' said Celia.

But the hoarseness was in his chest again. He coughed and spat out thick phlegm. But as always when this sickness was on him, he had hardly torn the purulent fungus from his bronchial tree when a new growth rose about it, blocking and strangling his breath.

'I'm a terrible nuisance to you,' he said, 'a silly awkward old man.'

'You're not,' said Celia, 'and you'll be better tomorrow. And there's a fine shed at Clett where you can mend boots. I'll ask Ronald to put a stove in it.'

The shoemaker was suddenly asleep, the way sleep comes to the very young and the very old. His cheeks flushed like two withered apples. He breathed as quietly as a child.

'Thank God,' said Celia.

She drew the blankets up to his chin and kissed him on the forehead.

The window paled with the end of the night.

The rain had stopped, as it often does before dawn. Celia closed the door of the shoemaker's room softly and unbarred the outer door and went out on to the pier. The first seagulls were screaming along the street, scavenging in the bins. She breathed the clean air of early morning. She stood at the pier wall and watched the sea moving darkly against the weeded steps and slipways. A rat in the seaweed squinnied at her and twitched its whiskers and went into the water with a soft plop. The sun had not yet risen, but light was assembling in broken colours over the Orphir hills. The first blackbird in the fuchsia bush under the watchmaker's wall faltered into song and then was silent again. Celia could see the boats in the harbour now and at the farm across the harbour black ploughed squares among green grass and brown heather. It would be a beautiful morning.

Then the sun rose clear of the Orphir hills and folded the girl in the light of a new day.

Brig-o-Dread

When thou from hence away art past
Every nighte and alle
To Whinny-muir thou com'st at last
And Christe receive thy saule

From Whinny-muir when thou may'st pass
Every nighte and all
To Brig-o-Dread thou com'st at last
And Christe receive thy saule

From Brig-o-Dread when thou may'st pass
Every nighte and all
To Purgatory fire thou com'st at last
And Christe receive thy saule

'I should say at once who I am, in case it is necessary for me to make a statement soon. My name is Arkol Andersvik. I have been married for twelve years to my dear good wife Freya. We have a son, aged 11, called Thord, a clever fair-haired boy whose craze, at the moment, is science fiction. His school reports are promising – I will say no more. We live in a fine old house in Hamnavoe, and I have a garden that slopes down from the hill to the street. My shop is in the town centre. Out of whalebone we – my brother and I – carve souvenirs and mementos and I deal in a variety of sealskin articles. We do a fair business in summer, when the islands are filled with tourists. I am a councilor. I am fifty years old.

'I try not to neglect the cultural side. For the past ten years I have imposed a discipline on myself. I have striven to acquaint myself with the best that has been sung and thought and written. You might call it a quest for truth and beauty. At the moment I am engaged on reading *Hamlet* for the third time. A poem that I chanced on last week really delighted me – the *Ode on a Grecian Urn* by Keats. It gave me a feeling of great purity and peace.

'My brother says this pursuit of culture is a substitute for the kirk pew. He may be right. I am not a religious man.

'Something strange has happened to me. That is why I am preparing this statement. I am not at home, nor in the shop. I don't know where I am, that's the truth. I am sitting on a bench in a bare room, like a prison cell. (But that is impossible.) Or it could be like a room where witnesses wait until they are called to give their evidence. It is worrying. I have never been involved in any kind of legal process. I intend to get to the bottom of it. It is a waste of my time, to put it mildly. I have a business to attend to. I have council work to see to this very evening. Freya will be very worried indeed.

'I have just discovered, with a certain relief, that I am not in prison; they have not removed my tie and bootlaces. I will go on writing in my notebook. That might help to clarify the situation in my mind.

'Wistan and I went seal-shooting yesterday afternoon, it being early closing day in the town. (Wistan is my younger brother.) We took our guns and motored four miles along the coast to a certain skerry[1] where the seals come and go all summer. Some people wax sentimental over these animals. They invoke all the old legends about the selkie folk, half man and half seal, and their fondness for music. They denounce those who slaughter them, forgetting that they are voracious beasts that eat half the fish in the sea. The legends are charming, but most of that kind of talk is slush. Every man has his living to make. (What about the beasts that are slaughtered for our Sunday joints?)

'Wistan and I got out of the van at the cliff top and, carrying our guns, made our way carefully down salt broken ledges to the sea, only to find that the skerry was bare. The seals were away at their fishing. That was disappointing. We decided to wait for an hour or so, seeing that it was a fine afternoon and still early. I laid my gun along a ledge of rock. Wistan said he would take a walk round the coast, to see if he could find some shells or stones that – properly decorated – might tempt the tourists in search of souvenirs. He offered me his whisky flask. I declined, of course.

'A word or two about Wistan. He helps me in the business. I might have made him a partner but the truth is that there is a certain waywardness about him, an unreliability. He went to sea as a lad – came home after two years. My father used his influence to get Wistan work in a lawyer's office in Kirkwall, but he left, saying he couldn't bear the thought of scribbling and copying all day and every day, maybe for the rest of his life. For the next year or two he was a ne'er-do-well, spending his mornings in the pub, his afternoons in the billiard hall. Most evenings he would take his flute to dances in this parish and that. Wistan's conduct clouded our father's last years – I am certain of that.

'In the end I employed him in the shop. What else could I do? He is my brother. I did not want to see him wasting his life entirely. Wistan has talents. No one can make more handsome sealskin bags and slippers than him, and the way he paints birds and flowers on stone is masterly. He, not I, is the whalebone carver. I pay him twelve pounds a week. He has a small house on a pier and lives there alone. (In case somebody should say, 'That is a poor wage to give a man,' I reply, 'That is all the business will stand. Give him more, he would simply squander it . . .' Besides, who but myself would employ him?)

'Poor Wistan! He is not highly regarded in the community. He was a delightful child, but

---

[1] A sea rock or islet.

some kind of raffishness entered into him at adolescence. It has never left him – the dreams, the deviousness. He drinks too much. Freya does not like him. I inflict him on her all the same – I insist that he comes to dinner every Sunday. In that way I can be sure that he gets at least one good meal in the week. He lounges about in the house all Sunday afternoon while I retire upstairs to my books and gramophone records.

'I thought to myself, between the crag and the skerry, 'How on earth can Wistan afford whisky, on his wage?' I am not a skinflint, I hope, and I have nothing against a dram in the evening – but to booze in the middle of a summer afternoon! So I shook my head at the offered whisky flask. Still holding his gun in the crook of his arm, Wistan took a sip or two.

'A sleek head broke the surface fifty yards out. Large liquid eyes looked at the hunters. I whistled. Wistan whistled, farther off. The creature stirred and eddied towards us. 'Come on, my beauty,' I remember saying. The water was suddenly alive with seals. And this is all I remember, until I found myself an hour ago in this cell-like room.

'It is very strange. Where am I? Where is Wistan? Where is the seal, the shore, the gun?'

★　★　★

Mr Andersvik had no sooner closed his notebook than he saw that the door of the mysterious room now stood open. It was a summer day: there was blue sky and white clouds. He was free to go, it seemed.

Outside a signpost pointed: TO THE MOOR.

The landscape was strange to Mr Andersvik. The moor stretched, a wine-red emptiness, from horizon to horizon. It was eerie, to say the least. 'Well,' he thought, 'I'm bound to meet somebody who can tell me the way to Hamnavoe.' Indeed, when he took the track that wound into the moor, he saw a few people and they too, like the landscape, had a remote dreamlike quality. They moved like somnambulists. Every heath-farer was solitary and did not appear to be going anywhere. The moor was a slow soundless dance of intersections and turnings. The faces were down-tilted and preoccupied. It was soon obvious that the moor-dwellers wanted nothing to do with Mr Andersvik. As soon as he tried to approach one or other of these lonely ones, to ask the direction, they held out preventive hands – they had nothing to say to him, they did not want to hear anything that he had to say to them. Mr Andersvik was a bit hurt to begin with at these rebuffs. But after he had walked a mile or two a kind of contentment crept through him.

It was quite pleasant out here on the moor. What contented Mr Andersvik particularly was the account he had written in his notebook in 'the court-room' – he had set it down defensively (as if he was actually going to be charged with some offence) in order to put a good face on things, to cover up certain shames and deficiencies in his life that were, after all, his own concern. But here, on this moor, the images and rhythms of his prose pleased him very much indeed; he could savour them with extraordinary vividness in the solitude and silence. The remembrance was all pleasant, a flattering unction. He began the cycle of his life again – Freya and love and the garden, Thord and promise, Wistan and irresponsibility, the shop and sealskins and money, the council and honour, the temple of culture where he was a regular devoted worshipper . . . The second round of meditation was if anything sweeter than the first . . . This delight, he thought, might go on for a long time. He very much hoped that it would.

Mr Andersvik discovered, by certain rocks and a certain gorse bush in the moor, that he had drifted round in two wide circles. He was learning to behave in the manner of the moor-dwellers. He halted.

'This will never do,' said Mr Andersvik to himself, breaking the lovely idyll. 'I must get back. These memories are not entirely true, I'm afraid. I must open the shop. There is this council meeting tonight.'

He turned. He strode on across the moor, frowning and purposeful. He was aware that his ankles had been rather badly scratched with gorse-thorns – he had not noticed the pain till now.

One of the moor people loomed close, with a tranced preoccupied face, drifting on, smiling, in a wide arc across the path of Mr Andersvik.

'Please,' said Mr Andersvik. 'One moment. I'm wanting to get to Hamnavoe. Could you tell me if I'm going in the right direction?'

'What's wrong with this place?' said the dancer on the moor. 'What greater happiness could there be than this solitude? If you leave the moor you'll never get back. Beware, man. Your journey will end in ashes and smoke' . . . The man drifted on, smiling, feeding deep on the honey of his past.

A finger of fear touched Mr Andersvik. To go on like that for ever, nourished on delusions! He was sure of one thing now, he wanted to break out of these endless self-flattering circles. He hurried on. Gorse tore at his ankles. Once he fell in a blazing bush – his hands bled and burned. He picked himself up and went on. Clumps of gorse blossomed here and there on the moor – it was impossible to avoid them entirely. Freya would have to put some disinfectant on a multitude of scratches.

He came over a ridge and saw with relief that the track gave on to a road.

It was strange. Mr Andersvik thought he knew every road in the island, but he had never been on this particular one. He came after a mile or so to a crossroads. The signpost said: TO THE BRIDGE. He walked on. Soon familiar hills and waters came about him. He recognised Kringlafield and the twin lochs with the prehistoric stone circle. And over there was the farm where his sister Anne had gone to live and toil when she married Jock Onness thirty years before. Alas, Anne had been dead for four years. That death had been a blow to Mr Andersvik; Anne was one of the few folk he had ever had affection for. He felt a pang as he looked at the widowed farm. Should he call in and have a word with old Jock? He thought, not today. The shop – souvenirs, sealskin – he was losing pounds. Besides, he did not feel in a mood to explain to the old man all the strange things that had happened to him. Jock was very deaf, and not too bright.

He walked on. Ahead was the little stone bridge that divides sea from loch, parish from parish. Under the triple arch salt water mingles with sweet water twice a day. A woman was standing at the hither end of the bridge. She beckoned to Mr Andersvik. Her face was tranquil, as if a quiet flame had passed through it.

It was his sister Anne.

He tried to speak, but his mouth locked on the words.

'Arkol,' she said, 'I've been expecting you. You've been on the moor a long time.'

'An hour or two,' he whispered.

'Longer than that,' said the dead woman. 'Oh, much longer. Well done, Arkol, all the same. Only a few folk have the strength to tear themselves away from that moor.'

Mr Andersvik took his first dark taste of death.

'I had to come and meet you,' said Anne, 'before you cross the bridge. Otherwise the pain would be too sudden and terrible.'

The half-ghost understood nothing of this. Death, in his understanding, was a three-day feast of grief, a slow graining and seepage among roots, the last lonely splendour of the skeleton – but all enacted within a realm of oblivion (except for a few fading fragrances in the memory of friends). An eternity of harps, or flames, had always seemed to Mr Andersvik an insult to the human intelligence.

He could not by any means accept his present situation. Yet here he was, in dialogue with a solicitous riddling ghost.

'Arkol, you've chosen the truth,' said Anne. 'That's splendid. But the truth is cruel, Arkol. A poor naked truth-bound ghost has a terrible journey to go.'

'What happened to me?' said Mr Andersvik after a time.

'A gun-shot wound. In the head. The court said 'Death by misadventure.' Poor Arkol.'

'My gun was six yards away on a ledge of rock!' cried Mr Andersvik. 'That's impossible!'

'Poor Arkol,' she said again. 'But that's only the start. Are you willing to be dead?'

'No,' he cried. 'I don't believe it. Don't touch me. I can't be dead! I have years of work in front of me. Thord must be given a good start. Freya must be provided for. There's the housing committee and the graveyard committee. I am going to extend the business. I haven't made a will.'

His sister soothed him. She spoke to him with all the tenderness and kindness that in the old days had persuaded Mr Andersvik that, for example, he must really not be so pompous, he must learn to laugh at himself a little; that he must give Freya a more generous house-keeping allowance, she was having to pinch here and patch there – it was a shame, him with all that money and all these pretensions . . . Now Mr Andersvik sensed a new depth in his sister's concern. He bowed his head. He yielded to her wisdom, there on the bridge between the dead and the living. Anne kissed him on the mouth, and so sealed his death for him.

Arkol crossed over the bridge then.

In darkness the dead man returned to the dimension he had left. Time is a slow banked smoulder to the living. To the dead it is an august merciless ordering of flames, in which the tormented one, in Eliot's words, must learn at last to be a dancer.

*　　*　　*

His fellow councillors were sitting in the council chamber. There was a new member seated in the chair he normally occupied – his brother Wistan. The provost was making some kind of formal speech . . . 'welcome our new councillor, Mr Wistan Andersvik, to this chamber. We welcome him doubly in that he is the brother of the late councillor Arkol Andersvik, who died in such tragic circumstances a month ago. The late councilor was a highly valued member of this assembly. His wisdom and his humanity will be greatly missed. Some said that maybe he was overcautious in this matter and that, but my reply to that was always, 'Arkol Andersvik is a true custodian of the public purse' . . . A more prudent man never walked the streets of this burgh. We trust, indeed we know, that his brother will be in all respects a worthy successor. He will bring imagination to our debates where the lamented elder brother gave us abundant practical sense. I will ask you, fellow-councillors, to be upstanding as a token of our respect for that good man who was taken so suddenly from our midst' . . .

They stood there, a lugubrious circle, and Wistan stood among them. Arkol felt for the first time the pain of the wound in his head. He cried out that they had taken a murderer into their fold, a brother-killer; but no one heard him. They passed on to the next business on the agenda . . .

*　　*　　*

Arkol shook himself clear of that flame. Darkness beset him again for a while (he did not know how long); then, far on, a new flame summoned, a white splash of time. He eddied like a moth towards it . . . What shuttered place was he standing in? Light sifted through slatted window blinds. Of course he soon recognised it: it was his shop. The clock ticked on the shelf, spilling busy seconds into his timelessness. It was a quarter past ten in the morning, and still the door hadn't been opened to the public. So, it had come to this. How had Freya ever allowed it! She ought to have sold the business as a going concern. It had been a small gold-mine. Plenty of folk would have given a handsome price for 'A. Andersvik – Novelties, Presents, and Souvenirs.'

The key shrieked in the lock. The street-door opened. A familiar shadow stood there, carrying a heavy bucket.

Arkol saw in the new light from the street that there were no longer any painted pebbles or sealskin on the shelves. In their place were pieces of baked hollowed-out clay, garishly decorated. So Wistan had set himself up as a potter? The shop was a shambles – it reeked of burnt earth.

'You killed me,' he said sternly. 'But you're too loutish and lazy to enjoy the fruits of murder. How dare you ruin a good business! Filthying my shop with your mud and fire!'

Wistan set his bucket of clay beside the warm kiln. He moved over to the bench. He began to knead a lump of clay with knuckles and fingers. He was humming happily to himself . . .

Arkol came out of that flame singed and trembling, and glad of darkness.

★   ★   ★

He stood on Celia's pier in the first light of morning . . . (Time here was, as always, surely, a limpid invisible burning.) The old women arrived with their cats and basins while the fishermen (just back from the west) handed up the steps baskets of haddocks. It was a famous place for gossip and opinion and elegy. Gulls, savage naked hungers, wheeled between the boat and the pier.

They were speaking about a death.

'Accident,' Maisie Ness was saying. 'That makes me laugh. You can't shoot yourself by accident. He was in trouble if you ask me. He was on the verge of bankruptcy. So I heard. There was nothing else for him to do but shoot himself.'

'Well,' said Andrina Moar, 'he isn't that much of a miss. The swank[1] of him! The strut of the creature along the street!'

Not one face on Celia's pier stilled with sorrow for the dead man. Instead, the women, old and young, began to tear at Arkol's death like gulls among fish guts.

The haddocks gulped and shrugged in their baskets: dying gleams. Cats mewed. Sea and sky and stone was an asylum of gulls. The voices went on and on in the sunlight . . .

The darkness wrapped him away, trembling, from the slanders of the living.

★   ★   ★

He emerged into fragrance and sweetness. A peaceful green rectangle sloped down from the hill to the clustered roofs of Hamnavoe: his garden. What man was that sitting on the bench under the sycamore tree? It was, again, Wistan. Years had passed. Wistan's face was thin and sick and grey. Was he perhaps on the point of accomplishing his suicide by alcohol (an end that Arkol had more than once prophesied)? Then Arkol saw that Wistan was somehow injured – his right hand (the one that had pulled the trigger) was white and thick with bandaging. Wistan looked very seedy indeed in that net of green wavering shadows. (So Freya, out of the foolish kindness of her heart, had taken the creature into her house. for cure or for death.)

Freya came out of the kitchen into the sunlight. There was an extra decade of flesh and capability on her now. She was carrying a tray with salves and bandages on it. Wistan looked up. Blackbirds sang here and there in the bushes. It was a marvellous summer morning. The man and the woman smiled at each other. But immediately the shadow fell on Wistan's face again.

Freya set down the tray on the bench. She bent forward and kissed him on the forehead.

The ghost stirred in its flame.

'So, dearest,' said Freya, 'this is one of your black days, is it?' . . . She knelt on the grass and began to undo the bandage on Wistan's hand.

There was a passionate outpouring of song from the rosebush at the bottom of the lawn.

'It was an accident,' said Wistan in the shivering silence that followed. 'The gun went off in my hands. But, dear, he'd done such terrible things, anything he could think of – you know – to make me eat dirt, that sometimes I think' . . .

'We've been through all that before,' said Freya the comforter. 'I know. You've told me hundreds of times' . . . She kissed the scarred hand. 'There, if it helps you. Of course it was an accident. Just as you didn't mean to put your hand in the kiln last Friday. You were aiming for the seal that day. You might as well argue that I killed Arkol. If I didn't particularly want him to die, that was just because I'd got used to him. I realise that now . . . You wedged the gun into his arms – that's all you have to reproach yourself with, love. It was nothing. It was

---

[1] Athletic, well set forth, here apparently with a connotation of ostentation; showing off.

clever of you, in fact. It saved a lot of trouble, a lot of fuss and anger and suspicion.'

Wistan closed his eyes. Freya began to spread the unguent over his charred palm.

Freya said, after another blackbird interlude, 'I don't think now, looking back, that I ever really liked Arkol. The meanness of him, the arrogance! That horrible flesh lying beside me all night and every night! But you, dear, the first time I ever saw you . . .'

The ghost smouldered in the garden, among the sievings of birdsong. It glowed. It reeked. It longed to be anywhere, in any darkness, away from this incestuous place. Then it remembered, and acquiesced in the stake. The flames thickened. The ghost burned terribly. Yet it forced itself to look while Freya wrapped Wistan's wound in new bandages, swiftly, delicately, tenderly; and even afterwards, when the man and the woman enfolded each other on the long bench.

If only a ghost could die . . . It bore into the darkness terrible new scorchings.

*   *   *

Arkol came to a room that had a stale smell in it. It was the study where he had sought to improve his mind with good music and books. A reproduction of Van Gogh's *Sunflowers* hung over the mantelpiece. Freya, it seemed, had sealed the place off like a mausoleum. The dust whispered to him from shelf and record-player, 'What good was it to you, after all? You went through life blind and dense and hoodwinked. Here we are, Chopin and Jane Austen and Shelley, and we tried to tell you many a wise and many a true thing, but it only served to bolster your self-importance. Go and look for some peace now, poor ghost, if you can . . .' No one ever entered the study. *Hamlet* was lying on the table, just as he had left it the day before his murder, and *The Oxford Book of English Verse*, open at 'The Grecian Urn.' The ghost bent over the grey page. The poem was, as never before, a cold pure round of silence; a fold; a chalice where, having tasted, a man may understand and rejoice.

*   *   *

Arkol passed deeper into the charred ruins of his life. In another room a youth was sitting at a table, making notes of some kind. Thord had grown into a pleasant-looking young man. Bits of *Hamlet* drifted through the ghost: 'Thy father's spirit' . . . 'He took me grossly full of bread' . . . 'Avenge his foul and most unnatural murder' . . . The ghost smiled, in spite of its pain. As if this ordinary youth could ever be roused to such eagle-heights of rage, assoilment, passion! What had Thord done with his life? Arkol had had high hopes of the shy eager boy with his pile of science fiction books on his bedside table. Thord, he had thought, might well become a physicist, or a writer, or even a seeker among the stars. The ghost bent over the warm shoulder. Thord was filling up a football pools coupon. On the door-hook hung a postman's cap. To this favour the clever little boy had come: knocking at doors with white squares of gossip, propaganda, trivia. It did not matter. The ghost drank the beauty of his son's face – and saw, without rage, how like his mother he was now. He longed to linger out his time in this flame. But, shadow by slow shadow, he was folded in oblivion once more . . .

*   *   *

This was the rock, right enough. Coldness and heaviness and poise lay across the ghost, a gun-shape. It oppressed him. He wished he were free of it. Another man was walking on the loose stones of the beach fifty yards away. The man stooped and picked up a stone or a shell every now and again. The man uncorked a flask and tilted it towards his mouth. A sleek head broke the grey surface – a seal, with large dark brimming eyes. The ghost whistled, but no smallest sound was added to the wash of the waves, the sliding of stones, the click of a bolt. There was another louder whistle farther along the shore. Suddenly the bay was musical with seals; they clustered about the offshore rock; their sea-dance was over, they clambered awkwardly on to the stone. 'Come on, my beauties' . . . Whitman's song came on the wind:

I think I could turn and live with animals,
They are so placid and self-contained.

A line of Coleridge flowered: 'he blessed them in his heart' . . . The ghost raised an invisible hand seaward. He greeted the clean swift beautiful creatures of the ocean. He acknowledged the long wars of man against that innocent kingdom. He whispered for forgiveness. Then he turned calmly to face the blaze and the roar.

*   *   *

The day began with streams of blood. All the village followed the white-robed priest and the heifer whose horns were hidden under wreaths and clusters of blossom. Children danced and shouted. The throng of people disappeared beyond the last house of the village.

The only man who did not go to the ceremony sat in his cell and waited. The door had been open since first light.

He heard, after a long loaded silence, a whisper on the hillside, a fierce flailing of hooves, a surge and a spattering; then a wild ecstatic cry.

Presently the folk returned to the village. The lonely celebrant went with his red arms into a small house at the shore. The village street was soon empty. Family by family, purified, was eating its morning meal.

Not long afterwards the prisoner was summoned out to the village square.

A court of some kind was assembled and waiting. The square brimmed like a well with light. People of all ages sat here and there. Arkol was invited to station himself beside a sun-warmed stone.

The interrogator faced Arkol. Four people sat apart from the others, against the wall of the pottery maker. Arkol took them to be a panel of judges. They consulted together. Occasionally one looked across at him and smiled.

The interrogator began with a reading out of the statement that Arkol had originally made: 'trust of the townsfolk' . . . 'quest for truth and beauty' . . . 'intend to get to the bottom of this' . . . The interrogator was interrupted every now and again by wondering laughter.

The older men and women sat in their doorsteps. Children – hidden voices – shouted in the gardens behind the street. The sound of the sea was everywhere. A young man went round the people in the square carrying a tray with a pitcher and tankards. An old man nodded approval over the white blown fleece of foam. An old woman shook her head reprovingly at all the raised tankards.

The voice of the interrogator – austere, measured, and melodious – reached into the bright morning. The villagers were rather bored with the proceedings, on the whole. Arkol could tell by their faces that they would much rather have been down at the fishing boats, or on the hill with their sheep, than wasting the day with such a trivial case. But at the end, he supposed, the villagers would have to give some kind of a verdict in the square.

Some young folk had got out of it by bathing. Arkol could hear shouts along the beach and the splash of bodies in the surf. There were mocking harp-like cries, then a sudden silence. A young man, gleaming with sun and water, passed hurriedly through the square and entered a small steep alley. Children shrieked at the sea drops that shivered and showered over them. Voices from the rocks called for the insulted one to come back. A girl with wet hair appeared at the mouth of a seaward close. 'We're sorry, Adon,' she called. 'Please come back. Please.'

'Silence,' said the interrogator sternly. 'Go back to the sea. We are considering an important case.'

The girl withdrew bright hair, bright shoulders.

The case suffered no more interruptions. The interrogator paused upon this phrase and that: . . . 'a word or two about Wistan' . . . 'I am not a skinflint, I hope.' An old man laughed above his ale. Arkol smiled ruefully.

A boy called from a hidden garden that he had caught a butterfly – he had – but it had wriggled out of his fingers and was free in the wind once more.

What intrigued Arkol more than anything that morning were the faces of the four judges who, he supposed, would finally decide whether his application should be granted or no. They sat on a long bench in front of the interrogator. It was as if old woodcuts and frontispieces and dead music had trembled and quickened. These were the jurors: a man with wild hair and a wild mouth – a young woman who in spite of merry mischievous eyes looked rather prim – a man with a russet beard and a scar at one ear – long lank hair over a lank dark cheek, a velvet jacket, lank fingers: the hollows and shadows scattered whenever the man smiled, which was often.

There was silence in the square. The reading of the statement was over.

The cup-bearer had spread a white cloth on a long trestle table. He reappeared in the square now, carrying a tray with steaming fish on it, and bread. He set the tray on the table. He began to arrange seats.

'The statement, it is a tissue of lies,' said the hollow-cheeked juror in a foreign accent. All the jurors nodded. They looked at Arkol and smiled.

'The wonder is how he ever managed to escape,' said Van Gogh. 'I took him for a typical moor-dweller as soon as he arrived here last night.'

'He is a hero,' said a girl in a doorway who was feeding a baby at her breast.

The bathers came up from the sea, white-shrouded and shivering. The girl whose face had been glimpsed for a moment between the houses looked anxious now. Her companions tried to reassure her. They went in an agitated troop up one of the alleys.

The cupbearer carried from the inn a huge pitcher – both his arms were round it – some wine slurped over on to the cobble-stones. An old man cried out in alarm. But the pitcher was safely deposited at last among the fish and the bread.

'As one of the villagers,' said a man who was leaning against a wall smoking a pipe, 'I think he must at least do this before we give him the stones to build a house – he must alter the account of his life so that it comes a bit nearer the truth.'

The villagers shouted their approval.

'You can't eat or drink with us, you understand,' said the interrogator to Arkol, 'or stay here in this village, until you have paid your debt to the truth. You must revise your statement in certain important respects. You will be given pen and paper. Now that you've crossed the bridge and been through the fire, I think you may enjoy doing it.'

The villagers turned away from Arkol. They began to gather round the table. The bathers, all but two, came down the alley and joined the others. Mugs and pieces of bread were passed round – there was a mingling of courtesy and banter. Three seats were empty.

Arkol sat on a sunlit step. He poised his pen over the paper. He wondered how to begin.

The children's voices drifted down from the hillside. They were filling baskets with blackberries. Pure echoes fell into the square. The children shouted that they would not be home till sunset.

The lovers who had quarreled on the sea verge stood in the mouth of the close. They were tranquil and smiling now. They moved into sunlight. Folk rose up at the table to let them pass on to their places.

Arkol wrote. Phrases with some beauty and truth in them began to come, with difficulty. He longed to sit among the villagers, and share their meal. But the feast was eternal. He hoped that he might be able, before it was over, to present to the elders the poem of his life.

Derick Thomson (1921 –)

Thomson is one of the best modern Gaelic poets. However, the poems below, which are Thomson's translations of his own Gaelic originals, have been selected for inclusion here on their own merits as English-language poetry.

The Well

Right in the village there's a little well
and the grass hides it,
green grass in sap closely thatching it.
I heard of it from an old woman
but she said: 'The path is overgrown with bracken
where I often walked with my cogie*,   wooden pail
and the cogie itself is warped.'
When I looked in her lined face
I saw the bracken growing round the wall of her eyes,
and hiding it from seeking and from desires,   10
and closing it, closing it.

'Nobody goes to that well now,'
said the old woman, 'as we once went,
when we were young,
though its water is lovely and white.'
And when I looked in her eyes through the bracken
I saw the sparkle of that water
that makes whole every hurt
till the hurt of the heart.

'And will you go there for me,'   20
said the old woman, 'even with a thimble.
and bring me a drop of that hard water
that will bring colour to my cheeks.'
I found the well at last,
and though her need was not the greatest
it was to her I brought the treasure.

It may be that the well
is something I saw in a dream,
for today when I went to seek it
I found only bracken and rushes,   30
and the old woman's eyes are closed
and a film has come over their merriment.

The Herring Girls

Their laughter like a sprinkling of salt
showered from their lips,
brine and pickle on their tongues,
and the stubby short fingers that could handle fish,
or lift a child gently, neatly,
safely, wholesomely,
unerringly,
and the eyes that were as deep as a calm.

The topsy-turvy of history had made them
slaves to short-arsed curers,   10
here and there in the Lowlands, in England.
Salt the reward they won
from those thousands of barrels,
the sea-wind sharp on their skins,
and the burden of poverty in their kists*,   chests
and were it not for their laughter
you might think the harp-string was broken.

But there was a sprinkling of pride on their hearts,
keeping them sound,
and their tongues' gutting-knife   20
would tear a strip from the Lowlanders' mockery –
and there was work awaiting them
when they got home,
though they had no wealth:
on a wild winter's night,
if that were their lot,
they would make men.

'Who Are the Scots?'

The Spring cold
penetrated our old bones,
our knuckles reddened
and our hands shook a little,
and not knowing why
we began to talk about our youth,
and the hunting we did that autumn,
the reel we danced beneath the harvest moon,
the velvet cloth
and the hard grip we had   10
before this pneumonia
gripped our lungs.

Turning the beads
on the old velvet
with shaky hands,
the blood thinning,
taking a pride in enamel.

Clifford Hanley (1922 –)

Hanley is best known for his novels and for his autobiography, *Dancing in the Streets* (1958). He also writes crime stories as 'Henry Calvin'. The sketch below is taken from *A Skinful of Scotch* (1965), and is part of a very long, distinguished tradition of pieces in which the Scots guy themselves. Given Hanley's satiric bent, his authorship of the anthem, 'Scotland the Brave', is especially intriguing.

The Orange and the Green

So there was this fella that went into a pub near Ibrox Park, and he has an alligator walking beside him on a lead, and he says to the barman, 'Here, mac, do you serve Catholics in this pub?' So naturally the boys might have been annoyed in the normal way, but they didny fancy the look of this alligator, and they kept well back and looked respectful, and the barman says, 'Sure, sirr, it's quite all right,' so the man says, 'Aye, right, a pint for me and a Catholic for my pal here.'

And then there was this other fella on a Saturday night bus to Castlemilk, and he thought the fare was sixpence, but the Pakistani conductor says it was eightpence, so they argued the toss for a while because the fella had a good bucket in him, but he finally paid up, but here, as the Pakistani was walking back down the bus, the fella turns round and shouts, 'Away, ya durty Orange get!'

There was also these two Rangers supporters that went to the Odeon to see *Quo Vadis*, and Charlie says to Hughie, 'Here, I'll have to get out, these Christians getting mutilated and flung to lions and that, I can never stand cruelty, it makes my blood curdle.' But Hughie says, 'Sit down there, you've paid your money, and anyway, in these days all the Christians were Catholics.' So Charlie peers at the screen again, and says, 'Hey, what's that lion supposed to be up to, sittin' there doin' *nothin'*?'

Then there was the drunk man standing on the parapet of the Stockwell Bridge, and a crowd collected, and he said he was for committing suicide, so a kind-hearted man went up to him and said, 'I know you've got your troubles, but stop, for the sake of your family.' 'I've got no family.' 'All right, then, for the sake of the good old Rangers.' 'I don't support Rangers.' 'Okay, well,' says the man, 'I'm not prejudiced. For the sake of Celtic.' 'I don't support Celtic either,' says this bloke on the bridge. 'Right, jump, ya rotten atheist!'

I once took two American jazzmen into Denholm's Bar, just down the street from the Glasgow Central Hotel, and they said they loved Scotland because they had just come from Texas, and it was a delight to be in a country where nobody gave a damn about a man's colour.

'I accept your compliment on behalf of my native country,' I said with old-world courtesy, 'and you'll be fine as long as you keep your mouth shut about religion.' They laughed like anything. At least religion doesn't *show*.

It doesn't, either, because I've tried out the Glasgow theory that you can tell a Catholic by looking at him. What kind of a city would develop a superstition like that?

Come to think of it, I suppose Birmingham, Alabama, could do exactly the same thing. The more I think of it, in fact, the more I realise that we don't shoot people in the back in Glasgow or set fire to them because they have the wrong colour or the wrong religion. We only throw bottles now and then, and only under stress of deep emotion, as when the Protestant Rangers are playing the Catholic Celtic at a game derisively described as football. But you can live all your life in Scotland without ever going to see Celtic and Rangers, and this is the way most people in Scotland plan their lives.

It's the lousy old history that accounts for religious feuding in the West of Scotland, naturally. We blame the whole thing on the Irish, a notably convenient people for blaming things on. The Irish started everything. The name Scot was imported to this country by a wandering tribe from Ireland, the Scoti, who immediately started feuding with the local Picts, or Picti (the people who wore blue paint) and since those days we have never been short of an excuse for another punch-up. In the nineteenth century, the British Government was faced with the Irish potato famine, and by exercise of thought and ingenuity, succeeded in converting this into a national disaster which cut back the population by two million. Some of the Micks who still had the strength to stagger to the coastal towns and sixpence left for boat-fare, fled to Scotland and set up a minority problem. By that time, thanks to John Knox and other stubborn subversives, Scotland had gone Protestant, and the Irish immigrants were all hot and strong for Popery. They went in for mumbo-jumbo with crucifixes and painted idols, and this was viewed with panic suspicion not only by native Scotsmen, but by other immigrants from Ireland who had fought with William of Orange to put down the Irish Catholic Rebellion some time before – or who *would* have fought with King Billy, if it had been convenient.

Some of the Catholic immigrants had joined a foul secret society, the Fenians, dedicated to the independence of Ireland, and pretty soon every Catholic of any nationality was known positively to be a treasonous Fenian. That's how it all started, and the top witchhunters were Irish-oriented Protestants of the Orange movement, an interesting historical society which holds a big Walk every year and takes a dram in the name of religious purity.

Most of the time, you never notice this at all, but occasionally you have to tread a thin line. I was coming out of Tom's Bar one day with Jimmy Donnelly, the crime reporter of the Glasgow *Evening Citizen*, and we were talking about something very high-toned, like Kierkegaard or the *Kama Sutra*, something intellectual like that, when a jovial member of the artisan classes approached silently from behind and patted us both on the back and said,

'Aye, us crowd has to stick thegither, eh?'

'Eh?' we said.

'Ach, you know, boys?' And he made a stylish drop-kick movement *with the left foot*. That's a sure sign, you see. Catholics kick with the left foot.

'Aye, sure.' we said, which is the formula for avoiding any trouble in Glasgow no matter what anybody has said. And we parted with furtive thumbs-up signals.

'He thinks the pair of us are Fenian gets,' Jimmy said to me, and my amiable features turned stern.

'That's all right for you,' I said. 'You *are* a Fenian get.' The trouble with me is the name Hanley, which was brought from County Roscommon two generations back and can label a man. It was brought by a devout Catholic too, but the faith sort of diluted itself as the generations went on till it reached me as Calvinism and left me as nothing at all. Mind you, life was always dangerous around a man like Donnelly, who has an earnest chubby face and means no harm whatever, but can attract crises like a magnet. When he wrote a kindly piece about the death of the last of the Protestant gangsters, the king of the Billy Boys, he started getting anonymous phone calls, threatening him with death, and this is even more remarkable since he didn't have a telephone at the time.

One day I was out in the city with Donnelly, going about lawful occasions, in company with another Irish-sounding thug, Brian Feeny, a history teacher who keeps playing the piano and singing 'In the Good Old Summer Time' and who in spite of the name is a strictly non-Pope man, and everything happened to Donnelly that can happen to a man who is minding his own business. First of all we went into a bookshop and Donnelly picked three Penguins and paid for them, but Feeny and I were still browsing and he came back in to wait for us. On the way out, an assistant ran round the counter and accused Donnelly of trying to steal three paperbacks. It did no good when Feeny and I backed up his claim that he had paid for them – we were obviously a large-scale criminal outfit, and they had to fetch the manageress to adjudicate, and she didn't believe us either. She let us go because she didn't want the shop wrecked.

Brooding, we went round to a pub in Hope Street and Feeny and I kept patting Jimmy on the back and telling him we knew he was an honest man. All the time a stranger at the far end of the bar kept trying to catch my eye, and I turned on my glassy stare and I looked past him, and Jimmy said he was an obvious moocher. No sooner had the words been spoken than this moocher's mate materialised at our elbows, grabbed Jimmy by the arm, and said,

'Are you sneerin' at my pal?'

Donnelly, already embittered by fate, threw the stranger's arm off, but people in pubs get very persistent, and this one was looking for retribution.

'Right, outside!' he snarled. Outside, I ask you – in the middle of a main street at ten past five. Donnelly was blowing twin jets of steam down his nostrils, and, acting as his friends, we elbowed the stranger aside and urged him away from the trouble area.

'You would think I had the evil eye or something,' Jimmy said bitterly, glaring at the traffic in Hope Street, and dead on cue, a Morris Minor passed under his nose and its front nearside wheel fell right off.

One night in Barcelona, on a secret mission, I fell into the company of a middle-aged doctor from New York State who was doing the grand tour on his own, being a widower. His name was Edwin Shea, and for want of anybody more fascinating, we joined up for the evening, and I may say we got clipped for eleven quid for buying four Coca-Colas for two lassies in a night-club, so don't tell me anything about the low cost of living in Spain. However, Ed would have no part in this narrative except that he visited Glasgow on his way home and I picked him up at noon one Saturday to buy him a cheap nasty lunch. He was in a condition of bewilderment because he had spent the morning failing to get through the crowds in a city which he had always thought to be old, folksy and quiet. It only then dawned on me that this agreeable Catholic foreigner had somehow picked the day of the Orange Walk to be in Glasgow, and not only that, he was due to sail for Ireland the same night. In his place, I would have simulated appendicitis and stayed underground till the following week, but these Americans are tough travellers, hungry for experience.

On the day of the Orange Walk, the native enthusiasts are swollen by a really fervent contingent which comes over from Ulster, the home of Orangery, and those of them who are sober enough to find the dock, travel back to Ulster on the same night. Doctor Shea got his cheap lunch and we exchanged some corn, and then he vanished from human ken temporarily, but I had a letter from him in America describing the educational night he had spent on the Belfast boat, listening to the songs and thuds through the thin walls of his cabin and making rapid diagnoses all night as limbs scrunched on companionways and stomachs were hurled into the Irish Sea, and then covering his face with the blankets and possibly praying, for all I know. He complained philosophically that he had ended up minus a new camera which he had bought in Italy, and I wrote him a brusque note advising him to be thankful, and telling him to count his fingers, toes and heads if he didn't agree with me.

William Neill (1922 –)

Wild Places

They who are used to walking the wild places
are not to be driven mad by a raven's croak,
the beak that stabs the carrion's last traces,
the mistletoe that sucks life from the oak.

The dead lamb's maggots meet with a calm eye;
acorns are strewn before the oak-tree's fall.
Among the rocks wherein the corpses lie
the rising-trumpet is the raven's call.

Mr Burns for Supper

Once a year, Robin, they will remember you
in a word or two beyond your actual name.
The fatuous speeches will scarcely encumber you,
the maudlin tear, the exaggerated claim.
Who love what you love measure your true fame
in a kind of silence the foolish find too great.
They take your measure by their own puffed state.

You who remembered Fergusson's smothered grave
when all but you had consigned him to oblivion;
placing his image in its proper frame   10
honoured the seed of your own inspiration:
the common urge to teach in song a nation
not merely sold but deliberately retarded
by those whose place enjoined on them to guard it.

In your occasional sploring they will seek
solace for their own indulgences to find,
but few enough of them will ever read,
that they may penetrate into the mind
hidden beneath that aching urge to rhyme
and scan in song this land's life and your own   20
wherein man is and will be made to mourn.

The true admirer wonders how you did it . . .
scribling away in the midst of the Elect,
who seeing joy would hasten to forbid it,
suspicious of all but their own miserable respect
for a stone-age merciless god of their own construct
totally without love, an idol Christ did not know,
made from a kind of prurience welded into law.

Two worlds, the patient hoof and the ploughshare,
the high-fashion Dunedin drawing-rooms.   30
But you were happy neither here nor there.
The brief encounters of sex, the Sabbath glooms,
whisky and hypocrites, the Presbytery of Ayr.
Coining your verses in the snirt* and sneer   snigger
of peasant envy and the Yahweh-fear.

Still, you survived the capital's delights,
a Hesiod in the Athens of the North.
They came between your vision and the light:
a curiosity, not seeing your true worth
more than the western men of your own sort.   40
You found few listeners in either place:
the growing deafness of a sinking race.

Now, poets write books that Scotland does not buy,
shrink, in their eyes to the status of eccentric;
poetry's drowned out by every parrot-cry
feeding the multitude the latest cantrip*.   magic trick
They value verses less than a clownish trick;
once a year only within a phantom nation
they shrink your head to fit a social occasion.

Parochial

The learned poets chide me, saying
I must not write verses about Scotland
because this is racialistic, nationalistic, chauvinistic
and all their other mystic-istics.
Thistles and kilts are out.

So I will forget the weeping moor,
sad shells of houses in the mountain shadows,
the fetid, soul-rotten slums of the central belt.

I will write instead of Eros
and Picadilly bunny shows.   10
The great all-white Statue of Liberty
and all the other kinds of universal truth
enlarged to an enchantment by remoteness
from my old parish pump.

For such things are international
not hysterical-calvinistical-papistical
and all the other Jock-tickles[1]
too tedious to mention.

[1] 'Jock' is a nickname for a Scotsman (cf. 'Paddy' for an Irishman).

I will no longer rhyme tartans and partans★ crabs
for they are not a vision of the great eternal   20
which is exclusive of all Caledonian
particularity, insularity, vulgarity and Jockularity.

Then and Now

I can see Wallace now
A man who burned like a flame
Stand in their perjured court[1]
His pride and glory sold to mockery;
See the cold Norman sneers
The hollow advocates
The secret envy in each Quisling★ heart   traitor
And one who saw his duty stark and clear,
Watching, regretful of past infamy.[2]

This is now as it was;   10
Time stills no truth,
No less obliged to answer for our blood
We stand condemned.
Our limbs and sinews feel the pain he felt
But gain no honour in dismemberment.

Yon steadfast, mighty man,
Whose torture stained their loud proclaimed nobility,
Is like our Scotland; with the same mind again
They draw the living bowels from our country;
Not now our manhood, but our nationhood   20
Emasculate.

Weekend Patriot

High, high I see the Castle banner
Flaunting in a Friday sky . . .
I like the military manner
It gives to Edinburgh's Lie.

For Friday night is Beltane Night
Though no fires burn on Pentlands' rim;
Perhaps the Malt will set alight
My Druid blood, however thin.

---

[1] The Scots patriot, William Wallace, betrayed by some of his countrymen, was tortured and executed by his English enemies in a particularly brutal manner.
[2] The 'one' of line 8 may refer to Robert the Bruce, who up to this point had largely sided with the English, but who was afterward to take the lead in the defence of his country's liberty.

I'll go down to the street behind
The Noblest, Proudest Thoroughfare   10
In Europe, and I'll speak my mind
To every clan and sept that's there.

When strengthened by the Malt I feel
A hidden army at my call,
The rust is wiped from Fingal's[1] steel
And Gaeldom breaks its weekday thrall

On the bare puritanic boards
I'll take an Export and a Nip
Defiance of proud Edward's hordes
Bestirs my soul with every sip.   20

O slainte mhath and slainte mhor
I'll raise up schiltroms[2] in the mind . . .
Believe that Wallace breathes once more
His spirit through my sleeping kind.

O great the spell of usquebae,
I see my forbears' honour clear . . .
I see again the Noble Way
And wash my soul in Heavy Beer.

I lose the guilt that haunts my day
Says love of country is a sin . . .   30
Bewail Culloden's dowie★ day   sad
In Celtic teardrops clear as gin.

There's literary gents abound
Among the Hanoverian Squares,
Who pipe a Caledonian sound
To Gaelic and to Lallans airs . . .

. . . Rub shoulders with the hoi-polloi;
In cheery howffs★ we get their crack★,   taverns/conversation
They burst our hearts with hopeful joy
And ancient glories summon back.   40

But comes the morn, I die the death,
The dream as shattered as my head . . .
A bleary eye and stinking breath
Drive Fingal, weeping, back to bed.

---

[1] Mythical Gaelic champion, celebrated in Macpherson's eighteenth-century prose poems.
[2] In military usage, Scottish spear formations.

Gallowa Spring

The gowd is back upon the brae
Millyea has tint★ the snaw;   lost
lown★ is the northart sough the day   gentle
an warm the wastlin blaw.

Blythe nou wha tholed★ the wintertide   suffered, endured
its crannreuch★ cauld an lang.   frost
Green, green the shaws★ on braw Kenside   groves
an sweet the laverock's sang.

The Millman

October's moon over the evening yard,
rumble of wheels upon the rutted road,
breaking the earth for all the frost was hard
under that iron load.

Steam tractor, threshing mill and caravan,
come there to part their straw and chaff and grain,
the final fruiting of the peasant plan,
reward of labour's pain.

Into the firelit room the millman came,
with a hook for a hand, a face as pale as death;   10
the child, who saw all grown men as the same,
drew in a frightened breath.

The millman only grinned and waved his hook,
stuck down his corpse's face to the boy's head:
I'm more alive, my laddie, than I look.
It's just my hand that's dead . . .

and buried too, for it was never found
when the engine skidded on the bank and fell.
I often sit and think about that hand,
waiting in heaven or hell.

G. F. Dutton (1924 –)

Clach Eanchainn

that great stone
the shape of a brain
twisted and left there

out on the moor,
crystals and fire
fisted within it,

often has seen
forests go down
their soil squandered,

seeds blown in   10
blown out again,
ashes and iron

beneath it surrendered.
it was begun
with the first star

is now a stone
sheltering foxes
out on the moor.

often have men
marched through the dawn   20
to give it a name.

As So Often in Scotland

as so often in Scotland
the sun travelled
dyke over dyke, burning
dead grass golden and ending,
after a wallow of foothills,
on one brown summit;
that flared its moment, too,
and was gone.

Ticket

There has been
no summer and the road has ended
at a broken cliff. that hut

should have been the ferryman's
but he is out
and no one in

but an old woman talking to hens
and her son
has a good job in the town

will not be back   10
maybe the second week maybe
december, that was his car

I did not see
on this bare island with one road,
cliffs at both ends.

Return

I come from the sea.
there is salt on my lip.
I have lain on the sand
in the waves' retreat,
I have raised myself up
and trembled, been met
by battering light,
untouchable air;
and still stand here
bearing my weight,   10
trying to re-gather
trying to command
foot after foot
to climb the shore,
persuade my mind
to understand
why I must suffer
myself to land.

Flat

like much of Scotland
this is a flat land,
stretched between

mountains and shore,
grey cloud grey haar★   sea mist
most of the year

and no doubt
has often been
as flat

though shrugged about   10
various seas,
dipped and raised

time again,
kindled, braised
iced to the bone;

yet nevertheless,
smoothed with pale green
under a weak sun

and offered to
shall we say man,   20
it had its attractions.

whether or no
any remain
or any new

have come in
is less certain.
these constructions

dot it sadly, though
big at the feet,
for this is not   30

climate for concrete
and mud
too rapidly succeeds

ideas of grass.
people and weeds
have to thrive here

roots and seeds
have to explore
momentary silt

have to cherish
leaf or even flower
of the one result.   40

Carmen Mortis

Wha gangs alane
gangs free.

Wha's for companie,
gangs wi me.

Pensioners

In various parts of the garden
you meet them,
the admirers
of flowers.

It is the colours
the freshness, you see,
particularly
the freshness.

The rain just gone
the gravel dry   10
enough to walk on,
and the sun, the sun.

Each year it gets harder
each year to wander
drinking the freshness
back to the bone.

Each year to wonder
if the gates of the garden
after the winter
open again.   20

Bulletin

The glaciers have come down,
dead white
at the end of the street. All over town

cold mist of their breath,
and along gutters
water runs

freezing beneath. But
the machines are out, lined up,
beautiful, their great lights

tossing back darkness. And the engineers   10
have promised to save us,
they have left their seats

for a last meal, when they return
all will be well, under control,
it is their skill, listen –

already upstairs
they are teaching their children
to sing like the ice.

Ken Morrice (1924 – 2002)

Flight

One day off-handedly her sister told her
she was fat. Sixteen years old,
construing her adolescence in the mirror
and deciding she objected to the mould
and curve of breast and thigh,
she took to muesli, oranges and lettuce,
lost thirty pounds in sixty days,
tucking in jeans instead of food. 'Don't fuss,'
she told her mother, who called it 'Just a phase.'
Father, table-thumping, predicted she would die.   10

Thin as a sparrow, secretive as a water-rail,
with pointed nose and elongated toes,
she pecked her food, grew pale,
sprouted fingered wings and rose
one day from family noise and bother
to flutter through the open kitchen window,

circling and soaring high into the sky.
Father preoccupied failed to see her go.
Mother remarked, 'I'm not surprised. Our Di
ate just like a bird.' 'How absurd!' said Father.   20

Mother it was who missed her most, pattering
round the house beslippered every evening,
leaving the cage-door open and scattering
bird-seed on a plate. But too little and too late.

Murder in the Morning

Clock screams its shrill alarm. I reach out
in cold and dark blindly to cut its throat.
Wife stirs lazy, reluctant; and half-asleep
I turn awkwardly in bed to hold and keep

the consolation of her warmth and love.
But time intransigent must prove
(ticking and tocking) its regular demands.
Clock whirs, splutters, and points its hands

accusingly. Winter is come. Time to rouse and rise.
Culpable, contentious, I open bloodshot eyes.   10

Ian Hamilton Finlay (1925 –   )

Orkney Lyrics

(One)
Peedie Mary Considers the Sun

The peedie sun is not so tall
He walks on golden stilts
Across, across, across the water
But I have darker hair.

(Two)
The English Colonel Explains an Orkney Boat

The boat swims full of air.
You see, it has a point at both
Ends, sir, somewhat
As lemons. I'm explaining

The hollowness is amazing. That's
The way a boat
Floats.

(Three)
Mansie Considers Peedie Mary

Peedie Alice Mary is
My cousin, so we cannot kiss.
And yet I love my cousin fair:
She wears her seaboots with such an air.

(Four)
Mansie Considers the Sea in the Manner
of Hugh MacDiarmid

The sea, I think, is lazy.
It just obeys the moon
– All the same I remember what Engels said:
'Freedom is the consciousness of necessity.'

(Five)
Folk Song for Poor Peedie Mary

Peedie Mary
Bought a posh
Big machine
To do her wash.

Peedie Mary
Stands and greets*.   weeps
Where dost thoo
Put in the peats?

Silly Peedie
Mary thoo   10
Puts the peats
Below, baloo.

Peedie Mary
Greets the more.
What did the posh paint
Come off for?

(Six)
John Sharkey Is Pleased to Be in Sourin at Evening

How beautiful, how beautiful, the mill
 – Wheel is not turning though the waters spill
Their single tress. The whole old mill
Leans to the West, the breast.

Black Tomintoul

To Scotland came the tall American
And went to stay on a little farm
Oh it was a Scotch farm set in the wild
A wee Scotch burn and a stony field

She came to a corner, it was raining
And the little trees were all leaning in
This was Scotland the way she had thought of it
Care, not gravity, makes them lean
The rain falling Scotchly, Scotchly
And the hills that did not soar up but in   10
But most she looked at the bull so wild
She looked at the bull with the eyes of a child
Never in New York did she see such a bull
As this great Scotch one, Tomintoul
She called him secretly, the great Scotch bull

He was black all over, even for a bull
And oh he had such a lovely hide
She saw him follow one cow aside
Tell me, please, is that cow his bride?
No, they are all his lawful br-r-ride   20
There were twenty-four cows on the Scotch hillside

It was almost too much for the tall American girl
She watched him stand on his opposite hill
Black Tomintoul, and he always bellowed
But afterwards something in her was mellowed.

Alastair Mackie (1925 –)

Adolescence

Gin they wid leave me alane!

Whit ails me
I dinna ken.

Look ahin my een, ye'll fin
het saut and love-stounds★.   blows, throbs

Thae days it cams easy
like – dinna greet lassie –

A beast mum and tethert
to a stound.

The soond o the guitars   10
and me dwamin* thro them.   swooning

And did he nae smile to me?
But he did smile to me!

The keekin-gless is my frien
I tell it aathing jist lookin.

It says neathing the haill time
but – 'Ye'r bonny, quine.'

I fill up its laneliness
wi my ain dowie* face   sad

and when my een crack   20
it shares my hert-brak,

cut gless lookin at cut gless.

Scots Pegasus

Oor Scots Pegasus
is a timmer* naig   timber (wooden)
wi a humphy back and cockle een.

He ettles* to flee   tries
but his intimmers* are fu o the deid-chack.   insides
Gin he rins ava
he pechs* sair.   pants
And skelbs* drap aff like sharn*.   splinters/dung

He's fed on bruck*   scraps
scranned fae aa the airts.   10
This gies him the belly-thraw
and yon etten and spewed* look.   pasty-faced

Makars* whiles   poets
fling a leg ower his rig-bane
and crank the hunnle* on his spauld*.   handle/shoulder
He taks a turn roon the park
but never gets aff the grun
or oot o the bit.
This mishanter's caad
in some stables –   20
'A new voice in Lallans*.'   Scots

Ithers, brither Scots
gie him the hee-haw.

The hert o the nut is this –
naebody, dammt, kens the horseman's word.

Primary Teachers

My primary teachers o the Thirties
maun aa be middle-aged skeletons by nou,
Aa weemin they were.
    The early snaw in their hair.
They pit up wi impetigo, flechy★ heids,   louse-ridden
and bairns that couldna pey their books –
    the fathers were on the broo
And yet they did learn us, yon auld wives,
We chantit tables like bairn-rhymes
to keep aff the inspectors or the heidie.   10
And when we spelled the classroom skriechit
sclatey music fae oor soap-scoured slates.
Their scuds★ were murder – the Lochgelly soond.   straps
'Don't turn on the water-works' they girned★.   grinned
    (they spoke English)
They kent naething o new methods
but in their fashion they were as teuch
as gauleiters, ramrods withoot breists.
They did their T. C.'s★ prood.   training colleges
    I salute ye nou,   20
Miss Smith, Miss Tough, Miss McIvor –
steam-hemmers somebody maun hae loved.

Lochan

A lochan in the hert o the hills.
By day-time het kye drink at your edges.
At nicht, the keekin-gless★ o the galaxies.   mirror
The-day your cauld clarity gars me grue★.   feel horror

Youthheid likes itsel best.
Twa laddies cam here aince.
Whit gaupit back at them was an ee o ice.

Alastair Reid (1926 –)

A Lesson for Beautiful Women

Gazing and gazing in the glass,
she might have noticed slow cotillions pass
and might have seen
a blur of others in the antique green.
Transfixed instead,
she learned the inclinations of her neat small head
and, startling her own surprise,
wondered at the wonder in her jewelled eyes.

Gardens of rainbow and russet might have caught her
but, leaning over goldfish water,   10
she watched the red carp emphasize her mouth,
saw underneath
the long green weeds lace in
through a transparency of face and skin,
smiled at herself smiling reflectively,
lending a new complexion to the sky.

In service to her beauty
long mornings lengthened to a duty
patiently served before the triple mirror
whose six eyes sent her many a time in terror   20
to hide in rows of whispering dresses;
but her glass soul her own three goddesses
pursued, and if she turned away,
the same three mouths would breathe 'Obey, obey!'

And in procession, young men princely came,
ambassadors to her cool perfect kingdom.
Set at a distance by their praise,
she watched their unspeaking eyes adore her face.
Inside, her still self waited. Nothing moved.
Finally, by three husbands richly loved   30
(none of them young), she drifted into death,
the glass clouding with her last moist breath.

Changed into legend, she was given rest;
and, left alone at last,
the small mim* servant shuttered in her being   prissy
peeped mousily out; and seeing
the imperious mirrors glazed and still,
whimpered forlornly down the dark hall
'Oh, grieve for my body, who would not let me be.
She, not I, was a most beautiful lady.'   40

Scotland

It was a day peculiar to this piece of the planet,
when larks rose on long thin strings of singing
and the air shifted with the shimmer of actual angels.
Greenness entered the body. The grasses
shivered with presences, and sunlight
stayed like a halo on hair and heather and hills.
Walking into town, I saw, in a radiant raincoat,
the woman from the fish-shop. 'What a day it is!'
cried I, like a sunstruck madman.
And what did she have to say for it?   10
Her brow grew bleak, her ancestors raged in their graves
as she spoke with their ancient misery:
'We'll pay for it, we'll pay for it, we'll pay for it!'

Ghosts' Stories

That bull-necked blotch-faced farmer from Drumlore
would never dream (or so we heard him boast
to neighbours at the lamb sales in Kirkcudbright)
of paying the least attention to a ghost.

Were we to blame for teaching him a lesson?
We whored his daughter, spaded all his ewes,
brought a blight on his barley, drew the sea
rempaging over his sod . . .

If we had any doubt that deserved it,
that went when we heard him stamp his ruined acres   10
and blame it all on God.
When we went on and frightened Miss McQueen
for keeping children in on Halloween,
and wailed all night in the schoolhouse, she, poor woman,
sent for the Fire Brigade.
And so we made
fire lick from her hair, till they put her out.

The children knew what it was all about.

The Figures on the Frieze

Darkness wears off, and, dawning into light,
they find themselves unmagically together.
He sees the stains of morning in her face.
She shivers, distant in his bitter weather.

Diminishing of legend sets him brooding.
Great goddess-figures conjured from his book
blur what he sees with bafflement of wishing.
Sulky, she feels his fierce, accusing look.

Familiar as her own, his body's landscape
seems harsh and dull to her habitual eyes.   10
Mystery leaves, and, mercilessly flying,
the blind fiends come, emboldened by her cries.

Avoiding simple reach of hand for hand
(which would surrender pride) by noon they stand
withdrawn from touch, reproachfully alone,
small in each other's eyes, tall in their own.

Wild with their misery, they entangle now
in baffling agonies of why and how.
Afternoon glimmers, and they wound anew,
flesh, nerve, bone, gristle in each other's view.   20

'What have you done to me?' From each proud heart,
new phantoms walk in the deceiving air.
As the light fails, each is consumed apart,
he by his ogre vision, she by her fire.

When night falls, out of a despair of daylight,
they strike the lying attitudes of love,
and through the perturbation of their bodies,
each feels the amazing, murderous legends move.

The Day the Weather Broke

Last out in the raining weather, a girl and I
drip in the splintered light while cars slur by,
and the single drizzling reason
of rain in an alien season
turns us to each other till a train arrives
to share, by bond of wetness, our wet lives.
Although at first we can find to put our thumb on
only the rain in common,
is this not what love is? That we draw together
in the inhuman weather,   10
strangers, who pool our sheltered selves and take,
for the grey heavens' sake,
this luck, caught without our usual cloak
the day the weather broke?

'Burns Singer' (James Singer, 1928 – 1964)

Peterhead in May

Small lights pirouette
Among these brisk little boats.
A beam, cool as a butler,
Steps from the lighthouse.

Wheelroom windows are dark
Reflections of light quickly
Skip over them tipsily like
A girl in silk.

One knows there is new paint
And somehow an intense   10
Suggestion of ornament
Comes into mind.

Imagine elephants here
They'd settle, clumsily sure
Of themselves and of us and of four
Square meals and of water.

Then you will have it. This
Though a grey and quiet place
Finds nothing much amiss.
It keeps its stillness.   20

There is no wind. A thin
Mist fumbles above it and,
Doing its best to be gone,
Obscures the position.

This place is quiet or,
Better, impersonal. There
Now you have it. No verdict
Is asked for, no answer.

Yet nets will lie all morning,
Limp like stage scenery,   30
Unused but significant
Of something to come.

To Marie

For Half a Year of Happiness
November 6th: 1956

For half a year of happiness
Between us two
These small barefooted words must run
Along my pen to you.

They whisper secretly in one
Another's secret ear:
Heavy black-booted thoughts patrol,
But cannot hear.

This mob of children from the streets
Where love is young and we   10
Playing pavement games, chalk clumsy signs
And riddle-ree.

O do not be deceived my dear.
Sing me a song.
These little gangs, in secret gay,
Have beaten down those long

Vocabularies, squads of words,
In sulky navy-blue.
There's half a year of happiness
Between us two.   20

Africa

Africa happened a long time ago.
It was merely the scent of coffee
Inhaled through thin nostrils
That made it happen to me
But at that moment it seemed to appear
On my right hand side, twenty degrees left,
And it entered my bloodstream with huge lunges
Which I couldn't shift.
The black and white were merry at once
And I couldn't agree which was which.   10
The white had stolen molasses from me
And the black was a bitch.
They entered, both right, and began to grapple
Until they were all on the floor.
I looked about carefully and discovered
That a corridor led to a mirror.
There black and white transplanted were
And worth emerged the victor.
I thought it sad, in many ways mad
And I hid behind the door.

Iain Crichton Smith (1928 – 1998)

Iain Smith is perhaps the most admired Scottish poet of recent years. An opposite of his contemporary, Edwin Morgan, Smith has limited himself in both subject matter and technique. He was born on the island of Lewis and is bilingual. He has written much in Gaelic and has translated from that language. Scottish history, the rhythms of the countryside, a concern for country people, a sense of isolation, and a (rather ambiguous) nostalgia for a passing age (i.e., of rural simplicity and of the Gaelic tradition) are never far from him. The astonishing group of five poems printed below, all with the same title, 'Old Woman', demonstrate his tendency to return to favourite themes, his humanity, and a classical economy of means. He is the master of the quiet style – simple but exact, elegant and expressive.

Smith is also one of the best short story writers of our age. Two of his finest are given here. 'The Adoration of the Mini' is in the understated vein of much of his verse. 'The Crater', on the other hand, while also basically realistic, is a terrifying, hallucinatory glimpse into the world of the unspeakable. He is an admired novelist. *Consider the Lilies* (1968), a novelette, may be his most praised fiction.

The Clearances

The thistles climb the thatch. Forever
this sharp scale in our poems,
as also the waste music of the sea.

The stars shine over Sutherland
in a cold ceilidh of their own,
as, in the morning, the silver cane

cropped among corn. We will remember this.
Though hate is evil we cannot
but hope your courtier's heels in hell

are burning: that to hear   10
the thatch sizzling in tanged smoke
your hot ears slowly learn.

Highlanders

They sailed away into the colored prints
of Balaclava, or at tall Quebec
you'll see them climbing almost native rock
in search of French and not of cormorants.

Abroad, they fought the silks and bright coats
while to their homes the prancing dandies came
on horses like Napoleon's, in the calm
(but clouds of snuff) of all their ruined boats,

them high on Nelson's topmasts looking over
a coloured sea at evening coming up   10
with complex tackle and harmonious rope
from pictured oceans and a roaring fire.

Culloden and After

You understand it? How they returned from Culloden
over the soggy moors aslant, each cap
at the low ebb no new full tide could pardon:
how they stood silent at the end of the rope
unwound from battle: and to the envelope
of a bedded room came home, polite and sudden.

And how, much later, bards from Tiree and Mull
would write of exile in the hard town
where mills belched English, anger of new school:
how they remembered where the sad and brown   10
landscapes were dear and distant as the crown
that fuddled Charles might study in his ale.

There was a sleep. Long fences leaned across
the vacant croft. The silly cows were heard
mooing their sorrow and their Gaelic loss.
The pleasing thrush would branch upon a sword.
A mind withdrew against its dreamed hoard
as whelks withdraw or crabs their delicate claws.

And nothing to be heard but songs indeed
while wandering Charles would on his olives feed   20
and from his Minch of sherries mumble laws.

Old Woman

And she, being old, fed from a mashed plate
as an old mare might droop across a fence
to the dull pastures of its ignorance.
Her husband held her upright while he prayed

to God who is all-forgiving to send down
some angel somewhere who might land perhaps
in his foreign wings among the gradual crops.
She munched, half dead, blindly searching the spoon.

Outside, the grass was raging. There I sat
imprisoned in my pity and my shame   10
that men and women having suffered time
should sit in such a place, in such a state

and wished to be away, yes, to be far away
with athletes, heroes, Greek or Roman men

who pushed their bitter spears into a vein
and would not spend an hour with such decay.

'Pray God,' he said, 'we ask you, God,' he said.
The bowed back was quiet. I saw the teeth
tighten their grip around a delicate death.
And nothing moved within the knotted head   20

but only a few poor veins as one might see
vague wishless seaweed floating on a tide
of all the salty waters where had died
too many waves to mark two more or three.

Old Woman

Your thorned back
heavily under the creel
you steadily stamped the rising daffodil.

Your set mouth
forgives no one, not even God's justice
perpetually drowning law with grace.

Your cold eyes
watched your drunken husband come
unsteadily from Sodom home.

Your grained hands   10
dandled full and sinful cradles.
You built for your children stone walls.

Your yellow hair
burned slowly in a scarf of grey
wildly falling like the mountain spray.

Finally you're alone
among the unforgiving brass,
the slow silences, the sinful glass.

Who never learned,
not even aging, to forgive   20
our poor journey and our common grave

while the free daffodils
wave in the valleys and on the hills
the deer look down with their instinctive skills,

and the huge sea
in which your brothers drowned sings slow
over the headland and the peevish crow.

Old Woman

Overwhelmed with kindnesses and you have nothing.
They bring you roses to refresh their hearts
and still the bitter voices.
They greet you sweetly, you are now their child,
they flatter you completely,
and you have nothing to present to them
objects to objects just your used self.
Only a god I think could take such gifts
and not feel hatred. Only a god could bear
such manifold penances, and be the vase   10
for all these guilty roses.

You are no god and therefore should you snap
suddenly out at them between old teeth
like a fox dying in a sweet country
I should not turn from that poor twisted face
bayed in its autumn by solicitous smiles.

Old Woman

'The Old Age Pensioners,' she said,
'are to be granted an extra pound.
It was stated by the Government.'
And this, I knew, had made her proud.
Now she'd more easily afford
residence in her own son's house.
And I, who had more than enough
to buy whatever she should choose —
her prudent spare necessities —
must in that luxury pretend   10
to be gladdened by such marvellous news.

For dignity is what we crave
when all else has been pared away
and we must sit each single day
or lie, as ready for the grave.
It is a way of being brave
and a diminished happiness
seems only diminished to the strong.
Tonight the tears came to my eyes
unbidden as I thought of this.   20
It was the ending of the day
and a white moon was in the skies.

Old Woman

Your face is wrinkled
with the roads you have travelled
The vows you have made
to the crockery
Your beauty
shines through old age
like an old boat in a strait
fishing in the blaze
of a last sunset.

The Cemetery Near Burns' Cottage

Tombs of the Covenanters nod together
grey heads and obstinate. They saw them come
the silver horsemen meditating murder
but stood there quietly to the beating drum
of God and psalm, the heart's immaculate order.

So now I see them as the churchyard turns
red in the evening light. They did not know
that moral milk turns sour, and something churns
inside the stony cask. This churchyard now
flickers with light, untameably with Burns,   10

the secret enemy within the stone,
the hand which even here stings its hot whip
in glittering rays from socketed bone to bone.
In such fixed Eden did his changing shape
unlock their teeth from what they'd bravely won.

Johnson in the Highlands

A reasoning mind travels through this country.
In these sad wastes a Londoner by choice
sees water falling, and some meager deer.

Examines with his tough reasoning mind
lochs, deer, and people; is not seduced
by Mrs Radcliffe's green hysteria

from a musical prose we've never once achieved,
whose fences cannot reach between the words
whose arguments are broken-backed with exile.

A classical sanity considers Skye.   10
A huge hard light falls across shifting hills.
This mind, contemptuous of miracles

and beggarly sentiment, illuminates
a healthy moderation. But I hear
like a native dog notes beyond his range

the modulations of a queer music
twisting his huge black body in the pain
that shook him also in raw blazing London.

At the Highland Games

Like re-reading a book which has lost its pith.

Watching the piper dandying over a sodden stage
saluting an empty tent.

The empty beer glasses catch the sun,
sparkle like old brooches against green.

Fur-hatted, with his huge twirling silver stick
the pipe-major has gypsy cheekbones, colour of brick.

Everything drowses. The stewards with aloof eagle stare
sit on collapsing rock, chair on brown chair.

Once the pibroch showed the grave 'ground'   10
of seas without bubbles, where great hulks were drowned,

meat with mustaches. The heroic dead lie
over and over the sea to misty Skye.

Past the phantom ivy, bird song, I walk
among crew-cuts, cameras, the heather-covered rock,

past my ancestry, peasants, men who bowed
with stony necks to the daughter-stealing lord.

Past my ancestry, the old songs, the pibroch
stirring my consciousness like the breeze a loch.

Past my buried heart, my friend who complains   20
of all the crime, 'their insane violence.'

Stone by stone the castles crumble. The seas
have stored away their great elegies.

'Morag of Dunvagen.' Dandy piper
with delicate soft paws, knee-bending stepper,

saluting an empty tent. Blue-kilted stewards
strut like strange storks along the sodden sward.

Finished. All of it's finished. The Gaelic
boils in my mouth, the South Sea silver stick

twirls, settles. The mannequins are here.   30
Calum, how you'd talk of their glassy stare,

their loud public voices. Stained pictures
of what was raw, violent, alive and coarse.

I watch their heirs, Caligulas with canes
stalk in their rainbow kilts towards the dance.

By the Sea: Dunoon and the Holy Loch

The huge sea widens from us, mile on mile.
Kenneth MacKellar sings from the domed pier.
A tinker piper plays a ragged tune
on ragged pipes. He tramps under a moon
which rises like the dollar. Think how here

missiles like sugar rocks are all incised
with Alabaman Homer. These defend
the clattering tills, the taxis, thin pale girls
who wear at evening their Woolworth pearls
and from dewed railings gaze at the world's end.   10

The Exiles

The many ships that left our country
with white wings for Canada.
They are like handkerchiefs in our memories
and the brine like tears
and in their masts sailors singing
like birds on branches.

That sea of May running in such blue,
a moon at night, a sun at daytime,
and the moon like a yellow fruit
like a plate on a wall,   10
to which they raise their hands
like a silver magnet
with piercing rays
streaming into the heart.

You Lived in Glasgow

You lived in Glasgow many years ago.
I do not find your breath in the air.
It was, I think, in the long-skirted thirties
when idle men stood at every corner
chewing their fag-ends of a failed culture.
Now I sit here in George Square
where the War Memorial's yellow sword glows bright
and the white stone lions mouth at bus and car.
A maxi-skirted girl strolls slowly by.
I turn and look. It might be you. but no.   10
Around me there's a 1970 sky.

Everywhere there are statues. Stone remains.
The mottled flesh is transient. On those trams,
invisible now but to the mind, you bore
your groceries home to the 1930 slums.
'There was such warmth,' you said. The gaslight hums
and large caped shadows tremble on the stair.
Now everything is brighter. Pale ghosts walk
among the spindly chairs, the birchen trees.
In lights of fiercer voltage you are less   20
visible than when in winter you
walked, a black figure, through the gaslight blue.

The past's an experience that we cannot share.
Flat-capped Glaswegians and the Music Hall.
Apples and oranges on an open stall.
A day in the country. And the sparkling Clyde
splashing its local sewage at the wall.
This April day shakes memories in a shade
opening and shutting like a parasol.
There is no site for the unshifting dead.   30
You're buried elsewhere though your flickering soul
is a constant tenant of my tenement.

You were happier here than anywhere, you said.
Such fine good neighbours helping when your child
almost died of croup. Those pleasant Wildes
removed with the fallen rubble have now gone
in the building program which renews each stone.
I stand in a cleaner city, better fed,
in my diced coat, brown hat, my paler hands
leafing a copy of the latest book.   40
Dear ghosts, I love you, haunting sunlit winds,
dear happy dented ghosts, dear prodigal folk.

I left you, Glasgow, at the age of two
and so you are my birthplace just the same.
Divided city of the green and blue
I look for her in you, my constant aim
to find a ghost within a close who speaks

in Highland Gaelic.
      The bulldozer breaks
raw bricks to powder. Boyish workmen hang
like sailors in tall rigging. Buildings sail   50
into the future. The old songs you sang
fade in their pop songs, scale on dizzying scale.

For My Mother

You have so little and that I have more
(money, I mean) angers me. As well,
I had four years at University where
I sipped good learning under a proud bell.

You on the other hand were gutting herring
(at seventeen) on a hard Lowestoft quay
with glassy hands to which dark blood would cling
while the red clouds would lighten on the sea.

Angrily I watch you from my guilt
and sometimes think: The herring in my hand,   10
bloody and gutted, would be far more solid
than this more slippery verse, but that cold wind

appals me as a voluntary price to pay,
the lonely figure in the doubtful light
with the bloody knife beside the murmuring sea
waiting for the morning to come right.

By Ferry to the Island

We crossed by ferry to the bare island
where sheep and cows stared coldly through the wind –
the sea behind us with its silver water,
the silent ferryman standing in the stern
clutching his coat about him like old iron.

We landed from the ferry and went inland
past a small church down to the winding shore
where a white seagull fallen from the failing
chill and ancient daylight lay so pure
and softly breasted that it made more dear   10

the lesser white around us. There we sat,
sheltered by a rock beside the sea.
Someone made coffee, someone played the fool
in a high rising voice for two hours.
The sea's language was more grave and harsh.

And one sat there whose dress was white and cool.
The fool sparkled his wit that she might hear
new diamonds turning on her naked finger.
What might the sea think or the dull sheep
lifting its head through heavy Sunday sleep?   20

And later, going home, a moon rising
at the end of a cart-track, minimum of red,
the wind being dark, imperfect cows staring
out of their half-intelligence, and a plough
lying on its side in the cold, raw

naked twilight, there began to move
slowly, like heavy water, in the heart
the image of the gull and of that dress,
both being white and out of the darkness rising
the moon ahead of us with its rusty ring.   30

Home

To have to stay
in spite of scorn, hatred,
in spite of shattered
illusions also. To be unable
to break cleanly away
since this is truly home
simple, imperishable,
since otherwhere is chill,
dull-breasted, dumb.

Since this too is hated,   10
loved, willed to be perfect, willed
to a finer yield,
fiercer, less barren, richer,
its harvests be completed.
Since to have seen tall men
moving in light and fire
yet human too is more
grace than can be given

this (one says) is tragic
(to be fixed on a wheel   20
implacable, internal,
as tears break, as roses
bowed gravely down to rock
proliferate endless versions)
is not tragic but cause
of fresh honours, horses
impelled by used reins.

The Hills Are Stony As They've Always Been[1]

The hills are stony as they've always been
with narrow roads and wide blue lochs between
and the bowed women carrying peats in creels
and tourists spread on grass at picnic meals
and buzzards hunched on fence posts bent on prey
and boys on bicycles and girls at play.
No houses now are thatched. Museums show
the curtained beds, and byres* of long ago,   animal barns
the tall old lamps, the griddles, and peat fires,
the wooden cart wheels before rubber tyres,   10
oars for the hands of giants, and low chairs
made from rough planks washed up on earlier shores.
Cows munch among the buttercups, and sheep
lie at the roadside almost sunk in sleep.
Tinkers subdued to council houses learn
to live as others do, earn as they earn
and English growing as the Gaelic dies
describes these vast and towering island skies.
God is surrendering to other gods
as the stony moor to multiplying roads.   20
Folk songs and country westerns in the bars
displace the native music sweet and harsh
which dilettantes soon will learn to prize
when the last real brutal singer dies,
too zealous and too tearful. Ah, those eves
of fine September moons and autumn sheaves
when no one knocked on doors, and fish was free,
before the Bible faded to TV
and tractors ground the bones of horses down
into bone-meal well suited to the town,   30
and girls were simple who drink brandies now
and wear mascara who would milk the cow.
But times have changed, and steamers bring to shore
cargoes of cars, that brought just men before,
and drivers in black glasses burn the miles
between waning townships and diminished schools
where children learn what education's for –
to look from elsewhere to a well-loved shore
and leaving home wave to the tourists who
set off each summer into hopeful blue.   40

---

[1] This is the first poem on a sequence called 'Return to Lewis'. The poem which follows is its fourth section.

This Is the Place I Grew In

This is the place I grew in. Barefoot, I
would run to school under a summer sky
on the grass beside the road. Today I see
far larger houses each with its TV
aerial on the roof and at most doors
or in their garages new glittering cars.
The moor smells heavy as it used to do
and skylarks rise from nests. My town-made shoe
squelches among the moss. I've travelled far
from this small village by its sandy shore   10
with its ruins of thatched houses, roofless walls.
The girls I knew are wearing women's shawls.
The fields seem smaller, and the Standing Stones
diminished now against less wide horizons
which once were bounds to simpler, slower minds.
The grass is waving now in stranger winds
and I feel sorrow more than I feel joy
as all must do who see the phantom boy
that they once were, scrambling among the pools,
in his breeze-filled jersey, or among sea shells   20
entirely concentrate. No one can return
ever again to the place where he was born
who once has left it. Perhaps better so.
My feet accelerate to swift from slow
as if pursued by ghosts that in the breeze
seethe like the fish in these rich northern seas.

In Your Long Skirts

In your long skirts among the other girls
you stand beside the barrels, leather-gloved,
in 1908 or so, with severe lips.

The girls are all dead and you are dead.
Two wars have happened since and many fish
have bred and died in the cold North Sea.

In that brown picture you all look very old
for twenty-year-old girls and you're all gazing
to a sun that's off the edge and is made of salt.

The Shadows

'I think,' she said, 'we shall not see again
each other as we did. The light is fading
that was once sunny in the April rain.
Across the picture there appears a shading
we didn't notice, but was in the grain.'

The picture shows two people happily smiling
with their arms around each other, by the sea.
Whatever they are looking at is beguiling
themselves to themselves. There is a tree
with orange blossoms and an elegant styling   10

but they are lost quite clearly in each other.
They do not see the landscape, do not hear
the stream that tinkles through the azure weather.
It's as if really the clear atmosphere
were a creation of two souls together.

But at the back there steadily grow two shadows
one for each lover that they can't evade.
They emerge threateningly from the coloured meadows
as if they were a track the two had made
and they were ignorant of, their changeless natures.   20

And as they move the shades intently follow
growing steadily darker, spreading as they go
as the wings' shades pursue the flying swallow.
My dearest love, if these should make us slow
remember late the first undying halo.

My Brother

My brother, today the rain is falling,
I haven't heard from you for twenty years.
When you left first you were so confident,
riding your new horse from coast to coast.
Then after a while you stopped writing.
My letters never reached you for you changed addresses.
Were you ashamed that your new horse never lasted?
Sailors from the old country have seen you in bars
but you don't speak to them.
Success is demanded of the exile.   10
Today as the rain falls it occurred to me
that I do not know where you are.
How the world comes between even two brothers!
All I can see is the horse you wrote of
standing in a cage of rain somewhere
with the burrs of twenty years on its skin.

Kilnave Churchyard, Islay

In this calm place the graves are very old,
the writing almost illegible. Many men
are lying here with their wives and children,
families reconciled in stone
under the earth's green billows. As we read
in the loud sound of the Atlantic
a lark flies straight up singing. There's a grave
newly open with a spade inside it.
A large hare leaps from behind a stone
and dashes crazily from us. The sky holds   10
us and the dead, our flesh and the old stones,
some of which are bare of writing.
Imagine how in winter the wind howls
round the unwritten stone, unglamorous, poor.
But now the world is totally calm.
The Atlantic glitters gaily. My hand is warm
leaning on this stone. My shirt is rippling.
The hare has gone to ground, the lark is singing.
The dead knew this joy, they are part of this joy now.

The Adoration of the Mini

It was an old people's hospital and yet he wasn't old. As she stood at the door about to press the bell she looked around her and saw beside a shrouded wheelchair some tulips swaying in the white March wind. Turning her head into the cold bright sun, she saw farther down the road a fat man in blue washing a bright red car. She felt joyous and sad by turns.

She pressed the bell, and a nurse in white and blue came to the door. Visiting hours were two to three, but she thought she could call at any time now. The nurse was stony-faced and middle-aged and glancing at her quickly seemed to disapprove of the roundness of her body: it was not the place for it. She pushed back her blonde hair which had been slightly disarranged by the wind. She asked for Mr Mason, and the nurse showed her the door of the ward. Here and there she could see other nurses, but none of them was young; it would have been better if at least one or two had the expectancy and hope of youth. It would make the place brighter, younger, with a possible future.

She walked into the ward. The walls were flaked with old paint, and old men, propped on pillows, stared ahead of them without recognition or care. One old man with a beard, his eyes ringed with black as if from long sleeplessness, looked through her as though she had been a window pane beyond which there was no country that he could love or desire. By one or two beds – the bedside tables bearing their usual offerings of grapes and oranges, and bottles of yellow energy-giving liquids wrapped in cellophane – there were women talking in whispers.

She walked through the main ward, not seeing him, and then through into a smaller one. And there he was, on his own, sitting up against the pillows as if waiting. But he could not be expecting her. He might be expecting her mother or her brother or her other sister, but not her.

The smell of imminent death was palpable and distinct. It was in the room, it was all round him, it impregnated the sheets, it was in his face, in his eyes. She had seen him ill before, but not like this. His colour was neither yellow nor red, it was a sort of grey, like old paper. The neck was long and stringy, and the knotted wrists rested meagerly on the sheet in front of him.

She stood at the foot of the bed and looked at him. He looked back at her without energy. She said,

'I came to see you, father.'

He made no answer. It was as if he hadn't heard her or as if (if he had heard her) she wasn't worth answering. She noticed the carafe of water at the table at the foot of the bed and said,

'Do you want a drink?'

He remained silent. She began again:

'I came up by train today. It took me eight hours.'

She shook her yellow hair as if to clear her head and said, 'May I sit down?' He still didn't speak and she sat down on the chair. He spoke at last:

'How do you think I look?'

She replied with conscious brightness,

'I had thought you would be worse.'

'I think I'm dying,' he said tonelessly and almost with cunning, 'I've had strange visions.' He shut his eyes for a moment as if to rest them.

'What do you want?' he asked without opening his eyes.

'I wanted to see you.'

'What about?'

'I . . . '

'You left a good job and went off to London and you're pregnant, isn't that right,' he said slowly, as if he were carving something with a chisel and hammer. 'You had a good brain and you threw it all away. You could have gone on to university.'

'We're married now,' she said.

'I know that. You married a Catholic. But then Catholics breed a lot, don't they?' He opened his eyes, looking at her in disgust, his nose wrinkling as if he could smell incense. She flared up, forgetting that he was dying.

'You know why I left, father. I didn't want to go to university. I'm an ordinary person.'

'You had an I.Q. of 135. I shouldn't be telling you this but I saw it on your school records.'

'I didn't want to go to university. I didn't want to do Science.'

'I didn't care. It didn't need to be Science. It could have been any subject. You threw yourself away. You went to work in a wee office. And then you got pregnant. And now you say you are married. To a Catholic. And you'll have to be a Catholic too. I know them. And your . . . ' He couldn't bring himself to say that her child would be a Catholic.

She couldn't stop herself. 'I thought a scientist wouldn't care for these things. I thought a scientist would be unprejudiced.'

He smiled grimly. 'That's the kind of remark I would have expected from you. It shows that you have a high I.Q. You should have used it. You threw it away. You ignored your responsibilities. You went off to London, to see the bright lights.' She sensed envy in his voice.

After a while she said,

'I couldn't stand school. I don't know how I can explain it to you. The books didn't mean anything after a while. It was torture for me to read them. Can you understand that?'

'No.' His mouth shut like a rat-trap.

'I tried,' she continued. 'I did try. But they didn't mean anything. I would look at a French book and a Latin book and it didn't connect with anything. Call it sickness if you like, but it's true. It was as if I was always tired. I used to think it was only people in non-academic classes who felt like that. I was all right in the first three years. Everything seemed to be interesting. And then this sickness hit me. All the books I read ceased to be interesting. It was as if a haze came down, as if the words lost any meaning, any reality. I liked music but there was nothing for me in words. I'm trying to explain. It was a sickness. Don't you understand?'

'No, I don't understand. When I was in the upper school I wasn't like that. I read everything I could lay my hands on. Books were treasures. When I was in university it was the same. I read because I loved to read. I wanted to have as much knowledge as possible. Even now.' He paused.

She probed: 'Even now?'

But he had stopped speaking, like a watch run down. She continued,

'Yes I admired that in you, though you were narrow minded. I admired your love of books and knowledge and experiments. I admired you for thinking out new ways of presenting your subject. I admired your enthusiasm, though you neglected your family. And then too you went to church. What did you find in church?'

'In church? I found silence there.'

'It was different with us,' she continued. 'It wasn't that I didn't try. I did try. I would lock myself in my room and I would study my Virgil. I would stare at it. I would look up meanings. And then at the end of an hour I hadn't moved from the one page. But I tried. It wasn't my fault. Can't you believe me?'

'I don't understand.' Then he added mercilessly, 'It was idleness.'

'And there you would be in the other room, in your study, preparing your lesson for the following day, smoking your pipe, thinking up new ideas like the time you made soap. You were the mainstay of the school, they said. So much energy. Full of power, boyish, always moving, always thinking. Happy.'

A smile crossed his face as if he were looking into another world which he had once loved and in which he had meaning and purpose.

'Yes, I gave them a lot,' he said. 'A lot. I tried my best with you as well. I spent time on you. I wanted you to do well. But I couldn't make a favourite of you. And then you said you were leaving.'

'It happened one night. I had been doing some exercises in English. I think it was an interpretation passage. I was sitting at the table. There was a vase with flowers in front of me. The electric light was on, and then I switched on the radio and I heard this voice singing 'Frankie and Johnny.' It was Lena Horne. I listened to it. At first I wasn't listening to it at all. I was trying to do my exercise. Then, after a while, the music seemed to become more important than what I was doing. It defeated what I was doing. It was about real things and the interpretation wasn't about anything. Or rather, it was about the lack of trade unionism in Japan. I'm not joking: that's what it was: How the bosses wouldn't allow the workers any unions and how they kept their money for them. It had no meaning at all. It was like . . . It was like some obstacle that you pushed against. Like a ghost in a room. And I laid down my pen and I said to myself, What will happen if I stop doing this? And then I did stop. And suddenly I felt so free. It was as if I had lightened myself of some load. I felt free. I listened to the song and I didn't feel any guilt at all.'

He looked at her almost with hatred.

'If you didn't feel any guilt why are you here then? Why didn't you stay with your Catholic? By the way, what does he do?'

'He has an antique shop. Actually, he's quite scholarly. He's more scholarly than you. He knows a lot about the Etruscans. He's very enthusiastic. Just like you. He's got a degree.' She laughed, bubbling.

'In that case,' he said, 'why didn't you stay with him?'

'I came to ask you,' she said, 'what it all means.'

He said, 'I remember one morning at a lecture we were told about Newton. It was a long time ago and it was a large lecture room, row upon row of pupils, students stretching to the very back and rising in tiers. There was sunlight and the smell of varnish. And this bald man told us about Newton. About the stars and how everything was fixed and unalterable and the apple falling to the ground in a garden during the Plague. Harmony. He talked about harmony. I thought the sky was full of apples. And that the whole world was a tree.'

There was a long silence. In it she felt the child turning in its own orbit.

'What use are the books to you now?' she said. The words sounded incredibly naive almost impudent and inhuman but she didn't mean them like that. And yet . . .

'You mean,' he said, 'that my life was useless. That I spent my days and nights on phantoms. Is that what you want? Did you come to gloat?'

'No, I want to know, that's all. I want to know if it was something wrong with me. Perhaps it was something wrong with me all the time.'

She imagined him walking in the middle of the night, listening to the silence of the wards, watching the moonlight on the floor. She imagined him looking into the eyes of nurses for reassurance, without speech. She imagined him imagining things, the whispers, the rumours, the laughter. Sometimes a man would die and his bed would be empty. But there would always be another patient. She imagined him thinking: At what hour or minute will I die? Will I die in pain? Will I choke to death?

She thought of London and of this small place. She thought of the anonymity of London, the death of the rainy days. The lostness. The strangeness. Had she chosen well? She thought of Sean, with his small tufted beard, vain, weak, lecherous. He was her only link with that brutal city. All else flowed, she could only follow him, the indeterminate atom.

'You don't know what duty is,' he said at last. 'You live on romance and pap. I've seen you reading *Woman's Own*. You think that the world is romantic and beautiful.' (Did she think that? Was that why she had run away? Did she think that now? What had she not seen? Into the heart of the uttermost darkness in that room where at night the lights circled the ceiling, and nothing belonged to her, not even the flat, not the Etruscan soldiers with their flat, hollow sockets.)

'You don't know about trust and loyalty. You knuckle under whenever any difficulty crops up. Your generation is pap and wind. You owe allegiance to nothing. I have owed allegiance to this place. They may forget me, but I served. What else is there to do?'

She said in a low voice, 'To live.' But he hadn't heard her.

'To serve,' he said. 'To love one's work. Oh, I was no Einstein but I loved my work and I think I did good. You, what do you do?'

Nothing, she thought, except to live where the lightning is, at the centre where the lightning is. At the disconnected places. At the place where our truth is to be found on the rainwashed blue bridges. At the place without hypocrisy. In the traffic. Where she would have to fight for everything including her husband, not knowing that at least this she could keep, as her mother had known. In the jungle.

She stood up and said, 'Goodbye, father.'

Defiantly he said, 'You refused your responsibility.'

It was like standing on a platform waving to a stranger on a train. For a moment she couldn't make up her mind whether he was leaving her or she leaving him.

He relapsed into petulance. 'I shouted for the nurse last night but she was too busy. She heard me right enough but she didn't come.'

She thought to herself: 'There is a time when one has to give up, when nothing more can be done. When the connection has to be cut. It is necessary, for not all things are retrievable.'

As she stood up she nearly fell, almost upsetting the carafe of water, herself full of water.

He had closed his eyes again when she turned away and walked through the ward head down, as if fighting a strong wind. She paused outside the door in the blinding March light where the tulips were.

The man she had seen before had finished polishing his car and was looking at it with adoration. She thought: The Adoration of the Mini, and smiled.

The child stirred. The world spun and took its place, the place that it must have as long as she was what she was. She had decided on it. And what she was included her father. And she thought again of her child, loving and pitying it.

The Crater

In the intervals of inaction it had been decided by the invisible powers that minor raids were feasible and therefore to be recommended. In the words of the directive: 'For reasons known to you we are for the moment acting on the defensive so far as serious operations are concerned but this should not preclude the planning of local attacks on a comparatively small scale . . . '

Like the rest of his men on that particular night, Lieutenant Robert Mackinnon blackened his face so that in the dugout eyes showed white, as in a Black Minstrel show. He kept thinking how similar it all was to a play in which he had once taken part, and how the jokes before the performance had the same nervous high-pitched quality, as they prepared to go out into the darkness. There was Sergeant Smith who had been directed to write home to the next of kin to relate the heroism of a piece of earth which had been accidentally shattered by shrapnel. His teeth grinned whitely beneath his moustache as he adjusted the equipment of one of the privates and joked, 'Tomorrow you might get home, lad.' They all knew what that meant and they all longed for a minor wound – nothing serious – which would allow them to be sent home honourably. And yet Smith himself had been invalided home and come back. 'I missed your stink, lads,' he had said when he appeared among them again, large and buoyant and happy. And everyone knew that this was his place where he would stay till he was killed or till the war ended.

'I remember,' he used to tell them, 'we came to this house once. It was among a lot of trees, you understand. I don't know their names so don't ask me. Well, the house was rotten with Boche and we'd fired at it all day. And the buggers fired back. Towards evening – it might have been 1800 hours – they stopped firing and it got so quiet you could hear yourself breathing. One of our blokes – a small madman from Wales, I think it was – dashed across and threw a grenade or two in the door and the window. And there wasn't a sound from inside the house, 'part from the explosion of course, so he kept shouting, 'The Boche are off, lads,' in that sing-song Welsh of his. So we all rushed the place and true enough they'd mostly gone. Run out of ammunition, I suppose. We went over it for mines but there wasn't none. So we stood in the hall, I suppose you'd call it, all of us with our dirty great boots and our rifles and bayonets and there was these stairs going up, very wide. The windows were shot to hell and there was glass all over the place. And suddenly – this is God's truth – an old woman come down the stairs. Dressed in white she was, a lovely dress like you'd see in a picture. And her lips all painted red. You'd think she was dressed for a ball. Her eyes were queer, they seemed to go right through you as if you wasn't there. She came down the last steps and our officer stepped forward to help her. And do you know what she did? She put her arms around him and she started to waltz. He was so surprised he didn't know what to do – the fat bugger. And all the time there was this music. Well, in the end he got away from her and some people took her away. Well, we could still hear this music, see? So we goes upstairs – there was a dead Boche on the landing, he'd been shot in the mouth – and we goes into this room. There was a bed there with a pink what-do-you-call-it over it. And beside the bed there was this big dead Boche. And do you know what – there was a dagger with jewels in it stuck in his breastbone. And beside him on the floor there was this phonograph playing a French tune, one of the officers said. He said it was a dance tune. Someone said it was bloody lucky the little fat fellow wasn't wearing a grey uniform.'

'All present and correct, sir,' said Sergeant Smith.

'All right, let's go then,' said Lieutenant Mackinnon.

Down the trench they went, teeth and eyes grinning, clattering over the duckboards with their Mills bombs and their bayonets and their guns. 'What am I doing here?' thought Robert, and 'Who the hell is making that noise?' and 'Is the damned wire cut or not?' and 'We are like a bunch of actors,' and 'I'm leading these men, I'm an officer.'

And he thought again, 'I hope the guns have cut that barbed wire.'

Then he and they inched across No Man's Land following the line of lime which had been laid to guide them. Up above were the stars and the air was cool on their faces. But there were only a few stars, the night was mostly dark, and clouds covered the moon. Momentarily he had an idea of a huge mind breeding thought after thought, star after star, a mind which hid in daylight in modesty or hauteur but which at night worked out staggering problems, pouring its undifferentiated power over the earth.

On hands and knees he squirmed forward, the others behind him. This was his first raid and he thought, 'I am frightened.' But it was different from being out in the open on a battlefield. It was an older fear, the fear of being buried in the earth, the fear of wandering through eternal passageways and meeting grey figures like weasels and fighting with them in the darkness. He tested the wire. Thank God it had been cut. And then he thought, 'Will we need the ladders?' The sides of the trenches were so deep sometimes that ladders were necessary to get out again. And as he crawled towards the German trenches he had a vision of Germans crawling beneath British trenches undermining them. A transparent imagined web hung below him in the darkness quivering with grey spiders.

He looked at his illuminated watch. The time was right. Then they were in the German trenches. The rest was a series of thrustings and flashes. Once he thought he saw or imagined he saw from outside a dugout a man sitting inside reading a book. It was like looking through a train window into a house before the house disappears.

There were Mills bombs, hackings of bayonets, scurryings and breathings as of rats. A white face towered above him, his pistol exploded and the face disappeared. There was a terrible stink all around him, and the flowing of blood.

Then there was a long silence. Back. They must get back. He passed the order along. And then they wriggled back again avoiding the craters which lay around them, created by shells, and which were full of slimy water. If they fell into one of these they would be drowned. As he looked, shells began to fall into them sending up huge spouts of water. Over the parapet. They were over the parapet. Crouched they had run and scrambled and were over. Two of them were carrying a third. They stumbled down the trench. There were more wounded than he had thought. Wright . . . one arm seemed to have been shot off. Sergeant Smith was bending over him. 'You'll get sent home all right,' he was saying. Some of the men were tugging at their equipment and talking feverishly. Young Ellis was lying down, blood pouring from his mouth. Harris said, 'Morrison's in the crater.'

He and Sergeant Smith looked at each other. They were both thinking the same: there is no point, he's had it. They could see each other's eyes glaring whitely through the black, but could not tell the expression on the faces. The shells were still falling, drumming and shaking the earth. All these craters out there, these dead moons.

'Do you know which one?' said Robert.

'I think so, sir, I . . . Are you going to get him?'

'Sergeant Smith, we'll need our rifles. He can hang on to that if he's there. Harris, come with us.' They were all looking at him with sombre black faces, Wright divided between joy and pain.

'Sir.'

Then they were at the parapet again, shells exploding all around them.

'Which one is it?' And the stars were now clearer. Slowly they edged towards the rim. How had he managed to break away from the white lime?

They listened like doctors to a heartbeat.

'Are you there, Fred?' Harris whispered fiercely, as if he were in church. 'Are you there?' Lights illuminated their faces. There was no sound.

'Are you sure this is the right one?' Robert asked fiercely.

'I thought it was. I don't know.'

'Oh, Christ,' said Sergeant Smith.

'We'd better get back then,' said Robert.

'Are you going to leave him, sir?' said Harris.

'We can't do anything till morning. He may be in one of the shallower ones.' His cry of 'Morrison, are you there?' was drowned by the shriek of a shell.

'Back to the trench again,' he said, and again they squirmed along. But at that moment as they approached the parapet he seemed to hear it, a cry coming from deep in the earth around him, or within him, a cry of such despair as he had never heard in his life before. And it seemed to come from everywhere at once, from all the craters, their slimy green rings, from one direction, then from another. The other two had stopped as well to listen.

Once more he heard it. It sounded like someone crying 'Help.'

He stopped. 'All right,' he said. 'We're going for him. Come on.'

And he stood up. There was no reason for crawling any more. The night was clear. And they would have to hurry. And the other two stood up as well when they saw him doing so. He couldn't leave a man to die in the pit of green slime. 'We'll run,' he said. And they ran to the first one and listened. They cried fiercely, 'Are you there?' But there was no answer. Then they seemed to hear it from the next one and they were at that one soon too, peering down into the green slime, illuminated by moonlight. But there was no answer.

There was one left and they made for that one. They screamed again, in the sound of the shells, and they seemed to hear an answer. They heard what seemed to be a bubbling. 'Are you there?' said Robert, bending down and listening. 'Can you get over here?' They could hear splashing and deep below them breathing, frantic breathing as if someone was frightened to death. 'It's all right,' he said, 'if you come over here, I'll send my rifle down. You two hang on to me,' he said to the others.

He was terrified. That depth, that green depth. Was it Morrison down there, after all? He hadn't spoken. The splashings came closer. The voice was like an animal's repeating endlessly a mixture of curses and prayers. Robert hung over the edge of the crater. 'For Christ's sake don't let me go,' he said to the other two.

It wasn't right that a man should die in green slime. He hung over the rim holding his rifle down. He felt it being caught, as if there was a great fish at the end of a line. He felt it moving. And the others hung at his heels, like a chain. The moon shone suddenly out between two clouds and in that moment he saw it, a body covered with greenish slime, an obscene mermaid, hanging on to his rifle while the two eyes, white in the green face, shone upward and the mouth, gritted, tried not to let the blood through. It was a monster of the deep, it was a sight so terrible that he nearly fell. He was about to say, 'It's no good, he's dying,' but something prevented him from saying it, if he said it then he would never forget it. He knew that.

The hands clung to the rifle below in the slime. The others pulled behind him. 'For Christ's sake hang on to the rifle,' he said to the monster below. 'Don't let go.' And it seemed to be emerging from the deep, setting its feet against the side of the crater, all green, all mottled, like a disease. It climbed as if up a mountainside in the stench. It hung there against the wall. 'Hold on,' he said. 'Hold on.' His whole body was concentrated. This man must not fall down again into that lake. The death would be too terrible. The face was coming over the side of the crater, the teeth gritted, blood at the mouth. It hung there for a long moment and then the three of them had got him over the side. He felt like cheering, standing up in the light of No Man's Land and cheering. Sergeant Smith was kneeling down beside the body, his ear to the heart. It was like a body which might have come from space, green and illuminated and slimy. And over it poured the merciless moonlight.

'Come on,' he said to the other two. And at that moment Sergeant Smith said, 'He's dead.'

'Dead?' There was a long pause. 'Well, take him in anyway. We're not leaving him here. We'll take him in. At least he didn't die in that bloody lake.' They lifted him up between them and they walked to the trench. 'I'm bloody well not crawling,' said Robert. 'We'll walk. And to hell with the lot of them.' He couldn't prevent himself swearing and at the same time despising himself for swearing. What would Sergeant Smith think of him? It was like bringing a huge green fish back to the lines. 'To hell with them,' he shouted. 'This time we'll bloody well walk. I don't care how light it is.' And they did so and managed to get him back into the dugout. They laid him down on the floor and glared around them at the silent men.

'Just like Piccadilly it was,' said Harris, who couldn't stop talking. 'As bright as day.'

'Shut up, you lot,' said Sergeant Smith, 'and get some sleep.'

Robert was thinking of the man he had seen reading a book in a flash of light before they had gone in with their bayonets. He couldn't see properly whether it had been a novel or a comic. Perhaps it was a German comic. Did Germans have comics? Like that green body emerging out of the slime, that fish. He began to shiver and said, 'Give the men whisky if there is any.' But he fell asleep before he could get any himself, seeing page after page of comics set before him, like red windows, and in one there was a greenish monster and in another a woman dancing with a fat officer. Overhead the shells still exploded, and the water bounced now and again from the craters.

'The bloody idiot,' said Sergeant Smith looking down at him. 'He could have got us all killed.' Still, it had been like Piccadilly right enough. Full of light. It hadn't been so bad. Nothing was as bad as you feared.

Gael Turnbull (1928 –)

For many years a resident of Canada or the U. S., the cosmopolitan Turnbull is usually considered a 'British' poet. He has been an important publisher and has helped make available the works of a number of his fellow poets.

By the Tweed

Who called me 'Tuppenny' and took
me fishing, tried to teach
how to pierce worms, minnows
'so they dinna die too quick'
or rip throat, guts from fish,
not scornful but 'whit's wrang?
ye're queerways, there's nay harum'

and there was none in him,
gone to the kirkyard now
with all the life he 'heyked'   10
from that flashing river
where I'm still snagged
floundering on the bank and he
the one that's got away for ever.

The next two poems are 'panels' of a longer verse sequence, 'Impellings'.

Through What We Seek, What Comes to Hand

met, begging near Tollcross, no coat,
summer jacket 'grew up in children's homes . . .
four months on the street . . . sleep
where I can . . . bus shelters, doorways . . .
'til shifted on' where the sheddings
of affluence are disposed by a wind
that slashed across the Meadows as if
direct from the stars, and where the mark
of each foot is dark against the frost

and on a shimmering screen: vagaries   10
of snowflakes on the wind, men cheering
at shipyard gates, with image of a man,
his tatar profile, crashing into rubble, who
'did nothing by halves,' shifted history,
laughed once at irony, 'sat down to chess

unwillingly' and before dying spoke again
'somewhat sadly' of an old comrade from whom
he had, by much necessity, parted

Sometimes Fearful with Splendour

Her face alight, a young girl, fingertips
on ivory keys, rising, falling,
the music driving forward, gathering
to a pitch, toward a gap of stillness
under the dome of a concert hall
with orchestra assembled, converging,
every movement, her each breath
as we hold ours, feeling a halt
in our throats, a flare of sound

while the prow of a warship lifts,   10
drops upon the swell, dividing forward,
rimmed by foam, making its course,
assembled with others, converging,
strained to a pitch, alert, until
in a moment, throbbing out of stillness
'orange streak . . . ball of light . . . a roar . . .
my fingers numb . . . then rush of heat . . .
couldn't breathe . . . saw men on fire . . . '

C[ecil] P. Taylor (1929 – 1981)

C. P. Taylor is the most successful Scottish playwright since James Bridie. His masterwork is surely *Good*, probably the most internationally celebrated Scottish play of the last thirty years. The author writes frequently of his Jewish identity, and he dedicated this play to his father, Max Taylor, 'a refugee from anti-Semitism in Czarist Russia'. *Good* was first performed in London in September, 1981. C. P. Taylor died three months later.

Good

A Tragedy

ACT ONE

Thirties dance band ensemble. The band is playing: 'I'm Always Chasing Rainbows'.

HALDER *(to the audience)* The bands came in 1933. So you can't say they came with the rise of the Nazis, exactly. The Nazis were on the rise long before that. To some extent, it was a device that was with me from childhood. Bringing music into the dramatic moments of my life. But from '33, they became an addiction. Jazz bands . . . cafe bands . . . tenors . . . crooners . . . symphony orchestras . . . Depending on the particular situation and my mood. . . . A strategy for survival? Turning the reality into fantasy? . . . It was a dance band, that day. What they were playing was an English song . . . or an American. Is there any difference?

SISTER *(impatiently)* Doctor Halder?

HALDER Yes. I'm coming.

The CROONER is into the middle section.

CROONER Why should I always be a failure? Why should I never get the breaks?

HALDER *(to the audience)* Stolen, of course, from Chopin . . . *Fantasie Impromptu* . . . Nice, wallowing-in self-pity kind of thing.

HALDER *and the band approach the* SISTER.

SISTER Visiting hours are between seven and eight, Doctor Halder.

HALDER I live in Frankfurt, you see . . .

SISTER I see.

HALDER Long journey to Hamburg . . . Busy time at the University, just now. Coming up to examinations.

SISTER You can go and see her for ten minutes or so. But we are about to serve lunch.

MOTHER *is wheeled towards* HALDER *in an invalid chair.*

MOTHER Johnnie. Listen to me. Get me out of here. Another day, and I'll go out of my mind. Get a chair for Helen. *(To where she imagines* HELEN *is:)* Helen, have pity on me.

HALDER Helen's not there, Mother . . . *(The band is about to play again.* HALDER *waves them away. They put down their instruments.)*

MOTHER Will you get your wife a chair. This isn't the time or place for jokes, son.

HALDER Mother, you're imagining it. She's not here.

MOTHER She's not standing beside you?

HALDER It's just you're confused, just now. That's all.

MOTHER Listen, are you trying to make me mad altogether? Helen, tell him. He has to get me out of here . . . Have pity on me.

HALDER You've been in a coma, mother. A thyroid deficiency . . . one of the effects . . .

you see things.

MOTHER Helen's not there? Are you not there, Helen? Wait a minute. Do you think I'm going out of my mind? If I'm going out of my mind . . . that's a bad business.

HALDER It makes you confused . . . That's all.

MOTHER Wait a minute. Last night. Did that happen? You were drunk . . . and banging at the door all night to get in?

HALDER Imagination.

MOTHER John . . . Come closer to me, a minute. *(Looking round to make sure nobody's listening.)* Is anybody listening to us?

HALDER No one is near us . . .

MOTHER *(whispering)* You're not a communist?

HALDER You know that. I could never accept Marxism. Parts of it . . . yes.

MOTHER I'm *talking* to you, son. You're not a communist and Hitler's not going to put you in prison. Your trial's this afternoon.

HALDER For God's sake, mother!

MOTHER Oh, thank God . . . Thank God . . . You're *not?*

HALDER Mother!

MOTHER Listen . . . I'm going out of my mind . . . Johnnie, I've got to go home.

HALDER You can't *see*, mother.

MOTHER What about your house?

HALDER With the children and Helen . . . I couldn't cope with you, mother. *I* would . . . but how can I ask the children and Helen . . .

MOTHER Listen. Is that my imagination too? This place, it's a *front*. Men come up here to go with the women . . . That sister, there . . .

HALDER This hospital's a front for a brothel?

MOTHER Is it not? . . . Johnnie, this is a bad business . . . I'm going out of my mind.

HALDER I could cope with you for a week, mother . . . We'd *like* to have you for a week or so . . . But you know what Helen's like. She can't even organise the house with just *us* in it . . . You wouldn't be happy . . . You never are there . . .

MOTHER The best thing is to take twenty or thirty of my pills and finish myself off once and for all . . .

HALDER You could do that. It's against the law, but . . .

MOTHER What have I got to live for? I can't see. My eyes are finished. Nobody wants me . . . I'm better out of it . . . What have I got to live for, for God's sake!

HALDER *(looks round . . . lost . . .)* A difficult question, that.

A CLERK comes to him.

CLERK Can I help you?

HALDER This is Tiergartenstrasse Four . . . I'm looking for the Committee for Research into Hereditary Diseases . . . Over-Leader Philip Bouller . . .

CLERK You've come down the wrong passage . . . I'll show you where his office is, Herr . . .

HALDER Professor Halder . . . Is this some new committee . . . ? I've never heard of it before.

CLERK It's just been set up, Herr Professor . . . You have an appointment with the Over-Leader?

HALDER I have an appointment. Yes . . . Pleasant place . . . To work in.

CLERK Professor . . . It used to be one of the best residential areas in Berlin. Charlottenburg . . . I'll see if the Over-Leader is free Herr Professor . . . *(He goes.)*

HALDER *paces up and down waiting.*

MAURICE Will you stop bloody wandering around, man. Sit down . . . . *Bands!*

HALDER Have you *got* to be a doctor, Maurice?

MAURICE I *am* a doctor. It's an automatic response. Somebody comes to me as a doctor. I'm a doctor. Listen. What do you want to do? Pull me into your neurosis? I've got my own, thanks.

HALDER Maurice, how could I come to you as a doctor, for God's sake? The question I am putting to you – as my closest friend. *(To the audience.)* My *only* friend. *(To* MAURICE:*)* Should I see a psychiatrist?

MAURICE *Bands?*

HALDER Music, generally. Not very big bands. Odd times, the Berlin Philharmonic . . . Last Senate meeting, it was the Phil. Playing the Storm Movement from The Pastoral . . . Not just the bands, Maurice . . . I want to try and throw off this neurosis I've been living with all my life . . . To give my work and my family relationships a more healthy basis . . .

MAURICE What does *that* mean? That's *words*, Johnnie. Johnnie . . . That's verbal shit you're giving me . . . *We* don't work like that, for Christ's sake! *You* and *me*.

HALDER I want to try. All my work so far has been based on this bloody anxiety neurosis. I do. I want to see what work I can do, free of it.

MAURICE What's he talking about? What's this man talking about? People don't go to analysts to streamline their lives . . . They go to free themselves from agony. Listen, I know. You're suffering . . . You have to tell me about it. I'm your friend for Christ's sake . . . Just now . . . If you want to know about suffering . . . My agony, just now . . . My neuritic track . . . That wakes me up four o'clock in the morning in a panic . . .

HALDER I can't get *lost* you see? I can't lose myself in people or situations. Everything's acted out against this bloody musical background.

MAURICE *Objectively. Intellectually* . . . The Nazis . . . That's just flag-waving to get hold of the masses . . . This anti-Jew hysteria . . . Now it's got them where they wanted to go . . .

HALDER Could it be some sub-conscious comment on my loose grip of reality? The whole of my life is a performance? Is that too glib, do you think, Maurice?

MAURICE If you knew the unconscious like I do . . . Nothing's too glib for that bastard. What I'm saying to you . . . Listen to me . . . It's interesting, sometimes, listening to other people . . . You don't need to make too big a habit of it . . . but odd times.

HALDER I'm *listening*.

MAURICE I'm telling you . . . I know, for Christ's sake . . . The Nazis are politicians above everything else. Realists . . . I know that . . .

CLERK *(coming to* HALDER*)* Professor Halder?

HALDER I'm slightly early. I can never time appointments. I'm sorry.

CLERK Over-Leader Bouller has someone with him at present. He will see you shortly.

HALDER That's all right. That's fine. I have my book here . . . This is a new committee . . . I gather . . .

CLERK *(going)* You will have to excuse me. Heil Hitler . . .

HALDER Yes, of course. Heil Hitler . . . *(Political gesture.)*

MAURICE Politicians are practical people. I *know* that. They're realists . . . They live in the world as it is . . .

HALDER Let's just have some coffee, Maurice. Forget about *my* problems.

MAURICE Listen. Is it sex, Johnnie? I'm *asking* is it sex . . . Of course it's sex . . . Everything's sex . . . Sex is very difficult, Johnnie . . . I don't personally know anybody who doesn't find sex difficult, Johnnie . . . If that's any comfort . . . Listen . . . If it's potency problems . . . Or maybe some taste you've developed . . . Bondage, for example . . . That's no problem if you can find somebody with mutual interests . . . Or tranvestism . . . You'd be amazed how common tranvestism is . . .

HALDER I've never been attracted to bondage or flogging or anything like that, Maurice . . . Probably, my sexual imagination is very limited . . .

MAURICE Listen, I know how much Germany depends on Jewish brains . . . Jewish business . . . Hitler's got all the power he needs now. They're bound to drop all that racial shit they had to throw around to get their votes . . . They can't afford not to. I know that . . . But I can't *believe* it. − You see what I'm getting at . . . I'm sorry . . . I'm developing an obsession . . . I'm in a bloody panic state . . . Look at me . . .

HALDER I'll get you a drink, Maurice . . . Relax . . . You're right . . . All that anti-Jew rubbish . . . You're right . . . Just balloons they throw up in the air to distract the masses . . . You're right.

MAURICE I *know* I'm bloody right. I'm telling you . . . But my blood anxiety neurosis has fixed on to it . . . and I can do shit all about it . . . Listen . . . What do I want to run off to England for . . . Or Shanghai . . .

HALDER Shanghai might be interesting. China . . .

MAURICE This is my home. I love Frankfurt. I love Hessen. I love the whole bloody place . . .

HALDER Take a bit of cheesecake, Maurice.

MAURICE I'm a German. I was born here. Look at me. I don't look Jewish. It could well be my grandmother had it off with some Bavarian peasant or plumber or something . . . Who the bloody hell knows . . .

HALDER Maurice . . . You're right . . . The racialist programme is not practical . . . They'll drop it . . . They'll have to drop it . . .

MAURICE I said I *know* I'm right . . . I *know* . . . *I* don't want any cheesecake. This is my *home* . . . Every morning . . . Before breakfast . . . I take a walk in Nizza Park . . . Along the river

HALDER Yes . . . You're right . . . talking about impotence complexes . . . I might have a bit of . . .

MAURICE I'm telling you about my feelings for Frankfurt . . . ! Walking about Frankfurt in the morning. Looking at the river and the trees . . . and the wonderful buildings. The *pride*. For Christ's sake . . . You are . . . You're proud to be a German . . . To live in a city like this . . . Walking by the cathedral . . .

HALDER *(to* himself:*)* He's a nice man. I love him. But I cannot get involved with his problems. So in the next few months they might kick in his teeth. But just now, he's all right. What's he worried about? I bet you *he* has no problems in bed with his wife. *I've* got problems now. Me. My problem is *immediate*. It's an urgent problem . . . *(To* MAURICE:*)* You're right Maurice. It's a beautiful city to live in.

MAURICE Was that you having a visitation from one of your bands just now?

HALDER I do that from time to time. I talk to myself in my mind. That's another addiction.

MAURICE About me?

HALDER More or less.

MAURICE Negative − resentment?

HALDER Negative *and* positive, Maurice.

MAURICE This morning . . . Walking along Deer's Ditch . . . Passing Goethe's house . . . I thought about you. What a worthwhile man that is . . . Johnnie Halder . . . Good! I love him.

HALDER You know Goethe refused to send Beethoven money when he was desperate . . . Dying . . .

MAURICE Listen. Don't talk about Beethoven, Johnnie . . .

HALDER I never knew that till a few weeks ago. The week Hitler became Chancellor, I happened to be going through some papers in the library . . . I found this letter . . . Beethoven writing to Goethe for a few marks . . . Desperate . . . Last days before he died. The swine wouldn't send him a penny! Ignored his letter . . .

MAURICE *(watching* HALDER − *sudden insight)* Do you know what's happened? It's just come to me John . . . Hitler has perverted the whole nature of our relationship. Buggered up one of the few friendships I valued . . . That's not *good*, Johnnie.

HALDER *(to* himself:*)* Failing. I don't like failing . . . Failing throws me into a panic state . . . It's not good.

MAURICE I'm envious . . . I'm bloody envious.

HALDER Of my *state*, Maurice?

MAURICE You're *safe*. That's what I'm talking about. You can stay in Frankfurt for the rest of your life. End up Professor – Vice-chancellor . . . *I* cannot predict what pillow I'll be resting my head on tonight . . .

HALDER That's panicking, Maurice. That really is.

MAURICE It is . . . You're right. *Next week.*

HALDER Maurice, we've established that . . . They've got to drop the Anti-Jew programme . . . In the long run . . . For the survival of the bloody state . . .

MAURICE *I* know that . . . and *you* know that . . . But does bloody *Hitler* . . . That's what's worrying me . . . That's it – not neurosis at all . . . It's bloody reality . . .

HALDER The night the girl turned up at my house, I turned it into an opera . . . There was a Cafe Trio . . . Playing Wagner . . .

Cafe trio playing 'Star of Eve' from 'Tannhauser.'

HALDER *(stepping over the debris of his living-room . . . To the audience:)* I had difficulties stepping through the debris of Helen's battle with the day . . . Helen was lying in front of the fire reading a biography of Telemann, waiting for me to cook the supper for the kids . . . *(To the accompaniment of the trio: Recitativo to* HELEN:*)*

> I bought some smoked ham,
> Panhas and bread.
> You need not trouble,
> Your pretty head.
> Everything's cold,
> No need to wait,
> Just take your seat,
> And fill your plate.

HELEN *(recitativo:)*

> Darling, I want to talk to you seriously.
> Your mother phoned,
> Very disturbing.
> And my father,
> We had a long conversation.
> I hate nagging at you,
> But really you can't hang on any longer.
> You'll have to shake yourself,
> Out of this apathy.

HALDER *(with the food, recitativo:)*

> Will you have it at the fire,
> If I clear the newspapers
> And scores?
> I think I can get down to the carpet.
> I quite like eating on the floor.

HELEN *(recitativo:)*

> I had mother pick up the children,
> From school and take them home for a meal.

HALDER *(recitativo:)*

> Should we try a maid,
> Once more.
> I know you find it hard
> Having strangers living with us.

HELEN Johnnie . . . I'm useless . . . I spent all afternoon trying to play these triplets against crochets in that Beethoven sonata , . . My whole life . . . Everything . . . Look at the state this house is in. I didn't even clean my teeth this morning. I'm a slut. I've no idea why you love me. Do you, love?

HALDER Yes. I love you.

CLERK Over-Leader Bouller will see you now, Herr Professor.

HALDER Thank you. *(Going to* BOULLER.*)* Heil Hitler.

BOULLER Heil Hitler. Please sit down, Herr Professor . . . Make yourself comfortable . . . Please if you wish to smoke, be at ease to do so.

HALDER Thank you, Over-Leader . . . I don't smoke . . .

BOULLER Before we begin, I wish this to be clearly understood. Everything that is discussed between us in this room is absolutely Top Secret. This is understood?

HALDER Absolutely, Over-Leader . . .

BOULLER Apart from knowing something of your work and your record since you joined us, your superiors have recommended you without reservation as a person of total loyalty to the state and National Socialism . . . Would you consider this an accurate description of your position and commitment?

HALDER I've written about this, Over-Leader . . .I am committed to use whatever abilities and talents I might have for the betterment of the lives of the people round me . . .

BOULLER Are you warm, Herr Professor? It's a hot day.

HALDER Slightly . . . Yes.

BOULLER Please . . . Take your jacket off . . . Make yourself comfortable . . . We have called you here in the role of a consultant . . . A comrade who we can trust and who is, at the same time, something of a figure in the academic world . . . We have been reading your novel . . . As you see . . . About life in a home for the aged . . . You raise very interesting moral questions in it, Herr Halder . . . Some of your conclusions . . . *Fascinating . . . Profoundly . . .*

HALDER It was a subject close to me . . . at the time . . .

BOULLER I have coffee at two-thirty. Would you like coffee?

HALDER Please . . . Yes . . .

BOULLER I'll arrange to have an extra cup brought in . . . In the meantime, this is a letter I would like you to read. It was sent direct to the Chancellory for the attention of The Leader . . . It's from the father of a deformed child . . . *(Going.)* Even your wife, Herr Professor . . . Not a hint of what is discussed here must be communicated to even your wife . . . Not a word . . . This is a direct order from the top Leadership . . . You understand this . . . ?

HALDER Fully, Over-Leader . . . Yes . . .

HELEN *(calling to him)* John, I'm sorry . . .

HALDER Why should you be sorry? I don't mind living in chaos. It's all right. The children are used to it.

HELEN You come back from a hard day at work, and I overwhelm you with self-pity.

HALDER Yes.

HELEN You shouldn't stand this. Me turning your house into a shithouse, Johnnie.

HALDER Tell you what. After tea, we'll clean it up.

HELEN *(with a pastry)* I wish you wouldn't buy these pastries. It's just indulging my greed and making me fat . . .

HALDER Don't eat them.

HELEN For Christ's sake, why do you love me?

HALDER I don't know why I love you. Have you got to?

HELEN I can't even look after your bloody kids . . . Father rang . . .

HALDER *(to the audience:)* Behaviourist psychiatrist . . . Losing clients left, right and centre to Jewish Freudians . . . All right now, Hitler was in . . .

HELEN He wants to speak to you. Tonight. He says the time is long past for being pure and self-righteous. For the sake of your children and me . . . You must make a definite decision to join the National Socialists . . . With your army record, they'll welcome you with open arms . . . Actually, he heard from somebody very high up, Goebbels has read your *Faust and Goethe in Weimar* . . .

HALDER I was thinking about Hitler, on my way home.

HELEN He's right. You'll get nowhere in the university now, unless you join the party, Johnnie . . . Father says you could even lose your lectureship . . .

HALDER *(going to her, holding her)* Listen, you are not to leave me. You understand. Whatever it is. You and the kids. They're the whole basis of my life.

HELEN Yes. I know . . . I know that, dear. I'll never leave you. You'll never leave me.

HALDER I thought I'd tell you.

HELEN I'm sorry . . . I'm tired, Johnnie . . .

HALDER I'll come up soon . . . I'm waiting for this student . . .

HELEN I love you.

HALDER I love you. *(To the audience:)* I had to keep saying that to her. For *my* sake. Not to pacify her.

MAURICE And the girl turned up with Richard Tauber.

HALDER It's very complex. Unless you bear with me, Maurice and follow every strand . . . You won't get anywhere near the core of what is happening to me . . . If you will anyway . . . If there's anything to get to the core of, anyway . . . She had an appointment with me that morning . . . So the tenor turning up in my office was clearly related to her coming to see me . . . *Could've* been Richard Tauber . . . He was singing 'You Are My Heart's Delight' . . .

> *The music comes up and the* TENOR *appears on stage, singing.*

Yes . . . Probably *was* Tauber.

ANNE That's what I find hard, Herr Doctor. Trying to find what it has to do with my life. Faust . . . or practically everything on the literature course . . . Goethe, especially, though . . . obviously he's Germany's greatest writer . . . There must be something missing in me.

HALDER Tell me about your troubles in your lodgings.

ANNE You see . . . It's ridiculous . . . I find what happens to me in my digs . . . I don't know why . . . profound . . . *important*, anyway . . . and what happens in Faust banal . . . trivial . . . How am I going to get a degree, with an attitude like that . . .

HALDER That's what worries you, then.

ANNE We're all in this flat in the Altstadt . . . I thought when I first went there . . . Wonderful, living in the old town . . .

HALDER Next door to where Goethe was born.

ANNE There's a dozen of us . . . And we're all alone. In this flat with Frau Stagl. She runs it for some capitalist.

HALDER Jew.

ANNE Probably . . . Anyway, they're all so pathetic and interesting. There's a man who has an obsession with trains . . . He plays them all night. A couple of days ago one of the lodgers smuggled a woman into his room. You should've seen her. At least forty-five . . . I thought . . . Poor soul, you must be desperate . . .

HALDER I can see that . . . Yes . . . Faust with his deep abstract thoughts . . . In his study . . . Conjuring up rather tedious depressing spirits spouting poetry . . . and the Devil with his cheap conjuring tricks. And your fellow lodger with his train set.

ANNE Herr Doctor, what am I going to do? I'm never going to get through my exams like this, am I?

HALDER You didn't find my book on Goethe helpful?

ANNE I found your two novels more *real* . . . I'm sorry . . . It's just me . . .

HALDER And this man who keeps knocking at your door?

ANNE It's understandable. He gets confused. You see . . . there are a couple of prostitutes in the house, too . . .

HALDER Listen. I'd like to think about this. You've raised an important point . . . The contemporary significance of Faust . . . To your generation . . . Why don't we have another one to one seminar . . . Very soon . . . This evening. Are you bush this evening?

ANNE Actually he's quite nice, this man who keeps knocking at my door. Very tall. Lovely white teeth. It's just . . . He gets on my nerves . . . Waking me up. I mean, he's not a rapist or anything. He takes 'no' for an answer very calmly, you know. 'Well, if you're not inclined . . . That's all right. Pity. Sorry for troubling you.' I'm doing it again . . . I'm sorry . . . Why am I coming out with all this rubbish, Herr Doctor?

HALDER *(to himself:)* She touched my hand! No. Our clothes accidentally brushed together . . . My jacket and her cardigan . . . That was all . . . I liked her in the matching cardigan and jumper . . . I admit that . . .

ANNE Yes . . . I'd like to come tonight. Very much. If you can spare the time, Doctor . . . That would be wonderful.

MOTHER John . . . It's like a prison here. I want to get back to my own house.

HALDER I'm organizing everything, mother . . . There was a burst pipe . . . The whole house is damp, just now . . .

MOTHER It doesn't matter . . . If there's food . . . As long as I can get back to my own bed.

HALDER I've got the plumbers coming in . . .

MOTHER Why can't I come to *you* for a week?

HALDER You can come to me for a week. What happens *after* the week?

MOTHER No . . . The best thing is to do away with myself . . . That'll be a finish to the whole problem.

HALDER *(checking his watch)* She's late.

MAURICE Your mother turned up. This girl . . . And the band. You had a crowded evening.

HALDER Richard Tauber came back for a final chorus, too . . . Maurice . . . Listen . . . What it could be . . . Is nothing I touch real? . . . Is it? . . . My whole life is like that . . . I do everything, more or less, that everybody else does . . . But I don't *feel* it's real. Like other people. On the other hand, it could be other people probably feel the same thing . . . For Christ's sake, maybe I *am* in a bad way . . . So I'm entitled to pity myself a bit . . . There's the door bell. *(To the audience:)* She was very pale and lovable. That was my first impression. Standing in the doorway . . . Wet . . . Her hair was dripping . . . And her coat . . . Soaked through. I'll put some more coal on the fire . . . Are you soaked through? . . . Take my dressing-gown.

ANNE I don't mind being wet.

HALDER I'm going to give you a cognac . . . Will you take it?

ANNE Yes, please . . . Thanks.

HALDER Frau Halder's gone to bed. That doesn't mean you're late. She goes to bed early. One of her pleasures is reading in bed.

ANNE Frau Stagl kept me back. She had an accident . . . Nothing much. She burned her arm . . . Cooking . . . I took her to hospital to get it dressed. She's fine now . . . but it took up all the evening . . . Waiting around.

HALDER Would you like some smoked ham . . . and bread . . . I was going to have some, myself . . . Just before you came . . .

ANNE Actually, I am hungry. Please . . . Shall I help you . . .

HALDER I've got everything here . . . *(To himself:)* That girl is definitely after me. Am I after her, that's the question . . . Could be . . . *(To* ANNE:*)* Listen, you can't go all the way back to your digs tonight . . . It's still pouring . . . I'll bring you down some blankets . . . That couch is very comfortable . . . I've slept on it myself.

ANNE Herr Doctor, I couldn't sleep *here*.

HALDER And a pillow . . . We haven't got to the core of the problem yet, anyway.

ANNE You see, I don't believe in evil. Not like Goethe seems to . . . Do you?

HALDER That's what we have to talk about. It could be a way into Faust for you. While the examiners generally are looking for the same old stock answers to the stock questions . . . If a student does come up with a really original approach . . . Showing that he's taking a work they take so seriously as seriously himself . . . *(To himself:)* She's rousing me . . . Christ! She is! Where there's life, there's hope. . . I've always thought there was a major flaw in me. Love . . . I never thought it was in me to love . . . To really love . . .

ANNE If you get me the blankets . . . I'll make up the bed, Herr Doctor . . .

HALDER Yes . . . I'll get them for you . . . Do you like two pillows or just one?

ANNE I'd like two, please . . .

THE MAJOR, later known as FREDDIE *(coming to meet* HALDER *– outstretched hand)* Herr Doctor . . . Delighted to meet you . . . Please . . . Come in . . . You wish to join us . . . First class . . . Your father-in-law, Doctor Brunau telephoned me . . . He speaks so highly of you . . .

MAURICE You joined the Nazis! You . . . For fuck's sake.

HALDER I told you I joined the Nazis . . .

MAURICE The reality is coming to me . . . Jesus . . . Johnnie . . . God in heaven.

HALDER Facts of life . . .

He goes to ANNE.

Anne . . . I think I'd better tell you this. The last few months . . . You've been coming to me for seminars . . . What's happened is I've been getting emotionally attached to you . . .

ANNE Have you? . . . Honestly?

HALDER I don't know how it happened. I have.

ANNE *(going to him. Putting her arms round him. Kissing him passionately)* John . . . I love you . . . I can't believe it . . . I love you . . . I've loved you for months . . . And you love me . . .

HALDER I love you.

MAURICE And you lost your erection?

HALDER I was a bit overwhelmed by her response . . .

MAURICE Panic?

HALDER A bit . . . Yes . . . Yes . . . I was frightened. In a panic. What was I letting myself in for? I've got a first-class job. Peace of mind. Wife . . . kids . . . And I'm suddenly jumping into the sea . . . I was bloody terrified . . . The last person I wanted to see was Marlene Dietrich . . . I never fancied her anyway . . .

Marlene Dietrich sings 'Falling in Love Again.'

I have a good wife . . . Reasonably attractive . . . Three first-class children . . . A home . . . A growing reputation as a critic and a novelist . . . I'm on the brink of committing myself to the National Socialists and a completely new phase of my life . . . To get myself involved in an affair with a woman . . . You understand? . . . What was I going to do? I had with a couple of sentences unleashed the floodgates of a woman's heart as Goethe might have said . . . Two women loved me . . . In these days, that was a problem . . . My God! My children! . . . What was going to become of them . . . Where could I go? Where would we live? Anne and I . . . In that sordid lodging house . . . It didn't even have a proper garden . . . I needed a garden . . . And Helen . . . How could I leave Helen . . . You know how you get when you jump into the sea for the first time like that . . . with a combination of guilt, brandy, over-fatigue and general tension on top of ever present anxiety neurosis . . . I fell asleep. When I woke up, Helen was up, reading some new book on keyboard technique . . .

HELEN I woke up and couldn't get to sleep again. Did I wake you?

HALDER That student turned up, last night. Soaking wet. It was pouring. So she's downstairs. In the lounge. I gave her some blankets.

HELEN That's all right. Will she be warm enough?

HALDER I gave her some blankets. Helen I want to talk to you. I've decided to join the Party. I had a long talk with your father. He's right. Basically . . .

HELEN You told me that. Who's going to give her breakfast?

HALDER *I'll* give her breakfast . . . I didn't tell you about my decision.

HELEN I *assumed*, in the end, you'd be sensible.

HALDER I'm doing it because I love you . . . You know that. If it was just myself, I'd take a chance. I'm not one hundred per cent sure about Hitler . . . You understand that . . . I love you and the children . . .

HELEN I know that.

HALDER That's the whole foundation of my life.

HELEN That's good.

HALDER I'll never leave you.

HELEN Why should you?

HALDER You won't leave me?

HELEN Why should I?

HALDER Plenty of people leave each other.

HELEN Plenty of people get knocked down by buses.

HALDER That's a good observation.

HELEN Well, they do. I'm glad. Father'll be glad, you joining the Party. It's a real commitment . . . You're not just joining to keep your job or get on in life . . .

HALDER Am I not?

HELEN You see . . . I don't do anything well . . . Do I? I'm useless . . .

HALDER You're a good wife.

HELEN I don't think I am.

HALDER You are. You're the best wife in the world. I love you.

HELEN *Do* you?

HALDER You're my sweetheart, aren't you?

HELEN Am I?

HALDER You are. What are you?

HELEN Your sweetheart . . .

BOULLER *enters with coffee.*

BOULLER I brought the coffee in myself . . . To avoid interruptions . . . Halder, would it surprise you if I said Doctor Goebbels himself had suggested your name to us? He drew our attention to your novel . . . He was profoundly moved by it . . . 'Objectivity,' he said, 'combined with compassion and humanity' . . .

HALDER *(to the audience:)* They got me at a bad time. With my mother in the state she got herself in . . . And the state I got in at her state . . . I had to write all the guilt out in a pro-euthanasia novel . . .

BOULLER You read the letter?

HALDER You read the letter? *(Forgetting.)* I've read it. Yes . . . Moving.

BOULLER *(taking up* HALDER*'s novel)* The Leader himself has looked over this. Do you know that? Would you like to read his comment. *(Showing him.)* Look . . . In his own writing . . .

HALDER *(to the audience:)* God forgive me . . . The human bloody being! The surge of pride in me! Reading that scrawled sentence in Adolf's shaky hand – It said: 'Written from the heart!'

A Bavarian trio.

MAURICE A Bavarian mountain *band*?

HALDER *(to the audience:)* While Anne was in the bathroom and the Bavarian Mountain Ensemble were singing their hearts out, I kept moving from panic to romantic plans of going back to nature with my beloved.

HALDER With the band, in songspiel. We'll go to Schwarzwald . . . Anne and I . . . Between Bernau und Wehr . . . There's a stretch of forest there, nobody goes into . . . We'll build a rough hut. Dry. Warm. What do a man and a woman need to live? . . . Now and then – I'll buy a rifle, of course – I'll shoot wild boar, deer . . .

HALDER *stops singing.*

It was irresponsible of me in my position to encourage her . . .

HALDER *starts again.*

A goat . . . We'll keep a goat . . . *(He falters and stops. The band falters, but then goes on:)*
Can you keep a goat in the forest? Why shouldn't you? . . . I'm not talking about
illegally living in the forest. Obviously, I'll have to buy some land . . . Four or five
acres . . . I'd sell the house . . . Split the money two ways, between Helen and I . . .
(With sarcasm:) I could gather folk tales from the natives and make a book out of
them . . . Everything under the pure sky . . . We eat, sleep, make love under the sun . . .
or stars . . . whichever is about at the time of the activity . . . *(With sarcasm:)* To the
accompaniment of the Bavarian Mountain Ensemble . . .

The band stops.

I'm not sure if – *(To* ANNE, *who wanders in wearing his dressing-gown:)* Are you musical?
Do you play anything?

ANNE I don't play anything. No. I like music but I never seem to be able to stand more
than about the first movement of anything . . . I can sit through all the movements of
Beethoven's Fifth . . . I don't mind that . . . Do you play? Obviously somebody
does . . . with all that music around . . .

HALDER No . . . I don't play. Look, will I take you into the university with me, this
morning. Or do you want to go back to your lodgings first . . .

ANNE *(looking at him . . . drinking him in . . . in love)* I still can't believe it! All the time I
have been thinking 'He'll never look at me.' And I've been in your mind . . . All the
time . . .

HALDER *(to* ANNE:*)* You stood out, you see . . . As an exceptional person . . . That is what
drew me to you . . . You are . . . There's no question about it . . . I'm drawn to you . . .
I like you very much . . . But you have to understand . . .

ANNE *(frightened now waiting)* Yes . . . I want to understand. I want to understand everything
about you . . .

HALDER *(to* ANNE:*)* When I said to you, last night, how much I liked you . . . You might
have got the wrong impression . . . Sometimes I can be very inarticulate . . .

ANNE Honestly . . . I feel it . . . You love me . . . Last night, I felt it . . . This morning,
you're fighting it . . . I know. It must be frightening for you . . . I know that . . . Are
you frightened, love?

HALDER I don't know where I am . . . No . . .

ANNE Last night . . . You said you were emotionally involved with me . . . You loved
me . . .

HALDER *(to himself:)* How could I not love you, my beautiful darling . . . *(to* ANNE:*)* You
see . . . It's the children . . . I love them . . . I could never leave my children . . . Being a
father . . . you see . . .

ANNE No. I can see that. You love them. They love you . . . I suppose your wife being
what she is . . . not being able to cope . . . You have to be father and mother to
them . . .

HALDER They love their mother too . . .

ANNE Do *you* love her, do you think? . . . Do you still love her . . .

HALDER Outsiders might think . . . with all the rubbish littering the floors . . . My having
to cook meals and send the children to school . . . I don't say the pigsty here doesn't get
on my nerves at times . . . and not being able to invite people to the house . . . without
having a major cleaning operation . . .

ANNE John . . . You're drowning . . . I'm not saying that because I love you and I need
you . . . You're drowning . . .

HELEN comes in, in her dressing gown.

HELEN I came down for more coffee. Is there any hot? *(To* ANNE:*)* Has he fed you?

ANNE Yes thank you. He made me eat a proper breakfast . . .

HELEN I'm sorry the place is such a pigsty. I haven't been coping with things.

ANNE It's all right.

HELEN Did you tell me her name, John?

ANNE Anne. . . You have lovely children . . . The girl's beautiful, isn't she?

HELEN Did you make anything for me, John?

HALDER I've fried you Liverwurst . . . I was just going to do an egg for you.

HELEN Were you warm enough here?

ANNE It was wonderful. John had to wake me.

HELEN You look very young. How old are you?

ANNE I'm older than I look . . . I'm nearly twenty.

HELEN I'm happy at thirty. I don't worry about not being young any more. If I'm thirty. I'm thirty . . . I'm not all that bad looking am I? What do you think?

A street musician, HILTER, *dressed in tweed plus-fours takes up his stance, watched by* MAURICE *and* HALDER. *He plays the first few bars of a Yiddish folksong.*

MAURICE Jewish Wedding song. *(He sings:)* Came along Mrs Bloom, brought along the handsome groom. Fine, fine, Mrs Bloom, brought along the handsome groom. . . . *Hitler?*

HALDER I *think* it was Hitler. Might've been a bit of Charlie Chaplin. I'm standing in the square by the fountain. Paralyzed. Not physically. Whatever part of me is responsible for decision taking. That seemed to have gone out of action . . . On my way to join the Party.

HITLER *(putting down his violin and addressing the world)* Understandable. Totally understandable. You make a deal with yourself one minute, you totally repudiate it the next. *(To* MAURICE, *conversationally:)* Quite right. Absolutely naive to think you can guarantee the minute you set yourself on a course that you're going to hold it over the next sixty seconds.

MAURICE Sounds more like Chaplin than Adolf.

HITLER *(to the world:)* The complexity of the human central nervous system alone. All the forces playing on the human organism . . .

MAURICE Shit!

HITLER (to the world:) Basically, what have we in a human being? A complex electrical network. No. Even more complex – a complex electrical and *chemical* network. *(To* MAURICE:*)* Can you *get* chemical networks?

MAURICE That's *conscious* shit. . . You don't need the sub-conscious to handle scientific shit. It deals with *real* shit.

HITLER *(to the world:)* Man does not live by bread alone.

HALDER I'm not sure about that.

HITLER *(conversationally)* I'm not sure about anything. That's the human condition. 'Man you are born to uncertainty. You can be sure of nothing.'

MAURICE Sounds more like Chaplin than Adolf to me.

HITLER *(to the world:)* For the first time in my life I am breaking free from the emotional/physical umbilical cords that tied me to my mother.

MAURICE Now *that's* Hitler. *Pure, unadulterated* Hitler shit.

HITLER Ring of the truth, but, Maurice.

MAURICE Shit *has.*

HITLER *(to the world:)* Breaking through to manhood. Completing myself as a human being . . . Establishing new emotional and physical umbilical strands with a woman I have chosen in my manhood. *(To* MAURICE:*)* Yes. I'm being pretentious and heavily profound. But it does happen. From time to time, you are confronted by profundities.

(To himself:) I have to get out of this . . . Apologizing for any profound universal statement that comes to me.

MAURICE *(to* HALDER:*)* You see . . . My fellow Jews. I can't stand them. My best friends are gentiles and Nazis.

HITLER *(to the world:)* What is the objective reality? The objective reality is there is no objective reality. I don't know. *Who* knows?

How do I bring about a balance of the electrical and chemical forces in my body to make for something like the optimum functioning of myself as an organism?

HALDER By joining the Nazis?

HITLER But now I am moving to a soul union . . . *(To* MAURICE:*)* What the fuck else is it, for Christ's sake? That's what it is. That's what I'm looking for. A soul union . . . *(To the world:)* Now I am moving to a soul union. . . Joining the Nazis is no longer a simple case of my own electrical and chemical state. It is hers too.

HALDER *(to* HITLER:*)* That's what I'm telling you. I have to see Anne, first. Before I can make a definite decision.

HITLER *(to himself:)* Yes. Now I understand why I have to see her.

HALDER Do I?

MAURICE This is a classic neurotic relationship. My best-loved friend is a Nazi!

HALDER I had to talk to you about it first.

ANNE You see . . . I'm not a political person. I wish I could help you more . . . I've never been able to get involved with politics . . . Just now . . . whatever you do would be all right to do . . .

HALDER I couldn't make the move, you see . . . Till we talked about it . . .

ANNE I'll try to help you . . . As much as I can . . . I hate them . . . being so down on the Jews . . . I hate that . . .

HALDER Their ideal might be a Germany without Jews . . . But the *reality* is Jews are part of Germany . . . It's not real, a Germany without Jewish doctors, scientists, chemists . . . and *capitalists* for Christ's sake . . . Without Jewish capitalists.

ANNE I think . . . you see . . . People just survive and live . . . It doesn't seem to matter what kind of government people have. They survived through all kinds of terrible times, didn't they? . . . You find somebody you love . . . and you have a family . . . and look after them . . . and try and not harm anybody . . . Isn't that what happens? . . . In the end you have to survive . . . And the less you harm people in surviving . . .

HALDER It's not only survival, is it? Joining the Nazis. If people like us join them . . instead of keeping away from them, being purist . . . And pushed them a bit towards humanity . . . Is that kidding yourself?

ANNE What if they push *us* the other way?

HALDER Yes . . . It could happen . . . Yes . . . If it did . . . I'd get out . . . No question about it . . . I'd pull myself away . . . I'd get out of the country . . . We'd get out of the country . . .

> ANNE *is obviously thinking of something else.*

What are you thinking about, sweetheart?

ANNE No . . . It's just . . . It's not good being frightened for yourself. When you're on your own. But being frightened for somebody you *love.*

HALDER *(arms round her)* We'll be all right. We'll help each other, won't we? As long as we are together . . . I feel that. That's the first time I've felt anything like that in my whole life . . . It doesn't matter what happens round us . . . As long as we have each other.

BOULLER *(with a letter)* Another letter we received only this week on the same theme.

> HALDER *taking the letter and reading it.*

The Chancellory is continually receiving requests from relatives of people with incurable mental illnesses, for the Leader's permission for mercy deaths for these patients . . . This is, of course, just another aspect of the way Germans are beginning to come to terms with the world and the human situation as it *is* . . . Throwing away superstition and mysticism and self-indulgent sentimentality.

HALDER Which does not always lead to humanity and compassion.

BOULLER Halder, we want a paper from you. Arguing along the same lines as you do in your novel, the necessity for such an approach to mercy killings of the incurable and hopelessly insane, on the grounds of humanity and compassion.

HALDER The novel came out of a direct experience . . . My mother's senile dementia.

BOULLER Exactly. This is what makes your analysis so potent. As the Leader says 'From the heart' . . . And I would add, from the mind. I take it the opinions so clearly expressed in your book, Halder, are firm personal convictions . . .

HALDER Below a certain level of the quality of human life . . . Yes . . . I can't see it worth preserving. From the individual sufferer's point of view and his family's . . . Yes . . .

BOULLER Look here, Professor . . . Let me be open and frank with you . . . I could rest much easier in my bed, with your participation in this project . . . You and I know how these things can get out of hand . . . There are certain elements in the party . . . And aside from that aspect . . . the inhumanities that can happen in hospitals and other medical institutions. . . . If we have you with us. You follow me? This would be for me, a guarantee that the whole question of humanity in the carrying out of this project would never be lost from the initial stages of planning, to the final implementation of the scheme.

HALDER I'll draft out a paper for you, Over-Leader . . . In the next week . . .

BOULLER That is *excellent*, Halder. First class . . . One copy only . . . And to be handed personally to me as soon as you have it.

A chorus of S. S. men . . . led by the MAJOR. *The* MAJOR *goes forward to put his arm round* HALDER. *All with tankards of beer in their hands.*

MAJOR *(singing to the tune of 'The Drinking Song' from the 'Student Prince':)* Drink, drink, drink,
> To eyes that are bright
> As stars when they're shining on me.
> Drink, drink, drink,
> To lips that are red and sweet
> As the fruit on the tree.
> Here's a hope
> That those bright eyes will shine,
> Lovingly, lovingly,
> Soon into mine.
> May those lips that are red and sweet,
> Tonight with joy my own lips meet.
> Drink, drink, let the toast start.
> May young hearts never part.
> Drink, drink, drink,
> Let every true lover salute his sweetheart.

HALDER *(to the audience:)* It could have been the atmosphere of the place. The Nationalist Socialist Office was in this great house that belonged once to some great nobleman. Marble Hall. Chandeliers . . . Turning everything into 'The Student Prince' . . . God forgive me! It was a wonderful feeling – joining. You have no idea, the emotional heights it lifted me to.

MAJOR Listen, we're old comrades.

HALDER Yes, I suppose we are.

MAJOR You went into the Hessian Life Guards first. Remarkable.

HALDER I'm not sure how I got in, you see . . . There was some confusion when I joined up in 1916 . . . *(To the audience:)* It's a terrible thing. But it's a wonderful thing getting into a uniform. When I first got into my uniform in 1916 . . . All the emotions came back to me now . . . now . . . For the first week, Martin and I – a quasi-emotional homosexual relationship to be frank about it . . .

CHORUS *(sings)* Drink, drink, *etc.*

HALDER This friend I had. Martin . . .

MAJOR *(sings)*

Here's a hope

That those soft arms will twine, *etc.*

HALDER *(to the audience:)* We went around for the first week in uniform. Looking for officers to salute . . . One of the most exciting experiences in my youth. Walking around Stuttgart, saluting officers . . . Some of the swine didn't even look at us . . . Turned their heads in the opposite direction . . . And now joining the Party . . . Not just joining. But being taken in like a brother.

MAJOR Herr Doctor . . . You can't just join the S. A. How can a man like you, join the S. A.? That amuses me. The modest opinion you have of yourself.

HALDER I hadn't . . . I'll be honest with you, Major . . . I hadn't heard of the S. S.

MAJOR The S. S., you see, Doctor . . .

CHORUS *(sings)* Drink, drink, *etc.*

MAJOR Let me tell you something. I never tell this to the usual applicants . . . You understand? But look here . . . John Halder . . . The Goethe man . . . My wife is a great reader . . . I'm sure she must have read several of your books . . . And your father . . . The Roman Man . . . Now . . . That book, I read . . . Obviously such a deep book as that, I just got the gist of it, but that wonderful discovery he made . . . 'The true and pure German culture can be found only in that part of Germany the Romans failed to contaminate' . . . You see, I still remember bits of it . . . Look here, I'm going to lunch shortly. Lunch with me . . . Please . . . I want to talk to you in detail about the S. S.

CHORUS *(sings)* Drink, drink, *etc.*

HALDER *(to the audience:)* They loved me. You see? I was an old soldier . . . and the Goethe Man . . . If they love you like that, you can't help loving them back. Freddie, the Major, gave me smoked ham and baked potatoes and Frankfurt Cyder . . .

MAJOR Better than wine, eh? Our Apfelwein . . . The Kaiser had his own elite regiment . . . as you know, The Imperial Guard, and, of course, now we have our elite. The S. S. Clearly, that is the only place for you. In the elite along with us.

HALDER *(to the audience:)* He was such a nice, open man . . . His father was a school teacher . . . So was his wife's father . . . He wasn't a cliché Nazi ex-jailbird thug . . . And he told me what Hitler had said to him . . .

MAJOR I can hear his voice, now. That Austrian accent. Pleasant, quiet, concerned. He was so concerned about us.

HALDER/HITLER I should like to make you two pledges. I will never give a command to march against the lawful government of Germany – that is, I will never attempt a second time to come to power by force.

MAJOR We all looked at him. Everybody was surprised. This is 1932 I am talking about. The terrible conditions. Inflation. Unemployment. Children in the streets in winter without shoes

HALDER/HITLER And I promise you, I will never give you an order which goes against your conscience.

MAJOR 'I will never give you an order which goes against your conscience' . . . And the way he said it, you see . . .

CHORUS *(sings)* Drink, drink, *etc.*

MAURICE *(grabbing* HALDER*)* Listen to me, Nazi cunt! I'm fucking talking to you! You hear me?

HALDER Maurice, I'm listening.

MAURICE For fuck's sake! This *obscenity*, Johnnie. I never use obscene language like this . . . I don't *need* to use obscene language . . .

HALDER *(to himself:)* I don't mind the obscenities and the abuse. It's understandable. But I want to get down to business and go home. The whole situation is throwing me into panic. Coming here, to a *Jewish house*. That's a highly dangerous action, for God's sake!

MAURICE What was I saying to you, Johnnie? I got so lost in abuse and obscenities, I've forgotten what I was saying to you.

HALDER *(to himself:)* The whole situation depresses me. That was one of the highlights of my week. A quiet, relaxing evening of communication with my one friend over a Jewish dinner . . . completely *destroyed*! I can't even *speak* to him on the telephone now, without being thrown into panic . . . *(To* MAURICE:*)* You're my *one bloody friend*. You know that . . . *(To himself:)* And he's got to be *Jewish*!

MAURICE Get me these exit papers, then, Nazi cunt. Fucking *do* something about this *fucking great friendship*, then for fuck's sake! . . . Jesus! What am I *doing*? Listen, Johnnie . . . Don't pay any attention to it . . . This is just my filthy unconscious coming to the surface . . . My whole defenses have totally collapsed . . . It's nothing to do with my real feelings for you . . . I love you . . . I *do* . . . Jesus . . . I do . . .

HALDER You know that, Maurice . . . How can I get you exit papers? If I could, I would . . . You know that . . . *(To himself:)* I love him. No question about it. I love him. But I am not going to prison for him. I couldn't stand going to a Nazi prison. *(To* MAURICE:*)* I'm looking at this meal we're sitting down to.

MAURICE You're a fucking Nazi S. S. officer, for fuck's sake. You can find some way of getting me out of this fucking country! For fuck's sake! Listen to the fucking language pouring out of me!

HALDER Maurice, this is a circular discussion, leading nowhere . . . You know that.

MAURICE Come with me, Johnnie. If you came with me, I could *stand* leaving Germany. That would make it bearable. If we were together. Listen. I know . . . Both of us . . . We don't take to all that many people . . . What kind of life would it be here, without me?

HALDER You're in an anxiety state, Maurice . . . You know that . . . Engulfed in a 'subconscious storm'. Your own words . . .

MAURICE I'm *lost*, Johnnie . . . *Totally, utterly lost* . . . Do *you* know what's happening to me?

HALDER Look at this meal, Maurice. We sit down to a meal that would cost a worker, if he's lucky, what he earns in a week . . . That's the *real* issue, just now.

MAURICE *More*! The wine alone is a week's wages.

HALDER We can't go on like this, can we? . . . You as a Socialist . . . Me as a Socialist . . . How long can you go on crying about the poverty of the workers while you are living off the fat of the land . . .

MAURICE Johnnie . . . Johnnie . . . This is my fucking home . . . I'm like in mourning . . . I'm bereaved . . . You know that? . . . The idea of being cut off for the rest of my life from my place in Burgsinn. I've put up nesting boxes for the spring . . . I went out and bought special nesting boxes . . . For woodpeckers . . . We were looking forward to woodpeckers nesting at the back of our cottage . . .

HALDER *(to himself:)* I want to talk to him about that cottage. *(To* MAURICE:*)* I want to talk to you about the cottage.

MAURICE I come *alive* there. The trees . . . And the green . . . I was bloody *born* here . . . My father was *born* here . . . My grandfather . . . Listen . . . I don't even *like* Jews . . . I like my wife and kids . . . But generally . . .

HALDER I don't like *anybody* all that much . . .

MAURICE That's true . . . Listen Johnnie, for Christ's sake . . . You've got to help me get out of here . . . Are you listening to me . . . ? You've got to *help* me! We've both got to get out of here!

MOTHER *(trapped in a corner – lost – frightened)* John . . . John . . . John . . . For God's sake . . . Where am I?

HALDER *(rushing to her)* Where do you think you are, mother?

MOTHER It's no use. Take me back to the hospital . . . I'll never manage to live here on my own. Take me back . . . I'm collapsing . . .

HALDER Just try, mother . . . Try to get a picture of your house in your mind . . .

MOTHER Am I in the kitchen?

HALDER No. You're in the bedroom.

MOTHER I'm in the bedroom? *(Groping about her.)* It's no use, son, I'm finished. I can't take it in . . . I'll go back to the hospital.

HALDER I'll take you over to the bed again. *(Leading her.)* Try to picture it in your mind . . . Your room. Put your hand on the bed.

MOTHER It's no use, I tell you I'm finished . . . You have got your own life to lead. Go back to Frankfurt, son. I'll go into some institution.

HALDER Follow the edge of the bed, mother . . . hand . . . Think . . .

MOTHER I can't think. It's all going from my brain.

HALDER Think of the room . . . You remember the room before you lost your . . .

MOTHER It's all going out of my brain, I'm telling you I can't . . . *(Desperately trying.)* This is the bedroom wall? *(Feeling.)* That's the bed cabinet . . .

HALDER Try again, mother . . . Work out what it is . . . How can that be the cabinet?

MOTHER *(feeling)* It's the table.

HALDER That's right.

MOTHER And that's the way to the door?

HALDER *(giving up – despairing)* That's the window.

> *A burst of flames at the rear of the stage. A bonfire is in progress. Jazz trio playing jazz 'Hold That Tiger'. BOK, carrying a load of books, turns to HALDER.*

BOK What about these? They're in French. Can't make them out.

HALDER *(looking at the titles)* 'Recherche du Temps Perdu . . . '

BOK Eh?

HALDER Remembering the past.

BOK Oh, well . . . They might as well go too. Don't want to waste any time on the past, do we? . . . Here you are, lads . . . *(He throws the books on the bonfire.)* Fancy French dish in for you bonfire.

> *S.S. MAJOR, now known as FREDDIE, bottle in his hand, calls to HALDER.*

FREDDIE Brandy, Johnnie?

HALDER *(going to him)* Good party. Freddie. We're both enjoying ourselves . . . (As he is talking, ANNE approaches with ELISABETH, FREDDIE's wife.)

ELISABETH Freddie, I want to talk to you for a minute. John, why didn't you *tell* us about your accommodation problem? *(To FREDDIE:)* These two poor children have nowhere to live.

ANNE We'll find somewhere. It's just that John has to live somewhere where there are fields and open spaces.

FREDDIE I'm just going to have a quick word with Johnnie, Liz, my love.

ELISABETH We're going to choose our May Queen. Where are you going?

FREDDIE Choose Anne. Look at her! Why can't *I* have women like that falling for me.

ELISABETH Freddie, they need somewhere to live . . . Desperately.

FREDDIE We'll organise that. Don't worry about it.

ELISABETH We will be choosing the May Queen and the May King at nine precisely.

FREDDIE I just want a minute with him, Liz . . .

HALDER *(turning to the* DOCTOR*)* What a pleasant place this is Doctor.

DOCTOR It hasn't been a private residence for many years.

HALDER All the courtyards and archways.

DOCTOR It was sold for an orphanage. Then it became a hospital, Herr Professor . . . Your field is literature then? . . . I see . . .

HALDER I think Berlin sees me as some kind of humanity expert . . . My role is to look round, assess the arrangements and make some recommendations on general humane grounds

DOCTOR Yes . . . I understand . . . I see . . . We had thought, of course, you were a medical man . . . What would you like to do first? Meet the staff?

HALDER I think I'll just wander around, if you don't mind . . .

DOCTOR I'll get someone to show you round. That's the best thing . . . One of our medical staff, I think . . . He can explain the medical ins and outs.

Fats Waller: 'My Very Good Friend the Milkman.'

FREDDIE *(opening a case)* I'm going to let you into this, to show I trust you, Johnnie . . . Both of us . . . Our records . . . We don't need to goose-step round the square, shouting 'Heil Hitler' to prove we're good Party people . . . Look here, there's an order come through for you. I'd rather we didn't make it an order . . . You know that . . . This particular order especially . . . Because I can understand how you'll feel about it . . . *(Opening a box.)* We all have our vices . . . Our private secrets . . . Not a man hasn't something he doesn't want anybody else to know about . . .

HALDER If it's an order – give it to me. It's all right, Freddie . . .

FREDDIE I'm letting you into my vice. Records. *(Drawing out a file . . . opening it.)*

HALDER Gramophone records . . . *(Clearly disappointed.)*

FREDDIE That's it.

HALDER Military marches . . .

FREDDIE That's what it says on the labels . . . See . . .

HALDER Jazz . . .

FREDDIE I changed all the labels. Took me weeks . . . You know the Party line on decadent Negroid swamp jungle music. Opium . . . I'll tell you something . . . I know this for a fact. The Great Man . . . Up in Berlin . . . You know his favourite film . . . ? Jew Charlie Chaplin . . . Watching Charlie Chaplin till midnight . . . every night . . . I can't help it. I've been playing Jazz since I was called up . . . Used to have a sergeant in my squad . . . Got killed in Verdun . . . He played the fiddle . . . He played the blues . . . Soothed me . . .

HALDER I'm trying to listen to the music.

FREDDIE . . . Soothes me that music . . . Christ knows you need *soothing* in this bastard job at times. Building up a country from fuck all. What did those Social Democrat shits leave us? A fucking shit heap . . . I'm sorry . . . I don't usually talk like that . . . But it's true.

HALDER It's a nice tune . . . *(to himself:)* What else can you say?

FREDDIE I haven't any *real* friends . . . I haven't . . . Have you? . . . Apart from your woman, I mean . . . Between you and me . . . Most of the comrades . . . They're good lads . . . But they piss me off, after an hour or so . . . Only one who doesn't seem to piss me off's you. Probably because you're educated . . . I don't know . . . At times, *you* piss me off, too, of course . . .

HALDER Mutual.

FREDDIE I know I piss you off . . . No question about that . . . *(He hands him a paper.)* That's the list.

HALDER *(studying it)* Oh . . . I like him . . . I like everybody . . . It's just books. It's a list of books. *(Reading:)* I see . . . I'm ordered to organise the Book Burning Ceremony at the university.

FREDDIE When it came through you see . . . I said to myself: 'Johnnie's got deep feeling about books . . . This is going to cut him deeply I can see that.'

HALDER Long list . . . Thomas Mann . . . Remarque . . .

FREDDIE I read that. *All Quiet on the Western Front.* Don't ask me why they've done a downer on that. That's exactly how it was at the front, wasn't it?

HALDER *(to himself:)* There's a positive aspect to all this. You've got to make a supreme effort and look positively . . . One of the basic defects of university life is learning from *books.* Not from *experience* . . . Life . . . *involvement* . . . *commitment* . . . agony and panic at being thrown into the storm that's the human condition . . .

FREDDIE Mind, I can see what they're getting at, burning Freud's filthy shit. Pervert, isn't he? Tried to make out everybody's as twisted and perverted as he is!

HALDER *(to himself:)* If you looked at it from the philosophical standpoint, that the burning is symbolic of a new healthy approach to university learning . . . Man does not live by books alone.

FREDDIE All right, Johnnie? Can I leave that to you?

HALDER As long as I can keep *my* copies, Freddie.

FREDDIE *I've* got my jungle music, haven't I?

Lieder SINGER *in evening dress.* HELEN *at the keyboard. Schubert's 'Standchen' . . .*

SINGER Gently floating, through the evening,
Hear this song for you.
In this quiet,
Grove below you,
Waits your lover true.

HALDER *(to the audience:)* You might think what a bloody ridiculous thing to be doing, writing out a recipe for goulash for your wife who you are about to leave. But if you think about it, it's sensible enough, if she can't *cook* . . . Anyway, it was something practical to do, while she was practicing Schubert . . . *(To* HELEN:*)* It's a simple recipe, Helen. You see . . . I've written it out in simple stages . . .

HELEN John, you're so pale. You don't look well.

HALDER *(to himself:)* That's a good approach. Excellent. Go on, make it really difficult. Be understanding. I am very sorry for that woman. All my compassion goes out to her. I'm failing her . . . I'm failing *myself* even worse.

HELEN Are you just going to leave me one *recipe* before you run off to the forest with her?

HALDER Helen, I don't know what I'm doing. *(To himself:)* Who says I'm running off? *(To* HELEN:*)* I don't know if I'm going anywhere . . . I'm just writing this recipe . . . Because it's easy . . . All you need is a tin of meat . . .

HELEN It looks easy enough on paper, but I'm not sure there's not something wrong with me. I don't seem to be able to co-ordinate things . . . I get obsessed with the wrong order. When I make a stew I get obsessed with the potatoes to be cooked and cook them . . . before the meat . . .

HALDER I don't know *what* I'm going to do . . .

HELEN I hate it when you suffer like this . . . Look at you.

HALDER Why have you turned so bloody understanding all of a sudden?

HELEN I don't know . . . Have I? . . . I'm just lost . . . That's all . . . The worst thing . . . You know what the worst thing is . . .

MOTHER *(shouting)* John! John . . . Helen . . .

HALDER I'll be up in a minute, mother . . .

MOTHER I need to go to the toilet.

HALDER What was the worst thing . . .

MOTHER John!

HALDER You've just been to the bloody toilet!

MOTHER I need to go again. Have I got to have set hours when I go and don't go . . .

HELEN I'll take her.

HALDER She's my mother . . . You take her all day . . . Stop being so nice to me will you . . . I'm coming . . . I'm here, mother . . .

MOTHER I'm very sorry. I can't get my bowels to make a timetable for me, son . . . Where's the seat?

HALDER (guiding her) There you are . . . I'll wait outside for you.

MOTHER Wait outside . . . Stay inside . . . What difference does it make to me now

HALDER I'll wait outside . . .

MOTHER John . . . What's going to happen to me if you run off with that prostitute from Altstadt? . . . Don't kid yourself, she's in love with you . . . She knows when she's got a mug . . . With a position and a good income . . . Where the toilet paper? My God. I can't find it. This miserable house . . . They don't even have any toilet paper . . . I knew it was an unlucky house the first time I stepped through the door . . .

HALDER There's the toilet paper, for God's sake. Mother . . . Why the hell did you have to tell Helen about Anne?

MOTHER Where's the wash-hand basin? I need to wash my hands . . .

HALDER Follow the wall . . . Use your imagination . . . You'll never be able to bloody live on your own if you don't give yourself a shake . . .

MOTHER I'm sorry, son . . . I can't perform for you . . . I can't take it in . . . and be independent, so you can run off with your prostitute and leave me on my own without feeling guilty . . . Where's the bloody tap . . .

HALDER Use your imagination . . .

MOTHER I can't wash my hands with imagination, son. Maybe you can. God in heaven . . . The women you pick . . . I told you from the beginning . . . Your father did . . . That woman is no good to you . . . Didn't we plead with you . . . The night before your wedding. To call it off . . . Where are you taking me now?

HALDER I'm taking you back to the bedroom.

MOTHER I've been stuck up there all day. I want to go downstairs . . . What are you going to do about the children?

HALDER They'll be all right . . . I'll look after them.

MOTHER That woman. Dear God, she can't even make a cup of coffee. She gave me bread and butter this morning . . . The bread was cut like doorsteps . . . I want to go downstairs . . .

HALDER Sit in your room a minute . . .

MOTHER Will you take me downstairs . . . What do you think you're doing . . . Torturing me here . . . Locking me up like a prisoner with not a soul coming to see me all day . . . If that is what you wanted to do . . . Giving me a holiday with you . . . You should never have taken me out of the hospital . . .

HALDER I'll come back in a minute . . . I need to go to the toilet . . . (To the audience:) Helen was in the kitchen. Trying to cook the recipe I'd written out for her. (To himself – watching her:) It could well be there is a vestigial brain damage. Not all that much. A trace. That stops her cooking and cleaning the house. And, of course, relating to me as deeply and fully as I need.

HELEN You fry the onions first?

HALDER You don't need to do it this minute, do you?

HELEN I'm doing it now. While you're here to put me right. Up till a few months ago . . . I wouldn't have felt it so much . . . You saying you love somebody else . . . Now when you say it . . . It's like a cold hand reaching into my intestines . . . I loved you a bit during our honeymoon . . . and after . . . Then just a few months ago . . . I really started falling in love with you . . . It surprised me . . . I don't know why . . . Did you notice?

HALDER Yes . . . *(To the audience:)* Well when your wife suddenly comes out with something like that for Christ's sake. *(To HELEN:)* I think so . . .

HELEN Probably my instinct told me I was losing you . . . So I began to realise what I was losing . . . *I* don't know . . .

HALDER *(to himself:)* She's not frying the *meat*. *(To HELEN:)* You have to fry the meat too, Helen.

HELEN That's right . . . The idea of losing you . . .

HALDER You're *not* losing me.

HELEN Just . . . My whole life really . . . It's round you . . . That's the basis of my whole life . . .

HALDER *(to himself:)* You're not losing me . . . I'll never leave you . . . *(To HELEN:)* I won't leave you.*(To himself:)* What do I mean by that . . . I won't . . .

HELEN Don't just say things to pacify me, John . . . will you not, love? . . . I couldn't stand that

MOTHER John . . . John . . .

HALDER Oh, Jesus . . . I cannot cope with that bloody woman just now . . .

MOTHER John . . .

HALDER I'm coming . . .

MOTHER I thought you were in the toilet.

HELEN What are you going to do with her . . . If you have any ideas, tell me . . .

MOTHER John . . .

HALDER *(going)* I'm coming.

HELEN I don't understand you, John. What do you mean . . . you're not leaving me?

HALDER I don't know . . . *(To himself:)* What do I mean? *(To HELEN:)* I'll be in every day to see you and the children . . . Make sure you're all right.

HELEN If you're living miles away . . . In the forest . . .

HALDER I've got to come into the university . . . I have Storm Meetings . . . All kinds of things to do in Frankfurt . . .

HELEN *(indicating the food)* Is this right?

HALDER That's fine.

MOTHER John . . . John . . .

HELEN I wish I could help you . . . I do . . . It's a shame for you . . . I know . . . It's me . . .

HALDER I'd better get that bloody woman downstairs . . .

HELEN I haven't any *friends* . . . I could never make friends . . . Never at any time . . . I never had any real friends . . . Except you . . .

MOTHER John . . .

HALDER I'm bloody coming! *(To HELEN:)* You still have me . . . As your friend . . .

HELEN When I started loving you . . . The children irritated me . . . Their continual bloody presence . . . I just wanted the two of us to be on our own . . . Just stupid fantasies . . . You know what I'm like . . .

MOTHER John . . . John . . .

HALDER I'll bring you down in a bloody minute!

MOTHER I don't *want* to go down. I need to go to the *toilet!*

A DOCTOR wheels in a severely mentally handicapped woman.

DOCTOR You have to ask yourself, as you did in your novel . . . Which moved me deeply, Herr Professor . . . When you come to this level . . . Is this *human* life? She has no control over her bladder or bowels . . . The dimmest awareness of her environment and what is happening round her . . .

HALDER We can take the arguments as read I think, Doctor. What we have to make sure of is that the procedure is carried out humanely . . . Their last hour must be absolutely free from any trace of anxiety . . .

DOCTOR Absolutely . . . Of course . . .

HALDER This room is adequate . . . But it needs to be much more ordinary and
reassuring . . . Could it be made to look like a bathroom, perhaps . . . So that the
patients are reassured and believe they are being taken for a bath . . .

DOCTOR Yes. So they come in here . . . Ostensibly for a bath . . . A normal daily
routine . . .

HALDER What about the families? This is very important . . . Exactly how the families are
informed will have to be carefully worked out . . . In detail . . .

DOCTOR Of course, Herr Professor . . . Of course, they'll be bound to accept the doctor's
word on the death certificate . . .

HALDER I'd like a meeting of everybody concerned, after lunch, Doctor, to discuss this in
detail . . . The families have had enough pain as it is, looking *after* poor souls like
her . . .

Music: 'Carolina in the Morning.'

MAURICE *(shivering)* What are we *doing* here? Sitting in the middle of a cold, freezing,
miserable fucking park in the middle of winter!

HALDER *(following the band)* The interesting thing, Maurice, is I am not consciously aware I
ever knew that song. 'Carolina in the Morning.'

MAURICE I don't know it . . . It's like lovers. Having secret meetings . . . In any case, I don't
think it's a good idea. It's suspicious, coming here. Who goes to parks in the middle of
winter!

HALDER No. I've established that as a regular routine. Every day about this time, I go for a
walk in the park.

MAURICE I'm *freezing*, for God's sake!

HALDER You should've brought a warm sweater, Maurice. *(To himself:)* This friendship. All
I get from it now, is pain, anxiety and panic. I know. This is not good. The shallowness
of my feelings for the one friend I have in the world. (*Looking at* MAURICE.) On the
other hand. I could be underestimating my love for him. My feelings may not be quite
as shallow as I imagine. I *have* gone out of my way to meet him here, just now . . . I
know. I'm after his cottage . . . But it's not entirely that . . . Is it? . . . *(To* MAURICE:*)*
Going to your house, Maurice. During this temporary racialist aberration. It's not a
sensible action . . . For your sake or mine.

MAURICE So how does the cat come over the water? *I* can't come to *your* house.

HALDER *Worse.* Coming to *my* house.

MAURICE Listen, Johnnie . . . I know . . . I can understand that . . . You can't get me these
exit papers . . . I know . . . It's asking too much of you . . .

HALDER *(to himself:)* What is coming clear to me, now . . . I had thrown away the concept
of cowardice and courage. I can see now. There is some meaning to them. To some
extent, there is an element of cowardice in my failing Maurice like this . . . At the same
time, All these people depending on me. *(To* MAURICE:*)* If it was just myself. But I have
two wives, two children and a blind mother, Maurice . . .

MAURICE *(handing him a parcel)* I brought you some cheesecake . . . Where will you get
Jewish cheesecake, when you've locked up all the Jews?

HALDER *(alarmed)* Is that somebody coming? Somebody's coming. Feed the pigeons,
Maurice.

MAURICE Nobody's coming . . .

HALDER Feed the pigeons, Maurice . . .

MAURICE I've nothing to feed the fucking pigeons with!

HALDER *(offering the cheesecake)* Here. Give them some cheesecake.

MAURICE I'm not feeding good, Jewish *cheesecake* to fucking *pigeons*!

HALDER There is somebody coming.

MAURICE They've come to listen to your band. It's an unusual attraction for the park in
winter.

HALDER It's all right. They've gone down the other path . . . Maurice . . . I don't want to push you about the cottage . . . But if we could have it even just for a few months . . . You're not using it anyway, just now . . . It would be exactly the right start for us . . . Somewhere like your cottage . . .

MAURICE Walking through the forest, hand in hand, with the love of your life . . . At dawn . . . The way the sun comes through the trees at dawn sometimes. The shafts of sunlight . . . Yes. It's a beautiful picture. It lifts the whole sexual element right up . . . You're right. It's a beautiful picture.

HALDER (to himself:) Yes. That was a superficial evaluation of my feelings for him. I still love him. Just for the moment, love has been obscured by panic and anxiety . . .

MAURICE You understand what I'm saying, Johnnie . . . It's too much to ask from you. The exit papers . . . Forget the papers . . . Just get me five tickets to Switzerland HALDER. Maurice . . . how can I go to the station and ask for five single tickets to Switzerland, for God's sake!

MAURICE Ask for *returns*.

HALDER Or returns. I'm a bloody officer in the S. S.

MAURICE That cheesecake. I bought it at Epstein's. I can't *stand* them. I can't stand Jews. I spent thirty-five Marks in there at one go, and they couldn't even give me a 'good afternoon' . . . You're right. There's something seriously wrong with Jews. I can see Hitler's point.

HALDER With people.

MAURICE That's what I said. With people . . . I'm talking about what kind of fucking neurotic am I? *Jews*, in the same boat as me, who have done me no wrong except they don't wish me a 'good afternoon,' I can't stand. Nazis, who want to crucify me, I buy cheesecake for!

HALDER Another word for a human being, Maurice. 'Neurotic' . . .

MAURICE Listen. A major insight like that! We should send a telegram to Freud! . . . Johnnie . . . Take the cottage. Use it in health and joy. I won't need it in Switzerland.

HALDER You don't need to go anywhere, Maurice. I don't want you to go anywhere . . . This is a temporary racialist aberration. Hitler's not going to survive another six months. You said that yourself . . . This is still a capitalist country. The real power is in the hand of the capitalists . . . They can't afford to have a mystic idealist running their country . . . You know that . . . This is a temporary aberration . . .

MAURICE It's a basic biological drive, you see, Johnnie . . . When people come after you with fucking machine guns, you start running . . . Look at me . . . I'm calm. I am looking at this cold and rationally . . . Yes . . . It's a temporary aberration . . . The trouble is, with all the machine guns in this fucking country, it's not going to take all that long a temporary aberration to finish off the whole Jewish population . . .

HALDER (to himself:) I love Jews. I'm attracted to their whole culture. Their existence is a joy to me. Why have they got to be a bloody problem to everybody? (To MAURICE:) You know that, Maurice . . . Nobody takes that metaphysical racialist rubbish in *Mein Kampf* seriously . . . Pure races and foul, perverted, spiritually-riddled-with-disease Jews . . . Nobody can even *read* it!

MAURICE He doesn't listen to people. I'm telling you. There is legislation coming in the next few days . . . In the next day. Today . . . Maybe *yesterday*. Against men without foreskins . . . I *know* that . . . Laws . . . I've got fucking hard information. *Now*, will you get me five tickets to Switzerland? No, you won't . . . You don't give a shit what happens to me . . . Understandable . . . (Turning to go.) Listen. It's cold. I've enough on my head without getting pneumonia . . .

HALDER When you're out of your anxiety state, Maurice, you'll see that for yourself . . . Hitler is not going to survive . . . They got rid of Rohm and they'll get rid of Hitler . . . It's going to be all right.

MAURICE Yes. For you, it'll be beautiful. For Nazi cunts it's going to be a beautiful, golden world.

HALDER We'll talk about it, when you're calmer, Maurice . . .

MAURICE Yes. When I'm lying on the ground, riddled with fucking Nazi cunt machine-gun bullets.

HALDER *(to the audience)* . . . *He* was cutting himself off from *me*. Good. I was free from him. Then he turned back and looked at me. No, I said to myself, watching him: 'I didn't think it would be as easy a parting as that.'

MAURICE Listen. You'll have to run from here. For your fucking life, Johnnie. As much as me . . . Maybe even more than me . . .

DOCTOR If you come in here, Herr Professor . . . You can meet some of the patients.

HALDER What is vital, Doctor, is to look fully into their families . . . The quality or lack of quality of their relationships to the patients . . . How often they visit them.

DOCTOR Absolutely, of course . . .

HALDER I'd like to talk to some of the relatives . . .

DOCTOR One or two, Herr Professor, have expressed strong views about the pointlessness of the existence of human parodies like these . . . I am using their words, of course . . .

HALDER *(to a patient:)* Hullo . . . Is that your doll? *(No response.)* What do you call it? . . . Does he behave himself? *(To the* DOCTOR:*)* I'd suggest something like the families being told the patients are being sent here for a new course of treatment.

DOCTOR Or perhaps a routine transfer . . .

HALDER The patients should not have the slightest grounds for alarm or anxiety . . .

DOCTOR We are planning to hold to the normal procedures, Herr Professor . . . On arrival, each patient would be examined by a doctor . . . A thorough examination . . .

HALDER And no delay . . . It would be intolerable if they stayed here any length of time . . .

DOCTOR Absolutely, Herr Professor . . . Once the decision has been reached to terminate . . .

Up bonfire.
The CHANCELLOR *touches the bonfire with his torch . . . a mass of flames . . .*
Music: Wagner.

ANNE What is in your mind, John? That is the most important thing, the beliefs in your mind . . . I don't know . . .

HALDER It's political hysteria for the minute . . . Hitler being in power . . . Getting drunk with success . . . Once the hysteria's over . . . I told Maurice this . . .

ANNE Do you *think* it is?

HALDER What about Freddie's summer house by the river?

ANNE Liz is taking me tomorrow to look at it . . .

HALDER It was a nice party . . . It was nice . . . When they crowned you May Queen . . . I know it's stupid . . . But I had this feeling of pride . . .

ANNE I looked as though I'd stepped out of 'The Rheingold' in that dress.

HALDER You're lovely.

ANNE I love you and you love me.

HALDER I do . . . But . . .

The bonfire flares up.

ANNE I don't know what it is . . . These books . . . When I think about them burning the books . . . I just say to myself: 'It's just a gesture. It doesn't mean anything. Most people. They're not even aware they exist.' I'm frightened.

HALDER I know . . . You're right. That's exactly the feeling . . .

ANNE Do you have it?

HALDER I went into a fever hospital when I was four . . . Scarlet fever . . . They came for me during the night . . . A nurse carried me away from my room . . .

ANNE *throws her arms round* HALDER. *They cling to each other.*

ANNE All we can do is hold on to each other. If we're good to each other. And the people round us . . . If we try to the utmost to be good . . .

The bonfire flares up.

What else can we do?

HALDER I haven't even read Einstein.

Up bonfire. The Bach fugue.

CROONER Day is ending. Birds are wending.
        Back to the shelter of
        Each little nest they love.
        Nightshades falling.
        Lovebirds calling.
        What makes the world go round.
        Nothing but love.

FREDDIE *carries in a load of freshly cut logs.* ELISABETH *is dancing.*

FREDDIE Two things I enjoy. I love polishing boots till you can see your face in them . . .
        And making fires . . . I'm a born hotel porter, aren't I?

CROONER When whipper wills call,
        And evening is nigh,
        I hurry to my
        Blue heaven.
        A turn to the night,
        A little white light,
        Will lead you to my
        Blue heaven.

ELISABETH It's a beautiful house, Anne.

ANNE It is a nice house. I like it.

FREDDIE It's a professor's house . . . Come up in the world since your little wooden hut by the river . . .

ANNE I loved that summer house . . .

CROONER You'll see a smiling face,
        A fireplace, a cosy room.
        A little nest that nestles where
        The roses bloom.

HALDER *(to himself:)* Life is sweet . . . For the next five minutes . . .

FREDDIE Johnnie . . . I want to talk to you . . . Come over here a minute.

HALDER Anne's cooking a duck for dinner . . . Specially for you . . .

FREDDIE Good woman . . . Christ, she's an excellent woman you've got, Johnnie . . . You want to hear the verdict . . . The verdict is we can't have any kids . . .

HALDER That's only one opinion, Freddie, for Christ's sake . . .

FREDDIE Johnnie, don't be nice to me, not just now . . . Do not be nice to me . . .

HALDER Nothing marvellous about kids, anyway . . .

FREDDIE I said don't be nice to me. I know you're a good nice man . . .

HALDER I mean it . . . There's nothing marvellous about having kids . . .

FREDDIE You can say that because you've got fucking kids . . . *(Tearing up paper to stuff in the fire.)* It's a good paper the *Frankfurter Zeitung* for lighting fires. Some papers are better than others . . .

HALDER Yes, you're right. I used to dream about having a kid, before I had any. You're right.

FREDDIE Look at us, for fuck's sake. Liz and me . . . They keep on at me at
        Headquarters . . . When are you going to start fucking breeding. A perfect Nordic pair

like you and Liz. This regime . . . It's obsessed with fucking breeding. I'm going to be stuck major . . . You know that . . . I might even be demoted . . . Till I breed some fucking kids . . . That's not why we want kids . . . That's the official line . . . I even had to go to Liz's uncle's doctor . . . In Wiesbaden, for fuck's sake . . . Just in case they tracked down my report . . . They'll probably still track it down . . . What am I going to do, for Christ's sake . . . We love each other. You know that . . .

HALDER It could be the doctor's wrong, Freddie. *(To the audience:)* What else can you say in a situation like that . . . I was getting to love him . . . And Liz . . . We both were . . .

FREDDIE I haven't been sleeping three nights running. Going round in circles . . . Talking about it . . . Liz and me . . .

CROONER You see a smiling face
A fireplace A cosy room
A little nest that
Nestles where
The roses bloom.
Just you and me
And my baby makes three
In my blue heaven.

FREDDIE It's *me*. Nothing to do with potency . . . That's all right as far as that's concerned . . . I used to think that was all that counted . . . Liz is all right . . .

HALDER *(to the audience:)* Then there was this screaming motorbike. They were always running around with screaming motor bikes . . . With despatch riders . . . Anne showed a young lad into the room . . . Tall . . . blond . . . beautiful in his S. S. uniform . . . He didn't say anything . . . Handed Freddie a sealed envelope.

FREDDIE All right. Thank you. Dismiss. Heil Hitler . . .

BOY Heil Hitler . . . The Jews have shot Von Rath, sir. In the Paris Embassy . . .

FREDDIE Dismiss . . .

BOY You're to go to headquarters.

FREDDIE I've got a car.

BOY Yes, sir . . . *(Going.)*

FREDDIE *(after him)* Von who?!

BOY A secretary in the Embassy . . . A polish Jew shot him. *(He goes.)*

FREDDIE *(reading his orders to HALDER:)* If I got desperate . . . If you were desperate . . . For your wife to have a kid . . . Would you get someone like that lad there . . . ?

HALDER Who's Von Rath?

FREDDIE Who the fuck knows or cares. Some fifteenth fucking secretary in the Paris Embassy . . . But the cunt's fucked up my whole night . . . I haven't had duck for months . . . I wanted to fucking talk to you . . .

HALDER Leave Liz here . . .

FREDDIE I'll leave Liz here . . . *(To the women:)* Women . . . I've got to burn down a few synagogues and arrest some Jews. I could be up all night.

ANNE I thought it was all finished. I thought they'd finished with the bloody Jews.

HALDER A Jew's shot somebody in the Paris Embassy.

FREDDIE *(embracing LIZ)* You stay the night here . . . All right, Liz? . . . You'll be all right?

ANNE You're not really going to burn down synagogues, Freddie?

FREDDIE Save some of the duck, Anne . . . Won't be the same heated up . . . Still . . . No . . . First thing is a briefing session to organise, down to the last detail, a spontaneous demonstration of the indignation of the people of Germany – for tomorrow night . . .

OFFICER Over-Leader Eichmann is ready to see you now, Professor Halder . . .

HALDER *(going to EICHMANN)* Thank you . . . *(To EICHMANN:)* Heil Hitler . . .

EICHMANN Heil Hitler . . . Sit down Herr Professor . . . I've just been going through your papers . . . Joined us in 1933 . . .

HALDER Early 1933, Over-Leader . . .

EICHMANN And been an excellent comrade, Halder, since your first days . . . As an officer and a university man. . . . I think we can work well together . . . The ingredients are all there . . . For an excellent working relationship . . . What do you think?

HALDER If the Leadership believe we can . . .

EICHMANN You haven't written specifically on the Jewish Question . . . Halder?

HALDER My field, as you'll see, is German literature . . .

EICHMANN I mean on the question from a racial point of view . . . At the same time, some of your papers here . . . And reports on some of your lectures . . . This paper on the reactionary, individual centred emphasis of the Jewish influence on Western literature . . . Very good, true, deep comment . . . first class.

HALDER I have to warn you, Over-Leader, I have had very little personal contact with Jews . . .

EICHMANN There's a note here referring to some kind of friendship with a Gluckstein . . . Maurice Gluckstein . . .

HALDER Mainly a professional relationship . . . As a doctor . . .

EICHMANN That's right . . . He was a doctor . . . I have it down here . . . But your paper on the corrupting Jewish influence on our literature . . .

HALDER (turning to students) I do not wish to get lost in speculation about such things as Jewish humanist writers' word orders . . . Or Heine's poetry . . . reflecting the structure of the Jewish palate . . . Whether this is objectively true or not seems, to me, trivial beside the consideration of the direction Judeo–Humanistic philosophy has pushed Western literature . . . There is a Talmudic quotation much used by Jewish writers and thinkers: 'If I am not for myself, then who is for me?' In certain aspects . . . of course, this is a valid question or statement . . . It is, however, in complete contradiction with the basic philosophical statement which is the foundation of the Third Reich: *The common interest before self.* In the course of these lectures, we will examine the highly individually centred philosophy of Judaism. The concept that God himself can be appealed to directly, without the need for priests or other intermediaries . . . We will look into the evolution from the basic individualistic philosophy – or degeneration – whichever we decide is the case at the end of our investigation – in the total preoccupation with self-fulfillment of much contemporary literature, influenced as it has been by the strong current of Jewish humanism . . . Proust . . . Kafka . . . Freud. It will be my thesis, that while this was a valid exploration of the human soul at the time, it pushed Western literature in a direction which almost entirely ignored man as a social animal. Man as an organism which, in fact, has no objective reality, no meaning, unless seen in relationship to his culture, the political and economic structure of the society he lives in and so on. This is not to say that writers have not touched on these aspects of humanity, but they have examined them only from the point of view of individual fulfillment, rather than the fulfillment of a culture, or a nation as a whole. The question I will be asking, is, can this be the only role of literature? The self-fulfillment of the individual? Can we not move in a new direction, reflecting that in which our political philosophy has moved . . . *The common interest before self.*

Slow movement of Mendelssohn's violin concerto.

HALDER (takes a spade. To the audience:) In the morning of 'The Night of Broken Glass,' I didn't have to go into the university . . . I went into the garden to dig the last of the potatoes. The air was sharp and all the scents of autumn were still fresh to me. Giving me the feeling I was in a different country . . . This Jew operation tonight. It weighed on me . . . along with the food I couldn't digest properly . . .I enjoyed the duck . . . at the same time . . . (To himself:) I am very happy. I love her. She loves me. I've got enough money. People recognise me for the brilliant man I am . . . Maurice came into the garden, playing Mendelssohn's violin concerto . . . (To MAURICE:) It's a very Jewish interpretation, Maurice . . . Of course . . . It's a Jewish concerto . . . That's true. Listen . . . This Jewish operation tonight . . . If you try to look at it in perspective . . .

Yes . . . Of course . . . It's not a good thing . . . For tonight . . . and next week . . . Coming down on a racial group like . . . Arresting Jews . . . Breaking into their houses and synagogues . . . No doubt – I'll be honest with you Maurice – kicking in quite a number of Jews' teeth and balls . . . You know the roughnecks in the Party . . . Excesses are bound to happen . . . I am not deluding myself . . . am I? Maurice? This is a regime in its childhood . . . It's social experiment in its earliest stages . . . You know what a child is like . . . Self-discipline isn't formed, yet a large element of unpredictability . . . It *could* be . . . if the Jews stayed here much longer . . . You see what I'm getting at . . . ? Some of the extreme elements in the regime, could get out of hand . . . Christ knows what they would do to the Jews next . . . I see tonight . . . As a basically humane action . . . It's going to shock the Jews into the *reality* of their situation in Nazi Germany . . . Tomorrow morning . . . They'll be running for their lives out of the country . . . A sharp, sudden shock . . . that is going to make those who still delude themselves they can stay here in peace to face reality . . . and . . .

The music stops.

Keep out of it . . . As much as possible. You can do fuck all about it. Tonight . . . what can I do about it? All over the country, they'll be marching against the Jews. It's a bad thing. No question about it. Work it out . . . Me . . . If I *died*. That would worry me . . . The idea of being snuffed out . . . If I got *cancer*. That would worry me. Or if they stuck me in one of these concentration camps and one of Himmler's perverts got at me . . . That worries me . . . If Anne stopped loving me and ran off with another man . . . that would worry me. I've got a whole scale of things that could worry me . . . The Jews and their problems . . . Yes, they are on it . . . but very far down, for Christ's sake . . . Way down the scale. That's not so good, the Jews being so low down on my anxiety scale. *Emotionally. Intellectually* . . . As an intellectual concept it's fairly high as a moral problem . . . The thing is, I am fundamentally a happy person . . . That's what it is. That's the problem. I'm a happy person . . . Absolutely . . .

HALDER'S MOTHER, *now in a state of senile dementia, is wheeled out in a wheelchair.*

We're growing marrows in the garden, mother. Dad loved marrows . . . Fried with sausage and onion. That time we went to Rugen . . . Remember that holiday house we had in Rugen . . . Listen, I have had a complaint about you . . . From the sister . . . Climbing out of your bed in the middle of the night . . . What do you say, mother? . . . I can't make you out . . . *(At last understanding.)* You were going home . . . Yes . . . I understand you, mother . . . I heard you . . . You were going home . . .

BOK *(calling)* Herr Professor . . . It's Bok . . .

HALDER I'm here . . . Out in the garden . . .

BOK What a house you've got. A mansion. Look at the garden . . . Acres.

HALDER Four acres.

BOK You deserve it. I'm delighted for you. Do you know that? That you've got a good woman like Frau Halder . . . and a house like this.

HALDER I've got some beer. Would you like some beer, chilled in the fridge?

BOK They sent me up with orders for you. I've got them here. I wouldn't mind a cold beer.

HALDER (to himself:) If they won't let me alone, they won't . . .

BOK It's a big show tonight. You heard? The Jew cunts murdered Von Rath.

HALDER Was he a friend of yours Bok?

BOK I like that, that's to the point, isn't it . . . That's a wonderful thing about you Herr Professor. You can get it straight up the hole . . .

HALDER gives him beer.

. . . Who gives a shit for Von Rath. You're right. It's the idea of a Jew having the cheek to shoot a German

HALDER Your beer all right?

BOK I've never had a garden . . . I thought about getting an allotment . . . Never got down
to it . . .

HALDER *(reading the orders)* We move into action 3 p.m. this afternoon.

BOK That's the orders. You should see the excitement in the university . . . The students
are making banners . . . organizing torches . . . Nobody's doing a stroke of work.

HALDER I was looking for a peaceful day in the garden. I wish they'd get these bloody Jews
out of their system. Why didn't they all get to hell out of here years ago, while they still
had a chance.

BOK Get the cunts out now, Professor.

HALDER Would that make you really happy, Bok? When there is not a single Yid left in the
universe?

BOK *Me?*

HALDER I'm talking about *you*? Would that make you really happy . . . Paradise . . . A Jew
free world . . . ?

BOK I'll put it to you this way. Hitler, now . . . he comes up with this stuff about the Jews.
He's thought about it, worked it out. The Jews are sucking the fucking lifeblood of the
country . . . Now . . . look at us . . . now . . . He's begun to shake the cunts out.
Everybody's got jobs. Holidays . . . Couple of years time, and everybody'll have their
own cars. Ordinary workers . . . Some people used to say he doesn't know what the
fuck he's talking about, Hitler . . . Just farts out of his mouth instead of his arsehole.
What do they know? He's delivered the goods, hasn't he? He knew what he was talking
about all along. Herr Professor . . . *You* didn't like living in a Jew Germany . . . Did
you? Now . . . You walk about in the streets. And you feel it . . . You know this is *our*
place now . . . Don't you? He's got us back our own country . . . Look at you, if you
don't mind me saying. You're laughing, now, Professor . . . You've taken over that Jew
shit Mandelstam's job . . . big house . . . The whole university's back to a German
university . . . You've got no complaints, what Hitler's done for you . . . have you?

HALDER *(to himself:)* I am very happy . . . I am . . .

EICHMANN Basically, your usual, clear objective reports . . . That's what we want from you,
Halder . . . On leadership, morale . . . amenities . . . the general situation of the camps
I've listed. I'll follow this up by a personal visit.

HALDER This order, Over-Leader, to re-settle all the Jews by the end of the year . . .

EICHMANN Sooner if possible . . .

HALDER Since we're going to work closely together . . . and I am in the role of some kind
of adviser . . . could I ask you how you feel about this direction of resources . . .
personally . . . I'm thinking of us fighting the war on so many fronts . . . the desperate
shortage of rolling stock for the offensive and so on . . . and re-directing so much of it
to transporting Jews . . .

EICHMANN Russia, we'll soon finish off . . . They're on their last legs, Halder . . . That'll be
one front less . . . In any case . . . that's our orders . . .

HALDER I was curious about the need for such urgency . . .

EICHMANN Your point about fighting on so many fronts . . . All the more reason to keep
the enemy within under tight control . . . You can see that can't you . . . From the
question of security alone . . . You'll make the arrangements then . . . You'll need to
base yourself in Berlin during your assignment with me . . .

HALDER I'll make the arrangements . . . Yes . . .

EICHMANN The leadership, of course, have ordered me that on no account are you to cut
yourself totally off from your university . . . Some sabbatical is being arranged for
you . . . But it is vital you are in Berlin within the next week . . . I look forward to us
working together . . .

ANNE Johnnie . . . Are you going to get changed, for God's sake . . . You've to report at
three o'clock . . .

HALDER *(putting away his spade)* I'm coming.

ANNE John . . . relax . . . All right, love?

HALDER I had the picture in my mind, out there in the garden . . . Germany's been turned
into one great prison . . . You don't think we should run away? It mightn't be too
late . . .

ANNE Too late for what? Run away where? Why do you have to make such a dramatic
thing out of everything . . .

HALDER No . . . Just sometimes I panic . . .

ANNE I know . . . Now listen here, that's exactly what you are doing. You're panicking . . .
Talking about prisons and running away . . . *(aware of him for the moment in his
underwear)* . . . Men look funny in their underwear, don't they?

HALDER Do I? Yes . . . I panic . . . Sometimes. In the garden, after Bok went off. I had this
wave of panic and guilt . . . I'd destroyed your whole life.

ANNE How have you done that? If it is destroyed . . . The *words* you use, love! If it is, *I* did
it myself. It was *my* choice. *You* . . . I wish you hadn't a wife and other children that
keep pulling you from me . . . But you have. I love *you*. It would've been easier if I
loved somebody without all these weights on them . . . But I love you. *(Helping him on
with his S. S. uniform.)* What exactly are you going to do tonight? Think about it . . .
You're going out on a police action. That's all. You're not going to *shoot* Jews . . . do
any violence to them. Your orders are to keep things under control. Stop people
burning down Frankfurt . . . That's *all*, for God's sake . . . Just try and think calmly
what you are really doing . . .

HALDER I am. You've got a good logical mind. That's good. You're right.

ANNE Somebody in the family needs to have one. Are you going to stop beating your
breast now about things you don't *need* to beat your breast about? You've got plenty of
real things to feel guilty about.

HALDER You're right. What real things? . . .

ANNE In any case, for God's sake . . . If I was Jewish I'd have got out of here years back . . .
The first year Hitler was in power . . . Any Jew with sense is out by now . . . The ones
that are left must be utterly stupid or desperate to hang on to their property . . . What
are they doing staying in Germany?

HALDER Listen. You're so clever. You're right. Everything you say is so logical and true.

ANNE You look lovely in that uniform. I think Elisabeth is after you. Do you know that?

HALDER *(fastening his holster belt)* So we won't run away, then? To California?

ANNE All right. We'll run away. I'll pack, and you can phone your children and tell them
you'll write to them every week.

HALDER I'd better go.

ANNE *(putting his cap on)* Is the revolver loaded?

HALDER I *think* so.

ANNE I'll see you when I see you, love.

HALDER I love you.

ANNE I love you . . . And no *prisons* or yawning chasms in front of you . . .

HALDER God, I love you sweetheart . . .

ANNE I know you do . . .

EICHMANN What do we do with them, Halder? The sick and the diseased . . . The volume
of Jews and anti-socials flooding into the camps . . .

HALDER I see . . . Yes . . . We're talking about the sick and diseased . . .

EICHMANN The Reich Leader has been into this personally . . . It is coming from him . . .
We need a centre in the east to carry out these actions that are now necessary.

HALDER We are concerned particularly, of course, with the highly infectious diseases . . .
Typhoid . . .

EICHMANN Halder, we're at war. Surrounded by enemies. How can anyone expect us to
bear the burden of millions of diseased, anti-socials, sucking the blood and strength of
the country . . .

HALDER I'm looking at the map. I see . . . Because of the railway?

EICHMANN It's a logical centre . . . We have psychologists and medical doctors and other specialists looking into this. But you are one of us, John . . . I need a report I can trust . . . An evaluation of the recommendations for the processing of the diseased and the unfit . . . We're not monsters, for God's sake . . . The order's out. It has to be obeyed . . . I am in total agreement with it, in any case. But I want the same human, without sentimentality approach that seems to be your particular strength . . . Understood, then?

HALDER I'll be on the train for Silesia tonight.

EICHMANN Total and absolute top secret. I agree, by the way, totally with your report on the accidents in the east. The procedure is not to be even considered. On grounds of humanity, among other things. I want any evidence you might find there, too, of unnecessary cruelty . . . indulgence in sadistic behaviour . . . Apart from anything else, these things have a disastrous effect on the general level of discipline.

HALDER I'll make a full report.

EICHMANN Directly to me. No copies, Halder!

HALDER Maurice came to me. With the Frankfurt Jewish Male Voice Choir *(singing 'Jesu Joy of Man's Desiring')* He had disappeared months ago. I don't know where to. One day he stopped meeting me in the park. But he came to me that night. Through the smoke of the burning buildings.

MAURICE The flames are aesthetic. Never seen Frankfurt look more like the set of 'Gotterdammerung' at Bayreuth.

HALDER *(to the audience:)* It was five o'clock in the morning and they were still at it. I was dizzy with the smoke and the violence was getting to my nerves. We were sitting on a scrap of wasteland. Although it was November, there was still flowers growing through the cracks in the concrete. *(To MAURICE:)* Maurice . . . It's just come to me . . . Our whole approach has been superficial and simplistic . . . The *Jews* the Victims – the *Nazis* the Persecutors . . . We've reduced the whole complex situation to this stock, simplistic construct. *(MAURICE takes this in.)* What do you think, Maurice?

MAURICE I'm trying to take it in, Johnnie. The effect seems simple enough . . . They mow me down with machine-guns, cut off my balls, rape my wife . . . no . . . I take that back . . . Most of the cunts couldn't rape a fucking sparrow.

HALDER What we are doing, Maurice . . . Listen to this . . . is we are allowing ourselves to be trapped by obvious, stock responses . . . Instead of daring to confront ourselves with reality maybe, Maurice, maybe . . . It's the Jews' fault . . . They are responsible for pushing Germany into this Jewish, moralistic, humanistic, Marxist total fuck up . . .

MAURICE *goes back to his choir.*

Maurice . . . I'm trying to communicate deep and profound truths with you . . . Will you stop conducting that choir . . . What is the Frankfurt Jewish Male Choir doing singing about Jesus, anyway . . .

MAURICE It's reformed. Converted . . .

HALDER No. I withdraw the word 'profound.' I accept that. Profundity has nothing to do with human beings . . . Whenever you imagine yourself soaring to profundity, remember the total banality of your existence and vision.

MAURICE That's true. That's a profound statement, Johnnie . . .

HALDER *(watching the flames)* You think we might be having a nervous breakdown. The whole thing is a national nervous breakdown?

MAURICE It's standard process. Evolution, isn't it? Animals go as far along the line of development as they can. And that's it. They become too big or too heavy . . . or too specialized . . . and they go extinct . . . Don't worry about it . . .

HALDER I don't accept that . . .

MAURICE All right. Don't accept it. Please yourself.

HALDER Maurice. We have to accept the consequences of your Jewish Humanism . . . The time's past for covering it up with pseudo-scientific smoke screens . . . I'm not blaming you . . . I forgive you, Maurice.

MAURICE What's he saying? What is this shithead talking about? It's my fault, his fucking machine-guns mowed me down?

HALDER I'm talking about objective moral truth, Maurice. What is an Objective Moral Truth? I'm not being profound, Maurice . . . I'm just coming to grips with reality . . . What has happened, is we have confused subjective fantasy concepts like good, bad, right, wrong, human, inhuman . . . as objective, immutable laws of the universe. Jews are bad, Germans are good . . . Like a stone falls to the ground . . . It is a moral act to get rid of the Jews. It's an immoral act . . . That's the kind of clouded, subjective thinking parading as objective truth that has totally disorientated the world and led us into this violence and chaos . . . There's something there, Maurice . . . Do you think there's something there?

MAURICE I'm confused . . . What are you saying! It's a good thing to have your balls cut off . . . It's a beautiful, uplifting experience being mowed down by machine-guns . . . Johnnie I'm confused . . .

HALDER It's what is happening. That is what human beings do . . . What happens. How the world is. Not what Jesus or Lenin or Moses or all the Jewish moralists would like it to be. How it is . . . If we could work on that basis of accepting the world as it is . . . What do you think?

MAURICE People fuck other people's wives, Johnnie . . . That's the world as it is. How does that fit in with your new approach, Boychical?

HALDER That's true . . . That's an important point . . . I don't like that . . . The idea of somebody stealing Anne . . . That's not good, Maurice. You're right . . .

MAURICE Listen. Don't worry about it . . . It's too complicated. There's too many people in the world to cope with . . . With too many problems.

HALDER Coping with all these *people*, Maurice.

MAURICE Two's difficult . . . Three's getting too many . . . Ten for a Minyan's impossible . . .

HALDER Listen . . . You're probably right, Maurice . . . The way things are going . . . That should be the end of us . . . You're right . . . I can't see people lasting much longer on this earth . . .

MAURICE Best thing. A finish to people torturing the earth. I'm telling you. Who needs us? Look at that – what is it? Ragwort? – Dandelion? Pushing its way through solid concrete.

MAURICE Through a crack.

HALDER That's right. It couldn't push it's way through concrete.

MAURICE Concrete rots in the end. It can wait.

HALDER It can wait. Plants are in no hurry.

MAURICE John my friend, let's go home.

HALDER You know what I could do with? A good thick slice of ham . . . two eggs . . . black bread and butter . . . hot mug of coffee . . . and seeing Anne . . . could do with my arms round Anne more than anything else just now.

MAURICE Let it all burn. Don't want to drag out the end too long.

HALDER (*bending to the flower*) So don't worry, ragwort or whatever you are . . . Won't be long, now . . . You'll soon have it all to yourself. (*To* MAURICE *as they go:*) Nice flower that, Maurice.

They walk towards ANNE, *waiting for them.* ANNE *goes to* HALDER *with his greatcoat . . . helps him on with it.*

ANNE We're mad. Some couples are separated for years . . .

HALDER I know.

ANNE I've never heard of Auschwitz.

HALDER In Upper Silesia . . .

ANNE Yes, you told me . . .

HALDER I should be back in a week or so . . . Two at the most . . . I'll phone you every day, if I can.

ANNE There is something wrong with us . . . The way we can't stand being separated.

HALDER I know . . .

ANNE Are you all right, now, love?

HALDER I'm fine . . .

ANNE John . . . Listen to me . . . Whatever happens . . . round us . . . However we get pushed . . . I know we're good people . . . both of us . . . It just isn't what's happened . . . You destroyed me . . . Pulled me down . . . It isn't . . . It's the other way round . . . You've pulled me up . . . I've done the same for you . . . From the first time we came together . . .

HALDER Yes . . . We probably are . . . good . . . Yes . . . Whatever that means . . .

ANNE You know what it means.

HALDER Yes . . .

ANNE Remember it then.

HALDER *(to the audience:)* I got into Auschwitz early in the morning. It was an ordinary dirty industrial town. Big station. Munition trains . . . sparrows on the platform poking at microscopic crumbs on the concrete. People going about their work. Like a normal town. I was sitting on the platform, feeling insecure like I always feel away from home . . . absolutely longing for Anne and the children . . . the comfort of her hand in mine. I'd taken out a book, while I was waiting for a car from the camp to pick me up. A German translation of *Don Quixote* . . . I could only read escapist literature like that in these days . . .

ANNE Remember it, then. And remember that I love you. And you love me . . . and we'll always love one another . . . Will you remember that . . .

HALDER *(kissing her eyelids)* I'll remember that.

Music: Schubert march.

(To the audience:) When we arrived at the camp, Hoss, the Commandant, was waiting at the gate for me.

HOSS *comes forward.*

(To the audience as he shakes hands with HOSS*)* Funny man . . . Poor soul . . . Something *wrong* with him. I was trying to work out what exactly it was, all the time he was welcoming me . . .

HOSS That's very kind. Reich Leader Eichmann sending his regards. Of course, please convey mine to him. My very kindest regards.

HALDER *(to the audience:)* He showed no emotion. That was it. Might have been some mental condition. On the other hand, just stress . . . The poor bastard had a hell of a job . . . He did make a supreme effort and *smiled*. The funny thing was . . . I heard this band. Playing a Schubert March. 'Oh,' I registered to myself. 'We're having Schubert, now.' . . . Then I became aware that there was in fact a group of prisoners . . . maybe in my honour. I'm not sure . . . The important thing was . . . The significant thing: the band was real.

Up band . . . HALDER *watching them . . .*

. . . The band was *real!*

Up music.

Alastair Fowler (1930 –)

The Fisherman's Wife

Offshore the hidden rocks
Are sharper than seems;
And harder than fishing boat
Can touch and stay afloat.

Three go down quick
Where nothing breaks
The green but crabs and flesh
And then more crabs and fish.

After a week the sea
Washes one   10
With sand all through its hair
Up on the shingle there.

Run and fetch her quick.
At the washing green
Hanging out his clothes.
When that is done she goes

And picks away the crabs
Frilling his wrists.
From a face unpicks what clings.
Those are his messed things.   20

Each crab she softly takes
And drops in a pail.
Then says to the fishermen
To put him out again
Lads: set him again.

Bits 5: Winds Sift Keenly

This is section five of a six-part imagistic poem sequence entitled 'Bits'.

Winds sift keenly:
some elected leaves
rose from mounds
up through dark snowflakes.

Carol Galbraith (1930 –)

Eftir Lang Years

Lachen amang freens
I turnt owrequik
an there ye war
quaiet
owre far
an yet
lik ae duimwatch robot
ayont controwlin aa my thocht.

Nae ither ee bar mine
thowlt the grup o yer een   10
nae ither soul bar mine
lowpt the warrls atween
nae ither life
lowst* an strupt awa   discarded
the lane leevin ye hanna seen

for luve lang smooert*   smothered
lowt* tae ivry airt   flares
kinnilin wi mine
its neebor hert.

Alex Hamilton (1930 –)

Dead Men Walk

'Orkney?' said Smithson, unbelievingly.

The Features Editor swiveled through 330 degrees and, thereby meeting the phone again, placed the receiver against his chest, as if he were staking his oath on the entire network. 'Orkney,' he mouthed.

'Why not send Flett? He was born there.'

'That's why.'

'And when I get there?' challenged Smithson.

'Mill about in the stuff. Under the skin a bit. Drag in some history, if you want.'

'Colour piece,' said Smithson colourlessly.

'Now listen,' said the Features Editor, absent-mindedly hanging up on his phone call, 'how often have you come in here . . . ?'

'All right, Orkney,' said Smithson quickly. 'Light and shade.'

'More of the latter, I think. You can bring out the darkness a bit if you want.'

'It's probably the wrong time of year for darkness, but all right. Only when I've got it, I hope you won't leave it lying round on overmatter until they declare their own U.D.I.'

'You should be so lucky. We'll want a newspaperman there then.'

'I am a camera,' intoned Smithson, on the way to the door, 'And also a quill, an I.B.M., a pair of ragged claws, scuttling across silent seas, a telex, a desk console, a dream of fair women . . .'

'A poove.'

'All these things for just the one salary. But don't thank me, thank the Imperial Packaging Company who sent me.' He saw that he had lost his audience, began to open the door, and then quietly shut it again. He cleared his throat.

The Features Editor looked up. 'I thought you were in Orkney.'

'Just to clear up one point before I go. I read a piece the other day by Linklater . . .'

'Eric?'

'Magnus, son of. Born there, like Flett. Wrote about the women there, how loving, how they came down to the boat, bearing gifts.'

'Reasonable expenses,' said the Features Editor. 'And by the way, Flett was telling me the other day how very reasonable expenses are up there.'

'Flett was born there,' said Smithson. 'That's always more reasonable.'

The phone rang. 'Ah. glad you got through again,' said the Features Editor. 'Some fool must have cut us off. I don't know how I get through the day with all the interruptions.'

'I'm not really at liberty to divulge,' said Smithson.

'I'm sorry for you,' said the elderly man on the boat. 'That's no life, to be keeping your fellow man at arm's length.'

'I'm going to stand in the middle of the boat,' said Smithson. 'They say it doesn't move about so much.'

'They blether that say it. The boat's all of a piece, and when it moves the middle moves with it.'

'I don't care to argue about it,' Smithson muttered. He calculated the middle and picked up his suitcase.

The elderly man moved off with him. 'Ye've no need to be taking the suitcase. It'll neither get sick nor stolen on a boat.'

'Do you mind?' said Smithson. 'I'm supposed to be looking at the scenery, not talking about suitcases.'

'Ye'll be a fillum executive no doubt. It's said fillum folk are aye searching for an island.'

'I am not, and I loathe islands. Islands have water round them, and I loathe water.'

'This bit water's placid enough today, so it is. I've seen the Pentland Firth when it was all one white agony, as though the de'il himself had gone into the lace business.'

'No doubt you had your work cut out handling your birch bark canoe?'

'There were no boats out that day, nor for many days after. But many men have been drowned hereinabout on days like it. That was their privilege, but that they risked the lives of the lifeboatmen too. Perhaps ye've a mind to visit the wives of the Longhope men whiles ye're in Orkney?'

'Does everybody visit them?' asked Smithson. 'Are they some sort of tourist attraction?'

'No, no. I'd no' go so far as that. But those from the television have been known to do so.'

'Television people fly,' murmured Smithson despondently. The old fellow crouched over to hear Smithson's words, and his coat tails stuck out like an insect's wings, as if he were about to take off himself. 'If I were to be sick now,' continued Smithson, 'I should have no choice but to spoil your shoes, which I see are of suede, and the nicest thing about you.'

The shoes moved a few prudent inches. 'It was better not to fly,' their owner remarked consolingly. 'This is the only true route into Orkney from the mainland. Ye'll aye remember the rocky wild profile of the Creator about you now.'

Smithson uttered nothing in reply but a sad little grunt, which altered in mid expression to a startled cry of pain, as the wizened little man smote him sharply between the shoulder blades. 'Look up, man!' cried his tormentor. 'Take your mind off yoursel' wi' a grand sight. The clouds are lifting off the brow of the cliffs. There they tower, in all their red majesty!'

Smithson jerked his head up, and gulped air. 'I suppose that stony stack all by itself is the Old Man of Hoy?' he forced himself to enquire. 'Didn't the TV people broadcast the first climb? A feat to rank with the sagas, took 'em days, nights, food and sleep on a dizzy ledge, wonderful stuff.'

'Aye!' replied the other. '*You* might call it that.'

'Didn't everybody?'

'More's the pity. For no sooner had they come down than three wee bairns ran up to the top and down again, wi'out a word of their intent to anybody. It's been a fright to every mother since every time she hears her weans talk of a picnic.'

'Still, you Orcadians must be glad to be able to boast that the old heroic blood of the Norsemen is still running in young veins.'

'Don't call me Orcadian. If you please,' snorted the old man. 'I'm from Perth. There's nothing in Orkney but fish. They fetch me up against my better judgment, and the fish when you think of it live in the sea. And weans are the same the world over.'

'As you say,' said Smithson, as the chainmail grey of Stromness hove into view on the port bow, 'the kids are entitled to be mad here like anywhere else. But do they grow up mad?'

'What brings you to Stromness, sir?' asked the hotel barman.

'I couldn't get in at Kirkwall,' said Smithson.

'I wonder at that,' returned the barman. 'There's nothing doing at Kirkwall. They'll not be that busy in Kirkwall that they could not take one more body in.'

'It has something to do with their experience of the Press. The last journalist in Kirkwall wrote the most terrible things about his hotel. Put them out of business, nearly.'

'Journalists are good company, but they get their facts wrong.'

'You have nothing to fear from me,' said Smithson. 'We aim to become a paper of record. We would much, much rather be dull than inaccurate. I take it that that moose was shot in about 1871, and the nickelodeon installed in the following year?'

'I could find out for you, Sir, but I would rather that my name were not brought into it.'

Smithson waved a deprecating hand. 'Oh, non-attributable, of course.'

'You'll be here to see Jo, perhaps?'

'Jo?'

'Jo Grimond. Leader of the Liberals, that was.'

'That's not a bad idea. Where's he to be found?'

'At Westminster, I believe. But if you took the bus, you could see his house from the road. But if you mean to get out of the bus, for a proper look, then take a tip – catch an early bus, or you'll find that the last bus coming back the way is already safe here in Stromness for the night.'

Smithson urged his glass forward for a refill. 'Safe from what?'

'I can't tell you that, Sir. It wouldn't be facts.'

'Things happen at night?'

'They say they do.'

'That's a relief,' said Smithson.

'The hotel's a bit quiet just now. You should have been here last week. The place was hotching[1] with facts.'

'And next week too, I suppose?'

'Packed out, Sir. The maids'll be doubling up next week. We'd not have been able to fit you in, not with a shoehorn wrapped in a five pound note.'

---

[1] Twitching, infested.

'Shows how astute they are in London,' said Smithson. 'Their only thought is that their reporters should bunk comfortably. Wherever possible we choose a quiet week. Do the waitresses double up too? That was a very pretty one with red hair that served me at dinner. Sharp too – recited the menu like a music hall turn.'

'That's very kind of you to say so, Sir. She's my daughter. Comes up from Edinburgh University for the season.'

'Does she, indeed? Well, I won't ask you about all the others. It's plain to see that they're your sisters.'

'Can you come up?' shrieked Smithson.

'You come on down!' roared back the painter.

Carried on the updraught, the words seemed to take physical shape as blobs and tatters of spume, wrenched from the yellow murk of the sea below.

'They said I might find you here,' temporised Smithson. Lying with only his head jutting out over the cliff edge, his vision swam with moving specks of black and white, in the remote background far below the painter. When the cramping vertigo relaxed its hold on him, he recognised them for kittiwakes, and puffins, and little auks and guillemots. The painter's head, pink and bald and nesting in a thick roll top sweater, looked like the egg of some huge extinct bird. Smithson looked nervously around him as the idea occurred to him, fearing some troll might show up, casting about the crags for materials for an omelette, and seeing Smithson-filler as a *bonne bouche*.

The egg revealed a physiognomy again, as the painter looked up. 'Ye needna be feart,' he insisted. 'I'm used to people watching over my shoulder as I work.'

'I can't fly,' yelled Smithson.

'There's a rope in my car. Make it fast to the bumper.'

When he had lowered himself to the painter's side, Smithson was pleased to find that the relentless wind pinned him closely against the rockface, while his feet seemed to shoot nerves out through the leather of his shoes, palpating every interstice in the stone – until suddenly they found what they were hunting and, with an involuntary click like a plug entering its socket, both feet thrust simultaneously into holes. He turned his head at right angles and observed that the painter's canvas was lashed to a sort of natural easel, formed by a couple of cradling bush stumps and a knob of rock above. The painter himself swung as cheerfully in his cloth belay as if he had been a metropolitan window cleaner.

'I heard of your arrival last night,' said the painter. 'It's a terrible hotel that for gossip. It's said ye've an eye on Cathie. Ye'll need to be discreet. Her father's a mercenary old devil.'

'Good God!' exclaimed Smithson. 'Gossip isn't the word. After the sermon her old man gave me last night on facts! I haven't spoken two words out of place to the girl, beyond asking for an extra portion of chips when the kitchen was closed.'

The painter shook his head. 'It's a bit late to undo all that now,' he said dubiously. 'It would cause ill feeling in the closes of Stromness if you went back in your shell after such a beginning. Besides, she's a good lass, Cathie, she and my second daughter were in school together, and I'd be as sorry to see the one with tears in her eyes as the other.'

The wind was whipping one continuous tear from the corner of Smithson's own right eye. 'I'll do my best to accommodate the common will,' he said.

The painter nodded and dabbed cloth at a mistake on the canvas. He walked up the rock a bit to tilt back and examine the result. 'You're a good lad,' he said. 'Well now,' he continued, lying almost horizontal, 'I suppose you're after an interview on the fisheries situation?'

'Yes and no,' replied Smithson, as casually as the tearing wind and his precarious balance would allow. 'I've not done the homework I should have on the fisheries situation.'

'I'll spoonfeed you. I'm just the man to do it. It's a scandal.'

'I can tell you have strong views on a number of subjects. Could we talk a bit about your painting first?'

'I paint what I see, you know, like any true artist.'

Smithson bent his head till it rested on the other's shoulder. He could now see the whole canvas. 'The intriguing thing is,' he said, 'that you don't . . .' A strange menacing sound rolled about in the painter's throat, like the sea booming in a cave. 'I mean,' continued Smithson hastily, 'it's like everything else since I came North, the real thing is just out of vision, or out of earshot. I mean, from where we are there's a whole lot of rock, and sky and sea and birds and some sort of inlet over there with what looks like a bashed-up boat. I don't see any of that on your canvas. You seem actually to be painting a croft, with a man coming home from work in the fields and a woman with a baby at her breast.'

'D'ye like it?'

'Yes, it's fine, but . . .'

'It's no' bad, is it? I've painted the subject a dozen times.'

'But you've gone to some considerable trouble to install yourself here, and I can't see anything remotely resembling a croft or these people for miles around. The whole landscape's different from your picture.'

'Och, I only come here for the privacy. It's like Friday at the butcher's at home. I used to come here for eggs when I was a lad. I've painted that too, as a subject, more times than I could count, but now the inspiration for it has left me.'

'And these crofters, where did you see them?'

'Nowhere, boy. Ye'll maybe see a few crofts about still, standing with their roofs stripped away to the elements, but the way of life has gone. On these islands, dead men walk.'

'Dead men walk,' repeated Smithson. 'I think my editor would like you to elaborate.' He ended the sentence on a panic-stricken squeal, as he perceived that he was voicing his request to the painter's boots. Then, as abruptly as he had descended, he felt himself rising again. As he passed the painter again, in a rapid ascent to the clifftop, the painter shouted after him – the words echoed weirdly as if they were spinning up from the sea itself – 'And the living can't keep their hands off other men's motorcars. But don't worry. They'll be frightened to death when they see you coming up like a genie from a bottle.'

'Dead men walk,' said Smithson into his pillow. 'But nobody's said anything about them dancing.'

'Hush up,' said the girl with red hair (which on closer inspection had turned out to be a sort of deliriously rich auburn) 'The dance isn't till the day after tomorrow, and you'll be all right by then, except for a few bruises.'

'Would you massage the small of my back again, please.'

'There's not a thing wrong with the small of your back,' said the girl with red hair.

'I think that may be why I enjoyed it so much. Most of the rest was excruciatingly painful.'

'Be brave. Think of childbirth.'

'I'll meditate on it for an hour, unbroken,' he promised, 'if you will just first indulge me this whim.'

'Somebody might come.'

'Somebody might have come earlier, while the agony was on.'

'But I should have had a clear conscience.'

'All right then, I give in. Just pour a whisky down my left ear-hole, and leave me to my dreams of a frowsty bedsitter in Fulham, London, England, the World.'

'I'll give you a whisky,' said the girl with red hair, 'if you invite me to have one with you.'

'Among various linctuses and old herbal remedies on my night table,' said Smithson, 'you'll find a bottle labelled, unless my taste nerve was shattered with my kneecap, Park Royal. Please pour two bumpers, beakers or toothmugs of that blissful hippocrene, one for you and one for me.' With his eyes closed he listened to the viscid gurgle, and did not open them when he felt the mug placed between his outstretched fingers. 'You know,' he remarked, 'ever since I came to these islands, I've had the impression that it is not enough to paint, or report, merely what you see, and that just out of sight is something wonderful, mysterious, terrifying, beautiful or downright Orcadian. Which with a little more subtlety or a little more speed, I might just be in time to see one of these days. I have the idea that if I were to open my eyes this second, and turn my head as quickly as a puppet, I would see behind me a gorgeous woman, with long red hair glowing as red as the flames of the beacons when Rognvald Kolson returned from dalliance in the Mediterranean.'

'*Don't* open your eyes, *nor* move your head,' she said. He felt another glass of whisky being given him, in his left hand, then the swift flutter of her lips all across the small of his back.

'It burns more there, now, than anywhere,' proclaimed Smithson.

'I'll leave you to drink both whiskies, I think,' said the girl with red hair, and closed the door behind her.

'They said I wouldn't find you here,' said Smithson. They said you were away to Glasgow. Others said Perth, others Edinburgh. They all said you were away – the shopkeepers, I mean.'

'I've not been away for twenty years,' said the poet, standing aside from the doorway of his council flat. 'Will you come in?'

'Why did they say that, then?' asked Smithson, entering.

'Perhaps they wanted to protect me from the unexpected. It's not within mortal compass, but they try.'

'They warned you I was coming?'

'They did,' said the poet, turning his back on Smithson, and gazing through the window, out over the shoulder of the museum towards Scapa. 'Jimmy Isbister told me in person.'

'Who's Jimmy Isbister?'

'He sells me things. He sold me that harpoon for half a crown. He found it in a dump, I believe. He keeps an eye out for things that might please me. You'll have met him in the closes, with his bicycle.'

'Of course. He pushes that bicycle everywhere. But I never see him riding it.'

'I believe he's still looking for the chain.'

'But it was he who told me where to find you.'

'He's my Public Relations Officer,' said the poet. He seemed, with a convulsive effort, to come to a decision. He wheeled round from the window and marched across the room, with his jaw thrust out, towards his little kitchen. 'You'll take a dish of coffee,' he ordered.

'Thank you kindly,' said Smithson, lowering himself with great care into a strawbacked rocking chair. For a rocking chair it was built on rather formal lines, and embraced him like a carnivorous mollusc. He instantly regretted his immobility, for he spied on the table by the window, held down by a porridge bowl, a marmalade pot and a sugar basin, sundry pieces of paper flapping in the draught. These should be the worksheets of a new epic concerning Vikings and Orkneymen, masons and crofters, fiddlers and bakers, before the Reformation corrupted the pure root of mythology which was the blood in the stone of the hard men of the North.

'I'd be sorry if I thought I was playing the person from Porlock,' called Smithson. But the poet was gazing down the sink, humming tunelessly. The person from Porlock would have made no impression on this one. When he had given Smithson his coffee, he turned away and communed with a picture of Rackwick on the wall.

'You're getting to be quite famous, even in America,' said Smithson at last. 'Are you never tempted to travel, out of Orkney?'

'Orkney exports whisky and eggs and professors,' replied the poet, 'but I . . .' he broke off as he saw Smithson pull out pad and pencil. 'You're not thinking of writing it all down?'

'Just a note or two,' said Smithson. 'It makes a better interview if I do.'

A look of utter dejection lengthened the poet's countenance. 'I wouldn't know how to talk in an interview,' he said.

'You made a very promising beginning,' Smithson encouraged him.

The poet rubbed his hands together fretfully. 'Let's see then,' he said in a pessimistic tone.

'You never even cross to the mainland of Scotland?'

'No,' said the poet warily.

'You're content to write only about your own people?'

'Yes.'

'Their legends and myths, their heroes – like St Magnus the Martyr.'

'He would be mentioned.'

'The clans that came out of the northern darkness? And put down roots of darkness in this earth?'

'If you like.'

'Perhaps as a reminder to the people today of what they are in danger of losing?'

'You might put it like that.'

'Do you have a sense that here dead men walk?'

'Dead men . . . ' The poet stopped. 'A sense . . . ' Perspiration stood out all over his brow. Smithson ostentatiously put pad and pencil back in his inside pocket. A faintly hopeful look lightened the poet's haggard expression. 'Is that all?' he asked.

'I think we've covered the main subjects,' said Smithson. 'I'll be in Orkney a few days yet. We might meet in one of the bars, and just drop in a few of the details.'

'We must, that,' said the poet enthusiastically, confirming the words with a vigorous twist of his head. 'But I hope you'll be getting into no more fisticuffs. You've had trouble enough with the Norwegians already, from the look of you.'

'Who told you that?' said Smithson. 'I haven't seen any Nor . . . '

But his denials went unheard. The poet had launched into a series of waterfront stories and anecdotes, reaching farther and farther back into the past. Smithson listened, spellbound.

'Don't you find it eerie, a place like this right in your backyard?' asked Smithson.

The farm girl said nothing. She reached out a hand and a small girl sprang from nowhere to attach herself to it.

'It's pretty deserted,' said Smithson. 'We might be alone in the world.'

The farm girl, already plump as a pigeon, seemed to swell further. She compressed her lips, as if she had difficulty in holding utterance back.

'A few trees would help,' said Smithson doggedly. 'But I suppose the wind doesn't give them a chance.'

The farm girl picked up a lantern and held it ahead of her as if she needed it to see the way ahead, although the sun was high in the sky. The mite held fiercely to a sheaf of postcards.

'I understand there's a tree in Kirkwall,' said Smithson.

With her little appendage skipping at her side, the sturdy wench forged briskly across the courtyard. Smithson caught up with them at the edge of the highway which ran past the farm, where his two guides examined the road in both directions. As far as each of its horizons, no vehicle of any sort could be seen. After a pause, the pair of them scuttled across. 'Why don't you agitate for a zebra crossing?' Smithson called after them.

On the far side they bounced across the springy turf towards the entrance of the burial mound. Every time Smithson came up with them they accelerated. 'All right, I won't talk any more,' panted Smithson. 'I'll save my breath to cool my porridge.'

At the beginning of the shallow cutting which led to the mouth of the grass-covered tomb, they stopped and the little one fished a key out of her knickers. With a great air of solemn officialdom she unlocked the iron gate, stood back to wave to her companion, then Smithson, and followed after into the vault. The elder girl put down her lantern and then stood as still as a graven image.

Standing erect under the dome, Smithson said, for the sake of a human voice, 'So this is the ancient Maeshowe, the chamber where the silent vanished races laid their chiefs to rest.'

There was a faint hiss from the farm girl at his elbow. Smithson turned in surprise from contemplation of the hieroglyphs around him, as he realised it was the prelude to speech. The farm girl then spoke for some ten minutes.

She delivered herself of her message in a high sing-song which, were it transcribed, could have no punctuation. She talked of highborn maidens and great heroes, of oppressors and defiance, of gold and jewels, mighty spirits and wretched vandals. She kept her head high all the time, never removing her eyes from a fixed spot at the apex of the ceiling. When she had come to the end, she lowered her head and for the first time her hitherto waxen features relaxed in a smile of sheer pride.

'Jolly good,' said Smithson. 'That sounded like word-perfect.' The little girl spread out a display of postcards on a slab for him to make a choice. 'They're sevenpence each,' she said. 'But some people give me a shilling.'

Smithson having aligned himself with some people, and effected several purchases, the farm girl said, 'Ye must accept my apology for remaining dumb. I canna concentrate on my history and the questions folk put to me all in the same while. But if there's anything ye want to know, ye can ask it now.'

'Well then,' said Smithson. 'Your great poet told me that on midwinter's day, just before the year's midnight, the last of the setting sun actually comes down that passage for an instant and shines on the wall. Now, have you ever seen that?'

'I have not. And I dinna ken if it's so. For in December I'm always up and away to Switzerland for the skiing.'

At that moment the sound of a malicious little chuckle came from the external end of the passage. The iron gate clanged to, and the key turned in the padlock. In the silence that followed the farm girl sighed. Smithson dropped to a crouching stance and hurried down the passage. 'Come back, you little blighter!' he shouted.

But the little girl had vanished into the outside world, hidden from view by the curve in the cutting. Smithson came snarling and crouching back, like Caliban, to the farm girl. 'She's scapa'ed,' he said. 'Come to think of it, I wish she would, and drown herself.'

The farm girl had sat herself down, carefully spreading her skirts on the stone slab. 'She gets bored,' she said. 'It's only a phase. She needs a skelping, I suppose.'

'We're buried alive,' shrieked Smithson. 'With a lot of prehistoric bones!'

'They might find us, I think,' said the farm girl.

'Yes, but when? You said yourself ten minutes ago that at one period nothing but ghosts came near the place for several centuries.'

'Aye, but there wasn't a regular bus service in those days. There's generally somebody wanting to see the Maeshowe on every bus in the summer.'

'When's the next bus?'

'It's a two-hourly service.'

'Two hours! That's an eternity, ravelled up in a pagan crypt.'

'Ye're no' verra gallant.'

'There's a time and a place for everything,' said Smithson. 'And let me tell you that if that lamp isn't still burning when they dig us out of here, I'll sue the head off every modern descendant of your ancient earls that still haunt the place.'

'You're sitting just now on the bones of a warrior that lost his heid,' said the farm girl. 'It's a guid story, so it is, for those wi' a strong stomach . . . '

'It's not the Maeshowe,' remarked Smithson sententiously, 'but it's a good site. I shouldn't think anything will disturb her there for a thousand years.' From the graveyard, on the other side of the wall, came the sound of the first sod being shoveled on to a coffin.

'She was in no hurry to come here, all the same,' observed the chemist.

'At 92?' exclaimed Smithson. 'There's a fair case for saying the angel of death must have passed her over a few times already.'

'Oh, I don't think she was greedy,' said the chemist. 'One more week, perhaps two, and she'd have been content. As it was, I regret to say her last words were notable for their mood of indignation and a sense of injustice.'

'Some dear relative on the high seas couldn't quite make it?' suggested Smithson.

'Oh, not at all,' replied the chemist. 'She'd been a widow for nigh on fifty years, and there's moss already on the headstone of the last of her family to be laid here. But you see, she took in lodgers to help the money along, and harvest celebration time, which falls next week, was always very fruitful for her.'

'From where we stand,' said Smithson, looking inward from the path which divided the cemetery from the sea, 'the harvest of death looks the richest of all. It's a beautifully kept estate. You're very conscious of death up here.'

'You're very conscious of our consciousness,' retorted the chemist. 'Furthermore the whisper says you spent a record four hours in the Maeshowe today, and it's even said there were tears in your eyes when you emerged.'

'Tears of desperation,' said Smithson. 'The first bus didn't even stop. I don't want to talk about it.'

'Yet here you are, straightaway down for the funeral of a poor old soul that spun out her history in a Stromness close. Did you follow the cortege down the hill from the kirk?'

'Pure accident,' said Smithson, who wished that he could believe that it had been woven in the loom of fate. 'I came round the shore looking for this wrecked freighter to take a photograph . . . ' They turned together to face the rusting hulk, which lay canted over against the rocks, with its mainmast like a tall extra cross above the cemetery. Smithson looked into his viewfinder. 'It makes a dramatic shot, but I came down not even knowing the graveyard was here, much less that it would be operational at this moment.'

'There's sea wrack all about the coast,' said the chemist, scornfully. 'Many that would make better spectacles in a photograph than this one. I'm interested in the art of the camera myself, and could take you round the coast for some pictures. If you happened to use any of mine in your paper I wouldn't want payment – it's the credit to your name that's important when you're building up a reputation.'

'Exceedingly kind offer,' said Smithson. The mourners were beginning to move away, and he worked the lever with great speed. 'I think you'd need to belong to the union before we used your work. And anyway it's only this wreck I want. You see, your great poet based a story on it. He seeded in this freighter, that was his phrase.'

'It's no story to make public,' said the chemist witheringly. 'The crew were all drunk, or they'd never have lost her on a rock marked with a buoy.'

Smithson lowered his camera. 'Come again,' he said. 'I don't see any rock with a buoy.'

'No. It's up the way a bit. A couple of hundred yards yonder, perhaps a bit more.'

'And the wreck was in the way of shipping? She was pulled in tight by the shore?'

'No. She found her own way.'

'To a *graveyard*,' said Smithson in a hushed voice. 'Did anybody see this happen?'

'It happened one night.'

'Fantastic! Who saw it?'

'Nobody saw it. There was nothing to see. The crew had been taken off a long time.'

'Nothing to see!' echoed Smithson despairingly. 'Nobody saw it!'

'It was a natural happening. I don't understand your emotion.'

'I can't explain it,' replied Smithson. 'But if I can't see anything myself, I wish to heaven I could see something obliquely at least, through somebody else's eyes.'

'For a chemist, he's not a bad fiddler,' said Smithson.

'For an invalid, you're not a bad dancer,' said the girl with red hair.

'I've learnt that in Orkney everybody has to play two roles.'

'What else have you learnt?' she enquired, leading Smithson by the hand away from the concourse dancing in the barn.

'Read all about it in Thursday's edition. This year, next year, sometime, never.'

They passed down the central aisle of the adjacent cowshed. Every cubicle seemed to be occupied by an amorous couple. She laughed when she saw the look on Smithson's face. 'Don't worry,' she whispered. 'I know you believe in A. A. comfort. Anyway, we're only going to fetch in the skog.'

The skog proved to be a dark brown liquid, getting its colour and viscid nature from a liberal ferment of sugar. They carried it back in small butter churns. She began to tell him the recipe but he stopped her after the first three items, 'Any moment you'll tell me it includes beastings.'

'It's very potent. It'll make them beastly drunk, but you can't have a barn dance without,' she said.

'A good many are three parts cut already.'

'They go on a pub crawl first,' said the girl with red hair.

'Yes, the poet showed me the way. I was afraid we'd soon run out of pubs, but he proved his genius by going in the public bar and saloon of each, thus doubling the number of stops.'

'You look sad. Is it because you're going tomorrow?'

'That of course,' said Smithson. 'And also because I didn't find what I was looking for, although I'm convinced it's here.'

'Perhaps you've been looking too hard. What were you looking for?'

'How can I put it?' wondered Smithson. 'Perhaps . . . what happens in the dark, only guessed at by most people.'

'You found a little of that, at least,' she said. 'Though I hope you won't write about it.'

'You have my word for that,' promised Smithson. 'But that's not what I meant.'

Three dances later the festival had become much noisier and the air was thick and sticky, as if it too were fermenting into skog. A young man and a girl were being pursued by shrill groups of youths, in and out of the barn, whooping and shrieking as they led their rout of pursuers. Both had their faces blacked.

'They've to be married tomorrow,' explained the girl with red hair. 'Tonight with their faces blacked they can do as they please and nobody knows who they are.'

'Everybody seems to know who we are,' said Smithson. 'At least, they keep looking. Perhaps we should have blacked our faces.'

'It doesn't work if you're not about to be wed.'

'Shall we just sit outside then?' suggested Smithson.

They sat on a knoll a hundred yards from the byre. The bare hills of Orkney lay all around in soft billows of charcoal, against a sky like polished eggshell. The dance behind them thumped and squeaked and skirled, with an occasional extra lift of irreverent, boisterous laughter. Sometimes a car door banged in the lane, and once a lad with a hip flask climbed on a metal roof and clanged out a solo dance, until he fell into the arms of his companions. The bride-to-be flashed by within a few yards of them like a firework, a small train of sparks still stubbornly after her, fizzed into a hollow, and was suddenly silent.

'But they won't sack you, will they?' asked the girl with red hair anxiously, 'if you didn't get what you came for?'

'Oh, Good Lord, no. I've got enough *copy*.'

'Then I don't understand.'

'Did you ever play Grandmother's Footsteps?' asked Smithson.

'Where one person stands with his back to everybody else, and they all try to creep up without being seen to move?'

'That's it. Exactly. Well, I haven't caught anybody moving. When I look directly, they're all standing like stone. As motionless as those stones, down there on the plain.'

The Standing Stones of Stenness, indecipherably ancient, were there in the bowl below, a wide circle of dolmens, on slightly raised turf between two tarns.

'This is the night when those stones are said to move,' she said quietly.

He sat and stared at the huge, roughly-hewn pieces of rock. It was impossible.

'They won't move if I'm looking,' he said.

'Would you be content if I saw them move?'

'Have you seen them?'

'No, never. But I've never had cause.'

'Yes, I'd believe you.'

'It's coming up midnight,' she said. 'Stand with your back to the stones.'

She rose with him, and faced him. They stood there, unmoving. The sound of a police jeep came to them, making its way up the hill to the barn. A cat wound its way round

Smithson's legs, but he did not look down. 'In the daytime you have green eyes,' said Smithson.

'Now! Now!' she cried. 'Don't look round!' In her eyes he saw the stones move. Then the vision trembled and was gone, as they filled with tears.

'I saw!' she said, swaying towards him.

'And I saw too,' said Smithson, catching her in a triumphant embrace.

'Most of it's padding,' said the Features Editor. 'And too damned dark at that.'

'You asked for darkness,' said Smithson.

'I don't know how you got that impression. We're not here to make people's flesh creep, except with facts. Anyway, it doesn't matter. The Editor's very pleased with the stuff on the Fisheries Problem. There was a question asked in the House yesterday, so you can put in another two hundred words on that, and it'll do nicely for tomorrow's paper.'

'And the rest?'

'Forget the rest. You know, you make quite a good reporter, when you stick to the facts.'

'Thanks,' said Smithson. At the door he said, 'You know it's true about the girls. They do come down to the boat, bearing gifts.'

'So?'

'It's a fact.'

'Damned boring fact,' said the Features Editor. 'And quite irrelevant in the context of the fisheries problem.'

Sheila Douglas (1932 –)

The Makar[1]

Ill-wrocht, ill-thocht, wis his daurk destinie:
Tae feel his bodie turnin intae stane,
While reid life's bluid wis stoundin* in ilk vein,   throbbing
His strang spreit dowsit wi fell crueltie.
Hoo cud he thole* sic a captivitie   endure
When in its dreichness* solace there wis nane?   dreariness
He hid nae lowe* tae warm him bit his ain,   flame
A cauld mune skinklet* on his miserie.   gleamed

Fule! Ye hinna reid weel whit he scrievit!
Nae malison cud ding a chiel sae swack*,   10   agile
An even daith itsel he laucht tae scorn.
He wis a makar, weel may ye believe it,
He scoured the universe upon his back
Wi dreams o lowpin like the unicorn.

---

[1] The reference is to William Soutar (1898–1943), the fine Scots poet who was bedridden the last thirteen years of his life (see page 429).

The Gangrel Bodie

She wis aye that sleekit
Ye niver kent
Whaur she hid come fae,
Whaur she wis bent.
Like a tod★ i the mirk   fox
That smools★ through the haar★,   slips/mist
She wis here an awa
An ye didnae ken whaur.

Tom Nairn (1932 –)

Festival of the Dead 1967

This article first appeared in the *New Statesman* 1 Sept. 1967. Nairn writes to the editor of a 'slight reservation'; his article may now appear dated, especially since 'history re-started' in 1998 (that is, when Scotland was granted its own parliament.)

This is the 21st Edinburgh festival. A time for serious questions as the *Scotsman* reminds us from its pulpit. More Drama, or less within the overall glory of the thing? Will Lord Provost Brechin and his cronies cut the Festival Grant by one third next year, to celebrate the majority in the Proper Presbyterian style? Time even to revive the hoariest nut of all: when, how will this songless city get its own Opera House?

   Huddled in the dense gentility of the Festival Club on a Sabbath afternoon, to the rhythmic strains of that genuine voice of bourgeois Edinburgh, the Freda Winston String Trio, dreadful doubts assail one. The sour anglicised whine of these polite cultural exchanges in the Edinburgh tongue puts such questions into much better perspective than the *Scotsman* can. Behind the appalling artificial waterfall and a thousand carefully-poised teacups, a truly serious question is forced upon one: what *is* this Festival after 21 years, what has it become? The answer is: it was Culture, it has become Scotland. It has not merely succeeded; it has turned fatally and permanently into another Scottish Thing, another structural element in the tiresome fantasy-life the Scots have been doping themselves with for the past three centuries to avoid their real problem. Festival time in Edinburgh seems to have joined tartanry, militarism, Burns and Scott – those 'mummied housegods in their musty niches,' as Edwin Muir put it – as a constituent of the Great Scottish Dream.

   The Scottish Dream is a function of the Scottish Neurosis. This collective neurosis was brought about in the 18th century by the partial suppression of Scottish nationhood in the Union Treaty of 1707. Nationality is of course the 'normality' in relation to which the basis of modern Scottish history must appear as pathology. Whatever its limitations – these are more evident every day now, and this fact is of importance to the Scots – the nation was the necessary framework of society throughout this time. Deprival of it inflicted an intolerable strain upon the Scots, and there has never been a real solution to the problem; consequently, there had to be a fantasy solution to make the situation tolerable, a dream-nationhood to take the place of the real one. A very great part of modern Scottish culture, and almost all of Scottish Nationalism has been poisoned at the root by this obsessive need. Essentially, it has been a magic incantation to raise the dead, a spell to recreate that whole social culture which – already deeply compromised and unsure of itself after the Reformation and the departure of the Stuart court – was finally decapitated in 1707.

A certain sense of identity, the convergence of thoughts and feelings around certain ideas, certain themes or attitudes, is a normal part of national society. The conditions of modern Scotland destroyed this self-image. The dilemma of the Scots has been to feel (again in Muir's words) that

> we are a people; race and speech support us, ancestral rite and custom, roof and tree . . . And something that, defeated, still endures

but to have lost all idea of *what* people they really are. Some societies could perhaps survive the loss of statehood, the political means to construct their own destiny. The precarious and bloody earlier history of Scotland made it absolutely vital to preserve these means. Hence, the loss of them was an insufferable void, and Scottish cultural history is the dismal record of the attempts to escape from this void – either by literal escape to the south, or by fantasy-escape a peopling of the emptiness with romantic shadows. This is why Scotland was so significant within European romanticism, as both subject and creator of myths: by its situation, it was made for the romantic posture. And to this day, a profoundly false, wish-fulfilling nostalgia remains the characteristic Scottish emotion.

The worst part of this insoluble problem lay in what *was* genuinely inherited and preserved, as the 'something that endures.' By and large, it was the odious hell-religion of Scottish Calvinism which endured, and still endures as the cultural substratum of the country.

The three-week Festival is exactly like an interminable church fete in atmosphere. People comment ceaselessly upon how little effect it has had upon the real, continuing life of the city – but what do they expect? The soil Scotland offers to this fragile festive culture is mildewed religiosity a mile deep, and what could thrive in this? Edinburgh's soul is bible-black, pickled in boredom by centuries of sermons, swaddled in the shabby gentility of the Kirk – what difference could 21 years of Festival make to this? In Edinburgh the iron age of Calvinism has long since turned into rust, and it is this rust which chokes and corrodes the eye and the ear.

The crisis of identity was rendered permanent – and even more insoluble – by the total impossibility of accepting the kirk as a national self-image. Every human being provided with a minimum of intelligence and sensibility has recoiled from this idea, as from a sentence of death. But the Kirk *was* reality. Consequently, in Scotland the real must become unreal, and the unreal be seen at all costs as real – to state the matter frankly the Scots Neurosis is absolutely incurable.

In Waverley Market there is an exhibition commemorating the 200th anniversary of Edinburgh's Georgian 'New Town.' Here one can study the plans for this Heavenly City of the 18th-century philosophers. Although the Nationalists naturally mention these giants in their trumpetings, they fail to see that this was in its day simply the most positive and brilliant escape from the tragedy of being Scottish. The great intellects of the New Town held elocution classes to expel dialect from their speech and Craig's 1767 plan refers to Edinburgh as 'the Ancient Capital of North-Britain.' The driving impulse of this great era was escape from the particularity of Scotland, on to the plane of the Universal – to an abstract truth and a cosmopolitan culture – owing nothing to their origins. In this moment of grandeur, Scotland discovered the right way of not being herself. When these conditions changed, and Romanticism took their place, she was doomed. Doomed to being merely herself, that is, to the intolerable contradictions mentioned.

Of course this had already been prepared during the Edinburgh Enlightenment itself, by the revived interest in popular and folk culture. The search for the past had already begun, in the time of Robert Burns's success, and was swollen to chronic dimensions by Walter Scott. Scotland had found herself. This, not the bracing of the Golden Age, was the definitive formula – the dream from which Scotland never recovered.

Now as ever, the only really popular part of the Festival is the Military Tattoo staged on the esplanade of Edinburgh Castle. Massed on this dominating height, the folk who have assembled from every part of Scotland turn their solid backs on the Music and Drama, and enjoy themselves. Intellectuals who slink in in search of High Camp will be richly punished. But they had better be prepared to join in the vociferous choruses of *Abide with me* and stand bolt upright for *The Queen*. This corking spectacle begins with massed pipes and drums, and mounts up colourfully with swelling enthusiasm through every known level of corniness to the great climax of the lone, spot-lit piper puffing a tearful farewell on the battlements.

This culture and its profound popularity reflect the most important footnote added to the Tartan Ideology after Scott. Within the context of an expanding English imperialism, the Scots discovered another sub-identity, as the pioneers and military servants of the Empire. They were not merely exploited into this role – they avidly appropriated it, as another solution to the perennial problem of how to exist.

Nowadays of course, the Nationalist intellectuals have to dismiss this in the way they have always dismissed the Kirk. That is, too easily. They fail to observe that the really ugly truth of the spectacle lies less in its hideous content than in its semantic relationship to reality. The dream *works*. The utter feebleness of Scottish political Nationalism is the consequence of this: political Nationalism in Scotland is a contradiction in terms, everyone feels this, and hence the subject is a joke.

In Milne's Bar, the crowds of poets come and go among the portraits of MacDiarmid, Goodsir Smith, MacCaig and the other heroes. The prominent part of alcohol in the National spiritual life is well-known. The function of the mental whisky that also flows at Milne's is less appreciated: poetry. Next to tartan and soldiers, poetry is the greatest curse of contemporary Scotland. It is the intellectuals' special form of dope, which they can indulge in with a good conscience while the crowds go mad up on the Castle esplanade.

The meaning of the extraordinary prevalence of poetry in modern Scottish literature is evident. Prose is too risky. After Scott's fantasies, Scotland parted company with the great mainstream of the European novel: this was a developing tradition of realism, based on the dialectical exploration of appearance and reality in society. Scottish society could not face this kind of exposure. Here, precisely where speech is needed, there is a zone of silence, guarded by the ceaseless babble of versifying. Poetry, which ought to arise out of a prose culture, instead has to be a *substitute* for it, as in MacDiarmid. Poetry has to conjure up the national culture, as well as the nation itself, through an impossible, encyclopedic lyricism. Devoted to this false task, the poets actually fail to disturb the real, terrible silence of Scotland.

The crowds troop in nightly to see Pop Theatre Shakespeare and Moliere, through the dank courtyard of the Church of Scotland's Assembly Hall, past the forbidding image of black Knox himself. As long as his tradition holds the tongue of Scotland in its grip, the sounds within the Hall will never have their proper resonance. This is the worst thing their twisted history has done to the Scots. Society is language; Scotland is silence.

The poet's wish is above all to burst through this heart of inarticulacy, to cry the Word which could restore all things whole. But the loss is far too deep for this. Presbyterianism appropriated the country's tongue and, merely by being what it is, killed it.

Scotland has no voice, and no present. This is the country of 'the dead, who lodge in us so strangely, unremembered, yet in their place,' while the 'common heels' come and go 'And are content, with their poor frozen life and shallow banishment.' Yet even Muir, the poet who could feel these truths, could go on to state the problem in these words:

> For how can we reject
> The long last look on the every-dying face
> Turned backward from the other side of time?
> And how offend the dead and shame the living
> By these despairs?

This distinctive, hopelessly nostalgic feeling is itself a trap. For Scotland, reality and speech obviously lie somewhere on the other side of rejection. The offence of the dead and the shame of the living are conditions of sanity. Hope, as that well-known Scotsman R.D. Laing might well have put it, can only be beyond absolute despair.

'I find it hard to believe,' pomps Magnus Magnusson in the *Scotsman's* centre page, 'that anyone could disagree that the Edinburgh International Festival has exalted Edinburgh into a real capital city after a lapse of centuries . . . ' Unerringly, he focuses upon the new element of delusion the Festival has permanently imported into Scottish life. Only a Scotsman who has suffered all, from the inside, and then despaired, can possibly measure the emptiness of these words.

Duncan Glen (1933 –)

The tireless publisher of the distinguished Akros Press from 1965 to 1983, Duncan Glen has been one of the most important supporters of modern Scottish poetry. An effective poet himself, he writes in a vivid and utterly convincing Scots. The first poem below, 'My Faither', has become a classic. Its last two words have a resonance that stays in the mind like the memory it describes.

My Faither

Staunin nou aside his braw bress-haunled coffin
I mind him fine aside the black shinin range
In his grey strippit troosers, galluses and nae collar
For the flannel shirt. My faither.

I ken him fine thae twenty or mair years ago
Wi his great bauchles and flet auld kep;
And in his pouch the spottit reid neepkin
For usin wi snuff. My faither.

And ben in the lobby abune the braw shoon and spats
Aside the silk waistcoat and claw-haimmer jaicket   10
Wi its muckle oxter* pouch, hung the lum[1] hat.   underarm
They caa'd him Jock the Lum. My faither.
And nou staunin wi thae braw shinin haunles
See him and me baith laid out in the best
Black suitin wi proper white aa weel chosen.
And dinna ken him. *My father.*

Aff the Nicht Shift

Wee grey men walk doon the street
withoot a word bein said. The sun's a reid glory
at the street end wi the Spring dawn brakin.

---

[1] Lum: a chimney; a 'lum hat' is a tall hat or a dress hat.

They turn up the closes
leivin reid dust frae their buits on the stairs.
He draps into a chair and stares at the oot fire.

'The Hert o Scotland'

I hae problems.

I would scrieve o Scotland
and mak a unity o it
but
ken nae word o Gaelic
though I've had three fortnichts in the hielants
and went on a boat to Lochboisdale
wi hauf an 'oor ashore. In Inverness I was that lanely
I went to bed early. In Fort William it rained
and though I sclimed Ben Nevis in record time   10
it was sae misty I could haurdly see the peth at my feet.

Dundee I hae forgotten frae an efternoon veesit
and Union Street Aiberdeen I've never seen to forget.
Perth I reached efter a lang bike ride
and had to turn back as soon as I got there
haein nae lichts.
Stirling Castle I hae stood on and surveyed the scene
but I mind the girl mair than the panorama.
The Borders I ken weill enterin or leavin by a sign
SCOTLAND   20
but I've never gote aff the train.

I hae problems.

Fife noo is different.
It I ken frae pushin an auld bike to the limits
and stood on baith Lomonds and Largo Law. I hae kent it
early and late wi the extremes o youth. And mony
girls
but aw the faces and names noo forgetten
but yin that coonts
in or oot o Fife and she was born in Mallaig   30
whaur I'd never been.
Fife is different.
I hae my Glesca voice and Fifers notice that.
And I've never played golf at St Andrews.

I hae problems.

Still there's Edinburgh
and that gies a bit o status if no unity
for aw that awbody kens Edinburgh
(they'd hae us believe!)
I had the advantage o digs in Marchmont   40

and days at the Art College
– but aye a visitor wi a time limit
as still
wi sae mony ithers.

I hae problems
being frae Lanarkshire.

It's true there's the hills by Symington
and orchards in the upper Clyde valley
and Kirkfieldbank. But
I was yin that never went to see the Spring blossom   50
steyin pit in grey streets
in the shadow o pits and bings* and steelwarks.   slag-heaps
The ugliest stretch in aw Scotland
those that ken their Scotland hae tellt us
and I only kent aboot as faur as I could walk.

I hae problems.

There's my Scotland. A wee corner o Lanarkshire
and Glesca (I should mention!)
whaur as message boy
at fifteen I kent aw the addresses   60
and short cuts. There I belanged

– till I left at echteen!

My Country

'This is my country,
The land that begat me,
These windy spaces
Are surely my own.'
    – ALEXANDER GRAY

It's a croodit train.
We are aw aff on oor holidays
to Fort William or Arisaig
or Morar or Mallaig
or owre the sea to Skye.

We are traivellin on the West Highland Line.

At Bridge of Orchy
we hae been invadit by a wheen* o maist polite   bunch
older children and their maters and paters
and aunts and uncles and cousins and visiting friends   10
I should guess. Aw are piled hie wi hampers
and bags ticht wi the maist unlikely claes
considerin they're near aw dressed in kilts
– to match their Received English voices no doubt.

Most obviously in 'Scotland'
for the 'Shootin and Fishin'
they swarm aw owre the train lookin for seats
that are no to be had
and makin mair noise than
would hae been thocht possible   20
wi such exaggeratit politeness.

We stop at Rannoch Station
and on the platform a tall, tall, thin, military-lookin man,
wi his lady wife and ghillies* further back.   retainers
He walks wi a bad limp and ae sleeve pinned onto his jaicket
in Nelson style. He walks wi a muckle shepherd's crook
and bent legs wi bony knees showin frae unner his kilt.
A plaid is owre his shoulder and he taks aff
a deerstalker hat
to shout a welcome in stiff-upper-lip voice.   30

He sees his equivalent among the horde
and hirples* furrit wi lang wobbly strides   limps
and haund outstreetched.

Afore they quite meet he shouts in formal nasal tones:

'Welcome to my country.'

Disbuddin

My faither is singin
a tune to himsel
in his gairden.

He's disbuddin
chrysanthemums
to create large
single blooms
he kens he'll ne'er see.

He's near tone deif
but likes hymn tunes   10
rendered wi gusto.

He disnae believe
in God

and has nae answers

but to accept
the disbuddin

wi a sang . . .

Edinburgh Autumn

It is September. There is a haar★   mist
driftin in frae the Forth
gien an air o mystery.
A cauldness in the air owre soon.

The soonds heard blurred.
It is haurd to tell from whaur
they cam. But the mist will clear
if a bite aye in the air

takin us into the beautiful
irony o autumn.   10

Alasdair Gray (1934 –)

Alasdair Gray is one of the most admired of modern Scottish writers, one who has achieved a truly international reputation. Mischievous, astonishingly versatile, learned, perverse, witty, entirely original, Gray is just *sui generis*. Gray's brilliant, bizarre science-fiction novel, *Lanark*, is one of the most amazing achievements in modern fiction. The two short stories which begin the Gray section, 'The Spread of Ian Nicol' and 'The Comedy of the White Dog', share its sometimes chilling oddness, its delight in metamorphosis, and its allegorical bent. *Lanark* itself is represented by 'The Oracle's Tale', a self-standing inset narrative which serves as a bridge between the novel's opening fantasy chapters and the realistic study of Glasgow life which follows. 'Mister Meikle' is an autobiographical sketch, though in the oddly deadpan style that only Alasdair Gray employs.

The Spread of Ian Nicol

One day Ian Nicol, a riveter by trade, started to split in two down the middle. The process began as a bald patch on the back of his head. For a week he kept smearing it with hair restorer, yet it grew bigger, and the surface became curiously puckered and so unpleasant to look upon that at last he went to his doctor. 'What is it?' he asked.

'I don't know,' said the doctor, 'but it looks like a face, ha ha! How do you feel these days?'

'Fine. Sometimes I get a stabbing pain in my chest and stomach but only in the morning.'

'Eating well?'

'Enough for two men.'

The doctor thumped him all over with a stethoscope and said, 'I'm going to have you X-rayed. And I may need to call in a specialist.'

Over the next three weeks the bald patch grew bigger still and the suggestion of a face more clearly marked on it. Ian visited his doctor and found a specialist in the consulting room, examining X-ray plates against the light. 'No doubt about it, Nicol,' said the specialist, 'you are splitting in two down the middle.'

Ian considered this.

'That's not usual, is it?' he asked.

'Oh, it happens more than you would suppose. Among bacteria and viruses it's very common, though it's certainly less frequent among riveters. I suggest you go into hospital where the process can complete itself without annoyance for your wife or embarrassment to yourself. Think it over.'

Ian thought it over and went into hospital where he was put into a small ward and given a nurse to attend him, for the specialist was interested in the case. As the division proceeded more specialists were called in to see what was happening. At first Ian ate and drank with a greed that appalled those who saw it. After consuming three times his normal bulk for three days on end he fell into a coma which lasted till the split was complete. Gradually the lobes of his brain separated and a bone shutter formed between them. The face on the back of his head grew eyelashes and a jaw. What seemed at first a cancer of the heart became another heart. Convulsively the spine doubled itself. In a puzzled way the specialists charted the stages of the process and discussed the cause. A German consultant said that life was freeing itself from the vicissitudes of sexual reproduction. A psychiatrist said it was a form of schizophrenia, a psychoanalyst that it was an ordinary twinning process which had been delayed by a severe case of prenatal sibling rivalry. When the split was complete, two thin Ian Nicols lay together on the bed.

The resentment each felt for the other had not been foreseen or guarded against. In bed the original Ian Nicol could be recognised by his position (he lay on the right side of the bed), but as soon as both men were strong enough to walk each claimed ownership of birth certificate, union card, clothes, wife and National Insurance benefit. One day in the hospital grounds they started fighting. They were evenly matched and there are conflicting opinions about who won. On leaving hospital they took legal action against each other for theft of identity. The case was resolved by a medical examination which showed that one of them had no naval.

The second Ian Nicol changed his name by deed poll and he is now called Macbeth. Sometimes he and Ian Nicol write to each other. The latest news is that each has a bald patch on the back of his head.

The Comedy of the White Dog

On a sunny afternoon two men went by car into the suburbs to the house of a girl called Nan. Neither was much older than twenty years. One of them, Kenneth, was self-confident and well dressed and his friends thought him very witty. He owned and drove the car. The other, Gordon, was more quiet. His clothes were as good as Kenneth's but he inhabited them less easily. He had never been to this girl's house before and felt nervous. An expensive bunch of flowers lay on his lap.

Kenneth stopped the car before a broad-fronted bungalow with a badly kept lawn. The two men had walked halfway up the path to the door when Kenneth stopped and pointed to a dog which lay basking in the grass. It was a small white sturdy dog with a blunt pinkish muzzle and a stumpy tail. It lay with legs stuck out at right angles to its body, its eyes were shut tight and mouth open in a grin through which the tongue lolled. Kenneth and Gordon laughed and Gordon said, 'What's so funny about him?'

Kenneth said, 'He looks like a toy dog knocked over on its side.'

'Is he asleep?'

'Don't fool yourself. He hears every word we say.'

The dog opened its eyes, sneezed and got up. It came over to Gordon and grinned up at him but evaded his hand when he bent down to pat it and trotted up the path and touched the front door with its nose. The door opened and the dog disappeared into a dark hall. Kenneth and Gordon stood on the front step stamping their feet on the mat and clearing their throats. Sounds of female voices and clattering plates came from nearby and the noise of a wireless from elsewhere. Kenneth shouted, 'Ahoi!' and Nan came out of a side door. She was a pleasantfaced blonde who would have seemed plump if her waist, wrists and ankles had not been slender. She wore an apron over a blue frock and held a moist plate in one hand. Kenneth said jocularly, 'The dog opened the door to us.'

'Did he? That was wicked of him. Hullo, Gordon, why, what nice flowers. You're always kind to me. Leave them on the hallstand and I'll put them in water.'

'What sort of dog is he?' said Gordon.

'I'm not sure, but when we were on holiday up at Ardnamurchan the local inhabitants mistook him for a pig.'

A woman's voice shouted, 'Nan! The cake!'

'Oh, I'll have to rush now, I've a cake to ice. Take Gordon into the living room, Kenneth; the others haven't arrived yet so you'll have to entertain each other. Pour yourselves a drink if you like.'

The living room was at the back of the house. The curtains, wallpaper and carpets had bright patterns that didn't harmonise. There was an assortment of chairs and the white dog lay on the most comfortable. There was a big very solid oval table, and a grand piano with two bottles of cider and several tumblers on it. 'I see we're not going to have an orgy anyway,' said Gordon, pouring cider into a tumbler.

'No, no. It's going to be a nice little family party,' said Kenneth, seating himself at the piano and starting to play. He played badly but with confidence, attempting the best known bits of works by Beethoven and Schumann. If he particularly enjoyed a phrase he repeated it until it bored him; if he made a passage illegible with too many dischords he repeated it until it improved. Gordon stood with the tumbler in his hand, looking out the window. It opened on a long narrow lawn which sloped down between hedges to a shrubbery.

'Are you in love with Nan?' said Kenneth, still playing.

'Yes. Mind you, I don't know her well,' said Gordon.

'Hm. She's too matronly for me.'

'I don't think she's matronly.'

'What do you like about her?'

'Most things. I like her calmness. She's got a very calm sort of beauty.'

Kenneth stopped playing and sat looking thoughtful. Voices and clattering dishes could be heard from the kitchen, a telephone was ringing and the noise of a wireless still came loudly from somewhere.

Kenneth said, 'She's calm when she's at home. They're all very nice folk, pleasant and sincere I mean, but you'll find all the women of this family – Nan, her mother and grandmother and aunt – all talk too loudly at the same time. It's never quiet in this house. Either the wireless is on loudly, or the gramophone, or both. I've been to one or two parties here. There are never many guests but I've always felt there are other parties going on in rooms of the house I don't know about. Do you want to marry Nan?'

'Of course. I told you I loved her.'

Kenneth laughed and swung from side to side on the piano stool, making it squeak. He said, 'Don't mistake me – there's nothing disorderly about the house. Nobody drinks anything stronger than cider. Nan's father and brothers are so quiet as to be socially non-existent. You only see them at mealtimes and not always then. In fact I'm not sure how many brothers she has, or how large this family is. What are you grinning at?'

'I wish I could talk like you,' said Gordon. 'You've told me nothing surprising about Nan's family, yet you've made it seem downright sinister.'

Kenneth began to fumble out the tune of 'The Lark in the Clear Air.' 'Anyway,' he said, 'you won't get a chance to be alone with her, which is what you most want, I suppose.'

Nan came in and said, 'Gibson and Clare will be here in half an hour . . . er . . . would you like to have tea in the garden? It's a good day for it. Mum doesn't like the idea much.'

'I think it's a fine idea,' said Kenneth.

'Oh, good. Perhaps you'll help us with the table?'

Gordon and Kenneth took the legs off the table, carried the pieces on to the back lawn and reassembled it, then put chairs round it and helped to set it. While they did so Nan's mother, a small gay woman, kept running out and shouting useless directions: 'Put that cake in the middle, Gordon! No, nearer the top! Did ye need to plant the table so far from the house? You've given yourself a lot of useless work. Well, well, it's a nice day. Where's my dog? Where's my dog? Aha, there he is below the table! Come out, ye bizum! No don't tease him, Kenneth! You'll only drive him mad.'

Gibson and Clare arrived. Gibson was a short thickly built man whose chin always looked swarthy. At first sight he gave a wrong impression of strength and silence, for he was asthmatic and this made his movements slow and deliberate. Though not older than Gordon or Kenneth his hair was getting thin. As soon as he felt at ease in a company he would talk expertly about books, art, politics and anything that was not direct experience. Clare, his girl-friend, was nearly six feet tall and beautiful in a consciously chaste way. Her voice was high-pitched, pure and clear, and she listened to conversation with large wide-open eyes and lustrous lips slightly parted. Her favourite joke was to suspect an indecency in an ordinary remark and to publicise it with a little exclamation and giggle. Kenneth had nicknamed the two Intellect and Spirit. He said there seemed nothing animal between them.

The tea was a pleasant one. Only Nan, her four guests and the dog were present, though. Nan's mother often ran out with a fresh pot of tea or plate of food. The sun was bright, a slight breeze kept the air from being too warm, and Kenneth amused the company by talking about the dog.

'There's something heraldic about him,' he said. 'It's easy to imagine him with another head where his tail is. Look, he's getting excitable! He wants to sit on a chair! Oh, I hope he doesn't choose mine.' The dog had been trotting round the table in a wide circle, now it came toward Kenneth, wagging its tail and grinning. Kenneth grabbed a plate of meringues and got down under the table with them. 'These at least he shall not have!' he cried in a muffled trembling voice. The others laughed, left their chairs and finished the meal sitting on the grass. All but Gordon felt that pleasant drunkenness which comes from being happy in company. Kenneth crawled about the lawn on his knees with a sugar bowl in his hand and when he came to a daisy peered at it benevolently and dropped a small heap of sugar into the flower. Gibson crawled after him, adding drops from the milk jug. Clare sat with the dog on her lap and pretended to cut it up with a knife and fork. Actually she stroked and tickled its stomach gently with the edge of the knife and murmured baby-talk: 'Will I be cruel and eat oo, up doggie? No, no, no, doggie, oo is too sweet a doggie to eat up.' Nan had taken needles and wool from her apron pocket and was quietly knitting and smiling to herself.

Gordon lay nearby pretending to sunbathe. He was worried. He really did not know Nan well. He had only seen her at the homes of friends, and had not even spoken to her much. His invitation to the party had been a surprise. Nan did not know him as well as several other people she might have invited. He had assumed she knew what he felt for her and was giving him a chance to know her better, yet since he arrived she had not paid him any special attention. Now she sat placidly knitting, sometimes glancing sideways at Clare with a slight ironic smile; yet he believed he saw in her manner a secretive awareness of him, lying apart and wanting her.

'Ach, the bitch,' he thought, 'she's sure of me. She thinks she can hurt me all she likes. Well, she's wrong.' He got up, went to the table and started piling the plates together.

'I'll take these indoors,' he said.

'Oh, don't bother,' said Nan, smiling at him lazily.

'Someone will have to shift them,' said Gordon sternly. He took several journeys to carry the table things into the kitchen. It was cool and dim indoors. Nan's father and three of her silent brothers were eating a meal at the kitchen table. They nodded to him. The mother was nowhere to be seen but he heard her voice among several shrill female voices in some other room. Gordon brought in the last table things and put them on the dryingboard of the sink, then stood awkwardly watching the four eaters. They were large men, with stolid, clumsily moulded faces. Some lines on the father's face were deeply cut, otherwise he looked very like his sons. He said to Gordon, 'A warm evening.'

'Yes, I prefer it indoors.'

'Would you like a look at the library?'

'Er, yes, thanks, yes I would.'

The father got up and led Gordon across the hall and down a short passage, opened a door and stood by to let Gordon through. The library had old glass-fronted bookcases on each wall. Between the bookcases hung framed autographed photographs of D. H. Lawrence, Havelock Ellis, H. G. Wells and Bernard Shaw. There was a leather-covered armchair, and a round tin labeled 'Edinburgh Rock' on a low table beside it.

'You've a lot of books,' said Gordon, looking round.

'The wife's people were great readers,' said Nan's father. 'Can I leave you now?'

'Oh yes. Oh yes.'

The father left. Gordon took a book at random from a shelf, sat down and turned the pages casually. It was a history of marine engineering. The library was on the opposite side of the hall from the living room, but its window also looked on to the back garden and sometimes Gordon heard an occasional shout or laugh or bark from those on the lawn. He told himself grimly, 'I'm giving her a chance. If she wants me she can come to me here. In fact if she has ordinary politeness and decency she'll be bound to look for me soon.' He imagined the things she might say and the things he would say back. Sometimes he consoled himself with a piece of rock from the tin.

Suddenly the door sprang open with a click and he saw coming through it towards him, not Nan, but the dog. It stopped in front of him and grinned up into his face. 'What do you want?' said Gordon irritably. The dog wagged its tail. Gordon threw a bit of rock which it caught neatly in its jaws, then trotted out through the door. Gordon got up, slammed the door and sat down. A little later the door opened and the dog entered again. 'Ye brute!' said Gordon. 'Right, here's your sweet; the last you'll get from me.' He escorted the dog to the door, closed it carefully, then pulled the handle hard. The lock held the door tight shut. There was a key in it which he turned to make double certain, then went back to the chair and the book.

After a while it struck him that with the door locked Nan wouldn't get in if she came to him. He glanced uneasily up. The door was open and the dog stood before him, grinning with what seemed, to his stupefied eyes, triumphant amusement. For a moment Gordon was too surprised to move. He noticed that the animal was grinning with its mouth shut, a thing he had never seen a dog do before. He raised the book as if to throw it. 'Grrr, get out!' he yelled. The dog turned jauntily and trotted away. After thinking carefully, Gordon decided some joker must be opening the door from outside to let the dog in. It was the sort of pointless joke Kenneth was fond of. He listened carefully and heard from the lawn the voice of Kenneth and the barking of the dog. He decided to leave the door open.

Later he found it too dark to see the page of the book clearly and put it down. The noises from the lawn had subtly altered. The laughter and shouting were now not continuous. There were periods of silence disturbed by the occasional shuffle of running feet and the hard breathing of somebody pursued, then he would hear a half-cry or scream that did not sound altogether in fun. Gordon went to the window. Something strange was happening on the darkened lawn. Nan was nowhere to be seen. Kenneth, Gibson and Clare were huddled together on the bare table-top, Clare kneeling, Kenneth and Gibson crouching half-erect. The white dog danced in a circle round the table among over-turned chairs. Its activity and size seemed to have increased with the darkness. It glimmered like a sheet in the dusk, its white needle-teeth glittered in the silently laughing jaws, it was about the size of a small lion. Gibson was occupied in a strange way, searching his pockets for objects and hurling them at the shrubbery at the far end of the garden. The white dog would run, leap, catch these in its mouth while they were in air, then return and deposit them under the table. It looked like a game and had possibly begun as one, but obviously Gibson was continuing in an effort to get the dog as far away as possible. Gordon suddenly discovered Nan was beside him, watching, her hands clenched against her mouth.

Gibson seemed to run out of things to throw. Gordon saw him expostulate precariously for a moment with Kenneth, demanding (it appeared) his fountain pen. Kenneth kept shaking his head. He was plainly not as frightened as Gibson or Clare, but a faint embarrassed smile on his face suggested that he was abashed by some monstrous possibility. Gibson put a hand to his mouth, withdrew something, then seemed to reason with Kenneth, who at last shrugged and took it with a distaste which suggested it was a plate of false teeth. Kenneth stood upright and, balancing himself with difficulty, hurled the object at the shrubbery. It was a good throw. The white dog catapulted after it and at once the three jumped from the table and ran to the house, Kenneth going to the right, Gibson and Clare to the left. The dog swerved in an abrupt arc and hurled toward the left. He overtook Clare and snapped the hem of her dress. She stumbled and fell. Gibson and Kenneth disappeared from sight and two doors were slammed in different parts of the house. Clare lay on the lawn, her knees drawn up almost to her chin, her clasped hands pressed between her thighs and her eyes shut. The dog stood over her, grinning happily, then gathered some of the clothing round her waist into its mouth and trotted with her into the bushes of the shrubbery.

Gordon looked at Nan. She had bowed her face into her hands. He put an arm round her waist, she laid her face against his chest and said in a muffled voice, 'Take me away with you.'

'Are you sure of what you're saying?'

'Take me away, Gordon.'

'What about Clare?'

Nan laughed vindictively. 'Clare isn't the one to pity.'

'Yes, but that dog!'

Nan cried out, '*Do you want me or not?*'

As they went through the dark hall, the kitchen door opened, Nan's mother looked out, then shut it quickly. In the front garden they met Kenneth and Gibson, both shamefaced and subdued. Kenneth said, 'Hullo. We were just coming to look for you.'

Gordon said, 'Nan's coming home with me.'

Kenneth said, 'Oh, good.'

They stood for a moment in silence, none of the men looking at each other, then Gibson said, 'I suppose I'd better wait for Clare.' The absence of teeth made him sound senile. Nan cried out, 'She won't want *you* now! She won't want *you* now!' and started weeping again.

'I'll wait all the same,' Gibson muttered. He turned his back on them. 'How long do you think she'll be?' he asked. Nobody answered.

The drive back into the city was quiet. Gordon sat with Nan in the back seat, his arm around her waist, her mourning face against his shoulder. He felt strangely careless and happy. Once Kenneth said, 'An odd sort of evening.' He seemed half willing to discuss it but nobody encouraged him. He put off Gordon and Nan at the close-mouth of the tenement where Gordon lived. They went upstairs to the top landing, Gordon unlocked a door and they crossed a small lobby into a very untidy room. Gordon said, 'I'll sleep on the sofa here. The bedroom's through that door.'

Nan sat on the sofa, smiled sadly and said, 'So I'm not to sleep with you.'

'Not yet. I want you too much to take advantage of a passing mood.'

'You think this is a passing mood.'

'It might be. If it's not I'll see about getting a marriage licence. Are you over eighteen?'

'Yes.'

'That's good. Er . . . do you mind me wanting to marry you, Nan?' Nan got up, embraced him and put her tear-dirty cheek against his. She laughed and said, 'You're very conventional.'

'There's no substitute for legality,' said Gordon, rubbing his brow against hers.

'There's no substitute for impulse,' Nan whispered.

'We'll try and combine the two,' said Gordon. The pressure of her body started to excite him, so he stood apart from her and started making a bed on the sofa.

'If you're willing, tomorrow I'll get a licence.' He had just settled comfortably on the sofa when Nan came to the bedroom door and said, 'Gordon, promise you won't ask me about him.'

'About who?'

'You can't have forgotten him.'

'The dog? Yes, I had forgotten the dog. All right, I won't ask . . . You're sure nothing serious has happened to Clare?'

'Ask her when you see her next!' Nan cried, and slammed the bedroom door.

Next day Gordon bought a marriage licence and an engagement ring and arranged the wedding for a fortnight later. The next two weeks were among the happiest in his life. During the day he worked as an engineering draughtsman. When he came home from work Nan had a good meal ready for him and the apartment clean and tidy. After the meal they would go walking or visit a film show or friends, and later on they would make rather clumsy love, for Gordon was inexperienced and got his most genuine pleasure by keeping the love-making inside definite limits. He wasn't worried much by memories of the white dog. He prided himself on being thoroughly rational, and thought it irrational to feel curious about mysteries. He always refused to discuss things like dreams, ghosts, flying-saucers and religion. 'It doesn't matter if these things are true or not,' he said. 'They are irrelevant to the rules that we have to live by. Mysteries only happen when people try to understand something irrelevant.'

Somebody once pointed out to him that the creation of life was a mystery. 'I know,' he said, 'and it's irrelevant. Why should I worry about how life occurred? If I know how it is just now I know enough.' This attitude allowed him to dismiss his memories of the white dog as irrelevant, especially when he learned that Clare seemed to have come to no harm. She had broken with Gibson and now went about a lot with Kenneth.

One day Nan said, 'Isn't tomorrow the day before the wedding?'

'Yes. What about it?'

'A man and woman aren't supposed to see each other the night before their wedding.'

'I didn't know that.'

'And I thought you were conventional.'

'I know what's legal. I don't much care about conventions.'

'Well, women care more about conventions than they do about laws.'

'Does that mean you want me to spend tomorrow night in a hotel?'

'It's the proper thing, Gordon.'

'You weren't so proper on the night I brought you here.'

Nan said quietly, 'It's not fair to remind me of that night.'

'I'm sorry,' said Gordon. 'No, it's not fair. I'll go to a hotel.'

Next evening he booked a room in a hotel and then, since it was only ten o'clock, went to a coffee bar where he thought he might see some friends. Inside Clare and Kenneth were sitting at a table with a lean young man whom Gordon had not seen before. Clare smiled and beckoned. She had lost her former self-conscious grace and looked an adult very attractive girl. As Gordon approached Kenneth stopped talking to the stranger, stood up, gripped Gordon's hand and shook it with unnecessary enthusiasm. 'Gordon! Gordon!' said Kenneth. 'You must meet Mr McIver. (Clare and I are just leaving.) Mr McIver, this is the man I told you about, the only man in Scotland who can help you. Goodnight! Goodnight! Clare and I mustn't intrude on your conversation. You have a lot to discuss.' He rushed out, pulling Clare after him and chuckling.

Gordon and the stranger looked at each other with embarrassment.

'Won't you sit down?' said Mr McIver, in a polite North American voice. Gordon sat down and said, 'Are you from the States, Mr McIver?'

'No, from Canada. I'm visiting Europe on a scholarship. I'm collecting material for my thesis upon the white dog. Your friend tells me you are an authority on the subject.'

Gordon said abruptly, 'What has Kenneth told you about the dog?'

'Nothing. But he said you could tell me a great deal.'

'He was joking.'

'I'm sorry to hear that.'

Gordon stood up to go, sat down again, hesitated and said, 'What is this white dog?'

McIver answered in the tone of someone starting a lecture: 'Well known references to the white dog occur in Ovid's "Metamorphoses", in Chaucer's unfinished "Cook's Tale", in the picaresque novels of the Basque poet Jose Mompou, and in your Scottish Border Ballads. Nonetheless, the white dog is the most neglected of European archetypes, and for that reason perhaps, one of the most significant. I can only account for this neglect by assuming a subconscious resistance in the minds of previous students of folk-lore, a resistance springing from the fact that the white dog is the west-European equivalent of the Oedipus myth.'

'That's all just words,' said Gordon. 'What does the dog do?'

'Well, he's usually associated with sexually frigid women. Sometimes it is suggested they are frigid because they have been dedicated to the love of the dog from birth . . . '

'Dedicated by who?'

'In certain romance legends by the priest at the baptismal font, with or without the consent of the girl's parents. More often the frigidity is the result of the girl's choice. A girl meets an old woman in a lonely place who gives her various gifts, withholding one on which the girl's heart is set. The price of the gift is that she consents to marry the old woman's son. If she accepts the gift (it is usually an object of no value) she becomes frigid until the white dog claims her. The old woman is the dog's mother. In these versions of the legend the dog is regarded as a malignant spirit.'

'How can he be other than malignant?'

'In Sicily the dog is thought of as a benefactor of frigid or sterile women. If the dog can be induced to sleep with such a woman and she submits to him she will become capable of normal fruitful intercourse with a man. There is always a condition attached to this. The dog must always be, to a certain extent, the husband of the woman. Even if she marries a human man, the dog can claim her whenever he wants.'

'Oh God,' said Gordon.

'There's nothing horrible about it,' said McIver. 'In one of Jose Mompou's novels the hero encounters a brigand chieftain whose wife is also married to the dog. The dog and the chieftain are friends, the dog accepts the status of pet in the household, sleeping by the fire, licking the plates clean et cetera, even though he is the ghostly husband of several girls in the district. By his patronage of the house in this ostensibly servile capacity, he brings the brigand luck. His presence is not at all resented, even though he sometimes sleeps with the brigand's daughters. To have been loved by the dog makes a woman more attractive to normal men, you see, and the dog is never jealous. When one of his women marries he only sleeps with her often enough to assert his claim on her.'

'How often is that?'

'Once a year. He sleeps with her on the night before the wedding and on each anniversary of that night. Say, how are you feeling? You look terrible.'

Gordon went into the street too full of horror and doubt to think clearly. 'To be compared with a dog! To be measured against a dog! Oh no, God, Nan wouldn't do that! No, it would be wicked, Nan isn't so wicked!' He found he was gibbering these words and running as fast as possible home. He stopped, looked at his watch, then forced himself to walk slowly. He arrived home about midnight, went through the close to the back court and looked up at the bedroom window. The light was out. He tiptoed upstairs and paused at the front door. The door looked so much the same as usual that he felt nothing wrong could be behind it; he could still return to the hotel, but while he considered this his hand was stealthily putting the key in the lock. He went softly into the living room, hesitated outside the bedroom door, then opened it quickly. He heard a gasp and Nan shrieked, 'Gordon!'

'Yes,' said Gordon.

'Don't put the light on!'

He switched the light on. Nan sat up in bed blinking at him fearfully, her hands pressed protectively on a mound between her legs under the tumbled bedclothes. Gordon stepped forward, gripped the edge of the bedclothes and tugged. 'Let go!' he said.

She stared at him, her face white with terror, and whispered, 'Go away!' He struck her face and she fell back on the pillows; he snatched away the bed clothes and the white dog sprang from between the sheets and danced on them, grinning. Gordon grabbed at the beast's throat. With an easy squirming movement it evaded his hand, then bit it. Gordon felt the small needle-teeth sink between his finger bones and suddenly became icy cold. He sat on the edge of the bed and stared at the numb bitten hand still gripped between the dog's grinning jaws: its pink little eyes seemed to wink at him.

With a great yell, he seized the beast's hind leg with his free hand, sprang up and swung its whole body against the wall. Nan screamed. He felt its head crush with the impact, swung and battered it twice more on the wall, leaving a jammy red stain each time, then he flung the body into a corner and sat down on the edge of the bed and stared at his bitten hand. The sharp little teeth seemed to have gone in without piercing any veins or arteries, for the only mark on the skin was a V-shaped line of grey punctures. He stared across at the smash-headed carcase. He found it hard to believe he had killed it. *Could* such a creature be killed? He got to his feet with difficulty, for he felt unwell, and went to the thing. It was certainly dead. He opened the window, picked the dog up by the tail and flung it down into the back court, then went over to the bed where Nan lay, gazing at him with horror. He began to undress as well as he could without the use of the numbed right hand. 'So, my dear,' he muttered, 'you prefer convention.'

She cried out, 'You shouldn't have come back tonight! We would all have been happy if you hadn't come back tonight!'

'Just so,' said Gordon, getting in bed with her.

'Don't touch me!'

'Oh yes, I'll touch you.'

Toward morning Gordon woke, feeling wonderfully happy. Nan's arms clasped him, yet he felt more free than ever before. With a little gleeful yelp he sprang from the nest of warmth made by her body and skipped upon the quilt. Nan opened her eyes lazily to him, then sat up and kissed his muzzle. He looked at her with jovial contempt, then jumped on to the floor and trotted out of the house, the shut doors springing open at the touch of his nose. He ran downstairs into the sunlit street, his mouth hanging open in a grin of sheer gaiety. He would never again be bound by dull laws.

The Oracle's Tale

This is an inset tale from the novel, *Lanark*. The central character, Lanark, who has lived for some time in the bizarre, futuristic country called 'Unthank' without knowing who he is or how he got there, has asked the 'Archives' to give him this information, and has been referred to a bodiless voice called the Oracle. The Oracle agrees to tell him his history. Lanark then asks, 'But how do you know this? Who are you anyway?' The following is the answer he gets. The lines in boldface are Gray's headers for the individual pages. This editor has kept them in the places they occupied in the original text. As here, they do not interrupt the sentences of the tale itself.

A Bleak Man Tells Why He Likes Bleakness

From an early age I only wanted to deal with what I was sure of and like all thinkers I soon came to distrust what could only be seen and touched. The majority believe that floors, ceilings, each other's bodies, the sun, etc. are the surest things in the world, but soon after going to school I saw that everything was untrustworthy when compared with numbers. Take the simplest kind of number, a telephone number, 339-6286 for example. It exists outside us for we find it in a directory, but we can carry it in our heads precisely as it is, for the number and our idea of it are identical. Compared with his phone number our closest friend is shifty and treacherous. He certainly exists outside us, and since we remember him he also, in a feeble way, exists in our heads, but experience shows that our idea of the man is only slightly like him. No matter how well we know him, how often we meet him, how conservative his habits, he will constantly insult our notion of him by wearing new clothes, changing his mind, growing old or sick or even dying. Moreover, my idea of a man is never the same as someone else's. Most quarrels come from conflicting ideas of a man's character but nobody fights over his phone number, and if we were content to describe each other numerically, giving height, weight, date of birth, size of family, home address, business address and (most informative of all) annual income, we would see that below the jangling opinions was no disagreement on the main realities.

On leaving school my teachers suggested a career in physics, but I rejected the idea. Science certainly controls the physical world by describing it mathematically, but I have already mentioned my distrust of physical things. They are too remote from the mind. I chose to live by those numbers which are most purely a product of the mind and therefore influence it most strongly: in a word, money. I became an accountant, and later a stockbroker. It puzzles me that people who live by owning or managing big sums of money are commonly called materialistic, for finance is the most purely intellectual, the most sheerly spiritual of activities, being concerned less with material objects than with values. Of course finance needs objects, since money is the value of objects and could no more exist without them than mind can exist without body, but the objects come second. If you doubt this, think which you would rather own: fifty thousand pounds or a piece of land valued at fifty thousand pounds. The only people likely to prefer the

It Seems a Strength but Proves a Weakness

land are financiers who know how to increase its value by renting or reselling, so either answer proves that money is preferable to things. Perhaps you will say that in some circumstances a millionaire would give his wealth for a cup of water, but these circumstances happen more in arguments than in life, and a better indication of how folk regard money is the instinctive reverence which all but ignorant savages feel toward the rich. Many deny this, but introduce them to a really wealthy man and see how unable they are to treat him casually.

I was thirty-five when I became really wealthy, but long before then I was living in a service flat, driving a Humber, playing golf at weekends and bridge in the evenings. People who did not understand financial reports thought my life a dull one: they could not see the steep determined climb from one level of prosperity to the next, the excitement of the barely avoided loss, the triumph of the suddenly realized profit. This adventure was purely emotional, for I was physically secure. I feared the greed of the working classes and the incompetence of governments, but only because they threatened some of the numbers in my accounts; I did not feel in danger of hunger or cold. My acquaintances lived like myself in the world of numbers rather than the muddle of seeable, touchable things which used to be called reality, but they had wives, which meant that as they grew richer they had to move into bigger houses and buy new cars and reproduction antique cocktail cabinets. These things naturally occurred in their conversation, but I also heard them gloat on other objects with an enthusiasm which seemed greater the more useless the object was.

'I see the daffodils are with us again,' they would say, or 'My God! Harrison has shaved his moustache off.' Where I saw a leaf they saw a 'lovely green' leaf. Where I saw a new power station they saw 'technological progress' or 'industry ravaging the countryside.'

Once at a party a couple started fighting. I was explaining something to a client and the noise made me raise my voice, but the other guests were greatly excited and began whispering and spitting adjectives: 'disgraceful,' 'pathetic,' 'ludicrous,' 'distressing,' 'inconsiderate.' I saw that most people had excessive funds of emotion which they got rid of by investing in objects they could not use. I had no excess emotion, my work absorbed it all, but now I know that these casual investments showed a profit. Like vain women, the objects postured before their admirers in light and colours

I was never allowed to see. They showed me just enough of themselves to let me know they existed. And one day they began to stop doing even that.

I was studying a document when my attention was nagged by some difference outside the printed paper. I examined the top of my desk. It had been polished wood with a slightly rippled grain, but now the grain had vanished and the surface was as blank as a sheet of plastic. I looked round the office, which was furnished in the modern manner for I detested fussy details. The white walls and plain carpet were as usual but the view through the window had altered. What had been a typical street in the business centre of an old-fashioned industrial city, a street of elaborately carved and pillared facades, was now bordered by blank surfaces punctured by rectangular holes. I saw at once what was happening. Not content with showing itself in poorer materials than it kept for others, reality was economizing further. Where I had once seen irrelevant details and colours I saw none at all. Stone, wood and patterned surfaces became plain surfaces. The weaves of cloths were indistinguishable, and all doors looked flush-paneled.

Yet I did not feel ill-treated, for there was still enough outer reality for me to work with and in some ways I could work better. On entering a room of employees before this I usually had to look at several before recognizing the one I wanted, which wasted time, especially if I felt obliged to smile or nod at the men I noticed first. Now, when I entered a room, everyone but the man I wanted was as faceless as an egg, so I knew him at once. And later I only saw the man I wanted – nobody else was visible, unless they were slacking or wanted to speak to me, in which case they displayed enough substance to let me deal with them.

You may wonder why I never collided with those surrounding me. Well, in my office it was other people's business to keep out of my way, and when driving there I noticed traffic signs and adjacent vehicles, though pedestrians and scenery were invisible. But one day I parked the car in the usual side street, opened the door to walk to the office and could see neither street nor pavement, just a clear general greyness, and leading through it to the dim silhouette of my office (there were no other buildings) a line of solid, pavement-coloured stepping stones, each the size and shape of the sole of my shoe. I could only leave the car by walking along these; each vanished as I took my weight

There's Nothing to Fall Back Upon

from it; I had spasms of vertigo and was in terror of what would happen if I stepped *between* the stones. On reaching the office doorstep (which was completely visible) I squatted and moved the palm of my hand experimentally down into the emptiness. A piece of pavement the shape of the hand appeared underneath it. Simultaneously three clerks solidified round me, asking if I felt unwell. I pretended, not convincingly, to tie a shoelace.

Later I sat on a swivel chair above fathoms of emptiness, grey emptiness all around except where, six feet to the right, a pencil moving on its point across an angled notepad showed where my secretary was taking down the words I dictated to her. My right hand felt as if it rested on my knee, but I could see nothing but the dial of the wristwatch. At half-past five a line of carpet-coloured stepping stones appeared which released me from the chair, but walking on them was hard for I could no longer see my feet, and when I reached the end, instead of the linoleum-coloured stepping stones of the lift floor I saw nothing: the emptiness before and behind was total and complete. I saw nothing, heard nothing and felt nothing but the soles of my feet pressing the floor under them. Suddenly I was too tired and angry to continue. I stepped forward and nothing happened, except that the pressure on my feet vanished. I neither fell nor floated. I had become bodiless in a bodiless world. I existed as a series of thoughts amidst infinite greyness.

At first I was greatly relieved. I have never been afraid of loneliness, and the previous days had been more of a strain than I had let myself believe. I slept almost at once, which means that I stopped thinking and the surrounding greyness went black. After a while it grew light again and for the first time in my life I was idle. Every life has blank moments when we stand waiting for a bus or a friend and there's nothing to do but think. In the past I had filled these moments by calculating how an unexpected war or election would affect the wealth entrusted to me, but I had no zest for calculation now. Money, even imaginary money, needs the future to give it force. Without future it is not even ink in a ledger, paper in a purse. The future had gone with my body. There was nothing to do but remember, and I was depressed to find that the work which had given my life a goal and a decent order now looked like an arithmetical brain disease, a profit-and-loss calculation lasting years and proving nothing. My memory

Returning to His Sensual Birth

was a catalogue of things I had ignored and devalued. I had enjoyed no definite friendship or love, no intense hatred or desire; my life had been stony soil in which only numbers grew, and now I could do nothing but sift the stones and hope one or two would turn out to be jewels. I was the loneliest and most impotent man in the world. I was about to turn desperate when a lovely thing appeared in the air before me.

It was a cream-coloured wall patterned with brownish-pink roses. A beam of early morning summer sunlight shone on it and on me. I was sitting in bed with the wall on one side and two chairs on the other. It seemed a very big bed, though it was an ordinary single one, and two chairs had been placed to stop my falling out. My legs were covered by a quilt on which lay a tobacco pipe with a broken stem, a small slipper and a book with bright cloth pages. I was perfectly happy and singing a song on one note: *ooloolooooloo*. When tired of that I sang *dadadadada* for I had discovered the difference between *loo* and *da* and was interested in it.

Later still, having tired of singing, I took the slipper and thumped the wall until my mother came. Each morning she lay in bed with a thin solemn young man on the other side of the roses. Her warmth reached me through the wall so I was never cold or lonely. I don't suppose my mother was unnaturally tall but she seemed twice the size of anyone else, and brown-haired, and regally slender above the hips. Below the hips she changed a lot, being often pregnant. I remember seeing her upper body rising behind the curve of her stomach like a giantess half-hidden by the horizon of a calm sea. I remember sitting on that curve with the back of my head between her breasts, knowing her face was somewhere above and feeling very sure of myself.

I can't remember her features at all. Light or darkness came from them according to her mood, and I am certain this was more than the fantasy of a small child. I remember her sitting very still in a room of chattering strangers and steadily reducing them to whispers by the sullen silent fury she radiated. Her good moods were equally radiant and made the dullest company feel gallant and glamorous. She was never happy or depressed, she was glorious or sombre, and very attractive to modest dependable men. The men I called father were all of that kind. Apart from loving her they had no peculiarities. She must have attracted them like an extravagant vice for she was a poor housekeeper; on coming to live with a man she tried to prepare meals and keep things tidy, but the effort soon waned. I think the first house

A Splendid Body Gives Him Worth

I remember was the happiest because it had only two small rooms and my first father was not fastidious. I believe he was a garage mechanic, for there was a car engine beside my bed and some huge tires under the recess bed in the kitchen. As I grew older my mother was less ready to come when I thumped the wall, so I learned to crawl or stagger to the bed next door and be pulled in. She would lie reading newspapers and smoking cigarettes while my father made a hill under the blankets with his knees and suddenly flattened it when I had climbed on top. Later he would rise and bring us a breakfast of tea and fried bread and eggs.

The house was in a tenement with a narrow, busy street in front and a cracked asphalt yard at the back. Behind the yard was the embankment of a canal, and on sunny days my mother dragged me up this by straps fastened to a harness round my chest and we made a nest in the long grass beside the mossy towpath. The canal was choked with rushes and leafy weeds; nobody passed by but an old man with a greyhound or boys who should have been at school. I played with the tobacco pipe and my slipper, pretending I was my mother and the pipe me and the slipper my bed, or pretending the slipper was a car with the pipe driving.

She read or daydreamed as she did at home, and I know now that her power came from these dreams, for where else could an almost silent woman without abilities learn the glamour of an enslaved princess, the authority of an exiled queen?

The place where we lay was level with our kitchen window, and when my father returned from work he would prepare a meal and call us in to eat it. He seemed a contented man, and I am sure the quarrels were not his fault. One night I was wakened by noise from the dark wall at my ear, my mother's voice beating like high waves over protesting mutters. The noise stopped and she entered the room and lay with me and hugged me hungrily. This happened several times, filling the nights with anticipation and delight and leaving me stupefied all day, for her thundering kisses exploded like fireworks in my ears and for long spells annihilated thought entirely. So I hardly noticed when she dressed me, and packed a suitcase, and took me away from that house. I don t remember if we travelled by train or bus, I only remember that as night fell we walked along a track between trees whose high branches crashed together in the wind, and the track brought us to a farmhouse where we lived for over a year. My sister was born soon after we arrived.

A Reckless Body Gives Him Worth

My mother's ominous attraction is shown by the fact that even in a visible state of pregnancy, with a two-year-old son, she was employed as a housekeeper by a thrifty farmer whose wife had died. For the first few weeks I was happy. We slept together in a small low-ceilinged room at the back of the house and ate by ourselves. I remember us sitting furtively in a corner of the cosy parlor while the farmer and his children dined before the fire. My mother was singing softly in my ear:

> 'Wee chooky birdy, tol-lol-lol
> laid an egg on the window sol.
> The window sol
> began to crack,
> Wee chooky bird roared and grat.'

Soon afterward we all began eating together and I slept in the little low room by myself. My mother spent most of the time in an upstairs room I could never visit and an old woman came each day to do the housework. I believe the old woman was first employed as temporary help while the baby was born, but she was still cleaning the house and making meals many months later, and carrying eggs and toast upstairs on a tray while the farmer, his children, and I breakfasted on porridge at the kitchen table.

All my memories of the farm have eggs in them. When exploring the barnyard one day I found a great cluster of brown eggs in a clump of nettles behind an old cart. It was a surprising sight, for our eggs usually came from wooden hen houses in a nearby field. I trotted into the kitchen to tell someone. The farmer was there, and he explained that hens sometimes laid astray in an effort to get their eggs hatched instead of eaten. I led him to the eggs; he gathered them in his cap, praised me and gave me a peppermint. Whenever I felt lonely after that I would crawl into a hen house through one of the tiny doors the hens used, steal an egg from under a sitting fowl and go to the stackyard or byre and pretend to find it under hay or among the cowcake. Then I took it to the farmer, who always patted my head and gave me a peppermint. I think he must have known where I got the other eggs, but it was friendly of him to pretend otherwise. He probably liked me.

His children did not. There was a garden of tangled grass and stunted fruit trees behind the house, and on warm summer evenings I played there, building nests in the ivy round my bedroom window. One evening the farmer's daughter came and said, 'What do you think you're doing?'

She may have been less than twelve but she seemed a grown woman to me. I said I was making a nest for a bird to lay an egg in. She said, 'A wee chooky birdy? That's daft. And where did you get the straw?'

I said, 'On the ground in the yard.'

'Then it belongs to my daddy and you stole it so put it back there.'

Since I continued building she gripped and twisted my wrists until I kicked her ankle, then she went off screaming she would tell my mother and I would be sent away. I ran crying to the hen house field, squeezed through a hen door on hands and knees and squatted in a corner of the grain-sprinkled floor till it grew dark. I meant to starve to death there but I heard my mother distantly calling, sometimes nearer and sometimes farther, and at last I felt that the misery in her breast and the misery in mine were the same thing. I squeezed through the door and moved among the black hen houses under a high ceiling of stars. An owl was hooting. Suddenly I found her and wrapped my arms round her big stomach and she was kind to me. A few nights later I was wakened by a great uproar and she entered the room and climbed into bed. This was less pleasant than it had been in town, for she brought my sister and the bed was overcrowded. The loving heat she baked me in was still deliriously exciting, but my mind was now too strong to be unmade by it. I was worried, because I liked the farm in some ways. A week later the farmer took us in his pony cart to a railway station, gave me a bag of peppermints and left us on the platform without saying a word.

I understand my mother now. She expected splendour. Most of us expect it sometime or other, and growing old is mainly a way of learning to do without. My mother could never learn to do without so she kept altering her life in the only way she knew, by shifting to other men. She shifted when pregnant because pregnancy made her more hopeful than usual, or because she feared that bearing a child when living with the father would fix her to one man forever. If this is so then I never saw my real father. The third substitute was a bank manager who lived with his widowed sister in a mansion in a small fishing port. He was a gentle, dismal, kindly man; she was an abrupt, unhappy, slightly acid woman, and my mother

Can Lanark Lead Him Out of Hell?

(with a four-year-old son, one-year-old daughter, five-month old embryo) charmed and dominated both of them. But three is the smallest number that can make a series, and she no longer dominated me. Perhaps she no longer wanted to. At any rate, when she moved on I was left with the bank manager. My life became calm and dependable. I went to school, was good at lessons, and every evening the manager and his sister developed my powers of concentration by playing three-handed bridge with me, for small stakes, from half-past six till bedtime. That was how I learned to dread the body and love numbers.

Having relived these memories I saw that the path from sunlit roses to the grey void had been inevitable, yet I was not content. I was appalled at having nothing to do but remember a life like that. I wanted madness to blot out the memories with the strong tones and colours of a delusion, however monstrous. I had a romantic notion that madness was an exit from unbearable existence. But madness is like cancer or bronchitis, not everyone is capable of it, and when most of us say, 'I can't bear this,' we are proving we can. Death is the only dependable exit, but death depends on the body and I had rejected the body. I was condemned to a future of replaying and replaying the tedious past and past and past and past. I was in hell. Without eyes I tried to weep, without lips to scream, and with all the force of my neglected heart I cried for help.

I was answered. A sullen, determined voice – your voice – asked me to describe *his* past. My experience of void had made me able to visualize things from very slight cues, and that voice let me see you as you were. From the pebble and shell in your hands I deduced the shore where you grasped them, and from the shore I saw a path stretching back through mountains and cities to the house where you were born. You know now why I am an oracle. By describing your life I will escape from the trap of my own. From my station in nonentity everything existent, everything *not me*, looks worthwhile and splendid: even things which most folk consider commonplace or dreadful. Your past is safe with me. I can promise to be accurate.

Mister Meikle – An Epilogue

At the age of five I was confined to a room made and furnished by people I had never met and who had never heard of me. Here, in a crowd of nearly forty strangers, I remained six hours a day and five days a week for many years, being ordered about by a much bigger, older stranger who found me no more interesting than the rest. Luckily the prison was well stocked with pencils and our warder (a woman) wanted us to use them. One day she asked us what we thought were good things to write poems about. The four or five with opinions on the matter (I was one of them) called out suggestions which she wrote down on the blackboard:

> A FAIRY
> A MUSHROOM
> SOME GRASS
> PINE NEEDLES
> A TINY STONE

We thought these things poetic because the verses in our school-books mostly dealt with such small, innocuous items. The teacher now asked everyone in the class to write their own verses about one or more of these items. With ease, speed and hardly any intelligent thought I wrote this:

> A fairy on a mushroom,
> sewing with some grass,
> and a pine-tree needle,
> for the time to pass.
> Soon the grass it withered,
> The needle broke away,
> She sat down on a tiny stone,
> And wept for half the day.

The teacher read this aloud to the class, pointing out that I had not only used every item on the list, I had used them in the order of listing. While writing the verses I had been excited by my mastery of the materials. I now felt extraordinarily interesting. Most people become writers by degrees. From me, in an instant, all effort to become anything else dropped like a discarded overcoat. I never abandoned verse but came to spend more time writing prose – small harmless items interested me less than prehistoric monsters, Roman arenas, volcanoes, cruel queens and life on other planets. I aimed to write a novel in which all these would be met and dominated by me, a boy from Glasgow. I wanted to get it written and published when I was twelve, but failed. Each time I wrote some opening sentences I saw they were the work of a child. The only works I managed to finish were short compositions on subjects set by the teacher. She was not the international audience I wanted, but better than nobody.

At the age of twelve I entered Whitehill Senior Secondary School, a plain late 19th-century building of the same height and red sandstone as adjacent tenements, but more menacing. The playgrounds were walled and fenced like prison exercise yards; the windows, though huge, were disproportionately narrow, with sills deliberately designed to be far above our heads when we sat down. Half of what we studied there impressed me as gloomily as the building. Instead of one teacher I had eight a week, often six a day, and half of them treated me as an obstinate idiot. They had to treat me as an idiot. Compound interest, sines, cosines, Latin declensions, tables of elements tasted to my mind like sawdust in my mouth: those who dished it out expected me to swallow while an almost bodily instinct urged me to vomit.

I did neither. My body put on an obedient, hypocritical act while my mind dodged out through imaginary doors. In this I was like many other schoolboys, perhaps most others. Nearly all of us kept magazines of popular adventure serials under our school books and when possible stuck our faces into *The Rover*, *Hotspur*, *Wizard* and highly coloured American comics, then new to Britain, in which the proportion of print to pictorial matter was astonishingly small. Only the extent of my addiction to fictional worlds was worse than normal, being magnified into mania by inability to enjoy much else. I was too clumsily fearful to enjoy football and mix with girls, though women and brave actions were what I most wanted. Since poems, plays and novels often deal with these I easily swallowed the fictions urged on us by the teachers of English, though the authors (Chaucer, Shakespeare, Jane Austin, Walter Scott) were far less easily digested than *The Rover* et cetera.

Mr Meikle was my English teacher and managed the school magazine. I met him when I was thirteen. He became my first editor and publisher, and a year or two later, by putting me in charge of the magazine's literary and artistic pages, enabled me to edit and publish myself. There must have been times when he gave me advice and directions, but these were offered so tactfully that I cannot remember them: I was only aware of freedom and opportunity. Quiet courtesy, sympathy and knowledge are chiefly what I recall of him, and a theatricality so mild that few of us saw it as such, though it probably eased his dealings with those inclined to mistake politeness for weakness. I will try to describe him more exactly.

His lined triangular face above a tall thin body, his black academic gown, thin dark moustache, dark eyebrows and smooth reddish hair gave him a pleasantly saturnine look, especially as the carefully brushed-back hair emphasized two horn-shaped bald patches, one on each side of his brow. While the class worked quietly at a writing exercise he would sit marking homework at his tall narrow desk, and sometimes one of his eyebrows would shoot up into a ferociously steep question mark, then sink to a level line again while the other eyebrow shot up.

This suggested he had read something terrible in the page before him, but was now trying to understand the writer's frame of mind. Such small performances always caused a faint stir of amusement among the few who saw them, a stir he gave no sign of noticing. Sometimes, wishing to make my own eyebrows act independently, I held one down with a hand and violently worked the other, but I never managed it. Outside the classroom Mr Meikle smoked a meerschaum pipe. He conducted one of the school choirs which competed in the Glasgow music festivals. His slight theatrical touches had nothing to do with egotism. As he paced up and down the corridors between our desks and talked about literature he was far more interested in the language of Shakespeare, and what Milton learned from it, and what Dryden learned from Milton, and what Pope learned from Dryden, than in himself.

Not everyone liked Mr Meikle's teaching. He did not stimulate debates about what Shakespeare or Pope said, he simply replied to any question we raised about these, explained alternative readings, said why he preferred one of them and went on talking. Nor did he dictate to us glib little phrases which, repeated in an essay, would show an examiner that the student had been driven over the usual hurdles. He let us scribble down what we liked in our English note-books. This style of teaching seemed to some as dull as I found the table of elements, but it just suited me.

While he told us, with erudition and humour, the official story of English literature, I filled note-book after note-book with doodles recalling the fictions I had discovered at the local cinemas, on my parents' bookshelves, in the local library. I was not ignoring Mr Meikle. While sketching doors and corridors into the worlds of Walt Disney, Tarzan, Hans Andersen, Edgar Allan Poe, Lewis Carroll and H G Wells I was pleased to hear how the writers of

Hamlet, *Paradise Lost*, *The Rape of the Lock* and *Little Dorrit* had invented worlds which were just as spooky. I was still planning a book containing all I valued in other works, but one of these works was beginning to be Glasgow. I had begun to think my family, neighbours, friends, the girls I could not get hold of were as interesting as any people in fiction – almost as interesting as me, but how could I show it? Joyce's *Portrait of the Artist as a Young Man* suggested a way, but I doubted if I could write such a book before I was seventeen. Meanwhile Mr Meikle's voice often absorbed my whole attention. I remember especially his demonstration of the rhetorical shifts by which Mark Anthony in *Julius Caesar* changes the mind of the mob.

My private talks with Mr Meikle took place before the class but out of its earshot. We could talk quietly because my head, as I stood beside his desk, was level with his as he sat leaning on it. I remember telling him something about my writing ambitions and adding that, while I found helpful suggestions in his teaching and in the music, history and art classes, the rest of my schooling was a painful hindrance, a humiliating waste of time for both me and my teachers.

Mr Meikle answered that Scottish education was not designed to produce specialists before the age of eighteen. Students of science and engineering needed a grounding in English before a Scottish university accepted them, arts students needed a basis of maths, both had to know Latin and he thought this wise. Latin was the language of people who had made European culture by combining the religious books of the Jews with the sciences and arts of the skeptical Greeks. Great writers in every European language had been inspired by Roman literature; Shakespeare only knew a little Latin but his plays showed he put the little he knew to very good use. Again, mathematics were also a language, an exact way of describing mental and physical events which created our science and industry. No writer who wished to understand the modern world should ignore it.

I answered that Latin and maths were not taught like languages through which we could discover and say great things, they were taught as ways to pass examinations – that was how parents and pupils and most of the teachers viewed them; whenever I complained about the boring nature of a Latin or mathematical exercise nobody explained there could be pleasure in it, they said, 'You can forget all that when you've been through university and got a steady job.' Mr Meikle looked thoughtfully across the bent heads of the class before him, and after a pause said he hoped I would be happy in what I wished to do with my life, but most people, when their education stopped, earned their bread by work which gave them very little personal satisfaction, but must be done properly simply because their employers required it and our society depended upon it. Schooling had to prepare the majority for their future, as well as the lucky few. He spoke with a resignation and regret I only fully understood eight or nine years later when I earned my own bread, for a while, by school-teaching.

This discussion impressed and disturbed me. Education – schooling – was admired by my parents and praised by the vocal part of Scottish culture as a way to get liberty, independence and a more useful and satisfying life. Since this was my own view also, I had thought the parts of my schooling which felt like slavery were accidents which better organisation would abolish. That the parts which felt like slavery were a deliberate preparation for more serfdom – that our schooling was simultaneously freeing some while preparing the rest to be their tools – had not occurred to me.

The book I at last wrote described the adventures of someone a bit like me in a world like that, and though not an autobiography (my hero goes mad and commits suicide at the age of twenty-two) it contained portraits of people I had known, Mr Meikle among them. While writing the pages where he appeared I considered several pseudonyms for him. (Strang? Craig? McGurk? Maclehose? Dinwiddie?) but the only name which seemed to suit him was Meikle, so at last I called him that. I was forty-five when the book got published and did not know if he was still alive, but thought he would be amused and perhaps pleased if he read it.

And he was alive, and read it, and was pleased. He came to my book-signing session at Smith's in St Vincent Street, and said so. It was wonderful to see him again, as real as ever despite being a character in my book. Of course his hair was grey now, his scalp much balder, but my head was greying and balding too. I realized he had been a fairly young man when I first saw him in Whitehill, much younger than I was now.

Three years ago I got a note from Mr Meikle saying he could not come to the signing session for my latest novel, as arthritis had confined him to his home. He had ordered a copy from the bookshop, and hoped I would sign it for him, and either leave it to be collected by Mrs Meikle (who was still in good health) or bring it to him myself.

I phoned and told him I could not bring it, as I was going away for a month immediately after the signing session, but I would inscribe a copy for Mrs Meikle to collect, and would phone to arrange a visit as soon as I returned. He said he looked forward to that.

I went away and tried to finish writing a book I had promised to a publisher years before. I failed, came home a month later and did not phone Mr Meikle. He was now one of many I had broken promises to, felt guilty about, wanted to forget. When forgetting was impossible I lay in bed remembering work to be finished, debts to be paid, letters to write, phone-calls and visits I should make. I ought also to get my false teeth mended, tidy my flat and clean the window facing my door on the communal landing. All these matters seemed urgent and I often fell asleep during efforts to list them in order of priority. Action only seemed possible when I jumped up to fend off an immediate disaster, which Mr Meikle was not.

Suddenly I decided to visit him without phoning. It seemed the only way. The sun had set, the street-lights shone, I was sure he was not yet abed, so the season must have been late in the year or very early. The close where he lived was unusually busy. A smart woman holding a clipboard came down and I was pressed to the wall by a bearded man rushing up. He carried on his shoulders what seemed a telescope in a felt sock. I noticed electrical cables on the stairs, and on a landing a stack of the metal tripods used with lighting equipment. None of this surprised me. Film making is as common in Glasgow as in other cities, though I did not think it concerned Mr Meikle.

It did. His front door stood open and the cables snaked through it. The lobby was full of recording people and camera people who seemed waiting for something, and I saw from behind a lady who might have been Mrs Meikle carrying round a tray loaded with mugs of coffee. Clearly, a visit at this time would be an interruption. I went back downstairs regretting I had not phoned first, but glad the world was not neglecting Mr Meikle. I even felt slightly jealous of him.

A while after this abortive visit I entered a public house, bought a drink and sat beside a friend who was talking to a stranger. The friend said, 'I don't think you two know each other,' and introduced the stranger as a sound technician with the British Broadcasting Corporation. The stranger stared hard at me and said, 'You may not know me but I know you. You arranged for a whole BBC camera crew to record you talking to your old school-teacher in his home, and did not even turn up.'

'I never arranged that!' I cried, appalled, 'I never even discussed the matter – never thought of it!'

'Then you arranged it when you were drunk.'

I left that pub and rushed away to visit Mr Meikle at once. I was sure the BBC had made a mistake and then blamed me for it, and I was desperate to tell Mr Meikle that he had suffered intrusion and inconvenience through no fault of mine.

Again I entered his close and hurried up to his flat, but there was something wrong with the stairs. They grew unexpectedly steep and narrow. There were no landings or doors off them, but in my urgency I never thought of turning back. At last I emerged onto a narrow railed balcony close beneath a skylight. From here I looked down into a deep hall with several balconies round it at lower levels, a hall which looked like the interior of Whitehill Senior Secondary School, though the Whitehill I remembered had been demolished in 1980.

But this was definitely the place where Mr Meikle lived, for looking downward I saw him emerge from a door at the side of the hall and cross the floor toward a main entrance. He did not walk fast, but a careful firmness of step suggested his arthritis had abated a little. He was accompanied by a party of people who, even from this height, I recognized as Scottish writers rather older than me: Norman MacCaig, Iain Crichton Smith, Robert Garioch and Sorley

Maclean. As they accompanied Mr Meikle out through the main door I wanted to shout on them to wait for me, but felt too shy. Instead I turned and ran downstairs, found an exit and hurried along the pavement after them, and all the time I was wondering how they had come to know Mr Meikle as well or better than I did. Then I remembered they too had been teachers of English. That explained it – they were Mr Meikle's colleagues. That was why they knew him.

But when I caught up with the group it had grown bigger. I saw many Glasgow writers I knew: Morgan and Lochhead and Leonard and Kelman and Spence et cetera, and from the Western Isles Black Angus and the Montgomery sisters, Derick Thomson, Mackay Brown and others I knew slightly or not at all from the Highlands, Orkneys and Shetlands, from the North Coast and the Eastern Seaboard, Aberdeenshire, Dundee and Fife, from Edinburgh, the Lothians and all the Borders and Galloway up to Ayrshire.

'Are all these folk writers?' I cried aloud. I was afraid that my own work would be swamped by the work of all these other Scottish writers.

'Of course not!' said Archie Hind, who was walking beside me, 'Most of them are readers. Readers are just as important as writers and often a lot lonelier. Arthur Meikle taught a lot of readers that they are not alone. So did others in this mob.'

'Do you mean that writers are teachers too?' I asked, more worried than ever.

'What a daft idea!' said Archie, laughing,

'Writers and teachers are in completely different kinds of show business. Of course some of them show more than others.'

I awoke, and saw it was a dream,
though not entirely.

Christopher Salvesen (1935 –)

History of Strathclyde

How earth was made, I might have had it sung,
How life began – hushed rocking of the tide
Lapping the sleepy margins of the world.

But – searching back into almost unsearchable
Time (and yet, the waters have always stirred) –
Footprints tell a different order of fact:
Three-toed, Batrachian, printed in the rocks,
In the flaggy sandstone of Euchan Water
In the upper reaches of Nithsdale – early
Exploratory steps as the moment passed;   10
Petrified, along with suncracks and ripples,
Like those of any casual hen or dog
On a wet concrete path – the same sun shone.

Ah but the earth, this grassy land, has changed.
These pitted marks I long to think are raindrops
More properly interpreted as sea-spray:

No fossil bones or plants remain to help us
But – carcasses and all organic debris
Devoured by scavengers and scouring tides –
It was a coast, the glaring salty shore   20
Where bushy banks run now and the rowans sway.

A kingdom in the history of man,
A Dark Age kingdom and in that well named –
So little known of family and fighting,
Thus easily guessed at but so hard to grasp –
It was a border, and a middle ground,
As the power of Rome withdrew: other tides,
Less tied to the moon's control, carried on
The moves of life, washed over them as well.

Today in the bright afternoon I saw,   30
As I walked a drove-road towards the north,
The black-faced ewes cropping the heathery hills,
One, by the track, seeming asleep: except –
A neat dark-red pit in the bony face –
The crows had pecked its eyes out: for a moment,
As the sun went on with its mindless work,
In that wool hulk, a history of Strathclyde.

Psychoscotia – A Complaint

The sunset – she made me watch,
A blackbird, listen
Lady my mother Macbeth.
Another day's boredom
Burnt out at the end:
In the branches rain-song, cold,
The beginnings of spring.
I have sucked ever since
Those rainy clouds
Those runs of song.   10

Sometimes I seem to be nothing
My Lady mother Macbeth
Or an idea, nothing but,
Turned up in a touring actor
A moorland shifting mist
On the way from there to here.
Or else my mother, bored with me,
Willed me into life
And almost, wailing, back again
To my reedy native shore.   20

Who wouldn't have a soldier father?
Guns he had fired – such batteries –
The river-hole he swam in
That summer afternoon,

They deafened him, confused his head.
Lady Macbeth my mother
He deserved his wound
The fields of Africa and France,
And Hannibal, a master, his marches
And – in the end – defeat.   30

Stewart Conn (1936 –)

Stewart Conn is one of Scotland's most skilled and wide-ranging poets, though he is often seen largely as the writer of the 'farm' poems which he featured early in his career. A sympathetic, if quite unsentimental, treatment of the natural world, or the rural one at least, does run throughout his poetry, but so do the themes of love, family relationships, the nature and power of art, and that time-honoured subject of poetry – the fragility and transitoriness of life itself. Like Iain Smith's, Stewart Conn's art is often the elegant understatement which seems to deny art, but which is in fact one of its highest forms. Conn, who was a BBC Radio Scotland drama producer for many years (1977–92) is also a major playwright, as witnessed by *The Burning* (1972), and *Play Donkey* (1977) among about twenty productions. In 2002, he was inaugurated as the first Edinburgh Makar (the capital's poet laureate).

Todd

My father's white uncle became
Arthritic and testamental in
Lyrical stages. He held cardinal sin
Was misuse of horses, then any game

Won on the Sabbath. A Clydesdale
To him was not bells and sugar or declension
From paddock, but primal extension
Of rock and soil. Thundered nail

Turned to sacred bolt. And each night
In the stable he would slaver and slave   10
At cracked hooves, or else save
Bowls of porridge for just the right

Beast. I remember I lied
To him once, about oats: then I felt
The brand of his loving tongue, the belt
Of his own horsey breath. But he died,

When the mechanised tractor came to pass.
Now I think of him neighing to some saint
In a simple heaven or, beyond complaint,
Leaning across a fence and munching grass.   20

'Harelaw'

Ploughlands roll where limekilns lay
Seeping in craters. Where once dense
Fibres oozed against gatepost and fence
Till staples burst, firm wheatfields sway;
And where quarries reeked, intense

With honeysuckle, a truck dumps load
Upon load of earth, of ash and slag
For the raking. Spliced hawsers drag
Roots out and wrench the rabbit wood
Apart as though some cuckoo fugue   10

Had rioted. On this mossy slope
That raindrops used to drill and drum
Through dusk, no nightjar flits nor numb
Hawk hangs as listening foxes lope
And prowl; no lilac shadows thumb

The heavy air. This holt was mine
To siege and plunder; here I caged
Rare beasts or swayed royally on the agèd
Backs of horses – here hacked my secret sign,
Strode, wallowed, ferreted, rampaged.   20

But acres crumple and the farm's new image
Spreads over the old. As I face
Its change, a truck tips litter; hens assess
Bright tins, then peck and squawk their rage.
The truck spurts flame and I have no redress.

In a Simple Light

Winter in this place
Is a tangerine sun.
Against the skyline
Nine Shetland ponies

Stand like cut-outs
Fraying at the edges.
Snow puffs and flurries
In weightless driblets

As they platter downhill,
Pink-hooved, chins   10
Stitched with frost, manes
Jiggling a tinsel trail.

They clutter and jolt,
Are pluff-bellied, biff
Posts, thrum their trough
With warm breathing, smelt

Ice. On the skyline
Again, part fancy, they
Freeze. In each eye
Is a tangerine sun.   20

Farm

The sun drills the shire through and through
Till the farm is a furnace, the yard
A quivering wickerwork of flame. Pitchforks
Flash and fall. Bales are fiery ingots.
Straws sputter like squibs. Stones
Explode. From the byre, smack on time,
Old Martha comes clattering out
With buttered bannocks and milk in a pail.

Todd, his face ablaze, swims back
In what shadow there is. Hugh and John   10
Stretch out among sheaves. Hens squabble
For crusts; a dog flicks its tail
At a cleg★; blueflies bunch like grapes.   horsefly
Still the sun beats down, a hammer
On tin. And high overhead vapour-trails
Drift seaward, out past Ailsa Craig.

The Yard

The yard is littered with scrap, with axles
And tyres, buckled hoops and springs, all rusting.
The wreckage of cars that have been dumped.

The hut is still there. In the doorway
Two men talk horses – but not as he did
In the days when the Clydesdales came

To be shod, the milk-wagons for repair.
The din of iron on iron brings it all back:
Rob beating the anvil, to a blue flame.

The beast straining, the bit biting in,   10
Horn burning, the sour tang of iron,
The sizzling, the perfect fit of the shoe.

In his mind's eye, the whole yard is teeming
With horses, ducking blackthorn, tails
Swishing, the gates behind them clanging . . .

The men have started to strip an old van.
In passing he takes a kick at the wing. No one
Notices. The dead metal does not ring at all.

Summer Afternoon

She spends the afternoon in a deckchair,
Not moving, a handkerchief over
Her head. From the end of the garden
Her eyes look gouged. The children stare,
Then return to their game. She used to take
Them on country walks, or swimming in the lake.
These days are gone, and will not come again.

Dazzling slats of sunlight on the lawn
Make her seem so vulnerable; her bombazine
Costume fading with each drifting beam.   10
As the children squall, she imagines
Other generations: Is that you, Tom,
Or Ian, is it? – forgetting one was blown
To bits at Ypres, the other on the Somme.

Momentarily in pain, she tightens
Her lips into something like a grin.
There comes the first rustle of rain.
Carrying her in, you avoid my eye
For fear of interception, as who should say
Shall we, nearing extremity,   20
Be equal objects of distaste and pity?

Yet desperate in the meantime to forbear
For the sake of the love this poor
Creature bore us, who was once so dear.

In the Kibble Palace

In the Kibble Palace with its dazzling statues
And glass dome, reading a poet I've just come across,
I learn that under ice the killer whale

Seeing anything darker than snow, falls away
Then charges, smashing the ice with his forehead,
Isolating seal or man on a drifting piece

Of the floe. Imagine those tons of blubber
Thrusting up; tail curveting
As the hammer head hits. What if the skull

Should split, splinters penetrate to the brain?   10
Nor will dry land protect us from the thudding
In the blood, these forces below. How can we conquer

Who cannot conquer ourselves? I shall think of this
When, fishing on frosted glass, I find
My line tightening against the swell;

Or hearing you moan and turn in your sleep
I know you are on your own, far out,
Dark shapes coursing below. Meanwhile

The horizon closes in, a glass
Globe. We will admit it is there   20
When it is too late; and blunder for the exits

To find them locked. Seeing as though through ice
Blurred forms gyrate, we will put our heads
Together and try to batter a way out.

Farm Funeral

His hearse should have been drawn by horses.
That's what he envisaged: the strain
And clop of crupper and chain, flashing
Brass, fetlocks forcing high. With below
Him, the frayed sheets turning slowly yellow.

On the sideboard a silver cup he had won,
Inscribed 'to Todd Cochrane', now a lamp;
And tinted prints of his trotting days,
Switch in hand, jockey-capped, the gig silky
With light, wheels exquisitely spinning.   10

For fifty years he was a breeder of horses;
Nursing them nightly, mulling soft praise
Long after the vet would have driven his plunger in.
Yet through them was his hip split. Twice
He was crushed by a stallion rearing.

Himself to the end unbroken. God's tool, yes,
That to earth will return. But not before time.
He ought to have been conveyed to the grave
By clattering Clydesdales, not cut off
From lark and sorrel by unseemly glass.   20

The shire is sprinkled with his ashes.
The fields are green through his kind. Their clay,
His marrow. As much as the roisterer, he: even
That last ride to Craigie, boots tightly laced,
His tie held in place by a diamond pin.

Under the Ice

Like Coleridge, I waltz
on ice. And watch my shadow
on the water below. Knowing that
if the ice were not there
I'd drown. Half willing it.

In my cord jacket
and neat cravat, I keep
returning to the one spot.
How long, to cut
a perfect circle out?   10

Something in me
rejects the notion.
The arc is never complete.
My figures-of-eight
almost, not quite, meet.

Was Raeburn's skating parson
a man of God, poised
impeccably on the brink;
or his bland stare
no more than a decorous front?   20

If I could keep my cool
like that. Gazing straight ahead,
not at my feet. Giving
no sign of knowing
how deep the water, how thin the ice.

Behind that, the other
question: whether the real you
pirouettes in space,
or beckons from under the ice
for me to come through.   30

'Kitchen-Maid'

Reaching the Rijksmuseum
mid-morning, in rain,
we skirt the main hall
with its tanned
tourists and guides

and, ignoring the rooms
we saw yesterday,
find ourselves heading
past Avercamp's skaters,
Brueghel's masses of flowers,   10

and even the Night-Watch
in its noisy arena
till, up carpeted stairs,
we are in a chamber
made cool by Vermeer.

For what might be hours
we stand facing
a girl in a blue apron
pouring milk
from a brown jug.   20

Time comes to a stop.
Her gesture will stay
perpetually in place.
The jug will never empty,
the bowl never fill.

It is like seeing
a princess
asleep, under ice.
Your hand, brushing mine,
sustains the spell: 30

as I turn to kiss you,
we are ourselves
suspended in space;
your appraising glance
a passionate embrace.

Visiting Hour

In the pond of our new garden
were five orange stains, under
inches of ice. Weeks since anyone
had been there. Already by far
the most severe winter for years.

You broke the ice with a hammer.
I watched the goldfish appear,
blunt-nosed and delicately clear.

Since then so much has taken place
to distance us from what we were.   10
That it should come to this.
Unable to hide the horror
in my eyes, I stand helpless
by your bedside and can do no more
than wish it were simply a matter
of smashing the ice and giving you air.

Ghosts

My face against the bars
of your cot, close to yours,

I listen while you whisper
urgently, telling me where

you want to go. Needless
to say, it is the Kibble Palace.

As soon as you are dressed
and have had breakfast

we set off; a fine
mist rising from the Kelvin.   10

We are alone in the Gardens.
Leaving the pram at the entrance

I take you to where the goldfish are.
For what seems hours, you peer

through the murky
water. Under the lattice-work

of white spars, whose
curved glass has

mirrored family upon family,
we too shall soon be,   20

like my father and grandfather,
ghosts in the empty air.

Cherry Tree, in December

The cherry tree outside my study window, heavy
With blossom, is an elaborate bouquet,
A celebration or renewal of vows, this December day.

In your white dress, you walked smilingly
Down the aisle, then were whisked away
To the reception, the remainder of the lives we,

Together, would share. I regret only
That the years have passed so speedily;
Each moment, rushing by,

Leaving less time to enjoy.   10
I thank you for your love, and pray
Death when it comes, may come gently.

Meanwhile on this December day I see
From my study window, with a new intensity,
The delicate blossoms on that cherry tree.

Over the Desert

Entering the Kalahari the pure waters
of the Delta, rather than form an estuary,
peter out in a depth of sand so great
even major earth tremors leave no trace

but are absorbed before reaching the surface.
Subjecting our lives, scarcely
more substantial, to varied analogy:
refreshment, or drought, of the spirit;

placing ourselves at others'
disposal; from this, to loss   10
of enlightenment over the centuries.
Below, a terrain *in extremis,*

dry valleys and fossil dunes
extending to the horizon and beyond;
the world's curve, billions of sandgrains.
Through a blur of condensation

imagine mirage-like, hazy and wavery,
an ancient Bushman and his wife, alone
in the thornveld, awaiting the hyenas
through whom they will join their ancestors.   20

White Tulips

Over the years, now decades, memories sporadically
surface for no seeming reason: among them one
of a classmate's sister who, playing one day
at the Creamery, must have tripped and fallen in.
I still shudder involuntarily, at the pain
encountered, the scalding of her skin; and can
but pray her engulfing was mercifully speedy.

As I sit in the garden this fragrant May afternoon
she comes to mind, incongruous light-years away.
First there's the shiver that coursed through us,   10
who at that age thought ourselves scatheless.
Only after this, do I consciously take in
these tulips beside me, their ghostly whiteness
grown suddenly diaphanous in the light breeze.

The following is taken from a fifteen-unit autobiographical
sequence called 'Above the Storm' (1995).

Again I Visit My Mother

Again I visit my mother. Her room brims
with the fragrance of unseasonal roses.
She sits as though tranced, in prisms
of light and shade. 'Is it time to go down?'
The blooms tremble, in their fluted vase.

A pair of gulls, swooping past, are mirrored
in the glass of a photo. An inner voice
similarly reduces her presence, and mine,
to no more than a fleeting reflection
of Life outside: a moment, then gone . . .   10

William McIlvanney (1936 –)

McIlvanney, a realist, is generally considered one of the two or three leading Scottish novelists, with *Docherty* (1975) perhaps his most praised. Notable also are the Laidlaw detective thrillers with their intriguing combination of pulp genre conventions, Glasgow realism and philosophical ambiguity.

How Many Miles to Babylon?

'Benny!' Matt O'Neill shouted up through cupped hands. 'Benny Mullen!'

In a moment, a broad, close-cropped head appeared, projecting beyond the uncompleted upper edge of the building, like a blueprint for a gargoyle. The wide mouth spouted words.

'What the hell is it?'

'Time up, Benny,' Matt O'Neill called up. 'Ah'm sendin' yer taxi for ye.'

He worked the pulley, and the wooden platform on its chains, normally used as a hoist for building materials, rose steadily till it stopped at the level where Benny was working. Benny had disappeared.

'Watch this,' Matt O'Neill said.

'That's Tank's job,' Johnny Rayburn said.

'Tank's job! Got a boy of ten could do it. Goin' to give Benny a wee thrill here.'

'You watch what ye're doin'.'

Matt was smiling.

'It'll be just like the Big Dipper. Benny says he can't remember bein' frightened. Should be no problem for a man of his calibre.'

He pronounced it jocularly, to rhyme with 'Khyber.' Wanting no part of it, Johnny Rayburn found a barrow that needed shifting but didn't shift it to where he couldn't see what was happening. Benny reappeared with his jacket over his shoulder and stepped out casually, maybe fifty feet above them, on to the platform, his free hand taking hold of one of the vertical chains. The platform started to descend smoothly with Benny gazing down upon them. Then Matt suddenly spun the pulley. The platform dropped sheer for about fifteen feet before Matt braked it dead. They could hear Benny bouncing on the wooden platform, and muffled cursing among the dancing rattle of the chains, and the worn work jacket, emptily bulbous at the pockets where Benny always carried his eight slices of bread and cheese, floated like an empty parachute to the ground. Benny's head came over the edge of the platform and said, 'Ya bastard! Wait till Ah get doon there.'

Matt was laughing helplessly.

'Ye'll need to be more polite than that, Benny, if ye want to get doon,' he said.

He was still laughing when he felt a grip manacle almost his entire forearm. He looked into a stare like burnished metal.

'What's the game?' Tank Anderson said.

'It's a bit of fun.'

'You're the only one that's laughin'.'

'Maybe Ah'm the only one wi' a sense of humour.'

'Ah've seen a man killed in one of these,' Tank said. 'You lose control of this, ye've got a man wearin' his pelvis for a hat. Ya bastard. Benny! You okay?'

'Okay, Tank.'

'You wait there till this man comes doon,' Tank muttered.

'That'll worry me,' Matt said.

Tank reset the pulley gently into motion. A few of the men had gathered to see what would happen. As the platform reached ground level, they could see how shaken Benny was.

'Okay' had been an attitude adopted, not a fact. Benny's face was trying to find an expression of hardness but the expression floated somehow uneasily on his features, wouldn't gel. Johnny had picked up his jacket and offered it to him. But Benny stepped off the platform and walked past him to face Matt O'Neill.

'Wait a minute, Benny,' Tank said and, spinning on his heel, hit Matt O'Neill on the jaw with a hand clenched into a club.

Matt sprawled among a pile of stone chips as if he was going to drown in them. He surfaced and spat a couple of chips. Tank had turned to Benny.

'Ah'm site foreman, Benny,' he said. 'It was ma instruction Matt ignored. So it's ma responsibility. And it's finished. Okay?'

Benny nodded. Tank crossed and held out his open hand towards Matt. Matt hesitated only briefly, for the hand extended to him had a local legend on the end of it. He clasped his hand in Tank's and Tank hauled him erect.

'Better than losin' yer job,' Tank said and winked.

'Aye, ye've had yer chips, Matt,' somebody said.

The laughter was a general amnesty. Tank brought Matt and Benny together to shake hands. Benny grimaced as they shook.

'That bloody chain,' he said.

He showed the palm of his hand, bruised where the chain of the platform had gnashed on it.

'Ah'm glad ye don't shake with yer jaw,' Matt said and rubbed his chin.

The crisis shared and averted developed a temporary camaraderie among them, like a small war survived with no serious casualties. Six of them made a little parade to 'The Market Bar.' Benny wasn't a regular there. He drank in 'The Akimbo Arms.' Usually he split off from the men and went there alone after his work. But tonight he felt himself part of them. He had been the centre of a small event and he innocently assumed that was what made them more than normally friendly towards him. It didn't occur to him that it was because they had seen him momentarily divested of the tough image he wore like a suit of armour. The fear floating on his face as he stepped off the platform had allowed him into their company. Their jokes were the admission charge.

'Bet that's cured yer constipation, Benny,' Johnny Rayburn said as they worked on their first pints.

His bowels were one of the site topics, like the government.

'You still as bad?' Deke Dawson asked.

'Ye kiddin'?' Frank Climie said. 'Ye could hire out Benny's arse for nestin'. A bird could rear a brood up there between performances.'

'It's all the cheese sandwiches ye eat,' Tank was suggesting.

The pub became busy. As the banter flew around him seeming, under the transforming effect of four pints of heavy beer on his growling stomach, like exotically coloured birds in a noisy aviary, Benny had a visionary experience. He didn't have them often. This one began in a slow, congealing realisation, a still point glowing in his mind like a steady light. He could have been killed. If Matt O'Neill's hand had slipped, if the pulley had snapped under the sudden pressure, if the brake hadn't held . . . he could have been killed.

He looked at Matt O'Neill nodding to Deke Dawson and laughing into his pint, and Benny felt not anger or a desire for revenge but a strange shivering thrill which his body contained comfortably like an overcoat, an overcoat he was still wearing. He saw Matt not with malice but with something oddly like gratitude, saw those very banal features take on a significance beyond themselves, as if Matt were a messenger from a dark force. The message was the grandeur of ordinary life. The warmth of the pub, the middle-aged barmaid's back bulging sensuously in two places beneath the strap of her brassiere, the uninhibited laughter of a man at the end of the bar, a whorl of smoke unraveling in air, the found gold that formed in a whisky-glass held to an optic, all were gifts of pleasure. They demanded a bigger expression of gratitude than he had been giving them. He needed a gesture.

Then he saw it, a sign the expansiveness of his own mood had created. A man beside him had the *Evening Times* half-folded on the bar. The headline seemed to point at Benny: The Flying Scots. The photograph beneath it showed three men at Glasgow Airport smiling self-consciously for the camera. They were flying out to Saudi Arabia. The story talked about the strangeness of modern life where workers caught a plane instead of a tram to go to their work. There was a reference to their wives waiting with rolling-pins if their wages were short when they got back. It occurred to Benny sadly that he wouldn't have had that problem. But the idea struck him like a revelation. The world was a small place. What need did he have to spend his life here? What reason did he have for staying? Time was running out. He didn't want to waken up at sixty and regret what he hadn't done. He was going to travel.

Like a sudden convert to the generous possibilities of life, he bought another round of drinks and included the man with the *Evening Times*, despite his embarrassed protestations. He slapped Matt O'Neill mystifyingly on the shoulder, as if he had saved his life instead of almost ending it. He said, 'Aye, Tank by name and Tank by nature,' so many times that Tank said, 'Actually, ma name's Harry.' He bought a carry-out of eight cans of export and had to be followed out of the pub by Johnny Rayburn because he had left them behind. Swinging the cans in their plastic bag as he walked, he brought his new dream up the road with him, singing 'Scotland the Brave' quietly to himself.

The house was a place he didn't like entering in the early evening. It wasn't so bad late at night because he had usually taken enough beer by then to numb the pain. But this evening was all right. Painlessness had come early. The thought that this council house was too big for him didn't settle its gloom around him as it normally did, didn't echo with the ghosts of the children he had wanted as if it were a castle rented for a clan that hadn't turned up, Mullen's Folly. He went through and dropped his jacket on the double-bed without noticing particularly how empty it looked. He still moved among dead dreams but already it was as if he had found something that for the moment was a small, if ludicrous, compensation, a dream of his own, a miraculous by-blow, like an illegitimate grandchild where there had been no children.

He still spent the evening almost entirely in the living room, though. It was the room that was the nearest thing to home he had. It was where Noreen and he had always sat. Sometimes, when the loneliness was bad, he even slept here, buttoning up the heavy army-style coat Noreen had bought for him in Milletts' Stores and dossing down in front of the coal fire both of them had agreed they would never change. On these occasions, the vague impulse in him was that by not sleeping alone in the bed he wasn't endorsing the fact of her death, as if he had a say in it.

Tonight he had first left the living room to go into the kitchen and put on two pork chops and then had come back through and drunk three cans of export, talking loudly to himself as had become his habit, and waited till the smell of the chops announced that they were burnt. He had salvaged some charred pieces of meat and chewed them into threads which he washed down with more export.

Having obeyed in his own way one of the several warnings that Noreen had handed down to him as her stoutness dematerialised relentlessly from leukemia ('See that you eat right'), he went on with the preferred part of his private communion, the drink. He chatted to the room like company. It was his favourite place for talking to himself, the only part of the house he felt furnished with his presence. The rest of it he couldn't afford psychologically to maintain.

'A close call right enough,' he said. 'It fairly makes ye think.'

He thought of Noreen. There had been no early warning system for her. Once they knew what she had, they knew what would happen. No chance to rethink their lives, no time significantly to make the most of what was left. The nature of the illness had meant that they couldn't. The best they had managed was the week in Morecambe after one of the treatments had given her a temporary boost. They had taken a room in a big hotel, at his insistence. He had wanted to take her everywhere, give her everything. But they had been like a one-legged man trying to dance. She had retained all her bantering warmth but instead of its enlarging him, as it had done before, he had shrivelled before it. He caught her looking at him secretly, looks that knew how lost he would be, and he had felt her receding from him and he was colder that week of hot weather than he had ever been before, like being slowly skinned. That week he had spent longer in the lavatory than at any other time. The men on the site might have found that funny. But he had needed a place to cry without being seen.

The conjured presence of Noreen made him admit the truth of himself, as it always did. She was the one who had found him out. She had provided a home for Benny's secret softness, a place where he could take off his muscles and let his shameful gentleness emerge. He might fool the citizenry with his deliberate swagger and the haircut that made his hair look like moss on a cannonball, but Noreen hadn't believed him. It was as if she had known him when he went first to the orphanage at the age of ten, very thin and with a bird-like capacity for panic.

Always frightened of feeling before, he had found himself after her death with a great load of affection like stolen goods and nowhere to fence it. He had started again to stash it in his muscles and hope that nobody would notice. Glancing drunkenly around the room, he saw it looking like a gymnasium. He had a bullworker leaning in a corner, a chest expander fixed to the door and assorted weights in the cupboard. It was as if he had been trying to intimidate his grief.

But to his sense of her he admitted the truth again. He couldn't quite believe in himself as a hard man. He had watched nearly every Clint Eastwood film several times, like taking a course in callousness, but somehow the treatment hadn't quite taken. No doubt he would go on trying, since out there he didn't know what else to do. Sitting in this room, however, he owned up to himself. He had been terrified on the platform. He had been glad when Tank Anderson settled the matter with Matt O'Neill, because Benny wasn't sure that he fancied his chances against Matt.

'A man's a man for a' that,' he said to his seventh can of export with his finger in the ring-pull.

The explosion of escaping gas was like faint applause. Benny loved Robert Burns, not just the poetry, which he could quote at great and sometimes pub-emptying length, but the man, the hard life, the democratic stance of him, the sense he gave of effortlessly incarnating Scottishness, the fact that he, like Benny, was an Ayrshireman. Scottishness was very important to Benny. He wasn't sure what it was but, whatever it was, it bit like lockjaw and the fever of it was in his blood. When he read Burns, he looked in a national mirror that told him who he was and forbade him to be diminished by what other people had. He was enough in himself. The greatest expression of his Scottishness that he could think of at the moment was to travel. It was what him to do.

> 'The hert's aye the pairt aye
> That maks us right or wrang.'

He would travel. He might even emigrate. Wasn't that what Scots did? He remembered a story he had heard.

Somebody in the pub had been talking about a book he was reading. It was about a man sailing round the world himself. That was something to do, except that Benny didn't know a gib-sail from a tablecloth. But the man had written a book about his trip. One place he stopped in South America, he met some natives and they told him about a primitive tribe up-country who had red hair. The man had visited them and, sure enough, they had dark skins and reddish hair. The man thought they were descendants of Scotsmen who had settled there. Panama, Benny thought it was. The idea of it made him shake his head in wonderment.

'Christ, we're everywhere,' Benny said, raising his beer can in a toast to the empty room. 'We are the people. Open an alligator's gub in the Congo an' a Scotsman'll nod oot at ye. We're everywhere. Australia, Canada, America, South America, Asia.' He paused, running out of places. 'Russia. There was always Scotsmen in Russia. An' all over Europe. For centuries. India. A lotta Scottish graves in India.' He started to sing. 'There was a soldier, a Scottish soldier. We are the people. Scotsmen can go anywhere. An' why no' me? Why not Benny Mullen? Ye can go anywhere. Ye could even go—' His mind eddied with the drink and he waited to find what exotic flotsam it would throw up. 'To Babylon.' The word shimmered in his head. 'Babylon.' He laughed and drained his can. 'Correct. Ye could even go to Babylon. How many miles wid that be?'

His laughter was a celebration of how simple life was. His eighth can gave him his vision complete. He would go to Babylon, not necessarily to stay there. He would see it first and then decide. But it was a beginning. He would need an atlas.

He referred the project to his memory of Noreen, like praying at a shrine before a journey. He felt her approval given. As if an oracle had spoken, he remembered another of her parting warnings, given from her hospital bed when her body hardly made a bump on the coverlet and families were murmuring all around them in the ward and her eyes had rekindled for a moment into their old liveliness:

'You've a life to live, Benny Mullen. Live it! Ye're thertyfive. Don't let me catch you skulkin' in coarners. Ah married a man, not a mouse.'

That had been three years ago and what had he done to justify her faith? He would do it now, for the two of them. He stood up suddenly.

'By Christ, ye're right, Noreen. You are right, ma bonny lass. An' say Ah've said it.'

He toasted himself with his can. It was empty. Wondering vaguely if there would still be a can left over in the fridge from his last carry-out, he made to move through there and slipped on an empty beer can. The can he was holding slithered across the floor. He landed on his hands and knees. He gave long thought to the problem of rising and slowly subsided on the carpet. He felt it was his first step on the way to Babylon. Trying to find a comfortable position for his right leg, he kicked another empty can. Just before he slept, doubts began to buzz like flies around his dying enthusiasm. How could he go? Where would the money come from? Would he feel the same in the morning? He hoped that Noreen would forgive him for the mess.

Robin Fulton (1937 –)

As well as a fine poet, Fulton has been a major critic. His *Contemporary Scottish Poets* (1974) is a major achievement in that field.

Gods

Between the sixth and the seventh days they came.

Myths, white-winged, infallible,
Struck tall fountains from the sea;
The goddess reclined on her shell; high tide
Laid dead dolphins on a mattress of weed;
At the resurrection of spring flowers a faun
Fathered his shadow with multitudinous spawn.

After it all, when the legend of trees had withered
And the wind's lawless fingers had ripped the leaves,
We came on the seventh day to the naked woods   10
Expecting vestals raped by their drunk gods

And corn-kings nailed on their trees. By dawn
We had found nothing but certain articles of sin.

Another history of gods was about to begin.

Museums and Journeys

An exhibition: a hundred years of Edinburgh life.
Coming out I move as heavily as a diver
on the ocean floor: one step, one breath
against the weight of the invisible dead. So many
yet the air is clear. And they've no time for me,
their view of the future blocked by giant headlines.

A journey: one I didn't want to take but took
shutting my eyes – a child again hoping the needle
wouldn't hurt. Lakes and forests, lakes and forests
pass with the weightless ease of delirium. So many.   10
My view of the past stays clear but hard to read
like a radio-map of a secret corner in the night sky.

Museums and journeys. We meet as strangers do
at the end of long ellipses over continents.
We exchange histories. Our view of the present is clear
but the landscapes go on sliding past. So many
memories, I try to say 'One at a time!'
They keep piling up like urgent unanswered letters.

The First Sight

As when the sun breaks through thick cloud
and our eyes wince and find shelter
among shades, so
at the first sight of your fresh grave

I tried not to look. I listened.
In the church across the river
an evening psalm was unwinding;
the river with its soft voice spoke;
up the hill around your own church
the sycamores were loud with rooks.   10

It's the first sight that won't let go:
as when the sun in a picture,
made relentless
by art, unblinking, stares and stares.

For Something like a Second

It's weeks now, I thought,
since they've noticed me.
The dead, I meant. That night, then –
I'm fifty but back
where once I was five.
From the manse window I watch
a flat-topped beech-hedge
(which was never there)
and beyond it the black pools
(which were) flooded up   10
from The Black Water.
Father, gone four years, is back
too, but not thirty,
more like seventy,
ruffled, tired in mid-morning.
We're out of time with
time and place, our years
slide, bits of broken mirror.
But for something time
would call a second   20
we're in time with each other.
Beyond the crisp hedge
the unmoved black pools
turn white, answering the sky.

Ellie McDonald (1937 –)

The Gangan Fuit

Whit ist that greets★ outby the nicht,   weeps
that fakes tae fin the sneck?
It's juist the wind, my bonnie lass,
gaen speiran★ i the daurk.   questioning

Whit ist that greets outby the nicht
that keens abuin the ruif?
It's juist the glaid★ my bonnie lass,   kite, buzzard
gaen seekin i the lift

The glaid gangs free, my bonnie lad
kens nocht o daith nor birth,   10
the wind but cairts aa human pain
tae ilka howe★ o yirth   hollow

Whit seeks tae come inby the nicht,
nae bield has ever haen,
but haiks its gangrel★ body, whaur   vagabond
eternities cry doun.

Widdershins

Our mither tongue wis dung doun
in Scotland bi John Knox.

Juist tae mak shair
it bided yirdit★   buried

the weans got thir licks
frae the dominie

for yasin the auld leid★   tongue
but it niver dee'd, though

a hantle★ o fowk hae trockit★   number/bartered
thir tongue for a pig in a poke   10

an a sicht mair ken nocht
but a puckle★ o words.   handful

Nou, the makars★ scrieve   poets
translations aneath thi poems

sae that edicatit fowk
can jalouse★ thir implications.   suspect, guess

James Aitchison (1938 –)

Antarctica

From the Journal of Patrick Napier
(Sub-Lieutenant Patrick Napier served on HMS Challenger which
sailed to the Antarctic in 1874 under the command of Sir John Murray.)
                                        – For Robert Nye

The weather continues calm but the terrain
Is more mountainous than our charts show
And we have travelled but seventy miles
From where the *Challenger* lies at anchor with half-crew.

Mountains, charts and compasses conspire
To make a phantasm of the natural world.
Some charts are false and all are incomplete;
Our compasses' erroneous reckonings
Suggest the Pole has fickle satellites
Whose only constant is inconstancy.   10

By tricks of distances and wind and light
The mountains seem to march across the land,
Shouldering their way through flying clouds.
Mountains enormous on the morning skies
Dissolve in minutes in a sea of mist.
The mountains come and go at will, as if
This land has not assumed a final shape.

───────────────

We have seen distant turmoils in the air –
Too far, too swift for our camera –
Like great flocks of birds startled in their flight.   20
And on the ground, towards the horizon,
We have seen upsurgings and scatterings of snows
As if creatures fled from us in panic.

And yet there are no other creatures on this land;
Only our small company of men and dogs.

At night when the dogs have ceased their howling
I hear the rending of the ice

And the land groaning under its burden of ice.
From the ratings' tent I hear the sounds of a melodeon.
Sir John allows the lamps to be kept lit all night   30
In the three principal tents and in the latrine.

───────────────

On the sixth day the skies were overcast.

The Esquimaux dogs were ill-tempered
And were whipped snarling to their traces.
The gale got up while we were travelling.
It lifted grains of ice from the ground
And hurled them in our eyes.
I could not walk against the force of the wind.
I felt the gale pressing my eyes into their sockets.
I could not see the sledge ahead of me   40
And tried to call out to Captain Russell
But the words were blown back in my throat.

The dogs lay down in the snow and would not go on.

───────────────

The gales have kept us to our tents five days and nights.
I fear the tents will not take the onslaught.

Last night Sir John said, 'Gentlemen,
I cannot believe this land is part of the Creation.
This world of ice is not of the Lord's making.
Perhaps another god . . . '

I could scarcely hear him speak above the gale,   50
Its long blasts like the harshest organ chords.

'Perhaps this everlasting wilderness
Is how the world was before there was God.'

The gales have lessened and we travel again.

Each day is a wailing twilight of winds and snow,
Each night a broken sleep of racing dreams.

I dreamed that great white apes
With swollen members glowing in the darkness
Ran round and round my tent.
I dreamed I stood engulfed in a wild storm   60
On the shore and cried out as I watched
The *Challenger* in fair weather set sail for England.

And all this time the clouds are come so close
We have seen neither sun nor moon nor stars
For seven days and nights.
I no longer hear the sounds of the melodeon.

The snow and ice lie so deep that we walk
not on the earth but on solid weather.
We walk on the weather of many centuries.
If engines could be brought to this land   70

We might sink mines down to the beginning of time
And to the way the world was before there was God.

Yesterday a man, a sledge and a team of dogs
Fell through the snow into an abyss.

Atkinson was lowered on the longest rope.
He saw nothing; heard no cries from man or dogs.
We tied together all our ropes
And lowered him down again for a full hour,
Calling out to him all the while.
When he came up again he said there was nothing.   80

Sir John said, 'The abyss is bottomless.
The creatures have fallen into infinity.'
Captain Russell said, 'No, but we have lost
William Carter, a most honest and willing man,
And with him one third part of all our food.'

That same night Russell said we must turn back.
Sir John said, 'My dear Russell,
I knew you lacked all sense of mystery
But I had thought you a bolder man than this.'

'Sir, we lack not mystery but food.   90
If we turn back tomorrow we may live.'

The men grow careless on the journey back
And inattentive from lack of sleep.
They are less companionable to each other.

Some do not wax their boots. One man
Has forgotten how to make fast both tent and sledge.
Another, Rawlins, acts as if the dead
Carter were still one of our company;
Greets him, stands aside to let him pass.

Captain Russell is intolerant;   100
He speaks sharply, insultingly, to the men.

'You think me harsh, Lieutenant,' the Captain said.
'Do you not see that each day we take longer
To make and break our camp?
Each day we travel less and less
And yet we eat the same quantities of food.
We may perish in this land.

'The men grow careless with their lives, Lieutenant.
I see in unwaxed boots an end to walking
But there are many miles between us and *Challenger*.   110
I see in an unfastened tent an unfastened mind,
Admitting the cold, admitting death.
Rawlins is not in mourning for his dead
Friend, Carter, but in love with death itself.
Rawlins is accompanied by death;
He has found that sweet delirium which, unchecked,
Will prove contagious.
Soon the men will lie down in the snow
And think themselves babes at their mothers' teats.'

I dreamed I had not left the *Challenger* but lay awake,   120
Waiting for daybreak and the order to disembark.

The dream warned me of a predatory beast
Which followed travellers and would not be eluded.
Those whom it chooses, the dream said, it takes.

I dreamed I could not sleep for fear of the beast
And listened to the *Challenger* at anchor
Sighing and whispering through the night.

When I awoke and saw the little lamp
And the shadows waltzing on the walls of the tent
I thought myself in God's waiting room.   130

And then I felt the joy of being alive,
Alive in this land, not the *Challenger*.
I walk in this vast mercilessness and survive.

I have not been chosen by the beast
Nor fallen in love with death.
I am in communion with every man
Who ever travelled this land.
We are a brotherhood of Antarctica.

I looked at Captain Russell lying asleep
And thought him the hardest and truest of friends.   140

I found Rawlins lying dead in the snow
With a smile frozen deep into his features.
We wrapped him in his sealskin coat
And heaped snow upon the body.

Captain Russell stepped forward and raised his hand.
Surely he cannot scold them now, I thought.
Another scolding will send these men to their deaths.

'We have lost another good man, a cruel loss,
For we are less than two days' march from *Challenger*.

Less than two days, and then I promise you   150
Hot mutton pies, hot dumplings, pints of rum.'

I saw the *Challenger* in the bay and felt no joy.
I heard the men speak of their deliverance
And hurrah the Captain and Sir John.
I watched the men dance a hornpipe on the shore;
They beckoned to me but I would not join them.

I have my journal but it does not catch
The pitiless majesty of this land,
The changing vastnesses and the many musics.
Memory will smooth away the mountains and abysses,   160
Diminishing the continent to a chart.

I pray that part of me is still falling
Through the bottomless abyss towards infinity.
And I pray that I have loved and feared
Antarctica enough to have its dreams.

Starlings in George Square

A black leaf on a leafless tree
begins to sing, and thousands more
join the harsh, high-pitched, off-key
November vespers in George Square.

They leap into the air and swirl
in a blizzard of false notes among
the leafless trees. George Square skirls
with shrill November evensong.

They wheel and screech, a multi-track
fast-forward scratch falsetto choir   10
of thousands, a November flock
of starlings singing in George Square.

Climber in the Nameless Places

Even in a huddled country like this
there are places without names.

maps print cairns of words on mountain tops
but there are chasms between the cairns,
there are plunging shadows
and the tracklessness of gouged
infinitely patient places of unnamable stone.

Trace the river back through the gorge
of roaring voices to the anonymous voice,
the fluctuating syllables   10
of muscled-water-over-stone
to the sheer silences above the beginnings of rivers.

All this can vanish in clouds of rain or sleet
for days on end. Sky vanishes.
Daubs of crusted lichen vanish.
Shadows are more solid than stone.
There are no names for these long darknesses.

Even in a little land like this
there are nameless, unknowable places.

Tessa Ransford (1938 –   )

Former director of the Scottish Poetry Library and editor of the influential *Lines Review*, Tessa Ransford has been an unflagging friend and support to contemporary Scottish verse. Her own poetry is notable for its intelligence and range.

Nocturne (Lewis)

It is raining on Lewis in the night
Darkness has brimmed over the hills
spilling upon the moor
and dropping into circles of inland sea.

Last night the moon was wildly shed
by mountain and cloud to reveal a sheer
countenance at the window
and blending with the water in bright festoons;

But tonight the dark is raining on Lewis:
on the black-house with its hunched thatch   10
on battered, abandoned buses
derelict cars and stacks of murky peat.

Boats are plying under the rain
and enormous eels under the boats
and fishing nets are lifted
up and under the tide like diving birds.

For thousands of years of nights the stones
have loomed in lonely communion
beneath the moon, the rain,
ritually aloof, cleansed and illumined.   20

And the white schist of my lasting self
safe and awake yet exposed to love –
its darkness and shafts of light –
takes up position in line with primeval wisdom.

Girl Raking Hay: 1918

She laughs in the hayfield, sixteen, slight,
over her shoulder a chestnut plait,
broad-brimmed hat
and long skirt,
summer, hay day, August heat,
1918, peace not yet.

The huge hayrake is twice her size,
her hands that wield it, like lilies;
death the news,
her brother dies.   10
While girls all yearn for armistice
the hay falls scythed about their knees.

Any Old Woman

'After a recitative
denoting her distress
Berenice sings an aria
in which she begs to die
rather than live
without the love of Titus.'

In dignified tones
a Radio Three announcer
introduces the theme:

I am on my knees   10
in the kitchen
as the flood of music over me
washes the despair
of Berenice
round my wall, my heart.

'Such emotion,' I think,
'should be trapped in art . . .
nor let loose
with all apparent nonchalance
into any old kitchen   20
any old women.'

My Troy

I am my own Cassandra and foresee
the fall of my own Troy –
        murder of the heroes
        destruction of her children
        women taken as spoils.

None can save Troy now – the very gods
are scuttling in retreat.
        She brought the dummy horse
        within her sacred space –
        it spilled out all its spite.   10

She was deceived and ransacked utterly
by Greek aggrandisement.
    Her altars now are fallen
    golden treasures stolen
    palaces in flames.

Helen now has lost her queenliness
her beauty and her youth.
    She lives to end her life.
    The brutal brothers both
    now lord it over us.   20

Cressida has been flung to and fro
between opposing warriors
    who mock her now, since she
    preferred their manhood
    to the cause they fought.

Your victory Achilles shall be short
but Troy's defeat eternal.
    Her suffering shall be sung
    whenever human worth
    is slain and trampled on.   30

I am my own Cassandra and foresee
my death in Mycenae.
    No place for the displaced.
    We dwell within our sorrow
    in every earthly kingdom.

D[avid] M[acleod] Black (1941 –)

D. M. Black was born in South Africa, arriving in Scotland in 1950. He has achieved a considerable reputation outside of Scotland. His poems are often said to occur in 'a country of the mind', where philosophy and psychology meet – psychodramas, in effect.

The Red Judge

We shut the red judge in a bronze jar
– By 'we,' meaning myself and the black judge –
And there was peace, for a time. You can have enough
Yowling from certain justices. The jar
We buried (pitching and swelling like the tough
Membrane of an unshelled egg) on the Calton Hill.
And there was peace, for a time. My friend the black
Judge was keen on whisky, and I kept

Within earshot of sobriety only by drinking
Slow ciders, and pretending   10
Unfelt absorption in the repetitive beer-mats. It was a kind of
Vibration we noticed first – hard to tell
Whether we heard it or were shaken by,
Whether the tumblers quivered or our minds. It grew
To a thick thudding, and an occasional creak
Like a nearby axle, but as it were
Without the sense of 'nearby' – the hard flag-
stones wriggled slightly under the taut linoleum.
I supported the black judge to the nearest door
 – Detached his clutched glass for the protesting barman –   20
And propped him against a bus-stop. Maybe
It was only a pneumatic drill mating at Queen Street,
Or an impotent motor-bike – the sounds grew harsher:
My gestures stopped a 24 that spat
Some eleventh commandment out of its sober driver,
But I was more conscious of the rocking walls,
The pavement's shrugging off its granite curb . . .

Quite suddenly the night was still: the cracks
In the roadway rested, and the tenements
Of Rose Street stood inscrutable as always. The black judge   30
Snored at his post. And all around
The bright blood filled the gutters, overflowed
The window-sills and door-steps, soaked my anyway
Inadequate shoes, and there was a sound of cheering
Faintly and everywhere, and the Red Judge walked
O thirty feet high and scarlet towards our stop.

An Epic of Self-Discovery

Experience never happens until you see
Your self. I used to go a-
round in a shining raincoat against the dull
Sleet; (even the bitterest winds
Glided apart, letting me walk warm
In their freezing flood). So too I shut my
Skin from heat, from the emollient
Syrup of summer – and it was probably years
Before my brittle-as-a-cricket self by rattling
Struck me. Unbuttoning the abdomen disclosed   10
Only a dried bean, and a tiredly-drifting
Tuft of vapour.
                    One's intestines are always unnerving:
I clutched the gap and went hugely extravert,
Stared after every blouse in Princes Street,
Pranced in a rapt operetta over vulgar linoleums,
Floated on tides of ballet
                    without call.
 – It was the dried bean
Upset me. Retiring,   20

I examined again the wrinkled glaucous skin,
That hard and pellet quality; how satisfying,
How utter; *how complete* –

I have never worn a raincoat or other clothes
Since then: except for the fig-
leaves of essential reticence: otherwise
Have let the sun and the snow iron seams across me,
The winds abrade me like the certain hills.

(And my resulting growth is remarkable, would you but notice
Me, as you clamber aloft up my sky-
scraping stalk to the heart's counties.)

At All Costs

You have to keep control, at all
costs. No one can refute a
stone, but a mush they slop
to whatever shape their sense of ridicule
cares to deride. I therefore
undressed my shivering flesh and built
piece by piece around it a rigid armour
of mudguards and circular saws and
nutmeg-graters, making it discreetly
size 15, so that within it   10
I could conserve the amorphous flesh. And on this
condition I stood firm at the scurrying cross-road:
no one troubled to mock, or appear bewildered; they knew me
by my toothless vacuum-feeder, my plume, and my fast location.

And it is there still, the monster; but inside
we have bred nations. Into the burrows
of life and death my swarms
turmoil, and I no longer clamber
up to the breadknife eyelashes and peer
out on the darkening cross-road: my attention   20
is adequately gripped by the goings-on
within, and I watch delighted
as every scurrying mite or fungoid scours
the waste places,
then stands so proudly in the robust highway
and hoods himself with toothpaste tube or eggshell.
That, at the least,
is one lesson learned.
Indeed so completely
learned, that you could search for days   30
along the enchanted roadway and would not find
a fleck of quivering flesh.

The Educators

In their
limousines the
teachers come: by
hundreds. O the
square is
blackened with dark suits, with grave
scholastic faces. They
wait to be summoned.
These are the
educators, the   10
father-figures. O you could
warm with love for the firm lips, the
responsible foreheads. Their
ties are strongly set, between their collars. They
pass with dignity the exasperation of waiting.

A
bell rings. They turn. On the
wide steps my
dwarf is standing, both hands raised. He
cackles with laughter. Welcome, he cries, welcome   20
to our elaborate Palace. It is indeed. He
is tumbling in cartwheels over the steps. The
teachers turn to each other their grave faces.

With
a single grab they have him up by the shoulders. They
dismantle him. Limbs, O
limbs and delicate organs, limbs and
guts, eyes, the tongue, the
lobes of the brain, glands; tonsils, several
eyes, limbs, the tongue,   30
a kidney, pants, livers, more
kidneys, limbs, the tongue
pass from hand to hand, in their serious hands. He is
utterly gone. Wide
crumbling steps.

They
return to their cars. They
drive off smoothly, without disorder;
watching the road.

St Andrews Poems

November

The Lade Braes in the glorious November
sunlight has a vitality that certainly
chilling age or the labyrinths of being
conscious will not extinguish. It informs her
oaks and beeches! In every leaf the colour
burns miraculously against the perfect
blue air; and where the broken ground is cumbered
with sawn boles it is present also, flooding throughout each trunk to the smallest corrugation   10
in the exterior bark. I turn and take the
track that leads from the bridge and holds for fifty
yards or so to the burnside, till a weir distracts the water; above it on the silent
pool two swans like a one contrivance flow toward me. White of entrancing purity! I
too participate in that self-existing
equanimity: and contain the macro-
cosm which plainly has solved our famous teaser,
the *perpetuum mobile*, and even put it to   20
maybe useful employment. For here in this
Buddha's Paradise with its jewel colours,
its pure light, and the air as ripe as *saké*,
truly nothing restrains my confidence or
knocks it from its alignment, so completely
am I held in the world and all its changing
weathers. And I retain that poise and would not
have it different as in the same sunlight I
saunter home to my glumly dying Father.

December   30

1970 comes to its undodgeable
final day. Bitter frost. The flawless winter
sunlight cannot obscure a single grain of the
poignant sandstone. A friend of mine once told me:
'This cathedral was build largest in Christendom,
save St Peter's.' By ruined ancient walls I
pass on: ground-plan of Mary's chapel, and what
once were fishermen's houses; then walk out on the
weathered blocks of the pier. O every facet
of the ponderous sea is visible, crumpled or   40
shining. And, for a counterpart, a sky so
filled with light that to think it blue would
be sheer indolence. At the further end three
boys run shouting away (and then return) beneath each splattering wave: one, soaked, attempts to
clasp his fellow for warmth but is disdainful-
ly hurled backward. A fight develops. I return the length of the pier; and as I go two
swans accompany me that one might think were
drifting over the ocean but are plainly   50

swimming positively for as fast as I they re-
gain the harbour. I think: perhaps their forebears
watched my clamorous ancestry arriving
round Cape Wrath, in the long beaked ships for which they
must have modeled; and no doubt too then equally
rode the water with perfect elegance, perfect
leisure, transiting unconcernedly that opaque and
formless cradle; and were as white as these are –

September

From my Mother's third house among the dahlias   60
I stride down to the castle; cross wet rocks to
St Rule's Cave; and alone staring out on the
self-same prospect that must have grabbed that bearish
eremitical fellow – skerries, gulls, and
filling sea – with a sense of all of Scotland
at my back, I could dream that some relation
quite aside from transmitted genes or dogma
can yet bind to the ancientry the current.
Fourteen centuries' lapse. The well-directed
gaze need take nothing in that was not present   70
even then, and the courage the Dark Ages
called-for when someone chose to accept abandoning
all security can have been no less than
we'd require. And for what? The whole scenario's
here before me: that storm-stained, ageing, brilliant-
eyed ascetic for whom high tides and nightfalls
clocked whatever routine his training specified;
and the reaching-out rock, the lifting seaweed,
the small birds. Let me not forget that God
exists as master of *maya* and not otherwise.   80
Yet the glib formulations do not close the
issue, which is expressed in days and weeks of
sun and squall and the skies that hurry for no man;
and transferred into words, evaporates, or
makes a poem or two, no doubt, and things of that sort –

Douglas Dunn (1942 –)

A major poet, critic and editor, Dunn spent many years of his life in England. His
rather celebrated return to Scotland in 1984 marked an increasing emphasis upon
Scottish themes. A member of the faculty at St Andrews, Dunn has written poetry
which has a subtle, restrained, intellectual exactness of diction and rhythm, which
when combined with the emotionally charged subject matter of his wife's illness and
death from cancer at 37 produced in *Elegies* (1985) some of the finest poetry in
recent years.

   His short stories may be even more impressive. Only James Kelman and perhaps
Iain Smith have produced short fiction of such consistency and quality.

The Patricians

In small backyards old men's long underwear
Drips from sagging clotheslines.
The other stuff they take in bundles to the Bendix.

There chatty women slot their coins and joke
About the grey unmentionables absent.
The old men weaken in the steam and scratch at their rough chins.

Suppressing coughs and stiffnesses, they pedal bikes
On low gear slowly, in their faces
The effort to be upright, a dignity

That fits inside the smell of aromatic pipes.   10
Walking their dogs, the padded beats of pocket watches
Muffled under ancient overcoats, silences their hearts.

They live watching each other die, passing each other
In their white scarves, too long known to talk,
Waiting for the inheritance of the oldest, a right to power.

The street patricians, they are ignored.
Their anger proves something, their disenchantments
Settle round me like a cold fog.

They are the individualists of our time.
They know no fashions, copy nothing but their minds.   20
Long ago, they gave up looking in mirrors.

Dying in their sleep, they lie undiscovered.
The howling of their dogs brings the sniffing police,
Their middle-aged children from the new estates.

Guerrillas

They lived on farms, were stout and freckled, knew
Our country differently, from work, not play.
Fathers or brothers brought them to school in cars,
Dung on the doors, fresh eggs in the back.
The teachers favoured them for their wealth,
Daffodils and free eggs, and we envied them
The ownership of all the land we roved on,
Their dangerous dogs and stately horses,
The fruit we had to steal, their land being
Income, and ours a mysterious provider.   10
They owned the shadows cast by every branch,
Chestnuts and flowers, water, the awkward wire.
Their sullen eyes demanded rent, and so
We shouted the bad words to their sisters,

Threw stones at hens, blocked up the foggy drains.
Outlaws from dark woods and quarries,
We plundered all we envied and had not got,
As if the disinherited from farther back
Come to our blood like a knife to a hand.

From the Night-Window

The night rattles with nightmares.
Children cry in the close-packed houses,
A man rots in his snoring.
On quiet feet, policemen test doors.
Footsteps become people under streetlamps.
Drunks return from parties,
Sounding of empty bottles and old songs.
The young women come home,
The pleasure in them deafens me.
They trot like small horses   10
And disappear into white beds
At the edge of the night.
All windows open, this hot night.
And the sleepless, smoking in the dark,
Making small red lights at their mouths,
Count the years of their marriages.

This next poem, and the five which follow it, are taken from *Elegies* (1985), written after the death of the poet's wife, Leslie Balfour Dunn, in March, 1981.

A Silver Air Force

They used to spin in the light, monoplanes,
Biplanes, a frivolous deterrent to
What had to happen. Silver-winged campaigns,
Dogfights against death, she blew, and I blew,
The mobile spun: Faith, Hope and Charity,
Wing and a Prayer, shot down, shot down in flames.
I watched, and thought, 'What will become of me
When she is dead?' I scramble in my dreams
Again, and see these secret Spitfires fly
As the inevitable aces of the sky,   10
Hanging from threads, a gentle violence.
But day by day they fell, and each plane crashed
On far, hereafter wheatfields in God's distance –
White strings of hope a summer blueness washed.

Pretended Homes

I am returning to that treeless drama
Where rock and sea and passionate distances
Invent an island. Ground and air congeal
Around phenomena that happen here.
A nightclub, penthoused high up on The Paps,
Is lit with pleasurable trivia.
Sheep graze up to its doors. The fishermen,
The electrician and the butcher's boy
Play Punto Banco in a private alcove.
The cinema, down on the tideline,   10
Is managed by a sour projectionist
In love with Myrna Loy. He lives his life
In the black-and-white of a standard flea-pit.
And this is an island of blind fiddlers
Where storytellers speak by pulsing oil-lamps,
Telling of kelpies and brownies, of the man
Who wed his spirit-sweetheart, under the hill.
I am making a place to the song of
Sorrow and wind and the man-eating seas
That writes itself on the guitars of marram,   20
On Aeolian dunes, on rippled sifts of the strand.
I am making my heart, wondering why
It pictures glamour in a wilderness,
And *glamourie*★, Ovidian and Gaelic.   magic
      The sea-circus is coming on its strange boats
With its elephants, clowns and saxophones,
With boxes of sawdust and baled canvas,
Its coils of rope, with its fire-eaters.
White ponies are hollow-hoofed on the jetty.
The harbour-master's wife sits at her mirror.   30
Lions and tigers in their wheeled cages
Displace the latitudes; the acrobats
Tumble and leap outside the bars. Already
The postman's daughter is in love with a
Blond boy who somersaults without a net
From a trembling swing. We will be there tonight
In all our finery, to watch the clowns
On their monobikes, and the seals that slip
Obediently out of our local seas,
And the lions, with their big teeth, zebras   40
In African stripes. Here is a conch. Listen
To the sea. It is the music of your love,
Whoever you care for. And this is also
A land of the uncomplicated sabbath
Where nothing happens on a Sunday other
Than dawn, the day, and simple pagan prayers,
A spreading of the charitable crumbs,
A bowl of curds and whey for the good neighbours,
The aborigines of these islands.
      The weary scholars in the Library   50
Have mastered everything there is to know.

Soon they'll begin their study of the sea
And sky, the physics of the open-winged
Feathery sea-eagle, and, when they have learned
To fly, the deities of the blue wind,
The black wind and the blow laden with rain.
Tonight these academic bachelors
Will dress for dinner and attend *Le Cirque*
De la Mer Bleue, come from Armorica
To fall in love with us and break our hearts.   60
For they are the servants of the sea, brought
On the happiness of a calm ocean,
Horizon after horizon, and over
Wet hills when the sun sets, like the whole world
Going down in its sufferings of pink,
Red, yellow, dark, and the light dimmed every day,
Complete and universal, wise and good
No matter present grief hurting your heart.
From this real house, I go beyond myself
Into imagined clarity, sorting   70
It out. I see her where the shingle sings
With salt, looking for pretty stones, her skirt
Held out of water's sea-lazy stroke and surge.
I am inventing here for one who's dead.
I am making a place for her. It is
On no map. It is out of my spirit.
Clowns, acrobats, a braided orchestra,
A zoo led by remembering elephants –
Their gaiety comes on a fictitious fleet
To play with northern marvels, which are sky,   80
Sea, rock, the pale sand an accordion
Crooning the wind and sifting its own sieves.
I wave; I shout. The cold sun sips the ocean.
I make a flat stone skid across the sea
And all my calling cannot bring her back
To this real house, she in so much of it.
Its artistry is cooling from her touch –
The yellow sideboards and ceramic boats,
Her miniatures, her objects for the hand,
A poetry of rooms spun from her heart.   90
So close, my love. Our dreams are cooling too.
We go beyond ourselves, beyond our deaths.

France

A dozen sparrows scuttled on the frost.
We watched them play. We stood at the window,
And, if you saw us, then you saw a ghost
In duplicate. I tied her nightgown's bow.
She watched and recognized the passers-by.
Had they looked up, they'd know that she was ill –
Please, do not draw the curtains when I die' –
From all the flowers on the windowsill.

'It's such a shame,' she said. 'Too ill, too quick.'
'I would have liked us to have gone away.'   10
We closed our eyes together, dreaming France,
Its meadows, rivers, woods and *jouissance*.
I counted summers, our love's arithmetic.
'Some other day, my love. Some other day.'

Empty Wardrobes

I sat in a dress shop, trying to look
As dapper as a young ambassador
Or someone who'd impressed me in a book,
A literary rake or movie star.

Clothes are a way of exercising love.
False? A little. And did she like it? Yes.
Days, days, romantic as Rachmaninov,
A ploy of style, and now not comfortless.

She walked out from the changing-room in brown,
A pretty smock with its embroidered fruit;   10
Dress after dress, a lady-like red gown
In which she flounced, a smart career-girl's suit.

The dress she chose was green. She found it in
Our clothes-filled cabin trunk. The pot-pourri,
In muslin bags, was full of where and when.
I turn that scent like a memorial key.

But there's that day in Paris, that I regret,
When I said No, franc-less and husbandly.
She browsed through hangers in the Lafayette,
And that comes back tonight, to trouble me.   20

Now there is grief the couturier, and grief
The needlewoman mourning with her hands,
And grief the scattered finery of life,
The clothes she gave as keepsakes to her friends.

December

'No, don't stop writing your grievous poetry.
It will do you good, this work of your grief.
Keep writing until there is nothing left.
It will take time, and the years will go by.'
Ours was a gentle generation, pacific,
In love with music, art and restaurants,
And he with she, strolling among the canvases,
And she with him, at concerts, coats on their laps.
Almost all of us were shy when we were young.

No friend of ours had ever been to war.   10
So many telephone numbers, remembered addresses;
So many things to remember.
The red sun hangs in a black tree, a moist
Exploded zero, bleeding into the trees
Praying from the earth upward, a psalm
In wood and light, in sky, earth and water.
These bars of birdsong come from another world;
They ring in the air like little doorbells.
They go by quickly, our best florescent selves
As good as summer and in love with being.   20
Reality, I remember you as her soft kiss
At morning. You were her presence beside me.
The red sun drips its molten dusk. Wet fires
Embrace the barren orchards, these gardens in
A city of cold slumbers. I am trapped in it.
It is December. The town is part of my mourning

And I, too, am part of whatever it grieves for.
Whose tears are these, pooled on this cellophane?

Loch Music

I listen as recorded Bach
Restates the rhythms of a loch.
Through blends of dusk and dragonflies
A music settles on my eyes
Until I hear the living moors,
Sunk stones and shadowed conifers,
And what I hear is what I see,
A summer night's divinity.
And I am not administered
Tonight, but feel my life transferred   10
Beyond the realm of where I am
Into a personal extreme,
As on my wrist, my eager pulse
Counts out the blood of someone else.
Mist-moving trees proclaim a sense
Of sight without intelligence;
The intellects of water teach
A truth that's physical and rich.
I nourish nothing with the stars,
With minerals, as I disperse,   20
A scattering of quavered wash
As light against the wind as ash.

At Falkland Palace

For L. J. B.

Innermost dialect
Describes Fife's lyric hills,
Life, love and intellect
In lucid syllables,
    Domestic air.
Natural play of sun and wind
Collaborates with leaf and mind,
The world a sentient
Botanic instrument,
    Visible prayer.   10
Everything's birth begins
On the moment of the May's
Creaturely origins
– I'll live for these good days
    Love leads me to
In gardened places such as this
Of the flower and apple-promise,
Lark-sung, finch-wonderful;
Edenic circumstance, not fall,
    Walking with you.   20
Balladic moments pass,
Tongue-tied, parochial,
A narrative of grass
And stone's hierarchical
    Scottish Versailles.
These native liberties propose
Our lives, rose by unbudding rose,
A song-crazed laverock
Whose melodies unlock
    Audible sky.   30
Dynastic stonework flakes,
Weathers and fails, withdraws
From shapely time and shakes
A gargoyle's severed claws
    At visitors.
Here wrinkled time's abolished house
Perpetuates a posthumous
Nation, monarchy's urn
In which the Stewarts mourn
    What once was theirs.   40
In a country like this
Our ghosts outnumber us:
A ruined artifice
Empty and sonorous,
    Malevolent
In how its past force-feeds with filth
Anachronism's commonwealth
And history bemoans
What history postpones,
    The true event.   50

In the hollows of home
I find life, love and ground
And intimate welcome:
With you, and these, I'm bound
    To history.
Touching your hair, holding your hand,
Your beauty blends with time and land,
    And you are loveliness
    In your green, country dress,
        So fair this day.   60

Going to Aberlemno

By archaeologies of air,
Folkways of kirks and parishes
Revised by salty haar*,   mist
You reach the previous
Country, the picturesque
And the essential east,
By a padlocked summer kiosk
And industry's ill-starred
Inlets, a breaker's-yard
A ruby sore of rust.   10
Here four roads intersect
Beside the tallest oak
And the best hawthorn
Where every step you take
Breaks on an acorn.
Through astral solitude
A Pictish dialect,
Above a bridged Firth, cries
For lyric nationhood,
And horsemen, in a stone disguise,   20
Ride through the Pictish wood.

Jig of the Week No. 21

Under optimum conditions – the room quiet
In fireglow, rain lashing on nocturnal glass –
I start an old American puzzle.
It smells like my Webster's dictionary;
It reminds me of the lesson in Latin
Translating Lincoln's *Gettysburg Address*
Into my Ciceronian of errors.
On junior versions of wet, wintry nights
Around Christmas, I tried to be patient,
A jigsaw on a white enamel tray   10

Encouraging pictorial wanderlust –
My father's ear close to the wireless set's
Hummed murmuring of Cold War '49,
My mother sewing, my brother fast asleep.
Posed by the artist in a daze of stunned
Courage, a wounded man waves in the paint,
A salutation from a grassy foreground.
Here is a piece of sky; this one's a hoof.
I give a man his legs, then rummage for
A clue of horse, a clump of grass. Slaughter's   20
Perfectionists, the North Virginian troops
March through the woods of Pennsylvania
Intent on orders and aesthetic war.
Omniscient history makes good puzzles:
This one is Pickett's *Charge at Gettysburg*.
Jigsaw research – whose side was Pickett on?
I look him up, then file a book away.
The man who painted this supported Blue;
My mind and fingers soldier with the Grey.
Three hundred fragments of American   30
Cardboard carnage! This old Bostonian box
Crossed the Atlantic sixty years ago;
Thousands went all over the United States
Shipped by the Universal Distribution Company.
A segment finishes the Stars and stripes
Carried before blue-trousered infantry.
A dozen pieces, more or less the same,
Assemble shell bursts, foliage and sky,
Turquoise and pink, a summer's afternoon
On Cemetery Ridge, the Butcher's Bill   40
Extortionate in fact but not in paint –
Invoices brought at night, slipped under doors.
A painter oiled his military bias,
For a good price, and then his work became
A reproduction of a reproduction
Issued in multiples, mail-ordered
All over childhood to the merry puzzlers.
You can open old wounds like a box,
That slow knitting of pictures and glory
In Tennessee and Massachusetts.   50
I hold an inch of space, the missing piece,
The notional and beautiful republic
Expressing what was fought for and who died,
'The last full measure of devotion . . . '
– Put hats on heads, place heads on fallen men
And resurrect the dead, the broken wheels:
A finished puzzle ends up in a dream,
A subterranean, consecrated picnic,
A hand waving in the fraternal paint.

The Penny Gibbet

Wearing a badge to prove his pauperdom's
Licensed, official, therefore no disgrace
To the parish and the marching kettledrums,
But grounded deep in lawfulness and place,

He chooses where to stand, a blue-gowned man
Between the barrowed cripples and the tall
Two orphaned daughters of the cateran
They hanged a year ago. Good copper dole

That day by the gallows, as soon as death
Startled the crowds and prophesied their own –   10
Post-mortem charity when strangled breath
Froze in the air, a daughter's Gaelic moan

Chilling the deed. Now there are other throats
Brought here to weight the frosted ropes today.
A loyal beggar, hungering for groats
In the morning, by the guarded carpentry –

'*God Save the King!*' – transacts his livelihood.
A garrison of Union marches up
On its dynastic tread, and gratitude,
Servility and hate, chink in the cup.   20

Queen February

She is no angel-wind, this
Orphan of orphans, kicked out
Thousands of years ago
From her mother's tragedies.

Poverty is all she's known,
Opulent squalor, rain-rags.
She has no complexion;
She is a child without skin

Fathered by distance on ocean.
Ancient ice, incarcerated water,   10
Squeaks on millennial centimetres
At the split, glacial cliffs.

She is northhood's daughter,
Victim first, now terrorist,
With her thin howls, emaciated
Chilled visions, refrigerated wrath

Broadcast on her spectacular
Bellows, her Golgothic breath.
Her special gift is to invade
Whole islands and to sweep them   20

To treeless hygiene, polished rock.
The government of shrubs and trees
Treats for mercy, but branches snap
Where her grey fingers throttle

And go flying as twigs become
Breakages, timber amputees
In the wintry leaflessness
Where light is a month's essence.

Distant trees on a ridge lean
In their submissive silhouettes –   30
Pale and sinister February,
A crippled slave-grove atop

Thrashed copses, frantic woods,
Shivering coniferous tips.
Her cries are thrawn* and vindictive;   twisted
She is a hemisphere's affliction,

Its malevolent waif.
I stare into her stormy eye
And her screams crest as I call
To her – '*I am not your enemy.*'   40

But she is witches' laughter.
There is no talking to her; she is
Colossal unforgiveness,
Mockery, anger, hysteria,

And a man on a ridge feels raped
By this Fury, this Amazon
Giantess with icy lips,
Innumerable flaxen-haired

Lady Viking faces, her shrieks
Exploding from female Valhalla   50
And lifetimes and lifetimes of wrongs,
From the Siberian Islands.

I'm her momentary plunder,
A psyche to be ransacked, buffeted
By weather that begins in ice.
Her booty's like that – lives,

The men and women she enlists
Or steals. Their bones stuff her caverns.
Their spirits fly with her.
She means to cause trouble, and does.   60

When I get home, she's there.
She comes in by windows and doors,
Through the plugged chinks in them,
This Lucifer-girl, this rebel

From the world's sculleries and brooms,
Its pantries, dust-pans and sinks,
Its deplorable circumstances,
Hostels, hovels and addictions.

She has no bed or birthday where she sleeps
Among her countless replicas,   70
Her acolytes, the frozen genders;
She is surrounded by herself

In her stronghold, by cold fire-flesh,
Entwined and sobbing in her streeted caves
As a blizzard whitens darkness
And glaciers pretend to shift.

Early Autumn

Last month, by this same window, moist dusks
Closed the light slowly by summer curtains
And the eye had its space to go flying
Through glassy corners of sky, land and water.

Now it is dark and mid-September breathes
Numberless whispers. After blue sky,
Still Firth and summer's dry appearances,
Night is quick, with shivers at its edges.

Moths in the lampshades set to their *maudit*
Radiant, nocturnal manias, last gasps,   10
Powdery suicides on whirring wings.
They drop dead from electric interrogations.

My fingers smell of a soap that is new to me.
I should close windows, but aromatic fires
Linger from stubble burning all over Fife
And nothing's left of black daylight smoke.

An insect scribbles its white signature.
The letter 'a' can be seen through a veined wing.
Through 'a' the beginning of time can be seen,
A serpent's tongue licking around an apple.   20

Something begins in me; but I don't know
What it is yet. I shall try to find out.
It could be some sort of inhuman benevolence
Made of moth-powder, wings, smoke and soap.

Long Ago

In a house I visited when I was young
I looked in through a partly opened door.
An old man sang 'Long Ago and Far Away'
To a rocking-horse, a friend's grandfather
Whose first-born son was lost at sea
Half-a-century before
In a ship whose name I have forgotten.

Whenever that sad song is played or sung
I'm in that house again, by that same door.
A woman tugs my sleeve. 'Come away,'   10
She says. 'Leave him alone.'
He sings, but he's no longer there.
The rocking-horse is rocking like the sea.
Ocean is everywhere
And the room is wind and rain.

The Canoes

Peter and Rosalind Barker began their holiday on Loch Arn on an evening in the first week of August. We were standing by the rail of what is known in our village of Locharnhead as the Promenade – a name that does no more than repeat the intent of the old Duke, who paid for its construction many years ago as a means of employing our fathers. It is just a widening of the pavement by the side of the road that runs along the head of Loch Arn and then peters out in an unpaved track a mile farther on. We have ten yards of Promenade, and that is not much of a walk. Our fathers used to lean on a low stone wall there. Now, as the old Duke considered this wall a symbol of our fathers' idleness, the job of knocking it down for good wages was meant to be significant. As a boy, I remember the old Duke's rage when, within a day of the work's completion, as he found our fathers loafing on the splendid new barrier they had just built, he craned from the window of his big car and cursed them to lean perpetually on a hot rail by the hearths of damnation. On summer evenings, therefore, we stand where our fathers stood, and one or two very old men sometimes stand beside their sons. For the most part we keep our mouths shut and enjoy the mild breeze that whispers across the water.

The Barkers looked a prosperous young couple. Mr Barker could have been no more than thirty years of age; his wife might have been a year or two younger. Their skins were already tanned, which I thought strange for two people at the start of their holiday. Mrs Barker wore a broad red ribbon in her fair hair, and I was pleased to see that her husband was not the sort of young man whose hair hides his ears and touches his shoulders. They both wore those modern clothes that, in my opinion, look so good on young, slender, healthy men and women. And I noticed that they wore those useful shoes that have no laces but can just be kicked off without your stooping to struggle with ill-tied knots as the blood rushes to your head.

Mr Barker parked his car in the place provided by the County Council, adjacent to the jetty. The jetty was paid for by the old Duke. It is announced as Strictly Private Property on a wooden notice board, though few people here can be bothered to read notices. The paint has long since peeled from it, and its message is rewritten in the badly formed letters of the new Duke's son's factor. Perhaps more would be done for the attractions of Locharnhead, which stands in need of a coat of paint throughout, if it was not the sort of place you can only get back from by returning along the arduous way you came.

Our eyes swung genially to the left to inspect the new arrivals – all, that is, except those of Martin MacEacharn, who is so dull of wit he proclaims himself bored with the examination of tourists. They are a kind of sport with the rest of us. Much amusement has been given to us by campers and hikers and cyclists in their strange garbs and various lengths of shorts and sizes of boots. We tell them they cannot light fires and pitch their tents where they are permitted to do so; and we tell them they may light fires and pitch tents to their hearts' desire where gamekeepers and bailiffs are guaranteed to descend on them once it is dark and there will be no end of inconvenience in finding a legal spot for the night.

Young Gregor remarked enviously on the couple's motorcar. It was low to the ground, green, sleek, and new, and obviously capable of a fair rate of knots. Magee, whose father was an Irishman, ambled over toward Mr and Mrs Barker, pretending he was too shy to speak to them. They were admiring the fine view of the long loch from the jetty. Mr Barker had his arm around his wife's shoulders and was pointing to various phenomena of loveliness in the scenery. They are a familiar sight to us, these couples, who look and behave as if they feel themselves to have arrived in a timeless paradise of water and landscape and courteous strangers in old-fashioned clothes. On fine summer evenings the stillness of the water may be impressed on all your senses to the abandonment of everything else. Our dusks are noted far and wide and remembered by all who have witnessed them. On Loch Arn at dusk the islands become a mist of suggestions. There are old songs that say if only you could go back to them once more, all would be well with you for ever.

Mr Barker noticed Magee beside him and said, 'Good evening,' which Magee acknowledged with his shy smile and slow, soft voice. 'You'll be looking for me, perhaps,' Magee said. All of us leaning on the rail of the Promenade – Muir, Munro, Young Gregor, MacMurdo, MacEacharn, and myself – nodded to each other. When the couple saw us, we all nodded a polite and silent good evening to them, which we believe is necessary, for they have heard of our courtesy, our soft-spoken and excellent good manners and clear speech. All except Martin MacEacharn extended them the thousand welcomes; he was undoubtedly thinking too hard in his miserable way about the Hotel bar behind us and for which he had no money to quench his thirst.

'If you're the boatman, then, yes, you're the man we're waiting for,' said Mr Barker to Magee. My, but he had a bright way of saying it, too, though we all thought that a couple who possessed two long kayak canoes on the trailer behind their motor car had no need of a boatman. He towered over Magee, who is short, wizened, bowlegged, and thin, though his shoulders are broad. Mrs Barker, too, was a good half foot taller than him.

'Well, I think I can just about more or less manage it,' said Magee, with a quick look at his watch, which has not worked in years. 'Yes,' he said, for he must always be repeating himself, 'just about. Just about, if we're handy-dandy.'

'Handy-dandy?' said MacMurdo with contempt. 'Where does he pick them up, for goodness' sake?'

Magee, as we all knew, was desperate for a bit of money, but a lethargic disregard of time is obligatory in these parts. Or that, at least, is the legend. What I will say is that if Magee is late for his dinner by so much as half a minute, his wife will scatter it, and probably Magee as well, before her chickens. Social Security keeps him and the rest of us alive, and I have yet to see a man late for his money. If it ever came to the attention of the clerk that Donal Magee turns a bob or two with his boat, then he would be in deeper water than the depths of Loch Arn, some of which, they say, are very deep.

It soon became clear why the Barkers couldn't paddle themselves out to Incharn. Gear and suitcases are awkward to transport by canoe. Magee, a lazy man, turned round to us with a silent beckoning. He was asking us to lend him a hand but was frightened to say so aloud for fear that our refusals might ruin the atmosphere of traditional, selfless welcoming he had created with such skill and patience. We turned away with the precision of a chorus line it was once my good fortune to see in one of these American musical films – all, that is, except Martin MacEacharn, who wasn't looking.

Once Magee had loaded his boat and tied the canoes to its stern, the flotilla set off in the dusk like a mother duck followed by two chicks. I treated them to one of my lugubrious waves, which I am so good at that no one else is allowed to make one while I am there. How many times, after all, have the holiday types said to us, 'We will remember you forever'? It is a fine thing, to be remembered.

Incharn is a small and beautiful island. That at any rate is how I remember it, for I have not stepped ashore there since I was a boy. A school friend of mine, Murray Mackenzie, lived on Incharn with his mother and father. Only one house stands there among the trees, with a clearing front and back, between the low knolls at each side of the small island. When the Mackenzies left for Glasgow, or whatever town in the south it was, Murray was given a good send-off at school. We had ginger ale, sandwiches, and paper streamers. The minister of the time presented him with a Holy Bible, in which we all inscribed our names in their Gaelic forms.

For a good few years the house lay empty. None of the Duke's men were inclined to live there and put up with rowing back and forth on the loch to get to work and come home from it. A childless couple took its tenancy. The man was a forester, and every day he rowed his boat to a little landing stage by the loch side and then followed the steep track over the hill. But his wife was visited by another boat, at whose oars sat Muir's elder brother, a self-confident and boastful lad who had spent four years at sea with the P & O Steam Navigation Company. Still, the poor woman must have been lonely on Incharn, all by herself most of the day, and she would have grown sick of it, especially in winter, waiting for her man to row back in the early dark; and it would have been worse if there had been a wind blowing or a bad snow. Muir's elder brother went back to sea without so much as a farewell to his fancy woman, and he has never been heard of since. She was found by her husband, standing up to her middle in the waters by the pebble beach, shivering and weeping but unable to take that last step – and one more step would have been enough, for it shelves quickly to the depths. They, too, left, soon after that, and the island and its house lay empty. To row past it used to give me the shudders. I was a young man then, and had been away, and would go away again.

For a number of years the house has been rented in the summer months. The Duke's factor will accept only those who are highly recommended by the solicitor in London who handles the Duke's English business.

Magee and his hirers were soon no longer visible to the naked eye. We lounged by the rail, which has been rubbed by our hands and elbows to a dull shine. Muir, I think, remembers his lost brother when he looks toward Incharn, though he is too sullen to say so.

'Another couple to Incharn, then,' said Munro. 'Now, there's been more folk through the door of that house in a couple of years than there have been kin of mine through the door of my mother's house.' He always calls his house his mother's. She has been dead for twenty years; but we are born in houses, as well as of mothers.

'It's a sad thing that no one will lend a man the price of a pint of beer,' said MacEacharn.

'If we wait for Magee returning,' said the cool, calculating, and thirsty MacMurdo, 'then we'll have the price of several apiece. A twenty-minute drag over the loch is worth a pound or two.'

'Aye,' said Young Gregor, 'and don't forget the twenty minutes back.'

Eyes tried to focus on Incharn as its form vanished into the dusk. Lips were wetted by tongues as we imagined the pints of beer to which Magee might treat us on his return if we behaved nicely toward him or threatened him with violence. But Magee was in one of his funny moods. He is not the man to stand up to a woman like his wife. Munro has said, 'I'm glad I am married to the woman who accepted my proposal, but I'm doubly thankful I'm not married as much as all *that*.'

Magee did not come back but illustrated once again how he has inherited from his father an aptitude for the evasion of responsibilities. He beached his boat a few hundred yards to the right of us, where there is a spit of sand, and then went home in the dark with his money, hoping perhaps to buy a few hours of peace and quiet through giving his wife a cut of his boatman's fee.

That Magee had been well paid is a matter of which I am certain. A couple of nights after the arrival of Mr and Mrs Barker, I had nothing to do, and Magee agreed that I go with himself and another English couple to Inverela, where there is another house on the new Duke's son's estates. It stands by the loch side and cannot be reached by road unless you park a mile from it and then walk along a narrow track. To go by boat is only sensible.

'Well, well, then,' Magee began as we were taking our leave of the Englishman on Inverela's tiny landing stage. His wife, by the way, was running around cooing about how wonderful it was, but we took no notice of that. 'I hope the weather stays fine and the loch remains as calm as a looking glass all the while you are here.' Highly impressed by this eloquent desire for their comforts, the Englishman gestured for his wife to come over and hear this, because it was obvious that Magee was far from finished. 'And may there be no drop of rain, except perhaps once or twice in the night, to make your mornings fresh and to keep the leaves as green as you wish to see them.'

They settled back before this recitation.

'And may your sleep be undisturbed and tranquil and you have no reminder whatsoever of the cares of the world, which I am told are the very devil outwith of Loch Arn. And, to translate from our Gaelic' – of which Magee knows one curse, two toasts, and a farewell – 'may your bannocks never freeze over or your hair fall out, and may you never forget to salt your potatoes.'

I imagined how that couple would say to each other, as soon as our backs were turned, that it was true after all: the people here speak better English than the English. In that matter, the explanation is to be found in the care with which our kinsmen of long ago, in their clachans[1] by the shores of Loch Arn, set about forgetting their original tongue so that their children, and their children's children, and all their posterity would converse in translation.

As Magee stepped into his boat, it was in the way of a man who expects to be paid nothing at all for his troubles. His grateful employer was shuffling in his jacket for money – a sight studiously avoided by Magee's little blue eyes, which are too close together. The Englishman had a look of prosperity about him and a willingness to be forthcoming. 'Ah . . . ah . . . ' The Englishman was a bit embarrassed. 'How much do I owe you?'

Now, there can be a long and historical answer to that one, but Magee thought for a moment with one hand on his chin while the other removed his hat and began scratching his head. 'How . . . how much would you say it was worth?'

'Would a fiver do?' asked the Englishman. His wife nudged him. Magee, like myself, was quick to notice that this woman, in a hat of unduly wide brim – dressed, it seemed to me, for a safari – was a touch on the overpaying side of humanity.

I was all for putting an end to Magee's playacting and stretching my own hand out to receive the note. But Magee began ponderously calculating: 'Now, then . . . It is thirty minutes out, after the ten minutes it took to get you aboard, and unloading you took another ten minutes, while it will take us another thirty to get back home . . . '

That was a fine stroke of obscurity, for the man was nudged once more by his grinning wife, and he produced another fiver. Two fivers together was more than the government gave you for having no job. Magee looked at the notes as if insulted.

'Now, that seems a lot to a man like myself . . . sir,' he said. 'How does the seven pounds strike you . . . sir? You see, it's the fair price.'

'A bit of a problem there,' said the gent. 'I haven't a single note on me.'

'Then, in that case,' said Magee, a bit too quickly, 'I'll take the ten pounds and I'll see you when you come to Locharnhead.'

'How will we get there?' asked the woman, who was already blinking in a soft hail of midges.

'By that boat there,' said Magee, who pointed to a beached rowing boat that belonged to the house. 'Or you may walk by the track, on your right.'

---

[1] Villages.

'Ah. I see. Yes, indeed. On the right, you say?'

'On the right, sir. But you will be quicker by the loch.'

I remember it took the Englishman four hours to row to Locharnhead the following day, for that canny son of an Irishman had been to Inverela that morning to hide one of the oars. Magee did well with a sort of contract for their subsequent transportation.

'Ten pounds for a night's work, Magee,' I said on our return voyage. 'Is it not a liberty to take so large a sum, even from an Englishman who looks as though he can well afford it?'

'Do you want a drink?' he asked. 'Or do you want a *good* drink?'

'You know me,' I said.

'Then hold your hush and don't whine at me for a hypocrite. Because daylight robbery is exactly what it is, and you and the rest of them will sup on the benefit of it. Though I'll tell you true enough that if he didn't look such a pig of a rich man in his pink shirt and white breeks, I'd have let him off with the three pounds the factor says is the fixed charge to Inverela.'

We passed Incharn on the return trip in the late dusk. I waved to its holiday tenants, who had lit a fire on the beach. That couple we'd just left at Inverela could not be imagined lighting a bonfire. I had a feeling the Barkers would have been glad of our company if we had called on them for a few moments, but the thirsty lads, we knew, would be waiting for us on the Promenade, and with me in the boat Magee would have no chance of getting up to his tricks. In the light of their bonfire Mr and Mrs Barker looked like people of the far long ago, when, we are told, there was great happiness and heroism in the world. Or it may just have been the way they carried their youthfulness that led me to think so.

'Now, I hope you didn't fleece that nice couple of the Barkers there.'

'What kind of a thief do you take me to be? I asked for the factor's fixed charge, and they were kind enough to pass me a fiver.'

'Aye, well, there will be no more work for you out of that pair. These two are water babies.'

A day or two later I was walking on the hill. My old pal Red Alistair was, I knew, reluctantly laying down a drain on the Duke's lower pastures – the one he was meant to do the year before but didn't get around to finishing. He is called Red on account of the political pamphlets he inherited from his father. He is annoyed by the nickname, being twice the Tory even than the new Duke's son, and he keeps his legacy of pamphlets in deference to his father's memory. As I was looking for Red Alistair, I found the minister scrutinising the loch through his spyglass.

'Now, there's a sight I've never seen on the loch before,' he said. 'There are two canoes on it today.'

He gave me his glass and I had a clear view of Mr and Mrs Barker in single line ahead. They wore yellow waterproof jackets and sensible life jackets as well, which was a relief to me.

'Is there any chance of that becoming popular?' I asked the minister, after I had told him who the two canoeists were and what nice people they had turned out to be.

'You should ask that of Young Gregor. He's the boy who's daft on boats round here, though if he ever opens that marina he does nothing but talk about, we will become a laughing-stock for our broken craft, and make no mistake.'

He was as disappointed in Young Gregor as we all were. 'Go, for God's sake, to a southern city,' we urged the boy. 'There's nothing here but old men and the bed-and-breakfast trade.' Lack of capital was what he complained of – that and the poor show of enthusiasm he received from the manager of the Bank, which comes twice a week to Locharnhead in a caravan.

'These canoes can fairly shift some,' said the minister. 'My, if I was young, I'd be inclined to try my hand at that. What an emblem of youth is there before our eyes.'

'We should encourage Young Gregor in it,' I suggested. 'These craft appear to have no engines at all.'

'That boy will break my heart. Is there nothing that can be found for him to do?'

'Can you imagine any woman from round here sporting about on the water like that?'

'Our women are not so much bad-natured as unpredictable,' he decided. 'By and large, though, it might be the bad nature you cannot predict. But we have known great joys in our time. There is no sweeter thing in this life than an harmonious domesticity. You know, I even miss the bad nature of my late wife.' He paused as he peered through his telescope. 'They are a tall couple, these English Barkers.'

'They tell me she is called Rosalind.'

'Now, that is a name from Shakespeare, I believe.'

'Then it's a fair English name,' I remember saying, 'for a young woman as handsome as Mrs Barker and with a true demeanour to go with it.'

'It makes a change from Morag, or Fiona, I'll say that much,' said the minister.

For many more minutes we stood there on the hill, exchanging the spyglass as we watched the two canoes.

'What day is it?' asked the minister.

'I think it must be Thursday, for I saw the women waiting on the fishmonger's van.'

Mr and Mrs Barker visited the Hotel bar in the early part of some evenings for a drink and a bite to eat. While they were inside, we took the opportunity of examining their Eskimo craft – not, of course, that there is much to look at in a kayak canoe. I studied them longer than the others had the patience for. A jaunt in one of them would have been very satisfying. To have asked Mr Barker might have been thought a bit eccentric of me, though I doubt if he would have taken it as an impertinence. Their canoes had a very modern look to them, as, indeed, had that bright and lively couple with their air of freedom.

'Aye,' said MacMurdo, who joined me on the jetty, 'that must be a fine and healthy outdoor sport for them – the sort of thing that could set you up for the winter and keep you well.' MacMurdo, fresh-faced as he is for his years, is housebound for three months of the calendar with the sniffles. When the Barkers came back, we stood to one side and said our soft 'Good evening' together, which they returned. Then we watched them slip into their canoes and paddle away into the early dusk.

'It's the best time of all to be on the water,' said MacMurdo. 'Just look at the beauty of it over there. The whole world is getting itself ready to settle down for the night.'

'Do you think he'd mind if I asked him – I mean, if he'd let me take his canoe out for a few minutes?'

'What's so special about one of these canoes?'

'They strike me for one thing as an exciting little sort of a craft, that's what. Now, look there, and see how close you would be to the water.'

'A man of your age . . . A boat like that is for young things.'

'It would be interesting to *me*.'

A man like myself might be expected to resent these folks who come up from the south like swallows to take their ease on a country that has brought me no prosperity. All the same, no one can tell me better than I tell myself that I am as lazy as any man born. Part of my trouble is that I have become content enough on plain victuals in modest quantities and two packets of Players a week. What jobs I've done in other parts than this one did not contribute much to my happiness. But there are things I've seen, and people I've met, I would not do without if I had my chance again. When the mobile library, which is a wonderful thing, calls at Locharnhead, I am the first man aboard and the last man out. That is not hard, as the only other reader in our community, apart from the youngest MacMurdo when he's at home, is Mrs Carmichael, wife of our stingy publican and the Hotel's cook. By the way, I once ate a large dinner there. It was not worth the money, and Magee and the rest of them watched me through the window for all five courses, screwing up their faces and licking their chops in an ironic manner. MacEacharn, I noticed, was there, too, but that obstinate man wasn't even looking.

But for all the large contrast between myself and the likes of Mr and Mrs Barker, it made me mellow and marvellously sad to watch them paddle in the still waters of Loch Arn at dusk, going toward Incharn, where the Mackenzies once lived, and that unhappy couple who followed them.

Incharn, as I have said, is a beautiful island. A good number of trees grow there, and on the side you cannot see from the head of the loch there is low ground and a growth of reeds of which nesting swans and water-fowl are appreciative. This is the most beautiful side of all, though you can only see it properly from the water, which means that it has been observed by few people. Facing Locharnhead, the beach is of fine pebbles, and it slopes quickly into the water. Crab apples grew there when my friend Mackenzie lived on it, and that bitter fruit made grand jelly in his mother's big copper pan. They had a black leaded stove of great size, which Mrs Mackenzie kept as spotlessly black as a Seaforth's boots, and we were famous for the spit and polish. Mrs Mackenzie would do her washing in a wooden tub on the beach, and her suds floated and spread as Murray and I threw stones at the scattering patches of foam.

People on holiday do no washing at all, I'm told. Sometimes I felt like telling Mr and Mrs Barker about Incharn, but I never got round to it. They might have been interested. Magee has been known to tell those he ferries to the island of the tragedy that befell there. In his story, the woman drowned herself, and her demented husband first slew her lover with his bare hands and then committed his own life to the chill waters, but it was not that way. For all I know, the Barkers heard that story from Magee; but if they did, they were too happy to pay it any heed.

At night you can see the small lights of the cottage if its blinds or curtains are not drawn. In our famous dusks and sunsettings, the lights seem to spread in the open and watery mist, and they float above the island like benedictions. A man can look toward Incharn and feel drawn toward it. Muir's brother may have felt that, too, for whether the beauty of a place discriminates among those who are to be compelled by it is not a subtlety I am prepared to go into. Incharn draws a charitable thought from me, at any rate. But then I was always a bachelor, though not because I wanted to be one; and so I am always glad of something that holds disgruntlements at bay. All winter long I look forward to the holiday couples. It would please me more if Mr and Mrs Barker were to come back, with their frail canoes, and the way they splashed each other with water off their paddles, and capsized and rolled over under the water and came back up again as my heart beat with admiration for them – and, above all, the way they just followed each other about on the still water.

Alan Bold (1943 – 1998)

As well as a poet, Bold has been an astonishingly fertile critic and editor, probably the most heard from in recent Scottish letters.

Grass

Grass basks greedily in the sun
As light penetrates each vein
Saturating the stem in the sheath.

Grass contains every gradation of green:
Loves both fiery sun and drenching rain;
Tugs the watcher downwards, underneath

Grass to crushing earth and stone.
Still the watcher comes to watch again,
To see the grass caress the gravel path.

The Auld Symie

Winter is deasie
An' ootside the snaw
Churns like a salmon
In its deid-thraw.

White gettin' mair white
Piled on the stanes
Folk look stark naked
Clad in their banes.

But still the auld symie*   devil
Wi' bent kipper-nose   10
Maks for the kirk where
God alane goes.

Harvest

By the frontiers of a farmer's field,
In shadow cast by the hawthorn hedgerow,
A body lies bleeding. Come close:
See the features growing old

While the barley brightens in the sun.
A body lies bleeding. The ground
Is stained with blood, red on brown
Supporting yellow stalks. The wound

Is fresh, still oozing as the sun
Shifts from pale yellow to blood-red   10
In a cloudless sapphire sky.
The body darkens in the shade.

Another body, running for its life,
Holds the horizon as the sunset dies:
A silhouette sharp as the scythe
That comes to the barley, bringing death.

Alexander Hutchison (1943 –)

Mr Scales Walks His Dog

The dog is so old dust flies out from its arse as it runs;
the dog is so old its tongue rattles in its mouth, its eyes were changed
in the 17th century, its legs are borrowed from a Louis Fourteen bedside cabinet.
The dog is barking with an antique excitement.
Scales dog is so old its barks hang in the air like old socks,
like faded paper flowers.
It is so old it played the doorman of the Atlantic Hotel in *The Last Laugh*,
so old it played the washroom attendant too.
Scales dog is so old he never learned to grow old gracefully.
Scales dog bites in stages.   10
Scales dog smells of naphtha.
Scales dog misjudges steps and trips.
Scales dog begs for scraps, licks plates.
Scales dog is seven times older than you think:
so he runs elliptically; so he cannot see spiders; so he is often distracted;
so he loses peanuts dropped at his feet; so he has suddenly become diabetic
and drinks from puddles; so there is bad wind in his system that came over
with the Mayflower; so he rolls on his back only once a week.
Scales dog is Gormenghast, is Nanny Slagg.
Scales dog is Horus, is Solomon Grundy.   20
His body makes disconnected music.
He is so old his eyes are glazed with blood;
so old wonders have ceased; so old all his diseases are benign; so old
he disappoints instantly; so old his aim is bad.
Scales dog is so old each day Scales urges him to die.
Scales dog puts on a show like a bad magician.
Scales dog squats as if he was signing the Declaration of Independence.
Scales dog is so old worms tired of him.
So old his fleas have won prizes for longevity.
So old his dreams are on microfilm in the Museum of Modern Art.
So old he looks accusingly.   31
So old he scratches for fun.
Scales dog was buried with the Pharaohs, with the Aztecs; draws social
security from fourteen countries; travels with his blanket; throws up on
the rug; has a galaxy named after him; Scales dog runs scared;
would have each day the same, the same;
twitches in his sleep,
wheezes.

Inchcolm[1]

This morning I saw
on the waters of the firth a diving
bird I never saw before, turning a nimble
loop to enter the wave, and the wonder
of green light filtering down.

What was it like
for the king – Alexander, when the boat
nearly foundered, and all might be tossed
in the swirl of the sea? Did he kick
his boots free? Did he call out by his   10
birth-right for men to assist him?
And how did they come to land?

None of these
things is reported with surety. But fear,
if he felt it, was followed by gratitude –
the gift of an abbey for the Inch of
St Colme. 'Lord, I was drowning. What
better can I build than this?'

Then chancel
and chapter-house rose on the island.   20
Stone flourished on stone. Upon the table
slab of the altar five wounds were cut
like stars.

'It is foolish
to shrink from what cannot be avoided.' Such
safety was the bread they broke to sustain
them. 'Quicquid mali finxerit lingua' –
whatever evil the tongue composes
conscience may overcome.

What warmth   30
of the spirit must have wound itself
round them – only one social fireplace
beyond that in the kitchen – though something
burned in the wall of the Choir, when
Richard the Bishop had his heart interred,
so his ardor became part of the fabric
of the building.

Today we have
come to the natural harbour on the lee
side of the isthmus, climbed iron rungs   40
to the pier-head, and followed a path
by the narrow neck of land to stand

---

[1] An island in the Firth of Forth.

in the grave-yard, the Relig Oran,
surveying what replaced Colme's
daub and wattle traces.

      Kings of Scotland
and Norway, Danes that were slain
at the 'bickering' of Kinghorn, all
have their rest here: some at a stiff
price, and some with due reverence.   50

      It is still broad
day when I take the night stair from
the ruins of the Church, and climb with my
sleeping child in my arms to the Dormitory,
talking and singing, though she sleeps,
and sitting for a while in the recess
at one of the windows.

        The last day of January,   58
and the weather being mild, the water will
offer no menace as we make our return, not even
when we pass by Aberdour, crossing the Deep of
that impious Mortimer, long consigned in his shroud
of lead, well short of the island for which
he possessed, by gift of his forebear,
the right of interment.

      But now there burns
in my arms a burden lightly borne – her
hair like a cresset or candle in the dark,
her hair like a badge or blazon – my
darling girl.   70

      Within this high-vaulted
chamber I show you to shadows: the dreaming
forms of those who sleep like mist, who looked
in their own way for what holds true beneath
the bewilderment of surfaces.

      It was a cold, uncertain,
isolate existence; lived besides in a tangle
of dogma, that wrapped in despite: rock,
grass, flesh, sea-thrift and sea-bird.

      I hold you here   80
against distortion; knowing that love
is work, is hard we know as breaking stones,
and desperate distance even when
the breath comes close.

      But patience
with yourself; patience with the love
of others is a law worth learning, a thread
of blood I give you as a bond; and the water

of the world to enter and feed there as in
your natural element, taking your place   90
and composure, folding life around you,
your father's breath like a tide
on the margin of sleep.

Roderick Watson (1943 –)

The Director of the Museum

I was on holiday in August,
the University year was ended,
but on that particular afternoon
when I walked into town
I saw that everything was changed
and it was time for me to find
(as so many had to do)
a technique for coming through.

So I numbered kerb-stones by the road,
and placed them in linen bags   10
carefully labeled and stitched from flour sacks
for use when I was a student
of geology (it was years ago)
I hardly thought I would need them again,
still, I kept them, and that is how
I started my collection.

It seems the fireball in the air
had spoiled the concrete slabs
used for the street, and metre by metre
you can see its print on the face   20
of the pavement – fused, cracked, or merely
burned, according to the distance from centre.
(I proved all this by later study
of my map and sample bags.)

Curiosities came to light:
a mechanic's spanner and hand
welded in the engine it was mending;
and you will all have heard
of the ball in the air that never came down
(I cut its shadow from a wall).   30
But the tea-cup that looks like a flower
seems duller on my shelves

and I hardly know it any more
for the jewel among the ashes
found on those concentric shores
where I moved in a mineralogist's dream;
until the time the cries died down
around me, and dazed and awake I stood
in the suburbs and knew that I survived
(and the collection was complete).   40

Beyond the Edge

I'm drawn to the moment on a blade when steel
fades out of self and into nothing, on a line
fine enough to defy even the gentlest touch.

There were seven chisels in my father's toolbox
laid top and tail about like sardines
(or packed on their sides like bottles of wine)
yet each one different suited and ground
to its own purpose and buffed
to a misty mirror-finish on the flat.

Unused for years they speak of when   10
preparation seemed all there was to do
and as important as the job itself
in the fight against encroaching dullness
with hands that shook on those clouded blades.
This was to be his last anthology of sharpness.

Each chisel was taken to the limit
honed on a strap and then laid by
keen to make even the dullest timber
flower – some other day perhaps.
I took them home and use them now   20
– and now and then I sharpen one. Thinking

nothing cuts forever. Thinking
of a molecular discrimination so refined
that you would feel nothing should the finger
slip to bone – beyond surprise
at how the blood has come to marry oil
on the cold black stone below.

So we work to carve shape from sense
trembling in the confusion of the wild woods
out there – where my father went to live   30
altogether away from sharp edges.
With a toolbox ready for every single thing
but that which came to pass.

Ian Abbot (1944 – 1989)

The Bestiary of Cortes

Mythical
we move like centaurs
through the fabulous wood.

They come to us
jewelled like birds:
their eyes are downcast, they look into the earth:
mould stirs under their feet.
They come to us
with shields made of feathers,
with armour   10
made of feathers,
with bones, with souls
made of feathers.

They look on our ships and are amazed: from every tree
their eyes stare down like pearls. I am their god.
None can believe
that everything I am is mortal. They deploy
about my feet their offerings of gold.
And now my pikes split bone from bone
like heavy bills; the sun gorges   20
on blood and broken plumes, steam
rises from the earth.
A wind stirs my cloak like wings,
my horse is trembling against my thighs.

I move like a centaur through the sullen green.
They see me now.
I am the one, the feathered one,
the black. My heavy bill clacks shut.
I am the raven of Christ.

Ariel [1]

A sudden breath, a dark sharp
whispered word, and I
go out into the world like dreams.

---

[1] One remembers that Ariel is the not-altogether willing spirit-servant of the magician, Prospero, in Shakespeare's *Tempest*. His name suggests his nature.

The earth below me
passes by like smoke, and as I turn
my head this way and that
there are those who sleep
and those
whom I bring out of sleep; those who are born   9
into the world and those from whom I draw the world away.

All night, all night
I work in whispers, dreams and air
until the morning brings me back here to your feet.

To feel your collar fixed about my neck
and my soul fastened to the iron in the earth.

A Crofter Buried

To wade at last
in the soft ocean of the earth, finally to see
how your every tentative step
has been preserved, infolded:
and to notice
how they form one singular, uncertain track
that leads back all the way to your beginnings.

Your children carry you above ground. Through stones
and over dark, low bushes.
Now you move   10
in wood and brass while under and between

your body and their solemn legs
the warm air trembles like a sheaf.

You thought to print the earth indelibly.
But now let down, and burdened
with the bare field's sullen weight,
you must lie still and be content.
The cairn begins to crumble
even as the final stone is being placed.

Your footprints are already blowing shut.   20
In time the earth accepts from you
the price of everything you borrowed from it.

Avoiding the Gods

They have come
to scald our blood, to call us out
from our bright houses to the twisted shadows under trees.
Let us not listen to them. Do not let them in.

There beyond the darkened garden, in the obscure forest,
the night expends itself in numberless small deaths.
That is the way of them, the way of predators. A kind
of innocent destruction
but destruction nonetheless.

Let us abandon them   10
to moulder on their crosses,
beat their iron wings; to redeploy their armies and invent
new forms of sinning and of guilt.

Let us remain here, calmly
taking bread, and wine, and speech.
And in the morning
take our limbs to work, and walk behind
the swaying, fuming breath of cattle.

And let us look for our salvation
in the language we have come to teach ourselves.   20

Shrapnel

It came to him, he said,
one white night in an empty,
frozen desert of his youth
as he stood lost beneath a sky
that fumed with clouds of seeding stars.

Some cometary debris,
flung outwards from
the great, elliptical orbiting of wars
brushed by him, pressed
its glittering needles through his flesh   10

and pinned him down.
But he remembered nothing of it
till he woke uneasily
among the charred bones
and the ruinous, subsiding light of fires.

Then later, someone drew
those tiny spittings out of him, except
for one deep splinter, just
too intimately-placed
to tease away with safety.   20

So now he bears it with him, inoffensive
for the most part, quiescent
other than on nights like this
when we sit by and watch again
his blank eyes flicker

as that old recording whirls in him,
spinning its terrible roll
of names, and sounds, and silenced voices.
His unforgetting needle twists and shifts itself; minutely
scratching, scratching at his heart.   30

Ga–Cridhe

A spear once passed among the hands of heroes.
It came to each one
hooded and laced in leather, thonged
and tightly bound about its shaft.
A monk-spear, a spear without a voice,
nevertheless it trembled imperceptibly
throughout the body of the man who carried it.

So that at a certain time, inexorably,
his fingers would unravel ancient knots
and slowly slip the hood   10
until the head emerged, barren
as the colour of the moon
and studded randomly with bright, barbaric rivets.

Then the voice of the spear would issue from his mouth:
a voice of ruin, hoarse
with the colour of blood. Tumultuous with destruction
it would shout in his mind like the sea
and drive him like an animal
while his companions gathered and stood by,
nodding their grey heads sadly.   20
Until at length, sated with calamity
the man and the spear lay down together,
and waited to be cowled again with piety and guilt.

And now this spear, or one of its descendants, lives with me.
I keep it hooded: day by day investigate
the safety of its thongs.
But late at night, in sleep
I feel that same spear tremble like a foetus. My dreams
are a complex maze of leather, filled
with patterns of interwoven lines. The thongs   30
whisper to me, and stained
with the mythical colour of blood
my hands rehearse a slow untying of the knots.

Harbingers

A friend once told me how, before
a great outbreak of cholera or yellow
fever struck his father's village into dust,
certain families had seen, outside
their windows or their doors
the figure of an angel trembling in the air at noon.

Its form, each one agreed, was of a beauty
almost beyond speech: a radiant innocence
haloed in chromatic light that seemed to murmur
soundless words of benison and peace.   10
Nonetheless, within ten days,
the remnants of these families
were broken with exhaustion after burying their dead.

And I recalled a day in August, on the burning moor,
when I watched lean, red dogs that quartered
to the right and to the left
before a straggled line of men.
Their bodies flowed like wine above the heather, every muscle
shaped in the fluidity of oils, each fibre
of their coats a blaze of russet lights.   20

They trembled as they smelled the nestling coveys.
Wrapped in intense innocence, they ignored
the dark oiled barrels swinging into place,
but floated forward, almost motionless;
the dazzling harbingers of a day of blood.

Alison Fell (1944 –)

For Myself

In her
thirty-three year old
long grown
prime,
still the gnarled
changeling
peeks from her
cot,
ugly as a turnip
sheep-gnawed,   10
little sprout
which grew

in the dark
lives hardy through
frost,
etched
with a breadknife,
lonely as
black Hallowe'en,
fire hungers   20
in her lantern
eyes

The Hallowe'en Witch

*(for the wire-cutters at Greenham Common,
31 October 1983)*

She who slips out
of doors in the hour
between blindness
and enchantment
must be flotsam or
trouble

After the moon goes down
and the cameras are asleep
she does butterfly-balance
on the turn of the night   10
where the weathers set sail

Safer than shuttered houses
in the space she waits
while soldiers in their muttering beds
suckle like cats at the blankets
and dream of a long eye entering,
the wall open wide

Only in the morning
she is busy and small and
they will not know her   20
as she wipes the scattered
sun like dust from her
black clothes
and hides in the city's
grinding eye

Desire

The wind is strong enough to move wasps.
This blowing branch is mine,
silvery thing, all mine,
my teethmarks swarm over it:
what sweet sap and small beetles racing.

Mother warns me I will get worms
from this zest
for chewing and digesting
fur buds and the satin
leaves of beech, from all this   10
testing and possessing.
'Stop that,' she says.
'Stop this minute. See the
wee eggs you'll swallow!'

My needle-bright eye is rash
and scans greedily,
sees pine-cones lose pollen
in yellow gusts;
the loch's rim has a
curd of it, the face of   20
the middle deeps is
skimmed with dust and wrinkles.

The birch trunk wears a
sleeve of paper, clear-layered,
like sunburned skin – a wrap.
It streams from my thumbnail
till the wind snatches it.

Heart-breaker

wheelchair lady
approaching 100 years old
in white straw hat
with pink petunia
and fine angry eyes on me
because she too
was once long as a lily
and in love
because today
they tucked her disastrous limbs   10
neatly sideways
and dressed her for holidays
and she thinks I don't know
petunia was her colour

the one she stung
and blistered in
and she thinks I don't know
what laughter seamed
her quartz and cunning face
and she thinks I don't know   20
what's coming to me

Rannoch Moor

Behind us, Glencoe of the Slaughter,
Achnacone, field of dogs,
Achtriachan, where the water-bull
lurks among thin fish tickled by weed,
and the Great Herdsman of Etive
over us like a black axe[1]

To pace the moor, and mark it,
like a cat bruises the grass
for its bed,
or be claimed instead –   10
scars of burnt heather, dead
weariness, the sheep paths
misleading, and the bogs
pitted with white water

Slow steps mark the line
on the moor sour with struggle,
where darkness is brought to the brim,
and the bog-cotton bursts
like puffs of smoke
after a musket,   20
and the broken bleached roots
of the old forest
are white bones under
the petrol shimmer of methane

Slow march in the whine
of telegraph wires,
while the wind chops
at my breath,
and the peat mud sticks to my feet
like rafts   30

---

[1] The Great Herdsman of Etive – *Buchaille Etive Mor* – is a mountain at the east end of Glencoe (AF).

Shena Mackay (1944 –)

Dreams of Dead Women's Handbags

It was a black evening bag sequined with salt, open-mouthed under a rusted marcasite clasp, revealing a black moiré silk lining stained by seawater; a relic stranded in the wrack of tarry pebbles and tufts of blue and orange nylon string like garish sea anemones, crab shells and lobster legs, plastic detritus, oily feathers, condoms and rubbery weed and clouded glass, the dry white sponges of whelk egg cases, and a brittle black-horned mermaid's purse. This image, the wreckage of a dream beached on the morning, would not float away; as empty as an open shell, the black bivalve emitted a silent howl of despair; clouds passed through its mirror.

Susan Vigo was much possessed by death. Sitting on a slow train to the coast, at a table in the compartment adjacent to the buffet car, she thought about her recurring dream and about a means of murder. A book and a newspaper lay in front of her, and as she inserted the word 'limpid' in the crossword, completing the puzzle, she saw aquamarine water in a rock pool wavering limpidly over a conical white limpet shell. Her own id was rather limp that morning, she felt; the gold top of her pen tasted briny in her mouth. The colour of the water was the precise clear almost-green of spring evening skies when the city trembled with the possibility of love. She wondered dispassionately if she would ever encounter such a sky again, and as she wondered, she saw a handbag half-submerged on the bottom of the pool among the wavering weeds, green and encrusted with limpets, as though it had lain there for a long time, releasing gentle strings of bubbles like dreams and memories. A mermaid's purse, she remembered her father teaching her, as she made her way to the buffet, was the horny egg case of a skate, or ray or shark, but to whom the desolate handbag in her dreams had belonged, she had no idea, only that its owner was dead.

The buffet car steward seemed familiar, but perhaps the painful red eyes were uniform issue, along with the shiny jacket spattered by toasted sandwiches; his hair had been combed back with bacon grease and fell in curly rashers on his collar, his red tie was as slick as a dying poppy's petal. As Susan waited in the queue she told herself that he could have no possible significance in her life, and reminded herself that she made many journeys and had probably encountered him before, leering over the formica counter of another train. Nevertheless she watched him, it was her habit to stare at people, with an uneasy notion that he was Charon ferrying her across the Styx – but Charon would not be the barman, but the driver of this Inter-City train, sitting at the controls in his cab, racing them down the rails to the Elysian fields, and she was almost certain that she and her fellow passengers were still alive and their coins were for the purchase of refreshments and not the fees of the dead.

The barman's years of bracing himself on the swaying floors of articulated metal snakes had given him the measure of his customers. The woman in the simulated beige mink, in front of Susan in the queue, asked for two gin and tonics, one for an imaginary friend down the corridor, and was given two little green bottles, two cans of tonic, and one plastic cup with a contemptuous fistful of ice cubes. Her eyes met the barman's and she did not demur. One of his eyes closed like a snake's in a wink at Susan as the woman fumbled her purchases from the counter. 'It takes one to know one,' thought Susan refusing to be drawn into complicity by the reptilian lid of his red eye as she ordered her coffee. Her face in the mirror behind the bar, her shirt, her scarf, her brooch, the cut of her jacket spoke as quietly of success as the fur-coated woman's screeched failure.

Failure. That was a word Susan Vigo hated. She saw it as a sickly plant with etiolated leaves, flourishing in dank unpleasant places, a parasite on a rotting trunk, or a pot plant on the windowsills of houses of people she despised. If she had cared to, she could have supplied a net curtain on a string as a backcloth and a plaster Alsatian, but she had a horror of rotting window frames and rented rooms, and banished the image.

Susan Vigo was not the sort of woman who would order two gins for herself on a train. She was not, like some she could name, the sort of writer who would arrive to give a reading with a wine-splashed book and grains of cat litter in her trouser turn-ups, having fortified herself with spirits on the journey for the ordeal, who would enter in disarray and stumble into disrepute. The books in her overnight bag were glossy and immaculate with clean white strips of paper placed between the pages, to mark the passages which she would read. She did not regard it as an ordeal; she had memorised her introductory speech, and was looking forward to the evening. She had done her homework, and would have been able to relax with a book by another author had consciousness of the delivery date of her own next crime novel not threatened like a migraine at the edge of her brain.

The irony was that the title of her book was *Deadline* and for the first time in her life, she feared that she would not meet hers. Notice of it had appeared already in her publisher's catalogue and she had not even got the plot. It was set on the coast, she knew that; it involved a writer – yes, and horned poppy and sea holly and viper's bugloss, stranded sea-mice leaking rainbows into the sand, and of course her Detective Inspector Christopher Hartshorn, an investigator of the intellectual, laconic school; a body – naturally; a handbag washed up on the beach – the sort of handbag that had foxtrotted to Harry Roy, or a flaunting scarlet patent number blatant as a stiletto heel, a steel-faceted purse, a gondola basket holding a copy of *Mirabelle* or *Roxy* – she didn't even know in which period to set her murder – a drawstring leather bag which smelled of raw camel hide, a satchel with a wooden pencil box, a strap purse, containing a threepenny bit, worn across the front of a gymslip – old handbags like discarded lovers. She sifted desperately through the heap of silk and plastic, leather and wicker – it had to be black, like the handbag in her dream.

Susan lived in Hampstead, on a staple diet of vodka and asparagus, fresh in season, or tinned. It made life simple; she never had to think about what food to buy except when she had guests, which was not very often; she was more entertained than entertaining. She loved her flat and lived there alone. She had once been given two lovebirds but had grown jealous of their absorption in each other and had given them away. Trailing plants now entwined the bars of the cage where the pink and yellow birds had preened, kissing each other with waxy bills; she preferred their green indifference. There was not a trace of a plaster Alsatian. The man who had seduced her had introduced her to asparagus, its tender green heads swimming in butter, with baked beans – her choice. Professor Bruno Rosenblum, lecturer in poetry who although his juxtaposed names conjured up withered roses on their stems, had once strewn the bed with roses while she slept. Waking in the scent and petals, she had wept. "'Ah, as the heart grows older, it will come to such sights colder",' she thought now, in the train, remembering, as the past, like the dried petals of potpourri exhaled a slight sad scent, and 'Perhaps G. M. Hopkins got it right – it is always ourselves for whom we are grieving – enough of this' she turned from the dirty window slashed with rain that obscured the flat landscape and the dun animals in the shabby February fields, to her book. She wondered if she could, perhaps, take its central situation or *donnee*, and by changing it subtly, and substituting her own characters, manufacture a convincingly original work. . . .

'If you want to know about a woman, look in her purse.' The detective dumped the clues to the dead dame's life into a plastic bag and consigned it to Forensic. Susan's own handbag, if studied, would have told of an orderly life and mind, or of an owner who had dumped all her old makeup in the bin and dashed into an expensive chemist's on the way to the station: no sleazy clutter there, no circle of foam rubber tinged with grimy powder, no sweating stubs of lipstick and broken biros leaking into the lining, or tobacco shreds or dog-eared appointment cards for special clinics or combs with dirty teeth or minicab cards acquired on flights through dawn streets from unspeakable crises.

Susan could see as clearly in her mind the contents of the handbag of the woman who had bought the two gins as she could see her black stilettos resting on the next seat, and the fall of fake fur caressing her calf. She saw her lean forward and open a compact the dark blue of a mussel shell, and peer into a mirror, and her imagination supplied a crack zigzagging across the glass, presaging doom.

The man directly opposite Susan was reading a report and was of as little interest as he had been at the start of the journey; on the other side of the aisle a family, parents and two children, finished their enormous lunch and settled down to a game of three-dimensional noughts and crosses, which involved plastic tubes and marbles, clack clack clack. The marbles bounced off Susan's brain like bullets. 'Why can't they just use pencil and paper?' she thought irritably: the extra dimensions added nothing but cost and noise to the game. She put her hands over her ears, and, resting her book on the table, tried to read, but her concentration was shot to pieces. She closed her eyes, and the handbag in her dream returned like a black shell, which if held to the ear would whisper her own mortality.

There was this handbag washed up on the beach – what next? She waited for a whole narrative to unwind and a cast of characters to come trooping out, but nothing happened. There was this crime writer travelling on a train, panicking about a deadline when suddenly . . . a single shot passed through the head of the buffet car attendant's head, shattering the glass behind him . . . Susan's fascination with firearms dated from a white double holster studded with glass jewels and two fancy guns with bluish shining barrels and decorated stocks; she had loved them more than any of her dolls, taking them to bed with her at night, loving the neat round boxes of pink caps. She could smell them now, and the scent of new sandals with crepe soles like cheese.

Dreams of dead women's handbags: the click of a false tortoiseshell clasp, the musty smell of old perfume from the torn black moiré lining, and powder in a shell, lipstick that would look as ghastly on a skull as it did on the mouths of the little white flat fish on the seaside stall, skate smoking cigarettes through painted mouths, the glitter of saliva on a pin impaling whelks. She saw a man and a woman walking on a cliff top starred with pink thrift, a sea gull's white scalloped tail feathers; the woman wore a dress patterned in poppies and corn and the man had his shirt-collar open over his jacket, in holiday style. A child skipped between them on that salty afternoon when the world was their oyster.

Amberley Hall, where Susan was heading, was a small private literary foundation where students of all ages attended courses and summer schools in music, painting and writing. She had been invited to be the guest reader at one of their creative writing courses, and was looking forward to seeing again the two tutors, both friends, and renewing her acquaintance with Amberley's directors whom she had liked very much when she met them the previous year when she herself had been a co-tutor. The house was white and stood on a cliff; reflections of the sea and sky met in its windows. Susan hoped that she would be given the room in which she had slept before, with its faded blue bedspread and shell-framed looking glass and vase of dried flowers beside the white shells on the windowsill, sea lavender faded by time, like a dead woman's passions and regrets. The clatter of marbles became intolerable. Susan strode towards the buffet car. The train seemed to be going very slowly. She began to worry about the time and wish that she had accepted her hosts's offer to meet her at the station.

'Going all the way?' the barman asked as he sliced a lemon with a thin-bladed knife. The other woman had not been offered lemon.

'I beg your pardon?'

'Going all the way?'

'No. Not quite.'

'Business or pleasure?'

Susan had never seen why she should answer that question, so often asked by strangers on a train.

'A bit of both,' she replied.

Again his eyelid flickered in a wink.

'Ice?'

'Please.' She hoped her tone matched the cubes he was dropping into her glass with his fingers, one of which was girdled with a frayed plaster. Stubble was trying to break through the red nodules of a rash on his neck; he looked as though he had shaved in cold water in the basin in the blocked toilet, with his knife. The arrival of two other customers brought their conversation to an end.

As she approached her seat with her vodka and tonic she stopped in her tracks. That woman in the fur coat had Susan's overnight bag down on the seat and was going through her things.

'What do you think you're doing?' She grabbed her furry arm; her hand was shaken from it.

'I'm just looking for a tissue.'

'But that's my bag. Those are my things!'

The woman was pulling out clothes and underclothes and dumping them on the seat while the noughts and crosses clicked and clacked, tic tac toe. She scrabbled under the books at the bottom of the bag.

'Stop it, do you hear?'

'She's only looking for a tissue,' said the man opposite mildly, looking up from his report.

'I'm going to get the guard. I'm going to pull the emergency cord.'

The other woman's full lips trembled and she started to cry.

The man took a handkerchief from his breast pocket, shook it out and handed it to her.

'Have a good blow.'

She did.

'I'll give you a good blow!' said Susan punching her hard in the chest, at the top of a creased *décolletage* where a gilt pendant nestled in the shape of the letter M. The lights went out. The train almost concertinaed to a stop.

'Now look what you've done, pulling the communication cord.'

'I didn't touch it,' Susan shouted. 'What's going on? What's the matter with everybody? I didn't go near it.'

She felt the woman move away, and sat down heavily on her disarranged bag, panting with affront and rage, the unfairness of it all and the fact that nobody had stood up for her. Tears were rolling down her face as she groped for her clothes and crammed them back into the bag. Marbles rolled across the table and ricocheted off the floor. The tips of cigarettes glowed like tiny volcanoes in the gloom and someone giggled, a high nervous whinny. Susan began to sweat. Rain was drumming on the windows like her heartbeats, and she knew that she had died and was to be locked for eternity in this train in the dark with people who hated her. This was her sentence: what was her crime? Battalions of minor sins thronged her memory. Her hand hurt where she had punched the woman; she sucked her knuckle and tasted blood. The lights came on. Susan screamed.

The barman stood in the doorway, his knife in his hand.

'Nearly a nasty accident,' he said. 'Car stalled on the level crossing.'

People started to laugh and talk.

'Could've been curtains for us all,' he said as the train brayed and the orange curtains at the black windows swayed as it started to move.

The woman in the fur coat came sashaying down the aisle, reeled on a marble, and plonked herself down beside Susan.

'Sorry about that little mistake, only I mistook it for my bag. They're quite similar. Here, let me help you put it up.'

They swung it clumsily onto the rack, next to a dirty tapestry bag edged in cracked vinyl. Susan looked into her eyes, opaque as marbles, and perceived that she was mad. She picked up her book.

'Like reading, do you?'

'When I get the chance.'

'I know what you mean. There's always something needs doing, isn't there? I expect you're like me, can't sit idle. What with my little dog, and my crochering and the telly there's always something, isn't there?'

'Crochering?' Susan heard herself ask.

'Yes, I've always got some on the go. I made this.'

She pulled open her lapels to show a deep-throated pink filigree garment.

'It was a bolero in the pattern, only I added the sleeves.'

Susan smiled and tried desperately to read, but it was too late: she saw in vivid detail the woman's sitting room, feet in pink fluffy slippers stretched out to the electric fire that was mottling her legs, the wheezy Yorkshire terrier with a growth on its neck, the crochet hook plying in a billowy sea of pink and violet squares; a bedspread for a wedding present to a niece, who would bundle it into a cupboard.

She almost said, 'I'm sorry about your little dog,' but stopped herself in time, and before she was tempted to advise her to abandon her bedspread, the guard announced that the train was approaching her station. She gathered her things together with relief and went to find an exit. As she passed the bar the steward, who had taken off his jacket and was reading a newspaper, did not raise his head. She saw how foolish she had been to fear him.

'Thank God that's over,' she said aloud on the platform as she took deep breaths of wet dark air which although the station was miles inland, tasted salty, and the appalling train pulled away, carrying the barman and the deranged woman to their mad destinations. She came out into the forecourt in time to see the rear lights of a taxi flashing in the rain. She knew at once that it was the only one and that it would not return for a long time. She saw a telephone box across the road, and shielding with her bag her hair that the rain would reduce to a nest of snakes hurried through the puddles. At least, being in the country, the phone would not have been vandalised. A wet chip paper wrapped itself around her ankles; the receiver dangled from a mess of wires, black with emptiness roaring through its broken mouth, like a washed-up handbag.

A pub. There must be a pub somewhere near the station that would have a telephone. Susan stepped out of the smell of rural urine and started to walk. She would not let herself panic, or let the lit and curtained windows sheltering domesticity make her feel lonely. Perhaps she could hire a car, from the pub. She imagined the sudden silence falling on the jocular company of the inn and a fearful peasant declaring, 'None of us villagers dare go up to Amberley Hall. Not after dark,' and a dark figure in a bat-winged cloak flying screeching past the moon.

Mine host was a gloomy fellow who pointed her to a pay phone. The number was engaged. Temporarily defeated, Susan ordered a drink and sat down. It was then that she realized that her overnight bag had been transformed into a grubby tapestry hold-all with splitting vinyl trim. A cold deluge of disbelief engulfed her and then hot pricking needles of anger. She drowned the words that rose to her lips; this wasn't Hampstead. How could it have happened – that madwoman – Susan was furious with herself; she would have scorned to use the device of the switched luggage in one of her own books, and here she was, lumbered, in this dire pub, with this disgusting bag, and worse, worse, all her own things, her books – the reading . . . She was tempted to call it a day then, and order another drink, and consign herself to fate, propping up the bar until her money ran out and they dumped her in the street, but she made another attempt at the telephone, and this time got through. Someone would be there to pick her up in twenty minutes. She thought of ordering a sandwich but the knowledge of the meal, the refectory table heaped with bowls of food awaiting her, restrained her, and she sat there half listening to the jukebox, making her drink last, wishing she was at home doing something cheerful like drinking vodka and listening to Bessie Smith, or Billie Holiday singing 'Good Morning Heartache'.

She thought she had found her murder victim, a blond woman with a soft white face and body and a pendant in the shape of the letter M and a stolen bag; she lolled in death, her black shoes stabbing skywards, on a cliff top lying in the thrift that starred the grass and was embossed on a threepenny bit, tarnished at the bottom of an old handbag. Threepence, that was the amount of pocket money she had received; a golden hexagonal coin each Saturday morning. The early 1950s: a dazzle of red, white and blue; father, mother and child silhouetted against a golden sunburst in a red sky like figures on a poster, marching into Utopia.

The dead woman's dress was splashed with poppies and corn – no, that was wrong – it must be black. Her mother had had a dress of poppies and corn, scarlet flowers and golden ears and sky-blue corn flowers on a white field; Ceres in white peep-toe shoes, the sun sparkling off a Kirbigrip in her dark gold hair. Her father's hair was bright with brilliantine and he wore his shirt-collar, white as vanilla ice cream, open over his jacket. Susan's hair was in two thin plaits of corn and gripped on either side with a white hair-slide in the shape of Brumas the famous polar bear cub. Susan sat in the pub, becoming aware that it was actually a small hotel and staring at a red-carpeted staircase that disappeared at an angle, leading to the upper guest rooms. In a flash she realized why the barman in the train looked familiar, and blind and deaf to the music and flashing lights she sat in a waking dream.

The child woke in the hotel bedroom and found herself alone. Moonlight lay on the pillows of the double bed her parents shared. The bed was undisturbed. They had come up from the bar to tuck her in. 'You be a good girl now and go to sleep. We're just popping out for a stroll, we won't be gone more than a few minutes.' Her father's eyes were red – she turned her face away from his beery kiss. Her mother's best black taffeta dress rustled as she closed the door behind them. She pulled a sweater over her nightdress and buckled on her holster and her new white sandals and tiptoed to the door. A gust of piano playing and singing and beer and cigarette smoke bellied into the bedroom. She closed the door quietly behind her and slid slowly down the banister, so as not to make any noise. She was angry with them for leaving her alone. She bet they were eating ice creams and chips without her. She crept to the back door and let herself out into the street. Although she had never been out so late alone, she found that it was almost light – girls and boys come out to play, the moon doth shine as bright as day – she would burst into the cafe and shoot them dead – Susan saw her in the moonlight, a small figure in a white nightdress in the empty street with a gun in each hand. The cafe was closed.

She turned onto the path that led to the cliffs. Rough grass spiked her bare legs and sand filled her new sandals and rubbed on her heels. She holstered her guns because she had to use her hands to scramble up the steep slope, uttering little sobs of fear and rage. She reached the top and flung herself panting onto the turf. At the edge of the cliff sat two figures, from this distance as black as two cormorants on a rock against the sky. The sea was roaring in her ears as she wriggled on her belly towards them. As she drew nearer she could see the woman's arms, white as vanilla in her black taffeta dress and the man's shirt-collar. She stood up and drew her guns and took aim but suddenly she was frightened at herself standing there against the sky and just wanted them to hold her, and shoved the guns back in the holster and as she did the man put his arm around the woman's shoulder and kissed her. The child was running towards them, to thrust herself between their bodies shouting joyfully 'Boo!' as she thumped them on their backs and the woman lost her balance and clutched the man and they went tumbling over and over and over and the woman's handbag fell from her wrist and went spiralling after them screaming and screaming from its open black mouth.

When the landlady, impatient at the congealing breakfast, came to rouse the family in the morning she found the child asleep, cuddling up to a holster instead of a teddy. The parents' bed was undisturbed. It seemed a shame to wake the little girl. She looked so peaceful with her fair hair spread out on the pillow. She shook her gently.

'Where are your mummy and daddy, lovey?'

The child sat up, seeing the buckle of her new sandal hanging by a thread. Mummy would have to sew it on.

'I don't know,' she answered truthfully.

'Susan. Hi.' Tom from Amberley Hall was shaking her arm. 'You look awful. Have you had a terrible journey? You must have.'

'Perfectly bloody,' said Susan.

'I'm afraid you've missed supper,' said Tom, in the car, 'but we'll rustle up something for you after the reading. I think we'd better get straight on with it if you don't mind. Everybody's keen to meet you. Quite an interesting bunch of students this time. . .

His voice went on. Susan wanted to bury her face in the thick cables of his sweater. As they entered the house she explained about the loss of her bag.

'Just like Professor Pnin, eh, on the wrong train with the wrong lecture?' he laughed. Susan wished then profoundly to be Professor Pnin, Russian and ideally bald; to be anybody but herself in her creased clothes with her hair snaking wildly around her head and a tapestry bag in her hand containing the crocheted tangle of that woman's mad life.

'It was the right train,' she said, 'but I haven't got anything to read.'

'I did get in touch with your publishers to send some books to sell, but I'm afraid they haven't arrived. Never mind though, some of the students have brought their own copies for you to sign so you could borrow one. Five minutes to freshen up, OK? We've put you in the same room as last time.'

'No bloody food. No bloody wine. Not even any bloody books,' said Susan behind the closed door of her room. She aimed a kick at the bookcase: each of those spines faded by sea air representing somebody's futile bid to hold back eternal night. Precisely five minutes later she stepped, pale, poised and professional, into the firelit room to enchant her audience.

When she had finished reading, a chill hung over the room for a moment and then someone started the clapping. As the appreciative applause flickered out, bottles of wine and glasses were brought, and the evening was given over to informal questions and discussion. A gallant in corduroys bowed as he handed her a glass.

'You're obviously very successful, Miss Vigo, or may I call you Susan? Could you tell us what made you decide on writing as a career in the first place? I mean I myself have been attempting to – '

'I wanted to be rich,' interrupted Susan quickly before he could launch on his autobiography. The firelight striking red glints on her hair, and her charming smile persuaded her listeners that she was joking. 'You see, I was always determined to succeed in whatever career I chose. I came from a very deprived background. My parents died tragically when I was young and I was brought up by relatives.' Her lip trembled slightly; a plaster Alsatian barked in corroboration.

'What was your first big breakthrough?'

'I was very lucky in that I met a professor at university, a dear old soul, who took an interest in my youthful efforts and who was very helpful to me professionally. He's dead now, alas.' She became for a moment a pretty young student paying grateful tribute to her crusty old mentor. Most of the audience were half in love with her now.

'What made you turn to crime, as it were, Susan, instead of to any other fictional form?'

Susan's slender body rippled as she giggled, 'I don't know really – I developed a taste for murder at an early age, and I've never looked back, I suppose.'

'Can I ask where you get your ideas from?'

The frail orphan sipped her wine before replying.

'From "the foul rag-and-bone shop of the heart".'

Robin Bell (1945 –)

The Wooden Curlew

She was the extra decoy,
the one who looked different
to make the others credible.
She served her purpose
in the first hour of October light
amid the guns, the wounded splashing
and the black ripples
of the swimming dogs.

As daylight grew stronger
the gunfire tailed away.   10
Its sharp smoke slipped from
the hanging willow branches
while the men packed up their gear
into the green Range Rover
and drove off. She was left,
forgotten in the lee of a birch root.
She wintered there with weathering paint,
attracting real wildfowl to the safety
of the shallows by the empty hides.

The March floods lifted her   20
from her black nest in the withered reeds.
Slower and heavier with the winter's weight
of water in her frost-sprung grain,
she bobbed across the lake
and in the false dawn saw
the headlights cross the misty ridge
and park beside the water.
She saw the men launch the punt
and lay the mallard decoys
in a floating line.   30
There was no wooden curlew
to make them real. Still,
uncertain of what she had become,
she kept her distance from the slanting guns.

Sawing Logs

My father, once in a while, would sit
beside the logpile as if to discover
how many days warmth were left in it;
and I'd say, while he still thought it over,
'It's a good day for sawing, isn't it?'

The sapling rowans by the gate were bare
and the deer down early from the hills.
We needed more logs; I'd sit and pare
an apple with my penknife till
he said, 'You're right: there's not much there.'   10

The saw-horse stood in the back yard
with a stack of split planks, barrel staves,
lopped limbs from trees, old stakes and spars
from the garden: all the spare wood saved
since the first signs that winter would be hard.

We'd check for knots or awkward grain
and lay wood firm across the forks.

Setting the saw, my father would explain
how to go steady, make the blade do all the work.
I'd rush and buckle, have to start again.   20

The wood is scored to guide the blade;
the wrists bear down, the shoulders brace.
I'd saw from the forearms, but my father said,
'You'll tire yourself out. Saw from the waist
and put your whole back into it instead.'

Only well seasoned wood is fit to burn;
anything green will wait a few weeks yet.
Once our stroke ran smooth, the stack was turned
into long-houred logs. He'd take a hatchet
and split some kindling when we'd done.   30

The saw did our speaking. The sharp air
drew out our breath. The wind was cold;
but we were warm and making warmth out there.
He was near seventy. I was twelve years old
and four hands on a saw was all we were.

Tantallon in Winter

To build a castle and defend it
is at the heart of what we are.
Against all enemies, even the King
and his drumbeat, 'Ding doon Tantallon. Ding
doon Tantallon.' Gunstone's jar
nor gnawing siege shall ever rend it.

But at the last it is a thing of walls,
of inward-seeking, buttress and red fire,
of keeping-out, of moat and precipice.
How many victories made of this   10
pass for a life? Would domes and spires
be better? Or no sanctuary at all?

They answer themselves like echoes from the wark,
these questions. Let the landward side
engage the world with its facade.
Let someone else build spires we never had.
May he have space to site them. Look, the tide
is running. It is almost dark.

The sea is white with turning. The broad fields
of Lothian are white with snow. The roads   20
to the hinterland glisten with black ice.
We have won. The world can take its own advice.
Down in the courtyard gulls compete with crows.
Look at the open sea. Has night concealed

new terrors, neither ancestors nor we
have turned away already? Snowclouds scud.
Birds on the Bass Rock settle down to sleep.
And why not us? Why is it that we keep
our senses trained on night, with quickening blood,
salt-lipped from vigil, pierced with victory?   30

The following is one of three 'Radio Poems' written to be performed over the airwaves; they were published in 1989.

Melville Bay

In the year 1838 a young ship's surgeon
tells the story of a whaling expedition
from Dundee to north-west Greenland.

1. Trying Out

Grey smoke rose through the Greenland sky all day
like surfacing breaths from an enormous whale.
On deck the cauldrons hissed and spat
while in the hold the cooling butts
thickened and slapped. The stiff folds of our sails
glistened with grease. In the crook of Melville Bay

a hard September sun set in the hills.   10
It coloured the snow red. The tryworks boiled,
as round the flames men spiked the strips
of blubber, filled the cauldrons up,
laughed and skated with their hooks where oil
had greased the deck. Black carcasses of whales

bobbed alongside in chains, all specked with snow,
till each was hauled on to the cutting stage.
The air hissed with flensing knives and claws;
bones squeaked and snapped beneath the saws.
The starboard bulwarks acted like a cage   20
for slippery flesh that slid towards the bows.

I was no sailor. It was my first time
on a whaleship. Captain Chalmers took me on
as his ship's surgeon because I
was half way through my medical degree.
Chalmers nodded: 'That's half more than the last one.
If you can set a bone, you'll do just fine.'

Five months out from Dundee, the fishy stench
no longer troubled me. Great ropes of smoke
twisted upwards from the cauldrons' mouths.   30
Hard by starboard, ice floes drifted south
or caught on headlands like white flowers on stalks.
Folco, the carpenter, stood at his bench

straightening saws and sharpening worked-out blades.
The owner's son, Paul Graham, smoked his pipe,
perched high up on the spare boat skids.
The boatswain Carey's baccy quid
bulged through his hare-lipped grin, each time we wiped
away the sweat, at the Indian streaks we made.

As it grew dark, we saw the esquimaux   40
venturing closer to the fiery glare.
Our masts and shrouds and close-furled sails
stood black above the molten whales.
Sparks flew like shooting stars through the night air.
Our fires drowned out the crackle of the floes.

A crescent moon watched as we hacked and hurled.
Sometimes we glimpsed beside the cabin stairs
two tall, cloaked women in fur hoods.
'Women don't bring a ship no good,'
muttered Folco. The captain's wife went to her prayers   50
and left the darkness to the other girl.

2. **Pack Ice**
In the morning, when the tryworks fires were out,
the sky shone twice as blue and twice as cold.
The yellow sun gave off no heat.
Frost crazed the deck beneath our feet.
Wisps of fishy steam seeped from the hold
for Reuben the cat to ruffle and sniff out.

We had the best catch. The rest of our fleet
had sailed from Melville Bay three days before
with holds half-empty. Graham had made us wait   60
till we had finished trying-out.
While Captain Chalmers rushed about and swore,
his wife rehearsed her hymns and stayed discreet.

The lower main hold was stacked high with casks
of whale oil and meat packed in layers of salt,
beside great bundles of baleen
for umbrella ribs and corset bones.
And in the fore 'tween decks lay sealskin pelts
coddled round heavy spermaceti flasks.

Paul Graham took a ledger round the holds   70
– his father's son – to tally all our catch,
checking it with his tall, young wife.
Folco ground out a ragged knife.
'Wives is bad luck,' he grunted to the watch.
'Aye, and not just at sea,' the cold watch growled.

The night had bound more ice-floes in the bay.
They creaked and tapped against the naked stem,
no longer fendered by our whales.

All morning we prepared to sail.
Five of us climbed down to hack ice from the stern.   80
Above, the ship's name glinted: *Mercury*.

We used the on-shore wind as best we could
and nosed our way between the grumbling floes.
The passage narrowed, disappeared.
Sun and wind dropped. The sky was clear
with gimlet stars. We felt our outer clothes
stiffen with frost as if we were made of wood.

The crew climbed down on to the ice with ropes
to haul the *Mercury* toward the sea.
The more we tugged, the more we slipped   90
and dragged ice up against the ship
till all our axes could not cut her free.
The silent women watched us climb back up.

3. The Whaleboats

Three days slipped by. Cracks opened in the ice
and sealed again more tightly. Hummocks rose.
The captain glumly led the men in morning prayers.
His wife's voice swooped through the air,
bearing our hymns across the echoing floes.
Paul Graham grew restless. At first his advice

was to keep trying to move the *Mercury*.   100
The captain told him that it was no use,
that we would have to winter here:
'We've stores to last us a whole year.'
'My father won't take that for an excuse,'
snapped Graham. 'He wants the oil. Who's going to pay?'

We'd little chance of catching up our fleet,
but Graham was determined to send word back home:
'Or, if we find a ship near here,
we'll transfer our cargo to her.
We've food enough, but we're too low on rum.   110
What will the men do when it runs out?'

The crew played cards. I cut some whaletooth dice.
Folco taught young Isles to make scrimshaw.
Graham and the captain argued in full view
while Reuben prowled and Carey chewed.
The captain gave in: 'Two whaleboats can go
and maybe find a ship beyond the ice.'

Graham and the captain both agree to go.
Neither trusted the other out of sight.
Graham insisted he bring his wife with him,   120
so Mrs Chalmers came with her hymns.
Folco and Isles prepared to man Graham's boat.
The captain took Carey and the third mate, Low.

Each chose two seamen, long-boned Stromness lads
and watched while the whaleboats were loaded up
with casks of water, salt meat and oatmeal,
candles, rum, ice-saws, warm wraps made from seals.
Folco made decks and nailed canvas on top
then bolted sledge runners to the whaleboats' sides.

They went on board. The davits rattled out   130
and lowered them to the ice. The ladies sat
while the men hauled the boats along.
They stopped, looked up at us. Something was wrong.
The captain walked back, hailed John Cramb the mate:
'The ship's listing. I can see it from the boat.'

Our deck seemed flat enough. I placed a penny
on its edge. The crew watched it slowly roll
to the port side and clatter down.
'I'm sending Folco back again'
the captain called. 'He'll need to brace the hull.   140
I'll take you instead.' He pointed at me.

4. The Journey South

I ran below and filled my ditty bag
with medical supplies. The rest I gave to Cramb.
I took Folco's rope. We made our way
south by south west on Melville Bay.
Although the ice was ridged where floes had jammed,
we'd no deep snow to make our runners drag.

Despite the cold, I soon worked up a sweat
and felt it stick and freeze on my eyebrows.
Crystals of ice, like frozen tears,   150
clung to my lashes and my beard.
The whaleboats handled like two clumsy scows.
We raised the masts but no wind filled our sheets.

The ice grew rougher. Jagged, rockswept slopes
forced us east to find a passable route.
One smooth field slithered down into a ditch.
Another petered out in treacherous brash.
Twice we had to carry the whaleboats
between locked bergs that frayed our frozen ropes.

When sun and moon stood in the same sky   160
we pitched camp in our boats. Mrs Chalmers asked:
'Whom would you like mentioned in your prayers?'
'I pray we meet no polar bears,'
grinned Carey. All night long the salt meat casks
creaked if we stirred, so close-packed did we lie.

Beside me lay an oilskin lucifer bag
and a box of maroons. The saltpetre smell
made me dream of Coronation Day

and the fireworks I saw as a boy.
Our sealskin wraps were cold as chestnut shells.   170
Mrs Graham's pillow was a folded flag.

The morning saw us stiff as marionettes.
Captain Chalmers was all for turning round:
'There's no point struggling on,' he said. 'We're not equipped.'
'We've come this far. Let's try to find a ship,'
Graham argued. 'Look! I can see an open sound.'
We hacked the runners free and off we set.

The ice grew smooth. A wind rose. The boats skimmed
and bumped across the ice with bulging sails.
We reached a channel, launched the boats.   180
Our legs felt strange to be afloat.
We saw no ships. An anvil-headed gale
struck towards us. The sky grew tallow dim.

The wind dropped suddenly. We tried to row
back to the shore. We heard a humming noise
that become a whistle. The sky had grown
a luminous blue-black. The air pressed down.
Waves pushed the boats apart. I heard my voice
shout to Mrs Graham lo keep down low.

5. **The Storm**
We dropped our sails and hugged the ragged shore,   190
but the storm clutched and tore us out to sea.
Our whaleboats seemed to shrink. The waves
became a seething labyrinth of caves.
I was hurled to the gunwales. Above me,
the Stromness men fought with the steering oar.

It sprang loose and was gone. The whaleboat yawed.
Disaster, when it came, came suddenly.
The captain's boat leaped at a floe
that sheared the mast, stove in her prow
and sucked her under. Paul Graham braced his knee   200
like a harpooner. He crashed overboard.

Our Stromness men drowned, trying to save him.
I tried to bale. A barrel crushed Isles' chest.
My lint was soaked and would not staunch his blood.
Breached stores clung to my boots like mud.
The whaleboat teetered on a great wave's crest
where screeching sleet tore at my eyelids' skin.

The whole weight of the wave dropped on the boat.
I grasped the steering-oar brace. Mrs Graham
clung to my waist. Isles' body flew,   210
like a doll with its head askew,
up through the water. The boat's frame
shuddered and righted. We began to float,

mastless and oarless on the rolling caps
as the storm died away. Mrs Graham and I
baled out the hull. Our stores were soaked.
Worst of all, our water casks were breached
and mingled with brine. Our own clothes seemed dry,
till we stopped working. We piled up the wraps

and huddled together. We could not speak.   220
I tried to keep myself from falling asleep.
I salvaged some oatmeal. It smelled of brine.
I made her eat it. The sun began to shine.
It gave no heat. 1 looked out for a ship,
but all that moved were icebergs' glittering peaks.

She gathered strength and talked. She had been wed
less than a year. Their families were close friends.
She had known him all her life,
Always assumed she'd be his wife.
She'd seen him sail away, come back again   230
'looking more like himself each trip he made,

less like his father,' she said. 'He'd always try
to teach me. This voyage to Greenland
was his idea. He wanted me to see
and not be like those women at the quay,
afraid of what they do not understand.'
I realised she was as young as I.

Five days we drifted, waterless. We ate
as little as we could of the salt food.
She became delirious. All I could do   240
was bleed her. I gathered her blood in a shoe,
mixed it with meal and fed her. The fresh blood
revived her. I bled myself and ate.

I dried the lucifers inside my shirt
and shook out powder from the wet maroons.
At dusk we saw a sail. I lit a fire,
fed it with damp pelts. The smoke rose higher
till we were seen. It was a Dutch ship, the Jan Boom.
They launched a boat and carried us on board.

6. **Laura Graham**
The Dutchman gave us warm, dry clothes.   250
His Malay cook made us a court bouillon,
laced with genever. We inhaled its heat
and told our story. He agreed
to take us to the port of Godhavn,
but wouldn't risk his ship in more rescues.

Two days of keen wind let us make good speed.
We rounded the bleak cliffs of Svarten Huk
and spied three whaleships nestling by the cape.

I took the captain's telescope,
read their names and called Mrs Graham to look: 260
Sidlaw, Chattan, Pointer — our own fleet.

I went aboard the *Chattan*. Even as I climbed
up the rope ladder, watched by the whole crew,
word spread that the Mercury was lost.
I told them, 'No.' Old James Buist,
the senior captain, called the other two.
He said, if we sailed now, there should be time

to take survivors off the *Mercury*
before fresh sea-ice blocked the shore again.
We sailed. The storm had scoured the coast.   270
changing its outline. Bergs and floes
slipped by. Buist insisted Mrs Graham
should take his cabin. For six nights she lay

burning with fever. She would talk and doze,
call Paul Graham's name, ask me not to leave her.
The *Chattan's* surgeon, Donald Grier,
looked at her once, would not go near,
mumbling, 'It could be scarlet fever,'
despite the violet frostbite on her toes.

By the time the fleet made Melville Bay   280
the worst of Laura Graham's illness was past.
She'd hardly strength to stir her sheets,
but joked about her bandaged feet,
'I shall not dance again with Mr Frost.'
I only smiled, unsure of what to say.

The five days' icy drift seemed far away.
Laura had the warmth of a real bed,
water to drink and the captain's best food.
Our sealskin huddle and the taste of blood
seemed like some indiscretion, best unsaid.   290
I rose to leave. She motioned to me to stay.

She seemed to take on her widow's role
as if she and Paul Graham had talked it through.
'My voyage,' she said, 'is already done.'
She raised her head, 'But yours is just begun.'
I'd been too close to say it wasn't true.
We were like twins, too bonded to console.

Her hands were cold. I laid her hooded cloak
over the bed, like the doctor I would be.
She drifted off to sleep again.   300
I heard the sound of anchor chains
and footsteps on the stairs. I went to see.
The captain's steward called me to the boats.

7. The Mercury

The three whaleships dropped anchor well off shore.
We took eight whaleboats, each manned with four men
to leave space for the stranded crew.
By the map we'd just four miles to go
across the ice. The black whaleboats began
to crawl like beetles on a dairy floor.

The sun set early. Through a cold, red mist   310
we heard a dull boom, then quick rifle fire.
As the haze sank, the *Mercury*
loomed like a wave of crystal spray.
These were no shots, but the crack of timber.
The pack had crushed her sides. The penny list

had heeled so far her yardarms scraped the floe.
The tryworks stared like blind eyes from the deck.
Davits curled down like walrus teeth
with tight-lipped chain plate mouths beneath.
As we drew close we made out, round the wreck,   320
oil-barrels stacked but no sign of the crew.

We hailed the *Mercury*. No answer came.
The hatches gaped like grizzled men struck dumb.
Then slowly from the barrel stacks
figures appeared; voices called back.
Folco was waving, and the mate John Cramb.
More cracks rang out round the port anchor chain.

Folco had built the barrels into huts,
lined with sail canvas. When we went inside
we found men huddled round a stove.   330
Folco embraced me with his tattered gloves.
Somehow they knew Captain Chalmers had died
before I told them. From the low roof struts

hung a lantern, unlit to save oil
amid the plenty. We bundled up in sealskin pelts,
afraid to fall too much asleep.
We rose before the sun came up.
Cramb gave the order to strike camp. I knelt
and helped lash up the sealskins into bales.

We loaded all we could into the boats: 340
whaletooth, seal pelts, spermaceti flasks.
Folco had made skids for the baleen
and rigged them up with a lateen.
We left behind most of the whale oil casks.
As we looked back, we saw the frail huts float,

like makeshift coracles, above the mist.
The Mercury's hull seemed a hummocked floe.
Folco, now that his work was done,

looked like an old man, small, withdrawn.
We reached the *Chattan* in a swirling snow. 350
Cramb and I made reports to Captain Buist.

I went to Laura. She sat up in bed
and asked me, one by one, about the crew.
She listened gravely, as her husband's heir,
inquired about the cargo, 'I declare,
when I go home, I'll have much work to do.'
She lay back down. I smoothed the patchwork spread.

I sat with Laura till she fell asleep
then went on deck and watched the moonlit clouds
massing. While the fleet prepared to sail 360
from Melville Bay, a school of whales
played under the full moon off the starboard bow,
silently sounding out our southbound ships.

Trevor Royle (1945 –)

The Children in the Apple Tree

At the source of the longest river
The voice of the hidden waterfall
And the children in the apple-tree
Not known, because not looked for
But heard. half-heard, in the stillness
Between two waves of the sea.

— T. S. Eliot *Little Gidding*

I knew that he was going to hit me even before the blow came. My feeble attempts to avoid the issue by argument had failed to impress him and there could be only one solution. His small muscle packed body tensed and he hit me with a sickening punch to the head. For the first time in my young life seeing stars stopped being a comic book illusion. Another punch hit me, and another, and my attempts to stop them were like a frigate taking on a pocket battleship. I was out-gunned and out-flanked and both of us knew it.

But I had enough gumption not to cry. It was bad enough being beaten but to have cried too would have been unthinkable and in any case would only have attracted further retribution. Satisfied that the fight as any sort of competition was over my assailant lost interest and left me alone to pick myself up and to consider my crime. I was English, lah-di-dah, useless, toffee-nosed, had spoken out of turn. Even if those thoughts were not in my nine-year-old head the pounding fists had certainly made the point.

Amidst my not inconsiderable pain and confusion I slowly became aware of two blue-rinsed, matinee-hatted ladies tut-tutting their disapproval of fighting in public, especially outside the Town Kirk. I looked to them for sympathy, but their frosty stare told me that I was as guilty as my attacker who was by then scuffing his way down the main street.

Two weeks later, at my first school in Scotland the lesson had been learned. An insult, real or imaginary, it didn't matter which, was thrown in my face. This time I knew what to do. A sudden fight and my taunter was so bewildered by the ferocity of my onslaught that victory in the morning break made me a hero by four o'clock. I was one of the lads, could use my fists in a fight, could be made a member of the gang dignified by a circle of chanting boys.

Not bad for an Englishman.

You could be forgiven for thinking that that little scene had its origins in a deprived post-industrial-Revolution urban centre. That would no doubt have been a more realistic scenario than the place where it really did happen – in St Andrews, a cold douce wee town in East Fife that would have been just like any other small Scottish town but for the dignity of its past and its university, both of which dominated the place to an exceptional degree.

St Andrews was not my home town, indeed I doubt that it ever will be. The journey from stranger to native lasts at least fifty years and unless your family is rooted in the neighbourhood, you are a newcomer. When we first went there I had spent most of my life in the Far East and my family had had little contact with post-war Britain. The world was white and those who were white were English. I am certain that I had never heard of Scotland or if I had, I probably thought of it as being a remote northern county of England. We came home (that lovely colonial euphemism for the long-lost country of one's youth) to my parent's glum separation; my father retired to his native England and my mother, brother and myself went to St Andrews where we had relatives who like us were strangers to the place. It was another world.

In the 1950s St Andrews was a very different sort of place than the busy town it is today. There was a train service but no Tay Road Bridge and the motor car had not then gained its universal ascendancy. It was a curiously remote town, not quite the same as the rest of Fife and yet firmly set on the edge of the rich farmlands of its Howe. Its history overshadowed the locality and everywhere one looked were the symbols of Scotland's past, a heritage so rich that it was easy to forget that St Andrews had languished for two centuries, a poor, church-ridden fishing town like many another East Coast neighbour.

The nineteenth century had been the town's salvation. The rise of a Scots bourgeoisie left a growing and rejuvenated medieval university and a summer holiday trade to be serviced. It was mainly a town of shopkeepers and hoteliers and remained so until it became a dormitory for the mobile professional middle classes of Dundee. There was (and is) very little poverty. Most people solidly voted Unionist and paid lip service to Scotland at countless Burns Suppers and St Andrews Nights Dinners. When I first went there, it soon became quite clear what the future would hold. The only way to get on would be to get out.

'Getting on' was the key phrase. It dominated my childhood and it was constantly dinned into me. There was a new world out there for the asking if you were prepared to work for it. I went to school (the local school, Madras College with its hungover Victorian pretensions to being a 'public' school) in the knowledge that work was all important, it being the only key to progress. Work to learn, work to understand what work means, work to know what authority is, what standards of behaviour and belief I had to respect. The primary means of learning were teaching by rote up to the age of eleven and I only have to hear the sonorous litanies of the eleven times table, a class conjugating in unison or the deliberate spelling of a-c-c-o-m-m-o-d-a-t-i-o-n to be taken back to the chalky atmosphere of a form-filled classroom.

The school had been founded in 1832 by Andrew Bell, a local boy who had made good by going out to India and collecting a small fortune. Of course, he went as a chaplain and did good works but that did not seem to have deterred him from making money too. He founded the monitorial system of education whereby the pupils themselves would be responsible for disseminating instruction at elementary level and for maintaining discipline.

'Give me twelve children and in twenty-four hours I shall give you twelve teachers.'

One hundred and twenty years had done an awful lot to dilute those fine ideals and the £120,000 that had financed them, and by 1956 Madras was part of the state system of education.

The children who went to Madras in the 1950s were divided into two groups – those who would do the 'Highers' and those who would not. There was a simple dividing line – the 'qualie' (qualifying exam or 11+) – which separated innocent eleven-year-olds into As and Bs, and apart from one or two promotions and relegations along the line those were the divisions for the six years we were to spend at secondary school. If you belonged to the A's the road of classics and science beckoned as far as the Golden Gates of the university. It was a quiet, solid, orderly road with few worries if, like myself, you kept to the middle. On the verges there were surprises, some pleasant, such as prizes, medals and a name on the dux board; others less so and primrose-covered at that.

For most of us the reward had been determined as a place at the university and preferably at the local university which occupied such a massive physical presence in the town. Even the spire of St Salvator, the university chapel, outstripped that of the Town Kirk in its praise of an all – providing and omnipresent deity. The red gowned students, black-robed professors, examination results in the local paper and the names of departments on the doors of quiet town houses were all a constant reminder of where the brightest and best of us would eventually go to complete our educations. But the students – thae students – seemed not to work but to have fun. Charities week, the Kate Kennedy Procession, the red-gowned Sunday walk to the end of the pier were all part of an unknown and mysterious world. The students spoke with different accents too and it was only when I was older that I realised that this was because the majority were in fact English. Which was confusing for a boy who was trying to do the right and proper thing by losing his own anglicised voice. I had just to take it for granted that everyone would acquire a wondrous new accent on going to university.

The University at St Andrews has often been described as second only to Oxbridge, and sometimes less politely as a haven for those who have to put up with it as a second choice. St Andrews certainly has the appearance, but the reality is often less than kind. Anyone who has stood in the face of a North-East gale with the wind gusting down from the northern polar wastes could ever compare the town with southern England in springtime. Where there is light in the south, there is sombreness and moderation in St Andrews. An English spring is always a surprise and a revelation, it impress the northerner with its rich and sleepy beauty, but in Scotland the winter slowly gives way to a grudging summer. It is a country made for autumn. The big sky to the west over Drumcarrow Craig, a fiery pitch of red reaching up to the golden upper layers of clouds and finally giving way to the blue of night, could never belong to the south. Autumn was the season that flattered St Andrews and bathed it in a rich melancholy which suited it perfectly.

As every schoolboy amongst us knew, the first college of Scotland's oldest universally was founded in 1411 as a strong beacon of learning in the north by the wealthy Bishop Wardlaw of St Andrews. It is Scotland's oldest and proudest university and yet, sadly, it has paid so little attention over the years to the land that nurtured it. St Andrews was and still is an English academic isle set in a Scottish sea. Perhaps it is too pretty a place, too reminiscent of Academe with its gracious quadrangle of St Salvator and the dainty chapel of St Leonard, too much like a collegiate university. Whatever the reason there are those who claim that it has sold its birthright too cheaply. At the time, I was innocent of such niceties and was much more concerned with the not insignificant problems of being an English boy in a predominantly Scottish school.

If the beginnings of my self-knowledge had their roots in my opening my mouth once too often then final acceptance was reached by learning a new tongue. The language surprised me. It was English undoubtedly, but of a sort, and it sounded strange and coarse to my ears. I was continually teased because I had a natural difficulty in saying 'loch' with the firm guttural sound needed to choke out the 'och'. In time this was to improve, to my own great joy but to my mother's consternation. Other words had to be learned and accepted.

'Aye' for yes, 'stanes' for stones, 'chuck' for throw, 'dyke' for wall, 'winnock' for window, 'smatter' for smash.

'Rin for it, lads he's done it noo, the great gomeril. Here comes the polis.'

Like all children we had one language for the playground and one for the classroom.

Some of the farmers' sons refused to honour even that distinction and used the East Fife tongue inside and outside school, paying concessions to no one. I soon built up a set of credentials that gave me further passports and passwords. I knew how to play chickie-mellie and chappie-knockie without being caught. I could jump well at peevers (playing hoppie-restie, of course) and I came to know the intricate rules needed for playing dodge-ba' and king-ba' in a crowded playground.

By the time I got to secondary school I had learned enough to get by and to survive and, more importantly from a child's point of view, to merge into the background. I remained on the outside, keen to get on but not willing to involve myself too deeply. I could never (and this *was* a test) feel the intense dismay and dislike of the English that my friends felt. And why should I have, being one myself? No matter how hard I tried, my innate (to my fellows soft) southern background betrayed me. I even felt my too obvious name to be some sort of treason and longed for the simplicity of a more usual name. I knew when it was necessary to hold my tongue and surely that is the supreme English vice?

Not that as schoolchildren there was any deep understanding of Scotland, her past, her traditions and her possibilities. North Sea Oil was still in the future and loyalties to Scotland owed more to Jimmy Shand and to the White Heather Club than to any social or political reality. That that should have been the case was partly due to the education system which was then rooted in the idea that a complete education based on the classics with a grounding in the sciences was the key that opened all doors. In their approach our teachers were more like the old village dominies who turned out lads o'pairts, pupils who had a solid factual grounding in the arts and sciences. Men like Thomas Chalmers, Duncan MacLaren or Thomas Guthrie, the great social reformers of the nineteenth century. In case any of my old teachers read this, let me say that I make this comparison not out of criticism, but out of an understanding of what they were trying to do. It was we their pupils, who were out of sympathy and growing away too quickly from a kind of Scotland that was gradually fading into memory.

But of Scotland's real past we knew little. Culloden was the necessary and probably deserved putting down of a rebellion against authority. Gaelic was a dead language spoken by the people killed at Culloden. The Clearances were part of the world movement of peoples. Bagpipe music was the school band. The Industrial Revolution was a good thing that gave work to all those Highlanders who had gone down to Glasgow. Maclean and Maxton? Didn't they play for Third Lanark? There was no essential grounding in the political facts of Scotland's past, no intellectual debate or analysis about what had happened, why it had happened and what might be done to prevent it from happening again. We knew more about the Risorgimento than we did about the Land League resistance on Skye.

Sport gave the best clue to patriotic feelings for Scotland and provided a national focus, especially when Scotland played England at football or at rugby. Then there was an overt necessity for the men in blue not only to defeat the white-shirted hard men of England but also to thrash them, to humiliate them and to outplay them with skill and arrogant superiority. The first game I ever saw at Hampden ended in a 1–1 draw (1960, the year before that terrible defeat, and disgrace for Frank Haffey), and in the dying seconds I knew what the braying crowd would choose if they were offered a second goal for Scotland or instant independence. Sure, self-government would be grand, but what could ever top the sweetness of victory over England, the Auld Enemy? It would have been Bannockburn all over again. The football writers went daft at that time of the year and sport and history mingled to make heroes of the players. Big Geordie Young, a second Bruce (Gallant Scotland defeat England's might); Billy Wright the Hammer of the Scots (Unlucky Scots fall to England's might).

Madras was a rugby-playing school albeit not a very distinguished one. The idea that football should be played as well had been discussed in the twenties but had been dismissed as a silly season aberration. Nevertheless it was the game that dominated most of our childhoods in one way or another. We supported teams which to us were only names, played twenty-a-side football on the damp corporation park on Saturday afternoons, headers against walls, kicking tennis balls along pavements and endless games of keepie-uppie and three and in. As far as I can remember there was no social differentiation about playing football or rugby and most of us played both, rugby for a school team in the morning and football for our enjoyment in the afternoon.

The greatest test though was at rugby and it came every second year at Murrayfield when Scotland played England (Wales and Ireland one year, France and England the next). Although it was expected of all of us to support Scotland with an undying devotion I cannot remember ever going to a match wholeheartedly expecting Scotland to win. Neither did many of my friends and we would sit gloomily in the train to Edinburgh forecasting yet another miserable defeat. Except against England. Then it was all bravado with myself keeping a wary silence or sporting a cocky indifference. It didn't matter who had won – on the return journey either I had to stifle my joy or I joined in the general despondency. Scotland never seemed to win in the fifties.

Looking back, I am sure that those were the heights of nationalism for me to climb and yet they were such gentle foothills that it would be wrong to give a bleak picture of a childhood spent in isolation because I had been, so to speak, born on the wrong side of the blanket. It would be convenient and perhaps half truthful to say that there was a sense of duality in my childhood. Living in Scotland, English but half Scottish and yet orphaned from the country to the south. Every year when my brother and I were dispatched to England to spend summer holidays with relatives a curious transformation took place. When we were in Scotland we were inescapably English, but in the south the mantle of the Scot was thrust upon us. Despite our surnames we were 'Scotties' or 'Jocks' and people smiled at the way we rolled our r's (how I tired of that sly joke).

After a week or two we became more Scottish than the Scots and in the absence of critical countrymen arrogantly boasted about our adopted country's superiority. I was constantly aware that Scotland was a different place and my links with both countries only served to make the disparities more clearly and sharply defined. I grew to understand my friends' gut reactions to England and their feelings of inadequacy when they looked back at the two centuries of political partnership between the two countries. The Union of 1707 had been an awkward way of doing things and many Scots still smarted with shame at the nature of the joining together of the two very different peoples.

My English relatives certainly didn't see it in that light and it was here that the Scotch comic had made such a mark on the British imagination. Scotland for the rest of my family was a country of quaint, hairy-kneed and parsimonious old men who went about muttering into their whisky: 'It's a braw bricht moonlicht nicht the nicht, ye ken.' Such smiling small talk was calculated to bring out in me feelings of intense moral indignation which never failed to amuse my uncles and aunts. I always rose to the bait, too.

At another level, living in Scotland was socially acceptable: it was like coming up from the country or having cousins in Devon – far enough away not to be an embarrassment and yet possessed of a rural respectability. There were too the memories of a superior Scottish education, a hangover from the days of the nineteenth century when it was the Scots who helped to administrate, police and govern an English world Empire. My father's family, a respectable middle class Lancashire manufacturing family who had made their fortune in the early years of this century by the supreme Victorian virtue of industry, felt that my brother and I must be in good hands if we were at a Scottish school. If our accents had changed somewhat, well that too was no bad thing as didn't some quite acceptable people not have a slight brogue?

For the rest of my school life I merged into a reasonably happy atmosphere of contentment and well-being. In those quiet days of the fifties and early sixties there was little noticeable social unrest or urban violence, kidnappings or hijackings, inflation or bankruptcy, and yet by our own complacency we were busy sowing their seeds. Because it was such a quiet and cut-off little place St Andrews shielded most of us from the crude outside world. There were times when I sensed that something bigger and bolder was going on elsewhere and that knowledge attracted and appalled me at the same time. After my first visit alone to Europe when I was sixteen I knew that I wanted to leave that warm haven, that my young muscles needed to be flexed and tried out. I made a point of telling myself and my friends that once I left school Scotland would no longer be able to hold me.

You might ask how fifteen years later I still find myself in Scotland, married with three sons about to go the same gait as me when several disbelieving school friends are scattered over the distant parts of the globe. St Andrews is after all only sixty odd miles from Edinburgh but the distance that I find myself from it now cannot be measured in man-made miles. I was grateful to the place for its security, its smallness and despite the weather its shy warmth. The education I received was sound in an old-fashioned way; it taught me little in any kind of depth but instead cluttered up my mind with obscure facts that I occasionally find useful for solving crossword puzzles. I was also taught self-confidence, and the unhappiness that I felt at the loss of my father was compensated for by the several friendships I made as a child and by my general liking for the town and the sleepy countryside that surrounded it.

But my real education began when I left St Andrews and that is what separates me from my past. I read voraciously, rediscovered Scotland, her past, and began to see through the romantic myths and legends that covered up Scotland's history and perpetuated divisions among the people. I realised that if there was to be any hope for the future the evils of the past had to be recognised and in a specifically Scottish context (to which my childhood bound me) that required an understanding of Scotland's relationship to England. This was not a neurotic concern, but I believed that it needed a better explanation than the memory of a small English boy being duffed up merely because he spoke differently.

Today I think I understand more about the effects of that connection – the Union of 1707, the effects of the Industrial Revolution and the continuing grip of an international capitalism, the cultural sell-out of Scottish standards. These are of course no longer directly related to the alliance but they were spawned by it. Without wanting to be pedantic, because I knew none of this at school, its revelation in maturer years was all the more telling. I am not denying that these problems are unique to Scotland but perhaps it is only in understanding one's own past first, that one becomes aware of the general human condition, or as Gramsci, the Italian Marxist, paraphrased it:

> Self-knowledge and knowledge of one's historical rights and duties do not come spontaneously, but by intelligent reflection, first by a few and then by the whole class on why certain conditions exist and how best to convert the facts of vassalage into the signals of rebellion and social reconstruction.

My formal education taught me one set of facts and my later education taught me not only about Scotland but (in doing so) also much about contemporary politics and the ways in which politics impinge themselves upon the lives of ordinary people.

From my present vantage point, almost half-way through the hoped-for allotted span, I can see that, in a sense, you can choose your own nationality. It is not a matter of blood, despite the grim nationalism of many Scots of my generation who keep alive a selfish feeling for the country for its emotional impact alone. It is too easy to summon up the half-true, half-phoney romantic spirit of long lost battles, or football matches, the two blending together so easily, against the Auld Enemy. By learning about the real past and the political conditions of their own country it may be that Scots at school today will have a greater compassion for the dispossessions and political imbalances in other further flung parts of the world. Scotland can become another country and, like the past, a different one from the place I knew as a child. There are other reasons too why I decided to stay in Scotland. I like it here, so does my family. Scotland is a country I grew to love as a child, and we feel at home in the north – it is as simple and domestic as that.

And yet underlying that complacency is the terrible sense of paradox in Scotland. On the one hand I can feel a strong empathy with a small country with its own indigenous culture being threatened by the processes of international big business. On a rational and political level that is comprehensible. On the other I have experienced a people torn by several emotions unable to express itself formally and yet in frightening detail able to display the whole gamut of passionate experience from extremes of anguished love to extremes of bitter violence. There were times when I felt that my forebears must have landed with St Regulus to plant the bones of the crucified saint and so give the town its name, such was my joy of St Andrews and my sense of acceptance by it. There were also those infrequent times, dark to the memory, when I bitterly resented the shame of being on the outside and cursed the Scots bigotry towards the English and all that they stood for. In Scotland there can be no middle way.

On the evening before I left St Andrews to go to another university in another part of the country I had gone drinking with a few friends to celebrate the parting of the ways. Walking back home after closing time we passed a group of Freshers who were waiting to go up to St Andrews University. Like us they were flushed with drink and new-found freedom. We heard them coming before they staggered into sight – loud braying English voices magnified by too many pints of beer. As they passed a group of local hoods standing outside the one cafe that kept late hours, to our horror, a scuffle broke out. One of the students fell with a well-aimed butt to the head and as he went down the boot went in.

As a piece of violence it was hardly remarkable and it was over in seconds. The lads sauntered off with scarcely a glance in our direction and the hapless Englishman was left to pick himself up and to consider his crime. As his assailant passed us he spat into the gutter and sneered: 'English student shite.'

The following day I went down to the station and left behind me the town that I had known for so long. There was to be no return.

James Kelman (1946 –)

Kelman, the voice of the working man, has been described in some places as the most important living Scottish writer and the finest since the War. The present editor once repeated this statement to the redoubtable poet and critic Edwin Morgan, rather expecting a show of protest at such a sweeping assertion. Morgan thought about it, and then answered in his quiet way, 'That's about right.'

Kelman is the major figure in the Glasgow School – the group of writers whose chief characteristics are realism, working-class sympathies (carried to the point of social protest), and a remarkable emphasis upon the vernacular (i.e. Glasgow 'Scots'). Kelman's stories are often interior monologues – at times a stream of consciousness – in which the realism is tempered by the protagonist's philosophical interests and insights and by a range of vocabulary rendered logical partly by the long Scottish tradition of working-class education, and partly just by literary convention. Also apparent are sizable dashes of 'surrealism,' which may be defined offhandedly as the use of sharply realistic detail within a strongly non-realistic premise. This appears in Kelman as his utterly believable characters' placement within sometimes monstrous social conditions – mistreatment by the police, the bosses, the welfare office. His crowning achievement may be his recent brilliant Booker Prize winning novel, How Late It Was, How Late (1994).

Throughout his fiction, Kelman shows a remarkable sympathy with his protagonists, their inner lives, frustrations, their rich Glasgow humor, and above all, their humanity. It has been suggested that the Kelman message is simply that working people – including the Glasgow 'riff-raff' – are worthy of our understanding and our respect.

Kelman's stories often seem plotless. That, plus the working-class dialect, emphasis upon the speaking voice (whether literal or internal) and what appears a certain garrulousness in his characters, lends to his stories a casualness which disguises a painstaking attention to style. His is remarkably exact writing.

Not Not While the Giro

> say not talkin about
> not analysin nuthin
> is if not not
>   – TOM LEONARD, 'Breathe deep, and regular with it'

of tea so I can really enjoy this 2nd last smoke which will be very very strong which is of course why I drink tea with it in a sense to counteract the harm it must do my inners. Not that tea cures cancer poisoning or even guards against nicotine – helps unclog my mouth a little. Maybe it doesnt. My mouth tastes bad. Hot and kind of squelchy. I am smoking too much old tobacco. 2nd hand tobacco is stiff, is burnt ochre in colour and you really shudder before spluttering on the 1st drag. But this is supposed to relieve the craving for longer periods. Maybe it does. It makes no difference anyway, you still smoke them 1 after the other because what happens if you suddenly come into a few quid or fresh tobacco – you cant smoke 2nd hand stuff with the cashinhand and there isnt much chance of donating it to fucking charity. So you smoke rapidly. I do – even with fresh tobacco.

But though the tea is gone I can still enjoy the long smoke. A simple enjoyment, and without guilt. I am wasting time. I am to perambulate to a distant broo. I shall go. I always go. No excuse now it has gone. And it may be my day for the spotcheck at the counter. Rain pours heavily. My coat is in the fashion of yesteryear but I am wearing it. How comes this coat to be with me yet. Not a question although it bears reflecting upon at some later date. Women may have something to do with it. Probably not, that cannot be correct. Anyway, it has nothing to do with anything.

I set myself small tasks, ordeals; for instance: Come on ya bastard ye and smoke your last, then see how your so-called will fucking power stands up. Eh! Naw, you wont do that. Of course I wont, but such thoughts often occur. I may or may not smoke it. And if it does come down to will power how the hell can I honestly say I have any – when circumstances are as they are. Could begin smacking of self pity shortly if this last continues. No, yesteryear's coat is not my style. Imitation Crombies are unbecoming these days, particularly the kind with narrow lapels. This shrewd man I occasionally have dealings with refused said coat on the grounds of said lapels rendering the coat an undesired object by those who frequent said man's premises. Yet I would have reckoned most purchasers of 2nd hand clothing to be wholly unaware of fashions current or olden. But I have faith in him. He does fine. Pawnshops could be nationalised. What a shock for the small-trader. What next that's what we'd like to know, the comer bloody shop I suppose. Here that's not my line of thought at all. Honest to god, right hand up that the relative strength of the freethinkers is neither here nor there. All we ask is to play up and play the game. Come on you lot, shake hands etcetera. Jesus what is this at all. Fuck all to do with perambulations to the broo.

Last smoke between my lips, right then. Fire flicked off, the last colour gone from the bar. Bastarn rain. The Imitation Crombie. And when I look at myself in the mirror I can at least blow smoke in my face. Also desperately needing a pish. Been holding it in for ages by the feel of things. Urinary infections too, they are caused by failing to empty the bladder completely ie. cutting a long pish short and not what's the word – flicking the chopper up and down to get rid of the drips. Particularly if one chances to be uncircumcised. Not at all.

In fact I live in a single bedsitter with sole use of confined kitchenette whose shelves are presently idle. My complexion could be termed grey. As though he hadnt washed for a month your worship. Teeth not so good. Beard a 6 dayer and of all unwashed colours. Shoes suede and stained by dripping. Dripping! The jeans could be fashionable without the Imitation Crombie. Last smoke finished already by christ. Smile. Yes. Hullo. Walk to door. Back to collect the sign-on card from its safe place. I shall be striding through a downpour.

Back from the broo and debating whether I am a headcase after all and this has nothing to do with my ambling in the rain. A neighbour has left a child by my side and gone off to the launderette. An 18 month old child and frankly an imposition. I am not overly fond of children. And this one is totally indifferent to me. The yes I delivered to the neighbour was typically false. She knew fine well but paid no attention. Perhaps she dislikes me intensely. Her husband and I detest each other. In my opinion his thoughts are irrelevant yet he persists in attempting to gain my heed. He fails. My eyes glaze but he seems unaware. Yet his wife appreciates my position and this is important since I can perhaps sleep with her if she sides with me and has any thoughts on the subject of him in relation to me or vice versa. Hell of a boring. I am not particularly attracted to her. A massive woman. I dont care. My vanities lie in other fields. Though at 30 years of age one's hand is insufficient and to be honest again my hand is more or less unused in regard to sexual relief. I rely on the odd wet dream, the odd chance acquaintance, male or female it makes no difference yet either has advantages.

Today the streets were crowded as was the broo. Many elderly women were out shopping and why they viewed me with suspicion is beyond me. I am the kind of fellow who gets belted by umbrellas for the barging of so-called 'infirm' pensioners while boarding omnibuses. Nonsense. I am polite. It is possible the Imitation Crombie brushes their shoulders or something in passing but the coat is far too wide for me and if it bumps against anything is liable to cave in rather than knock a body flying. Then again, I rarely wear the garment on buses. Perhaps they think I'm trying to lift their purses or provisions. You never know. If an orange for example dropped from a bag and rolled in my direction I would be reluctant to hand it back to its rightful owner. I steal. In supermarkets I lift flat items such as cheese and other articles. Last week, having allowed the father of the screaming infant to buy me beer in return for my ear, I got a large ashtray and two pint glasses and would have got more but that I lacked the Imitation Crombie. I do not get captured. I got shoved into jail a long time ago but not for stealing cheese. Much worse. Although I am an obviously suspicious character I never get searched. No more.

My shoes lie by the fire, my socks lie on its top. Steam rises. Stomach rumbles. I shall dine with the parents. No scruples on this kind of poncing. This angers the father as does my inability to acquire paid employment. He believes I am not trying, maintains there must be something. And while the mother accepts the prevailing situation she is apt to point out my previous job experience. I have worked at many things. I seldom stay for any length of time in a job because I cannot. Possibly I am a hopeless case.

I talk not at all, am confined to quarters, have no friends. I often refer to persons as friends in order to beg more easily from said persons in order that I may be the less guilty. Not that guilt affects me. It affects my landlord. He climbs the stairs whenever he is unwelcome elsewhere. He is a nyaff, yet often threatens to remove me from the premises under the misapprehension I would not resort to violence. He mentions the mother of this infant in lewd terms but I shall have none of it. Maybe he is a secret child molester. I might spread rumours to pass the time. But no, the infant is too wee. Perhaps I am a latent molester for even considering that. Below me dwells the Mrs Soinson, she has no children and appears unaware of my existence. I have thought of bumping into her and saying, Can I watch your television.

Aye, of course I'll keep the kid for another bastarn half hour. Good christ this is pathetic. The damn parent has to go further messages. Too wet to trail one's offspring. I could hardly reply for rage and noises from the belly and sweet odours from the room of a certain new tenant whom I have yet to clap eyes upon though I hear she is a young lady, a student no doubt, with middle class admirers or fervent working class ones or even upper class yacht drivers. I cannot be expected to compete with that sort of opposition. I shall probably flash her a weary kind of ironic grin that will strike her to the very marrow and gain all her pity/sympathy/respect for a brave but mis-guided soul. What sort of pish is this at all. Fuck sake I refuse to contemplate further on it although I only got lost in some train of thought and never for one moment contemplated a bastarn thing. I day dream frequently.

This infant sleeps on the floor in an awkward position and could conceivably suffocate but I wont rouse her. The worst could not happen with me here. Scream the fucking place down if I woke her up.

I am fed up with this business. Always my own fault with the terrible false yesses I toss around at random. Why can I not give an honest no like other people. The same last time. I watched the infant all Friday night while the parents were off for a few jars to some pub uptown where this country & western songster performs to astonishing acclaim. Now why songster and not singer. Anyway, they returned home with a ½ bottle of whisky and a couple of cans of lager so it wasnt too bad. This country & western stuff isnt as awful as people say yet there are too many tales of lost loves and horses for my liking although I admit to enjoying a good weepy now and then unless recovering from a hangover in which case – in which case . . . Christ, I may imagine things more than most but surely the mother – whom for the sake of identity I'll hereon refer to as Greta. And I might as well call him Percy since it is the worst I can think of at present – displayed her thigh on purpose. This is a genuine question. If I decide on some sort of action I must be absolutely sure of my ground, not be misled into thinking one thing to be true when in fact the other thing is the case. What. O jesus I have too many problems to concentrate on last week and the rest of it. Who the hell cares. I do. I do, I wish to screw her, be with her in bed for a lengthy period.

Oxtail soup and insufficient bread which lay on a cracked plate. Brought on a tray. Maybe she cant trust herself alone with me. Hard to believe she returned to lunch off similar fare below. I cant help feeling nobody would offer someone soup under the title of 'lunch' without prior explanation. Tea did of course follow but no further bread. I did not borrow from her. I wanted to. I should have. It was necessary. I somehow expected her to perceive my plight and suggest I accept a minor sum to tide me over, but no. I once tried old Percy for a fiver on his wages day. He looked at me as if I was daft. Five quid. A miserable five. Lend money and lose friends was his comment. Friends by christ.

Sucked my thumb to taste the nicotine. A salty sandish flavour. Perhaps not. In the good old days I could have raked the coal embers for cigarette ends. Wet pavements. I am in a bad way – even saying I am in a bad way. 3.30 in the afternoon this approximate Thursday. I have until Saturday morning to starve to death though I wont. I shall make it no bother. The postman comes at 8.20 – 7.50 on Saturdays but the bastarn postoffice opens not until 9.00 and often 9.05 though they deny it.

I refuse to remain here this evening. I will go beg in some pub where folk know me. In the past I have starved till the day before payday then tapped a handful on the strength of it and . . . christ in the early days I got a tenner once or twice and blew the lot and by the time I had repaid this and reached the Saturday late night I was left with thirty bob to get me through the rest of the week ie. the following 7 days. Bad bad. Waking in the morning and trying to slip back into slumber blotting out the harsh truth but it never works and there you are wide awake and aware and jesus it is bad. Suicide can be contemplated. Alright. I might have contemplated it. Or maybe I only imagined it, I mean seriously considered it. Or even simply and without the seriously. In other words I didnt contemplate suicide at all. I probably regarded the circumstances as being ideal. Yet in my opinion

No more of this shite. But borrowing large sums knowing they have to be repaid and the effects etc must have something to do with the deathwish. I refuse to discuss it. A naive position. And how could I starve to death in two days, particularly having recently lunched upon oxtail soup. People last for weeks so long as water is available.

Why am I against action. I was late to sign-on this morning though prepared for hours beforehand. Waken early these days or sometimes late. If I had ten pence I would enter supermarkets and steal flat items. And talking about water I can make tea, one cup of which gives the idea if not the sustenance of soup because of the tea bag's encrustation viz crumbs of old food, oose, hair, dandruff and dust. Maybe the new girl shall come borrow sugar from me. And then what will transpire. If

Had to go for a slash there and action: the thing being held between middle finger and thumb with the index slightly bent at the first joint so that the outside, including the nail, lay along it; a pleasant, natural grip. If I had held the index a fraction more bent I would have soaked the linoleum to the side of the pot. And the crux is of course that the act is natural. I have never set out to pish in that manner. It simply happens. Everyman the same I suppose with minute adjustments here and there according to differing chopper measurements. Yet surely the length of finger will vary in relation. Logical thought at last. Coherence is attainable as far as the learned Hamish Smith of Esher Suffolk would have us believe. I am no Englishman. I am for nationalisation on a national scale and if you are a small trader well

No point journeying forth before opening time.

It is possible I might eat with the neighbours as a last resort and perhaps watch television although in view of the oxtail soup a deal to hope for. But I would far rather be abroad in a tavern in earnest conversation with keen people over the state of nations, and I vow to listen. No day dreaming or vacant gazing right hand up and honest to god. Nor shall I inadvertently yawn hugely. But my condition is such company is imperative. I can no longer remain with myself.

And that includes Percy, Greta and the infant, let us say Gloria – all three of whom I shall term the Nulties. The Nulties are a brave little unit gallantly making their way through a harsh uncaring world. They married in late life and having endeavoured for a little one were overwhelmed by their success. The infant Gloria is considered not a bad looking child though personally her looks dont appeal. She has a very tiny nose, pointed ears, receding hair. Also she shits over everything. Mainly diarrhoea that has an amazingly syrupy smell. Like many mothers Greta doesnt always realise the smell exists while on the other hand is absolutely aware so that she begins apologising left right and centre. Yet if everybody resembles me no wonder she forgets the bastarn smell because I for the sake of decency am liable to reply: What smell?

Greta is a busy mum with scarce the time for outside interests. There is nothing or perhaps a lot to say about Percy but it is hell of a boring. The point is that one of these days he shall awaken to an empty house. The woman will have upped and gone and with any sense will have neglected to uplift the infant. Trouble with many mothers is their falling for the propaganda dished out concerning them ie. and their off-spring – Woman's Own magazines and that kind of shite. Most men fall for it too. But I am being sidetracked by gibberish. No, I fail to fit into their cosy scene for various reasons the most obvious of which is 3's a crowd and that's that for the time being.

But dear god I cannot eat with them tonight. They skimp on grub. One Saturday (and the straits must have been beyond desperation if Saturday it truly was) they sat me down and we set to on a plate of toast and tinned spaghetti. For the evening repast! My christ. But what I said was, Toast and spaghetti, great stuff. Now how can I tell such untruths and is it any wonder that I'm fucking languishing. No, definitely not. I deserve all of it. Imitation tomato sauce on my chin. And after the meal we turn to the telly over a digestive smoke and pitcher of coffee essence & recently boiled water; and gape our way to the Late Weather. I could make the poor old Nulties even worse by saying they stand for God Save The Queen Of The Great English Speakers but they dont to my knowledge – it is possible they wait till I have departed upstairs.

I have no wish to continue a life of the Nulties.

Something must be done. A decisive course of action. Tramping around pubs in the offchance of bumping into wealthy acquaintances is a depressing affair. And as far as I remember none of mine are wealthy and even then it is never a doddle to beg from acquaintances – hard enough with friends. Of which I no longer have. No fucking wonder. But old friends I no longer see can no longer be termed friends and since they are obliged to be something I describe them as acquaintances. In fact every last individual I recollect at a given moment is logically entitled to be termed acquaintance. And yet

Why the lies, concerning the tapping of a few bob; I find it easy. Never in the least embarrassed though occasionally I have recourse to the expression of such in order to be adduced ethical or something. I am a natural born beggar. Yes. Honest. A natural born beggar. I should take permanently to the road. The pubs I tramp are those used by former colleagues, fellow employees of the many firms which have in the past employed me for mutual profit. My christ. Only when skint and totally out of the game do I consider the tramp. Yet apparently my company is not anathema. Eccentric but not unlikeable. A healthy respect is perhaps accorded one. Untrue. I am treated in the manner of a sick younger brother. It is my absolute lack of interest in any subject that may arise in their conversation that appeals to them. I dislike debates, confessions and New Year resolutions. I answer only in monosyllables, even when women are present: Still Waters Run Deep is the adage I expect them to use of me. But there are no grounds for complaint. Neither from them nor from me. All I ask is the free bevy, the smoke, the heat. It could embarrass somebody less sensitive than myself. What was that. No, there are weightier problems. The bathwater has been running. Is the new girl about to dip a daintily naked toe. Maybe it is Mrs Soinson. Or Greta. And the infant Gloria. And Percy by christ. But no, Percy showers in the work to save the ten pence meter money. Petty petty petty. I dont bathe at all. I have what might be described as an allover-bodywash here in the kitchenette sink. I do every part of my surface bar certain sections of my lower to middle back which are impossible to reach without one of those long stemmed brushes I often saw years ago in amazing American Movies.

Incredible. Someone decides to bathe in a bath and so the rest of us are forced to run the risk of bladder infection. Nobody chapped my door. How do they know I didnt need to go. So inconsiderate for fuck sake that's really bad. Too much tea right enough, that's the problem.

No, Greta probably entertains no thoughts at all of being in bed with me. I once contemplated the possibility of Percy entertaining such notions. But I must immediately confess to this strong dislike as mutual. And he is most unattractive. And whereas almost any woman is attractive and desirable only a slender few men are. I dont of course mean slenderly proportioned men in fact – what is this at all. I dont want to sleep with men right hand up and honest to god I dont. Why such strenuous denials my good fellow. No reason. Oho. Honest. Okay then. It's a meal I need, a few pints, a smoke, open air and outlook, the secure abode. Concerted energy, decisive course of action. Satisfying gainful employment. Money. A decidable and complete system of life. Ungibberishness. So many needs and the nonexistent funds. I must leave these square quarters of mine this very night. I must worm my way into company, any company, and the more ingratiatingly the better.

Having dug out a pair of uncracked socks I have often made the normal ablutions and left these quarters with or without the Imitation Crombie. Beginning in a pub near the city centre I find nobody. Now to start a quest such as this in a fashion such as this is fucking awful. Not uncommon nevertheless yet this same pub is always the first pub and must always be the first pub in this the quest.

Utter rubbish. How in the name of christ can one possibly consider suicide when one's giro arrives in two days' time. Two days. But it is still Thursday. Thursday. Surely midnight has passed and so technically it is tomorrow morning the next day – Friday. Friday morning. O jesus and tomorrow the world. Amen. Giro tomorrow. In a bad way, no. Certainly not. Who are you kidding. I have to sleep. Tomorrow ie. tonight is Friday's sleep. But two sleeps equal two days. What am I facing here. And so what. I wish

To hell with that for a game.

But I did move recently. I sought out my fellows. Did I really though. As a crux this could be imperative, analogous to the deathwish. Even considering the possibility sheds doubt. Not necessarily. In fact I dont believe it for a single solitary minute. I did want to get in with a crowd though, surely to christ. Maybe I wasnt trying hard enough. But I honestly required company. Perhaps they had altered their drinking habits. Because of me. In the name of fuck all they had to do was humiliate me – not that I would have been bothered by it but at least it could have allayed their feelings – as if some sort of showdown had taken place. But to actually change their pub. Well well well. Perhaps they sense I was setting out on a tramp and remained indoors with shutters drawn, lights extinguised. My christ I'm predictable. Three pubs I went to and I gave up. Always been the same: I lack follow through. Ach.

Can I really say I enjoy life with money. When I have it I throw it away. Only relax when skint. When skint I am a hulk – husk. No sidesteps from the issue. I do not want money ergo I do not want to be happy. The current me is my heart's desire. Surely not. Yet it appears the case. I am always needing money and I am always getting rid of it. This must be hammered home to me. Not even a question of wrecking my life, just that I am content to wallow. Nay, enjoy. I should commit suicide. Unconsecretated ground shall be my eternal resting spot. But why commit suicide if enjoying oneself. Come out of hiding Hamish Smith. Esher Suffolk cannot hold you.

Next time the landlord shows up I shall drygulch him; stab him to death and steal his lot. Stab him to death. Sick to the teeth of day dreams. As if I could stab the nyaff. Maybe I could pick a fight with him and smash in his skull with a broken wine bottle and crash, blood and brains and wine over my wrist and clenched fist. The deathwish after all. Albeit murder. Sounds more rational that: ie. why destroy one's own life if enjoyable. No reason at all. Is there a question. None whatsoever, in fact I might be onto something deep here but too late to pursue it, too late. Yet it could be a revelation of an extraordinary nature. But previously of course been exhausted by the learned Smith of Esher decades since and nowadays taken for granted – not even a topic on an inferior year's O-level examination paper. He isnt even a landlord. I refer to him as such but in reality he is only the bastarn agent. I dont know who the actual landlord really is. It might be Winsom Properties. Winsom Properties is a trust. That means you never know who you are dealing with. I dont like this kind of carry on. I prefer to know names.

Hell with them and their fucking shutters and lights out.

It isnt as bad as all that; here I am and it is now the short a.m.'s. The short a.m.'s. I await the water boiling for a final cup of tea. Probably only drink the stuff in order to pish. Does offer a sort of relief. And simply strolling to the kitchenette and preparing this tea: the gushing tap, the kettle, gathering the tea-bag from the crumb strewn shelf – all of this is motion.

My head gets thick.

One of the chief characteristics of my early, mid and late adolescence was the catastrophic form of the erotic content. Catastrophic in the sense that that which I did have was totally, well, not quite, fantasy. And is the lack by implication of an unnatural variety. Whether it is something to do with me or not – I mean whether or not it is catastrophic is nothing to do with me I mean, not at all. No.

Mr Smith, where are you. No, I cannot be bothered considering the early years. Who cares. Me of course it was fucking lousy. I masturbated frequently. My imagination was/is such I always had fresh stores of fantasies. And I dont wish to give the impression I still masturbate; nowadays, for example, I encounter difficulties in sustaining an erection unless another person happens to be in the immediate vicinity. Even first thing in the morning. This is all bastarn lies. Why in the name of fuck do I continue. What is it with me at all. Something must have upset me recently. Erotic content by christ. Why am I wiped out. Utterly skint. Eh. Why is this always as usual. Why do I even

Certain clerks behind the counter.

I mend fuses for people, oddjobs and that kind of bla for associates of the nyaff, tenants in other words. I am expected to do it. I allow my – I fall behind with the fucking rent. Terrible situation. I have to keep on his right side. Anyway, I dont mind the odd-jobs. It gets you out and about.

I used to give him openings for a life of Mrs Soinson but all he could ever manage was, Fussy Old Biddy. And neither he nor she is married. I cant figure the woman out myself. Apart from her I might be the longest tenant on the premises. And when the nyaff knows so little about her you can be sure nobody else knows a thing. She must mend her own fuses. I havent even seen inside her room or rooms. It is highly possible that she actually fails to see me when we pass on the staircase. The nyaff regards her in awe. Is she a blacksheep outcast of an influential family closely connected to Winsom Properties. When he first became agent around here I think he looked upon her as easy meat whatever the hell that might mean as far as a nyaff is concerned. And she cant be more than fifty years of age, carries herself well and would seem an obvious widow. But I dispute that. A man probably wronged her many years ago. Jilted. With her beautiful 16 year old younger sister by her as bridesmaid, an engagement ring on her finger just decorously biding her time till this marriage of her big sister is out of the way so she can step in and get married to her own youthful admirer, and on the other side of poor old Mrs Soinson stood her widowed father or should I say sat since he would have been an invalid and in his carriage, only waiting his eldest daughter's marriage so he can join his dearly departed who died in childbirth (that of the beautiful 16 year old) up there in heaven. And ever since that day Mrs Soinson has remained a spinster, virginal, the dutiful but pathetic aunt – a role she hates but accepts for her parents' memory. Or she could have looked after the aged father till it was too late and for some reason, on the day he died, vowed to stay a single lassie since nobody could take the place of the departed dad and took on the title of Mistress to ward off would-be suitors although of course you do find men more willing to entertain a single Mrs as opposed to a single Miss which is why I agree with Womans Lib. Ms should be the title of both married and single women.

In the name of god.

Taking everything into consideration the time may be approaching when I shall begin regularly paid, full-time employment. My lot is severely trying. For an approximate age I have been receiving money from the state. I am obliged to cease this malingering and earn an honest penny. Having lived in this fashion for so long I am well nigh unemployable and if I were an Industrial Magnate or Captain of Industry I would certainly entertain doubts as to my capacity for toil. I am an idle goodfornothing. A neerdowell. The workhouse is too good for the likes of me. I own up. I am incompatible with this Great British Society. My production rate is less than atrocious. An honest labouring job is outwith my grasp. Wielding a shabby brush is not to be my lot. Never more shall I be setting forth on bitter mornings just at the break of dawn through slimy backstreet alleys, the treacherous urban undergrowth, trudging the meanest cobbled streets and hideously misshapen pathways of this grey with a heart of gold city. Where is that godforsaken factory. Let me at it. A trier. I would say so Your Magnateship. And was Never Say Die the type of adage one could apply to the wretch. I believe so Your Industrialness.

Fuck off.

Often I sit by the window in order to sort myself out – a group therapy within, and I am content with a behaviourist approach, none of that pie-in-the-sky metaphysics here if you dont mind. I quick-fire trip questions at myself which demand immediate answers and sometimes elongated thought out ones. So far I have been unsuccessful, and the most honest comment on this is that it is done unintentionally on purpose, a very deeply structured item. Choosing this window for instance only reinforces the point. I am way way on top, high above the street. And though the outlook is unopen considerable activity takes place directly below. In future I may dabble in psychiatry – get a book out the library on the subject and stick in, go to nightschool and obtain the necessary qualifications for minor university acceptance whose exams I shall scrape through, industrious but lacking the spark of genius, and eventually make it into a general sanatorium leading a life of devotion to the mental health of mankind. I would really enjoy the work. I would like to organise beneficial group therapies and the rest of it. Daily discussions. Saving young men and women from all kinds of breakdowns. And you would definitely have to be alert working beside the average headbanger or disturbed soul who are in reality the sane and we the insane according to the learned H.S. of Esher S. But though I appear to jest I give plenty thought to the subject. At least once during their days everybody has considered themselves mad or at least well on the road but fortunately from listening to the BBC they realise that if they really were mad they would never for one moment consider it was a possible description of their condition although sometimes they almost have to when reading a book by an enlightened foreigner or watching a heavy play or documentary or something – I mean later, when lying in bed with the lights out for example with the wife fast asleep and $8^1/_2$ months pregnant maybe then suddenly he advances and not too accidently bumps her on the shoulder all ready with some shite about, O sorry if I disturbed you, tossing and turning etc, but I was just wondering eh . . . And then it dawns on him, this the awful truth, he is off his head or at best has an astonishingly bad memory – and this memory, under the circumstances may actually be at worst. And that enlightened foreigner is no comfort once she will have returned to slumber and you are on your own, alone, in the middle of the night, the dark recesses and so on dan d ran dan. But it must happen sometimes. What must fucking happen.

The postoffice may be seeking reliable men. Perhaps I shall fail their medical. And that goes for the fireservice. But the armed forces. Security. And each branch is willing and eager to take on such as myself. I shall apply. The Military Life would suit me. Uplift the responsibility, the decision making, temptations, choices. And a sound bank account at the wind up – not a vast sum of course but enough to set me up as a tobacconist cum newsagent in a small way, nothing fancy, just to eke out the pension.

But there should be direction at 30 years of age. A knowing where I am going. Alright Sir Hamish we cant all be Charles Clore and Florence Níghtíngale but at least we damn well have a go and dont give in. Okay we may realise what it is all about and to hell with their christianity, ethics, the whole shebang and advertising but do we give in, do we Give Up The Ghost. No sirree by god we dont. Do you for one moment think we believe someone should starve to death while another feeds his dog on the finest fillet of steak and chips. Of course not. We none of us have outmoded beliefs but do we

I cannot place a finger somewhere. The bastarn rain is the cause. It pours, steadily for a time then heavier. Of course the fucking gutter has rotted and the constant torrent drops just above the fucking window. That bastard of a landlord gets nothing done, too busy peeping through keyholes at poor old Mrs Soinson. I am fed up with it. Weather been terrible for years. No wonder people look the way they do. Who can blame them. Christ it is bad, the weather, so fucking consistent. Depresses everything. Recently I went for a short jaunt in the disagreeable countryside. Fortunately I got soaked through. The cattle ignored the rain. The few motor cars around splished past squirting oily mud onto the Imitation Crombie. I kept slipping into marshy bogs from whence I shrieked at various objects while seated. It wasnt boring. Of yore, on country rambles, I would doze in some deserted field with the sun beating etc the hum of grasshoppers chirp. I never sleep in a field where cattle graze lest I get nibbled. The countryside and I are incompatible. Everybody maintains they like the countryside but I refuse to accept such nonsense. It is absurd. Just scared, to admit the truth – that they hate even the idea of journeying through pastureland or craggyland. Jesus christ. I dont mind small streams burning through arable-land. Hardy fishermen with waders knee-deep in lonely inshore waters earn my total indifference. Not exactly. Not sympathy either, nor pity, nor respect, envy, hate. Contempt. No, not at all. But I heroworship lighthousekeepers. No. Envy is closer. Or maybe jealousy. And anyway, nowadays all men are created equal. But whenever I have had money in the past I always enjoyed the downpour. If on the road to somewhere the rain is fine. A set purpose. Even the cinema. Coat collar upturned, street lights reflecting on puddles, arriving with wind flushed complexion and rubbing your damp hands, parking your arse on a convenient convector heater. But without the money. Still not too bad perhaps.

According to the mirror I have been going about with a thoughtful expression on one's countenance. I appear to have become aware of myself in relation to the field by which I mean the external world. In relation to this field I am in full knowledge of my position. And this has nothing to do with steak & chips

Comfortable degrees of security are not to be scoffed at. I doff the cap to those who attain it the bastards. Seriously, I am fed up with being fed up. What I do wish

I shall not entertain day dreams
I shall not fantasise
I shall endeavour to make things work

I shall tramp the mean streets in search of menial posts or skilled ones. Everywhere I shall go, from Shetland Oilrigs to Bearsden Gardening Jobs. To Gloucestershire even. I would go to Gloucestershire. Would I fuck. To hell with them and their cricket & cheese. I refuse to go there. I may emigrate to The Great Englishes – o jesus christ Australia & New Zealand. Or America and Canada.

All I'm fucking asking is regular giros and punctual counter clerks.

Ach well son cheer up. So quiet in this dump. Some kind of tune was droning around a while back. I was sitting clapping hands to the rhythm and considering moving about on the floor. I used to dream of playing the banjo. Or even the guitar, just being able to strum but with a passable voice I could be dropping into parties and playing a song, couple of women at the feet keeping time and slowly sipping from a tall glass, 4 in the a.m.'s with whisky on the shelf and plenty of smokes. This is it now. Definitely.

black and white consumer and producer parasite thief come on shake hands you lot.

Well throw yourself out the fucking window then. Throw myself out fuck all window – do what you like but here I am, no suicide and no malnutrition, no fucking nothing in fact because I am leaving, I am getting to fuck out of it. A temporary highly paid job, save a right few quid and then off on one's travels. Things will be done. Action immediate. Of the Pioneering Stock would you say. Of that ilk most certainly Your Worship. And were the audience Clambering to their feet. I should think so Your Grace.

The fact is I am a late starter. I am

I shouldnt be bothering about money anyway. The creditors have probably forgotten all about my existence. No point worrying about other than current arrears. The old me wouldnt require funds. A red & white polkadot handkerchief, a stout sapling rod, the hearty whistle and hi yo silver for the short ride to the outskirts of town, Carlisle and points south.

It is all a load of shite. I often plan things out then before the last minute do something ridiculous to ensure the plan's failure. If I did decide to clear the arrears and get a few quid together, follow up with a symbolic burning of the Imitation Crombie and in short make preparations to mend my ways I could conceivably enlist in the Majestic Navy to spite myself – or even fork out a couple of month's rent in advance for this dump simply to sit back and enjoy my next step from a safe distance and all the time guffawing in the background good christ I am schizophrenic, I never thought I acted in that manner yet I must admit it sounds like me, worse than I imagined, bad, bad. Maybe I could use the cash to pay for an extended stay in a private nursing home geared to the needs of the Unabletocope. But can it be schizophrenia if I can identify it myself. Doubtful. However, I regard

I was of the opinion certain items in regard to my future had been resolved. Cynical of self, this is the problem. Each time I make a firm resolution I end up scoffing. Yes. I sneer. Well well well, what a shite. That really does take the biscuit. And look at the time look at the time.

Captains of Industry should create situations for my ilk. The Works Philosopher I could be. With my own wee room to the left of the Personnel Section. During teabreaks Dissidents would be sent to me. Militancy could be cut by half, maybe as much as 90%. Yet Works Philosophers could not be classed as staff, instead they would be stamping in & out like the rest of the troops just in case they get aspirations, and seek reclassification within Personnel maybe. Gibberish. And yet fine, that would be fine, so what if they got onto the staff because that would leave space for others and the Dissident next in line could become the new Works Philosopher and so on and so forth. And they would stick it, the job, they would not be obliged to seek out square squarters whose shelves are crumb strewn.

I shall have it to grips soon. Tomorrow or who knows. After all, I am but 30, hardly matured. But fuck me I'm getting hell of a hairy these days. Maybe visit the barber in the near future, Saturday morning for instance, who knows what is in store. Only waiting for my passion to find an object and let itself go. Yes, who can tell what's in store, that's the great thing about life, always one more fish in the sea, iron in the fire; this is the great thing about life, the uncertainty and the bla

Jesus what will I do, save up for a new life, the mending of the ways, pay off arrears, knock the door of accredited creditors, yes, I can still decide what to do about things concerning myself and even others if only in regard to me at least it is still indirectly to do with them and yet it isnt indirect at all because it is logically bound to be direct if it is anything and obviously it is something and must therefore be directly since I am involved and if they are well

well well,

who can tell what the fuck this is about. I am chucking it in. My brain cannot cope on its own. Gets carried away for the sake of thought no matter whether it be sense or not, no, that is the last fucking thing considered. Which presents problems. I really do have a hard time knowing where I am going. For if going, where. Nowhere or somewhere. Children and hot meals. Homes and security and the neighbours in for a quiet drink at the weekend. Tumbling on carpets with the weans and television sets and golf and even heated discussions in jocular mood while the wives gossip ben in the kitchen and

Now then: here I am in curiously meagre surroundings, living the life of a hapless pauper, my pieces of miserable silver supplied gratis by the Browbeaten Taxpayer. The past ramblings concerning outer change were pure invention. And comments made about one's total inadequacy were done so in earnest albeit with a touch of pride. Even the brave Nulties are abused by me, at least in respect to grub & smokes. And all for what. Ah, an ugly sight. But this must be admitted: with a rumbling stomach I have often refused food, preferring a lonely smoke and the possible mystery of, Has he eaten elsewhere . . . and if so with whom. Yet for all people know I have several trunks packed full of articles, clothes and whatnot. Apart from a couple of clerks nobody knows a thing about me. I could be a Man About Town. They probably nudge each other and refer to me as a bit of a lad. I might start humping large suitcases plastered with illegible labels. Save up and buy a suit in modern mode. Get my coat dyed, even stick with its symbolic burning. Or else I could sell it. A shrewd man I occasionally have dealings with rejected this coat. But I did ask a Big price. Shoes too I need. Presently I have what are described as Bumpers. Whereas with real leather efforts and a new rig out I could travel anywhere and get a new start in life. I could be a Computer Programmer. But they're supposed to reach their peak at 21 years of age. Still and all the sex potency fucking peak is 16. 16 years of age by christ you could not credit that. Ach. I dare say sex plays more of a role in my life than grub. If both were in abundance my problems could only increase. Yet one's mental capacities would be bound to make more use of their potential without problems at the fundamental level.

But

the plan. From now on I do not cash giros. I sleep in on Saturday mornings and so too late for the postoffice until Monday mornings by which time everything will be alright, it will be fine, I shall have it worked out and fine and if I can stretch it out and grab at next Saturday then the pathway shall have been erected, I shall have won through.

Recently I lived in seclusion. For a considerable period I existed on a tiny islet not far from Toay. Sheep and swooping gulls for companions. The land and the sea. After dark the inner recesses. Self knowledge and acceptance of the awareness. No trees of course. None. Sheer drops from mountainous regions, bird shit and that of sheep and goats as well perhaps, in that kind of terrain. No sign of man or woman. The sun always far in the sky but no clouds. Not tanned either. Weatherbeaten. Hair matted by the salt spray. Food requires no mention. Swirling eddies within the standing rocks and nicotine wool stuck to the jaggy edges, the droppings of the gulls.

Since I shall have nothing to look forwards to on Saturday mornings I must reach a state of neither up nor down. Always the same. That will be miserable I presume but considering my heart's desire is to be miserable then with uncashed giros reaching for the ceiling I can be indefinitely miserable. Total misery. However, to retain misery I may be obliged to get out and about in order not to be always miserable since – or should I say pleasure is imperative if perfect misery is the goal; and, therefore, a basic condition of my perpetual misery is the occasional jaunt abroad in quest of joy. Now we're getting somewhere Sir Smith, arise and get your purple sash. And since ambling round pubs only depresses me I must seek out other means of entertainment or henceforth desist this description of myself as wretch. And setbacks and kicksintheteeth are out of the question. Masochism then. Is this what

Obviously I am just in the middle of a nervous breakdown, even saying it I mean that alone

But for christ sake saving a year's uncashed giros is impossible because the bastards render them uncashable after a 6 month interval.

Walking from Land's End to John O'Groats would be ideal in fact because for one thing it would tax my resistance to the utmost. Slogging on day in day out. Have to be during the summer. I dislike the cold water and I would be stopping off for a swim. Yet this not knowing how long it takes the average walker . . . well, why worry, time is of no concern. Or perhaps it should be. I could try for the record. After the second attempt possibly. Once I had my bearings. Not at all. I would amble. And with pendants and flags attached to the suitcase I could beg my grub & tobacco. The minimum money required. Neither broo nor social security. The self sufficiency of the sweetly self employed. I could be for the rest of my life. The Land's End to John O'Groats man. That would be my title. My name a byword, although anonymity would be the thing to aim for. Jesus it could be good. And far from impossible. I have often hitched about the place. Many times. But hitching must be banned otherwise I shall be saving time which is of course an absurdity – pointless to hitch. And yet what difference will it make if I do save time because it can make no difference anyway. None whatsoever. Not at all. And if it takes 6 weeks a trip and the same back up I could average 4 return trips a year. If I am halfway through life just now ie. a hundred and twenty return trips then in another hundred and twenty trips I would be dead. I can mark off each trip on milestones north & south. And when the media get a grip of me I can simply say I'll be calling a halt in 80 trips time. And I speak of returns. That would be twenty years hence by which time I would have become accustomed to fame. Although I could have fallen down dead by then through fatigue or something. Hail rain shine. The dead of winter would be a challenge and could force me into shelter unless I acquire a passport and head out to sunnier climes, Australia for example to stave off the language barriers yet speech need be no problem since communication will be the major lack as intention perhaps. No, impossible. I cannot leave The Great British Shores. Comes to that I cannot leave the Scottish ones either. Yes, aye, Scotland is ideal. Straight round the Scottish Coast from the foot of Galloway right round to Berwick although Ayrshire is a worry its being a very boring coastline. But boredom is out of the question. Ayrshire will not be denied. So each return trip might involve say a four month slog if keeping rigidly to the coast on all minor roads particularly when you consider Kintyre – or Morven by fuck and even I suppose Galloway itself to some extent. But that kind of thing is easily resolved. I dont have to restrict myself to mapped out routes from which the slightest deviation is frowned upon. On the contrary, that last minute decision at the country crossroads can only enhance the affair. And certain items of clothing are already marked out as essential items. The stout boots and gnarled staff to ward off country animals after dusk. A hat & coat for wet weather. The Imitation Crombie may suffice. Though an anorak to cover the knees would probably reap dividends. And after a few return trips – and being a circular route no such thing as a return would exist ie. I would be travelling on an arc – the farmfolk and country dwellers would know me well, the goodwives leaving thick winter woollies by the side of the road, flasks of oxtail soup under hedges. Shepherds offering shelter in remote bothies by the blazing log fires sipping hot toddies for the wildest nights and plenty of tobacco always the one essential luxury, and the children up and down the land crying, Mummy here comes the Scottish Coastroad Walker while I would dispense the homespun philosophies of the daisy growing and the planet as it revolves etc. A stray dog joining me having tagged along for a trip at a safe distance behind me I at last turn and at my first grunt of encouragement it comes bounding joyfully forwards to shower me in wet noses and barked assurances to stick by me through thick & thin and to eternally guard my last lowly grave when I have at length fallen in mid-stride plumb tuckered out after many years viz 12 round trips at two years a trip. Yet it might be shorter than that. While the hot days in central summer are the busloads of tourists arriving to see me, pointed out by their driver, the Legend of the North, the solitary trudging humpbacked figure with dog & gnarled staff just vanishing out of sight into the mist, Dont give him money Your Lordship you'll just hurt his feelings. Just a bite of your cheese piece and a saucer of milk for the whelp. Group photographs with me peering suspiciously at the camera from behind shoulders at the back or in the immediate foreground perhaps, It is rumoured the man was a Captain of Industry Your Grace, been right round the Scottish Coastroad 28 times and known from Galloway to Berwick as a friend to Everyone. Yes, just a pinch of your snuff and a packet of cigarette-papers for chewing purposes only. No sextants or compasses or any of that kind of shite but

By the Burn

Fucking bogging mud man a swamp, an actual swamp, it was fucking a joke. He pulled his foot clear but the boot was still lodged there like it was quicksand and it was going to get sucked off and vanish down into it forever. He felt the suction hard on his foot but when he pulled, curling his toes as firm as possible, out it came with a loud squelching sound. Thank Christ for that. He shook his head, studying the immediate area, these marshy stalks of grass were everywhere; fucking hopeless. He glanced back across the wide expanse of waste ground and up to where the blocks of flats were. But he had to go this way and go this way right now, he was late enough as it was, he just couldnt afford to waste any time. He continued on, steering clear of the clumps of long weeds, the kind that told you where the worst of it was, but it was bad and each step now his boot sunk in an inch or so, but still not as bad as before. Imagine if he had lost the fucking boot but Christ almighty, hirpling down the road for the train then into the interview office, trying to explain to the folk there how you had just lost your shoe in a fucking swamp. My God, a fucking joke right enough. He stopped to look ahead. Then the rain started again and this time it wasnt a passing shower, the sky was full of dark grey clouds, he turned up the collar of his suit jacket, it was going to get worse, nothing surer. And he would get bloody soaked. What the hell time was it? Aw for fuck sake who cares, he plunged on, veering off towards the banks of the burn. You could actually hear the roar of the water: so it was probably running awful high. So there was no chance of him crossing at the usual stepping stones, maybe have to skirt right the way round through the wood to get to the bloody bridge. Aw dear. He hated having to go that way. By this time he had reached the last of the marsh and there was the ordinary grass and the short clumps of bushes. He passed the wee tree, most of its branches half snapped and trailing onto the ground. A kid's sock dangled off one of them. Then the slope up to the bank of the burn. It was all slimy mud here and he had to steady himself by using his hand as a prop, stepping up in a kind of semi-circle. His hands were all muddy now and he had to pull off a couple of big docken leaves to wipe them clean. The roaring from the burn was really loud now, deafening. He waited a moment up on the bank, staring down at the swollen water, it came rushing, spray flying out, so high it looked set to overflow the banks. You couldnt even see the stepping stones where he would have crossed, probably about two feet of water were covering them. So that was it now there was no chance, the path across the bridge or nothing, that was for fucking definite, he just had no choice in the matter. He sighed, blowing out through his mouth. He felt a wee twinge across his shoulders and that was followed by a shiver. He actually did feel tired although it was only about half eleven in the morning, he felt a bit weak in fact. Then the rain on his head. He felt like going away home again, back to the fire, cup of tea and put the feet up. It was just a joke, the whole fucking thing. Away in the distance he saw a shape looming into view through the trees, then another one. Two blokes. They cut off but, taking a different route to get to the flats, up through the field. The rain now definitely getting heavier. He walked as fast as he could along the peak of the bank without slipping on the fucking mud, arse over elbow into the burn – probably he wouldnt have been able to save himself from drowning for Christ sake. Once upon a time aye, but no now. He glanced down as he went. The water was flowing that fucking fast. It was years since he had had a swim too, years. High time they extended the path along this way for the poor cunts living up the flats, the fucking council, it was out of order the way they didnt bother. They had been fucking talking about it for donkeys. He left the bank at the first opportunity, following a narrow trail into the wood and he took shelter beneath the first big tree. He started shivering again. Just the dampness maybe because it wasnt really cold. And he needed a coat. He really did need a coat man this was just stupid. He had one right enough he just didnt wear the fucking thing, he didnt like it. It was too big for him for a start, it was his brother-in-law's. You could have wrapped it round him twice. But still and all he should have wore it, he could have carried it over his arm and just stuck it on and off, depending on what it was doing, if it was raining or not, he didnt have to wear it all the time. His suit shoulder nudged against the tree trunk now and he moved from it, it was slimy, it was really fucking slimy. He gave the material a good rub but the stain still showed, the mud or whatever it was. He caught sight of his boots, all soaking wet and bits of grass and leaves sticking to them, nettles, the lot. Some picture. The wife would be pleased. Once they dried but they would be alright, brand new – except because of the damp they would turn white probably. They werent that old either, bastard. Just like it when you needed everything to be right, when you needed to be at your best, the way you looked. Fucking Jesus. My God. Never mind. Never mind. They would do for the time being, as long as they stayed damp they would pass inspection. If he ever got out of here! Because the fucking rain was pelting down and thick heavy blotches were dropping through the branches of the tree and landing on his nut. Still another half mile through the wood and he would have to start moving soon, he couldnt afford to wait any longer oh but Christ he didnt want to go he would just have to make a run for it, he would just have to make a run for it, just forget about the rain because it wasnt going to go off now, it was on for the bloody duration. The smell of the tree was in his nostrils, it was like decay or something like it was rotten. A lot of the bark had been cut from the trunk here, peeled off. Somebody with a knife. Wee boys probably. Maybe big ones. He studied the bark that was left, the thick dark green stuff, all criss-cross lines and it was like cobwebs inside it, a gauzy sort of stuff; it would be full of beetles, beetles and termites, maggots, all living off it, the bark was there to be eaten, they would eat it. He jumped suddenly out from the tree and started running, keeping his head down. At places the trail got really narrow and it took sharp angles and he had to slow down to avoid the traps, the bent branches and the roots and stumps of trees. It was a joke, it was just a joke. Then he was having to walk, he couldnt go any faster, it was just too thick, it was too thick. He had his hands in his trouser pockets. By the time he arrived in the office he wouldnt be in a fit state for the interview. They probably wouldnt even let him in the fucking door man they would send for the fucking polis, the way he was looking, the suit all fucking mud and the boots turned white because of the fucking dampness man it was just bloody out of order, you just had no fucking chance. He needed a car. Every cunt needed a car. That was what happened when you stayed out in the schemes, it was fine till you wanted to go someplace, once you did you were in fucking trouble. Stupid, it was just stupid. But it was a bastard, it really was a bastard, these bloody fucking bushes and swamps man what could you do, going for a fucking job, just when you needed to look right, it aye happened, that was the way it went, you just couldnt win, you just couldnt fucking win man never, you could never win. He glanced about him. Then he looked back over his shoulder. A funny feeling there. He walked on a few paces then slowed again, he stopped. He stopped and listened, he was feeling a bit funny, like somebody was watching him. It was like there was somebody watching him. He felt the twinge in his shoulders. There *was*. There was somebody watching him. What was it he felt so Christ almighty another shiver, somebody definitely watching him. It was gloomy and dark now with the trees high and affecting what light there was; shadows, all the bushes, all thick. He stood where he was, he just stood there.

Then he felt it again, right across his shoulders. It was a chill. He had caught a chill. Definitely. He was damp, he was bloody cold. He was oh Christ almighty and he felt it another time now right across his chest as well a sort of tremor and down his thighs to his knees it was, it was like a tremor, a spasm. But it was his daughter, it was his daughter. Like her ghost was somewhere. He knew it. He knew what it was exactly. Because it was the sandpit. It was right across the burn from where he was standing and if it was winter and the leaves had fell you would see right across and the sandpit was there, it was right there, just on the other side. Aw dear, the wee fucking lassie. Aw dear man aw dear it was so fucking hard so fucking awful hard, awful hard so fucking awful hard. Oh where was the wife. He needed his fucking wife. He needed her. He needed her close. He needed her so fucking close he felt so fucking Christ man the sandpit, where the wee lassie and her two wee pals had got killed. Hiding out playing chases. Aye being warned to steer clear but in they went and then it collapsed on them, and it trapped them, all these tons of earth and they had all got suffocated. Aw dear. Aw dear. He stepped in near a big tree and leaned his arms against it, his forearms, crossed, them shielding his eyes, he was greeting without any sound, he just couldnt handle it. He couldnt. He had never been able to. It used to keep him awake at nights. For ages, fucking ages. He could never get it out his mind. For Christ sake bloody years ago it was, bloody years ago. Oh Christ. She was stronger than him. The wife. She was. She really was. She could handle it. He couldnt. But she could. She could handle it fine. She got by on it. But he didnt. He couldnt; he just couldnt handle it. He never could. He had never been able to, he had just never been able to. He opened his mouth to breathe fresh air. The insides of his mouth ached. Throat dry. A wetness at the corners of his lips: he wiped them with the cuff of his suit sleeve. He had just never been able to handle it; he couldnt come to terms with it at all. These years. All these fucking years. And that wee fucking lassie oh God man he just could never fucking handle it. Plus as well he would have wanted to be one of them that carried her out. No just her but the other ones, her two wee pals. But he wasnt there. He didnt know. He just heard about it later. Him and the wife man they never fucking knew it had happened, no till too late, it was too late when they knew. It had been firemen done it and some other folk who went down. But him and the wife never knew about it till too late, there was nobody telt them. But it was nobody's fault, they didnt know who it was that was buried, no till they got them out. The firemen came and cleared out the rubble, then they found them, the wee souls, they lifted them and carried them. He would like even to have seen it He telt the wife that at the time as well, just from a distance, it would have been fine as long as he could just have seen them, the wee legs all spindly and them broken like that, their wee bodies. Ah dear, ah dear. He swallowed. The tears were running down his face again. He shut his eyes tight to stop it. He could feel rain down the back of his neck; his throat was so dry. He flexed his shoulders. Just seeing her would have been good, smoothing her head and hair, just smoothing her head and hair, that was all. God. Ah God he was feeling better, it was passed. Poor old wife but it was a shame for her, the missis. She had to carry on. She had to cope. Different for him. Different. He wasnt stuck in the house, he had a job at the time, but she was, she was stuck in the house. Plus she had to look after the other one. That was what kept her going. Christ almighty he could do with a drink. All this rain and he was dying of fucking thirst. It was past now, finished. He felt better. Aye he could do with a drink, of water just. The feeling was away, it had gone. There was another twinge now at his knees but it went as well. He shivered again. He was alone. He had to carry on now. He started walking, following the trail. One thing he did know but, see when he died, he was going to die of a heart attack, he was going to die of a heart attack and he was going to be alone, there wasnt going to be no cunt, no cunt, he was going to be fucking alone, that was the way he was going to die, he fucking knew it, it was a fucking racing certainty.

Street-sweeper

The sky was at the blueyblack pre-heavygrey stage of the morning and the gaffer was somewhere around. This is one bastard that was always around; he was always hiding. But he was somewhere close right now and Peter could sense his presence and he paused. It wasnt a footstep but he turned to see over his shoulder anyway, walked a few more paces then quickly sidled into a shop doorway, holding the brush vertical, making sure the top of his book wasnt showing out his pocket. This was no longer fun. At one time in his life it mightve been but no now, fuck, it was just bloody silly. And it wisni funny. It just wisni fucking funny at all. These things were beginning to happen to him more and more and he was still having to cope. What else was there. In this life you get presented with your choices and that's that, if you canni choose the right ones you choose the wrong ones and you get fucked some of the time; most of the time some people would say. He closed his eyes, rubbed at his brow, smoothing the hair of his eyebrows. What was he to do now, he couldni make it back to the place he was supposed to be at, no without being spotted. Aw god. But it gave him a nice sense of liberty as well, it was an elation, quite fucking heady. Although he would have to move, he would – how long can you stay in a doorway! Hey, there was a big cat watching him, it was crouched in beside a motor-car wheel. Ha, christ. Peter chuckled. He was seen by a cat your honour. There he was in a doorway, having skived off because he had heard about a forced entry to a newsagent shop and thought there mightve been some goods lying available to pilfer.

Objection!

Overruled.

Ah but he was sick of getting watched. He was. He was fucking sick of it. The council have a store of detectives. They get sent out spying on the employees, the workers lad the workers, they get sent out spying on them. Surely not. The witness has already shown this clearly to be the case your Honour. Has he indeed. Aye, fuck, he has, on fucking numerous occasions, that's how come he got the boys out on strike last March.

Ah.

Naw but he's fucking sick of it, he really is. High time he was an adult. Here he is forty-seven years of age and he's a boy, a wee lad – in fact, he is all set to start wearing short trousers and ankle-socks and a pair of fastrunning sandshoes (plimsolls for the non-Scottish reader). What was he to do but that is the problem, that is the thing you get faced with all the bloody time, wasnt it just bloody enervating. But you've got your brush you've got your brush and he stepped out and was moving, dragging his feet on fast, dragging because his left leg was a nuisance, due to a fucking disability that made him limp – well it didni make him limp, he decided to limp, it was his decision, he could have found some new manner of legmotoring which would have allowed him not to limp, by some sort of circumlocutory means he could have performed a three-way shuffle to offset or otherwise bypass the limp and thus be of normal perambulatory gait. This was these fucking books he read. Peter was a fucking avid reader and he had got stuck in the early Victorian era, even earlier, bastards like Goldsmith for some reason, that's what he read. Charles fucking Lamb, that's who he read; all these tory essayists of the prechartist days, that other bastard that didni like Keats. Why did he read such shite. Who knows, they fucking wreaked havoc with the syntax, never mind the fucking so-called sinecure of a job, the street cleaning. Order Order. Sorry Mister Speaker. But for christ sake, for christ sake.

Yet you had to laugh at his spirit I mean god almighty he was a spirited chappie, he was, he really and truly was. But he had to go fast. There was danger ahead. No time for quiet grins. Alright he was good, he was still doing the business at forty-seven, but no self-congratulatory posturing if you please, even though he might still be doing it, even though he was still going strong at the extraordinarily advanced age of thrice fifteen-and-two-thirds your honour, in the face of extraordinarily calamitous potentialities to wit said so-called sinecure. Mister Speaker Mister Speaker, this side of the House would request that you advise us as to the appertaining set of circumstances of the aforementioned place and primary purpose of said chappie's sinecure so-called. Uproar. A Springburn street. Put on the Member for Glasgow North. The Member for Glasgow North has fuckt off for a glass of claret. Well return him post-haste.

But the goodwife. Has the goodwife a word to say. Yes, indeed. The goodwife would bat him one on the gob. She thought all this was dead and buried. She thought the sinecure was not deserving of the 'so-called' prefixed reference one iota, i.e. sinecure *qua* sinecure in the good lady's opinion.

She wouldni think it was possible but, it's true, she thought it was all over as far as the problematics were concerned. Pussycats pussycats, I thought I saw. But there you are, getting to the doddering stage, being spotted by a crouching cat, so much for his ability to cope, to withstand the helter skelter, the pell mell, the guys in the darkblue and the bulky shoulders. Bejasus he was getting fucking drunk on the possibility of freedom, a genuine liberty, one that would be his prior to deceasement. What he fancied was a wee periscope from the coffin, so he could just lie there watching the occasional passersby, the occasional birdie or fieldmouse:

he was into another doorway and standing with his back pressed into the wall, his eyes shut tight, but lips parted, getting breath, listening with the utmost concentration. Nothing. Nothing o christ why was he an atheist this of all times he felt like screaming a howsyrfather yr paternoster a quick hail mary yr king billy for christ sake what was it was it a fucking footfall he felt like bellowing, bellowing the fucking place down, it would show them it would show them it would display it, it would display how he was and how he could bellow his laughter in the face of the fucking hidebound universe of them, fucking moribund bastirts – was it the gaffer? He pulled the brush in, held it like an upright musket of the old imperialist guard, India or Africa yr Lordship.

Carol thought it was all dead and buried. She did, she truly truly did. His eyes were shut and his lips now closed, the nostrils serving the air channels or pipes, listening with the utmost concatenation of the earular orifices. Not to scream. Not to make a sound. Another minute and he would go, he would move, move off, into the greying dawn.

He was safe now for another few minutes. It was over, a respite o lord how brief is this tiny candle flicker. Peasie Peasie Peasie. For this was his nickname, the handle awarded him by the mates, the compañeros, the compatriots, the comrades: Peasie.

It didni even matter the profit but this was the fucking thing! Maybe he got there and the newsagent turned out to be a grocer for god sake how many cartons of biscuits can you plank out in some backcourt! Fucking radio rental yr Lordship, Mind you the profit was of nae account, nane at all. Neither the benefits thereon. If there were benefits he didni ken what they were. He shook his head. Aright, aright me boy, me lad. There was a poor fucker lying on the grun ahead. There was. Peter approached cautiously. It was a bad sign. It was. If the security forces martialled, and they would, then they would be onto him in a matter of hours, a couple of hours, maybe even one; he would need a tale to tell. Diarrhoea. Diarrhoea, the saviour of the working classes. He had to go to the loo and spend some several minutes, maybe thirty, unable to leave in case the belly ructured yet again. But the body was a bad sign. Poor bastard.

Peter knelt by the guy. He was still alive, his forehead warm and the tick at the temple, a faint pulsing. But should he drag him into a closemouth No, of course not, plus best to leave him or else

but the guy was on his back and that was not good. Peter laid down his brush and did the life-saving twist, he placed the man's right arm over his left side, then raised and placed his right leg also over his left side, then pulled the left leg out a little, again gently, shifting the guy's head, onto the side: and now the guy would breathe properly without the risk of choking on his tongyou. And he would have to leave it at that. It wisni cold so he wouldni die of frostbite. Leave it. You'll be aright son, he whispered and for some reason felt like kissing him on the forehead, a gesture of universal love for the suffering. We can endure, we can endure. Maybe it was a returning prophet to earth, and this was the way he had landed, on the crown of his skull and done a flaky. He laid his hand on the guy's shoulder. Ah you'll be right as rain, he said, and he got up to go. He would be though, he would be fine, you could tell, you could tell just by looking; and Peter was well-versed in that. Yet fuck sake if he hadni of known how to properly move the guy's body then he might have died, he couldve choked to death. My god but life is so fragile; truly, it is.

And he was seen. The pair of eyes watching. The gaffer was across the street. The game's a bogie. He looked to be smiling. He hated Peter so that would be the case quite clearly.

Come ower here!

Peter had walked a couple paces by then and he stopped, he looked across the road. Giuseppe Robertson was the gaffer's name. Part of his hatred for Peter was straightforward, contained in the relative weak notion of 'age'; the pair of them were of similar years and months down even to weeks perforce days and hours – all of that sort of shite before you get to the politics. Fucking bastirt. Peter stared back at him. Yeh man hey, Robertson was grinning, he was fucking grinning. Ace in the hole and three of them showing. Well well well.

Come ower here! he shouted again.

He wasnt kidding. Yeh, Peter licked his lips. He glanced sideways, the body there and still prone; Robertson seemed not to have noticed it yet. He glanced back at him and discovered his feet moving, dragging him across the road. Who was moving his fucking feet. He wasnt, it had to be someone in the prime position.

The gaffer was staring at him.

I'm sorry, said Peter.

It doesni matter about fucking sorry man you shouldni have left the job.

I had to go a place.

You had to go a place . . . mmhh; is that what you want on record?

Aye.

The gaffer grinned: You've been fun out and that's that.

As long as you put it on record.

Ah Peter Peter, so that's you at last, fucking out the door. It's taken a while, but we knew we'd get ye.

You did.

We did, aye, true, true true true, aye, we knew you'd err. So, you better collect the tab frae the office this afternoon.

Peter gazed at him, he smiled. Collect my tab?

Yes, you're finished, all fucking washed up, a jellyfish on the beach, you're done, you're in the process of evaporating. The gaffer chuckled. Your services, for what they're worth, are no longer in demand by the fathers of the city.

That's excellent news. I can retire and grow exotic plants out my window boxes.

You can do whatever the fuck you like son.

Ah, the son, I see. But Giuseppe you're forgetting, as a free man, an ordinary civilian, I can kick fuck out you and it'll no he a dismissible offence against company property.

Jovial, very jovial. And obviously if that's your wish then I'm the man, I'm game, know what I mean, game, anywhere you like Peter it's nomination time.

The two of them stared at each other. Here we have a straightforward hierarchy. Joe Robertson the gaffer and Peter the sweeper.

Fuck you and your services, muttered Peter and thereby lost the war. This was the job gone. Or was it, maybe it was just a battle: Look, said Peter, I've no even been the place yet I was just bloody going, I've no even got there.

You were just bloody going!

Aye.

You've been off the job an hour.

An hour? Who fucking telt ye that?

Never you mind.

There's a guy lying ower there man he's out the game.

So what?

I just bloody saved his life!

Robertson grinned and shook his head: Is that a fact!

That means I've just to leave him there?

Your job's taking care of the streets, he's on the fucking pavement.

Mmhh, I see.

It was on the streets, past tense.

Aw for fuck sake man look I'm sorry! And that was as far as he was going with this charade, no more, no more.

It doesni fucking matter about sorry, it's too late.

It'll no happen again yr honour. . . Peter attempted a smile, a moment later he watched the gaffer leave, his bowly swagger, taking a smoke from his pocket and lighting it as he went. Death. The latest legislation. Death. Death death death. Death. Capital d e a

He continued to watch the gaffer until he turned the corner of Moir Street.

Well there were other kinds of work. They were needing sellers of a variety of stuff at primary-school gates. That was a wheeze. Why didnt he get in on that. My god, it was the coming thing. Then with a bit of luck he could branch out on his own and from there who knows, the whole of the world was available. Peter cracked himself on the back of the skull with such venomous force Aouch that he nearly knocked it off Aouch he staggered a pace, dropped his brush and clutched his head. O for fuck sake christ almighty but it was sore. He recovered, stopped to retrieve the brush.

It was bloody sore but christ that was stupid, bloody stupid thing to do, fucking eedjit – next thing he would be cutting bits out his body with a sharp pointed knife, self-mutilation, that other saviour of the working classes. O christ but the head was still nipping! My god, different if it knocked some sense into the brains but did it did it fuck.

Who had shopped him? Somebody must have. Giuseppe wouldni have been so cocky otherwise. One of the team had sold him out for a pocket of shekels; that's the fucking system boy no more street-sweeping for you. Yes boy hey, he could do anything he liked. Peter smiled and shook his head. He glanced upwards at the heavy grey clouds. He felt like putting on a shirt and tie and the good suit, and get Carol, and off they would go to a nightclub, out wining and dining the morning away. He liked nightshift. Nightshift! It was a beautiful experience. My god Robertson I'd love to fucking do you in boy that's what I would fucking like. But he had no money and he was eighteen years short of the pension. And he was not to lose control. That was all he needed. The whole of life was out to get you. There's a sentence. But it's true, true, the whole of life. Who had shopped him but for fuck sake what dirty bastirt had done the dirty, stuck the evil eye on him, told fucking Robertson the likely route. Och dear, I had a dream, I had a dream, and in this dream a man was free and could walk tall, he could walk tall, discard the brush and hold up the head, straightened shoulders and self-respect:

the guy was still lying there.

Ohhh. A whisky would be nice, a wee dram. Peter carried a hipflask on occasion but not tonight, he didnt have it tonight. Ohhh. He paused, he stared over the road, seeing the guy in that selfsame position. Perhaps he was dead, perhaps he had died during the tiff with the gaffer. Poor bastard, what was his story, we've all got them, we've all got them.

Morning has bro-ken.

Sheena Blackhall (1947 –)

Gloamin

There's a hole i the sky, at the back o the day
Tae gang til't, naebody daurs
For there, like a bar-fit bairn, stauns nicht
Wi his neive★ stap-fu o stars.   fist

The day creeps oot, wi a hirplin★ gait   limping
A gomeril★, spent, an dane   fool, rascal
Its lowe★ burned grey, as a ghaistie's goun   flame
An the gloamin glint, in its een.

An ben yon chink, at the back o the cloud
Far the settin sun sits reid   10
fleerichin★ up, till★ an unkent hame   sparking/to
Are the souls o the newly deid.

There's a hole i the sky, at the back o the day
A place far naebody's been
Till Daith, the lanely leerie★ man   lamplighter
Cams steekin★ their waukkrife★ een.   shutting/sleepless

Lament for the Raj

Mithers uncle Dougie, an faither's Cousin John –
Ane vrocht in Kuala Lumpur – the tither in Ceylon;
Twa hin-hochs o the Raj's rump . . . the tail-eyn o its reign
Milkin siller ooto rubber trees – the Fite Man's gravy-train.

Atap ma mither's mantle (Dougie's gift frae Singapore)
An ebon elephant wad raxx★ its muckle chouks an roar.   stretch
Three monkeys cocked abune the press: ane's lugs★ frae lees war stappit;   ears
Anither's mou wis steekt★ frae ill: the hinmaist's een war happit;   shut
An ben the hearth, on box o braisse, far★ granny's coal wis keepit,   where
Emblazoned wis a tiger, creepin forrit, fly an sleekit.   10

Johnny's keepsake? Twa braid oxen rugged a braisse cairt wi a reef
As princely's a pagoda, fit fur Rajah or Caliph.
In the firelicht o an evenin, foo yon oriental breets
Wided ben a bairnie's fancies, far the Real an Unreal meets!

Mither's Uncle Dougie, an faither's Cousin John –
O Aiberdeenshire fairmin stock, war eident★ an won on;   diligent
Twa sahibs brocht up on sowens★, cheengin kail fur vindaloo,   fermented oatmeal
Spikkin Hindi melled★ wi Doric on the roads frae Katmandu –   mixed
Oh, the schule buiks fu o mahouts an mongooses that I read!
Foo I yearned tae cross the coolie lines far Jumbos trumpeted!   20

Tae converse wi haly Saddhus, dusky Brahmins, warlike Sikhs
In the jungles an the temples far the slit-eed cobra keeks★!   peeks

Mither's Uncle Dougie, an faither's Cousin John –
The nearest tae their Eastern airts★ I reached wis Foggieloan.   quarters
Noo my quinie's pulse is quickened bi the TV's trashy trock –
Foo she yearns tae gyang tae Disneyland (the thocht o't gars me bock★)   vomit
Viewin Mickey Moose an Donald, ettin Super Macs an Cokes
Or tae traivel tae Australia, the surf-lan o the Soaps!

Following are the poet's English and Scots version of the same poem.

Ram on the Moor

Morag looked on the ram
The upward sweep of the hoof
Was that of a dancer
Suddenly smashed on stone
Caught in the lilt
Of a stately, slow Strathspey.
Dropped lace its fleece. The ribs
Were strung like a clarsach★   Celtic harp
The winds blew coronachs
Between each singing bone   10
A requiem, for a brute life at peace.

Niall looked on the ram
A severed knot
Of horn, hoof and hide
Of ripe red ochre, cream
And hill-hare grey
A feast of hues – Mortality's gay palette
The rich and riotous tapestry of rot
The hinged skull,
Repository of smells   20
With its hollows, holes and whorls
A sculptor's challenge
The horns were hard as shells.

Murchadh looked on the ram
A smuggler's keg,
Smashed open on the snow
The precious wine
Spilled, down the peat's dry throat
The pumping pulse was still
It was an old kill   30
Poor shards of flesh and skin
Where weaving mists
Snaked slyly out and in
Thin pickings, fit for a crow

The tatters of decay
Murchadh turned on his heel
And strode away.

Ceit looked on the ram
The silent ram . . . for nothing's as silent as death
Where had the bleat gone   40
And the glistening eye?
The warmth and the living breath?
What did it mean to die?
Like a shipwrecked boat it lay
Marooned on the heath
Its anchor, loosed and sundered.
Ceit looked on the ram
At the heart of the windblown moor
Long upon long with the wind lifting her hair
And wondered.   50

Ram on the Muir

Morag spied the ram
The upwird raxxin hoof
Wis thon o a dauncer
Caad tae smush on stane
Catched in the lilt
O a genteel, slaw Strathspey.
Drappit lace its fleece. Its ribs
War strung like a clarsach
The win blew coronachs
Tween ilkie singin bane   10
A requiem fur ae breet life at peace.

Niall spied the ram
The horn, hoof an hide
A cuttit knot
O ripe reid ochre, cream,
An ratten grey
A glut o hues . . . Mortality's bricht palette
The rich an reekin tapestry o rot
Far peat an sinew mells
The hinged skull   20
Wi 'ts crannies, neuks an furls
A scuptor's challenge
The horns war hard as shells.

Murchadh spied the ram
A smuggler's coggie
Caad tae crocanation in the snaw
The precious wine
Scaled doon the peat's dry thrapple
The plappin pulse wis still
Twis an auld kill   30

Puir scrats o flesh an skin
Far wyvin mists
Crept sleekit oot an in
Pot scapins, fit fur a craw
Murchadh turned on his heel
An strode awa.

Ceit spied the ram
The quaet ram, fur naethin's quaet as death
Far hid the bleat gaen
An the glimmerin ee?   40
The warmth, the leevin braith?
Fit★ did it mean, tae dee?   what
Like a shipwracked boatie
Ooto the warld's steer
Its anchor lowsed an sinnert.
Ceit spied the ram
At the hairt o the winblawn muir
Lang upon lang, wi the win heistin her hair
An winnert.

Colours

The Wee Fowk peinted the roses reid
The pheasant's lugs★ an the cockerel's heid   ears
They peinted the skyrie sunbeams gowd
They splytered broon far★ the brackens showd.   where

They steered the fite in the calfie's cream
They clarted★ yalla ower the meen   smeared
Siller they set on the snailie's back
An a daud o blaik on the hoodie's back.

They mirled★ the mavis, they strippit the brock★   variegated/badger
They skirpit green ower knowe an knock★   10   hillock
Pit blae on the sclate wi a doughty dicht
The Wee Fowk, makkin the warld bricht.

The Tryst

Twa lovers trysted bi the birk
The lass had munelicht in her een
Bit creepin saftly throw the mirk
The waukrife★ lad had nane   alert, sleepless

Warm wis his kiss, an strang his airm
The blin-sicht mowdie★ turned awa   mole
Nae lad sae fine could mean her hairm,
Her bridal guest, the hoodie craw.

A lass gaed up the ferny hill
A gowk★ cam back, wi feint★ a wird   cuckoo, fool/scarcely
The cankered wirm wis on its broo,
And in its wame★, the yird.   11   belly

Liz Lochhead (1947 –)

An electric reading/performance style has helped make Liz Lochhead one of the most popular of modern Scots poets. She is also one of the most praised of recent playwrights. Her *Mary Queen of Scots Got Her Head Chopped Off* (1987), has received especially enthusiastic notice.

Dreaming Frankenstein

She said she
woke up with him in
her head, in her bed.
Her mother-tongue clung to her mouth's roof
in terror, dumbing her, and he came with a name
that was none of her making.

No maidservant ever
in her narrow attic, combing
out her hair in the midnight mirror
on Hallowe'en (having eaten   10
that egg with its yolk hollowed out
then filled with salt)
– oh never one had such success as this
she had not courted.

The amazed flesh of her
neck and shoulders nettled
at his apparition.

Later, stark staring awake to everything
(the room, the dark parquet, the white high Alps beyond)
all normal in the moonlight   20
and him gone, save a ton-weight sensation,
and marks fading visibly where
his buttons had bit into her and
the rough serge of his suiting had chafed her sex,
she knew – oh that was not how –
but he'd entered her utterly.

This was the penetration
of seven swallowed apple pips.
Or else he'd slipped like a silver dagger

between her ribs and healed her up secretly   30
again. Anyway
he was inside her
and getting him out again
would be agony fit to quarter her,
unstitching everything.

Eyes on those high peaks
in the reasonable sun of the morning,
she dressed in damped muslin
and sat down to quill and ink
and icy paper.   40

What the Pool Said on Midsummer's Day

I've led you by my garrulous banks, babbling
on and on till – drunk on air
and sure it's only water talking –
you come at last to my silence.
Listen, I'm dark
and still and deep enough.
Even this hottest gonging sun
on this longest day
can't white me out.
What are you waiting for?   10
I lie here, inviting, winking you in.

The woman was easy.
Like to like, I called her, she came.
In no time I had her
out of herself, slipping on my water-stockings,
leaning into, being cupped and clasped
in my green glass bra.
But it's you I want, and you know it, man.
I watch you, stripped, knee-deep
in my shallows, telling yourself   20
that what makes you gasp
and balls your gut
is not my coldness but your own fear.

– Your reasonable fear,
what's true in me admits it.
(Though deeper, oh
older than any reason).
Yes, I could
drown you, you
could foul my depths, it's not   30
unheard of. What's fish
in me could make flesh of you,
my wet weeds against your thigh, it
could turn nasty.
I could have you

gulping fistfuls fighting yourself
back from me.

I get darker and darker, suck harder.
On-the-brink man, you   40
wish I'd flash and dazzle again.
You'd make a fetish of zazzing dragonflies?
You want I should zip myself up
with the kingfisher's flightpath, be beautiful?
I say no tricks. I say just trust,
I'll soak through your skin and
slake your thirst.

I watch. You clench, clench
and come into me.

Revelation

I remember once being shown the black bull
when a child at the farm for eggs and milk.
They called him Bob – as though perhaps
you could reduce a monster
with the charm of a friendly name.
At the threshold of his outhouse, someone
held my hand and let me peer inside.
At first, only black
and the hot reek of him. Then he was immense,
his edges merging with the darkness, just   10
a big bulk and a roar to be really scared of,
a trampling, and a clanking tense with the chain's jerk.
His eyes swiveled in the great wedge of his tossed head.
He roared his rage. His nostrils gaped.

And in the yard outside,
oblivious hens picked their way about.
The faint and rather festive tinkling
behind the mellow stone and hasp was all they knew
of that Black Mass, straining at his chains.
I had always half-known he existed –   20
this antidote and Anti-Christ his anarchy
threatening the eggs, well rounded, self-contained –
and the placidity of milk.

I ran, my pigtails thumping on my back in fear,
past the big boys in the farm lane
who pulled the wings from butterflies and
blew up frogs with straws.
Past throned hedge and harried nest,
scared of the eggs shattering –
only my small and shaking hand on the jug's rim   30
in case the milk should spill.

Rapunzstiltskin

& just when our maiden had got
good & used to her isolation,
stopped daily expecting to be rescued,
had come to almost love her tower,
along comes This Prince
with absolutely
all the wrong answers.
Of course she had not been brought up to look for
originality or gingerbread
so at first she was quite undaunted   10
by his tendency to talk in strung-together cliché.
'Just hang on and we'll get you out of there'
he hollered like a fireman in some soap opera
when she confided her plight (the old
hag inside etc. & how trapped she was);
well, it was corny but
he did look sort of gorgeous
axe and all.
So there she was, humming & pulling
all the pins out of her chignon,
throwing him all the usual lifelines   20
till, soon, he was shimmying in & out
every other day as though
he owned the place, bringing her
the sex manuals & skeins of silk
from which she was meant, eventually,
to weave the means of her own escape.
'All very well & good,' she prompted,
'but when exactly?'
She gave him till
well past the bell on the timeclock.   30
She mouthed at him, hinted,
she was keener than a T.V. quizmaster
that he should get it right.
'I'll do everything in my power,' he intoned, 'but
the impossible (she groaned) might
take a little longer.' He grinned.
She pulled her glasses off.
'All the better
to see you with my dear?' he hazarded.
She screamed, cut off her hair.   40
'Why, you're beautiful?' he guessed tentatively.
'No, No, No!' she
shrieked & stamped her foot so
hard it sank six cubits through the floorboards.
'I love you?' he came up with
as finally she tore herself in two.

Poem on a Day Trip

It's nice to go to Edinburgh.
Take the train in the opposite direction.
Passing through a hard land, a pitted
and pockmarked, slag-scarred, scraped land.
Coal. Colossus of pit-bings,
and the stubborn moors where Covenanters died.
Hartwood, Shotts, Fauldhouse, Breich –
Something stirs me here
where the green veneer is thin,
the black-gut and the quarried ash-red   10
show in the gashes.

But the land changes
Somewhere in the region of West and Mid Calder.
Greener and gentler, rolling Lothians,
Edinburgh. Your names are grander –
Waverley, Newington, Corstorphine,
never Cowcaddens, Hillhead or Partick.
No mean city,
but genteel, grey and clean city
you diminish me –   20
make me feel my coat is cheap,
shabby, vulgar-coloured.
You make me aware of your architecture,
conscious of history and the way it has
of imposing itself upon people.
Princes Street.
I rush for Woolworth's anonymous aisles.
I feel at home here
You could be anywhere –
even in Glasgow.   30

My Mother's Suitors

have come to court me
have come to call oh
yes with their wonderful world
war two moustaches their long
stem roses their cultivated
accents (they're English aren't they
at very least they're
educated-Scots).
They are absolutely
au fait with menu-French   10
they know the language of flowers
& oh they'd die
rather than send a dozen yellow
they always get them right & red.
Their handwriting on the florist's card
slants neither too much to the left or right.

They are good sorts.
They have the profile for it – note
the not too much nose
the plenty chin. The   20
stockings they bring have no strings
& their square
capable hands are forever
lifting your hair and gently
pushing your head away from them
to fumble endearingly at your nape
with the clasp of the pretty heirloom
little necklace they know their
grandmother would have wanted
you to have.   30
(Never opals – they know
that pearls mean tears).

They have come to call & we'll all
go walking under the black sky's
droning big bombers
among the ratatat of ack-ack.
We'll go dancing & tonight
shall I wear the lilac, or the
scarlet, or the white?

Alan Spence (1947 –)

Its Colours They Are Fine

Billy pulled on the trousers of his best (blue) suit, hoisting the braces over his shoulders, and declared that without a doubt God must be a Protestant. It was no ponderous theology that made him say it, but simple observation that the sun was shining. And a God who made the sun shine on the day of the Orange Walk must surely be a Protestant, in sympathy at least.

From the front room Lottie mumbled responses he couldn't quite make out, but which he recognised as agreement. Over the 23 years they'd been married, she had come to accept his picture of God as a kind of Cosmic Grand Master of the Lodge. It seemed probable enough.

Billy opened the window and leaned out.

The smell of late breakfasts frying; music from a radio; shouted conversations; traffic noises from the main road. A celebration of unaccustomed freedom. Saturday had a life and a character all of its own.

Sunlight shafted across the tenement roofs opposite, cleaved the street in two. A difference of greys. The other side in its usual gloom, this side warmed, its shabbiness exposed. Sun on stone.

Directly below, between a lamppost and the wall, a huddle of small boys jostled in this improvised goalmouth while another, from across the road, took endless glorious corner kicks, heedless of traffic and passersby.

One of the most noticeable things about a Saturday was the number of men to be seen in the street, waiting for the pubs to open, going to queue for a haircut, or simply content to wander about, enjoying the day. For them, as for Billy, a Saturday was something to be savoured. He would willingly work any amount of overtime – late nights, Sundays, holidays – but not Saturdays. A Saturday was his. It was inviolable. And this particular Saturday was more than that, it was sacred. In Glasgow the Walk was always held on the Saturday nearest the 12th of July, the anniversary of the Battle of the Boyne. It was only in Ulster that they observed the actual date, no matter what day of the week that might be.

Billy closed the window and went through to the front room, which was both living room and kitchen.

Lottie was laying out his regalia in readiness for the Walk – the sash, cuffs, white gloves and baton. She had laid them out flat on a sheet of brown paper and was wrapping them into a parcel.

'Whit's this?' he asked.

'Ah'm wrappin up yer things. Ye kin pit them oan when ye get tae Lorne School.'

'Not'n yer life! D'ye think ah'm frightened tae show ma colours?'

'That's jist whit's wrang wi ye. Yer never DONE showin yer colours! Look whit happened last year. Nearly in a fight before ye goat tae the coarner!'

'Look, wumman, this is a Protestant country. A Protestant queen shall reign.' He rapped on the table. 'That's whit it says. An if a Marshal in the Ludge canny walk the streets in is ain regalia, ah'll fuckin chuck it. Ah mean wu've goat tae show these people! Ah mean whit wid HE say?'

He gestured towards the picture of King William III which hung on the wall – sword pointing forward, his white stallion bearing him across Boyne Water. In a million rooms like this he was hung in just that pose, doomed to be forever crossing the Boyne. This particular ikon had been bought one drunken afternoon at the Barrows and borne home reverently and miraculously intact through the teatime crowds. Its frame was a single sheet of glass, bound around with royal blue tape. Fastened on to one corner was a Rangers rosette which bore a card declaring NO SURRENDER.

'An you're askin me tae kerry this wrapped up lik a fish supper!'

'Ach well,' she said, shoving the parcel across the table. 'Please yersel. But don't blame me if ye get yer daft heid stoved in.'

Billy grinned at the picture on the wall. Underneath it, on the mantelpiece, was the remains of what had been a remarkable piece of sculpture. One night in the licensed grocer's, Billy had stolen a white plastic horse about ten inches high, part of an advertising display for whisky. On to its back had been fitted a Plasticine model of King William, modeled by Peter, a young draughtsman who was in Billy's Lodge.

But one night Billy had come home drunk and knocked it over, squashing the figure and breaking one of the front legs from the horse. So there it sat. A lumpy Billy on a three-legged horse.

He picked up the splintered leg and was wondering if it could be glued back in place when there was a knock at the door.

'That'll be wee Robert,' he said, putting the leg back on the mantelpiece.

'Ah'll get it,' said Lottie.

Robert came in. He was actually about average height but he just looked small beside Billy. He and Billy had been friends since they were young men. They were both welders, and as well as working together, they belonged to the same Lodge. Robert was not wearing his sash. Under his arm he carried a brown paper parcel which looked remarkably like a fish supper.

'Is that yer sash?' asked Billy.

'Aye. Ach the wife thought it wid be safer like, y'know.'

'Well ah'm glad some'dy's goat some sense!' said Lottie. 'Ach!' Billy buttoned his jacket and put on his sash, gloves and cuffs. 'Great day orra same!' said Robert. He was used to being caught between them like this and he knew it would pass. 'It is that,' said Billy. He picked up his baton. 'Right!' he said. 'Ye better take this,' said Lottie, handing him his plastic raincoat. 'O ye of little faith, eh!' He laughed, a little self-conscious at setting his tongue to a quote, but he took the coat nevertheless. 'Noo mind an watch yersels!' Lottie watched from the window as they walked along the street and out of sight. At least this year they'd got that far without any trouble.

As they rounded the corner, in step, Billy turned to Robert.

'Ah'm tellin ye Robert,' he said. 'God's a Protestant!'

Emerging into the sunlight from the subway at Cessnock, they could hear some of the bands warming up. Stuttered rolls and paradiddles on the side drums, deep throb of the bass, pipes droning, snatches of tunes on the flutes.

'Dis yer heart good tae hear it, eh!' Billy slapped Robert on the back.

Robert carefully unwrapped his sash and put it on, then defiantly screwed up the paper into a ball and threw it into the gutter.

'At's the stuff!'

Billy caught the strains of 'The Bright Orange and Blue' and started to whistle it as he marched along.

'Ther's the bright orange an blue for ye right enough,' said Robert, gesturing towards the assembly of the faithful.

So much colour, on uniforms, sashes and banners. The bright orange and blue, the purple and the red, the silver and the gold, and even (God forgive them!) the green.

The marchers were already forming into ranks. It must be later than they'd thought. They hurried up to where their Lodge was assembled and took their positions, Billy at the side, Robert up behind the front rank, carrying one of the cords which trailed from the poles of their banner. Purple and orange silk, King William III, Loyal and True. Derry, Aughrim, Inneskillin, Boyne. These were the four battles fought by William in Ireland, their magic names an incantation, used now as rallying cries in the everlasting battle against popery.

They were near the front of the procession and their Lodge was one of the first to move off, a flute band from Belfast just in front of them.

Preparatory drumroll. 'The Green Grassy Slopes.' Sun glinting on the polished metal parts of instruments and the numerals on sashes and cuffs.

To Billy's right marched Peter, long and thin with a wispy half-grown beard. Billy caught his eye once and looked away quickly. He was still feeling guilty about ruining the Plasticine model that Peter had so carefully made. A little further on, Peter called over to him. 'The band's gaun ther dinger, eh!'

'Aye they ur that. Thull gie it laldy passin the chapel!'

It was as if they were trying to jericho down the chapel walls by sheer volume of sound, with the bass drummer trying to burst his skins. (He was supposed to be paid a bonus if he did, though Billy had never seen it happen.) And the drum major, a tight-trousered shaman in a royal blue jumper, would leap and birl and throw his stick in the air, the rest of the band strutting or swaggering or shuffling behind. The flute band shuffle. Like the name of a dance. It was a definite mode of walking the bandsmen seemed to inherit – shoulders hunched, body swaying from the hips, feet scuffling in short, aggressive steps.

Billy's own walk was a combination of John Wayne and numberless lumbering cinema-screen heavies. He'd always been Big Billy, even as a child. Marching in the Walk was like being part of a liberating army. Triumph. Drums throbbing. Stirring inside. He remembered newsreel films of the Allies marching into Paris. At that time he'd been working in the shipyards and his was a reserved occupation, 'vital to the war effort,' which meant he couldn't join up. But he'd marched in imagination through scores of Hollywood films. From the sands of Iwo Jima to the beachheads of Normandy. But now it was real, and instead of 'The Shores of Tripoli,' it was 'The Sash My Father Wore.'

They were passing through Govan now, tenements looming on either side, people waving from windows, children following the parade, shoving their way through the crowds along the pavement.

The only scuffle that Billy saw was when a young man started shouting about civil rights in Ireland, calling the marchers fascists. A small sharpfaced woman started hitting him with a union jack. Two policemen shoved their way through and led the man away for his own safety as the woman's friends managed to bustle her, still shouting and brandishing her flag, back into the crowd.

'Hate tae see bother lik that,' said Peter.

'Ach aye,' said Billy. 'Jist gets everyb'dy a bad name.'

Billy had seen some terrible battles in the past. It would usually start with somebody shouting or throwing something at the marchers. Once somebody had lobbed a bottle from a third-storey window as the Juvenile Walk was passing, and a mob had charged up the stairs, smashed down the door and all but murdered every occupant of the house. Another common cause of trouble was people trying to cross the road during the parade. The only time Billy had ever used his baton was when this had happened as they passed the war memorial in Govan Road, with banners lowered and only a single drumtap sounding. A tall man in overalls had tried to shove his way through, breaking the ranks. Billy had tried to stop him, but he'd broken clear and Billy had clubbed him on the back of the neck, knocking him to the ground. Another Marshal had helped him to pick the man up and bundle him back on to the pavement.

But this year for Billy there was nothing to mar the showing of the colours and he could simply enjoy the whole brash spectacle of it. And out in front the stickman led the dance, to exorcise with flute and drum the demon antichrist bogeyman pope.

They turned at last into Govan Road and the whole procession pulsed and throbbed and flaunted its way along past the shipyards. Down at the river, near the old Elder cinema, buses were waiting to take them to the rally, this year being held in Gourock. Billy and Robert found seats together on the top deck of their bus and Peter sat opposite, across the passage. As the bus moved off there was a roar from downstairs.

'Lik a fuckin Sunday-school trip!' said Robert, and he laughed and waved his hanky out the window.

They were in a field somewhere in Gourock and it was raining. Billy had his raincoat draped over his head. He was eating a pie and listening to the speeches from the platform, specially erected in the middle of the field. The front of the platform was draped with a union jack and like the banners it drooped and sagged in the rain.

Robert nudged him. 'Wher's yer proddy god noo!'

Proddy god. Proddy dog.

(A moment from his childhood on his way home from school – crossing waste-ground – there were four of them, all about his own age – the taunt and the challenge – 'A Billy or a Dan or an auld tin can' – They were Catholics, so the only safe response would be 'A Dan' – To take refuge in being 'An auld tin can' would mean being let off with a minor kicking. Billy stood, unmoving, as they closed round him. One of them started chanting –

'Auld King Billy
had a pimple on is wully
an it nip nip nipped so sore
E took it tae the pictures
an e gave it dolly mixtures
an it nip nip nipped no more.'

Jeering, pushing him. 'A Billy or a Dan . . . ' Billy stopped him with a crushing kick to the shin – heavy parish boots – two of the others jumped on him and they fell, struggling, to the ground. They had him down and they would probably have kicked him senseless but about half a dozen of Billy's friends appeared round a corner, on their way to play football. They ran over, yelling, and the Dans, outnumbered, ran off – and as they ran, their shouts drifted back to Billy where he lay – 'Proddy dog! Proddy dog!' fading on the air.)

On the platform were a number of high-ranking Lodge officials. One of them, wearing a dog-collar, was denouncing what he called the increasing support for church unity and stronger links with Rome.

'The role of the Order,' he went on, 'must increasingly be to take a firm stand against this pandering to the popery, and to render the strongest possible protest against moves towards unity.'

Billy was starting to feel cold because of the damp and he wished the rally was over.

'Wish e'd hurry up,' said Robert, rain trickling down his neck.

Billy shuffled. His legs were getting stiff.

The speaker pledged allegiance. Loyal address to the crown.

Applause. At last. The national anthem.

Billy straightened up. The blacksuited backs of the men in front. Long live our noble. Crumb of piecrust under his false teeth. Rain pattering on his coat. Huddled. Proddy god. Happy and glorious. Wet grass underfoot, its colour made bright by the rain.

Billy poured the dregs of his fourth half into his fourth pint. The discomforts of the interminable return journey and the soggy dripping march back to Lorne School were already forgotten as Billy, Robert and Peter sat drying off in the pub. Soon the day would form part of their collective mythology, to be stored, recounted, glorified.

Theirs was one of four rickety tables arranged along the wall facing the bar. Above them, rain was still streaking the frosted glass of the window but they no longer cared as the night grew loud and bright around them.

'Didye see that wee lassie?' said Robert. 'Cannae uv been merr than six year auld, an ther she wis marchin alang in the rain singin 'Follow Follow.' Knew aw the words as well. Magic so it wis.'

'Bringin them up in the Faith,' said Billy.

Over at the bar an old man was telling the same joke for the fifth time.

'So ther's wee Wullie runnin up the wing, aff the baw like, y'know. So ah shouts oot tae um 'Heh Wullie, make a space, make a space!' An he turns roon an says 'If ah make a space Lawrence'll build fuckin hooses oan it!''

A drummer from one of the accordion bands was standing next to him at the bar, still wearing his peaked cap. Addressing the bar in general, he said, 'Aye, if Lawrence will stoap tryin tae run Rangers like is bloody builders we might start gettin somewherr!'

Robert hadn't been listening. He was still thinking about children and the Faith. He turned to Peter.

'Is that wee burd ae yours no a pape?'

'Ach she disnae bother,' said Peter, and added quickly, 'Anywey, she's gonnae turn when we get married.'

'Ah should think so tae,' said Billy. 'See thae cathlicks wi weans. Fuckin terrible so it is. Tell'n ye, see at that confirmation, the priest gies them a belt in the mouth! Nae kiddin! A wee tiny wean gettin punched in the mouth! It's no right.'

'Soldiers of Christ for fucksake,' said Peter.

'D'ye know whit ah think?' said Robert.

'You tell us,' said Peter.

'Ah think it's because thur families ur that big they don't bother wae them. D'ye know whit ah mean? Ah mean it stauns tae reason. It's lik money. The likes a some'dy that hisnae goat much is gonnae look efter whit e's goat. Well! Ther yar then! It's the same wi families. Folk that's only goat wan or two weans ur gonnae take kerr ae them. But thae cathlicks wi eight or nine weans, or merr, they're no gonnae gie a bugger, ur they?'

'They eat babies an aw!' said Peter, mocking.

'You kin laugh,' said Billy. 'But ah'm tellin ye, that's how they huv such big families in the furst place. It disnae happen here mindye, but see in some a thae poor countries wher ye've goat famine an that, they widnae think twice aboot eatin a baby or two. Usetae happen aw the time in the aulden days. Likes a the middle ages, y'know.'

Peter didn't argue. It might well be true and anyway it didn't really matter.

'Whit d'ye make a that cunt this mornin then?' asked Robert. 'Cryin us aw fascists!'

'Ach ah've goat a cousin lik that,' said Peter. 'Wan a they students y'know. Wurraw fascists except him like. E wis layin intae me the other day aboot the Ludge, sayin it was 'neo-fascist' and 'paramilitary' an shite lik that. E says the Juveniles is lik the Hitler Youth an Ian Paisley's another fuckin Hitler. Ah don't know wher they get hauf thur ideas fae, neither ah dae. E used tae be a nice wee fulla tae. But is heid's away since e went tae that Uni. Tell'n ye, if is heid gets any bigger, e'll need a fuckin onion bag fur it!'

'Sounds lik mah nephew,' said Billy. 'Tryin tae tell me that King Billy an the pope wur oan the same side at the Boyne! Talks a lotta shite so e dis. Ah jist cannae understaun them ataw. Ah mean, if wurraw supposed tae be fascists, whit wis the war supposed tae be aboot?'

(Those old newsreels again. Nuremberg rally. Speeches. Drums. The liberation of Paris. VE Day.)

'Ach fuck them all!' said Peter 'Smah round, intit?' He made his way to the bar. 'Three haufs 'n three pints a heavy, Jim!' He made two journeys, one for the whisky, one for the beer, and when he sat down again Robert was telling a joke.

'Huv ye heard that wan aboot the proddy that wis dyin? Well e's lyin ther oan is death bed an e turns roon an asks fur a priest. Well, is family thoaght e wis gawn aff is heid, cause e'd always been a right bluenose. But they thoaght they better humour im like, in case e kicked it. So anywey the priest comes.'

'Impossible!' said Peter.

Billy shooshed, but Robert was carrying on anyway.

'An the fulla says tae the priest, 'Ah want tae turn father.' So the priest's as happy as a fuckin lord, an e goes through the ceremony right ther, an converts um intae a cathlick. Then e gies um the last rites, y'know, an efter it e says tae the fulla, 'Well my son, ah'm glad ye've seen the light, but tell me, what finally decided ye?' An e lifts imself up, aw shaky an that, an wi is dyin breath e turns tae the priest an says, 'This'll be another durty cathlick oot the road!''

'Very good!' said Billy, laughing. 'Very good!'

'Ah heard a cathlick tellin it,' said Peter, 'only the wey he tellt it, it wis a cathlick that wis dyin an e sent fur a minister!'

'Typical!' said Robert.

'Ah'll away fur a pee,' said Peter.

While he was gone, Billy asked Robert if he'd seen any of Peter's cartoons.

'Ah huv not,' said Robert.

'Great, so they ur. E's a bitty an artist like. Anywey, e goat this headline oot the paper – y'know how the pope's no been well – an this headline says something aboot im gettin up, an Peter's done this drawin a the pope humpin this big blonde. Ye wanty see it!'

Peter came back.

'Ah've jist been tellin Robert aboot that drawin a yours, wi the pope.'

'Ah think ah've goat it wae me,' said Peter. He rummaged through his wallet and brought out a piece of paper. Gummed on to the top was the headline POPE GETS UP FOR FIRST TIME, and underneath Peter had drawn the pope with an utterly improbable woman.

He passed it round the table.

'Terrific!' said Robert. 'Fuckin terrific!'

Peter put it back in his wallet.

The talk of Peter's artistic talent reminded Billy, yet again, of the ruined Plasticine model. He quickly slopped down some more beer.

He set down his glass and held it in place as the room swayed away from him then rocked back to rest. He was looking at the glass and it was suddenly so clearly there, so sharply in focus. All the light of the room seemed gathered in it. Its colour glowed. The gold of the beer. Light catching the glass and the glistening wet mesh of froth round the rim. He was aware of his glass and his thick red hand clutching it. The one still point in the room. And in that moment he knew, and he laughed and said, 'Ah'm pished!'

The group over at the bar were singing 'Follow Follow' and Billy shouted 'Hullaw!' and the three of them joined in.

'For there's not a team
Like the Glasgow Rangers
No not one
No not one.
An there's not a hair
On a baldy-heided nun.
No not one!
There never shall be one!'

The barman made the regulation noises of protest, fully aware that they would have no effect.

'C'mon now gents, a wee bit order therr!'

'Away an fuck ya hun!'

The accordion band drummer produced his sticks and somebody shouted 'Give us The Sash!' The barman gave up even trying as the drummer battered out the rhythm on the bartop and the drunken voices rose, joyful, and on past closing time they sang.

'Sure it's old but it is beautiful
And its colours they are fine
It was worn at Derry, Aughrim,
Inneskillin and the Boyne,
My father wore it as a youth
In the bygone days of yore
And it's on the twelfth I love to wear
The Sash My Father Wore.'

Billy was vaguely aware of Robert going for a carry-out and Peter staggering out into the street. He swayed back and aimed for the door, lurching through a corridor of light and noise, getting faster as he went, thinking he would fall at every step. Out of the chaos odd snatches of song and conversation passed somewhere near.

'C'mon now sir, clear the bar. . .'

'An ah didnae even know the cunt . . . '

'RIGHT gents!'

'So ah shouts oot tae um Make a space Make a space . . . '

'Ah'm gonnae honk . . . '

No not one.

Into the street and the sudden rush of cold air. Yellow haloes round the street-lamps. The road was wet but the rain had stopped. He leaned back against the cold wall and screwing up his eyes to focus, he looked up at the sky and the stars. All he knew about astronomy was what he had learned from an article in the *Mail* or the *Post* called 'All about the Heavens.' or 'The Universe in a Nutshell,' or something like that. Millions of stars like the sun making up the galaxy and millions of galaxies making up the universe and maybe millions of universes.

Robert came out of the pub clutching his carry-out under his arm. Peter emerged from a closemouth where he'd just been sick.

'Yawright son?'

'Aye Robert, ah'll be awright noo ah've goat it up.' Robert handed him a quarter bottle of whisky.

'Huv a wee snifter.'

'Hanks Robert.' He sipped some and shuddered, screwing up his face. Then he shook hands lingeringly with each of them, telling them they were the greatest.

'Ah fancy some chips!' said Robert. 'Me tae,' said Billy.

'Ah've took a helluva notion masel,' said Peter, and the three of them swayed off towards the chip shop, passing the bottle between them as they went.

At the next corner, Billy stopped to drain the last drops, head tilted back to catch the dregs. Tenements looming. The night sky. Dark. Galaxies. He looked at Robert and asked him, earnestly, if he'd ever smelt fall.

'Smelt whit?'

Recovering from a coughing spasm, he tried again, this time enunciating his words very carefully.

'Robert.'

'Aye.'

'Whit ah meant tae say wis, have ye ever felt small?'

Robert looked thoughtful for a moment, before replying, emphatically, 'Naw!' Grabbing Billy's lapel, he continued, 'An you're the biggest cunt ah know, so ah don't see whit YOU'RE worried aboot!'

'An neither dae ah!' said Billy, laughing. 'It's fuckin hilarious!'

And in all the stupid universe there was not a man like himself, not a city like Glasgow, not a team like the Rangers, not a hair on a nun, not a time like the present, not a care in the world

Telling it, he shouted. 'God Bless King Billy!'

'EE–ZAY!'

And he hurled his bottle, arching, into the air, into the terrible darkness of it all.

Margaret Elphinstone (1948 –)

Island

And how the land cries out to me:
The lowness of it, a strip
Suspended between air and water,
Earth precious as emerald;
Rainwashed, sheepshaven,
Sheer shores inviting me
To be responsible for my own death.

Life is a choice
Wrung out of a thin soil,
Wrested from an indifferent sea.   10
I watched waves tower against red cliffs
And the breaking of them
Shook my body, pressed against the thrift.
The island has been mine.
I have taken seisin★   possession
Rightfully. My lamp burned
Across the water, and by my presence
The boats were guided home.

An Apple from a Tree

You ask for the whole story, which seems a large return for the loan of a small towel, but since you helped me out when I needed it, I'll tell you what I think happened, which is, after all, as near to a whole story as anyone can get.

As with many significant changes, the story began in the Botanic Gardens. I have always enjoyed walking there, not only to commune with nature, such as it is, but also to watch people in the throes of conversations and encounters that are obviously about to change their lives. However, I always thought of myself as a mere observer. I thought I was as likely to become part of the drama as I was to start sprouting leaves in spring, or to receive a proposal under the lilac. Not only was I not expecting anything, I didn't want anything much either.

One day in early September, the gardens were almost deserted. It was a damp Monday evening and the place seemed separate and enclosed. After the weekend, the city had gone back to whatever it thought mattered, and a thick fog lay over it, obliterating the distinctive skyline. The muffled sound of traffic could have come from anywhere, and might as easily have been made by live creatures roaring in a wilderness of their own devising. Meanwhile in this oasis of calm, I wandered under the trees. The first leaves were beginning to come down. I wove to and fro across the grass, kicking as many leaves as I could, but they were still sparse. At least no one had attempted to rake them up. A balsam poplar grows just beside the gate, and when I reached it I scooped up a handful of leaves and held them to my face. Damp and yellow, they smelt exotic and flower-like. I wandered on through the mist.

Twice I circled the lawn at the top, which is itself encircled by an ancient hedge of yew. Then I slipped in through a gap, and found myself under the great beech trees at the end. Perhaps their tops were above the mist. I couldn't tell, but there seemed to be a wind up there that spoke of cleaner air, sighing as it did among the branches, sending the first brown leaves scudding into the sky. I looked up and saw the mist clearing, the sky turning blue, like seeing the sea from an aeroplane when the cloud breaks apart. Hearing the sea up there made me nostalgic. It was autumn, and I had a whole winter to face in the city. The Firth hardly counted. It was brown and smelly, and when the tide went down it left a thick black scum, like the tideline from a diabolic bath.

I went to and fro under the beeches, as though by waiting long enough I could make something happen. That was foolish, of course, but the wind up there seemed so real and so near, I almost expected the waves of it to come lapping at my feet. I don't know what I was thinking of but, as the leaves came down, I jumped and tried to catch them. Seven years' good luck, we used to say. I don't know who taught me that. You don't catch luck falling off a tree; at least, I never supposed so.

Something came down hard that was not a leaf, falling straight towards me. I re-acted instinctively, as though playing a celestial form of cricket. I cupped my hands together and caught it, letting my hands go with it so it didn't hurt me. It was round and solid, like nothing from a beech tree. I unfolded my hands slowly, and looked.

It was an apple.

Up I looked again, but there was nothing, only the beech trees tossing in a wind I could not feel. The last mist wreathed away like the tail of an unidentified creature whisking out of sight. Shadows that I had not known existed slid out of vision, and the leaves, both green and gold, were washed in sudden brightness.

I turned the apple over. It was not very big, greenish on one side, red on the other, hard and firm. There was a lack of emphasis about it I recognised as being old-fashioned. On a supermarket shelf it would have looked small and misshapen, and would probably have lain untouched until past its sell-by date. That gave me reason to suppose it might taste good. I smelled it cautiously. It smelled more like an apple than any apple I'd come across for years. It was more like the apple-scented bottles in the Body Shop. I'd forgotten that apple was astringent, sweet certainly, but almost as sharp as pine at the same time. I sniffed it again. Then, in spite of the fact that I'd no idea where it had been, I bit into it.

It seems tragic that a taste more subtle than anything we have come to know on earth should be wasted, but I hardly noticed it, for the very good reason that I was caught up in something that resembled, more closely than anything else I can think of, a Victorian steam roundabout. I once rode such a roundabout. I rode a great grey dapple horse with staring eyes and flaring nostrils; we tore up and down in strides like no horse ever made, faster and faster, with a wild music clinging to us that never dropped behind for all our speed.

This was not quite like that. There was no horse and no music. At least, I think there was not but, now I try to remember more carefully, I cannot say for sure. We did go round and round, in a spiral of leaves all caught up and rolled up, spun into a cone shape that whizzed over the lawn like a bobbin gone mad, until it fell apart in the long tall grass under the apple tree, flinging me down on knobbly ground that turned out to be wet soil strewn with windfalls. A painful landing, but I was too surprised to think about my bruises. I was still clutching my apple. I stood up, shakily, and realised that I was not alone.

The woman who stood watching me was quite naked. That was the first thing that I noticed about her. If that makes you think that I pay too much attention to trivia, you should read the regulations governing the conduct of visitors to the Botanics, and you will see at once why this should seem so startling. Also, it was September, and none too warm. She stood in thigh-high grass. Her dark hair fell right down her back, and was woven through with stems of bryony. She was brown, so evenly tanned that she might never have worn clothes at all, and quite slender, though not skinny. She seemed unmoved by my sudden appearance and stood regarding me without moving. It was a disconcerting gaze. Her eyes were so black they looked almost hollow.

'Hello,' I said.

'Hello,' she replied, so that it sounded like my own voice coming back at me. I thought she was mocking me and stiffened, but her gaze was not unfriendly. If she spoke English, I thought, it seemed all the odder that she should be naked. In case you think there is prejudice in that, let me remind you that it could mean only that she was able to read the regulations as well as I could. Assuming she could read, of course. I looked at her askance.

'Where have you come from?' she asked me next.

That flummoxed me. Surely she was taking the words from my mouth? 'Me?' I said. 'I was here all the time. Where have you come from?'

'I was here all the time.'

I don't like being mimicked. She even had the same accent, but she seemed to be using it quite innocently. I held out the apple.

'I caught it,' I said. 'Does it belong to you?'

'It came off the tree.' She pointed, and I looked.

The beech trees were gone, and the lawn, and the yew hedge. But it was still autumn and the leaves were still turning red and gold. This time they were apple leaves, for before me rose the hugest apple tree I ever saw, crowning the hill like a wreath of berries round an old man's head. The grass was long and unkempt, beginning to die back, but over it the apple-laden tree bent its branches low, so I could have reached up and picked and picked, though never got a tithe of all that lay beyond my reach. I never saw such a tree, nor so many apples, red and green and gold. I looked away, and saw a line of craggy hills across the skyline, softened by the ranks of trees.

'Where is this? What is that tree?'

She looked at me, apparently puzzled. 'This is the world,' she said, 'and that is an apple tree.'

'Thank you,' I said. I can be sardonic when I choose, but sarcasm seemed to wash over her like a summer breeze.

'That's all right,' she said, and then she asked a question of her own. 'What is wrong with you?'

'Me?' I was indignant. 'Nothing. Why? What should be wrong?'

'You're all wrapped about. Even your feet.'

I looked down at my feet. I was wearing trainers, somewhat damp and down at heel but perfectly respectable.

'My feet are fine, and so is the rest of me. I just happen to be wearing clothes. I'm surprised you managed to get here without, yourself.'

There was no doubt about it then. She was laughing at me. I would have walked away with dignity, but I had the disadvantage of not being sure any more where anything was. In fact, I didn't know where I was myself except that I hadn't left the Botanics and was, presumably, still in them.

'Are you upset? Don't you like the apple?'

I had almost forgotten the apple. I looked at it a mite suspiciously, not being quite sure how far it was responsible. I had an idea and held it out to her. 'Eat it yourself.'

'I was going to, but then you caught it.'

'Did you throw it?'

'No, he did.'

'He?' I looked round nervously. 'Who?'

'He,' she repeated with emphasis. 'Didn't you hear? I thought you said you'd been here all the time?'

'If I was, I wasn't listening.' I looked at the apple as though it might bite me, rather than vice versa. 'Why?' I asked, and failed to keep misgiving entirely out of my voice. 'Perhaps you'd better tell me what happened.'

'Nothing,' she said. 'After all that. I picked it, and I offered it to him. And he said, 'I'm not hungry,' and threw it. Then he went, and you came. That was all.'

'Where's he gone?'

'I neither know nor care. He showed a lamentable want of curiosity. I don't think he's ever really interested in anything but sex. And food, of course. I'm not sure whether he never had any imagination, or whether nameless fears subsequently drove it out of his head. What sex are you, incidentally?'

'Me?' For the third time I was indignant. 'I'm a woman, same as you. Can't you tell?'

'I thought so. It was the wrappings that confused me. What happened after you bit it?'

'I was here.'

'Damn.'

'I'm sorry?'

'I had hoped,' she explained patiently, 'that it might get one to somewhere else. Evidently not. Never mind. Shall we go now?'

'Go? Where?'

'Well, we can't stay here.'

She was right. At any moment there would be voices crying out 'Closing ti-ime' from one end of the gardens to the other. Such was the deception of the Botanics. Refuge seemed to be offered, a way out through the very heart of the city, then, just as the shadows lengthened and the truth seemed near at hand, policemen came shouting along the paths, expelling everybody, then closing the great iron gates behind them. I was never sure whether it was worse to leave before the expulsion began, or wait as long as possible, and be harried to the gates while the voices circled round me like sheepdogs driving an unwilling flock.

'Where do you live?' I asked her.

'In the world. Are you coming?'

If we passed through the gates, I never noticed. Once we left the apple tree behind, alone on the summit of the hill, we were down among the rest of the trees. The smell of balsam was still there, permeating the evening like a promise of something new. But the trees seemed to crowd more thickly than usual, pressing together and lining our route, like people watching a procession. We hardly made a procession, she and I, and there was no other human being to be seen anywhere. The path wound this way and that until quite soon I had lost all bearings. Golden leaves were strewn under-foot. They rustled as we walked. Where there were gaps in the trees, the long evening light broke through, bright on the fading leaves above, then speckled further down, where the leaves interrupted its path.

Brambles grew beside the way, thick with berries. She picked and ate them as she passed, absent-mindedly, as though browsing were automatic and her mind far away. But it slowed her down, and I was glad of that. The trailing stems caught my jacket, and I had to keep stopping to disentangle them. It was warm and humid among so many trees. I felt the sweat gather under my shirt, and trickle down my back. It was quiet in the wood, but not silent. The squirrels were everywhere, up and down the trees and running across the path in front of us, stopping when they saw us, and regarding us with bright eyes from about a yard distant, perched on their hind legs, jaws chattering. I was pleased to see them; they helped me to grasp that I was in the Botanics, which is the only place I know where squirrels are that tame and numerous. But when we saw the deer, I began to wonder again. I know there is more wildlife in city parks than ever meets the eyes, but a herd of roe deer? The little group we saw bounded away through the trees as we approached, disappearing among the birch stems in a pattern of brown and silver.

Presently we crossed a burn. Luckily there hadn't been much rain lately; even so, we had to wade. A curtain of willow hung down over the water, stems trailing even in the diminished flow. She waited while I took my shoes and socks off, and rolled up my trousers. My clothes seemed to amuse her. To distract her from that, and because our brief halt renewed the chance for conversation, I tried to pin her down a little more.

'What is your name?' I asked her.

'Nosila.'

I thought she might ask mine, but she didn't.

After that there was little opportunity for talk. We were ascending a steep hill, weaving our way through thick trunks and twining stems. The canopy was so dense here that the sun was quite blocked out. I would have said that it was getting darker, but it could not be less than an hour before sunset, for no one had called 'Closing ti-ime.' I wondered if I would wake up enough to hear them. I had had strange dreams in the Botanics before now, I told myself, and the police could surely be trusted not to ignore a sleeping body?

The hill hardly seemed to slow her down at all. I stopped even trying to think but stumbled after her, tripping over roots, and pulling myself uphill by thin stems. The forest badly needed clearing. No one had thinned out the young saplings, or cleared away the masses of fallen trunks and dead wood. Sometimes we climbed over these obstacles, sometimes we forced our way round, ducking under horizontal branches that were now pushing up new shoots from their sides, straight towards the sky. Even the sky shocked me; it was not pale, but a deep velvety blue, with one star showing. Even in the heart of the Botanics the dark could not look like that, even if one were allowed to stay and see. There had been times when I had circumnavigated the gardens at night, two sides of houses and two sides of endless iron railing, hoping for a glimmering of the night sky that might look down on the silent trees within. Shut out in an unremitting orange glow like tortured fire, I could only imagine it. The stars were lost to me. I could have clung to those railings and shaken them, hammered at the gates of the garden like a demented being, but I was afraid of the police, and of the danger of walking alone at night, so I walked quickly and never stopped.

Now there was no walking quickly, although the dusk filtered in soft and fast, swallowing up the tree tops, while the sky began to prick out stars, like the lighting of old-fashioned lamps. I could see better now. We were at the top of the hill and the slope below us stretched down to open ground. When I looked again I saw it was not ground but water. It was black in the half-light, uncannily calm, and on the far side it was lost in shadow where a great precipice towered over it. I found it weird, as though the place were full of hidden things I did not wish to think about.

'Where are we?'

'By the loch.'

It occurred to me that she could not help being completely literal. Although she spoke as fluently as I did, perhaps her grasp of language did not go so far. If she sought for nuances in anything, it was clearly not in words.

'Where are we going?' I asked patiently.

'There is shelter. It will soon be night.'

'I would rather go home.'

She looked at me with concern. A slight breeze blew up, and I heard the water lap on the shore below, invisible in the thickening air. I identified a difference then, which had been present from the moment when I bit the apple. The trees smelled so sharp they overwhelmed me. The air was full of scents: leaves, water, soil, a tinge of salt on the breeze. Just as when I tasted the apple, I felt I had never known such richness. I sniffed again; and the breeze was damp and resinous, heavy with tree smells.

She answered just as I was about to speak again. The rhythm of her conversation was quite different from mine. She left long pauses for thought between each statement as though the fear of interruption was quite unknown to her.

'Are you tired?' she asked. 'Are you hungry? You still have the apple.'

I remembered, and took it out of my pocket. I was not sure what that apple was responsible for, and I distrusted it. 'I'm not sure about it,' I said. 'You have it.'

She took it. 'You want to give it to me?'

She seemed to attach undue importance to my purpose. I only wanted to be rid of the thing, and it hardly seemed such a momentous gift. After all, she could have picked as many as she liked.

'Yes,' I said lightly. 'Why not?'

Her eyes widened and she looked at it almost fearfully, as though I had challenged her to something. I was about to explain that nothing was further from my thoughts, and she need feel herself under no imaginary obligations, when she bit into it.

There was a roar like an approaching train from somewhere deep below us, and the ground seemed to quiver and to shake. I heard rushing water, like a great waterfall bursting its confines and engulfing the whole forest. We were flung together, and I felt her flesh under my hands as I clung to her, whirling downwards as the sky vanished from over us, until we landed hard on concrete, crashing in a heap amidst a tumble of wet leaves.

'Christ,' I muttered, clutching my bruised head in my hands. There was an orange glow which hurt my eyes, and the roaring was still in my ears, with a stench like the pits of a furnace. I felt a clutching at my arm, which I gradually realised was becoming painful. I looked up.

We were sitting on the pavement at the foot of Waverley Bridge, and there were taxis turning in and out of the station. We must have just missed the iron railings that enclosed Princes Street Gardens behind us. It was dark in there, and silent, all locked away for the night. I found myself staring at a fat white airport bus, that ground towards us like a giant caterpillar.

Nosila screamed in my ear.

'Ow!' I tried to calm her, or myself, I wasn't sure which. 'Now hold on. At least we know where we are.' I turned and looked at her, and the appalling truth dawned on me: she was still stark naked.

I looked up and down the street in horror. There was no one on the pavement except an old wino huddled against the railings, and a shuffling woman weighed down with carrier bags. We were still unseen.

'Here,' I said, struggling out of my jacket. 'No, no, that won't do, it's too short. Oh Christ!' I thought desperately. 'You'll have to take my jumper. You can hold it down at the ends.' I tore it off.

'What are you doing?'

'Taking my clothes off,' I snapped. 'Here, put this on.'

She stared at it as though it might shrivel her up. 'Why? What is it?'

'It's a jumper.' I realised, even in my desperate embarrassment, that more explanation was going to be necessary. 'You have to wear it. Put it on. Like I did. You can't walk around here stark naked.'

She looked round, her eyes dilating with fear. 'What is naked?'

'I'll tell you when we get home. Now look, this is Edinburgh. Anywhere else, they'd probably take no notice. Put it on, for God's sake. Trust me.'

Well, I got it on to her, and explained the necessity for holding the ends down so that they reached to her thighs. She was puzzled, but docile. I put my jacket on again.

'Come on, quick.'

'Where are we going?'

'Home. It still looks most odd, though at least you're decent. But hurry.'

She didn't seem to have any idea what the trouble was. In Princes Street the shops were shut, and the crowds had gone, but the evening groups of kids with nowhere to go were just starting to assemble. We had to pass a gang of boys with motor bikes as we scurried through the shadow of the Scott monument, and sure enough they stopped and stared, and muttered as we passed. I'd rather they'd shouted something lewd, it would have meant they didn't intend to do anything else, but they just looked after us in silence. Nosila's bare feet left marks on the pavement, still being wet from the leaves. I didn't look at her. I didn't want my worst fears confirmed. But I remembered the wreaths of bryony, and shuddered.

In Hanover Street there were people passing to and fro, and cafes open, as well as long queues at the bus stop. I hesitated, wondering if a bus would be easier, but then, I thought, there was no way I could allow Nosila to sit down, and it would be light inside. I grabbed her elbow and hurried her on.

That's when I thought of you. The idea of walking all the way home appalled me but your house was quite close. True, I didn't know you very well then but I thought you'd be willing to help, and that was the most important thing. As we hurried downhill I tried to think how to explain it to you. You hadn't struck me as being particularly quick on the uptake, when we met. Perhaps the less said, the better.

Nosila broke into the tail of my thoughts. We were just passing Queen Street Gardens when she pulled away from me. The next thing I knew, she was trying to climb the railings, abandoning every vestige of decency in the process. I grabbed her by the tail of her jersey.

'What are you doing, for God's sake? Not that way!'

I had to prise her hands away from the railings. I couldn't have done it if she had gone on resisting, but she seemed to give in suddenly and turned to face me. She looked wild-eyed and desperate, like a sheep that has been separated from the rest of the flock being brought in by dogs. I would have preferred her to cry. It would have made her seem less alien.

'What are you trying to do?'

'I want to go back where it's dark!'

'You can't. It's locked up. And it would be dangerous. Come on, I'll take you home.'

'What is home?'

'Safe,' I told her, and hurried her on before she got the chance to argue. We reached your street, I pressed your buzzer and thank God you were in. I thought for a moment, then decided to leave her at the foot of the stairs. I just couldn't see myself explaining everything.

'I'll be right back. Stand against the wall and don't move. No one can get in without a key. If they do, just stand back against the wall and don't say anything.'

She stood at the bottom watching me. I tore up the five flights of stone steps as fast as I could, and found your door open at the top.

It would have been easier to explain if I hadn't been so out of breath, but I can't say you were helpful. The way you said, 'Trousers?' as if I'd asked you for a time bomb, I could have hit you. That's why I gave up. You seemed to have a bee in your bonnet about lending a simple pair of trousers, as if I were about to go off and do something diabolical or humiliating with them. For Christ's sake, I thought, he thinks it's Rag Week or something. Anyway, that's why I ended up just asking for a towel, and that was hard enough. I never met anyone as suspicious as you seemed to be that night. And when you did produce a towel, it wasn't exactly generous, was it?

Anyway, it served to get us home. I tied it round her like a kilt, and tucked it in. She looked as though she'd been interrupted in the middle of a sauna, but no one accosted us. I realised when I got home that I was completely shattered, and so was she. I fried up herring and tatties for supper, and that made the world seem slightly more tenable again.

About halfway through the evening the phone rang. It was Kate. 'Alison?' she said. 'I was just phoning to see if you wanted a lift tomorrow.'

'A lift to what?'

She was talking about that party at the gallery. I'd forgotten all about it. It was the last thing I felt like dealing with, but I can't afford to miss any possible opportunities, so I said I'd go.

I offered Nosila a bath, and that intrigued her. She seemed to think it was funny. I found her attitude slightly irritating, but at least amusement brought the colour back to her cheeks and restored her equanimity. After that I made a cup of tea and we sat down to discuss the situation. At least, that's what I'd planned to do. She didn't seem to know what a discussion was. She was more interested in my houseplants. I watched her wandering from one to another, apparently whispering sweet nothings into their leaves. It seemed like a caricature of myself going round with the Baby Bio, but I'd never behave like that if I were a guest in someone's house.

'Nosila, we have to talk about things.'

She ran her fingers along the mantelpiece. She might have been testing for dust, but I understood by now she was only intrigued by the feel of paintwork. 'You talk a lot,' she remarked. 'Does it make you happy?'

'I don't. In fact I'm remarkably anti-social. But we have a problem.'

She looked round, but evidently saw nothing that might be thus defined.

'Do you think one of us is dreaming?' I asked her next.

She shook her head helplessly.

'How do you think you got here?'

'Like you,' she said. Then she sighed. 'Perhaps he was right to be content.'

'I don't know what you mean. But think about this: if I bite the apple, we get where you were, and if you do, we get to where I was. Am. I mean we are.'

'Yes,' she said.

'But we can't either of us get back to where we were. Not both at once.'

She seemed to be listening carefully. 'Entwined,' she said.

'I beg your pardon?'

'Hold out your hand.'

I held out my right hand. She came round beside me and laid her own against it, palm to palm. Our hands were the same size, small but square and firm. Hers were more roughened than mine but there seemed to be no other difference. Moreover, her hand was quite real, flesh and blood. I could feel the warmth of it against mine.

'That's touching,' she said.

'I see it is.'

'You want to let go?'

'I'm torn.'

'Yes,' she said. 'We can't have two places at once.'

'Then we have to find a way of separating.'

'No.'

'What do you mean, no?'

'It's all one.'

I gave up then, and suggested that we went to bed.

The morning was sunny and hopeful. She was still there. I found her drifting naked round the kitchen, tasting the food from the jars.

'You can't eat raw flour. We'll have breakfast.'

I was in a practical mood and, as the major problem seemed no nearer a solution, I applied myself to the more immediate task of acclimatising her to the world as it was. I took her shopping, and explained to her about traffic lights, and crossing roads. She kept bumping into people, and I taught her to say 'Sorry' every time. I had cause to regret that, as it left very little opportunity for saying anything else. She just didn't seem to see people coming. There were other problems. She stopped and wept over the greengroceries displayed outside the shop on the corner and, when we passed a row of gardens, she kept trying to climb the low stone walls.

By the end of the morning I was ready to try anything to be rid of her, even if I had to bite that wretched apple all over again.

In spite of it all, I decided to take her with me to the party that night. I didn't dare leave her alone in my flat and I didn't want to miss the party. I was too desperate for work to miss such an opportunity: it was the opening of a new exhibition. I knew the people vaguely and the more they saw my face the more likely they were to employ me.

I don't know what I'd have done if you hadn't been there. You hadn't distinguished yourself over the towel episode, but that evening you saved me from social disaster. I still don't know whether that was just a ploy but I suppose I had some idea what you were hoping for. Anyway, in my eyes you redeemed yourself.

I was trying to talk to the person I most needed to impress, but I could hear your conversation out of the corner of my ear. It made my own somewhat disjointed.

'A friend of Alison's,' you were saying to her, 'I thought you must be a relative.'

'Yes,' she said.

'Are you involved with art too?' you asked her.

'What is art?'

'Help,' I heard you say. 'I don't know that I'm in the mood for intelligent conversation. Are you a student?'

'No,' she said. 'I'm frightened already. I don't want more.'

' . . . And of course,' the important person was saying to me, 'you'll know the work of so and so and such and such.'

'Well,' I said cautiously, 'naturally the names are familiar . . . Wasn't that . . . ? Oh, yes, when would it be . . . ?'

'1985.'

'Of course,' I said, 'a breakthrough.'

'You don't think that was mostly hype?'

'It's amazing what marketing can do,' I said.

I had to concentrate for a bit. When I heard you and Nosila again, you were talking about the sex life of plants. She looked relaxed and happy, almost as I had seen her first. I took a deep breath, and turned back to my own conversation. 'No,' I said, 'I haven't actually read it, but of course I saw the reviews . . . '

There was a hush, as the tape of soft music wound to an end, and for a moment conversation died with it.

Nosila's voice came loud and clear, 'Why do they sway together so, like trees in a gale? Why do they express anger and sex at the same time? What are they trying to do to one another? Do you know?'

There was a silence.

'We must all have asked those questions,' you replied easily. 'A highly ambiguous work of art. Everyone thought so.'

Nosila looked puzzled but I could have kissed you. A month later I did, of course, but by that time all was well.

'She must have seen the preview,' murmured my companion. 'It's booked out now, more or less until the millennium, I believe.' She chortled at her own joke. 'Luckily I was sent tickets.'

'What is?' I said, and realised that I sounded like Nosila.

'The performance to which that girl referred. Surely you've across it? It was reviewed everywhere.'

'Oh yes,' I said, subdued.

I had no idea what chivalrous impulse had prompted you but when I managed to get a word with you, just before I left, I said, 'Thank you for taking care of my friend. She really isn't used to this.'

'I admire her for it,' you said, and left me feeling confused.

I was even more confused when you phoned me three weeks later to say you'd been meditating in a tent in the Cairngorms ever since, and you wanted me to come and live on an uninhabited island with you to grow potatoes and study the ancient philosophers. However, I was tempted. I'm glad we came to a more reasonable compromise than that, but that's not part of this story.

I woke next morning from a deep sleep and saw that the day was drear and grey. I pressed my face into the pillow, trying to recapture the dark. There seemed to be no greater gift than oblivion. Evading me, it hovered at the corners of my consciousness, tempting me onwards into a desire for something too close to nothingness for me to pursue with any courage. Reluctantly I sat up and faced the day.

It was raining. That upset all my plans. But then again, why not? At least the gardens would be deserted. I got up and surveyed Nosila. She was sleeping flat on her back, the covers flung away, her hair spread over the pillow like a black halo. To my jaundiced eyes, she looked like something out of Aubrey Beardsley. Irritated, I nudged her with one slippered foot. 'It's morning,' I said. 'I'm going to make a cup of tea.'

She was fully awake at once, jumping up eagerly to look through the window at the rain. It evidently moved her: she began to chant and then to dance around the room, thumping on the floor in a manner calculated to get the man downstairs balanced on a chair, thumping back on the ceiling with the end of a broom handle.

'Stop! You can't do that here.'

'But it's raining.'

'You can't do that even if it's Noah's flood. Here, borrow my dressing gown.'

She didn't want to get dressed that day. She kept murmuring that it was raining and what was the point? She seemed to be in a fever to get outside and, sure enough, once we were on the pavement she went leaping down the street, banging her fists against her chest and ululating at the sodden sky. The curtains of the flat below mine were seen to twitch and to remain poised half held, like a blocked-in question mark.

'Nosila, stop. You can't do that here.'

Once we were on the path by the water, I let her go. She went dancing and leaping under the trees, her bare feet light as fallen leaves. I never did manage to make her wear anything on her feet, although otherwise I persuaded her to dress fairly normally. It was a relief when we finally turned in at the gates of the garden. I cast a doubtful glance at the policeman in his box as we passed, but he was reading the *Express* and didn't see us. Not that we were contravening anything, but Nosila certainly looked as if she might.

I felt I needed time to think, out of the rain, so I took her into the plant houses. Now, when I think of it, I am more satisfied about that than about any of the rest. I would like to think that she gained something from her experiences, and nothing else that I could provide seemed to make her any wiser or happier. But for her that place was enchanted. She touched everything, while I kept a wary eye out for patrols. She ran her hands up and down the stems of the palms, and poked her fingers gently inside the orchids. When she dabbled her hand in the pool, the carp came up and nibbled her fingers, and she laughed. The ferns astounded her. She stood in their house for a long time, as if she were listening. I was so near I could hear her breathing.

'But they are so old,' she said at last. 'Now there at last is a story worth the telling.'

'What story?' But she was away, her hands moving up the vines.

By the time I got her out of there, the clouds had cleared a little. We walked up to the crown of the hill, and stood beneath the beech trees. The sound of water dripping from trees was cold and mournful. Dew clung to the grass, so that we left green foot-prints over a lawn that had been white. Nosila took the apple from her pocket. It was wrinkled now, and the two bite marks had gone quite brown.

'You try first,' I said to her.

She bit, and screwed up her face. 'It's sour now.'

Nothing else happened.

'I was afraid of that,' I said, and held out my hand. The apple looked thoroughly unappetising. I was aware of a pit of fear yawning inside me, and I think my hand was shaking.

'There's no other way,' she said quietly. I sensed her desperation. I could refuse, I supposed, but then I'd feel responsible for her ever after. I hate responsibility, which left me no choice. I bit.

Since it was wet this time, it felt like being run through the rinse programme of an automatic washing-machine. We were caught up in a blur of spinning water, gyrating wildly. Sky, grass and trees melted away into rapids, all turning water-coloured. We were too entangled to keep our balance and when we fell we stayed entwined, like a four-legged monster gasping in its lair of thick grass, for the grass was long again.

When we sat up we could see nothing but feathered seedheads bending before the breeze above our heads. The broken stems gave us a softer landing than before. Once we had reclaimed our respective limbs, we stood up cautiously.

The rain had gone. Sun dappled the grass, patterned by the shadows of the leaves. The air was heady with the smell of apples. All round us the forest was turning golden under the morning sun. The sky was pale blue, with a thumbnail moon rising high over the ridge to the south. This time I studied the horizon more closely. There were precipices over there, surrounding a craggy bluff topped by trees and, further east, a higher hill whose shape was more than familiar. The expanse of forest in between set it far beyond my reach. A line of grey cliff, surmounted by autumn gold, all still untrodden. I touched Nosila's shoulder. 'Over there.' I pointed. 'You've been up there?'

She nodded, but her eyes searched the nearer woods restlessly and she hardly looked where I was pointing.

'What do you see from there?'

She glanced again. 'From there? The sea, of course. Beaches.'

'What colour is the sea?'

She laughed at that, as though it were a foolish question. 'All colours,' she said. 'Like the sky, like the forest, like the loch. All those. Changing.'

'I see.'

She cried out then, throwing back her head and making a sound that must have echoed almost to the crags, a long, yodeling call that threw back an echo, then left the woods more silent than they had been before.

I stood trembling, not understanding. There was a movement in the trees, shadows passing, and the flick of branches pushed back. Then a man appeared, standing in the clear space that surrounded the apple tree, naked as the day he was born and brown as a naturist back from the Riviera. Nosila left my side and flung herself upon him.

I turned my back, and tried to steady my pulse by reciting all the regulations governing behaviour in the Botanics, from beginning to end. I had just reached the part about no sketching, painting or picnicking, for the third time, when various animal-like sounds behind me heralded the end of my ordeal. I counted to three hundred and turned round.

Nosila was on her feet again, watching me anxiously. 'Are you ill?' she asked me.

'No,' I said, 'I don't know what I want.'

'No?'

'I want both,' I said, suddenly understanding, 'but I don't know how.'

'Let me think.' She turned back to the man and began to talk to him in a low voice. I hardly listened. The apple was still in my hand. After the three bites we had already taken there was not much left. My time was running out. Was this my world, or hers? I only knew that I wanted to keep it, more than I had wanted anything in my life. I couldn't stay; I thought of you, without intending to. I wanted what Nosila had, but not here. I couldn't inhabit her whole world. There was no place for me in it. I glanced up at the apple tree.

There was my answer, staring me in the face.

'Nosila!'

She looked at me, still troubled. 'What is it?'

'The apples,' I said. 'I'm going back now, but I want my apple.'

She was puzzled for a moment, then she laughed, suddenly understanding. She pulled a branch down until it was level with my face. It was heavy with apples, two or three on every spur. I selected one, and twisted it off.

The man touched her on the shoulder, and muttered something. I wished he would stop hovering around, and leave us in peace.

'Why not?' said Nosila out loud. 'She's free to do what she likes. Who's got the right to stop her?'

He shrugged.

My apple was smooth and sweet-smelling, red and gold and green. I put it carefully in my pocket.

She watched. 'That's the first good reason I've seen for them.'

'For what?'

'Clothes.' She waved her hands in an effort to explain. 'A way of carrying apples. That's all.'

'Yes,' I said, and hugged her.

'Are you ready?'

I nodded.

'Then give me the first apple.'

The man said something incoherent, and she shook her head at him. 'No, it's all right. We'll only be a few minutes.'

He frowned.

'I promise,' she said, and took the remains of our original apple from me.

I was elated, excited by my own cleverness. I could have both. I had an apple of my own, and so all the worlds I wanted were now open to me. I would go home and Nosila would be here, also at home. Separated, but entwined. I took her hand. She bit the apple.

The whirlwind that followed was nothing to the power I felt inside. I was drunk with it, my head still spinning like a top long after the rest of me had fallen with a thud upon the neat mown turf. I hardly noticed that Nosila had lost all her clothes, and here we were back in civilisation. It didn't matter. The familiar Botanic Gardens were all around me, and imprinted on my mind was the image of the wilderness they hid.

Nosila held my hand and we walked quietly down the hill. People stared at us, as well they might. We crossed a shrub bed. Luckily no uniformed official was in sight. There were railings in front of me. Eight-foot-high black railings and the road below. I felt the curve of the apple in my pocket and was reassured. I could see the Christian Science Church opposite, and the line of country to the south all blurred by rain.

'If I hold on tight,' I said, 'whatever happens, when it starts, you go. But I'll hold on. I think it'll work, if you hold the apple.'

Her black eyes looked hollow again, as they had the first time I saw her. I would miss her physical presence, in spite of what I knew. I realised I was crying for the loss of it, although I knew it was illusory. She shed no tears. Perhaps she had none. I looked through the bars to the world outside.

She followed my gaze. 'You belong there,' she remarked. 'Hold tight.'

She held the apple to my lips.

I bit, and spat.

The world flung away from me. The bars bucketed like a boat in a storm. The apple was wrenched away, and something else, splitting away from my side like my heart being torn out, but I went on holding. I held so hard the iron bit into me, and I heard someone scream. It was I, and someone other, spinning away from me out of the world. Through the bars I saw a forest turning, leaves torn before a driving gale, and the sky circling below. Then slowly the grey road subsiding, the squat church and a skyline of spires and defenses. I sank to my knees, soaked, and exhausted.

When someone touched my shoulder I swung round, not knowing what to expect.

It was a policeman. Looking down, I saw his black polished shoes sinking into the newly dug soil. For a moment I was disorientated, then I felt the apple in my pocket, firm and real.

'You all right, hen?' he asked me.

I stood up slowly. 'Yes,' I said, without attempting to explain, and smiled at him, secure in my own knowledge.

Valerie Gillies (1948 –)

Fellow Passenger

Mister B. Rajan, diamond buyer,
crystallises from this travelling companion.
He goes by rail, it seems, by criss
and cross, Hyderabad to Bangalore
to Madras, Madras, Madras,
seeking the industrial diamond.

He brings new orient gems from hiding.
Himself, he wears goldwealthy rings
of ruby, and, for fortune,
another of God Venkateswaran.   10
His smile is a drillpoint diamond's,
incisive his kindness.

Sparrowboned, he walks unstable passageways,
living on boiled eggs and lady's-fingers
with noggins of whisky to follow.
He dreams of his house, the shrineroom picture
of Sai Baba, corkscrew-haired young saint.
And he has at home beautiful hidden daughters.

Roadgang Women

Here come the stonebreakers,
these little skeletons of the roadgang women
with their long strands of hair
knotted high at the back of their skulls.

They take a moment
to wipe sweat from around their eyes
with a corner of torn sari.
The road waits for their hands.

They carry stones in baskets on their heads,
like apricots marked by a bird's beak,   10
wizened and bruised:
both heads and stones.

A raised track on a country without limit.
A big sun beating off any shade.
A woman stitches a piece of shadow
with an upright stick and sacking.

She breaks stones below it.
Once, she eats from a shallow tin dish
with not much in it;
some steamed riceflour cake. 20

Old women of thirty
work in the day's quickforge.
Nobody can work like them,
though they pause to quarrel or laugh.

They must find fire nourishing,
as the salamander does, who is meant
to live in the flames,
where others would die, she lives happily.

Asian in Edinburgh

Far off
in the crowd
a sleek oriental head –
assumption of calm
not borne out
when the traffic closes
with grave foglamps
in the puritan manner
And nearer
their wolfskin caps. 10

Through
an alien street odour,
its reticent fumes,
the stranger moves
all gold
his nape delicate
inclined towards the station steps;
each step a slight regret
below the quietest of suns.

The Old Woman's Reel

She is at the small deep window
looking through and out:
the Aran islands, rock and seawater,
lie all about.
A face strong in poverty's hauteur
is hers, then and now.

Being a young woman in Flaherty's film
'Man of Aran',
she nearly drowned in the undertow
by the boat where she ran.   10
He kept on filming even though
he thought her dead on the rockrim.

A body plaited by water twine
they carried ashore:
partnered in the ocean's set dance
by two men or more.
The sea had had its chance
to peel her off by the shoreline.

Now in her great old age
toothless and tough,   20
the island music still delights her:
one dance is not enough.
The tunes of a people poor and cut off there
have a special power to engage.

Drawn upright, her stiff bones
already dancing,
she spins, not on one foot
but on her stick, tap-balancing.
While to one side like a pliant offshoot
a little girl mimics her, unbeknown.   30

In a Galloway Wood

By the alley of limes
                          along the way
crowd ancient tombstones
                              carved angel heads.
Moss and mildew
                   eat away the words.

Barred ruined transept
                            of the roofless chapel
named for the knights,
                          St John of Jerusalem: 10
here kings and queens came
                                to cross at the ford.

A great grey-green stone
                             in a Galloway wood
with the hollow pool
                          quite perfect
filled with rainwater
                           and red rowan-berries:

a holy water basin
                        on the border of the walk.   20
'Keep away,' the minister
                            warned his villagers,
'in this a lost child
                    lay and drowned.'

But the sun suddenly
                        shining on shadows
hollow and throaty
                    sound the hooves
fording by the old way
                        paved under the water.   30

And the sun works
                    as the snow does
on a wisp of green corn
                                in workaday clothes,
in sweatshirt, shorts
                    and muddy sandals,

a little lass
                laughs near the stone
with her crown
                    of tawny hair,   40
an incarnation
                    of the pilgrims' way.

Sunlight clothes her
                        in a timeless space,
endows a Galloway wood
                            with a new Devorgilla,
a young sweetheart
                    again for Scotland.

The Crook-maker

One day it would come into my grandfather's mind
to make a crook and staff.
A shepherd friend had sent
rams' horns for him to give the proper shape.

First, he looked through Scotland's woods
for the single stock in a spread of trees
as far as Blair Atholl, rejecting stick after stick,
looking for the straightest hazel bough.

Then there were days, maybe three,
of turning the incurved twists of the horn   10
into the single crooked claw of their hooked form:
to one smooth bend like a unique curl of hair.

It unbent through steeping in hot water.
He used his vice-grip to hold it to the curve.
He carved and whittled it to an adorned head,
a curving salmon-leap or a fluffed thistle-top.

He bound crook and staff with loops
of a thick turk's-head knot,
a red turban of twine. All this time
he had never noticed his other walks or work.   20

But the longest time of all was to come,
smoothing and polishing the crook,
adding each day to its sheen, from
the first emery paper to the last chamois leather.

It changed from angry ruts to fondled silks.
He put on the ferrule last,
tipped the wood with a metal tip,
signing it as of a man's making.

With the finishing stroke put to the work
there sprang up before our eyes   30
a bough with new proportions,
sprouting a curly horn, blossoming a carving.

The heap of shavings
was still fresh at his feet:
my grandfather not a moment older
through all these days of crook-making.

The Negative

He's come for the pipe-band,
being just big enough
to put on his sporran.
My son is a scrap
of his own tartan:
he is all kilt, save for his brown knees
and the bloodied old scars on them.

It's his everyday kilt, but here, today,
it makes a tourist trample through the crowd:
'Move *there*, little boy.'   10
She fires the camera, conspires
to steal his virtue into a picture.
He flashes a dour and warring glance
that must be perfect for her.

Now that it's taken, he ought
to spring to life,
flash out a knife,
ask for her money or the negative.

Yet he must know
that will develop into something   20
different from the youthful Lachlan.

No,
the negative will show
a stony moor,
a twisted tree,
and all around them
the ragged map
of Scotland.

Letter to Scotland

The hill has a life of its own.
Fish! fish! it whales its way
through the sky,
dashing clouds off
with the temper
of a granite fin.

The hill owns its life.
Dog! dog! it ripples a collar
of pine-studs,
bristles its hipbones   10
through bracken;
mist froths its jowls.

The Piano-tuner

Two hundred miles, he had come
to tune one piano, the last hereabouts.
Both of them were relics of imperial time:
the Anglo-Indian and the old upright knockabout.

He peered, and peered again
into its monsoon-warped bowels.
From the flats of dead sound he'd beckon
a tune on the bones out to damp vowels.

His own sounds were pidgin.
The shapeliness of his forearms   10
lent his body an English configuration,
but still, sallow as any snakecharmer

he was altogether piebald.
Far down the bridge of his nose
perched roundrimmed tortoiseshell spectacles;
his hair, a salt-and-pepper, white foreclosed.

But he rings in the ear yet,
his interminable tapping of jarring notes:
and, before he left,
he gave point to those hours of discord.   20

With a smile heavenly
because so out of place, cut off from any home there,
he sat down quietly
to play soft music: that tune of 'Beautiful Dreamer',

a melody seized from yellowed ivories
and rotting wood. A damper
muffled the pedal point of lost birthright. We eaves-
dropped on an extinct creature.

The Rock of Hawthornden

At the rock of Hawthornden,
steep outcrop well-loved by men
since the day they first fortified its crag,
put a hand to the rockface,
it is magnetized in place
by the fiery core of the old magma.

Marked with clefts and caves,
ferns and trees within its waves,
sewn with deadwood petrified in seams,
crystals and glittering stones embed   10
shining eyes upon this head
while through its ivy wreath there darts a wren.

In India such rocks
worshipped like beasts or gods
are visited by pilgrims walking on the plain;
only here in Scotland
it takes a solitary stand
among discords of chainsaw and firing range.

River Esk so far below
turns sunwise in its flow   20
round the rock and the house on its rampart,
where wooded shades sun never clears
keep dark four hundred years
since the man of Hawthorndon lived at its heart.

His was a white melancholy
suspended on this promontory
washed by weathers high above the wooded valley,
a house rich in angled shapes,
turrets and crow-step gables:
for the art of thinking he rebuilt his sanctuary.   30

Now Drummond of Hawthornden
once wrote to a true friend,
'Where I love, there I love for years'
and from this place he loved
his spirit cannot now remove;
he is at last his own rockform here.

Ron Butlin (1949 –)

One of the most talented of contemporary Scottish poets, Butlin is also one of the most skilled writers of short fiction. The short story given here, 'The Child and the Man', reveals a typical combination of the realistic and the grotesque that amounts almost to surrealism, and to a consistent theme, the missing or destabilising father figure.

Descriptions of the Falling Snow

I described a flight of imaginary birds
across an imaginary sky in words
that played out every laboured game of skill
involving consonants and vowels, until
sufficient universal truths obeyed
the cadences of my trade.

I argued love and metaphysics through
by sound, resolving dissonance into
a line of formal spontaneity:
a passionate description of, let's say,   10
the falling snow. These were not dreams
but calculations for what seems

a well-constructed winter sky. Neatly
stammered syllables of discreetly
quantified despair described the view:
some fields of hardened grass and mud; a few
abandoned tractors; a waterfall's cascade
stiffening into ice. I made

events from over twenty years ago
translate into each metaphor – as though   20
a door slammed shut, or someone's name
had set the limits to my suffering.
(And if the phrase read awkwardly I'd pause.
checking each effect for flaws.)

The qualities of light through falling snow;
the patterns made by frost; the fields below
my house – I scanned and stressed a thousand words
describing everything I saw. The birds
in flight across the imaginary skies
sang what I set down – my lies   30

were coming true. And yet, I cannot live
uncorrupted by the narrative
I tell. All things are mine to name:
there is no innocence, no shame;
nothing is, that is not of my own
and of my incantation.

My fingers claw at imaginary birds.
My tongue stutters over lists of words
I've learnt by heart. Such passionate pretence!
It is almost five o'clock. I sense   40
the hammer strike the bell and cancel-out
each pitiless belief and doubt.

Indian Summer

As though time passes. Drenched in silver
and pale gold an ocean seems to break
beneath us; it brings together night
and day imperfectly.

As though each sliding contour of the sky
has paused, the colours of the clouds
saturate the ocean.

As though it is a late September afternoon
we sit drinking wine outdoors;
the dusklight falls between our hands   10
and soaks into the grass.

Soon, moonlight will stain the ocean-floor:
sea-creatures will take fright
and turn away.

Two Women

The room is stacked high with caged birds.
Feathers cover the floor.
One woman brings out tequila
while another, almost a child,
brings lemon, salt and a small sharp knife.

The old woman's songs are slovenly,
she makes herself cry. Then,
kicking up feathers, she makes the child dance through down-
drifting scarlet, vermilion and gold:
desert-colours for her lips, her breasts and her thighs;   10
the deadness of desert-light in her eyes.

My Grandfather Dreams Twice of Flanders

My grandfather dreamt he was trying hard to die
and no one would help him.
He dreamt he went walking across Flanders field,
and he saw the companies of dead men
whose screaming he still hears night after night.

The countryside was a woman dressed in red.
He saw her courted briefly by a million men
carrying bayonets and mortars; her face
turning towards his, turned his to stone
and made the white clouds whirl dizzily overhead.   10

My grandfather dreamt that he was six years old
and a woman decked in flowers or blood
was guiding him to Flanders field:

he saw ungathered poppies scattered on the floor
and the ceiling tilting crazily
and the lights swaying;
shadows tumbling out of the darkness
beckoned him everywhere.

He saw her heaping flowers into a bed.
Then one by one she took the shadows   20
to lie with her, and one
by one he saw them disappear.

Portrait of a Shadow-sailor

At thirty-five years old
he's halfway round his lifetime's only world
– quite at sea. (*That* at least, is true).
By day he plays the captain and the crew
Whose rank and medals have been tattooed on
– gentle pinpricks cutting to the bone.
At night he lies and listens: the crow's nest sways
almost audibly above, and weighs
out silence for the darkened scene below
– letting the slightest measure only, flow   10
into his sea-crazed mind.

Tightening his grip upon the helm
(in 'lock-position') the shadow-sailor calms
approaching storms by will-power. He reshapes
the cliffs and waves according to his maps;
their tears and creases mean what *he* decides
in terms of shallows, hidden reefs. He prides
himself upon a life's experience
of reading charts long out of date: he glides
across the wind-scarred surface, making sense   20
of every ocean-contour (this one hides
a bogeyman within its childish scrawls,
and that one traps a god). Such reverence!
In these deserted sea-lanes he collides
with ghost-ships – their slow and soundless passage falls
shadowless across his decks and hull.

Sea-wraiths and the demons who preside
upon the ocean-floor advise him; coral
(saturated with the sudden cries
of drowning men) signifies their power.   30
These are his familiars; their histories
are his; their voices he alone can hear;
their silence is the elemental measure
of despair.
            Thus his world has taken shape:
a place of terror, clashing rocks, the hiss
of cross-run currents, undertows to rip
his soul apart . . .

His log's kept neat for he believes that this
– i.e. the mastery of words, and clear
calligraphy – improves the truth. His fear,   40
therefore, must complement the sentence-structure
or be dropped. Each entry's much the same;
new page, top left: 'The heat, the chill, the heaving
sea beneath are everything I know . . . '
Yet sometimes he can sense a tide whose flow
runs greater, and carries to a farther shore:
Too briefly, then, he'll glimpse and recognise

what lies beyond this shadow-sea, these shadow skies.
    As evening falls he watches ocean-colours
and the sun dissolve into each other,   50
letting their transparency reveal
the night sky and the ocean-floor:

The heavens' slow creation and destruction
the shadow-sailor takes into himself,
letting constellations drift at random:

– until he's made, of stars and minerals,
the darkness his imagination spills
unearthly light upon.

Note: Butlin subsequently revised this fine poem, under a slightly different title. Following is
his second version, as it gives a fascinating glimpse into the poet's craft.

The Shadow-sailor

1

He's quite at sea (*that*, at least, is true).
By day he plays the captain and the crew
with rank and medals tattooed on –
gentle pinpricks cutting to the bone.
By night the empty crow's nest sways
between the cold moon and himself, and weighs
out stillness for the darkened scene below
letting the slightest measure only, flow
into his sea-crazed mind.

A tightened grip upon the helm and steering blind   10
he navigates by will-power, shapes
the changing waves according to a map
long out of date and precious. Ink-blots, tears and scrawls
mean 'Danger – hidden reef', 'cross-currents', 'rip-tide',
'wreckage'. Sea-wraiths advise him. Ghost-ships glide
through his, each unsounded passage falls
shadowless across his decks and hull.
He shuts his eyes to ward off the invisible.

2

He's more than halfway round his lifetime's only world:
to north and south the cries of drowning men   20
have turned to ice;
to east and west the ocean and the sun
dissolve into each other.

It's time to voyage further: to see what lies
beyond this shadow-sea, these shadow-skies.
It's time to take into himself the heavens'
own creation and destruction:
to make, of stars and minerals,
the darkness his imagination spills
unearthly light upon.   30

Coming of Age

You're waiting for a train that isn't late,
or glancing out the window at the street
before the curtain's pulled.

Some broken glass, a child's ball bouncing
down a flight of steps, the threat of
rain, a ploughed field,
the colour of a passing car —
each in turn betrays the man you are.

Take care, your heartbeat's stilled
and still you do not die. No delegate   10
can take your place or answer to your name:
when the curtain's closed the world's shut out.
Your train arrives on time.

Beginnings of the Ice Age

An ocean hardens into Linton Valley as line
on line the winter geese fly south — tidemarks
on a farther shore.

The ocean's freezing over: wind, scratching its surface
here and there, suggests what might have been.
Someone's voice, another's glance, the taste a woman's skin has
as she wakes — all these remain, and are
the brittleness of shells.

The geese trail silence after them until the shoreline
disappears. This is the ground we stand on —   10
dark sand and darker water.
A rowan tree takes root beside our house;
a stone bridge hump-backs over Linton burn;
the hill we'd planned to walk across today
is turning green. Creation of the world seems easier
than a change of heart.

African Sunlight

A man is riding a slender camel, a woman
carrying a jar – two lives that give a human scale
to the empty landscape and open skies.
Their faces lack expression. Unspoken truths
and lies suggest a husband with his wife,
a king and his slave, strangers even.
The jar she offers him contains cold water
tasting of exhaustion or desire:
the words of greeting he will never speak
will never bring her peace.   10

The artist threads his needle, pulls tight,
bites off what isn't needed, spits
and then begins upon the same two lives again.
Beneath his fingers the wax-embroidered sun remains at noon;
the desert-sand raised up as darkness, catches fire.

The following poem is the seventh in an eight-unit sequence 'in memory of my
mother' called 'Ryecroft' (1995).

The Curtains Were Closed

The curtains were closed when I entered her room:
the day was shut out, the night was shut out
and she wasn't there.

I looked down at her face, her mouth and her eyes:
I tried to remember her mouth and her eyes.

The walls were as mist when mist disappears,
the door falling rain that no longer falls;

the corridor ran the length of the world
and she wasn't there.

The Child and the Man

When I was fourteen I fell in love for the last time. And then one night I was awakened by
the sound of tapping on my window. Thinking it was the wind I turned over and tried to get
back to sleep; but how quiet everything was – no rattling of slates nor roaring in the chimney,
just this tap-tap on the window-pane. After several minutes of complete wakefulness I got out
of bed. The tapping became more insistent as I went over to the curtains. I hoped to see my
mother when I opened them – that is, I hoped to see the spirit of my mother, for she had
been dead for fourteen years.

I had been brought up by my aunt Vera, a woman in her late forties, both my parents having been killed in a car-crash shortly after I was born. She was my mother's sister, and as degenerate a woman as I am ever likely to meet. Is her kind dying out now? I sincerely hope so, if there is to be any hope for my generation. My earliest memories are of her thick fingers prodding my stomach to assure herself that I was growing fat. She had a horror of thinness and was herself a remarkably stout woman.

When I was five years old, each evening I would dutifully get up from my toys when it was time to go to bed, then get changed into my pyjamas by myself and under her direction. She insisted that I was never to be completely naked but do the top half first and then the bottom half. Gradually I accustomed myself to the method and speed of undress she wished. Sometimes she would say, 'Not so fast Paul, careful now, you might tear that shirt,' meanwhile her finger-nail would impatiently scratch the side of the arm-chair until I had adjusted to the desired rate. Soon the whole operation could be performed in complete silence but for the scratching of her finger-nail to slow down my actions, and let her linger over any detail that particularly appealed to her that evening. To speed up any part that seemed to cause her momentary impatience, she repeatedly slapped the chair-arm with the palm of her hand, gradually slowing down until my process of undress arrived at the next detail she wished to study, any finer adjustments then being made by her finger-nail. And all the while with her free hand she conveyed marshmallows to her mouth and chewed noiselessly, and gazed at me. If she wanted me to turn round she would give me a marshmallow.

We lived in a basement, and my aunt, when she wasn't eating marshmallows, would often smoke woodbines. She warned me not to smoke for then I would never grow big and tall like my father, but sometimes I used to go into the garden and smoke until I was nearly sick. I also used to smoke in the bathroom, leaving the window open. I frequently wondered what my father had looked like and so I would wet my hair and part it as he had in his photographs. Then, with a cigarette in my mouth, I would look at myself in the mirror. If my aunt came knocking at the door asking what I was doing in there all day, I would quickly recomb my hair, put out the cigarette, put my father's photo up my jumper, and having made sure all the smoke had cleared, I would flush the toilet and leave.

When I came out she would often ask me if I had been 'up to anything.' I'd reply that I didn't know what she meant, and then she'd say that I wasn't normal. Usually though she would just pat me on the stomach, saying that at least I wasn't thin and that was a blessing. One day, however, I risked taking in the whole family album which had some photographs of my mum and dad together with me, taken when I was very small. I spent ages trying my dad's various partings and expressions, and even some of my mum's smiles and ways of tilting her head. When I came out my aunt asked if I'd been looking at pictures. My expression must have given me away immediately, because she said 'Aha!'

That evening while I was going through the customary ritual of getting ready for bed, although I was almost ten years old by this time, she asked me if I liked looking at pictures. I didn't say anything. Then she asked me if I'd ever seen 'the real thing' or just pictures. I answered that of course I had, but I couldn't remember anything as I was very young at the time. To this she smiled with lascivious pleasure and remarked that I was a smart one. Then she asked if I would like to see the real thing, but added that I would not see everything, not just yet anyway. At this I broke out in a big smile. I was very happy because I thought she meant that somehow I was going to see my mum and dad and that I had misunderstood what being dead meant, for really they were just away somewhere for a while and waiting for me to grow up from being a small boy.

When she noticed how excited I was, her face became flushed and she said that I really was a smart one and no mistake. Then she unbuttoned her blouse and exposed her very large breasts. I was rather puzzled by this turn of affairs and was uncertain what was happening. 'Don't be afraid,' she said, 'it's alright seeing that I'm not your mother or sister. Look at them, they're real, not pictures.' I felt cheated as this was not at all what I'd expected; I wanted to see my mum and dad. Then she asked me if I wanted to touch them. I didn't want to touch them, and said so. She kept on asking if I wanted to, saying how soft they were and so nice to touch.

Finally she grabbed my hand, and they did feel nice to touch. She said again that I was a smart one and I should soon grow up big and tall like my father – then I burst into tears. She comforted me and sent me to bed with my mouth full of marshmallows.

As can be imagined, things did not stop there, and over the next few months she introduced me to many kinds of intimacies. She began taking me to her bed sometimes where I would have to lie close beside her in the darkness. Then one night she said I wasn't to be afraid but she was going to make me grow big and tall like my father. I became afraid. But soon I felt a strange thrilling and shivering sensation run all over me for the first time – and this I took to be the spirit of my father being raised within me.

As I said, when I was fourteen I fell in love for the last time and, considering the way aunt Vera brought me up, it's nothing short of miraculous that I fell in love at all. She used the word 'love' when ever we were in bed together saying, 'You do love me, John, don't you?' (John was my father's name) – to which I had to reply, 'Yes, Vera, I love you.'

The first time that this happened, along with my father's spirit being raised, proved too much for me: I went to the bathroom afterwards and cried and tried to smoke a woodbine; then I went to my own bed even though I knew it would be cold. Soon however I stopped crying afterwards and would smoke my woodbine in bed beside her – she liked that, though it was the only time she ever let me smoke.

She always made me go and sleep in my own bed afterwards. At first, as I said, I really wanted to get away from her as soon as possible, but as it was always so cold by myself I asked her once if I couldn't stay and sleep with her instead. At this she became quite angry, and as she was seldom even cross with me really, I never asked her again. What she wanted me to do it seemed, was to smoke my woodbine then, without saying goodnight or anything, just slip out of her bed and go through to my own. The only exception to this was on the night of my fourteenth birthday. I had had some friends round for tea and when they'd gone she got very drunk. After I left her bed she came through to my room and climbed in beside me, then she put her arms tightly about me and immediately fell fast asleep. She snored so loudly that I'm sure I didn't sleep all night but lay there trapped. In the morning when she woke up she just looked at me, bit her lip and said, 'Oh, Paul!' Then she got up and rushed through to her own room; later I heard her crying. That was the only time we really slept together, though, as I said, I did very little sleeping.

For a short time after that she did not take me to her bed to do 'real things,' as she called them, as often as before; but when she did she was in a real frenzy, demanding that I tell her how much John loved her, and then that I prove it 'to her complete satisfaction' as she would say. It was at this time that I started going out with Margaret, a girl at my school. Though I had seen her every day for years one day I seemed to see her for the first time. I felt as if she was all around me and within me. At last I summoned up enough courage to ask a friend of mine to ask a friend of hers to ask her if she fancied me at all. And in no time we were skipping school together to sit all afternoon in cafes or cinemas holding hands. We didn't say we were in love, of course, in fact we didn't say very much at all; just held hands and squeezed them occasionally depending upon what record was playing or what the hero and heroine were saying or doing.

I was afraid of my aunt finding out about Margaret. Somehow I thought it would be better if she did not know. Life continued at home very much as it had always done: she took me to her bed about once a fortnight and, excepting that, I suppose things were perfectly normal. But once I started going out with Margaret I dreaded my aunt's caresses and endearments.

Then one night she wanted me to come to her and I wouldn't. I didn't say anything but just lay there in my bed very, very tense. She pleaded with me, shouted at me and eventually she slapped me across the face before stalking back to her room. When she'd gone I relaxed and started drifting back into dreams about Margaret where we kissed lingeringly and spoke tender words to each other over and over again. I was falling asleep when the door opened once more and in walked Aunt Vera. I was ready to scream to her to get out, to leave me alone, when she said she'd come to apologise. After a moment I replied that it was alright, and then she remarked that it was time we had a serious talk. I didn't know what she wanted to talk about, but I was afraid that somehow she had found out about Margaret and wanted me to stop seeing her.

She sat on the edge of my bed and began talking to me about schoolwork and what kinds of jobs I might get when I left. As she didn't seem to be going to say anything about Margaret and as I was very tired anyway, I started falling asleep and so lost much of what she was saying until I became aware of her voice calling, 'John, John,' softly but firmly. Before I realised what was happening, she had begun to raise the spirit of my father. Again I felt that delicious thrill run over my body, and I reached for and pulled her in beside me saying, 'John loves you, John loves you.' Afterwards when I had finished my woodbine and aunt Vera had gone back to her room, I thought about Margaret. I fell asleep trying to picture her as she had looked that day sitting next to the window in class.

Lately I had noticed that I was growing more and more to resemble my father as he looked in some of the photographs. Did this mean, I wondered, that his spirit was growing stronger and stronger within me? Did it mean that when I had grown to resemble him completely, his spirit would completely take over and I would no longer exist? Then quite suddenly I understood everything: I was the child and he was the man; and now that the child was growing up the man was taking over. When aunt Vera raised his spirit within me for the first time she said that I was not to be afraid; but his spirit frightened me, and each time since it seemed stronger and stronger. People sometimes said, 'he's only a child,' and now I understood what they meant. I thrilled every time my father's spirit was raised within me. I was exhilarated and frightened at the same time. For a few moments I sensed what it was to be a man, and at the same time I sensed my own death.

Then one night I heard that gentle tapping on my window and I knew my mother had come to see my father, whose spirit her presence would further strengthen within me. I opened the curtains expecting to see her as in the photographs, but I saw nothing, just an empty street. My aunt must have heard me walking about for she came into the room at that moment and asked if anything was the matter. I told her that I had just been closing the window which had woken me by its rattling. This seemed to work for she said goodnight and went back to her room.

I lay in bed listening to hear if the tapping would start again. Several times I even got out of bed and went over to the window to check that there was no one there. By this time I was too disturbed to sleep and lay there wide awake. My father's spirit had been raised and he was angry. Then he began to speak to me for the first time. Why hadn't I gone to the window quicker? Didn't I want to see my mother? Didn't I care about her? I was too afraid to reply. I lay there in the darkness without moving while his voice continued, shouting inside me. Eventually he calmed down. I told him that I was very tired. I did not tell him that I had missed him all these years and that now I was terrified of him.

He said that we had much to talk about having been apart for so long, so I told him all I had done as far back as I could remember. I told him about my aunt and the evening rituals, the marshmallows – which he thought very amusing, about the photographs, and how my aunt showed me what was 'real,' and how at those times I had felt his spirit rise within me. And he said that that was good, but now we could talk together at any time of the day or night, I wasn't to go to aunt Vera unless he said so.

Then he told me about my mother and what the family had done together when I was just a baby. He told me where we'd been when the photographs I knew so well had been taken. He then went on to describe how he had met my mother when he had been doing his National Service, and that was why in some of the photographs he was dressed as a soldier. When I asked him what it was like being in the army, he began telling me the most fantastic stories of tanks and battles, and gradually I fell asleep.

Next day as I was on my way to school he began speaking to me again. He was asking about Margaret and I told him that he would see her soon in class, and also that I was going a walk with her at lunchtime. He kept asking about her. I had to tell him how I first met her, what she looked like, what she was wearing, had I ever seen her naked? He made me angry and I shouted to him to shut up, but he just laughed. I tried to explain to him that with Margaret it was different because I wanted to be able to fall properly in love with her, not just do with her the things I had to do with my aunt.

All through the morning lessons he kept on at me. He wouldn't let me concentrate on my work. Didn't I want to see her naked? Didn't I want to touch her? He just would not shut up. Did I know the facts of life? he asked me. I tried to ignore him. Then he began telling me that many women are almost as different physically from each other as they are from men. Just as they have different kinds and colours of hair, so they have different kinds of bodies under their clothes. I could not help looking round the class at some of the girls and I felt his spirit getting restless inside me. That's what people mean, he continued, when they say they suit each other. You don't know if you and Margaret suit each other yet, do you? That's the danger about falling in love, he remarked after a short pause, especially for the first time, that if people find out too late that they don't suit each other, then sometimes they are so unhappy that they kill themselves.

Even though I'd heard people talk like that, especially in the films or on TV, I felt he was trying to trick me into doing something that he wanted to do and I didn't. He wanted me to do with Margaret all the things I did with Aunt Vera so that his spirit would grow stronger and stronger, and eventually take control completely and I would no longer exist. He said that he was warning me about falling in love, for, if she and I didn't suit each other, then perhaps I might kill myself, and he and I would be parted again, this time forever. Maybe he was telling the truth but I wasn't sure. I knew that he and I would part soon because I could not remain both a man and a child for long. What I hoped was that if Margaret loved me then together our love might be strong enough to resist him. Even though I doubted there being any truth in the matter, I began to worry whether we did suit each other or not.

I met Margaret at lunchtime and suggested we went for our walk down by the river. As we left the school she began to tell me what had happened at her home the previous night, and what she had seen on television. Then she asked me if a boy in the class called Steve fancied Helen, a friend of hers. She was in the middle of chattering about this when we turned off the street to go down to the river. I interrupted her to say that I loved her. I took her in my arms and looked deep into her eyes as I had seen them do in the pictures. When she didn't reply I kissed her softly on the forehead and said that I hoped she loved me. She blushed and squeezed my hand, but said nothing.

I smiled, but inside I was frantic. Why didn't she just answer a simple yes or no like in the films? So I asked her again. This time she replied that we were really going steady, weren't we? Then she paused for a moment and added that, yes, she thought she was in love with me but she wasn't sure yet; she would have to think about it, and would let me know after school. When she said this, my father told me that I would have to find out if we suited each other. I would have to find out now, he urged, before it was too late.

We walked further down the river, onto a long stretch where the path was hidden from the road by a line of trees. Margaret started asking me about Steve again, and I said that I'd no idea if he fancied Helen or even if he fancied anyone at all. I tried to speak normally but a fierce dialogue was raging inside me between my father and myself. At length I interrupted her again to ask her if she thought we would suit each other. She kissed me, then said that she thought we would. We kissed again for a long time, and didn't say anything.

Make certain, before it's too late, my father broke in fiercely. I felt certain that he was setting a trap for me. I wanted to resist him. He began to bully me saying, touch her breast, that will relax her. Caress it gently, he whispered. You must. You must find out if you suit each other. You're lying, I said to him, you're trying to trick me. But he ignored me. Let your hand slide gently from her breast, he urged, move it gradually down her jersey and try to put it up her skirt.

She wouldn't let me do that, however, and began pushing my hand away. But she has not stopped kissing you, he said. You can try again. She pushed my hand away. You can try once more. Then she began kissing me very hard, she was letting my hand slide up her thighs. I became afraid because I felt his spirit was growing stronger within me. She pushed me away again. His spirit was growing stronger and stronger and I had to try again, and again she pushed me away – this time, however, she stopped kissing me as well. I was not going to try any more no matter what he said, for I could feel him raised very strong within me and he was tense.

Again she pushed me away very firmly, saying that perhaps we should be getting back to school. I told her that I was sorry, but I had just wanted to know for certain that we suited each other. She said that it was alright really and, though she was sure that we did suit each other, she didn't want to rush things. Now, he said, now.

And already I was watching him, whose spirit now filled my whole body so that it was tingling and stinging, use my hands to force her legs apart and rip off the tights she would not let me place my fingertips inside. I watched in horror as Margaret's face was pushed backwards by my hand and held to the ground by my fingers gripping her hair. I tried to speak to her to tell her not to be afraid, not to struggle or I was sure my father would kill her so strong did he feel within me. I wanted to avert my eyes, to stop my ears but he would not let me, saying that I had to listen and I had to look to make certain that she and I suited each other. When he was at his fullest strength my whole body shook and thrilled – and then he was gone.

Margaret lay on the ground in tears. Her face was smeared with dirt and blood but that did not matter because I loved her. When I told her that I loved her, she tried to stand up; she seemed very weak so I held onto her in case she fell. Then she said I was never to touch her again or to speak to her again. I watched helplessly as she stumbled off along the bank. Then my father began speaking to me again. She has refused your love and you will be very unhappy, but do not worry because I will be with you, he said. He was trying to sound comforting but I knew he was exulting. Now that Margaret would have nothing to do with me he thought that my love for her was of no consequence – that I would soon kill myself and so give way to him completely.

'But I love you,' I cried after her as she staggered towards the end of the line of trees. 'I love you, I don't want to hurt you.' She said nothing. Then she stumbled, and I ran towards her to help her all the while crying that I loved her. I was in tears now and desperate; inside me my father's spirit was laughing. I caught up with her and she tried to shake me off, but she was too weak.

Then my father became serious: this is not the woman you love, he said. 'Yes she is, she is,' I stammered. She was staring at my face and looking far into the distance; she was very frightened. The tears were streaming down my cheeks as I held her, my hands on her shoulders. 'I love you. can't you understand?' I pleaded.

Then my father began gripping her shoulders more tightly in my hands. He must have been very strong because he lifted her up off her feet and threw her onto the ground. This is not the woman you love, he said, look at her. And though her face was all dirt and blood I said yes it is, this is Margaret whom I love. Then he picked up a stone in my hand and struck her face with it, and still I said I recognise her because I love her so deeply. Again and again he struck her until at last I could no longer recognise her, then he stopped. Do you know who she is? he asked. No, I answered. Come with me, he said.

We went home. The house was empty. My aunt was out. I spread the family photographs out on the table. There is my mother. But I can't recognise her. She was killed in a car-crash. I know that I am dying as well. I am her child. The spirit of the man she loved is growing stronger and killing me. He killed Margaret the girl that I love. He was driving the car when my mother was killed. He ran it into a wall killing her like this and like this and like this – my finger-nail scratches across her photograph. I am looking at the photograph now, it is torn – and all at once I do recognise my mother. I saw her today in fact, when I was returning from a walk by the river. She was lying on the bank.

. I keep hearing myself differently, my voice is changing all the time – it is my father's voice speaking more and more. He is saying Aunt Vera will be coming home soon and I must put away the photographs. I must not tell her about recognising my mother today – that is to be a secret. I must not tell her about Margaret who does not want me to touch her or to speak to her again.

I saw my mother today and I stood beside her while she was asleep. I wondered what she was dreaming about. Tonight she will come to me in secret; she will tap on the window-pane; she will take me away to be with her for always. My aunt will know nothing of this.

My aunt is here. My father's voice is speaking to her, and he will always speak to her from now on. My voice is a whisper that only my mother will hear. He is joking with her and I can hardly hear what he is saying. She is laughing. I can see her teeth and her tongue. She is patting my stomach and I cannot hear what she is saying. His spirit is everywhere as my fingers undo the buttons on her blouse; he is laughing. Knowing that my mother is coming for me I am no longer afraid.

Now she is breathing awkwardly, quickly. Her eyes stare into the distance. I want to approach where my father is now; I want to feel what he is touching now with my hands. Everything is different to him. He is telling her that it is different, he is telling how it is different. She is getting more excited than she has ever been before. Now he is telling her that he loves her; at last he is speaking for himself, at last he is saying that he loves her and has always loved her.

She is pulling him closer and closer. She whispers hoarsely and excitedly into his ear, 'Who loves me, tell me who loves me?' Then I hear him reply, 'Paul loves you, Vera, Paul loves you.'

Morelle Smith (1949 –)

Deep-water Terminal

You like names like that, you said,
The day we went to the James river,
Drove along the Old Gun Road,
Sun hot and heavy,
Trees coloured like a child's paint-box.
I stepped in the mud,
And it oozed between my toes,
So I waded in the river, to clean them.
Big steamers come miles up the river, you said,
As far as deep-water terminal.   10

We went to Babe's restaurant, before I left,
To drink some wine.
The waitress hugged two men at the next table,
She almost skipped across the floor,
Her eyes were blue and bright.
She put candles on all the tables.
It was getting dark, and we were talking
About dreams, supernatural things,
And inexplicable connexions between people.
You said you didn't believe in 'all that' anyway,   20
And your face was jumping in light and shadow.

You look to the side of people, when you talk,
You rarely catch their eyes.
Hidden by so many jokes and stories,
I imagine voyages in all your dreams,
Circling within the limits of your laughter.
I never dared to step within your boundaries
Although I thought I heard you calling
As if you thought that I was far away.

Highland

Snow on the high mountains
Is smoothed by the wind.
The white folds of winter
Fray into yellow grass
And sleeping heather.

There is no tree between me and the mountain.
Only the wind combing the marsh grass.
A ledge of snow forms a step to the house
And the sunlight trips, on its way to the ground.

Catherine Czerkawska (1950 –)

Being Me

Roughly once a month
The leaves framed by my
Kitchen window crawl
Over the sky.
They are black
Like currants
Or (more menacingly) insects perhaps
And there are shiny gaps
Where the light comes between.
I perceive how we   10
Talk in metaphors mostly
And hardly know that
We and all our days
Consist of them.

Roughly once a month
The world and its straight ways
Aggravates.
Instead there is this
Ill-at-easiness with things,

This crookedness of things.   20
Odd details of shape
And colour and sound intrude,
Odd connections that the mind makes,
Odd affinities it knows.
Things are other and the same at once.
Anything is possible.

Roughly once a month
I think that maybe
I could put
This faculty to some good use   30
Being me.
As long as I am reassured that
You will not hedge it with
Fearful rationality
And call it madness.
Well I will defy you:
Not insane but sometimes seeing.

For Annot and John

In the years 1250 to 1300
The summers were finer than before or since.
Some poet before me wrote of
Cyngyure and sedewale and the gylofre
By which he meant that these were
His little Anne. Ginger, valerian and the
Gillyflower you understand were precious.
Some living breathing walking man
Whose name was John has left us
A pot pourri of words,   10
For the sunlight to shine upon. It dried
And dried the fallen petals around his pen.
Her name was in a note of the nightingale.

In his garden when he wrote of singing birds
It is possible to smell the garden in his words.

Silverfish

This man always lived
On the far side of a book
Lived second hand.
So when the wild world finally

Stepped in with a drunken song
To touch his numb senses
He slid quietly between the pages
And did not come out again.

Book and all they moved him
Into a library stacked him and   10
Catalogued him by courtesy of
The Dewey Decimal System.

No one has touched his tome for years.
He scuttles between the pages still.
One crush and he will
Dissolve into a little grey dust or
Merely a smear.

I hear now the heavy attendant
Moving up and down
With his trolley,   20
Junketing along the
Black metal stacks.
Strip lighting buzzes on off on.
Books crash together with a muffled thud.

Old Soldiers Never:

Forgive me.
I had not realized you were
Old until today.

You are a straight
Handsome man still.
I look at your face
Its surfaces and shadows
Not at your premature
And therefore ironic
Silver halo.
I listen and   10
Your voice your verse
Is economic still.
Your astringency
Shrivels the unwary.

Age went unconsidered
Until you receded behind your eyes
And beyond your words today
Into places I had not
Come to.
God help me   20
I had not realized
You were old.

A Bad Year for Trees

It had been a bad year for trees. The elms in the deer park were the first to go. They were diseased and there was no help for it. Martin mourned them like old friends, stooping over their fallen carcasses and cursing under his breath so that the forestry workers called in to do the felling should not hear him and think him foolish. In late spring there came freak gales from the wrong direction. The prevailing winds here were Easterly and the trees had long ago learned which way they ought to bend. The sudden change, this onslaught from the West, brought many casualties: a tangle of fallen hazel and beech in the plantation that sheltered garden from shore. Now, looking up at the birch grove that divided precise terraces from conifers striding in serrated ranks up the hill above the house, he saw that the birches too were growing old and could not be expected to last for much longer.

Martin was the head gardener in this small country park where visitors came to walk and picnic each summer. But it was already late October and the gardeners could go about their business in peace. He did not like summer visitors, seeing them as a necessary evil. They parked their cars where they should not. They dropped litter and picked flowers and etched their initials into tree trunks. Earlier that year he had come across a hedgehog staggering blindly along a gravel path with its head firmly jammed into a tin can, cutting a ludicrous little figure. Anger rose in him as he caught the terrified animal and freed it from its encumbrance.

He had moved to a small cottage on this estate some twenty years before while his daughter Rosemary was a baby and his wife still alive. But she had died young and suddenly, and after her death, his work in the small enclosed world of the park had begun to intrude upon him to an intolerable degree. He saw the growing and dying, the preying of parasitic plant upon plant or bird upon small animal with a searing clarity. If so much as a rose tree in the walled garden withered he felt something wither and die in him also. Last winter he had found birds on the beach, unfamiliar birds that he learned later were cormorants, staggering ashore their wings black with oil. At the time he had raged around the cottage that seemed too small to contain his passion. He frightened his daughter and was sorry for it later. But the tragedies of land and sea ate into him and there was nothing he could do to remedy them.

On this fine autumn morning he was working with a group of men combing the lawns with strong, long handled rakes to rid them of loose grass. He paused to rest his back which was often painful these days, and saw his daughter walking up the terraces towards him, shading her eyes against the sun. She raised a hand in greeting, smiling.

'What are you doing here at this time?' he asked accusingly. 'I woke you before I went out. You should be at work.'

'You forgot your flask. I brought it.'

She was a big girl, standing awkwardly, holding out his flask over the fence. He saw that her dress was too small for her, clinging to heavy breasts and thighs. That it was too thin for the day. She embarrassed him.

'Put it down. Leave it there,' he said, quickly. 'I can't take it now, can I?'

'No. I'm sorry.'

She was always sorry. He felt impelled to say 'Thanks for bringing it.'

'No trouble.'

'Why aren't you at work?' He looked at her suspiciously.

'I was sick.'

'Were you?' She seemed very robust and healthy: an outdoor girl with apples in her cheeks, her mother would have said. She was a tree in bloom, sturdy and handsome. All unconscious of the cold, she stood, rubbing one foot up and down her leg, leaving a smear of mud. Mouse shy, she was afraid to go, afraid to stay.

He turned back to his raking and in doing so, noticed the other men watching Rosemary with sidelong, covetous glances.

'Dad?'

'Well?' He looked over his shoulder and she was reminded of a horse, eyes wild, ears laid back. 'Go away. Go away' he thought desperately.

'Nothing,' she said. 'I'll get off to work then.'

He watched her go down the hill and shrugged in exasperation. He was not a bad man. The men who worked for him thought him very calm and quiet. He aroused no antagonism in them. His speech was usually gentle with the occasional glimpse of an oblique, wry humour which they appreciated. He was always tactful with strangers. Only with his daughter could he allow the mask of his customary civility to slip. Consequently it was at once a relief and an irritation to be with her.

She went down the track to the cottage. Looking in her purse to see if she had change for the bus, she was irresistibly drawn to the photograph in the card compartment. At least once a day she found herself staring at it. It was a cheap one taken in a station booth. There had been four for twenty pence. Her own face seemed large and vacant to her, like a full and witless moon. Her companion was a good-looking boy with a clever, beaky face. He was screwing up his mouth and crossing his eyes for the camera. She remembered the sensation of his arm around her, fingers deftly squirming up inside her nylon blouse, his too-long nails catching at the fabric, catching at her flesh. 'A nice warm girl' he had said, chuckling in her ear. What was his name? Johnnie? Bobby? She had met him at a dance. Later he had taken her to a pub, a city pub with carpets and soft music and little tablets of pink soap in the ladies. She remembered all that but she could not remember his name. In his small flat with its debris of wet towels, cigarette ends, dirty clothes, her mind had been fuzzy with unaccustomed alcohol; too happy, overwhelmed by his welcome attention. Her body, hungry for affection, had clung much too closely to this stranger. She almost smiled at the memory. Then the cool ascetic face of her father came into her mind. 'Why aren't you at work?'

'Because I'm sick. Because I think I'm pregnant.'

How could one say such things? How could such things be? They must not be. She began to walk blindly around the little kitchen, her hands pressed to her temples as though something were hurting her there. He had carried her on his shoulders when she was small, showing her birds and trees and flowers. He had walked with his hands holding her small feet, firmly. Her mother had been alive. She had been safe. How could she ever tell him? She stumbled against the table and banged her legs. Then she sat down and resting face in her hands, began to cry. Presently she dried her eyes, washed her hot cheeks at the sink and went out to catch her bus. She was embarrassed. The conductor would see that she had been crying.

In the park, Martin raised his eyes to the birches. They were his favourite tree with their white paper bark, their drooping twigs that fashioned the spring-time leaves into veils of coined light, a dazzling gold. And now they were golden again but with the deeper nostalgic yellow of autumn.

Rosemary had been a gentle child. But adolescence had not favoured her. She had become clumsy, heavy, diffident. Even her name seemed too light and pretty for her solid, reproachful presence. 'I'm sorry' she told him all the time. He had no sympathy for her. He no longer knew how to speak to her.

'These birches' he said, 'They'll have to come down sometime. Getting past it.' The trees were so old that their bark had grown very dark, gnarled and irregular.

'Not much you can do with birches' said one of his companions. 'They make good kindling. No heartwood though. One way and another it's been a bad year for trees.'

Tom Pow (1950 –)

Voices: Four Meditations and a Lament
(On words scratched on the windows of Croick Church in Ross-shire)

1. GLENCAL PEOPL WAS IN THE CHURCHYARD HERE
From Maeshowe to Pompey; from Lascaux to Tobruk:
the ancient mark of momentary presence,
the signature of ghosts. With their absence they paid
for this gaunt landscape, those who sought shelter
in the churchyard, too pious to enter the church itself.
Lit by small fires in the damp, tented graveyard,
the peat-cutting hand cut into the glass. He signed
in another tongue to reach another shore:
they had been broken on their own, their name, a song   10
already fading. I can still catch his breath
as fist and flint loop across the small diamond pane.
This is harder than breaking rocks! But it must be said.

2. MURDER WAS IN THE YEAR 1845
Call a spade a spade. There are many ways to skin
a rabbit and none knew more of them than they did.
First you must kill it. Deal in facts as the graveyard does:
birth, death – murder. This voice is the bitter whisper
in the wind: you can't shake it this end of the glen.
Though the murder written of here didn't happen here,   20
as the lament that sings in Wounded Knee was composed
many years before it, and the murder of Kurds
driven like deer was in someone's eyes long before it.
Ten years before Thoreau split the godless world –
on one hand there is suffering, on the other
the 'quiet desperation' through which we live our lives –
this, painfully, was scratched into the wind.

3. GLENCALVIE PEOPLE THE WICKED GENERATION
As if they were another species, someone
from *The Times* spoke for them to the wider world,   30
told of the wretched spectacle they'd made leaving
their land at last, refugees with carts of children,
the poor supporting the helpless poor. Anon wrote:
If such as happened here transpired in the south
there would be outrage. (His pen; their flint.) But they
being damned, damned themselves. Though they grew like rowans
in the rock of the land, their spirits cracked
like firs without it. This voice is the saddest fiction
and they took it to the grave. The wretched of the earth –
shaking the journalist's hand, he thought, like children.   40

4. GLENCALVIE IS A WILDERS
Passing over a swell of lonely hills that sap
the earlier green of the strath, black cloud shadows
like lids in the sky, close on clear runs of sunlight.

The rubble of an ancient broch can give no shelter here,
nor the ruined sheepfolds pinned to the hills.
The faint light still catches the last of their voices
muted by horse chestnut, sycamore and ash,
though the wind soughing through the tall spruce bites
back the last word. Their backs turn from you now, their carts
move off and they fade, leaving not the pristine world   51
of Walden, but a hard land that once gave shelter
turned into a land of ghosts, a wilders . . .

CODA: LAMENT
It is above all and beyond all doubt a doleful song,
characterised by a melismatic note, a monotonous tone,
appearing to involve a repetitive attempt
at a drone-like narration of some overwhelmingly sad and disturbing events
which seem to have affected the home.

The singer's inner agitation is clearly shown   60
in the way his face appears drained and drawn,
with a fixed smile as ironic accompaniment for such a doleful song.

One is left with the lasting impression
of a man who has been battling with tears too long;
but who, even in exhaustion, cannot cease his lament.
His is the haunting voice of peoples whose futures are rent,
whose stolen past cannot come again.
          It is above all a doleful song.

(From the observations of a musicologist
on an untranslated song by an Aché
Indian whose tribe faces systematic
genocide in Paraguay.)

Love at the (Bronx) Zoo

We walk the icy paths
past frozen ponds, snowed-in enclosures,
where reeds like drifting porcupine
and black huts are all that show.

In the dim warmth of an animal house,
we linger by a tank
with a sandy-coloured,
soft-shelled turtle, the size
of my spread hand. From the long spoon
of its head, nostrils stick out   10
like tiny binoculars. Eyes,
two silvery stains. When it rises
from the dark green weed, its fins,
like sycamore seeds, brush the window
we peer through. So close is it
and so angled, we see

the thin loop of its down-turned mouth;
almost fancy it would speak . . .

Back in the Bronx, we don't know
which blind-eyed alley to turn down;   20
eventually are wrong anyway. We ride around –
a fly caught in deadly nightshade – trying
to reclaim the rim of the highway
past burned-out buildings, waste-ground;
a brazier licking the chill
off some winos.

A battered blue cadillac jerks
to a stop in front of us. Rusted panels
shake; red tail lights glare
from corroded fins. We sit tight   30
as the black man's black curses plume
into the winter air. We turn to each other –
sudden neophytes, who might – sleepless, speechless,
in the dark cage of night – hold their soft bodies
close; fear
for love's survival.

Raymond Vettese (1950 –)

Prologue

Ae nicht I sat by mysel at the fire
and thocht. Nae soond in the street forbyes★   except
the wun blawin thro the telephone wire.
A quarter-muin gied but sma licht, starns,
in clood, barely shone: a dour compromise
'twixt soond, silence, dairk, licht –
the ootward cast o the state o my harns★,   brains
catched in a swither, whiles★ shair o the richt,   sometimes
whiles thrawed★ wi doot . . . this maitter's fasht★ me lang, twisted/troubled
th' uprisin o Scots, och, I micht be wrang.   10

Mebbe aa this cuid but connach★ braith.   waste
There's monie a gow★ gaed aifter a wile,   fool
fu-shair o't, yet fun', disjaskit★, sair daith,   dejected
no hecht★ o life. Ay, and sae it micht be   promise
wi mysel, and my foot'rin phraisie★ style: flowery
snashgab★, nocht mair, a silly dashelt★ screed,   snarling/exhausted
bummlin aboot, barmy on words, skinkin★ orra bree –   pouring, mixing
ach, the thocht o the waste is whit I maist dreid,
waste o span hundin a deein cause,
my thick bluid dreepin clause by clause.   20

Whit's the point in this dootsum* endeavour   doubtful
tae bring back whit's lang gane, whit purpose?
Mebbe the fowk wha say it's gane forever
are richt, and mebbe I should turn awa
frae sic daft notions. Yet I'm thirlt* til this,   bound
I canna gie it owre, it's stuck in me
like faith, ayont reason. It's my weird's* caa*,   fate's/call
or sae I blaw, tae shaw whit it micht be,
this leid*, yased aricht. That's mebbe a fraik*   language/whim
but's the brag that sets me oot on this raik*.   30   path

I hae a vision o Scotland set free
and freedom and language tae me is ane.
I hae a vision that Scotland micht be
itsel again, its present and its past
souderet* for the future's sake, tho the pain   united
o Freedom's no easy nor wantin doot
and whiles I dae nocht but staun aghast
at the thocht o't, feel the strength sypin oot
frae sickerness, as I dae this hauf-nicht
fu o gloamin unease, an' dootsum licht.   40

The toon is quiet, only noo and then
swippert* feet dunt* in the tuim* street ayont.   nimble/pound/empty
I sit and think on the likely again,
speir* the chances o mendin, the chances   question
o hinmaist decline, a doonfaa no alunt*   lit
wi ae laist leam, but dairk wi dreich* smirr   dreary
o lichtless silence. Nae gleg* hope dances   sharp
on sic a nicht whaun nae sunk life can stir,
yet I maun rise abuin the lair o wanrufe*   unease
or slutter* in't, wae-gowpin, a slottery coof*.   50   flounder/fool

I set my compass tae a fremmit* airt,   foreign, strange
reenge* aifter yon driven starn, let it lead   search
whaur it will, ayont stoundin fearfu hairt;
fling aff my trauchelt* thochts and stramp oot   tired
on the lang traik til the truth in my heid
that winna be lowsed* save in words like these.   released
It's aiblins* daft, this ploiter* o pursuit   perhaps/floundering
owre bitter acres whaur the braith micht freeze,
but it's the ae gait*, I doot, for me.   way
Somewhaur the bield* and the green maun be.   60   shelter

My Carrion Words

In deep
o dairk sleep
I dreamt my words
gaithert like stairvin birds
on a bare tree
and skreiched owre me

wi carrion hoast★:   cough
Lost! Lost!

And syne
I ran, wad tine★   10   lose
that greetin
o things forleeten★   lost
i the muckle dairk,
but aye the cark★   concern
souched ahent★:   behind
Tak tent★! Tent!   care

Whaun I woke
the day spoke
wi anither voice
that croodled douce★ choice: 20   pleasant
give up this nonsense,
this pretence;
what's gone is gone, here's
English for contemporary ears.

But ach, I doot
I'm no cut oot
for sic mense★   gentility, honour
(that's dowit★ leid★ for 'common sense');   low/speech
the auld coorse Scotland's in me,
an' the bare tree   30
an' the stairvin birds:
frae sic as them, frae yon, my carrion words.

Andrew Greig (1951 –)

Annie, in Spring

Life a dream? They're misinformed
who never laid a finger on your skin.

When you wake in spring
the fuzz on the pussy willow
and the willow itself are one:
nothing out of focus here.

The sun on our shoulders blooms, passes,
what more should we ask of light?
What is seen, is.
The eyes have it.   10

Now the sheen on the chestnut
and the chestnut itself
embrace in her hair,
there is no further waking.

Annie, in November

A last pibroch in South Queensferry

Enough fourteen-bar compressed & gurgling
pibrochs for you, Annie, whoever you were
(I mythed you). There are affairs
more pressing than love, say they who have it.

So look around, The satellite disc
shines on the new deli; library hours are cut;
my neighbours roof leaks into mine
(would we were separate, or one) . . .

The Chancellor parks his belly on TV,
proclaims Auld Scotia is a bag of wind   10
squeezed in History's oxter*. Behind my town   armpit
the fields are burning, it is time to leave.

Rush hour. The trucks point North and whine
the wild notes, the low sun splits
the Road Bridge like a reed.

Aide Memoire

Being eighteen,
light-headed, hormonal, daft,
there is much to be said for it.
I said it at length
on the Fife coast that winter.

I donned my Doric cap,
took a stiff whisky,
walked out the door.
In town the lights were blazing
but no one was at home.   10

What of the white line
I toed by the sea?
The wind blew apart
the clouds round the moon
and I stepped through.

Billy Kay (1951 –)

Lambing in Easter Ross

Anither day's dawin
on the stibbled parks
abuin Dornoch's caller★ watters.   fresh
In the park o the new born,
brockie★ faced lambkins   black and white
loup, stacher an totter
ahint the buirdly★ shanks   solid
o hooseproud yowes
playin an soukin.

Glisked abuin the   10
muirlan braes o Struie
a formation
o sea gulls
splicin white stucco
in the mornin blue o the lift★.   sky

The faa wes free
the wings wes swept
an the crack
o the brockie's craig★   throat
wes quaet   20
claught
in a forlorn frisk
that landit
gralloched★   disemboweled
wi the ruggin★   tearing
o six beaks,
fleain awaa
caain
in a flauchter
o reid, white an yella.   30
Twa scarlet trails
belly an thrapple★,   throat
efterbirth, efterlife.

In the park of the unborn
aa is still.

Frank Kuppner (1951 –)

Kuppner is the most playful of modern Scottish writers, endlessly ready to subvert his reader's expectations. Sometimes this takes the guise of a Lawrence Sterne-like mocking of literary form, sometimes a Lewis Carroll-ish assault on logic and language themselves. Whether this gamesmanship is at the service of a serious, insightful view of our irrational universe the reader may decide for himself. Kuppner has made his distinctive mark in the novel as well as in verse.

The Intelligent Observation of Naked Women

i.

Unable to sleep, I have turned the bedside lamp on.
Did she too once catch sight of that photograph above her?
That picture of stars above my bed was surely there three years ago;
She must have lain beneath that picture of the stars.

ii.

As they were before the creation of the earth,
Apparently the furthest galaxies yet photographed;
It is clear to me she must have seen that picture then;
Did she not react to the picture pinned beside it?

iii.

An exquisite-faced beauty culled from a chance old magazine;
Hungarian, I think; 1965; showing a tiny breast in profile.   10
At one point she reared up, which was impressive, but puzzled me;
I realised later she was imitating that other woman.

iv.

Surely because her own breasts were so much bigger,
I did not understand that till months had passed;
On the day when someone pouted towards a man on the continent,
How many dark-haired, unbreasted girls were walking down our streets?

v.

But that night she was for a long while motionless;
Lying back against a pillow, in quiet, grown display;
Of course my eyes never lifted to the stars,
Not to the stars, not to pictures of stars.   20

vi.

And a few sighs from a tossed head, in the absence of words,
Filled through the universe I was present in
Beyond the whispers of the nuclear stars
Breaking through their long inaudibility.

vii.

A sort of starlight in a little room that night –
A small bed, salmon pink walls, heaps of books everywhere –
And particles drifting in from neighbourly galaxies,
Through the walls, through those lying on the bed. onwards –

viii.

Uninfluenced, unimpressed, not stopping for the least look,
Out through my red curtains and into the universe,   30
Through blackness, through other rooms, through blackness
Through blackness, through blackness, through other planets,

ix.

Other rooms containing a near identical joy,
Or the last representatives of some taller race;
Ah, these interludes in the prevailing emptiness!
Such brief interruptions in the blackness, like us.

x.

Not remembering the leading-up events,
But that suddenly she lay in such a giving attitude,
Her face lit by an unaccustomed confidence,
Nor how it ended, two or three minutes later.   40

xi.

And when, enchanted by so many details,
I reached out to touch a part of her body –
A swelling cleft formed between her thighs at the sheet –
The universe trembled, and tried to end, but did not.

xii.

A tentative voice from beneath the stars said 'please don't';
I brought back my insane, exploring hand,
Back into its own small world, landing dizzily on a sheet,
Amazed that such vast distances could be covered so easily.

xiii.

The explosion at the centre of our galaxy,
Which (some say) has for long ripped relentlessly outwards,   50
Hesitated in its progress for a few moments,
Letting a slight shock ripple by in the opposite direction.

xiv.

I think the room right next to me at that time was still empty;
I do not know who, if anyone, was in the room directly above us;
Why do I feel that, in a southern suburb of the town,
your mother was lying awake during those moments?

xv.

My past self wandered blithely through the room next to us,
Narrowly avoiding bumping into loud furniture;
It tore a picture of stars from a magazine;
It gasped, put it upon the wall, then largely forgot about it.   60

xvi.

A sort of happy terror in gazing at such a sight,
Of course entirely unlike the joy of looking at you,
Who are not a star, more complex than a star,
But somehow this joy reminds me of that terror.

xvii.

For how long did the interiors of stars
Labour to produce their earliest complexities?
A quick glance into my eyes, and then away;
There were no quick glances during that long cooling.

xviii.

The structure of the female cannot but be an object of wonder;
As might befit the daughters of the stars,   70
Expertly inheriting the family enchantment,
Losing the sheer size, but little of the brightness.

xix.

Or that exquisite entrance through which any daughter of hers
Would emerge into this world of light and textbooks,
Where most stars are still hurrying away from her,
And infinite nearer ones still come towards.

xx.

But a lifetime's acceleration will not bring them into sight,
Even if such possible daughters do reach a lifetime;
I will not talk of them as being imprisoned within her;
Are thoughts of me imprisoned inside her head?   80

xxi.

Behind her fringe; behind her delightful brow;
If every spark caused by me from nerve to nerve
Were to be turned loose into that other space as stars,
Would the sky above our house that night have been any brighter?

xxii.

Would anyone at that silent hour of the morning,
Crossing the high bridge nearby, beside the church,
Have been amazed by a sudden luminance in the sky,
And rush home trembling, to listen to music I love?

xxiii.

Or anyone caught on that stairway not far away,
Whose picturesqueness she remarked on once, months afterwards,
Have been disturbed by a sudden overwhelming blackness,   91
And forget for a moment his or her own ecstasy?

xxiv.

Oh, hydrogen, hydrogen, why do you so assail me?
To produce helium is no doubt within your sphere,
But why produce transparent nail varnish too?
Why were the stars a preparation for this?

xxv.

That lightness should become such tactile flesh;
That a whirl of plasma should smile at me;
That the throwing out of metals by a dying star
Should sit down on my chair in the morning, to put on her tights.

xxvi.

The stars beyond pulsing their various hues,   101
And her wine-coloured bra resting on heaps of my papers;
That which has cradled her breasts scenting the flickers of my imagination;
Far away from this, they grow too fully.

xxvii.

The intelligent observation of naked women
Is, besides, to glimpse an alternative universe;
The outline of her breasts is confirmation enough
That distances are not the only distances.

xxviii.

Within touching distance is also infinity;
Her clothes discarded like our neighbour galaxies;   110
The ease with which she and the morning reassemble them;
The ability to open a closed door.

xxix.

She left behind her cigarettes and a lighter;
I found them and, against instructions, ran after her;
I met her at the bus-stop, and we talked,
Moving back into the doorway of a shop.

xxx.

The sky was blue, and feigned an absence of stars;
The pictures did not whimper inside my locked room;
My fingers weaved figures in the cool air,
Beside her body, but now only beside.   120

xxxi.

The captain of the spacecraft passing nearby
Scrutinized the scene casually in his viewfinder,
Decided there was no sign of intelligent life,
Re-examined his charts, and went on for better places.

xxxii.

Inside my room the air particles danced for joy;
The sheets ecstatically re-arranged themselves;
I bought a newspaper and took it back to my room;
Sitting in the chair where she had sat, I began to read it.

xxxiii.

And the same eyes which had so caressed her body,
An arms length to the right, long hours ago,   130
Now ran over reports from the other world,
Seeing wars refracted by the shape of her navel.

xxxiv.

I thought myself stationary in my little room;
Herself travelling back to a nearby room;
The planet moving, and its motion moving;
All things moving much as they always have.

xxxv.

Sitting on a chair, reading a newspaper;
The low, soft chair on which she had sat earlier;
Which had been in that room since first I rented it;
My happiness the aftermath of who knows what feelings.   140

xxxvi.

What grey divorces have lapped against the walls of his room?
What seas have slowly rotted into intelligence?
Where were her various sighs already by my reading?
Reverberations still rippled from wall to wall.

xxxvii.

Oh, in the background to the sound of stars,
There still exists a faint remnant of noise
From the first explosion which may have started all this;
Which some believe was not the first explosion.

xxxviii.

After all, I twice heard her sharply intaking breath;
So why should the universe not also breathe twice?   150
Space so large and dark and her arm-bangle so precisely placed;
How do we ever overcome the distances involved?

xxxix.

Nearness is nearness only up to a point;
Although better by far she should be in the same room
Than lost unspoken to elsewhere in this city,
It is still a private cosmos whose foot I touched.

xl.

It is still a sort of star lying beneath stars;
A star put into human, breathing shape;
A star which could choose who should enjoy its light;
A star that could think and laugh and be hurtful.   160

xli.

A star which could disappear for over a year,
Then pass by suddenly in a street significant to us,
Throwing a normal visit to the theatre
Into a few hours of shaken recovery.

xlii.

I am using her to overpraise the stars,
For no star ever had such liquid eyes;
And words developed from their careless fusion,
Some of which I wish could be unspoken.

xliii.

That night we talked below a picture of stars;
A little turning planet took us into the morning;   170
On less than a dot to the nearest other such planet,
I whispered endearments approximately into her ear.

xliv.

In whatever direction I turn there is such richness:
In the numbers of planets caught in the curves of stars;
In the number of rooms in this not very long street;
The number of hairs in the scented galaxy I drifted into.

xlv.

How nonchalantly the wind rearranges her hair;
As nonchalantly as it turns into flame
Different visitors from beyond the earth;
Is there no light where her hair was strewn across my pillow?

xlvi.

Or was it her whom I saw in that building yesterday,   181
Or one of the phantoms I mistake for her;
Her face much changed, about the mouth particularly,
But the architecture of that face remaining.

xlvii.

If, on that morning, I thought of the future at all,
It was as the present continued, something miraculous;
What sort of inappropriate world is this
Where so much misery follows such a night?

xlviii.

Is it three years, nearly, which have altered that face?
Something of the tiredness of her morning features   190
Might thus have been imitated by misfortune;
How much I would have preferred her morning features.

xlix.

So much space around us, and yet we lie to each other;
So much silence, and yet we add silence onto it;
On so many mornings when I could have watched her face,
I have woken up to the pictures on the wall.

l.

And I have ignored the pictures on the wall too;
I have passed days beside pictures of the galaxies
Without too great a thought of the worlds involved,
As once I spent a night, a few nights, too few nights.   200

Brian McCabe (1951 –)

The Blind

The blind old men who come arm in arm
On good-smelling days to the park,
Grateful to the girl who brings them
Since they seldom have the chance
Of a slow, recollective game of bowls,
The sun that signs their faces
With smudge-like marks where eyes were
Suggests to their memories a notion
Of green, and summer days ago.
Taking pleasure from the silence of grass   10
And the weight of the wood in the hand,
They engross themselves in the game
They play by sound intuition:
The girl is young, sighted.
She stands at the far end of darkness
And claps her hands – once, twice –
And then the first bowler stoops,
As if about to kneel and be blessed,
Then throws to her clapping hands.
As the dark wood is travelling the green   20
She waits, motionless, and waits
As if by any slight move she might alter
The swing and slowing of the bowl.
When it halts, she bows, she measures,
Then calls its distance, its 'time':
'Seven feet, at four o'clock.'
Again she claps her hands.
Another player stoops, lets go . . .
This time it comes closer, close enough
To enter the young girl's shadow.   30
When it kisses the jack, there's a 'cloc'.

The old men smile.

It Was Not Just

a denuded tree a ravaged forest
an eye locked in a socket of ice
not just those delicate horrors
skeletons of birds for example
glued to the iron earth no
it was not just our winter
baring its teeth in the usual way
what was it then what was it
that bowed our heads as we waited

clung like a cold sweat to our coins   10
made us less than naked in our clothes
between our eyelids it slid
veiled our sight with its ignorance
inevitably it leaked into our minds
blotting thought
it seeped at last into our hearts
extinguishing feeling

                        what was it

it was not just that winter no
that winter did not cause it   20

call it our poverty our hardship
in any case it was not just that

The Face

He didn't want to see the face.

It was like a railway tunnel, except this tunnel sloped down the way, down through the dripping darkness, down into the deep, dark ground. He could see the dark shine of the rails and he could feel the ridges of the wooden sleepers through the soles of his gymshoes. It was very dark. He was glad his father was there with him.

It would be good to go back up to the daylight now, where the miners were sitting round a brazier, eating their pieces and drinking hot tea from big tins with wire handles. One of them had given him a piece and let him drink some tea from his tin and had pointed to different birds and told him their names, while the other miners talked about the pit and how it was closing. One of them had said he'd be quite happy never to see the face again.

He remembered the first time he'd heard about it: his father came in late from the pit and walked into the kitchen very slowly and sat down still with his coat on. Then he took off his bunnet and looked at it and put it on the kitchen table and talked to his mother in the quiet voice not like his usual voice. Like he couldn't say what he had to say, like when some of the words get swallowed. Because somebody had got killed at the face, John Ireland had got killed at the face, so he'd had to go to Rosewell to tell his wife. That was why he was late. Then his mother took a hanky from her apron pocket and sat down and started crying and his father put his hands on her shoulders and kissed her like it was Christmas except this was a different kind of kiss. Then his father looked up at him and nodded to him to tell him to go through to the other room, so he went through and watched TV and wondered how the face had killed John Ireland, the man who ran the boxing gym for boys, and how something terrible could make people need to kiss each other.

He could hear the water dripping from the roof of the tunnel and trickling down the walls and the scrape and crunch of his father's boots on the ground. They sounded too loud, but in the dark you had to hold on to sounds, like when you shut your eyes and pretended to be blind, hold on to them to stop yourself hearing what was behind them, where it was like the darkness was listening.

Every few steps he could see the wooden props against the walls, but they were nearly as dark as the walls. And he could just make out the shapes of the wooden sleepers and the rails, but he didn't like the darkness between the sleepers and between the props. If you looked at darkness like that too long you started seeing things in it: patterns, shapes, faces . . .

He listened to his father's voice. It sounded too loud, and crackly like a fire, but you could hold on to it. He was telling him about the bogies that used to run up and down on the rails in the old days, taking the coal up to the pit-head. It was good to hear his father's voice talking about the old days, but he didn't like the sound of the bogies. He asked what a bogie was and listened as his father told him it was sort of like a railway carriage on a goods train. He knew that anyway, but he wanted to hear his father telling him again, just in case.

There were other bogeys-bogeymen. He asked if there were bogeymen down the pit. His father laughed and said that there weren't. But he knew different, he knew that it was dark enough down here for bogeymen, especially now the word had been said out loud.

Sometimes if you said a word over and over again it started to sound different. It started to mean something else, to mean what it sounded like it meant. Then, if you kept on saying it over and over again, it started to not mean anything, the word started to be a thing. And the thing didn't mean anything except what it was.

He tried it now, saying it under his breath over and over again . . . But before the word could lose its meaning, his father had stopped walking. He stopped too and turned, glad that they were going to go back up to the light, to the ordinary world.

'You go on.'

At first he wondered what his father meant, then he knew: he wanted him to keep on walking down into the dark. Alone. He pretended not to have heard and took a step towards the start of the tunnel, then he felt his father's hand on his shoulder and his heart pounding in his chest.

'Down ye go.'

He didn't move. He didn't say anything, hoping his father would lose his patience with him and change his mind.

'Are ye feart?'

'Naw, but . . . '

But what? He turned to the darkness. He could still see the rails and the props and the sleepers, but only just. He didn't want to see the face.

'Go on.'

He started walking down into the darkness. He had sometimes seen it in his dreams, after his father had come home late and spoken in the quiet voice to his mother about John Ireland: at first there was just the dark, the pitch-black dark that was blacker than coal, because even coal wasn't always black, because sometimes it was blue or grey, and sometimes it had a dark shine to it, like the cover of the Bible, and sometimes the coal had seams – of fool's gold, or the thin, brittle, silvery seams of mica – but the darkness in the dream had no shine to it, no seams, it was pure black. Then you felt it there like a shadow in the dark, a shadow that went long and went wide, went thick like a wall and went thin like a thread, then the shadow had the shape of a man and the man had a face and the face was the face of John Ireland.

He stopped walking, turned around and looked back at his father. He called to him and asked if he'd gone far enough.

'Further.'

It was good to hear his father's voice behind him, but it didn't last long enough to hold on to. Why didn't his father walk down further too? Why did he have to walk down on his own? Sometimes his father liked him to walk in front of him along the street. 'Walk in front,' he'd say, 'where I can see you.' Like the time he'd taken him to the gym to see John Ireland and he'd seen John Ireland's face. It looked like a bull-dog's, with a flattened nose and a crushed ear and big, bloodshot eyes. In the dream it looked worse. In the dream, somehow you forgot it was the face of an old boxer. John Ireland had given him a pair of boxing gloves. He'd tied them together and put them round his neck on the way home. And his father had told him to walk in front, where he could see him. But that wasn't the reason, not the real reason he wanted him to walk in front. It was because he wanted to dream about his son being a champion boxer. He hadn't gone back to the gym because his mother had put her foot down, but he still put the gloves on sometimes and pretended to be a champion boxer. Now there wasn't a gym because of what had happened at the face.

Maybe it wouldn't be like the face in his dream, but he still didn't want to see it. He stopped and turned around. He could still see the dark shape of his father against the light from the start of the tunnel. He shouted to him and waited.

'Go on.'

His father's voice faded to an echo.

He turned and walked further down into the dark, the pitch-black dark even blacker than coal, then he felt it there, a shadow in the dark . . . He stopped, turned and shouted to his father. He could still see the dim greyish light from the start of the tunnel, but now he couldn't see his father. He shouted out again. His own voice echoed and he heard the fear in it, then all there was was the listening darkness all around and the pounding of his heart. The shadow had the shape of a man and the man had a face . . .

As he turned to run away he was lifted in the air and his father's laughter filled his ear. He was laughing and saying he was proud, proud of him because he'd walked down on his own, proud because now he was a man.

He rubbed the bus window with his hand and looked out at the big black wheel of the pit. He watched it getting smaller as the bus pulled away, till it was out of sight.

'Da? Why are they gonnae shut the Pit? Is there nae coal left in it?'

'There's plenty coal.'

'How then?'

'The government wants it shut.'

'Where'll ye go tae work then?'

'Mibbe in Bilston Glen.'

'Is that another pit?'

His father nodded. He waited a minute, then he asked:

'Da? Has it got a face as well?'

'Aye, it's got a face.'

'Is it like the face in your pit?'

His father shrugged.

'Much the same.'

'Da . . . Ah *saw* it.'

'What?'

'The face.'

His father shook his head and smiled at him, the way he did when he thought he was too young to understand something.

'Ah did see it!'

'Oh ye did, did ye? What did it look like then, eh?'

'It looked like the man who ran the gym.'

And he knew he'd said something very important when his father stopped smiling, turned pale, opened his mouth to say something but didn't say anything, then stared and stared at him – as if he couldn't see him at all, but only the face of the dead man.

From the Diary of Billy Bible

MONDAY

Today I am in Therapy again it being Monday. I am in Therapy five days a week now because I am good. On Saturday and Sunday I am in the ward because Therapy is shut. There is nothing to do in the ward so I do nothing except what the nurses tell me. If I had a friend like Peter in the ward it would be better but I have no friend like Peter in the ward. In Therapy I do pictures mostly of Christ Our Saviour on the cross. Mister Cuthbert calls them crucifixions. I did so many Mister Cuthbert had to put them in the store room. Then he said I was to stop doing those crucifixions and do something else. Then I started doing the tunnels. Mister Cuthbert said they all look the same but when I do one I remember something different from the last one. Mister Cuthbert says I am a born artist. I think I will do another tunnel today.

TUESDAY

I have been reading the Bible my father sent me a long time ago being a minister of God. He sent me the Bible and a letter and a steel clip to stop wet dreams. It was just after I came here. I started putting the steel clip on like I did at home before I went to bed at night. Because I am good I am good. But I showed it to one of the male nurses and asked him to guess what it was for like I asked my friend Peter a long time ago. The male nurse took it away from me when he found out what it was for and ever since then it has been hard to be good. But I still have the Bible and I always take it with me everywhere in my jacket pocket. Once I lost it but I got it back again. It has my name on the page before Genesis. The part I like to read most is the Creation. I am always reading it so the nurses call me Billy Bible. It says the earth was without form and void and darkness was upon the face of the deep. Peter is like that now without form and void now that he is dead. I think I will do another tunnel today.

Mister Cuthbert says if I do more tunnels he will have to put them in the store room with the crucifixions. I don't like the pictures I do being put in the store room. When I want to look at them I have to get a key from Mister Cuthbert. I don't like going into the store room because of the darkness upon the face of the deep and the rats. Mister Cuthbert tried to kill the rats with cobalt blue poison but they ate the poison and got stronger. They eat anything the rats. They eat the wool and the paper in the store room and the foam rubber the sewing women put inside the soft toys they make. Sometimes you are in the bathroom and when you go to wash your hands you see their teethmarks in the bar of soap. It is light in the bathroom but in the store room there are no windows. When you switch on the light in there it takes a little while to come on. It is called a strip light that light in the store room. I don't like being in the store room with the darkness and the rats before the light comes on. I don't like the no windows darkness you get in the store room and some other places for instance the ward. The ward has great big windows but you still get the no windows darkness when you wake up in the middle of the night after a wet dream. Then it is all around you everywhere all over the face of the deep. Then you see a torch coming down between the beds and the night nurses come and say keep it quiet. I takes me a while to know it is the night nurses. I am talking to my friend Peter then I hear them saying to me it's all right Billy the train isn't coming tonight. They don't know it already has.

The tunnel has no windows. It is deep and dark in there and I am running out of black.

WEDNESDAY

Today I was taken out for an outing because I am good. Mister Cuthbert took me and four others in Therapy to an art gallery. In the art gallery Mister Cuthbert showed me a picture with three parts called a TRIPTYCH. This is what the TRIPTYCH was like. In the middle part it was Christ Our Saviour on the cross like some of mine but with details. Mister Cuthbert showed me all the details for instance the hair and the crown of thorns and the blood just above the eye. In the side parts there were a lot of little soldiers and a lot of little women all crying. On the way back to the mini-bus I saw a butcher's shop. There were dead beasts without heads hanging from steel hooks on a big steel rail.

This afternoon I did Christ Our Saviour on the cross with details for instance the hair and the steel hooks and the blood above the eye. Mister Cuthbert put it up but he took it down again because it made one of the sewing women scream out loud and throw her felt-work snake on the floor. Mister Cuthbert took it down again and put it in the store room with the others. I am worried because if the rats eat Christ Our Saviour on the cross they will get stronger than people. I saw one today it was big and brown like burnt sienna with a long tail. It ran along the wall in therapy and I think it went into the store room.

Tomorrow I think I will do a TRIPTYCH with three parts. In the middle tunnel I will do the inside of a church with the minister of God reading the Bible. In the side parts the night nurses coming down between the rails and me and my friend Peter all crying.

THURSDAY

Today Mister Cuthbert brought a mirror into Therapy. It was lying on a table in the pottery room when I came in. When I looked at it I saw my head dark with the light on the ceiling behind it. Mister Cuthbert says it is his mirror from his home. It has three parts like a TRIPTYCH. He brought it over to my table and he said do a self portrait Billy. He put it on my table against the wall and it is still there. He took away the three tunnels and he brought me a clean sheet of paper. I said I have never done a self portrait of anyone before so he showed me all the details in the mirror.

I don't look the same as before. I have not looked in a mirror for a long time and now I look different. I am still neat and tidy. I put water on my hair before I comb it and I wash myself every night and every morning and I fold my clothes because I am good. But now my shirt is torn at the collar and my jacket is dirty. One leg of my glasses is held on with a piece of elastoplast and now they don't sit right on my nose. My eyes are staring and dark like the cover of the Bible and my face has no details for instance the hair. The head has no blood no crown of thorns and my face is without form and void.

I think I will do a self portrait with three parts like a TRIPTYCH. In the side parts a lot of little sewing women making soft toys and a lot of little Mister Cuthberts all crying.

FRIDAY

Mister Cuthbert said to finish the self portrait but I am doing a tunnel. I did the eyes the hair and the mouth the ears then I saw it was my friend Peter not me in the mirror. I told Mister Cuthbert but he said it looked quite like me and to finish it. So I started the tunnel on top of it. You can still see Peter's face in the tunnel it is the face of the deep. I can't remember anything before the tunnel but when I do one I remember something more. This time I remembered something more about the tunnel and the steel clip to stop wet dreams.

It is harder to be good now without the steel clip before you go to bed and you wake up in the middle of your sleep. The steel clip had little teeth that cut into you where you were dreaming the wet dream and it woke you up before the train came. But our suffering is nothing to the suffering of Christ Our Saviour on the cross.

One of the male nurses took it away when I asked him to guess like Peter and I have never seen it again.

I wasn't supposed to go where the tunnel was my father said not to go there being a minister of God.

Peter did not want to go through the tunnel because of the darkness and the rats. Then I showed him the steel clip and I said guess what it is for. I told my friend Peter I would tell him about the steel clip and what it was for if he came through the tunnel. I liked my friend Peter because he was scared of my father.

I was bad in the tunnel when the train came I pushed my friend Peter into the deep and now that is where he is.

I am in hospital to make me good again. Christ Our Saviour is with me on the cross in the store room with the darkness and the rats. Peter is with me in the tunnel where I put his face instead of the mirror.

Mister Cuthbert came over to see the self portrait and when he saw it he shook his head.

MONDAY

Today I am in Therapy again it being Monday. Last night I had a dream and I woke up in the middle of the tunnel. I saw a torch far away and I thought it was the men coming for Peter. It was the night nurses coming down between the beds to tell me to keep it quiet. They said it's all right Billy the train isn't coming tonight. They don't know it already has.

I have been reading the Bible my father sent me a long time ago. And a letter and a steel clip to guess what it is for. I have still got the letter in my inside jacket pocket but I spilled the paint water on it and the words ran. It said be good and keep yourself neat and tidy Billy do what the nurses tell you Christ Our Saviour will help you read the Bible and put the steel clip on before you go to bed.

The letter is all yellow now like a piece of skin and I can't read it. I was reading the part about the Creation so the nurses call me Billy Bible. It said the earth was without form and void and darkness was upon the face of the deep. I always stop reading when I get to the deep.

Mister Cuthbert says I am a born artist. I think I will do another tunnel today.

John Glenday (1952 –)

A Dream of Gliders

Father built an airfield in the garden yesterday,
And I,
(Having ceased playing the enthusiastic child),
Laughed at him;
Told him the garden was too small.
He just pointed at the sky
Where silver wings drifted against
The bright blue air.
The hot air held them, and only held them;
Softly rocked them.   10
My brother caught two gliders with a magnet.

A curse on the dog in our dirty alley,
Which woke me rudely with its stupid bark;
Which dragged me back to
This building in an empty sky;
Which forced me to admit
Our garden could never have been big enough
After all.

Distant Relations

Great Uncle Jim ran off to sea;
but he didn't sail far. He stepped

head first from his whaler, blind drunk
on rum, in a dirty squall; and sank

through the tassled carpet of God's
infinite grey room, never to be smelled again.

My Grandmother wept into her embroidery
for her brother's short, cold life;

thinking nothing of the voyage
she was doomed to make   10

through the mouths of worms
in a ship of grass, with her name

and times carved in the sail
no winds would bend; no gust could fill.

Snow

Carefully, snow invaded,
From out of its own country,
Hidden behind the air.
All through the long night in drifting silence
The grey parachutes had come to seize my land.
Now they have turned it to their own ends,
And I am powerless but to do their will.
See how this place is made
As strange as sleep
By the enforced beauty of their gentle war.   10
Still, the faultless cycle will defeat them,
When their bones, once weightless starfish,
Round into allies for the slanted rain;
Though the memory of that doomed conquest will prevail
All sunlight long,
As the motes go tumbling through an empty house,
And drift to the farthest corners of my heart.

Making Things Dark

A dark wind lifts
the pages from my desk,
and scatters them through the open window
to the pine woods,
and the unlit fields.
There is no point in chasing after them.
I go back to my desk and begin again.

The shadow of the poem
darkens the paper.
The meaning darkens   10
in the shadow of the word.
Time absolves me
from the burden of the truth.

Why do I write? I write
to weight the pages
of my life.
I write to give the shadows depth.

Why do I write?
I write to make things dark.

Edie's Room

for Mary Stewart

Just before dawn, I was woken
by the soft hush of the dead about their work.
It was cold in her room, so cold

I could see the half-bright cloud of my life
hung out in the air between the darkness
and the moon. I can't help but fall

for the dark each time it has to go.
Its death, like any other death, leads on
from mystery towards brighter mystery.

Fire-Damp

And yet, I believe something
must sing in the heart.
I once read that when canaries
were taken underground

they would often sing back
towards what little light there was.

The Loom

What held him suspended, grey fathoms
above sleep?

Not the silent wife beside him,
two decades into strangeness,

nor the sullen youth kicking
dust into moonlight,

nor the familiar, evaporating dream
of oars threshing corn in a kingdom

without sea.
Only a hank of darkness on the untouched   10

loom, weaving a shroud
which would not be undone.

Alba

Some say she looks like an old witch,
a dark caillich★ with a cat's-tail of islands for hair.   old woman
Brine sluices the words from her cracked lips.
I say no. I say she's as fresh as these flakes
of schist and quartzite I gathered yesterday.
Some say she's barren: *'Look how they scoured*
her bairns from her womb with a dab of wool,' they say,
'and them scarce halfways down the road to birth.
The four airts★ buried them.   quarters, directions
Their cries will circle the earth like little storms.'   10
I say no. I say she's poor but whole and strong
and I've heard her children sing out in our half dark street,
barely a whisper before night.

Some say she's bad news, a temptress, a whistler on ships,
that the man who sleeps with her will wake one morning
at dusk on a hillside under the brisk rain, his pockets weighted with sand.
I say no. I say, look at me: I've slept with her all the nights of my life
and still each morning when I wake I find her tongue in my mouth.

Angus Martin (1952 –)

Malcolm MacKerral

MacKerral, that was one hard winter.
Your father died on the moor road,
his bag of meal buried under snows.
Death relieved him of his load.

Raking wilks★ with freezing fingers,   whelks
your little sisters crawled the shore,
scourged by gusting showers
until their knees were raw and sore.

Your few black cattle, thin and famished,
lay and died at the far end   10
of the draughty common dwelling.
There was little else you owned.

In the factor's oaken-panelled room
that the shafting sunlight glossed
you looked for your reflection:
you had become a ghost.

That month a stranger entered
the green cleft of the glen.

You watched him coming, from a hill,
and stabbed the earth again.   20

When he returned he brought the sheep.
At the house where you were born
you closed a door behind you.
Two hundred years had gone.

There was no end to the known land.
You looked, and there were names
on every shape around you.
The language had its homes.

Words had their lives in rivers;
they coursed them to the sea.   30
Words were great birds on mountains,
crying down on history.

Words were stones that waited
in the silence of the fields
for the voices of the people
whose tenures there had failed.

You knew those names, MacKerral;
your father placed them in your mouth
when language had no tragic power
and you ran in your youth.   40

You ran in the house of the word
and pressed your face upon the glass
and watched the mute processions
of your grave ancestors pass.

Look back on what you cannot alter.
Not a stone of it is yours to turn.
All that you leave with now:
lost words for the unborn.

Forest

For Sid Gallagher

Since I lately came to live
in an old house with a fire in it,
wood has got into my vision.

I put my saw to wood
and glance a nick, and then I cut
wood into bits that please me.

Weight and form may please me,
and I am pleased to own
what at last I have to burn.

I am a Scottish wood-collector;   10
I belong to a great tradition
of bleeding hands and thick coats.

Wood accumulates about me;
I build it into piles,
I bag it and I lug it.

I love the look of wood:
its surfaces are maps and pictures,
and staring eyes and voiceless mouths.

Wood to the end is unresisting:
it lets me lift and drag it   20
far from the place that it lay down.

Wood will never fight
the blade's truncating stroke
or scream when fire consumes it.

But I had dreams of wood.
I was alone in a high forest,
sun and seasons banished.

The trees bent down their silent heads
and closed their branches round about
and I was gathered into air.   30

I burn in my dreams of wood,
a melting torch suspended
in the dark heart of a silent forest.

Hugh Ouston (1952 –)

Redshanks

The adults screamed their springy warnings up
And down the salt-marsh grass as if language
Could change what it complained about. An hour
And inch of life, crouched in its shallow cup –
The pole round which they swung like loud brown stars –
The bony chick designed its camouflage
From silence. Only its white eyelids' flick
Admitted my caress might be the last
Sensation of these senses' life, this quick
Visit, unregretted because unasked.   10

A fortnight later, a few yards away,
The wings, the shrieks spun to a single djinn
Could not stop the killer I never saw.
The chick was warm, the still reflecting eye,
A trace of blood damp on the skull, no more
Immobile than before. Later that day
The rain had parted, flattened the unpreened
Down and the dull beak was entangled in
Grey stems, releasing the parents to fly
In widening circles to a silence learned.   20

Gannets

Position: ten miles south of Mingulay.
Night. Breakers on our port bow. Course: north-west.
The hull flexes and yaws that way. Each crest
Through slow rise, shock and endless fall away
Buries us deeper in the loud black ocean.
The wriggling heiroglyphics which the motion
Of the swell compels the masts to write appeal
To a still rose of stars from the turning wheel.

Yet by deceit we use the wind and trick
Our tacks by cheek and shoulder where we will.   10
The slow accretion of our species' skill
Through boat and man is knotted in this thick
And awkward crabwalk clawed across the chart.
Iberian patience, Viking flair, the art
Of Arab sailmakers can just devise
A progress from Atlantic waves and skies.

Dawn gives the sea not colour but contour
That rides beneath us its rough slides and swings.
There in the hollows, folded in their wings,
Float sleeping gannets. Leisurely and sure,   20
Containing the entire grace of its kind,
Each opens itself to the empty wind,
Dynamic-soaring out from troughs of night
To luff into its element and write
In unlearned, fine italic script how we
Must calculate our inadequacy.

The Hermitage of Braid

O wealthy men of Morningside,
Your Labrador-eyed daughters ride
And learn to drive the car and dance,
Buy records, spend a month in France . . .
But I have seen their souls arrayed
Along the Hermitage of Braid

Among the fleeing leaves, alone,
To some new prince or fancy blown,
Warm in their Jenner's anoraks,
But always, always at their backs,   10
Discovering surprising things
Within them, from elsewhere, the wind,
Inciting motion, moving sense
On sense until omniscience
Alone the wind will satisfy
And like the leaves they leap and fly
To find some revolution's cause.
You whistle for their running paws
Among the leafy sky in vain
Then home to tea-time turn again.   20
They wonder that they ever tried
To see from just the morning side.
You, in the quiet, unfortunate
And apple ringing autumn, wait
With golf and whisky grown forlorn:
All children are to folly born.

Ronald Frame (1953 –)

The Camelhair Jacket

'It isn't a proper story at all,' the man began. 'Nothing very much happens.' He shrugged. 'Still, for what it's worth.'

The event took place one afternoon when the man – another man not the one telling me the story – was in the house and his wife was returning in the car with the three children, from school. The husband worked at home; he was an architect.

'As I said, nothing "happens" really. Although possibly it just *might* have. It begins with the car pulling into the road and the children getting out, then the man's wife . . . '

It was the husband's claim that he was sitting at the desk upstairs, that he heard the car draw up and the doors slamming and the children's voices as they chased each other up the garden path. followed by the clacking of his wife's heels. He heard the front door open and the children come running into the hall, and the front door bang shut. He called out something, and then concentrated again on what he was doing.

Another ritual of sounds began – piano scales, the bath taps gushing, feet jumping up and down on the spot – and everything was just as it normally was. As normally happened too, the man's wife came upstairs about ten minutes later with a tray of tea things for him. He smiled over his shoulder as the door opened, then he got up and walked across to take the tray from her.

'Oh,' she said, 'you've changed.'

'Have I?' he asked her, sounding surprised.

'You must have done,' she told him.

'I believe,' he said, meaning to be jocular about it, 'I am the man I was when you left.'

'No,' his wife told him. 'That's not what I meant.'

'No?' he repeated.

'You were wearing your camelhair jacket.'

'Was I?' he said, not concealing his surprise. 'When?'

'Earlier.'

'Not when you left?'

'No,' she said. 'Not when I left.'

'Well, when?' he asked.

'Just now.'

'No, I wasn't,' he said.

'Ten minutes ago.'

'No,' he repeated, and laughed. 'No, I wasn't.'

There was no possibility of confusion about the jacket they were discussing: it had been a recent purchase, an expensive one, worn on 'special' occasions.

'Of course you were wearing it,' the man's wife said. 'I saw you from the car.'

The husband, dressed in a navy blue guernsey jumper, crossed his arms.

'It wasn't me,' he told her, 'whoever it was you think you saw.'

'You were standing at the window,' she said.

'But I haven't been away from this desk,' he told her.

'Weren't you?' she asked, and sounded and looked disbelieving.

'No,' he said, and said it – he wasn't sure why – quite firmly.

'*Weren't* you?'

'Of course not.' He uncrossed his arms and dug his hands into his trouser pockets. 'And I didn't put on the camelhair jacket either. Why on earth should I have done that?'

His wife shrugged. 'I didn't make it up.'

'But why should I say I haven't worn it if I really did have it on,' he said. 'That doesn't make sense.'

His wife looked lost for an answer. The pair of them stared at each other for several seconds.

'You were mistaken,' he told her.

She shrugged again. 'I don't think so. I don't see how.'

'You must have been,' he said. 'Mistaken.'

'Not if it's what I saw.'

'*If* it was . . . '

'If it's 'if' for me,' she said, 'then it should be 'if' for you too. Surely.'

'But it didn't happen like that. None of it happened.'

'I'd tell you I was mistaken if I really felt like that, that I *was*,' his wife said, her voice unsteady.

'Well, you were.'

'But – to my eyes – I did see you. You were – over there, standing at the window – you were wearing the camel jacket.'

'There's only *one* camel jacket. I've nothing else like it.'

'Yes, I know that.'

'I always wear a jumper to work in.'

'I know that too.'

'And there aren't *two* of me,' he said. 'Are there?'

His wife seemed disturbed. She shook her head.

'I can't explain it,' she said.

'Of course not,' her husband told her. He considered himself a man of rational and sound reasoning. 'For the very good reason that I was in here all the time. At the desk, not at the window. And I wasn't wearing the camelhair jacket.'

'There must be *some* reason,' the wife said. She certainly didn't consider herself an irrational person.

'Some reason why you *think* you saw me in the jacket?'

'My eyes are better than yours. You're always telling me.'

'I know,' he said.

'Well, then?'

'"Well, then" what?'

'You probably want this tea anyway,' his wife said. 'I think you'll find *it's* real enough.'

And then, without another word, she made for the door and left the room.

They referred to the matter later, but only once more, in the evening, before they ate. The husband asked his wife if she'd thought of an explanation. No, she replied, *she* hadn't, not at all, the situation seemed exactly the same to her. Then, the husband said, she must have *imagined* she'd seen him, mustn't she?

'Oh no,' she answered. 'Not at all. I didn't *imagine* it.'

'What other explanation *is* there, then?' the man asked her.

'It's you who's telling me there *has* to be an "explanation",' the wife said.

'It's *your* word, *you* used it. Upstairs. But it's because you don't really believe me,' the man said. 'You don't, do you?'

They tacitly agreed not to talk about it. Supper was eaten in silence, except for the din of the children of course; or rather, beneath their noise the two of them ate without speaking, without communicating, while the voices and clatter of cutlery was like a rising tide of sounds.

'Either nothing happened,' the man telling me the story said, 'or perhaps something of great significance in the circumstances did. In future, you see, the man never wore the camelhair jacket again.' He repeated that it had been an expensive purchase, one the couple had discussed for at least three or four weeks beforehand. Now the husband chose to leave it hanging in the wardrobe, and his wife said nothing when she saw that he wasn't wearing it, even on those occasions when they'd planned he would wear it.

After six months or so he still couldn't bear the thought of putting it on. It was as if some harm belonged to the jacket and existed in the cloth: something contrary. Moreover, ever since the incident he and his wife had separately been conscious of a remoteness gathering. It hadn't been there before, or rather not to the same degree: but when they did look back, separately (they both told their own version of the story, and seemed equally sure of what they said), each of them understood that there had been lurking dangers, that they'd already sensed crosscurrents and undertows pulling beneath the supposedly harmonious and settled waters of marital life.

It caused both of them to consider the question, just how much one person ever completely knows of another: and a second question quite naturally followed out of that one – to what extent do we create our own versions of other people?

It set the husband wondering how his wife saw him, in her mind's eye, or how she wished to see him, how she wanted him to be – since it was she who'd been responsible for at last insisting on the indulgence of the expertly-tailored camelhair jacket. And *she* wondered if it wasn't now the case that she relied on distinguishing between the two images in her head, and that on that particular afternoon she'd been depending on seeing the 'other' man at the window – the husband he claimed he wasn't.

'Perhaps someone would tell you that domesticity frightened her, it frightened them both,' the man said to me, 'someone who's got the right words and theories, that is. I don't really know myself all that happened afterwards – if the wife and her husband continued faithful to each other, or even if they *had* been all the time before. I only know that he never wore the jacket again, and that eventually it disappeared from the wardrobe. They both admitted as much to *me*, a stranger, but they didn't discuss the matter with each other, not at all. I suppose it had to do with an absence of some kind,' the man said, finishing his story that he'd told me wasn't going to be a 'proper' story, 'it had to do with some lack they never confessed to, which they never even referred to together. If you like, call it a wanting.'

Sue Glover (1953 –)

The Bondagers

CHARACTERS

LIZA, a very young farm worker (or 'bondager'), facing her first 'hiring' away from home
MAGGIE, a woman with numerous children, married to one of the farm workers
SARA, Maggie's age or a good bit older. Works on the farm with her daftie daughter
TOTTIE, Sarah's daughter, about fifteen. A daftie
ELLEN, the farmer's wife. Formerly a farm worker like the others, now risen to the status of
    a lady
JENNY, another young farm worker, slightly older than LIZA
TWO WARDERS (non speaking). These could be played by the actors who play LIZA and
    JENNY

Note: Bondagers were the women workers of the great Border farms in the last century. Each farm worker was hired on condition he brought a female worker to work alongside him – if not his wife or daughter, then some other girl that he himself had to hire at the Hiring Fair, and lodge and feed alongside his own family in his tiny cottage.

It is also a play about the land . . . and the misuse of land . . .
The play is set on a Border farm of 1860. Act One – with the exception of the opening scene (the 'Hiring') – takes place in the summer; and Act Two in winter.

The set should be minimal. There should be one area of the acting space that represents MAGGIE'*s house – but not defined so definitely as to be intrusive during those passages of the play in which it does not figure. The cradle is in this area – it is a statement, and should be visible. Possibly there should also be an 'area' of the acting space that represents* SARA'*s house (when required – again not intrusive). But the 'house' area(s) could simply be used as part of the field, the barn, whatever, during other scenes, they can 'come and go' as it were.*

The bondagers' dress was distinctive, almost a uniform, and something approximating it is necessary: boots or clogs; full skirts with two or three petticoats; 'headhankies' – i.e. kerchiefs that covered their heads, and could, when work required, be tied over the chin, or even over the whole lower part of the face when the dust and dirt was really flying; and black straw bonnets with red ruching (trimming). Muddy and sometimes shabby, maybe, but beguiling.

ACT ONE / SCENE ONE

LIZA, SARA, JENNY, TOTTIE *in the market place, for the hiring Fair.* MAGGIE *at home.*
VOICES *(all the cast, cutting in on each other's phrases, some of the phrases can be repeated. Low whispers at first, growing louder)* The Hiring, the Hiring, the Hiring . . . Hiring Fair,
    Hiring Fair, Hiring Fair . . .
    What a folk/ What a crowd/ What a carts/ What a people/ What a noise!
    Ye get a' the clash at the Hiring.
    Ye get a' the fun at the Fair.
    I'm blythe to see ye
    Tam/Andra/Jenny/Meg/William/Neil/Geordie/Joe/Jane/Jack.
    What fettle? Fine fettle. How's the cow? Doing grand. How's a' wi you? How's the
    bairns . . . and the cow? How's the wife . . . and the cow?

Did you ken about Davie/Jockie/Tam/Sandy/Nathan/Ned/Mary/Betsy/Bob?
What's the crack?[1] / Heard the crack from
Langriggs/Redriggs/Smiddyhill/Smiddyford/Horsecleugh/Oxencleugh/Whitehas/
Blacksheils/East Mains/Westlea.

> *During this* LIZA *is wandering, jostled by the crowd, looking for a place to stand.*

VOICES *(these phrases more distinct)* The Hiring, the Hiring Fair.
First Monday in February.
Coldest Monday in February.
Eight o'clock. Soon as it's licht.
See the farmers bargain wi the hinds.
See the hinds bargain wi the bondagers.
See the bonny bondagers stand in a row.

> LIZA *has chosen her place, waits to be hired.* SARA *and* TOTTIE *are also standing now together, waiting to be hired.*

FIRST VOICE *(low whisper)* The coldest Monday. Soon as it's licht. *(Louder, taunting.)* No
bondager worth a puckle's left after ten o clock.
LIZA *(outwardly defiant – not in answer to the voice, and never speaking directly to the audience)* I'll
be gone long afore ten. Bound over. Hired. See if I'm not. Broad shoothers, short back,
strong legs.
SARA Stand here Tottie, stand still now.
LIZA – I'll not take the arle from the first that comes,
I'm only going to a well-kent hind.
I can shear come harvest. I'm good with the horses.
I'll fettle the horses – but not your bairns.
I'll redd[2] up the steading – but not your house,
I'll work a' day – but not in your bed.
SARA Tut, lass, dinna talk that way.
LIZA – Broad shoothers, short back, strong legs.
The good name of Tam Kerr, deceased, to live up to,
And my brother Steenie, over the seas.
JENNY No bondager worth a puckle's left after ten o clock.
LIZA I'll be hired by ten of the clock . . . I'll take the arle by ten of the clock.
SARA Stand straight, Tottie, dinna look sweer.
JENNY No cottar wife's hired till the back o twelve. *Gin* she's hired.
SARA *(to* TOTTIE*)* Look sonsie,[3] can't you?
TOTTIE I'm hungry.
SARA Maybe we'll buy a tuppenny loaf after?
TOTTIE After what?
SARA After we're hired.
JENNY *Gin* she's hired!
TOTTIE There's the Maister o Langriggs – maybe we'll get to Langriggs.
SARA Maybe. Look sonsie, now.
VOICES *(each line spoken singly, in turn, by the cast)*
Ten bolls of oatmeal
Fifteen bushels barley
Six bushels pease
Twelve hundred yards potatoes, planted
A peck of lint, sown

---

[1] Gossip, chat.
[2] Tidy, straighten up.
[3] Pleasant.

Three pounds sheep siller
Grass for the cow
The privilege of keeping hens
Four carts of coals

FIRST VOICE It is customary to give them their meat during one month of harvest. They may keep a pig. Their wives must shear in harvest. The hinds are also bound to hire and keep a field worker, a female servant called a bondager, commonly paid ten pence a day. (. . .) The hinds complain of this; the wives even more so.

MAGGIE *(at home. Very busy. Washing clothes, churning butter – or knitting – she knits on the hoof, whilst she's watching a porridge pot, or rocking the cradle. Not directly to audience)* Coldest Monday since Hallowe'en. I should have put straw in his shoon. He's well respected, my man Andra. Any farmer would be thankful to hire him. He was up afore dawn to be there for the Hiring. Kirk claes. Kirk shoon. And a shave like he hasnae had since the kirn. Three things a hind depends on: a good wife, a good cow – and a good razor.

FIRST VOICE A good hind needs a good maister.

MAGGIE He can take his pick o maisters.

FIRST VOICE A good hind needs a good bondager.

MAGGIE He can take his pick o bondagers . . . gin he knows how. But some o those lassies wear two faces – one for the hiring, and another for the farm! Just so long as the lass can shear – I can't work harvest, not with the bairns. Just so long as she takes to the bairns!

LIZA I'm not going to any place hoatchin wi bairns!

SARA *(to LIZA)* Tuts, lassie – there's bound to be bairns!

MAGGIE See and pick right, Andra. Pick a good maister! Dinna say yes to the first farmer that slaps your hand and offers a dram. There's questions to be asked! Two rooms! I'd like a house with two rooms. The maister at Langriggs bigged a new row of houses – all with the two rooms . . .

SARA We don't hope for much, Tottie and me. Day and way.

LIZA I want a place on a big farm. Plenty lassies for the crack. Plenty plooman for the dancing!

MAGGIE A house near the pump. A roof without holes.

SARA *(coming in on MAGGIE's line)* A roof without holes.

SARA *and* MAGGIE Good pasture for the cow.

SARA Kindness for Tottie – she's slow – she has days.

TOTTIE Bad days! Bad days!

LIZA No bairns underfoot.

MAGGIE And if it's a good place – maybe we'll stay – not just the year . . . longer. Same house, same farm, same kirk, same neighbours . . . *(Realising it's an unlikely notion.)* Aye! Well! – so long as it's dry for the flitting.

SARA *(coming in on her last line)* So long as it's dry for the flitting.

TOTTIE I doubt it'll rain for the flitting, Mammy!

LIZA I'll buy a new hat for the flitting.

SCENE TWO

LIZA, TOTTIE, ELLEN. LIZA *walking away from the fair,* TOTTIE *comes after her.*

TOTTIE *(to LIZA)* You, you, you. What farm are you going to? What farm?

LIZA *not answering, doesn't think much of* TOTTIE.

TOTTIE *(insistent)* What farm?

LIZA Blacksheils.

TOTTIE So are we. Which hind will ye work with?

LIZA Andra Innes.

TOTTIE We're on our own. Mammy and me. *(Trying to keep* LIZA's *attention.)* There's ghosts at Blacksheils. Up on the moor.

LIZA *(not impressed by ghosts)* Is it still Maister Elliott farms Blacksheils?

TOTTIE The one that married Ellen. Ellen Rippeth that was. She worked with us at Blacksheils. Not last year. Before. Before she set her cap at the maister.

LIZA I know.

TOTTIE *You* weren't there.

LIZA I was at Billieslaw. Over the hill. I was bondager to my brother.

TOTTIE Set her cap at him, and married him and a'. That's how we got hired. For the sake o lang syne.

LIZA Ellen Rippeth never gave any favours.

TOTTIE Ay, she does. She's the mistress now.

ELLEN *(practicing using a fan, elegantly, expertly)* Learn to use a fan? I can single turnips in the sweat; shaw them in the sleet – I can surely use a fan! Take tea with the gentry? They talk about turnips. Yield, rotation, manure. They know about turnips. Their shoes are shiny, clothes clean, shoothers dry. We were soaked to the skin by half past eight, in the mist, in the morning. Frost, snow, sun, wind, rain; single, shaw, howk, mangle, cart. Aye. We kenned about neeps!

SCENE THREE

LIZA *and* MAGGIE. MAGGIE *is busy, very. (The baby and the porridge pot both at once.)* LIZA *arrives with her bundle of worldly goods.*

LIZA I'm Liza. The bondager.

MAGGIE I'm Maggie, his wife. You'll have seen the bairns, they're playing round the doors.

LIZA Which are yours?

MAGGIE All of them, nearly.

LIZA The wee laddie that kicks?

MAGGIE *(serene)* Kicks? Oh, no, never – you must have got in the way. My bairns wouldna kick. Now. Then. *(Proudly.)* We've the two box beds. So you can share the other one with the bairns.

LIZA I'll not. I'll not sleep with bairns. I'll sleep in the roof.

MAGGIE *(serene)* The older bairns sleep in the roof.

LIZA A couple of bairns, he said, at the Hiring!

MAGGIE *(serene)* Andra said that? No, no – you'll have got it wrong. Andra would never deny his ain bairns! You were gabbing to some other hind, nae doubt! Here – see to the pot while I see to the babby. *(She is busy with the baby.)* Lisa Kerr? Steenie Kerr's sister? There were only the two of you after Tam crossed the Jordan. And a whole house to yourselves? But lassie – naebody round here has a bed to hisself! I dinna ken anyone that sleeps alone – save the plooman up in the steading – mind you, from what I hear, there's one of the dairymaids – still, it's early days yet to pass judgement. You'll soon love the bairns. You're a lassie, after all – you're bound to love them. *(Sharp appraisal.)* Can you shear?

LIZA Aye.

MAGGIE You'll do!

SCENE FOUR

All of them, except ELLEN. *They are singling turnips. In their large hats and head-hankies tied over their chins, they are not individually recognizable. The five of them are part of a larger squad; 'the field' on-stage is part of an enormous field – thirty or forty acres. They work fast, each moving along her own drill, keeping more or less in pace with the others.* (TOTTIE *is slower, maybe much slower.) The dialogue, when it comes, is fast, fragmented, overlapping. It comes in spurts, with pauses between. And they never stop working. Obviously the gist of the dialogue is important, equally, though, every phrase does not have to be heard. The only lines that have to be spoken by particular characters are* JENNY's *and* LIZA's. *(Two of them sing.)*

Woo'd and married and a'
Kissed and carried awa
And is no the bride well off
That's woo'd and married and a'

I'd bind more rags round your hands, if I were you lass!

I've nane.

Straw, then, Rope. We'll have to mak mair.

The saddler's come! That's him just passed the gate!

Aw, now, there's a bonny callant![1]

He'll no be staying more than a week!

That's what makes him bonny!

I'll get a bit crack with him when I redd up the stables!

I'll redd up the stables.

No, you'll no!

Saddler's mine!

Laughter. Pause.

Is he married, the saddler?

No.

Can he dance?

Can he dance!

Fiddle and dance all at once — as good as yon dancing maister frae Jeddart!

We'll hae a bit dance, then!

I'll hae a bit dearie!

Laughter.

Ye're an awful lassie, Jenny!

A'body wants the saddler!

A'body want a bit dearie!

(Singing)

Woo'd and married and a'
Kissed and carried awa
Was she nae very well off
Was woo'd and married an a'

Was Sara married?

Dinna ken. Was Sara married?

Dinna ken.

She was going to marry Wabster, my mother said.

She was never married.

She was never neglected.

JENNY *and* LIZA *together:*

JENNY Can ye spin, Liza — ye get to work up at the Big House if ye can spin.

LIZA Don't want to spin.

JENNY It's good work on a rainy day. Better than being laid off. And you get your meat, sitting down in the kitchen.

LIZA I can't spin.

Ye ken yon plooman with the curls?

Kello?

By, he can dance! Tappity with his clogs — and a kind of singsong he makes all the while — right there in the glaur,[2] at the tweak o a bonnet.

Is he a Gyptian?

Dinna ken. His eyes are black!

Of course he's a Gyptian!

---

[1] Young man.
[2] Mud.

A mugger!
A tinkler!
Maister Elliott hiring Gyptians!
The maister's brown as a peat bog himself
Maister's a gentleman!
Married one of us, though!
He's still a gentleman!
Maybe the other gentry don't think so!
Nellie makes a braw lady!
Aye – the besom![1]
Mistress Ellen.
Mistress *Elliott*!
Was she no very well off
Was woo'd and married an a'
(Shouts coming from the far end of the field.) Ye can stop now, stop at the end of the drill. We're stopping – Jenny! Liza!
They rest on their hoes, flex their backs, leave the field. JENNY *and* LIZA, *slightly apart from the others. Stop to talk.*
JENNY You're lucky biding with Maggie. She keeps a good kitchen.
LIZA I'm aye starving all the same. And I sleep with the bairns.
JENNY So do I – I'm glad of the bairns!
LIZA Could you not sleep in the roof?
JENNY And have him creeping all over me?
LIZA Who?
JENNY Who! Who do you think? *(As* LIZA *gapes, astonished.)* Close your gob, Liza, the
    flies'll get in!
LIZA But – his wife?
JENNY It's his bairns keep me safe, not his wife. I can teach ye to spin, Liza. If you're
    wanting work up at the Big House.
LIZA *(suddenly irritable)* I'm not wanting work at the house.
JENNY Oh, well – ! *(Walking off, then stops to call back at* LIZA.*)* Besom you!

SCENE FIVE

LIZA *and* TOTTIE. LIZA *on her own. She slumps, tired, leaning against or sitting on something, starts unwinding the rags that were bound round her hands.* TOTTIE *comes on; stands and stares at her.* LIZA *still uncertain of* TOTTIE.
LIZA Go away! Shoo!
This has no effect. Tries a frightening face or gesture.
    Aaaaaargh!
TOTTIE *for a moment impassive, then, grinning, copies her.*
TOTTIE Aaaaaargh! *(Gives* LIZA *a shove.)* Maggie says to come and mind the babby for it's
    girny[2] and she has to milk the coo.
LIZA If it's girny, it's wet, if it's wet it's likely mingin'[3]. *(Sweetly.)* You mind the babby,
    Tottie. Go on. Go and sing to bee-baa-babbity.
TOTTIE Don't you like babbies? You're a motherless bairn. *And* a fatherless bairn. And
    you've no brother either, for he's gone to Canada.
LIZA *tries to ignore her. She lies or slumps, wanting to rest, pulling her headhankie right up and forward, hiding her face.*
TOTTIE My daddy's gone to Canada. My daddy's been away for a hundred year. *(The word is
    a talisman for her.)* Sas-katch-e-wan. Sas-katch-e-wan. *(A silence.)* There's dancing

---

[1] Witch.
[2] Peevish, whinning.
[3] Stinking.

tonight.

LIZA Where?

TOTTIE In the turnip shed. The saddler's fetching his fiddle. Maybe ye'll hae a bit dearie.

LIZA What's that supposed to mean?

TOTTIE That's what Jenny always says. 'A'body needs a bit dearie.'

LIZA Away and see to the babbity![1]

LIZA *walks away.*

TOTTIE Where are you going?

LIZA To the pump. To wash off the glaur.

TOTTIE *goes over to the cradle.*

TOTTIE Bee-baa-babbity. Are ye wet? Ugh! Are ye mingin'? UUUUgh! *(Hastily, in case she sets it howling.)* Don't cry, don't cry. *(Very matter-of-fact, as if to someone much older.)* I'll tell you a story. I'll tell you about the ghostie. It's true. I was up on the moors. The maister sent me. With a message for the herd. And the mist came doon – and roon – and doon. I was feared. And I shouted for the herd. But the mist smoored my words. And then I heard, very close: 'Shoough . . . shoooough . . . shoooough . . . ' – a plough shoughin through the ground, and whiles whanging a stane or twa. And a man, calling to his beasts: 'Cooooop, coooooop.' Like a crow. I could feel the beasts on the ground, I could feel them through my feet. Oxen. I could smell them. I wanted to walk with the plooman till the mist parted. I shouted. But the mist swirled roon and smoored a'thing. After, Jock the herd said: *(She copies his patronizing tone.)* 'Naebody ploughs there, Tottie – the only rigs there are the lang syne rigs. Ye can see the marks still. Hundreds of year old. But ye'll no see ony plooman, and ye'll no see ony plough.' Aye. But I heard him though . . .

VOICES *(low whispery)* Lang syne ploughman
Lang syne rigs, rigs, rigs, rigs
Lang syne barley, barley, barley, barley
Barley means bread, oats means bread, pease means bread
Bread of carefulness
Never enough bread

CHILDREN'S VOICES *(or the cast on stage as children; loud, matter-of-fact, unkind)* Tottie's seen a bogle, Tottie's seen a ghostie. Tottie's a softie, Tottie's a daftie.

TOTTIE *(cutting into these lines)* I'm not. Stop it. I'm not.

FIRST CHILD Sixpence in the shilling

TOTTIE Stop it! No!

SECOND CHILD No all there.

TOTTIE I am! *(Upset, blundering about, wanting to shove, shout down her tormentors.)*

CHILDREN *(jeering, laughing)*
Your mammy lay with Wabster
Gat ye in the corn rigs
Cleckit in the barley rigs
Coupled
Covered
Ploughed

TOTTIE Married! *(Upset, aggressive – she has blundered into or pushed the cradle, it's rocking wildly.)*

FIRST CHILD In the corn rigs?

TOTTIE Yes.

SECOND CHILD In the *corn rigs*?

TOTTIE Yes. Yes. She had a babby. It was me.

FIRST CHILD *(soft, sly)* And where's your daddy now?

TOTTIE *(whisper)* Sas-katch-e-wan . . . Sas-katch-e-wan.

---

[1] Also refers to a children's game and (see later) a country dance.

She goes to the cradle, blundering, whimpering. She has to steady the cradle, and in doing so quietens herself.

SCENE SIX

SARA, TOTTIE, ELLEN, LIZA. *TOTTIE is maybe still by the cradle.* SARA *busy cleaning horse tack, or patching/sewing sacks, or winding the home-made straw rope into neat oval balls: any wet-weather work.* ELLEN — *adjusting, admiring her clothes, hat? umbrella? — half pleased at her elevated status, but half laughing at herself:*

ELLEN Sweet wheaten bread, and tea, and cream and sugar and ham! All this for breakfast! Brought by a servant girl better dressed than I ever was till now. A table like snow, a floor like a looking-glass; china, lace. Great wide windows to let in the sun — to look out on the fields. Every field fifty acres square. Hedges trim. No weeds. No waste.

TOTTIE stares at her, delighted to see her. Admires and is fascinated by ELLEN. ELLEN *has always tolerated* TOTTIE, *with an offhand but genuine acceptance.*

ELLEN I saw you hoeing the fields this morning. I watched till you left off because of the rain.

TOTTIE We don't know what to call you now.

SARA We must call her Mistress Elliott now.

ELLEN Aye. That's what you cry me.

Seeing TOTTIE's *grinning welcome,* ELLEN *goes to her, hugs her.* TOTTIE's *reciprocating hug is uninhibited, wholehearted.*

SARA *(fearful of* ELLEN's *gown)* Mind now, Tottie.

ELLEN I wear this one to take tea.

SARA There's no tea here, Nell!

ELLEN I have just taken tea — at Langriggs.

An awkwardness. She sits down very carefully. TOTTIE *gapes at her happily.* SARA *motions to* TOTTIE *to start work.*

TOTTIE *(still with her eyes on* ELLEN*)* Ellen Rippeth-that-was. Like a lady now. She sits like a lady.

ELLEN It's the stays. Can't bend forrard. Can't bend back. I'm tied up every morning — let loose at bedtime.

TOTTIE Who ties you — the maister?

ELLEN *(to* SARA*)* D'you mind Betty Hope? The maister's auld mither hired her for my maid.

SARA She's got the sort of face that comes in useful for a wake.

ELLEN Nae crack from Betsy. It's hot in here.

TOTTIE It's wet out there!

SARA Too wet for work. The lassies are throwing their money at the packman. The lads are in the stables, larking.

TOTTIE Larking!

ELLEN By, it rained for the flitting. I watched the carts from the window, coming down the loan. Bung fu': beds, bairns, clocks, dressers, grandpas, geraniums — a'thing drookit.[1]

SARA I've a hundred rheumatisms since the flitting. Maggie's bairns have the hoast yet.

ELLEN My shoothers are always dry now. If my stockings are soaked, or my shoes, someone fetches another pair.

SARA 'And was she no very well off — / That's woo'd and married an a'!'

ELLEN Here, Tottie — let loose my stays! *(Shows* TOTTIE *where to loosen the laces under the bodice.)*

SARA *(shaking her head at Nell's old ways)* Mistress Elliott!

ELLEN *flops on the straw.* TOTTIE *imitates her.* SARA *never stops working.*

TOTTIE Bad Nell!

ELLEN Not now! I'm a married lady now!

---

[1] Drenched.

TOTTIE Are you having a baby? Is it in there yet?

ELLEN No . . . Not yet.

SARA *(after a pause; softly)* There's time enough.

ELLEN A hind wouldn't think so! Some of them would have you swelled before they called the banns, even!

SARA Och, now, Ellen.

ELLEN Well, it's true!

SARA Not at Blacksheils. The maister wouldn't stand for it. He's stricter than the minister.

ELLEN He's – he's – a fine man. Keeps his passion under hidlings, though!

SARA And his mother, the widow?

ELLEN She calls me 'the new blood'. 'No sense growing prize turnips, Gordon, without prize sons to mind them!'

SARA Well, you know what they say: the bull is half the herd.

ELLEN *lolls in the hay. More like the bondager she used to be.*

ELLEN Is that true for folk, as well as beasts?

SARA Must be. Surely.

ELLEN He had a son. It died before it got born. It killed its mother before it was even born.

TOTTIE How could a baby kill you?

SARA The Elliotts have farmed here since I don't know when. His grandfather drained those cold fields of clay. He died before they were ever first cropped. Look at them now. Tatties, clover, the finest neeps in Europe. People come from all over – Germany, England – just to look at Blacksheils, and talk with the maister.

ELLEN A son for Blacksheils. Of course he wants a son.

TOTTIE *(tormenting ELLEN, pulling at her)* How could a bull be half the herd? How could a baby kill you?

ELLEN Babies are mischief. Like you, Tottie! No telling what they'll do.

LIZA *appears.*

SARA It's Liza, Mistress Elliott. Liza Kerr. Andra's bondager.

TOTTIE *(to LIZA)* You must cry her Mistress Elliott, now.

LIZA *gives a bob.*

ELLEN *(getting up, brushing off the straw – but not put out at being caught lolling there by a servant)* I would hardly have known you. You've grown. (ELLEN *is going.*)

LIZA Steenie's in Canada.

ELLEN Yes, I heard. I hope he's well?

LIZA *doesn't answer.* ELLEN *goes.*

LIZA *(muttering after her)* No thanks to you if he's well. No thanks to you!

TOTTIE *(softly)* Sas-katch-e-wan.

LIZA Steik yer gab, you!

Gives TOTTIE *a shove, as she goes.*

TOTTIE Sas-katch-e-wan.

SCENE SEVEN

ELLEN, MAGGIE, SARA. *They are not 'together', but in their separate areas.*

ELLEN Steenie Kerr. He was only a bairn. Lovesick loon! Heart on his sleeve. Scratching my name on the steading walls.

SARA Poor Steenie. I felt heart-sorry for him.

ELLEN He played on pity. Punished me with other folk's pity. Used me.

MAGGIE She led him a dance.

SARA Well, he wouldn't take no.

MAGGIE She drove them a' wild, the plooman.

SARA Such a beautiful summer.

MAGGIE Not for Steenie.

SARA They were a' mad for dancing – danced every night. Till the first field was cut. And the night of the kirn[1] – the moon was so bonny, a real harvest moon.

ELLEN I was angry. I'll show you, I thought. Steenie, all of you. I felt angry. Wild. The maister was there in the fields every day, keeping an eye on things. In the fields. At the kirn . . . Ye'll hae a dance, maister? . . . Anither dance, maister? . . . And ye'll hae a bit mair dance, maister . . . He looked that modest! He made me laugh. He made me want. Stricter than the minister, a'body said. I'll have him in the hay, efter, I thought. Why not? A'body needs a bit dearie. And then I thought – never mind the hay, Nell – ye can mak it tae the bed. Ye can mak the Big Hoose. Ye'll can cry the banns. I could see it in his eyes. Feel it in his bones. (. . .) He cried out when he loved me. Not blubbing like Steenie, not like I wasn't there at the end, but like he was wanting to take me with him . . . Just a bit dearie. And what do I get? A'thing. I got a'thing.

SCENE EIGHT

MAGGIE, SARA, LIZA, JENNY.

MAGGIE Did you hear about Marjie Brockie? Buckled up wi Jamie Moodie! Buckled up at Coldstream Brig. Ca' that a wedding?

SARA It's legal.

MAGGIE The minister wouldn't say so. Folk should marry in kirk with the full connivance of the Almighty. A lad and lass walk into the inn, and someone says 'Who's the lass, then?' and the lad says 'O, she's my wife!' Ca' that a wedding?

SARA Well, it's legal!

MAGGIE It's a scandal!

SARA It's cheaper that way. Kirk weddings cost. No wonder they run off to Coldstream under hidlings. After the fair. Or after the kirn.

LIZA Did you run away to Coldstream?

SARA No, Liza. We were handfasted, Patie and me. We lived together, man and wife, for nearly a year, to see how we would do.

MAGGIE Handfasting! And who's left holding the bairn?

SARA But that's what they're waiting for, often as not, to see if there's a bairn. It's the baby leads them to the kirk, eventually.

MAGGIE Or sends the man fleeing. To Canada, for instance.

SARA Patie loved the baby. She was a queer bit babby, wheezy and choky. He knew she wasn't quite natural. But he loved her, you mustn't think he didn't, she was ours. He was restless, though. He wanted – something, adventure, Canada. It was me said no, I wouldn't go. This parish was my calf-ground: Langriggs, Blackshiels, Billieslaw; the fields, the river, the moor up yonder with the lang syne rigs. Patie loved the land. 'Her.' But maybe I loved her more. When it came to the bit. When it came to Greenock – and even there the land seemed foreign. And the sea; and the ships. A sad, sad place. A great crush of folk, all quiet, and a highland lass singing. Then a voice cried out, loud: 'Hands up for Canada! Hands up for Canada!' A rushing, like wings, all the hands held high. And the baby screamed like she'd never grat[2] before. Such a stab in my heart it made the milk spurt from me. I couldn't step forward. I couldn't go on. And Patie couldn't stay. I knew he couldn't stay. He crossed the ocean; I looked for the carter to take us back home. Patie Wabster. I think of him every day, many times every day.

MAGGIE Fourteen years! He'll have bairns of his own now.

SARA I hope so surely. He was made for happiness, Patie.

LIZA and JENNY are all ears, gripped by all this.

MAGGIE Well! (She hasn't heard so much of this story before, is shocked, disapproving, of SARA.) Well, you've made your bed, you must lie on it.

SARA (laughs easily) I've no leisure for my bed!

---

[1] Harvest home (celebration of the completion of the harvest).
[2] Wept.

MAGGIE As ye sow, shall ye reap! A cottar wife's bound to be hard-wrought!

SARA *(serenely)* Day and way!

MAGGIE *(annoyed, and shows it in the way she is working, with thumps and bangs – feels* SARA *should be regretful and guilty about this)* Well, it takes all sorts! . . . There's naught so queer as folk! . . . *(Exasperation.)* A kirk wedding would have bound you both! . . . *(More to* LIZA *now.) You* have to bring them to account. Andra wouldn't ask me. He *wouldn't.* He was never going to ask. So when he was standing with a crowd of the lads, I flew to his neck and measured him for the sark. His wedding sark.

LIZA *and* JENNY *start to giggle at this.*

MAGGIE Once word got round I was sewing him the sark, well, he had no choice, he had to call the banns. And not before time.

MAGGIE *either goes offstage, busy on some errand, or busies herself with some work; has left* SARA *and* LIZA *on their own.*

SARA *(to* LIZA *and* JENNY*)* She doesn't understand. And neither do you, I daresay. And neither did I, at the time. Patie was lovely, like no one else. Happy, clever. But he needed to wander, he wanted the world. I have to bide still, I have to stay where I am.

JENNY But you don't bide still – you flit every year!

SARA *(laughs)* Aye, so I do! But I never flit far. I've never been further than the three, four farms; never been further than – oh – twenty miles, maybe.

LIZA But you went as far as Greenock once.

An assent from SARA.

LIZA *I* could go to Canada.

SARA Well, you could. And join your brother.

LIZA Saskatchewan. I could go there. Is it a big place?

SARA It's a place I think about every day. But I don't know what it's like. I wonder: do they have peewees. Patie loved the peewees, he'd never plough a peewee's nest, he'd steer the horses round it. We understood each other. Tottie's part of that, part of Patie and me. That makes her special.

SCENE NINE

JENNY, LIZA, TOTTIE. *Night. Candlelight. They have a candle, a looking-glass, an apple. With lots of shushing, they arrange themselves, so that* TOTTIE *has the candle,* JENNY *the glass,* LIZA *the apple.* LIZA *places herself in front of, and not too near, the glass. A clock begins to strike twelve. This is what they've been waiting for. Immediately, solemnly,* LIZA *bites into the apple, throws the bitten-out chunk over her left shoulder.* TOTTIE *wants to retrieve the bite of apple –* JENNY *restrains her. They take the apple from* LIZA, *hand her a comb. Ceremoniously she combs her hair, staring all the while into the mirror, peering into the space over her shoulder in the mirror. The others are waiting expectantly,* TOTTIE *tries to look in the glass, obscuring* LIZA*'s own view of it, they signal* TOTTIE *to move away. Suddenly* LIZA *bursts into excited laughter, doubles up, dances around, gives a 'hooch' of delight.*

TOTTIE *and* JENNY *crowding, cutting each other's lines, in a rush:*

JENNY Did you see him, Liza?

TOTTIE Which one, Liza?

JENNY Was it the Gyptian?

TOTTIE Was it Kello?

JENNY Black-eyed Kello?

LIZA *still dancing about, laughing, nodding 'yes,' clutching at* JENNY.

TOTTIE Do me! My turn!

JENNY *(sternly)* No!

TOTTIE I want to see my man! Give me an apple! *(She looks for the apple piece that* LIZA *threw over her shoulder.)*

JENNY Sump! It's past twelve o the clock! You can't tell fortunes now!

She or LIZA *blows out the candle.* You can't see anyone now!

LIZA, MAGGIE, SARA, TOTTIE, JENNY . . . *and later,* ELLEN. *They are stopping for a piece-break, milk or water, and bannocks of some kind.* MAGGIE *has brought the food along to the field for them.*

TOTTIE *He was shouting – in the turnip shed. Shouting at the neeps. Nobody there, just neeps.*

MAGGIE It's a speech. For the meeting! He'll be practicing his speech.

JENNY For the Soiree!

LIZA *(the title – an official one – sounds glamorous to her)* The Plooman's Soiree!

SARA Go on, then, Tottie, tell us – what did he say?

TOTTIE He said – we are not penny pies.

LIZA 'Gentlemen! We are not penny pies; We must continue to press for the six-pound rise!'

TOTTIE Yes, that's what he said.

SARA Six pound!

MAGGIE Rowat of Currivale gives farm servants a grand wage, and lost time.

SARA Lost time?

LIZA What's that?

MAGGIE I dinna rightly ken. But he gives them it.

SARA Dunlop of Smiddyhill's promised to mend up his houses. Planks on the floor. *And* in the loft.

MAGGIE Every year the maisters promise to mend up the houses! But syne it's time for the Speaking, and syne the Hiring, and syne the Flitting – and where are the promises?

MAGGIE *and* SARA Snowed off the dyke!

SARA If we didn't flit every year, they'd have to mend up the houses.

MAGGIE If the houses were mended up, we wouldn't want to flit ae year.

SARA *(quite cheerful)* Tinklers, that's all we are!

TOTTIE Penny pies. We are not penny pies.

MAGGIE A six-pound rise would do me fine, and a new house even finer – but what we really need is an end to the bondage.

Surprise from the others.

MAGGIE *(slightly abashed)* Lots of folk are beginning to speak out against the bondage.

Others not convinced.

MAGGIE I've barely a shilling a week to spare for her.

LIZA I earn my keep!

JENNY A shilling! Is that all we're worth?

MAGGIE Barely a shilling for all that food –

LIZA – I'm aye starving –

JENNY Even a horse can't work without food!

MAGGIE She takes the bed from my bairns, and the warmth from my fire –

LIZA *(furious)* Where d'you expect me to –

SARA *(restrains her)* She doesn't mean you – *(To* MAGGIE:*)* Maggie! – *(To* LIZA:*)* It's the bondage she's angry at!

MAGGIE Flighty, giddy bits o lassies! Pay no heed to the hind, or his wife!

LIZA I'm not *your* servant!

MAGGIE I'm not *your* washer woman!

SARA This'll never do now, fraying like – tinklers!

TOTTIE Penny pies!

MAGGIE Remember Rob Maxwell two year ago at the Hiring? Pleading with a bondager – a woman he didnae ken from Eve – begging her to take the arle as if his very life depended on it!

SARA Well, but it did. For his ain wife had bairns, and without a female worker who would have hired him? No maister round here.

MAGGIE And remember how that young bondager turned out? Remember a' that?

LIZA What?

MAGGIE Never you mind. But a poor unsuspecting hind shouldn't have to hire by looks. A sweet face won't shift the sharn[1].

LIZA And what about us? It works both ways.

JENNY Ay, both ways. How can we choose a decent hind by his looks?

MAGGIE That's just it – the farmer should hire you lassies, not the hind.

LIZA We'd still get picked by our looks.

MAGGIE Andra's picked by his looks too, come to that.

LIZA They'd still pinch our arms and gawp at our legs!

JENNY We'd still have to sleep with the bairns – or worse!

MAGGIE The maister should hire all the bondagers himself – aye and lodge them too.

SARA Now, where could he lodge them, Maggie?

LIZA In the Big Hoose!

JENNY In the big bed! Oooh-ooh!

LIZA We should have a meeting!

SARA Who?

LIZA Us! The lassies! There's as many of us as them! More lassies than men, come harvest!

MAGGIE *and* SARA *shrug off her anger, won't see the point.*

LIZA We should make the speeches!

MAGGIE What do you want? A six-pound rise? And what would you spend it on? Ribbons, ruching? *(To* SARA.) Do you know how much this besom owes the draper?

LIZA We don't get much!

MAGGIE I wish I had it. I hunger my bairns, whiles, to feed you! And you spend your money at the draper's!

JENNY We don't get much compared to the men.

MAGGIE A man's got a family.

LIZA Sara's got a family.

SARA Oh, but we're not doing men's work. We canna work like men.

ELLEN 'Don't be ridiculous, Ellen,' says the maister. 'We can't do away with the bondage. I can't employ a man who hasn't a woman to work with him. One pair of horse to every fifty acre, one hind for every pair of horse, one bondager for every hind. That's the way it's done,' he says. 'I'm all for progress,' he says, 'but I won't do away with the bondage,' he says. 'We need the women. Who else would do the work? . . . Women's work, for women's pay.'

LIZA *(or all, taking phrase by phrase, in turn. She is kirtling up her skirts, putting on the sacking apron)* Redd up the stables, muck out the byre, plant the tatties, howk the tatties, clamp the tatties. Single the neeps, shaw the neeps, mangle the neeps, cart the neeps. Shear, stook, striddle, stack. Women's work.

ELLEN Muck. A heap of it – higher than your head. Wider than a house. Every bit of it to be turned over. Aired. Rotted. Women's work.

LIZA *(forking the dung)*
Shift the sharn, fulzie, muck
Sharn, sharn, fulzie, muck
Shift the sharn, fulzie, muck . . .

ELLEN *(on top of* LIZA'*s words)* Muck is gold, says the maister.

LIZA *(forking, digging)*
Sharn, sharn, fulzie, muck
Sharn, sharn, fulzie, muck

ELLEN Muck's like kindness, says the maister, it can be overdone.

LIZA *(to* ELLEN) You mind what it was like, cleaning your claes after this? My new bonnet – it stinks. My claes, my skin.

---

[1] Dung.

SARA It's Maggie who washes your claes.

LIZA *(to* ELLEN*)* What was the job you hated most?

ELLEN Howking tatties. I'm long – here – in the back. At the end of the day I used to scraffle on all fours. I couldn't get to my feet till I was halfway down the loan. Can you shear?

LIZA Aye.

ELLEN Striddle?[1]

LIZA Aye!

ELLEN Are you good?

LIZA Aye. It's the corn I love best. It's the whisper it gives when it's ripe for the sickle.

ELLEN I love the speed of it all, the fury. Faster, faster, keep up with the bandster[2]; faster faster, and better your neighbour. I felt like yon Amazon in the Bible. No one could stop me, if Mabon himself had stood before me, I'd have cut him in two with a swipe o my sickle. I gloried in the shearing. I'll miss the hairst.

LIZA *and* ELLEN *smile at each other.*

SARA I remember my mother and her neighbour each had a rig of corn on the village allotment. My mother was gey thrang, all her life. Too much to do, no time to do it. On night, when the corn was ripe, she couldn't sleep. The moon was full. So she went out to shear her corn. And as she sheared, every now and then, she'd take just a bitty from her neighbour's rig, just as much as would make bands to tie her sheaves. Syne she went home and slept the last hour or two till day, glad the work was done. But in the mornin passing the field, she saw she'd reaped the wrong rig, her neighbour's rig. The corn she'd stolen to bind her sheaves was her own corn – and she still had her own rig to shear. O, but she grat! It was a punishment, she said.

SCENE ELEVEN

MAGGIE, LIZA, SARA. *Evening.* SARA *is working quietly – in her garden or her house (sewing? hoeing?), near enough to hear/overhear* LIZA *and* MAGGIE. MAGGIE *is busy (so is her tongue, she scarcely draws breath during the first part of this scene.) She could be churning butter – it calls for steady rhythmic movement, she wouldn't be able to leave her work till the milk was turned.* LIZA *is not so busy: adding ribbon to her petticoats, or ruching to her bonnet.*

MAGGIE You must draw all the milk off each milking. Well, I've told you before, it's no use milking if you don't milk her right – she'll draw all the milk that's left back into herself, and come next milking she'll give a bit less –

LIZA Coo, coo, I'm sick o the coo.

MAGGIE – you'll only get the same next time, as you took from her the time before. We need all the milk she can give. I can't bake flourocks without good cream –

LIZA I could eat a coo, I'm starving!

MAGGIE – Andra's fond of flourocks. *You* eat them fast enough – And what about the teats, Liza? I said wash the teats with alum and water –

LIZA Horses – aye. Coos – no.

MAGGIE – I said to wash the warts on her teats. Poor coo. A' you bondagers are the same. You know nothing of coos, or kitchens or bairns –

LIZA Bairns – never!

MAGGIE The milking's important, Liza, can't you see. I can't feed the family without it!

LIZA You've plenty of your own if your coo runs dry.

MAGGIE *(stops short, at last, for a moment anyway)* Aye, I have. And don't think I'm not proud of it. Oh, you wait. Wait till you're wed. Wait till you've a man to feed –

LIZA Oh, wait. You wait. You'll ken! You'll see!

MAGGIE – Wait till you've bairns. You'll ken. You'll see! Canna bake, canna milk, canna

---

[1] While standing on a corn-stack, passing sheaves to the stack-builder.
[2] The sheaf binder.

sew, canna spin. Wait till you're wed!

LIZA I'm not getting wed. I'll be a cottar wife like Sara.

SARA *(more to herself than to them)* You want to be like Sara? It's day and way for Sara. Every year gets harder for Sara.

LIZA *(coming in over* SARA's *words)* I'm not getting wed. Not yet. Not for years. The sooner you wed, the more bairns you get.

MAGGIE That's what you wed for – bairns!

LIZA Why?

MAGGIE Why? Why! *(Can't think what to say, can't see why she can't think what to say.)* Why, they keep the roof over you when they're older, that's why. They keep things going. Wull and Tam will soon be half-yins, getting half pay, and when they're grown there'll be Jim and Drew, and the girls will make bondagers in time. Meg can work with her daddy. Netta can work with Wull or Tam. It'll be grand. We'll can take our pick at the Hiring. Ay, we'll be easy then. Soon enough.

LIZA All in the one house – all in the one room? And what about him *(indicating the cradle)*, he'll not be grown, and Rosie's still wee – and how many more? Easy! You'd be easier without.

MAGGIE Without what?

LIZA Bairns.

MAGGIE Fields aye need folk.

LIZA Bairns for the maister?

MAGGIE What's a hoose without bairns?

LIZA If you think they're so bonny, what are you greeting for?

MAGGIE Me?

LIZA What do you greet for nights?

MAGGIE No, not me – it must have been one of the wee ones – Rosie cries –

LIZA 'Bake, cook, sew, spin, get wed, have bairns.' Natter, natter. Nothing about fighting him off in the night!

MAGGIE *(a gesture: meaning 'you're havering')* Now . . . where was I . . . what was I going to do next . . .

LIZA I hear you! I hear you nights! Do you think I don't hear you?

MAGGIE Now, what was I doing . . .

LIZA You sit on by the fire, hoping he'll sleep. You fetch moss from the peat moor to stuff up your legs. I've seen.

SARA *(calling out from her own house, or garden)* Liza, fetch me some water, would you?

LIZA It's bad enough listening when folk are – happy. But when they're pleading, crying – giving in –

SARA Liza! Go to the pump for me, there's my lass!

MAGGIE *(very upset, loathe to admit it to herself)* What's day is day . . . and night is night.

SARA Liza!

LIZA *insouciant, unrepentant, fetches some receptacle for water, and goes off to the pump.*

MAGGIE . . . and the bairns are my days! *(She starts – or resumes – some piece of work, then stops, goes to the cradle.)* Aye . . . wee lamb . . . my wee burdie . . . *(Picks him up.)* She doesna ken ought. Just a muckle great tawpie, that's all she is. *(Begins to nurse the baby.)* Dinna go to sleep my burdie. Tak your fill. *(It is she who is being comforted by the nursing, rather than the baby.)* Now . . . Now . . . I ken where I am now. I canna feel dowie[1] when you tug like that. A' the bairns at the breast. A' the folk in the fields. A' the bonny folk. A good harvest is a blessing to all. Aye. That's right. Tak yer fill, burdie, I ken who I am when you're there.

---

[1] Sad.

LIZA, TOTTIE, *all.* LIZA *is waltzing – humming, or lala-ing the tune ('Logie o Buchan'). Then starts to make up words for the tune, dancing hesitantly, searching hesitantly for words. Sings some or all of this.*

LIZA O, the plooman's so bonny wi black curly hair
    He dances so trig and his smile is just rare
    His arms are so strong as he birls me awa
    His black eyes are bonny and laughing and bra
    His name it is Kello, the best o them a'
    His name it is Kello, the best o them a'

Waltzing with an imaginary partner now, more confident, repeating the song more confidently . . . A laugh heard from TOTTIE, *who has been hiding, watching. She appears, kissing her own arm with grotesque kissing noises, sighing, petting noises.* LIZA, *annoyed, gives her a shove or tries to –* TOTTIE *shoves back, hard.*

TOTTIE Tinkler, tailor, beggar – Kello! *(More kissing noises.)* Tinkler, tailor, beggar – *lover!*

LIZA Tak yer hook, you – go on.

TOTTIE I looked in the glass. I looked in the glass too. It was twelve o clock, so I saw. I saw my man. You know who I saw?

LIZA You haven't a glass. Jenny's the only one with a glass. Away wag yer mou somewhere else. Go on!

TOTTIE Jenny went with the saddler. I saw them in the rigs. Not our rigs. The lang syne rigs up by the moor. You can hide up there, the furrows are deep. The ghosts'll get them if they don't watch out. Her claes were way up. Woosh! She's getting wed to the saddler. That's what you do! Woosh! *(. . .)* I've seen you too. You went with the Gyptian. In the turnip house.

LIZA I never did. I was dancing, that's all. He was showing me the steps. And he's not a Gyptian.

TOTTIE Woosh!

LIZA Daftie! Come on, I'll show you the steps. Come on, come here.

TOTTIE I know the steps!

LIZA I want to go over the steps. If you don't know them right, no one will ask you. You want to dance at the kirn, don't you?

LIZA *holds out her arms, but* TOTTIE *declines to dance with her.* LIZA *starts waltzing again, singing.* TOTTIE *watches for a while, then suddenly breaks into a raucous clog (or boot) dance, in fast reel or jig time: rough, spirited, noisy. And, like* LIZA, *sings her own accompaniment:*

TOTTIE Liza loves the plooman
    Bonnie black-eyed plooman
    Kello is the plooman
    O, he's no a tinkler
    O, he's no a mugger
    O, he's no a Gyptian
    He's a black-eyed plooman
    Bonnie black-eyed plooman, etc.

Which kills LIZA's *waltz. She stares amazed –* TOTTIE's *dancing may lack finesse, but it's wholehearted, makes you want to dance with her. The others appear, join in. Someone bangs the ground with a graip (or hoe) handle, beating time, they are all singing* TOTTIE's *rhythm now, same tune, same lines, but each singing different lines to each line of the music. The dance is becoming the kirn, has led into the kirn. It stops abruptly:*

VOICES *(toasts, asides, conversation)*
    The kirn, the kirn, the kirn, the kirn
    What a folk/ a'body's here/ mind the bairns
    A good harvest/ best for years/ best in my time

TOTTIE *(listing the repertoire of dances)* Reel o Tulloch, ribbon dance, pin reel, polka

VOICES All the corn standing and none to lift I can't stay late because of the bairns Will you
    look at Marjie's petticoats! The saddler's shed his hair doon the middle!
TOTTIE Tullogorum, petronella, strathespey, scotch reel
VOICES
    A good harvest's the envy of none
    And a blessing to all
(Toast.) Welcome to the maister
(Toast.) Thanks to the maister for the harvest home
    And the use of the barn
    And the beer and the baps
    We've a good maister
(Toast.) To the maister
    And a better mistress
(Toast.) To the mistress
    Health and Prosperity
    A good harvest is a blessing to all
    And the envy of none
They shush each other to silence as someone starts to sing (maybe Burns, the song entitled 'Somebody.')
        My heart is sair – I darena tell
        My heart is sair for somebody;
        I could wake a winter night
        For the sake o somebody.
        Ohon! for somebody!
        O-hey! for somebody!
        I could range the world around,
        For the sake o somebody!
        Ye Powers that smile on virtuous love,
        O, sweetly smile on somebody!
        Frae ilka danger keep him free,
        And send me safe my somebody.
        Ohon! for somebody!
        O-hey! for somebody!
        I wad do – what wad I not?
        For the sake o somebody!

SCENE THIRTEEN

JENNY, LIZA, MAGGIE, TOTTIE, SARA. *Dawn, or just after, the morning after the kirn.* JENNY *and*
LIZA *arriving home, fits of giggles. High from lack of sleep and the night's events.* MAGGIE *has heard
them coming, she's already up – splashing her face with water? fetching water? something – and 'nursing
her wrath.'*
MAGGIE I'll thraw¹ your neck when I come to you, lass. I'll dadd your lugs². I'll skelp you
    blue.
LIZA We were only dancing!
MAGGIE Dancing! He was dragging you down the loan!
JENNY He'd had a drop! They'd all had a drop.
MAGGIE Gyptians! Steal the clothes off your back – and a whole lot more!
LIZA Kello's not a Gyptian.
JENNY It was the kirn, Maggie.
LIZA We were dancing!
MAGGIE Where to? Coldstream?

----

¹ Twist.
² Ears.

Renewed giggles.

And for the love of the Lord, stop that laughing. You cackled and screeched all through the kirn!

JENNY She wasn't going to Coldstream *really*! She wasn't getting wed or anything!

LIZA *(mockingly)* Oooh-ooh! Buckled up at Coldstream!

MAGGIE You weren't? Were you? By, you'd see – !

LIZA You'd lose your bondager if I got wed. That's all that bothers you.

MAGGIE Get ready for work, go on, the pair of you. The steward won't brook lateness after the kirn. Especially not after the kirn. He'll have a thumping head on him this morning. And not the only one. Gin you were mine – I'd shake you, lass!

SARA *has appeared, been milking her cow or fetching water or firewood.*

SARA Is Tottie not up yet?

They stare at her blankly.

SARA Still sleeping with the bairns, is she?

MAGGIE *shakes her head, is about to say 'no.'*

SARA I left her last night dancing with the bairns.

MAGGIE Well, she wasn't with me, Sara.

SARA *(worried, but not unduly)* I thought she was sleeping at your place. Now where can she be?

MAGGIE The hayloft, probably.

JENNY *and* LIZA *exchange looks.*

SARA She didn't want to leave with me. She wanted to dance.

JENNY She followed us a way.

SARA You've seen her then – ?

JENNY Last night.

SARA Well, but now, where is she now?

MAGGIE *(angry, to* LIZA *and/or* JENNY*)* You should have kept an eye on her.

JENNY Why?

LIZA She's a pest.

JENNY Traipsing after us.

MAGGIE She's been girny lately. Thrawn.

SARA She's been having bad days.

LIZA What's the fuss? She never goes far. She's too daft to get far.

They catch sight of TOTTIE.

SARA Tottie, burdie, where have you been? Come here. You're a bad girl, going off like that, where have you been?

TOTTIE *(triumphant, but wary too – keeps her distance)* I've been married.

Ooh-ing or giggles again from LIZA *and* JENNY.

SARA Oh, it's a notion she takes. Like the dancing.

MAGGIE *(to* JENNY, LIZA*)* She was with you, then?

SARA Where have you been, Tottie?

TOTTIE I've been with my man. Getting wed. Liza wouldn't go. He didn't want her anyway.

Each time they approach her she withdraws.

JENNY You've never been to Coldstream and back, not without wings.

LIZA You can't wed, you're not sixteen.

TOTTIE I'm not the bairnie now! I know things. I'm wed.

MAGGIE It's their fault, putting ideas in her head.

LIZA Us!

JENNY She wasn't with us!

TOTTIE I was! I was. They were going to Coldstream brig, they were laughing and dancing, they were having a wedding. I wanted to go too. But they shouted at me, Liza and Jenny and Kello and Dave, and Dave threw a stone. So I hid. Then I heard them running across the field, Liza and Jenny, running and stopping to have a bit laugh, and running and stopping and laughing and running. But the ploomen didn't run cos they'd had too much ale, they couldn't loup the dyke, they stayed in the loan. So I went and asked them could I go to Coldstream instead, and Kello said yes.

LIZA Kello.

JENNY You've never been to Coldstream!

LIZA She's making it up, she talks like that all the time.

TOTTIE I'm going to have a clock and a dresser and a bed. And a baby.

The silence gratifies her.

LIZA Who said?

TOTTIE *starts laughing, almost dancing (or lolling about in the hay, as* ELLEN *did earlier), hugging herself with satisfaction – at last night's, as well as this morning's, attention.*

MAGGIE What did he do? Tottie? Which one was it, and what did he do?

SARA There's blood on her skirt.

MAGGIE *(slapping at, or shoving at* JENNY *or* LIZA, *whichever is nearest)* Your fault, bitches!

As she speaks the farmyard bell – maybe just two iron bars banged together – is heard in the distance.

MAGGIE That's the steward in the yard. You're late. Go on, The pair of you, hurry up, on. No sense everyone being late.

SARA Tell the steward we're both sick, Tottie and me. Tell him we're sick.

MAGGIE And Jenny – both of you – keep your gob shut!

LIZA *(to* TOTTIE*)* Was it Kello?

MAGGIE Tak your hook, Liza!

TOTTIE *(calling after her in triumph)* You're the bairnie now, Liza!

LIZA *and* JENNY *go slowly towards the field, collect their hoes, tie on their head-hankies, aprons, etc.*

TOTTIE It was Kello I saw in the glass. Yon night I took a loan of Jenny's glass.

MAGGIE *and* SARA *say nothing, don't know what to say – to* TOTTIE, *to each other.*

TOTTIE He said we hadn't got all night, we'd never get to Coldstream, we should go in the rigs. We were wed in the rigs. Lift your claes! Woosh! I wanted a look at his prick, but I couldn't see right, it was still half dark. And he never lay me doon at all, he pushed me agin the stack. 'We'll smoor the fleas together,' he says. 'It canna hurt if we smoor a wheen[1] fleas.' But it hurt. I'm hurt. *(But just when she seems distressed and ready to be comforted, she starts laughing again, excited, gleeful.)*

LIZA They'll tell the steward and the maister.

JENNY *(to* LIZA*)* What'll they do to that Kello, eh? What'll they *not* do!

MAGGIE There's always trouble after the kirn!

JENNY *(looking to the fields)* They're ploughing already. I can see the horses. *He's* turning up the stubble, your Kello –

LIZA Not mine!

MAGGIE Go to work, Sara. I'll see to her now. Leave her here with me. If you don't work, you don't get paid. And the steward'll be angry if you're not in the field, it'll mak him angrier at Tottie.

SARA *(more angry than sad, for once)* At *Tottie?*

But SARA *can't go.*

JENNY *(to* LIZA*)* What'll you say when you see him, Kello?

LIZA I won't see him – I won't look!

JENNY If he speaks to –

LIZA I'll spit!

MAGGIE *(looking to fields)* They're ploughing already. Ploughing for winter.

SARA Come home now, bairnie!

TOTTIE Not the bairnie now!

MAGGIE Trouble – it comes like the first nip of frost. Sure as frost after harvest.

LIZA I wish it was last night again. I wish it was the kirn still.

---

[1] Few.

MAGGIE Sure as winter.

JENNY I wish the summer would last for ever.

LIZA I wish we were still dancing!

ACT TWO / SCENE ONE

It is dark, at first we barely see the characters on stage. The different sections of chorus here come fast on top of each other, sections actually overlapping – until MAGGIE *and* SARA *speak individually, in character.*

A SINGLE VOICE *(tune: traditional)*

>Up in the morning's no for me
>Up in the morning early
>When a' the hills are covered in snow
>Then it is winter fairly . . . *(last line more spoken than sung)*

VOICES *(in a spoken round)*

>When a' the hills are covered in snow
>Then it is winter fairly . .

As the round finishes, voices still saying 'Winter . . . winter . . . winter . . . '

A burst of noise: a rattle of tin cans, or sticks clattering together, or a stick drumming on tin – or something like. (It was Hogmanay, not Hallowe'en, when kids went guising[1] in the Borders.)

A CHILD *(calling out in a mock scary way)* OOooooh!

A CHILD *(calling out, merry)* We're only some bits o bairns come oot to play Get up – and gie's oor Hogmanay!

Some laughter, children's laughter. The rattle/drumming noise. If possible an impression of the laughter fading to distance – as if the children have retreated, and the adults, and adult worries, are coming to the centre of the stage.

VOICES *(singly, in turn)*

>Cold wind: snow wind
>Small thaw: mair snaw
>The snow wreaths
>The feeding storm
>The hungry flood

SARA's *and* MAGGIE's *speeches here more definite, more individual.*

SARA The dread of winter. All summer long, the dread of it. Like a nail in the door that keeps catching your hand. Like a nip in the air in the midst of the harvest.

A voice *(whispery, echoey)* Cold wind: snow wind.

MAGGIE *(brisk, busy)* There's beasts to be fed, snaw or blaw!

Voice Cold. Ice. Iron.

MAGGIE *(with a certain satisfaction)* A green yule makes a fat kirkyard!

As TOTTIE *starts speaking, light comes on her. Her voice gets louder. She is brandishing a graip – maybe there are tin cans or something else tied to it that make a noise when she brandishes. She is swathed for winter (as are the rest of the cast here, but not quite so wildly) – straw-rope leggings, her arms covered in extra knitted over-sleeves; fingerless mitts, shawl, the headhankie pulled protectively well around the face. A right tumshie-bogle.*

TOTTIE *(voice becomes less childish, harsher, more violent as she recites)*

>Get up auld wife and shake your feathers
>Ye needna think that we're a' wheen beggars
>We're only some bits o bairns come oot to play
>Get up – and gie's oor Hogmanay!

Aggressive now, hitting out maybe – whanging the straw bales/stack/hedgerow with the graip or just beating about with it, or beating the ground.

---

[1] Masquerading.

Hogmanay-Hogmanick

Hang the baker ower the stick

When the stick begins to break

Take another and break his back

TOTTIE, LIZA, SARA — *and* MAGGIE, *who talks with them, but has work to do in her own 'home area.'*

SARA Tottie!

TOTTIE No!

SARA We'll be late for the field, Tottie.

TOTTIE I want to play.

MAGGIE Don't be daft, now.

TOTTIE *(with menace)* Not!

MAGGIE The maister'll be after you.

TOTTIE A' the men are after Tottie!

SARA Tie up yer claes, we're going to the field.

TOTTIE I'm playing!

SARA We've to work, Tottie. No work, no shillings.

MAGGIE You're too big to play!

TOTTIE I'm married now!

MAGGIE Leave her be. What's the use when she's this way?

SARA If I leave her be she'll go deaving[1] the men.

TOTTIE I'm going guising. Going to guise the ploomen in the chamber.

SARA No, you're not. You're not to go there, Tottie. Leave the men alone.

TOTTIE *(violent. She's still apart from them, by herself)*

'Hogmanay, Hogmanick

Take another and break his back' . . .

A'body wants Tottie. A' the men are after Tottie.

LIZA *watching all this, watching* SARA *and* TOTTIE, *miserable for herself and them.*

MAGGIE Best leave her for now. Best get moving. You'll make the steward angry if you're late — aye, and the maister. No work, no pay.

SARA *goes towards the field.* TOTTIE *sulking.*

MAGGIE *(with venom, she's meaning* LIZA*)* Dirt! . . . Dirt!

LIZA, *utterly miserable, follows* SARA *towards the field.*

SCENE TWO

TOTTIE *by the stacks/bales.*

TOTTIE *(a slow, sour version of her former jig/song)*

Tottie loves the plooman

Tottie's black-eyed plooman

Kello is the plooman

Throws herself against the stack, beats at it a bit with her body, her arms, her fists . . .

Not fair. Wasn't there. Not fair. Didn't come . . .

'Away up the moor, Tottie,' he says. 'I'll meet you up on the moor.'

But he didnae. Kello.

There was a man there, but it wasnae him.

Twixt me and the sun. Just the one man.

He was stood in the rigs, the lang syne rigs.

'A week's work done in a day,' he cries.

'We don't need you now!

We don't need folk. We don't need horses.

---

[1] Deafening; annoying.

Machines without horses.
We've plenty bread now,' he cries.
'Too much bread.'
He was pleased. He was laughing.
But I wasnae feared. *(She's laughing a bit, it pleases her.)*
For he wasnae the ghost.
I was! I was the ghost!

VOICES *(whilst speaking these lines, they are moving into position, still muffled in headhankies, mitts, etc., still 'hauden-doon' by winter. Spoken quite matter-of-factly, either singly, turn by turn, or in unison)*
Barley means bread
Pease means bread
Oats means bread
Wheat means bread
Corn means bread

TOTTIE *(in the middle of the above, on top of their words – the voices do not pause)* 'We've plenty bread now,' he cries. 'Too much bread.'

VOICES
Never enough bread
Give us this day our daily bread
The bread of carefulness

TOTTIE 'Too much bread now! Mountains!' he cries.

VOICE(S) The bread of progress!

SCENE THREE

ELLEN *(polite teatime voice – a teapot or cakestand? – she's talking to the foreigners visiting the show farm of Blacksheils)* Progress? Progress! The key to progress is rotation: Maister Elliott's six-course rotation. Famed throughout the land; throughout Europe. Corn, potatoes, turnips, and swedes, clover, and rye grass, with a good stock of sheep and cattle. Sixty tons of farm manure. Twelve hundredweight of artificials. Wheat yields – up! Potato yields – up! The rent? – up! – naturally. Raised by the Marquis according to our yields. Rotation! Rotation of course applies also to the work force. On farms of this size we have to be exact. Twenty men and eight women in winter, eighteen extra women and boys in summer. The steward can't do with less, the master can't pay for more.

(Not talking to the visitors here.) If Jimmy Eagan's too frail now to work,
Then he and his family must move elsewhere,
For his house is needed for a younger hind,
And his wife and three daughters are surplus to requirements.
If Tam Neil's lad is ready for the fields,
The family will have to seek a new place at the Hiring,
We've too many young boys at Blacksheils already,
We don't need more half-yins, We need more hinds,
We need more bondagers and unmarried ploughmen.

(To the visitors again.) Of course, they never move far . . . ten, fifteen miles . . . They're used to it. Some welcome it . . . 'So long as it's dry for the flitting!'

(No longer addressing the visitors.) 'Please God: Keep them dry for the flitting' . . . He's a fair man, the maister. He'd have built a new row of houses by now – if it wasn't for the Marquis raising the rent. 'I overlook small faults in a good workman,' says the maister. 'I've lived here all my life,' he says. 'I know this place like I know my own hand. I know the Border peasant: honest, industrious, God fearing . . . '

He never knew me, never knew my name even, till I set my cap at him. The first year of marriage, I still had the face of a bondager: white below, where the kerchief had been tied, the top of my cheeks and my nose dirt brown. The ladies stared, and smiled behind their fans. But I'm all pale now, I'm a proper lady now.

Not once has he asked me what it was like: to live in the row, to work in the fields. Not once . . . They've made a lady of me now.

SCENE FOUR

MAGGIE, TOTTIE, SARA, LIZA . . . and ELLEN *later. All working, or about to.* MAGGIE *working in, or for, her own house.* LIZA *filling buckets or a barrow with neeps to feed the beasts (or crushing the neeps in the crusher).* SARA *helping* TOTTIE *to 'breech her claes,' i.e. kirtle up her skirts, so that they're almost like trousers, ready for work.*

SARA Has he spoken to Andra, the maister?

MAGGIE No. Not yet. Has he spoken to you?

SARA *(shakes her head)* No. Not yet. Not to anyone yet. Not that I've heard. *(Without conviction.)* Well. there's time . . .

LIZA There's hardly any time. It's past Hogmanay.

A pause. Uneasy.

SARA Maister Elliott always speaks well before the Hiring. He's good that way.

MAGGIE Not long till the Hiring now.

LIZA First Monday in February.

Uneasy pause.

MAGGIE He's bound to keep some on. The steward; the herd. And he's well pleased with Andra, he'll be speaking to Andra. *(To* SARA.*)* Ellen'll see that you're kept on, don't fret.

SARA Tottie's had bad days. Too many bad days.

MAGGIE And who's to blame? Kello. Well, they won't keep him on, that's for sure. It's a wonder he wasn't sent packing before – straight after the kirn! Mind, the same could be said for some other – dirt!

SARA That's not right, Maggie, that's not fair!

MAGGIE You don't know the half of it. Don't know the half of her! Flaunty piece of – dirtery!

SARA *wants to smooth this, but can't.*

MAGGIE, SARA, LIZA, *all speaking and shouting at once here:*

MAGGIE *(to* LIZA*)* Her father must be turning in his grave. Dirt. If the maister only knew, he'd send her packing. Dirt – that's all she is.

LIZA *(incoherent, upset)* My father – aye, he must – at you – at you and your man. What do you expect me to do – what? If my father knew – if Steenie was here – he'd – if it's not right – it's not.

MAGGIE Just like her mother. Maisie Kerr – no better than she should be. Tinkler trash!

SARA That's not true, Maggie, that's not true at all!

LIZA Liar! That's a lie!

ELLEN What's all this? All this noise? Haven't you work enough to keep busy? The maister's sick of all this clamjamfray. Where's Tottie – Tottie? – Tottie, come here –

TOTTIE *comes, without enthusiasm.* ELLEN *hugs her, but she doesn't reciprocate.*

ELLEN Why haven't you been working? Bad girl. Wild girl! *(Says this nicely, cajolingly, but* TOTTIE, *sulky, is tying to break away.)* You used to be a good worker, Tottie. You've got to be good. Hey, now, promise me, now – you'll be a good girl now.

TOTTIE *retreats to stack, bale, somewhere.*

ELLEN *(to* SARA*)* The steward's been grumbling to the maister. She deaves all the men, she throws herself at Kello.

MAGGIE Kello shouldn't be here. They should have sent him away.

ELLEN Yes. I know.

MAGGIE Then why did they not?

ELLEN Because she wouldn't say. Tottie wouldn't say. *(To* TOTTIE.*)* You should have told them, Tottie, you should have told them what happened to you.

MAGGIE She said it all to us. Don't they believe it? There was blood on her claes.

ELLEN I know.

MAGGIE He should have been punished.

ELLEN *(knowing how feeble this is)* They did punish him, the men.

MAGGIE Oh – they douked him in the trough, and kicked him round the yard. But they feel sorry for him now. Some of the lads admire him, almost, some of the lassies even. It's Tottie they're angry at now.

LIZA *very silent, very subdued – and very resentful.*

SARA He changed Tottie. He stole her.

MAGGIE They laugh and swear at her now.

ELLEN 'I keep a steward to manage my workers.' That's all the maister says, that's all he'll say. 'I won't keep a dog and bark for myself.'

MAGGIE He barks when it's lassies causing the trouble. He sent Minnie packing . . . almost before we'd time to find out why!

ELLEN And the steward won't budge. 'It takes two,' he says. 'Takes two to smoor the fleas.' You know how they are – maisters, stewards – they leave things be, till the turn of the year. They leave it till the Speaking, and let the bad ones go. Leave it till the Hiring, and let them go.

MAGGIE *(with some satisfaction)* No one'll hire Kello. That's for sure!

ELLEN I wouldn't be so certain. He's good with the horses, he's a hero with horses.

MAGGIE *(with a venomous look at* LIZA*)* Folk like that are left till last at the Hiring! Lads or lassies!

SARA It's us who'll get left, Tottie and me.

ELLEN You won't need to go to the Hiring, Sara. You can stay on here, you know that surely. But see she behaves. If she won't do any work, at least keep her quiet – and away from the men. For the maister won't stand for all this – nonsense.

SARA *obviously feels this is easier said than done.*

ELLEN She throws up her skirts, she rushes at Kello, the other men have to pull her away.

SARA *(very quietly)* He changed Tottie, he stole her.

MAGGIE If she hated him now – if she feared him, even – well, that would make sense.

SARA She's angry at him – but not that way.

ELLEN You know what they say? 'Well, no wonder,' they say. 'No wonder what happened, just look at the way she behaves, poor Kello, poor man, it wasn't his fault, he'd had a few, mind, why not, at the kirn, and what was she doing there out in the field – asking for it.' That's what they say.

SARA I know.

MAGGIE *(going off, brisk, busy)* Not the only one asking for it. And not just in the fields, either! Sleekit piece of dirtery!

SARA *(to* TOTTIE*; as she talks, she fetches* TOTTIE, *and ushers her reluctantly off)* We'll spoil a few moudies[1] in the far field, Tottie, eh? You like doing that. Fetch your hoe, we'll give the moudieworps a gliff.

ELLEN *(she has been aware of* LIZA's *reactions, and the vibes from* MAGGIE *throughout this scene)* Liza!

LIZA I've the beasts to feed.

ELLEN *(signals* LIZA *to come nearer)* There's Mary and Jenny to see to the beasts. Tell them I needed you up at the House. It's no more than the truth – there's flax to be spun!

LIZA *(miserable, awkward, won't meet* ELLEN's *eye)* Can't spin. I don't want to spin.

ELLEN *(though never sentimental, touched now by* LIZA's *misery)* Don't listen to Maggie, what she said about your mother, it isn't true. She's jealous, that's all. Your father was fierce but a'body liked your mother.

LIZA How would you know?

ELLEN Steenie told me. Over and over.

---

[1] Moles.

LIZA *wants very much to go.*

ELLEN Liza. It wasn't your fault. About Kello and Tottie. You're not to blame. Don't let them blame you. Jenny's not blamed. She holds up her head. Don't let them blame you.

LIZA *(frustrated, near to tears)* It's not just that . . . It's *her*!

ELLEN Maggie?

LIZA *Him!*

ELLEN Kello?

LIZA *shakes her head.*

ELLEN Andra?

LIZA *nods.*

ELLEN *(incredulous)* Andra!

LIZA *(blurting this, chopping it up)* It's not my fault. It's not. Just because I – because because of Kello – since the kirn – Maggie – they all think – they all think I'm – word gets round – it's not my fault – I haven't done anything . . .

ELLEN *(disbelief – not tragically shocked, because she can't take Andra all that seriously – maybe a hint of mirth already in her voice)* Andra.

LIZA *(upset)* She won't – I can't help hearing them at night – and then he – I hate it, hearing them – she won't let him, she won't touch him – and then he – he comes and stands by the other bed. I keep the curtains drawn, I hug the bairns close, the two on the outside, and the wee one between me and the wall – but they sleep like the dead – he stands there, I can hear him – she can hear him, that's the worst, she can hear him, I hear her listening – but it's not my fault – it's not my fault – it's not . . .

ELLEN But he doesn't – does he? – Andra? What does he do?

LIZA Nothing. He stands there. Breathing.

ELLEN *can no longer hold in her laughter, fairly snorts with mirth.*

LIZA *(outraged at this response)* It isn't funny. It isn't my fault.

ELLEN Andra! It would be like going to bed with a tumshie[1]! *(Beginning to laugh again.)*

LIZA *(in self-defence)* He isn't in my bed. *(Almost in defence of him.)* I don't think he's a tumshie! He's got awful bonny legs.

ELLEN Oh?

LIZA I've spied them through the curtains.

ELLEN Ah.

LIZA I like working with Andra. That wall-eyed mare, the one that kicks, she was ramming me tight against the stable wall, I was losing my breath, but Andra came along and roared and whacked her, he showed me how to roar and whack, she's been quiet with me since.

ELLEN *(laughter threatening again)* Ummm.

LIZA I don't want him in my bed, whatever Maggie says. I don't want him at all. I'm not a bad girl.

ELLEN I know that, Liza. I know you're not bad. *(Without remorse, quite fondly.)* Ellen Rippeth was bad, Ellen Rippeth-that-was . . . I was douce[2] with Steenie, though, I wasn't bad to Steenie . . . Have you heard from Steenie?

LIZA *shakes her head.*

ELLEN Saskatchewan. Are they douce there, I wonder?

LIZA You sent him away.

ELLEN *(brisk)* Thistles!

LIZA Steenie left because of you.

ELLEN Bonnets! He set off for Canada like you set off for Coldstream brig – he never made up his mind – he'd no mind to make up. You're two of a kind – you and your brother – fresh pats of butter still waiting on the stamp. He was ower young, Steenie. I didn't love him, Liza.

---

[1] Turnip.

[2] Pleasant.

LIZA *(muttering) You* don't love the maister, either.

ELLEN What?

LIZA But you love the maister, do you?

ELLEN *(very quietly)* Almost. Almost.

A pause. Each lost in her own thoughts – of the maister; of Kello.

LIZA Kello can ride the maister's black mare – make it dance, and turn in a ring. He stands on its rump, whilst it circles around, he keeps his balance, he takes off his jacket, his waistcoat, his kerchief. *(She is moving, dancing really, as she recalls watching Kello, in the summer, in the paddock.)* . . . A red-spotted kerchief. He aye keeps his balance, the mare canters round, and around, and around, and when Kello jumps off, he turns in the air, right round in the air, and lands on his feet . . . A red-spotted kerchief . . . His eyes are aye laughing, he dances so trig. He showed me the steps. He stroked my hair.

ELLEN Tinkler, sorner,[1] seducer – thief!

LIZA *(taken aback; then braving it out)* I know.

ELLEN That's all right then, so long as you know. The maister locks the doors at night to keep him away from the dairymaids. So now he meets with the hedger's wife instead when he's not walking over to Langriggs at night. The parlourmaid there – they meet in the woods. Bella Menteith. Huh! Who would have thought! Well, she's no chicken – and so perjink![2]

It's a kick in the teeth for Liza. ELLEN *didn't mean to say so much.*

LIZA *(face-saving; lying)* I knew all that! A'body kens that!

LIZA *goes.*

SCENE FIVE

ELLEN, MAGGIE, TOTTIE. TOTTIE *appears – maybe been hiding nearby for a while.*

ELLEN *(softly; taking account of* TOTTIE*'s presence, but not directly to her)* A'body kens that. Don't they, Tottie?

TOTTIE *(ditto: not directly to* ELLEN *at this point)* 'I'll meet you,' he says. He keeps on saying 'Away up the moor – down by the mill – along by Craig Water – I'll meet you there, soon – I'll meet you there later.' But he doesnae.

ELLEN You don't want to see Kello, Tottie. He's a bad man.

TOTTIE Yes, he is.

ELLEN Then you must leave him alone.

TOTTIE *still has her hoe, she's been hoeing down molehills. She attacks the ground, or something, hay bale, something, with her hoe.*

TOTTIE Foxton field's plagued with moudies – moudie hillocks all over the field. Ten, two, a hundred moudies!

    Hogmanay, Hogmanick
    Find the moudie and break its neck
    Find its hillock and ding it doon
    Ding! Dang! – BANG!
    – Seven hillocks, seven moudies!

(Well aware of ELLEN*, half an eye on* ELLEN*.)*

    Moudiewort, moudiewort, run to the Tweed
    For your hillock's danged doon, and we all want you dead
    Ding, dang – damn!

(Repeats this with quieter pleasurable concentration.)

    Damnation! Damn! Damn!

But ELLEN *is walking away (maybe not right offstage).*

    Hell! Damn! A hundred moudies! Yes, he's bad. I know where he bides. He bides in the

---

[1] Extortionist, beggar.
[2] Neat, fussy.

chamber up above the new stables. He's to fetch me a clock, still. And a bed. *(She's by the cradle now.)* Hasn't he, babby? Eh? Wee babby. Bee-baw-babbity.

MAGGIE *bustling in:*

MAGGIE Now then, Tottie, keep away from wee Joe. You shouldn't be here – you've work to do. Mind what Mistress Ellen told you.

TOTTIE I'm minding the babby.

MAGGIE No, no. Not now. Take that hoe out of here. You're not to mind the babby any more, he's – he's too big for you to mind now.

TOTTIE He's not. I'm bigger.

MAGGIE *(losing patience; has the baby in her arms now, waiting for* TOTTIE *to go)* Away you go now, Tottie, get that hoe out of here!

TOTTIE *gives the cradle a push, maybe with her hoe, and goes, leaving the cradle rocking.* MAGGIE, *still holding the baby, follows* TOTTIE *a little way, but not offstage, to make sure she's really going.*

SCENE SIX

ELLEN, MAGGIE, SARA.

ELLEN *(not talking directly to* SARA *yet – nor to* MAGGIE*)* I like the idea of a winter baby. Swaddled in shawls. I'd feed him in bed by the light of the fire. I'd keep him safe from the feeding storms. When spring burst on us, he'd be fat as a lamb, he'd laugh at the leaves.

MAGGIE *(muttering)* Lie in bed? All right for some! *(Busy, busy . . . self-righteousness increasing.)* Lying in bed! With a baby to look after? *(Seems to calm down . . . and then it gets to her again. With scorn and envy.)* Lying in bed! Huh!

She goes. Meanwhile SARA *appears, with some quiet kind of work, maybe knitting (she would be knitting as she walked).*

ELLEN *(to* SARA*)* What do I have to take, Sara? What do I have to do? Don't say: 'Time enough!' Don't say: 'Be patient!' I need a child now! Not for me – well, not for me only for the maister! *(. . .)* Sara?

But SARA *can't think what to say.*

ELLEN It was your mother brought me into the world. She knew all the cures. My mother always said she did. You know them, too, don't you?

SARA Be happy, Nell. You were happy as a lark, once. And so was the maister.

ELLEN He has things on his mind. Yields per acre, tiles for drainage . . . mortgage for mortgage . . . I don't know what. I'm useless in that great house! Dressing up; pouring tea. His mother minds the house, Betty Hope minds me. I'd shift the sharn if it'd help; mangle the neeps, feed the beasts. I watch him at his desk, writing, counting. He doesn't even know I've come into the room. He breaks my heart. I only want it for him. I'm plump, I'm greedy, I'm healthy! Damn it, why can't I swell? It happens soon enough for those who don't want it, who don't even think about it!

SARA Then don't think about it, Nell.

Exasperation from ELLEN.

There's time.

More exasperation.

Be patient!

ELLEN Sara!

SARA And don't let him sit at his desk all night. You can't fall for a baby while he sits at his desk!

They laugh.

ELLEN *(. . .)* There's a herb. It cures a'thing, my mother used to say. It grows round these parts. I don't know its name. But it looked like a docken. I remember she said that.

SARA *shakes her head very slightly, as she continues knitting or whatever.*

ELLEN You know about it, don't you? You know where it grows?

SARA It cured cuts and wounds. We put the leaves on the wound, and bandaged them round. I never knew it to fail for things like that. For sickness too, and fevers, and wasting.

ELLEN Barrenness?

SARA *(gently)* Nell –

ELLEN Tell me where it grows. I'll fetch some. I'll dig it up. Tell me what to do with it. Eat it? Wear it? I'll wrap myself in it from head to heel.

SARA It used to grow at Craig's Pool. It never had a name. 'The leaves by Craig Water,' that's what we cried it. But – I'm not sure it would have cured barrenness, Nell –

ELLEN I could try.

SARA You aren't barren, Nell – you're spun dizzy with nerves. You just need to –

ELLEN Craig's Pool – on the crook of the river?

SARA The leaves don't grow there now.

ELLEN Where else do they grow?

SARA That's the only place we ever knew of. But they don't grow there now. The maister had a wall built, some years ago – to keep the river from flooding the fields. He had the bank raised. They moved tons of earth. And build a braw dyke, and a paving on the bank so we could wash the linen. *(. . .)* Nobody thought. We used the leaves all the time – your mother was right, we used them for a'thing . . . well *(partly her sensible opinion, and partly tying to comfort* ELLEN *in her dismay)* not so much for babies, Nell, some women tried, but I don't –

ELLEN I could have tried. I could have tried.

SARA Nobody thought to save any of the roots. Nobody gave it any thought . . .

SCENE SEVEN

All (except ELLEN*).* TOTTIE *brandishing a letter,* LIZA, *desperate, furious, tying to get it back. A silent, quite vicious struggle, shoving, wrestling, pinching, kicking. And* TOTTIE *wins.*

LISA Give it me.

TOTTIE No.

LISA It's mine.

TOTTIE No.

LISA It's not yours.

TOTTIE Sas-katch-e-wan.

LIZA It's not yours.

TOTTIE My daddy's been away for a hundred year.

LIZA You can't read anyway.

TOTTIE I can so, I can. Collop Monday, Pancake Tuesday, Ash Wednesday, Bloody Thursday, Lang Friday, Hey for Saturday afternoon; Hey for Sunday at twelve o clock, Whan a' the plum puddings jump out o the pot.

Throughout this recitation LIZA *is trying to shut her up, shout her down:*

Lisa That's not reading. You can't read. Daftie! You can't read, Tottie!

TOTTIE *is upset.* LIZA *beginning – slightly – to take pity on her, but still irritated and fearful for her letter. A moment's pause.* TOTTIE *gets out the letter – keeping it well away from Liza's snatching hands, begins to 'read' it:*

TOTTIE *('reading' letter)*

    'Here's tae ye a' yer days
    Plenty meat and plenty claes
    Plenty porridge and a horn spoon
    And another tattie when a's done.' *(. . .)* I can so, I can read.

LIZA Here. I'll read it to you. *(. . .)* It's a story. There's a story in the letter – from Steenie, my brother. I'll read you the story.

Very slowly TOTTIE *gives in, gives* LIZA *the letter. As* LIZA *opens the letter* TOTTIE *suddenly changes mood, all excitement, all smiles, jumps, dances about, laughing, yelling, yelling at the top of her voice.*

TOTTIE Hey-ey! Oooo-oh! Hey-ey! Liza's got a letter. Liza's reading a letter. A letter. A story. A story. A letter. Sas-katch-e-wan!

They all come forward, as for a story (it is, for them).

LIZA *(reads)* 'Dear Sister: I am writing letting you know I am in good health. The country is good if a man keeps his health. The land costs eleven shillings and thruppence an acre, but we must take up our axes and cut down the trees. Should he not take land, a man gets four shillings a day and his meat which is no bad wage. Donald McPhail is here, I am staying with him still, he has sixty acres, and Walter Brotherston from Coldstream, one hundred acres.

'The winter here is long. The ice floats in the lake like so many peats, and some the size of a house. The Indians say that Hell is made of snow and ice, and they say that heaven is alive with buffalo. There is buffalo everywhere for eating, they belong to no master. There are no masters here, and no stewards, and no pride. If a man be civil he is respected. I have dined with gentlemen and been asked to say the grace. My – *(She stops dead, astonished.)* my wife – '

They wait for enlightenment, amused, curious.

LIZA *(reads)* 'My wife Emily joins with me in her best respects to you. This letter is brought by her father, Mr Monroe, who is going home to Edinburgh owing to his health.'

They wait – surely there's more?

LIZA *(reads)* 'Your loving brother, Steenie.'

But surely there's more?

LIZA *(reads)* 'PS. Tell John Mackintosh if he comes he need bring no axes, just the clothes for the voyage.' *(LIZA stares at the letter, nonplused, lonely.)*

TOTTIE *(softly)* Buffalo . . . Buffalo . . .

MAGGIE Men!

SARA But it's a grand letter, Liza, and grand news of Steenie. You must write to the wife, you'll get more crack from his wife.

JENNY *(suddenly, merrily, jigging about)*
Woo'd and married and a'
Kissed and carried awa!

She and TOTTIE *jigging about, tying to get* LIZA *to jig/dance also – but* LIZA *is still taking in the news of the letter, half-thrilled at the news, at any news, half let-down . . . bewildered . . . at the gaps in the news, at the fact that Steenie, now married, belongs to her less.* TOTTIE *and* JENNY *dance around her, jostle, even push her, but she doesn't join in.*

TOTTIE, JENNY And is no the bride well off
That's woo'd and married and a'!

They're all thinking over the news. LIZA *is silent, holding her letter, tracing the seal, the writing, with her finger. She pays only intermittent attention to the ensuing conversation, goes off to some quiet corner to sit with her letter, or goes offstage.*

SARA Walter Brotherston! A hundred acres! *(She starts to laugh.)* Well, he was a young limmer[1] and no mistake! Remember the night of that kirn at Westlea?

MAGGIE *(frosty)* I certainly do.

SARA *(enjoying herself)* There were half a dozen bairns – the wee ones, just babies sleeping in the hay at the farthest end of the barn. Oh, they were good as gold, not a cheep out of them, and of course around dawn everyone started for home, and the mothers were tired out, and the babies sleeping like the dead. So it wasn't till later, till they were all home, that they found out what Walter had done!

MAGGIE He should have been whipped!

SARA It wasn't just him, it was Jamie as well. They'd changed the babies round. They'd changed all the clothes, the bonnets and shawls. Six babies! – and all of them home with the wrong mother!

JENNY But they'd notice, the mothers!

---

[1] Rascal.

SARA *(laughing)* Eventually! What a squawking and screeching across the fields – it sounded like a fox had got amongst the hens.

MAGGIE *(muttering under* SARA's *words)* A swearing scandal, that's what it was!

SARA The blacksmith's bairn was away up the hill with the shepherd and his wife! And Maggie's wee Tam ended up in the village, who was he with again, Maggie, was it Phoebe?

MAGGIE *(grim)* I went to feed and change my bairn – and he'd turned into a lassie! Oh, you can laugh. But there's many a baby been changed by the Gyptians – so what was I to think? He was never a Christian that Walter Brotherston – and neither's that scoundrel Jamie Dodds. They aye watch him at the kirk! He'll more likely take money out the plate than put anything in.

JENNY And when he does put something in, it's only a halfpenny.

SARA There's plenty he gives that no one knows of. He gives to the needy. Many a time.

MAGGIE *(grudgingly)* He's a grand worker, I'll grant you that.

SARA Ay. *(. . .)* The maister will be keeping *him* on, likely.

A pause. These days they are all nagged by the same thought.

SARA Has he spoken to Andra yet, the maister?

MAGGIE No. Not yet. Has he spoken to you?

SARA No.

JENNY You don't need to fret, Sara. Ellen said you were biding on.

SARA Well, he hasn't spoken yet.

MAGGIE Maybe he's waiting till he's paid his rents. He'll be paying the rents on Friday down at the inn. They say the Marquis'll be there to collect in person this year. And the usual grand dinner for the tenants.

JENNY Hare soup. And goose. And plum pudding. And whisky 'as required.'

They dwell on this in silence. The conversation is becoming desultory, the scene ends (and light fades) quietly, conventionally.

JENNY The chimney piece at the inn takes up most of one wall. I've seen it from the yard, I've keeked through the window. They don't need candles with a blaze like yon.

They dwell on this too.

TOTTIE Plum pudding. Buffalo.

JENNY I wish I was a hedgehog . . . or a frog . . .

TOTTIE You're a cuckoo!

JENNY I wish I was. A frog. A cuckoo. I don't know what they do in the winter, those beasts. But you never see them working the fields.

Everyone has left by now, except TOTTIE.

TOTTIE Buffalo, buffalo, run up to heaven

For they want you all dead

And you'll soon be all gone.

(Suddenly boisterous.) Hey for Sunday at twelve o clock

When all the buffalo jump out the pot!

I can read, I can. I can write, too. I can write a grand letter. 'Dear Kello, What fettle? I am in good fettle, hope this finds you in the same. Did you see me in the glass? I saw you in the glass when the clock struck twelve. I want a clock that strikes twelve. I want to lie down right, not leaning up agin the stack. I want a plaidie on the bed, it canna hurt that way. 'Come under my plaidie, the night's going to fa'.' *(She is maybe almost half-singing the next lines, very softly, very low.)*

Come in frae the cold blast, the drift, and the snaw

Come under my plaidie, and lie down beside me

There's room here, dear lassie, believe me, for twa.

SCENE EIGHT

VOICES/CHORUS. LIZA, MAGGIE, SARA, JENNY, TOTTIE. *Couple of days since previous scene.*

Winter afternoon/evening. Already dark. Lamps or candles. From the beginning of the scene TOTTIE *hears and is aware of the commotion, but keeps separate from it . . . as if, by ignoring it, the commotion might simply disappear. As the lights go up, there is a great howl from* LIZA. *Then:*

LIZA Sara! Andra! Jenny! Maggie! Davie! Sara! Andra!

All this goes fast:

Voices What now?/ In the name of heaven?/ It's only Liza! Is that Liza?/ What a racket!/
 Where's the fire? What's happened?/ These lassies!/ What's wrong?

LIZA Get the maister – Oh – God! – someone – doctor – he's hurt. He's lying all – He's
 lying all crooked. Bleeding. Dying.

VOICES *(coming in halfway through* LIZA*'s last speech)*
 Who's hurt?/ Where?/ Who's hurt?
 What's happened?/ Shush now!/ Calm down
 Who's hurt?/ Lying?/ Dying?/ Bleeding?
 Where is he? Where?
 There, lass, shush now
 Let her speak

LIZA It's Kello. It's Kello. He's lying all crooked on the stable floor. At the foot of the ladder
 that leads to his chamber. Bella found him. Bella –

VOICES
 Bella Menteith!
 Bella Menteith?
 Huh, well – ! Shush, let her speak!

LIZA She shouted on me. She's there with him now. He's – It's Kello.

VOICE(S) Why didn't you run to the house?

LIZA There's no one there.

VOICE(S) Jenny, run to the house.

LIZA There's no one there.

VOICES It's the day for the rents
 They're down at the inn
 They're all at the inn
 The steward
 The maister
 But where's the mistress?

LIZA There's no one there.

VOICE(S)
 Fetch water
 Whisky
 Lineament
 Prayer . . .

A pause. Fearful.

LIZA *(quietly)* There's blood coming out of him. Out of his head.

SARA *(to* JENNY, *in fact, but as if to several)* Fetch the trap. For the doctor. Go on now.

MAGGIE Yes. Fetch the trap. Go and harness the mare.

MAGGIE, LIZA, SARA *are now watching 'the others' (i.e.,* JENNY*) go.* LIZA *obviously not keen to go back to the stables.* TOTTIE *still ignoring it all.* SARA *can't move – neither towards the stables to help nor towards* TOTTIE, *whom she is acutely aware of:*

MAGGIE *(going now too)* I'll follow them on. If you'll mind the bairns. Keep the bairn safe
 from – *(She means from* TOTTIE.)

SARA Yes, Maggie.

MAGGIE *(on her way)* Lying all crooked! That's rich – for a Gyptian! *(A dart at* LIZA.)
 Nothing but trouble!

All this time TOTTIE *has been determinedly tying to ignore the rumpus, tying not to care (and not to be noticed), birling the handles of her hoe or graip to and from one hand to the other, or fiddling, doodling, in some other way.*

LIZA *(in shock, really)* Bella Menteith. I was going to the dairy. She called from the yard, from the stable door.

SARA Who else was there?

LIZA No one.

SARA *She* found him?

LIZA He fell. There's blood coming out of him where he fell.

SARA She saw him fall?

LIZA She found him. I don't know. Kello. He's dying.

SARA Oh, now, you don't know that. I've seen several given up for dead. Why, my own *(Breaks off, looks at* TOTTIE; *very softly.)* my own . . .

LIZA Bella Menteith. She's no chicken!

SARA Are you sure there was no one else there?

LIZA There was no one about. I went to the Big House. There was no one about.

SARA *(she's comforting* LIZA, *calming her)* It's the day for the rents. They'll still be at the inn. They'll sit long at the dinner. The Marquis is there.

LIZA But Andra, and Tam, and —

SARA They'll be playing pitch-and-toss at the back of the inn. With the stable boys. There'll be whisky going spare from the tenants' dinner. If the farmers drink, why shouldn't the men?

LIZA But not Kello . . . Kello was here . . . Bella Menteith . . . Maggie thinks . . . I wasn't going to the stables, I was going to the dairy . . .

SARA *(ushering* LIZA *over to the cradle)* Go and sit with the bairns, my burdie. Go on now, till Maggie gets back. Look after wee Joe. *(Takes her arm, pats her, soothes her — but it's* TOTTIE *who's on her mind.)* Tottie?

TOTTIE No.

SARA Where have you been?

TOTTIE No.

SARA Where have you been?

TOTTIE Nowhere.

SARA You went to the stable?

TOTTIE No.

SARA Then where have you —

TOTTIE NO.

Big and strong, or small and wiry — she's more than a match fur SARA *when roused, as now — she pushes, or threatens* SARA, *and moves away. But she's scared . . . and she doesn't move all that far, stays on-stage somewhere.* SARA *turns away, but stays on-stage somewhere.*

SCENE NINE

MAGGIE *is summoned before the maister. He's tying to piece together what really happened. She is answering his questions. The others are present, also summoned to the maister's 'Inquiry.' There are whisperings before/just as* MAGGIE *speaks — Bella Menteith's name being whispered.*

MAGGIE Bella Menteith! Well, she's wrong, Maister Elliott. It wasn't like she said. Tottie wasn't — Tottie wouldn't —

Listens to the maister's questions.

Yes, sir. Well: Liza came screaming, and I ran to the stables, and Kello was lying at the foot of the ladder, and Bella Menteith —

Listens to the maister's questions.

Yes, sir. It was dusk. It was getting on for dark. But there was a light in the stables and another in the chamber. But they were all down at the inn, the men, so why would Kello — ?

Listens to the maister's questions.

No, sir. I never saw Tottie. I saw Bella Menteith. Kneeling over Kello. There was straw in her hair.

Listens to the maister's questions.

Yes, sir, I know that, sir. I know what she says. She said it all to me too, right there in the stables: she said she happened to be passing and she heard an argy-bargy and saw Tottie on the ladder, and that Tottie must have pushed him and that all Tottie said was 'it serves yourself right!' She said Tottie laughed and laughed up there on the ladder and yelled 'it serves yourself right.' I don't believe her, Maister Elliott. It wasn't like she said.

Listens to the maister.

Yes, sir – I know Tottie deaves all the men – Yes, sir, I know she's always after Kello, but she never wished him harm, sir, she's only a bairn. That night of the kirn – there was blood on her claes. He got off scot-free. She thought she was married –

But the maister cuts her short.

Yes, sir. (. . .) Thank you, sir.

She is dismissed, turns away, and her next words are not for the maister, but to herself, or maybe for SARA *and the others.*

Bella Menteith! It wasn't like she said. There was straw in her hair.

As MAGGIE *goes,* SARA *is putting on a black shawl, picking up a bible.*

CHILDREN *(or children's voices)*

Doctor, doctor, quick, quick, quick!

The black-eyed ploughman's sick, sick, sick!

Look at the blood coming out of his head!

Doctor, doctor, surely he's – ?

SARA So he died, and was waked. With pennies on his eyes and salt on his breast . . . Poor Kello. He was daft himself, if the truth be known. But he had that knack – horses, women – they softened at the very sound of his voice. And yet . . . no heart . . . no thought . . . no soul. That's what was wrong. If the truth be known. He wasn't all there. Poor young Kello. He was the one who wasn't all there.

CHILDREN *(or their voices. They are running around, playing at ghosties, laughing, enjoying scaring each other)*

Oooooooh! Here's Kello!

Here's a ghostie! Here's a bogle!

Oooooooh! Here's Kello!

Kello's coming to get you!

Tottie's seen a ghostie, Kello's ghostie!

Tottie's a daftie!

No all there!

Here's Tottie – Ooooh!

Shrieks of delighted fear. If they are present, and not just voices, they are flapping cloths – aprons, headhankies? – as they dart for TOTTIE, *then dart away again in fear.* TOTTIE *trying to catch them, or hit at them.*

Hideaway, hideaway! Hogmanay, Hogmanick! Hang the baker! Hang Tottie! Tottie's going to jaaaail! Stone walls, iron bars. They're going to put you awaaay! Hang the baker ower the stick. Hang the rope round Tottie's neck.

TOTTIE *lunges at them. They shriek – and run away. They are hiding somewhere, giggling, whispering, shushing.*

MAGGIE'S VOICE *(insouciant, without serious censure)* Now then, my burdies, what are you up to? Eh?

CHILD'S VOICE Tottie's in a swither!

SCENE TEN

TOTTIE, TWO WARDERS, MAGGIE, SARA. MAGGIE *and* SARA *are working somewhere, preferably in the field, away from the rest of the action.* SARA *knows what is about to happen, but can't bear to be there.*

TOTTIE, *still upset, relieved the taunting bairns have gone. Approaches the cradle, but warily since nowadays she's not allowed near. She picks up the baby's cane rattle – the old type with a bell inside the cane ball. Plays with it a bit . . . goes on playing with it while she's talking – her story seemingly less important than her concentration on the toy, as children seem, when they're trying to impart something that deeply troubles. She doesn't look at the baby, wrapped in her own world.*

TOTTIE *(not so maternal to the baby as she used to be)* I'll tell you a story if you like – it's true . . . He was up there in the chamber. He heard me coming up the ladder. Creepy, crawlie up the ladder. 'We don't need you!' he shouted. 'We don't need you now! Tak your hook, you!' He tried to kick me off the ladder. He hadn't any boots on, but I fell off, he made me fall. Ding! And the ladder fell. Clatter! – Bang! And he fell, Kello, from the top, from the trapdoor . . . dunt!

Two figures in grey cloaks – WARDERS – are creeping up on her. One of them is holding a blanket, or sheet – or maybe they are holding it between them.

He wasn't hurt bad – he didn't make a noise. Then she started to scream up there in the chamber. Her! Huh! She couldn't get down – and it served herself right – he was giving her the clock and the dresser and the bed – he was giving her the baby – Whoosh! – I heard. Creepy, crawlie up the ladder –

She breaks off somewhere in the last line as she senses the two behind her, turns round sharply. They have the sheet ready for the capture.

(Faltering, placating, retreating.) What fettle? Do you want a story? I'll tell you a story. I'll tell you a story of Jackanory.

They have taken hold of her, one on each side. She is paralyzed with fear, so doesn't struggle, at first. They wind the sheet around her.

TOTTIE No!

SARA *(she stops work, she's in pain, TOTTIE's anguish is piercing her)* Oh, no!

The WARDERS make a straitjacket of the sheet; in two or three well-practiced movements, that take TOTTIE by surprise, they have made her their prisoner.

TOTTIE No! No!

The two WARDERS are hustling TOTTIE away.

SARA *and* TOTTIE *both cry out 'NO' two or three times – not in unison – but we can hardly tell which cries come from whom.*

MAGGIE *(has been watching SARA anxiously)* Sara?

SARA *(flatly, not speaking to MAGGIE)* No.

MAGGIE Sara?

SARA No.

MAGGIE *(not directly to SARA. Even MAGGIE realises SARA is beyond conventional comfort at a time like this)* You can't keep your eyes in the back of your head. She'll be looked after where she's going. Poor maimed creature. The sheriff was right – she'll be better off there. Lucky it's not the jail. *(Lower.)* Lucky it's not the noose! And you won't have to pay for her keep. The well-off pay, but not the poor. There's a ward for the paupers –

SARA No!

MAGGIE I didn't mean ought. Be sensible, Sara – look at it this –

SARA I'll pay for my daughter, Patie's daughter. I'll pay.

ELLEN *has appeared by now.* LIZA *also – but not with* ELLEN.

SARA *(turning to ELLEN, a plea:)* I'll work.

But ELLEN *doesn't speak.*

MAGGIE *(to ELLEN, a reminder:)* It's only ten days till the Hiring. The maister hasn't spoken yet.

ELLEN The maister's out. The Elliotts are out. The lease is up – out – terminated. The great Lord Marquis has had enough: the foreign visitors, the mortgages, the politics. Maister Elliott got above himself, it seems: he supports the six-pound rise, he's standing for parliament. The Marquis is angry, very angry. The lease is up and not to be renewed. There'll be no Speaking at Blacksheils. Not this year. We'll be moving on too. Like the rest of you. *(. . .)* Will you come with us, Sara? I won't keep Betty Hope on. I'd rather have you.

SARA *(she is still in shock at* TOTTIE*'s incarceration)* But where will you go?

ELLEN *(a gesture – where indeed?)* We'll not get a lease round these parts. The Marquis owns all the farms round here.

SARA *(refusing the offer)* These fields are my calf-ground.

ELLEN *(softly)* Mine too.

SARA I've nothing else now.

ELLEN *turns away, goes.*

MAGGIE *(getting back to work again, picking up a bucket to feed or milk the cow)* It'll be cold for the Hiring. Bound to be. It's been a long winter – and more snow to come! *(Wistfully.)* I'd like a house with the two rooms. Maybe we'll get to Langriggs . . . *(*MAGGIE *goes off.)*

SARA She would tell me these stories, she said they were true.
She 'saw' them, she said, on the moor, in the mist.
In a hundred years – more
We'll be ghosts in the fields,
But we'll cry out in vain,
For there'll be no one there.
Fields without folk.
Machines without horses.
A whole week's harvest
All done in one night,
By the light of great lamps.
Not the light of the moon,
They won't wait for the moon . . . no need for the moon.

LIZA Sara? . . . We'll maybe both get to the same farm, Sara. If we do – will you teach me to spin?

Tony McManus (1953 –)

The Warld Cowps Lichtlie Ower Intil Black Nicht

The warld cowps★ lichtlie ower intil black nicht.	upends
The maik o nocht is discernibil.	
The yird is toom★. The wunds o ilka airt★	empty/quarter
Are still. The maik★ o nocht is sensibil.	form
Senses, theiveless★ as a tippit urn,	worthless
Black emptiness arises an faas doun,	
An aathing, envelopit, ceases tae be	
In touch or taste, sicht, smell or soun.	
An wi whit ferlie★ een, syne, dae I see	wonder-struck
Rise quick in the gowden mid–day sun, 10	
The reid glent in my dochter's wund–flaucht★ hair?	wind-blown
An frae whit marvellous, ayebidin★ sea	eternal
Dae aa thae bane-white, rowin★ brekkars run,	rolling
Faemin, gushin in the fresh, saut air?	

Neil MacCallum (1954 –)

Recognition

There will come a time
When ye will ettle★   struggle
Tae disregaird thae gloves
Deliberatlie tae lay thaim aside.
Barin til the bleffarts★   storm
The sleet and the rain
And craunreuch★ tae   frost
Throu weet and dry,
Yer haunds, alane
White and unprotectit.   10

By its ain
Will come a time
Chosen o itsel,
By its ain uncontestable instinct
The wey the weill wrocht gairdner kens
Frae luikin owre his grund,
Thon instant will hae arrived
Deemed ripent wi sufficiencie.

Dilys Rose (1954 –)

Every age has its stars, and its rising stars. For the prose-writing generation born in the fifties and sixties, Janice Galloway and A. L. Kennedy have been awarded much of the attention. But Dilys Rose has probably written Scottish short stories as well as anyone since James Kelman (b. 1946). Included also is her dramatization of one of her stories.

Figurehead

The fog thickens.
I see no ships.
The gulls left days ago

Ebbing into the wake
Like friends grown tired
Of chasing failure.

I miss their uncouth snatch and grab
Their loud insatiable hunger.
I see nothing but fog.

Before my ever-open eyes   10
The horizon has closed in
The world's end dissolved.

I lumber on, grudging my status –
I'm purpose-built to dip and toss
My cleavage, crudely carved

To split waves
My hair caked with salt
My face flaking off.

Fertility Doll

I'm nearly done – the belly
like a hand thrown bowl swells
with a homespun lack of symmetry
I swerve off-plumb.

I'm warm brown, a baked–clay shade
glazed to the sheen
of egg-brushed bread. A wholesome loaf
proving in the sun.

My days are numbered. All the same
my indolence is huge, my balance   10
precarious. This taut bulk
threatens to topple.

The man who made me cut me short
lopped off my legs, stuck
to the stumps two tiny feet –
his last caprice before dusk.

I was a laborious task. Now
my crammed mass is stilted,
pegged to the earth's crust
expecting dawn.   20

No Name Woman

All day she feeds the drunken menfolk
on the terrace. Between meals they gamble,
quarrel and groom their fighting cocks.
With one eye on her youngest child
(grubbing in the dirt for bugs)
she stirs the rice, ladles broth
from spoon to bowl, fans back
the ubiquitous flies. Steaming pots
and hot fat spit their hiss at her.

She wears the same rags constantly   10
a hand-me-down print wrap, the pattern
washed away, the hem a tatter
eats her dinner standing up
then clears and lays more tables
cradling plates to hush their clatter.

When only the rats nag for more
she sweeps the dirt floor clean.

Friendly Voices

I have been here too long. The city has shrunk into a village. *Incestuous* is a word bandied about the place by the stretching web of people I know. Not that I have a wide circle of friends – I have never been especially liberal with my affections and intimacy is something for which I have always had a certain reserve. Incestuous is not an exact description but close enough. Unwholesome enough. Yet we are not people who wish to be associated with the dirty underside of life, the margins of existence, the underdog, subculture. We talk about it, of course; we are all too aware of our tenuous position and ambiguous relationship and sympathise with those who, through no fault of their own, have found themselves on the fraying edge of our society.

It's the dug. Feart for it. Doesny say, like, but Raj knows well enough. Raj can smell the fear on her. Dirty big bastard that he is, makes straight for the crotch, pokes his wet nose into her baggy jeans. Ah let him sniff about a bit until she starts to get panicky, then ah call him aff and slap his arse so the both of them know who's boss around here. But ah'm an animal lover, a big softy where Raj is concerned. Love me love ma dug.

We talk about it, about them, but keep our distance. We have created areas of safety for ourselves or at least put in speak-entry systems and requested unlisted telephone numbers from British Telecom. We take certain routes through the city, avoid others. We know well enough what those other routes are like. We've seen them all before; in our student days when everything was briefly, falsely equal and later, as young professionals, early in our careers when we preached and practised a hands-on approach. Grass roots. We got down to grass roots. Not that grass was a particularly common feature of the landscape.

Once Raj has settled at ma feet, the doctor crosses her legs and clutches the top knee. Funny, never seen the wummin in a skirt. Probably a policy no tae send them up here showing a leg, in ease us lot, us *animals* get funny. Funny peculiar but. No supposed tae come up here on her ain, anyway, supposed tae have a mate wi her, for protection like. Ah tellt her she should get a dug. Hours a fun and guaranteed tae keep trouble at bay. That's unless trouble's got a dug of its ain.

There's no need to be reminded. It doesn't do any good to be reminded of things we can't change. We're not heartless but practical, having learned from experience that we can only function efficiently by maintaining a certain distance. We have our own problems – who doesn't – but we are, at heart, solvers, not sinkers.

When she comes in, she gies out this big sigh, like she's been holdin her breath all the way up in the lift. Probably has because the lift stinks. No all the time, no every single day. You might be lucky and catch it just after it's been washed, in which case you just about choke on the disinfectant. Me, ah'm used tae it. Doesnae mean ah like it, but some things you just put up wi.

Anyway, after Raj has had his wee thrill, ah let her settle intae the comfy chair and look around. She checks tae see how ah'm keeping the place, see if she can find clues as tae how the medication's workin afore she starts asking questions. No daft, this one, knows fine I'm a bloody liar, knows I'll say the first thing that comes intae ma heid tae confuse her. Tries tae get an idea of her ain, tae read between the fuckin lies ah spin her.

Shouldny come up here by hersel. Tryin tae make out she's brave and that, but she's crappin it all the same. She's all edgy, hingin aff the chair an that, eyes poppin out, kinda glaikit[1] like, crossin the legs one way an the other. Her jeans rub thegither at the crotch and the denim makes a kinda scrapin sound. She gies a wee kid-on cough and pretends to be dead interested in ma latest picture a Christ on the Cross. Crucified in a field full a sheep. Quite pleased wi that one when ah done it but now ah'm nae sure. Ah've got hunners a crucifixions anyway. She looks at ma picture and ah look at her crotch. The dug has left a damp patch on her jeans.

We've looked over the edge, know what lies there. We keep ourselves under control, in check, watch out for the signs, of losing the place, letting things slip. We know what to look out for. We're trained to spot the signs, like the weatherman is trained to read the clouds. It's what we do; spot the signs, make a forecast, though we like to think that meanings are not fixed, that there are options involved, possibilities.

No ma type at all, very plain. Nae make-up, jewelry – bet she's got plenty jewellry but leaves it at hame in case somebody gies her a doin – cropped hair, wee tits – ah mean, no a lot going for her, tae ma mind. Money but, she'll have plenty a that, plenty dosh for putting hersel out for the likes a me. Nice car. Nifty wee two-seater. Seen it last time she came. Frae the windae. Pale blue convertible. Can just picture her on a sunny day – the sleeveless dress on, something loose and cool, the open-toed sandals – pulling down the hood and belting out tae Loch Lomond. Bet she's a fast driver. Bet she gets a buzz frae rammin the accelerator intae the flair. Wouldnae mind a whirl in her motor masel. All ah ever get's the fucking ambulance or, for a treat, the paddy wagon. Ah'm no complainin, but. Never say no tae a wee bit drama.

Of course, everything's relative. One only has to pick up the paper to be re-minded just how much worse is daily life elsewhere: the Brazilian goldmine, say, where there is more malaria than gold; the bloody streets of Jerusalem or Johannesburg; the duplicitous back alleys of Bangkok or Rio, the hungry pavements of Bombay, New York, London. There are no goldmines on our doorstep, or war zones, no tin and board barrios, food queues. Yet.

She gets the chat goin so she can start tae suss out the state a the hoose. Sometimes ah clean up for her comin, sometimes ah dinnae. Depends. The place is a pure tip the day. Even if ah'm feeling no bad ah sometimes let the mess lie anyway, just tae see how she takes it. Like tae keep her on her toes. Dinnae want tae make her job too easy for her. Thinks she can tell the state a ma heid frae whether I've washed the dishes or no. And the chat's all geared tae pick up clues. Thinks she can earn her dosh by droppin in for tea and chitchat. Tries tae guess how ah'm daein frae what videos ah've watched, what magazines ah've read. Ah like it when she gets on tae that. Ah get a chance tae use ma imagination. Make up some brilliant titles, all horror and porn. Ah like tae get a wee blush goin on her, see that pulse start up at her throat. It's no a lot a response but she's no meant tae respond at all. It's her job tae stay neutral.

She's no bad, but. Means well. Heart in the right place and all that guff. Wants tae help. Ah mean, she could've gone for one a they plum jobs in the private sector, analysin the rich

---

[1] Foolish.

and famous in some plush place down south. The nurse who comes tae gie me ma drugs, ma monthly jab, he tellt me she's top notch, expert in her field. Could've been rakin it in, sinkin the excess intae a second hame, somewhere aff the beaten track, far away frae the hurly-burly a Harley Street, or wherever they doctors hing about these days. But no, she's chosen tae make her livin frae the likes a me.

We complain, particularly about the larger issues, particularly on behalf of others. We are outraged by what is happening in the world, indeed the state of the globe is one of the most popular subjects for conversation amongst people like us. We lie awake at night and worry about the depletion of the ozone layer, preservatives in food, the destruction of the rain forest, the incidence of cancer near nuclear sites and the latest epidemics, about religious fundamentalism, neo-fascism, wars, riots, strikes, demonstrations, disasters natural and man-made – hurricanes, droughts and floods, about aphids, wild dogs and mad cows.

But we get up in the morning, the sun is shining, a scent of blossom is in the air, the grass is fresh and green beneath the litter and dog-shit we are growing accustomed to in the municipal parks. Under a clear sky, joggers, dogwalkers, cyclists, down-and-outs, students and parents of young children take the air together, at their own speeds. There are cycle lanes, walking lanes and jogging tracks. A bird sings. Blossom drifts in pink clouds above our heads. A man on a tractor cuts the grass and cleans up yesterday's mess. Another day passes without event, without people like us overstepping the boundary between the solvers and the sinkers. We have accumulated the life-skills required to keep our individual globes turning fairly smoothly. We stay clear of the edge but don't allow ourselves to forget what lies beyond it. We care. People like us care.

She's near drunk all her tea by the time she gets on tae the voices. Just about time for her tae get goin when she brings them up. Have they been friendly? she says. Eh? Your voices . . . she says. Aw aye. Have they been friendly? she says. Aye, ah says, nae bother. Ah'm gonnae tell her about the state a ma heid, when the singin starts up. Ma ears go that plugged-up way like when you've got headphones on and the singin loups round ma heid. It's that kinda auld folky stuff, nae many words you can make out, just a miserable kinda moany sound but sorta nice wi it, soothin like. The doctor's askin me somethin. Ah cannae hear what she's sayin, ah just know it's a question cos she's got her heid cocked tae the side, like a budgie. Raj is sittin at ma feet, lookin up at me wi big sad eyes, daft dug that he is. Sometimes ah think he hears ma voices tae. Ah give him a clap and tickle his belly. Loves a good tickle, so he does.

My office is bright, sunny. The walls are painted a pale, buttery yellow. On the wall facing the door is a small watercolour of a decorative plate and some pearly mussel shells. Behind my desk, above a shelf where I keep a constantly updated selection of leaflets (and my shade-loving ferns) is a calm abstract painting: *Contemplation 4*. There were three other remarkably similar paintings in the small gallery where I bought it. Any of them would have done just as well. Buying paintings is not a particular interest of mine. But I like those I have and they brighten up the office, give my patients (we call them clients) something to look at while they try to untangle their troubles, sort them into words, order the chaos of their minds into sensible phrases. People don't like to look you in the eye when they tell you their troubles.

It's no ma kind a singin but ah'm sittin here, hearin it, nae moving a muscle, an ah've got this amazin glow all over, ah'm feeling pure brilliant. Ah cannae explain it, ah've just got this kinda swellin in ma chest, like ma lungs is blowin up wi pure clean air, no the usual muck we suck in up this way. It's a gloomy auld tune, right enough, but it cheers me up no end. Here's this doctor, this consultant, sittin in ma chair, ma hoose, which may be a tip the day but isnae always. Next time she comes ah'm gonnae show her. I'll straighten it up, clean, aye well sometimes it doesnae seem worth the bother just for me and the dug.

Just like me she is, this doctor, on her ain. Naebody tae cuddle in the night. Least ah've got the dug if ah'm desperate. What's she got? What does she snuggle up tae on a cauld night?

A hot water bottle, a teddy bear, a sex toy? Nae sae young neither tae he alane. Better get the skates on if she wants tae tie the knot. But then maybe she's one a they solitary types by choice, christ. Or queer, aye that's a possibility. Ah mean she's no what ah'd call a man's wummin.

Considering the design of the surgery, I'm fortunate to have a window. I've lined the sill with plants, the hardier varieties, those which require the minimum of attention. When I'm there, I play music, Vivaldi mostly, at low volume. I read somewhere about experiments on house plants to see how they responded to different kinds of music. Rock music made the plants wilt whereas Vivaldi made them flourish and wrap themselves lovingly around the sources of the music. I try to give a client the same opportunity to flourish. I listen, offer tea, an old but comfortable armchair, now and then a sympathetic nod. Mostly I listen until my client has told me the first version. It's usually a slow, tiresome process, for both of us. I ask a few more questions and the client redrafts the problem.

I try to give people an opportunity to flourish but don't claim a high level of success. The nature of the task being what it is and nothing being absolute, even an accurate assessment is rarely possible. My plants do better, when I'm around to tend them though. I'm rarely in the office these days. In the catchment area served by our practice, those who need me rarely come looking.

It's that singing. Ah just get this overpowerin . . . ah just get this feeling that she could really dae wi a big hug. Ah get tae ma feet, cross the room and lift her aff the chair. Ah'm staunin there, huggin her, fair away wi masel till ah see the look in her eyes and Jesus fuckin christ it's pure terror, the wummin's scared rigid, like a big cauld stane in ma hauns afore ah let go a her. And then the singing stops. Just like that. Like a tape being switched aff. Nae mair glow. That fuckin singin.

Doesny say anything about it, no a fuckin word. Just picks up her briefcase, tells me tae mind and be in for the nurse themorra, and goes. Raj chucks hissel at the door then slinks aff tae the kitchen. Needin fed but he'll have tae wait. Ah'm in nae mood for the fuckin dug. Ah hear her panicky wee steps as she hurries alang tae the lift. She'll no notice the stink on the way down, she'll be that happy just tae get the fuck out a here.

There she goes, marchin aff tae her motor, aff tae her next patient. Maybe she'll need a wee pit-stop somewhere, tae pull hersel thegither, get hersel nice and neutral again. When she's through wi us lot, put in her time, done her bit, she's gonnae nip back tae the surgery, tae her cheery wee office, take out ma file and bang in a new prescription. She's gonnae up the dosage, up it enough tae take away ma voices allthegither, blot them out, kill them aff. Didnae mean her any harm for fuck's sake. Christ, ah was tryin tae be nice but she'll no see it that way, will she? She'll see it as a fuckin problem, and up the dosage. Tae bring me back tae ma senses, back tae The Real World. Tae this. The morra. Jab day themorra. Ah get the feelin ma voices areny gonnae be fuckin friendly the night.

Glancing

Rain glances off shiny pavings at a crazy angle, wind slashes her face, her city clothes useless against the unrestrained elements of this wild, exposed island; she should turn back, make a dash for the green door with its B & B sign swaying above it, take the steep narrow stairs two at a time to her tasteful, verging-on-twee accommodation, strip off the wet clothes, snuggle up and listen to the racket the rain makes on the roof and the sea makes on the window, try and get used to it so it doesn't keep her awake like it did the night before. But she's been in the room enough, too much, and the solitude hasn't been soothing, in spite of bland little abstract collages on the walls, perky pot plants, an efficient heater, a sea view.

The people she's come out to meet haven't arrived yet and the place is so dreary it would have been funny, had there been anybody to share the joke with. Six lone lads hunch on barstools and mutter curses. At home, it's the kind of place she'd walk into and out of again and feel relieved to be standing in the rain. But she's here to meet people more prone to the animated huddle than the lonely line – and who should arrive shortly – so she buys a drink and takes it to the table facing a dormant juke-box. Even silent, the juke-box is better than nothing: modern, hundreds of songs to flip through, the casing dayglo pink and yellow; as out of place here as happiness. A deserted pool-table fills the back room. Above it, a lamp with a fringed shade casts a thin, smoky beam across the baize. The wallpaper is a repeat pattern of interlocking coffins.

She didn't think to bring anything to read, so reads the bar, which has been hammered together from fish-crates: ABERDEEN, WICK, THURSO, 2 doz COD 2 doz. WHITING. Reading the bar involves craning her head sideways and attracts attention. One of the boys at the bar glances round, his head swivelling slowly from the neck. Surreptitious. Reptilian. She concentrates on not meeting his eyes. To do this without obviously looking away and maybe setting up some unspoken game of chase, she stares at the gap between him and his neighbour.

Her purse is heavy with coins, the juke-box enticing. She leaves her seat, feeds in a handful of change and begins to read the song titles, taking her time, reading slowly, re-reading, becoming deliberately engrossed in the business of choosing, flicking the card index forward and back again, making a pastime of indecision.

She must have pressed the wrong buttons. The juke-box plays nothing she chose, though the selection it thumps out could have been worse. The element of surprise is a distraction. The volume alone improves the place, for her if not for the others. It's good to be filling the dull air with the illusion of somewhere else. She doesn't blame the locals for being gloomy. The day has gone from sodden grey to bruised blue. Who'd fancy the prospect of darkness for months on end? In a place like this, an island off the scrag[1] end of the country, weather matters, makes a difference. There's a lot of it about, and when the sky's bright enough to see anything at all you see the weather coming. Rain clouds wheel, snow flurries shear over the hills, greybacks wail across this exposed, battered island and there's nothing to be done but stick it out.

Her drink's nearly done. She's going off the prospect of meeting people. Friends of friends. Theatre people on tour. Nothing to do with her. She could go now, skip out and miss them. She's come all the way here for peace and quiet, after all. Many do, in summer, and clutter up the narrow streets. Off season, she's one of a handful of visitors. The tourist shops are deserted or closed. What she'd wanted. But peace and quiet haven't been having the desired effect, the juke-box is still playing and she hasn't had her money's worth yet.

The lad with the lank, sandy fringe is getting bold, letting his eyes linger, willing her to look at him, to adjust the angles of her eyes just a fraction, and meet his. Eye contact, coinciding lines of vision, that's the game, but she's not playing. After two more random selections and several failed attempts to catch her eye, he cracks down his glass, scowls in her direction and lurches out into the rain. Behind him the door bangs, predictably.

Another lad strolls over to the juke-box. Smallish, dark tidy hair, white shirt, denims. The disc drops, clicks into place, makes a couple of scratchy revolutions. A piano mourns, brushes drag over a drum, lead in to Joe Cocker's melancholy squeal:

I looked out over nowhere, there was nothing at all . . .

– I like this one, he says.

He shifts his hips to a couple of bars then turns to face her. A pinkish baby face, squint smile, bright eyes. Clean-cut. Fresh-faced.

---

[1] Shriveled, dried up.

She liked the song too. Hadn't chosen it. A song for the lonely, the heartbroken, and she wasn't that.

– Come and play pool, he says. It'll cheer you up.

She makes excuses to stay put – doesn't need cheered up, wants to hear the music, can't play pool – but he's persistent and points out, in a light, easy way that she can do what she's doing, feel what she's feeling and still knock some balls across the table.

He chalks cues. Big smile.

– What's your name?

– Joanne.

– And where're ye frae, Joanne?

– Edinburgh.

– Edinburgh, eh? Ah've a half-brother doon there. Muirhoose. And whit're ye daein here?

– Getting away from Edinburgh.

He draws in his breath, lines up his cue, fires at the racked balls, sends them rocketing across the table.

– And whit're ye daein in the pub? Ah'm nosey by the way.

– Having a drink and playing pool.

Big smile again. Shirt-sleeves pushed up to the elbow.

– Aye, ah ken. But aboot here lassies dinna come intae pubs on their ain.

– I'm meeting people.

– Local folk?

– City people. In a show at the town hall.

– Ach well.

He's got an appealing, wee-boy cheekiness about him, and dimples.

She hasn't played pool for years but begins to enjoy the game, the geometry, the way you could see one action causing another, the contrast between a direct hit and the knock-on effect of a duff shot. If you could lay your life on a table, work out the angles of contact, predict the knock-on effects . . . And circling the table fills time better than staring at the juke-box or the fish-crate bar.

– Ah'm a butcher, he says. Wis on the fishin but oot a work mair than in it. It's a job. Jimmy's in Muirhoose, like ah said. Except he's no there that much ah don't think. No that ah ken how he comes and goes. No seen him in five year. In the forces, like, been all over the place. Belfast. Falklands. The Gulf. In the paras now. A hero, he is. Medals and everything. Shot! Tch, and you said you couldna play!

– Cracked up one time. Lost the place he did. Hit the deck every time a bloody car backfired – thought it was gunshot, ken. And a pure mental temper he had, raging. Put a boy in hospital and himself in the cells. Better now, ken. Been asked to go into the flying squad, S.A.S., like.

He goes for hard shots, spinning out the game.

– If he goes for it, if he signs up, they give him this contract which says – ah'm no supposed tae ken this, top secret like – but if something happens to him, if he gets done in, all his faimily mither, faither, wife, bairns – they'll all be taken care of. A pension, ken. And protection. No that he's got wife or bairns yet.

She's taking her time too, eyeing up possible angles. The dreary little backroom is warmed by the boy's soft island voice, easy smile, his ready confidences.

– No me, like. Half-bloods dinna coont. Last time ah saw him, ah wis in the shop – new tae the trade then but an auld hand noo – ah was standin at the coonter and this big laddie – a full six inches taller'n me – is standin on the ither side, sayin: 'Get a fuckin move on there, Alex,' – that's my name by the way – and ah'm thinking, How does this lad ken ma name? ah says to him, 'Do ah ken you?' And he says, 'You fucking should, you cunt. Ah'm your fucking brother.'

– Excuse the language but you shoulda seen me. Stopped in ma tracks, rigid ah wis. The cleaver above ma heid and ma mooth wide open, like ah'd seen a bloody ghost. If there hadna been the pork chops and the big high coonter atween us ah'd have thrown ma airms roon him right there and then. When ah got off ma shift we came doon here, drank pints and pints, then staggered up the brae, huggin each other and greetin like bairns. Hadna seen each other since primary school.

He misses a shot. Still grinning, he points the tip of his cue at an easy ball.

– There you are. Ah'm giving you a chance . . . He hung aboot awhile, hiked over every incha the toon in his DMs – it was pissing rain the whole time he was here, like tonight. Liked the place, so he did; slagged[1] it off, ken, but jokin like. He was a laugh. Ah miss him. Dinna really ken him, like, but ah miss him.

A lucky shot wins her the game. The remaining balls are returned to their pockets. Without their rolling geometry, the click of contact, the room resumes its usual dreariness.

– Are ye for another lager? he says, but she's ready to go, to get out before the theatre people arrive . . .

– Ach well. At least you're smiling now. When you came in, ken, you had a face like thunder.

The room is warm. She wraps a towel round her wet hair, pushes her toes into thick, dry socks, cups her hands around a mug of steaming tea. She'd missed the theatre people, after all, missed them on purpose. As she turned back along the street, she'd heard them straggling down the brae, their sharp city voices cutting through the island storm. Lowering her head into the rain, she'd kept on walking.

It is a good room. She was lucky to find such a good room. More home comforts than home, in some ways. Simple. A clean calm room in the midst of a storm. She wipes the condensation off the window, looks past crooked chimney stacks and sagging walls, looks through shifting masses of darkness towards the rain-streaked lighthouse beam way out in the bay.

Red Tides

This day there's no swimming because of the red tides. At the town end, First Beach is covered with noxious algae the colours of rust and blood. A thick band of the stuff clings to the high-tide line like a scarf or a bandage. A big stretch of sand is messed up by clots and spatters. Sunbums have moved further along, making our patch less private than usual.

But it's a good day for the beach: hot, with a fresh breeze blowing off the water. Lois, Carla and I are face down, flat out on our towels. We're lying in a row, like a tanning chart – Before, During and After. I'm white and pink in bits, Lois is light honey, Carla is olivey bronze. We could soak up the sun all summer and our skin tones still wouldn't even up. We're different, that's all. Around us is the usual litter of clothes, tanning oil, snacks, cold drinks, cigarettes, books. We've been coming here between shifts since the good weather began. We've got our beach needs sorted out.

Carla and I do other things together when Jimmy's out of town. Lois stays home and waxes her furniture or her legs. Or dates Andrew who's definitely a hot number. The girl wriggles when she says his name, stretching the A around her mouth like gum. His name comes up a lot. Doesn't matter what we're gabbing about, Andrew has seen it, done it, or got an opinion on it. You can see the *frisson* rip through the girl every time she stretches that A. No problem in that, I mean, everybody likes a little jolt. But when you're between men the eternal mention of somebody else's really gets to grate and right now that's my story.

_____

[1] Criticised, mocked.

There's a piano-player in one of the wharfside cafes who's kinda cute – plays moody Van Morrison numbers and smiles to himself while he's tickling the ivories. Sometimes I drag Carla down there after the beer bars but I know she hates it. The decor's repro deco, straight lines everywhere, nothing fancier than the odd triangle, and that goes for the clientele as well. Basically, Dorothy's is full of jerks, but because it's pricey it's never so bombed you can't get a seat, and at the end of a shift that's something. I guess I'd have settled for the crush at the beer bars if it hadn't been for the little blond guy with the nimble fingers. Looks good in his tux. So who doesn't? Carla says. And you've only seen him late-night. This is true and I've been fooled before by candlelight, dimmer switches and booze.

The reason Carla and I don't go places with Lois – apart from the beach – is basically Andrew. She keeps the guy out of sight but can't shut up about him. We know his height: six/two; hair colour – chestnut (not just brown for God's sake, chestnut); eye colour – hazel – Andrew the nut, as Carla says. We know what kind of car he drives, what he likes to eat: littlenecks and bloody beef; how many times he brushes his teeth, what he likes about Lois – her body, hair, clothes, apartment, personality, in more or less that order. Lois tells all. Can't help herself. Andrew is way up on her priorities. Otherwise, she keeps her business under wraps. Like what she did before she moved to the coast. One time Carla asked her straight out. Lois closed her eyes, turned her neat nose to the side, blew a slim line of smoke through neat, glossy lips and said, Streetwalker – dead serious – Fall River.

We got the message. Sure there are places to be a streetwalker but Fall River is not one of them. Stinks of sulphur from the mills when they're open and hard times when they're shut down. This girl wouldn't drive through the streets of that town, never mind walk them. Her favourite slogan is a store sign outside a dry cleaners: GRIME DOESN'T PAY. And does she believe it. Her apartment has surfaces which glow like the heavenly bodies are supposed to and her soft furnishings have a nurtured look, like pets.

Lois has manicured blonde hair which turns into her neck in a single wave and looks metallic in the sun. She's pretty in a regular front-of-house way – even-featured, nothing lop-sided, nothing too big or too small, medium height, leggy, looks good in clingy T-shirts, skimpy sun-dresses and the high-cut frosted bikini she's wearing. She's undone the back strap and halter neck so she won't have any paler strips of skin around her tits. In case Andrew doesn't like it.

There are things we don't know about the girl. We do know she's recently divorced. Alan (another A name), the husband she ran after for years, ran off with a girl the spit of Lois but younger and with money. Lois threw all the frozen dinners she had prepared – a month's supply of planned, balanced meals – into the waste disposal and moved to the coast for fun, sun and fucking. What she got was Andrew.

After our shift at Neptune's, Carla and I sometimes go drink beer, listen to the band, bitch about this and that – the slow eaters, cheap tippers, the pains and the real assholes. Maybe we'll let some guys buy us a beer. But Carla won't fool around. It's not safe and she knows it, she's no fool. Jimmy drinks Old Bushmills and sings slushy Irish songs with some touring band, Retro – or Repro-something they call themselves and it's what they are, old-style fake. Jimmy's never been within a thousand miles of the Emerald Isle but turns on a brogue at the merest sniff of whisky. And gets punch-drunk and jealous in a big way. Carla's a whole lot better than he deserves.

Our place in the sun is at the end of the comfort zone. Further along the coast it's too rocky for stretching out. There's a big cruising scene down by the changing huts but where we are, next to the big rock and high, scratchy dunes nobody can just stroll by and parade their tan and muscle tone. They have to say something and better have some good lines. Carla gets off on crucifying cruisers. She's right, sure. But sometimes when it's hot like this and there's nothing to do and the sand chafes the bikini line and grinds its way under the swimsuit legbands, mixing with slicks of tanning oil, sweat and other body fluids, I'm personally not in such a hurry to chase away an okay guy.

But here we three are on our own little tail of beach and who's there in the distance but

Monsignor Zyw. The black skirts of his coat wing out as he picks his way over the wounded-looking beach. The Monsignor is a regular at Neptune's and everybody's favourite customer. What a treat he is, a real sweetie. And so easy – orders the same meal every time.

– The Scrod, bless your heart.

(Scrod – no such thing. It's a made-up name for baby cod, a restaurant fiction.)

But this little guy with his tinkly voice – who gets the giggles halfway through his second Martini – makes us all try to be a bit nicer than we really are. Even Gus. His usual cynicism crumples like a dishrag at the sight of old Zyw perched tidily at his table for one, hands clasped round each other, bird eyes sparkling.

And how are you tonight, Father? says Gus.

He dips his voice to the carpet and tips a two-fingered salute at the worry waves rolling across his forehead.

– Wonderful, my son, Zyw answers every time, Bless your heart.

While Monsignor Zyw chews at his Scrod and the Ballams pick at their lemon-dressed salad and probe sensitive areas of their marriage, blind Bill likes to give us girls a hard time. We forget to turn our heads when we speak to him. Thinks we don't bother. Look at me, goddammit, he says. You think, what's he getting at? He can't see. But Bill can say exactly where your voice hits the wall. Tunes pianos. Looks like Roy Orbison.

– Take a look at who's cruising, says Carla to Lois, Doesn't it kill ya?

Lois takes forever to see the vertical buttoned-up Monsignor among the horizontal bodies. When she does, instead of going coy and cutesy – like she does when she waits on him – her face goes kinda cloudy. I mean, I'm looking up thinking the weather's about to break but no, the sky is pure blue – then she's twisting about on her towel, hooking up the backstrap and halter, squeezing into a tight T-shirt (Lois doesn't own any baggy ones). Then she's stashing the book she's been reading, in her bag.

– Must be raunchy stuff, says Carla. Lend it to me when I'm feeling deprived.

– I could use it right now, I say.

Lois ignores us. She lies down on her back. A frothy red scarf lifts and ripples and veils her face.

We always bring books and read for a bit before we get too hot and sticky, before the print starts to jump in the sunlight and it becomes too much effort to turn a page. Carla picks racy new fiction and crime stories set in exotic locations. Lois goes in for sex disguised as romance or romance disguised as sex. Me, I never know what I'm looking for and never seem to find it. I get through a load of books. Don't read them. Start plenty but mostly give up quick. Short attention span. Or something.

– So what's the story? says Carla. Picking up tips on a new way to fuck, or what?

– I wish you wouldn't call it that, says Lois – who's no stranger to the word. It sounds so ugly.

– You want it to sound like eating ice-cream?

– I gotta go.

– No you don't.

– Ice-cream sounds good. Black walnut with blueberry ripple.

– Butterscotch fudge.

– Who's going to stand in line?

– Think you could give up sex if you had a constant supply of ice cream?

– Think you could give up ice-cream if you had a constant supply of sex?

– Really girls, I gotta go.

– Things to do

– People to see.

– Anyone in particular?

– No prizes for guessing.

– Please, says Lois, will you please knock it off?

Some nights just don't work out. however you look at it. It's like there's something in the air, some kind of virus which hits out at everybody. A hot day, a hotter sweaty night, the cooks stripped down to their vests, Gus running out of ice and running off at the mouth at blind Bill's sister. Somebody screwed up on the reservations. It happens. So what's the big deal? Everybody gets their goddamn dinner sooner or later but regulars don't like it, regulars get ratty real quick about folks from out of town taking their tables. The Ballams get stuck by the kitchen and jeez do they bitch and bicker and hassle us girls, sticking a fork in the air every time we go by. Monsignor Zyw gets wedged between the crabtank and the airconditioner and the kitchen runs out of Scrod just before his order goes in. The night is lousy all round. By the time we get our aprons off we're ready to kill or sink some drinks and think about it. I'm speaking for me and Carla. Lois has other plans.

This town is too small. I mean first we meet the Monsignor on the beach – he finally gets through all those bodies to us, raises his hat, bows and walks around the rock, to peace and quiet and an empty stretch of shingle. Carla and I wave, Lois crosses herself. Chrissakes, we should have known something was up with the girl. I mean, it's just not something you do when you're wearing a bathing suit. After the dinner shift, our feet are burning up, I persuade Carla to start out at Dorothy's instead of ending up there and who do we meet but blind Bill. He's sitting right by the piano, alone at the best table, on the prawn-pink sofa. He picks up on our voices and calls us over.

Bill orders highballs for us without asking, pats the sofa on either side of him in invitation. Carla stays on her feet. I sit. The guy doesn't bother me. He's got some good stories about old jazzers he's tuned pianos for in New York City, I like his line about seeing with his ears, he doesn't say stupid things about what you're wearing or how you've fixed your hair. And I get to see the piano-player.

Carla sucks down her drink. – I'm out of here, she says. Jimmy's doing a spot at O'Malleys. I've heard Jimmy's band enough to know I can miss it. And O'Malley's has the worst seating in town – high-backed pews some nut saved from a burning chapel and stuck in the bar when old-style was new. After tonight's shift, I'm happy to stick with the sofa.

Maybe Lois tried calling the bars, she knows where we go. Maybe she tried a couple and gave up. It's always the same, isn't it, I mean, where's anybody when you need them? More likely she couldn't get near a phone. On the beach, at work, she said nothing and Lois never liked to be asked. She'd tell you a thing in her own time, if at all. We should have known. But say she'd come looking for us, what would she have found?

Jimmy going loco with a broken bottle, carving up Carla's ex for buying her a beer. Me out of it on the beach with Bill and the piano-player – Lyall – all three of us blind drunk, stumbling, lurching, swaying into another kind of craziness. Carla at the hospital, me on the beach, Lois out of her mind in her glossy apartment. Some night. Must have been a full moon or something, but I wasn't paying much attention at the time.

* * *

The sea is warmer than earlier in the summer, the beach clean and swimming good. These days, mostly, I'm alone, though once in a long while Carla joins me. Carla doesn't get out much and when she does, all she wants to do is sit in the dingiest corner of some tired, empty bar and worry about Jimmy. Something's got to give.

Her ex now has a ragged scar across his neck and he's been spreading the word that Jimmy better quit town, which of course he won't do while he can still camp out at Carla's place, eating her food, drinking her booze etc. I reckon she'll go south at the end of the season, if she's still got it in her to make the break.

The red tides haven't been back and neither has Lois. She quit Neptune's and got herself some kind of day job. Andrew doesn't like her working nights and what Andrew doesn't like, goes. Her name comes up from time to time. Gus says she's giving out to half the cops in town. Andrew's father is chief of police. Andrew admires and fears his father. Andrew has a Dobermann, a shotgun and a taste for pain games. That day on the beach, the girl was reading de Sade. Nobody could say she wasn't prepared, but still. Lois. I reckon she's gone over the limit.

I miss the company down here, by the black rock. Just me and the gulls is getting kinda dull. I've given up books. Too much trouble. I eat, sleep and cool off in the water. The gulls clean up my crumbs before the breeze blows them away. We had some good times, the three of us, and when times were bad we kept each other from going under. Laying around, flaked out in the sun, it seemed like no matter what was happening in anybody's life – if we could just laze around and talk it through, or just talk, about anything, it didn't matter, almost any kinda mess could be straightened out. At the end of an afternoon, we'd take home our garbage, our oily, gritty towels, our hot tight skins. Also some kinda plan for the future: no big deal – some way to get by for a night, a week, month, season. A season at the outside.

I miss the girls. Don't miss blind Bill or the piano-player much.

Don't remember much. There's a blank where there should be a weekend. Bill's eating someplace else these days and I steer clear of Dorothy's. Not much to miss, I reckon, either of them. Nothing I couldn't find elsewhere. But I don't know for sure and right now I've nobody to talk it over with. Maybe I should move further along the beach, meet some new people. Or on. Maybe move on.

Dilys Rose and Jack Wyper (1947 –)[1]

Friendly Voices

A short screenplay by Dilys Rose and Jack Wyper,
based on a short story by Dilys Rose.
10th draft. March 23, 1997.

Open on a black screen and the sound of applause from an enthusiastic studio audience.

Fade up from black to . . .

1. INT. 15TH FLOOR TOWER BLOCK, GLASGOW. ALEC'S FLAT. DAY.
The pixellated image of a television screen. A grinning TV chef, the host of a typical daytime show is describing a recipe for lobster thermadore. The sights and sounds of this show will provide a background counterpoint throughout the scene that follows.

[1] This film was produced for the series *Prime Cuts* by Simon Mallinson, MTP (Mallinson Television Production) and jointly funded by Scottish Film Production fund, Scottish Television, British Screen, and SAC Lottery Fund. Its first screening was July 26, 1997, at the Glasgow Film Theatre.

Cut to c/u of the back of ALEC'*s head, TV in background. Cut to c/u* ALEC . . .

ALEC 'It's the dug. Feart for it. Disnae say, like, but Raj knows well enough . . . Raj can smell the fear on her.'

We're in a down-at-heel flat. ALEC *is in his forties, unshaven, wearing a moth eaten pullover, old corduroy trousers and trainers. He's sitting in an armchair by the television, eating a plate of corned beef and spaghetti hoops. His concentration is mainly on his food, but between mouthfuls, he talks to camera . . .*

ALEC 'Dirty big bastard that he is, aye makes straight for the crotch, pokes his wet nose intae her skirt.'

His large Alsatian dog RAJ *has been lying on the floor, but is now sniffing up towards* ALEC'*s dinner plate. At first,* ALEC *pushes the dog away, then when it resists he crouches down and tickles the dog . . .*

ALEC 'Ah let him sniff about a bit til she starts to get panicky, then ah call him aff an' slap his arse. Let 'em baith know who's boss.'

ALEC *wipes some food from his chin with his sleeve, grins down to the dog, and tickles it more vigorously . . .*

ALEC 'But ah'm an animal lover where you're concerned, eh pal? . . . Love me. Love ma dug.'

Cut to black screen. Fade up title –

FRIENDLY VOICES

Fade o black.

Cut to . . . 2. INT. Dr BLACK'S SURGERY. DAY.
Overhead view of JOAN *in close up, thinking aloud.* JOAN *is in her forties, with short hair and 'lived in' features. Her manner is very deliberate, as she pauses regularly to digest a thought, or consider a phrase . . .*

JOAN ' . . . In my student days and when I was a young professional, I had faith.'

JOAN *is lying on an analyst's couch in an upmarket surgery.* JOAN'*s analyst,* DR ANGELA BLACK *is out of her view, sitting at an oak desk at the head of the couch, listening . . .*

JOAN 'I got down to "grass roots"' . . .

She smiles ruefully to herself . . .

JOAN ' . . . not that grass was ever a particular feature of the landscape.'

At her desk, DR BLACK *listens and takes notes, still out of* JOAN'*s line of sight. Having waited in vain for* JOAN *to elaborate,* DR BLACK *prompts her . . .*

DR BLACK 'And now?'

JOAN 'Now . . . Now we function by maintaining a distance . . . we install speak entry systems, request unlisted numbers from British Telecom . . . '

DR BLACK *waits patiently.* JOAN *stares at the ceiling as she wrestles with her thoughts. She eventually continues . . .*

JOAN 'Sometimes I think it's my emotions that are ex–directory . . . We're never allowed . . . we never allow ourselves . . . contact.'

Cut to . . . 4X. INT. ALEC'S FLAT. LIVING ROOM. DAY.
An old snapshot of ALEC *in his teens on the mantelpiece.*

RAJ is licking ALEC's dinner plate.

> Cut to . . . 4. INT. ALEC'S FLAT. KITCHENETTE. DAY.
> ALEC *is at the sink, nervously lighting a cigarette. We still hear the television, but the chat show has been succeeded by a quiz show, complete with laughing studio audience.*

ALEC 'Sometimes ah clean up, sometimes ah dinnae . . . Depends. Even if ah'm feeling no bad ah sometimes let the mess lie anyway.'

> *He glances to camera . . .*

ALEC ' . . . Keep her on her toes.'

> *As* ALEC *removes cups from his kitchen cupboard,* JOAN *calls from his hallway . . .*

JOAN *(o/s)* 'Mr Doyle?' . . .

> Cut to . . . 4X cont. INT. ALEC'S FLAT. LIVING ROOM. DAY.

RAJ looks up expectantly.

> Cut to . . . 4 cont. INT. ALEC'S FLAT. KITCHENETTE. DAY.
> ALEC *calls back from the kitchenette . . .*

ALEC 'Aye, in ye come . . . ahm just gettin' the kettle. Lift workin' awright was it?'

> Cut to . . . 5. INT. ALEC'S LIVING ROOM. DAY.
> JOAN *comes into the living room and immediately receives* RAJ's *unwelcome attentions . . .*
> JOAN *(as she tries to push* RAJ *away)* 'Yes . . . yes, fine . . . thank you.'

> Cut to . . . 6. INT. ALEC'S KITCHENETTE. DAY.
> ALEC *knows well about* RAJ's *tricks, but he replies as though ignorant of* JOAN's *predicament.*

ALEC 'Aye, well ye were in luck the day.'

> *As* JOAN *continues fighting off* RAJ's *advances in the living room,* ALEC *smiles to himself.*

> Cut to . . . 7. INT. ALEC'S LIVING ROOM. DAY.
> *Eventually* ALEC *comes through to* JOAN's *assistance, giving the dog a sharp smack.*

ALEC 'You should get a dug yersel, doctor. Hours a fun an' guaranteed tae keep trouble at bay.'

> Cut to . . . 8. INT. ALEC'S KITCHENETTE. DAY.
> *As he drags the dog into the kitchenette,* ALEC *shuts the door behind himself and the dog and adds . . .*

ALEC ' . . . unless trouble's got its ain dug.'

> Cut to . . . 9. INT. ALEC'S LIVING ROOM. DAY.

JOAN *is wiping herself down and trying to recover her composure as she examines the state of the room. Dirty clothes are thrown over an armchair, sweet wrappers and newspapers are strewn on the carpet, fag ends are lying in saucers and on the floor. Also on the floor, a child's watercolour paint box lies open alongside several brushes and pencils.*
She picks up an 'occult' video tape from the top of the telly.
Across the room, JOAN *scrutinizes one of* ALEC's *paintings – A brightly painted watercolour painting, very amateurish, but very vigorously painted, pinned to the wall with just one drawing pin. An erratic representation of the Christ on the Cross, surrounded by sheep. As he brings the tea from the kitchenette,* ALEC *looks round the room. His expression acknowledges the mess, but refers only to the painting . . .*

ALEC 'Quite pleased wi that yin when ah done it but now ah'm nae sure.'

ALEC *clears a space on the cluttered coffee table, puts down the cups and sits down at the end of the settee. He doubts the sincerity of her interest, and is suitably self deprecating.*

ALEC 'Ah've got hunners o' crucifixions anyway.'

JOAN *smiles, then notices some forlorn cacti shrouded in dust and fag ends.*

JOAN 'I've been neglecting my plants at the surgery lately . . . They do need attention, don't they?'

She picks up a fag end, blows some of the dust from the cacti and turns round.

JOAN 'So, how have you been? . . . '

JOAN *picks up her cup and saucer, but chooses to stay on her feet. They seem uncomfortable in each other's presence.*

ALEC 'Ach, the usual . . . Up and down.'
JOAN 'Have you been getting out and about?'

ALEC *is stirring his tea with a pencil he's picked up from the table.*

ALEC 'Aw, the dug aye gets me oot.'
JOAN 'Good . . . that's good.'

The armchair is covered in dirty laundry, so JOAN *sits down at the other end of the settee from* ALEC.

ALEC 'Disnae want tae go far mind . . . A trip tae the shop and he's whingin' tae get back hame.'
JOAN *(tentatively)* 'And the voices . . . ?'

He's now stabbing his hand with the pencil.

ALEC 'Eh?'
JOAN 'Have the voices been friendly?'

ALEC *breaks the pencil point on the back of his hand. He clearly doesn't want to talk about this.*

ALEC 'Aye, aye, nae bother.'

JOAN *decides to change the subject . . . for the moment. . .*

JOAN 'And visitors? Have you had any visitors?'
ALEC 'Bloke frae the water board. Roofs leakin'. Aw aye, an ma sister wis o'er last week.'
JOAN 'Do you get on well with your sister?'
ALEC 'She's awright. Means well . . . Mind you, ah wouldnae . . . want . . . tae see . . . wouldnae want . . . tae see.'

Suddenly ALEC *seems confused. He struggles to concentrate on what he's trying to say . . .*

ALEC ' . . . eh, wouldnae want tae . . . eh . . . too much . . . '

JOAN *closely scrutinizes* ALEC's *predicament. Embarrassed and agitated,* ALEC *quickly gets up from the settee and goes through to the kitchenette.*

Cut to . . . 10. INT. ALEC'S KITCHENETTE. DAY.
ALEC *leans back on the door. He stands there motionless, eyes heavenwards, in a world of his own. Having forgotten that* RAJ *is in the kitchenette, he only notices the dog when it rubs itself against his leg, whining its concern.* ALEC *smiles and looks down.*

ALEC 'It's okay pal . . . They're good . . . They're good this time . . . '

He pats the dog on the head . . .

ALEC 'Sometimes ah think you hear ma voices tae.'

As RAJ *looks up at him,* ALEC *crouches down and cuddles the dog . . .*

ALEC 'Least ah've got you eh? Whit's she got? Whit does she snuggle up tae on a cauld night? A hot water bottle? . . . a sex toy?'

Through the glass door panel we see JOAN *on the settee sitting with her back to the kitchen.* ALEC's *'voices' are obviously heightening his sense of well-being.*

ALEC 'Here's this doctor . . . this consultant . . . Just like me she is . . . on her ain.'

Cut to . . . 11 INT. ALEC'S LIVING ROOM. DAY.
Feeling composed enough to return to the living room, he directs his next words to JOAN, *but they are as much to himself. He seems in a trance . . .*

ALEC 'Ah've got this . . . glow. Ah just get the feelin' that . . . '

JOAN's *look of professional concern turns to one of apprehension. As* ALEC *moves towards her, the action slows down and all sound is lost.*

In a silent, slow-motion sequence, ALEC *clumsily attempts to hug* JOAN, *who freezes, then tries to stand up, causing them both to topple back on to the settee. Her spectacles are knocked across her face. Seeing the terror in* JOAN's *eyes,* ALEC *jumps up from the settee, accidentally knocking the coffee table. The silent slow-motion sequence ends with a clatter when* JOAN's *teacup topples into its saucer, spilling over one of* ALEC's *drawings.*

Behind the closed kitchenette door, we hear RAJ *whining and frantically pawing at the door to be let back into the living room.* JOAN *is now gathering up loose papers which have fallen on the floor, trying to mask her distress. At the other side of the room,* ALEC *is staring blankly at the wall.*

Time lapse to the same, locked off shot, now at dusk. On the television, the crass quiz show has been replaced by a Gaelic cartoon. JOAN *has now gone, but* ALEC *is still standing in the middle of the room . . .*

ALEC *(bewildered)* ' . . . Ah just thought . . . she could dae wi' a cuddle.'

He wanders to the table, picks up the TV remote control and mutes the sound.

ALEC 'She'll no huv noticed the stink on the way doon . . . She'd be that happy just tae get tae fuck out o' here . . . Maybe a wee pit-stop . . . Get hersel' nice an' neutral again.'

ALEC *starts to tidy up the living room, picking up his dinner plate from the floor, some sweet wrappers and the tea cups from the table, then takes them to the kitchen.*

ALEC 'Then back tae her surgery, tae bang in a new prescription. Up the dosage . . . up it enough tae take away ma voices awthegither. Kill them aff.'

Back in the living room, he picks up the soaking drawing and crumples it up . . .

ALEC 'Christ, ah was just tryin' tae be nice. But she'll just see it as a fuckin' problem . . . an up the dosage. Tae bring me back tae ma senses.'

He puts the crumpled ball into a cup on the window sill and stares out of the window.

ALEC 'Back tae the Real World.'

He looks around the room . . .

ALEC 'Tae this.'

RAJ *is at the window, standing on its hind legs, front paws on the window-sill. As* ALEC *joins the dog, it licks his hand, while alec voices his thoughts to the darkening city skyline . . .*

ALEC 'Jab day themorra . . . Ah get the feelin' ma voices areny gonnae be fuckin' friendly the night.'

Pull focus to the metal grill on his balcony.

Cut to the vast, grim wall of windows on the Red Road flats. We can hear children playing and the faint strains of an ice-cream van playing 'My Darling Clementine'.

Fade slowly to black.

Roll end credits.

Valerie Thornton (1954 –)

If I Were a Dog

She has come back from the dead,
she, whom they took away
at peace and ready for death.

Our grief is unspent
our funeral thwarted
as, unwanted, we welcome her home.
We, too, had tasted freedom.

Dressed and fed
she re-lives alone in the living room
sitting in grudged sunlight.   10
She is too good
or too bad for homes.

We crush her with news
of her cataracts.
She wishes she were dead.
'If I were a dog
I would have been put down.'

She drops the cake plate
into the potato basket;
earth on the cake,   20

fear in her eyes.
She is inconsolable.

Slight and frail
she creeps to communion
helped gently all the way
up the long slow aisle.

Change

They will become you,
my old love,
these chilling silver hairs.

You with golden hair
who slipped through my fingers
like quicksilver
from a broken game.

For you,
my lost and golden boy,
silver is second best.   10

For me,
small change
until this bright pain
can tarnish.

Nearly Ben Venue

In the time it took to pass
and park at the lochside,
the eight-foot gate
became closed and PRIVATE.

Black on yellow letterfangs:
BEWARE WILD BOAR.

Nearly forbidding,
it swung sweetly open
and we crunched past
a snowfield black with cattle   10
clustered low against the cold.

Nearly unnoticed
as we approached the rise,
cliché silhouettes of boar
dark against the snow
scuttled far from us.

BEWARE THE BULL
on the next gate
into a field of highland cows.
We skulked fast up the fenceline 20
and still they flounced away.

KEEP CLOSED
raved the highest gate,
wide open and inviting us to climb
past great caterpillars of ice
past their herd of timid goats
scattering rank scent
on the still air.

Higher yet and we follow
the deep track of a hare 30
nearly perfect
but for scarlet granules
in its floral pawprint
and a score of snowpain
between each bound.

Nearly sunset
and we make it
almost to the top.
Creag a Bhealaich has to do;
the distant Arran Hills are set 40
against a gilded sky
and our shadows fall
purple and long.

Such a slog
to this frozen cairn
beyond drifts like dunes
and curtains of icicles,
I nearly gave up, often.

But the return
was in the descent 50
bounding hysterical
down snowdrifts
holding your shoulder
while every leap plunged
or crested
with separate caprice.

By Loch Ard our moon is bright
and broken on black ripples.
I make my way
behind you 60
nearly.

Familiar

When I lie on the rug
the cat settles
in the small of my back
and we are a camel.

When I sit on the chair
in my big woolly jumper
the cat burrows under
and we're seven months gone.

When I stand by the window
longing to fly   10
my wings are rolled up
purring, across my shoulders.

When I'm trying to sleep
on a cold winter's night
I am near stifled
by a rumbling fur hat.

When I'm cooking our fish
and she tries to be slippers
I am a stumbling monster
she, a mouse under the dresser.   20

Esha Ness

Turning my back on you
I am seduced by the assault
of the north-westerly gale
on my face. Far below,
great plains of aquamarine
churn against implacable mansions
of brown rock which shred the surge
to long fingers of white froth, falling.
Explosions of spray erupt
far above my horizon   10
and from a shifting skin of scum
clumped like a cream fleece
the wind whips flocks of foam.
Such sucking and hissing,
such roar and retreat.
The yellow-green of the grass clashes.
Soaring there, a fulmar
vaunting its freedom above such a drop
that I too want to fly
but, like a fool,   20

I keep to the windward edge
of the cliff top. When I look over
I lie flat like a seal,
or a fish out of water.

Armageddon

Armageddon sleeps in the church and lives in the park where he is walking to Sullom Voe.

The church where he sleeps is long since abandoned by all but the god on the wall. This is a Jesus, in blue and gold mosaic, high above Armageddon's head. His open arms are inviting Armageddon to be blessed. 'Come unto me' is cut into the red sandstone to his right, with 'Blessed are the poor' on his left.

When the wind whips through the ragged lace of the stained-glass windows, Armageddon curls below the hood of his mousy duffel coat, sheltering beneath the shattered ribs of the upturned organ. He knows if he uncurls and stares for long enough at the pale pointed oval on the end wall of the transept, his Jesus will materialise in the gloom and bless him, because he is poor.

Armageddon makes fairly regular sacrificial offerings to his god of polo mints, dog food and El Dorado. The polo mints are a luxury. It is enough that the god, who cannot eat, can see them. Armageddon eats them for him.

Armageddon knows the whore of Babylon lives behind lace curtains in a tenement flat opposite his church and that if he doesn't melt into his church, shadowy as the night, then the bitch will call the police.

They pick their way over the rotten floorboards, their torches staggering over the peeling walls until they pluck him out and put him on the street. They're okay though. After the whore of Babylon lets fall her evening velvet curtains with a heavy rustle of self-righteousness, Armageddon walks around the block and back home again.

Armageddon belongs to the church as much as the church belongs to him. He will tell you this as you walk through his park.

He is a slight figure, pale, with fine skin drawn over his features which are sharpened by many hungers. His chin sticks out like the man in the moon, with a tiny mouth above it. Only the slightest of dark hairs above the corners of his thin lips suggest he's male. He has lost all his teeth, and his voice, light as a bird, gives nothing away.

'Bless you, Joseph!' he says, falling into step with you, however many you are, and whatever sex.

'Bless you, Joseph!' he says again, struggling to extract a new map of Scotland from the pocket of his duffel coat. 'I'm walking to Sullom Voe. It's just over there,' he says pointing in a northerly direction, towards the far side of the park. 'You been there, Joseph?'

'No, it's a bit far for me. Why are you going there?'

'I am about my father's business,' he announces, folding the map all against the preset creases and stuffing it into his pocket.

His eyes are a little sticky and there are cobwebs on the hood of his duffel coat, but his fine black hair is clean and soft.

'My name is Armageddon. I have bone in my head which doesn't belong to me. Look!'

And from his pocket he takes a grubby bird skull, small, like a thrush or black-bird. His slender pale fingers turn it this way and that, with careful knowledge of its delicacies.

'Look at it and it will be in your head too, and you will be blessed. When the circles of the years are complete, you will be on the inside too, with the rest of us. See over there, Joseph?' He points to the far side of the river, to a dark space below a mossy stone lintel, with water lapping at its lip. 'That's where I was shut behind the stone. With Mary, my mother.'

He swerves from your side to a bed of purple crocuses at the edge of the path and picks up a pebble.

'This is the same stone. It has become small with the passing of years. Soon, when the centuries turn around, it will be nothing. It is accursed from the beginning of time.'

Armageddon hurls the stone into the river.

'The trees have all been killed too,' he says.

'Yes, but they'll soon get their leaves again, in the summer, won't they?'

'Maybe, I don't know. I'm not of this time. I don't see things the way you do,' he waves his thin fingers up and down the river. 'I don't know the day or the month or the week or the decade or the season. They've taken my brain away. I'm old. Very, very old. In fact, I'm mummified. Yet underneath, I'm still wrapped in my swaddling clothes. This, my raiment, was once white.'

It's difficult to know what to say, so you say nothing.

'See that sand bank over there?' he continues.

It doesn't look like a sand bank. It's covered in last year's long grass, combed pale by the winter. It supports several leafless trees.

'When I was little my father was a carpenter. He made a basket of rushes and floated me on the river.'

'That must have been fun!'

He laughs and nods at the memory of it.

'He called me Armageddon.'

'Doesn't that mean the end of the world?'

'No, the world can't end. It says world without end.' Up ahead, leaning against the railings, staring at nothing in the river below, is an old man. His face is dark as autumn, his black clothes shabby and indistinguishable. As Armageddon draws level with him, he falls out of step and approaches the old man.

'How're you doing, Joe?' he says, offering him a polo mint.

Armageddon spends a long time, even in his timeless wilderness in the park, looking for Sullom Voe. By the time he gets back to his church, late in the evening, it has shrunk almost to nothing. There, instead of a roof to shelter below, instead of the narrow passage up to the broken way-in window, there is nothing but a big empty muddy space.

It is almost the end of the world for Armageddon, but for some reason, Jesus is still waiting for him. The transept wall, which adjoins the tenements next door, still stands, like a bookend, with a few feet of red sandstone walls on either side of Jesus, who is now opening his arms for the whole poor world to see. There is no roof, but the remainder of the wall, projecting on either side, provides some shelter. The whore of Babylon's curtains are drawn tight shut.

It is a night for Noah and by morning Armageddon is chilled to the bone. Above him, his Jesus looks over his head to the repair garage down the road, secure and smug with its white pebble-dash walls.

Armageddon, his clothes stiff with mud and many rains, is walking through the park talking to no one in particular.

'I'm a fully qualified architect, you know, Joseph. Without papers. They've taken everything away. Car, bank cards, credit cards, stocks and shares. They've taken my brain too. Left me with nothing.'

He has a fine beard curling around his chin, and his duffel coat is stained and torn. Most of his map has long gone except for the Shetland Isles which he ate.

'I have a castle in my kingdom over there,' he says, pointing south, towards the distant towers of the hospital. 'But I have to be in the wilderness now. For forty days and forty nights until Sullom Voe comes to pass. That old man's in my castle; he had a heart attack. They wouldn't have taken him in if they'd known he was related to me. No one'll take me in.'

Beside Armageddon prances a white charger, reduced to the form of a small mongrel which he is feeding with dirty polo mints.

'I am old enough to see now,' he continues, 'and I can see many homes in my head. Many little homes inside my church. For all the whores of Babylon who will be left behind when the years turn around.'

And while these things were coming to pass, Armageddon slept within the scaffolding, within the shells of flats which were rising from the ashes of his church. There was no more Jesus to come unto him, they had knocked him off the wall to make way for many bricks. But now it didn't matter. Jesus was in Armageddon's head, bright as remembrance, below the hood of his duffel coat.

When all the whores of Babylon were installed in their new quarters, when the years had turned around from the time when the poor were blessed, yet another casualty was found huddled cold as stone below his duffel coat in the park. His name was unknown, as was his age, and the message in the grey crumbs of bone and polo mint in his pocket was indecipherable.

John Burnside (1955 –)

Agoraphobia

My whole world is all you refuse:
a black light, angelic and cold,
on the path to the orchard,
fox-runs and clouded lanes and the glitter of webbing,
little owls snagged in the fruit nets
out by the wire

and the sense of another life, that persists
when I go out into the yard
and the cattle surround me, obstinate and dumb.
All afternoon, I've worked at the edge of your vision,   10
mending fences, marking out our bounds.
Now it is dusk, I turn back to the house

and catch you, like the pale Eurydice
of children's classics, venturing a glance
at nothing, at this washed infinity
of birchwoods and sky, and the wet streets leading away
to all you forget: the otherworld, lucid and cold
with floodlights and passing trains and the noise of traffic,
and nothing like the map you sometimes
study, for its empty bridlepaths,   20
its hill-tracks and lanes, and roads winding down to a coast
of narrow harbours, lit against the sea.

Children Sledding in the Dark, Magdalen Green

We have studied the colours of night:
loan-path ambers, hedges dipped in bronze,
jade-tinted snow

and nothing is wholly true
till we believe:
the sky is glass, the distance is a train.

angels are sealed in the gaps
of walls, their fledged wings
spreading through mortar,

and under the lamps, possessed by the pull of the dark,   10
these children hold the glow
of the imagined,

perfect and hard, arriving at copper or gold
by guesswork; trusting what's contrived in flesh
to echo in the rooms of gravity.

Anstruther

Watching the haar★ move in   mist
I think of the times we came out here, as children,

and disappeared like ghosts
into the fog:

ghosts for ourselves, at least; we were still
involved with substance

and swallows flickering along the rim
of light and sand

avoided us, no matter how we tried
to be invisible.   10

The far shore, that I used to think
was somewhere strange,

the lighthouse that once seemed large
and fishing boats beneath the harbour wall

are forming anew
within this fold of mist,

more real than ever, harder and more precise,
and nothing ghostly in the way

the cold welds to my skin
and lets me know   20

how quick I am, how quick I have to be
to go on walking, blindly, into silence.

Shekinah

I've heard how the trawlermen harvest
quivering, sexless fish
from the ache of the sea;
how they stand on the lighted decks and hold
the clouded bodies,
watching the absence form in those buttoned eyes
and thinking of their children, home in bed,
their songless wives, made strange by years of dreaming.
I've heard that seal-folk drift in from the haar
through open doors,   10
the cold that strokes your lips while I am gone,
probing your sleep and stealing a little warmth
to mimic love
– so, driving back, it's always a surprise
that coming home is only to the given:
old gardens in Lochgelly, thick with privet;
still-pools of oil and silt at Pittenweem;
lights on the Isle of May; the low woods
filling with salted rain beyond Markinch.
It's always a surprise: the stink of neeps;   20
the malt-spills of autumn fields, where floodlit tractors
labour and churn;
the last few miles of wind and scudding clouds,
or starlit silence, hung around the house,
as vivid as the angel who attends
all marriages.
                    Its shimmer on our bed
is subtle, but it keeps us to itself,
learning the make-believe of granted love,
and this is all we know, an angel's gift: 30
that weddings are imagined, love's contrived
while each of us has one more tale to tell,
the way you feel the turning of the tide
beneath the house, or somewhere in the roof,
or how I sometimes linger on the stairs,
listening for nothing, unconvinced,
less husband than accomplice to the dark,
beguiled by the pull of the moon
and the leylines of herring.

Heimweh

Remembering the story of a man
who left the village one bright afternoon,
wandering out in his shirt sleeves and never returning,
I walk in this blur of heat to the harbour wall,
and sit with my hands in my pockets, gazing back
at painted houses, shopfronts, narrow roofs,
people about their business, neighbours, tourists,
the gaunt men loading boats with lobster creels,
women in hats and coats, despite the sun,
walking to church and gossip.   10
It seems too small, too thoroughly contained,
the quiet affliction of home and its small adjustments,
dogs in the backstreets, barking at every noise,
tidy gardens, crammed with bedding plants.
I turn to the grey of the sea and the further shore:
the thought of distance, endless navigation,
and wonder where he went, that quiet husband,
leaving his keys, his money,
his snow-blind life. It's strange how the ones who vanish
seem weightless and clean as if they have stepped away   20
to the near-angelic.
The clock strikes four. On the sea wall, the boys from the village
are stripped to the waist and plunging in random pairs
to the glass-smooth water;
they drop feet first, or curl their small, hard bodies to a ball
and disappear for minutes in the blue.
It's hard not to think this moment is all they desire,
the best ones stay down longest, till their friends
grow anxious, then they re-emerge
like cormorants, some yards from where they dived,   30
renewing their pact with the air, then swimming back
to start again. It's endlessly repeatable, their private game,
exclusive, pointless, wholly improvised.
I watch them for a while, then turn for home,
made tentative, half-waiting for the day
I lock my door for good, and leave behind
the smell of fish and grain, your silent fear,
our difficult and unrelenting love.

Ports

Pas de port. Ports inconnus.
               – Henri Michaux

I HAVEN
Our dwelling place:
                              the light above the firth;

    shipping forecasts; gossip;
    theorems;

the choice of a single word, to describe
the gun-metal grey of the sky, as the gulls
flicker between the roofs
on Tolbooth Wynd.

                       Whenever we think of home   10
we come to this:

the handful of birds and plants we know by name,
rain on the fishmonger's window, the walleyed plaice

freckled with spots
                 the colour of orangeade.

We look for the sifted light
that settles around the salvaged

hull of the *Research*
                    perched on its metal stocks
by the harbour wall   20
its smashed keel half-restored;
                      the workmen
caged in a narrow scaffold
                    matching the ghosts
of umber and *blanc-de-Chine*.

We notice how dark it is
                 a dwelling place
for something in ourselves that understands

the beauty of wreckage
                 the beauty   30
of things submerged

II URLICHT
              – our
dwelling place:
            a catalogue of wrecks
and slants of light –

never the farmsteader's vision
of angels, his wayside shrines
to martyrs and recent saints
                  the rain   40
gleaming on wrapped chrysanthemums
                      forced
roses and pinks –

here we have nothing to go on
                  or nothing more
than light and fog
             a shiver in the wind
or how the sky can empty
all at once

when something like music comes   50
                                        or rather
something like the gap between a sound
and silence
            like the ceasing of a bell

or like the noise a tank makes as it fills
and overflows

              how everyone expects
that moment, when a borrowed motor stalls
half-way across the channel, and you sit
quiet, amazed by the light   60
                        aware
of everything
              aware of shoals and stars
shifting around you, endlessly

entwined.
            Our neighbour
                        John
who spends his free time diving

plumbing the sea for evidence and spilt
cargoes   70

            who has burrowed in the mud
to touch the mystery of something
absolute

              can tell you how
                        out in the Falklands
he walked inland
climbing a slope where blown sand turned to grass
the emptiness over his head
like a form of song.
He still has the pictures he took   80
                        of backward glances
of whale bones on the shore
                        the wind exact
and plaintive in the whited vertebrae.

He'd been out diving
                        finding the shallow wrecks
of coalships from Wales
                        and one old German
sail-boat, whose quick-thinking crew
had scuppered it just offshore   90
to douse a fire

its cargo of beer and gunpowder
still in the hold,
each stoppered bottle
sealed with water weed.

He'd walked less than a mile
when, settled upon its haunches
                            as if it had recently
stopped to rest

he found a carcass: one of those feral   100
cattle that wander the dunes
                    a long-forgotten
ghost of husbandry.

It might have been there for years
                            but it looked alive
the way it had been preserved
in the cold, dry air
and he stood in the wind to listen
                            as if he might hear
radio in the horns   110
                    or ancient voices
hanging in the vacuum of the skull.

He had his camera
                    but couldn't take
the picture he wanted
                            the one he thinks of now
as perfect
            he couldn't betray
that animal silence
                    the threadwork of grass through the hide,
the dwelling place   121
                    inherent in the spine

                                        that

III Moorings
kinship of flesh with flesh.

                            When we go walking
early
        at the furled edge of the sea

we find dark webs of crabmeat
                            herring-bone   130
                                    wet
diaphragms of stranded jellyfish;

spring water mingles with salt
                            beneath the church
where Anstruther's dead
                            are harboured in silent loam;
sea-litter washes the wall where the graveyard ends
a scatter of shells and hairweed
                            and pebbles of glass
made smooth   140
            in the sway of the tide.

From here
               amongst the angel-headed stones
we see the town entire:
                              the shiplike kirk;
the snooker hall above the library;
the gift-shop on the corner
                              windows packed
with trinkets of glass
                              and pictures of towns like this;   150

a rabble of gulls;
                    the scarlet and cherry red
of lifebelts and cars:
                       the bus that will wait by the dock
for minutes
            before it returns
to Leven.

               By evening the harbour belongs
to men at work.
They're swaddled in orange or lime-green   160
overalls
          their faces sheathed
in perspex:
                crouched to the blue
of their torches
                they are innocent
of presence
                flashes and sparks
dancing in the blackness of their masks
as if in emptiness.   170

Sometimes we stand in the cold
and watch them for hours
                         the way
they bend into the flame
like celebrants
                immune to everything
that moves or falls around them
                                 isolates
suspended in the constancy
of fire.   180
        This time of year
it's night by five o'clock

and as we walk
               we harbour something new
                              the old pain
neutral and stilled in our blood
like a shipwreck observed from a distance
                                   or one of those
underwater shapes we sometimes glimpse   190
through hairweed and clouded sand
                         a shifting form

that catches the eye for a moment
then disappears.

At dusk, above the street
                          above the painted
shopfronts and roofs
and children walking home in twos and threes

it starts to snow.
                          At one end of the quay   200
a boat is docked

it's mostly fishing vessels here
                          but this
is tusk-white
                with a terracotta keel

a pleasure boat
                          a hope pursued through years
of casual loss.

It's unattended now
                          but you could guess   210
its owner from the writing on the hull

a stenciled row of characters that spell
against the painted wood
                          the word
S E R E N I T Y.

In daylight, it would seem
almost absurd:
too sentimental
                gauche
                          inaccurate   220
a weekend sailor's image of the sea

but now
          as snow descends into the rings
of torchlight
                and the sky above the harbour
darkens
          it is only what it seems:
a name for something wanted
                          and believed

no more or less correct than anything   230
we use to make a dwelling in the world.

Carol Ann Duffy (1955 –)

Born in Glasgow, Duffy moved to England as a young girl and went through the process of feeling strange and accent-marked among the English children. Perhaps as a consequence, a search for identity and a fascination with language are two of her major themes.

Plainsong

Stop. Along this path, in phrases of light,
trees sing their leaves. No Midas touch
has turned the wood to gold, late in the year
when you pass by, suddenly sad, straining
to remember something you're sure you knew.

Listening. The words you have for things die
in your heart, but grasses are plainsong,
patiently chanting the circles you cannot repeat
or understand. This is your homeland,
Lost One, Stranger who speaks with tears.   10

It is almost impossible to be here and yet
you kneel, no one's child, absolved by late sun
through the branches of a wood, distantly
the evening bell reminding you, *Home, Home,*
Home, and the stone in your palm telling the time.

Originally

We came from our own country in a red room
which fell through the fields, our mother singing
our father's name to the turn of the wheels.
My brothers cried, one of them bawling *Home,*
Home, as the miles rushed back to the city,
the street, the house, the vacant rooms
where we didn't live any more. I stared
at the eyes of a blind toy, holding its paw.

All childhood is an emigration. Some are slow,
leaving you standing, resigned, up an avenue   10
where no one you know stays. Others are sudden.
Your accent wrong. Corners, which seem familiar,
leading to unimagined, pebble-dashed estates, big boys
eating worms and shouting words you don't understand.
My parents' anxiety stirred like a loose tooth
in my head. *I want our own country,* I said.

But then you forget, or don't recall, or change,
and, seeing your brother swallow a slug, feel only
a skelf* of shame. I remember my tongue   splinter
shedding its skin like a snake, my voice   20
in the classroom sounding just like the rest. Do I only think
I lost a river, culture, speech, sense of first space
and the right place? Now. *Where do you come from?*
strangers ask. *Originally?* And I hesitate.

In Mrs Tilscher's Class

You could travel up the Blue Nile
with your finger, tracing the route
while Mrs Tilscher chanted the scenery.
Tana. Ethiopia. Khartoum. Aswán.
That for an hour, then a skittle of milk
and the chalky Pyramids rubbed into dust.
A window opened with a long pole.
The laugh of a bell swung by a running child.

This was better than home. Enthralling books.
The classroom glowed like a sweet shop.   10
Sugar paper. Coloured shapes. Brady and Hindley
faded, like the faint, uneasy smudge of a mistake.
Mrs Tilscher loved you. Some mornings, you found
she'd left a good gold star by your name.
The scent of a pencil slowly, carefully, shaved.
A xylophone's nonsense heard from another form.

Over the Easter term, the inky tadpoles changed
from commas into exclamation marks. Three frogs
hopped in the playground, freed by a dunce,
followed by a line of kids, jumping and croaking   20
away from the lunch queue. A rough boy
told you how you were born. You kicked him, but stared
at your parents, appalled, when you got back home.
That feverish July, the air tasted of electricity.

A tangible alarm made you always untidy, hot,
fractious under the heavy, sexy sky. You asked her
how you were born and Mrs Tilscher smiled,
then turned away. Reports were handed out.
You ran through the gates impatient to be grown,
as the sky split open into a thunderstorm.   30

November

How they can ruin a day, the funeral cars proceeding
over the edge of the Common, while fat black crows
leer and jeer in gangs. A parliament all right.

Suddenly the hour is less pleasant than it first appeared
to take a walk and post a harmless, optimistic letter.
Face up to it. It is far too hot for November

and far too late for more than the corpse stopped
at a red light near the Post Office, where you pause
wishing you could make some kind of gesture

like the old woman who crosses herself as the hearse moves on.

The Way My Mother Speaks

I say her phrases to myself
in my head
or under the shallows of my breath,
restful shapes moving.
The day and ever. The day and ever.

The train this slow evening
goes down England
browsing for the right sky,
too blue swapped for a cool grey.
For miles I have been saying   10
What like is it
the way I say things when I think.
Nothing is silent. Nothing is not silent.
What like is it.

Only tonight
I am happy and sad
like a child
who stood at the end of summer
and dipped a net
in a green, erotic pond. *The day*   20
and ever. The day and ever.
I am homesick, free, in love
with the way my mother speaks.

In Your Mind

The other country, is it anticipated or half-remembered?
Its language is muffled by the rain which falls all afternoon
one autumn in England, and in your mind
you put aside your work and head for the airport
with a credit card and a warm coat you will leave
on the plane. The past fades like newsprint in the sun.

You know people there. Their faces are photographs
on the wrong side of your eyes. A beautiful boy
in the bar on the harbour serves you a drink – what? –

asks you if men could possibly land on the moon. 10
A moon like an orange drawn by a child. No.
Never. You watch it peel itself into the sea.

Sleep. The rasp of carpentry wakes you. On the wall,
a painting lost for thirty years renders the room yours.
Of course. You go to your job, right at the old hotel, left,
then left again. You love this job. Apt sounds
mark the passing of the hours. Seagulls. Bells. A flute
practising scales. You swap a coin for a fish on the way home.

Then suddenly you are lost but not lost, dawdling
on the blue bridge, watching six swans vanish 20
under your feet. The certainty of place turns on the lights
all over town, turns up the scent on the air. For a moment
you are there, in the other country, knowing its name.
And then a desk. A newspaper. A window. English rain.

Hugh McMillan (1955 –)

Anglophobia

Sometimes, after ten pints of Pale in Mather's,
my pals and I discuss, with reasoned calm,
the origins of Anglophobia.

The philosophy was mother's milk to me.
Our cat was called Moggy the Bruce.
In 1966 my uncle Billy died on his knees
before the telly screaming 'It didnae
cross the line ye blind bastard!'
I remember my Grandad, seventy five
and ridged with nicotine, sitting, grimly watching 10
a schoolgirls' hockey match. Hands like shovels,
he'd never even seen a game with sticks
but he was bawling 'Bully up, Fiji,
get intae these English!'

An expression of lost identity, they say.
Some identity.
We were the most manic crew of cutthroats
out, never happy unless we were fighting,
preferably each other; any venue,
Turkestan to Guadeloupe. 20
It was only after the Pax Britannica
that any of us had a free minute between rounds
to contribute to the culture of the world.

By some strange alchemy we had however found
the untapped source of arrogance and up
to our arses in mud we could thumb our noses
at the Florentines and all the other poofs
of the Renaissance and take some solace
from thumpings by our betters by claiming
moral victory; a piece of turf from Solway   30
Moss and the crossbar from Culloden.

But despite all that, and sober, the limp
red lions stir the blood and in a crowd of
fellow ba-heids I'll conjure up the pantheon
of Scotland's past and jewel it with lies.
Unswerving stubbornness.
I suppose that in the graveyard of nations
Scotland's epitaph will not be a volume
like the French but a single line:
Ye'll be hearing from us.   40

An American Dream

Reading Bukowski,
drinking Michelob
and watching the sky
bounce away to the wide lapels
of the world
I was moved by a vision of America,
a pandemonium of blue and prairie gold
snapping past my eyes like film,
and I sniffed a freedom
born of space, or its illusion,   10
then the Guard announced 'Kilmarnock,'
a sound like softly closing doors,
and when an old man asked
Is this us then? I had to say yes it was.

Christmas 1992

No sooner is your exhaust smoke gone
than it is Christmas
and easy to be sad.
There is a choir gulping under the clock
and a man seasonally abusing his wife.
Will you shut the fuck up, he asks her,
as the Herald Angels hark.
No one is smiling anywhere,
I know because I look.
Only a shop assistant smiles –   10
and it is one she made up earlier –
as I pluck from a barrel of teddy bears
a last thoughtful Christmas gift.

Robin Robertson (1955 –)

Tokens

Roofs folded in and stepped against
the sea's retaining wall:
where the gulls creak
in the knocking wind
and the sea is climbing the stones of the stair.
Stood
counting waves in the dark:
the seen pulse of a hidden drum.
Spinning out the six white stones to her,
the tokens.   10

Walking widdershins[1] to a cold curve,
sea brink and stone collide: the coming night
become drenched rock, the churning wind;
waves become faces, their cries
becoming tide.

In Memoriam David Jones
1.xi.1895–28.x.1974

The first day of winter
and the sun's long shadows
cover the leaves on the river path to the sea.
Fleeing moorhens drill across the water,
homeless now for the year's cold quarter;
it was a wild night put their reeds among these trees.

The river's speed prevents its freezing:
the hard thread of the undertow gives one more twist
and coasts out to the bay.
The path follows at a distance, rising   10
as the land is pulled up short, forced into cliff.
In this, as in all things, the ocean has its way.

The sun's slow burn is glazing the sky,
turning birds on its rim into glass.
From this high rock the sea is signal:
shaking saucers of light on water
lap like lanterns, shatter
into white-caps, into lifting gulls

---

[1] At an angle oblique to the sun.

that tilt at the sun and drop from its height,
laughing like indulgent fathers   20
down to the chopping sea;
they go fluent over wave and spray:
sleights of wing, beautiful deceits for each corrugation,
each new world in their way.

Cloud darkens the sea like gathering shoal
and a grey seal surfaces, astonished,
on a scene that stays the same;
sinks back phantom and is towed under –
has never tired,
will never tire of this.   30

At Dusk

Walking through the woods
I saw these things:
a cat, lying, looking at me;
a red hut I could not enter;
the white grin of the snared fox;
the spider in a milk bottle,
cradling the swaddled fly,
rocking it to sleep;
a set of car keys, hanging from a tree;
a fire, still warm, and a bone   10
the length of my arm, my name
carved on it, mis-spelt.
The dog left me there,
and I went on myself

The final two Robertson poems are taken from 'Camera Obscura', a series of poems and prose pieces on the life of David Hill (1802–1870), 'Pioneering photographer in Edinburgh in the mid-19th century'. The title of the first poem is that of a famous 18th-century Scots song, also quoted therein. The second poem describes the death of Hill's infant daughter.

The Flowers of the Forest

Shouldering my daughter
like a set of pipes
I walk her
to a dead march
and counterpoint her crying
with my hummed drone:
the floo'ers o' the forest
are a' wi'ed awae

my cracked reed
blanking
on the high note,
the way a nib runs dry
in the rut it makes,
and splays.

10

She Put Her Hand on Me

She put her hand on me,
the bud of her hand on mine,
and in my withering hands she died.

Janice Galloway (1956 –)

Janice Galloway is regarded as one of the most important of contemporary
Scottish prose writers. Notable among her characteristics is an uncanny eye
for detail and a sensibility that has been called 'gothic.'

Fearless

There would be days when you didn't see him and then days when you did. He just appeared
suddenly, shouting threats up the main street, then went away again. You didn't question it.
Nobody said anything to Fearless. You just averted your eyes when he was there and laughed
about him when he wasn't. Behind his back. It was what you did.

Fearless was a very wee man in a greasy gabardine coat meant for a much bigger specimen
altogether. Grey-green sleeves dripped over permanent fists so just a row of yellow knuckles,
like stained teeth, showed below the cuffs. One of these fisted hands carried a black, waxed
canvas bag with an inept burst up one seam. He had a gammy leg as well, so every second step
the bag clinked, a noise like a rusty tap, regular as a heartbeat. He wore a deceptively cheery
bunnet like Paw Broon's over an escape of raw, red neck that hinted a crewcut underneath;
but that would've meant he went to the barber's on a regular basis, keeping his hair so short,
and sat in like everybody else waiting his turn, so it was hard to credit, and since you never
saw him without the bunnet you never knew for sure. And he had these terrible specs. Thick
as the bottoms of milk bottles, one lens patched with elastoplast. Sometimes his eyes looked
crossed through these terrible specs but it was hard to be sure because you didn't get to look
long enough to see. Fearless wouldn't let you.

There was a general assumption he was a tramp. A lot of people called him a tramp
because he always wore the same clothes and he was filthy but he wasn't a tramp. He had his
own house down the shorefront scheme; big black fingerstains round the keyhole and the
curtains always shut. You could see him sometimes, scrabbling at the door to get in, looking
suspiciously over his shoulder while he was forcing the key to fit. There were usually dirty
plates on the doorstep too. The old woman next door cooked his meals and laid them on the

step because he wouldn't answer the door. He sometimes took them and he sometimes didn't. Depended on his mood. Either way, there were usually dirty plates. The council cut his grass, he had daffodils for christsake – he wasn't a tramp. He was the kind that got tramps a bad name: dirty, foul-mouthed, violent and drunk. He was an alkie all right, but not a tramp: the two don't necessarily follow.

The thing about Fearless was that he lived in a state of permanent anger. And the thing he was angriest about was being looked at. Sometimes he called it MAKING A FOOL OF and nobody was allowed to get away with it. It was a rule and he had to spend a lot of time making sure everybody knew it. He would storm up and down the main street, threatening, checking every face just in case they were looking then if he thought he'd caught you he would stop, stiffen and shout WHO ARE YOU TRYING TO MAKE A FOOL OF and attack.

Sometimes he just attacked: depended on his mood. Your part was to work out what sort of mood it was and try and adjust to it, make the allowance. It was what you were supposed to do. Most folk obliged, too – went out of their way to avoid his maybe-squinty eyes or pointedly NOT LOOK when they heard the clink and drag, clink and drag, like Marley's ghost, coming up the street. Then the air would fall ominously silent while he stopped, checking out a suspicious back, reinforcing his law. On a bad day, he would just attack anyway to be on the safe side. Just in case. You couldn't afford to get too secure.

There was even a story about a mongrel stray he'd wound into a half-nelson beause it didn't drop its gaze quick enough, but that was probably just a story. Funnier than the catalogue of petty scraps, blows that sometimes connected and sometimes didn't that made up the truth. It might have been true right enough but that wasn't the point. The point was you were supposed to laugh. You were meant to think he was funny.

Fearless: the very name raised smiles and humorous expectations. Women shouted their weans in at night with HERE'S FEARLESS COMING, or squashed tantrums with the warning YOU'LL END UP LIKE FEARLESS. Weans made caricatures with hunchback shoulders, cross-eyes and a limp. Like Richard the Third. A bogey-man. And men? I have to be careful here. I belonged to the world of women and children on two counts, so I never had access to their private thoughts voiced in private places: the bookie's, the barber's, the pub. Maybe they said things in there I can have no conception of. Some may have thought he was a poor old soul who had gone to the bad after his wife left him. Romantics. I suppose there were some who could afford to be. Or maybe they saw him as an embarrassment, a misfit, a joke. I don't know.

What I do know is that I never saw any of them shut him up when the anger started or try and calm it down. I remember what women did: leaving food on the doorstep and bottles for him to get money on; I remember women shaking their heads as he went past and keeping their eyes and their children low. But I don't remember any men doing anything much at all. He didn't seem to touch their lives in the same way. They let him get on with what he did as his business. There was a kind of respect for what he was, almost as though he had a right to hurl his fists, spit, eff and blind – christ, some people seemed to admire this drunken wee tragedy as a local hero. They called him *a character. Fearless is a character* right enough they would say and smile, a smile that accounted for boys being boys or something like that. Even polismen did it. And women who wanted to be thought above the herd – one of the boys. After all, you had to remember his wife left him. It was our fault really.

So we had to put up with it the way we put up with everything else that didn't make sense or wasn't fair; the hard, volatile maleness of the whole West Coast Legend. You felt it would have been shameful, disloyal even, to admit you hated and feared it. So you kept quiet and turned your eyes away.

It's hard to find the words for this even now. I certainly had none then, when I was wee and Fearless was still alive and rampaging. I would keek out at him from behind my mother's coat, watching him limp and clink up the main street and not understand. He made me sick with fear and anger. I didn't understand why he was let fill the street with himself and his swearing. I didn't understand why people ignored him. Till one day the back he chose to stop and stare at was my mother's.

We were standing facing a shop window, her hand in mine, thick through two layers of winter gloves. The shop window was full of fireplaces. And Fearless was coming up the street. I could see him from the other end of the street, closer and closer, clinking the black bag and wheeling at irregular intervals seeing if he could catch somebody looking. The shouting was getting louder while we stood, looking in at these fireplaces. It's unlikely she was actually interested in fireplaces: she was just doing what she was supposed to do in the hope he'd leave us alone – and teaching me to do the same. Fearless got closer. Then I saw his reflection in the glass: three days' growth, the bunnet, the taped-up specs. He had jerked round, right behind where we were standing and stopped. He looked at our backs for a long time, face contorted with indecision. What on earth did he think we were plotting, a woman and a wean in a pixie hat? What was it that threatened? But something did and he stared and stared, making us bide his time. I was hot and cold at once, suddenly sick because I knew it was our turn, our day for Fearless. I closed my eyes. And it started. A lot of loud, jaggy words came out the black hole of his mouth. I didn't know the meanings but I felt their pressure. I knew they were bad. And I knew they were aimed at my mother. I turned slowly and looked: a reflex of outrage beyond my control. I was staring at him with my face blazing and I couldn't stop. Then I saw he was staring back with these pebble-glass eyes. The words had stopped. And I realised I was looking at Fearless.

There was a long second of panic, then something else did the thinking for me. All I saw was a flash of white sock with my foot attached, swinging out and battering into his shin. It must have hurt me more than it hurt him, but I'm not all that clear on the details. The whole thing did not finish as heroically as I'd have liked. I remember Fearless limping away, clutching the ankle with his free hand and shouting about a liberty, and my mother shaking the living daylights out of me, a furious telling off, and a warning I'd be found dead strangled up a close one day and never to do anything like that again.

It was all a long time ago. My mother is dead, and so, surely, is Fearless. But I still hear something like him, the chink and drag from the close-mouth in the dark, coming across open, derelict spaces at night, blustering at bus stops where I have to wait alone. With every other woman, though we're still slow to admit it, I hear it, still trying to lay down the rules. It's more insistent now because we're less ready to comply, look away and know our place. And I still see men smiling and ignoring it because they don't give a damn. They don't need to. It's not their battle. But it was ours and it still is. I hear my mother too and the warning is never far away. But I never could take a telling.

The outrage is still strong, and I kick like a mule.

After the Rains

think

it is too warm here and my heart is racing think where was I I was

in the bus shelter.

Dripping in there with the rest of them out of the rain.

It must have been shortly after ten because the bus to the Cross had just drawn up, the brakes still squealing and when they stopped there was a sound of nothing. That was what was different. I remember distinctly, the silence. The sound of people listening to each other listening. We peered, curled pieces of ourselves beyond the perspex, testing from under rain-mates for what it was. I watched an elder bush, the nearest of the seven planted by the council to represent nature on the estate. Its leaves dripped still. But I could swear the drops were less assured now, visible seconds lurching between one drop and the next as I watched. A child standing near me ducked and looked up, suddenly suspicious. With a muffled grunt that could have been apology, a large woman shoved by me and out into the middle of the road to make sure for all of us. We watched her stand there, face upturned. The slow, steady smile. In that moment, we knew. It had stopped raining. After nine solid months, it had stopped raining. Folk normally so wary, so shy of ridicule it hurt, we blossomed. We cracked jokes and spoke to perfect strangers, we embraced

like warm soup to remember it, the touch of human skin

while the bus sat like a ruin on the road. There was laughing and cuddling and general pagan revelry. Some of the passengers got off the bus and joined us as we emerged from the shelter, one shaking a bottle of lemonade with his thumb over the neck, spraying it like champagne. The driver was out too. Even given the mood that was remarkable since he was usually such a bloody minded big bastard. He looked, he saw, he made a hammy mime of looking at his watch. Right, he said. The rain was off. We'd seen what there was to see. If anybody's goin to the Cross they better come wi me, he said. Some of us have got schedules to keep. Nobody minded. We came, good-natured to spite him: we drifted back. Then, as I straggled on, I noticed something in the corner of the shelter: a wee girl, huddling in on herself, keeking out between her fingers. I watched her as the bus began to move, indistinct behind too much hair. Something in my stomach fluttered but that was all. Maybe I should have been more curious, taken time. The bus picked up speed, though. With the rest I let myself be taken and my excitement eclipsed her.

The road itself was interesting now the rain had stopped. Commonplaces became significant as we noted with genuine feeling it was 'turning out nice' or 'taking a turn for the better.' Puddles in the gutters seemed just as full but elsewhere, tarmac was surfacing. You could see boys on the crest of the road, in the middle of the traffic path, for the novelty of standing there without water tugging at their shoes. As we entered the town, a gang of youths were kicking planks away. Everyone hated the planks. Stretched kerb to kerb by selfish old people too afraid of the road tides to attempt crossing without them, they caused accidents, cost limbs, the lives of children. It was like a blessing, a sign of something better to come to see those boys kicking the planks away. Someone sang a hymn. The rest of us pointed and waved, rubbing with cuffs at the windows streaming with our too close breath, the damp smoking from our clothes. Talk seemed abnormally loud: it wasn't just that we had more to say, but that the noise of drizzle no longer deadened everything. Too much for some, maybe. Too soon. A few near me were in tears and a low groaning could be heard from the upper deck. I thought it had nothing to do with me. I thought it would pass. When the bus stopped at the terminus, I left without giving it further thought.

Only half an hour later, the sky had lightened considerably. Offices and shop windows were framed with workers looking out. I could see rows of them from my bench at the corner of the pedestrian precinct. I was
what was I doing?
just looking too looking up I was

looking up when suddenly, without warning, the sun came out. A great rip in the cloud and there it was: one whole, flaming presence. And with it came the colours. Colours. With a catch of emotion, I realised how much we had forgotten, how ashen everything had been for so long. The low light, the constant smurr – we had encouraged it. For some children, greyness was all there ever had been, was all we were entitled to. Now everything returned, yellows, greens, reds, oranges and wild blues shaming in their brightness. From all over the Cross came a sigh of relief and wonder. We realised how little we had fought. Yet the sun had come out. The sun had come out.

Those of us in the street found the windows of the television showrooms: we were, after all, only ordinary folk and untrusting of the evidence of our own eyes. For a moment or two, there was only a cookery demonstration, a chopping of knives. Then the first news flash. Words typed themselves over sliced vegetables as we watched. Letter by letter it spelled out what we had hoped. The sun had come out. Reassured, as though we knew it all along, we cheered. Laughter died away as a blender mushed solid matter to a pulp behind the printout. A huge pair of hands pulled the top off the glass canister, spilling its dark contents into a bowl before the food disappeared altogether and a man appeared, keen to explain with radiating lines and velcro symbols about the weather. He did that for five minutes, then read cheerfully from a slip of paper. Scientists were confident this was the end of the rain for some considerable time, he said. There would be a full report later and news flashes throughout the day. The Queen was preparing a statement. A picture of her shaking hands with the Prime Minister flickered over the monitor briefly. Both were smiling. Satisfied, we turned away from the tv and shone our faces upwards, crunching our eyes against the unaccustomed sky. I remember my scalp tingling, the back of my neck rippling with a warmth. On all sides, shop workers clustered in open doorways, filled their display windows with faces tilting towards the light. As if it had been waiting for this moment, a massive, seven-coloured arch appeared, pouring itself above the buildings and the town to prickle ready tears. We applauded. We applauded the rainbow and its promise. We were radiant.

By the afternoon it was hot. I hadn't moved much: the length of the street, a little shopping, then back to the bench at the Cross to watch the day unfold along with others who had the time. The streets were misty and dry patches had squared out on the paving. We remarked on the speed of the change of events, but not overmuch. It was enough it was happening at all. City bakeries sold out of sandwiches as people lunched al fresco. Bright dots of tee-shirts began to appear among the crowds. Sloughing off rain clothes allowed us to look at ourselves afresh and become dissatisfied with what we saw. Those who lived close enough went home to change: canvas trousers, summer dresses, short-sleeved shirts with bleachy angles poking out. Some improvised, rolling up trouser legs in a jokey but serviceable imitation of Bermuda shorts, fit for the tropic the Cross had become. Almost everyone wore a hat, sunglasses or visor against the glare. More news flashes confirmed it: the country was in the grip of a freak heat wave. Temperatures were rising by the minute. The huge plastic thermometer in the travel agent's window bled steadily upward as we rolled up our sleeves and loosened collar-buttons. I went to the riverside walkway seeking cooler air.

cooler there
did I fall asleep? I must have slept
I slept and awoke and

By late afternoon, the Cross was much less crowded. Many had drifted off out of the punishing light and gone back indoors to work. Novelty was passing. The crowd under the shade of the Co-op canopy were silent, merely waiting for the bus home. The news agent's on the corner was shutting, the women who worked there clashing security mesh in place, jangling keys into the stillness. As they crossed the tarmac to the shelter, something pale and smoky billowed out from under their slow-moving soles. It took me a minute to work out it wasn't smoke at all. It was dust. Dust rising up from gutters that had churned with running water for so long. My head thumped. The heat and windlessness of the street was surely intensifying. Workers who had poked their heads from windows earlier to feel the sun on their faces had long since retreated. I couldn't help thinking of them in there – all that glass.

A solitary blind cord tapped listlessly against an overhead pane. Just then the plump woman who owned the flower shop appeared at her open door, wheezing and gasping, the effort of her lungs making her very red about the face and chest in her short summer frock. The OPEN sign swung behind her as she fought for space among the carnations and dahlias. Some other shops were near closing now there was no one to buy and a few individuals were lowering shutters, keen, I supposed, to get out of the thickening air. The bus queue swelled, sweating. The absence of the hiss of rain had left a vacuum. Cars had quit long since and there was no thrum of flies. It was sickly quiet. Seething. Something

something

was coming. A stretching sound, like a mass intake of breath over our heads was its announcement. Then a low rumble along the horizon, hollowing the ear: distant thunder like men clearing their throats. Ready. It was ready to begin. There was an earth-rippling crack and I looked up. The rainbow was growing, inflating to fill up every stretch of blue till none remained as a touchstone for the sky. At the same time, a huge rushing sound spreading from ear to ear as though some invisible hand were unzipping the hair from my skull. I threw up my hands for protection, seeing others doing the same, some falling on their knees. *Too late for that . . .* There were children too, the odd one or two dancing on the pedestrian walk-way while others were running or clapping their hands. *We are not all seeing the same thing,* I thought, *we are all of us experiencing something far outside the normal run, but,* and the thought horrified me in its obviousness, *but not the same thing.* A glance confirmed it: the faces around me, behind the glass, in doorways and on the road varied extremely. There was barely time to digest the idea when the sound, a terrible sound of high sudden screaming took all attention for itself. Heads turned to find its source. There, still struggling in her own front doorway, was the florist. She appeared to be trying to pull a shoot *no*
several green shoots she appeared to be trying to pull
several green shoots and leaves from her dress as we watched. More and yet more leaves burst out despite her efforts, and I realised suddenly they were not attached to her dress. They were attached to her elbow, to her arm. I looked harder. They were her arm. *They were her arm.* Greenery surged up her neck and into her hair, buds clustering in a pink halo all around her head. Huge roses ripened at her armpits and elbows; camellias and magnolias fanned out of her cleavage. Seconds or whole minutes, I could not say how long it took. When chrysanthemum petals began falling from somewhere beneath her skirt, the woman stopped struggling. Enough of her face remained however to let me see she was smiling. She was, I realised, welcoming the garden she had become. I felt a twinge of outrage, but as I looked again at the woman's smile and her pleasure, I was moved with compassion. I had to admire it too. The scent was overpowering. It carried all the way from the other side of the road.

In the commotion, we had not noticed a lesser transformation. Her assistant, formerly a girl of about seventeen, now a living display of hyacinth and spring ferns, stepped out from behind the older woman's shadow. At the next doorway, the grocer watched a cabbage foresting the front of his overall. He saw me gaping, hesitated, then pointed at it shyly with his ladyfingers, ears coiling with pea tendrils. The reaction of the crowd to his bravado was enthusiastic. Some cheered and one elderly woman shuffled over for a closer look, muttering endearments. From the back of the bus crowd, a check-out boy I recognised from Tesco's pushed forward to give himself room. The pregnant bulge at the front of his coat was elongating as he came, squaring out to make a trolley complete with front wheel to balance the projection from his body and toddler straps. He did not smile but lowered his shopping into it with great dignity. At the same time, the electrical goods manager of the Co-op displayed a shiny transparent door in the centre of his chest, eager for us to see the bright whorls of washing tumbling inside and receive congratulations on his achievement. All the while the sun grew hotter.

it is too warm here

My arms still cautiously hugging my head, I walked the length of the street to find some shade where I could more comfortably continue to observe. I thought I could see a pattern and wanted to watch it unfold. Though some might have longer gestation periods than others, the transformations would keep going. Loud snickering and the dull rustle of used notes emitted from the bookies as I went past: a squashy bundle emerged from the wool shop. Before long, it would be unstoppable. A whisper was mouthing in my head, half formed. Perhaps I remembered the child in the shelter from the morning. Something like realisation prickled its beginnings up the back of my neck. I recalled the moaning I had heard on the bus, partial glimpses of things I had chosen to ignore. Without knowing why, I panicked. I ran round the corner, maybe in the hope of escaping, but something blocked my path. An enormous white grub spread the length of the pavement, bulbous tips waving in what looked horribly like appeal. Beyond this nerveless thing, a three-headed phantom groped forward on its hands and knees. Where features should have been was only tight, smooth skin, blanket-grey and eyeless. As another of its kind fumbled from the council offices, nail-less hands foraging for something to give it a sense of its bearings, I drew back, repulsed, fearing the thing it might touch would be me. In so doing, my back touched the wall of the Job Centre, rebounded again at the ripping cold of its walls against my shirt. Even in this heat, frost had feathered the windows and a faint haar issued from the open doorway. I knew nothing would come out of there. Then I was sure. There would be others like this too. Not flowers, not harmless eccentricities, but other things, terrible other things. At that moment, a pitiful screeching forced me to turn. I was facing the butchers'. The howling and the bloody trail at their doorway. The awful death stench and low weeping of children, childish voices seeping under the door of the church.

I would not look in there
I did not want to see

I began to run then. Faster. Curiosity pushed my glance down despite the urgings of reason. My hands were very pale and whitening still. Thinning.

They were stark white.
I kept on running.

George Gunn (1956 –)

The Blue Boat

The blue boat sits as plump as an eye
beside the dilapidated pier
from which some boys fish
There are no lobsters for the boat
or its owners to catch
only the vast sheer ocean
for it to mingle its blueness with
for it to bob & fathom the essential
moonbound sucking of the sea

Some scruffy crows on the beach   10
beside you, blue boat, peck & caw
at each other & a dead skate
& the boys land a velvet crab & a cudeen
& the finger of Portmahomack points east
Behind us, blue boat
the mountains are shrugging
their shoulders at the sky
& history puts on its boots
& takes the dynamite path
to Bheinn a' Bhraggie   20
ah, blue boat, you wink at me
the shape of melancholy

Ravens

(Looking Back from 1964)

As bairns half blind
we were taken to London twice
to be shown Tower Hill
Buckingham Palace, Victory
& many another tribal totem
which in their tongue
of adoption warned us
'No longer will your kind
take freshly stolen bulls
to Thurso to be traded   10
& no horses will take you back
home to the deep strath
when drink & ceilidh
overcome you'

The clipped wings of the ravens
flapped at us then
like the capacious heat
of history windmilling its way
through the uncut pages
of a dropped bible   20
not pure before or after
& if we took risks
they were sold like cattle
beneath the oaks
so all these things emerge
as Ireland twenties
into Scotland nineties
find a home

The Conversation of the Mountains

Young I was & sleepier then
from bed one morning
a hard try I could not make
my father bellowing about the need

for rising & I arose then
& came down stairs
'Are ye glued til thon mattress
boy?' he asked, I shrugged & said

'Let me tell you about the conversation
of the mountains' 'What's   10
'at? Ay conversation
oh ay mountains? Ye'll be tellin

us next ye'r a bloody poet!'
Breakfasting in the afternoon
my beans firmly on my toast
I replied 'Yes, it's true & it goes like this'

& he listened surprisingly & I said
'Ben More Assynt raised her grey
eyebrow one morning & said
'It's good to be here' A thousand   20

upon a thousand years passed
& Suilven stirring her rump
agreed, saying 'yes, it is good
to be here but we must never say it'

The universe expanded & Time caught
the magic bus & came back again
'Yes' agreed Ben More Assynt
'We must never say it, never'

& the lassoo of several centuries
tightened & loosened on the neck   30
of the world, 'Will you two stop
your squawking' growled craggy Stac Pollaidh

'Or I'm clearing out of here!'
'This,' I concluded 'is the conversation
of the Mountains' 'I've never
heard sae muckle troc' replied my father

'an can ye no eat decent like?'
& went out to feed the hens
I yawned & turned on the radio
to hear someone lying about trains   40

Helen Lamb (1956 –)

Married Bliss

That night, she lay awake and listened to
the traffic going home past her window
and she listened to the clock
and she listened for a click in the lock
and listened to the neighbours talking through the wall
and listened for a footfall
and listened to her heart beat faster
and the meter in the hall clocked another unit
and she counted the units
and the heart beats   10
and the tick tocks
and every time she missed
she said – so this is married bliss.

Peter McCarey (1956 –)

Space permits only a representation by his shorter poems here, but McCarey has
moved steadily toward more expansive forms. In 1998 *Lines Review* published his long
poem *Tantris*, which the poet/critic Tessa Ransford calls 'the most exciting and
rewarding long Scottish poem since *A Drunk Man Looks at the Thistle*'.

Home Movie

Raindrops crowd onto the glass
in perfect silence.
Engine room noises travel up
to the eighth floor of the library
through the air conditioning system.

And this might be a nautilus
in sonar quiet
The glass – a ciné screen projection
of a flatwash and graphite Glasgow
where the frames flicker between light and lens   10
with the sound of steady rain.

Shipley

In drystane crannies snowflakes flock
and sheep with stain of moss and stone
on snowy fells.
Ice makes dice from dalebones.
shivered whins are fivestanes
the sky plays.
It rocks stones,
collapses crouching arches,
in rage attacks the stellar slide
within stone,   10
and rugs at baffled, battled hearts.

Eugene's Dream

Nurse. Nurse. Sister.
What?
You got five minutes?
As it happens. I know what it was.
We were waiting for a train
At night in a big station.
We sat on a suitcase, we ate some cheese.
The pigeons drifted in
Down from the girders,
Along the rails;   10
Looked at us with one eye
And with the other eye.
One had a severed leg;
We tried to feed him, but by and by
Each one displayed it was missing a claw
Or two, tailfeathers or wing.
The bitter blind and the halt, come down
Like drops of rusty water, oil or brine
Or blood through the ceiling
Angel reptiles from aerials,   20
Slates and clay tiles, scaffolding
Flat roofs strung with slackwire
The frontier, slivers and spikes,
Between the conurbation and the sky
Glazed rain no mans land
Slopes and stacks diagonal
Rain rain rain rain
Bubble in the gutters and
Roan down the urban bypass
Under the asphalt.   30
Eugene.
What?
That's five minutes.

Elizabeth Burns (1957 –)

The Poem of the Alcoholic's Wife

Not just the endless empty bottles
the beery taste of kisses;
not just the stench of the bedroom
where his vomit smears the floor;
a cupboard stuffed with secrets
smashed china
photographs ripped from their frames

But, somehow, as well as this
a memory of myself once
in a yellow cotton dress   10
a breeze off the sea
and his hands gently touching my face;
and of my mother in a corner of the kitchen
writing her journal

and now, a woman who brings me oranges;
a poem thought up in the night
forgotten over breakfast
as the nuzzling child tells of her nightmare
then dragged back by a bunch of lilacs
plucked in the rain   20
and quickly recorded on a typewriter
balanced on the lap

The Oddity

She is a crooked planet: does not fit
in the thin universe of this house
that peoples itself with gentlefolk
who blink as though they do not see her
when she asks to use the library.

There is a clanking housekeeper
whose spiked mouth, licked, would give off poison,
and a cluster of maidservants
who, in the mothballed linen cupboard,
will gossip on the newcomer.   10

It's whispered that she's delicate
is delivered of bowls of sopped bread
bland milk puddings
but Cook sees her, the little witch,
sneaking herbs from the kitchen garden.

This household's under the thumb
of the chimes of the grandfather clock
Nothing here is tainted by imagination's kiss
and nothing queer-eyed or peculiarly skinned
gets out to roam the corridors   20

so that she, with her silences and pencils
her barefoot tiptoeing over the flagstones
in her old grey muslin dress
that billows out in draughty stairwells
feels freak: hears laughter

frothing in the steamy kitchen
whispers bubbling under doors,
is trailed by soft footsteps, rustling silks,
but reaches the room a fastness:
turns the brass key in the lock behind her.   30

Soon there will be apron-smothered giggles
outside her door: she will rise
stuff the keyhole with a handkerchief
to block the peering eyes
then draw the shades against the lilac sky

and in thin dusk-light, take ink,
begin, in copperplate,
though hot tears plop, and blot the page,
and voices batter at her head
like scatty moths, to write.   40

Gordon Meade (1957 –)

Last Quarter, Fallen Leaves

Tonight, the trees have started
To lose their leaves. Old men, they
Stand half-naked in the shadows and shiver
In the autumn breeze. Through

Their thin fingers we can see
The moon, only half the woman she
Used to be. Face powdered white, lips blue,
She turns away from her reflection.

Seeing her dying, we walk indoors,
Our feet rustling through the fallen   10
Leaves like rats' feet leaving a sinking
Ship and swimming for the shore.

Brighter Morn

At night, just seeing her
Leaving, her lit interior disappearing
Beyond the quay, is enough

To want to join her,
Uprooted and restless for silver,
Stalking the moonlit sea.

At dawn, just watching her
Unloading, her icy stomach overflowing
With fish, is enough

To want to quit   10
The land, and greet the morning sun
With silver in your hand.

The Scrimshaw Sailor

for Desmond and Trude

In the belly of a ship
On a storm-tossed sea, a sailor
Carves out the figure of a polar bear
From the jaw-bone of a whale.

Delicately, with cut–
Throat razor and sail-maker's awl,
His nimble fingers etch in the pupils
Of its eyes, the talons on

Its shaggy paws. Outside,
The ocean batters at the ship's   10
Stout timbers as the tempest blows.
Inside the ship's dank hold,

The man becomes, himself,
A scrimshaw sculpture, fashioned
In the sea's own image by the ship's
Thrown pitch and tumbling roll.

Alan Riach (1957 –)

The Blues

The lights are on all over Hamilton.
The sky is dark, blue
as a stained glass window in an unfrequented church
say, by Chagall, with grand and glorious chinks
of pinks and purples,
glittering jewels on those glass fronted buildings
where the lifts are all descending
and the doors are
being closed.
        You're out there somewhere,   10
going to a concert in wide company or maybe
sitting somewhere weaving a carpet
like a giant tapestry, coloured grey,
pale brown, weaving the wool
back in at the edges of the frame, your
fingers deft as they turn the wool in tight and
gentle curves.
        Or somewhere else.
        What do I do
        except imagine you?   20
        The river I keep crossing
        keeps going north. The trains
        in the night cross it too.
        Their silver carriages are blue.

The Heron

To you who are long gone
and far away
        I send
these words. rolling down and round the world.

For answer,
you'll send midnight to me from your distant place
and I'll return it.
And nothing more will ebb away.

Like the heron Diarmid heard
that had landed on a rock off Ireland   10
(when Grania at last overtook him
they heard it cry at break of day
in the tidal air while the sea swept past
in the bitter cold, and she asked him why
it gave that cry?

    – It is frozen to the rock, he said.
    – I stand rock-hard in this stony place
and the soft diurnal sift
that will ash rock
strains me to you, and I lean   20
but do not loosen.

A Short Introduction to My Uncle John

Nulla placere diu, neque vivere carmina possunt,
quae scribuntur aquae potoribus.[1]

My Uncle John kept corks.
He kept the corks out of all the bottles of wine that were drunk in his
        apartment.
He kept them in a wickerwork basket, a laundry basket,
high as your thigh. It was two-thirds full
of corks. Oh, he had a use for them. He's
an artist; he paints pictures, portraits, landscapes,
mainly in oils. Over each painting on the walls of his studio
there's a light shining down, and he'd put two corks
under the frame of each painting at the bottom, just to
bring it out that extra inch from the wall,   10
so that the light wouldn't strike the glass directly.
But there were only so many paintings in the studio.
And there are always more bottles of good wine to draw
corks out of.
        Well, one day my Uncle John's wife Yvonne
discovered this laundry basket and saw
how it was two-thirds full of corks. They hadn't
been married long and John hadn't told her before
that he kept corks. So she thought up a way
to get rid of the corks, because,   20
really, what is a grown man doing
with a laundry basket two-thirds full
of corks?
        In their kitchen there's a window
that opens out onto the garden. Except that
their kitchen, studio and the whole apartment is on the top floor
of Albany Mansions at Charing Cross in Glasgow,
and the building itself curves around Charing Cross,
so the garden, which is tucked in, inside the curve or the V of the building,
is deep down there in a concrete canyon.   30
It gets very little light all day
and it's usually covered in a thick layer of soot and grime
and the air is often dense with exhaust fumes and other
exhalations of the city not conducive to
vegetable growth. Nevertheless, my Uncle John has taken pains
in gardening this little plot. He has planted

---

[1] No poems (or songs) can please long and live that are written for water-drinkers.

many things and hoped that they would grow,
even almost rushing downstairs to replant in the afternoon
the plants that he'd planted that morning, to get
the afternoon light on them, as it shifted in the shadows of the buildings.
       Anyway,   41
this window in their kitchen on the top floor of the building was opened by
being lifted *up* before it was swung *back*, into the room, on its
hinges on its left-hand side. So, Yvonne devised a plan to get rid of the corks.
She left the window open in the summer, just a little,
before they went to work, John to teach at the Art School,
and Yvonne to an estate agent's. She wedged a single cork in between
the window-frame and the lintel, and left it there.
Now, when it got cool in the evening after they were home from their work,
they would have to lift the window an inch before swinging it back
to close the frame flush with the lintel, and,   51
when they did that, the cork would fall
out of the niche it was wedged in, and into the dark canyon of the garden below,
where it would be lost, forever.
Yvonne began doing this one Tuesday morning.
It took until Thursday. On
Thursday evening she came home to find
John, already sitting there, at
the kitchen table, writing a letter, and having a glass of wine.
She noticed something out of the corner of her eye   61
over at the kitchen window,
so she went over to have a look.
And what she saw was this: the cork
was just as she'd left it that morning, wedged
between the frame and the lintel, but firmly stuck in
to the cork was a small pin. Attached to the
pin was a thread, which stretched down and around to the wooden paneling
next to the pantry door, whore it was securely tied to a second small pin,
which was in its turn stuck tightly in   70
to the wood.
       'What,'
Yvonne said, 'is this?'
(When they closed the window now, the cork would fall, attached to its thread,
daintily, back into the kitchen, and dangle there between
the window-frame and the doorway, waiting and ready for use again
when the time came next morning.)
         'Ah yes,' my Uncle John replied, glancing round:
      'I rigged that up   80
just this afternoon. I was
losing
too many corks.'

Urlar

    It's one of those sodden, Sunday afternoons
    in a wet New Zealand winter: everything is green
    and soaked right through. The bush falls
    over itself down on the walls of the garden.

I'm listening to bagpipes, another explanation of
the origins of pibroch: the human voice, and
all the limitations of the actual instrument.
It will return to the ground-bass, or urlar.
I'm thinking of elsewhere, another ground, Rachmaninoff,
and a drone of feeling fear that cold and wet   10
will raise blue mould on spines of books, of
relatively worthless books: my grandfather's collection –
the works of S. R. Crockett. The nature of inheritance.
That fear. There is another urlar playing now,
sounding with the surge of waves. Scotland
might seem not so far but near; surely
there's as much rain here. And music.

Chris Dolan (1958 –)

Sleet and Snow

She sat on the bed and he knelt in front of her. He took her left foot in his hands, which were big enough to go right round her from ankle to toe, and he pulled like billy-o. The boots weren't that tight, but his arms ached. He had no strength left in his grip. It always took him by surprise, this powerlessness. His arms didn't *feel* weak on a day-to-day basis. Only when he had to pull at something – like the heavy saucepan from the bottom of the cupboard, or the toilet door when the carpet rode up and stuck it – then they felt like they were half empty. Like his veins were too big for the dregs of blood that sloshed around inside them.

– What's with the tight shoes anyway, Missus? Trying to make your feet look thin?

– I've squeezed and squashed every bit of myself half me life. Why stop wi' me feet?

He used to like that – seeing all that soft flesh crammed into hard, tight clothes, like a spongy cushion stuffed into a leather cover. Breasts siphoned into boned bras, buttocks jacked up into ribbed pants, stomach squeezed into girdles. Then looking forward to it all springing back into life again at the end of the day. Now her getting dressed served the opposite purpose – to make it look as if there was some flesh left beneath the clothes. That, and to cover up the pain. She had more pain than flesh now.

Their lives had become very physical in their old age. All this helping each other on and off with shoes and jerseys, rubbing on ointments, clutching each other on stairs:

– Can't seem to keep our hands off each other these days, Missus.

They both wore the same kinds of clothes, now. Slip-on jerseys and trousers with elastic waists that didn't require the use of strong fingers. She'd laugh and tell him:

– No point in you getting kinky all of a sudden and trying on all my clothes. We're unisex now.

She pulled off the whole geriatric show much better than he could. A dab of lipstick, a water-colour rinse, taking the supporting arm like it was a lady's prerogative and not the result of aching bones. All her life she had been the independent one, doing her own thing whenever it came up her hump. Now she was the lady who expected to be waited upon.

She'd got into his taxi one day outside Central Station wearing a skirt and cardigan and slippers when the snow was piled six inches high.

– Where to?

– Eh, Dennistoun, I think.

– Couldn't be a bit more specific, could you?

– Dumbarton Road.

– Dumbarton Road's not in Dennistoun.

– Is there a Dennistoun Road in Dumbarton then?

– Came out for your ciggies and forgot where you live, did you?

She looked at him for a minute, then threw her head back laughing.

– And I don't even smoke.

She was English. Chubbier, taller than most women he knew; her hair different. Not blonde, not brunette. Honey, she would tell him later. Honey in some lights, strawberry blonde in others. This was just after the war when you couldn't get a decent pot of jam. Strawberry and honey sounded very tempting.

– So what do we do now then, Missus?

– How do you know me name? And she started laughing again.

It stuck for the rest of their lives. He still called her Missus. Fifty years later there was still somrthing of the stranger about her. Just some missus that stepped off a train into his cab.

When her wheezy laugh had run out of steam – he could have sworn blind it was a smoker's laugh – she didn't open the door to get out, or give him any new instructions, but just sat there, like she was in the living room of her own house. He felt like he was being cheeky, bringing up the subject of where to go.

– That's what they told me. Dumbarton Road. Dennistoun. Or t'other way round.

She stated it like the problem was his.

– Who did?

– These friends of mine.

– Close, are they?

That laughter again, filling up the taxi like a window had been left open.

– They'd bloody better live there. I've been sending their Christmas cards there for ten years.

The row of cabs behind him started blasting their horns. He turned on the engine and moved the car slowly through a red light round the corner. There was something in that decision. Why not just tell her to stop wasting his time? Why go out of his way for a woman who didn't even know where she was going?

The boots finally removed, pyjamas and dressing gown on, she went off out to the loo. He quickly grabbed a handful of tissues to wipe his crotch and the tops of his legs. He'd had a bit of bleeding for a few days now and didn't want her to know. For a start she'd worry her head off. And anyway, he'd already had one operation down there and had no intention of having another. He stuffed the hankies smeared with blood into his pyjama pocket. She came back in and sat in front of the mirror to comb her hair like she'd done every night for the last forty-five years.

– You'll comb that hair out. He used to tell her.

– On the contrary. Combing preserves the hair. You're the one that'll be bald before you're fifty.

Turned out she was wrong. His hair was thicker than hers. But his was grey, and had been since well before fifty. Somehow the combing had helped her keep her colour, though. She wasn't exactly strawberry blonde anymore, but she wasn't grey either. The honey had turned to syrup – a bright thin silvery sheen that perfectly coated the shape of her head, the way their sons' hair did when they were about a year old. She used the brush they had bought for Simon, the first one, forty-six years ago, with soft bristles that straightened the single layer of hair without scratching the skull. Nowadays, all it took was one sweep of the brush over the head, and her hair was sorted. But she did it over and over again, as if her hair was still thick.

He'd never expected to see her old. Every morning in life he'd gone off in his cab fully expecting her to be gone by the time he got back. She walked into his life in cardigan and slippers and might just as easily walk out of it.

– You just went into the station and got on the first train? He had turned round in the driver's seat to talk to her.

– Don't be daft. The first train out would've taken me straight back to Chorley. I'd just got off the bus from there. Anyway, Glasgow seemed just right. All those nice Scottish people. And then there was Molly and Jim.

– Dumbarton Road, Dennistoun?

– Or t'other way round.

– Molly and Jim what?

– Macdonald. Think you can find them?

– You must be joking. Everyone here's called Molly and Jim Macdonald.

– So what now?

He knew it should really have been him asking *her* that. He suggested an hotel, but she'd barely enough money on her for the hire out to Dennistoun. He suggested she go to the police and try and locate the Macdonalds, but she didn't like that idea at all. He wondered if she was on the run.

– Yeh. The Great Escape.

– Who from?

– Me old man. I didn't mean to, like. I just upped and offed, before he got home. I was sittingdown to do my Christmas cards . . .

– In January?

– Better late than never.

For the next forty years they made a point of sending out their Christmas cards in January, as a kind of celebration. Some years it got even later. She thought you couldn't send out cards until there was snow – it was really the snow – she was celebrating. Once, their cards didn't go out until the end of February. This year, she hadn't worked up the energy for it at all yet. It was nearly March now. He had written, addressed and stamped the cards back in December, and was still waiting for her to post them. The fact that she hadn't, worried him. Maybe this was it. The signal. He would find her one of these days hobbling out the door in her slippers and elasticated trousers. He bought her a Damart body stocking, just in case. Not that he wanted her to go, but he didn't want her catching her death either.

In the taxi cab, she'd laid her head back against the window and closed her eyes.

– I'd had enough.

– Of what?

– Don't know rightly. Albert's a gent. Nothing he wouldn't do for me. Works hard, and buys me everything I want. Bought me one of those new Hoovers. First house in the street to have one. Works a treat too. But this morning I took the Hoover and hawked it round the neighbours. Got enough for the bus to Preston, and a ticket to here.

He could see poor Albert getting in from work, finding his wife and Hoover gone. Maybe he never found out she sold it, imagined his wife and Hoover rambling round the country together, leaving him alone in an empty house with dirty carpets.

He never bought her a Hoover. Not even when they became vacuum cleaners and everybody had one. They beat their carpets, hung them out the back, like in the old days. The boys never noticed, until they got married. Then their wives made them see that a house without a proper carpet cleaner is not a home. The girls didn't like their mother-in-law. Thought she neglected her motherly duties. In a way, it kind of kept the family together. The four wives, who had nothing else in common, ganged up, meeting regularly to discuss her shortcomings and how to make up for her to their menfolk. She never noticed. She wasn't what you'd call a woman's woman. It was only when Eddie, their second, split up with his wife that she took the slightest notice of any of her daughters-in-law. She sent her a letter with her birthday card every year, and another with the Christmas card.

He'd started up the engine.

– Where are we going?

– I'll see you all right for the night, at least.

She started to open the door as the car moved off.

– You've got it wrong, mister. I'm not in the market for hows-yer-father.

He stamped on the accelerator, pissed off at that and thought if she wants to jump, let her.

But she closed the door again.

– I'm taking you to my sister's. She'll put you up. But you'll have to give her a sob story. Tell her your old man was thumping you or something. She likes a sad story, does Meg.

Meg died twenty-two years ago last June, and it was almost a relief. She'd been coming round to their house at least twice a week for over twenty-five years, just to make sure he wasn't thumping her. If Missus strained her ankle or whatever, Meg'd ask for all the details. If she jabbed herself on a thorn when she was out in the back doing the rose bushes, Meg looked in the sink and the cutlery drawer for a fork or a skewer with dried blood on it. Whenever he got fed up with it he'd shout a bit. Not at Meg, at her. Then she'd remind him the whole cock-and-bull story about her being bashed up was his idea in the first place.

The brushing routine finished, he helped her off with her dressing gown and into bed. He pulled the duvet back and held her hand to help her balance as she moved first one leg, then the other on to the bed, and sunk her frail body slowly down on to the sheet. Now they would talk, like they always did.

He'd tried his best never to let their lives get into routines, but with hindsight he had to admit they were riddled with them. Like talking before going to sleep. Every night since they were married, she would ask him about all the places he had been that day, and he would recount his tales, like an explorer back from the North Pole. He told her about the corners of the city he had poked about in in his little black cab, reeling off destinations like a Willy Nelson song: Ruchazie, Arden, Whitecraigs, Shettleston.

Until not so long back, the talking came after sex. Even in their seventies, they had managed a regular session. But it had eventually become a strain on their memories – each of them making love to the bodies they used to have – and on their tired limbs. She never said anything, but he realised how painful any kind of movement was becoming for her. Her moaning began to sound different. He stopped hearing the grunts of pleasure and the slap of spare flesh, and heard instead the scrape and whine of bone and pain. Anyway, his op had put paid to any inclinations in that direction.

So now they just lay side by side, in a way that, if anyone had come in the room, it would have looked like they had just been doing it. She stroked the hair on his chest, as she had always done, and he told her about the day's adventures. Not cabbying any more, of course. He had to retire at 65. But he still drove, taking the grandkids here and there, or just driving around. He sought out streets he had never been hired to go to. He thought if he kept on driving, he might stop himself turning into Albert; coming in at regular times, expecting to find her there, and then one day coming back to an empty house.

He never met Albert. And she never mentioned him. Except once when she had to file for a divorce before they could get married, and he had to sign a paper in a lawyer's office, stating that he had had an adulterous affair with Mrs Albert Critchly. Some hope. It had been two years since she stepped into his taxi, and he'd got no more out of her then French kissing. It took another two years before they got married. But poor Albert must have sat appalled in his house in Chorley, his wife running round the country with his Hoover, having it off with Scotsmen.

Her pain was bad tonight. She didn't have to say anything. Grimace or moan or anything like that. He just knew it was bad. She couldn't prop herself up on her elbow any more to face him when they were talking. She lay flat on her back, with her head turned towards him, smiling. Even the smile hurt. He could tell.

– You want a rubbing?

He leaned over her to get her Tupperware box full of medicines and ointments, but she shook her head and pushed his arm gently away. It was the pain, he knew that. But, still, she was quieter these days. More distant, lost in her own thoughts. He wondered if she was thinking it was time she went back and explained to poor old Albert Critchly. If he was still alive. He turned out the light, and lay thinking in the dark. There was nothing he could do to make her stay. If only she'd send the damned Christmas cards, he'd feel easier.

She wasn't sleeping either. The pain was keeping her awake. She didn't move, but her breathing didn't change rhythm. He wanted to ask her if she was all right, but she got fed up with him asking that. He lay facing away from her, imagining that if he turned he'd see that strawberry blonde woman in cardigan and slippers. She touched his arm, and it reminded him of when she'd leant forward and touched his back when he was driving her that first day to Meg's.

— Thanks, love. She'd said. — See? I knew I could depend on you nice Scottish folk.

Her fingers on his back had felt warm despite the cold.

Now they were cold against his arm, even though the heating was up full blast.

— You really want to know why I left? she said. Out of the blue, picking up a conversation started in a taxi half a century ago.

— There was no point in being there. Albert and Vera. The Critchlys, 14 Pendle Street, Chorley. Like Jim and Molly Macdonald. Too many of them.

— And here? John and Vera Murdoch, Ivanhoe Terrace, Cumbernauld?

— That's what I'm saying. I shouldn't be here. What am I doing being called Murdoch? I should never've got on that train. Shouldn't have sold that nice Hoover.

She coughed and laughed, squeezed his arm and turned around, settling into sleep.

The next morning, he woke. As usual, she'd got up before him and brought them both a cup of tea which they never drank. It was snowing outside. Well, sleeting. Big grey flecks of shredded cloud slid down the window pane. He reached out for his cuppa, and nudged her as she lay, still there and grinning that smoky grin of hers, beside him.

— Tea's getting cold, Missus.

He nudged her again, but she was gone.

Irvine Welsh (1958 –)

Irvine Welsh is the rising star. His stories of the disaffected young of Edinburgh, chock full of youthful sex, drugs, profanity, scatology, violence, irreverence, wit and style have become best sellers. One of his most respected, *Trainspotting*, has been made into a well-received, if controversial movie. Essentially an offshoot of Glasgow realism, his works have also a style which combines the racy dialect of the streets, a 'speaking voice' narrative and a surprisingly sophisticated philosophical bent which is both humorously inappropriate and touching. The style is not original to Scotland – one can find it in the dialect humorists of many nations – such as Damon Runyan or Joe Orton – but it has become remarkably prevalent in Scotland in recent years. Tom Leonard and James Kelman would seem to be the major influences there, but Welsh has made himself a master of the form.

The Acid House

Something strange was happening over Pilton. Probably not just Pilton, Coco Bryce considered, but as he was in Pilton, the here and now was all that concerned him. He gazed up at the dark sky. It seemed to be breaking up. Part of it had been viciously slashed open, and Coco was disconcerted by what appeared to be ready to spill from its wound. Shards of bright neon-like light luminated in the parting. Coco could make out the ebbs and flows of currents within a translucent pool which seemed to be accumulating behind the darkened membrane of the sky, as if in readiness to burst through the gap, or at least rip the wounded cloud-cover further. However, the light emanating from the wound seemed to have a narrow and self-contained range; it didn't light up the planet below.

Then the rain came: at first a few warning spits, followed by a hollow explosion of thunder in the sky. Coco saw a flash of lightning where his glowing vision had been and although unnerved in a different way, he breathed a sigh of relief that his strange sighting had been superseded by more earthly phenomena. Ah wis crazy tae drop that second tab ay acid. The visuals ur something else.

His body, if left to its own devices would tend towards rubber, but Coco had enough resources of the will and enough experience of the drug to remember that fear and panic fed off themselves. The golden rule of 'stay cool' had been mouthed by wasters down the decades for good reason. He took stock of his situation: Coco Bryce, tripping alone in the park at roughly three o'clock in the morning, lightning flashing from a foreboding sky above him.

The possibilities were: at the very least he'd be soaked to the skin, at worst he'd be struck by lightning. He was the only tall thing around for a few hundred yards, standing right in the middle of the park. – Fuck sakes, he said, pulling the lapels of his jacket together. He hunched up and stole quickly down the path that split the massive canine toilet which was West Pilton Park.

Then Coco Bryce let out a small whisper, not a scream, just a murmur, through a soft gasp. He felt his bones vibrate as heat surged through his body and the contents of his stomach fell to displace those of his bowels. Coco had been struck by something from the sky. Had his last vision before he let go of consciousness not been one of the concrete path rising to meet him, he might have thought: lightning.

Who   *What*   *Where*   *How*   *WHAT AM I?*

Coco Bryce. Brycey fae Pilton Brycey: one ay the Hibs Boys. Coco Fuckin Bryce, ya radge, he tried to shout, but he had no voice with which to make himself heard. He seemed to be blowing limply in a wind, but he could feel no currents of air nor hear their whistle. The nearest he could approximate to any sensation was that of being a blanket or a banner, floating in a breeze, yet he had still no sense of dimension or shape. Nothing conveyed to his cauterised senses any notion of his extent; it seemed as if he both encompassed the universe and was the size of a pin-head.

After a while he began to see, or sense, textures around him. There were images alright, but there was no sense of where they were coming from, or how they were being processed, no real sense of him having a body, limbs, a head, or eyes. Nonetheless these images were clearly perceived; a blue-black backdrop, illuminated by flickering, sparkling shapeless objects of varying mass, as unidentifiable as he was himself.

Am ah deid? Is this fuckin deid? COCO FUCKIN BRYCE!

The black was becoming more blue; the atmosphere he was moving around in was definitely getting thicker, offering more resistance to his sense of momentum.

Coco Bryce

It was stopping his movement. It was like a jelly, and he realised that he was going to set in it. A brief panic gripped him. It seemed important to keep moving. There was a sense of a journey needing to be completed. He willed himself on and could make out, in the distance, an incandescent centre. He felt a strong sense of elation, and using his willpower, travelled towards this light.

This fuckin gear isnae real. Eftir ah come doon, that's it, that's me fuckin well finished!

*   *   *

Rory Weston's hands shook as he put the receiver down. He could hear the screams and shouts coming from the other room. For a moment, no more than a few seconds, Rory wished he wasn't occupying this particular space and time. How had all this happened? He began to trace the sequence of events that led to this, only to be disrupted by another violent shriek from through the wall. – Hang on, Jen, they're on their way, he shouted, running through towards the source of the agonised cacophony.

Rory moved over to the swollen, distressed figure of his girlfriend, Jenny Moore, and crushed her hand in his. The Parker Knoll settee was soaked with her waters.

Outside, the thunder roared on, drowning out Jenny's screams for the neighbours.

Jenny Moore, through her pain, was also thinking about the cumulation of circumstances which led her to be in this condition in this Morningside flat. Her friend Emma, also pregnant, though a month less advanced than Jenny, had caught sight of their waddling figures reflected in a shop window in Princes Street. – God sakes, Jen, look at us! You know, I sometimes wish, looking back to that cold winter's evening, that I'd given Iain that blow job instead, she exclaimed.

They had laughed at this; laughed loudly. Well, Jenny wasn't laughing now.

I'm being torn apart and this bastard sits over me with that stupid fucking expression on his face.

What did it take out of them physically? It was just another fuck for those bastards. We had it all to do, but there they all were telling us how to do it, controlling us – gynaecologists, fathers to be, all men; together in a sickly pragmatic conspiracy . . . the scumbags have already disengaged emotionally from you; you're just the receptacle to carry the precious fruit of their sweaty bollocks into the world, through your fucking blood . . . But you're being hysterical darling . . . it's all those hormones, all over the place, just listen to us, we know best . . .

The bell went. The ambulance had arrived.

Thank god they're here, the men. More bloody men. AmbulanceMEN. Where the fucking hell were the ambulance WOMEN?

– Easy Jen, there we go . . . Rory said with what was meant to be encouragement.

There WE go? she thought, as another wave of pain, worse this time than anything she had known, tore through her. This time the thunder and lightning of the freakiest freak storm to hit Scotland simply couldn't compete. She was almost blacking out with the pain as they got her on the stretcher, down the stairs and into the van. No sooner did they start up than they realised they wouldn't make the hospital.

– Stop the van! shouted one of the ambulancemen. – It's happening now!

They stopped the van by the side of the deserted Meadows. Only the flashing bolts of lightning; strange, persistently luminous and following awkward, uncharacteristic trajectories, lit up the starkly darkened sky. One of these bolts struck the ambulance parked in that deserted road as Jenny Moore was trying to push the offspring of her and her partner Rory Weston out into the world.

★   ★   ★

AW THIS IS NOWT TAE FUCKIN DAE WI ME

COCO

COCO BRYCE

BRYCEY

COLIN STUART BRYCE

```
        C              T        BR   Y   C   E         Y
        O              R                               A
        L        A                                     F
        I        U                                     U
        N      S T                                     C
                                                       K
                                                       I
                                                       N
```

How long dae ah go oan fir

IN STUUUUUAAAAARRRTTTTTTT B R
COLINSTUARTBRYCE

Colin Stuart Bryce, or Coco Bryce, the Pilton casual, as he perceived himself to be, although he could not be too sure anymore, floated in the heightless void of gel, toward its white luminous centre. He became aware of something racing toward him at great speed, approaching from that far off central point he had sensed. While the now thick and solidifying gel had begun to constrain the life force that was Coco Bryce, this other energy source negotiated it with the ease of light travelling through air. He could not see this, only gain a notion of it through some strange, indefinable conglomeration of the senses.

> Hi bees here
> Hi-bees there
> Hi-bees every

It seemed to sense him too, for it slowed down as it approached him, and after hesitating, shot past him at speed and was gone, vanishing into the indistinct environment around him. However, Coco had a chance to sense what it was, and it was like nothing he'd witnessed before, an elongated blue, glass-like, cylindrical-shaped force, yet in a bizarre way it felt human; just as he, Coco Bryce, still considered himself to be human.

> fucking where
> na na na na na
> na na na na

> we scored one
> we scored two
> we scored seven
> more than you

> Dad's comin back tae us, Colin. He's better now son. He's changed, Colin. We'll soon be thegither again son. Yill see a big difference, you mark ma words. Dinnae be frightened son, yir Ma widnae lit um hurt us again. Ah widnae lit um back in the hoose unless he'd changed, son

He felt elated as the light grew closer, more powerful, beckoning him. He felt that if he could get to it, everything would be all right. Hopeful, he willed himself on through the rapidly thickening gel. Propulsion, achievable purely through the exercise of will, was becoming increasingly difficult. No idea of where he was, of his shape, size, or his senses in the discrete categories of sight, touch, taste, smell, hearing, these seeming obsolete, yet him somehow able to experience the exploding kaleidoscope of colours beyond the gel that engulfed him; to feel the movement and the resistance to that movement.

> There is one nasty, malignant little creature in this class, an odious young fool of a boy who spreads

It was growing darker. As soon as that awareness hit him, he noted it was pitch black. Coco felt fear. He had slowed down completely now, grinding to a halt. His will no longer served as a driving mechanism. The light was closer though. The Light. It was upon him, around him, in him. LIGHT LIGHT

> his poisonous influence to other, keener pupils. I am referring, of course, to

LIGHT LIGHT LIGHT LIGHT LIGHT
LIGHT LIGHT LIGHT LIGHT LIGHT
LIGHT LIGHT LIGHT LIGHT LIGHT
LIGHT LIGHT LIGHT LIGHT LIGHT
LIGHT LIGHT LIGHT LIGHT LIGHT
LIGHT LIGHT LIGHT LIGHT LIGHT
LIGHT LIGHT LIGHT LIGHT LIGHT
LIGHT

> Colin Bryce, the most common and disgusting little man I've ever had the displeasure of teaching in one of my classes. Step forward, Colin Bryce! What have you to say for

LIGHT LIGHT LIGHT LIGHT
LIGHT LIGHT LIGHT LIGHT
LIGHT LIGHT LIGHT LIGHT

> YILL DAE IS YIR FUCKIN WELL TELT, COLIN, YUH WEE CUNT! AH SAIS TWINTY FUCKIN REGAL! NOW! MOVE IT!

LIGHT LIGHT LIGHT LIGHT LIGHT LIGHT LIGHT LIGHT
LIGHT LIGHT LIGHT LIGHT LIGHT LIGHT LIGHT LIGHT
LIGHT LIGHT LIGHT LIGHT LIGHT LIGHT LIGHT LIGHT

Yir a tidy cunt, mate. Coco, is it no? Welcome tae the family. Fuckin main man!

LIGHT LIGHT LIGHT LIGHT LIGHT
LIGHT LIGHT LIGHT LIGHT LIGHT

Kirsty, ah really like ye, ken? Ah mean, ah'm no much good it talkin like this, bit ye ken whit ah mean, likesay you n

LIGHT LIGHT LIGHT LIGHT LIGHT LIGHT LIGHT LIGHT
LIGHT LIGHT LIGHT LIGHT LIGHT LIGHT LIGHT LIGHT

Ye shag that burd Coco? Fill hoose? Tony's been up it likes. C'moan Coco, dinnae git stroppy. Oly sayin likes! Hey boys, Coco's in luurrve! Hi! hi! hi!

Too much fuckin ridin, too many fuckin collies n no enough fuckin swedgin. That's whit's wrong wi us these days.

LIGHT LIGHT LIGHT LIGHT LIGHT LIGHT LIGHT LIGHT

You're on a slippery slope, Bryce. It's no game, son. I kid you not. The next time I get a hold of you, the key gets thrown away. You're vermin, son, pure vermin. You think you're a gangster, but you're just a silly wee laddie to me. I've seen them all come through here. Oh, they aw think they're so hard, so cool. They usually die in the gutter or the lodging house or rot their miserable lives away in a cell. You've blown it Bryce, totally blown it, you silly little toe-rag. The saddest thing is you don't even realize it, do you?

LIGHT LIGHT LIGHT LIGHT LIGHT LIGHT LIGHT LIGHT
LIGHT LIGHT LIGHT LIGHT LIGHT LIGHT LIGHT LIGHT

The thing is that ah'm a fuckin. businessman. Right? The demolition business.

LIGHT LIGHT LIGHT LIGHT
LIGHT LIGHT LIGHT LIGHT
LIGHT LIGHT LIGHT LIGHT
LIGHT LIGHT LIGHT LIGHT

LIGHT LIGHT LIGHT LIGHT LIGHT LIGHT LIGHT LIGHT
LIGHT LIGHT LIGHT LIGHT LIGHT LIGHT LIGHT LIGHT
LIGHT LIGHT LIGHT LIGHT DARKER DARKER DARKNESS.

Heaven or hell, wherever this is, ah'm fuckin closin in! Thir's gaunny be some changes aroond here, ya cunts! Coco Bryce. Pilton. Distinguished honours at Millwall (pre-season friendly), Pittodrie, Ibrox and Anderlecht (UEFA Cup). Coco Bryce, a top boy. A cunt that messes is a cunt that dies. See if any cunt . . . if any cunt gits . . . if any cunt . . .

His thoughts trailed out insipidly. Coco was frightened. At first the fear was an insidious quease, then it became brutally stark and raw as he felt great forces on him, crushing and pulling at him. It felt as if he was in the grip of a vice while simultaneously another power tried to tear him from its grasp. These forces, though, enabled him to define his body for the first time since this strange journey had begun. He knew he was human, all too human, too vulnerable to the powers that crushed and wrenched at him. Coco prayed for a victor in the struggle between the two great and evenly matched forces. The torture lasted for a while, then he felt himself being torn from the void. He had only sensed THE LIGHT before, but now he could actually see it, burning through his closed eyelids, which he could not open. And then he realised there were voices:

– It's a beauty!

– A wee laddie for ye, hen, eh's a wee cracker n aw.

– Look, Jen, he's wonderful!

Coco could sense himself being held up; could sense his body, where his limbs were. He tried to shout: Coco Bryce! Hibs Boys! What's the fuckin score, ya cunts?

Nothing came from his lungs.

He felt a slap on his back and an explosion of air within him, as he let out a loud, wrenching scream.

★   ★   ★

Dr Callaghan looked down at the young man in the bed. He had been comatose, but now that he had emerged into consciousness, he was displaying some strange behavioral patterns. He couldn't speak, and writhed around in his bed thrashing his arms and legs. Eventually he had to be constrained. He screamed and cried.

Cold.
Help.

– Waaahhh! screamed the youth. At the foot of his bed, had a name tag: COLIN BRYCE.

Hot.
   Help.
   – Waaahhh!

  Hungry.
  Help.
  – Waaahhh!

  Need hug.
  Help.
  – Waaahhh!

  Want to pish, shite.
  Help.
  – Waaahhh!

Dr Callaghan felt that, through his screaming, the youth was perhaps trying to communicate: though he couldn't be sure.

★   ★   ★

On the ward Jenny held her son. They would call him either Jack or Tom, as they had agreed, because, she considered with a sudden surge of cynicism, that's what people like them tended to do. They were located in an eighties English-speaking strata where culture and accent are homogenous and nationally is a largely irrelevant construct. Middle-class, professional, socially aware, politically-correct people, she reflected scornfully, tended to use those old proletarian craftsperson names: ideal for the classless society. Her friend Emma had announced her intention to call her child Ben, if it was a boy, so the choice had been narrowed to one of two.

How's my little Jack, Rory said to himself, his index finger touching the baby's doughy hand.

Tom, Jenny thought, cradling her son.

What's the fuckin story here then, ya cunt?

★   ★   ★

Over the following few days the family of Colin Bryce became resigned to the fact that their son seemed to alternate between the vegetative and the rambling lunatic states after the accident. Friends testified that Coco had taken not one, but two tabs of acid, Supermarios to boot, and the press seized onto this. The youth in the hospital became a minor celebrity. The newspapers posed the same rhetorical question:

DID COLIN BRYCE GET HIS BRAINS FRIED BY
LIGHTNING OR LSD?
COLIN BRYCE – A VICTIM OF A FREAK ACCIDENT OR YET
ANOTHER OF OUR YOUNGSTERS DESTROYED BY
THE DRUGS MENACE?

While the press seemed to know for sure, the doctors were baffled as to the nature of the young man's condition, let alone the possible causes of it. However, they could see signs of improvement. There was growing eye contact over the weeks, definite indications of intelligence. They encouraged friends and family to visit the youth, who it was felt would benefit from as much stimulation as possible.

$$\star \quad \star \quad \star$$

The baby was called Tom.
 Coco, ya radge cunts! Coco Bryce! Brycie! CCS! Hibs boys smash all fuckin opposition. Too true. Becks then, cunt.
Jenny breastfed her baby.
 Phoah, ya fucker! This'll fuckin dae me. Coco Bryce, who he? Ma name's Tam, eh Tom!
The child fed greedily, sucking hard on Jenny's nipple. Rory, who had taken some holiday time on top of his paternity leave, observed the scene with interest. – He seems to be enjoying himself. Look at him, it's almost obscene, Rory laughed, concealing the growing feeling of unease which swept over him. It was the way the baby looked at him sometimes. It actually seemed to focus on him and look, well, contemptuous and aggressive. That was ridiculous. A small baby. His baby.
He reasoned that this was an important issue to share with some of the other Persons Of The Male Gender at his men's group. It was, he reasoned, perhaps a natural reaction at the inevitable exclusion of the male partner from the woman-parent and child bonding process.
 Phoah, ya cunt ye! Some fuckin jugs oan it!
Jenny felt something small and sharp pressing on her stomach. – Oh look, he's got a stiff little willy! she exclaimed, holding up the naked baby. – Who's a naughty little boy? she kissed his plump stomach and made quacking noises.
 Lower, ya big fuckin pump-up-the-knickers! Git yir fuckin gums roond it!
 – Yes, interesting. . . Rory said uneasily. The child's face; it looked like a leering, lecherous old man. He'd have to see about this terrible jealousy, talk it through with other men who were in touch with their feelings. The thought of having a genuine hang-up to share with the rest of the group thrilled him.
That night Rory and Jenny made love for the first time since she'd come home with the baby. They started gently, warily testing the tenderness of her sex, then became increasingly passionate. Rory, though, was distracted during his performance by sounds he thought he heard coming from the cot at the side of the bed. He looked around and shuddered, sure that he could see the outline of the baby, this baby only a couple of weeks old, standing up in the cot watching them!
 Ya dirty cunts! Doggy style n aw! Phoah . . .
Rory stopped his strokes.
 – What is it Rory? What the fuck is it? Jenny snapped, angry at the interruption as she was chasing her first post-birth climax.
They heard a soft thud from the cot.
 – The baby . . . it was standing up, watching us, Rory said weakly.
 – Don't be bloody stupid! Jenny hissed. – C'mon Rory, fuck me! Fuck me!
Rory, however, had gone limp, and he spilled out of her. – But . . . it was . . .

– Shut up for fuck's sake! She moved around, angrily pulling the duvet over them. – It's not an it, HE is a HIM. Your own bloody son! She turned away from him.

– Jen, he put his hand on her shoulder, but she shrugged it off, its limp creepiness sickening her.

After that, they decided it was time to put the baby in the room they'd made into a nursery. Jenny found the whole thing pathetic, but if Rory was put off that much, well, so be it.

The following night the baby lay silently awake in its new location. Rory had to concede that he was a good baby, he never seemed to cry. – You never seem to cry, do you, Tom? he asked wistfully as he stood over the child in the cot. Jenny, who'd had a panic attack in the night due to the child's silence, had sent Rory through to check on him.

Ah'm feart ay nae cunt. Whin ah goat cornered by they fuckin cunts at Cessnock whin wi pissed aw ower thum at Ibrox, ah jist goes: Come ahead then, ya fuckin weed-jie cunts. Ah'm no exactly gaunny burst oot greetin cause some specky cunt's five minutes late wi ma feed now, um uh? Fuckin tube.

Could handle a fuckin Becks.

★   ★   ★

There was still no change in the condition of the youth in the hospital, although Dr Callaghan was now sure that he was using attention-seeking behaviour to meet his basic needs of food, changing and body temperature regulation. Two of his friends, young men in hooded sweatshirts, came to see him. They were called Andy and Stevie.

– Fuckin shame, man, Andy gasped, – Coco's fucked. Jist lyin thair greetin like a bairn, eh.

Stevie shook his head sadly, – Tell ays that's fuckin Coco Bryce lyin thair, man.

A nurse approached them. She was a pleasant, open-faced, middle-aged woman. – Try to talk to him about some of the things you did together, things he'd be interested in.

Stevie stared at her with open-mouthed bemusement; Andy gave a snigger followed by a mocking shake of his head.

– You know, like discos and pop, that sort of thing, she cheerfully suggested. They looked at each other and shrugged.

Too warm.

– Waah!

– Right, Andy said. – Eh, ye missed yirsel the other day Coco. The semi, ken? Wi wir waitin fir they Aberdeen cunts at Haymarket, eh. Booted fuck ootay the cunts, man, chased thum back doon tae the station, back ontae the train, doon the fuckin tracks, the loat! Polis jist fuckin standin thair n aw, didnae ken what tae fuckin dae, eh no. How good wis it Stevie?

– Fuckin barry, ya cunt. Couple ay boys goat lifted; Gary n Mitzy n that crew.

– Waah!

They looked at their screaming, unresponsive friend and fell into silence for a while. Then Stevie started: – N ye missed yirsel at Rezurrection n aw, Coco. That wis too mad. How radge wir they snowballs, Andy?

– Mental. Ah couldnae dance, bit this cunt wis up aw night. Ah jist wanted tae spraff tae ivray cunt. Pure gouchin the whole night, man. Some fuckin good Es floatin aroond the now, Coco, ye want tae git it the gither man, n will git sorted n git some clubbin done . . .

– It's nae fuckin use, Stevie moaned, – eh cannae hear us.

– This is fuckin too radge, man, Andy conceded, – cannae handle aw this shite, eh.

Feed.

– Waah! WAAAHHHHH!

– That's no Coco Bryce, Stevie said, – no the Coco Bryce ah ken anywey.

They left as the nurse came in with Coco's food. All he would eat was cold, liquidised soup.

★   ★   ★

Rory reluctantly started back at work. He'd grown worried about Jenny, concerned about how she was coping with the baby. It was obvious to him that she was suffering from some form of post-natal depression. Two bottles of wine had been taken from the fridge. He'd said nothing to her, waiting for her to raise the matter. He'd have to keep his eye on her. The men at the group would support him; he'd have their admiration, not just for being in touch with his own feelings, but also for his unselfish responsiveness to his partner's needs. He remembered the mantra: awareness is seventy percent of the solution.

Jenny had a bad fright on Rory's first day back at work. The baby had been very sick in his cot. There was a strange smell coming from him. It was like . . . alcohol.

We do not carry hatchets, we do not carry chains, We only carry straws to suck our lemonade.

Oh, ya cunt ye. . . ma heids fuckin nippen wi that vino. Cannae drink as much as ah used tae, no as a sprog . . .

The horrible truth dawned on Jenny: Rory was trying to poison their baby! She found the empty bottles of wine underneath the bed. That sick, warped, spineless fool. . . she would take the child to her mother's. Though perhaps it hadn't been Rory. A couple of workmen had been in, young lads, sanding and staining the wood-work: the doors and skirting boards. Surely they wouldn't have tried to give a new baby alcohol. They wouldn't be that irresponsible . . . she'd get onto the firm. Perhaps even contact the police. It could be Rory though. Whatever, Tom's safety was all that mattered. That inadequate fool could bleat piteously about his sick little problems to the insipid like-minds in his pathetic group. She was leaving.

– Who did it, Tom? Was it bad Daddy? Yes! I bet it was! Bad Daddy's tried to hurt little Tom. Well we're going away, Tom, we're going to my mummy's down in Cheadle.

Eh? What?

– That's near Manchester, isn't it Tom-Tom? It is! Yes, it is! And she'll be so pleased to see little Tom-Tom, won't she? Won't she?! Yes, she will! Will Will Will Will Will! She smothered the baby's doughy cheek with wet kisses.

– *Git tae fuck, ya daft cunt! Ah cannae go tae fuckin Manchester! Goat tae pit this fuckin sow in the picture. Ah'm no her fuckin bairn. The name's Coco Bryce.*

– Look, eh Jenny . . .

She froze as she heard the voice coming from that small mouth which twisted unnaturally to form the words. It was an ugly, shrieking, cackling voice. Her baby, her little Tom; he looked like a malevolent dwarf.

Fuck sakes. Ah've done it now. Stey cool, Coco, dinnae freak this daft hoor oot.

You spoke! Tom. You spoke . . . Jenny gasped in disbelief.

– Look, said the baby, standing up in his cot, as Jenny swayed unsteadily, – sit doon, eh sit down, he urged. Jenny obeyed in silent shock. You'd better no say nowt tae nae cunt aboot this, right? the baby said, looking keenly and sharply at its mother for signs of understanding. Jenny just looked bemused. – Eh, I mean, Mother, they would not understand. They would take me away. I would be treated like a freak, cut up oan a laboratory table, tested by aw they specky cunts . . . eh, the people in white coats. Ah'm a sortay, eh, a sort of phenomenon, I've got eh, special intelligence n that. Right?

Coco Bryce was pleased with himself. He thought back to the videos of *Star Wars* he'd watched avidly as a kid. He had to act cosmic to keep this gig going. He was doing alright here. – They'd want tae take ays away . . .

– Never! I'd never let them take my Tom away! Jenny screamed, the prospect of losing her baby galvanising her into some sort of sense. – This is incredible! My little Tom! A special baby! But how, Tom? Why? Why you? Why us?

– Eh, jist the wey it goes. Nae cunt kens, ah mean, it's just the way I was born, Mother, my destiny n that.

– Oh, Tom! Jenny scooped up the baby in her arms.

– Eh right! the child said with embarrassment. – Eh listen, Ma, eh, Jenny, one or two wee things. That scran, eh, the food. It's no good. I want what grown-ups get. No aw that veggie stuff that yous eat. Meat, Jenny. A bit ay steak, ken?

– Well, Rory and I don't . . .

– Ah'm no giein a fuck aboot you n Rory . . . ah mean, eh, yous have no right to deny me my free choice.

This was true, Jenny conceded. – Yes, you're right, Tom. You're obviously intelligent enough to articulate your own needs. This is amazing! My baby! A genius! How do you know about things like steak though?

Oh, ya cunt. Dinnae fuck up here. This is a good fuckin doss yiv goat.

– Eh, I picked a lot of it up from the telly. I heard they two joiner boys that ye hud in daein yir woodwork bletherin. Ah picked up a lot fae them.

– That's very good, Tom, but you shouldn't talk like those workmen. Those men are, well, a little common, probably a bit sexist in their conversation. You should have more positive role models.

– Eh?

– Try to be like somebody else.

– Like Rory, the baby scoffed.

Jenny had to think about that, – Well, maybe not, but, oh . . . we'll see. God, he's going to be so shocked when he finds out.

– Dinnae tell um, it's oor secret, right.

– I have to tell Rory. He's my partner. He's your father! He has the right to know.

– Mother, eh Jenny, it's jist this ah git a vibe offay that radge. He's jealous ay me. He'd shop ays, git ays taken away.

Jenny had to concede that Rory had been unstable enough in his behaviour towards their child to suggest that he wasn't emotionally equipped to handle this shock. She would go along with this. It would be their secret. Tom would just be a normal little baby with others around, but when they were alone he'd be her special little man. With her guiding his development he would grow up non-sexist and sensitive, but strong and genuinely expressive, rather than an insipid clown who clings to a type of behaviour for limp ideological reasons. He'd be the perfect new man.

★   ★   ★

The youth they called Coco Bryce had learned to speak. At first it was thought that he was repeating words parrot fashion, but he then began to identify himself, other people and objects. He seemed particularly responsive to his mother and his girlfriend, who came to visit regularly. His father never visited.

His girlfriend Kirsty had cut her hair short at the sides. She had long wanted to do this, but Coco had discouraged her. Now he was in no position to. Kirsty chewed on her gum as she looked down at him in the bed. – Awright, Coco? she asked.

– Coco, he pointed at himself. – Cawlin.

– Aye, Coco Bryce, she said, spitting out the words between chews.

His heid's finally fried. It's that acid, they Supermarios. Ah telt um, bit that's Coco, livin fir the weekends; raves, fitba. The week's jist something tae get through fir him, and he'd been daein too much fuckin acid tae get through it. Well, ah'm no gaunny hing aboot waitin fir a vegetable tae git it thegither.

– Skanko n Leanne's suppose tae bae be gitten engaged, she said, – that's what ah heard anywey.

This statement, though it elicited no response from Coco, sparked off an interesting line of thought for Kirsty. If he could remember nothing, he might not remember the status of their relationship. He might not remember what a pain in the arse he could be when it came to talking about their future.

Toilet.

– Number twos! NUMBER TWOS! the youth screamed.

A nurse appeared with a bedpan.

After he had shat, Kirsty sat on the edge of her boyfriend's bed and bent over him. – Skanko n Leanne. Engaged, she repeated.

He pushed his mouth towards her breasts and began sucking and biting at them through her t-shirt and bra. – Mmmmm . . . mmmm . . .

– Get the fuck offay ays! she shouted, pushing him away. – No here! No now!

The sharpness in her voice made him wail. – WAAHH!!

Kirsty shook her head scornfully, spat out her gum, and left. If, though, as the doctors were suggesting, he was a blank piece of paper, Kirsty had realised that she could colour him in as she liked. She'd keep him away from his mates when he got out. He'd be a different Coco. She'd change him.

⋆ ⋆ ⋆

All Jenny's material on post-natal care hadn't quite prepared her for the type of relationship she and her baby were developing.

– Listen Jenny, ah want ye tae take ays tae the fitba oan Setirday. Hibs-Herts at Easter Road. Right?

– Not until you stop talking like a workman and speak properly, she said. The content of his conversation and the tone of his voice concerned her.

– Yes, sorry. I thought I'd like to see some sport.

– Em, I don't know much about the football, Tom. I like to see you express yourself and develop interests, but football . . . it's one of those terribly macho things, and I don't think I want you getting into it . . .

– Aw aye, I mean, so I can grow up like that wanker! Eh, my father? C'mon Mum, wise up! He's a fuckin toss!

– Tom! That's enough! Jenny said, but she couldn't help smiling. The kid was definitely onto something here.

Jenny agreed to take the child onto the East Terracing at Easter Road. He made her stand over by a heavily policed barrier which divided the rival sets of fans. She noted that Tom seemed to spend more time watching the youths in the crowd than the football. They were moved away by startled police who remonstrated with Jenny on her irresponsible behavior. She had to admit the grim truth; great freak of nature and genius he may be, but her baby was a yob.

Over the weeks, though, Coco Bryce grew happier in the new body. He would have it all. Let them think that the old body in the hospital was the real Coco Bryce. He was fine here; there were opportunities. At first he thought that he missed shagging and drinking, but he found that his sex drive was very low and that alcohol made his baby body too sick. Even his favourite food was no longer palatable; he now preferred lighter, runny, easily digested stuff. Most of all, he felt so tired all the time. All he wanted to do was sleep. When he was awake, he was learning so much. His new knowledge seemed to be forcing out much of his old memories.

⋆ ⋆ ⋆

An extensive program of reminiscence and recall therapy had failed the youth in the hospital. Educational psychologists had decided that rather than try to get him to remember anything, he would learn everything from scratch. This programme paid instant dividends and the young man was soon allowed home. Visiting the surroundings he had seen in photographs gave him a sense of who he was, even if it was a learned rather than a recalled concept. To his mother's shock, he even wanted to visit his father in prison. Kirsty came round a lot. They were, after all, as good as engaged, she had told him. He couldn't remember, he remembered nothing. He had to learn how to make love all over again. Kirsty was pleased with him. He seemed eager to learn. Coco had never been one for foreplay before. Now, under her instruction, he discovered his tongue and fingers, becoming a skillful and responsive lover. They soon became formally engaged and moved into a flat together.

The papers took an occasional interest in Coco Bryce's recovery. The young man renounced drugs, so the Regional Council thought that it would be good publicity to offer him a job. They employed him as a messenger, though the youth, continuing and rapidly progressing with his studies, wanted to get into clerical work. His friends thought that Coco had gone a bit soft since the accident, but most put it down to his engagement. He had stopped running with the casuals. That was Kirsty's idea; it could get him into bother and they had their future to think of. Coco's ma thought this was great. Kirsty had been a good influence.

One evening, around eighteen months later, the young man known as Colin Bryce was travelling on a bus with his wife Kirsty. They had been visiting her mother and were now heading back to their flat in Dalry. A young woman and her chubby infant sat in front of them. The child had turned around and was facing Colin and Kirsty. It seemed fascinated by them both. Kirsty jokingly played with the toddler, pressing his nose.

– Tom, the baby's mother laughed, stop disturbing people. Sit round straight.

– No, he's awright, Kirsty smiled. She looked at Coco, trying to gauge his reaction to the child. She wanted one. Soon.

The infant seemed mesmerised by Coco. His daughy hand reached out and played over the youth's face, tracing its contours. Kirsty stifled a laugh as her husband pulled his head back and looked self-conscious.

– Tom! The baby's mother laughed in mock exasperation, – You little pest. C'mon, it's our stop.

– KOKORBIGH! KOKORBIGH! the child squealed as she scooped him up and carried him away. He pointed back at the youth, tearfully wailing as they left the bus,

– KOKORBIGH!

– That's not Kokirbigh, she explained, referring to the dream demon that persistently plagued her son Tom, – that's just a young man.

Kirsty talked about babies for the rest of the journey, engrossed in the subject, never noticing the fear and confusion on her husband's face.

Robert Crawford (1959 –)

Also an important scholar and critic, Crawford writes some of the wittiest of modern Scottish poetry.

Scotland in the 1890s

'I came across these facts which, mixed with others . . . '
Thinking of Helensburgh, J. G. Frazer
Revises flayings and human sacrifice;
Abo of the Celtic Twilight, St Andrew Lang
Posts him a ten-page note on totemism
And a coloured fairy book – an Oxford man
From Selkirk, he translates Homer in his sleep.

'When you've lived here, even for a short time,
Samoa's a bit like Scotland – there's the sea . . .
Back in Auld Reekie with a pen that sputtered   10
I wrote my ballad, 'Ticonderoga' or

'A Legend of the West Highlands,' then returned
To King Kalakaua's beach and torches –
You know my grandfather lit Lismore's south end?'

Mr Carnegie has bought Skibo Castle.
His Union Jack's sewn to the stars and stripes.
James Murray combs the dialect from his beard
And files slips for his massive *Dictionary*.
Closing a fine biography of mother,
Remembering Dumfries, and liking boys,   20
James Barrie, caught in pregnant London silence,
Begins to conceive the Never Never Land.

Scotland

Semiconductor country, land crammed with intimate expanses,
Your cities are superlattices, heterojunctive
Graphed from the air, your cropmarked farmlands
Are epitaxies of tweed.

All night motorways carry your signal, swept
To East Kilbride or Dunfermline. A brightness off low headlands
Beams-in the dawn to Fife's interstices,
Optoelectronics of hay.

Micro-nation. So small you cannot be forgotten,
Bible inscribed on a ricegrain, hi-tech's key   10
Locked into the earth, your televised Glasgows
Are broadcast in Rio. Among circuitboard crowsteps

To be miniaturised is not small-minded.
To love you needs more details than the Book of Kells –
Your harbours, your photography, your democratic intellect
Still boundless, chip of a nation.

Alba Einstein

When proof of Einstein's Glaswegian birth
First hit the media everything else was dropped:
Logie Baird, Dundee painters, David Hume – all
Got the big E. Physics documentaries
Became peak-viewing; Scots publishers hurled awa
MacDiarmid like an overbaked potato, and swooped
On the memorabilia: Einstein Used My Fruitshop,
Einstein in Old Postcards, *Einstein's Bearsden Relatives*.
Hot on their heels came the A. E. Fun Park,
Quantum Court, Glen Einstein Highland Malt.   10
Glasgow was booming. Scotland rose to its feet
At Albert Suppers where The Toast to the General Theory
Was given by footballers, panto-dames, or restauranteurs.

In the US an ageing lab-technician recorded
How the Great Man when excited showed a telltale glottal stop.
He'd loved fiddlers' rallies. His favourite sport was curling.
Thanks to this, Scottish business expanded
Endlessly. His head grew toby-jug-shaped,
Ideal for keyrings. He'd always worn brogues.   19
Ate bannocks in exile. As a wee boy he'd read *The Beano*.
His name brought new energy: our culture was solidly based
On pride in our hero, The Universal Scot.

Ghetto-Blastir

Ghetto-makars, tae the knackirs'
Wi aw yir schemes, yir smug dour dreams
O yir ain feet. Yi're beat
By yon new Scoatlan loupin tae yir street

Wi a Jarre-lik puissance, ghetto-blastin
Auld sangs crooned doon
Yir reedy beaks, wastin an tastin
O deid pus. See us? We're foon

Wi whit's new, wi aw that's speerin oot
An cummin hame tae roost, tae set the feathirs   10
Flyin in yir kailyard. Scoot
Tae yir hales, tak tae yir heels, blethirs,

Wee naethins aye feathrin yir ain nests
O douce semis! Yir psychadelic tartan's
Shite tae oor white nichts an aw the guests
Oor laughtir's aftir. Sook yir fozie cartons

O guttir music, mak the Muse seik uttir-
lie wi yir gabbin, stabbin, sabbin
Ochones. Gang tae the Gents' an muttir.
Ladies tae! Bicoz we're grabbin   20

Whit's left o the leid★ tae mak anither sang   language
O semiconducters, Clydes aw dancin fastir
Than yir feart shanks. Ye'll scraich tae hear amang
Pooer-clubs an cliques, twee pubs o freaks,
When cockiedoodlin doon yir beaks

The raucus sweet soon o oor Ghetto-Blastir.

Opera

Throw all your stagey chandeliers in wheelbarrows and move them north
To celebrate my mother's sewing-machine
And her beneath an eighty-watt bulb, pedalling

Iambs on an antique metal footplate
Powering the needle through its regular lines,
Doing her work. To me as a young boy
That was her typewriter. I'd watch
Her hands and feet in unison, or read
Between her calves the wrought-iron letters:
SINGER. Mass-produced polished wood and metal,   10
It was a powerful instrument. I stared
Hard at its brilliant needle's eye that purred
And shone at night; and then each morning after
I went to work at school, wearing her songs.

Bhidhio

They walk towards us in blue overalls, tiny
Millionaires of the rain,

Peat poets, a fiddler with a hacking cough.
They speak what it says on the roadsigns,

But to us always English. Their smiles and glances
Are what gets lost in translation.

After centuries of practising
Australia and Canada, these survivors blockade their lives

Beautifully with abandoned cars and rich
Theological silence. Neighbours   10

Peg their families' souls on washing lines
In a close surveillance society

Where ministers' noble, orgasmic voices
Say the Evil One is near as he was in Eden

Flying in under the radar. We
Sweep past their bungalows, heading back for the mainland.

They drive slowly to their prayer-meetings, different.
They watch us on their television.

Iona

Doctor Johnson feels seasick. The small man who
As the years twitch past will slowly overtake him
Has gone off to scrabble for green stones.

Those bearded boatmen who rowed him here
Mutter in Gaelic. Johnson noticed their powder-red eyes
When they offered him oatmeal. He likes them

Knowing all along their abbey is full of pigshit;
This place of beginnings is cold, bare, muddy.
He is starting to get tired of London.

A Scottish Assembly

Circuitry's electronic tartan, the sea,
Libraries, fields – I want the lot

To fly off and scatter, but most of all
Always to come home to roost

In this unkempt country where a handicapped printer,
Engraver of dog collars, began with his friends

The ultimate encyclopedia.
Don't expect any rhyme or reason

For Scotland remaining an explosion reversed
Or ordinariness a fruited vine   10

Or why I came back here to choose my union
On the side of the ayes, remaining a part

Of this diverse assembly – Benbecula, Glasgow, Bow of Fife –
Voting with my feet, and this hand.

The Ticket

We're careful, trying to save – replacement windows,
A flat roof by the North Sea, paying back over

Two thousand pounds non-statutory pay.
Today while I was left holding our baby

You nipped out just to get some Christmas stamps
And got a parking ticket. You came home anxious,

'I shouldn't have chanced it.' Right,
But now I love your tiny criminal record,

Your scar, our tiny needle's-eye of risk.
Blessed are we who slip from moderation   10

The way our baby girns* and scowls and quickly   grimaces
Just laughs and laughs and laughs out of sheer badness.

Barra

At night you are a collie stretched on the waters.
Kisimul Castle is your dish.

The plane that growls across the cocklestrand
Would hold the Presbyterians of this Catholic island

Each of whom was eagerly praying on Sunday
For the conversion of India and China.

In the Craigard men talk fish through the news,
There is silence for the weather forecast.

Drams vanish down a boilersuited Rembrandt
Who works on the Vatersay road,   10

First asphalt on this continent that begins with Gaelic,
Playing snooker, trussing sheep in the back of a van.

Out there in that dog's dish of a castle
Is where the herald proclaimed from the battlements,

'Macneil of Barra has had his dinner.
The rest of the world may now dine.'

Baptism

Only this morning he had not been arrested;
It was Lowlanders did it as a practical joke

He still can't quite understand.
He just wanted work, and now here he is

Bundled into the back seat of a Baby Austin
By two big Glasgow constables.

'Right, then, Donald, aff tae the station.'
Neither of the constables has the Gaelic.

Consul

You were a stranger in Greenock at a Burns supper
The night the shipyards were axed.

'There are more statues of Robert Burns
In Australia than anywhere outside Scotland,'
You heard yourself saying. Then an ex-
Crane-driver sang 'Scots Wha Hae.'

You saw his wife, standing with an orange juice,
Saying nothing, dignified as a heron
At a polluted pool who can't understand
She'll see no fish there again.   10

Graham Fulton (1959 –)

Commuter

Raggedy man on the
slippy station floor

seems to avoid the spaces left
by blank evening people

who left five minutes before;
seems to carefully tear

strips off GLASGOW HERALD
wrapped around his chest

under his purple shirt
in time to piped muzak,   10

smooth niggling strings.
Like a reptile

shedding skin,
leaving a wake

of ruined life,
scrunched paper moons.

The Fall of the Ferguslie Mills

Like a displaced House of Usher
about to sink in the tarn.

The wind dies at the KEEP OUT gate.
There is nothing

to stir the surface
of the gangrene water lying beside
the shell of Spinning Mill Number 1
that stands like something, almost, dead.
A twitchy fly in sticky web.

Spindles, bobbins, rollers, frames.   10
The thread has snapped. Machines have stopped.

The last of the twilight shift have gone, swiftly
along Maxwellton Road to catch
the bus at Maxwellton Park,
leaving behind a bandage of frost
that silently wraps itself around
red brick-skin slashed and peeled
exposing ancient bones beneath.

Window sockets, fire escapes.
Proud towers and scarred carved faces   20
gaze across the scrub-ground at
a modern toyland housing estate.

Satellite dishes, burglar alarms,
small snipped lawns and car-wash men
ignore the eyesore over the fence,
and all that's left of the Paisley canal
full of bricks, half-bricks, charred
timber, buckets, mudguards, wheels,
metal, wrappers, barrels, bags,
hardhats, cookers, bedsprings, upturned   30
armchairs, boxes, soft porn pages,
cartons, bottles, quarter-bottles,
cans and cans and
cans
        and
                cans
and sodden dumps of fashion cloth.
Twisted rags frozen strange. A smashed
burnt-out rusty van, perhaps

a Mill girl's ghost, or two.   40

Deaf Mo with callused thumbs,
gallus Jackie who worked the hoist
becoming fluff on the fabric of time.
And kids crack puddles with their heels.
The last of the twilight shift have gone
to wash the cotton-dust from their pores.
There is nothing to disturb

a graffiti skull on the counting-house door.
Pillared chambers, crumbled roofs
where Heaven drips, a slow torture.   50

History's heart, buried alive,
waiting for the demolisher's fist
to punch it softly into sleep.

Crows flap to dark rafters.

The Furniture

The air in THE OLD CURIOSITY SHOP
furniture restorers is sweet
with Radio Three.
Walnut and teak stand in line for treatment.
The owner, blissfully, sits in his office
sneaking a peek at Miss October,
waiting for orders to roll in.
He has grasped the concept of delegating work.
On the shopfloor at the sink
a YTS boy, three weeks   10
out of school and keen to make
his way in the world, is bursting into flames.
His skin is blistering, fiercely. He is holding
a varnish-dipped brush in his hand, his mouth
is stretched wide to accommodate
the size of the scream as he stumbles
among the shavings and kettle.
Another, calmer, who has poured
methylated spirits over him then set him
alight with his Ronson, a gift, is screwing   20
the top, carefully, back on the bottle.
He has grasped the concept of economy.
Employees: old, young, happy to be active,
scratch away with sandpaper strips,
rub, smooth, french polish, plane.
They have grasped the concept of conscientious toil.
A golden pollen dusts their hair,
biscuits and mugs are strategically placed.

David Kinloch (1959 –)

Second Infancy

'We've washed her,' said the nurse.
And then we met a bank of sour carbolic air,
My grandmother hovering in a tiny wicker basket,
A gossamer mesh of rib and hair
Caught on its interstices.
Suddenly I remembered that trip with her
To Greenock, the smack she gave me
For imprinting a ring of muck around my eye
When I pressed it to whorls in the pier,
Trying to see the sea.   10

And later, on the boat, as I pulled towards me
Her cats-cradle, the game that always made
The shape of her forgiveness,
She kissed me, as I kiss her now.

Looking down through the criss-cross cot,
She seems to gently see-saw
As we did once on disused gangways,
And in the evening light, threaded
Between the latticework, I briefly see
Cold waves through the dark rings of my eyes.   20

Revolution

Revolution
brought a thaw to the silver structure
of snow in Glasgow

and my father climbed
the hill of our garden
carrying a tree.
Its branches antlered him,
warlock with a broom he planted
upside down.

We planted a pear tree   10
under which our moles
spun grass into still
whirlpools of blade and seed.
My feet just small enough to fit
tripped on their volcanic lips.

Revolution:
this morning my father swallowed
sixteen coloured pills from bottles
and pointed to a pear tree
bearing fruit he cannot go to pick.   20
His arms which carried trees
have dimples at their elbows,
moles hills of flesh
with wrinkled lips,

his head as smooth
as the youngest pear leaf.

fruitfall in the grass
drowns the faintest footfall
going to gather earth

Donny O'Rourke (1959 –)

Essentially a poet, O'Rourke has also done first-rate work as a critic and editor. His anthology, *Dream State: The New Scottish Poets* (1994), may be the finest collection of contemporary Scottish verse.

Parallels: For PC Stephen O'Rourke

In the temporary mortuary
at the ice rink, you spent Christmas Day
body bagging those the pathologist's knife
had gourded. You'd asked us round and Life

Goes On . . . I carved the turkey in your absence
shirking comparisons. Dorothy was tense
the children muted – the crackers they pulled
imploding like a Boeing's pressurised hull

in the dead air space over Lockerbie.
While we scoured the floor for the debris   10
of a shattered toy, your colleagues searched
the Galloway Hills for bomb fragments. Perched

on the edge of your empty seat we passed the day
resisting the emblems of Tragedy:
in cinnamon scented candles and kitchen smells;
the reek of putrefaction – parallels.

The Rooming Houses of America

I'm the Stranger
the locals call Himself
holidaying wryly
off season in Donegal
sporting tweeds
reading detective novels
being found fascinating.

I'm the Poet
with hair en brosse
idling over pastries   10
in the Cafe Sperl
gossiping about the Opera
considering an intrigue
with a Frau in furs.
I'm the Drifter
in loose bruised jeans
riding blue rails

stealing guitar licks
from the widows of jazzmen

my only luggage
a pre war Remington
for the novels I tap out drunk
in the rooming houses of America.

W. N. Herbert (1961 –)

Pictish Whispers

What are the serrations down the tongue,
stitchings in the tissue of the language,
half-forgotten graftings of two strains
of rose, like a border between nations
that may tear
                            grandfather grammar from
the noise my mother tried to make
my playground larynx take
that now my lover hears as me?

There is a golf course, we laugh to learn,   10
that lies on the line between
being Danish or a Finn,
so that a ball, once driven, must cross
time's borders too,
and therefore spends an hour aloft
and lands a little altered, part–
meteor, part–albatross.

And sometimes on our alluvial lawn, on
the very green of our domesticity,
a little vowel will putt back to the past,   20
dislocating my identities like
the vertebrae of the neck,
suggesting that small congeries collect
like Pictish whispers, beneath
such incongruities as language can detect.

The act of translation is always with us,
touching us like love; why else
would the Italians crowd their ages
beneath the labial curtains
of a Madonna della Misericordia?   30
Why would they mingle with
their saints' Roman robes,
the modernity of armour on a frightened soldier?

Tintoretto paints his *Resurrection* in
sure knowledge that
such lightning can only strike us
now, cracking causality's mould:

all ages leap back from his Christ
as I did, at our kitchen sink,
when the thunderbolt seemed   40
to enter the room,
and suddenly, at my fingers' tips,
like a
                          word unwantedly passing your lips,
I saw the spider.

The Land o' Cakes

(for Alec Esplin)

Perched in their multi-storey flat
like a well-fed eagle, the skin
around my small aunt's eyes splintered
with staring into needless distances.

As if her countryside was made of cakes
she swept up great trays for us,
while my uncle disgorged awful jokes
with Eric Morecambe-like insouciance.

A glass cabinet held miniature beers,
dustless undrunk guinnesses, light ales.   10
Once someone jumped from an upper floor
like jam on her spotless tablecloth.

She had diabetes suddenly; leaving
a ripped-off toe she plummetted too
in the hospital bed, grabbing onto us
like washing on the flashing balconies,

but she fell through pain like Alice
to me, and I thought she was constantly
halving her distance toward death
and would never smash, or like   20

an eagle losing its nerve, would pull
out of that dive. These days my uncle
stares at the distant bottles, stirs
his tea with a sugarless spoon.

Dingle Dell

There is no passport to this country,
it exists as a quality of the language.

It has no landscape you can visit;
when I try to listen to its vistas

I don't think of that round tower, though
only two exist in Scotland, though

both are near me. There are figures on
an aunt's old clock, cottars; Scots

as marketed to Scots in the last century: 10
these are too late. I seek something

between troughs, a green word dancing
like weed in a wave's translucence,

a pane not smashed for an instance
through which the Dingle Dell of Brechin

sinks into the park like a giant's grave
from which his bones have long since

walked on air. Into this hole in
the gums of the language I see a name

roll like a corpse into the plague pits:
Bella. It is both my grandmothers'.   20

Beauty, resilient as girstle, reveals
itself: I see all of Scotland

rolling down and up on death's yoyo.
There is no passport to this country.

Bluebottle Bella

(for Isobel Neil)

Thi ainguls waulk upon
Heaven's flair wi sookie-feet,
wi galaxies fur een
as oan thi Earth they leet★.   tell

Thi gress hiz jist been mown
an Granda muves atween
thi roseis an thi palm trees,
tweelin★ grey thru green.   weaving

Thi bakiry gees aff a gust
o breid lyk a spang-new cod*   10   pillow
an aa thi ainguls trummil,
caucht i thi wab o Gode.

Thi gless ut treetuls doon thi fremm*   world?
thi gulls slip owre thi rivir,
thi rowld-up Tully* ut descends   'Evening Telegraph'
an blauds thum oot furivir.

Winter Prayer

Gowd maun gleet ablow thi groond
inna lang saft blintir* as   gleam
a waatirgaw* waulks ower Fife,   rainbow
follyin thi train Eh'm lukein frae.

Ma haunds muve thigithir smooth
as saut waatir mellin* wi fresh: mixing
Lord, therr issa spidir
drinkin at meh hert's quaich*.   cup

She has a pearl o meh aynd*   breath
caucht i thi starnie o'ur lends*,   10   loins
waash hir awa wi a pirl*   touch
fae yir fingir's prisum.

Fill ma lungs wi toyts* o braith   pearls
ma hert wi rubyellie bluid
and oan ma tung pit gowd,
since Eh maun sing.

Logantime

The seagod's arms held the clashing rocks
apart, like fingers between the bells
of an alarm clock, while the Argo sped
beneath, into myth's hourless world.

It was the New Year's Day movie in
Dave Logan's house and he was one
of the clan of uncles my father gave me
just by working in Timex: all

the children of sub-managers watched
the film whilst the parents of our   10
extended family got pished, picking food
up from a round tupperware dish

divided into hour-big triangles filled
with chipolatas, cheese cubes and pickled
onions on cocktail sticks, button biscuits.
We sipped cordials like little gods

as Jason drew his sword in terror
at the sowing of the Dragon's teeth,
the springing up of skeletons
that clacked their jaws and cut down   20

uncle after argonaut, advancing from
the eternal seventies into the slow
retreat from factory to factory,
the bony tick of recession's feet.

Roadkill

That summer I kept hitting gulls
off the top of my windscreen
like breasting a white-hatted wave
as I sped down the country roads:
herring gulls mainly, and
their brown-speckled young,
bulky birds all, that
looking in my mirror I'd see
drop, vertically, from
an already distant impact point,   10
and smack upon the tarmac.

Roadkill had been bad that year:
I kept passing smears of pheasant,
well-parted rabbits' ears,
the odd pigmy mammoth, hunched by
the verge, obviously dead;
then there was the gutted angel,
small, malnourished, and
various eohippi.

On the road to Buckie one blustery day   20
when the sun tried bursting out
of hill-big rain-clouds, I saw
a series of creatures, half-squid, half-skate,
pale and lurid in that orangey light,
too battered to identify.

Gradually my small white car began
to alter: a membrane-like look
crept over the bumpers
as of a seabird's foot;
the hint of a pale eye glinted back   30
from the side mirror.
Once as I drove along

the undulant lane to Lhanbryde,
there was a rippling off the bonnet
as of feathers in a fierce breeze.

After the fifteenth gull
the seats seemed to be covered in shagreen,
a seaweed smell came off the wheel
onto my hands, and
there was an isinglass flash   40
to the windows.
Obviously, the car, under the impact of
so many souls, had begun to adapt.

I started slipping whitebait in
the petrol tank as a treat,
visiting the coast nightly, until
a spirit of the sandstone cliffs
by Burghead told me what to do.

That night, having strewn the back seat
with haddock and tangles, I drove   50
to the end of Grant Street, that looks
past the Pictish fort to the Firth,
and there asperged the dashboard
with fifteen year-old Ordiequish.
Slipping the car into first I drove,
door open, past the last houses,
lighter in my lap.

Just before the drop
I jumped, dropped the flame:
the fire quickly filled the interior   60
with a flicker of white wings
as the car hit the dark waters.
I watched it tumble and sink
the fifteen feet or so to liberty.

Gordon Legge (1961 –)

A Blues

She tells me she has three kids and that her husband's in prison. She doesn't seem too bothered. She sounds like she means it when she says he could be dead for all she cared.

She doesn't talk fast but she doesn't need to. I'm not the interrupting type. She says my name when she speaks. She's friendly. She's not a stupid wee lassie.

I didn't want any of this. I just went down the pub to make sure Doc was getting my ticket for Saturday. There was a gang of them and she was there. She was a bit drunk when I arrived and she's what you'd call merry now. We're back at my flat. I've made the coffee and she's sitting beside my electric fire, her hands caressing the imitation coal. She put the fire on.

I never knew about the kids or the husband. I hardly know her at all, really. She was just that lassie that used to work behind the bar. I think Alec fancied her. I could have guessed about the kids, mind you. There's a standing joke with our lot about the pregnant barmaids.

She isn't feeling sorry for herself. She takes an interest in what I say. Occasionally she stops and I remember how drunk she is. I get worried she's going to cry or be sick or fall asleep or something. She gets up from the fire and I can see that two middle buttons on her shirt are undone and the zip at the back of her skirt is halfway down.

She planks herself on my settee and invariably we get round to talking about school. I work out she's the same age as my sister. We talk further then remembering each other. We all went to a disco once. I had glitter round my eyes and she wore a tartan waistcoat. They were good times. I fill her in about my sister then I ask about her husband. I don't know him but she's sure I'd recognize him. He was a mistake, she says. She tells me how he got arrested for armed-with-a-penknife robbery, and how he made pots of tea in the middle of the night as an apology for being hopeless in bed. Only one of the kids is his, she confides; though not I suspect for the first time.

I ask about the kids. She tells me they're with her mother. Her mother left her father and moved in with them at the start of the year . . . Her father beat her mother . . . Her expression is anxious as though bad memories are threatening to take over. She collects herself and tells me one day they stole half his furniture while he was out at work.

She laughs and says the female side of her family are all thieves. She tells me about the time she 'borrowed' keycards from an ex-boyfriend and emptied his accounts. She says that to this day he has no idea it was her who did it – and she still has his doorkey so she could do it again.

She starts slagging me. She's teasing and I tell her so. She says all women tease. The room is boiling and I'm very tired. That tired I know I won't sleep. She asks if I'm religious. I shake my head. She shakes hers in disappointment. She starts talking about God. She goes to church and her faith is strong. Her faith in God.

I tell her I have work in the morning. She tells me so does she but that one of the kids has to go to the health centre and they need her signature, so she'll get a lie-in and the morning off. Her mum sees to the kids at breakfast time.

She asks what I'm thinking about. I get a bit flustered. She says she just said that to make me blush. She adopts a West Indian accent and says, 'I like to see white people blush.' I laugh and tell her I think mostly about my work.

She relaxes and looks peaceful. Like she's had a big meal or a long journey . . . or too much to drink. I can hear her breathing. She declares that she is drunk. I nod and nick one of her cheeky faces to show that I'd noticed.

I go to the toilet. I hate myself for thinking she might be stealing something. When I return she's kneeling by my records. The zip on her skirt is all the way down allowing a bulge of underwear to jut out. She slags my records and asks if I've got any Bryan Adams. No. She gets up and falls flat back onto my settee. I can see her sweaty armpits as she flings her arms back.

I ask if she's taking the kids on holiday. This dumbfounds her. She tells me how much it costs to look after the kids, not forgetting her mother. No matter how much she makes it all goes on the kids. She says that she has great battles with the kids – and that she always wins. She blows on her fingertips and brushes her chest. It all sounds like work because it is work, she says.

She asks if I'm still hung up on Frances. I tell her that situation's a bit up in the air at the moment. I'm surprised she knew about me. I think she'll know a lot about a lot of people. She tells me never to marry or live with anyone. She says she made the same mistake twice.

She says she has to go. I'm glad. I tell her it's because I've only got two fags left. She gives me hers and says it's okay cause she'll nick her mam's. The thief smiles. She stands at my window and slags off this town. I knew that was coming and tell her so. She smiles again and asks if Doc had my ticket. Yeah, sort of. She says that when she gets home she will kneel by the beds of her children and pray. She tells me that she prays every night and that her prayers come true. I ask what she prays for. She prays for the children: for their health and their future. She says nobody'll take her with three kids but she doesn't care. She says that she'd go through everything again just to have the children. She says she'll mention me in her prayers.

I offer to see her home. She says it's all right. She just lives in the next court. The flat with the purple curtains. Every room has purple curtains. I tell her I don't notice things like that.

She thanks me for the coffee and apologizes for being a pain in the bum. She looks attractive now. Her skin is soft and her eyes are alert. She lets herself out into the close and the smell of booze, fags and heat gives way to a freshness. I tell her to take care of herself . . . and her kids . . . and her mam. She points to her flat. The light's still on. She laughs and says the stupid old bitch is still waiting up for her.

Kathleen Jamie (1962 –)

For good or for ill, it has been this fine writer's fortune to be labelled, along with Liz Lochhead, as Scotland's preeminent feminist poets.

Things Which Never Shall Be

I shall be your wife.
Behind the doors of our house
which are wooden, and plentiful:
dogs and other animals, eager to play.
Rooms of grasses and flowers give out
to further rooms, our house
will be settled among woodland and hills.
So go. And take the dogs with you.
Leave me to work and fecundity in everything:
trees, hedgerows, weather-signs, poetry,   10
quirks you'll love and mock
only in jest. Our bedroom
will gather bouquets of sunshine,
we'll be home there in winter, I'll play
the spirit and you'll catch your breath.
We'll inhabit a huge place,
where I could move between rooms
with books in my arms,
and our home will be home to all comers.
We'll become skilled in art and endurance,   20
experts in love, and each other.

Den of the Old Men

C'mon ye auld buggers, one by one
this first spring day, slowly down
the back braes with your walking sticks
and wee brown dugs, saying: *Aye, lass*
a snell* wind yet but braw. Ye   fierce
half dozen relics of strong men
sat in kitchen chairs
behind the green gingham curtain
of yer den, where a wee dog grins
on last year's calendar – we hear ye   10
clacking dominos the afternoon for pennies.
And if some wee tyke
puts a chuckie* through the window   stone
ye stuff yesterday's *Courier*
in the broken pane, saying
jails too guid fur them, tellys in cells!
– We can see your bunnets nod
and jaws move: what're ye up to
now you've your hut built,
now green hame-hammered benches   20
appear in the parish's secret soft-spots
like old men's spoor?
Is it carties? A tree-hoose?
Or will ye drag up driftwood;
and when she's busy with the bairns
remove your daughters' washing-lines
to lash a raft? Which,
if ye don't all fall out and argue
you can name the 'Pride o' Tay' and launch
some bright blue morning on the ebb-tide   30
and sail away, the lot of yez,
staring straight ahead
           like captains
as you grow tiny
out on the wide Firth, tiny
as you drift past Ballinbreich, Balmurnie, Flisk
with your raincoats and bunnets,
           wee dugs and sticks.

The Queen of Sheba

Scotland, you have invoked her name
just once too often
in your Presbyterian living rooms.
She's heard, yea
even unto heathenish Arabia
your vixen's bark of poverty, come down
the family like a lang neb*, a thrawn* streak,   beak/twisted

a wally dug¹ you never liked
but can't get shot of.

She's had enough. She's come.   10
Whit, tae this dump? Yes!
She rides first camel
of a swaying caravan
from her desert sands
to the peat and bracken
of the Pentland hills
across the fit-ba pitch
to the thin mirage
of the swings and chute; scattered with glass.
Breathe that steamy musk   20
on the Curriehill Road, not mutton-shanks
boiled for broth, nor the chlorine stink
of the swimming pool where skinny girls
accuse each other of verrucas.
In her bathhouses women bear
warm pot-bellied terracotta pitchers
on their laughing hips.
All that she desires, whatever she asks
She will make the bottled dreams
of your wee lasses   30
look like *sweeties*.

Spangles scarcely cover
her gorgeous breasts, hanging gardens
jewels, frankincense; more voluptuous
even than Vi-next-door, whose
high-heeled slippers
keeked★ from dressing gowns   peeked
like little hooves, wee tails
of pink fur stuffed in the cleavage of her toes;
more audatious even than Currie Liz   40
who led the gala floats
through the Wimpey scheme
in a ruby-red Lotus Elan
before the Boys' Brigade band
and the Brownies' borrowed coal-truck;
hair piled like candy-floss;
who lifted her hands from the neat wheel
to tinkle her fingers
at her tricks
        among the masons and the elders and the police. 50

The cool black skin
of the Bible couldn't hold her,
nor the atlas green
on the kitchen table,
you stuck with thumbs

---

¹ Wally dugs are porcelain dogs meant for display, usually in pairs.

and split to fruity hemispheres –
yellow Yemen, Red Sea, *Ethiopia*. Stick in
with the homework and you'll be
cliver like yer faither.
but no too cliver,   60
no *above yersel*.

See her lead those great soft camels
widdershins¹ round the kirk-yaird,
smiling
as she eats
avocados with apostle spoons
she'll teach us how. But first

she wants to strip the willow
she desires the keys
        to the National Library   70
she is beckoning
        the lasses
        in the awestruck crowd . . .

Yes, we'd like to
        clap the camels,
to smell the spice,
admire her hairy legs and
bonny wicked smile, we want to take
PhDs in Persian, be vice
to her president: we want   80
to help her
        ask some Difficult Questions

she's shouting for our wisest man
to test her mettle:

        Scour Scotland for a Solomon!

Sure enough: from the back of the crowd
someone growls:
        whae do you think y'ur?

and a thousand laughing girls and she
draw our hot breath   90
        and shout:

THE QUEEN OF SHEBA!

---

¹ Oblique to the sun, usually part of a magic ritual.

Wee Wifey

I have a demon and her name is
                    WEE WIFEY
I caught her in a demon trap – the household of my skull
I pinched her by her heel throughout her wily transformations
until
          she confessed
                    her name indeed to be WEE WIFEY
and she was out to do me ill.

So I made great gestures like Jehovah: dividing
land from sea, sea from sky,   10
                    my own self from WEE WIFEY
(There, she says, that's tidy!)

Now I watch her like a dolly
keep an eye,
          and mourn her:
For she and I are angry/cry
                    because we love each other dearly.
It's sad to note
          that without
                    WEE WIFEY   20
I shall live long and lonely as a tossing cork.

Swallows and Swifts

Twitter of swallows and swifts:
'tickets and visas, visas and tickets' –
winter, and cold rain
clears the milky-way of birdshit
where wires cross the lane.

James Meek (1962 –)

Bonny Boat Speed

When I see Arnold I remember the woman who could walk. I think about Jenny too of course, not that she looked anything like her dad. I haven't seen her for a long time now. That was why I stopped the woman who could walk, to find out when the healing would be over and Jenny would come out. I didn't go inside. I had nothing that needed healing then. Nothing that you would stand up and say you believed in Jesus for, or that you'd know if you'd been healed of. Praise the Lord! I can love the ones I didn't love before, and stopped loving the ones that didn't love me! Hallelulia! I walked up to the hall entrance slowly, early, and I was reading the curved red letters on fresh pasted white paper about Pastor Samuel's Ark of

Salvation when the woman who could walk walked out. I knew she could walk because she told me. She was big and mobile in skirt and sweater and her hands stuck in the pockets of her open raincoat which was flying behind her in the warm wind over the car park, her face was white and her mouth slightly open and she was staring straight ahead. She had a crutch tucked under her right arm. I had to catch her by the elbow to stop her.

Excuse me, d'you know how much longer it's going on? I said.

She stopped, one foot lifted, balanced by my hand resting on her elbow – it was a soft, round elbow – and looked at me long enough to say: I can walk! before she walked, then ran, to her car and drove away. It was a straight slip road to the M8, a busy enough evening with no roadworks, and as far as I could understand from the paper next morning it happened within a couple of minutes of her merging with the flow that the juggernaut swung easily through the barriers and hit her car head on, with a combined speed of 150 miles per hour. I suppose Pastor Samuel might have said Well, I healed her, so the least she could've done was to have stayed to the end of the meeting. Now she walks, nay drives, with the Lord.

I was concerned for myself. I kept her back for half a second and the juggernaut hit her. In half a second a truck travelling at 70 miles an hour travels its own length twice – that's what Arnold told me when I shared this with him, a free sample. From her side she could have avoided the truck by being more polite. We were both in the wrong. I suffered by not knowing I'd have to wait quarter of an hour for Jenny to come out. The woman who could walk suffered by being conscious for at least 30 seconds of the sensation of the destruction of her body by an oncoming lorry (spontaneous Arnoldism). Usually when I think about the woman who walked the thought is: I didn't summon up the juggernaut, did I. You don't guess the instant when northbound and southbound collide, like a single bolt of lightning. Only when I see Arnold I think about how maybe everything is equaled out in the end, not in a good way, and how easy it is to summon up an irresistible opposing force, after all.

What Siobhan said this one time, and the tenner pointing at my empty tumbler was sharp and fresh as a new razor, was even more ominous than Arnold lurking round the pub as he was: Same one again? she said. Not Same again? but Same one again?

Ah, better not, last ferry and all. I looked down into the glass and dodgemed the sleek humps of ice around the bottom. The unnecessary One hung in the air.

Go on, said Siobhan. You sold a house today, didn't you? Take a cab.

I sell a house most days. I sold one yesterday.

It was a big one, you said.

It was a big one. I felt like rewarding myself with a third g & t. But the taxis skin you for a ferry trip and it's no better picking up a second one on the other side.

I can't drive after three, I said.

Take a cab. Two gin and tonics please, she said. She'd seen the weakness in my face and got the order out the way so we could argue about it over a drink.

I don't want to take a cab, I said, looking over at Arnold sitting by himself at the table by the cigarette machine. He was working, he had the yellow pad out in front of him. He turned and smiled at me. I looked at Siobhan.

It's not the money, I said. I don't like being screwed. I've got to take the car across. I've got a season ticket.

Well drive then, she said, holding the two glasses out in front of her.

But I can't if I have a third drink, I said. I took one of the glasses from her.

Don't drink it, she said.

I won't, I said, and took a mouthfill of the stuff and swallowed it down.

You're so weak, she said, smiling and touching her earring.

You make it sound as if that's good.

Oh, I love weak men.

So how do I get home?

I'll give you a lift back.

I was very happy. It was easy to make me happy. Maybe I'd have four drinks and all in Siobhan's company, and a free ride all the way to Kirkcaldy on the big white ship. There'd be time for one on the moon deck bar on the way over and we could sit there studying the constellations, talking. I was grinning too much too close into Siobhan's heroic delighted face and turned again to Arnold. We smiled at each other and waved, I raised my glass to him. He raised his. It looked like water.

Great, I said to Siobhan. In the rush of it I almost said I love you, not meaning it like that, but instead said: Why did you say Same one again?

Confusion sluiced darkly into her face.

You said Same one again instead of Same again.

Did I?

Yes.

She looked into the middle distance, frowning, quiet for a while. So what? she said eventually.

I took a deep drink and went under, groping for something good.

We're like sister and brother, you and me, I said.

She looked at me without saying anything for a few seconds, then put her drink in my free hand. Arnold'll give you a lift, she said, and walked out the door.

I finished my gin, sat on a bar stool and started in on hers, raising the side without lipstick to my mouth, turning it to the side with lipstick. It tasted pretty much the same. I was watching Arnold. He was scribbling away with a pencil. The bar was full but the only person I knew was Arnold, sober as an ayatollah and his car parked outside.

Once there was a group of merchants who returned to the borders of the empire after months spent crossing the great wilderness. Everyone wanted to know what it had been like. Och, it was all right, the merchants said. Hot deserts of course, cold mountains, wet jungle – still, we made it.

Folk listened to them politely, clapped them on the back and drifted back to their affairs. Some time later another group of merchants arrived. The locals gathered round – what was it like? Incredible, the merchants answered. Absolutely unbelievable. It was so hot that the beaks of the vultures would soften and fuse together and they would die of starvation if they were careless enough to close them. It was so cold that we had to breathe on each other's eyes every five minutes to stop our eyeballs freezing solid. It was so wet that a cup held out would fill with rain faster than a man could drink it.

A huge crowd gathered round the second group of merchants, stood them drinks for a year, offered them their daughters in marriage and secured them pensions for life.

Arnold was making a good living on the discovery that folk hungered after apocryphal facts like drinkers hunger after salty snacks. He had a name. The editors would ring him up: Death Valley, Arn, they'd say, give me ten by six. And he'd sit around and write: In Death Valley in August, you can toss an ice cube in the air and it will have melted before you can catch it. Nine more like that. Or: Dead composers this week mate, say a dozen. And he'd write: If the Italian composer Vivaldi was alive, he would be the richest man on the planet, earning an estimated £1 million a minute from royalties on the use of The Four Seasons on telephone switchboards. The secret lay in the utter lack of research and confidence that anyone who could be bothered to challenge his published facts would be rejected as a nitpicking wanker. Besides, whenever one of his jobs appeared, it was so quickly plagiarized that it immediately took on the veracity of gospel – more so, in fact, since every second of every day somewhere in the world an average of 6.5 people challenge the authenticity of the New Testament (6.5 – what Arnold calls the precision principle in successful apocrypha) whereas no one, not even the Vatican, had ever taken the trouble to complain about Arnold's assertion that, for liturgical reasons, the Pope never flies in aircraft that can land on water.

He never said but I reckon it was something about the six months he did for dangerous driving that got him on the apocrypha thing. He'd been terrified of getting beaten up or abused or whatever in jail and tried to keep in with the authorities on both sides by writing pornographic stories to order. And maybe after a while the sex fantasies began to fray and it began to show that there was a hunger for something else, tiny legends of a world outside, and he began to slip them in: that it wasn't just the smooth slender bodies twining over the sheet which got the screws and lifers going but the insistence in parenthesis that the ancient Egyptians had abandoned goat-hair duvets for duck-down ones when they discovered the aphrodisiac qualities of the now extinct Nilotic eider.

Almost everyone had been amazed he got sent down, he was so middle class, even the advocate was embarrassed, he hurried away afterwards and didn't speak to anyone. I wasn't surprised, though. Arnold was a dangerous driver. He's a dangerous driver now. Whatever they did to him in prison, it didn't change his overtaking habits. It was a gamble on a blind summit and he lost, collided with a car full of students from England. He killed two of them. Arnold went into an airbag but his wife in the passenger seat didn't have one. She wasn't wearing a seatbelt. Perhaps she'd been as unhappy as that. I don't know. Anyway she went through the windscreen head-first. Straight away you imagine it happening in slow motion but it doesn't, of course, you don't see it like that any more than you see the flight of a shell from a gun. There's a loud noise and in an instant, like a badly edited film, it jumps, it's all arranged across the road, perfectly, peacefully, the broken cars, the glass, the bodies and the wheels spinning slowly.

Arnold was 36, same as me. His wife died about the time my divorce came through. Since the trial he'd seen even less of Jenny than I had. She didn't think he'd killed her deliberately, no one did. Before the accident Jenny said she liked the way he drove. Afterwards she didn't hate him: nothing so passionate. She went off him. She'd just started at art college and got a flat and never went round to see him any more, in jail or out. When they paroled him I expected him to take to drink, I don't know why. He went teetotal and as soon as he got his licence back he was driving worse than before. That's to say he was a good driver, very skillful, but always found a way to drive that was out beyond the edges of his skill and relied on luck to fill the space between.

I'd left my watch at home. The clock above the bar said 10.25 and the last boat was at 11. Someone'd told me that the landlord always set the clock ten minutes fast, so that left a good three quarters of an hour to get to Queensferry. You couldn't rely on Arnold to use that time well, though. Of course everyone ran the risk that they might die on their way home from the pub. A loose slate might fall on their heads, or they might have a heart attack, get stabbed. What else could happen? There could be an earthquake. A predator could escape from the zoo. A predator could escape from his mates. But the chances were infinitesimal. It wasn't something you thought about: Better watch on my way home from the pub in case I get killed. Driving with Arnold it was. Even if the chances of death doubled at the third decimal place, you wouldn't put money on it, there was only one life. To have four gin and tonics and then go out the door thinking and now, perhaps, the afterlife, now, even before morning.

Arnold was coming over. Need a lift? he said.

No thanks.

He nodded at the door. I don't think Siobhan's coming back. Did you say something?

Yes.

Arnold jiggled his car keys. Last boat at 11, he said.

I'll get a cab.

Come on.

No really Arnie, it's great of you, I appreciate it, but I'm fine, I'm doing all right, taxis are good, they're cheap, they're reliable, they're fast. Fast enough, I mean. Not too – yeah, fast enough. Don't want to have you going out of your way.

He looked hurt. He fidgeted with his keys and looked around. He did seem astoundingly calm and sober for an Edinburgh pub on a Friday night. Con, he said, I don't understand you. We've been drinking in this place for the past two years and we both know where we go at closing time. It's not like we're strangers. What is the deal with these taxis? D'you not get embarrassed when you're getting out of the cab on the quayside and you see me driving up the ramp? D'you think I avoid the moon bar on a Friday night cause I like the Stoker's Lounge better?

I had wondered about that. My face went the colour of the carpet in the Stoker's Lounge. It'd been stupid to think he hadn't noticed me trying to avoid him on the boat all this time.

I'm sorry, Arnie, I said. I don't like the way you drive.

I hadn't meant to say that. Anyway, he was alive, was he not?

I know, said Arnold. But I'm more careful now.

No you're not. I've seen the way you go down the Queensferry Road.

That's just the way it looks. That is me being careful. I don't hit anything. I never hit anything. I make sure now. I've made sure ever since that time. It's a science, it's dynamics. Anyway, there's plenty of time, there's no need to hurry.

The clock said 10.35, i.e. 10.25, so he was right, there was plenty of time. And even though I'd seen him shoot past and slot his car at 60 through a space you wouldn't try to park in, I'd never actually driven with him.

If you're so worried about the taxi, said Arnold, you can give me a fiver if you like. He grinned.

A fiver? To Queensferry? I could get to Inverness on a fiver.

And still have money left over for a deep fried Brie supper and a chilled Vimto.

Make it ten then.

We went out to the car. We hadn't got there before he'd hit me with some new apocrypha which might've made me change my mind if I hadn't been thinking along the same lines, so much that I was hardly aware he'd said it.

The dice you'd need to roll to reflect the chances of your being involved in a car accident on any one trip, he said, would have so many faces that without a powerful microscope it would be indistinguishable from a perfect sphere.

What was that? I said, fastening the seatbelt. He repeated it while he started the car.

Bet you didn't sell that to News International, I said.

No, I just thought of that one. It's not for sale.

Private apocrypha, eh.

He didn't say anything. That didn't bother me because I was looking at the digital clock on his dashboard. We were out on the road and moving. Arnold was driving at just under the speed limit in built-up areas. Cars were passing us. The clock said 10.35.

Your clock's wrong, I said.

I know, he said.

Right.

They were going to change the name to Kingsferry, said Arnold. In honour of the king who died falling off the cliff, you know, trying to catch the boat late at night.

That's not such a good one, Arnie. Don't think you'd get far with that.

It's true! I'm off work now. No apocrypha in my free time. It's true.

Why would they call it Kingsferry? They didn't start calling Dallas Dead Presidentville after Kennedy got shot there.

Because that's what it's about. It's not about folk crossing the river.

It is as far as I'm concerned. They could call them South Ferry Ferry and North Ferry Ferry and that'd make sense to me.

No, Con, said Arnold, turning to look at me, and even though we were still trundling along at 30, I wanted him to turn back and keep his eyes on the road. He looked worried for me, as if I was about to go out alone into the world without the things I needed to know to survive. If it was about folk crossing the river there'd be a bridge. A Forth road bridge. They could easily build one. It'd be open round the clock and no one would ever have to be racing to get the last boat again.

We're not racing, though, cause we've got plenty of time.

OK, but folk do. And they're supposed to be all into public safety. I tell you what it is, it's put there deliberately. It's a deliberate exception. Because they know you can't resist it. You want it. You want a place in the country where you can be provoked into taking a risk without going out and looking for it too hard.

No you don't.

You do, Con. You know you do. There just aren't enough real risks on the go, and you don't want to go rock climbing or bungee jumping or kayaking, cause you're getting on, and it's too much trouble, and they take all the risk out of it anyway, it's like a fairground ride, and you don't want to go out looking for a fight, and violence in the pictures is just a wank . . . so you sit in the pub and you wait until you're about to miss the ferry.

Don't talk this way, Arnie, it's not good.

It's not that you want to die. You want to live. More than anything, you want to live, you want to have even just the next five minutes of your life, never mind seeing the sun come up again. Only there's something that comes in between wanting one and wanting the other, it's like a separation, you start believing two different things at the same time, that if you die, it'd be the end, and that you can die without actually dying. That you can watch it. That you can do it again. That it'd be interesting. You really believe that. It's strange. I don't understand it. D'you understand it?

A horn opened up behind us and headlights flared through the rear windscreen. The car behind pulled out sharply and overtook with a roar of contempt. Our speed had dropped to 25. So far the only way we were going to die tonight was getting spannered by a fellow motorist. I wanted to talk about going faster. I wanted to talk about what happened to Arnold's wife. I didn't want to upset him.

I'm not into the risk, I said. I was really wanting to get a lift with Siobhan and sit with her in the moon deck bar in the big white ship and go home.

Arnold didn't say anything. I hadn't thought it was possible to drive any slower in high gear but it seemed we were slipping back to about bicycle pace. I remembered he'd been after Siobhan just after he'd got out, and I remembered he'd been sitting down there in the yeasty fug of the Stoker's Lounge for two years while we'd been up there watching the lights of passing ships through the rain on the glass roof and the moon wax and wane over the flint-coloured water of the firth.

We passed the Kwik-Fit garage. I turned round to check the time on the digital clock they had.

Arnie, I said. Let's talk about time.

Despite his mastery of the laws of space and time, said Arnold, Albert Einstein never owned a watch and relied on friends to tell him what year it was.

When we left the pub it was 10.25 by the clock, I said, which was ten minutes fast, so it was 10.15. Your clock said 10.35, but you agreed that was wrong.

Stonehenge tells the time more accurately than the most sophisticated atomic clock.

The Kwik-Fit clock we've just passed says 10.50.

The landlord of the Faulkner Arms always sets his clock 10 minutes fast to make sure none of his customers misses the last boat to Fife.

Christ, was it you told me that?

I didn't think you'd believe that one, said Arnold. He's a landlord, isn't he? His clock's slow. So's mine.

I looked around. Accurate timekeeping by: Kwik-Fit. Arnold's car had central locking, controlled from the driver's seat. Traffic was shooting past. I had the impression we were standing still. But we must have been going at least as fast as a strong freestyle swimmer. Ten minutes to cover seven miles. Not at this rate. Siobhan would be on board already. She was great but it upset her that all I wanted to do was talk to her and loiter in her presence for as long as she happened to be around. She wanted love, or sex, or both, I wasn't sure, which made it strange she'd put up with me for so long. One time we did come across Arnold on the big white ship, just when Siobhan was crying over something I'd said. There are people who treat crying as like sighing or yawning but I hate it, it's a catastrophe. Once when I was wee there was a primary school trip to the city reservoir and we were walking along the foot of the dam wall and I saw some drops of water dribbling down the concrete by my head and I screamed to the teacher that the dam was about to burst. Everyone laughed and the teacher, who never missed an opportunity for a bit of child-battering, gave me a thump on the back of the head. I was relieved. I really had thought the dam was going to burst. What got me wasn't so much the thought of all of us and Mrs Swynton getting swept away by a wall of water but the chest-hollowing innocence of the first little driblets, the inadequacy of the warning they were of the thousands of tons of dark, cold, merciless water pressing against the concrete. They did warn you, but they told you nothing of how deep and overwhelming their source was. I hadn't cried since I was a boy. That was something I could have asked Pastor Samuel about.

Arnold had tried to comfort her. It'd been terrible. She kept coming up against not liking him as much as she felt she should and he kept coming up against the fucking apocrypha every time something more than inane pleasantries were called for. He hadn't been like that before. When I heard him telling her, instead of not to pay any attention to the crap I'd said, that 60 per cent of single women in their thirties were in stable relationships by the time they were forty, the thought of him scribbling away about fantasy women in his cell, struggling to meet some deadline for fear he'd get his head kicked in, and getting infected with the spores of instant harmless wee fictions for instant meaningless wee rewards, almost set me going without the pastor's help.

We were quiet up to the city boundary, him crawling along, leaning back in the seat, one hand on the wheel, ignoring the cars overtaking us, staring ahead, placid and blinking, and me trying to work out how to open the door, the effect on the fabric of the jacket of rolling and skidding for a few yards, the effect on the fabric of me, the result of grabbing the hand brake and pulling it sharply upwards, calculations of time, distance and speed, and what about going by Kincardine, a place of great and famous beauty by night.

The moment the dual carriageway came in sight Arnold stamped on the accelerator and we were away. We had five minutes to get to the terminal. Once we were up to 90, I started to think we'd make it. By the time the needle shook on 110, I was thinking we wouldn't.

We'll just fly across, then, I said.

Arnold didn't say anything. We came up behind a Mercedes dawdling along in the fast lane at 80 or so. With two sharp movements of the wheel, we slid into the slow lane and back again in front of the Merc, missing a rusting hatchback by the thickness of paintwork.

Don't do this, Arnie, I said. It's not important. Slow down. We'll get there.

I thought you liked it, said Arnold. Just to see what happens.

I never did anything to give you that idea.

You fucked my daughter without wearing a condom, said Arnold.

People get older suddenly. It builds up and comes breaking through. One instant the age you've been for years, the next, the age you'll be for years to come. A dream one night, a drink, a cloud crossing the sun, a word, a thought, and you lurch backward into the next age like a drunk going over the balcony. I felt as if I'd been seized by eight relentless hands and had clingfilm pressed down over my face and body and I couldn't fight it, it was becoming part of me and that was me for the rest of my life with this extra, unwanted, itching skin.

As things stood the rest of my life was being measured out in red cat's eyes beaded along the A90, and the vision of the long cat of after dark expired at the water's edge, if not sooner. Arnold, I said, Arnie, wait, OK. Whatever you think, let's talk. Let's take time to talk. We'll go down the waterfront and get a carryout and sit up all night and talk it over. All weekend if you want. I can't talk when you're driving like this. It's putting the wind up me.

Arnold laughed. Putting the wind up you! he said. Good. Scientists say thirty per cent of the human brain is set aside exclusively to react to fear.

Bollocks, I said. Sixty.

The laugh went out of Arnold's face. He was leaning forward, his chin almost over the wheel, staring ahead. I don't know I want you to talk, he said.

Come on Arnie. She was 17, she knew what she was doing.

She was 16.

OK, she was 16 at the beginning, but she was very self-possessed.

It's interesting you talk about possession, said Arnold.

Christ, you're the one who was doing the my daughter my daughter bit! I was working up an anger because I could see we were going to make it to the terminal and up the ramp no bother. She was old enough to be living by herself. It's not like I was the first.

Arnold's left hand came swinging off the wheel and I flinched. But he was just changing down from fifth to fourth.

What are you doing? I said. We swung off the dual carriageway onto the back road into Queensferry, the long way round to the terminal, narrower, slower, and with great opportunities for head-on collisions.

You're such a bastard, Con, said Arnold, and you never bother to remind yourself of it.

I had a tight hold of the door-grip with one hand and my seatbelt with the other. We came up behind a Capri tanking along at 70 and Arnie took it on a blind bend just as something bright and screaming came round in the other direction. I closed my eyes, bent down and wrapped my arms around my head. There was a shrieking sound and horns, the Capri must have melted its brake pads to let us in, and we lived to fight another second.

Whatever it is I've done to upset you, Arnold, I'm sorry, I shouted.

No need to shout, said Arnold, frowning.

Slow down. There's a bend – Jesus.

How d'you think it feels when your wife's just died and they put you in jail for it and the daughter you raised for sixteen years stops seeing you cause she's getting screwed by a man the same age as you are?

Not good. Bad. There's a ffffff . . . there was no connection! She didn't want to see you any more. Nothing to do with me. We were in love for a while, it was good for both of us, and then we drifted apart.

We were accelerating into absolute darkness on the wrong side of the road. There was nothing to overtake any more. Like the wrong side was smoother. I could see the orange glow of Queensferry ahead and a pale scimitar of headlights rising and falling through the trees before we got there, the car we were about to go head to head with, though we knew it, and they didn't, they'd dip their headlights and slow down a little, voodoo steps to safety, they would never know. Apart from the apocryphal 30 seconds. He'd almost convinced me with that one.

There's a car coming, I said.

It's OK. We won't hit it. You know, Con, 95 per cent of teenage girls who have relationships with men twice their age or more say love was never a factor.

I remembered reading that in *Marie Claire* when I was still seeing Jenny and worrying about it.

You're talking shite, Arnold, I said. You're starting to believe your own apocrypha. There aren't any facts about love. Would you move to the right side of the fucking road?

It was over before I had time to wet myself, and when we'd swung round the bend into the blaring glaring squealing ton of glass and metal and flesh hurtling towards us, and there'd been no contact, I realised he'd done this before. Everyone else would swerve at the last moment, at exactly the same time as the other car, but he kept on on the wrong side, letting the other car swerve, so we missed.

Stop, I said. I'm sorry. You're right and I'm wrong. I repent. Could you stop the car? I meant it. I would have knelt in the Stoker's Lounge all the way across with my lips pressed to his ringpiece just to be out in the open and not moving. It was 10.59 by his clock, we were just coming down the hill to Queensferry, and I knew he'd try to clear the High Street narrows and all the rest in 59 seconds.

You're not making any sense, Con, said Arnie. You know better than I do what incidental risk's all about, the danger that comes with getting where you want to go when you can't wait. When you were screwing Jenny it was the hell with the crash, maybe you will, maybe you won't. What's the difference? You know you crashed. You do know, don't you? You couldn't stop yourself. You knew you might, and you did. You knew a kid would only be trouble for her and she didn't want one.

I'm not with you. Just stop, eh. Stop. Stop.

I'm not intending to stop. It's hard to stop when you're almost there. You didn't stop. And there are some accidents Pastor Samuel couldn't help her with. He threw up his healing hands and said: If you don't want his child, girl, cast it out.

STOP!

And she did cast it out. Six weeks gone. She really didn't tell you, did she?

I pulled hard on the hand brake. We both went quiet for what seemed like a long time, watching the masts of the yachts fly past, like little children watching a conjuror, it seems to me with our hands folded across our laps, but I suppose not. For a certain time, memory, the present and apocrypha became the same thing, a trinity, like the Father, the Son and the Holy Ghost. I remembered the car flying off the end of the pier before it actually happened, and I felt it skim three times across the waves like a stone as if it really did, though I knew I was feeling, with every bone and muscle, the apocryphal version of what truly took place, and the vague, imaginary sense of hitting the water once and going down was what was real.

Arnie had the sunroof open and was out of it before the top of the car sank below the water. He braced his legs on the roof and plunged his arms down for me through the flood that was beating me down into the seat and tried to pull me out, forgetting about the seatbelt. We went down into the black firth together, me struggling with the belt and gulping down a gallon of salt water before I shut my mouth, him clinging on to the edges of the sunroof with one hand and tugging on my jacket shoulder with the other. I got free just as a part of me I never knew I had started to try to rationalize the death experience into something negotiable but only making it worse. We were trying to kick off our shoes and jackets and our faces were in the air. We were treading water. The ferry was steaming out of harbour a few hundred yards away. It whistled. Arnold was swimming away from me towards the pier with strong breast strokes. I paddled my feet and coughed. I hate it when folk cry. It's never good, and when it's someone you thought you were fond of, like yourself, it's a disaster. It was too late anyway. There was too much water all around. There was so much of it.

Ali Smith (1962 –)

Cold Iron

What can I tell you? The sea and the snow and the wind.

Earth and then grass and then snow settling on the grass. Snow choking the narrow gravel paths, nestling into the neck and filling the stone eyes of a praying angel, silently mittening the leafless branches of trees, muffling the spruces. Over the iron railings, outside the great gate the sounds of a city bound and gagged by a few inches of snow, the soft blur of car wheels and engines. Above the city and above the grey snow clouds, more dark night sky; go up further into black space, the darkness broken only by the lumps of rock that (our stars, our futures) promise us light, wonder, constancy. Not visible tonight from below. Beneath, back on the ground and into the earth – through it, cold, hard – below snow grass soil packed tight the dead are lying quiet in their boxes holding their breath, waiting to be opened, like disappointed presents.

Snow falls, nothing happens.

I'm telling you. My mother died while the closing credits of 'Eastenders' rolled on the portable colour television my father had put up in the corner of the room where they'd set up the special bed with the special cushions. That's what my brother told me on the phone, I mean about the credits, so that made it a couple of minutes before eight, he said. I was six hundred miles away and I had been out of the house for the first time that day to get something to eat, going to the shops in the dark. The phone must have rung in an empty house. When I opened the door it was ringing, and there was the distance. We hadn't known when, but then it was, and there was nothing to do but sit, nothing to do but hang on till the morning and get the train along the coast-line through the snow.

The first dream I ever had was full of snow. Perhaps it wasn't my first, there were surely others, babies dream all the time. But this I think is the first one I remembered when I woke up. I was very young, two years old, and in the dream I'm standing outside our front garden and outside our front gate, I'm wearing my new red coat, my mother had bought it for me because we were going to Ireland to see her mother. That's real, that's not just the dream. We didn't go in the end; a couple of days before we were due to leave her mother died so I never met her. What I can remember is not really knowing what Ireland meant, or what Granny meant, wondering in my head were they interchangeable words.

In the dream I'm dressed in red standing outside our front gate in deep snow, and I look up at all the houses on our street, along both sides. All along the street people are leaning out of the upstairs windows of the houses, looking down at me and smiling, waving. They're paper people, paper cut-outs, they flap their thin arms when they wave, they're all coloured in with crayons, very bright colours, yellows and blues. They've got thick black lines that mark their clothes and their outlines, and the colours go over the lines like they do when you can't yet get the crayons to stay inside the lines. Their faces are black lines too but not coloured in, still paper-white, and they're smiling. And then this thing happens. A great wind blows, I hear it behind me and it blows past me. It gathers all the people up out of the windows and the people blow away into the sky. I watch them disappearing over the rooftops.

What I was telling you. My brother is older than I am, he works at the BBC so things like how many minutes to eight 'Eastenders' finishes have some meaning for him. I had been home visiting two days before at the weekend, and had helped her to get up and go through to the bathroom, had watched, stunned yet not in the least surprised, as my mother struggled out of the circle of two of us holding her up and somehow made her way through into the kitchen demanding that we light her a cigarette, her bones almost visible through her skin.

So I travelled back down on the Monday, and when I got there the phone rang and my sister told me things were worse, suddenly, but that still we didn't know when, still she was remarkably strong, though of course the drugs. And to hang on, no point in coming all the way back up. So I phoned next morning at half past eight and my father, harried, the phone had been ringing constantly and he'd been having trouble forcing my mother to swallow the several types of painkiller, passed the phone to her, a portable phone, one of those that crackle so you can't hear anything if they're held a certain way, and my mother spoke to me but I couldn't hear. So I went back to bed, and slept, and tried to work in the afternoon until someone phoned about the coma.

I walk around the streets and it feels like I'm always walking against a tide, all sorts of rubbish floating on it, my head full of stuff, packed like a junk shop. When I sleep I'm wakened by the murmuring of something round my head, worrying at me like fruitflies round a windfall.

My mother's ear, dainty and perfect in profile as she eats at the dinner-table, cutting up food pensively with her fork.

Once we watched a programme about Irving Berlin and how he put two basic formulae together to make one song, once she even stayed up and watched a late night film with me, it was good, I think it was *Metropolis*.

The day I was waiting for a lift to the station to go back down south and she was ironing and talked about the war, the men who went up and didn't come back from the air, saying cheery goodbyes to people in the canteen and knowing you might never see them again.

That's when she told me the story of when she was on a weekend's leave *staying with your aunty, but I was due to go back on at 4.30 and had to get the bus down in the morning, so I was ironing my skirt, we had this horrible sergeant who would slap you on report without so much as look at you if your buttons weren't sparkling or your shoes. So I was getting ready to go, I was ironing my uniform, I was singing away, my head in the clouds, or looking at the sky out of the window or something stupid, and the next time I looked down there was this great burn in the skirt, I'd burnt it! And I only had a couple of hours before the bus, and I didn't know what to do. So I pulled on my coat and I ran as fast as I could, I used to be able to run quite fast you know, to the tailor's on Queensgate, and the man looked at the skirt, and he looked at me like this, oh no he said, I don't think I can do anything with this, look at the state of it. And I said please could he try, and that I had to get the bus at lunchtime, so he said to me go home and have a cup of tea and come back and I'll see what I can do. And when I went back, there was my skirt, and you couldn't see that there had ever been a burn, you couldn't even see where he'd done any mending. And the tailor wouldn't take any money, he wouldn't take any money from me.*

Warne's Observer's Picture Cards. 32 Cards in Full Colour with Descriptive Text. I: British Birds II: Wild Flowers. Every set consists of 32 cards, each of which bears on one side a picture in full colour of an individual breed or species and on the back a panel of clear descriptive text explaining the distinguishing features of the subject. Frederick Warne & Co., Limited, London and New York. I found them in the bureau under the birth certificates and old official letters, and took them away with me without telling anyone, complete sets, yellowing a little. I don't remember ever having seen them before. Tiny browned holes, drawing-pin marks, at the top of some of them. Blackbird, swallow, chaffinch, house martin, house sparrow, mistle thrush, hedge sparrow, robin. Primrose, red poppy, wood anemone, cowslip, buttercup, forget-me-not, bluebell.

Post Office, Inverness, Telephone Inverness 600 Extension 1, 13 January 1949. Dear Miss Ann MacGregor, In connection with your recent interview regarding employment as a Temporary Telephonist, I have to inform you that you successfully passed the suitability test. I regret however, that in view of your engagement to be married in the near future, it would not be in the interests of the Department to incur the expense of training an operator whose services may be available for a limited period only. It is with reluctance, therefore, that I am unable to offer you the position. Yours faithfully, William C Forsyth, Head Postmaster.

I was fourteen, I was walking along the road at the back of the canal going to the fair illicitly with Caroline and Christine, and we had been talking and laughing about boys, then somehow we were serious with that carefulness about real things, asking Caroline what she could remember of her mother. I don't really remember much, she said, but I do remember her coming into my bedroom one night to show me her dress before she went out to a dance. It was really beautiful, I remember that, it was really beautiful, it was white.

The little toy dog is covered with dust, Something something something, The little tin soldier is covered with rust. Two little orphans a boy and a girl, Sat by an old church door. An Irish boy was leaving, Leaving his native home. Laughing under her breath at me crying at them, all toweled up after my bath.

I've come to the conclusion. There was driftwood along the beach I went to last week, but it was oily. There were shells whose ridges were stained with dirt from the sea, where the waves were black, that's not what you expect of waves. But I put the shells in my pocket anyway and only tossed away the dirtier ones, throwing them back into the sea, tricking the seagulls though not on purpose that it was food I was throwing. I walked out along a stone sort of pier, like a broad wall sticking right out into the sea with a railing running the length of it for people to hold on to against the wind, the sea on either side. On the left side the water lapped on the stones leaving a line of wet leaves, on the other the water was that filthy colour I was talking about; where the white bubbles usually form from the waves' movement, on this sea the spume was grey.

I didn't just find shells. I found a piece of that pottery that's blue and white, and the thing about it was that it had been shaped into a smooth triangle by the sea, and that on it in blue were printed circular and triangular shapes, the pattern was almost as if it was meant to just be that small triangle though it wasn't, it was a broken piece of something, it had been smoothed into its shape by sheer chance. I found a piece of glass too, made round, green and made smooth, like a bit of one of those old thick-glass bottles. The good thing was that these weren't blackened by the oil or whatever.

Because things don't make the shape we expect them to. Because there's never the conclusion we imagine, not really. After I hung up the phone I sat down to wait for whatever it was and my head filled suddenly with green and the vision of a girl I'd never seen before, smiling, laughing actually, and the place was in the sun, and this laughing girl took me as far into it as I could go, but that wasn't very far, it wasn't a place for me to know. She had as casually as you unzip, untie, undo the last buttons of the shapes you leave behind, stepped out, and as casually as a forties filmstar that people all know and love but can't remember the name of, waved goodbye, said it was all all right, the war would end soon. And that's where the credits rolled, and the screen went blank (the end of the reel) then white as the lights came back on.

It's then you're left on the outside, a mere member of the audience, one of millions, and the thing you saw, the thing you were part of has gone, it was just the play of light and movement through tiny frozen images.

That's when the murmuring starts eating at you. That's when you're at sea.

I put the shells in a bowl on top of the television when I got home from the coast, and put the piece of pottery on the mantelpiece, and I gave the bit of glass to a friend who put it on her bookshelf. Her way of doing it is different from mine. She says her father disappeared one day, went to sea in a sieve and, not surprisingly, it sank, but that the villagers put it down to the fact that he must have met a woman (possibly a witch) on the way to the harbour, or he must have got his feet wet before he got on to the boat. Or a witch must have rowed out to sink him in an eggshell someone hadn't smashed through the bottom of with a teaspoon. Or maybe, she says, he'd been foolish enough to speak out loud the forbidden words on board, the words that summon the devil, words like pig or salmon or rabbit, then forgotten to touch cold iron to lift the curse.

That's what she thought. Myself I'm hanging on, leaning on the rail that over-looks the sea on either side of me, I'm picking up bits and pieces for my house. I'm thinking it out, I'm working out the story.

Don Paterson (1963 –)

Paterson is the most original and important Scottish poet of his generation. His second book of verse, *God's Gift to Women* (1997), may be the most significant verse publication of the last fifty years. 'Joycean' is the term which comes to mind – both for its complexity and its stylistic range. Its verses at times seem to pack in almost more poetry than they can bear. So discriminating a critic as Robert Crawford has called Paterson both the most intelligent and most consistently 'surprising' of contemporary Scottish poets.

Amnesia

I was, as they later confirmed, a very sick boy.
The star performer at the meeting house,
my eyes rolled back to show the whites, my arms
outstretched in catatonic supplication
while I gibbered impeccably in the gorgeous tongues
of the aerial orders. On Tuesday nights, before
I hit the Mission, I'd nurse my little secret:
Blind Annie Spall, the dead evangelist
I'd found still dying in creditable squalor
above the fishmonger's in Rankine Street.   10
The room was ripe with gurry and old sweat;
from her socket in the greasy mattress, Annie

belted through hoarse chorus after chorus
while I prayed loudly, absently enlarging
the crater that I'd gouged in the soft plaster.
Her eyes had been put out before the war,
just in time to never see the daughter
with the hare-lip and the kilt of dirty dishtowels
who ran the brothel from the upstairs flat
and who'd chap to let me know my time was up,   20
then lead me down the dark hall, its zoo-smell,
her slippers peeling off the sticky lino.
At the door, I'd shush her quiet, pressing
my bus-fare earnestly into her hand.

Four years later. Picture me: drenched in patchouli,
strafed with hash-burns, casually arranged
on Susie's bed. Smouldering frangipani;
Dali's *The Persistence of Memory*;
pink silk loosely knotted round the lamp
to soften the light; a sheaf of Penguin Classics,   30
their spines all carefully broken in the middle;
a John Martyn album mumbling through the speakers.
One hand was jacked up her skirt, the other trailing
over the cool wall behind the headboard
where I found the hole in the plaster again.

The room stopped like a lift; Sue went on talking.
It was a nightmare, Don. We had to gut the place.

Exeunt

(i.)

DROP SERENE

He poured the warm, clear guck into the mould
in which he'd already composed, with tweezers,
dead wasps on an everlasting flower
or ants filing over a leaf. When it was cold
he slaved at the surface, softening the camber
till it sat with the row of blebs on his mantelpiece,
each with its sequestered populace
like a hiccup in history, scooped out of amber.

As if it might stall the invisible cursor
drawing a blind down each page of his almanac   10
or the blank wall of water that always kept pace,
glittering an inch, half an inch from his back.
He was out in the garden, digging the borders
when it caught him, in a naturalistic pose.

(ii.)

CURTAINS

You stop at the tourist office in Aubeterre,
a columbarium of files and dockets.
She explains, while you flip through the little leaflets
about the chapel and the puppet-theatre,
that everything is boarded up till spring,
including – before you can ask – the only hotel.   20
A moped purrs through the unbroken drizzle.
You catch yourself checking her hands for rings.
She prepares a light supper; you chat,
her fussy diction placing words in air
like ice in water. She leads you to her room
but gets the shivers while you strip her bare;
lifting her head, you watch her pupils bloom
into the whole blue iris, then the white.

(iii.)

BIRD

The wind baffled lightly as they filled the grave
and a queasy flutter left us, the last faint   30
ripple of the peristaltic wave
that ushered her out. In eight months, her complaint
had whittled her down to the palsied sylph
who filched the car-keys from her snoring spouse
and went out to prove a point; then found herself,
like Alice, on the wrong side of the glass.

Later, back at the house, I overheard
the disembodied voices in the hall
where George, who'd only last another year,
was trying to be philosophical: 40

Ach, there was nothin' o' her. She was nae mair
than a sparra, nae mair than a wee bird.

(iv.)

THE ELECTRIC BRAE

For three days and three nights, he has listened
to the pounding of a terrible jug band
now reduced to a wheezy concertina
and the disinterested thump of a tea-chest bass.
It seems safe to look: wires trail on the pillowcase,
a drip swings overhead; then the clear tent
becomes his father's clapped-out Morris Minor,
rattling towards home. The windscreen presents   50
the unshattered myth of a Scottish spring;
with discreet complicity, the road
swerves to avoid the solitary cloud.
On an easy slope, his father lets the engine
cough into silence. Everything is still.
He frees the brake: the car surges uphill.

00:00: Law Tunnel

*(leased to the Scottish Mushroom
Company after its closure in 1927)*

(i)

In the airy lull
between the wars
they cut the rails
and closed the doors

on the stalled freight:
crate on crate
of blood and earth
the shallow berth

of the innocents,
their long room   10
stale and tense
with the same dream

(ii)

Strewn among
the ragged queue –
the snoring king
and his retinue,

Fenrir, Pol Pot,
Captain Oates
and the leprechauns –
are the teeth, the bones   20

and begging-cup
of the drunken piper.
The rats boiled up
below the sleepers

(iii)

The crippled boy
of Hamelin
pounds away
at the locked mountain

waist-deep in thorn
and all forlorn,   30
he tries to force
the buried doors

*I will go to my mother
and sing of my shame
I will grow up to father
the race of the lame*

The Chartres of Gowrie

for T. H.

Late August, say the records, when the gowk-storm
shook itself out from a wisp of cloud
and sent them flying, their coats over their heads.
When every back was turned, the thunder-egg
thumped down in an empty barley-field.

No witness, then, and so we must imagine
everything, from the tiny crystal-stack,
its tingling light-code, the clear ripple of tines,
the shell snapping awake, the black rock
blooming through its heart like boiling tar,   10

to the great organ at dawn thundering away
half-a-mile up in the roof, still driving
each stone limb to its own extremity
and still unmanned, though if we find this hard
we may posit the autistic elder brother

of Maurice Durufle or Messiaen.
Whatever, the reality is this:
at Errol, Grange, Longforgan, and St Madoes
they stand dumb in their doorframes, all agog
at the black ship moored in the sea of corn.   20

11:00: Baldovan

Base Camp. Horizontal sleet. Two small boys
have raised the steel flag of the 20 terminus:

me and Ross Mudie are going up the Hilltown
for the first time ever on our own.

I'm weighing up my spending power: the shillings,
tanners, black pennies, florins with bald kings,

the cold blazonry of a half-crown, threepenny bits
like thick cogs, making them chank together in my pockets.

I plan to buy comics,
sweeties, and magic tricks.   10

However, I am obscurely worried, as usual,
over matters of procedure, the protocol of travel,

and keep asking Ross the same questions:
where we should sit, when to pull the bell even

if we have enough money for the fare,
whispering, *Are ye sure? Are ye sure?*

I cannot know the little good it will do me;
the bus will let us down in another country

with the wrong streets and streets that suddenly forget
their names at crossroads or in building-sites   20

and where no one will have heard of the sweets we ask for
and the man will shake the coins from our fists onto the counter

and call for his wife to come through, come through and see this
and if we ever make it home again, the bus

will draw into the charred wreck of itself
and we will enter the land at the point we left off

only our voices sound funny and all the houses are gone
and the rain tastes like kelly and black waves fold in

very slowly at the foot of Macalpine Road
and our sisters and mothers are fifty years dead.   30

A Private Bottling

So I will go, then. I would rather grieve over your absence than over you.
    — Antonio Porchia

Back in the same room that an hour ago
we had led, lamp by lamp, into the darkness.
I sit down and turn the radio on low
as the last girl on the planet still awake
reads a dedication to the ships
and puts on a recording of the ocean.

I carefully arrange a chain of nips
in a big fairy-ring; in each square glass
the tincture of a failed geography,
its dwindled burns and woodlands, whin-fires, heather,   10
the sklent of its wind and its salty rain,
the love-worn habits of its working-folk,
the waveform of their speech, and by extension
how they sing, make love, or take a joke.

So I have a good nose for this sort of thing.

Then I will suffer kiss after fierce kiss
letting their gold tongues slide along my tongue
as each gives up, in turn, its little song
of the patient years in glass and sherry-oak,
the shy negotiations with the sea,   20
air and earth, the trick of how the peat-smoke
was shut inside it, like a black thought.
Tonight I toast her with the extinct malts

of Ardlussa, Ladyburn and Dalintober
and an ancient pledge of passionate indifference:
Ochon o do dhóigh mé mo chlairsach ar a shon,
wishing her health, as I might wish her weather.

When the circle is closed and I have drunk myself sober
I will tilt the blinds a few degrees, and watch
the dawn grow in a glass of liver-salts,   30
wait for the birds, the milk-float's sweet nothings,
then slip back to the bed where she lies curled,
replace the live egg of her burning ass
gently, in the cold nest of my lap,
as dead to her as she is to the world.

   * * *

Here we are again; it is precisely
twelve, fifteen, thirty years down the road
and one turn higher up the spiral chamber
that separates the burnt ale and dark grains
of what I know, from what I can remember.   40
Now each glass holds its micro-episode
in permanent suspension, like a movie-frame
on acetate, until it plays again,
revivified by a suave connoisseurship
that deepens in the silence and the dark
to something like an infinite sensitivity.
This is no romantic fantasy: my father
used to know a man who'd taste the sea,
then leave his nets strung out along the bay
because there were no fish in it that day.   50
Everything is in everything else. It is a matter
of attunement, as once, through the hiss and backwash,
I steered the dial into the voice of God
slightly to the left of Hilversum,
half-drowned by some big, blurry waltz
the way some stars obscure their dwarf companions
for centuries, till someone thinks to look.

In the same way, I can isolate the feints
of feminine effluvia, carrion, shite,
those rogues and toxins only introduced   60
to give the composition a little weight
as rough harmonics do the violin-note
or Pluto, Cheiron and the lesser saints
might do to our lives, for all you know.
(By Christ, you would recognise their absence
as anyone would testify, having sunk
a glass of *North British*, run off a patent still
in some sleet-hammered satellite of Edinburgh:
a bleak spirit, no amount of caramel
could sweeten or disguise, its after-effect   70
somewhere between a blanket-bath and a sad wank.
There is, no doubt, a bar in Lothian
where it is sworn upon and swallowed neat

by furloughed riggers and the Special Police,
men who hate the company of women.)

O whiskies of Long Island and Provence!
This little number catches at the throat
but is all sweetness in the finish: my tongue trips
first through burning brake-fluid, then nicotine,
pastis, *Diorissimo* and wet grass;   80
another is silk sleeves and lip-service
with a kick like a smacked puss in a train-station;
another, the light charge and the trace of zinc
tap-water picks up at the moon's eclipse.
You will know the time I mean by this.

Because your singular absence, in your absence,
has bred hard, tonight I take the waters
with the whole clan: our faceless ushers, bridesmaids,
our four Shelties, three now ghosts of ghosts;
our douce sons and our lovely loudmouthed daughters   90
who will, by this late hour, be fully grown,
perhaps with unborn children of their own.
So finally, let me propose a toast:
not to love, or life, or real feeling,
but to their sentimental residue;
to your sweet memory, but not to you.

The sun will close its circle in the sky
before I close my own, and drain the purely
offertory glass that tastes of nothing
but silence, burnt dust on the valves, and whisky.   100

21:00: Baldragon

The first kneels in a circle of brown grass,
locked on the highest sun, drawing its rays
into the mirrored furnace of his body.
For days, hardly a crumb has passed his lips,
the quicker to advance his dark enquiries.
He mouths a name, and notes that he has turned
half his right hand gold with nicotine.

                    ★

Inside the middle sun's projection-beam,
a rosy aisle from here to Templelands,
the middle boy is basking in his fame,   10
and lets his luck break over him in waves.
The girl has hooked her thumb in his back pocket.
The leaves stir. Her image flickers slightly.

                    ★

The light deserts the War Memorial
where the eldest brother crouches like a beggar,
one hand to his face, the other out to catch

the rain, scattering black coins at his feet.
There is a tiny blaze on Gallowshill.

★

Three suns are going down over Baldragon
on three brothers, each born three months apart.   20
Here is wisdom: explain to me, if you can,
the parable concerning the three brothers.

Buggery

At round about four months or so
– the time is getting shorter –
I look down as the face below
goes sliding underwater
and though I know it's over with
and she is miles from me
I stay a while to mine the earth
for what was lost at sea

as if the faces of the drowned
might turn up in the harrow: 10
hold me when I hold you down
and plough the lonely furrow

14:50: Rosekinghall

(Beeching Memorial Railway,
Forfarshire Division)

The next train on Platform 6 will be the 14:50
Rosekinghall - Gallowshill and Blindwell, calling at:

Fairygreen – Templelands – Stars of Forthneth – Silverwells –
Honeyhole – Bee Cott – Pleasance – Sunnyblink –
Butterglen – Heatheryhaugh – St Bride's Ring – Diltie Moss –
Silvie – Leyshade – Bourtreebush – Little Fithie –
Dusty Drum – Spiral Wood – Wandershiell – Windygates –
Red Roofs – Ark Hill – Egypt – Formal –
Letter – Laverockhall – Windyedge – Catchpenny –
Framedrum – Drumtick – Little Fardle – Packhorse –
Carrot – Clatteringbrigs – Smyrna – Bucklerheads –
Outfield – Jericho – Horn – Roughstones –   10
Loak – Skitchen – Sturt – Oathlaw –
Wolflaw – Farnought – Drunkendubs – Stronetic –
Ironharrow Well – Goats – Tarbrax – Dameye –
Dummiesholes – Caldhame – Hagmuir – lug of Auchrannie –
Baldragon – Thorn – Wreaths – Spurn Hill –
Drowndubs – The Bloody Inches – Halfway – Groan,
where the train will divide

Duncan McLean (1964 –)

Fire, Blood, Wine

We were working on a site near the old Leith canal. Half a street of warehouses had been demolished a couple of years before, but it was only now that anything was being done with the land. We'd been sent there before anyone else, old Carl, me, and the new YTS. Her name was Chris and she knew nothing about the job. Or at least she wasn't letting on that she knew anything. In fact she wasn't saying much at all, so Carl had plenty of time to yap away; Chris wasn't interrupting – maybe she wasn't even listening – and I was having to do most of the work.

See what he's doing now? Carl said. He's cleared a space there, kicked the bricks out of the road, trampled down the weeds and that, and now he's putting up the structure, the skeleton of the thing. Three decent timbers, that's all you need: good thick branches if you're in the parks, or sleepers maybe if you're by the railway, or like here we've just looked around and found this old door, and we've got out the hatchet and took out three of these good thick planks.

I paused in smashing up an ancient tea chest. *I* looked around, I said, *I* got out the hatchet.

What's he doing now? said Carl.

Chris shrugged.

I'm working, I said, Do you mind what that is Carl?

What you have to do next is get a good substructure, a kind of heart to the thing inside the main frame there. Smaller bits of wood or board, big bits of the right kind of rubbish, a tyre or two, cardboard boxes maybe if you fold them down . . .

I walked up and stuffed an armful of crumpled newspaper and assorted crap into the middle.

See? said Carl, Just about anything can go in at this stage, anything as long as it burns.

Aye, but you have to be careful with some things, I said. Some of the furniture you find, old settees and that, you have to watch out for the fumes they give off, stand upwind, ken, well upwind.

I glanced at the girl to see if she was taking it all in. She was staring at her boots. I looked over at Carl, and he looked back. He took his pipe out of his pocket and tapped it against his leg, then gazed into the bowl and poked around in it with his pinkie.

Away and show her where the petrol is, he said.

I sniffed. Are you sure the strain won't fucking kill her?

He looked up. Watch your language in front of the lassie, he said.

For fuck's sake Carl, I said, I never asked to have a lassie put on with us! It's those cunts up in city chambers who're to blame for that. Why should I change my way of talking all of a sudden? I'll talk how I fucking like. Christ, you're so worried about the girl . . . I haven't heard *her* fucking complaining!

You haven't exactly been fucking listening, have you?

Both of us looked at her in amazement. It was just about the first thing she'd said all morning. Carl started to say something, but she carried on speaking over him.

I am fucking complaining, she said. I'm fucking fed up of yous calling me a lassie, going on about mind the girl and all that: I'm not a fucking girl!

There was a pause. You could've fooled me, I said.

I'm seventeen years old, she said, I'm a fucking woman!

Carl chuckled, stuck his pipe in his mouth. Oh aye hen, he said. Right enough. Sorry.

I started to walk off towards the van. Come on then woman, I called back, Come and give us a hand with this petrol. She didn't come after me.

Five minutes later, I'd poured a measure of petrol into the base of the structure, and splashed some over the sides and top too.

Carl cleared his throat. Stand back! he said. I looked at him. We'd been working together for three years, and he'd never said stand back before. Since when did he tell me what to do? I took a pace away anyhow. I always did, it was common sense. The girl stepped back too. Carl nodded at me, then at her. He struck a match and lifted it in cupped hands to the bowl of his pipe, hunched over slightly till he worked on that and got it going, then, just before the match burnt out, he threw it into the base of the fire, almost without looking, as if it didn't matter, like he was just chucking it away, and in an instant the whole structure streaked into flames.

Carl had jumped away the moment he'd dropped the match. Now he settled down on his hunkers, gazing at the fire, watching how it was going. I took a few steps round the far side to check it was burning evenly, then went over and stood beside him. Chris came over too.

See how the orange flames are dying down now? said Carl. That's the petrol burnt out. But there's others coming through, red and yellow and bits of blue and that: that's the wood and stuff catching. This is the important time. If the fire's going to take it takes now.

We all looked at the fire. It was doing fine.

If the heart's too tightly packed the flames don't catch, I said. On the other hand, if the insides are too loose they'll blaze up and be ashes in half a minute, and still you'll be left with the bones of the thing standing there.

I looked over at Carl and the girl. He was ricking on his pipe, she was holding her hands out to the heat.

But it looks like I put it together pretty fucking well, I said. There was a pause.

So what do we do now? said Chris.

Well . . . we just watch this one for a while, said Carl, Feed it up a bit. Then it might well be dinnertime. Then this afternoon we're away down to the docks.

What is it there the day? I said, A skip?

Carl took his pipe out of his mouth, shook his head. Line says three oil drums.

Drums of oil? said Chris.

I doubt it, said Carl. They're meant to take oil and chemicals and that away to some furnace somewhere.

But it wouldn't be the first time they haven't, I said.

Carl knocked his pipe out on the ground, then brought it up to his mouth and blew through the stem. Aye Chris, he said, That's one thing about this job: you start a lot of different kinds of fires.

Different fires for different folks, I said.

The girl looked over at me. Her face was blank.

At dinnertime Carl sat in the van as usual, eating his sandwiches and listening to classical music on the radio. I remembered from when we'd been in this part of the world before that there was a good cafe closeby, so I headed off for that. As I reached the top of the steps from the canalbank to streetlevel, I heard somebody running up behind me. It was Chris. I kept on walking. Twenty yards down the street she caught up with me, then for half a block she walked along two paces behind me, till I stopped.

Is this it? she said.

Oh, are you coming with me are you?

Well nobody told me I would need sandwiches. I mean I thought I'd be close enough to home to . . .

Look, if you're coming with me, come with me; don't hang around my arse like a . . . like a bad fucking penny.

She looked at me for a second, and I thought she was going to greet, but all of a sudden she burst out laughing. You really hate me, don't you? she said, then started laughing again.

Christ, I'm just needing my dinner, I said, Is that so fucking much to ask?

She started walking again, and so did I. Okay, she said, Where is this cafe?

Just across there, I said and nodded to the other side of the street.

Where?

That red place, I said, With the steamy window.

I thought that was a sauna. Could they not afford a sign or something?

Fuck knows. Why don't you ask them if you're so interested.

Okay, I will.

Don't.

We went in. It was just like somebody's front room, except four kitchen tables had been crammed in, and there was a serving hatch across a door in the far side. Three of the tables were more or less full, and everybody glanced up as I came in and threaded my way over towards the hatch. I heard the door shut with a bit of a bang, then suddenly there was total silence, everybody stopped talking and eating and stared at Chris as she crossed the cafe behind me. All men. Fuck. Obviously it wasn't the done thing to bring females into the place. They'd be blaming me for the intrusion as well. I was beginning to wish I'd never mentioned the cafe to her, and wondering if I could just turn round and walk straight out. Then I thought, Fuck it, where else am I going to get my dinner?

A middle aged woman with a big bosom and a big belly under her housecoat came over towards the serving hatch from the depths of the room behind it. Now son? she said.

What've you got?

We've got a menu. She leaned through the hatch and pointed to a paper plate pinned to the wall. It had writing on it in felt pen: BEEF STEW 90p, COD £1, RHUBARB CRUMBLE 50p.

I'll have the stew, I said, And a mug of tea and the crumble as well.

Custard or milk?

Custard with the crumble, milk with the tea.

She jerked her head hack, half closed her eyes and looked me up and down, then let out a loud hoot. I stared at her. She hooted again. It was laughter, I hadn't recognised it for a minute.

Give us a shout when it's ready, I said.

Hooh!

I turned and squeezed back across the room. As I was sitting down at the free table, I heard Chris talking at the hatch: Have you nothing vegetarian?

Once again, all conversation in the cafe stopped.

I'll have the fish then, said Chris.

Somebody whistled. A few folk looked over at me. I picked something up from the table. It was an old Pepsi bottle that had been filled up with sauce. I unscrewed the top, then picked some dried brown stuff out of the thread with my fork. Chris sat down on the bench opposite me. I put the bottle down.

So you're a veggie are you? I said. She shrugged. So is cod a vegetable then? She looked at me. I smiled. She looked away. So what do you reckon so far? The job I mean . . .

Is there a bog? she said.

What? I leant towards her.

She cleared her throat. A bog, she said loudly, Is there a toilet in here?

Christ's sake, no, I said. What do you think this is, the fucking Ritz?

There must be a bog, otherwise where does the old woman go when she needs a pish?

Don't ask me. Maybe she does it in the fucking stew for all I know.

I'm going to ask her.

Oh fuck.

Chris went over to the serving hatch and leaned over it, saying something to the woman in the back. After a few seconds, she lifted the counter and walked through. There was a general shaking of heads and complaining, then everybody went back to eating or what they were talking about before.

At one table somebody was saying, I heard of a woman who fed her man Kittikat and chips for tea one night, and he died.

Shite man!

It's true enough.

Kittikat wouldn't kill you!

Och, the cat food didn't kill him; he broke his neck when he bent down to lick his arse! STEW!

The woman was shouting from the hatch. I got up and went over. As I lifted the plate off the counter, she said, Oi, here's the fish for your dame as well.

She's not my . . .

Before I could finish, another door in the back room opened, there was the sound of a cistern filling, and Chris stepped out with a big grin on her face. When she saw me at the hatch, she threw her arms up in the air and shouted, Yeaahhh! I've got my chatties! No more abortions for me!

The cafe behind me went quiet, but for some reason this time I wasn't worried. I was standing there, a plate of stew and peas in one hand, fish and chips in the other, watching Chris dance around the backshop, shaking her hips, throwing her hands in the air, shouting and laughing. And I couldn't help myself, I was laughing too. I laughed till I got jabbing pains in my sides and I had to put the plates down for fear of dropping the lot.

You're a daft cow, I said, in a gap in my laughter.

She put her hands up to her ears like horns, and prancing about making mooing noises.

The woman who ran the place was laughing too. I'd kill for a glass of what she's on, she said.

Come on Chris, I said, Come and get your grub before it's time for work again.

She looked over at me, grinning. Fuck work! she said.

We ate quickly, not speaking, then I took the plates up to the counter, told the woman not to bother about the crumble, paid, and made for the door. Chris was waiting outside. As I came out, she started walking further up the street. I followed her.

They'll be talking about us for weeks in there, I said.

Ach, who cares! she said, striding on ahead.

Eh, where are we going?

She stopped in front of a Paki shop. Well, is this place licensed?

I pressed my face against the window and looked in. There's cans on a shelf there.

Right, wait here.

Half a minute later she came out with a big green bottle, and led back the way we'd come.

What's that?

Sherry.

Sherry?

Aye, this is a celebration.

How can we celebrate? We've got to start work again in fifteen minutes . . .

Forget it! if you're so worried about the time, stop talking and start drinking.

She made to pass the bottle, then took it back, unscrewed the top, and put it in her jacket pocket. She took a quick drink, then handed me the sherry. As the bottle was in my mouth, she spoke again.

I owe you a quid for dinner, right? Well the wine was one-eighty, so if we more or less halver it, that's us squared up, okay?

I held the bottle out to her, wiped my mouth on my sleeve, and was away to say something, but already she'd taken a swig and was talking again.

Christ, who wants a kid, eh? Who'd bring one into this world? Not me, anyhow. I mean, do you ken what this government's done to family allowance? Bastards! It's fucking atrocious, ask anyone, ask my mum. She took a quick drink,

YIPPEE! she shouted.

We went down the same steps we'd come up earlier. When she got to the canal-bank, Chris turned right and walked in the opposite direction to where the van was parked. I followed her. A few yards on, she sat down under a tree, balanced the bottle on a rock by her side, then got out a packt of Marlboro and lit up.

I never knew you smoked, I said. You never lit up all morning.

I thought I was pregnant, didn't I. She exhaled. Sit down and shut up.

I sat down. Already the two or three drinks of sherry were making me a bit unsteady. I leaned against the treetrunk as I went down, but once sitting I felt fine again, and lifted the bottle to take a drink. I looked at Chris as I was drinking. She was smiling, and blowing smoke out between her lips in a long jet.

I was beginning to worry this morning to be honest, I said. I mean I thought me and Carl had got stuck with a right miserable bitch – you hardly opened your mouth! – so, Christ, it's a relief to find out it was just the old PMT . . .

She turned slowly to look at me. What? she said quietly.

Well it affects lots of dames like that, eh no? Makes them a bit depressed, a bit weepy and that. Christ, I sympathise, I mean cutting yourself shaving's bad enough, but all that buckets of blood? Yous are welcome to it!

You ignorant bastard! She snatched the bottle out my hand.

What? I said.

I wasn't prefuckingmenstrual, I was worried in case I was going to be bringing a bairn into a world full of arseholes like you! Jesus, is that any reason to be cheerful?

She got to her feet and started walking straight for the canal. I jumped up, staggered slightly and fell back against the tree, then pushed myself upright and went after her. She'd stopped at the edge and was looking down past her feet into the dark, thick water. The bottle, still quarter full, dangled from her right hand. I stood slightly behind her, and to one side.

Don't do it, I said.

I'm going to.

Don't.

She bent the top half of her body back the way, then snapped it forwards, at the same time bringing her arm up and letting go of the bottle. It flew out over the canal and smacked into the water half way across, bobbed up once, then went under.

A few bubbles came to the surface. I watched them float off downstream. A tune came into my head. It was going round and round. I started to sing it: Come on baby light my fire, come on baby light my fire . . .

Chris took a step back from the edge and turned to face me. Is that supposed to be funny? she said.

What? I said. Is what supposed to be funny?

She was staring at me. I smiled. She looked beyond me and nodded to where the van was parked

Come on, she said, Let's get to work. I feel like burning a whole load of things.

Angela McSeveney (1964 –)

The Lump

Rolling over in a hot June night
I cradled my breasts in my arms
and felt a hard knot of tissue.

I was fifteen.
My life rose up in my throat
and threatened to stifle me.

It took three attempts to tell my mother.
She promised that my appointment would be
with a woman doctor.

A nurse called my name.   10
I didn't have cancer.

The stitches in my skin reminded me
of a chicken trussed for the oven.

I felt ashamed
that the first man to see me
had only been doing his job.

The Pictures

To avoid distracting the workers
the mill windows were set in the roof.

Consequently my mother never saw sense
in spending an evening in the cinema
with no air and not even light.

But she did go to see *Gone With The Wind*
when it first came out.

It was the same day Bessie Henderson's hair
caught in her loom and she was scalped.

The men came running   10
but they were no use, fainting and going on.

A woman had to hold Bessie up
while an engineer cut her loose.
The worst of it was she didn't faint.

Bessie should have been one of the girls
who went to see *Gone With The Wind*.

My mother tried
but she couldn't like it much.

Bouquet

He brought me roses unexpectedly
on our third date
because it was my birthday I thought.

He dropped the knot into my lap casually;
a posy from his garden,
hand-picked, the stems bound in tin foil.

There was a full headed red,
three yellows just budding,
one white curled like a soft shell.

Real roses: 10
thorns, patches of rust,

leathery leaves pocked by insects
and ohh that scent.

I stood them in a glass
at the corner of my bedroom.

In that heavy Summer night
the petals parted without a sound and let go
such a perfume from their discreet pores.

By morning the room
was sweet with it,   20
the first red petals scattered on the floor.

Alan Warner (1964 –)

Car Hung, Upside Down

The car hung, upside down high above the earth, in the leafless sycamore tree. Spunkhead was still strapped into his seat. Donald John had ended up kneeling on the squeezy black roof-padding. The loud, fast music kept playing.

Spunkhead, blond fringe hanging, his paleness flushed, reached out an inverted hand for the cassette eject button; then there was a roaring of blood in Spunkhead's ears, the sputtering hiss of upside-down-bust-radiator steam and another broke barrier fell away, past them from up on the hairpin above. Gatherings of naked winter twigs were violently twisted, shoved up against still-intact windscreen.

'Houston, we have a problem,' Spunkhead announced, his hair floating from side to side in space.

Donald John let out a yelp of laughter then went silent with a gulped breath. The roof he kneeled on was scattered with loose unmarked cassettes, empty beer bottles, sealed contraceptive foils, one or two pence pieces, cigarette butts and old *Playboy* and *Hustler* magazines. Some pages had flopped open.

'I wondered where that one had gone,' Donald John says quietly, moving out a hand to touch the girl on the shiny page.

'You okay?' Spunkhead let his arms dangle and placed both palms on the car roof.

'Watch it! Throw that seatbelt lock . . . '

'Aye. We get out. You first. The car gets lighter.'

'This is, we are agreed, a good thing?'

'Affirmative.'

'I'll get out first. Less weight in the car.'

'And the cradle *will* rock Donny ma man! Fuck, what if the whole kit and caboodle comes a-tumbling down?'

Donald John turned back from the door, creased his forehead at Spunkhead hanging there, then picked up a copy of *Hustler* that he rolled into a tube and slid down the front of his breeks. 'I snap a branch, I want her with me, all the way down, to break my fall.' Donald John coories on the upside down car roof and used both hands to gingerly wind the window handle the wrongish way, as if he was stirring a real big, thick pot of porridge oats. He looked at the digital clock, fitted into the dash:

$$\text{ƐƐ:0Ɩ}$$

Spunkhead was thoughtful. 'Hoi, Donny. No think, when yon Macpherson, the sergeant, finally gets this car down, its gony be a bit of a brasser . . . it being full of scud mags, flunkies, beer bottles; you gave The Argonaut a hurl back from the dance Saturday night so there must be roach ends in your fucking ashtray here.' Upside down, Spunkhead yanked the ashtray further out: a fresh confetti-ing of tumbling ash sprinkled down, butts pattered on the back of Donald John's leather jacket.

'I'll destroy all evidence . . . ' Donald John stopped winding the window. A few twigs had sprung in the gap the window had created. ' . . . Turf some of this shite out then.' Donald John reached about him, gathering the magazines, bunching the metallic contraceptive packets in his fist, rolling the Beck's bottles nearer with his fingertips.

'Yup. *That's* it.' Spunkhead encouraged from above.

Donald John shoved the cassettes and coppers to one side, revolved the window handle more, then started thrusting out and away the porno mags, into the spriglets, till they flappered and turned, then each of the beer bottles went out. Spunkhead and Donald John could hear the green glass bottles bump the high, thick boughs and clash through the twig clusters downwards or leap out, then the painful longness of the bottles' freefall in open air, before they hit the heavily rooted ground without smashing. 'Must be what Richard bloody Branson does as yet another balloon plummets earthwards,' Donald John muttered.

Spunkhead's laugh sounded different upside down. More strained.

Donald John says, 'Ample roach-ends here – every fucking butt's a joint. Fucked if I got to smoke half of it either. Every cunt've had in this car must've been spliffing away.'

'Hey now Donny! Got to watch you don't get a three year ban. Like me! C'mon now, get a move on, so's I can get down from here. Funny isn't it? When you're a kid, you can't get enough of being upside down; all the bloody time you're aye doing handstands just to see what the world looks like the other way up . . . here, look at the steering wheel fucks sake!'

The normally top of the steering wheel, now the lower section, was bent over almost as far as the plastic covering on the dash speedo. Spunkhead's tone went serious. 'Donny. You have a seatbelt on, ya daft cunt?'

'No. But that's just my weight on the wheel. I'd my two arms stretched out and the top of the wheel just took my weight was all.' Donald John cupped the contraband butts in his hands, swung his arms out the window, and set the little scraps free, as if he was releasing a trapped bird. He changed the subject. 'You mind I don't unbalance this thing when I get out.'

'You're unbalanced enough.'

Donald John wound on up the window, though when the car was the correct way up, this would be called winding *down* the window. He started shoving his legs out through the bunch of twigs; angrily, he snapped a persistent, inward-shoving one – the buff bark strained pale green then cracked backwards, revealing the powder-white innards beamed with a green tubering, so bright in the air. His legs dangled in space; he had to lean back to wriggle outwards through the window, so his face lay close to Spunkhead's.

'Careful for fucksake,' Spunkhead says.

'Mmm.' Donald John caught the door molding and swung his outside feet about, feeling for branch or bough. 'Fucking grab me if I cant get something here.'

He got the angle of a solid bough below him, where it joined into the main trunk. He grimaced as he let his canvas shoe take more weight and get squeezed into the branch's emerging angle. Donald John reached, got a grab where the twigs were thickening into a branch, shoogled to test, then shoved himself away from the car. He was out. He was stood, one foot canted up high on the jutting branch, the other foot wedged where the bough was moulded from the main green-barked trunk. Donald John edged his other leg down and this adjustment dropped his head to just below the dunted-up car roof. He smelled the smoke.

'Okay champion?' Spunkhead called. He held the roach to his hung-upside-down face and blew out a cloud. Holding the joint in his mouth, he sprung the seatbelt lock and walked backwards on his hands then fell softly, his legs curling him onto the roof. Spunkhead's face appeared in among the sprung-back twigs. 'Where'd my joint go? I dropped my joint there.' He crawled back around the roof, in frantic little circles that made the car creak and shift a bit. His face appeared again. 'I cannae find it.'

'Fucking get down here,' Donald John snapped. 'Watch it though. Hoor of a difficult getting balanced, but with having the extra height you should manage. If you're no too stoned. See, yon branch there – just use that springy one to tug out then, once your legs are secure here, heave over on that. I'll climb down to make room.'

Very gingerly, Donald John swiveled, trembling a little, stepping one canvas shoe over another, pushing his palms onto the cold wood trunk. He kneeled, placed an arm out behind him and lowered one foot to the next branch down. His leg jellied a bit . . . nervous . . . but he stretched out then got his arse down on the bough he'd been on. He slipped through the fanning of branches, arms locked secure behind so he could get those feet solid in that belowness there.

Meanwhile above, Spunkhead was wriggling from the car then placing his Nikes on wood near Donald John's left ear.

Donald John used this moment of pause in their onward, downward movement to a terrestrial base to take greater account of their surroundings.

The sycamore's upper boughs and reachings were almost as elevated as the broken barriers of the missed hairpin. Thinking back, Donald John could accept the tree as something of a landmark in the undulating lochside lands. The sycamore had always been there, in summer its lather of leaves shimmering before the waters of Loch Feochan by the raised beach. Up on the school bus, back when he was fifteen, you could see further down the tree than from a car on the hairpin. The cliff was sheer from the road. The fall from the verge to down there through the tree to all its roots, embedded in the earth . . . you would need to stop your vehicle, get out on that blind corner and peek down to see the muddied underside of the car. Donald John peered up in his imaginings, expecting some hesitant but concerned faces keeking downwards – their features hidden by chins compressed into chests – toes on the lip of the cliff.

There were no faces up there on the bluff above. As he was swallowing, looking skywards, Donald John heard the downgrading gears of a vehicle approaching the hairpin. He turned himself to survey beyond the main trunk and across the cultivated gowan fields to where the main road reached the waterside. The vehicle, a high-sided van, moved along round the trees, its white sides attracting the pinkish light. The van rounded the trees, its angular shape broken and divided up among the fat boughs, and it was gone.

Donald John now turned himself towards the raised beach and shoreline across the flat patchwork of fields. The redness of the morning was slicked on the loch surface. The actual stone beach, where land met water, out of sight, was concealed below the raised fields which ended in a puff of sand among some small dunes.

Donald John squinted at those little anchored boats, the factory ship with its trembly arc lights, brighter than anything, and then the shorecast bulk. Donald John says, 'Look,' then his eyes moved from the beaching out to the widening waters of the delta and open oceans. 'Look for fuck's sake.'

'Jesus Christ all fuckity, is that no a sight?' Spunkhead shook his head. 'That's fucking bizarre.'

From there, in their perch, they could see the grill-like grin ranged up the side where the cutting had begun. The tail's upper fin fallen hugely to one side, hung over in resignation.

'Lets get down there, Chavvy,' Spunkhead laughed, looking out onto the red sea loch, the low swell crests letting sunlight razor down their lengths. The same beauty of a shepherd's warning had been reflected in each oncoming windscreen Donald John had met on their homeward race before the hairpin, their trajectory to the tree, and the beginning of their descent . . .

Spunkhead was locked, spread-eagled among the boughs, twigs and branches a couple of steps up from Donald John. The looming of the upside-down car darkened his surroundings as Donald John began to climb to another bough, way down through the twig canopies.

'I'm fucking knackered,' Spunkhead piped up.

'Aye?' Donald John concentrated on getting a foot down.

'Aye. *I* need my seventeen or eighteen hours a night.'

Donald John looked up at the Spunkhead profile, then gazed out to the red-tinged loch. Donald John lifted a finger to his forehead, saw the thick sparkly sweat on the fingertip. He could feel the pinheads up in his hairline. He looked down – how the boughs grew thicker, lower in the tree.

Down at the next level Donald John looked back up to see Spunkhead stood on a thicker bough, leaned into the trunk, working into the bark with a Swiss army knife.

'Whatre you doing?'

'Carving my initials. Cant be all the way up here and not make ma mark.'

Donald John began to notice how all the porno mags seemed to have got snared up there in the clusters and branches, pages hung open and draped over branches, or splayed out on twigs so these naked, flesh-coloured little women seemed to sprout over the whole tree, sitting up in the branches like leopards, holding themselves open for the dumb stretches of farmland and the moss-strewn clutter of boulders and fenceposts below.

'The loch's so fucking red,' Donald John murmured, and more to himself than to Spunkhead. He could see the wee slivers of bright, creamy bark with green, tickering down from aboveness. He squinted up, knowing Spunker would carve also:

+

DEIRDRA

:Irish chick the both of them shagged in the toilets of the plane coming back from Alicante, her wee daughter was with her.

Donald John let out a smile, an awful long smile – a smile that took in the years – oh, the years, oh aye, so many years all gone. Donald John looked up at the car hung, upside down, then laughed then stopped, coughed.

'Whatre you getting off on, Chavvy?' Spunker muttered, concentrating.

Donald John wearily sat, fished the mag out of his Levis. He tried to read a story. It was an art form, how quick they got onto the boning. Some had perfected the introductory necessities to a single sentence:

> On Tuesday, the sexy, long-legged new assistant in the office said the photo
> of my husband on my desk really had her running to the toilet; so I said,
> 'Friday at 8, here's the address,' so on Friday my husband put his long tongue

in her throbbing mouth as soon as she walked in; I lifted her skirt from behind and . . .

Aye. Donald John tossed the mag away forward and at least saw this one turn on itself, then the heavy-thumbed spine, splat the ground amongst the beer bottles of the earth.

Donald John began to slide lower. He went, pensively, 'Weird, ain't it? I was talking to these townie lads when I was at the heliport in Eh-berdeen there, and the cunts were going on about the intra-caseys of how a lassie gets fucked by an Alsatian, or how she sucks a donkey's dick, or how about this scene where two chicks were getting a snake's head up them and that, yet these are the same pricks that every day call you and me fucking sheep shaggers. These twisted wanks watch so many porn movies they know the manual on animal intercourse . . . eh?'

Spunkhead blew onto his completed tree trunk carving. A little silence of satisfaction immediately followed.

'Know what I mean? I wouldnt know the first thing about how to get it on with a beast, but these cunts from the city are fucking experts! Even know what size of tea-chest you need to stand on to shag a horse up its ass.'

'Pervy town cunts,' tutted Spunkhead. 'When I was at primary, there was a cunt, Beamer McKechnie. Fat fuck. Says he found a sheep, drowned upside-down in a river pool with its sheep's fanny lips all open, like a chubby girls, so he fucked it.'

'Fucked a dead sheep?'

'Aye.'

'Ohh ya cunt ya.'

'I mind his big beaming happy fucking face the Monday morn. Aye. That fat cunt fucked the dead sheep okay.'

Donald John thought, then says, 'Walking back from the Turbines Bar, one nighty there, freezing as fuck; been on the drams all day. So fucking cold, the new loch had frozen solid. Im stalking along the shore road, singing to myself, and I hear this scraping, this manic slide-sliding. It's way *out* there. Out in the dark on the ice flow. Well I'm scared, deep scared man; I can hear this living being, this animate life form, *out* there . . . moving. So I climb down the road embanking and I step onto the ice. Its so thick, I feel more solid on it that I do on the floor of my flat. I'm walking out there, walking through the night, on the solid deep-water ice. Below a star, towards this mad, circulary scratching. When I get close Im scared – I can hear it snorting, breathing, knocking with its free hoof – cause it's a stag, a big fucking deer with horns, back legs stuck solid into the ice, one front leg right deep into the solid ice. Must've gone through the surface just before nightfall when it was thinner, then got all froze solid into it, as nightcold descended. I'm thinking to myself: if a big hoor of a stag can go through this ice so can I, and the bastard can see me, smell me too, so near, struggling on the ice. I just start tip-toeing back to the shore and I leave the bastard there.'

'So? You never shagged it then, you poof? Buggered it from behind while it was helpless?' says Spunkhead.

Donald John slowly looked upwards. 'Nay. But yon city cuntsdve been out gang-banging all fucking night, gang-bang on ice spectacular! The old Torvill and Dean.'

Donald John wiped more sweat off of his forehead and was about to restart his descent when he smelled it and looked up. Smoke was gushing out the open window of the car, hung upside down above them.

Donald John and Spunkhead stopped observing the morning and quickly began lowering themselves from branch to branch.

'We cannae do it. You and your fucking joints. We cannae make it. Drop's too far,' Donald John shouted.

'Here.' Spunkhead was quicker on the tree, he was right behind him, swinging off his jacket and dangling one leather arm down to Donald John's fingers.

A flame puffed out the open car window high above them, and then some burning thing fell down past. A swirl-trail of grey smoke was going off, turning over across the fields towards the red shoreline. Donald John knotted two arms of his own jacket and Spunker's together. There was a whoosh of combustion up there. Spunkhead giggled nervously above.

Donald John tied the arm of a joined-together-jacket round a bough and, as if he was a parachutist, tipped off the branch. He yelled in pain, the tied-together-jackets took the weight and swung him in the shore direction. Donald John let go, bicycled his legs in the air, hit, rolled on the hard earth. He stood up immediately and began striding towards the loch that was now lit up all white by the sun.

'Hey. Chubber, wait!' Spunkhead was down.

But Donald John wasn't waiting. He was walking onwards, till he crossed the first fence, palms digging into the wired barbs, and he reached the lip of raised beach, where he saw the two gulliver ships from the marine laboratory at Dunbeg anchored offshore there, and saw the lilliput men around the slab-peeled blubber, saw the loch.

'No.'

Far behind, Spunkhead was calling. Then the guts of the burnt-out car began to crash down through the cindered sycamore, exploding in a column of orange sparks. Ahead lay the gassed-up bulk of the shored whale, its blunt snout up-shore near the dune-grass, the loch slicked red with blood from the stripped white, fleshed flanks. Blood the same colour as the black glut of bloods hupping into Donald John's back throat from his rib-ripped innards.

Donald John: unbelieving that his last minutes should only have had ridiculous concerns in his mind . . . his mind where he'd prepared so long, only to have this humiliating trash, jumble and mess up there. Unbelievable.

He'd fallen. Eyes close to the grass were dead. Maybe. Splendid morning reflected in the black pupils. Maybe not. The day only just started and dead!

Far across the fields, above the buzz of chainsaws' dull impacts on the whale, Spunkhead was running, screaming, first in this direction, then in that.

A[lison] L[ouise] Kennedy (1965 –)

Friday Payday

Waiting here, with nothing to sit on was a bugger. You could sit, if you wanted, on the brick edge of the flower bed, but that would make you dirty; earth and chewing-gum and that. Folk stubbed out their chewing-gum on the bricks, it was disgusting.

Because of the rain, it was muddy this evening and she would have to watch herself more than usual, because she had on the fawn skirt and the cream-coloured jacket. They were nice, but they showed the slightest thing and she liked to keep clean.

Later, she would be tired, but just now, she felt very settled and quiet inside. She was here.

A block of faces came out to the sunlight, coats and hair rising in the breeze and she watched them. She knew how to watch.

Sometimes, there was a girl who was a dancer. This station must be near to where she lived. It was only a guess, but she ought to be a dancer. You could see in the way she walked, as though clothes were unnecessary. She was too thin, but she had a lovely face and, if she was stripped bare naked she probably wouldn't look even a wee bit undressed. Her skin would be enough, better than clothes.

It would always be a good night if you saw her. The dancer was lucky.

The faces passed more quickly than you would think. That was always the way. From the top of the steps until they reached her, she could count to seven slowly. Up to nine and they were beyond her, crossing the road and turning, going away.

No one had stopped this time. No one had really seen her, or hesitated. But they would. It was early yet, and the dancer hadn't come.

It was funny how people could tell why she was waiting. In the way she could tell the dancer was a dancer. It was the same. Some people would see her waiting here and they would be able to tell.

At first, she had only noticed them, noticing her, and hadn't known why, or who they were. Now she could recognise all the types before they had moved from the shadow of the entrance and walked past the poster for young persons' travel cards. Some of them did nothing. They looked at her or looked away, smiling, frowning, pretending she wasn't there. Some of them did what she needed. Needing wasn't hoping or wanting, but if they did what she was needing, then that was enough.

By the time it was fully dark, the first one had come and gone. They had walked together to the car park and stayed in his car. without driving away. Then she walked back alone to the station and stood. She waited.

Twenty pounds, ten minutes. He had been English, which she preferred. The Arab-looking ones had more money, but they frightened her. Scots were always somehow rougher, although she was Scottish too.

She was Scottish and here was London, Whittington's place, fucking Dick's place, but it didn't make much of a difference – most people she met didn't seem to come from here. They were all strangers together.

It did feel different, though. Out in this bit, the houses were all small with their own tiny gardens, too tiny to be any use. White walls and square, little windows looking over grass like green paper and stupid dots of flowers all of it only there to make a point. The people walked past her in the street and didn't like her, but she wasn't sure of why that was. They might be able to tell that she was Scottish; they might not like her waiting. They should have been nicer to her, really; she was only wee. And a stranger. Folk were dead unfriendly here.

Of course, this was a Friday night and the amateurs were out – just school kids making money for the weekend. She didn't like to wait near them – get messed up. Soon she'd go into the station and ride to town. The town was more like Glasgow – a proper city. Big, glass buildings and hamburger places and lights. Very bright, but very strange where the lights were and very black over everything else. She just dreeped down in between the two. The black to hide and the bright to show. The city was very ideal for her lifestyle.

Going down the escalator she passed the dancer who looked tired.

The underground could be scary. Not because of people – because of itself. She didn't like the push of wind when the train came up to the platform. She didn't like the noises. Even in the Glasgow underground, which was wee, she had been scared and this one would go where that fire had been – all those people underground and burning – like the coal in the shut-down mines. She closed her eyes as the carriages slid beside her. They opened their doors.

MIND   THE   GAP.

Sometimes, that was a tape-recording, but sometimes it was a real person, trying to talk like a tape-recording, she'd noticed that.

Inside, when it started moving, she sat away from either end, in case there was a crash, or else she stood near a door and held on with her feet apart which made you more steady, even with heels.

She wasn't frightened often. Sometimes they would ask her if she was scared. Scared of them. If they wanted her to say so, she would tell them she was, but she wasn't. For a person of her age, she was very brave. For a person of her age she was fucking older than anyone she knew.

The Hotel Man had believed she was scared of him but that was just because she let him; it wasn't true. Not really true. Also, she'd known he would have had to make her frightened if he hadn't thought she was frightened and she'd known he would like to do that. Just for peace and quietness, it was best if she made him think she was already scared.

She'd known he was going to be that way from the beginning – breathing and looking at her and trying to make her afraid. He came to her room in the morning on the fifth day she was there and said she would have to pay her bill or clear off out of it. He shouted and spoke about policemen and what they would do. Send her home, or lock her up and bodysearch her.

Locking up would be better than home. The same, but better.

Whenever he spoke to her, the Hotel Man breathed funny, through his mouth. He looked at her and breathed the way her mother had told her she ought to if she had onions to chop. If you breathed through your mouth, they wouldn't make you cry.

The Hotel Man breathed like you should for chopping onions when he told her about the polis and asked about her money and what could she suggest she ought to do. In her silence, he watched and breathed. Nobody was crying then and when she did, the following day, she was crying because of her mother, not because of him or being scared. She couldn't help crying, she was sad. She knew she would never be as good as her mother was now. Her skin would never be as nice, or her fingers – her Ma'd had clever hands. She couldn't even cook, it didn't work. It didn't taste good. It wouldn't matter if she practised, there would always be something missing from what she did and now she wouldn't be able to practise any more. Cooking had seemed dead important then, she didn't know why.

The Hotel Man was stupid, he hadn't understood. He was just satisfied with believing he'd made her cry. But he couldn't ever do that, wouldn't know where to begin.

Coming up out of the station, the wind was rising, growing unpredictable. Different parts of a newspaper were diving and swinging in the air and there were whirls of smaller rubbish scraping the foot of the walls. It felt like something starting, maybe a hurricane again.

The last hurricane in London had come when she was still in Glasgow. In school, they'd had to write about it and she'd been sad because of all the ruined trees. Her father had said there'd been a hurricane once in Glasgow, but nobody'd cared.

That was all in the autumn, after the third time she'd run to other places and before the fourth. The fourth time, she'd made it to London and the Hotel Man.

He'd been like her father. Only he'd called it testing the goods when he did it and he'd made her take him out of herself and rub him. He'd put it in her throat so she'd thought she would die, couldn't breathe, didn't know how to manage yet. Her father had been more sleekit. He'd climbed through the window from the street one afternoon and showed himself to her by accident on purpose. That was badness, she just had to accept that there was badness in people, like that.

Their sitting-room windows were opened right up and into the street and she could see other folk she knew, by their windows, sitting on the pavement or standing in their rooms. Her father was wearing shorts and trainers, nothing else, and he sat astride the window frame and smiled at her, let his shorts ride up.

It didn't seem right that all those people were there, just beyond the window.

Father called it having a cuddle and said it was her mother's fault. He'd used to do this with her mother but then she'd gone to somewhere else and he still needed someone because he was a normal man.

From then she'd always wanted to be somewhere else. It made you need a different place to be, getting stuck with a normal man. Then you got a different place and you were still wrong, because you were wanting a different time and to be a different person.

This was payday Friday, end of the month, which was usually the busiest time. After the fifth or sixth, she had a wee sit and something to eat. The gale was getting worse. It wasn't cold especially, but some of the gusts were so strong that when you faced them, you couldn't breathe.

Watching through the big glass panel with her coffee, she saw everything turning unsteady, losing control. It didn't feel dangerous now she was out of it, just weird. Like being drunk without drinking.

She had a choice of places to go to for a bit of peace: chicken places, or pizza places, hamburger places, all kinds of places. She preferred to go where they sold doughnuts because doughnuts had no smell. If you kept them in the napkin, your hands stayed clean and when you'd finished, your mouth was sweet. Folk didn't mind a wee bit sweetness on your lips. If you smelled of grease and vinegar, curry sauce or something, you'd get nowhere. Not with the ones who noticed these things and those were the ones you should want.

She had seen women talking to men they met in the doughnut place, but you couldn't do that, they might not let you in again. She wouldn't do work here, anyway, this was her place, where she could rest. That was a decision she'd made. She could have let ones take her in here and let them look like they could have been her father or her uncle – these would be ones who had thought she looked hungry, or cold, or wanted feeding up. They would take her here and feed her, be her daddy for a while, and then they would take her away and be strangers again. They were probably really poofs or something. She preferred to be here on her own.

A little crowd gusted in, on the way home from something, almost falling, hair wild, laughing. She smelled their mixture of perfumes, examined their clothes. One of the women looked at her and smiled, as the party sat down, then the man next to her whispered something short and she turned away.

Along the wall and away from the window, there were boys in tracksuits, drinking coffee. You could tell they all knew each other although they were sitting split up between different tables. Once they were outside, they would get louder and walk together, filling the street. She didn't look at them and didn't avoid them, she just accepted they were there. You couldn't tell what people like that might do. You couldn't tell what a group of them might wait outside to do. They weren't bad; only nosy. You didn't want to be something they had to find out about.

Danny wouldn't be pleased about this; her sitting around on her arse all night and not making him money. That was his fault for needing a lot. He said it was for medicine, but any cunt knew what kind of medicine that was.

She had nothing to do with that. Up at home, you were always getting offered that, anything, their mammy's tablets, anything, and she hadn't touched it then and she wouldn't now except for when her nerves were nipping. It was fucking stupid. He was just boring now. She could dress any way she wanted, he didn't care any more – he didn't even talk to her, or eat the food she got. She tried to look after him properly, but he didn't want it, he only wanted the money and the shite he was using now. He'd made love to her before – not the other stuff – and he'd been different and really lovely. He'd used to hold her and kiss and say the nice places in Scotland where they'd live when everything was fixed. Ha ha.

They were going to go back home with their money. It would be great to go back with money, old enough for folk to hear you and with money. She would have a baby and she would take excellent care of it and call it James or maybe Mary, like her mother. Ha ha ha.

Now Danny was shooting up, she wouldn't have his fucking baby. Couldn't be putting up with that shite altogether. She'd been so fucking careful, making people take precautions, trying really fucking hard to make all of them take precautions, and he didn't even know what she was talking about and now he was sticking needles anywhere he'd seen a vein. Sometimes she hoped he would just die, better if they all did – if they all lay out with the folk who were skippering and then in the morning the polis would come and brush them all away.

The last of her coffee tasted bogging. She might as well leave it. It was alright to do that here, there were unfinished doughnuts and napkins, paper cups across most of the tables. The floor wasn't clean, either. Every now and then, a girl would come and clear things away. She looked crabbit and sick, very yellow – doing the kind of job you took when you couldn't get anything else.

Most of the staff here were black. She couldn't get over that. Every time you went to places here, the people who served you and cleaned up after you were black. It must be like this in South Africa.

The times when she thought of stopping it, of really doing something else, she always imagined having to work in here. If she was lucky, she would work in here. In two years' time, she would be old enough to get a fucking dirty job in here and work all week to earn what she could in a day, just now. So what's the point of that? All right, she didn't get the money herself. You didn't ever get the money, but you earned it, you were close to it, you knew it was yours.

And all these folk that wanted her to change and to take her away from it – they talked about qualifications and training and then they just stopped. They couldn't make sense of it either. They asked you what you wanted to do and then stopped – just lies or nothing because nothing they could give you would be better than what you'd got.

She knew what she was qualified for – hand relief or up the kilt. That's what the Hotel Man called it – up the kilt – because she was Scottish and he wasn't. Fancied himself as a comic. Fancied himself like they all did, saying they were being careful but cheating all the same, still treating you like a wean.

Something hard clattered against the window and birled[1] away. It seemed to wake her from something. Like she'd been staring at the street without seeing for ages. Everything outside that could be was in flight, floating by, and it reminded her of looking at the dentist's fish tank and of feeling scared over what was coming next.

It was past the time when she should be out there, earn Danny some more, but she felt a bit sick again, a bit hot. If she bought another coffee and sat it would pass away. She hadn't felt right since she'd left the Hotel Man. Not since she'd had his present for going away.

A man in a nice jacket turned back from the counter and smiled. It was that daft, private smile that went between two, always ugly really, even if it was for you. The woman already at the table returned it with a friendly, wee shake of her head. She was much younger than him. Probably he wouldn't mind if she was younger still. A lot of them liked their girls little which was lucky for her. Or lucky for Danny, it depended how you looked at it.

A man like that had told her she should stop it and get out. Not a man, a customer. He'd looked like a social worker when you saw him up close – the same kind of pathetic face. Trying to understand you, as if he was the only one that could.

She'd got in his car as usual and then known he was weird. He was too relaxed. There wasn't much you could do with the weird ones, except to wait and see. He'd seemed harmless.

He'd told her he would pay her but he didn't want anything. She told him that nobody didn't want anything. He just patted her knee and smiled.

'I made that myself. It has two secret drawers in it and a secret panel.'

He'd grinned like he was completely stupid and passed her a heavy, wooden box, with a sloping lid. The wood was pale with little pieces of darker wood, set in. She'd liked the smell of it, and the smoothness.

You shouldn't ever let them take you home. Not take you anywhere unknown, because that wasn't safe. But she let him drive her to his home and take her in, made her steak and beans and baked potato, because that's what she felt like asking for. He gave her wine when she'd asked for voddy, but she drank it. Then he gave her the box.

'See if you can find the drawers.'

'I'm not a kid.'

'OK. Don't. I've got a video I want to watch. If you don't mind.'

'Canny sleep?'

'Not now, no. I want to see this film. Then you can tell me all about yourself.'

He smiled, as if that was a funny thing to say.

When she woke up, he was looking at her. He told her she must have been tired and she nodded. The TV wasn't on, which meant he must have been watching her instead of the video. So he was pervy, like she'd thought.

---

[1] Whirled, moved rapidly.

'You're not too well, are you? Do you know why?'

She shook her head, thinking that of course she knew why. She didn't eat like he did, or have a clean bed like he did, or live in a nice flat. She wasn't well because of rats and damp and dirtiness in Danny's squat, because there wasn't a toilet there, not even water to wash or anything. London wasn't like 'My Fair Lady' but you could tell, just by listening to him, that he thought it was and he was going to try and be Rex Harrison or some shite like that. Looked nothing like him.

The man kept on looking at her. You could see he was concentrating on being kind and getting her to talk, people liked to hear about things sometimes, but she wasn't going to tell him anything. It was none of his business, not even if he had paid for her time. Was this him trying to check if she was clean? Stupid if he was.

'Don't you think you deserve a bit better than this? Someone your age? You shouldn't be stuck with this. You need a future.'

No she did not. A future? All that time all the same? She didn't need that.

'I'm nineteen, I can do what I like.'

'I didn't ask how old you were. I could tell you how old I think you are. Maybe fifteen. I could tell you how much older you already look, but you know that.'

She watched him think of something else to say.

'You're not from round here. Where are you from?'

Maybe if she lifted her skirt that would shut him up. Then he wouldn't feel sorry for her. Then he'd stop trying so hard to respect her.

Not even the Hotel Man had done that – he'd only shown her the way things had to be done. When he'd found out she was leaving him, he'd locked her in her room. She'd been there for almost a day when he took her down to the where the boilers were. It was night and the hotel above her was quiet. The men sitting round the walls were quiet too, drinking and waiting for her. The Hotel Man did it first, and then he left.

It was maybe the following afternoon when she knew he'd come back again. Except she was in a different place then, in her room on top of the bed. She was dirty into her bones, stiff with it. Bastards. Only some folk were bastards but she'd met the whole fucking pack of them at once.

He told her she had half an hour to leave. She was going because he'd decided she would – that was the way it worked – she did what other people decided, just accept it.

She looked along the couch at the man. He was still staring at her.

'I've got nothing to tell you. You want me to go?'

'No, that's alright. Now you're here, you might as well stay.'

Which meant he'd decided what to do.

When they'd finished he brought sheets and stuff to the sofa. He tucked her in. Well, she hadn't expected he'd let her sleep in his bed, she wasn't clean. But he kissed her a lot, on the mouth and on the stomach – like she'd thought, pervy.

In the morning, he gave her cereal and toast for breakfast and coffee which she didn't drink. She didn't let him drive her back, because she felt sad again and that should be private. When she left, he squeezed her hand and watched until she'd turned the corner of the street. She wished he'd gone inside straight away.

It had took her ages to walk back to town. Danny hadn't been there when she got in and it was better without him. She knew that she wanted to stay where she was and have Danny go somewhere else. That would make her lonely but it would be best.

With the money that she'd kept from Danny and what she'd earned tonight, she could go back home. She could go up for a while and stay and then come back when she felt different. She wouldn't do this in Glasgow, only here, so she could only stay for a short while and then come back, because you had to work, look after yourself. Sometimes she just got dead homesick – adverts on the underground for Scotland, they lied like fuck, but they still made you think.

Stuart A. Paterson (1966 –)

The Leaving of Scotland

News at Ten,
January 1st 1997.

The news breaks on the eve of another
Border-summit, Scotland has asked for

Political asylum from Parliament Square.
They're putting up fences and putting out fires

In Motherwell, chaining the trawlers to
Each other in Fraserburgh as black-clad

Fish-terrorists riot and threaten a cod
War with Iceland, rushing the Secretary

Of State to a live TV broadcast in
Glasgow where, it's been reported, red   10

Kelvinsiders are demanding a
Fortune for Pat Lally's release from the

National Concert Hall. Poets are marching
To Fergusson's statue on the Mound singing

Venceramos, keeping police at bay with
Metaphors for educational cut-backs

In *Sabhal Mor Ostaig*. University
Students in Dundee are demanding the release

Of Douglas Dunn from a police cell in London
Where, in a *Scottish Books Special* emergency   20

Broadcast from the South Bank Centre, he
Called for the reintegration of

Scottish regiments. The news has broken,
Ayrshire has declared its independence

And littered the road to Glasgow with glass.
Up north, an organisation

Of Aberdeen radicals calling itself
The Scottish Offshore Republican Army

Has captured an oil rig in the name of
Ravenscraig. The Military are making a   30

Giant jail of the Highlands, repopulation
Of the Islands has begun and Gaelic

Is compulsory, English forbidden,
The Daily Record has barricaded itself

By the Broomielaw and blamed it all on
Dissatisfied Mirror Group Pensioners

In collusion with the Scottish Office.
Michael Forsyth has returned and instituted

A four-year plan for dissident writers
When it's discovered that 'Mac' is old Pictish   40

For 'comrade of.' McLeod, McLean,
MacIlvanney (and Massie for the sake of it)

Are rounded up to work crofts on only sixteen pounds
Each a week, deliver the mail, start spinning new cottage

Industries, teach their children the Works of
Walter Scott and Teatime Tales by Molly Weir.

All over Scotland, town halls
Are giving out free paper and copies of

Dwelly's English-Gaelic Dictionary.
The Herald has made Tom Shields Editor   50

And called for Pat Lally's release but his
Corpse is thrown from the roof of the Concert

Hall an hour later, tidied, bewigged
And flown to an all-expenses-paid
Funeral junket in Chicago.
The border-summit breaks up again,

No sign of agreement on extradition
For convicted heroin smugglers,

I'm sorry, I'll read that again,
convicted *herring* smugglers.   60

English embassies, packed with Inverness
Publicans and time-share owners, appeal

To the European Community for help.
But the oil's run out and so has Scotland.

Political asylum denied, it leaves.

John's Christmas, 1992

He chapped the doors of all our rooms
round four o'clock that afternoon.
Diane, an agoraphobic
depressive said she heard him knock
but couldn't answer, and Martin
spent his Saturdays losing lines
at William Hill's. I caught the four
fifteen for Troon drunk as a lord,
armed to the teeth with cheap presents,
filled with the homing instinct of Tennent's.   10
He got no answer, in or not,
went quietly to his attic flat
with just the one small carrier bag.
From which he took three lengths of wire,
a pen and notepad, two cans of beer,
scrawled down some lines 'to Stuart,' drank
one can, tied three tough knots then sank
down near the knees, all six foot three
of him in roofspace really
meant for children and for keeping things   20
boxed five high you'd not be using
in your time there. I found the note,
a few lines anyone might write
to say they'd been round, you weren't in,
no call-back time, but have that tin
of heavy on the mantelpiece,
that's yours Stuart, and if you'll please
turn round you'll see the cupboard doors
are open and my half-kneeled corpse
prays silently that you, of all   30
the lodgers, are testimonial
to knots I hope held true and tight.
knees necessary inches from
the floorboards and my arms still firm
behind the back, my wrists tied so
that when I drop there's absolutely no
chance of me missing that required
fine balance between there and here.
The depressive agoraphobic
wouldn't come out for the paramedics   40
even, and if I read her file
I'm sure I'd see, added, *denial*,
highlighted by red marker pen.
The distance between now and then
I still can't judge as well as one
small backstep to oblivion;
and then, you know, from there to here,
and soberness with one tin of beer,
has never come so awfully quick.
I drank the beer. Of course I did.   50

Achiltibuie

Where is it then, this Achiltibuie?
Today I received a poem about a
hen yard there, and remembered a friend's
praising of a particular inn which
sheltered her one wild night, in Achiltibuie.
And there on the *Scottish* pages of the paper,
I read of brave Achiltibuiean crofters
driving off the evil Southron lairds.

All the omens point to a long grey road north.

I will take my big green rucksack,   10
point a thumb up to imagined villages,
and there it will lie, amongst heather and bracken,
smoking gently low in the hills, a homely
peat-fire of scattered lights. Of all
the coasts, I hope it lies to the west
with a view of islands, tartan-shaded ranges,
and there will be a Gaelic name for it,
translating to *meeting place of the two streams*
or *big Iain's shebeen*. I'll mimic the tongue
never mine, practise soft vowels whispered   20
by forgotten ancestors in the golden time,
step humbly in lowland townie clothes over
rich-earthed boots and wary collies to a hearth,
order the water of life in a room full of fiddle,
put up a prayer in the Celtic Twilight Zone.
We Scots, even, must have our Brigadoon.

In a bothy near Arisaig, a fisherman
will be picking up, splitting a shingle-scratched
bottle, pulling out a single rolled-up page,
rubbing his eyes at the sight of 'Kilmarnock in Summer'
And trying to mouth a poem by Burns.   31

Richard Price (1966 –)

Tree-bird

I'm lending you this poem –
it's yours.

Do you remember the owl-hawk, white as a guiser –
the dusk's sucky blanket tucked round our caravan
and the bird rid of us

like, at break-ripe, the fruit of the tree-bird tree,
the applefist which splits
into a beak and feathers,
a yellow tern
before Newton can say   10
Golden Delicious.

(It's a legend, you know, among fishers
who ken damn few trees
and they all shrubbery
in this world, geese crack out of barnacles,
crabs lisp, and jellyfish are wedding veils
for mermaids who've vetoed
shivering grooms
in the wide aisle of a low ebb.)

I want to be the bird that's my hand in your hand,   20
to be the osprey that can dismember itself
like the lines of a poem,
climb the sky, dive, fish
and come back to itself
like a trick,
like the end of work.

Facts About Trout

trout prefer
to stay underwater

the trout that can breath
is a crocodile

there are two kinds of trout:
one lives among mountains,
the other in still water

farmed locally in large numbers,
trout have important duties
abroad   10

trout are influential
at tables
the world wide

trout never cry

they love the sky
for its flies

Highland

Snow on the high mountains
Is smoothed by the wind.
The white folds of winter
Fray into yellow grass
And sleeping heather.

There is no tree between me and the mountain.
Only the wind combing the marsh grass.

A ledge of snow forms a step to the house
And the sunlight trips, on its way to the ground.

Kenneth Steven (1968 –)

The Long Silence

On Iona the last Gaelic speaker has died.
Last winter when the gales battled each roof and window
He was blown out and into the wind.

Once upon a time he was a tall man,
Leaning at the porch of his weaver's cottage,
His eyes like pools of the sea.

Now in the summer when the tourists come
You will hear the languages fast and loud –
But never a word of Gaelic there.

All over the western islands, the last ones are going   10
Like candles tonight, falling across the wind,
Their last words drowned and lost in time.

But everyone is talking, busy talking,
The radios and televisions are loud all night
And no one is listening to the long silence.

For Calum Macleod of Raasay

News of your dying came to me
Like a branch withered and white
Carried on distant tides,
Like the salt-whip of sea-wind that grieves the eyes.

You cut the stone of your years,
Laid an unwritten song in the road to Arnish.
Not the fine or faceted song
Of the cold demeanor of cathedrals
But the pulsing vein of a people's struggle,
The clenched furrow that is roughened by storm,   10
Its prow against the plough of history.

You did not carry the snarl of the bayonet
Into the cowering jabber of war
Nor was your burial bronzed by some salute of splendour;
More pure the lament over Raasay,
The peewits that wept.

Gaelic

It lies in pockets in the hills,
A wink of gold that has not been panned
From the older veins and the worn faces.

And sometimes on a dark river of night
I imagine it returning from the seas in its struggle
Like salmon to the birthright of the springs.

Highland Bull

He is just an ornament on the moorland
Made of heather roots, too tough for meat
A piece of old machinery with handlebars
Left out to rust in all weathers.

Americans will stop their cars
In a force ten August, iron rain –
Looking for the bull's front end
And a snatched picture.

Yet in him somewhere is an engine room
Quite capable of firing.   10
Tickle the bracken beast
With care, with a little Gaelic.

Acknowledgements

Thanks are due to the following writers, or their indicated heirs or literary executors for kind permission to reprint materials in this book. In some instances publishers or agencies are co-holders of copyright, in which case they are acknowledged separately below.

'Bridie, James' (by Ronald Mavor)
Abbott, Ian (Frances Abbot)
Aitchison, James
Annand, J. K. (Rosemary Mutch)
Bell, Robin
Blackhall, Sheena
Bold, Alan
Brown, George Mackay (Archie Bevan)
Bruce, George
Burnside, John – for 'Ports'
Butlin, Ron
Conn, Stewart
Corrie, Joe (Morag Corrie)
Czerkawska, Catherine
Davie, Elspeth (George Davie)
Diack, Hunter (Elsie Diack)
Douglas, Sheila
Elphinstone, Margaret
Fell, Alison
Finlay, Ian Hamilton
Friel, George (Brian Elliot)
Fulton, Graham
Fulton, Robin
Galbraith, Carol
Gillies, Valerie
Glen, Duncan
Glenday, John
Graham, W. S. (Nessie Graham)
Gray, Alasdair
Gray, Alexander (John Gray)
Gunn, George
Gunn, Neil (Dairmid Gunn)
Hamilton, Alex
Hanley, Clifford (Jane Hanley)
Hay, George Campbell (Mrs Mary Hill)
Henderson, Hamish
Hutchison, Sandy – for 'Inchcolm'
Jacob, Violet (Malcolm Hutton)
Jamie, Kathleen
Jeffrey, William (Maeve Kinloch)

Jenkins, Robin
Kay, Billie
Kelman, James
Kinloch, David
Lamb, Helen
Law, T. S. (John Law)
Lindsay, Maurice
Lorimer, William (Priscilla Lorimer)
MacCallum, Neil
Mackie, Alastair (Bet Mackie)
Martin, Angus
McCabe, Brian
McCarey, Peter
McDonald, Ellie
McLean, Duncan
Mclellan, Robert (John McLellan)
McManus, Tony
McMillan, Hugh
McSeveney, Angela
Meade, Gordon
Meek, James
Mitchison, Naomi – for 'Five Men and a Swan'
Monro, Harold (Mrs Freda McGregor)
Montgomerie, William (Dian and Ian Montgomerie) – for 'Daft Jenny'
Morrice, Ken
Munro, Neil (Lesley Bratton)
Nairn, Tom
Neill, William
O'Rourke, Donny
Ouston, Hugh
Paterson, Neil (Rose Paterson)
Paterson, Stuart
Pow, Tom
Price, Richard
Raine, Kathleen
Ransford, Tessa
Reid, Alastair
Riach, Alan
Robertson, Robin
Rorie, David (David Rorie Society)
Rose, Dilys – for the poems and screenplay
Royle, Trevor
Salvesen, Christopher
Scott, Alexander (Catherine Scott)
Scott, Tom (Heather Scott)
Service, Robert (Mrs Iris ServiceDavies)
Smith, Iain Crichton – for the short stories
Smith, Morelle
Smith, Sydney Goodsir (Hazel Smith)
Spence, Alan
Taylor, Rachel (Louise and Walter Annand)
Thomson, Derick
Thornton, Valerie
Todd, Ruthven (Christopher Todd)

Turnbull, Gael
Vettese, Raymond
Warner, Alan
Watson, Roderick
Wood, Wendy (Cora Cuthbert)
Young, Andrew (Alison Young)
Young, Douglas (Clara Young)

Thanks are also due to the following publishers, literary agencies, or arts associations for kind permissions to reprint the following writers or works or selections from the indicated collections.

A. P. Watt, Ltd. on behalf of The Lord Tweedsmuir and Jean, Lady Tweedsmuir – for John Buchan *(Collected Poems,* Scottish Cultural Press, and *Complete Short Stories,* Thistle)

Anvil Press: – for Norman Cameron *(Collected Poems and Selected Translations,* Warren Hope and Jonathan Barker, eds, 1990), Carol Ann Duffy (five poems from *The Other Country,* 1990, and 'Plainsong' from *Selling Manhattan,* 1987)

Bloodaxe Books – for G. F. Dutton, Andrew Greig, Kathleen Jamie, W. N. Herbert

Calder Publications and The Calder Education Trust – for Sydney Smith *(Collected Poems,* 1975)

Carcanet – for Frank Kuppner, Hugh MacDiarmid, Edwin Morgan, Iain Smith (poems)

Chapman – for Tom Scott *(The Collected Shorter Poems)*

Canongate Books – for Olive Fraser *(The Wrong Music: The Poems of Olive Fraser,* 1909–1977), Edward Gaitens ('The Minodge' from *Dance of the Apprentices),* Alasdair Gray ('The Spread of Ian Nicol' and 'The Comedy of the White Dog' from *Unlikely Stories Mostly,* and 'The Oracle's Tale' from *Lanark),* Naomi Mitchison ('The House of the Hare' from *The Cleansing of the Knife),* William Montgomerie (Time to Time: Selected Poems)

Curtis/Brown – for Ronald Frame ('The Camelhair Jacket' from *A Long Weekend With Marcel Proust,* Bodley Head), William McIlvanney ('Walking Wounded' from *How Many Miles to Babylon,* Hodder and Stoughton, 1989)

David Rorie Society – for David Rorie

Faber and Faber – for Douglas Dunn (Collected Poems), Edwin Muir (Collected Poems), Don Paterson *(Nil Nil* and *God's Gift to Woman)*

Gordon Wright – for 'David Toulmin' ('Hardwood' from *Harvest Home,* Paul Harris)

Hodder and Stoughton, Ltd: William McIlvanney ('Walking Wounded' from *How Many Miles to Babylon,* 1989)

John Murray, Ltd – for George Mackay Brown

Little/Brown – for Ali Smith ('Cold Iron' from *Free Love,* Virago Press)

Macmillan and Co. – for Robin Robertson *(A Painted Field,* 1997)

Mercat Press – for J. K. Annand *(Selected Poems)*

Moyer Bell – for Shena Mackay ('Dreams of Dead Women's Handbags' from *Dreams of Dead Women's Handbags,* Heinemann)

National Library of Scotland – for William Soutar

Oxford University Press – for Edwin Muir (American rights – *Collected Poems)*

Penguin – for Algernon Blackwood ('The Wolves of God' from *The Wolves of God & Other Stories,* Blackwood)

Peters, Fraser & Dunlop Group, Ltd – for Douglas Dunn ('The Canoes' from *Secret Villages),* Eric Linklater ('The Goose Girl,' from *Sealskin Trousers)*

Polygon – for D. M. Black, Elizabeth Burns, Robert Crawford ('Ghetto Blastir' from *Sharawaggi),* Chris Dolan, Alastair Fowler ('Winds Sift Keenly' from *Catacomb Suburb),* Gordon Legge, Liz Lochhead

Ramsay Head Press – for Janet Caird

Random House – for John Burnside (Feast Days, Secker and Warburg), Robert Crawford

(*A Scottish Assembly and Talkies,* both Chatto & Windus, and *Masculinity,* Jonathan Cape), Alastair Fowler *(Domaine of Arnheim,* Secker and Warburg), Janice Galloway ('After the Rains' from *Where You Find It,* Jonathan Cape and 'Fearless,' from Blood, Secker & Warburg), Sue Glover *(The Bondagers,* Methuen), A. L. Kennedy ('Friday Payday' from *Now That You're Back,* Jonathan Cape), Norman MacCaig *(Collected Poems,* Chatto & Windus), Dilys Rose ('Glancing' and 'Red Tides,' from *Red Tides,* Secker & Warburg), Burns Singer *(Collected Poems,* Secker and Warburg), C. P. Taylor *(Good,* Methuen), Irvine Welsh ('The Acid House' from *The Acid House,* Jonathan Cape)

Routledge – for J. F. Hendry (The Bombed Happiness, 1942, and The Orchestral Mountain, 1943), Edwin Muir ('Language' from Scott and Scotland, 1936)

Saltire Society – for Robert Garioch *(Complete Poetical Works,* 1983), Raymond Vettese *(The Richt Noise)*

Samuel French – for James Barrie

Scottish Cultural Press – for Kenneth Steven (*The Missing Days*)

Sheil Land Associates, Ltd – for Sydney Tremayne *(Selected and New Poems,* Chatto and Windus, 1973)

The Agency, Ltd – for 'James Bridie' *(The Anatomist,* first published by Constable & Co. Ltd, 1931)

University of Massachusetts Press – for Alexander Hutchison ('Mr Scales Walks His Dog' from *Deep-tap Tree,* 1978)

Every effort has been made to trace all holders of copyright, but we have been unable to locate some of the estates whose works are reprinted in this book, for which omission, our sincere apologies. Should we be notified of these missing names, the publishers will be very pleased to give appropriate credit in future editions.

★ ★ ★

It would be impossible to thank individually all of the Scottish writers (or their families), critics, publishers and scholars who have contributed not just their works but their time to this volume over the several years in which it has developed. Nor would it be possible to respond properly to the generosity of the writers who gave permission to have their works included here. Not a single writer represented in this book who had control over his or her own copyright (as most did) ever asked for a permission fee, and very many of them were endlessly generous of their time in evaluating the proposed Vol. III Table of Contents. I refrain from listing those who were especially helpful only because they are almost all represented in this volume and I would wish no reader to imagine any given writer had been included or his listing affected by personal rather than aesthetic criteria. The best I can do is to affirm that Scotland well deserves its reputation for hospitality and generosity. Thanks to all.

Back in my own country, I offer special thanks to Mim, who proofread the entire three-volume manuscript, to Shay McC, who proofread many hundreds of pages, to Erik Thurin and Martha Wallen, who helped with the translations, to Mike Levy, whose knowledge of fantasy literature has been constantly useful in the preparation of these volumes, and of course to the University of Wisconsin-Stout for sabbatical leaves, travel and study grants and its endlessly patient library staff.

Index of Authors and Titles